Y0-BDY-909

THE IDEA OF FREEDOM

Volume II

THE IDEA
OF FREEDOM

Volume II

A Dialectical Examination
of the Controversies about Freedom

by

MORTIMER J. ADLER

for The Institute for Philosophical Research

GREENWOOD PRESS, PUBLISHERS
WESTPORT, CONNECTICUT

The Library of Congress has catalogued this publication as follows:

Library of Congress Cataloging in Publication Data

Adler, Mortimer Jerome, 1902–
  The idea of freedom.

  Reprint of the 1958-61 eds.
  Bibliography: p.
  CONTENTS: v. 1. A dialectical examination of the
conceptions of freedom.--v. 2. A dialectical ex-
amination of the controversies about freedom.
  1. Liberty. I. San Francisco. Institute for
Philosophical Research. II. Title.
  [B105.L45A32]   323.44   72-7872
  ISBN 0-8371-6547-4

Originally published in 1961
by Doubleday & Company, Inc., Garden City, New York

Reprinted with the permission
of Doubleday & Company, Inc.

First Greenwood Reprinting 1973

Library of Congress Catalogue Card Number 72-7872

ISBN 0-8371-6547-4 (Set)
ISBN 0-8371-6738-8 (Vol. II)

Printed in the United States of America

to

ARTHUR A. HOUGHTON, JR.

and

ADOLPH SCHMIDT

Contents

PREFACE TO VOLUME II *ix*

BOOK III
THE CONTROVERSIES ABOUT FREEDOM 1

PART I. INTRODUCTION AND
    RECAPITULATION 3

 1. *The Five Freedoms* 3
 2. *The Construction of the Controversies* 17

PART II. THE GENERAL CONTROVERSY 32

 3. *The Kinds of Freedom* 32
 4. *The Issue Concerning the Freedom of Self-Realization* 35
 5. *The Issues Concerning the Freedom of Self-Perfection* 91
 6. *The Issues Concerning Political Liberty* 135
 7. *The Issues Concerning Collective Freedom* 184
 8. *Introduction to the Issues Concerning the Freedom
   of Self-Determination* 223
 9. *Self-Determination: The Existential Issue Concerning
   Causal Initiative* 253
 10. *Self-Determination: The Existential Issue Concerning
   Causal Indeterminacy* 331
 11. *The Theological Issue Concerning Man's Freedom
   of Self-Determination* 464
 12. *A Possible Conceptual Issue Concerning Self-
   Determination: Chance, Responsibility, and Freedom* 488

PART III. THE SPECIAL CONTROVERSIES 526

 13. *Introduction* 526
 14. *The Conceptual Issues Concerning the Freedom of
   Self-Realization* 533
 15. *The Existential Issues Concerning the Freedom of
   Self-Realization* 562

16. The Normative Issues Concerning the Freedom
    of Self-Realization   603
17. The Issues Concerning the Freedom of Self-Perfection   621
18. The Issues Concerning Collective Freedom   626
19. The Issues Concerning the Freedom of Self-
    Determination   634

PART IV. EPILOGUE   648

20. Concluding Observations   648

BIBLIOGRAPHIES   653

ANALYTICAL TABLE OF CONTENTS   723

INDEX OF AUTHORS IN THE
GENERAL CONTROVERSY   733

INDEX OF AUTHORS IN THE
SPECIAL CONTROVERSIES   749

PREFACE

With the publication of this volume, the Institute for Philosophical Research completes the work on freedom which it began in 1952. During the academic year 1960–61, while seeing this volume through the press, the staff of the Institute has initiated a second study in the field of ideas, this time on the idea of love. Employing the same method and pursuing the same objective which guided its dialectical clarification of the idea of freedom, the Institute hopes to produce a comparable treatment of the idea of love; but it has also undertaken to accomplish this in a shorter time and, therefore, the projected work on love will necessarily be less comprehensive in scope and detail than the work on freedom. Similar briefer treatments of other ideas—progress, justice, property, equality—are planned.

Like Volume I of *The Idea of Freedom*, Volume II is the product of a sustained collaborative effort. Based on researches conducted by the staff of the Institute, its formulations were developed through conferences and consultations and represent the pooling of contributions from many sources. As successive drafts of this book were written, they were reviewed by the staff and submitted to the Institute's consultants for criticism and emendation. The final product is, therefore, truly the work of many hands. However, the Director of the Institute, to whom the task of writing this book fell, must assume final responsibility for its content and for whatever faults in style or substance represent the decisions of his individual authorship.

As Director of the Institute since 1952, I wish to express my great indebtedness to all the men and women who have been associated with me in this enterprise, as members of the Institute's resident staff or as its consultants. Their names are listed in Volume I, as are the names of the Institute's Board of Directors. I wish to take this occasion to thank the members of the Board for the counsel and guidance they have given me in the conduct of the Institute's affairs. To two of them—Mortimer Fleishhacker, Jr., and Arthur Rubin—and to Richard Bentley, I am especially grateful for the help they have given by reading the manuscript and commenting on it.

Above all, I want to convey my deep sense of personal gratitude to my two closest associates in the preparation and writing of Volume II—Peter Wolff and Robert G. Hazo. I cannot detail the manifold contributions they made to this work at every stage of research and writing, nor can I fully express my appreciation of the help and encouragment their constant collaboration has given me, but I can say, without the slightest exaggeration, that the completion of this work would have been impossible were it not for their efforts.

In the name of the Institute and of its Board of Directors, I wish to express the gratitude of its staff and its consultants to the sources of financial support which made it possible for the work on freedom to be completed in the years 1958–61 and which also make it possible for us to undertake similar work on other ideas in the years that lie immediately ahead. The following foundations and persons have made substantial contributions to the Institute: the Old Dominion Foundation, the Houghton Foundation, the General Service Foundation, the Belvedere Fund, Kenneth M. Harden, Mortimer Fleishhacker, Jr., and Helen Potter Russell. The Institute is also grateful to all those men and women who, as friends of the Institute, have made small individual contributions to its support.

These acknowledgments would not be complete without special mention of the fact that the Institute owes its continued and future existence to the unwavering faith and generous commitments of four men in particular—Paul Mellon, Ernest Brooks, Jr., and Adolph Schmidt (of the Old Dominion Foundation) and Arthur A. Houghton, Jr., (of the Houghton Foundation). To two of these men—Arthur A. Houghton, Jr., and Adolph Schmidt—this volume is gratefully dedicated.

MORTIMER J. ADLER

San Francisco
May 1961

Book
III

THE CONTROVERSIES
ABOUT FREEDOM

PART I

Introduction and Recapitulation

Chapter 1

THE FIVE FREEDOMS

As the subtitle of this volume indicates, Book III of *The Idea of Freedom* is concerned with a dialectical examination of the controversies about freedom. The two preceding books, published in Volume I, have prepared the way for this attempt to construct the issues that have been joined and debated in the course of twenty-five centuries of recorded discussion.

Book I set forth the nature and method of the dialectical enterprise in which the Institute for Philosophical Research has been engaged. That undertaking was there described as "an effort to take stock of Western thought on subjects which have been of continuing philosophical interest from the advent of philosophy in ancient Greece to the present day." We called such an effort "dialectical" in order to distinguish it both from the history of ideas and from philosophical thought about them.

We also used the word "dialectical" to refer to the Institute's method of dealing with differences of opinion in an objective and neutral manner. Employing this method, we approach the discussion of basic ideas from the standpoint of an observer rather than a participant. Our task is to order and clarify a wide diversity of views without taking sides or judging their soundness or truth. The dialectical approach, thus conceived, is generally applicable to the whole range of basic ideas.

The first steps in the application of this method to the idea of freedom were accomplished in Book II. A dialectical examination of the diverse conceptions of freedom had to precede any attempt to deal with the controversy.

Before this or any other complex field of controversy can be clarified—before genuine issues can be formulated and arguments set against arguments—it is necessary to discover whether there is only one or several distinct subjects involved in controversy. In the case of freedom, we found that there were five, each the focus of many differences of opinion. In Book II, we (i) identified these five distinct subjects of controversy, (ii) classified the major writers on freedom according to the conceptions or views they held on one or more of these subjects, and (iii) formulated that common understanding of freedom which would justify relating the subjects and the controversies as having something more in common than just the name "freedom."

Now, in Book III, we shall attempt to complete the dialectical task, taking the remaining steps called for by the method; namely, the formulation of the issues and the presentation of the arguments that constitute each of the controversies about freedom.

Because of their bearing on the present book, some recapitulation of Books I and II would appear necessary. (1) We must acquaint the reader with the descriptive formulas we have used to identify the five freedoms, with the tag names we have employed in referring to them, and with a list of the major authors who hold conceptions of each of the freedoms. (2) To prepare the reader for the way in which the various controversies shape up, it is also advisable to repeat the summary classification of theories of freedom, which was given at the end of Book II. (3) Finally, a word ought to be said about the common understanding of freedom which underlies all the diverse meanings of the term, and which makes possible one general controversy about the kinds of freedom.

1. FIVE SUBJECTS OF CONTROVERSY

We have used the words "circumstantial," "acquired," and "natural" to identify a freedom according to the way in which it is possessed by men. To complete the identification of freedoms that are distinct subjects of discussion, we have used the words "self-realization," "self-perfection," and "self-determination" to signify the mode of self in which a freedom consists.

In Book II we presented evidence for the identification of three main subjects of controversy: (i) a circumstantial freedom of self-realization, (ii) an acquired freedom of self-perfection, and (iii) a natural freedom of self-determination. In addition, we identified two other subjects which, while distinct from these three, are not co-ordinate with them, for each is a special variant of one of the principal subjects: (iv) political liberty, a special variant of circumstantial self-realization, and (v) collective freedom, a special variant of acquired self-perfection.

Each of these five subjects is discussed in the literature on freedom under a variety of conceptions which have enough in common to be grouped together. To enumerate the common traits of each is simply another way of stating the descriptive formula for identifying the freedom which is defined in different ways by the divergent conceptions in each group. Even though the authors who hold these divergent conceptions disagree about how that freedom should be defined, they agree implicitly on the descriptive formula by which we identify the subject of their disagreement. Such agreement about the identification of a subject of discussion—or disagreement—we have called a "minimal topical agreement."

What follows is a recapitulation of the minimal topical agreements for which we presented documentary evidence in Book II. For each of the five subjects that we have identified we shall state the brief descriptive formula which we have used to summarize our identification. We shall then list in alphabetical order the major authors who were shown in Book II to hold conceptions of the freedom named and who affirm it either as man's only human freedom or as, in some way, one of the freedoms man enjoys, or at least as a distinguishable aspect of human freedom. Finally, we shall comment briefly on the points in each topical agreement which constitute the understanding of freedom that is common to a given family of conceptions and which serve to distinguish it from the others.

CIRCUMSTANTIAL FREEDOM OF SELF-REALIZATION

Descriptive formula: a freedom which is possessed by any individual who, under favorable circumstances, is able to act as he wishes for his own good as he sees it.

Major authors: Aquinas, Ayer, Bentham, Burke, Dewey, Edwards, Freud, Hale, Hayek, N. Hartmann, Hobbes, Hobhouse, Hume, Kelsen, Knight, Laski, Locke, Macmurray, Malinowski, Mannheim, Maritain, J. S. Mill, Montesquieu, Nowell-Smith, Pareto, Priestley, B. Russell, Schlick, Yves Simon, Spencer, Adam Smith, Stevenson, Tawney, Voltaire.

Comment: The foregoing authors are in topical agreement on the following points about the freedom named:

(a) that it is a freedom which the individual possesses *only* under favorable circumstances, i.e., circumstances which do not prevent him from acting as he wishes or do not coerce him into behavior contrary to his wishes;

(b) that the circumstantial character of such freedom lies in the fact that the individual's ability to carry out his wishes, plans, or desires is a *circumstantial ability*, i.e., an ability wholly or partly dependent on propitious circumstances;

(c) that "acting as one wishes" or "doing as one pleases" expresses the meaning of self-realization only when two conditions are fulfilled: first, *execution*, whereby the individual's wish is translated into action; and second, *individual fulfillment*, wherein the individual's own good, as he sees it, is achieved by the action performed.

ACQUIRED FREEDOM OF SELF-PERFECTION

Descriptive formula: a freedom which is possessed only by those men who, through acquired virture or wisdom, are able to will or live as they ought in conformity to the moral law or an ideal befitting human nature.

Major authors: Ambrose, Anselm, Aquinas, Augustine, Marcus Aurelius, Barth, Bellarmine, Boethius, Bosanquet, Bradley, Calvin, Cicero, Dewey, Duns Scotus, Epictetus, Epicurus, Fouillée, Freud, Green, Hegel, Kant, Leibniz, Locke, Luther, Maimonides, Marcel, Maritain, Montesquieu, Philo, Plotinus, Rousseau, B. Russell, Santayana, Seneca, Yves Simon, Spinoza, Suarez, Tillich, Whitehead.

Comment: The foregoing authors are in topical agreement on the following points about the freedom named:

(a) that it is a freedom which, even under circumstances most favorable to the execution of what a man wills, is possessed only by those men whose state of mind or character enables them to will as they ought;

(b) that the acquired character of such freedom lies in the fact that the individual's ability to live in conformity to an ideal befitting human nature, or to obey the moral law willingly, is an *acquired ability*; i.e., an ability which represents a relatively stable change in the constitution, make-up, or inner workings of a human being;

(c) that "willing or living as one ought" expresses the meaning of self-perfection only when three conditions are present: first, the *objectivity and universality of the moral standards or goals* which determine what ought to be willed; second, the *autonomy of the individual* insofar as the moral standards, goals, or laws to which he conforms become, through acquired virtue or wisdom, to some extent his own rather than wholly external impositions; and third, the *spontaneity of his voluntary compliance* with such moral standards, goals, or laws.

NATURAL FREEDOM OF SELF-DETERMINATION

Descriptive formula: a freedom which is possessed by all men, in virtue of a power inherent in human nature, whereby a man is able to change

his own character creatively by deciding for himself what he shall do
or shall become.

Major authors: Anselm, Aquinas, Aristotle, Augustine, Barth, Bellarmine,
Bergson, Berkeley, Boethius, Burke, Calvin, Cicero, Descartes, Dewey,
Duns Scotus, Epicurus, Fichte, Fouillée, Green, N. Hartmann, Hegel,
William James, Kant, Knight, Leibniz, Locke, Lucretius, Luther,
Maimonides, Marcel, Maritain, Montesquieu, Philo, Renouvier, Rous-
seau, Santayana, Sartre, Secrétan, Yves Simon, Adam Smith, Suarez,
Tillich, Weiss, Whitehead.

Comment: The foregoing authors are in topical agreement on the following points about the freedom named:

(a) that it is a freedom which all men possess because every man,
simply in virtue of being a man, always has the power to decide
for himself what he wishes to do or to become;

(b) that the natural character of such freedom lies in the fact that
the aforesaid power is a *natural ability,* i.e., an ability inherent in
the native constitution or make-up of the members of the human
species;

(c) that "deciding what one wishes to do or to become" expresses
the meaning of self-determination only when at least two of the
three following conditions obtain: (i) the decision is *intrinsically
unpredictable,* i.e., given perfect knowledge of all relevant causes,
it cannot be foreseen with certitude; (ii) the decision is *not
necessitated,* i.e., it is always one of a number of alternative
possible decisions any one of which it was within the power of the
self to cause, no matter what other antecedent or concurrent
factors exercise a causal influence on the making of the decision;
(iii) the decision flows from the *causal initiative* of the self, i.e.,
on the plane of natural causes, the self is the *uncaused cause* of
the decision it makes.[1]

Before we attempt to summarize the topical agreements about the two
remaining subjects—political liberty and collective freedom—it may be useful to recall certain contrasts which we have found helpful in distinguishing
the three freedoms we have so far considered.

It is distinctive of authors who affirm a circumstantial freedom of self-

---

[1] Most of the authors who affirm man's natural freedom of self-determination hold
conceptions of it that involve all three of the conditions stated above. A few authors,
notably Bergson, Dewey, and Weiss, hold conceptions that involve the first two
conditions but not the third. (See Vol. I, pp. 492–94.) The conceptions to be found
in Aquinas, Hegel, and Fouillée do not require the first two conditions to be present
in all cases of self-determination; but for Aquinas they are normally present, and
for Hegel and Fouillée they are present at imperfect stages of self-determination.
(See Vol. I, pp. 531–39 and pp. 551–55.) Leibniz is the one author for whom
self-determination involves only the third of the three conditions stated above. (See
Vol. I, pp. 539–45 and pp. 549–51.)

realization that they advocate social reforms or changes in the environment as ways of increasing or decreasing the amount of freedom men enjoy or the number of men who enjoy it. In contrast, authors who affirm an acquired freedom of self-perfection look to the moral improvement of men, rather than to alterations in the institutions under which they live. For them, freedom is a development in the inner life of the individual.

Another point of contrast between these two groups of conceptions lies in the positions their exponents take on the relation of liberty to law. For those who affirm a circumstantial freedom of self-realization, it is not the individual's state of mind or character, but the amount of legal regulation or the compatibility of particular laws with what the individual wishes to do that affects the degree of his freedom. But for those who affirm an acquired freedom of self-perfection, freedom under law rests wholly on the harmony between the rightness of what the law requires and the rectitude of the individual's will, making his compliance with the law a voluntary act of obedience.

As contrasted with both of the foregoing, authors who affirm man's natural freedom of self-determination attribute it to power which is inherent in human nature and does not depend upon any alterable conditions whatsoever, neither upon the individual's external circumstances of life nor upon his moral state.

These contrasts can be stated in another way by reference to the typical questions that one would ask to discover whether a man exercised one or another of these freedoms in a particular act. In the case of self-realization, one would ask whether a man's behavior is uncoerced or unconstrained, whether it proceeds from his own wish or desire, and so on. In the case of self-perfection, one would ask whether an act is morally right and whether it is done through wisdom or virtuous inclination, and thus done willingly. But in the case of self-determination, one would ask whether the act is intrinsically unpredictable, whether it flows from the causal initiative of the agent, or whether the individual could have chosen to act otherwise, since he was under no necessity to make the choice he did.

We turn now to a summary of the topical agreements about political liberty and collective freedom, and to the contrasts which we have found helpful in distinguishing them from self-realization and self-perfection, of which they are, respectively, the variants.

POLITICAL LIBERTY

> *Descriptive formula:* a freedom which is possessed only by citizens who, through the right of suffrage and the right of juridical appeal against the abuses of government, are able to participate in making the positive law under which they live and to alter the political institutions of their society.

Major authors: Aquinas, Aristotle, Hobhouse, Kant, Locke, Maritain, Montesquieu, Yves Simon.

Comment: The foregoing authors are in topical agreement on the following points about the freedom named:

(a) that it is a freedom which is conferred on men by constitutional government and which is possessed only by those who are citizens with suffrage, i.e., those who through their constitutionally granted political rights and privileges are full-fledged and active members of a self-governing community;

(b) that the political character of such freedom lies in the fact that the individual's ability to participate in making laws and shaping political institutions is a power conferred on him by the *political status* he enjoys, together with all the rights and privileges which appertain thereto;

(c) that "self-government" expresses the meaning of political liberty only when two conditions obtain: (i) the public or legislative will to which the individual is subject is *not a will wholly alien to his own*, but one to the formation of which he, as a citizen, has contributed through his suffrage; and (ii) the individual as a citizen has the opportunity and power to say what is for the common good *from the point of view of his own particular interests.*

That political liberty is a variant of circumstantial rather than of acquired freedom is evident from the fact that it is possessed only by individuals who are favored by certain circumstances, regardless of their moral condition. The citizen with suffrage has political liberty whether or not, in exercising it, his will is directed by acquired virtue or wisdom.

That political liberty, while circumstantial, is not identical with the freedom of self-realization is equally clear from the fact that those who lack political liberty (i.e., all disfranchised persons) may have in varying degrees the circumstantial ability to act as they wish, while, on the other hand, those who have political liberty (i.e., enfranchised citizens) may be subject to coercions or constraints which eliminate their freedom of self-realization, but not their political liberty.

As we have seen, authors who affirm a circumstantial freedom of self-realization see in the amount of legal regulation to which an individual is subject or in the compatibility of particular laws with his individual wishes two conditions that affect the degree of his freedom. In sharp contrast, neither of these conditions is regarded as having any effect on political liberty by those who affirm it as a distinct freedom. Political liberty, they maintain, does not consist in obeying oneself alone or in not being subject to the will of others. It suffices for political liberty that the public will, by which the law is made, represents each citizen's own will together with that of every other citizen who has exercised his suffrage. So long as the law is made with his consent through constitutional processes in which he participates, the citizen remains politically free whether he is in the minority or the majority.

COLLECTIVE FREEDOM

> *Descriptive formula:* a freedom which will be possessed by humanity or the human race in the future when, through the social use of the knowledge of both natural and social necessities, men achieve the ideal mode of association that is the goal of mankind's development and are able to direct their communal life in accordance with such necessities.

> *Major authors:* Bakunin, Comte, Engels, Marx.

> *Comment:* The foregoing authors are in topical agreement on the following points about the freedom named:

> (a) that it is a freedom which will be acquired by mankind only when human life and social organization are directed by man's knowledge of natural and social necessities, and do not involve man-made rules or coercive force of any sort;

> (b) that the collective character of such freedom lies in the fact that it accrues to the individual only when it is *acquired by mankind,* and will be enjoyed by him as a member of the human race only when men have *collectively achieved* an ideal form of association;

> (c) that "being subject to scientifically established necessities and to these alone" expresses the meaning of collective freedom only if it is understood that mankind has reached that point in its development where, through putting to social use its knowledge of the inviolable laws of nature and of society, it directs all human affairs solely by reference to these acknowledged necessities.

Like the freedom of self-perfection, collective freedom is acquired, but, unlike the freedom of self-perfection, it is acquired by the human race in the course of its historical development, not by the human person in the course of his individual life. In addition to being acquired, collective freedom is akin to the freedom of self-perfection in that it involves compliance with law or necessity. But it is precisely at this point that they also differ.

According to the self-perfection authors, the moral laws or obligations to which a man should be able to conform in order to be free are *violable.* Since he can either obey or disobey them, his freedom is thought to lie in his being able to comply with them *willingly rather than against his will;* and such voluntarily compliance is thought to stem from his acquired virtue or wisdom. In contrast, according to theories of collective freedom, the scientifically discovered laws of nature and society are *inviolable*. They cannot be disobeyed, but they *can be put to beneficial social use or not*. It is when men, through achieving an ideal form of association, come to govern themselves solely by reference to these acknowledged necessities that they become collectively free.

2. GENERAL AND SPECIAL CONTROVERSIES

Precisely because they are minimal, the topical agreements we have just summarized identify subjects of controversy. Once we go beyond the minimum description that serves to identify each of these freedoms, we find many differences of opinion among the authors who affirm a particular freedom, and also that some authors reject a freedom which other writers affirm, or accept it only with modifications that others would deny. These findings were set forth in Book II and documentary evidence of them was given there.

When we formulate the disputed issues about freedom, we shall find it necessary, in the case of each of the five subjects, to distinguish those issues which constitute the special controversy about it from those issues which belong to the general controversy about the kinds of freedom. Each freedom is, in short, the subject of two quite different kinds of controversy. A brief recapitulation of our classification of theories of freedom will explain why this is so.

If the reader will look back at the lists of authors who are cited in the preceding section as affirming this or that freedom, he will see that some authors appear in one enumeration only, whereas others appear in two or more. This fact gives us the first significant division among all theories of freedom: they are either (i) theories which affirm one and only one of the freedoms we have been able to identify, or (ii) theories which affirm two or more of these freedoms. Each group of theories can be further subdivided in ways that are critically significant for the position which their authors take in the controversies about freedom. It is necessary to say a word about these subdivisions before we summarize our classification of theories.

(i) Theories which affirm one, and only one, of the five freedoms

Not all the writers who affirm one and only one freedom also explicitly deny or reject the others; nor do all explicitly assert of the one freedom which they do affirm that it is man's only freedom. Many of them simply ignore or neglect to discuss freedoms which are affirmed by other writers.

(ii) Theories which affirm two or more of the five freedoms

As in the preceding case, this group of theories must, first of all, be divided into subgroups according to which freedoms are included. There are two further differentiations of great significance here: (a) some writers attribute a number of distinct freedoms to man, whereas others conceive human freedom as a unitary thing, yet as having a number of distinguishable aspects; (b) of those authors who attribute a number of distinct freedoms to man, some affirm them without qualifications of any sort, whereas others find it impossible to combine them without imposing restrictive qualifications on at least one of them.[2]

The classification of theories which follows takes account of all these differentiations except one.[3] It does not indicate, in the case of theories which affirm less than all five freedoms, whether the omitted freedoms are explicitly rejected or simply ignored. However, in the enumeration of authors under each class of theories, an asterisk is placed after the names of those who either maintain that a particular freedom is man's *only* freedom or who explicitly reject one or more of the freedoms which other writers affirm.

Theories which affirm one, and only one, of the five freedoms

A. *Circumstantial Freedom of Self-Realization*
   Ayer,* Bentham,* Edwards,* Hale, Hayek, Hobbes,* Hume,* Kelsen,* Laski,* Macmurray, Malinowski, Mannheim, J. S. Mill,* Nowell-Smith,* Pareto, Priestley,* Schlick,* Spencer, Stevenson,* Tawney, Voltaire*

B. *Acquired Freedom of Self-Perfection*
   Ambrose, Marcus Aurelius, Bosanquet, Bradley,* Epictetus,* Plato,* Plotinus,* Seneca, Spinoza*

C. *Natural Freedom of Self-Determination*
   Bergson, Berkeley, Descartes, Fichte, William James, Lequier, Lucretius, Renouvier, Sartre,* Secrétan, Weiss

D. *Collective Freedom*
   Bakunin,* Comte, Engels,* Marx*

---

[2] In addition, the point that was made with respect to the first group of theories must be repeated here. Writers who affirm less than the five freedoms may not explicitly deny all of the others. They may simply neglect to discuss the rest or, while ignoring some of the freedoms they do not affirm, they may explicitly reject one or more of them.

[3] This classification was presented in Chapter 26 of Book II: see Vol. I, pp. 592–94. It covers only those authors who had been treated in the preceding chapters of Book II. In the course of the present volume, we shall examine the writings of additional authors and also take into account additional research on authors already examined.

Theories which affirm two, and only two, distinct freedoms, without restrictive qualifications on the affirmation of either

E. *Circumstantial Freedom of Self-Realization and Acquired Freedom of Self-Perfection*
   Freud,* Russell*

F. *Natural Freedom of Self-Determination and Circumstantial Freedom of Self-Realization*
   Burke, N. Hartmann, Knight, Adam Smith

G. *Natural Freedom of Self-Determination and Acquired Freedom of Self-Perfection*
   Anselm, Augustine, Barth, Bellarmine, Boethius, Calvin, Cicero,* Duns Scotus, Epicurus, Green, Leibniz, Luther, Maimonides, Marcel, Philo,* Rousseau,* Santayana, Suarez, Tillich, Whitehead

H. *Natural Freedom of Self-Determination and Political Liberty*
   Aristotle*

I. *Circumstantial Freedom of Self-Realization and Political Liberty*
   Hobhouse*

Theories which affirm three, and only three, distinct freedoms, with restrictive qualifications on one of these

J. *Natural Freedom of Self-Determination, Acquired Freedom of Self-Perfection, and Political Liberty*
   Kant*

Theories which affirm four, and only four, distinct freedoms, with restrictive qualifications on one of these

K. *Natural Freedom of Self-Determination, Acquired Freedom of Self-Perfection, Political Liberty, and Circumstantial Freedom of Self-Realization but only as subordinate to and circumscribed by Acquired Freedom of Self-Perfection*
   Aquinas, Locke, Maritain, Montesquieu, Yves Simon

Theories which affirm one human freedom having two or more distinguishable aspects, as follows:

L. *With Natural Freedom of Self-Determination distinguishable from Acquired Freedom of Self-Perfection only in the initial or preparatory phase of freedom's development, but fused with the latter in the terminal or ultimate phase*
   Fouillée, Hegel*

M. *With Natural Freedom of Self-Determination and Circumstantial Freedom of Self-Realization together subordinate to Acquired Freedom of Self-Perfection in freedom's development*
   Dewey

In the light of the foregoing classification, we can now state the criteria by which we shall determine whether authors who disagree are parties to the general controversy about the kinds of freedom or parties to one of the special controversies about a particular freedom.

Let us use the circumstantial freedom of self-realization to exemplify these criteria. Authors who disagree about the circumstantial freedom of self-realization are parties to the special controversy about that freedom (i) if they affirm that freedom and that alone, or (ii) if they affirm it as a distinct freedom even though they also affirm one or more other freedoms. Thus, for example, we shall find such writers as Hobbes, Locke, Hume, Bentham, J. S. Mill, Spencer, Laski, Hobhouse, Tawney, Freud, Russell, Ayer among those who disagree on points at issue in the special controversy about the circumstantial freedom of self-realization.

In contradistinction, disagreements between some of the authors just mentioned and such authors as Aquinas, Locke, Maritain, Montesquieu, and Yves Simon will belong to the general controversy to whatever extent the views of the latter about the circumstantial freedom of self-realization *as subordinate to other freedoms* leads them to deny that the circumstantial freedom of self-realization is unconditionally a human freedom. Since this is precisely what authors such as Hobbes, Hume, Bentham, J. S. Mill, etc. affirm, the two sets of authors are at issue about the kinds of freedom and so are parties to the general controversy.

The illustration we have just employed sets before us an issue in the general controversy on both sides of which we find authors who affirm the circumstantial freedom of self-realization but who nevertheless are in disagreement, because those on the one side affirm it without any restrictive qualifications while those on the other side insist upon such qualifications. Disagreement about the circumstantial freedom of self-realization may also occur between authors who affirm it (with or without restrictive qualifications) and those who reject it entirely as being a false freedom or a counterfeit of freedom (e.g., Plato, Aristotle, Kant, Hegel).

There is still one other type of disagreement which belongs to the general controversy. This can best be illustrated by reference to the natural freedom of self-determination. Here one side of the issue is taken by authors who affirm that freedom exists (e.g., Aquinas, Descartes, Kant, Bergson, William James, Sartre), and the other side by authors who deny its existence (e.g., Hobbes, Spinoza, Edwards, Hume, Priestly, Freud).

From these illustrations we can draw the criteria we shall use to determine whether two authors disagree in a way that makes them parties to the general controversy about the kinds of freedom: (i) if one author unqualifiedly affirms the freedom in question as a genuine human freedom and the other accepts it only with certain restrictive qualifications; (ii) if one author affirms the freedom in question as a genuine, human freedom, either unconditionally or with certain qualifications, and the other rejects it entirely as no freedom at all; (iii) if one author affirms the freedom in question as really existent and the other denies that it has any reality or existence.

3. A UNIFIED SET OF CONTROVERSIES

The foregoing section explains why we have projected five special controversies, each centering on a particular freedom, and one general controversy about the kinds of freedom. We have also seen the conditions under which each of the freedoms which is a subject of special controversy may also be a subject in the general controversy, i.e., when authors give contrary answers to such questions as whether or not it is genuinely a human freedom or one that has real existence. But if the five special controversies whose subjects we have identified have nothing in common except the name "freedom," we have little reason to associate them as members of a unified set of controversies. Furthermore, the diverse theories we have classified cannot be regarded as offering conflicting views about the kinds of freedom unless the five subjects, each of which may be defended or challenged as a *kind*, have something more in common than the name "freedom."

We faced this problem at the end of Book II. We saw there that its solution depended on our being able to give an answer to the following question: "What is that generic meaning or general understanding which is common to all the authors who write about a subject they call 'freedom' and whose theories involve one or more of the subjects we have been able to identify?" The solution we proposed can be briefly summarized here.[4]

Self and *other*, we found, are the basic common terms in the general understanding of freedom. These terms are present in the understanding of self-realization, self-perfection, and self-determination, as well as in the understanding of political liberty as a variant of self-realization and collective freedom as a variant of self-perfection. But in each of these, *self* and *other* are differently specified: each involves a different mode of *self* and a different *other* as the opponent of its freedom. In each the *ability to act in a certain way*, which is present in all conceptions of freedom, is differently specified as the power whereby *the self is exempt from the power of another*.

In every conception of freedom, we pointed out, the free act is that which proceeds from the self, in contrast to such behavior on a man's part

[4] For the reasons and documentary evidence that support this solution, see Vol. I, pp. 601–20.

which is somehow the product of another. It is *his own act* and the result it achieves is a *property of his self*—the realization of his self, the perfection of his self, the determination or creation of his self. A man lacks freedom to whatever extent he is passively affected, or subject to an alien power, the power of another rather than his own. In every conception of freedom, the self is the principle of freedom through possessing the power to be actively the source of whatever kind of activity is thought to manifest human freedom.

Let us recall the descriptive formulas by which we identified the three freedoms that are the main subjects of controversy. What is common to all conceptions of the freedom of self-realization can be expressed as follows: *a man is free who is able, under favorable circumstances, to act as he wishes for his own individual good as he sees it.* What is common to all conceptions of the freedom of self-perfection can be expressed as follows: *a man is free who is able, through acquired virtue or wisdom, to will or live as he ought in conformity to the moral law or an ideal befitting human nature.* What is common to all conceptions of the freedom of self-determination can be expressed as follows: *a man is free who is able, by a power inherent in human nature, to change his own character creatively by deciding for himself what he shall do or become.*

A descriptive formula for identifying freedom in general would obviously have to be indeterminate enough to allow for all the specifications introduced by the foregoing identifications of self-realization, self-perfection, and self-determination; and it would also have to be determinate enough to express what is common to all conceptions of human freedom. The required formulation can be stated as follows: *a man is free who has in himself the ability or power to make what he does his own action and what he achieves his own property.*

Chapter 2

THE CONSTRUCTION
OF THE CONTROVERSIES

In Volume I we outlined the problems to be solved in developing and testing our dialectical hypothesis about the controversies concerning freedom.[1] In accord with our hypothesis that the discussion of freedom involves a number of distinct but unrelated controversies, we enumerated the following problems to be solved in developing that hypothesis in detail:

(1) to identify the distinct freedoms which are the subjects of special controversies
(2) to identify the subject of the general controversy about the kinds of freedom, i.e., freedom in general
(3) to formulate the questions which raise the issues that constitute the controversies about each of these subjects
(4) to formulate the positions taken on each issue, together with the arguments pro and con that constitute the debate of these issues
(5) to describe the form or structure of each controversy by reference to the ways in which its constituent issues and arguments are related

As the reader can see from the summary of Book II given in the preceding chapter, we have completed only the first two tasks. A certain number of disagreements or issues were necessarily foreshadowed in our exposition of the differences of opinion underlying which we discovered the minimal topical agreements. Such foreshadowing prepared the ground for the construction of the issues and the controversies in Book III. The last three problems mentioned above remain to be solved and are the tasks we shall undertake in the present book.

To pass from the identification of a subject of controversy to the construction of the disagreements or issues about that subject requires, first of all, going beyond a *minimal* topical agreement to what we have called *complete* topical agreement. The difference between these two degrees of topical agreement is as follows: two men who agree about the identification of a subject under discussion are in *minimal* topical agreement; if, in

[1] See Vol. I, p. 52.

addition, they agree about a question to be answered concerning that subject (i.e., if they share a common understanding of the question), then they are in *complete* topical agreement. If, beyond this, they agree about the answer to that question, this further agreement is *categorical*, not topical, since, unlike agreement about the subject or the question, it involves them in the assertion of a position or view which they claim to be sound or true. Should they give contrary or contradictory answers to the agreed-upon question, they are in categorical disagreement; for then the claim each makes for the truth of his own position involves him in denying the truth of the view held by the other.[2]

The construction of issues obviously involves three steps, of which only the first has been accomplished: (i) establishing minimal topical agreement through identification of the subject; (ii) establishing complete topical agreement through the formulation of one or more commonly understood questions about that subject; (iii) establishing categorical disagreement by stating two or more incompatible answers to each question, i.e., the conflicting positions which have been taken on each issue. If more than two authors are parties to an issue, an additional step may be necessary —the establishment of the categorical agreement which obtains among those who stand together on each of the several sides of the issue.

If, by the foregoing steps, we do no more than construct a set of issues having a common subject, we have done the very minimum that is required to set forth the controversy about that subject. We can go beyond that minimum only to the extent that we are able to formulate the arguments pro and con that constitute the debate of the issues and are able to relate the issues to one another in order to exhibit the form of the controversy.[3]

The problems we shall try to solve in this book, and the steps we shall take, should now be clear. By way of introduction to the chapters which follow, it remains only to indicate some of the difficulties we shall meet with in our effort to make clear and explicit the controversies which are present, for the most part in an implicit fashion, in the literature on freedom. But before we mention the difficulties involved in constructing issues and establishing agreements and disagreements on the basis of the concurrent and divergent opinions to be found in the literature, it is necessary to explain briefly what we mean by "constructing" issues and "establishing" agreements and disagreements.

The easiest way to do this is perhaps by reference to the dialectical constructions which were completed in Book II, i.e., the identifications of the subjects of controversy. What was said about those constructions will apply to the constructions that remain to be made.

---

[2] See Vol. I, pp. 10–17.
[3] See Vol. I, pp. 32–35.

In saying of the descriptive formula which we employed to identify the circumstantial freedom of self-realization that it was *our own* dialectical construction, we stressed two points: (i) that it was stated in the strictly neutral language which we had devised for this purpose, rather than in the doctrinal language of this or that author, and consequently (ii) that, as expressed by us, it could not be found in the literature on freedom. In speaking of this identifying formulation as expressing a minimal topical agreement which could be established as obtaining for a certain group of authors, we had three further points in mind: (a) that it was based on what this group of authors actually said about freedom, being drawn therefrom by a process of discerning common elements in their diverse opinions; (b) that its neutrality made it unprejudicial to the views of any of the authors concerned; and consequently (c) that our constructed identification *would be* or *would have been* acceptable to them. Finally, we pointed out that in referring to this construction or any other dialectical formulation as hypothetical (or as a part of our whole dialectical hypothesis about the discussion of freedom), we were, in effect, inviting the reader to test its correctness by reference to the literature from which it was derived.[4]

Let us apply what has just been said to the dialectical construction of an issue about circumstantial freedom. If two authors whom we have found to be in minimal topical agreement about this subject explicitly formulate a particular question about this freedom and, addressing themselves to this question commonly understood by both, give incompatible answers to it, we can simply *report* the issue and their disagreement about it. But if they do not thus explicitly join issue and disagree by giving opposite answers to the same question, then it may still be possible to *construe* them as joining issue and as being in disagreement if, implicit in their expressed views, we can find ground for interpreting the positions they hold on freedom as answering the same question and answering it in opposite ways. Then, instead of reporting the issue as one which can be explicitly found in the literature, we will be constructing it on the basis of what is only implicitly there.

To do that, we will, of course, have to construe what the authors mean from what they say. In the light of such interpretation, we will have to formulate the question at issue in our own neutral language. We will also have to formulate the answers that are given to it, each, perhaps, shared

[4] See Vol. I, p. 49. For the whole treatment of dialectical constructions as hypotheses drawn from "data" in the form of the actual writings on freedom, and tested by reference to this body of materials, see *ibid.*, pp. 46–51 and 98–105. For the part played by a neutral language in the making of dialectical constructions, see *ibid.*, pp. 65–68.

by a number of authors who express that position each in his own language and style. The construction of the issue will thus represent construed agreements and disagreements—construed topical agreement on the question and construed categorical disagreement or agreement about the answers to the question.

To present this construction as a sound hypothesis is to claim that we have correctly interpreted the documentary evidence offered in its support. This, of course, is open to challenge or criticism. If we were reporting the issue as one actually and explicitly joined in the literature, direct quotation could completely substantiate the matter.

Compared with reporting, constructing is a creative process. To the extent that controversies exist implicitly in the literature on freedom, they take the explicit form we as dialecticians shall try to give them only as, drawing on these materials, we recreate them in the formulations that we are able to construct. Yet, as we have pointed out, these constructions are not pure fictions,

> for each has merit only insofar as it is faithful to the original materials and is certifiable by reference to what writers have explicitly said about freedom. Just as a portrait painter aims to present a likeness which is not only faithful to the original but also reveals the innermost character of his subject, so the dialectician should try to portray a discussion, like that of freedom, with fidelity to what is explicitly said, but in a way that also most fully and clearly exhibits the intellectual structure of all the implicit controversies.[5]

Let us now consider some of the difficulties to be faced in trying to construct issues and, beyond that, the debate which is the heart of controversy.

1 . THE FORMULATION OF QUESTIONS AT ISSUE

The first difficulty to be overcome in constructing the issues that are only implicitly present in the literature is for the most part obviated by the minimal topical agreements we have established through the identification of the several subjects under discussion.

This can be strikingly illustrated in the following manner. Anyone examining the analytical index to Book II will find, for example, that, in enumerating Ayer's views about freedom, the phrase "consistent with causal necessity" is employed, whereas, in enumerating the views of Aquinas, the phrase "inconsistent with causal necessity" is used. The phrases obvi-

[5] Vol. I, p. 35.

ously express contrary or conflicting views. It might be thought, therefore, that Ayer and Aquinas are opposed on an issue about freedom which could be formulated by the question, "Is freedom consistent with causal necessity?" But in fact Ayer and Aquinas do not join issue.

Looking more closely at the index, we find that Ayer's affirmation of the compatibility of freedom and causal necessity has for its subject the circumstantial freedom of self-realization, whereas the subject of Aquinas's denial of the compatibility of freedom and causal necessity is the natural freedom of self-determination. Since the two authors are considering different subjects, they are not even in minimal topical agreement, and so cannot be in the complete topical agreement which is prerequisite to genuine disagreement. There are, thus, two questions here, not one. Ayer is answering the question, "Is the freedom of self-realization consistent with causal necessity?" and Aquinas the question, "Is the freedom of self-determination consistent with causal necessity?" The fact that Ayer answers *his* question affirmatively and Aquinas *his* question negatively does not bring them into real disagreement.

The disagreement which we might have supposed to exist between Ayer and Aquinas was apparent, not real. That these authors hold different opinions about freedom is plain enough; but to constitute a real disagreement, their differences must be about the same subject. Further study will reveal that the difference of opinion before us does involve a genuine disagreement. But the precise shape which the real issue takes is concealed rather than revealed by the question, "Is freedom consistent with causal necessity?"

As we shall see in a later chapter, the question on which Ayer and Aquinas take opposite sides might be stated as follows: "Does the natural freedom of self-determination have existence?" Aquinas answers affirmatively, Ayer negatively. Their opinions about freedom and causal necessity point to what might be the reasons for their opposed answers: Ayer denies the existence of the freedom of self-determination because it involves exemption from causal necessity precisely because such exemption is required for the existence of such freedom, while Aquinas does not find that requirement an obstacle to affirming its existence.

The foregoing illustration shows us two things: first, the importance of identifying the subjects being considered by authors whose differences of opinion make them appear to disagree; and second, the importance of formulating the question in such a way as to disclose a real disagreement between the authors, *if one is implicit in their differences of opinion.* We saw that the question, "Is freedom consistent with causal necessity?" failed to do this because of the ambiguity of the word "freedom." Nor will it do to ask, "Is there any kind of freedom that is consistent with causal necessity?" This question would give rise to no issue between Aquinas and Ayer, for Aquinas might also answer this question affirmatively if he had the freedom of self-realization in mind. Hence, to bring out the real issue between them, the question must specify the same subject for both (i.e., the freedom of self-determination); and about that same subject, it must make the issue hinge on a point which both authors understand in the same way, which in this case is the real existence of such freedom.

Since the identifications we have constructed and the minimal topical agreements we have established in Book II enable us to overcome the first difficulty in the way of formulating the genuine issues which are implicit in differences of opinion about freedom, let us turn to the second difficulty —one that we shall encounter in the chapters to follow. It has to do with the question that raises an issue about a given subject.

In order to be able to establish the complete topical agreement that is necessary for the formation of an issue, we must be able to present documentary evidence that authors, whom we suppose to be in disagreement from the ways in which they differ, are addressing themselves to the same question about a given subject. But except for those instances in which the authors themselves explicitly joined issue (in which cases, of course, we have no problem of construction), such documentary evidence is not available in direct form. Whenever the issues we are trying to construct are merely implicit in the literature (as is usually the case), we seldom find questions about freedom formulated in such a way as to provide direct evidence that a number of authors are facing one and the same question about a given subject.

What we find on the surface by comparing the writings of authors who differ are mainly different opinions about freedom, different views, different theories, different arguments, usually expressed in vocabularies or idioms characteristically different for each author; and we find such differences in language even when we compare authors who express similar views and who, we therefore suspect, may be in doctrinal agreement. Nevertheless, we have found it possible to quote the actual language in which the authors express their apparently similar or different opinions as evidence for inferring their minimal topical agreement on one or another of the identifying formulas, couched in our own neutral language. In other words, by calling attention to the common elements in a number of differing views about freedom, or even similar views expressed in differing terminologies, we can point to a common understanding underlying the expressed differences, state it neutrally, and use it to identify the common subject of the various views considered.

Let us now suppose that we have found a number of authors who are in minimal topical agreement about a common subject, i.e., one of the identified freedoms. Since we do not find them all explicitly asking the same questions about this freedom, how can we infer from what they do say that certain of them face, at least implicitly, a question which they commonly understand, no matter how they answer it? Or to put the matter another way: if, in the light of what they do say, we formulate a question which we think they are, at least implicitly, facing and understanding in the same way, what documentary evidence can we offer to establish their complete topical agreement?

An actual example will help to explain our solution of this difficulty.

In the analytical index to Book II, a number of authors are recorded as holding apparently opposed positions about the freedom of self-realization, a freedom all these authors affirm. Thus, to take the clearest examples first, we find, in the case of Hobbes, the view that self-realization is "consistent with fear," whereas, in the case of Tawney, we find the view that it is "inconsistent with fear." If we were to turn to the pages of Book II to which the index refers us on these points, we should find a quoted statement by Hobbes and a quoted statement by Tawney which verbatim express these opposite opinions.[6]

Little if any interpretation is required to construe these opposite statements as conflicting answers to the question, "Is the freedom of self-realization consistent or compatible with fear?" That question is our construction *only* in the sense that we impute it to Hobbes and Tawney in virtue of interpreting the statements they make as answers to it. The question as formulated is not explicitly found in their writings.

The problem of interpretation is only slightly more difficult if we consider the views of other writers and attempt to construe them as answers to a question about the effect of fear upon a man's being able to do as he wishes. Thus, for example, we find Sidgwick writing that while freedom "signifies primarily the absence of physical coercion or confinement," nevertheless, "in another part of its meaning . . . 'freedom' is opposed not to physical constraint, but to the moral restraint placed on inclination by the fear of painful consequences resulting from the actions of other human beings."[7] And Schlick regards the individual who is forced "at the point of a gun to do what otherwise he would not do" as a man who suffers loss of freedom under compulsion as much as the man who "is

---

[6] Hobbes says flatly that "fear and liberty are consistent: as when a man throws his goods into the sea for *fear* the ship should sink, he doth it nevertheless very willingly, and may refuse to do it if he will; it is, therefore, the action of one that was *free*" (*Leviathan*, Part II, Ch. 21, p. 162). Tawney's opposite statement is equally explicit on the point: "Of all emotions the most degrading and the least compatible with freedom is fear" ("We Mean Freedom" in *The Attack and Other Papers*, p. 90).
[7] *Elements of Politics*, p. 45.

locked up, or chained."[8] Hence these authors can also be construed as giving, with Tawney, negative answers to the question, "Is freedom of self-realization consistent or compatible with fear?"

But in the following instances we are confronted with statements that require more extensive interpretation. Can we regard Jonathan Edwards as facing the question that we have formulated and giving an affirmative answer to it, on the basis of the following passage? Having said that a man's "power and opportunity . . . to do . . . as he will, or according to his choice, is all that is meant by [liberty]," Edwards declares that no consideration at all need be given to "the cause or original of that choice; or . . . how the person came to have such a volition."[9] And, on the opposite side, can we regard Knight as giving a negative answer to the same question on the basis of his statement that freedom "refers negatively to the absence of some more or less abnormal interference with acting in some normal way in which the individual would otherwise be able, would possess the power, to act."[10]

In order to construe Edwards as facing and answering the question we have formulated, we have to interpret him in the following manner. We must assume that Edwards would acknowledge that fear may cause a man's volition or decision to act in a certain way. But he says that a man is free if he is able to carry out his volition or choice, *no matter what its "cause or origin."* Does it not follow that Edwards would say that a man is free if he is able to carry out his volition or choice, *even when it is caused by fear?* Are we not justified then, in interpreting Edwards as in doctrinal agreement with Hobbes on the point that a man is free when no external impediment prevents him from executing whatever desire happens to be dominant at the moment, no matter how it becomes dominant? If so, it would seem fair to interpret Edwards as standing with Hobbes on the affirmative side of the issue raised by the question, "Is the freedom of self-realization consistent with fear?" even though Edwards nowhere explicitly discusses the effect of fear on a man's freedom to do as he wishes.

A similar process of interpretation is involved in construing Knight as facing that question and giving an answer that places him on the negative side along with Tawney and Schlick. Here we must assume that Knight would regard fear (i.e., the fear at "the point of a gun" which, as Schlick

[8] *Problems of Ethics,* p. 150.
[9] *Freedom of the Will,* p. 164.
[10] "The Meaning of Freedom" in *The Philosophy of American Democracy,* p. 64. Cf. also the statement made by the University of California Associates in Philosophy: "A man's acts are voluntary or free when they are determined by his own desires, motives, or intentions; they are involuntary or constrained when they are determined by desires, motives, or intentions other than his own" (*Knowledge and Society,* p. 238).

says, forces a man "to do what he otherwise would not do") as a "more or less abnormal interference with acting in some normal way in which the individual would otherwise be able . . . to act." Since Knight holds that freedom, at least negatively, consists in the absence of such interference, it would seem fair to interpret him as standing on the negative side of the issue raised by the question, "Is the freedom of self-realization consistent with fear?" even though Knight, like Edwards, nowhere explicitly discusses the effect of fear on such freedom.[11]

The foregoing illustrative instances enable us to distinguish three degrees of interpretation involved in the construction of questions at issue. They are as follows:

(i) The language of the authors (e.g., Hobbes, Tawney) is such that the question formulated does no more than put into interrogative form the *very words* used declaratively by the writers themselves. Thus, Hobbes says that "fear and liberty are consistent" and Tawney that "of all emotions . . . the least compatible with freedom is fear." The question, "Is freedom consistent or compatible with fear?" uses those very words. That question is, therefore, a construction *only* in the sense that we, not they, have phrased it as a question. In the light of their declarations we have also construed them as being in topical agreement about it, as well as in topical agreement about the identification of the freedom in question.[12]

(ii) The language of the authors (e.g., Sidgwick, Schlick) is such that it is necessary to interpret the *intent* of their declarations if we are to construe them as facing and answering the question we have formulated. As we have seen, this step of interpretation may be very slight. Sidgwick says that freedom is "opposed" to "the moral restraint placed on inclination by fear"; and Schlick offers us the example of a man who is forced to do something at gun point by the fear aroused in him, and says of such a man that he is deprived of freedom. While the *words* these writers use are not identical with those of Tawney, nor with the words of the question we have formulated, their *direct intent* seems to be the same. On the basis of their intent, rather than their actual words, we can construe them as facing and answering the question, "Is the freedom of self-realization consistent or compatible with fear?"

---

[11] The statement by the University of California Associates in Philosophy, quoted in fn. 10, *supra*, permits a similar interpretation. In that case, we need only assume that, according to their view, if a man acts at the point of a gun, his act is not determined by his own desires, motives, or intentions, but rather by those of the man who is pointing the gun.

[12] The documentary evidence that these authors are talking about the freedom of self-realization and that alone has been given in Book II and need not be repeated here.

(iii) The language of the authors (e.g., Edwards, Knight) is such that it is necessary to discern *implications* of the intent of what they actually say. This may involve, as we have seen, making certain assumptions about what they would say, such as the assumption, in the case of Edwards, that he would acknowledge that the fear induced by a gun may cause a man's will to act in a certain way; or the assumption, in the case of Knight, that he would regard such fear as a more or less abnormal interference with acting in some normal way in which the individual would otherwise be able to act. These are hardly violent assumptions. In the light of them, we can draw from the actual statements made by Edwards and Knight their *implied* views on the point in question. Here the question we construe them as facing and answering in opposite ways is furthest from the actual words they use and cannot be derived from the *intent* of those words, but only from views which we can attribute to them on the basis of what the intent of their remarks implies.

In the construction of questions at issue, we shall sometimes, as in the case before us, confront documentary materials which involve us in all three degrees of interpretation. But sometimes we shall be involved in only the latter two, and sometimes in only the third. In these cases, the difficulty of making the construction is increased by the total absence of documentary materials whose *actual language* can be employed in the formulation of the question. This is especially true of the cases in which we do not even have language where *direct intent* justifies our construction.

There are several other sources of difficulty which complicate the problem of construction. Ayer, for example, is an author who, like Schlick, affords us passages the direct intent of which warrants our construing him as standing with Schlick on the negative side of the question, "Is freedom consistent with fear?" But these passages also reveal that Ayer is concerned not only with the kind of fear which is induced by threatening external circumstances but also with neurotic anxieties which are not immediately aroused by external events.[13] Hence, what Ayer means by "fear" is not in all cases identical with what Schlick, Hobbes, and others mean by "fear" when they refer to cases in which external circumstances induce a man to act or not act in a certain way through the fear they directly arouse. This necessitates a more precise formulation of the question, as follows: "Are external circumstances of the sort which induce fear (with regard to acting or not acting in a certain way) in the class of circumstances that are unfavorable to the freedom of self-realization?" Or, perhaps, as follows: "Is the individual who acts in a certain way, from circumstantially induced

---

[13] See "Freedom and Necessity" in *Philosophical Essays*, pp. 279, 281. Cf. our discussion of Ayer's views in Vol. I, pp. 119–20 and 207.

fear, acting freely, i.e., doing as he wishes for his own individual good as he sees it?"

Our choice of the latter formulations would, in this particular case, be dictated by the desirability of making the point at issue clear, unambiguous, and explicit, in a neutral and unprejudicial phrasing, while including no more in the question than is warranted by the opposing views. In simpler cases, there may be nothing decisive at stake in this matter of alternative formulations of the question. But in more complicated cases, additional criteria may become decisive.

One way of phrasing the question may enable us to formulate a many-sided issue in which three or more affirmative answers, each incompatible with the others, constitute the conflicting positions, instead of a two-sided issue in which the sides are constituted by a single affirmative and a single negative answer.

If the reader will look back at the classification of theories presented in Chapter 1, he will see that there are three positions on the question whether circumstantial self-realization is genuinely a human freedom: (i) the position of Hobbes and Hume, (ii) the position of Aquinas and Locke, (iii) the position of Plato and Kant. The question at issue here can therefore be formulated in three ways.

(a) "Is circumstantial self-realization unqualifiedly a human freedom?" In this case, Hobbes and Hume would answer affirmatively and Aquinas and Locke, together with Plato and Kant, would answer negatively.

(b) "Is circumstantial self-realization, with or without certain restrictive qualifications, a human freedom?" In this case, Aquinas and Locke, together with Hobbes and Hume, would answer affirmatively and Plato and Kant negatively.

(c) "Under what conditions is circumstantial self-realization a human freedom?" In this case, Hobbes and Hume would give one answer (i.e., under all conditions); Aquinas and Locke would give another (i.e., only under certain conditions); and Plato and Kant would give a third (i.e., under no conditions).

What dictates the choice among these alternative formulations of the question? In the case before us, the third formulation will prove to be the most satisfactory because it enables us to reveal all of the doctrinal agreements and disagreements instead of leaving some of them concealed. Here one way of formulating the question is more clarifying than the rest, as well as more faithful to the documentary materials from which the construction must be derived. But, in other cases, resorting to a number of alternative formulations may be the most satisfactory solution.

One further source of ·difficulty remains to be considered. We some-times find that authors are completely silent on matters about which we suspect that their theories might have led them to take a position contrary to that taken by other writers. The problem we face is particularly trouble-some when the views of certain authors plainly indicate a position on freedom which could be one side of a possible issue. The total absence of authors who can be construed as taking the opposite side leaves the issue a merely possible one. It is not even implicitly present in the literature. If we were to construct it, we would have to fill the lacunae by imagining what might have been thought, instead of by interpreting what has been said.

In such cases, the temptation is strong to imagine how authors, mostly in the inaccessible past, would have stood on questions which they give no evidence of facing, even by implication. But we have decided that it is not our business to provide authors with reasonable answers to questions they failed to consider and answer. To do so, we explained in Book I,

> would be to substitute the role of the philosopher for that of the dialec-tician. The dialectician cannot furnish missing answers unless they are clearly implied by what the authors explicitly said. He must resist the temp-tation to go beyond the data and to imagine what he cannot construct as part of his hypothesis. He must allow the controversy to remain fragmen-tary and even unreasoned at certain points if that is the way the actual discussion left it.

On the other hand, we also pointed out that

> the limitations the dialectician's method imposes upon him do not pre-vent him from criticizing the controversy he constructs. There is no reason why he cannot expose its weaknesses and blemishes. In fact it is his duty to do precisely that, so far as it can be done without forsaking dialectical neutrality and without judging the truth or falsity of any of the philosoph-ical positions represented in the controversy. . . . He has done his part when he has constructed the controversies that most adequately and faith-. fully represent what was implicit in the whole discussion of a basic idea.[14]

The difficulty just referred to is more frequently encountered in the task of constructing the debate of issues than in that of formulating the issues themselves. But what the dialectician can do when faced with lacunae in the dispute remains very much the same.

[14] See Vol. I, pp. 50–51. "If such controversies are deficient in any respect," then, in our view, "the work of improving them must be done by others. We believe that if the dialectical work has been well done at a given time the philosophers of sub-sequent generations will thereby be both stimulated and prepared to carry the dis-cussion forward with somewhat more clarity and with a little better chance of reaching the truth" (*ibid.*, p. 51).

2. THE CONSTRUCTION OF THE DEBATE

There are a number of issues with respect to which the literature provides us with instances of authors who actually engaged in debate with one another. For example, we have the recorded disputation between Hobbes and Bishop Bramhall, the correspondence of Priestley and Price, and the interchange between Campbell and Nowell-Smith which has appeared in current journals. In these we find not only arguments for opposite sides of the issue about the real existence of a natural freedom of self-determination but also replies to arguments in the contrary tenor.

This does not relieve us of the task of having to construct this issue and its debate, since it is necessary to construe, in the case of many authors who appear to be involved, the question they are addressing themselves to, the positions they take, and above all the arguments they advance in support or defense of that position. But it does provide us with a model or standard by which to measure the completeness or adequacy of that part of the controversy which is not explicit in the literature, but must be constructed by us from what is implicitly there.

Judged by that standard, there are a great many issues which fall far short of what one might expect in the way of argument or disputation. In the general controversy, for example, on the issues concerning the freedom of self-realization and the freedom of self-perfection, we shall find little or no debate explicitly afforded by actual interchanges between those whom we construe as taking opposite sides by virtue of their views on the genuineness or reality of the freedom in question. Furthermore, the documentary materials will enable us to construe mainly, if not exclusively, arguments *against* self-realization or *against* self-perfection as a kind of freedom, but they will not enble us to construe arguments in reply, defending a particular freedom against such attacks, nor even, in many cases, positive arguments in support of it. Those who affirm it appear to assume that its reality or genuineness as a kind of freedom is unquestionable or unquestioned, and so there is no need to give reasons for affirming it.[15]

These lacunae do not affect the authenticity or clarity of the particular issue at the level of opposed assertions and denials, but they leave it regrettably incomplete and lopsided at the level of argumentation where one would hope that the parties on each side would give reasons for what they assert, reasons for denying what their opponents assert, and reasoned replies to the objections offered by their opponents.

[15] The state of the general controversy is even weaker on the side of debate with regard to the two special variants—political liberty and collective freedom.

Where there is documentary evidence of argumentation on one or another side of an issue, the problem of constructing the debate so far as it exists in the literature (explicitly or implicitly) does not differ from the problem of constructing the issue itself. Here as before, we encounter documentary materials which require more or less extensive interpretation on our part. The three degrees of interpretation that were enumerated above also represent the order of difficulties to be surmounted in the task of construing authors as arguing for a position, defending it against attack, or attacking the position of their opponents. In order to construct the debate, we must usually engage in extensive interpretation of the documentary materials and develop a series of implications from what we interpret to be the direct intent of actual statements. Here, much less frequently than in the case of constructing questions at issue, we can rely simply on what the authors actually said or on the readily interpreted direct intent of their remarks.

In each of the special controversies about one of the five freedoms, we shall find no signs of even implicit debate with regard to some of the issues that we are able to construct. While the actually expressed views of the authors enable us to construe them as taking opposite sides on certain questions, there is no evidence at all of argumentation on either side.

One explanation of this may be that the issue is merely verbal in the following sense. Each side on a question (let us say, about whether the freedom of self-realization should be conceived in one way or another) may regard its answer as asserting no more than that the way it advocates using the word "freedom" represents the way in which the word "freedom" is ordinarily or customarily used. It may be thought by each side that the common usage is so obvious that nothing more need be said. In other instances, the issue may be verbal in the sense that each side simply asserts that its position on the question represents the only right or proper way to use the word "freedom."

When debate is totally lacking on an issue, i.e., when no reasons are advanced on either side, we shall be obliged to decide whether we are dealing with a verbal issue in either of the senses indicated above or are dealing with an issue that could have been debated on grounds other than established or preferred usage, but was not. In some cases, it may be extremely difficult or even impossible to tell which is the case.

In general, our task is to report the debate so far as it exists explicitly in actual interchanges, to construct it to whatever extent it can be drawn by interpretation from documentary materials in which it is implicitly present, and to point out the lacunae—the unrealized possibilities in each controversy.

In carrying out this task, we shall proceed as follows. In Part II, we shall construct the general controversy about the kinds of freedom, dealing in successive chapters with questions at issue about each of the five freedoms. In Part III, we shall construct the special controversies, each of which centers on one of these freedoms.

PART II

The General Controversy

Chapter 3

THE KINDS OF FREEDOM

The controlling question in the general controversy concerns the kinds of freedom. The classification of theories summarized in Chapter 1 has already shown us how the major authors are divided on this matter. Some maintain that there is only one kind of freedom—that one or another of the freedoms which we have been able to identify is man's only freedom. Others maintain that two or more quite distinct freedoms can be attributed to man; and they differ, of course, with regard to the freedoms they include in their enumeration. And still others maintain that while freedom is a unitary thing, it nevertheless has several distinguishable aspects; and these often differ with regard to the aspects they distinguish.

One other difference divides those who affirm two or more distinct freedoms or distinguishable aspects of freedom: For some, each of the kinds or aspects may be thought of as independent or unaffected by its relation to other freedoms. For others, one kind or aspect may be thought of as subordinate to another or otherwise affected by its relation to that other. The subordinate kind or aspect will be affirmed by such authors only with certain restrictive qualifications that are not admitted by writers who affirm the freedom in question as man's only freedom or who regard it as independent of other freedoms or aspects of freedom.

When all these differences are taken into account, we have thirteen different answers to the question about the kinds or aspects of freedom.[1] If we were to use some formulation of that question to construct a single

[1] See Vol. I, pp. 596 ff.

issue, the general controversy about human freedom might consist of one issue involving thirteen sides, each one opposed to all the rest. But while this might be done, the complexity of the issue would defeat rather than serve the purpose of clarifying the many-sided dispute about the kinds of freedom.

We propose, therefore, to break that complex issue up into a number of simpler issues, each about a particular freedom that certain authors affirm and others reject as a distinct kind or aspect of freedom. In addition, with respect to a particular freedom, we may find it necessary to construct not one issue, but several, in order to separate the question about the real existence of a freedom from the question about its genuineness.

This difference in the questions at issue led us to distinguish, in Book I, between what we called "existential" and "conceptual" issues in the general controversy.[2]

In existential issues, the conception of the freedom in question is involved to the extent that it stipulates one or more elements which must have reality in human life—in the physical, psychological, or moral order—if the freedom thus conceived is to have real existence. The existential rejection of the particular freedom turns on denying the existence of one or more of these elements, the reality of which is asserted, and sometimes argued or defended, by those who take the opposite side.

In conceptual issues, the conception of the freedom in question is itself directly attacked. The reality of the elements it stipulates may be conceded by the adverse party who, nevertheless, takes the position that what is thus conceived does not conform to the general idea of human freedom. It is maintained that what is called "freedom" is not freedom at all, but a counterfeit of it. Here the opposite position must be that it is a genuine freedom, properly conceived according to the general understanding of freedom in human life. It is in this way that the generic idea of freedom enters into the general controversy and is, in a sense, its ultimate subject.

There are special logical problems to be solved in the construction of each type of issue, but consideration of them can be postponed until we are dealing with the materials to which they are germane. With regard to certain subjects, such as the circumstantial freedom of self-realization, we shall find a basis in the literature for constructing only conceptual issues. With regard to other subjects, such as the natural freedom of self-determination, both existential and conceptual issues arise.

The successive chapters of Part II will attempt to set forth all the issues, of either type, which are supportable by documentary evidence and which, taken together, constitute the whole controversy about the kinds of free-

[2] See Vol. I, pp. 28–30. Cf. *ibid.*, p. 598.

dom. Where these issues are disputed, we shall set forth the debate. In some cases, we shall call attention to merely possible issues, and also to the possibilities of debate which have not been realized.

We shall treat the subjects of the general controversy in the following order: Chapter 4, circumstantial self-realization; Chapter 5, acquired self-perfection; Chapter 6, political liberty; Chapter 7, collective freedom; and Chapters 8–12, natural self-determination.

Chapter 4

THE ISSUE CONCERNING THE
FREEDOM OF SELF-REALIZATION

There is no existential issue about the circumstantial freedom of self-realization. We have found no author who challenges its reality.

To readers who are considering this matter for the first time, it might also seem to be unquestionable that being able to do as one wills or wishes is genuinely freedom. While it might not appear equally obvious to them that this is man's only freedom (which, as we have seen, a large number of authors maintain), they might reasonably wonder how anyone could doubt that it is at least one of the freedoms which men normally want as much of as possible. Is it not the freedom that almost every child feels deprived of under parental regulation? Is it not the freedom that is taken away from the prisoner behind bars or from the slave who must do what another man wills? And when we think of the emancipation of children, prisoners, or slaves, is it not this freedom that we think of as being restored?

To these questions, the common-sense or everyday usage of the word "freedom" would appear to require an unqualifiedly affirmative answer. As that word is ordinarily used, it certainly connotes the absence of coercion, constraint, or other external interference that tends to prevent the individual from doing as he himself wishes. It would, therefore, appear to be farfetched or even preposterous to say that the meaning of the word in its most widely accepted usage is completely mistaken—that, in short, most people who use the word "freedom" in this ordinary sense are simply not speaking of freedom at all but of something else.

The same judgment might be made by readers who have become acquainted with the generic meaning of the word "freedom," i.e., the meaning which underlies or is common to all other meanings, whether manifested in the recondite conceptions of the philosophers or in our common-sense notions. That generic meaning, we have seen, can be expressed as follows: *a man is free who has in himself the ability or power to make what he does his own action and what he achieves his own property*. It certainly says that a man is free in those acts which proceed from himself instead of from another.[1] How, then, can anyone say that doing as one pleases or realizing one's own desires is not genuinely freedom— or not even a kind of freedom?

The prior question is, of course, *Does anyone?* Have we found any major writers who maintain that circumstantial self-realization is not a human freedom at all, nor any part of human freedom? Superficial evidence for the immediate affirmative answer might be summoned by reminding the reader of authors who distinguish between liberty and license and who, in the light of that distinction, call doing as one pleases license rather than liberty.

Unfortunately, the word "license," like the word "freedom" itself, is used in many ways. Some writers who hold that doing as one pleases is genuinely human freedom, or even man's only freedom, nevertheless use the word "license" for a part of such freedom—that part which, in their opinion, society would be justified in taking away from its members. Other writers, on the contrary, deny that men are ever free by virtue of being able to do as they please and use the word "license" to signify what they regard as an entirely false conception of freedom. There are, in addition, authors who appear to take a middle ground between these extremes. For them, acting as one wishes in contravention of the moral or civil law is license or a counterfeit of freedom, but in matters on which the law is silent, a man's true freedom consists in being able to do as he pleases.

Before we attempt to construct the issue that involves these three points of view, let us examine a representative sampling of the documentary evidence which most plainly points to the existence of this issue in the literature on freedom. In the course of doing this, certain preliminary clarification of language and thought can be achieved.

1. LIBERTY AND LICENSE: A PRELIMINARY CLARIFICATION

In Book VIII of Plato's *Republic,* where the perverted forms of government and the analogous degradations in the human soul are being described, Socrates speaks of the life of the democratic man as having "neither law nor order; and this distracted existence he terms joy and bliss and freedom."[2] Such freedom, which thrives on the absence of laws, he also refers to as "the libertinism of useless and unnecessary pleasures."[3]

[1] See Ch. 1, p. 16, *supra.*
[2] *Op. cit.,* 561D.
[3] *Ibid.,* 561A.

This would appear to be but another way of saying "the licentiousness of unrestrained self-indulgence." As democracy in its most extreme form, according to Plato, inevitably degenerates into tyranny, so the licentious man or libertine becomes a slave. "The excess of liberty, whether in States or individuals, seems only to pass into excess of slavery."[4]

On the face of it, the language used in the last statement quoted permits the interpretation that doing as one pleases is truly freedom, even though an excess of such freedom results in a man's being no longer master of himself.[5] What appears to be a verbally more explicit rejection of doing as one pleases occurs in Aristotle's *Politics*, again as in the *Republic* in the context of criticisms of democracy. "In democracies of the more extreme type," Aristotle says, "there has arisen *a false idea of freedom* which is contrary to the true interests of the state." He tells us that those who harbor this false idea think "that freedom means the doing of what a man likes." He leaves us in no doubt about his own view of the democracies in which "every one lives as he pleases, or in the words of Euripides, 'according to his fancy.'" After saying that "this is all wrong," he adds pointedly that "men should not think it slavery to live according to the rule of the constitution."[6]

Calvin echoes the above view when he refers to "fanatics, who are pleased with nothing but liberty, or rather licentiousness without any restraint. . . ."[7] He dismisses those who give the title of freedom to a man's ability to do what he wants in the absence of constraint

---

[4] *Ibid.*, 564A.

[5] We reach the opposite interpretation only if we take into consideration Plato's identification of the free man with the temperate man, in whom reason governs the appetites. In contrast, the man who gratifies his desires instead of following the dictates of reason is not master of himself and so is not free. See *ibid.*, Book IV, 430E–431B.

[6] *Op. cit.*, Book V, Ch. 9, 1310^{a}25–35. (Italics added.) Those who think it slavery "to live according to the rule of the constitution" make the mistake of thinking that to live lawlessly is freedom. This tends to confirm the earlier statement that "doing what a man likes" or "living as one pleases" is a false conception of freedom. A closely similar view is expressed by one of the speakers in Cicero's *Republic*, who, speaking of democracy, declares that "if the people hold the supreme power and everything is administered according to their desires, that is called liberty, but is really licence" (*op. cit.*, Book III, Ch. 13, pp. 201–3). We also find Spinoza repeating critical points made by Plato and by Aristotle. Having said that the duty of subjects is to obey the commands of the sovereign power, he adds: "It will, perhaps, be thought that we are turning subjects into slaves: for slaves obey commands and free men live as they like; *but this idea is based on a misconception*, for the true slave is he who is led away by his pleasures and can neither see what is good for him nor act accordingly: he *alone* is free who lives with free consent under the entire guidance of reason" (*Theological Political-Treatise*, Ch. XVI, p. 206). (Italics added.)

[7] *Institutes of the Christian Religion*, Vol. II, p. 771.

by asking: "What end would it answer to decorate a thing so diminutive with a title so superb?"[8]

The same points are made by later writers. Jonathan Boucher, speaking against the revolutionary party in the American colonies, quotes with approval Locke's statement that "where there is no law there is no freedom." In his own view, "liberty consists in a subserviency to law." If there ever were men who existed in a completely lawless state of nature, they would have been, according to Boucher, completely unfree. "There mere man of nature . . . has no freedom," even though he has the power, and circumstances allow him to do as he pleases.[9]

In Locke's view, natural liberty (i.e., freedom in a state of nature) is impossible precisely because there is a law of nature whereby men can govern their actions. But for Rousseau, who in certain passages pictures the state of nature as completely lawless, natural liberty is at best an animal or brutish freedom. The individual's power to do as he pleases, which is limited only by his strength or cunning set against that of others, does not differ in any way from the kind of freedom which the beasts of the jungle enjoy. When men deprive themselves of such freedom by entering into the social contract, they gain in its place the truly human freedom that, according to Rousseau, is at once a moral and a civil liberty, "which alone makes [a man] truly master of himself; for the mere impulse of appetite is slavery, while obedience to a law which we prescribe to ourselves is liberty."[10]

The transition from a state of nature to a state of civil society is, there-

---

[8] *Ibid.*, Vol. I, p. 287.

[9] *A View of the Causes and Consequences of the American Revolution*, XII, p. 509. Against the false conception of freedom as doing what one pleases, Boucher sets what he regards as the true conception: "True liberty," he writes, "is a liberty to do everything that is right, and the being restrained from doing anything that is wrong" (*ibid.*, p. 511).

[10] *The Social Contract*, Book I, Ch. 8, p. 19. Kant describes in similar fashion the transition from the anarchic condition of man in a state of nature to the juridical condition of civil society. He speaks of man as having "abandoned his wild lawless freedom wholly, in order to find all his *proper* freedom again entire and undiminished, but in the form of a regulated order of dependence, that is, in a civil state regulated by laws of right (*The Science of Right*, p. 437). (Italics added.) Cf. also the following statement by John Winthrop: "There is a twofold liberty, natural . . . and civil or federal. The first is common to man with beasts and other creatures. By this, man, as he stands in relation to man simply, hath liberty to do what he lists; it is a liberty to evil as well as good. . . . The other kind of liberty I call civil or federal; it may also be termed moral, in reference to the convenant between God and man, in the moral law, and the political covenants and constitutions amongst men themselves. This liberty is the proper end and object of authority and cannot subsist without it; and it is a liberty to do that only which is good, just, and honest" (*History of New England*, Vol. II, p. 229).

fore, not to be interpreted as involving the exchange of one kind of *human* freedom for another, but rather as the elevation of man from a brutish to a human condition. Exchanging a lawless for a lawful life, Rousseau explains,

> produces a very remarkable change in man, by substituting justice for instinct . . . and giving his actions the morality they had formerly lacked. Then only, when the voice of duty takes the place of physical impulses . . . does man, who so far had considered only himself, find that he is forced to act on different principles, and to consult his reason before listening to his inclinations.[11]

Only then, also, does man rise above the merely animal freedom of doing as he pleases and acquire the truly human freedom of doing as he ought. In Rousseau's mind, "these two things are so different as to be mutually incompatible," and he suggests calling the former "independence" in sharp contradistinction to what is properly called "liberty."[12]

According to Hegel, "the definition of freedom [as] ability to do what we please . . . can only be taken to reveal an utter immaturity of thought." He also speaks of freedom so defined as "freedom of a low and limited order."[13] However, in the larger context of his writings, it is certainly clear that, for Hegel, self-indulgence or self-will (i.e., doing as one pleases) is the very antithesis of freedom.[14] The very things which restrain the individual from doing as he pleases are the indispensable conditions of his freedom.[15] The limitation imposed on the individual by the state "is a limitation of the mere brute emotions and rude instincts; as also in a more advanced stage of culture, of the premeditated self-will of caprice and passion." But, as Hegel sees it, "this kind of constraint," far from being

---

[11] *Ibid.*, p. 18. If in civil society an individual persists in following his own individual inclinations instead of obeying the general will, then, in Rousseau's opinion, he must be compelled to obey. "This means nothing less than that he will be forced to be free" (*ibid.*).

[12] *Letters from the Mountain*, Part II, Letter VIII, pp. 437–38. It is possible for men to be independent in a state of nature apart from law or justice, but "liberty without justice is . . . truly a contradiction" (*ibid.*, p. 438); for "it is to law alone that men owe justice and liberty" (*Political Economy*, p. 294). Cf. *Emile*, p. 437.

[13] *Philosophy of Right*, Par. 15, p. 27.

[14] "Duty," he writes, "is a restriction only on the self-will of subjectivity. . . . Thus duty is not a restriction on freedom, but only on freedom in the abstract, i.e., on unfreedom. Duty is the attainment of our essence, the winning of positive freedom" (*Philosophy of Right*, Addition 95, pp. 259–60).

[15] The limitations imposed by duty and law, Hegel tells us, constrain "impulse, desire, and passion" and exclude "caprice and self-will." Such limitations are not "a fettering of freedom" but rather an "indispensable proviso of emancipation" (*Philosophy of History*, Introduction, p. 41).

destructive of freedom, is indispensable to the attainment of it "in its true—that is, its Rational and Ideal form."[16]

We know from ample evidence adduced elsewhere that the writers quoted in the foregoing paragraphs and footnotes affirm a freedom of self-perfection that is acquired only by the virtuous or the wise.[17] The passages quoted are offered to show that they also dismiss as no freedom at all a freedom other writers affirm. They speak of it as a false or illusory conception of freedom; they regard it as the antithesis of freedom—as unfreedom or slavery; they treat it as a freedom appropriate to animal but not to human life; they oppose it to freedom by calling it "license." Of these various ways of denying that circumstantial self-realization is genuinely freedom, only the last may be the cause of some confusion, in view of the fact that the word "license" is also used by self-realization authors to signify an exercise of freedom for purposes or in ways which they regard as socially undesirable.

Many of the authors who maintain that doing as one pleases is truly freedom (or even that it is man's only freedom) also maintain that certain limits must be set to the exercise of such freedom on the part of individuals living together in society. When they condemn the attempts of some men to go beyond these limits, they are censuring what they regard as excessive freedom, but in their view such excesses are still truly freedom. They are simply saying that if some men arrogate too much freedom to themselves, the freedom of others will be infringed. They never mean that the man who has too much freedom or acts licentiously thereby becomes himself less free or unfree.

This is the sense of Bentham's famous question: "Is not the liberty to do evil liberty?" Society must, of course, restrain men from the abuses of liberty, but in doing so does not society "take away liberty from idiots and bad men, because they abuse it?"[18] To say that what is being taken away is license, *not* liberty, is, from the point of view of Bentham and other self-realization authors, to mistake the distinction between a good and evil use of liberty for a distinction between what is freedom and what is not. Declaring that "the liberty to kidnap or engage in violence which

---

[16] *Ibid.* Cf. the opinion expressed in a recent essay for François Bourassa: "There is only . . . one single *true* liberty to which every man aspires from the depth of his being, one single liberty which is viable and salutary from human society; and that is liberty under law." ("*La liberté sous la loi*" in *Enquête sur la liberté*, p. 29). "Every human liberty which pretends to set itself apart from the law, and from the obligation it imposes on its activity, is an illusory liberty" (*ibid.*, p. 34). (Italics added.)
[17] See Vol. I, pp. 250–80.
[18] *Theory of Legislation*, pp. 94–95. "The price we pay for [liberty]," writes Hobhouse, "is that so far as a man is free to do right he is also free to do wrong" (*Elements of Social Justice*, p. 71).

the state represses is not a liberty which anyone would openly condone," Hale criticizes those "who say that when the state represses such activities, it is not repressing liberty at all, but license." What should be said, in his opinion, is that "the state undertakes to repress [the] liberty to commit 'license' "—that use of liberty which, if permitted, would "destroy . . . liberties which ought to be protected."[19]

The intent is similar in Knight's remark that "freedom does not mean unregulated impulse, or 'license,' "[20] and in Malinowski's statement that "to speak about the criminal's freedom to murder, to rape, or to steal is simply an abuse of words," by which he means no more than that "criminal tendencies to murder, to rape, and to steal should have no freedom."[21] The principle of limitation in these and many similar passages is one that draws a line between desires which society should permit men to realize and tendencies or impulses which it should restrain them from carrying out. When the restraint is successfully imposed by law or government, some men are deprived of freedom whether or not it is also called "license" because it is a liberty which should be taken away from them.[22]

Authors who conceive freedom as self-realization and who agree on the need for limiting freedom give somewhat different reasons for doing so. Some make the avoidance of injury the principle. Thus Mill writes:

> The sole end for which mankind are warranted, individually or collectively, in interfering with the liberty of action of any of their number, is self-protection.[23]

Some look to the maximization of freedom itself. Bertrand Russell, for example, maintains that

> there will be more liberty for all in a community where some acts of tyranny by individuals are forbidden than in a community where the law allows each individual free to follow his every impulse.[24]

[19] *Freedom through Law*, pp. 3–4.
[20] *Freedom and Reform*, p. 372. See the comment on this passage in Vol. I, p. 197.
[21] *Freedom and Civilization*, p. 82.
[22] According to Fosdick, "license connotes merely certain liberties which are deemed dangerous. They are still liberties" (*What is Liberty?*, p. 88). And referring to those who "bid us . . . distinguish liberty from license," MacIver declares that what they mean by license is nothing but "the liberty to do the things they disapprove" ("The Meaning of Liberty and Its Perversions" in *Freedom: Its Meaning*, p. 284).
[23] *On Liberty*, Ch. 1, p. 72. Cf. Adam Smith, *Wealth of Nations*, Book IV, Ch. 9, p. 65; Calhoun, *Speech on the Oregon Bill*, in *Basic Documents*, p. 293; Bentham, *Anarchical Fallacies*, Art. IV, in *Collected Works*, Vol. II, pp. 505–6; and Laski, "Liberty" in *Encyclopaedia of the Social Sciences*, Vol. IX, p. 444.
[24] *Roads to Freedom*, p. 123.

Knight holds that no coercive law, restrictive of freedom, is justified unless "it really adds more to freedom in some way than it directly subtracts."[25] And Spencer would have "every man . . . free to do that which he wills, provided he infringes not the equal freedom of any other man."[26]

From the point of view of authors who conceive freedom as self-perfection and who deny that there is any freedom in doing as one pleases, only those who have a false conception of freedom would give such reasons for limiting it. Hegel explicitly takes this point of view when he writes:

> Nothing has become . . . more familiar than the idea that each must *restrict* his liberty in relation to the liberty of others: that the state is a condition of such reciprocal restriction, and that the laws are restrictions. To such habits of mind, liberty is viewed only as casual good-pleasure and self-will.[27]

In this perspective, it is just as wrong to suppose that the individual is genuinely free in those cases in which no law governs his conduct, and so he can do what he wishes, as it is to suppose that any genuine freedom has been taken away from him in those cases in which some law prevents him from doing as he pleases.

We have seen that all the writers who affirm a circumstantial freedom of self-realization would dissent from both of the points made in the foregoing statement.[28] But not all who affirm an acquired freedom of self-perfection would agree to both; for, as we have seen, Locke and Montesquieu, together with Aquinas and his followers (e.g., Maritain, Yves Simon), would acknowledge the presence of true freedom in the enactment of individual desires wherever the moral or civil law is completely silent on whether the action desired should or should not be performed.[29]

These writers occupy a middle ground. On the one hand, unlike authors who affirm self-realization to the exclusion of self-perfection, they do not think that any freedom is taken away by the restrictions of law. On the other hand, unlike authors who affirm self-perfection to the exclusion of self-

[25] *Freedom and Reform*, p. 196.
[26] *Principles of Ethics*, Vol. II, p. 46. Cf. Sidgwick, *Elements of Politics*, p. 47; Hobhouse, Liberalism, pp. 23–24; Tawney, *Equality*, p. 220; Hayek, *Individualism and Economic Order*, Ch. I, Sect. 5, pp. 16–17; and Dewey, "Liberty and Social Control," in *The Social Frontier*, Vol. II, No. 2, p. 41.
[27] *Philosophy of Mind*, Sect. 539, p. 265. Cf. *Philosophy of History*, Introduction, p. 38.
[28] See Vol. I, pp. 171–244.
[29] See Vol. I, pp. 244–49, 318–27, and 351–59. Considering only acts which fall within the sphere of law, Aquinas contrasts "perverse freedom, when one abuses it to commit sin" with "true and spiritual freedom which is the freedom of grace, i.e., being without crimes" (*Commentary on St. John*, Ch. 8, Lect. 4, Sect. 4).

realization, they maintain that men are free when circumstances permit them to do as they please in all matters on which the law is silent as well as when virtue enables them willingly to act as the law commands.

"For in all the states of created beings capable of laws," writes Locke, "where there is no law there is no freedom."[30] Boucher, who quotes this statement with approval, interprets it to mean that men are free *only* in willing obedience to law. But, according to Locke, man is free to "follow [his] own will in all things where [law] prescribes not."[31] He has

a liberty to dispose and order as he lists, his person, actions, possessions, and his whole property, within the allowance of the laws under which he is, and therein not to be subject to the arbitrary will of another, but freely follow his own.[32]

Locke does not, therefore, wholly disagree with the statement he quotes from Sir Robert Filmer that freedom consists in "a liberty for everyone to do what he lists, to live as he pleases, and not to be tied by any laws." *Insofar as one is not tied by any laws,* freedom for Locke does consist in acting as one wishes; but he rejects that part of the statement which makes it consist in *not being tied by any laws.* On the contrary, he holds that a reasonable man enjoys freedom in willing compliance either with laws of nature or with the laws of the commonwealth that have been "established by consent."[33]

Whether in a state of nature or in a civil society, the reasonable man has, through willing compliance with law, a freedom of self-perfection; but he can also enjoy a freedom of self-realization in all matters where the law does not prescribe, to whatever extent favorable circumstances permit him to act in accordance with his own desires. Precisely because the law of nature lays down the things a man ought to do and leaves all other matters to his own discretion, the state of nature is "a state of liberty" and "not a state of licence,"[34] His freedom in both respects, i.e., in obeying the law of nature and in acting on his own discretion, "is grounded on his having reason, which is able to instruct him in that law he is able to govern himself by." Take away his reason and he would not have *human* freedom in either respect. "To turn him loose to an unrestrained liberty" would be

---

[30] *Civil Government*, Ch. VI, Sect. 57, pp. 36–37.
[31] *Ibid.*, Ch. IV, Sect. 22, p. 16.
[32] *Ibid.*, Ch. VI, Sect. 57, p. 37.
[33] *Ibid.*, Ch. IV, Sect. 22, p. 16. For a man to be guided by the judgment of his reason in all things, Locke holds, is no "restraint or diminution of freedom" (*Essay Concerning Human Understanding*, Vol. I, Book II, Ch. 21, Sect. 49, p. 345).
[34] *Civil Government*, Ch. II, Sect. 6, p. 6.

"to thrust him out amongst the brutes, and abandon him to a state as wretched, and as much beneath that of a man, as theirs."[35]

For Montesquieu, as for Locke, the "unlimited liberty" of acting entirely as one pleases is not human freedom. In a state of nature, men, like animals, may follow their own impulses so far as they have the power to do so and nothing external hinders them, but, according to Montesquieu, there is a great "difference between [such] independence and liberty. . . . [Men] acquired liberty" only when they gave up "their natural independence to live under political laws."[36]

In saying this, Montesquieu would appear to agree with Rousseau that the independence which men may enjoy in a state of nature is an animal, not a human, freedom.[37] But, unlike Rousseau and other self-perfection authors, he does not make human freedom, or freedom in civil society, consist entirely in doing what the law of the state or the general will commands. In societies directed by laws, "liberty does consist (i) "in the power of doing what we ought to will, and in not being constrained to do what we ought not to will";[38] but at the same time it also consists (ii) "in not being forced to do a thing where the laws do not oblige."[39] In these two statements, we find Montesquieu affirming, side by side, (i) a freedom of self-perfection and (ii) a freedom of self-realization, the latter limited to matters on which the laws are silent.

The foregoing pages present sufficient evidence to show the existence of a three-sided issue about whether circumstantial self-realization is a genuine or truly human freedom. In addition, they show that the question at issue here cannot be formulated in terms of liberty as contrasted with license. Nor can it be formulated by asking whether or not freedom should be limited or, more specifically, limited by law.

As we have seen, each of the typical parties to this issue would speak against license, just as each would speak for the limitation of freedom by law, *in some sense of these terms*. To construct the issue, then, it is necessary to state the question in other terms. They must be terms which are at once sufficiently neutral and sufficiently precise so that all parties can be brought into topical agreement about the question to be answered as well as about the freedom in question. We shall attempt to do this in the section immediately following and, at the same time, we shall submit additional evidence for construing particular authors as taking one or another position on the issue constructed.

[35] *Ibid.*, Ch. VI, Sect. 63, p. 40.
[36] See *The Spirit of Laws*, Book XI, Ch. 3, p. 180, and Book XXVI, Ch. 13, p. 570.
[37] See fn. 12, on p. 39, *supra*.
[38] *The Spirit of the Laws*, Book XI, Ch. 3, p. 180.
[39] *Ibid.*, Book XXVI, Ch. 17, p. 574.

2. THE QUESTION AT ISSUE

In an earlier chapter, we proposed three ways of formulating the question about the circumstantial freedom of self-realization.[40] The three formulations were as follows:

(i) Is circumstantial self-realization unqualifiedly a human freedom?

(ii) Is circumstantial self-realization, with or without certain restrictive qualifications, a human freedom?

(iii) Under what conditions is circumstantial self-realization a human freedom?

We have already seen that the authors with whom we are concerned are in minimal topical agreement about the subject in question. This holds true for those who challenge the genuineness of circumstantial self-realization as well as for those who affirm or defend it. The freedom that is being challenged and defended is commonly understood by all parties in the minimal terms of the following identifying description: *a freedom which is possessed by any individual who, under favorable circumstances, is able to act as he wishes for his own good as he sees it.* This identifying description might seem to beg the question by using the word "freedom." But we can avoid this difficulty by using the phrase "circumstantial self-realization" as shorthand for "the ability of an individual, under favorable circumstance, to act as he wishes for his own good as he sees it." About what is thus named, we can then ask, quite openly and without prejudice to any point of view, whether or not it is truly or really a human freedom.

Let us consider, first, what is intended by asking whether circumstantial self-realization is truly or really a human freedom.

Certain authors maintain, we have seen, that circumstantial self-realization represents a false or illusory conception of human freedom, that it is either no freedom at all or at best an animal freedom but not one proper to man as man. What is commonly intended by all of these negations is covered by saying that circumstantial self-realization is *not* truly a human freedom. The contradictory statement, that it *is*, also covers a variety of affirmations, viz., that it is a true or valid conception of freedom, that it is properly a human freedom, and either man's only freedom or at least one of his freedoms.

To cover the contradictory views indicated above, either the first or second formulation of the question would seem to be satisfactory. But

[40] See Ch. 1, pp. 14–15, *supra*.

neither of these formulations adequately reflects the opinions of those who accept circumstantial self-realization as a true human freedom *under certain conditions, but not unqualifiedly.* Hence, we shall adopt the third formulation of the question to distinguish the position held by this group of authors from those, on the one hand, who unconditionally affirm circumstantial self-realization, and from those, on the other hand, who unconditionally reject it.

We have seen that certain authors (e.g., Aquinas, Locke, Montesquieu) distinguish between two spheres of human conduct: (a) the sphere of actions which are prescribed by law, either the natural or moral law, or the positive law of the state, and (b) the sphere of actions which are morally or juridically indifferent, i.e., actions which no valid law either commands or prohibits. In their view, circumstantial self-realization is genuinely a human freedom *only* when the desires which favorable circumstances permit or enable the individual to realize can be realized by actions that are morally or juridically indifferent—things about which the law is silent or about which, to use Locke's phrase, the law prescribes not.

With regard to actions or matters which the law prescribes, a man possesses genuine freedom only when he is able to will as he ought in accordance with law, and this ability depends on his acquirement of a certain virtue, wisdom, or reasonableness. If circumstances permit a man to do what he wishes in contravention of law, his being able to realize his desires is not a genuinely human freedom, in the view of these writers; nor, in their view, is he free if he obeys the positive law merely to avoid its coercive force, or if he conforms to moral rules or customs merely to avoid social disapproval. Even in the case in which moral obligations or positive laws make demands which happen to coincide with what the individual wishes to do anyway, his willingness to act in that way, according to these writers, does not make him free; for, since such a man would obey only from fear of the consequences when what is required of him did *not* coincide with his own desires, he clearly does not have the virtue or wisdom that is indispensable to the only genuine freedom a man can have in relation to moral obligations or positive laws.

The foregoing paragraphs make explicit both the positive and negative effect of the restrictive qualification which certain authors impose on their affirmation of circumstantial self-realization as a human freedom. This constitutes their answer to the question, "Under what conditions . . . ?" For purposes of brevity, we shall summarize it as follows: *Only in matters on which the natural, moral, or civil law is silent.*

Let us now try to make similarly explicit, first, the position of those who affirm circumstantial self-realization without any qualifications, and who would therefore say "under *all* conditions"; and, second, the position of those who deny circumstantial self-realization with or without qualifications, and who would therefore say "under *no* conditions."[41]

Certain authors (e.g., Hobbes, Bentham, J. S. Mill, Spencer, Laski, Tawney, Russell) maintain that a man is genuinely free *whenever* circumstances permit or enable him to do as he himself wishes, *regardless* of the moral or legal quality of the actions that realize his desires. These writers would respond to the distinction between the sphere of acts which are regulated by law and the sphere of acts on which the law is silent by saying that the individual can have the same freedom in both spheres. In either sphere, he is unfree only when circumstances prevent him from doing as he himself wishes. To complete the picture, four subsidiary points must be mentioned.

(i) Some of the authors in this group (e.g., Hobbes, Edwards) differ from others (e.g., Sidgwick, Tawney, Schlick) in holding that the law destroys freedom when we are physically coerced or constrained by it, but not when we merely act from fear of punishments imposed by the law. But this difference does not affect their agreement on the point that a man's freedom is infringed whenever the institutions of law and government prevent him from doing what he wishes.

(ii) The authors in this group are also divided as follows. Some (e.g., Hobbes, Bentham, Mill) hold that any act which the individual performs in compliance with law is an unfree act, whereas some (e.g., Laski, Knight, Kelsen) hold that such acts are unfree only if what the law requires does not happen to coincide with what the individual wishes to do anyway.[42] But this difference between them does not affect their agreement on the negative point that the freedom of circumstantial self-realization is not restricted to matters on which the law is silent; for both contend that, given favorable circumstances, a man can be free to do as he wishes in matters regulated by law, *either* because what he wishes to do anyway happens to coincide with what the law prescribes *or* because he executes his wish in contravention of law.

(iii) With few, if any, exceptions, the authors in this group agree that men living together in civil society cannot be allowed to do whatever they please. Some limit must be set and enforced by law on the extent to which any individual should be granted such freedom. But this agreed-upon limitation of individual self-realization in society draws a line between the freedom which the individual should be granted and the freedom of which

---

[41] The third—or middle—position is the one which says "only under certain conditions," the conditions being specified by the qualification imposed. The three positions can also be summarized as follows: one holds that circumstantial self-realization is *never* freedom, one that it is *always* freedom, and one—the middle position—that it *sometimes is* and *sometimes is not* freedom.

[42] See Vol. I, pp. 224–25, 232–44, and 351–56.

he must be deprived. It does not distinguish between that which is properly or truly freedom and that which, in excess of the limit, is the very opposite of freedom.

(iv) With no exceptions, the authors in this group agree that in every instance a man's having freedom depends entirely on whether his acts realize his desires and, therefore, on circumstances which permit or prevent the enactment of his desires, *never* on the moral quality of his desire, will, or intentions. Stated another way, these authors agree that, by whatever standards a man's state of mind or character can be judged to be good or bad—wise or unwise, reasonable or unreasonable, virtuous or vicious— favorable circumstances confer the same freedom on good and bad men alike; given such circumstances, each can do as he pleases.

These four points, together with the main point to which they are subsidiary, make explicit what is involved in the view that circumstantial self-realization is genuinely human freedom under all *conditions* or *unconditionally*. The unconditional denial that it is genuinely human freedom rests, first of all, on a denial of the last of these points; for all the authors who would say that *under no conditions* is circumstantial self-realization genuine freedom agree in maintaining that *only* the good man— *only* the wise or virtuous man—is free. They differ among themselves about the bearing of favorable circumstances upon freedom: some (e.g., Rousseau, Hegel) think circumstances which permit a man to enact his right will are essential; some (e.g., Spinoza) think that such circumstances render the virtuous man's freedom more complete; and some (e.g., Philo, Epictetus, Kant) think circumstances totally irrelevant. None thinks that circumstances alone, not even the most favorable, confer freedom on men *regardless of their state of mind or character*.

Consequently, the authors in this group see no *human* freedom in the acts of a bad man who does as he wishes, whether or not what the bad man wishes to do happens to conform to the requirements of the moral or positive law. Nor would they say that the bad man is unfree because he is somehow prevented by just laws from doing as he pleases. The law takes no freedom away, either by threatened coercion or by the actual constraints it enforces. Furthermore, in their view, the law does not limit freedom in the sense of drawing a line between the freedom a man can be safely allowed in society and the freedom he must be asked to sacrifice for the benefits of social life. On the contrary, these authors maintain that the sphere of law and the sphere of freedom are perfectly coextensive: there is no freedom outside the sphere of the things a man ought to do; for only in respect to such things can a man achieve the freedom of being able to will as he ought.

Only in this sense do just laws limit freedom—the sense in which it is the indispensable ground or condition of freedom. Hence, for the authors in this group, *if* there are any matters which do not fall within the sphere of moral obligation or legal regulation, the actions which men take with respect to them in carrying out their individual wishes are neither free *nor* unfree. Since they are without moral quality, they are also indeterminate with respect to freedom. The foregoing "if" introduced a supposition seldom if ever entertained by these authors; but in any case the point to be made clear is that these authors, if they were to recognize the position of those who *conditionally* affirm circumstantial self-realization (i.e., as genuine freedom in matters on which the law is silent), would oppose it as firmly as they oppose the position of which they explicitly take cognizance (i.e., the position of those who *unconditionally* affirm circumstantial self-realization).

We have now explicated the positions which constitute the three mutually incompatible answers to the question, "Under what conditions is circumstantial self-realization genuinely a human freedom?" That explication of the meaning of the three answers—(A) "Under no conditions," (B) "Only under certain conditions," and (C) "Under all conditions"—shows that authors who, respectively, give these answers take opposing positions on the question in issue about the subject being considered.[43] The question is formulated with the requisite neutrality, so that it does not prejudice any of the positions on the issue; and since it does nothing more than cover those positions, that it is a commonly understood question for the adherents of those positions is vouchsafed by the positions themselves.

The complete topical agreement required for the existence of an issue is thus assured. But to complete the construction of the issue, one further step is necessary. We must show on what grounds or by what evidence we construe particular authors as taking sides on this issue.

3. THE PARTIES TO THE ISSUE

Of the authors whose theories we have examined in Book II, the following would appear to take sides on the issue that is formulated in the preceding section. Their names are listed, roughly in chronological order, under the positions they take.

POSITION (A): Under no conditions is circumstantial self-realization genuinely a human freedom.
    Plato, Aristotle, Cicero, Philo, Seneca, Epictetus, Marcus Aurelius, Spinoza, Rousseau, Kant, Boucher, Hegel, Bradley

[43] Authors who take Positions (A) and (B) stand together insofar as they reject the unconditional affirmation of Position (C); and authors who take Positions (E) and (C) stand together insofar as they reject the unconditional denial of Position (A).

POSITION (B): Circumstantial self-realization is genuinely a human freedom only under certain conditions, i.e., when the desires to be realized concern matters on which the natural and positive law is silent.

Aquinas, Locke, Montesquieu, Maritain, Yves Simon

POSITION (C): Circumstantial self-realization is genuinely a human freedom under all conditions.

Hobbes, Voltaire, Edwards, Hume, Priestley, Adam Smith, Burke, Bentham, Calhoun, J. S. Mill, Spencer, Pareto, Freud, Hobhouse, B. Russell, Tawney, Kelsen, N. Hartmann, Schlick, Hale, Malinowski, Knight, Macmurray, Laski, Mannheim, Hayek, Stevenson, Ayer, Nowell-Smith

It seems sufficiently clear that the following authors would oppose Position (C):

Ambrose, Augustine, Boethius, Anselm, Maimonides, Duns Scotus, Luther, Calvin, Bellarmine, Suarez, Leibniz, Green, Fouillée, Bergson, Barth, Tillich, Marcel

But the exposition of their views on freedom does not provide us with sufficient grounds for construing them as taking Position (A) rather than Position (B), or conversely. Hence, we can consider them as parties to this issue only insofar as the adherents of Positions (A) and (B) join forces against Position (C).

The foregoing classification of writers calls for a number of further comments.

(i) None of the enumerations is intended to be exhaustive. In each case, those named are among the major writers on the subject of freedom. The manner in which they take—or fail to take—a position on the issue can be regarded as typical or representative of the views of many others who have not been named.

(ii) The division of the authors into those who can and those who cannot be regarded as taking one of the three positions on the issue must not be interpreted to mean that those who are named under the three positions explicitly recognize the question at issue, whereas all the rest ignore or neglect it. Since none of the authors poses the question we have framed, none explicitly recognizes the question at issue.

(iii) Only a few of the writers listed under each position give explicit evidence of holding that position, either by the actual language in which they express their views or by the intent of their remarks. Of these, even a smaller number explicitly mention by name writers who take positions to which they are opposed. Bosanquet mentions Bentham, J. S. Mill, and Spencer, and Hobhouse, Laski, and B. Russell mention Rousseau and

Hegel; and Laski, in addition, mentions Bosanquet. As for the rest, their taking this or that position must be construed inferentially from what they say, the intent of their remarks, and certain reasonable assumptions about the views they hold.

The foregoing comments add up to the conclusion that the issue as stated cannot be explicitly found in the literature on freedom. We have found no authors who explicitly adhere to one of the three positions and at the same time explicitly recognize both of the other two positions. Nor have we been able to find even a single pair of authors (not to mention a triad of them) who actually confront one another in their writings as acknowledged opponents on the question at issue.[44] The lack of such evidence does not mean that the issue is fictitous. There is sufficient evidence to show that it is implicitly present in the literature, on the basis of which we can construct it and construe authors as being parties to it.

Finally, a word must be said about the minimum condition to be satisfied before we are justified in asserting that this issue—or any other— exists or is real and that it can be constructed from what is implicit in the literature. To establish the reality of the issue and the documentary basis for its construction, we must be able, for each of the positions set forth, to offer *at least one author* who can be construed as taking that side of the issue. It is not necessary for us to substantiate the adherence of more than one author to each of the positions; nor, in the case of that single author, is it necessary for the substantiation to be direct rather than inferential. Should the literature enable us to go beyond satisfying this minimum requirement, everything additional goes to show, not the reality or constructibility of the issue, but the extent to which major writers about freedom have engaged in this phase of the general controversy and the degree to which their participation as parties is more or less directly evidenced by what they wrote.

This last point must be borne in mind by the reader as he considers the reasons that we shall now try to give for regarding particular authors as parties to his issue. In some cases, the grounds will be quite plain and strong; in others, much weaker and less obvious. But it will suffice, in the case of each position, if the reader is persuaded that at least one of the authors dealt with holds views that make him an adherent of that position on the question at issue.

---

[44] The nearest approach to this is to be found in the fact that, on the one hand, Bosanquet, who allies himself with the views of Rousseau and Hegel, directly criticizes the views of Bentham, Mill, and Spencer, and that, on the other hand, Laski, Hobhouse, and Russell, who directly criticize the views of Rousseau and Hegel, themselves hold views which resemble those of Bentham, Mill, and Spencer. In addition, Laski criticizes Bosanquet.

We shall proceed as follows. Considering Positions (A), (B), and (C) in the order named, we shall for the most part begin with authors who approximate a direct espousal of the position, and then turn to those who can, with varying degrees of assurance, be inferred to hold it. In each case, we shall offer documentation by quoting an author only if such evidence has not already been presented. Otherwise, we shall refer the reader back to earlier sections of this work where such evidence was presented. Any other procedure would involve a mountainous repetition of materials which have been adduced in other connections. Where inferential interpretation is required, we shall state the criteria or signs on the basis of which authors can be construed as adhering to a certain position. In these cases, the evidence either quoted or referred to will be relevant to one or more of the indicated criteria or signs.[45]

POSITION (A)

Logically, the unconditional denial which constitutes Position (A) brings anyone who takes this position at once into conflict with those who either conditionally or unconditionally affirm circumstantial self-realization to be genuinely a human freedom. Nevertheless, the grounds for interpreting authors as being opposed to Position (B) are not the same as the grounds for interpreting them as being opposed to Position (C). As we shall see, interpretation in the latter case tends to be more direct. It involves no more than noting the intent of statements they make.

The following authors—Plato, Aristotle, Spinoza, Boucher, Rousseau, Kant, and Hegel—have already been quoted as making statements the direct intent of which is to deny the genuineness of circumstantial self-realization as human freedom; for they speak of it as a false or illusory conception, as the antithesis of freedom, or as an animal, but not a proper human, freedom.[46] But we have not quoted, nor can we quote, any statements by them, the direct intent of which is to deny that circumstantial self-realization is genuinely a human freedom *even in those instances in which the desires to be realized involve actions not prescribed by law.* However, it is a relatively easy and sure inference that the aforementioned authors would answer negatively if they were asked whether men enjoy human freedom in doing as they please in all matters on which the law is silent.

These authors maintain that the sphere of law and the sphere of liberty

[45] Cf. what was said about degrees of interpretation in Ch. 2, pp. 25–26, *supra*.
[46] See Section 1 of this chapter, pp. 36–40, *supra*.

are co-extensive; that the free act and the dutiful or lawful act are one and the same; that law and duty are the foundation or substance of freedom.[47] Their views imply that the morally or juridically indifferent act (if there is such a thing) is either entirely outside the sphere of freedom (i.e., is neither free nor unfree) or is at most an instance of animal but not human freedom.[48] We can make this inference with relative assurance in the light of the whole theories which these authors hold. Therefore, we feel justified in construing them as opposed to Position (B) as well as to Position (C).[49]

We turn next to authors in whose writing we find no statements the direct intent of which denies that circumstantial self-realization is genuinely a human freedom. Nevertheless, Stoic philosophers, such as Cicero and Epictetus, together with such writers as Philo, do give us a basis for inferring their unconditional rejection of the freedom in question. From their point of view, independence of everything beyond the power of the self is essential to freedom. Accordingly, they explicitly place man's freedom in the power of virtuous or wise men to will as they ought, for this is a power men can possess and exercise without dependence on anything adventitious or fortuitous, over which they have no control. By implication, they exclude from the realm of freedom the fulfillment of desires which depend for their satisfaction on external circumstances of any sort. It is in this way, as we shall presently see, that such authors argue for Position (A) and against the other two positions. The documentary evidence which supports this interpretation of them is given in Section 3 on the debate of the issue.[50]

Finally, we come to two groups of writers who require special consideration. They are, on the one hand, such British Hegelians as Bradley and Bosanquet, and, on the other hand, such exponents of collective freedom as Bakunin, Marx, and Engels. Each presents special problems of interpretation.

---

[47] See *ibid.*, and also Vol. I, pp. 224, 249 fn. 92, 262, 284–86, 290, 293–99, 342 fn. 43. Plato and Aristotle are much less explicit than Boucher, Rousseau, Kant and Hegel on the point mentioned above. Spinoza makes the point explicitly enough, but in terms of the rule of reason rather than in terms of law and duty.

[48] See Section 2 of this chapter, p. 48, *supra.*

[49] It may be worth-while to point out once again that even if this interpretation should be incorrect for certain of these authors (e.g., Plato, Aristotle, or even Spinoza), it suffices for the purpose of constructing and documenting the issue if the inference we have to make is valid for just one author (e.g., Rousseau, Kant, or Hegel). The only serious error of interpretation would be one which incorrectly attributed to certain authors a position that none of them could rightly be construed as holding; for then the issue itself would not have been correctly constructed as an explication of what is implicit in the literature.

[50] See pp. 68–71, *infra.*

The opponents of self-realization, whom we have so far considered, are all exponents of acquired self-perfection as true freedom. In this respect, Bradley and Bosanquet do not differ from them.[51] But in addition to being Hegelian, they are also English philosophers who are sensitive to the long tradition of English thought from Hobbes and Locke to Bentham, Mill, and Spencer, in which freedom is conceived as exemption from external coercion or constraint and as the power to do as one pleases. They recognize that this conception of freedom has the merit of conforming to the common-sense meaning of the word in everyday usage. Bosanquet, for example, even goes so far as to say that

> the juristic meaning of the term liberty . . . we may set down as its literal meaning, and so far the English writers . . . are on solid ground when they define liberty as the absence of restraint, or perfect liberty as the absence of all government (in the sense of habitual constraint by others).[52]

In another place, he speaks of "the literal or elementary sense of liberty as the absence of constraint exercised by one upon others"; and he admits that, "in going beyond it, we are more or less making use of a metaphor."[53] This is the metaphor, Bosanquet explains, which Plato first introduced when he described the free man as one in whom the higher principle or self controls the lower and who is, therefore, not enslaved by alien forces within himself.[54] What Bosanquet here calls the metaphorical sense of liberty is, as we have seen, the conception of it held by a long line of thinkers from Plato to Rousseau, Kant, and Hegel, a conception in which the *true* self, the *real* good, and the *right* will are the essential principles of human freedom.[55]

The question, therefore, is whether Bosanquet not only acknowledges the reality of the two kinds of freedom—circumstantial self-realization as well as acquired self-perfection—but also concedes that the former is, in a sense, the more real. If so, and if in addition, as seems to be the case, he recognizes that both the literal and the metaphorical sense are rooted in

---

[51] See Bradley, *Ethical Studies*, pp. 56–57; and Bosanquet, *The Philosophical Theory of the State*, Ch. VI.

[52] *The Philosophical Theory of the State*, p. 126. Cf. Bradley's first response to the question "Well then, what is freedom?" He begins by quoting the traditional English conception and the common-sense notion: " 'It means not being made to do or be anything' "; and, he continues, according to this notion "to be quite free is to be free from everything—free from other men, free from law, from morality, from thought. . . ." (*Ethical Studies*, p. 56).

[53] *The Philosophical Theory of the State*, p. 128.

[54] *Ibid.*, pp. 129–34.

[55] See Vol. I, pp. 250–80.

the same generic meaning of freedom,[56] how can we regard him as taking Position (A) against Position (C)? The fact that he calls the metaphorical sense "the higher sense," and the literal "the lower," does not obviate the fact that both would seem to be for him legitimate meanings of freedom.[57]

If we interpret him as accepting both meanings of freedom, Bosanquet cannot be regarded as an adherent of Position (A). On the other hand, it is perfectly clear that he does not take Position (C). His criticisms of such self-realization authors as Bentham, J. S. Mill, and Spencer, which we shall report in the next chapter, explain his rejection of the view that being able to do what one wishes is always, or unconditionally, freedom.[58] It would seem, therefore, that Bosanquet can be interpreted as being sympathetic to the qualified acceptance of circumstantial self-realization which characterizes Position (B). But there is no positive evidence to support this interpretation.

We are left with two alternatives. One is to recognize that Bosanquet clearly disagrees with Position (C), even though we cannot, with any assurance, treat him as an adherent of Position (A) or Position (B). In the debate of the issue, he is one of the principal sources of explicit argument against Position (C). The force of those arguments *against* Position (C) are not weakened by the fact that we remain in doubt about which of the other two positions Bosanquet would argue for.

The other alternative is to interpret Bosanquet as favoring Position (A) in spite of his apparent acceptance of circumstantial self-realization as "the lower sense of liberty," in contrast to acquired self-perfection as "the higher liberty." There is some evidence that, in one passage at least, he reverses

[56] "The metaphor . . . depends upon the same principle as the literal usage from which it is drawn. In the case of Liberty, conceived as a condition of the mind, just as in the case of Liberty, conceived as the absence of physical menace or coercion on the part of other persons, the root of the matter is the claim to be determined only by ourself" (*The Philosophical Theory of the State*, p. 133)—the difference being that, in the metaphorical conception, we "place the true self in something which we rather want to be than actually are" (*ibid.*, p. 134).

[57] "The higher sense of liberty, like the lower," Bosanquet writes, "involves freedom *from* some things as well as freedom *to* others" (*ibid.*, p. 128). There is a passage in Philo which might seem to raise the same problem. "Slavery is applied in one sense to bodies," Philo writes, "in another to souls; bodies have men for their masters, souls their vices and passions. The same is true of freedom: one freedom produces security of the body from men of superior strength; the other sets the mind at liberty from the domination of the passions" (*Every Good Man Is Free*, Ch. III, Sect. 17, p. 19). Like Bosanquet, Philo here seems to be acknowledging two freedoms, one of which is denied by Position (A). But Philo's immediate comment is that "no one makes the first kind a subject of investigation"; and the rest of his theory suggests that the reason for thus summarily dismissing it is that the body's exemption from physical constraint is a freedom that is common to stones and brutes as well as men, and so is not a specifically human freedom.

[58] See pp. 73-75, *infra*.

his earlier judgment. That is the passage in which he speaks of himself as having followed, *so far,* "the usual course of English thought . . . in admitting that the lower sense of liberty is the literal sense, and that the deeper meaning may be treated as metaphorical." He then adds:

> It is worth while to observe that the justice of this way of looking at the matter is very doubtful. . . . It is . . . in truth the sense of the higher liberty—the greatness and unity of life—that has communicated uncontrollable force to the claim for the lower; and if the fuller meaning is the reality and the lesser the symbol, it would be nearer the truth to say that *the reality is the liberty of a moral being whose will finds adequate expression in its life, of which liberty the absence of external constraint is only an elementary type or symbol.* The claim of the dictionary-maker that the earlier or the average meaning is also the truest or the "proper" meaning of words has no foundation.[59]

The italicized statement certainly appears to indicate a complete reversal with regard to which of the two liberties is the real freedom, and which is nothing but a metaphorical sense of the term. When we read it that way, does it not also reveal Bosanquet as an author who is saying that there is *no real freedom* in circumstantial self-realization, in spite of the common-sense opinion to the contrary and in spite of the tendency of English thought to accept this popular notion? If so, then Bosanquet is more nearly in sympathy with Bradley than he is with Green and accordingly can be aligned with Bradley on the side of Position (A).[60]

The problem of interpretation is somewhat different in the case of Bakunin, Marx, and Engels. The one freedom these authors affirm as real

---

[59] *The Philosophical Theory of the State,* pp. 134–35. (Italics added.)

[60] The case of Bradley is easier, for he makes short shrift of the common-sense notion that to be free is to be free from other men, free from law, from morality, etc. "To be free from everything," he writes, "is to be—nothing. Only nothing is quite free, and freedom is abstract nothingness" (*Ethical Studies,* p. 56). Green, on the other hand, whom Bosanquet regards himself as following, never qualifies or retracts his acknowledgment of two distinct types of freedom, both quite real and quite genuine—on the one hand, "freedom in the primary or juristic sense of power to act according to choice or preference" (i.e., the circumstantial freedom of self-realization); and, on the other hand, the freedom conceived by Plato, St. Paul, the Stoics, Kant, and Hegel, which is enjoyed only by those who are able to make the right choice (i.e., the acquired freedom of self-perfection). See his essay "On the Different Senses of 'Freedom' as Applied to Will and to the Moral Progress of Man" in lectures on the *Principles of Political Obligation,* pp. 2–27. The description, given in Vol. I, of Green's theory, as including the freedoms of self-perfection and self-determination, but not of self-realization, needs to be amended. His theory includes all three freedoms, but Green does not definitely relate the freedom of doing as one pleases to the freedom of willing as one ought by reference to matters which are or are not prescribed by law. Hence it is impossible to determine the choice he would make, as between Positions (B) and (C) on this issue. Cf. *Liberal Legislation and Freedom of Contract,* in *Works,* Vol. III, pp. 370–73.

or true is, as we have seen, a variant of the acquired freedom of self-perfection—collective freedom.[61] But this by itself does not seem to be sufficient ground for treating them as parties to this issue on the side of such self-perfection authors as Spinoza, Rousseau, and Hegel, with whom they have certain striking affinities.[62] Nor can we appeal simply to the fact that the one freedom they affirm involves things which should lead them to regard doing as one pleases as an illusory or false freedom. That fact would be more persuasive if we could find some evidence that they took cognizance of the freedom which is the subject of this issue and expressed some opinion about it, either in so many words or at least by implication.

Marx says clearly enough that "the realm of freedom does not commence until the point is passed where labor under the compulsion of necessity and of external utility is required."[63] This postpones the real existence of human freedom until some future time when all oppressive class divisions are abolished. Then and only then will a real community come into existence and "in place of the old bourgeois society, with its classes and class antagonisms, we shall have an association in which the free development of each is the condition for the free development of all."[64] Then also, as Engels points out, freedom will consist "in the control over ourselves and over external nature which is founded on the knowledge of natural necessity."[65]

What of the condition of men prior to the dawn of the classless society and the withering away of the state? One passage in *The German Ideology* provides an answer. It speaks of "the personal freedom [which] has existed only for the individuals who developed within the relationships of the ruling class and only in so far as they were individuals of this class."[66] Their power to do as they please is, at best, an illusion of freedom, not only because the class to which they belong is itself an "illusory community" but also because by having to belong to it they are inevitably fettered by it. Only in real community with others, unmarred by the barriers or fetters of class interest, "has each individual the means of cultivating his gifts in all directions"; only in such a community, therefore, "is personal freedom possible," and individuals are able to "obtain their freedom in and through their association," i.e., collectively.[67]

Bakunin's rejection of individual self-realization is less direct, but it is clearly enough implied. As we have seen, the exponents of such freedom

---

[61] See Vol. I, pp. 370–98.
[62] See *ibid.*, pp. 390–91.
[63] *Capital*, Vol. III, Part VII, Ch. XLVIII, Sect. III, p. 954.
[64] *The Communist Manifesto*, p. 343.
[65] *Anti-Dühring*, Part I, Ch. XI, pp. 128.
[66] *Op. cit*, p. 74.
[67] *Ibid.*, pp. 74–75.

all admit that, among men living together in society, the liberty of each must be limited to protect the liberty of others.[68] But, according to Bakunin,

> the only liberty worthy of that name is . . . a liberty which does not recognize any other restrictions but those which are traced by the laws of our own nature, which, properly speaking, is tantamount to saying that there are no restrictions at all . . .

It is a freedom which, "far from finding itself checked by the freedom of others, is, on the contrary, confirmed by it and extended to infinity."[69] Such freedom—the only real freedom—has never existed and does not yet exist; for "like humanity, of which it is the purest expression, [such] freedom presents, not the beginning, but the final moment of history."[70]

It remains to be seen that Bakunin, Marx, and Engels would reject Position (B) as well as Position (C). According to these authors, the only kind of rule to which free men, through acquired knowledge, should collectively submit are the scientifically ascertained laws of the physical world and of social life. When they submit, whether voluntarily or not, to the rules of traditional morality or the coercive enactments of the state, they are enslaved.[71] Since Position (B) affirms that men are free in their voluntary compliance with the moral and the civil law, as well as in doing what they wish in matters not prescribed by law, it is clear that the exponents of collective freedom take issue with it as well as with Position (C).[72]

---

[68] See Sect. 1 of this chapter, pp. 40–42, *supra.*

[69] *The Political Philosophy of Bakunin,* p. 341. Bakunin declares that *"to be free collectively* means to live among free people and to be free by virtue of their freedom" (*ibid.,* p. 340). Cf. *ibid.,* p. 270.

[70] *Ibid.,* p. 341.

[71] See Vol. I, pp. 373 ff. and 393 ff.

[72] As an exponent of collective freedom, Auguste Comte shares the antipathy of Marx, Engels, and Bakunin for arbitrary rules of morality and positive law. See Vol. I, pp. 371–73, 391–92. "The only way to reconcile independence with social union, and thereby reach *true liberty,*" Comte writes, "lies in obedience to the objective laws of the world and of human nature" (*Positive Polity,* Vol. I, p. 296; italics added). But while Comte tells us that man's "true liberty" will begin only when the arbitrariness of man-made rules has been totally eliminated from human life and society, he does not, like Marx, Engels, and Bakunin, indicate that, in his opinion, men have no real freedom at all under present conditions even when they succeed in evading arbitrary restraints and do as they please. Hence, we cannot construe him as standing with Marx, Engels, and Bakunin on the Position (A) side of this issue.

POSITION (B)

The adherents of Position (B) are in conflict with both Position (C) and Position (A): with Position (C), insofar as they maintain that virtuous, wise, or reasonable men are free when they will as they ought in conformity with the moral and civil law; and with Position (A), insofar as they maintain that any man, good or bad, is free when he does whatever he wishes in matters totally outside the sphere of law. Accordingly, the grounds for interpreting an author as an adherent of Position (B) must include evidence of two distinct affirmations, one in favor of acquired self-perfection as freedom under law and one in favor of circumstantial self-realization as freedom from law.

Both sorts of evidence are clearest in the case of Locke. In the case of Aquinas and his followers, ample direct evidence of the first sort is available; but on the second count we must resort to inference. However, the inference required is not too difficult to make. Only in the case of Montesquieu do we have a serious problem of interpretation.

The statement already quoted from Locke, that the freedom of men in society and under civil rule includes "a liberty to follow my own will in all things where that rule prescribes not,"[73] amounts to an explicit affirmation of the qualifying condition under which circumstantial self-realization is a genuine part of human freedom.[74] On the other side of the picture, we have the following statement:

> Law, in its true notion, is not so much the limitation as the direction of a free and intelligent agent to his proper interest, and prescribes no farther than is for the general good of those under the law: could they be happier without it, the law, as a useless thing, would of itself vanish; and that ill deserves the name of confinement which hedges us in only from bogs and precipices.[75]

When this is placed in the context of Locke's opinion that reasonable men, and they alone, enjoy freedom under law, in their voluntary compliance with all the rules that direct them to their proper interest and the common good, it amounts to an equally explicit affirmation of acquired self-perfection as part of human freedom.[76] Furthermore, these two parts are kept

---

[73] *Civil Government*, Ch. IV, Sect. 22, p. 16.

[74] For the full exposition of Locke's views about this part of man's freedom, see Vol. I, pp. 115–16, 118, 177, 191–92, 208–10.

[75] *Civil Government*, Ch. VI, Sect. 57, p. 36. This holds, Locke adds, for "all the laws a man is under, whether natural or civil" (*ibid.*, Sect. 59, p. 37).

[76] See Vol. I, pp. 248–49, 323–27.

separate, and so prevented from coming into conflict with one another, by virtue of the line that Locke explicitly draws between matters which fall within and those which fall outside the proper scope of law.[77]

There can be no question that Aquinas, and such twentieth-century followers of his as Maritain and Yves Simon, holds the view that virtuous men enjoy perfect freedom under the moral or civil law. In complying with its commands, they are not submitting to purely external impositions, for even though the law is of external origin, their virtue enables them to interiorize it and make its precepts the maxims of their own conduct. They thus retain their spontaneity in obeying it.[78]

There may be some question, however, about the grounds for interpreting Aquinas and his followers as extending human freedom to include the circumstantial ability of men to do what they wish in all matters that lie outside the scope of the moral and the civil law. No text can be quoted directly on the point. The only relevant texts are ones which reserve to the individual a certain latitude of choice in matters that are morally indifferent or in cases in which one means may be better than another but neither is morally bad.[79]

According to Thomistic doctrine, then, the divine law and the natural moral law leave alternatives open to individual discretion; an even larger area of unprescribed conduct is left open by the positive law of the state. So far, the intent of the texts is clear. The further step of interpretation involves the inference that in this area of unprescribed conduct the good man can enjoy the additional freedom of acting as he wishes. Such freedom cannot be open to good men without being open to bad men as well. Support for this interpretation can be found in the Thomistic view of the tyrant as an invader of the freedom of *all* who are subject to his unjust and illegal use of force.[80]

We have two problems of interpretation in the case of Montesquieu. One focuses on the intent of the words "liberty is a right of doing *whatever the laws permit*."[81] Does the phrase "whatever the laws permit" mean for Montesquieu what Locke means by matters about which the law "prescribes not?" An affirmative answer to this question seems to be warranted by Montesquieu's praise of moderate governments in which there is no abuse of power and in which "no [man] is *compelled* to do things to which the

[77] See *ibid.*

[78] See Vol. I, pp. 259–60, 266–67, 286–88, 311, 317–21, 341–46.

[79] See Aquinas, *Summa Theologica*, Part I, Q. 62, A. 8, Reply 3; Part I–II, Q. 96, AA. 2 and 3; Part III, Supplement, A. 47, A. 6, Objection 3 and Reply and cf. John of St. Thomas, *Cursus Theologicus*, Disp. IX, Art. 4, Vol. VII p. 449; Yves Simon, *Community of the Free*, pp. 17–21.

[80] See Vol. I, pp. 319–21, 342–46.

[81] *The Spirit of the Laws*, Book XI, Ch. 3, pp. 180–81. (Italics added.)

law does not *oblige* him, nor *forced to abstain* from things which the law *permits.*"[82] The italicized words, by equating that which the law does not require with that which the law allows, indicate an area of conduct not prescribed by law, in which the individual is free to do as he wishes *unless* extralegal factors *compel* him to act contrary to his desires or *force* him to abstain from acting in accordance with them. The fact that Montesquieu says, in another place, that "liberty consists principally in not being forced to do a thing where the laws do not oblige" not only confirms this interpretation but even suggests that he regards circumstantial self-realization as the major part of man's freedom in civil society and under civil government.[83]

The other problem of interpretation turns on the intent of the words "liberty can consist only in the power of doing what we ought to will, and in not being constrained to do what we ought not to will."[84] Does this statement mean for Montesquieu what Locke and Aquinas mean when they say that reasonable or virtuous men are free under the government of just laws because their reason or virtue directs them to will as they ought in conformity to such laws, always, of course, on condition that circumstances do not force them to act otherwise than as they will? The fact that Montesquieu says that "*only* as they are governed by the civil laws; and because they live under those laws . . . are [men] free"[85] might seem to suggest that he holds a view of freedom which is espoused by self-perfection authors. But that interpretation rests on shaky grounds unless we can find indications that Montesquieu also maintains that men are free in obeying the civil law *only if they do so out of virtue and quite willingly.* Since we do not find him making freedom under law the exclusive property of good men, it is quite possible to interpret him to be saying, as other self-realization authors do, that civil law and government secure a limited freedom for men in society (i.e., to do as they please to a certain extent) by taking away the unlimited independence they had in a state of nature.[86]

Before we turn to Position (C), one other writer remains to be consid-

---

[82] *Ibid.* (Italics added.)

[83] See *The Spirit of the Laws*, Book XXVI, Ch. 17, p. 574, and cf. Vol. I, p. 323, where it is pointed out that Montesquieu, in the very next sentence, declares that men have such freedom "only as they are governed by civil laws, and because they live under those laws."

[84] *Ibid.*, Book XI, Ch. 3, p. 180.

[85] *Ibid.*, Book XXVI, Ch. 17, p. 574.

[86] See *ibid.*, Book XXVI, Ch. 13, p. 570; and cf. what is said about this problem of interpretation in Vol. I, pp. 321–23, namely, that in the light of Montesquieu's writings as a whole it would appear that virtue in the individual is as essential to freedom under law as is justice in the laws to which men are subject.

ered. From his point of view, the question at issue is worded in an improper, even perhaps prejudicial, fashion. The question, "Under what conditions is circumstantial self-realization genuinely a human freedom?" covers alternative answers, all of which are unsatisfactory; and it provides no room for an additional alternative that might be satisfactory to him. Dewey's position as against others can be fairly treated only under a question that might be worded in the following way: "Is circumstantial self-realization in and of itself a kind of freedom?" To this question, his answer, as we have seen, would be negative.

We listed a large number of authors under Position (C).[87] With few exceptions, they are authors who affirm no freedom except circumstantial self-realization.[88] The exceptions fall into two groups: on the one hand, Hobhouse, who affirms political liberty, together with Adam Smith, Burke, N. Hartmann, and Knight, who affirm man's natural freedom of self-determination; on the other hand, Freud and B. Russell, who attribute to man an acquired freedom of self-perfection.

We shall consider these exceptional cases presently. The remaining authors would seem to raise no especially difficult problem of interpretation. Some of them, such as Hobbes, Voltaire, Edwards, Hume, Priestley, Bentham, J. S. Mill, and Laski, afford us documentary evidence that circumstantial self-realization, in addition to being the only freedom which they treat, is also the only one which they are willing to accept as real or valid. While such evidence is not available in the case of Calhoun, Spencer, Pareto, Tawney, Kelsen, Schlick, Hale, Macmurray, Mannheim, Stevenson, Ayer, and Nowell-Smith, the general tenor of their views raises a strong presumption that they, too, not only exclusively treat circumstantial self-realization but also regard it as man's only freedom.[89]

It is on the basis of the implied rejection of acquired self-perfection that we interpret all of the SR authors just mentioned as taking Position (C) on the present issue. To deny, as they do, that there is any freedom in willing compliance with duty or law is to assert that being able to do what one wishes is unconditionally freedom, i.e., not to be qualified in any way by reference to duties or laws. They are, therefore, opposed to Position (B) as well as Position (A).

The same interpretation can be made in the case of those writers

---

[87] See p. 50, *supra*.
[88] See Vol. I, pp. 250–51, 314, 592–93.
[89] Ch. 5 to follow deals with the issues concerning acquired self-perfection. In that chapter, the authors mentioned above will be seen to reject acquired self-perfection either on existential or conceptual grounds. The evidence or presumption for interpreting these authors on this point is more appropriately treated here. See Ch. 5, pp. 108 ff., *infra*.

who constitute an exception because they do not hold circumstantial self-realization to be man's only freedom. But the additional freedom that is affirmed by Hobhouse, Adam Smith, Burke, N. Hartmann, and Knight is not acquired self-perfection. We have reason to think that N. Hartmann and Knight reject it on existential grounds.[90] And we shall be able to offer explicit evidence of Hobhouse's argument against it.[91] As for Adam Smith and Burke, their rejection of it can be presumed from the whole tendency of their thought, though the presumption may be weaker in their case than it is in regard to such writers as Spencer, Kelsen, Schlick, Hale, Macmurray, and Ayer.

The remaining two authors who constitute an exception raise a more serious problem of interpretation. Freud and Russell affirm an acquired freedom of self-perfection in addition to a circumstantial freedom of self-realization.[92] In this respect, they differ from all the other writers listed under Position (C), who either regard self-realization as man's only freedom or at least do not also affirm self-perfection as a distinct freedom.

The problem to be faced arises from the fact that an unconditional affirmation of circumstantial self-realization is inconsistent with an espousal of acquired self-perfection. The only way we have found in which these two kinds of freedom can be consistently combined in a single theory involves the distinction made by the adherents of Position (B)—between matters prescribed by law and matters on which the law is silent. But Freud and Russell do not employ this distinction to relate the two freedoms they affirm. In fact, we have not been able to find in their writings any awareness of the problem involved in relating them to one another as distinct parts of human freedom.[93]

This may in part be explained by the atypical character of the conceptions Freud and Russell hold with regard to an acquired freedom of self-perfection. Freud's ideal of mental health and Russell's ideal of wisdom do not carry with them the kind of moral law or duty which requires that a man, to be free, must be able to will as he ought in all matters prescribed by law.[94] Hence, the fact that these writers affirm an acquired freedom of self-perfection does not affect their adherence to the unconditional affirmation of circumstantial self-realization that constitutes Position (C).[95]

90 See Ch. 5, pp. 109–10, *infra.*
91 See Ch. 5, pp. 113–14, *infra.*
92 See Vol. I, pp. 113, 133, 177, 263–64, 271–72, 276–77.
93 See Vol. I, pp. 212 fn. 25, and 317.
94 See Vol. I, pp. 263–64.
95 The same cannot be said for Green, since his conception of acquired self-perfection closely resembles that of Kant and Hegel, and so creates a problem in regard to his affirmation of circumstantial self-realization. See fn. 60, on p. 56, *supra.*

4. THE DEBATE OF THE ISSUE

We are satisfied that a three-sided disagreement exists about the genuineness of circumstantial self-realization as a human freedom. But so far we have seen nothing more than assertions and counterassertions by the authors who are parties to this issue. Do they, in addition, offer reasons for the positions they take or against the views of their opponents? Can we find evidence which tends to show something like rational debate of this issue?

A number of the authors, considerably less than half of those we have listed, do advance arguments, either in support of their own views or against views to the contrary. We shall be able to present documentary evidence that something like rational debate of this issue is implicit in the literature. But before we undertake to do this, it is necessary to comment briefly on the fact that what we shall find is at best only a rough approximation to rational debate. The reality falls far short of the ideal.

According to the logical requirements of the ideal, we should expect to find not only affirmative arguments for each position but also arguments in rebuttal, i.e., attempts by each position to refute the arguments advanced against it, or to meet objections and to answer difficulties raised. In fact, the literature affords us evidence of much less than this. We find only the following lines of argument: (i) reasons for the unconditional denial of circumstantial self-realization as a genuine human freedom, and (ii) some answers to these arguments by those who unconditionally affirm the genuineness of the freedom in question. Adherents of Position (C) do not offer any reasons for their unconditional affirmation beyond such as are discernible in their answers to attacks by adherents of Position (A). Nor do adherents of Position (B) present any arguments for their own position.

Logically, any argument for Position (A) also functions as an argument against Position (C) and against one part of Position (B). Whatever reasons can be given for asserting that under *no conditions* is circumstantial self-realization a genuine freedom are necessarily also reasons for denying that it is a genuine freedom under *all conditions*, as well as for denying that there are *only certain conditions* under which it is genuine —one part of the view held by Position (B). Conversely, whatever reasons support the assertion that circumstantial self-realization is a genuine freedom *under all conditions* also provide grounds for denying that there are *no conditions* under which it is a genuine freedom, as well as for denying that there are *only certain conditions* under which it is genuine— the other part of the view held by Position (B). Position (B) is, in a sense, caught in the cross fire between the two more extreme positions; for it agrees in part with Position (A) against Position (C), and in part with Position (C) against Position (A).

As we have pointed out, adherents of Position (C) do not offer reasons for their view apart from those contained in their attempt to rebut the arguments advanced by adherents of Position (A). However, these arguments in rebuttal often involve counterattacks on acquired self-perfection which the principal adherents of Position (A) affirm to the exclusion of circumstantial self-realization. It is often difficult to separate these counterattacks on acquired self-perfection from the defense of circumstantial self-realization. But we must try to keep them separate, for acquired self-perfection is not the subject of the issue we are here considering but will be the subject of the issue to which we turn in the next chapter. Hence, we shall try so far as possible to reserve until then the arguments advanced by Position (C) which go beyond the defense of circumstantial self-realization.

The summary just given reveals two things about such debate as can be found in the literature.

In the first place, the debate is asymmetrical rather than balanced. Considering for the moment only Positions (A) and (C), the motion of the debate involves an attack by adherents of Position (A) on circumstantial self-realization and the defense of it by adherents of Position (C). As the issue is framed, Position (C) is the affirmative position and Position (A) the negative. That may explain why we do not find adherents of Position (C) leading off with arguments against Position (A).

In the second place, the debate is deficient with respect to the arguments for or against Position (B). On the one hand, adherents of this position share the reasons given for opposing the view that circumstantial self-realization is without qualification a genuine human freedom, as, on the other hand, they have a certain sympathy with the reasons given for opposing the view that circumstantial self-realization is not a genuine human freedom under any conditions. But they do not argue affirmatively for the middle ground they hold between the two more extreme positions. Nor do those who either unconditionally affirm or unconditionally deny circumstantial self-realization argue against the middle position, except, of course, insofar as reasons for an unconditional affirmation or an unconditional denial operate against the view that there are certain conditions under which circumstantial self-realization is genuinely human freedom and certain conditions under which it is not.

In examining the arguments pro and con, we shall apply the usual standards of relevance and cogency. For example, arguments to the effect that circumstantial self-realization is a *lower* form of human freedom would be irrelevant, since the point at issue concerns its being a *genuine* form of *human* freedom. Argument must avoid question begging by tacitly assuming the correctness of the position affirmed or the incorrectness of the position denied. Where we find that such assumptions take the place of reasons, we cannot admit the cogency of what is offered. Argument, by definition, always involves something more than the mere assertion or denial of a position.

We shall, first, deal with the arguments for Position (A) and against Position (C). We shall then turn to the arguments in defense of Position (C) against attacks by adherents of Position (A). Finally, we shall consider the part that Position (B) plays in the debate, especially on the side of arguments against the unconditional denial of circumstantial self-realization. In each case, we shall project the general pattern of the argument before we attempt to present documentary evidence that authors have argued along these lines.

(1) *Arguments for Position* (A) *and against Position* (C). Arguments that doing as one pleases is not freedom under any conditions appeal to the generic meaning or common understanding of freedom. The effort is to show that *being able, under favorable circumstances, to act as one wishes for one's individual good as one sees it* does not conform to the idea of freedom, according to which a man must *have in himself the ability or power to make what he does his own action, and what he achieves his own property*. If it can be shown that the formulation of what is common to all conceptions of circumstantial self-realization does not fall under the most general formulation of what freedom is, that would provide adequate ground for asserting that circumstantial self-realization is no freedom at all, which is the contention of Position (A) against Position (C).

On the face of it, this line of argument might appear difficult to advance or sustain. The difficulty does not consist in establishing the relevance of the generic meaning of freedom to the question at issue. On the contrary, as we shall see, adherents of Position (C) also refer to something they call the common, or universal meaning of freedom. From their point of view, that meaning clearly shows that every instance of circumstantial self-realization is an instance of freedom; for in every case of acting as one wishes the individual's action *proceeds from himself* rather than from another, and what it achieves for him is *his own individual good*, something quite proper to himself.

How, then, can the generic meaning or common understanding of freedom provide the ground for concluding that no instance of circumstantial self-realization is ever an instance of freedom, because in no case of acting as one wishes does the action represent the self, nor does such action achieve a good that is proper to the self?

The answer to that question lies in the *interpretation* which is placed on the generic meaning by adherents of Position (A). According to that interpretation, circumstantial self-realization fails to conform to the generic meaning on two counts. This gives rise to two arguments against circumstantial self-realization, one based on the nature of the *self*, the other on the fact of *circumstantiality*.

(i) From the point of view of Position (A), the self which is the principle of freedom must be the *true* self, the self which *rightly* wills what is for the person's *real* good. The individual person as a whole includes forces or inclinations which are antagonistic to the true self and its real good. These elements in a man's make-up lie outside his true self and constitute the other within him which that self must control or dominate. Unless it does, he does not have self-mastery, i.e., mastery by his true self over the rest of himself.

No one is free who is not thus master of himself. But, so the argument runs, no one is master of himself who does whatever he pleases, for the true self is not in command when any wish or desire that the individual may have is the controlling source of his conduct. The true self is in command only when a person's conduct is controlled by what that self wills in accordance with the precepts of law or duty. Law or duty, not wish or desire, is the principle of every action that flows from the true self and is directed toward that self's proper or real good. Hence, "doing as one pleases" expresses an utterly false notion of freedom, the very opposite of self-mastery, since it acknowledges wish or desire, *without any qualification*, to be the ultimate principle of action.

Self-realization only *appears* to conform to the generic meaning of freedom. The counterfeit takes on a certain plausibility precisely because it appears to make the self the principle of freedom. But, it is argued by adherents of Position (A), the deception is unmasked as soon as we see that it is only the true self—the lawful or dutiful self—which can be the principle of true freedom. To use "self" as nothing but a covering or collective name for individual desires or wishes is to set up an impostor in place of the true self, and it is precisely this imposture which makes self-realization a counterfeit of genuine freedom.

(ii) The additional fact that self-realization is dependent on external circumstances which are favorable to the enactment of an individual's wishes or desires furnishes another argument against its being genuine freedom. Here again the ground lies in an appeal to the generic meaning of freedom. But now the argument turns on an interpretation which requires that the self be independent of the other. Freedom worthy of the name is not only self-mastery but also self-dependence, the opposite of which is dependence on the other.

No one is free so far as he depends on factors outside himself to make what he does his own action. But, so this argument runs, the individual's ability to enact his desires or wishes is said to depend wholly or partly on external circumstances. He does not have this ability in himself through the power of his own mind or character. Favorable circumstances confer on him the power to do as he pleases, and unfavorable circumstances leave him powerless to act as he wishes.

Hence, a man can hardly be called free or unfree in respect to those aspects of his behavior which are controlled by things other than himself. The circumstantial character of self-realization deprives it of the self-dependence or independence that is required for freedom. To call "freedom" that which involves dependence on the other is to use the word in a fashion that contradicts its generic or common meaning. In violation of that meaning, circumstantial self-realization is, therefore, a false conception and represents the very opposite of true or genuine freedom.

These two lines of argument are exemplified, sometimes separately and sometimes mingled, in the following passages drawn from the writings of authors whom we have construed as taking Position (A). Many of the authors whom we have interpreted as maintaining that circumstantial self-realization is never genuine freedom appear to assume the truth of their position; or, if they think it can be argued, they give us no clue as to their reasons. But the writers to whom we now turn do provide evidence, ranging from slight hints to more substantial indications, that the lines of argument we have constructed are actually resorted to and that this side of the debate is present in the literature, more or less explicitly.

The Stoic philosophers give a special turn to these arguments by twisting the language of self-realization to their own purpose. Taking cognizance of such expressions as "doing what one pleases" or "living as one wishes," they first treat them as if they conveyed the most generic sense of what freedom is, according to which all freedom lies with the self as against the other. They then proceed to exclude the sense of freedom which runs through all self-realization conceptions of it by the interpretation they place upon the very phrases they borrow from such conceptions to express the generic meaning.

"Who is it," Cicero asks,

> who has the power to live as he wishes, if not only those who follow right reason; whose pleasure consists in discharging their duties; who have planned their lives after giving much thought to it; and who, thereafter, never stray from this plan?

The question is obviously intended rhetorically to elicit the answer that only such men have the power (in which freedom consists) to live as they wish. "Such a person," Cicero continues, never does, nor says, nor thinks anything except as a consequence of sovereign freedom to which he brings his full will. Such a person has his actions and purposes rooted in his *true self*; and these actions never have as end aught but the *true self*. Such a person is truly *master of himself*.

Only such a man, Cicero concludes, "can truly be called free."[96]

Epictetus begins his discourse on freedom with a statement from which no self-realization author would dissent. "That man is free," he declares, "who lives as he wishes, who is proof against compulsion and hindrance and violence, whose impulses are untrammelled, who gets what he wills to get and avoids what he wills to avoid."[97] He repeats this again and again:

> Whenever a man can be hindered or compelled by another at will, assert with confidence that he is not free.[98]
> He is free whom none can hinder, the man who can deal with things as he wishes.[99]
> He is free for whom all things happen according to his will and whom no one can hinder.[100]

In all these statements, Epictetus appears to accept being able to do what one wishes as true freedom. But his purpose is just the opposite, i.e., to show that the man who is dependent upon external circumstances or anything beyond his innermost self for the power to gratify his wishes is a stranger to freedom.

Just as Cicero asks, "Who is it who has the power to live as he wishes?" so Epictetus asks, "Who is he whom none can hinder?" His answer, like Cicero's, excludes the man to whom self-realization authors attribute freedom. Only "the man who fixes his aim on nothing that is not his own" is free in the sense of being unhindered, uncompelled, a man who is able to live as he wishes, a man for whom all things happen according to his will. Epictetus immediately recognizes that the critical question then is, "What does 'not his own' mean?" This he answers as follows:

> All that does not lie in our power to have or not to have. . . . The body then does not belong to us, its parts do not belong to us, our property does not belong to us. If then you set your heart on one of these as though it were your own, you will pay the penalty deserved by him who desires what does not belong to him. The road that leads to freedom, the only release from slavery, is this, to be able to say with your whole

96 *Paradoxa Stoicorum*, Ch. V, 34, pp. 284–86. (Our italics and translation.)
97 *Discourses*, Book IV, Ch. 1, p. 406.
98 *Ibid.*, p. 410.
99 *Ibid.*, p. 418.
100 *Ibid.*, Book I, Ch. 12, p. 247.

soul: "*Lead me, O Zeus, and lead me, Destiny, Whither ordained is by your decree.*"[101]

The only thing which is wholly within man's power and entirely "his own," according to Epictetus, is a man's own will and the control it can exert over his judgments, impulses, and desires. Everything else is at the mercy of adventitious circumstances or can be hindered or controlled by the power of others. The man who sets his will on being able to walk in a certain direction can obviously be hindered; but, as Epictetus points out, it is only his body that is impeded "as a stone is hindered." He has made the mistake of thinking that there is freedom in unimpeded bodily motion, but such things are not *within his power* nor are they *his own.* "Who told you," Epictetus asks, "that it is your business to walk unhindered?"

> The only thing I told you was unhindered was your impulse; as to the service of the body, and its cooperation, you have heard long ago that it is no affair of yours.

The same reasoning applies to other bodily conditions, pleasures of every sort, and all forms of wordly goods. "Am I then not to will to get health?" The answer Epictetus gives summarizes his reason for rejecting circumstantial self-realization as something which lies entirely outside the sphere of human freedom. "Certainly not," he says, "nor anything else that is not your own."

> For nothing is your own that it does not rest with you to procure or to keep when you will. Keep your hands far away from it; above all, keep your will away, or else you surrender yourself into slavery, you put your neck under the yoke, if you admire what is not your own, and set your heart on anything mortal, whatever it be, or anything that depends upon another.[102]

That freedom involves independence is clearly the nerve of the argument. The circumstantial character of self-realization excludes it from being freedom. Whatever things shifting circumstances allow a man at one moment and take away at another cannot belong to his freedom. The sphere of a man's independence is the sphere of things which are *always* in his power.

It is this point about "always" which other adherents of Position (A) rely on in arguing against there being freedom in anything that is fortuitous or circumstantial. Thus, according to Ambrose, only the wise man can *always* do what he wishes, and so only he is truly free.[103] And Philo writes:

---

[101] *Ibid.*, Book IV, Ch. 1, p. 418.
[102] *Ibid.*, pp. 412–13.
[103] See *Letters*, pp. 291–95.

He who always acts sensibly . . . will have the power to do anything and to live as he wishes, and he who has this power must be free. But the good man *always* acts sensibly, and, therefore, he *alone* is free. Again, one who cannot be compelled to do anything or prevented from doing anything, cannot be a slave. But the good man cannot be compelled or prevented; the good man, therefore, cannot be a slave. That he is not compelled nor prevented is evident. One is prevented when he does not get what he desires, but the wise man desires things which have their origin in virtue, and these, being what he is, he cannot fail to obtain.[104]

In all of the foregoing passages, the denial that circumstantial self-realization is genuine freedom rests on an acceptance of "living as one wishes" or "doing what one pleases" as a general statement of what freedom is. None is accompanied by explicit recognition that these very phrases are used by self-realization authors to express their conception of freedom. Nor is any self-realization author named or referred to. Nevertheless, the intent of the passages is plain enough; for by restricting the ability to act as one wishes to matters wholly within the power of the self or, as Cicero says, "to purposes rooted in [the] true self," these passages argue in effect that circumstantial self-realization does not conform to the generic sense of freedom.

Writers such as Rousseau, Hegel, and Kant do not couch their arguments in terms of "living as one wishes" or "doing what one pleases." They rely solely on an interpretation of the generic meaning of freedom as involving *independence*. The self is the principle of freedom only in that realm of acts in which it is sovereign and autonomous—dependent on nothing but itself, even for the law which it obeys.

We find this form of the argument implicit in Rousseau's statements to the effect that the free man, in obeying himself alone, is secure from all personal dependence on others. "There are two kinds of dependence," Rousseau writes:

dependence on things, which is the work of nature; and dependence on men, which is the work of society. Dependence on things, being non-moral, does no injury to liberty and begets no vices; dependence on men, being out of order, gives rise to every kind of vice, and through this master and slave become mutually depraved. If there is any cure for this social evil, it is to be found in the substitution of law for the individual; in arming the general will with a real strength beyond the power of any individual will.[105]

Those who obey the general will do not obey other men, but themselves alone; and such "obedience to a law which we prescribe to ourselves is

---

[104] *Every Good Man is Free*, Ch. IX, Sect. 59–60, p. 45. (Italics added.)
[105] *Emile*, Book II, p. 49.

liberty."[106] Even the man who is compelled to obey the general will is thereby "forced to be free," for he is thus secured "against all personal dependence."[107]

Speaking in terms of the will instead of the self, Hegel equates freedom and independence. "Only that will which obeys law is free," Hegel writes, "for it obeys itself—it is independent and so free."[108] But Hegel goes further than Rousseau in excluding every form of dependence from the realm of freedom.

> The Will is Free only when it does not will anything alien, extrinsic, foreign to itself (for as long as it does, it is dependent), but wills itself alone —wills the Will.[109]

Circumstantial self-realization generally involves bodily motions for the enactment of the individual's wishes or the realization of his desires. But the physical realm of bodies in motion is one of dependent existences, each thing dependent for its being and its motions upon other things. Hence, according to Hegel, we cannot find any freedom there, but only in the realm of spirit, for "spirit is *self-contained existence*" and "this is Freedom exactly. For if I am dependent, my being is referred to something else which I am not; I cannot exist independently of something external. I am free, on the contrary, when my existence depends upon myself."[110]

For Kant also, there is no freedom without complete independence. For him, as perhaps not even for Rousseau and Hegel, the autonomy of the free man is absolute or unconditional.[111] The free man, who obeys himself alone, obeys laws of his own making—the legislative enactments of his own practical reason. He knows no constraint except *self-constraint*, no mastery except *self-mastery*, no government except *self-government*.[112]

---

106 *The Social Contract*, Book I, Ch. VIII, p. 19.

107 *Ibid.*, Ch. VII, p. 18. To complete the argument, it is necessary to remember that what Rousseau calls "natural liberty"—the power a man has in a state of nature to do as he wishes—is the very opposite of true liberty, precisely because it involves personal dependence, i.e., the dependence of the individual on his own strength as against the strength of others. See *ibid.*, Ch. VIII, p. 19.

108 *Philosophy of History*, Introduction, p. 39.

109 *Ibid.*, Part IV, p. 442. The self-enclosed will must be completely reflexive. It must be "related to nothing except itself and so . . . released from every tie of dependence on anything else" (*Philosophy of Right*. Par. 23, p. 30). The epitome of freedom for Hegel is "the free will which wills the free will" (*ibid.*, Par. 27, p. 32).

110 *Philosophy of History*, Introduction, p. 17.

111 See Vol. I, pp. 288–91. Hegel and Rousseau, we observed, do not, like Kant, conceive the free man as a self-contained whole, almost a world unto himself; in their view, he is only free as belonging to the larger world of the state.

112 See *Preface to the Metaphysical Elements of Ethics*, pp. 290–92, 307–8, 318–19.

Though Kant does not himself explicitly complete the argument, the implicit inference can be easily drawn from the premise he gives us. If the complete autonomy of the self is required for freedom, and if that can be achieved only by a self which is imbued with laws or duties that it gives itself, then circumstantial self-realization is the very opposite of freedom: first, because, in contrast to the true and lawful self, what we have here is nothing but desires or inclinations of external origin, and, secondly, because such desires are completely dependent on external circumstances for their realization.

The foregoing line of argument is slightly more explicit in Bradley, at least with regard to the true self as the self which is imbued with law. Independence is not stressed, as it is in Rousseau, Kant, and Hegel; but Bradley, nevertheless, appeals to the generic notion of freedom as involving the assertion of the self. "What," he asks, "*is* this self, the assertion of which is freedom?" The colloquy he then conducts in the following passage` outlines the argument:

> "My self," we shall hear, "is what is mine; and mine is what is *not* yours, or what does not belong to anyone else. I am free when I assert my private will, the will peculiar to me." Can this hold? Apart from any other objection, is it freedom? Suppose I am a glutton and a drunkard; in these vices I assert my private will; am I then free so far as a glutton and drunkard, or am I a slave—the slave of my appetites? The answer must be, "The slave of his lusts is, so far, not a free man. The man is free who realizes his *true* self." Then the whole question is, What is this true self, and can it be found apart from something like law?[113]

Finally, we come to a most explicit presentation of the argument and one that is accompanied by specific reference to writers who hold the view which is being argued against. In *The Philosophical Theory of the State*, Bosanquet devotes a whole chapter to criticizing the self-realization theories of freedom to be found in Bentham, J. S. Mill, and Spencer, and follows that, several chapters later, by a series of reflections on the meaning of liberty, on which he then bases his rejection of these counterfeits of true freedom.

Bosanquet acknowledges that the self-realization authors use the term "freedom" in a sense that *appears* to conform to its generic or essential meaning. Their insistence that freedom consists in the absence of constraint, or in the exemption of the self from coercion or obstruction by others, would seem to be a correct insistence on the self as the principle of freedom. Their understanding of freedom, Bosanquet tells us, seems to

---

[113] *Ethical Studies*, p. 57; cf. Plato, *Republic*, Book IV, 430E–31B.

grasp its "literal meaning" if we do not try to go beyond a "first look" at the subject.[114]

But when we take a second look, we find, according to Bosanquet, that these authors have a false conception of freedom because they mistake an appearance of the self for the real self. If you ask them what they mean by constraint, their "answer is founded on the current distinction between myself and others as different minds attached to different bodies."[115] But this, Bosanquet tries to show, is an utterly superficial, inadequate, and even somewhat contradictory notion of the self. The self must be properly understood if we are to understand the truth about freedom as "obeying only yourself" or as "being determined only by ourselves."

The identification of the self with the individual as a psychophysical whole leads Bentham, in Bosanquet's opinion, into irresolvable difficulties. Referring to Bentham's theory that every law is a restriction of liberty and a necessary evil which can be justified only in the case of those laws which prevent injury to others or which somehow maximize freedom, Bosanquet writes:

> But if this is so, the restrictive influences of law and government, which are the measure of the constraint imposed, cannot be alien to the human nature which they restrict, and ought not to be set down as in their own nature antagonistic to liberty or to the making the most of the human self. The root of the difficulty lies in assuming that the pressure of the claim of "others" in society is a mere general curtailment of the liberty of the "one," while acknowledging, not contrary to fact, but contrary to the hypothesis of that curtailment, that the one, so far from surrendering some of his capacity for life through his fellowship with others, acquires and extends that capacity wholly in and through such fellowship. . . . Government is made an evil of which it is impossible to explain how it ministers to the self which stands for the good. So long as to every individual, *taken as the true self*, the restraint enforced by the impact of others is alien and a diminution of the self, this result is inevitable.[116]

In treating Spencer's similar theory of the antagonism between law or government and freedom, Bosanquet again criticizes the fact that "liberty and the self are divorced from the moral end. . . .

[114] See *op. cit.*, p. 134, where Bosanquet refers to the self-realization authors as "theorist of the first look," and p. 126, where he speaks of "the juristic meaning of the term liberty, based on the normal distinction between one self-determining person and another . . . as its literal meaning."

[115] *Ibid.*, pp. 125–26. Cf. *Ibid.*, p. 133–34, where Bosanquet speaks of "the given self" as nothing but the set of "wishes, of feelings and ideas, associated from time to time with my particular body."

[116] *Ibid.*, p. 55. (Italics added.)

Selves in society are regarded as if they were bees building their cells, and their ethical character becomes comparable to the absence of encroachment by which the workers maintain the hexagonal outline due to their equal impact on each other as they progress evenly from equidistant centers. The self, which had ranked throughout these views as the end, to whose liberty all is to be sacrificed, turns out to be the non-ethical element of life.[117]

Finally, after criticizing Mill's "extraordinary demarcation between the sphere of morality and that of liberty," Bosanquet points to certain passages in which "Mill recognizes a principle wholly at variance with his own." One is the passage in which Mill says that no one should be allowed to abdicate his liberty by selling himself into slavery.[118] Here, according to Bosanquet, Mill shows himself aware

> that it may be right, according to the principle of liberty, to restrain a man, for reasons affecting himself alone, from doing what at the moment he proposes to do.

Bosanquet thinks that this acknowledges the soundness of the argument against self-realization theories: for it admits that

> we are entitled to argue from the essential nature of freedom to what freedom really demands, as opposed to what the man momentarily seems to wish. [Just as] "it is not freedom to be allowed to alienate his freedom," [so] it is not freedom to be allowed to walk over a bridge which is certain to break down and cause his death. Here we have in germ the doctrine of the "real" will, and a conception analogous to that of Rousseau when he speaks of a man "being forced to be free."[119]

According to Bosanquet, that doctrine, as found not only in Rousseau but also in many other writers from Plato to Hegel, gets at the truth about freedom as self-assertion and as absence of interference by others, because it properly identifies the true self which is the principle of freedom. The other, from whose interference the self must be exempt, consists of all those forces within a man that stand in the way of his willing what is really for his good. What at first appears to be only a metaphorical version of freedom, as contrasted with the "literal meaning" advanced by "the theorists of the first look," becomes upon closer examination the whole reality of freedom. This reality fully embodies the essential meaning of

[117] *Ibid.*, p. 68.
[118] "The principle of freedom," Mill writes, "cannot require that [a man] should be free not to be free. It is not freedom to be allowed to alienate his freedom" (*On Liberty*, Ch. V, p. 158).
[119] *Philosophical Theory of the State*, pp. 64–65.

freedom. Circumstantial self-realization, which always involves "the absence of external constraint," is nothing but "an elementary type or symbol" of freedom—the appearance of it, in short, not the reality.[120]

(2) *Arguments in defense of Position (C) against attacks from Position (A).* Against the reasons advanced by adherents of Position (A) for their unconditional denial that circumstantial self-realization is genuinely a human freedom, there are several arguments in rebuttal. Let us consider the general pattern these take before we look to the literature for specific exemplifications of them.

One form of rebuttal attacks the substitution of the *true* self for the actual self as the principle of freedom, and the consequent substitution of the *right* will for any wish or desire which the individual may have, and of the *real* good for whatever thing the individual judges to be good for himself. The charge is made that only by such illicit substitutions can it be argued that circumstantial self-realization does not conform to the generic idea of freedom. In addition, it is pointed out that many of the adherents of Position (A) begin by admitting that "being able to do as one wishes for one's own good as one sees it" expresses the common understanding of freedom, which is evidenced by ordinary or everyday speech. Some of them even go so far as to concede that this is the primitive, the elementary, or the literal meaning of the word. Hence, they can avoid the consequences of such acknowledgments only by playing tricks with the terms used.

According to the defenders of Position (C), the term "self," in its normal and literal meaning, refers to the individual as a whole—to everything that constitutes one human being and distinguishes him from other men and from everything else in his environment. The *other* which can oppose the *self* is to be found in anything and everything that lies outside or surrounds the existent individual, that psychophysical whole which includes all the bodily members and motions of the human organism as well as all the impulses, desires, emotions, thoughts, and judgments which enter into the organism's behavior. In its literal meaning, "circumstances"

---

[120] See *ibid.*, pp. 128–36. In the concluding lines of the book, Bosanquet indicates once more that the argument against self-realization rests on an understanding of freedom which the adherents of self-realization implicitly acknowledge, but which they misapply because they fail to recognize the true self, the right will, and the real good. "Freedom—the non-obstruction of capacities—is to be found," he writes, "in a system which lays burdens on the untamed self and 'forces us to be free.' What we feel as mere force cannot as such be freedom; but in our subtle and complex natures the recognition of a force may, as we have tried to explain, sustain, regularize, and reawaken the operation of a consciousness of the good, which we rejoice to see maintained, if our intelligence fails of itself to maintain it, against indolence, incompetence, and rebellion, even if they are our own" (*ibid.*, pp. 310–11).

refer to all the *surrounding* factors that condition the existence of the self and its behavior. Once admitted that *self* and *other* are the basic terms in the generic meaning of freedom, and that, accordingly, a man is free whenever what he does or becomes *flows from himself instead of from some other*, only unjustifiable restrictions on or perversions of the meanings of "self" and "other" can lead to the conclusion that circumstantial self-realization does not conform to the idea of freedom. In fact, it perfectly embodies the general understanding of freedom, for it adequately expresses the common notions that men have about self and other.

When the opponents of self-realization replace the actual self—identical with the individual as a whole—by the "real self" which they admit is only one part of the individual, and set this against another part of him which they then treat as the "interfering other," they are indulging in metaphors. Far from being the reality, the "real self" is a fiction of their own invention. Some of the adherents of Position (A) admit that it is metaphorical speech to speak of freedom as involving a relation between the component parts of a single individual by converting these into self and other. They then attempt to justify treating the metaphorical self as the real self, but they can do this only by treating man as if he were a disembodied spirit, not a biological organism, or as if he were a soul using a body as a driver uses an automobile, not a psychophysical unity.

Their substitution of the "real will" or the "right will" for the actual wishes or desires of the individual, and their replacement of the good as it appears to each individual by the "true good" or the "real good" which all men should seek, is equally illicit and unjustifiable. It is nothing more than a completely arbitrary attempt to impose upon everyone else the wishes or goals of those who happen to hold or share certain philosophical views about what is good for all men, whether they know it or not, and what they should seek, whether they wish to or not. It is hardly a tenable argument against self-realization theories of freedom to say that "acting as one wishes for the good as one sees it" truly represents freedom only if the individual who is doing the wishing can bring his wishes and his opinions concerning what is good for him into line with the wishes and opinions of the philosophers who are advancing the argument.

Most of the authors whom we have listed as adherents of Position (C) do not take any cognizance of attacks on their own views. Quite apart from efforts at rebuttal, most of them do not even argue affirmatively for the position that circumstantial self-realization is genuinely a human freedom. They either assume that there can be no question about this or, if they entertain the question, they simply assert that "being able, under favorable circumstances, to do as one pleases for the good as one sees it" expresses the common, the universal, or the literal meaning of the term "freedom."

However, a few self-realization authors go further than this. Such writers as Bentham, Laski, Hobhouse, and Russell, among the principal authors in this group, do take cognizance of contrary views and arguments and attempt to rebut them. The form their rebuttal takes is that outlined. They challenge the substitution of the "real self" for the actual self, and of the "real will" or the "real good" for actual desires and actual goals. They call attention to the metaphorical or fanciful, and even perverse, twists which their opponents give to the basic terms in which freedom is generally understood. They reject as illicit and unjustifiable such attempts to impose restrictive interpretations upon the general or common meaning, to the exclusion of circumstantial self-realization as no freedom at all.

In the context of arguing for his own view that every coercive law encroaches on some portion of freedom, Bentham refers to "those among the friends of liberty who are more ardent than enlightened [and who] make it a duty of conscience to combat this truth." This reference certainly covers adherents of Position (A) insofar as they maintain the very opposite, namely, that law is the foundation of freedom and that those who are compelled to obey the general will which it embodies are thereby forced to be free. Of them, Bentham writes:

> They pervert language; they refuse to employ the word *liberty* in its common acceptation; they speak a tongue peculiar to themselves. This is the definition they give of liberty: *Liberty consists in the right of doing everything which is not injurious to another.* But is this the ordinary sense of the word? Is not the liberty to do evil liberty? If not, what is it? What word can we use in speaking of it? Do we not say that it is necessary to take away liberty from idiots and bad men, because they abuse it?[121]

In similar vein, Bertrand Russell declares:

> I do not think it desirable to use words in fancy senses. For instance, Hegel and his followers think that "true" freedom consists in the right to obey the police, who are generally called "the moral law." In practice, the adherents of this view argue that the State is essentially and by definition impeccable. This notion is inappropriate in a country where there is democracy and party government, since in such a country nearly half the nation believes the Government to be very wicked. We cannot, therefore, rest content with "true" freedom as a substitute for freedom.

Russell then asserts the self-realization meaning for freedom as itself the generic meaning of the idea. " 'Freedom' in its most abstract sense," he

[121] *Theory of Legislation,* pp. 94–95.

writes, "means the absence of external obstacles to the realization of desires."[122]

A number of other writers echo this refrain. Barbara Wootton, for example, asserting that "freedom may be simply defined as ability to do what you want," then goes on to deny the validity, for all practical purposes, of any distinction between what people want to do, and what they 'really' want to do."[123] Robert MacIver makes the same point at greater length.

In an essay "The Meaning of Liberty and Its Perversion," he asserts that in saying what freedom is,

> we are merely identifying a meaning, not defining it. It is a meaning we must simply recognize, simply accept. The universality of usage sets it for us. It is understood by the child and by the savage as well as by the civilized man. It is a meaning we cannot do without, and thus we find that when people offer us some alternative and different meaning, they nonetheless imply that it is equivalent to the universally accepted meaning. Here, as we shall see, is the root of the worst perversions. On this account much that is written on the subject of liberty is worse than futile.[124]

What is the universal meaning of freedom which everyone recognizes and everyone employs, even those who distort or pervert it? "This universal meaning [about which] there can be no doubt," MacIver puts before us in the following examples:

> The child knows it who is forced to work when he wants to play. The savage knows it who is prevented from following his tribal custom. The criminal knows it who is put behind prison bars. The property-owner knows it who is not allowed to use his property as he pleases. Everywhere in human society, for better or worse, there are hindrances and prohibitions set by the will of others to that which we want to do, and everywhere the condition of which we are deprived is called liberty.[125]

[122] *Skeptical Essays*, p. 169. It will be remembered that Russell has a theory of freedom which includes an acquired freedom of self-perfection as well as a circumstantial freedom of self-realization. But as we pointed out earlier in this chapter, his conception of acquired self-perfection deviates from the typical theory of this matter to such an extent that he need have no embarrassment in attacking the more nearly typical theory of it to be found in Hegel. See p. 63, *supra*.
[123] *Freedom Under Planning*, p. 5.
[124] See *Freedom: Its Meaning*, p. 280.
[125] See *ibid.*, p. 285. "The meaning of the term," MacIver continues, "may be extended to include the absence of other obstacles to action than those that depend on the will of men to prevent our acting. . . . Or again it may be extended to include the absence of hindrances in ourselves to the fulfillment of the things our hearts desire. Thus we speak of men as being 'slaves to their habits.' But this is clearly an analogical variant, not to be pressed too far, *certainly not to be made the ground for a redefinition of a term so necessary, so widely used, so unmistakable in its primary applications*" (*ibid.*, italics added). In the italicized part of the last sentence, MacIver calls attention to the metaphorical sense of freedom in which the roles of self and other are played

Having thus declared the universal meaning of freedom to be the meaning embodied in circumstantial self-realization—negatively, the absence of restraints; positively, the ability to realize one's desires, whatever they are—MacIver then attacks two ways in which this meaning gets perverted. One way derives from the distortion of the meaning that results from placing exclusive emphasis on certain types of restraints or on certain types of desires to be realized. But at least those who do this "profess to mean by liberty that which is its universal meaning." Their fault consists in restricting its scope too narrowly in accord with their own special interests. What MacIver calls the worst or "final perversion" is committed by those who completely redefine freedom so that it becomes the very opposite of what is universally meant by the term. They, nevertheless, try to make it appear to be the only real embodiment of that meaning, so that they can "appeal to the emotions generated by the universal meaning . . . and transfer to [their] new meaning the values that properly attach to the original meaning."

This offense, which he calls "the lie in the soul," MacIver tells us has been made the fashion by a long line of philosophers.

> In the modern world it was set by Rousseau and it attained its philosophical culmination in Hegel. Today it is exploited most notably, though far from exclusively, by the apologists of antilibertarian forms of government. For the curious thing about these final perversions is that they enable men to justify in the name of liberty the most extreme suppressions of liberty.

Then, in the following passage, MacIver specifically enumerates the restrictive interpretations which are imposed on the generic meaning in order to distort or pervert its meaning beyond all recognition.

> Our modern sophists draw a distinction between real liberty and apparent liberty. They proclaim that we are free only when we do what we *ought* to do—or rather what they think we ought to do; only when we desire what we *ought* to desire—what they think we ought to desire. They say that liberty is self-realization, the realization of the true self. . . . So Bernard Bosanquet, for example, contrasted our "actual" will and our

---

by conflicting parts of one and the same man; but at the same time he argues against using this metaphorical sense to redefine the term in a way that would exclude its primary meaning, which is that of circumstantial self-realization. Dorothy Fosdick, a student of MacIver, calls attention to the fact that writers like Bosanquet admit that it is metaphorical speech to "use the term liberty to describe the inner relation between elements of a man's nature." She then uses this admission as sufficient refutation of his view. "While Bosanquet justifies the 'metaphorical application of the term "liberty" to a state of the individual mind,' his admission that it is a metaphor," Fosdick contends, "gives away his case" (*What is Liberty?* p. 104).

"real" will. With sublime Hegelian arrogance they confer reality on what they think ought to be, and degrade to unreality that which they think ought not to be.

So it is not surprising that they often end by merging liberty with its own contradiction. It is the supreme example of having one's cake and eating it too. Rousseau again led the way when he spoke of men being "forced to be free." He was not content with saying "forced to be good," "forced to be rational." He gloried in what seemed to him only a paradox—instead of a perversion. In this he has had a multitude of followers. They transmuted liberty into self-surrender, self-abnegation, obedience, subjection. Hegel reconciled the opposites by announcing that they were one. The individual who is "forced to be free" might protest, but of course it is not his true self that protests. Hegel knows better. . . .

These apologists will not face the issue that they value other things more highly than liberty and that they reject liberty for the sake of those other things. That position would at least be honest. Instead, they pervert the universal meaning of liberty in order to deny the most obvious of facts. They would destroy the meaning of liberty because they are afraid to admit its meaning. They call it something else, hoping that thus no one will claim it for what it is.[126]

The two writers who remain to be considered offer us the most explicit and detailed critique of Position (A) from the point of view of Position (C). In his *Metaphysical Theory of the State*, Hobhouse attacks what he calls the "idealist" theory of freedom, as he finds it expounded by Rousseau, Hegel, and Bosanquet; and Laski, in *Liberty in the Modern State*, devotes considerable space in his introductory chapter to a further statement of the arguments against the idealists, which, he says, were "put in classic form by the late Professor Hobhouse."[127] The major part of their effort is directed against the freedom of acquired self-perfection as that is conceived by Rousseau, Hegel, and Bosanquet, rather than to a defense of circumstantial self-realization as a genuine freedom. Intermingled with it, however, are the following indications of the argument in rebuttal that challenges the notions of "true self," "right will," and "real good."

What Hobhouse has to say in rejoinder to Bosanquet's *Philosophical Theory of the State* applies as well to the authors on whom Bosanquet most relies—Rousseau and Hegel. He quotes at length the passage in which Bosanquet attempts to distinguish between the real will and the actual will.[128] His summary comment is as follows:

[126] See *ibid.*, pp. 286–87.
[127] *Op. cit.*, p. 61.
[128] See *The Metaphysical Theory of the State*, pp. 41–42. Following this quotation, Hobhouse says: "According to Dr. Bosanquet, then, there is underlying the actual will, of which we are aware, a deeper real will, which is the actual will reorganized and made

The essence of the position is now before us. . . . The real will is the general will and is expressed in the social fabric. . . . The state, therefore, is the true self in which the mere individual is absorbed. . . . We are morally free when our actions conform to our real will, our real will is the general will, and the general will is most fully embodied in the state.[129]

This leaves us, Hobhouse points out, "with the paradox that our real will may be something which we never really will because we do not even know it and could not recognize it if it were set before us."[130] Not only does Bosanquet fail to explain away this paradox "but," according to Hobhouse, "there is a more fundamental objection to the term 'real will.'"

Strictly there is no part in me which is more real than any other part. There are elements in me which are more permanent, and if the self is permanent, there are, let us say, moods or actions which really belong to myself more than others do, but one mood is not more real a mood or one act more real an act than another. The term "Real" is in fact in such passages as these used rhetorically. . . .[131]

Hobhouse similarly criticizes the substitution of the real good for the actual goals that individuals set themselves.

. . . the will which Bosanquet calls real and which I would call rational, harmonious, or simply good, is not real in the average man, nor even in its completeness in the best of men. Bosanquet's own description of course shows that he is perfectly aware of this, yet he confuses the whole issue by the use of the adjective "real." It is misleading to contrast real with transitory, trivial aims. It is not merely one's superficial or casual interests that clash with others and exhibit contradiction with one another so that they interfere with the best life, it is also the deepest passions and sometimes the most fervid conscience. A man may feel, and the feeling may be no illusion, that a personal passion goes to the very foundation of his being, and yet the passion may be lawless or it may collide with the entire bent of his life in other directions, his devotion to public duty, for example, or perhaps deeprooted obligations of family and friendship. If the real self means that which goes deep, we cannot deny that it contains possibilities of contradiction far more serious than the collision between permanent interest and passing desire.[132]

---

completely consistent or coherent. It is in fact that organized system of purposes which we found in the Hegelian will, and in a later passage Dr. Bosanquet adopts the Hegelian phrase—'the will that wills itself' " (*ibid.*, pp. 42–43).

[129] *Ibid.*, p. 43.
[130] *Ibid.*, p. 44.
[131] *Ibid.*, p. 45.
[132] *Ibid.*, pp. 47–48.

Hobhouse, then, summarizes what he takes to be the four assumptions underlying Bosanquet's position.[133] Against the real will and the real self which these assumptions posit, he asserts the view that

> the self is a continuous identity united by strands of private memory and expectation, comprising elements of feeling, emotion and bodily sensation, which are its absolute exclusive property. No such continuity unites distinct selves, however alike, or however united to their objects. So at least it seems to those whom Dr. Bosanquet dismisses with contempt as "theorists of the first look." For them human individuality is and remains something ultimate. To Dr. Bosanquet on the other hand individuality is only a particular case of the distinct contribution offered by parts within a system which he calls the universal. The differences within the self are for him in their essential nature identical with the differences between selves. . . . This makes me, as popular metaphor has always recognized, a kind of miniature state; and for Bosanquet this metaphor expresses the real truth.[134]

Confronted by the idealist theory, common sense, according to Hobhouse, "has a feeling of outrage which makes it disinclined to argue. It is inclined to say that the difference between self and another is as plain as the difference between black and white, and that if a man does not see it, there is nothing plainer to appeal to." But Hobhouse does not feel that it is "quite satisfactory to leave the argument at this point. We must trace the roots of the fallacy."[135]

He traces "the foundations of Dr. Bosanquet's identification of individuals"—i.e., his fusion of individuals into one real self—"to a confusion in the use of the word 'experience.'"

> Experience as meaning a world of objects may be common to many selves. Experience as that which each self enjoys or suffers is absolutely private. In the former sense different minds can enter into a single experience; in the latter never, though they may know about one another's experience.[136]

Stemming from this confusion, Bosanquet's "denial of individuality leads [him] to repudiate the view that force, or generally speaking state inter-

---

[133] He states them as follows: "(1) There is in me a real self, my real will, which is opposed to what I very often am. (2) This real will is what I ought to be as opposed to what I very often am. (3) There is in you a real will and in every other member of society a real will. All these real wills are what you and every other member of society ought to be. In quality and character these real wills are indistinguishable. They are therefore the same. (4) This sameness constitutes of all the real wills together one self" (*ibid.*, p. 50).
[134] *Ibid.*, pp. 50–51.
[135] *Ibid.*, p. 51.
[136] *Ibid.*, p. 54.

ference, lies in the intrusion of others upon the self. To him in principle
there are no others."[137] He, therefore, fails to see how "the use of force is
subject to great abuse," precisely because "it is an intrusion on one set of
people by others."[138] Only in this way can Bosanquet explain how "in an
ordered society I am free, though under compulsion, because the will of
society is my will, and the compulsion is exercised by myself upon myself."
Hobhouse's comment is that, however attractive on the surface such a
theory may be, "these are mere words."[139] To speak of the self exerting
force upon itself is just metaphor which belongs "to the sphere of play-
acting with our moral nature."[140] And in the case in which "the law
prevents me from drinking or compels me to serve in the army, it is absurd
to maintain that it is in these very respects augmenting my freedom."[141]

Like Hobhouse, Laski presents an extended summary of the idealist
view that "conformity to a code, and even compulsory obedience to it, is
the very essence of freedom. So startling a paradox needs, at the least, an
explanation."[142] That explanation, he finds, requires all the assumptions
about the true self, the right will, and the real good which Hobhouse
enumerated and criticized.[143] It is precisely on these assumptions that one
argument against circumstantial self-realization is based. For those who
make them, "true liberty is . . . so far from being an absence of restraint,"[144] that it is the very opposite: I must regard myself as "most
fully free when I am most suffused with the sense of compulsion."[145] But,
according to Laski, "a true theory of liberty . . . is built upon a denial of
each of the assumptions of idealism," which add up to a view that
"contradicts all the major facts of experience."[146]

Laski then proceeds, in the following passages, to rebut the assumptions
on which is based the denial that circumstantial self-realization is true
liberty.

My true self [he writes] is not a selected system of rational purposes
identical with those sought by every member of society. We cannot
split up the wholeness of personality in this way. My true self is all that
I am and do. It is the total impression produced by the bewildering variety
of my acts, good and bad and indifferent. All of them go to the formation

[137] *Ibid.*, p. 57.
[138] *Ibid.*, p. 58.
[139] *Ibid.*, p. 59.
[140] *Ibid.*, p. 58.
[141] *Ibid.*, p. 60.
[142] *Liberty in the Modern State*, p. 56.
[143] See *ibid.*, pp. 56–58.
[144] *Ibid.*, p. 56.
[145] *Ibid.*, p. 58.
[146] *Ibid.*, p. 58. Cf. *The Grammar of Politics*, pp. 29–35; and also *The State in Theory and Practice*, pp. 37–85.

of my view of the universe; all of them are my expression of my striving to fulfill my personality. Each, while it is, is real, and each, as real, must give way only in terms of a judgment I make, not of one made for me by some other will, if I am to remain a purposive human being serving myself as an end. This attempt, in a word, at the extraction of a partial self from the whole of my being as alone truly myself not only denies that my experience is real, but, also, makes me merely an instrument to the purposes of others. Whatever that condition is, surely it cannot be recognized as freedom.[147]

Furthermore, he continues,

I see no reason to suppose that this assumed real will is identical in every member of society. The ultimate and inescapable fact in politics is the final variety of human wills. There is no continuum which makes all of them one. Experience suggests common objects of desire, but each will that wills these common objects is a different will in every sense, not purely metaphorical. . . . There is, therefore, no single and common will in society, unless we mean thereby the vague concept, entirely useless for political philosophy, that men desire the good. Each of us desires the good as he sees it; and each of us sees a good derived from an individual and separate experience into which no other person can fully enter. . . . We remain ourselves even when we join with others to attain some common object of desire. The ultimate isolation of the individual personality is the basis from which any adequate theory of politics must start.[148]

On this basis, which identifies the self with the isolated individual as a whole, Laski rejects "the idea of a real will, and, still more, the idea that there is a common will in society."[149] The same ground that Laski employs to rebut the attack on circumstantial self-realization he also uses to assert that self-realization represents the only true sense of self-mastery, and thus embodies the essence of freedom.

Man is one among a many obstinately refusing reduction to unity. His separateness, his isolation, are indefeasible. . . . If he surrenders it to others, he surrenders his personality. If his will is set by the will of others, he ceases to be master of himself.

With the generic meaning of freedom in mind, Laski concludes by saying, "I cannot believe that a man no longer master of himself is in any meaningful sense free."[150] We see here a striking confirmation that the adherents of Positions (A) and (C), in arguing against one another, appeal to the idea of freedom itself in its most abstract form as the ultimate touchstone to be used in separating true from false conceptions of it.

[147] *Ibid.*, pp. 58–59.
[148] *Ibid.*, pp. 59–60.
[149] *Ibid.*, p. 60.
[150] *Ibid.*, p. 62.

The foregoing represents the arguments in rebuttal which we have found in the literature. But it will be remembered that two different lines of argument are advanced against Position (C) by the adherents of Position (A)—one based on the nature of the self, and one based on the fact of circumstantiality.[151] The arguments in rebuttal that we just examined deal only with the first of these. We find no evidence of any attempt to meet the second line of attack upon circumstantial self-realization, the one which stems from the insistence that the generic meaning of freedom entails the absolute or unconditional independence of the self.

As we have seen, those who argue in this manner exclude all dependence on the other, and hence exclude from the sphere of freedom anything in which the self is dependent on external circumstances. They restrict freedom to that which is completely within the power of the self or to those things which the self is always able to do, no matter what the circumstances. How might such arguments be challenged or countered?

It is of interest to speculate about the form the rebuttal of them might take. The following is offered as a possible response.

Argument in rebuttal might begin by pointing out that the restriction of freedom to that which is *completely* within the power of the self is another illicit and unjustifiable contraction of the generic meaning. It violates one of the basic terms of the issue itself. The question at issue concerns the genuineness of self-realization as a *human* freedom, not as a superhuman or divine freedom. Man is a finite being and, like every finite being, suffers limitations in existence, power, and action. Human freedom, like every other aspect of human existence and behavior, is finite, not infinite, which means that it cannot take the form of absolute or unconditional independence. Precisely because they recognize that the ability of the individual to do as he wishes depends on circumstances, self-realization theories properly conceive human freedom. To reject these theories on the ground that such freedom does not give the self complete independence is to demand a freedom that exceeds man's finite condition and power.

Furthermore, this line of argument might proceed, it is false to say that because something is not wholly within the individual's power, it is not in his power at all. A man has in himself the power to walk, the power to acquire certain possessions, the power to strive for health, even if, in attempting to exercise such powers, he is prevented by adverse circumstances. The fact that favorable circumstances enable him to do these things does not warrant saying that the ability to enact his wishes is wholly conferred on him by external conditions or factors.

Granted that a man cannot always do as he wishes, because being able

[151] See pp. 67–68, *supra*.

to do so depends in part on circumstances and in part on his own capacities, it does not follow that he can *never* do as he wishes, but only that sometimes he can and sometimes he cannot. Here as before, to reject circumstantial self-realization on the ground that it is not enough for the individual to be able to do as he wishes some part of the time and under certain circumstances is to demand an absolute and superhuman freedom in place of one that is relative to human nature and is the condition of man as a dependent and finite being.[152]

(3) *The role of Position (B) in the debate.* In this chapter, we have indicated evidence that Aquinas, Locke, Montesquieu, Maritain, and Yves Simon assert the propositions which constitute Position (B).[153] And in Book II, we gave evidence that such writers as Aquinas, Maritain, and Yves Simon hold a conception of acquired self-perfection which differs from that held by such writers as Rousseau, Kant, and Hegel, as well as from that held by the Stoic philosophers, with regard to the degree of autonomy or independence involved in such freedom.[154] But we can find no evidence that the adherents of Position (B) take part in this debate by arguing against the views held by the adherents of the other two positions. It is clear that a three-sided disagreement exists in the literature, but a three-sided debate does not.

Nevertheless, it is of interest to speculate on the manner in which Position (B) might make itself felt in the debate of this issue. What follows is offered as a statement of possible arguments. Opposed as they are to each of the more extreme positions, involving respectively an unconditional denial and an unconditional affirmation of circumstantial self-realization, the adherents of Position (B) would have to argue against each of them separately: against Position (A) upholding the view that it is genuine freedom to be able, under favorable circumstances, to do what one wishes; and against Position (C) upholding the view that it is genuine freedom *only* in regard to matters on which the law, divine, moral, or civil, is silent.

It might look at first as if the defense of circumstantial self-realization against the unconditional rejection of it by Position (A) might be argued in the same way or on the same grounds from the viewpoint of Position (B) as it is argued from the viewpoint of Position (C). But upon closer ex-

---

[152] This argument in rebuttal might also point out that two of the main adherents of Position (A) themselves regard circumstances favorable to the enactment of the individual's will as *essential* to his freedom. While Rousseau and Hegel insist that only the good man is free, they also insist that living in a well-constituted state is indispensable to the freedom of even the wisest and most virtuous of men. See Vol. I, pp. 252–53, 306–9, 315, 346.

[153] See pp. 59–62, *supra.*

[154] See Vol. I, pp. 281–312, 315–27.

amination there is a difficulty about this; for the arguments in rebuttal made from the viewpoint of Position (C) are to the effect that there are no grounds whatsoever for denying that doing what one wishes is genuine freedom, or, in other words, that there are no conditions under which it should be rejected as a false conception. But what distinguishes Position (B) from Position (C) is that its adherents do reject circumstantial self-realization as license, not liberty, under certain conditions.

It might also appear that, in arguing against Position (C), the adherents of Position (B) might share the grounds employed by the adherents of Position (A). But this is not the case either; for arguments against circumstantial self-realization made from the viewpoint of Position (A) are to the effect that there are no conditions under which doing what one wishes is genuine freedom. In contrast, the ground which might be employed by Position (B) would have to support the view that it is genuine freedom under certain conditions, but not under others.

What might such ground be? As in the case of the arguments so far examined, appeal might be made to the common understanding of freedom and to self and other as the basic terms in that meaning. But instead of replacing the actual self by the real self and treating the latter as the principle of true freedom, which is the point argued by Position (A), and instead of asserting that, with regard to everything the individual wishes or desires, his actual self is the principle of freedom, which is the point argued by Position (C), the critical point in the argument for Position (B) might be that the self is the principle of freedom in two different ways according as what it wills or wishes does or does not concern matters subject to law.

In relation to matters not regulated by law, the self and the other are respectively the individual man and the external forces blocking the carrying out of his wishes. In relation to matters prescribed by law, the self is represented by the individual's right or reasonable will to conform to the rules of virtue or wisdom which he has adopted, and here the interfering other consists of the forces within the individual which hinder or prevent him from willing as he ought.

It might be argued, accordingly, that the self in each of these two aspects or relations is actual or real in the same sense. One is not the literal self and the other the metaphorical self, as adherents of Position (C) argue; nor is one a mere appearance of the self and the other the only real self, as adherents of Position (A) argue.

Since, in one aspect, the self is the principle of a freedom that is circumstantial, whereas, in the other aspect, the self is the principle of a freedom that is acquired, it might thus be concluded that both of these freedoms are genuine or true freedom, and that they are analogues of one another under the broadest meaning of freedom, which is not *universal* or *generic* in the usual sense, but *analogical.*

This would amount to a rebuttal of the view, held by certain adherents of Position (C), that circumstantial self-realization is the literal, elementary, or primitive meaning, or even that, by itself, it fully embodies the common understanding of what freedom is, in contrast to which acquired self-perfection is freedom only in a metaphorical (as distinguished from an analogical) sense. It would also amount to a rebuttal of the view, held by certain adherents of Position (A), that acquired self-perfection is the full reality of freedom, the perfect embodiment of the universal idea, despite its apparently metaphorical character, in contrast to which circumstantial self-realization is only a conventionally accepted symbol or image of freedom.

Finally, the argument for Position (B) might explain that since circumstantial self-realization and acquired self-perfection are both true freedoms in strictly analogous senses, the degree of dependence or independence involved need not be the same. Both are human, not superhuman or divine, freedoms. Both, therefore, are finite freedoms; in both, man is dependent for his freedom upon something other than himself, while at the same time he has some power in himself whereby he is free.

In circumstantial self-realization he is dependent on external circumstances which enable him to do what he, in himself, has a capacity to do. In acquired self-perfection, he is dependent on the law which, whether it is divine, moral, or civil, is not a law he gives himself, but one which is laid down for him. Here the power he has in himself is his acquired ability to adopt that law as his own rule of conduct and to obey it willingly. Here he is more independent, for he is not dependent on fortuitous circumstances to be able to will as he ought, though he may still depend on them to be able to make his freedom more complete by enacting what he wills.[155]

The foregoing possible arguments against Positions (A) and (C) are conceived in the spirit of Position (B). We might, therefore, expect to find some traces of them in the writings of the leading authors who hold that position. But we have not been able to assemble passages which exemplify these lines of argument, of the sort we were able to adduce in the case of the two arguments advanced by Position (A) against Position

---

[155] This part of the argument would in effect constitute an objection, from the viewpoint of Position (B), to the absolute or unconditional independence that is insisted upon by certain adherents of Position (A). It would also be in effect an objection to the view of certain adherents of Position (C) that the individual never has any freedom except under favorable circumstances.

(C), or in the case of one argument in rebuttal by Position (C). This constitutes the most serious deficiency in the debate of the issue with which we are here concerned. It is much more serious than the absence of argument of any sort by many of the adherents of Positions (A) and (C).[156] The fact that these authors do not engage in the debate of the issue does not leave the positions they espouse unsupported by argument. But Position (B) is left totally unsupported.

Attention must be called to two other lacunae which represent deficiencies that are almost as serious. Adherents of Position (A) usually argue against Position (C), but take no cognizance of the middle ground held by the adherents of Position (B). Similarly, adherents of Position (C) may rebut the arguments advanced from Position (A), but they rarely take cognizance of Position (B). This, combined with the fact that adherents of Position (B) do not engage in either affirmative argument or rebuttal, leaves the debate in an unsatisfactory condition.

In effect, the result of all these deficiencies reduces such debate as there is to argumentation on a somewhat different issue. It is as if the question at issue had been, "Is circumstantial self-realization a genuine human freedom?" instead of the question, "Under what conditions is circumstantial self-realization genuinely a human freedom?" The latter question frames a three-sided issue which, as we have just seen, is really not debated, since the critical point at issue concerns the *conditions*—none, some, or all. Such arguments as we have found in adherents of Positions (A) and (C) do not touch this critical point, and adherents of Position (B) fail to argue it.

On the other hand, the question, "Is circumstantial self-realization a genuine human freedom?" frames a two-sided issue, with regard to which the arguments we have found given by adherents of Position (A) advance grounds or reasons for a negative answer, and the arguments we have found given by adherents of Position (C) advance grounds or reasons for an affirmative answer. That is the question being debated, so far as evidence of actual argumentation goes. But to make that the question at issue would be to ignore the existence of Position (B), of which there can be no doubt. That a three-sided disagreement concerning the genuineness of circumstantial self-realization exists in the literature remains a plainly evidenced fact, even if the literature affords no evidence at all of the debate of the issue constituted by that disagreement.

---

[156] On the side of Position (A), we have found little or no trace of argument by Plato, Aristotle, Plotinus, Seneca, Marcus Aurelius, Spinoza, Boucher; nor by the exponents of collective freedom—Comte, Bakunin, Marx, and Engels. On the side of Position (C), we have found no argument by Hobbes, Voltaire, Edwards, Hume, Priestley, Adam Smith, Burke, Calhoun, Spencer, Pareto, Tawney, Kelsen, N. Hartmann, Freud, Schlick, Hale, Knight, Macmurray, Mannheim, Stevenson, Ayer, Nowell-Smith.

Chapter 5

THE ISSUES CONCERNING THE
FREEDOM OF SELF-PERFECTION

With few exceptions, the authors who affirm an acquired freedom of self-perfection also assert the existence of moral obligations or duties, moral standards or rules, and ethical ideals or goals, all of which have their foundation in universal laws of reason, of nature, or of God. They hold certain typical views about a fundamental conflict in man, between his reason and passions, between a sense of duty and sensuous inclinations, or between his higher and lower nature. To be able to will or live as one ought depends, in their view, upon having the power to follow the dictates of reason or duty and to overcome the promptings of passion or appetite. Hence, for them only the morally good man—the man who has attained virtue or wisdom—has the self-mastery in which the acquired freedom of self-perfection consists.

A freedom so conceived is subject to attack on two quite distinct grounds.

As in the case of circumstantial self-realization, the question can be raised whether or not acquired self-perfection fits the common understanding or the generic meaning of freedom. To say that it does not is to reject a whole family of conceptions as false conceptions of freedom, i.e., to say, in effect, that what is being conceived is not freedom at all, but something mistaken for freedom. The conceptual issue which would result from this type of rejection is not only like that concerning circumstantial self-realization treated in the preceding chapter but it is also in large part the reverse face of that issue and involves the same arguments in reverse perspective.

Acquired self-perfection, however, is subject to another type of attack. Questions can be raised about the validity of its ethical and psychological presuppositions. If they are not valid, then conceptions of freedom as acquired self-perfection are conceptions of a freedom which simply has no existence in human life, man and the world being what they are. If, in other words, there are no universal laws of reason, of nature, or of God which give rise to moral obligations, standards, precepts, or goals that are the same for all men and binding on all in the same way, then to say that men are free when they are able to comply willingly with moral requirements having such origin is to propound a mythical or fictitious freedom, not one that has reality or existence in the world as it is. To reject acquired self-perfection on such grounds is to reject a whole family of conceptions as existentially false, i.e., to deny, in effect, the existence of anything corresponding to the conceptions in question.

These two types of rejection are logically independent of one another; one does not necessitate or imply the other.

On the one hand, it can be admitted that conceptions of acquired self-perfection conform to the common understanding or generic meaning of freedom, even though it is held that the presuppositions underlying such conceptions are invalid. This is tantamount to saying that, if the various elements stipulated by such conceptions did exist, then what they conceive could not be rejected on the ground that it was in no sense freedom. To make this concrete, let us consider a particular conception of acquired self-perfection, one that involves the existence of God, a revealed divine law, a supernatural and eternal goal for man beyond the precincts of this earthly life, and the operation of divine grace as the source of the power which redeems man from sin, and one that enables man to love God, obey his commandments, and thus enjoy the freedom of being able to will as he ought. The existence of the things mentioned can be denied without thereby denying the truth of a hypothetical statement involving a condition contrary to fact, namely, that if such things did exist, then the freedom attributed to those who are raised to a superior life by God's grace would be unquestionably a genuine freedom.

On the other hand, the existence of the things stipulated by conceptions of acquired self-perfection can be conceded, even though it is held that what is being conceived is not freedom in any recognizable sense. The common understanding of freedom, as that is manifested in the generally accepted use of the term, would then be the ground for the rejection of these conceptions, just as in the other case the ground would be the nonexistence of one or more of the things they posit.[1] The fact that those who affirm acquired self-perfection assert the validity of their conceptions of freedom on both grounds does not require those who deny it to reject

---

[1] As we shall subsequently see, whereas the attack on acquired self-perfection appeals primarily to common usage, the defense of it appeals primarily to the meaning which underlies the usage of philosophers, i.e., the generic meaning described in Ch. 1, pp. 15–16, *supra*. Nevertheless, we shall find that, on the one hand, the argument against acquired self-perfection takes some account of the generic meaning and that, on the other hand, the argument in rebuttal pays some attention to the common usage of the term. See Section 3, pp. 114–17, *infra*.

such conceptions on both grounds. They can do so on either ground exclusively, or on both together.

When the ground of rejection is the meaning of freedom itself, the resultant issue is conceptual; when it is the non-existence of things stipulated or presupposed by a conception of freedom, it is existential.[2] It should be clear at once that the existential type of issue involves disagreement about things other than freedom, whereas in the conceptual type of issue nothing is in dispute except what is or is not freedom. Hence, it may be thought that in the general controversy about freedom the conceptual type of issue is always more fundamental. If what is being conceived is not freedom, then there is no issue about freedom, regardless of what is conceded to exist or not to exist. But the existential type of issue is equally important for the same reason: if the things essential to a certain conception of freedom are denied existence, then only a hypothetical or fictitious freedom can be in issue.

In the first section of this chapter, we shall deal with the existential issue concerning acquired self-perfection. In the next two sections, we shall deal with the conceptual issue: we shall formulate the question at issue in Section 2 and there indicate the authors who take the affirmative and the negative sides on it, and in Section 3 we shall consider the arguments pro and con in the debate of the issue.

1. THE EXISTENTIAL ISSUE

To clarify the problem with which we are here concerned, it will be helpful to look briefly at the logical structure of an existential issue about a particular freedom.

Let SP stand for the particular freedom in question. Let X, Y, Z stand for the factors which are posited or presupposed by typical conceptions of SP. Let F stand for freedom in general. And let (A) represent authors who affirm SP, and (N) the authors who reject or deny it.

In the general controversy, the question about SP is whether or not it is a kind or aspect of human freedom. To affirm that it is involves two assertions: (i) that SP conforms to the meaning of F and (ii) that the presuppositions X, Y, Z are valid; in other words, that all the factors posited have real existence. To deny that SP is a kind or aspect of human freedom involves either one or both of the following assertions: (i) that SP does not conform to the meaning of F; (ii) that one or more of the presup-

---

[2] See Ch. 3, pp. 33–34, *supra;* and cf. Vol. I, pp. 28–30. These issues remain distinct in type even when the rejection as well as the affirmation of the freedom in question is based on both grounds.

positions X, Y, Z are invalid; in other words, that at least one of the factors posited does not exist.

To isolate the existential from the conceptual issue about SP, let us now assume that (N) concedes that SP, as conceived by (A), conforms to the meaning of F. But SP, as conceived by (A), presupposes the factors X, Y, Z. The existence of these factors is denied by (N). Genuine disagreement obtains between (N) and (A) concerning the factors X, Y, Z only if (A) and (N) are in complete topical agreement about X, Y, Z. Let us assume that such complete topical agreement is present, i.e., (A) and (N) have the same thing in mind when they refer to X (or Y or Z), and they both accept the question "Does X (or Y or Z) really exist?" and understand it in the same way. That question, by the way, might alternatively take the form "As a matter of fact, is there any X?" or the form "Is the assertion of X valid?"

The issue which is joined when (A) and (N) give opposite answers to this question is, as we have already observed, not in itself an issue about freedom, the kinds of freedom, or SP as a kind of freedom. It is an issue about the existence of X (or Y or Z). However, the opposed positions in the issue about the existence of X entail opposed positions with regard to the existence of SP; for if the existence of SP presupposes the existence of X, Y, and Z, then to deny the existence of X is to deny the existence of SP. Hence, we can picture the logical situation in the following manner:

(A) asserts
   Presupposition 1: X *exists*
   Presupposition 2: Y *exists*
   Presupposition 3: Z *exists*
      and, therefore, can defend the proposition: *SP exists.*

(N) denies one or more of the foregoing presuppositions
      and, therefore, must deny the reality of SP, i.e., must assert: *SP does not exist.*

At the point at which (A) and (N) reach opposite conclusions about the existence of SP, we have an existential issue in the general controversy about the kinds of freedom. As we have already seen, (N) might be quite willing to admit that SP as conceived by (A) conforms to the meaning of F and would, therefore, be a human freedom in a world in which its requisite presuppositions could be validly asserted, i.e., in a world in which X, Y, and Z exist as a matter of fact. But the facts are otherwise according to (N), and so for him SP is not actually a human freedom. Since (A) is not content to maintain that SP is a possible freedom, but insists that it is a freedom actually possessed by man in the world as it is, (N) and (A) are in existential disagreement about SP as a kind of freedom in consequence of their disagreement about the existence of X, or Y, or Z.

The debate of a conceptual issue in the general controversy centers on the meaning of freedom itself. In contrast, the debate of an existential issue, such as the one we have pictured occurring about SP, centers on subjects other than freedom. The disagreement between (A) and (N) concerning the existence of SP is immediately consequential upon their disagreement about X (or Y or Z). Hence the debate of the existential issue about SP would necessarily involve the reasons which can be given for antecedently asserting or denying the existence of X (or Y or Z).

But such subjects, precisely because they are connected with freedom *only as presuppositions,* are capable of being discussed or argued without any reference to freedom, and that, for the most part, is the way they are treated. This explains why, for the existential issue concerning SP, we have found no evidence of debate in the literature of freedom. Since the evidence in the case is so scattered and inseparable from the other issues,[3] we shall have to limit ourselves to indicating how this issue takes shape. In the light of such evidence as we have found, we can do no more than suggestively outline the disagreement about the presuppositions of SP and indicate some of the authors who can be interpreted as coming into disagreement in this area.[4]

We shall proceed as follows. Dealing first with the affirmative side of the issue, we shall state the presuppositions common to typical conceptions of SP and name the authors for whom we have already offered evidence that they assert the things presupposed.[5] Turning next to the negative side, we shall indicate the views or doctrines which are incompatible with the presuppositions of SP and which, therefore, lead to the denial of its existence. Here as before, we shall name the authors who, in the light of

[3] To get at the arguments for or against the validity of the presuppositions of SP would involve the study of bodies of literature much more extensive than the literature of freedom—books and writings in the field of ethics or moral philosophy and on certain fundamental matters in psychology, metaphysics, and theology.

[4] We shall not be in the same plight when we come to the existential issue about the natural freedom of self-determination. In that case, we shall find the debate of the issue amply evidenced in the literature of freedom. In addition, there we shall be able to formulate the precise questions at issue in the light of some dialectical clarification of the terms involved. We cannot do that here because the area of the disagreement is one that is less intimately connected with the subject of freedom. A dialectical clarification of the terms involved in the existential issue about SP would require research into the literature of a great many fundamental subjects other than freedom.

[5] While all typical exponents of an acquired freedom of self-perfection must uphold the presuppositions upon which the existence of this freedom depends, the evidence that they do so is not equally clear in all cases.

evidence already presented, can be interpreted as rejecting SP on existential grounds.

(a) *The affirmative side.* The presuppositions common to typical conceptions of acquired self-perfection were set forth in Chapter 15 of Book II, in the course of formulating the topical agreement which obtains among a large group of authors who hold that men are free when, through wisdom or virtue, they are able to will or live as they ought.[6] Some indication of these presuppositions is given in the opening paragraph of the present chapter. What follows is a more complete summary of them.

The first presupposition concerns the *ought*. It asserts the existence of moral obligations or moral laws that are the same for all men and are binding on all in the same way. These moral rules or laws prescribe specific conduct and require a definite way of life. They define duties to be performed or virtues to be developed and practiced. The moral standards they establish, it is claimed, are not relative to the institutions of particular societies, the customs of particular cultures, or the temperamental differences of particular men. They are not offered merely as pragmatic or utilitarian recommendations of the things which it may be expedient to do, subject always to the individual judgment of what *appears* to be right, good, or pleasant in particular cases. On the contrary, what is being asserted is that, regardless of how they may appear to the individual, certain things are right or wrong, good or bad, and that the individual can be morally judged by reference to them.

The second presupposition concerns *willing as one ought*. It asserts the existence in man of a *rational* will or a *natural* desire to do or seek the very things which are morally obligatory or prescribed by the moral law. What every man ought to do or seek is something which each individual, *as rational*, wills to do, or which, by tendencies inherent in his nature, he desires to attain. It is not asserted that every man always acts in accordance with his rational will or his natural desire, but only that there exists in every man a principle which makes it possible for him to act as he ought *willingly*.

The third presupposition concerns *being able to will as one ought*. It involves a twofold assertion. The first assertion is the existence in all men of conflicting elements, variously designated as reason and the passions, a sense of duty and sensuous inclinations, the higher and the lower nature, etc.; of these, the second one named in each case represents the source of impulses to act as a man ought not. The second assertion is the existence in some men—the wise, the virtuous, the righteous, the holy—of an acquired power to resist or overcome the impulses to violate or transgress

[6] See Vol. I, pp. 250–80.

the rules of the moral life. Since this acquired power gives predominant strength to a will that is rational or that accords with natural desire, it enables those who possess it not only to will as they ought but also to do so willingly and, hence, freely.

Unless these three presuppositions are valid, i.e., unless what they assert to exist does in fact exist, typical conceptions of acquired self-perfection do not correspond to anything real in human life. Documentary evidence has already been presented (in Book II, Chapter 15) to show which authors can be interpreted as holding conceptions of freedom that involve these presuppositions. We shall name them presently. But before listing the names of those who assert the existence of the three things requisite for the existence of an acquired freedom of self-perfection, several points must be made clear.

(i) the foregoing summary of the three presuppositions is offered as a statement of what is common to all typical conceptions of acquired self-perfection. Like the descriptive formula which identifies that freedom as a subject of discussion, the foregoing summary is intended to be neutral with regard to all the more detailed differences of opinion among authors who are in topical agreement about the subject identified. Thus, for example, Stoic philosophers, Christian theologians, and modern thinkers, such as Spinoza, Kant, and Hegel, differ significantly in the way in which they conceive the moral law, its source, its sanction, its specific content; they also differ significantly about the nature of man and about the conditions under which men acquire virtue and wisdom. We have examined these and other differences of opinion at some length in order to point out that, while they may constitute disagreements in the special controversy about acquired self-perfection, they can do so only because such differences leave intact an underlying topical agreement about certain elements which are commonly present in diverse conceptions of this subject.[7] What is true of the topical agreement holds true also of the foregoing neutral summary of the presuppositions of acquired self-perfection.[8]

[7] See Vol. I, Ch. 15 (pp. 250–80); and also Ch. 16, pp. 281–312, on the forms of self-perfection.

[8] The presuppositions shared by all the SP conceptions need not be *materially* but only *formally* the same. Thus, for example, Epictetus, Aquinas, and Hegel all assert the existence of the moral law, but they hold quite divergent theories of it. We cannot say that what they have in common is that each of them acknowledges the existence of the moral law *no matter how it is conceived*. On the contrary, each of them insists upon one conception of the moral law as the only right conception of it and asserts the reality of it only as thus conceived. The same holds true of the other presuppositions. But this does not prevent the SP authors who hold quite divergent theories concerning these presuppositions from standing together against the opponents of SP. For example, against those who deny the moral law *in any sense*, the SP authors are formally united by their affirmation of it *in some sense*, while they

(ii) It is possible for an existential issue concerning acquired self-perfection to occur in the special controversy about that subject as well as in the general controversy about the kinds of freedom. The distinctive mark of this type of issue in the general controversy is that what is there being existentially denied is the whole set of conceptions which belong to one family by virtue of their all having acquired self-perfection as their object. In constructing this issue in the general controversy, it is, therefore, logically necessary to state the three existential presuppositions of SP in a manner that is neutral and common to the diverse conceptions of SP. The reason for this can be explained as follows.

Let X_1, Y_1, and Z_1 represent the specific form which the existential presuppositions of SP take in one typical conception of it (e.g., the Stoic conception) and let X_2, Y_2, and Z_2 represent the specific form which they take in a divergent typical conception (e.g., the Christian conception). Now let us suppose that all we know about a certain author is that he denies the validity of X_2, Y_2, and Z_2. From that fact alone, we are unable to tell whether the existential issue raised by his denial belongs to the general or to the special controversy regarding SP.

Sometimes we can tell from the context of the denial, or from the arguments used to support it, that X_2, Y_2, and Z_2 alone are being rejected; but in other cases it is evident that X, Y, and Z in general are being rejected. The psychological and ethical views of an author are often helpful in deciding whether the rejection applies generally to SP conceptions or is limited to one or another particular form of SP.

It is possible that he denies X_2, Y_2, and Z_2, not because he denies the validity of X, Y, and Z in general, but only because he rejects the specific form they take in Christian theology. If the Stoic conception of SP were called to his attention, he would find it as congenial to his views in ethics and psychology as he finds the Christian conception incompatible with them. In that case, the fuller understanding of his position would reveal him as existentially rejecting the Christian conception of SP while affirming the Stoic conception of it. Hence, he would be party to an existential issue in the special controversy about SP, but not to the existential issue in the general controversy about it.[9]

---

are *materially* divided by the different senses in which they affirm it. The relation between the different senses in which a given presupposition is affirmed and what is formally common to them all is the same as the relation between different conceptions of SP and what is formally common to all SP conceptions. For an analysis of this relation, see Vol. I, Ch. 27, pp. 606–7.

[9] In addition to the Stoic and Christian conceptions of SP, we need think only of such other typical conceptions as the Spinozist, the Kantian, and the Hegelian to realize the possibility of a complex existential issue in the special controversy about SP.

It follows, therefore, that in order to construct an existential issue about SP that belongs to the general rather than the special controversy, it is necessary to state the existential presuppositions of SP in their most general form and in a way that is *formally* common to diverse conceptions of SP. On the affirmative side of that issue, we know, of course, that particular authors, holding this or that typical conception of SP, assert the validity of these presuppositions in one or another specific form; but while those who assert them in the form X_1, Y_1, Z_1 may reject them in the form X_2, Y_2, Z_2, and conversely while those who assert them in the form X_2, Y_2, Z_2 may reject them in the form X_1, Y_1, Z_1, both groups of authors subscribe to the validity of X, Y, Z, which each group regards as simply a more general statement of the presuppositions involved in its own conception of SP. But on the negative side of the issue, the situation is different. Authors who take this side are joining issue with all the typical adherents of SP, not just some of them. To do that they must deny X, Y, Z—the existential presuppositions common to all forms of SP.

(iii) In the preceding pages, we have repeatedly referred to *typical* conceptions of acquired self-perfection. The stress on that word was necessary to exclude certain conceptions which are *atypical,* and atypical precisely because they depart from the presuppositions which, as stated, are common only to the typical conceptions. The atypical conceptions held by Freud, Russell, and Dewey have been discussed elsewhere.[10] We need not review them here, since our only point in calling attention to their atypical character is to exclude these three authors from the affirmative side of the existential issue in the general controversy.

We are now prepared to enumerate the authors who take the affirmative side of the existential issue concerning acquired self-perfection in the general controversy. We shall not include here all the authors classified in Volume I as affirming this freedom, either as man's only freedom or as one of various freedoms he possesses.[11] We shall restrict the enumeration to those SP authors with regard to whom we have relatively clear documentary evidence that they subscribe to the general presuppositions on which the existence of acquired self-perfection depends.[12] With this restriction, the enumeration is as follows:

[10] See Vol. I, pp. 262–64, 271–73. Dewey, in addition to differing from other self-perfection authors with regard to the general character of moral obligation and the moral law (in which respect he keeps company with Freud and Russell), also differs from all the rest in one respect that is uniquely true of him, namely, that for him acquired self-perfection is not one of several distinct human freedoms, but only a distinguishable aspect of the one freedom man possesses.

[11] See Vol. I, pp. 250–51, 314, and 592–94.

[12] We are referring here to the evidence presented in Vol. I, especially in Ch. 15 of Book II, but also in Ch. 6 and 16. Comparison of the lists presented earlier with

Plato, Philo, Seneca, Epictetus, Marcus Aurelius, Augustine, Anselm, Aquinas, Luther, Calvin, Spinoza, Leibniz, Rousseau, Kant, Hegel, Maritain.

Of course, other writers might be added, but no more are needed in order to have all the typical conceptions of acquired self-perfection represented on the affirmative side of this issue.

(b) *The negative side.* Our general knowledge of divergent approaches and of doctrinal differences in the fields of ethics and psychology enables us to say with some assurance that none of the presuppositions common to all typical theories of acquired self-perfection has gone unchallenged. In each case, contrary views have been held.

The famous statement by Protagoras, for example, that "man is the measure of all things" represents an approach to morals which, early in the tradition, challenged the view that judgments of right and wrong or good and bad can be more than personal opinions relative to the individual or to the society in which he lives. "Fire burns in Greece as it does in Persia," the sophists are often quoted as saying, "but the laws and customs of the Greeks differ from those of the Persians." This again represents the familiar doctrine of the sophists that opinions about the good or the right vary with time and place and that there is no criterion for deciding which, among such opinions, is objectively and universally true. It is against this skeptical view on the part of the sophists that Plato and Aristotle advance the distinction between the real and the apparent good, specify the things in which human happiness really consists, and try to argue for universal principles of justice and other virtues as providing a moral code that is the measure of the good man and the good life.

The foregoing example suggests one approach to moral questions which denies the validity of the first of the three existential presuppositions of acquired self-perfection. It is the approach that Montaigne, centuries later, found congenial to his general skepticism; and in our own day it has been widely adopted by sociologists and anthropologists who, on the basis of much more detailed evidence of the diversity of tribal customs, maintain that the *mores* of one social group do not provide any valid standard for judging the values enshrined in the customs of another. Still another

---

the enumeration given here will show that the present list does not even include all the authors who, unlike Dewey, Freud, and Russell, and perhaps also Epicurus and Santayana, hold typical conceptions of SP. In addition, there are authors who, like Aristotle and Burke, share the existential presuppositions common to all typical conceptions of SP, but whose theories of human freedom do not include a conception of acquired self-perfection.

variation on this point of view is to be found in the sharp distinction that is currently made between value judgments and judgments of fact, accompanied by the declaration that the former, unlike the latter, cannot be scientifically tested or empirically verified and must therefore be treated, in part at least, as expressions of emotional prejudice or purely personal predilection.

Anyone who takes some variety of the skeptical approach to moral matters, would deny the existence of moral obligations or moral laws that are the same for all men and binding on all in the same way. He would deny the existence of moral standards that are not relative to the institutions of particular societies, or to the customs of particular cultures, or to the temperamental differences of particular men. If, in addition, he were acquainted with the view that, since all men are duty-bound to behave in certain specific ways, those alone are free who are able to discharge their moral obligations willingly, he would reject the freedom described in this way as mythical or non-existent.

It would be possible to draw up a fairly long list of authors who, taking the approach indicated above, would deny the first (i.e., the ethical) presupposition common to all typical conceptions of acquired self-perfection. But since we are here concerned with issues relating to acquired self-perfection, we must confine our attention to authors who oppose this freedom on existential grounds. They constitute a much smaller group than the whole array of those who, whatever their theme may be, reject the presuppositions of SP. They are authors whom we have already construed as holding views incompatible with the views shared by typical self-perfection authors on moral principles and the moral nature of man.

In formulating what is common to all typical conceptions of self-realization, we emphasized two points: self-realization, we said, is commonly understood by the proponents of circumstantial freedom to consist in (i) *execution,* whereby the individual's wish is translated into action and (ii) *individual fulfillment,* wherein the good as he sees it is accomplished by the action performed.[13] It is the second of these two points which is relevant here insofar as it involves the realization of the aspirations that constitute an individual's own estimation of what is good for him. In this connection, we wrote as follows:

> The individual is the final arbiter of what is good and bad, for that is relative to his individual temperament and tastes. He is the sole judge of what his individual happiness consists in. Whether he calls his goal in life "happiness" or gives it some other name, the things he strives for are all parts of a goal that he deems best for himself. It is an individual goal,

[13] See Vol. I, p. 174.

a goal uniquely his own, in the sense that it has validity for him whether or not it is shared or approved by anyone else.

The fact that other persons of similar temperament or inclination may follow paths that lie in the same general direction does not make the path he takes any less his own. Nor does the fact that the concrete goal he pursues happens to be generally approved make it the right one for all men to strive for, any more than the fact that no one else accepts the goal he has set himself make it the wrong one for him to pursue. Each man is judge of what is best for him. He can be mistaken about how to achieve it and, through error as well as misfortune, he may fail or be defeated in the pursuit of his individual goal. But he cannot be mistaken about the goal he seeks, unless he misunderstands or miscalculates his own actual desires.[14]

Before presenting the evidence that certain authors share this view of individual fulfillment, we enumerated three points to which such evidence would be relevant. They were stated as follows:

(i) The desires which give content to the goal the individual seeks are the desires he actually has, not those he *should* have or *would* have if he were different than he is. Nor are they the innate tendencies or natural inclinations common to all men; for such desires, if they existed, would set the same goal for all men to achieve. . . .

(ii) What each individual deems to be good for himself is determined by what he himself actually and consciously desires. The good is that which pleases him or satisfies his desires. Hence, according as men differ in their desires, they differ not only in their goals but also in their judgments about what is good or evil. . . . To say that desire alone gives things their value is to say that there is no value or goodness inherent in things apart from their being actually desired—no fixed order of *real* goods that all men *should* desire as contrasted with *apparent* goods that men actually do desire and which each man orders according to his own scale of values as dictated by his own desires.

(iii) Negatively, the foregoing means that the wish or desire whose enactment contributes to self-realization need not conform to standards of right desire or rules of conduct that prescribe the things a man *should* desire or the duties he *ought* to perform whether he desires to do so or not.[15]

---

[14] *Ibid.*, p. 184. This understanding of individual goals, it was pointed out, "is shared by authors who affirm man's circumstantial freedom of self-realization, and most typically by those who hold that this is man's only freedom"; to which we added: "There are . . . some exceptions to the typical view. They are authors who, while recognizing the freedom that lies in self-realization, also affirm the existence of universal moral standards or ideals which set rules binding on all men regardless of their individual differences." Aquinas, Locke, Montesquieu, and Maritain are among the notable exceptions.

[15] *Ibid.*, pp. 186-87.

We shall not repeat here the documentary evidence which was offered to show that such authors as Hobbes, J. S. Mill, Hobhouse, Laski, Knight, and Hayek share an understanding of self-realization that involves the foregoing points.[16] The very same evidence also tends to show that the writers named hold views which are incompatible with one or more of the presuppositions common to typical conceptions of acquired self-perfection, especially the first presupposition, which asserts the existence of moral obligations or moral laws that are the same for all men. It is not quite so clear that these authors reject the other two presuppositions; but this does not matter since the rejection of any one entails the rejection of SP.

Moreover, two of the authors mentioned—Hobhouse and Laski—advance arguments which can be interpreted as denying all the existential presuppositions of acquired self-perfection as well as denying that it conforms to the common meaning of freedom. The passages from their writings which we quoted in the preceding chapter reveal that their view of the roles played by reason and desire in human life and their insistence on the integrity of the self (i.e., on the unity of the individual as a whole, comprising all his tendencies and aspirations) deny the existence in man of principles (such as a rational will or natural desires) which, when made to prevail over lower impulses by the power of virtue, enable the individual willingly to will as he ought. Here, then, we have some evidence of denials of the second and third presuppositions which are involved in conceptions of acquired self-perfection.[17]

The authors whom we have mentioned so far are the ones who can be most surely interpreted, in the light of evidence, as taking the negative

[16] See *ibid.*, pp. 189–201. In these same pages it will also be found that Freud, Russell, and Dewey have a similar understanding of individual fulfillment. This is consistent with their quite atypical conceptions of acquired self-perfection. On the other hand, the passages quoted from Locke, which seem to be of similar intent, must be reconciled with his conception of freedom under the moral as well as the civil law, possessed only by the reasonable man who voluntarily acknowledges the authority of rational principles of conduct. For the handling of this problem, see *ibid.*, pp. 245–49 and 323–27.

[17] See Ch. 4, pp. 81–85, *supra*. Since he affirms a circumstantial freedom of self-realization and casts doubt on the existential presuppositions of an acquired freedom of self-perfection, Sir Isaiah Berlin might be placed in the company of Hobhouse and Laski, were it not for the fact that he also appears to admit that SP is a tenable conception of freedom. In an extensive analysis of the differences between SR and SP (in both its individual and its social forms), Berlin affirms that both conceptions conform to the common meaning of freedom. See *Two Concepts of Liberty*, p. 43. Nevertheless, in the course of his exposition of what is involved in the whole theory of SP, he questions "the underlying assumptions" of its advocates. See *ibid.*, pp. 33, 39, 56. He therefore concludes that SR is a "truer" conception of freedom than is SP. See *ibid.*, p. 56; and cf. pp. 16–19, 32–33, 43, 47, 54.

side of the existential issue. A few others can be singled out as most likely to be on the negative side of this issue. They are N. Hartmann, because of his theory that free choice occurs in the realm of the *ought* and with respect to ultimate moral values;[18] Sartre, because of his theory that all the values or ends to which an individual is dedicated stem from projects of his own making;[19] and Bakunin, Marx, and Engels, because of their adverse criticism of traditional moral rules or codes of behavior.[20] Of these authors, only Hartmann affirms a circumstantial freedom of self-realization. For Sartre, man's only freedom is that of self-determination; for Bakunin, Marx, and Engels, it is the collective freedom which mankind does not yet enjoy, but will in the future.

We thus have a fairly representative set of authors on the negative side of the existential issue:

Hobbes, J. S. Mill, Bakunin, Marx, Engels, Hobhouse, N. Hartmann, Knight, Laski, Hayek, Sartre

This list could, of course, be greatly extended if we waived the restriction that limited it to authors who not only challenge the validity of one or more of the presuppositions of acquired self-perfection but also address themselves to the central question in the general controversy about freedom—the question about the one or more kinds of freedom that man actually possesses.

2. THE CONCEPTUAL ISSUE: THE POSITIONS AND THE PARTIES

Those who affirm that being able to will as one ought is genuinely freedom assert this without any qualifications. Those who deny that men are free when they bring their will into line with duty or with law also enter this denial without any qualifications. We find no intermediate group here who take the view that being able to will as one ought is freedom, *but only under certain conditions.* Hence, the conceptual issue concerning acquired self-perfection is simpler than the similar issue about circumstantial self-realization. It involves a two-sided disagreement stemming from contradictory positions, namely, the affirmative and negative answers to the question: "Is acquired self-perfection a kind of freedom?"

[18] See Vol. I, pp. 529–30.
[19] See *ibid.*, pp. 517–19.
[20] See *ibid.*, pp. 373–76, 393–95.

In thus wording the question at issue, we are using the phrase "acquired self-perfection" as shorthand for "the ability of an individual, through acquired virtue or wisdom, to will or live as he ought in conformity to the moral law or an ideal befitting human nature."

Topical agreement about the subject thus identified unites all the self-perfection authors, including those whose conceptions of it are atypical, such as Freud, Russell, and Dewey. These authors, too, affirm a freedom which is enjoyed only by men who have attained a certain state of mind or character, even though they do not share one of the presuppositions underlying typical conceptions of such freedom, namely, the existence of moral obligations or moral laws that are concretely the same for all men. The alternative phrasing in the identifying formula for acquired self-perfection—"in conformity to the moral law *or* an ideal befitting human nature"—was introduced precisely in order to allow for this basic difference of opinion between the typical and atypical self-perfection authors. This difference in their understanding of acquired self-perfection excludes Freud, Russell, and Dewey from the affirmative side of the existential issue about SP, but not from the affirmative side of the conceptual issue about it.

It is, of course, necessary for all the authors who take the negative side of this issue to be in topical agreement with their opponents about the subject in question. This requirement severely limits the number of writers whom we can interpret as joining issue about this subject. We must have clear evidence that the subject which they are denying to be freedom is identical with the common subject being affirmed by all self-perfection authors. In many cases, as we shall see, that which is being attacked is one or another particular conception of acquired self-perfection, not acquired self-perfection in all its diverse forms. In such cases, the possibility remains that if the writer were acquainted with other conceptions of SP, he might find them acceptable; and in that case, he would be a party to some issue in the special controversy about SP, but not to this issue in the general controversy.[21]

Complete topical agreement, requisite for genuine disagreement, involves a common understanding of the question at issue as well as of the subject in question. There would seem to be no difficulty in that respect with regard to the question as to whether SP is a kind of freedom. What is being asked is whether SP, as commonly conceived by all its adherents, conforms to the common understanding of freedom. The same evidence which shows certain authors maintaining that SP does conform and other

---

[21] Cf. what was said on pp. 98–99, *supra*. The same critical point that was made there in connection with the existential issue about SP in the general controversy applies with equal force here.

authors maintaining that it does not also indicates that all these writers are in topical agreement about the question.

We turn now to the problem of naming the writers who can be interpreted as joining issue on the question, dealing first with those who take the affirmative side and then with those who take the negative side.

POSITION (A)

We might justifiably list here all the authors whom we have already classified as exponents of acquired self-perfection and who either maintain that it is man's only freedom or that it is one of the freedoms man possesses.[22] But since the number of authors who can be cited as parties to an issue does not affect the genuineness of the issue, we shall restrict our enumeration to writers for whose views we have the clearest evidence. The bulk of the relevant evidence was presented in Volume I, though with respect to certain authors (e.g., Green, Bradley, Bosanquet) additional evidence was presented in the preceding chapter of this volume.[23] Pursuing the policy indicated above, the following writers can be named as clear adherents of Position (A):

> Plato, Cicero, Philo, Seneca, Epictetus, Marcus Aurelius, Ambrose, Augustine, Anselm, Aquinas, Luther, Calvin, Spinoza, Locke, Leibniz, McTaggart, Montesquieu, Rousseau, Kant, Hegel, Green, Bradley, Bosanquet, Freud, Maritain, Yves Simon

In the foregoing enumeration, the typical varieties of SP are well represented: the Platonic and Stoic conceptions in antiquity; the Christian conception, not only in the Middle Ages but also in modern times; and in modern times such divergent conceptions as the Spinozist, the Kantian, and the Hegelian. It is not claimed, however, that this exhausts the variety

---

[22] The complete list can be drawn from the classification given in Vol. I on pp. 592–94. Of all the authors there named, the only one about whom there might be some question here is Dewey, on the ground that he does not conceive SP as a distinct freedom, but only as an aspect of the one freedom man possesses.

[23] See Vol. I, pp. 134–47, 250–327; and also Ch. 4, pp. 73–76, *supra*. J. M. E. McTaggart should also be added to the group of affirmative authors. "A man is said to act freely," he writes, "when he acts according to the ultimate ideal of his nature." Continuing, he says: "We often regard reason and conscience as more truly parts of our nature than desires or passions, which we speak of as though they were forces acting on us from outside. When I act according to a passion it is said to master me. When reason or conscience prevents me from doing so, I am said to master my passion. Thus virtuous and reasonable action will appear, by the suggestion of such phrases, as more truly self-determined than other action" (*Some Dogmas of Religion*, pp. 141–42).

of SP conceptions. For example, Croce and Berdyaev might be added. Each of them proposes a conception of this freedom which is distinctively his own.[24] But including these variations in our treatment would add nothing new in principle.

POSITION (N)

There is a large group of authors whom we can construe, with varying degrees of assurance, as taking the negative side of this issue. The group includes

> Hobbes, Voltaire, Edwards, Hume, Priestley, Bentham, Calhoun, J. S. Mill, Spencer, Pareto, Hobhouse,* Tawney, Kelsen, Schlick, Hale, Malinowski, Macmurray, Laski, Stevenson, Ayer, Nowell-Smith

All are writers whom, in the preceding volume, we classified as attributing only one freedom to man, namely, circumstantial self-realization.[25] To them might be added such writers as

> Burke, N. Hartmann, Knight

who affirm natural self-determination as well as circumstantial self-realization;[26] such writers as

> Descartes, Renouvier, William James, Sartre

who place all of man's freedom in his inherent power of determining for himself what he will do or will become;[27] and such writers as

> Comte, Bakunin, Marx, Engels

for whom the only true freedom mankind will ever possess is the collective freedom it will enjoy in the future when society is organized entirely on the basis of our knowledge of natural and social necessities.[28]

Of the writers named above, only a few take explicit cognizance of the conception of freedom advanced by writers on the affirmative side

[24] See Croce, *My Philosophy*, pp. 97–99, 107–8; Berdyaev, *Freedom and the Spirit*, Ch. 4, pp. 117–34.
[25] See Vol. I, pp. 314 and 592. An asterisk is placed after Hobhouse's name to signify that he also affirms political liberty, which is a variant of circumstantial self-realization.
[26] See *ibid.*, p. 593.
[27] See *ibid.*, p. 592.
[28] See *ibid.*, p. 592.

of the issue. They are Bentham, Hobhouse, Laski, Macmurray, Knight, and Malinowski.[29] The rest can be interpreted as denying that acquired self-perfection is a valid conception of freedom only by virtue of what is implied by their *exclusive* affirmation of some other freedom or freedoms. To assert, for example, that being able to do as one pleases is the only freedom men possess is to deny, by implication, that men have a freedom which consists in being able to will as they ought.

The interpretation that certain authors by implication deny acquired self-perfection to be a human freedom can be made with varying degrees of assurance. For many of the authors who can be placed on the negative side of this issue only when they are thus interpreted, that interpretation must rest upon the whole tenor of their approach to and treatment of the problems of human freedom rather than upon any explicit statement to the effect that being able to do as one pleases is the only freedom which can be properly attributed to man.

It is one thing for a writer to treat only one of the various freedoms that have been discussed in the literature of this subject, and quite another for a writer to indicate, more or less explicitly, that the one freedom which he does affirm is also the only one he thinks can be properly affirmed. It would be incautious to conclude that, because an author affirms only one freedom, he rejects the others. The absence of reference to other freedoms is negative evidence and by itself quite insufficient.

However, we need not rely on merely negative evidence in the case of the authors whom we have mentioned. Some of them, as we have seen, do take cognizance of acquired self-perfection, explicitly reject it, and argue against it on conceptual grounds. With respect to them, we have clear positive evidence of their views. It will be presented in the next section of this chapter which deals with the debate of the issue. With respect to the rest, who are more numerous, either we can (a) allocate them to the negative side on the basis of a presumption, suggested by the general tenor of their thought, that they would align themselves on this side, or we can (b) present positive evidence that they assert some freedom other than acquired self-perfection to be man's *only* freedom.

Proceeding according to (a) above, we think the presumption is fairly strong in the case of the following authors: Calhoun, Spencer, Pareto, Tawney, Kelsen, Schlick, Hale, Stevenson, Ayer, Nowell-Smith, and Sartre. In contrast, we think it fairly weak in the case of Descartes, Burke, Renouvier, N. Hartmann, and William James. As for the authors who can be treated according to (b) above, we have already given evidence in some detail that Comte, Bakunin, Marx, and Engels look to the collective

---

[29] As we saw in the preceding chapter, a number of other writers, whom we did not treat in Vol. I, must be grouped with them: Wootton, MacIver, and Fosdick.

freedom which mankind will enjoy in the future as the only true freedom men can ever possess.[30] We have also given evidence that Hobbes, Edwards, Hume, Voltaire, Priestley, and J. S. Mill more or less explicitly assert that the freedom of being able to do as one pleases is the only freedom which conforms to the common understanding of the term and its everyday usage.[31] Nevertheless, it will be useful to call attention to passages in the writings of this last group of authors, in which that point is briefly though plainly made. But before we quote the passages mentioned, three things should be noted.

In the first place, it must be recognized that, if our interpretation of certain authors is correct (namely, that the only freedom they would acknowledge is circumstantial self-realization), then what is implied is their rejection of natural self-determination as well as of acquired self-perfection. Such authors as Hobbes, Edwards, Hume, Voltaire, Priestley, and more recently such writers as Ayer and Schlick, give some indication that their intent is to exclude natural self-determination (or what they call "free will") when they restrict freedom in any real or meaningful sense to circumstantial self-realization.[32] We cannot find in their writings any similar indication of intent to exclude acquired self-perfection.

In the second place, we know that some of the authors with whom we are here concerned reject acquired self-perfection on existential grounds, because they regard its presuppositions as invalid. They are Hobbes, J. S. Mill, Hobhouse, Laski, Knight, Hayek, and also N. Hartmann, Sartre, Bakunin, Marx, and Engels.[33] While the conceptual and existential rejections of a particular freedom can always be analytically separated, they are often commingled in the attack that certain authors make on it. We must conclude, therefore, that the writers just mentioned would maintain that acquired self-perfection is not an acceptable conception of freedom, even if its presuppositions were tenable as existing in fact.[34]

In the third place, a few of the authors who explicitly recognize acquired self-perfection appear to concentrate their attack on one or another particular version of it. Thus, in one place, Macmurray says that "the stoic

[30] See Vol. I, pp. 370–99.

[31] See Vol. I, pp. 171–201.

[32] For evidence of this, see Vol. I, pp. 218–23.

[33] See pp. 103–4, *supra*.

[34] Hayek, for example, refers to SP conception as one of "inner freedom"; and having made it clear that he does not think it conforms to the common meaning of freedom, he puts the reader on guard against the "sophism that we are free only if we do what in some sense we ought to do." His rejection of self-perfection as a genuine kind of freedom is clearly implied in his remark concerning a slave, that no "degree of 'inner freedom,' [will] make him anything but a slave—however much idealist philosophers have tried to convince us to the contrary" (*The Constitution of Liberty*, pp. 16, 20). Cf. *ibid.*, pp. 12, 15.

ideal of a freedom to be achieved by getting rid of desire and 'willing what happens' is the apotheosis of subjectively illusory freedom. Kant's effort to equate freedom with moral obligation," he continues, "falls into the same category. Desires which are suppressed do not cease to exist; they are at best inactive in consciousness."[35] And Knight, in a critique of the political doctrines of Maritain, comments adversely on "the Christian view of freedom."[36] The passages referred to can hardly be used as evidence that the writers reject all SP conceptions as invalid. Since such passages limit themselves to comments on one or another particular version of SP, they do not tell us what their authors would say about other conceptions in the same family.[37]

We turn now to the evidence which shows that certain authors maintain that being able to act as one wishes is the only freedom which exemplifies the generally accepted meaning of the term. In the following passages, we have italicized the critical words.

"By liberty," Hobbes tells us, "is understood, *according to the proper signification of the word*, the absence of external impediments."[38] And, again, he says: "Liberty, or freedom, signifieth (*properly*) the absence of opposition . . . and *according to this proper and generally received meaning of the word*, a free-man is he that in those things which by his strength and wit he is able to do, is not hindered to do what he has a will to."[39] Similarly, Jonathan Edwards writes that "*the plain and obvious meaning of the words 'freedom' and 'liberty' in common speech* is power, opportunity, or advantage that anyone has, to do as he pleases."[40] And Hume writes as follows:

---

[35] "Freedom in the Personal Nexus" in *Freedom, Its Meaning*, p. 511.
[36] *Freedom and Reform*, pp. 275 ff.
[37] We are here appealing to the same critical point that was made on p. 26, *supra* That point applies to a number of other writers: to Erich Fromm's remarks about Christian conception of SP (*Man for Himself*, Ch. V, pp. 245–46); to Lewis Feuer's remarks about the Spinozist conception of SP(*Spinoza and the Rise of Liberalism*, pp. 84–85, 241–42); to Morris Ginsberg's remarks about the Kantian conception of SP (*On the Diversity of Morals*, pp. 139–40); and to Karl Popper's more extended attack on the Hegelian conception of SP (*The Open Society and Its Enemies*, pp. 239–44).
[38] *Leviathan*, Part I, Ch. 14, p. 99. (Italics added.)
[39] *Ibid.*, Part II, Ch. 21, p. 161.
[40] *Freedom of the Will*, p. 163. (Italics added.) Edwards goes on to point out that only two things—coercion and restraint—"are contrary to [what] is called *liberty in common speech*," and concludes by declaring: "What has been said may be sufficient to show what is meant by liberty, *according to the common notions of mankind, and in the usual and primary acceptation of the word*" (*ibid.*, p. 164). He then attacks the misuse of the word when it is applied to "a self-determining power in the will, or a certain sovereignty the will has over itself" (*ibid.*); therefore, even though his reference to the common notions of mankind and the primary acceptation of the word is explicitly intended only to exclude self-determination from the realm of human freedom, it also implies the exclusion of self-perfection.

By liberty, then, we mean *only* a power of acting or not acting according to the determinations of the will; that is, if we choose to remain at rest we may; if we choose to move, we also may. Now this hypothetical liberty is *universally allowed* to belong to every one who is not a prisoner and in chains.[41]

In the same vein, Priestley declares: "I allow to man all the liberty, or ower, that is possible in itself, and *to which the ideas of mankind in neral ever go*, which is the power of doing whatever they will or ease."[42] In another place, he lays stress again on the common under-anding of what freedom is to support his contention that doing whatever man pleases is the only thing which can properly be called freedom.

In acknowledging in man a liberty to do what he pleases, I grant not only *all the liberty that the generality of mankind have any idea of, or can be made to understand*, but also all that many of the professed advocates of liberty, against the doctrine of necessity, have claimed.[43]

1 Voltaire and J. S. Mill, we find statements to the same effect. Voltaire sserts that "liberty . . . is not and *cannot be anything but* the power of oing what we will."[44] And Mill declares that "the *only* freedom which eserves the name is that of pursuing our own good in our own way,"[45] nd reinforces this later by saying that "liberty consists in doing what one esires."[46]

In contrast to these blanket rejections of SP are the rejections of it that 1ake specific reference to it and are accompanied by arguments against it. entham, Hobhouse, Laski, Malinowski, MacIver, Wootton, and Fosdick ive reasons for saying that acquired self-perfection is not acceptable as a ind of freedom.

3. THE DEBATE OF THE CONCEPTUAL ISSUE

The conceptual and existential issues concerning acquired self-perfection re, as we have seen, analytically separable.[47] But in the minds of those uthors who affirm that being able to will as one ought is genuine freedom, 1at affirmation is never found separate from the assertion of the existential resuppositions of such freedom or the assumption of their validity. This

1 *Enquiry Concerning Human Understanding,* Sect. VIII, Part I, Div. 73, p. 95.
2 *The Doctrine of Philosophical Necessity,* p. 2. (Italics added.)
3 *Ibid.,* p. 4. (Italics added.)
4 "Free-will" in *Philosophical Dictionary,* Vol. V, p. 133. (Italics added.)
5 *On Liberty,* p. 75. (Italics added.)
6 *Ibid.,* p. 152.
7 See pp. 92–93, *supra.*

fact must be borne in mind when we consider the affirmative arguments fo
SP as a conception that clearly conforms to the generic meaning of free
dom.

We have examined these arguments in other connections. They appea
to a generic sense of freedom as consisting in self-mastery (Plato), obeyin
oneself alone (Rousseau, Kant, Hegel), or obeying laws which, while no
originating with the self, are at least adopted by the self as rules it volun
tarily accepts as its own (Philo, Epictetus, Cicero, Augustine, Aquinas
Spinoza, Leibniz, Bradley, Maritain, and Yves Simon).[48]

The phrase "living as one pleases" is sometimes used, as by the Stoi
philosophers and others, to express the generic sense of freedom; and it
meaning is then equated with *being able to will as one ought* by thei
insistence that only the virtuous man, who wishes what is really good fo
him, is able to live as he pleases. In saying that freedom is self-assertion
Bradley regards himself as stating a meaning for freedom that is common t
every use of the term.[49] The phrase might, of course, be used by othe
writers to argue that self-realization or self-determination exemplify th
common meaning of freedom, but Bradley uses it to argue that, whe
the true self is known, the essence of freedom is to be found in sel
perfection and in that alone.[50]

All these ways of arguing that acquired self-perfection conforms to th
generic meaning of freedom presuppose the existence of moral obligation
or laws that are the same for all men. They also presuppose the existenc
of principles in human nature that make it possible for men to be maste
of themselves by subduing whatever forces within them are alien to th
ideal of their true selves; to do what they really wish—rationally or naturall
—when they will as they ought; and to achieve the full satisfaction of sel
assertion when they act for the fulfillment of goals that represent the tru
perfection of their being.

If these presuppositions are granted to the self-perfection authors, it ma
be wondered how their conclusion can be denied. In other words, i
there are moral obligations or laws which are binding on all men in th
same way; if, through wisdom or virtue, some men are able to comply wit
them willingly; and if, in doing so, they are acting in accordance wit

[48] See Vol. I, pp. 254–56, 264–67, 269, 284–91; and cf. Ch. 4, pp. 68–72, *supr*
[49] See *Ethical Studies*, pp. 56–57. If we understand Bradley to be calling our attentio
to the fact that freedom in every sense of the term refers to that which proceeds fro
the self rather than from the other, then "self-assertion" is one way of expressing th
generic meaning of freedom which, in the concluding chapter of Vol. I, we showed t
be common to all the conceptions of it which we have been able to discover in th
literature.
[50] See Vol. I, p. 614; and also Ch. 4, p. 73, *supra*.

their own real (i.e., rational) will or in accordance with their own real (i.e., natural) desires, then how can it be said that they are not free? How can it be said that to call them "free" is to depart from an acceptable meaning for that word?

The answer cannot be that the men in question are not free because restraint is imposed on some of their desires or impulses; for, according to the theory of freedom being challenged, restraint is self-restraint, not restraint by another. It is precisely such self-restraint which enables the virtuous man to will as he ought instead of yielding to contrary inclinations. Without it, he would be a slave to his passions, not master of himself and free.

Of course, to those who deny the validity of the presuppositions underlying this conception of freedom, the so-called virtuous man appears to be the very opposite of free. He is fundamentally other-controlled when, in doing what he calls his duty, he does what is expected of him by others; and, even if he voluntarily submits to extrinsically imposed rules of conduct, his freedom is infringed in every impulse that is frustrated.

The validity of such remarks depends upon disproving the presuppositions asserted by the exponents of acquired self-perfection. By denying those presuppositions, opponents can conclude that the freedom attributed to the virtuous man is mythical or non-existent. But that leaves the question at issue here untouched. To isolate this question from the question raised in the existential issue, we must grant the presuppositions involved in typical theories of acquired self-perfection and, granting them, still ask: even if they are true, is the virtuous man, who is able to will as he ought and to restrain his contrary impulses, free in any acceptable sense of that term?

There may be many authors, especially self-realization authors, who would say no to this question. But, as we have seen, the number with regard to whom we have found satisfactory documentary evidence on the point is smaller than the number whom we should reasonably suspect of giving a negative answer. In the case of such authors as Hobbes, Edwards, Hume, Voltaire, Priestley, and Mill, we have already presented evidence which shows that they explicitly assert circumstantial self-realization to be man's only freedom. It alone, they insist, fits the commonly accepted understanding of what freedom is. But certain authors—Bentham, Hobhouse, Laski, Malinowski, Wootton, MacIver, and Fosdick—go further than this. They explicitly argue against acquired self-perfection as departing from or violating the universally accepted sense of the term.

The arguments set forth by Hobhouse, Laski, and Fosdick commingle reasons for the existential rejection of acquired self-perfection with reasons for its conceptual rejection.[51] But it is not difficult to separate the one from the other, since the argument for the negative position in the con ceptual issue so plainly reveals its ground to be the meaning established by the general usage of the term freedom. That argument says, in effect. that even if the things presupposed by acquired self-perfection did exist. the virtuous man who is able to will as he ought cannot properly be called "free" in any sense which fits the commonly accepted meaning of the term.

To this argument, there is some response on the part of two self perfection authors—Green and Bosanquet. We shall, first, present evidence of the argument for Position (N) and against Position (A), and then pre sent evidence of the argument in rebuttal—in defense of Position (A). When we have summarized the opposed arguments for which we find some evidence in the literature, we shall consider briefly the possibility of other arguments which might have been advanced but which do not seem to have been made.

(i) *Argument for Position (N) and against Position (A).* As we have just pointed out, the common meaning or universally accepted sense of the term "freedom" is appealed to by those who take Position (N). This holds true both for those who imply that acquired self-perfection does not exhibit that meaning by their assertion that *circumstantial self-realization alone exemplifies it,* and also for those who refer to acquired self-perfection but explicitly reject it because *it does not exemplify that meaning.* Having already offered evidence of the implied rejection of SP, we turn now to evidence of argument for its explicit rejection. But, first, two things should be noted about the argument for Position (N).

(a) One concerns the relation between the meaning of "freedom" that is discovered by observing the common usage of the term in ordinary speech and the generic meaning which we have constructed by discovering what is common to all the more specific meanings of freedom that we have been able to identify in the literature of this subject. Both meanings claim to be the common meaning, but they are not common in the same sense. Thus, for example, writers such as Hobbes, Hume, Voltaire, and Priestley

---

51 These writers explicitly deny the presupposition that there exists a "real" self, "real" will, or a "general will" in which all actual wills can be united. See Hobhouse *The Metaphysical Theory of the State,* pp. 44–59, 71–87; Laski, *Liberty in the Modern State,* pp. 56–60, *The Grammar of Politics,* pp. 29–35, *The State in Theory and Practice,* pp. 37–85; and Fosdick, *What is Liberty?* pp. 110–22. We have also given evidence for thinking that Hobhouse and Laski, along with Hobbes, J. S. Mill, Marx, Engels, Bakunin, N. Hartmann, Knight, Hayek, and Sartre, deny the primary presup position of acquired self-perfection, namely, the existence of moral obligations or moral laws that are the same for all men. See pp. 100–4, *supra.*

may be right in asserting that, as the word "freedom" is used in ordinary speech, it means *being able to do as one pleases* and only that. But they would not be right in asserting that this is the only meaning of the term in the discourse of philosophers. Nor do they assert this. On the contrary, it is precisely because they are aware of philosophers who have used the term in other senses that they cite the authority of common sense and accepted usage against them. These writers and others who appeal to the commonly accepted meaning are, therefore, not discountenanced by reference to the *constructed* generic meaning.

It is of critical importance to note this, since, as we have seen, the authors who take Position (A) on this issue appeal to the latter meaning as their ground for thinking that acquired self-perfection plainly conforms to the common understanding of freedom, granted the validity of its presuppositions.[52] But the common understanding they refer to is the generic meaning that we have found common to all conceptions of freedom, i.e., exemplified in self-realization, self-determination, and self-perfection theories. All conceptions of freedom stress the self as against the other and regard only such acts as free which flow from the self rather than from the other. Each of the three major conceptions of freedom specifies in a different way the self which is the principle of freedom, and also the other which can be the source of unfreedom.[53] No one of these specifications, in itself, excludes the others. But this fact does not prevent the authors who affirm a conception of freedom in which *self* and *other* are specified in a certain way from excluding other specifications as untenable.

Thus, some self-perfection authors argue for the exclusion of the specification involved in the self-realization conception of freedom on the ground that the self referred to is not the real or true self.[54] Such arguments are countered by arguments in which some self-realization authors maintain, on their part, that no tenable distinction can be drawn between the individual's actual self, as constituted by his whole person, and some part of him which is elevated to the status of his "real" or "true" self.[55]

Here, then, we see both sides appealing to the generic meaning, at least insofar as each makes its argument turn on the specification of the self which is the principle of freedom. But this must not lead us to overlook the difference in the way the argument proceeds on each side.

While the self-perfection authors appeal primarily to the generic meaning which can be constructed from philosophical discourse about freedom, they

[52] See pp. 111–13, *supra.*
[53] See Vol. I, pp. 608–16.
[54] We saw this in the arguments of Bradley and Bosanquet which were reported in Ch. 4, on pp. 67–68, 73–76, *supra.*
[55] See the arguments in rebuttal by Hobhouse and Laski, reported in Ch. 4, on pp. 76–77, 81–85, *supra.*

sometimes also refer to the ordinary usage of the term, as, for example, when such writers as Cicero, Epictetus, Ambrose, and Philo not only recognize that "living as one wishes" or "doing as one pleases" expresses what men generally mean by "freedom" but also see in such common parlance an expression of what freedom essentially is.[56]

Similarly, while such self-realization authors as Hobbes, Hume, Priestley, and Voltaire appeal to common usage as their primary ground for excluding the self-perfection conception of freedom from the realm of significant discourse about that subject, they are not totally ignoring the generic meaning; for it is their implied contention that when an individual can do as he wishes, he is free not only in the commonly recognized sense of the term but also in the sense which is common to all philosophical conceptions, i.e., the generic sense of the term which we have constructed. The fact that they look upon all forms of external coercion and constraint as destructive of freedom shows that they understand being able to do what one wishes as the individual's ability to make what he does *his own act*, i.e., something that proceeds from himself rather than from another.[57] In this, they are acknowledging the self to be the principle of freedom and to that extent they are assimilating the generic meaning of freedom to the meaning of the term in ordinary usage. Yet their mode of argument contrasts sharply with that of the Stoic philosophers mentioned above and of others such as Ambrose and Philo. The latter refer to the meaning of the term in ordinary usage only for the purpose of assimilating it to the generic meaning.

The pivotal difference between the two modes of argument does not lie merely in which of the two meanings is primarily emphasized and which is assimilated to the other. Since both meanings are acknowledged in each case, and since in each case they are related by the assimilation of one to the other, each side might be construed as maintaining no more than that its conception is valid by virtue of conforming to *both* the philosophical and the ordinary sense of the term (i.e., to both the constructed generic meaning and the meaning attested by ordinary usage). If that were all each maintained, no disagreement or debate would result: to say that the SP conception of freedom is valid for these reasons is not to say that the SR conception is invalid, or conversely.

But, as we saw in the preceding chapter, there are writers on the SP side who go further and insist that the SR conception is invalid because it does not conform to the generic meaning of freedom, or, for that matter to the ordinary sense of the term *when that is assimilated to the generic meaning*. And, as we have seen in this chapter, there are writers on the SR

---

[56] For evidence of this, see Ch. 4, pp. 68–71, *supra*.
[57] See Vol. I, pp. 174–76, 255–56, 610–13.

side who also go further and insist that the SP conception is invalid because it does not conform to the ordinary sense of the term or, for that matter, to the generic meaning of freedom *when that is assimilated to the meaning established by common usage.* Genuine disagreement and debate then result between the authors just described, because each group is maintaining not only that its conception does conform but also that the conception held by the other does not conform to the two meanings of freedom which supply a basis for arguing that a particular conception is valid or invalid.

(b) The second point to be noted concerns the difference between the form which the argument against the SP conception takes in those authors (e.g., Hobbes, Hume, Priestley, and Voltaire) whose rejection of it is implied and the form which it takes in those authors (e.g., Hobhouse, Laski, MacIver, and Fosdick) whose rejection of it is explicit.

When the rejection of SP is implied by the assertion that the SR conception *alone* conforms to the common meaning of freedom, the argument for the negative position in the conceptual issue concerning SP involves no more than two premises: one to the effect that being able to do as one pleases *is* the common meaning of freedom as primarily determined by the common usage of the term, and one to the effect that the conception of freedom as circumstantial self-realization is the *only* conception which conforms to that meaning. Consequently, according to this view, acquired self-perfection cannot have the meaning of freedom.

However, when it is explicitly said that the self-perfection authors misappropriate the word "freedom" for what they are talking about, the argument usually involves an additional critical point. It can be summarized as follows. Not only do the self-perfection authors depart from the common meaning of freedom in their use of the term but they also try to conceal this with a metaphor designed to counterfeit the literal meaning.

To describe the so-called virtuous man, as the self-perfection authors do, as an individual whose true self or rational will is able to follow its own bent in the direction of the *ought* (because, having overcome contrary impulses or inclinations, it is exempt from the inner coercion they exercise in the opposite direction), is to concoct an image of freedom in the inner contest between "self" and "other" that bears a similitude to the fact of freedom in the world of external relations between individual things. It is the fact of freedom, so the argument runs, which gives the word its literal meaning. This is another way of saying that the only actual freedom an individual has is in relation to others wholly external to himself—other men or natural forces.

While it can be admitted that there may be something *like* freedom in the inner life of a man, or at least that there may be some poetic truth in the metaphorical attribution of freedom to one part of an individual as against coercion from another part of himself, concern for the scientific or philosophical truth of the matter requires the metaphor to be plainly labeled as such. When that is done, no one will mistake virtue for freedom because the power it confers on a man in his inner life is thought to resemble the freedom that favorable circumstances confer on him in the outer world of his actions.[58]

Granting all the ethical and psychological presuppositions of the self-perfection authors, but excluding their metaphorical use of the term "freedom," the critics point out in effect that the literal description of the man who is able to will as he ought would be that he is wise, or virtuous, or righteous, or dutiful, but never that he is as such free. Since these other terms are available for the self-perfection authors to use in expressing their various conceptions of the morally good man, there is no excuse for their misuse of the term "freedom" in this connection. And the argument in this form usually concludes by adding that the misuse not only puts a counterfeit conception of freedom into circulation but also leads to practical recommendations and policies that are deeply inimical to the cause of freedom.

We turn now to the authors in whom we have found this form of argument for the negative position. It is less explictly developed in Bentham, Wootton, and Malinowski than in Hobhouse, Laski, MacIver, and Fosdick. It should be noted also that Hobhouse and Laski concentrate their attack on a few typical conceptions of acquired self-perfection (those advanced by Rousseau, Hegel, and Bosanquet), whereas MacIver and Fosdick make reference to the whole tradition of self-perfection authors from antiquity to the present day. Fosdick particularly, in mentioning Plato, Epictetus, St. Paul, Rousseau, Hegel, Green, Bosanquet, and Maritain, takes account of most of, if not all of, the diverse typical conceptions of acquired self-perfection.[59] However, her attack on the SP conception in all its variety makes exactly the same critical points that Hobhouse and Laski make in their more limited attacks on Rousseau.

[58] The form of this argument has an ancient prototype in Aristotle's manner of dismissing the conception of justice advanced in Plato's *Republic*. Plato conceives justice as present in the soul when its various parts are properly related to one another. (See *Republic*, Book IV, 441B–44A.) Aristotle, on the contrary, insists that justice exists *only* in the relation of one man to another; and he refers to the common use of the term to support his conception of justice as the proper one. Admitting the possibility of a certain resemblance between an inner relation of one part to another and the external relation of one man to another, Aristotle disposes of Plato's conception by labeling his use of the word "justice" as metaphorical. (See *Nicomachean Ethics*, Book V. Ch. 11, 1138b5–7; and cf. Aquinas, *Summa Theologica*, Part II–II, Q. 58, A. 2.)
[59] See *What is Liberty?* Ch. IV, pp. 98–105, 110–22.

Hegel, and Bosanquet. This suggests that Hobhouse and Laski can be interpreted as arguing against the whole family of SP conceptions, in spite of their application of the argument only to the SP conceptions advanced by certain authors.

Of writers who insist that only the morally right act is free, Bentham says: "They pervert language; they refuse to employ the word *liberty* in its common acceptation; they speak a tongue peculiar to themselves."[60] According to Wootton, "Freedom may be simply defined as the ability to do what you want." This, in her view, is the "earthy commonsense view of the nature of freedom." To depart from it is to play on words or, worse, to deprive the word "freedom" of all meaning. It is in this context that she specifically attacks the SP conception of freedom, referring to the distinction such conceptions make between the things men actually desire and what they really wish when their wishes accord with their deepest natural aspirations or their rational will. "We deny the validity," she writes,

> . . . of any distinction between what people want to do and what they "really" want to do. Any such distinction is extremely dangerous, and may be the cloak for some of the most wicked, because the most insidious, attacks upon freedom. For sooner or later what I "really" want to do turns out to be a polite paraphrase of what you think I ought to want to do. But freedom means freedom to do what *I* want and not what anybody else wants me to want—*or else it has no meaning at all.* How my wants come to be what they are is, no doubt, the result of a complex social and personal process which had best be left to the psychologist to explore. *So far as freedom is concerned what people want to do must be taken as something to be discovered, not changed.*[61]

Like Bentham and Wootton, Malinowski charges that the proponents of SP are playing with the word "freedom" or, worse, perverting its meaning; but, unlike them, he specifically refers to a variety of representative self-perfection authors. He considers Plato, Cicero, Montesquieu, Rousseau, and Hegel, as well as Stoic and Christian conceptions in general; and he contrasts what he calls their "antinomic definition of freedom" with the common understanding of it. In his view, the "antinomic definition" not only departs from the accepted meaning of the term but also involves a contradictory use of it.

"The intuitive emotional subjective meaning of freedom, as felt rather than formulated by the man in the street," Malinowski begins, "conceives of freedom as the ability to do what one likes or to do nothing." This conception of liberty as the absence of restraint "is also the common

---

[60] *Theory of Legislation*, p. 94.
[61] *Freedom Under Planning*, pp. 4–5. (Italics added.)

semantic measure of all dictionary or encyclopedic definitions."[62] But we find Cicero telling us that "we are all the law's slaves, that we may be free"; Rousseau, that we can "be forced to be free"; Montesquieu, that when we do what the laws forbid, we are "no longer possessed of liberty." We are told by Plato and Hegel that freedom consists in submission to reason and law; by Stoic philosophers, that it consists in submission to fate; by Christian teachers, that it consists in the restraint of desires.[63] All such conceptions, which identify freedom with restraint, with obedience, with submission to reason, to law, or to fate, are, in Malinowski's view, "contradictions in terms of 'freedom as complete lack of restraint.' "[64] As measured by the standard or generally accepted meaning of the term, "freedom as willing submission to restraint—any restraint and every restraint—is obviously a perverted concept."[65]

Criticizing Bosanquet's use of the term "real will" to give *willing as one ought* the appearance of *willing as one really wishes*, Hobhouse maintains that strictly, or literally, "there is no part in me which is more real than any other part."[66] Only by using words rhetorically, he declares, can "freedom" be said to lie in what a man "really" wills, as contrasted with what he actually wishes. If we are guided by the common usage of terms, "we cannot . . . accept the definition of freedom suggested by Dr. Bosanquet." It is "mere words" to say that, in willing as I ought, I am free because "the compulsion is exercised by myself upon myself."[67]

Following Hobhouse, Laski argues in the same vein against what he calls "the idealist view of liberty" to be found in Rousseau and Hegel and defended by Bosanquet and Green.[68] As such authors use words, Laski points out, there is no sense to the problem of individual liberty, as that is ordinarily understood. They regard the individual as "free" in fulfilling his obligations, by insisting that when he "is constrained in this way he is in fact willing only what his true self desires." To talk this way is to play with the words that, in ordinary speech, express the accepted

---

[62] *Freedom and Civilization*, Part III, Ch. 1, p. 45.
[63] See *ibid.*, pp. 46, 48–50.
[64] *Ibid.*, p. 46.
[65] *Ibid.*, p. 47.
[66] *The Metaphysical Theory of the State*, p. 45.
[67] *Ibid.*, p. 59. According to Hobhouse, "the only sense . . . in which I am conforming to my own will, in obedience, is that of two evils I prefer the lesser. If in this I am free, it is . . . simply because I am *master of my own actions* and can choose, if I will, to abide by the penalties which disobedience will entail" (*ibid.*, italics added). The italicized words indicate that Hobhouse appeals not only to the everyday use of the word of "freedom" to mean "doing as I please" but also to the generic philosophical sense of the term, which is conveyed by the phrase "self-mastery."
[68] It is worth pointing out that Green's defense of the SP conception extends beyond the theories of Rousseau and Hegel to the views of Plato, St. Paul, the Stoics, and Kant. See his *Lectures on the Principles of Political Obligation*, pp. 3–18.

meaning of freedom, according to which any experience of constraint marks a loss of liberty. Those who try to tell a man "that he is made free when he is prevented from fulfilling the purpose he regards as the *raison d'être* of his existence . . . deprive words of all their meaning."[69]

According to MacIver, there can be no doubt that the "universal meaning" of liberty is exemplified by every instance in which an individual is prevented from doing as he pleases.[70] This meaning, he says, "we must simply recognize, simply accept. The universality of usage sets it for us. It is understood by the child and by the savage as well as by the civilized man. It is a meaning we cannot do without."[71]

There are "people who offer us some alternative and different meaning," but even they, according to MacIver, "imply that it is equivalent to the universally accepted meaning." Here, he points out, "is the root of the worst perversions" which culminate with the sophistry of turning "liberty into its own contradiction."[72] The greatest sinners in this respect are found in the long line of philosophers "from the time of Plato to the present day" who have defined freedom in terms of willing as one ought and given wide currency to this worst perversion of the term's obvious meaning. While MacIver pays special attention to Rousseau and Hegel, he clearly has the whole family of SP conceptions in mind.[73] All, in his view, substantiate the charge that "they enable men to justify in the name of liberty the most extreme suppressions of liberty."[74]

MacIver is willing to concede that the word "freedom" can be applied metaphorically to a man's exemption from inward obstacles to the fulfillment of his desires, but he cautions us against allowing the metaphor to replace the literal meaning of the term, "so unmistakable in its primary applications."[75] He would not object if such writers as Rousseau and Hegel were to say, on the one hand, that willing as one ought is good, and, on

---

[69] *The State in Theory and Practice*, p. 44. See *ibid.*, pp. 37–85; and cf. *The Grammar of Politics*, pp. 29–35; and also *Liberty in the Modern State*, pp. 56–62. It should be noted that Laski, like Hobhouse, appeals not only to the common-sense understanding of freedom but also to the generic conception of it as self-mastery. Unless the individual is able to follow his own will, i.e., lead a life entirely of his own choosing, "he ceases to be master of [himself]. I cannot believe," Laski concludes, "that a man no longer master of himself is in any meaningful sense free" (*Liberty in the Modern State*, p. 62).

[70] See "The Meaning of Liberty and Its Perversions" in *Freedom, Its Meaning*, p. 285.

[71] *Ibid.*, p. 280.

[72] *Ibid.*

[73] He refers to Dorothy Fosdick's book, *What is Liberty?*, in which other representatives of this tradition are considered, and recommends it as "the best analysis of the subject within my knowledge." See *ibid.*, p. 280, fn. 1.

[74] *Ibid.*, p. 286.

[75] *Ibid.*, p. 285.

the other, that liberty is good, and then "seek for some relation between them." But when "they say that the one *is* the other," MacIver charges them with misappropriating the term "freedom" for an ulterior purpose. Instead of speaking "of men as being 'forced to be free,'" Rousseau should have said "'forced to be good,' 'forced to be rational,'" for thus he could have avoided a paradoxical or, worse, a perverse use of terms. Such writers, MacIver concludes,

> will not face the issue that they value other things more highly then liberty and that they reject liberty for the sake of these other things. That position would be at least honest. Instead, they pervert the universal meaning of liberty in order to deny the most obvious of facts. They would destroy the meaning of liberty because they are afraid to admit its meaning. They call it something else, hoping that thus no one will claim it for what it is.[76]

The literal meaning of liberty, according to Fosdick, is not to be "estopped from doing what one desires and is able to do."[77] In this literal meaning, the only things that can take away a man's freedom are external obstacles that interfere with the realization of his desires. But men can *feel* inwardly free even when they *are not* free externally. It is this which, in Fosdick's opinion, leads them to accept a counterfeit of freedom for the reality. Unaware of the "necessary distinction between feeling free and being free," they equate "the inner experience of feeling free with the condition of being free."[78] The literal meaning of the word "free" is then replaced by a purely metaphorical use of it.

It is precisely this illicit and confusing substitution, she maintains, which has been perpetrated by a long line of writers from Plato, St. Paul, and Epictetus to Rousseau, Hegel, Bosanquet, and Green. They identify freedom with "the inner personal experience of having one's will unified through devotion to objects considered worth-while." But while conceding that the term "feeling free" can be justifiably applied to such experience, Fosdick insists that "being free refers to an outer environmental condition," in the absence of which the individual who feels free has no freedom.[79]

---

[76] *Ibid.*, pp. 286–87.
[77] *What is Liberty?* p. 16. Cf. *ibid.*, p. 122.
[78] *Ibid.*, p. 99.
[79] *Ibid.*, p. 106. If one wishes to avoid confusing fact and feeling, the literal and the metaphorical, one must not use the phrase "'being free' . . . to describe both an inner release from the bondage of a divided will and an outer release from the compulsion of other people." The "absence of tyranny by an alien impulse or habit, that one feels to be foreign, unworthy, or harmful" may make one "feel free," but it should not be called "having liberty," if one is to avoid the confusion that results from using "the word liberty to refer both to the relation of one man to another and to the relation of one impulse to another" (*ibid.*, p. 100). Cf. *ibid.*, p. 131.

Once the metaphor is plainly recognized for what it is, the meaning of freedom is secure from adulteration. Bosanquet's attempt to justify the metaphorical application of the term liberty to a state of the individual mind is an admission on his part that "the use of the term liberty to describe the inner relation between elements of a man's nature" is metaphorical; and this, Fosdick thinks, "gives away his case."[80] Bosanquet and others may be able to explain how the metaphorical meaning arises, but no explanation can justify forgetting that it is metaphorical and treating it as literal. While the metaphor may give meaning to the word "freedom" as the self-perfection authors use it, it does not validate that meaning. On the contrary, its fanciful character is thereby exposed.[81]

(ii) *Argument in rebuttal: in defense of Position* (A). Of the twenty-five authors who can clearly be construed as taking an affirmative stand on this issue, only Green and Bosanquet reply to the argument against acquired self-perfection that being able to will as one ought does not conform to the generally recognized meaning of freedom. Only they meet the charge that the self-perfection authors are using the term in a metaphorical sense without acknowledging their substitution of it for the literal meaning of freedom, which is exemplified in the conception of it as circumstantial self-realizaton. And Green alone defends a wide variety of representative authors on the affirmative side of this issue— Plato, St. Paul, the Stoics, and Kant, as well as Rousseau and Hegel.[82]

With the two exceptions just indicated, none of the authors mentioned, nor others in that tradition from Plato to Hegel, show the slightest awareness that there does or may exist a point of view from which their conception of freedom is denied validity. They assume the truth of the ethical and psychological presuppositions underlying their conception and further assume that, once these presuppositions are granted, it should be obvious that being able to will as one ought is genuine freedom. Some of them, Plato and Hegel, for example, recognize that freedom is popularly thought to consist in doing as one pleases; and they may regard their

---

[80] *Ibid.*, p. 104. The passage that Fosdick quotes from p. 129 of Bosanquet's *Philosophical Theory of the State* is as follows: "The mind, then, is treated by a metaphor as if it were two or more persons; and the term 'liberty,' which applies *prima facie* to the non-constraint of one person by another, is applied to the non-constraint of something within an individual mind by something else within it."
[81] See *What is Liberty?*, p. 105. "Giving meaning does not necessarily imply giving a valid meaning," Fosdick writes by way of comment on a statement she quotes from p. 18 of Green's *Lectures on the Principles of Political Obligation*, to the effect that ". . . the feeling of oppression, which always goes along with the consciousness of unfulfilled possibilities, will always give meaning to the representation of the effort after any kind of self-improvement as a demand for 'freedom.' "
[82] Bosanquet, in contrast, confines his defense to the theories of Rousseau and Hegel.

dismissal of this vulgar notion as a sufficient defense of the conception which they set in sharp contrast to it. However, no authors in this group except Bosanquet and Green consider the grounds on which freedom in any meaningful sense can be denied the individual for whom it is claimed by reason of his ability to will as he ought.[83]

The argument in rebuttal does not attempt to deny that being able to do as one pleases in the absence of external constraints is the commonly accepted meaning of freedom, and the only one employed in everyday speech. Nor does it deny that this is the primary or primitive sense of the term, insofar as the common-sense approach to the nature of freedom precedes the philosophical analysis of it. Green, and Bosanquet following him, affirm these things and go even further in their admission that any other use of the term must *at first* appear to be purely metaphorical.

"It must of course be admitted," Green writes, "that every usage of the term to express anything but a social and political relation of one man to another involves a metaphor."[84] He then reviews the various ways in which writers from Plato to Hegel have applied to the relation of elements in man's inner life "a term borrowed from relations of outward life."[85] None of these applications, he concedes,

> is at all implied in "freedom" according to the primary meaning of the term, as expressing that relation between one man and others in which he is secured from compulsion. All that is so implied is that a man should have the power to do what he wills or prefers. No reference is made to the nature of the will, or preference, of the object willed or preferred; whereas according to the doctrines we have just been considering, it is not constituted by the mere fact of acting upon preference, but depends wholly on the nature of the preference, upon the kind of object willed or preferred.[86]

Green even goes so far as to wish that the word "freedom" had never been used in any sense except that which applies to an individual's exemption from coercion or constraint by others, which he calls the "juristic sense" of the term. He says:

[83] It should be noted that Bosanquet and Green propose to themselves the possibility that acquired self-perfection may be charged with being freedom only in a metaphorical sense of the term. The actual charge that it is only a metaphor is made by authors who refer to their writings, but to whom they, in turn, do not refer. Of the three self-realization authors whom Bosanquet specifically criticizes—Bentham, J. S. Mill, and Spencer—only Bentham explicitly attacks the SP conception on the ground that its exponents pervert language and refuse to employ the term "liberty" in its common acceptation. But Bosanquet does not refer to this attack.

[84] *Lectures on the Principles of Political Obligation*, p. 3.

[85] See *ibid.*, pp. 3–9.

[86] *Ibid.*, p. 9.

If it were ever reasonable to wish that the usage of words had been other than it has been . . . one might be inclined to wish that the term "freedom" had been confined to the juristic sense of the power to "do what one wills," for the extension of its meaning seems to have caused much controversy and confusion.[87]

Nevertheless, at this point Green turns in the opposite direction to defend the views of freedom which have extended the meaning of the term from the individual's outer relation to other men and his environment to the relation of factors within his inner life. "After all," he writes,

> this extension does but represent various stages of reflection upon the self-distinguishing, self-seeking, self-asserting principle, of which the establishment of freedom, as a relation between man and man, is the expression. The reflecting man is not content with the first announcement which analysis makes as to the inward condition of the free man, viz., that he can do what he likes, that he has the power of acting according to his will or preference. In virtue of the same principle which led him to assert himself against others, and thus to cause there to be such a thing as (outward) freedom, he distinguishes himself from his preference, and asks how he is related to it. . . .[88]

What is of critical importance for us to note in this statement is that Green is here appealing to the generic meaning of freedom as against the commonly accepted sense of it in ordinary speech. His reference to the self-asserting principle is a reference to the generic meaning, according to which the assertion of the self as against the other is the principle of freedom. In the light of this principle, he then proceeds to argue that the common-sense meaning of freedom (i.e., the juristic sense in which it is applied to the actions of men in relation to one another) involves the "self-asserting principle" and participates in the generic meaning of freedom *neither more nor less* than does the meaning of freedom which develops from philosophical reflection (i.e., the moral sense in which it is applied to man's inner or spiritual life).

When this is seen, the fact that the common-sense meaning may be earlier in the order of development of our notions of freedom does not give it primacy among the various conceptions, all of which conform equally to the generic meaning of freedom; nor need we concern ourselves any longer with the propriety of using the word "freedom" in senses different from that employed in everyday speech.

Green makes this last point quite clear in the following passage, in which he considers not only the SR and the SP conceptions of freedom

[87] *Ibid.*
[88] *Ibid.*, pp. 9–10.

but also the SD conception (i.e., the conception of the freedom of a man's will in determining what he shall do or shall become).

> The propriety or impropriety of the use of "freedom" to express the state of the will, not as directed to any and every object, but only to those to which, according to the law of nature or the will of God or its "idea," it should be directed, is a matter of secondary importance. This usage of the term [i.e., in the SP sense] is, at any rate, no more a departure from the primary or juristic sense [i.e., the SR sense] than is its application to the will as distinct from action [i.e., in the SD sense]. . . . And certainly the unsophisticated man, as soon as the usage of "freedom" to express exemption from control by other men and ability to do as he likes [SR] is departed from, can much more readily assimilate the notion of states of the inner man described as bondage to evil passions, to terrors of the law, or on the other hand as freedom from sin and law, freedom in the consciousness of union with God, or of harmony with the true law of one's being, freedom of true loyalty, freedom in devotion to self-imposed duties [SP], than he can assimilate the notion of freedom as freedom to will anything and everything [SR], or as exemption from determination by motives or the constitution by himself of the motives which determine his will [SD].[89]

It may still be asked how Green rebuts the charge that the SP meaning of freedom is metaphorical, a charge he himself appears to have conceded at the beginning of this essay "on the different senses of 'freedom' as applied to will and to the moral progress of man." The answer is that he admits the metaphorical sense of the word "freedom" as applied to the inner state of the virtuous man *only when the juristic sense of the word, as applied in ordinary speech to the outer relation of one man to another, is taken as the whole and essential meaning of freedom.* Then, of course, any other sense of the term must depart from that meaning or borrow from it for the sake of applying the word to that which *is not freedom,* but only *something like it.* The juristic or social sense of the term (SR) being taken as the literal sense, the borrowed sense, adapted to the inner, moral life (SP), cannot help appearing to be metaphorical.

But when the ultimate source of meaning for any use of the word "freedom" is seen to be the generic sense of the self-asserting principle, and when the SR and the SP (as well as the SD) use of the term are all seen to be specifications of that generic sense, one no more primary than another, then none is a metaphor. In their common derivation from the

[89] *Ibid.,* p. 16. Green then goes on to say that, in his judgment, there is much less "to justify the extension of the usage of the term" to the self-determination of free will or to a self-realization which consists in being able to enact anything one pleases to will than to justify its extension to cover the virtuous man's ability to will as he ought.

generic meaning of freedom as self-assertion, none borrows from the meaning of the others. All share equally in the generic meaning, and each must be assimilated to it.

If the meaning of "freedom" in everyday speech could not be assimilated to the generic meaning, it would be questionable in spite of the facts of usage. However, Green, while questioning the extension of the common-sense meaning which occurs in conceptions of self-realization that place no limits on what a man should be able to do according to his pleasure, maintains that "there is a real community of meaning" between the circumstantial freedom of self-realization and the acquired freedom of self-perfection—"between 'freedom' as expressing the condition of a citizen of a civilized state, and 'freedom' as expressing the condition of a man who is inwardly 'master of himself.' "[90]

Since, according to Green, the essence or nature of freedom is the self-seeking or self-asserting principle which gives us the generic meaning that is common to every kind of freedom, he thinks that " 'freedom' is the natural term" to use for acquired self-perfection as well as for circumstantial self-realization and natural self-determination. He thus brings his argument in defense of Position (A) to a conclusion in the following passage:

> . . . just as the demand for an attainment of freedom from external control is the expression of that *same self-seeking principle* from which the quest for such an object proceeds, so "freedom" is the natural term by which the man describes such an object to himself—describes to himself the state in which he shall have realized his ideal of himself, shall be at one with the law he recognizes as that which he ought to obey, shall have become all that he has it in him to be, and so fulfill the law of his being or "live according to nature."[91]

[90] *Ibid.*, p. 16. "That is to say," Green continues, "the practical conception by a man . . . of a self-satisfaction to be attained in his becoming what he should be, what he has it in him to be, in fulfillment of the law of his being—or, to vary the words but not the meaning, in attainment of the righteousness of God, or in perfect obedience to self-imposed law—this practical conception is the outcome of the *same self-seeking principle* which appears in a man's assertion of himself against other men and against nature . . . [which] is the demand for freedom, freedom in the primary or juristic sense of power to act according to choice or preference" (*ibid.*, p. 17, italics added).

[91] *Ibid.*, pp. 17–18. (Italics added.) Furthermore, Green not only insists that "freedom" is the natural and proper term for being able to will as one ought but he also suggests that this conception of freedom is shared by people generally, and not just by a small group of philosophers. "To any popular audience interested in the work of self-improvement (e.g., a temperance-meeting seeking to break the bondage to liquor), it is as an effort to attain freedom," he writes, "that such work can be most effectively presented. It is easy to tell such people that the term is being misapplied; that they are quite 'free' as it is, because every one can do as he likes so long as he does not prevent another from doing so. . . . Still the feeling of oppression,

The argument in rebuttal as presented by Bosanquet follows the general tenor of the reasoning we have just examined.[92] Like Green, Bosanquet says that if we accept "the absence of constraint exercised by one upon others" as "the literal or elementary sense of liberty," then "we may admit that, in going beyond it, we are more or less making use of a metaphor."[93] And, like Green also, Bosanquet argues that what at first appears to be only a metaphor is seen really not to be one when we recognize that the SP conception of freedom, no less than the SR conception, is rooted in a generic meaning according to which the self is the principle of every kind of freedom. But where Green refers to this principle as the "self-seeking" or "self-asserting" principle, Bosanquet speaks of it as the "self-determining."

> In the case of Liberty, conceived as a condition of the mind, just as in the case of Liberty, conceived as the absence of physical menace or coercion on the part of other persons, *the root of the matter is the claim to be determined only by ourself.*[94]

In what follows, Bosanquet continues to use the word "literal" in order to remind the reader that he is referring to what Green called the "juristic sense of 'freedom'" which is exemplified in an individual's exemption from interference by others. Similarly, he continues to use the word "metaphorical" for the sense of freedom which is being questioned. Bearing this in mind, we shall not misunderstand the point he intends to make in the following passage.

> In the literal case, what we mean by ourself is the given self, the group of will and wishes, of feelings and ideas, associated from time to time with my particular body. . . . In the metaphorical case, we have made so much progress in self-criticism as to know at least that our "self" is something of a problem. We know that the given self, the mind from day to day, is not satisfactory; and we throw the center of gravity outside, and place the true self in something which we rather want to be than actually are. . . . And it is for this reason that we feel so confident, in proportion as we at all lay

which always goes along with the consciousness of unfulfilled possibilities, will always give meaning to the representation of the effort after any kind of self-improvement as a demand for 'freedom'" (*ibid.*, p. 18). It is precisely this passage on which Fosdick comments by saying: "Giving meaning does not necessarily imply giving a valid meaning." See fn. 81 on p. 58, *supra*. To which Green might reply that his reference, in the immediately preceding paragraphs, to the self-seeking or self-asserting principle which gives us the generic meaning of freedom, provides his warrant for asserting the validity of the SP meaning.

[92] Bosanquet acknowledges his debt to Green. See *The Philosophical Theory of the State*, p. 128, fn. 1.

[93] *Ibid.*, p. 128.

[94] *Ibid.*, p. 133. (Italics added.)

hold upon a life which can thus distinguish and identify us, that we have here the grasp of what is in its nature our true self. Here then, as in the literal case of liberty from personal constraint, we are putting in act the principle of "being determined only by ourself."[95]

Since both cases fall under or belong to "the same principle," it can be argued that the so-called "literal case" and the so-called "metaphorical case" stand on exactly the same footing as kinds of freedom, i.e., both are cases of "being determined only by ourself."

Bosanquet, however, is unwilling to accord them the same standing. In his view, being able to will as one ought has a stronger claim to be recognized as embodying the essence of freedom than being able to do as one pleases. He questions the justice of the treatment accorded these two freedoms in "the usual course of English thought," and even questions "the example of a writer [Green] whose caution equalled his enthusiasm, in admitting that the lower sense of the term Liberty is the literal sense, and that the deeper meaning may be treated as metaphorical." He thinks not only that, in full justice, these epithets should be expunged but also that the "deeper meaning" must be accorded primacy.

Bosanquet, therefore, concludes by asserting that what he calls "the lower sense of the term Liberty" (i.e., doing as one pleases) participates in the generic meaning of freedom only through the reflected light cast on it by "the higher liberty" (i.e., willing as one ought). Saying that it is "the sense of the higher liberty . . . that has communicated uncontrollable force to the claim for the lower," he declares:

> . . . if the fuller meaning is the reality and the lesser the symbol, it would be nearer the truth to say that the reality is the liberty of a moral being whose will finds adequate expression in its life, of which liberty the absence of external constraint is only an elementary type or symbol.[96]

He then finishes off his argument in rebuttal by ruling out as unfounded any claim for the primacy of the lower meaning (i.e., doing as one pleases) by reason of its earlier appearance or its popular acceptance. "The claim of the dictionary-maker that the earliest or the average meaning is also the truest or the 'proper' meaning of the words has no foundation."[97]

(iii) *Other possible arguments.* The number of authors who engage in the debate of this issue is much smaller than the number of authors who can be construed as taking opposite sides on it.

---

[95] *Ibid.*, pp. 133–34. (Italics added.)
[96] *Ibid.*, pp. 135–36. Cf. the interpretation of this passage that was given in Ch. 4, pp. 55–56, *supra.*
[97] *Ibid.*, p. 136.

When the writers on each side are listed in chronological order it is at once apparent that the case against acquired self-perfection is explicitly argued only by the more recent writers. The same is true on the other side of the case. Two relatively recent writers are the only ones who offer explicit arguments in defense of the proposition that being able to will as one ought is genuine freedom, and they are not typical SP authors in the way they treat the commonly accepted meaning of freedom as doing what one pleases. Furthermore, as we have already noted, the defense offered by Green and Bosanquet precedes in time the most explicit attacks —those made by Hobhouse, Laski, Malinowski, MacIver, and Fosdick.

It is surprising not to find any response to these attacks from twentieth-century writers who were in a position to answer them directly. In contrast, it is much less surprising to find that, prior to the nineteenth century, the affirmations and denials of acquired self-perfection were unaccompanied by explicit argument either in support of or in defense of the views held.

Whatever the causes of these deficiencies may be, they lead us to speculate about whether, if there had been more participants in the debate of this issue, both earlier in the tradition and in our own day, other arguments might have been advanced than the ones we have found. Considering the philosophical views of certain authors who might have taken part in the debate on the affirmative side but did not, as well as certain additional views held by authors who have taken part and who might have introduced them on the negative side, we can suggest three possible arguments, one in support of Position (N) and two in defense of Position (A).

The connection between the ideas of freedom and of responsibility, it might be argued in support of Position (N), reveals that being able to will as one ought does not conform to the idea of freedom. In the popular as well as the philosophical understanding of these matters, the self is both the principle of freedom and the principle of responsibility. On the one hand, it is generally recognized that no act of a man can be called free unless he himself and not another is the author of that act. On the other hand, it is generally recognized that no one is to be held responsible, answerable, or accountable for an act of which he is not himself the author. Accordingly, the spheres of freedom and responsibility are held to be coextensive, and a man cannot be blamed for an act unless it is one which he has freely performed. Hence, it can be argued that any attribution of freedom to a man which must be divorced from the attribution of responsibility to him is questionable.

It is precisely on this ground that the so-called freedom of self-perfection must be questioned. Its exponents claim that it is a freedom possessed only by morally good or righteous men, for only they, through acquired wisdom or virtue, have the ability to will as they ought. But how in this case, the argument might then continue, can the man who is *not* morally good be held responsible for not willing as he ought?

If the exponents of acquired self-perfection acknowledge the inseparability of freedom and responsibility, they must say that, since only good men have the freedom of being able to will as they ought, only good men are responsible in their free compliance with duties or laws. It must follow, then, that bad men, who do not have the freedom of being able to will as they ought, cannot be held responsible for the violation of moral obligations or laws, since they lack the requisite freedom. This would be an absurd conclusion for them to reach, especially in the light of their own views about moral obligations or laws.

Nor can they avoid this reduction to absurdity by replying that, in the moral realm, all men are free to choose between good and evil, right and wrong, obedience and disobedience. The freedom of choice to which they refer is the natural freedom of self-determination, which, its exponents claim, is inherent in all men, not the acquired freedom of self-perfection which, its exponents admit, is not possessed by all men, but only the wise or virtuous. The fact that a man's responsibility for his bad or wrong moral choices is thought to be connected with his natural freedom of self-determination in no way alters the fact that no responsibility in the moral realm can be connected with his acquired freedom of self-perfection, without at the same time embracing the absurdity of saying that those who lack such freedom also lack responsibility. That both virtuous and vicious men can be held responsible for their moral character or the moral state of their will, while only the virtuous are said to be free, plainly shows that the freedom which is connected with virtue is not freedom in any proper or literal sense of the term.

In defense of Position (A), it might be argued that, though the self is the underlying principle in the generic meaning of both freedom and responsibility, it does not follow that the ideas of freedom and responsibility are inseparably connected. There is, furthermore, good reason to think that they are not inseparably connected. We say that men are responsible because they are free, but we do not say that men are free because they are responsible. In other words, responsibility presupposes freedom, but not freedom responsibility.

Hence, the argument might continue, from the fact that acquired self-perfection or the lack of it does not provide a basis for holding men responsible or not, it does not follow that acquired self-perfection cannot be regarded as freedom. Nor from the fact that responsibility is connected with the freedoms of self-realization and of self-determination, but not that of self-perfection, does it follow that the latter cannot be freedom in a proper or literal sense. The error here can be construed as resting on the supposition that the generic meaning of freedom must be exemplified *in the same way* in all the more specific conceptions of freedom.

In the hands of certain authors, notably Maritain and Yves Simon, who embrace the Thomistic theory of a basic difference between analogical concepts and all other universals, the argument in defense of Position (A) might then attempt to expose the error involved in treating the idea of freedom as if it were an ordinary universal concept, such as corporeality or animality. The generic meaning of such concepts is exemplified in the same way in all the species that fall under it. But freedom does not have a generic meaning of this sort. Rather, like the analogical concepts of being or of unity, the meaning of freedom is exemplified diversely in all the particulars that fall under it, and therefore that meaning is strictly analogical, and not generic in the ordinary sense of the term.

It is all right to call the underlying meaning of freedom "generic" in order to call attention to the fact that this meaning is *common* to all conceptions of freedom, but, in stricter or more careful speech, it is necessary to say that the underlying meaning of freedom is *analogically* shared by all conceptions of freedom, and to point out that they do not participate in it as diverse species do in a common genus.

The foregoing possible argument not only bears on the problem of freedom and responsibility but also, quite apart from that, tends to confirm the argument actually advanced by two adherents of Position (A)—Green and Bosanquet—to the effect that there is a "real community of meaning" among the various senses of freedom, which embraces acquired self-perfection along with circumstantial self-realization and natural self-determination. When the adherents of Position (N) exclude *being able to will as one ought* from this "community of meaning," they treat *being able to do what one pleases* as if it were the perfect and only proper exemplar of the common meaning of freedom. By doing so, they can argue that *being able to will as one ought* participates in the common meaning of freedom only by borrowing the meaning to be found in its proper and primary exemplar, in the manner in which a term used metaphorically borrows its meaning from the literal use of that same term.

Thus, when a king is called the father of his people, the word "father" applied to a king is a metaphor based on a certain similitude between the relation of father to child and the relation of king to people. In this case, it is clear that "father," in its primary and literal meaning, applies only to the biological progenitor of offspring. The metaphorical use of "father" employs a derived meaning. But in the case of freedom, the similitude which exists between the free man in relation to other men and the free man in relation to parts of himself indicates that being able to do as one pleases (in the world of external action) and being able to will as one ought (in the inner moral life) are analogous types of freedom.

Extending the consideration to the third of the major freedoms, it might, in addition, be pointed out that each of the analogous types is both alike and different from the other two. Self-perfection is unlike self-realization and self-determination in a respect in which the latter two are alike, namely, the connection of freedom and responsibility; and self-determination is unlike self-perfection and self-realization in a respect in which the latter two are alike, namely, the compatibility of freedom and necessity.

None of the three, the argument would then continue, is the primary or perfect exemplar of freedom. All share in the analogically common meaning and exemplify it in quite diverse ways. Hence, the argument would conclude, it is erroneous to judge the validity of one exemplification by reference to the other, *as if it were the measure of what freedom truly is.* When that error is corrected, no foundation remains for the charge that acquired self-perfection is freedom only in a metaphorical sense.[98]

So far, we have considered an argument in defense of Position (A) that is available to authors who affirm both SR and SP as genuine freedoms. It is, as we have seen, the argument that is actually advanced by Green and Bosanquet in their rebuttal of the charge that SP is freedom merely in a metaphorical sense.[99] The possible argument that such followers of Aquinas as Maritain and Yves Simon might have employed, had they engaged in this dispute, goes further in the same direction; for they maintain that there is a common meaning of freedom in which both SR and SP participate equally—neither having primacy, neither being metaphorical.

[98] This argument to the effect that self-realization, self-perfection, and self-determination are all analogous exemplifications of the meaning of freedom can be advanced only by authors who, so far as SR and SP are concerned, affirm them both. As indicated in Ch. 4, pp. 88–89, *supra*, it is an argument that might have been employed in defense of the middle position in the three-sided issue about the conditions under which self-realization is truly freedom, i.e., the position held by Aquinas, Locke, Montesquieu, Maritain, and Yves Simon. From the point of view of these authors, to say that acquired self-perfection is the perfect and proper exemplar of the generic meaning of freedom, and thereby to exclude circumstantial self-realization as an illusory freedom, is to make the error mentioned in the text above, but in the opposite direction. It is the error of judging the validity of one exemplification (in this case, SR) by reference to another (in this case, SP), *as if the latter were the measure of what freedom truly is.*

[99] See pp. 123–24, *supra.*

We turn now to one other possible argument in defense of Position (A). This is the argument that might have been advanced by SP authors who deny that SR is a genuine form of human freedom. They are the authors who, in the controversy concerning circumstantial self-realization, take the extreme negative position, namely, that circumstantial self-realization is not freedom under any condition.[100] From the point of view of such writers, the SR sense of the term, far from representing the literal meaning of freedom, does not express the meaning of freedom at all. Since that is the case, they might conceivably argue, the meaning attached to freedom by the SR authors, which these authors also claim is the common usage of the term, cannot possibly provide a basis for the charge that the SP conception of freedom represents a metaphorical sense of the term.

While it is true that some of these SP authors, such as the Stoics, use the phrase "doing as one pleases," they never use it without at once giving it a meaning that expresses their conception of freedom as acquired self-perfection. Freedom, for them, does not consist in being able to do *anything* one pleases, but rather in being able to do that which one's true self rightly desires. By their insistence on the true self and on right desire, they, together with other SP authors, exclude from the realm of freedom any exemption from external coercion or impediment which is not accompanied by the true self's mastery over whatever inner forces work against its willing as it ought.[101]

[100] See Ch. 4, pp. 52–53, *supra.*
[101] See Ch. 4, pp. 66–76, esp. pp. 68–71, *supra.*

Chapter 6

THE ISSUES CONCERNING
POLITICAL LIBERTY

Concerning the liberty which individuals have or lack in relation to the state and to the institutions of government, there are striking differences of opinion. But when we examine these differences, we find no real disagreement to constitute an issue about political liberty in the general controversy.

That there is no issue about this subject—i.e., no issue which can be constructed on the basis of documentary evidence of real disagreement that is at least implicit in the literature—calls for some explanation, in view of the widely shared impression that this is one of the major subjects of controversy in the discussion of freedom.

Freedom is certainly one of the major subjects in political philosophy. There are few theories of the state or of government which do not consider the effect of political institutions upon freedom. The demands which the state makes upon its members, the power which civil government exerts over their lives, the regulation of their conduct by positive law—all these as well as the protection which the state gives to individuals, the moral tutelage or discipline it affords them, and the elevation to a higher plane of life have obvious implications for theories of freedom.

It is, therefore, natural to expect that basic disagreements in the philosophy of the state, of government, and of law should carry with them basic disagreements about freedom in relation to the state, government, and law. In view of this, the absence of issues about political liberty appears incredible and inexplicable. Yet it can be explained and made credible.

It must be noted, first of all, that we did not say that there are no real disagreements about man's freedom in relation to the state, to civil government, and to positive law. We said only that there is no issue about political liberty in the general controversy. To understand the meaning as well as the truth of that statement, we must recall the way in which issues in the general controversy about the kinds of freedom differ from issues in the special controversies about particular forms of freedom, such as the circumstantial freedom of self-realization or the acquired freedom of self-perfection. As we have seen in the preceding chapters, an issue about SR or SP in the general controversy consists in a disagreement about the existence or genuineness of the freedom in question, i.e., it involves the affirmation and denial that it is a distinct kind of freedom.

Similarly, for there to be an issue in the general controversy about political liberty as a distinct freedom, the subject of that issue would have to be a form of freedom which, as affirmed by certain authors, can be identified as distinct from SR, SP, and SD. In Book II, we offered documentary evidence to show that certain authors do conceive of a freedom which does not consist in being able under favorable circumstances to do as one pleases, nor in the acquired ability of the virtuous or wise man to will as he ought, nor in man's inherent power to determine for himself what he shall do or shall become. We thought it appropriate to call this freedom "political liberty" in view of the fact that it is attributed only to those men who, living under constitutional government, have the status of citizenship and, with that, the power which suffrage confers on them, i.e., the power to participate in the formation of the public will, in the shaping of the political institutions, and in the making of the positive law, of the society in which they live.

According to the conceptions we examined, an individual can enjoy such freedom only when it is conferred on him by the favorable circumstances of living under constitutional government and being admitted to citizenship with suffrage. Given these favorable circumstances, good and bad men alike possess a freedom that consists in the power which the individual has to realize his private will in public affairs. We, therefore, treated political liberty as a circumstantial freedom rather than an acquired one, and as a variant of self-realization rather than of self-perfection. While a variant of self-realization, it is nevertheless distinct from it. Proof of this is seen in the fact that authors such as Aristotle and Kant affirm political liberty as thus identified *but deny self-realization;* and also in the fact that authors such as Hobhouse and Sidgwick affirm both political liberty and the freedom of self-realization, *but assert that one is quite distinct from the other.*[1]

[1] See Ch. 18 on political liberty in Vol. I, pp. 329–67. The authors there treated as holding a conception of political liberty in addition to as well as distinct from other forms of freedom were Aristotle, Aquinas, Locke, Montesquieu, Kant, Hobhouse, Maritain, and Simon. See *ibid.,* pp. 593–94 for an enumeration of the diverse conceptions included in the theories of freedom held by these authors. In the present chapter, we shall cite a number of other writers who can also be construed as affirming political liberty: in addition to Sidgwick mentioned above, such writers as Marsilius of Padua, Alexander Hamilton, Karl Jaspers, and Barbara Wootton. It should be said at once that the conception of political liberty, while shared by all these writers, is most clearly expounded by relatively recent authors such as Hobhouse, Sidgwick,

Not all writers who attribute to citizens alone a special freedom conferred on them by their franchise to participate actively in political affairs use the phrase "political liberty"; and many use it who have in mind only the freedom of self-realization or the freedom of self-perfection, *considered in relation to political institutions* (e.g., Hobbes and Rousseau). However, the use or non-use of the phrase ceases to obscure the actual situation as soon as we are able to identify the form of freedom which particular authors have in mind when they discuss liberty in the context of political considerations. This can be illustrated by five typical answers to the question, "How can individuals be free when they are subject to the power of civil government and to the coercive force of the laws of the state?"

(i) The answer given by Hobbes, Bentham, Spencer, Hayek, and others is that men who are subject to civil government can be free *only in that portion of their conduct which is not prescribed by positive law*. In matters not regulated by law, they can do as they please, at least to whatever extent other circumstances are permissive. The form of freedom these writers have in mind is clearly that of circumstantial self-realization. Such freedom is sometimes called "political liberty" when it is considered in relation to the special set of circumstances consisting in the power of government and the laws of the state, to which the individual is subject. Hobbes, for example, refers to it as "political liberty" or as "the liberty of subjects," in order to contrast it with "corporal liberty," which is the freedom of being able to do as one pleases in the absence of merely physical (i.e., non-political) impediments.[2]

(ii) The answer given by Laski, Hobhouse, Knight, Kelsen, and others is that men who are subject to civil government can be free in that portion of their conduct which is not prescribed by positive law *and, in addition, also in matters regulated by law to whatever extent the prescriptions of law happen to coincide with their individual wishes*. Clearly, these writers have the same form of freedom in mind as do Hobbes, Bentham, Spencer, and Hayek, namely, circumstantial self-realization. To the favorable circumstance which is the absence of legal regulation, they add, as another favorable circumstance, the coincidence between what the law prescribes and what the individual himself wishes to do. They, too, sometimes call such freedom "political" in order to contrast it with self-realization under favorable circumstances that are not political in character.[3]

Jaspers, Maritain, and Simon. Earlier writers, such as Aquinas, Locke, and Montesquieu, leave us in doubt on certain points.

[2] See Vol. I, pp. 232–36.

[3] See *ibid.*, pp. 237–44 and 352–56. Among the writers mentioned above, Hobhouse is the only one who also affirms a freedom that resides in the possession of citizenship and the exercise of suffrage.

(iii) The answer given by Rousseau, Hegel, and others is that men who are subject to civil government can be free in obeying the laws of the state, *but only (a) if the laws express the general or objective will and (b) if the subjects are men who, through acquired virtue, are able to will as they ought, so that in their willing obedience to law they are, in effect, obeying themselves alone.* The two conditions mentioned show that the form of freedom these authors have in mind is that of acquired self-perfection. That such freedom is sometimes called, as by Rousseau, both "civil liberty" and "moral liberty" indicates the fusion of the political and ethical aspects of this form of freedom, which can be enjoyed only by the morally good man in the politically well-constituted state.[4]

(iv) Closely resembling the preceding answer, yet differing from it, is one of the two answers given by such writers as Aquinas, Locke, Montesquieu, Maritain, and Yves Simon.[5] It is that men who are subject to civil government can be free in obeying the laws of the state, *but only (a) if, deriving from the natural moral law, these laws provide just regulations for the common good and (b) if the subjects are men who, through acquired virtue, are able to obey the law from a willing acknowledgment of its authority and not from fear of its coercive force.* These writers have the same form of freedom in mind as do Rousseau and Hegel, namely, the freedom of acquired self-perfection which consists in being able to will as one ought; but they differ in the way they specify the two conditions under which men have such freedom politically. The crux of that difference lies in the fact that, for Aquinas, Locke, Montesquieu, Maritain, and Simon, the virtuous man who wills as he ought in compliance with the civil law is not conceived as free because he thereby obeys himself alone, but rather because, in view of the justice of the law made by another, he voluntarily adopts it as a rule of his own conduct.

(v) Quite different from all the foregoing answers is another answer given by Aquinas, Locke, Montesquieu, Maritain, Simon, together with Aristotle, Kant, Hobhouse, and others. It is that men who are subject to civil government can be free when, through citizenship and the right of suffrage, they have the power to participate in shaping the political institutions and laws under which they live. Such freedom, as we have already pointed out, is circumstantial rather than acquired, and akin to self-realization rather than self-perfection; for he who has the good fortune to be an enfranchised citizen can realize his individual will politically by contributing to the formation of the public will of the self-governing community

---

[4] See *ibid.*, pp. 292–300 and 349–51.

[5] See *ibid.*, pp. 244–49, 287–88, and cf. p. 290. See also *ibid.*, pp. 341–46, where it is shown that Aquinas, Locke, Montesquieu, Maritain, and Simon give not only this answer but also the one outlined in (v) below.

in which he, together with other citizens, is an active participant. Many of the authors mentioned above use the term "political liberty" for this form of freedom. Since it is quite distinct from other freedoms which they affirm or deny, it is this freedom to which we have attached the name "political liberty" in order to distinguish it from self-realization and self-perfection when these forms of freedom are considered in relation to political institutions.[6]

Let us use PL as the symbol for political liberty in the special sense just indicated in the last of the five answers to the question; and let us use SR(PL) for the self-realization sense of political freedom as indicated in the first two answers, and SP(PL) for the self-perfection sense of political freedom as indicated in the third and fourth answers. With these symbols, we can now briefly summarize how political liberty, in quite different senses, is a subject of controversy.

First, there are issues about SR(PL). Thus, for example, the writers who were cited in connection with answers (i) and (ii) above—Hobbes, Bentham, and Spencer, on the one hand, and Laski, Knight, and Kelsen, on the other—disagree about the political circumstances under which men are free to do as they please. There are other points of disagreement about SR(PL), raised by such questions as whether the political circumstances favorable to this freedom include living under constitutional as opposed to absolute government, or living in a democratic society, or having suffrage. Such issues belong to the special controversy about circumstantial self-realization in its political aspect.

Second, there are issues about SP(PL). Here, for example, the writers who were cited in connection with answers (iii) and (iv) above— Rousseau and Hegel, on the one hand, and Aquinas, Maritain, and Simon, on the other—disagree about the character of the autonomy which the virtuous man possesses in his willing obedience to the just or rightful laws of the state. Here, too, there are other points of disagreement, which concern the bearing of different forms of government on SP(PL) and the significance for such freedom of citizenship and suffrage. Issues of this sort may appear in the special controversy about acquired self-perfection.

Third, there are issues about PL. One illustration will suffice. The writers cited in connection with answer (v) above do not all agree about the principle of universal suffrage or the right of every man to be an enfranchised citizen. While they all maintain that *only* the citizen with suffrage can have PL, they disagree about *who* is qualified to exercise such freedom. This issue and similar ones belong to the special controversy

[6] See *ibid.*, pp. 242–43, 330–39, 343–46, 356–58, 359–67.

about political liberty as a freedom quite distinct from both SR(PL) and SP(PL).

Fourth, political freedom enters into the general controversy about the kinds of freedom insofar as SR(PL) is rejected by authors such as Aristotle, Kant, Rousseau, and Hegel, who, denying validity to all self-realization conceptions of freedom, also reject such freedom in its political aspect.[7] It also enters into the general controversy insofar as SP(PL) is rejected by authors such as Laski and Hobhouse, who, denying validity to all self-perfection conceptions of freedom, also reject such freedom in its political aspect.[8]

While we can find evidence to show that SR(PL) is rejected by writers who either affirm SP(PL) or PL, and, similarly, evidence to show that SP(PL) is rejected by writers who either affirm SR(PL) or PL, we cannot find equally clear-cut evidence to show that PL is rejected by a single writer who, being acquainted with *this form of freedom as conceived by authors who affirm it*, explicitly denies its existence or challenges its genuineness as a distinct form of freedom. Nor can we find any implied denials of this sort. That precisely, and that alone, is what we meant, at the beginning of this chapter, by saying that there are no issues about political liberty (i.e., PL) in the general controversy. It is necessary to add that such issues are *possible* with regard to PL. That possibility has not been realized in any actual disagreement for which there is evidence, explicit or implicit, in the literature of freedom.

But, it may be asked, does not the affirmation of SR(PL) or of SP (PL) imply the rejection of PL as a distinct freedom in the sphere of man's political life? It certainly would if SR(PL) or SP(PL) were inconsistent with PL. However, this is not the case. Hobhouse, for example, maintains that man has two quite distinct freedoms in the political sphere, one that is SR(PL) in form, and one that is PL in form. Similarly, Yves Simon attributes SP(PL) to the virtuous man who willingly obeys just laws for the common good and, quite distinct from such freedom, he also attributes PL to the citizen who has suffrage and who, whether or not he is a virtuous man, exercises a voice in his own government. The distinct freedoms that each is affirming may belong to different men under different conditions, or both may belong to the same man in different connections. Hence, there seems to be no ground for thinking that the affirmation of either

---

[7] It should be noted here that, of the writers mentioned above, two (Aristotle and Kant) affirm PL while rejecting SR(PL) and two (Rousseau and Hegel) affirm SP(PL) while rejecting SR(PL).

[8] Again, it should be noted that of the two writers mentioned above, one (Hobhouse) affirms PL while rejecting SP(PL) and one (Laski) affirms SR(PL) while rejecting SP(PL).

SR(PL) or SP(PL) logically entails the denial of PL as a distinct free-dom.[9]

Nevertheless, we can formulate a question which PL authors answer affirmatively and to which we think both SR(PL) and SP(PL) authors would give the opposite response, provided that such authors affirm SR (PL) and SP(PL) respectively as man's only political freedom. Is a man free in relation to a particular law (a) if his suffrage is involved in the making of that law, (b) even though the law does not coincide with his own wishes because it represents the will of the majority to which he does not belong, and (c) even though he, not being a virtuous man, obeys that law only from fear of its coercive force? According to PL con-ceptions of individual freedom viewed politically, the existence of con-dition (a) suffices for an affirmative answer. On the other hand, the consideration of condition (c) would elicit a negative answer from authors who affirm SP(PL) as man's only freedom in the political sphere, and condition (b), either by itself or with (c), would similarly elicit a negative answer from authors who affirm SR(PL) as man's only freedom in this sphere.

The foregoing question not only indicates the possibility of an issue about PL in the general controversy but it also helps us to say which, among the authors who affirm SR(PL) or SP(PL), would most probably deny PL as a distinct form of freedom. However, before we turn to the documentary evidence which enables us to assess that probability in the case of particular authors, it may be clarifying to analyze the actual rela-tionship that exists between PL authors, on the one hand, and authors who exclusively affirm either SR(PL) or SP(PL), on the other. If that relation is actually neither agreement nor disagreement about the form man's freedom takes in the sphere of political life, what is it?

[9] Nor does the affirmation of PL logically entail the denial of SR(PL) or of SP(PL). Though Aristotle and Kant, who affirm PL, reject SR(PL), they do so on grounds which have nothing to do with their affirmation of PL. The same holds true for Hobhouse who affirms PL and rejects SP(PL). Furthermore, authors such as Locke and Montesquieu quite consistently affirm all three forms of freedom: SR(PL) in matters on which the civil law is silent, SP(PL) in the case of the virtuous or reason-able men living under just laws, and PL on the part of the citizen who is governed with his own consent and with representation of his individual will in the making of the laws under which he lives.

1. INDETERMINATE RELEVANCE WITH RESPECT TO POLITICAL LIBERTY

In Book I we described the logical relation which obtains between two writers who, so far as we can tell from the views they hold, are neither in agreement nor in disagreement about a given matter, and yet with regard to that matter cannot be regarded as holding views which are completely irrelevant to one another.

When being in complete topical agreement about a subject under consideration and about the question concerning that subject which is to be answered, two writers either agree or disagree in the answers they give; that agreement or disagreement constitutes the *determinate relevance* of the view held by one to the view held by the other. When, on the other hand, even minimal topical agreement is lacking, and the two authors are dealing with different and unrelated subjects, their relation is one of *complete irrelevance*. Between these two extremes, there is a middle ground which we described as a zone of *indeterminate relevance*. In the absence of complete topical agreement, two authors cannot be construed as actually agreeing or disagreeing in their doctrinal assertions; but the fact that some sort of minimal topical agreement exists between them establishes the potentiality of such agreement or disagreement. The view held by one may have some inferential connection with the view held by the other.[10]

We called attention to two ways in which writers may be in a state of indeterminate relevance to one another. The first occurs when, considering the same specific subject, each is answering a different question about it. The second occurs when each is considering a different subject, but the two subjects, while specifically distinct, have something in common, i.e., fall under the same general subject.

In the second case, their minimal topical agreement consists in their both having the same general subject in common. As a result of this, they are both moving in the same general area of discourse and, therefore, the views they hold may, by implication, bring them into a doctrinal agreement or disagreement which they themselves had not envisaged. We are concerned here only with the second case, for, as we shall presently show,

[10] See Vol. I, pp. 12 ff. This relation of indeterminate relevance can also be described as one of *non-agreement*. Thus, for example, SR(PL) and SP(PL) authors who take no cognizance of PL as a distinct freedom neither agree nor disagree with PL authors about it.

hat is the way in which the authors who have something to say about
reedom in its political aspect are in a state of indeterminate relevance
ind, consequently, in at least potential agreement or disagreement with
egard to political liberty, i.e., with regard to PL as distinct from SR(PL)
ind SP(PL).[11]

It may be helpful to consider some examples of indeterminate relevance
>f the type with which we are here concerned. Let us begin with one that
ve have already mentioned.[12] Faced with the question "Is freedom con-
istent with causal necessity?" Hobbes and Ayer would give an affirmative
inswer, Aquinas and Sartre a negative one. But, as we pointed out, their
lisagreement is seen to be merely apparent as soon as we realize that
Iobbes and Ayer are asserting that the freedom of self-realization is con-
istent with causal necessity, whereas Aquinas and Sartre, far from denying
his, are asserting that the freedom of self-determination is inconsistent
vith causal necessity. Since they are about different subjects, the two as-
ertions are not incompatible. A writer such as Aquinas, who affirms both
orms of freedom, is not contradicting himself when he says that one form
>f freedom involves exemption from causal necessity and that another form
nvolves exemption from coercion rather than from necessity.

While the apparently contrary assertions about freedom in relation to
:ausal necessity do not constitute a real disagreement, they do place the
ipparently opposed authors in a state of indeterminate relevance to one
inother. Since these authors are all concerned with freedom in general as
vell as the particular form of freedom that is the immediate subject of
heir apparently contrary assertions, their theories of freedom are certainly
iot irrelevant to one another. Their potential disagreement lies near the
urface.

We can easily make the potential disagreement actual by a slight change
n the question with which we confront them. Instead of asking, "Is
:reedom consistent with causal necessity?" let us ask, "Is there any form
>f freedom that is inconsistent with causal necessity?" Our knowledge of
:he doctrines of Hobbes and Ayer tells us that when they answer this
question negatively, they are in fact denying the existence of self-determi-
iation as a form of freedom. We also know that an affirmative answer to
:he same question by Aquinas and Sartre is, in effect, an affirmation of the
eality of natural self-determination. Thus we see that Hobbes and Ayer
oin issue in the general controversy with Aquinas and Sartre on the exist-

[11] In what follows, we shall always use the term "political liberty" to stand for the
pecial form of freedom which is a variant of circumstantial self-realization and which
:ertain authors affirm as distinct from SR(PL) or SP(PL), which we shall refer to as
'self-realization in its political aspect" or as "self-perfection in its political aspect."
[12] See Ch. 2, pp. 20–22, *supra*.

ence of natural self-determination as an actual form of human freedom.
Their statements about different subjects—SR, on the one hand, and SD,
on the other—do not constitute a disagreement, yet the views they hold on
these subjects imply a disagreement, i.e., about the existence of SD as a
form of freedom. Only a slight alteration in the question is needed to
move them from a state of indeterminate to a state of determinate relevance and to disagreement.

Now let us take an example that is nearer to the problem of political
liberty. Suppose we ask, "How is freedom related to the law of the state?"
The answer which would be given by Rousseau and Hegel, that freedom
has its foundation in the law of the state, appears to be incompatible with
the answer which would be given by Bentham and Spencer, that freedom
exists only in areas that are exempt from legal regulation by the state. As
before, the disagreement is merely apparent. Rousseau and Hegel are asserting that the freedom of *willing as one ought* has its foundation in the
law of the state, whereas Bentham and Spencer are asserting that the freedom of *doing as one pleases* exists only in areas that are exempt from legal
regulation by the state. Authors such as Locke and Montesquieu do not
contradict themselves when they make both assertions, affirming that SP
(PL) and SR(PL) are both genuine forms of freedom.

Here again our knowledge of the doctrines of Hegel and Bentham
tells us that we need not leave them in a state of indeterminate relevance
which exists between them only so long as we regard them as concerned
with different though related subjects—SP(PL) and SR(PL). We know
that, confronted by a slightly altered question, "Is there any form of
freedom which has its foundation in the law of the state?" Bentham
would say "no" and Hegel "yes," and thus be in disagreement about SP
(PL) as a genuine freedom. Similarly, confronted by the question, "Is
there any form of freedom which exists only in areas that are exempt
from legal regulation by the state?" Hegel would say "no" and Bentham
"yes." Here they take opposite sides on the issue about SR(PL) in the
general controversy about the kinds of freedom.

That Bentham and Hegel are opposed to one another in the general
controversy, both on the issue about self-realization and also on the issue
about self-perfection, has been amply evidenced in Chapters 4 and 5.
Nevertheless, they would be in a state of indeterminate relevance if all
we knew about them were the fact that, in giving apparently opposed
answers to the question, "How is freedom related to the law of the state?"
Bentham's answer is about the freedom of self-realization and Hegel's is
about the freedom of self-perfection. If, *in addition*, we could not find in
Bentham's or in Hegel's writings any trace whatsoever of acquaintance

with the form of freedom being affirmed by the other, then we should have to leave them in a state of indeterminate relevance. Since that involves potential agreement as well as potential disagreement, we could do little more than speculate about which might be more probable.[13]

We turn now to a question which bears directly on the state of indeterminate relevance that exists with regard to political liberty. That question can be formulated as follows: "Does the possession of freedom depend upon the possession of suffrage?" To this question, we should expect a number of different answers from different authors. The answers and the conceptions underlying them are:

(i) The possession of suffrage is essential to the possession of freedom, i.e., PL. HOBHOUSE

(ii) The possession of suffrage is essential to the possession of freedom, i.e., SP (PL). ROUSSEAU

(iii) The possession of suffrage is not in any way germane to the possession of freedom, i.e., SP(PL). HEGEL

(iv) The possession of suffrage is not in any way germane to the possession of freedom, i.e., SR(PL). SPENCER

(v) The possession of suffrage is not essential to the possession of freedom, but it may increase the amount of freedom an individual enjoys, i.e., SR(PL). LASKI

Since they are talking about different forms of freedom, we know that the statements of Hobhouse and Rousseau do not represent an agreement between them; and this, for a similar reason, holds true for the statements of Hegel and Spencer. Nor do the apparently incompatible statements of Hobhouse, Laski, and Spencer or Hegel represent a three-sided disagreement about freedom in relation to suffrage, since Hobhouse's state-

---

[13] The suppositions we have made above, which are contrary to fact in the case of Bentham and Hegel, are not contrary to fact in the case of other writers. Thus, for example, if we confronted Burke instead of Bentham with the question about the relation of freedom to the law of the state, his answer might be, like Bentham's, that it exists only in areas that are exempt from legal regulation. We should know, of course, that his answer referred not to freedom in general, but to the specific freedom that he attributes to man in the political sphere, i.e., SR(PL); and so we should know that his answer only appears to be opposed to Hegel's answer, the subject of which is SP(PL). So far, then, Burke is only potentially in disagreement or agreement with Hegel. We cannot tell what his actual relation to Hegel is, since, from our knowledge of Burke's theory of freedom, we cannot tell how he would answer the question "Is there any form of freedom which has its foundation in the law of the state?" Hence, we have no way of bringing Burke and Hegel out of a state of indeterminate relevance and into actual agreement or disagreement with regard to the latter's SP(PL) conception of freedom in relation to law.

ment is about PL, Hegel's is about SP(PL), Laski's and Spencer's about SR(PL).[14]

Given these writers in a state of indeterminate relevance with regard to freedom and suffrage, our next step is to alter the question we put to them, as we did in the preceding examples of indeterminate relevance. Since our interest here is in discovering whether, in the general controversy there is an issue about PL, for we already know that there are issues about SR(PL) and SP(PL), the altered question is as follows: "Is there any form of freedom for which the possession of suffrage is not only essential but also the one indispensable prerequisite?"

It might appear at first that this question would bring the authors into disagreement, for would not Hobhouse answer this question affirmatively while all the rest would answer it negatively? But the opposed answers would still represent only an apparent disagreement if the correct interpretation of what is being said is that Hobhouse, in answering affirmatively, is affirming that PL is a distinct form of freedom, to which suffrage is the one essential prerequisite, while Rousseau and Hegel, or Laski and Spencer, in answering negatively, are merely reiterating that suffrage is not essential or is not the one indispensable prerequisite of the form of freedom—either SP(PL) or SR(PL)—which they have in mind.

We did not meet with a similar difficulty in the case of the two preceding examples of indeterminate relevance. Why do we meet with it here? The reason lies in an important difference between this last case and the preceding examples, and it goes a long way toward explaining why we can find no evidence of an actual issue about PL in the general controversy.

In the first example, which presented Hobbes and Aquinas as being initially in a state of indeterminate relevance with regard to freedom and causal necessity, we could easily resolve that indeterminate relevance into actual disagreement, because our knowledge of Hobbes's doctrine enabled us to interpret a denial by him of any form of freedom that involves exemption from causal necessity as tantamount to a denial that natural self-determination has any reality as a form of freedom. We know that Hobbes was acquainted with the form of freedom which Aquinas affirms and which he holds to be inconsistent with causal necessity. Hence, we know that Hobbes, in asserting that freedom is consistent with necessity, is really asserting two things: *first*, that the SR form of freedom is consistent with causal necessity; and *second*, that the SD form of freedom cannot exist precisely because it is inconsistent with causal necessity.

In the second example, which presented Bentham and Hegel in a state

---

14 By the same token, we know that Hegel and Rousseau are in disagreement about SP(PL), and that Laski and Spencer are in disagreement about SR(PL).

of indeterminate relevance with regard to freedom and the law of the state, we were similarly able to resolve that indeterminate relevance into actual disagreement. Knowing that Bentham is acquainted with the form of freedom affirmed by Hegel, i.e., SP(PL), we can interpret his denial that there is any form of freedom which has its foundation in the law of the state as more than a reiteration that SR(PL), as he conceives it, exists only in areas exempt from legal regulation by the state. His intention is to deny that SP(PL) is an acceptable kind of freedom. So, too, knowing that Hegel is acquainted with the form of freedom affirmed by Bentham, i.e., SR(PL), we can interpret his denial that there is any form of freedom which exists only in areas exempt from legal regulation by the state to be a rejection of SR(PL).

But when we come to the third case, few if any of the authors who might say "no" to the question (whether there is any form of freedom to which suffrage is the one indispensable prerequisite) manifest any acquaintance with the form of freedom, i.e., PL, which is being affirmed by the authors who answer that question affirmatively. In the elaboration of their own positive or negative views about freedom in the political sphere, they do not have in mind the conceptions of political liberty proposed and developed by Aristotle, Marsilius, Aquinas, Locke, Montesquieu, Kant, Hamilton, Hobhouse, Sidgwick, Maritain, Jaspers, Simon, and others.

As we have seen in Chapter 4, numerous SP authors are acquainted with SR conceptions of freedom. They can be interpreted as rejecting SR(PL) when they maintain that SP(PL) provides the only right answer to the question about freedom in relation to the law of the state. And in Chapter 5 we found numerous SR authors who are acquainted with SP conceptions of freedom and who can be interpreted as rejecting SP(PL) when they maintain that SR(PL) provides the only right answer to the same question.

Among the first group are authors such as Kant who, in addition to affirming PL as a form of freedom distinct from SP, also reject SR(PL) as a genuine form of freedom; and among the second group are authors such as Hobhouse who, in addition to affirming PL as a form of freedom distinct from SR, also reject SP(PL) as a genuine form of freedom. But while this places some authors who affirm PL in opposition to either SR(PL) or SP(PL), it does not create an issue about PL on which they are opposed by SR or SP authors. We are unable to interpret authors of the latter sort as opposing PL because we cannot detect in their writings clear evidence that they are acquainted with political liberty as it is conceived by those who regard it as a form of freedom quite distinct from self-realization and self-perfection in their political aspects.

The reason for this may be that, among the exponents of political liberty, only very recent writers, such as Hobhouse and Sidgwick, explicitly differentiate PL and SR(PL) as distinct forms of freedom in the political sphere. No writers make a corresponding effort to differentiate PL and SP (PL) as distinct forms of freedom in the political sphere.[15] This may explain why writers whose treatment of freedom in its political aspect stems from their SR or their SP conceptions of freedom do not take cognizance of political liberty as a form of freedom distinct from the form which they espouse in the political sphere.

But whatever the reason, the situation remains the same. With regard to political liberty, writers who appear to be opposed are really in a state of indeterminate relevance.

How, then, shall we proceed with regard to potential, if not actual, disagreement about the genuiness of political liberty as a distinct form of freedom? The importance of the subject calls for an effort to examine those authors whose writings lead us to suspect that, were they to become acquainted with the conception of political liberty, they would probably take a negative, or perhaps an affirmative, view of it and so pass from the state of indeterminate relevance into one of actual disagreement or agreement with the adherents of PL. By examining the evidence that raises such probabilities and, in the light of it, assessing the probabilities, we shall be doing as much as can be done on the basis of the recorded discussion. Beyond that, we can only speculate about possibilities.

It will be useful to begin in the next section with a brief summary of the conception of political liberty as it is found in the authors whom we treated in Chapter 18 of Book II,[16] attaching thereto additional evidence not there given or drawn from writers not there treated. Then, in Section 3, we shall consider the authors who would *probably* reject this conception as invalid, and, in Section 4, authors about whom there is unresolved doubt as to whether they would accept or reject it. Finally, in Section 5, we shall undertake to project the possibility of arguments pro and con in the debate of the issues about political liberty that are at least potentially present in the literature.

---

[15] Kant refers to the political liberty of the enfranchised citizen as "external freedom" and contrasts it with what he calls the "internal freedom" of the virtuous man in the sphere of the moral life. But he does not treat the virtuous man's freedom of self-perfection in its political aspect, and so he does not differentiate PL from SP(PL).

[16] See Vol. I, pp. 329–69.

2. THE CONCEPTION OF POLITICAL LIBERTY
AS A DISTINCT FREEDOM

In the preceding pages, we have mentioned two things which enter into the identification of political liberty as a distinct form of freedom, affirmed by certain writers and, to a large extent, ignored or unacknowledged by others. According to those who affirm this freedom, the possession of political liberty depends upon two circumstances: having the good fortune to live in a society that is constitutionally rather than despotically governed, and, in such a society, having the additional good fortune to be admitted to citizenship with all the rights and privileges belonging thereto, especially suffrage. These two points by themselves show that political liberty is inseparable from the status of citizenship and also that such freedom is exercised not in any and every type of human activity, but only in those specifically political activities through which the individual *qua* citizen participates in the business of government.

To be a citizen in the sense required by the foregoing statements involves more than being an inhabitant or resident of the state, or even being granted certain rights and protection by its laws, or enjoying certain of the benefits which a benevolent government provides for the general welfare of its people. Before they were enfranchised, women were not citizens in the sense intended; and this holds true for all those who, under existing constitutions, are disbarred from suffrage for whatever reason, e.g., infancy, insanity, criminal turpitude, indigence, race, nativity, etc. Clearly, all such persons may enjoy one or another form of personal freedom. They may be free to do as they please in matters not prescribed by law, or even in such matters, should the law require them to do what they would do anyway. They may be free in obeying laws which run contrary to certain of their inclinations because, being virtuous or wise, they acknowledge the authority of the law and bring their own will into harmony with it. But, not being enfranchised citizens, they do not enjoy political liberty in the precise sense of the conception we are here considering.

While being enfranchised separates the citizens with political liberty from those who are often called "citizens" but are merely inhabitants or subjects of the state, political liberty involves more than the right to vote in elections or the exercise of that right. No one has suffrage who does not have that right, but suffrage involves other forms of participation in government and political affairs. It includes all the ways in which a citizen is empowered or given the opportunity to register his individual will effectively, though often indirectly, in the shaping of the political institutions, the public policies, and the positive laws of his society. It usually includes such things as the right to be a candidate for public office, the right of juridical appeal for the redress of grievances, the right to form and belong to political associations or parties, the right to assemble for political purposes, etc.

Through the exercise of suffrage in this broad sense, each individual citizen shares in the sovereignty, and the will of each citizen contributes to the formation of the public will. The public will represents his individual will in the sense that he has taken part in the process of forming it, not in the sense that it is identical in substance or direction with his own will. On the contrary, when he is in the minority, the public will represents his individual will only in the sense that he has consented to the procedures established by the constitution, including the principle of decision by a majority.

Accordingly, the political liberty of the citizen is invaded or set at nought only by those acts of government which are unconstitutional and, being determined and imposed without due process of law, are despotic in procedure, no matter how benevolent in substance or aim. Laws, policies, or administrative acts that issue from despotic procedures do not express a public will which reflects the suffrage of the citizens. In regard to anything which is done by methods or means to which they have not consented and in the doing of which they, therefore, could not exercise their suffrages, the citizens are deprived of their political liberty.

It follows, of course, that under a wholly despotic regime no man has any political liberty whatsoever, for none is governed as a citizen who, by his consent to the constitution and by his participation through suffrage in the procedures it sets up, actively takes part in the government of his society. Despotic government proceeds wholly from the will of another.

In contrast, there is that type of constitutional government, especially in republics, which stems ultimately from the suffrages of the citizens and, consequently, from the pooling of their wills. From the point of view of any particular citizen, the public will thus formed may be contrary to his individual will on this or that matter, but it is never wholly alien to his will insofar as he has helped to form it and has consented to the process by which it has been formed.[17]

---

[17] As we pointed out in Book II, Ch. 18, the fact that other citizens try to shape the law in the light of their particular interests does not prevent an individual from bringing his own particular interests to bear on the formation of the law and other political institutions. Each citizen has the opportunity and power to say what is for the common good from the point of view of his own particular interests. His suffrage enables him to do that, and therein lies the special freedom he has as a citizen. See Vol. I, pp. 365 ff.

Suffrage enables each man to register his preference for things of particular interest to him as an individual, and yet also to regard them as means to the common good in which he as an individual shares. To the extent that he has the opportunity of getting his individual good considered, along with the particular goods of interest to others, he is able to realize his individuality and his personal aspirations as a member of the body politic. Since such self-realization is not accomplished by any form of action, but only by action that is strictly political in character, the political liberty which is peculiar to the citizen is a quite special variant of the freedom of self-realization.

The foregoing summarizes the main points that are common to the conceptions of political liberty which we found in the writings of Aristotle, Aquinas, Locke, Montesquieu, Kant, Hobhouse, Maritain, and Yves Simon. Not all these writers are equally explicit on all points. Nor are they in agreement on subordinate points, such as whether all men, as a matter of natural right, are entitled to be enfranchised citizens. But with variations in emphasis and in detail, these authors all affirm a form of freedom that is inherent in and inseparable from citizenship with suffrage.[18]

Before we turn to a number of other writers who give evidence of affirming the form of freedom thus identified, let us quickly run over the statement which one of the aforementioned authors makes of the main points in the summary just given. In Hobhouse we find not only a typical expression of the doctrine but also one of the clearest explications of political liberty as a distinct form of freedom.

"Political freedom," Hobhouse writes, "implies active citizenship. The claim of the free individual is not the impossible one that the common decision should coincide with his own, but that his decision should be heard and taken into account." Hobhouse is emphatic on the point that the citizen is just as free, through the exercise of his suffrage, when he is in the adversely affected minority as when he is in the majority. All that the citizen claims, he declares, is to have a voice in the common councils.

---

[18] This statement is, perhaps, most questionable in the case of Aquinas and Locke who, though they were constitutionalists, were not republicans and were not as clear as other writers in this group on the necessity and nature of suffrage. See fn. 1 on p. 136, *supra*. It should also be observed that for those in this group who also affirm man's freedom of self-perfection, political liberty is distinct from that freedom in its political aspect: the latter belongs only to virtuous men, whether or not they are citizens; the former belongs only to citizens, whether or not they are virtuous. And for those among them who also affirm man's freedom of self-realization, political liberty is distinct from that freedom in its political aspect: the latter belongs to men insofar as they are exempt from coercion or duress, whether or not they are citizens; the former belongs to citizens insofar as they are exempt from despotic government by the wholly alien will of another, whether or not they are subject to certain forms of coercion or duress by a government and laws of their own making.

Insofar as he makes his claim effective he contributes to the common decision even though in a particular case it goes dead against him. He is free, *not because the social will is his own, but because he has as much scope for expression as any one man can have if all are to have it and yet live and act together.* More than this is the beginning of tyranny, less is the beginning of slavery.[19]

In another place, Hobhouse reiterates this basic point in his understanding of "political freedom in the narrower sense," the sense in which it is quite distinct from being able to do as one pleases in matters not regulated by law or in matters where what the law prescribes happens to coincide with the individual's own will, i.e., the freedom of self-realization in its political aspect. In this special sense of political liberty, the freedom enjoyed by the citizen consists, according to Hobhouse, in

> the right of contributing by voice and vote to the explicit decisions, laws, and administrative acts, which bind the community. To say that in virtue of this contribution the collective decisions express the will of each citizen even if he has done his best to prevent it is a highly misleading piece of rhetoric which may be turned to harsh and cruel purposes. Political freedom, precisely because it is the common freedom of many, gives no such absolute liberty and therefore no such responsibility to any one man. *Political freedom is just the right of every man bound by decisions to contribute whatever it is in him to contribute to the making and remaking of those decisions.* It by no means guarantees that he will be bound only by his own will. *It guarantees that his will is to count among the rest in making the decisions,* and that the community as a whole will be bound by the main current of will flowing within it, the resultant of all the wills and brains of everyone concerned in proportion to the energy and intelligence which he brings to bear.[20]

In the ordinary sense in which self-realization is "the freedom of man in society," individuals are free to follow their own bent "without mutual encroachment"; but the political liberty which is a distinct aspect of man's freedom in society does not "mean that every man is to have his own way."[21]

Of the writers now to be added to those whose conceptions of political liberty we examined in Book II, only Sidgwick, like Hobhouse, explicitly distinguishes between political liberty and self-realization in the ordinary sense. The others, however, indicate their affirmation of political liberty as a form of freedom that belongs only to citizens who have a voice in the government of their society.

[19] *Metaphysical Theory of the State,* p. 61. (Italics added.)
[20] *Elements of Social Justice,* pp. 88–89. (Italics added.) Cf. *Liberalism,* pp. 227–35.
[21] *Elements of Social Justice,* p. 186.

Marsilius of Padua declares that men who are subject to laws imposed upon them by others suffer "despotism, that is, slavish dominion." Those who "by their own authority [make] the law over the whole body of citizens . . . [are] despots over the others." In contrast, when the law "is made through the hearing and command of the entire multitude of the citizens," the citizens enjoy free dominion, for they live under laws 'which each one seems to have imposed upon himself."[22]

According to Alexander Hamilton, "the only distinction between freedom and slavery consists in this: in the former state, a man is governed by the laws to which he has given his consent, either in person or by his representative; in the latter, he is governed by the will of another."[23] Hamilton calls such freedom "civil" rather than "political" liberty, but it is for him a freedom which "cannot possibly have any existence where the society, for whom laws are made, have no share in making them."[24] To be a free agent, in the strictly political sense of "free agency," a man must be a citizen with suffrage.

No Englishman, who can be deemed *a free agent* in a *political* view, can be bound by laws, to which he has not consented, either in person, or by *his* representative. . . . Every *free agent*, every free man, possessing a freehold of forty shillings per annum, is, by the British constitution, entitled to a vote in the election of those who are invested with the disposal of his life, his liberty, and property.[25]

A constitutional state, according to Jaspers, "is one in which laws come into being and are altered exclusively along a legal path."[26] It is always one "in which every citizen shares in knowledge and participates in action."[27] Only in such a state does political liberty exist and in such a state the citizens alone enjoy such freedom. It becomes the possession of all men only when all are admitted to citizenship "through *democracy*, that is, where it is possible for everyone to play a part in forming the

---

[22] *The Defensor Pacis*, Vol. II, p. 47. Alan Gewirth, the translator, in commenting on this passage, says that for Marsilius "political freedom consists in self-government, in the sense that the laws under which men live derive from their own wills or consent" (*ibid.*, Vol. I, p. 220).
[23] *The Mind of Alexander Hamilton*, p. 56.
[24] *Ibid.*, p. 89.
[25] *Ibid.*, p. 90. "It is therefore evident, to a demonstration," Hamilton continues, "that unless a *free agent* in America be permitted to enjoy the same privilege, we are entirely stripped of the benefits of the constitution, and precipitated into an abyss of slavery. For, we are deprived of that immunity which is the grand pillar and support of freedom. And this cannot be done without a direct violation of the constitution, which decrees to every *free agent*, a share in the legislature" (*ibid.*, pp. 90–91).
[26] *The Origin and Goal of History*, p. 158.
[27] *Ibid.*, p. 153.

collective will" and where "everyone enjoys the same right to make hi
influence felt through his vote at elections."[28]

While Jaspers introduces his discussion of political liberty by suggestin;
that it is something quite different from "social freedom, personal free
dom, economic freedom,"[29] he does not, like Hobhouse, specifically cal
attention to the way it differs from the other freedom of man in society
Sidgwick, however, as we have already mentioned, attempts to draw a lin
between the liberty that is the special possession of the enfranchisec
citizens in a constitutional state and the freedom which men enjoy i
such a state, or for that matter in any society, when they are not preventec
by physical or moral coercion from doing as they wish. His name for th
latter is "civil freedom"; and instead of "political" he speaks of "constitu
tional liberty" when he wishes to refer to the freedom "attributed to th
citizens of a state, not because the governmental coercion applied to then
is restricted to the prevention of private coercion, but because it is exercisec
with the consent of a majority of the citizens in question."[30]

Sidgwick observes that, while political, or what he calls constitutional
liberty "has had a very prominent place in political discussion," the term i
subject to misunderstanding. "It may be fairly affirmed that a *body* o
persons is 'free'—*in the ordinary sense*—when the only rules restrainin;
them are in accordance with the corporate will of the body; but it is *only ir
a very peculiar sense*—liable to collide markedly with the ordinary meanin;
of the term—that 'freedom' can be therefore affirmed of every member o
the body."[31] For, as he points out, even "under a government of whicl
the supreme control is vested in the mass of the citizens," the individual'
"inclinations may be restrained to any extent, and in the most annoyin;
way," especially if he has "the misfortune to belong to the minority o
this body," whereas "under a despotic government, [he] may be subjec
to no further coercion than is necessary to prevent worse coercion b
private persons."[32] But such variations in the degree of civil liberty enjoyec

---

[28] *Ibid.*, p. 161. Cf. *ibid.*, pp. 162–70. See also Barbara Wootton's statement that
"the essential political freedom [is] the right at any time to remove by constitutiona
process and not by force the persons holding supreme political power, and to put other
in their place" (*Freedom Under Planning*, p. 153). She also gives the following
enumeration of the elements of political freedom: "the right freely to express criticisn
of the Government and its works; the right to form opposition political parties; the
right to replace one Government and legislature by another, without resort to force'
(*ibid.*, p. 130). The things mentioned are but diverse ways in which the citizens are
able to participate actively in shaping the political institutions, the policies, and the
laws of their own society.
[29] See *The Origin and Goal of History*, p. 153.
[30] *The Elements of Politics*, pp. 46–47.
[31] *Ibid.*, p. 46. (Italics added.)
[32] *Ibid.*

by the individual under constitutional and under despotic government do not alter the fact that he possesses constitutional, i.e., political, liberty only as a citizen of a constitutional state.

In another place, Sidgwick comments on the difficulty with such phrases as "free government" and "free institutions," which results from the tendency to confuse the two meanings of freedom that he has been at pains to distinguish. By these phrases "a writer . . . sometimes means to imply that the government leaves the individual alone to look after his own affairs: sometimes that the private members of the community collectively exercise an effective control over the government: sometimes he seems to imply both together, apparently assuming a necessary connection between the two facts, which we may conveniently distinguish as 'civil' and 'constitutional' freedom, respectively." But, in Sidgwick's own view,

> there is no certainty that a representative legislature, chosen by universal suffrage, will not interfere with the free action of individuals more than an absolute monarch would: the essential difference is merely, that under absolute monarchy a majority of sane adults may be forced to submit to laws that they permanently dislike, whereas if a popularly elected assembly is supreme in legislation, this coercion can only be applied to a minority. To this extent constitutional freedom affords a security for civil freedom.[33]

But even when, in the case of members of the minority, their exercise of suffrage does not secure their freedom from coercion by laws which they dislike, they nevertheless remain, as citizens, politically free men.

In the light of the foregoing evidence, together with the evidence presented in Chapter 18 of Book II, we can be reasonably sure that a certain group of authors would understand the meaning of the question, "Is political liberty a distinct form of freedom?" or the equivalent question, "Is there a form of freedom for which the possession of citizenship with suffrage is not only essential but also the one indispensable prerequisite?" Were that question used, in either phrasing, to formulate an issue about political liberty in the general controversy about the kinds of freedom, we can be equally sure of an affirmative answer to it from the following authors:

Aristotle, (Aquinas), Marsilius, (Locke), Montesquieu, Kant, Hamilton, Hobhouse, Sidgwick, Maritain, Jaspers, Simon, Wootton[34]

But that question cannot be used to define an actual issue unless there are other writers who are in sufficient topical agreement with the aforemen-

[33] *Ibid.*, pp. 375–76.
[34] The parentheses around the names of Aquinas and Locke reflect the uncertainty mentioned in fn. 18 on p. 151, *supra*.

tioned authors to be able to disagree with them, i.e., writers who, in answering the question negatively, would have in mind the form of freedom which the aforementioned authors affirm. As already pointed out, we have found no writers who clearly and fully satisfy these requirements. But in the next section we shall examine evidence on the basis of which we can interpret certain writers as *probably inclined toward the negative side of this possible issue.*

3. PROBABLE OPPONENTS OF POLITICAL LIBERTY[35]

A number of authors, in the course of discussing freedom in the political sphere, deny that republican institutions and the enfranchisement of citizens comprise conditions peculiarly favorable to freedom in its political aspect. Since the things denied are regarded by the exponents of political liberty as indispensable prerequisites for the possession of such freedom, it may be thought that their denial is tantamount to the rejection of PL as a form of freedom. But we cannot be certain that this is the case, since the denial can be interpreted in another way. These authors may simply be maintaining that the aforementioned political conditions are not essential nor even favorable to the existence of circumstantial self-realization or acquired self-perfection in their political aspects, i.e., SR(PL) or SP(PL).

In the case of all the authors we are now about to consider, we are left with some degree of uncertainty about which interpretation is correct; and in proportion as we are more or less uncertain on this point, we can assess the probability that, were they to take explicit cognizance of political liberty, as that is conceived by other writers, they would reject it.

Since SR or SP authors might, of course, (i) deny that republican government and suffrage are required for SR(PL) or SP(PL), whether or not in addition they (ii) deny that PL is a distinct form of freedom, the following is, perhaps, a more precise statement of the case. The probability that a given author is an opponent of political liberty corresponds to our uncertainty whether the correct interpretation of his views should

[35] In the pages to follow we shall frequently use the phrase "opponents of political liberty." It must always be understood as short for "opponents of the conception of political liberty as a distinct form of freedom." It would be burdensome to repeat this longer phrasing over and over again; but it would also be unfortunate for the reader to interpret the shorter phrase as meaning that the authors referred to oppose political freedom, or the freedom of men in relation to law, government, or the state, in every sense of the term. As we have observed, they may affirm SR(PL) or SP(PL) while denying PL. See p. 139, and fn. 11 on p. 143, *supra.*

attribute *only* the first of the above denials to him. To the degree that we can overcome our doubts about the soundness of attributing the second denial to him as well as the first, his being an opponent of political liberty will be more probable in our judgment.

In the pages of this section, we shall treat only those authors whose opposition to political liberty appears, in our judgment, to be highly probable. We shall proceed as follows. We shall first treat (a) authors who discuss the bearing of political institutions on freedom from the point of view of acquired self-perfection, which is their own conception of freedom; then (b) authors who approach these matters from the point of view of circumstantial self-realization; and finally (c) authors whose point of departure is their own conception of collective freedom.

(a) *From the point of view of acquired self-perfection.* Of all the writers we shall consider, from this or any other point of view, Hegel is clearly one of the most probable opponents of political liberty. In his view, a freedom that springs from the individual will alone or which fulfills only individual desires is merely a subjective freedom; and that, as contrasted with the objective freedom which is founded on the universal and rational will, is for him an imperfect or counterfeit freedom. Hence, the notion that the constitution or government should derive its authority from the consent of the governed and the notion that the laws or decisions of government should be determined, even indirectly, by the suffrages of all the citizens appear to him to offer the individual nothing but the subjective aspect of freedom.

Hegel refers to this as a misconception of political liberty. It, therefore, looks as if he takes cognizance of the PL conception that involves suffrage and the consent of the governed. But Hegel supposes that unanimity is required by the conception which he is criticizing. "If . . . Freedom is asserted to consist," he writes, "in the individuals of a State all agreeing in its arrangements, it is evident that only the subjective aspect is regarded." And when the subjective will of the individual members of the state is made the principle of freedom, "the natural inference from this principle is that no law can be valid without the approval of all"; for otherwise the members of the minority are deprived of freedom.[36]

This shows that Hegel has the SR(PL) rather than the PL conception in mind; for, according to certain self-realization authors, men are not free in relation to the laws of the state unless what the laws prescribe happens to coincide with what they individually wish, whereas the exponents of political liberty, i.e., PL as quite distinct from SR(PL), maintain that the freedom which resides in the exercise of suffrage is enjoyed by citizens

[36] *Philosophy of History, Introduction,* p. 43.

who belong to an adversely affected minority as much as it is by members of the majority group.

We must, therefore, interpret Hegel's attack on the theory that political participation promotes the freedom of the individual in relation to government as an attack on the doctrine that through such participation the individual may be able to maximize his freedom of self-realization. In rejecting SR(PL) as a merely subjective and illusory freedom, he turns at once to what he thinks is the only real alternative, i.e., SP(PL), the objective freedom which rests on the universal and rational will that is embodied in the State.[37] He does not recognize PL as a form of freedom distinct from both SR(PL) and SP(PL). Nevertheless, insofar as political liberty is a variant of self-realization rather than of self-perfection, Hegel's attack on the freedom of self-realization, as that is conceived in relation to law and government, warrants us in thinking that he probably would also reject political liberty, and for the same reasons, namely, that it caters exclusively to the individual or subjective will. That probability is increased by the fact that the very things which are held to be essential to political liberty are the targets of his attack.

"The term political liberty," Hegel writes,

> is often used to mean formal participation in the public affairs of state by the will and action even of those individuals who otherwise find their chief function in the particular aims and business of civil society.[38]

But, in his view, this usually involves a misunderstanding of the reason for such participation, and consequently it involves a false conception of man's freedom in relation to the state.

> The aggregate of private persons is often spoken of as the *nation*: but as such an aggregate it is *vulgus*, not *populus*: and in this direction, it is the one sole aim of the state that a nation should *not* come to existence, to power and action, *as such an aggregate*. Such a condition of a nation is a condition of lawlessness, demoralisation, brutishness: in it the nation would only be a shapeless, wild, blind force, like that of the stormy elemental sea, which however is not self-destructive, as the nation—a spiritual element—would be. *Yet such a condition may be often heard described as that of true freedom.*[39]

And, in the following passage, Hegel illustrates concretely what he has in mind.

---

[37] See *ibid.*, p. 39 ff.

[38] *Philosophy of Mind*, p. 266. Cf. *ibid.*, p. 265, where he refers to "the participation of all in political affairs and action" as "an *assumed* definition of liberty." (Italics added.)

[39] *Ibid.*, p. 271. The italicization of the last sentence in the above passage has been added to call attention to the implied dismissal of a misconception of freedom.

Take the case of *England* which, because private persons have a predominant share in public affairs, has been regarded as having the freest of all constitutions. Experience shows that that country—as compared with the other civilized states of Europe—is the most backward in civil and criminal legislation, in the law and liberty of property, in arrangements for art and science, and that objective freedom or rational right is rather *sacrificed* to formal right and particular private interest. . . . The desirability of private persons taking part in public affairs is partly to be put in their concrete, and therefore more urgent, sense of general wants. But the true motive is the right of the collective spirit to appear as an *externally universal* will, acting with orderly and express efficacy for the public concerns.

Furthermore, Hegel points out,

it is not in the inorganic form of mere individuals as such (after the democratic fashion of elections), but as organic factors, as estates, that [the people] enter upon that participation [i.e., participation in the sovereignty]. In the state a power or agency must never appear and act as a formless, inorganic shape, i.e., basing itself on the principle of multeity and mere numbers.[40]

The high probability that Hegel would reject the conception of political liberty to be found in such writers as Locke, Montesquieu, Hobhouse, and Sidgwick can be inferred from the fact that whereas they look upon the English constitution as the source of the freedom which the enfranchised citizens of that state enjoy, he regards it as the very antithesis of true constitutional government and of the only true (i.e., objective) freedom which the members of a state can enjoy. In Hegel's view, the truly constitutional state is a constitutional monarchy of the Prussian, not the English, type. A purely republican constitution in which the ultimate authority rested with the citizens would be, *a fortiori*, even more remote from his ideal of the one right form of government that can assure freedom to men as organic members of the state.

It has "become usual," Hegel declares, "to give the title constitution only to the side of the state which concerns [the formal, not organic] participation of . . . individuals in general affairs, and to regard a state, in which this is not formally done, as a state without a constitution."[41] As against this false view, he asserts that

if the principle of regard for the individual will is recognized as the only basis of political liberty, viz., that nothing should be done by or for the State to which all the members of the body politic have not given their sanction, we have, properly speaking, no *Constitution*.[42]

[40] *Ibid.*, pp. 271–72.
[41] *Ibid.*, p. 266.
[42] *Philosophy of History*, Introduction, p. 43.

According to this false notion of political liberty, he goes on to explain,

> the only arrangement that would be necessary, would be, first, a center having no *will* of its own . . . and, secondly, a contrivance for calling the members of the State together, for taking the votes, and for performing the arithmetical operations of reckoning and comparing the number of votes for the different propositions, and thereby deciding upon them.[43]

Such an arrangement provides no constitution at all and tends to replace government with anarchy, and true freedom with license. A constitution exists only where "the necessity that the laws be reasonable, and their actualization secured, lies in the collective spirit of the nation. . . . The constitution presupposes that consciousness of the collective spirit, and conversely that spirit presupposes the constitution." Hence, there can be as little sense to the question, "To whom . . . belongs the power to make a constitution?" as to the question, "Who has to make the spirit of a nation?"

> A constitution only develops from the national spirit identically with that spirit's own development, and runs through at the same time with it the grades of formation and the alterations required by its concept. It is the indwelling spirit and the history of the nation . . . by which constitutions have been and are made.[44]

To suppose that constitutions are made by the consent of the people as a multitude of voting constituents, or that they can be altered by the will of a majority expressing itself in an election, is to substitute the fiction of popular sovereignty for the true notion of sovereignty. It is not in the people, but in the monarch, that the sovereign power resides. When the government is "regarded as [an] organic totality," the monarch's will represents "the all-sustaining, all-decreeing will of the state, its highest peak and all-pervasive unity." And, Hegel continues,

> in the perfect form of the state, in which each and every element . . . has reached free existence, this subjectivity is not a so-called "moral person," or a decree issuing from a majority . . . but an actual individual,—the will of a decreeing individual,—*monarchy*. The monarchical constitution is therefore the constitution of developed reason: all other constitutions belong to lower grades of the development and realisation of reason.[45]

In no real constitution, even one less perfect in form, does the suffrage of the citizens, whether they are the few or the many, decisively determine the laws or acts of government.

43 *Ibid.*
44 *Philosophy of Mind*, pp. 266–67.
45 *Ibid.*, p. 269.

All those forms of collective decreeing and willing—a common will which shall be the sum and the resultant (on aristocratical or democratical principles) of the atomistic or single wills, have on them the mark of the unreality of an abstraction.[46]

This comes close to a denial of political liberty, for if individual participation in government has "the unreality of an abstraction," then the freedom which is thought to reside in such participation must also be unreal. Hegel's attack on "atomistic suffrage," especially in its democratic extension to all, as contrasted with the corporate representation of the estates that compose society, tends to confirm this impression.[47]

The probability of Hegel's being an opponent of PL can be weighed by considering how he would answer the following question: "Is the individual's will free in relation to laws in obedience to which the individual does not obey himself alone?" Citizens, according to the exponents of political liberty, are free if they have a voice in making the laws, even though, in obeying them, they may be submitting to the will of the majority, not their own. But, according to Hegel, "only that will which obeys law, is free"; for in obeying law—the objective, universal, and rational will of the State—"it obeys itself."[48] Hegel is thinking only of SR(PL). If he had PL in mind, and not SR(PL) alone, he could doubtless be construed as an opponent of PL also.

What is true of Hegel holds true, for somewhat different reasons, of other writers whose political theories place them in opposition to the very notions of constitutional government based on the consent of the governed and on the right of citizens to participate actively in the political life of a self-governing community.

Bodin, for example, upholds the view that government is by its very nature absolute: its power or sovereignty must always be concentrated in the hands of a single person. But this monarch may govern in a manner which Bodin calls "despotic, royal, or tyrannical." If a king governs despotically or tyrannically, those who are subject to his rule are enslaved, rather than politically free men, for their good is not the object of his rule. In contrast, the true king, i.e., the royal monarch, "is one who observes the laws

---

[46] *Ibid.*
[47] "To hold that every single person should share in deliberating and deciding on political matters of general concern on the ground that all individuals are members of the state, that its concerns are their concerns, and that it is their right that what is done should be done with their knowledge and volition, is tantamount," Hegel declares, "to a proposal to put the democratic element without any rational form into the organism of the state, although it is only in virtue of the possession of such a form that the state is an organism at all" (*Philosophy of Right*, Par. 308, p. 200). Cf. *ibid.*, Par. 309–11, pp. 201–3.
[48] *The Philosophy of History*, Introduction, p. 39.

of nature as punctiliously as he wishes his subjects to observe his own laws, thereby securing to them their liberty, and the enjoyment of their own property."[49]

This liberty, according to Bodin, belongs only to those subjects of the king who are citizens, for, unlike slaves, they alone are "free subjects." Their freedom consists entirely in the fact that, under a royal monarch, they are obliged to obey only just laws made for their own good. Slaves, on the other hand, have neither freedom nor property; for they are the property of their masters and are used as instruments for their master's good. Hence, it is clear, Bodin declares,

> why a citizen is to be defined as a free subject who is dependent on the sovereignty of another. I use the term *free subject*, because although a slave is as much, or more subject to the commonwealth as is his lord, it has always been a matter of common agreement that the slave is not a citizen, and in law has no personality. . . . We can say then that every citizen is a subject since his liberty is limited by the sovereign power to which he owes obedience. We cannot say that every subject is a citizen. This is clear from the case of slaves. The same applies to aliens. Being subject to the authority of another, they have no part in the rights and privileges of the community.[50]

In contradistinction to slaves and aliens, Bodin regards the citizen as free even though the sovereignty of the prince is more absolute than that of the slave owner.[51]

> It is not the rights and privileges which he enjoys which makes a man a citizen, but the mutual obligation between subject and sovereign, by which, in return for the faith and obedience rendered to him, the sovereign must do justice and give counsel, assistance, encouragement, and protection to the subject.[52]

As citizenship consists in "the submission and obedience of a free subject to his prince, and the tuition, protection, and jurisdiction exercised by the prince over his subject,"[53] so the freedom of the free subject, whom

---

[49] *Six Books of the Commonwealth*, Book II, Ch. 3, p. 59. "In defining royal monarchy," Bodin continues, "I have said that the subjects should obey the king, to make it clear that sovereign majesty is vested in him, and I have said that the king should obey the laws of nature, to show that he should govern in accordance with the principles of natural justice, which are as obvious, as clear and illuminating as the light of the sun" (*ibid.*).

[50] *Ibid.*, Book I, Ch. 6, p. 19.

[51] "Princes," he writes, "are not subject to any jurisdiction which delimits their claims over their subjects, as are lords and masters in respect of their vassals and slaves" (*ibid.*, p. 21).

[52] *Ibid.*, pp. 20–21.

[53] *Ibid.*, p. 21.

Bodin calls a citizen, derives entirely from the justice of the government to which he is subject, and in no part from his participation in that government.

Bodin's definition of the citizen is, on the face of it, diametrically opposed to the conception of citizenship that is involved in political liberty, for the latter is completely incompatible with subjection to absolute government. So, too, Bodin's holding that the freedom of the citizen depends solely on the justice and benevolence with which his sovereign exercises absolute jurisdiction over him makes him appear to be clearly opposed to a conception of political liberty that places the citizen's freedom entirely in his own exercise of a share in the sovereignty.

All that is lacking for certitude about this interpretation of Bodin is the absence of explicit recognition on his part of the theory to which we are construing him as an opponent. Yet even this seems to be supplied by the following passage.

> It is a very grave error to suppose that no one is a citizen unless he is eligible for public office, and has a voice in the popular estates, either in a judicial or deliberative capacity.[54]

This, says Bodin, "is Aristotle's view,"[55] as indeed it is. In addition, it further involves the view that the political liberty of those who are citizens *in this sense* consists in their belonging to the ruling class, who rule and are ruled in turn. But Bodin does not refer to the freedom that Aristotle attributes to citizens as he understands citizenship, which is obviously quite different from the freedom of Bodin's citizen. Hence, we are left with some residual doubt about where Bodin would stand if he had come to terms with Aristotle's conception.

It is Bodin's theory, of course, "that the origin and foundation of commonwealths was in force and violence," and that, in consequence, sovereignty must be absolute and a "free subject" must be one "who is dependent on the sovereignty of another."[56] On the basis of this theory, Bodin would probably have denied the existence of political liberty as

---

[54] *Ibid.*, p. 20.

[55] *Ibid.* Bodin goes on to say that Aristotle "corrects himself when he observes that it only applies to popular states." This, according to Bodin, is a damaging admission, for Aristotle "himself said in another place that a definition is valueless unless it is of universal application" (*ibid.*). Yet, as we have seen, it is only in constitutional states, whether these are popular (i.e., democratic), oligarchical, or aristocratic, that Aristotle thinks citizenship exists. Under absolute government, whether that is royal or despotic, no man is a citizen. Citizenship comes into existence with the transition from royal or despotic to constitutional or political rule. See *Politics*, Book I, Ch. 12, and Book III, Ch. 1–5.

[56] *Op. cit.*, p. 19.

Aristotle conceived it. It is on an existential, not a conceptual, issue about political liberty that Bodin can be regarded as likely to be on the negative side. Unlike Hegel, Bodin does not give us reason to suppose that he would reject political liberty as a matter of principle or by reference to the very meaning of freedom. But there is relatively clear evidence that he does reject, as non-existent in fact, the conditions prerequisite to the existence of political liberty.[57]

Boucher shares with Bodin the view that all government must be absolute, but he does not think that absolute sovereignty must necessarily be vested in one man. "All government," he writes, "whether lodged in one or in many,

> is, in its nature, absolute and irresistible. It is not within the competency even of the supreme power to limit itself, because such limitation can emanate only from a superior. For any government to make itself irresistible and to cease to be absolute, it must cease to be supreme, which is but saying, in other words, that it must dissolve itself or be destroyed.[58]

Furthermore, he maintains that "kings and princes (which are only other words for supreme magistrates) were doubtless created and appointed . . . for the sake of the people committed to their charge; yet are they not, therefore, the creatures of the people." On the contrary, he continues,

> so far from deriving their authority from any supposed consent or suffrage of men, they receive their commission from Heaven; they receive it from God, the source and original of all power. . . . [The] supreme magistrate, whether consisting of one or of many, and whether denominated an emperor, an archon, a dictator, a consul, or a senate, is to be regarded and venerated as the vicegerent of God.[59]

Holding this view of the source and character of the sovereignty which every government exercises for the sake of the people committed to its charge, Boucher maintains that "in the only rational sense in which the term can be used . . . liberty consists in a subserviency to law." His emphasis upon law, as opposed to the "mere arbitrary will or wills, of any individual, or any number of individuals," suggests that he, like Bodin, thinks that freedom depends upon the justice of the laws. Because, in his opinion, "true liberty . . . is a liberty to do everything that is right, and

---

[57] The only existential presuppositions of political liberty are the institutions of constitutional government and citizenship with suffrage. The *existence* of these institutions is seldom, if ever, challenged. Bodin and, perhaps, also Boucher and Hobbes, whom we shall presently consider, constitute the rare exceptions.

[58] *A View of the Causes and Consequences of the American Revolution*, VII, pp. 545–46.

[59] *Ibid.*, p. 534.

being restrained from doing anything that is wrong," he insists that it is only "by being included within the pale of civil polity and government" that the natural man "takes his rank in society as a free man," free through "being governed by law and by law only."[60]

By his denial that governments derive "their authority from any supposed consent or suffrage of men," Boucher would appear to be denying the very things that are prerequisite to political liberty. But while he attacks Locke's doctrine of the compact whereby men consent to a constitution of government which obliges them to submit to the determination of the majority,[61] he does not take cognizance of the conception of political liberty that is contained in that doctrine. He does not understand the sense in which Locke regards men as free through having a voice in their own government, and as still free, even when their own will does not prevail, because they consent to the process by which a decision contrary to their own was reached. What he explicitly rejects, as a false alternative to the "liberty [which] consists in a subserviency to law," is one that is thought to consist in "making our own wills the rule of our own actions," or doing exactly as we please. This, he says, is license, and not liberty at all.[62] But what Boucher here calls license is, as we know, the SR form of freedom which, in its political aspect, thrives on exemption from law rather than on subserviency to it. It is not political liberty, i.e., not PL as distinct from SR(PL).

That Boucher would probably deny the existence of political liberty is as clear in his case as in that of Bodin. Being like Bodin an absolutist in his theory of government, he denies the existence of the political institution upon which political liberty depends. Where Bodin appeals to the facts of history in support of his theory of the origin of commonwealths, Boucher appeals to the divine origin of the absolute sovereignty of all legitimate governments. But the effect is the same, so far as the denial of republican institutions is concerned.[63]

---

[60] See *ibid.*, pp. 509, 511. "The more carefully well-devised restraints of law are enacted, and the more rigorously they are executed in any country," Boucher declares, "the greater degree of civil liberty does that country enjoy" (*ibid.*, p. 510).

[61] See *ibid.*, pp. 514–21, 534.

[62] See *ibid.*, p. 509. "So far from our having a right to do everything that we please, under a notion of liberty, liberty itself is limited and confined—but limited and confined only by laws which are at the same time both its foundation and its support" (*ibid.*, p. 511).

[63] It should be observed that Aquinas also thinks that God is the source of all power, but he speaks of the appointed ruler in a free society as "vicegerent of the whole people," and not directly the vicegerent of God. See *Summa Theologica*, Parts I–II, Q. 90, A. 3. The theory that God is the ultimate source of all power is, therefore, not necessarily inconsistent with the view that officeholders in a constitutional state represent the people and are responsive to their will.

It might be supposed that Boucher's remarks about license as contrasted with true liberty indicate that he would reject PL, as he does reject SR (PL), and for the same reason, namely, that it represents a false conception of freedom. But since he does not distinguish between SR(PL) and PL, we cannot be sure of this. One further consideration creates doubt that the conceptions of freedom held by Boucher and Bodin would necessarily lead them to reject political liberty as an untenable conception.

Their conception of the freedom of men who are subject to government is very close to one conception of it advanced by Aquinas. Quite apart from active participation in lawmaking and the other acts of government, men can be free even under absolute government, according to Aquinas, if two conditions are fulfilled: first, that the laws to which they are subject are just and for their own good; second, that they themselves are virtuous enough to obey such laws willingly and not just from fear of coercion.[64]

We have interpreted Bodin and Boucher as insisting upon the first requirement. To this extent at least, their conception of freedom in political life approximates the conception of it as acquired self-perfection in relation to the law of the state, i.e., SP(PL). But Aquinas, in addition to holding this conception of freedom in the political sphere, also appears to hold a conception of political liberty which resembles that of Aristotle.[65] He holds both conceptions without inconsistency, applying one to men who live in societies that have not yet achieved self-government, or even to men in such societies who have not yet been admitted to citizenship, and applying the other to men who live in constitutional states or self-governing communities.

Hence, in the case of Bodin and Boucher, the conceptual rejection of PL does not follow as a matter of logical necessity from their affirmation of SP(PL) or something like it. That they appear to affirm the latter as if it were the only freedom possible in the political sphere stems from their existential denial of constitutional or limited government and, in Boucher's case, from his rejection of SR(PL) as license rather than liberty.

(b) *From the point of view of circumstantial self-realization.* Of the writers we shall consider here, Hobbes is the clearest case of a probable opponent of political liberty from the point of view of circumstantial self-realization. From that point of view, his conception of the liberty of subjects is also opposed to the views we have just examined in Bodin and Boucher. Yet he shares with them the view that all civil government is, by its nature and origin, absolute. For him as for them, this means that the subjects of government are not citizens in Aristotle's sense of men who

[64] See Vol. I, pp. 341–42.
[65] See Vol. I, pp. 333–34.

share in the sovereignty and who rule and are ruled in turn. Whether the commonwealth is instituted by covenant or set up by conquest, "the essence of the commonwealth . . . is *One Person*"; and "he that carryeth this Person is called Sovereign, and is said to have *Sovereign Power*; and everyone besides, his Subject."[66]

In a passage just preceding the chapter in which Hobbes considers "the Liberty of Subjects," he reiterates that the sovereign power is, in all commonwealths, absolute, or almost absolute.

> . . . it appeareth plainly, to my understanding, both from Reason and Scripture, that the Sovereign Power, whether placed in One Man, as in Monarchy, or in one Assembly of men, as in Popular and Aristocratical Commonwealths, is as great as possibly men can be imagined to make it. And though of so unlimited a Power men may fancy many evil consequences, yet the consequences of the want of it, which is perpetual war of every man against his neighbor, are much worse.[67]

Against this background, Hobbes then continues:

> But as men, for the attaining of peace, and conservation of themselves thereby, have made an Artificial Man, which we call a Commonwealth; so also have they made Artificial Chains, called *Civil Laws*, which they themselves, by mutual covenants, have fastened at one end, to the lips of that Man, or Assembly, to whom they have given the Sovereign Power; and at the other end to their own Ears.

It is "in relation to these Bonds only," Hobbes declares, "that I am to speak now, of the *Liberty* of *Subjects*."[68]

That liberty, Hobbes tells us, consists "only in those things, which in regulating their actions, the Sovereign hath pretermitted"; and he immediately adds that "we are not to understand that by such Liberty, the Sovereign Power of life and death, is either abolished, or limited."[69] However, certain natural rights, such as the right of self-defense, cannot be

---

[66] *Leviathan*, Part 2, Ch. 17, p. 132. See also Ch. 18 and 19, pp. 133–52, in which Hobbes describes the unlimited extent and indivisible unity of the sovereign's power, upon which his subjects can impose no limitations, against which they have no juridical appeal or redress, and from which they cannot escape except by breaking their covenant and returning to the state of war and violence.

[67] *Ibid.*, Ch. 19, p. 160. See *ibid.*, Ch. 19, p. 142, where Hobbes denies that there is any real difference between the traditionally distinguished good and bad forms of government; "for they that are discontented under *Monarchy*, call it *Tyranny*; and they that are displeased with *Aristocracy*, call it *Oligarchy*: So also, they which find themselves grieved under a *Democracy*, call it *Anarchy*." The traditionally pejorative names, Hobbes here declares, "are not the names of other Forms of Government, but of the same Forms misliked."

[68] *Ibid.*, Ch. 21, pp. 162–63.

[69] *Ibid.*, p. 163.

alienated to the sovereign by the mutual covenants men make with one another to institute a commonwealth; and insofar as they retain such rights, they also have the corresponding liberties.[70] With these few exceptions, all others liberties of the subject "depend on the Silence of the Law. In cases where the Sovereign has prescribed no rule, there the subject hath the Liberty to do, or forbear, according to his own discretion."[71]

So far we can interpret Hobbes as affirming that the *only* liberty of subjects under government, which is *always* absolute, consists in their being able to do as they wish in all matters on which the law is silent, or in the few exceptional matters to which the natural law gives them an unalienable right, i.e., SR(PL). Is this sufficient evidence on the basis of which to construe him as denying the reality or validity of the freedom which other writers attribute to citizens who, under limited or constitutional government, participate in lawmaking and other acts of government, i.e., PL? We know that Hobbes was acquainted with Aristotle's *Politics*, and we are, therefore, impelled to look for some reference on his part to Aristotle's treatment of political liberty. Could we find that, and find that it reveals an explicit awareness of the conception in question, we should be warranted in saying, almost with certitude, that Hobbes rejects political liberty as an illusory conception of man's freedom in civil society and in relation to civil government.[72]

What we find, however, is something less than perfectly clear. In his first reference to the liberty which is so much praised by the political writers of antiquity, Hobbes points out that they have in mind the freedom of the state itself, not the freedom of the men who are its inhabitants. The sovereignty of an independent state carries with it the same kind of freedom which men originally had when they were in a state of nature; for, like men in that condition, sovereign states or princes are in a state of anarchy and war as regards each other.[73]

"But it is an easy thing," Hobbes then observes, "for men to be deceived,

---

[70] See *ibid.*, pp. 167–68. These rights and liberties are severely limited to matters of self-preservation. Thus, for example, Hobbes tells us that "to resist the Sword of the Commonwealth, in defence of another man, guilty or innocent, no man hath Liberty" (*ibid.*).

[71] *Ibid.*, p. 168.

[72] It should, of course, be added that Hobbes might be construed as an opponent of PL simply from the fact that, being so largely concerned with freedom in the political sphere, he says that "the only proper significance" of the term liberty is SR, and consequently SR(PL).

[73] See *ibid.*, pp. 164–65. In this sense, Hobbes declares, "the *Athenians* and *Romans* were free, that is, free Commonwealths: not that any particular men had the Liberty to resist their own Representative," i.e., the sovereign commonwealth itself. Whether the commonwealth is republican Athens and Rome or despotic Constantinople, "the Freedom [of Subjects] is still the same" (*ibid.*).

by the specious name of Liberty," as they were, in his opinion, by the ancient political writers, especially Aristotle. By him "the Athenians were taught . . . that they were Freemen, and all that lived under Monarchy were slaves"; for Aristotle "puts it down in his Politics (*lib.*6, *cap.*2): *In democracy, Liberty is to be supposed: for 'tis commonly held that no man is Free in any other Government.*"[74] If we can take this single reference to Aristotle's conception of political liberty as sufficient evidence of Hobbes's recognition of what such freedom involves, then, perhaps, we need have no doubt that it is Hobbes's explicit intention to reject that form of freedom as specious, i.e., no real alternative to the "true Liberty of a Subject." This, according to Hobbes, is the same under a monarchy and in a democracy, for, despite appearances, the sovereign power is equally absolute in both and equally unshared by those who are subject to civil government.

On the other hand, the reference to Aristotle leaves us in some doubt whether Hobbes is explicitly joining issue about a form of freedom which he understands in the sense in which it is affirmed by its proponents. Nevertheless, we can be almost certain that his theory of absolute and indivisible sovereignty *as the only possible political reality* excludes from even possible existence a form of freedom that cannot exist except under a limited or constitutional government, in which those who are subject to its power also participate in determining its acts.

The problem of interpreting Spencer as an opponent of political liberty is somewhat different. It is perfectly clear that he conceives freedom as the individual's ability to do as he pleases in the absence of coercion by anyone, whether private persons or the public personages who wield the power of government. In relation to the state and government, Spencer not only affirms man's freedom of self-realization, i.e., SR(PL) but also thinks that such freedom can be maximized *only* by diminishing the power of government and reducing the area of legally prescribed conduct. So far, he is giving us no more than his view of the conditions under which, vis-à-vis the state, individuals can most fully enjoy the freedom of doing as they please. This, by itself, does not constitute a denial of political liberty as a quite distinct form of freedom; for, as we have seen, writers such as Hobhouse and Sidgwick affirm the political liberty of the enfranchised citizen in addition to the freedom any member of society has to do as he pleases in the absence of legal or extra-legal coercion.

However, if the following passages can be taken to indicate some cognizance on Spencer's part of the view that citizenship and suffrage confer upon men a special form of freedom, then they also indicate that he thinks such a view to be false.

[74] *Ibid.*, pp. 165–66.

Is the individual, he asks, "any the less coerced because the body coercing him is one which he had an equal voice with the rest in forming?"[75] To this, the exponents of political liberty might reply, along with Spencer, that he is not. Political liberty, they maintain, does not involve the citizen's exemption from coercion by the government in which he has a voice. The very terms of the question raise some doubt that Spencer is talking about the form of freedom they have in mind.

The same doubt remains, and for the same reason, with regard to the following passage:

> . . . the liberty which a citizen enjoys is to be measured, not by the nature of the governmental machinery he lives under, whether representative or other, but by the relative paucity of the restraints it imposes on him; and . . . whether this machinery is or is not one he shared in making, its actions are not of the kind proper to Liberalism if they increase such restraints beyond those which are needful for preventing him from directly or indirectly aggressing on his fellows—needful, this is, for maintaining the liberties of his fellows against his invasions of them: restraints which are, therefore, to be distinguished as negatively coercive, not positively coercive.[76]

This can be interpreted to mean no more than that Spencer regards citizenship and suffrage as having no effect upon the degree to which individuals enjoy freedom from coercion by government or by other private individuals. Not all who affirm SR(PL) agree with him on this point; e.g., Laski, Knight, and Kelsen think that democratic institutions and processes tend to increase freedom of self-realization for a large number of citizens.

Such disagreement is about self-realization in its political aspect, not about political liberty. An exponent of PL might take either side of this issue about SR(PL). Conversely, those who take either side of this issue about SR(PL) may or may not be authors who would reject PL if they took explicit cognizance of it. All that can be said is that an SR(PL) author such as Spencer is more probably an opponent of PL than writers such as Laski, Knight, and Kelsen, because the one sees no significance for freedom in constitutional government and suffrage, whereas the others do. The evidence that Spencer takes cognizance of political liberty, as that is conceived by Aristotle, for example, is too unclear to warrant the judgment that the probability is high in Spencer's case.[77]

[75] *The Man vs. the State*, p. 17.
[76] *Ibid.*, pp. 18–19.
[77] The same judgment must be made of Dorothy Fosdick. She does not evidence any recognition of political liberty as a special form of freedom. For her, all genuine liberties are simply diverse ways in which individuals can realize their own desires. "One cannot identify freedom with one institutional arrangement as compared with

(c) *From the point of view of collective freedom.* The writers to whom we now turn can, of course, be viewed as opponents of political liberty, as well as of other forms of freedom, merely on the basis of their contention that collective freedom is the *only true freedom* men will ever enjoy and one that still lies in the future. The coming to be of collective freedom awaits the day when human association is emancipated from the oppressive forces of state and government, as these have existed so far in the history of mankind. That day will dawn when mankind achieves and puts to social use knowledge of the natural and social necessities, and when, in the light of that knowledge, men are able to live together under forms of association determined entirely by reference to scientifically formulated laws of nature and of society.[78]

To regard these writers as taking the negative side of the issue about political liberty, we need specific evidence that they address themselves to the question about the validity or reality of such freedom. Do they have in mind a conception of freedom in terms of which other writers maintain that the enfranchised citizen of a constitutional state enjoys a liberty peculiar to his status? With this in mind, do they, then, deny that such freedom has ever existed, can exist, or, if it did exist, would be truly freedom rather than illusory?

We cannot find evidence that they do, but in this respect they are not very different from other writers whom we have considered as in varying degrees probable opponents of political liberty, such as Hegel, Bodin, and Boucher, or Hobbes and Spencer. On the other hand, they, like those other writers, do refer to the institutions which the exponents of political liberty think essential to the form of freedom they affirm, i.e., such things as republican government and suffrage. Unlike Hobbes, Bodin, and

---

another," she writes. "Any institutional arrangement inevitably sustains some liberties and abridges others. It makes it possible for some people to do as they like and by so doing deprives others of choices they desire" (*What is Liberty?*, p. 80). It is in the sense of the foregoing statement that she then says of democracy that it "gives one type of liberty to a large number of people. Within a democracy a great majority may freely register their opinion on the policy of the government under which they live. They are free to state what they want enacted into law. While to many this is a very important liberty, it is no guarantee against the enaction of laws by a majority depriving large numbers of citizens of what they prize as important freedoms" (*ibid.*). It could be that Fosdick is here acknowledging participation in government to be a special type of liberty, i.e., one that is open to all who are citizens in a democracy. But another interpretation is suggested by the context of Fosdick's theory of freedom; namely, that the freedom of the citizen consists in nothing more than his opportunity to "voice [his] opinion and to criticize," *if he so desires.*

[78] Thus, for example, Bakunin refers to collective freedom thus envisaged as "the only liberty worthy of that name" (*The Political Philosophy of Bakunin*, p. 270). For the affirmation of such freedom by Comte, Engels, and Marx as well as Bakunin, see Vol. I, pp. 391–98. Like Bakunin, the others speak of it as the only true freedom.

Boucher, they do not deny the existence of these institutions. Nor do the even deny that, in mankind's march toward collective freedom, suc things as constitutional government, democracy, and suffrage play a part. But they do deny that these institutions by themselves can secure an genuine freedom for men, even for those who have been made citizen and granted the rights of suffrage.

This last point suffices as a basis for interpreting them as probabl opponents of political liberty. Were they explicitly confronted with th proposition that constitutional government and citizenship with suffrag are the only conditions needed for a certain form of freedom, i.e., PL we can have little doubt that, in the last analysis, they would dismiss i as false. The only doubt that remains is whether they would treat PL a an imperfect stage of freedom in mankind's development instead of re jecting it as entirely illusory or no freedom at all.

Thus, for example, Engels points out that, while universal suffrage ma someday work for the emancipation of the laboring class, it does not alway and necessarily contribute to their freedom. This is not only true i republican "America, the latest French republic . . . and honest littl Switzerland"; for "a democratic republic is not essential to [the] brotherl bond between government and stock exchange." This, Engels declares

> is proved not only by England, but also by the new German Empire, where it is difficult to say who scored most by the introduction of universal suffrage, Bismarck or the Bleichröder bank.

The point he wishes to make is that

> the possessing class rules directly by means of universal suffrage. As long as the oppressed class—in our case, therefore the proletariat—is not yet ripe for its self-liberation, so long will it, in its majority, recognize the existing order of society as the only possible one and remain politically the tail of the capitalist class, its extreme left wing. But in the measure in which it matures towards its self-emancipation, in the same measure it constitutes itself as its own party and votes for its own representatives, not those of the capitalists.

[79] On this point, see Comte, *Positive Philosophy*, p. 691; and Lenin, *The State and Revolution*, p. 98, where it is said that "the fundamental idea which runs like a red thread through all of Marx's works [is] that the democratic republic is the nearest approach to the dictatorship of the proletariat," as that in turn is the prelude to the completely communist society in which the state has withered away." Cf. *ibid.*, p. 137–38, where Lenin says: "Democracy is of enormous importance to the working class in its struggle against the capitalists for its emancipation. But democracy is by no means a boundary not to be overstepped; it is only one of the stages on the road from feudalism to capitalism, and from capitalism to Communism."

In his opinion, "universal suffrage is thus the gauge of the maturity of the working class. It cannot and never will be anything more than that in the modern state; but that is enough."[80] It is enough, in other words, if universal suffrage eventually contributes toward the attainment of collective freedom. We must not expect more from it, certainly not that by itself it confers a special freedom on those who are enfranchised.

Bakunin is much more explicit in his attitude toward representative government and suffrage. These institutions may lull men into thinking that they have freedom, or have come nearer to having it, but they will never really possess it until they have completely done away with all "the political and juridical laws, imposed by men on other men, whether with the right of might, violently, or hypocritically in the name . . . of the fiction, the democratic lie, which is called universal suffrage."[81] In Bakunin's opinion, "the citizens are slaves as long as they obey the official representatives of the law, the leaders which are imposed on them by the state—even if these leaders were confirmed by universal suffrage."[82]

He explicitly maintains that men are no freer when they are governed by officials of their own choosing than when they are subject to the will of a despot.[83] He says again and again that "universal suffrage is no guarantee of freedom."[84] He refers to it as "the most extensive and at the same time the most refined manifestation of the political charlatanism of the State . . . the surest means of making the masses cooperate in the building of their own prison."[85] So long as that prime enemy of freedom exists—the state—no form of political organization can ameliorate or do more than disguise its oppressive tyranny.[86]

In all this, of course, Bakunin has his own ideal of collective freedom in mind. It is that freedom which can never be attained as long as the

[80] *Origin of the Family*, p. 158. "On the day when the thermometer of universal suffrage shows boiling-point among the workers," Engels adds, "they as well as the capitalists will know where they stand" (*ibid.*). Cf. *Critique of the Gotha Programme*, pp. 17 ff.
[81] *Oeuvres*, Vol. III, pp. 213–14.
[82] *Ibid.*
[83] Whether political decisions and legislation "emanate from the will of a sovereign, [or] whether they result from the votes of a parliament elected by universal suffrage," he tells us, "[they] . . . are equally disastrous and contrary to the liberty of the masses, because they impose on them a system of laws which are exterior and consequently despotic" (*ibid.*, p. 51).
[84] *Political Philosophy of Bakunin*, p. 209. "A republican State, based upon universal suffrage, could be exceedingly despotic," he writes, "even more despotic than a monarchic State, when, under the pretext of representing the will of everyone, it bears down upon the will and the free movement of every one of its members with the whole weight of its collective power" (*ibid.*).
[85] *Ibid.*, p. 217. Cf. *ibid.*, pp. 220–24.
[86] See *Oeuvres*, Vol. I, pp. 143–44 and 283–84.

state exists; nor, in his view, which differs from that of Marx and Engel in this respect, can it even be gradually approached through the machiner of democracy and universal suffrage, at least not while the institution o private property survives.

> *So long as universal suffrage is exercised in a society where the people, the mass of workers, are ECONOMICALLY dominated by a minority holding in exclusive possession the property and capital of the country, free or independent though the people may be otherwise, or as they may appear to be from a political aspect, these elections held under conditions of universal suffrage can only be illusory, anti-democratic in their results, which invariably will prove to be absolutely opposed to the needs, instincts, and real will of the population.*[87]

At one point in this passage, Bakunin seems to be taking cognizance o. the notion of political liberty, i.e., in conceding that the enfranchise citizens of a democracy are "free and independent" or at least "appea to be from a political aspect," even if, being propertyless, they are no economically independent. If that interpretation is tenable, it increase the probability that Bakunin can be construed as an opponent of politica liberty as a distinct form of freedom.

We have now examined the evidence for treating a number of writer as probable opponents of political liberty. Their views can be taken as typical of the diverse points of view from which political liberty woulc *probably be* rejected as a distinct form of freedom, *if, as conceived by its adherents, it were clearly before the minds of those who would have reason to deny it.* But that, as we have seen, is seldom if ever the case.

Of all the writers whom we have considered, only three—Bodin, Hobbes, and Boucher—refer by name to an author who is one of the proponents of political liberty, i.e., Aristotle in the case of Bodin and Hobbes, Locke in the case of Boucher. Their references, as we noted, fall far short of being an accurate or an adequate representation of either Aristotle's or Locke's theory about the freedom of the citizens of a constitutional state. It is highly significant that no other adherents of political liberty are mentioned by name in conjunction with explicit reference to the conception they propose, not even by Hegel, who was acquainted with the works of Kant and Montesquieu, or by Spencer, Marx, Engels, and Bakunin, who were in a position to take account of the political theories of such authors as Aristotle, Aquinas, Locke, Montesquieu, and Kant.

By the requirements which we regard as the only reasonable ones for determining that writers actually join issue on a particular subject (namely, that they give evidence of addressing themselves to that subject and of

[87] *Political Philosophy of Bakunin*, p. 213.

nswering the same question about it in opposite ways), we are compelled
o say that, in the general controversy, no issue is joined on the subject of
political liberty in answer to the question whether such freedom has or
an have real existence or in answer to the question whether it is genuine
ather than illusory. While there are authors who give us sufficient evidence
or interpreting them as affirmative on both counts, there is none who can
be construed as definitely confronting the proponents of PL or addressing
imself to either question.

That being the case, we cannot be *certain* that any author is definitely
in the negative side of the possible issues raised by these questions. Never-
heless, the documentary evidence we have just examined does make it
ighly probable that such writers as Bodin, Hobbes, and Boucher, on the
ine hand, and such writers as Hegel, Engels, and Bakunin, on the other,
vould take a negative view of political liberty, where they to take explicit
cognizance of it as conceived by its proponents.

The reason for grouping the aforementioned writers in this way is that
he first group would be on the negative side of an existential issue about
political liberty, whereas the second group would be on the negative side
of a conceptual issue about it. The political theories of Bodin, Hobbes,
and Boucher, in excluding the possibility of anything but absolute government, also exclude the two conditions prerequisite to the existence of
political liberty. The conceptions of freedom held by Hegel, Engels, and
Bakunin are the basis for their dismissing as false or illusory the form of
freedom which is thought to inhere in the possession and exercise of
suffrage under constitutional government.

4. FOR OR AGAINST?

We turn now to writers of another sort. Unlike Bodin, Hobbes, and
Boucher, they hold that the difference between absolute and republican
or constitutional government is fundamental and has the most important
bearing upon human freedom. Unlike Hegel, Engels, and Bakunin, they
hold that such things as republican government and citizenship, or democracy and universal suffrage, are crucial for freedom in the political sphere.
Nevertheless, we find in their theories of freedom no cognizance of political
liberty as distinct from the freedom of self-perfection or of self-realization
n its political aspect; and so we remain quite uncertain whether they
would be on the affirmative or negative side of a conceptual issue about
PL in the general controversy.

The writers we have in mind fall into two groups. On the one hand,
there are Spinoza and Rousseau whom we have interpreted as exponents

of SP(PL).[88] On the other hand, there are J. S. Mill, Laski, Knight and Kelsen, whom we have interpreted as exponents of SR(PL).[89] The question we find it difficult to answer is the same for both groups. If these writers squarely confronted the conception of political liberty as that is expounded by Aristotle, Kant, Hobhouse, or Sidgwick, would they accept or reject it? Would Spinoza and Rousseau, like Kant, affirm PL as a freedom distinct from SP(PL)? Would Mill, Laski, Knight, and Kelsen, like Hobhouse, affirm PL as a freedom distinct from SR(PL)?

The fact that these writers are for republican institutions and for constitutional provisions which provide for the participation of citizens in government does not by itself constitute evidence that they would espouse PL as a distinct form of freedom. On the contrary, everything they explicitly say fits much more readily into the interpretation that they are in favor of these political institutions because they promote SP(PL) or SR(PL) as they conceive it. When Spinoza says that democracy is "of all forms of government the [one] . . . most consonant with individual liberty,"[90] we know that he has in mind the virtuous man's freedom of self-perfection which in relation to the laws of the state is SP(PL), not PL.[91] We know that Rousseau also has SP(PL) in mind when he explains why the republic instituted by the social contract is essential to what is for him at once the "civil" and the "moral" liberty of the citizen who, in obeying the commands of the general will, obeys himself alone in willing as he ought.[92] And we know that Mill, Laski, Knight, and Kelsen are in favor of democratic institutions, and especially universal suffrage, because the citizen with

[88] See Vol. I, pp. 292–97, 347–50.

[89] See *ibid.*, pp. 237–44, 351–58.

[90] A *Theological-Political Treatise*, Ch. XVI, p. 207. Cf. *ibid.*, pp. 206–7, and see also A *Political Treatise*, Ch. XI.

[91] See Vol. I, pp. 347–49, where attention is called to the crucial sentence in which Spinoza says that in a democracy or, for that matter, any state in which the laws are "founded on sound reason," every man "*may, if he will, be free, that is, live with full consent under the entire guidance of reason.*" The italicized words indicate that Spinoza attributes freedom in even the best state only to those who are themselves virtuous enough to live with full consent under the entire guidance of reason. Democracy or citizenship confers no freedom on men who follow their passions.

[92] See *ibid.*, pp. 292–97 and 349–50. As we pointed out in the latter pages, Rousseau does not say that men are free in virtue of being citizens, but rather that they are both citizens and free in virtue of the sovereignty of the general will. He tells us that if individuals, whose particular interests are contrary to the general will, happen to be in the majority, they would enact a law that is not consonant with the general will and "in that case [they would] not have been free" (*The Social Contract*, Book IV, Ch. 2, p. 106). See also the passage in *Emile* (p. 437) in which Rousseau compares the condition of the wise man and the knave in republican Geneva and in despotic France: "The vile man," he says, "bears his slavery in himself; the one would be a slave in Geneva [even if he were a citizen], the other free in Paris [even as a subject of the Bourbons]."

voice in his own government stands a better chance of living under laws
that harmonize with his own desires. Such laws augment his freedom of
self-realization in the sphere of political life, i.e., SR(PL).[93]

The fact that they are exponents of the freedom of self-perfection or of
self-realization in the political sphere does not preclude their acceptance
of PL as well. As we have pointed out before, Kant's theory of freedom
which includes PL as distinct from SP(PL) and Hobhouse's theory which
includes PL as distinct from SR(PL) show that the espousal of SP(PL)
does not in itself prevent Spinoza and Rousseau from affirming PL; nor are
Mill, Laski, Kelsen, and Knight prevented from affirming PL by their
espousal of SR(PL). But mere possibility is one thing, and probability
based on evidence is another.

In general, it can be said that these authors, by the main tenor of their
political theories, are more inclined to be for than against political liberty
as a form of freedom possessed only by enfranchised citizens who can take
an active part in their own government. But in the case of two of them—
Spinoza and Rousseau—we think that the probability of their affirming PL
as distinct from SR(PL) is very slight. We base this on the following
observations.

Of all the SP authors who also affirm PL as a distinct form of freedom,
Kant alone unconditionally rejects the freedom of self-realization. For him,
as we have seen, there is no genuine freedom at all in an individual's being
able to do as he pleases or to realize his individual preferences. The others
—Aquinas, Locke, Montesquieu, Maritain, and Simon—maintain that,
under certain conditions, there is genuine freedom in the individual's
being able to act on his desires.[94]

Among these authors, only Kant has any difficulty in fitting political
liberty into his whole theory of freedom. He does so by sharply dividing
man's freedom into an "internal freedom," which belongs to man's inner
or moral life, and an "external freedom," which belongs to his outer or
political life.[95] As a result of this dichotomy of the moral and the political
spheres of human freedom, Kant does not consider the freedom of self-
perfection in relation to the laws of the state or the acts of government,
for such considerations apply only to the external freedom proper to the
political sphere. In other words, Kant does not attempt to combine political
liberty with the freedom of self-perfection in its political aspect. For him
the latter has no political aspect.

However, for Spinoza and Rousseau, SP does have a political aspect;

---

[3] See *ibid.*, 237–44, 352–58, and 368.
[4] See Ch. 4, pp. 42–44, 59–61, *supra.*
[5] See *Metaphysical Elements of Ethics*, pp. 374, 378. Cf. *Science of Right*, pp. 397–8, 401.

and for Rousseau, as we have seen, the political and moral aspects c
acquired self-perfection are almost fused. This fact, together with the fa
that Spinoza and Rousseau, like the Stoic philosophers and like Hege
show little or no tolerance for individual self-realization in either the mor.
or the political life of man, makes it unlikely that they would endor:
the special form of political self-realization which suffrage is thought to co
fer upon citizens, no matter what their moral character or the moral quali
of their political preferences.

As for J. S. Mill, Kelsen, and Knight, all of whom are exponents c
self-realization, both in general and in its political aspect, the probabilit
is naturally much greater that they would combine PL with SR(PL), a
do Hobhouse and Sidgwick, with whom they otherwise share the sam
general approach to political problems and to the problems of freedon
Of these writers, the probability seems greatest in the case of Mill.

In our earlier consideration of Mill with regard to political liberty, w
found it extremely difficult to decide whether or not he belonged to th
group of those who affirm it as a distinct form of freedom. We foun
passages in his writings which suggest that he does, along with passag
of a contrary tenor.[96] We had no comparable problem in the case c
Laski, Kelsen, and Knight. In spite of their being, like Mill, advocates c
democratic institutions and especially universal suffrage, we found no pa
sages in their writings which suggest their espousal of political liberty as
freedom which belongs to the citizen simply in virtue of his enfranchise
ment and his exercising the rights and privileges of political participatior
The reason for our uncertainty about where Mill stands on the questio
of political liberty is also our reason for thinking it somewhat likely tha
were the question explicitly put to him, he might answer it affirmativel

One other writer, whom we have associated with Mill, Laski, and Knigh
as an exponent of SR(PL), remains to be considered. Like them, Tawne
advocates political liberalism and democratic institutions as conduciv
to individual self-realization.[97] But, unlike them, Tawney gives us som
ground for thinking that, in his view, the individual's active participatio
in the management of affairs which concern him provides a form of free
dom that is distinct from his being exempt from legal regulations or othe
constraints which interfere with his doing as he wishes.

In calling for "the extension of liberty from the political sphere . .
to [the sphere] of economic relations,"[98] Tawney indicates that the typ

[96] See Vol. I, pp. 357–58, which presents the evidence that Mill does not have
conception of political liberty as a distinct freedom; and cf. fn. 121 on p. 367, whic
presents the evidence that he does.
[97] See Vol. I, pp. 229, 237, 241.
[98] *Equality*, p. 225.

of liberty which he wishes to see extended consists in having a voice in one's own affairs. Just as the citizen is able to participate in the formation of policies and decisions that are of concern to him in the political sphere, so the worker should be able to exercise some control over the organization and administration of the industry in which he is engaged.[99] Protesting that freedom is too often exclusively "interpreted in political terms," he even says in one place that, in such terms, "it is regarded as belonging to human beings as citizens, rather than to citizens as human beings."[100] If the tendency of this statement is merely to suggest that citizens, as human beings, have need of freedom in other than the political sphere, but not to deny that their specifically political liberty belongs to human beings *as citizens*, then it almost amounts to an affirmation of political liberty. The fact that Tawney appears to be proposing an analogous freedom of participation for the human being *as worker* in the sphere of industrial life adds to rather than subtracts from the probability of this interpretation of his views.

5. POSSIBLE DEBATE OF THE POSSIBLE ISSUES

By considering the probable opponents of political liberty, we have seen the shape that two possible issues might take on that subject in the general controversy about the kinds of freedom.[101]

One is an existential issue that arises from the question whether such things as constitutional or limited government, with effective participation in lawmaking and other acts of government by an enfranchised citizenry, has or ever can have any political reality. Since these institutions are indispensable to political liberty, the denial of their existence is a denial of its existence.

From the point of view of political history and experience during the last three hundred years, and also with memory of the republics of antiquity, the question may seem to be a forced one. Such things as constitutional government and an effective suffrage appear to be such plain matters of fact that it is difficult to understand how their existence can be questioned. Yet it is also the fact that Bodin, Hobbes, and Boucher do question them; and while they lived too early to fit their theories of absolute government to the political phenomena of modern republics or democracies,

[99] See *The Acquisitive Society*, p. 129.
[100] *Equality*, p. 224.
[101] We have chosen to call these issues possible rather than actual because on their negative side we can do no more than suggest the probable opponents of political liberty. See p. 148, *supra*.

they had knowledge of the republics of Greece and Rome and were acquainted—Bodin and Hobbes, at least—with Aristotle's views on constitutional government and citizenship.

As we have seen, Bodin and Hobbes are not at all disturbed by what appear to be contrary views on Aristotle's part. Bodin charges him with being inconsistent in his use of the term citizen, and Hobbes charges him with trying to deceive himself and his compatriots about the difference between the subjects of kings or despots and the citizens of a republic. Similarly, Boucher charges Locke with harboring and perpetrating illusions about the derivation of political authority from the consent of the governed and about setting limits to the sovereign's power.

From this we can infer how Bodin and Hobbes would handle political phenomena which seem to challenge their thesis that all governments are, both *de jure* and *de facto*, absolute. Republics, ancient or modern, may appear to be limited governments, may appear to be creatures of popular sovereignty and the consent of the governed, may appear to provide for the direct or indirect participation in all affairs of state by the enfranchised citizens. But these are only the *appearances*—the surface phenomena which, unanalyzed, can deceive us into thinking that there are facts that challenge the thesis which they advance and which they would defend by dismissing the supposed facts as mere sham and delusion.

If, as Bodin, Hobbes, and Boucher charge, Aristotle misinterpreted the political phenomena of his day, or Locke in his, so can we in ours, and in the same way, i.e., by allowing a false political theory to prevent us from seeing the facts as they are. They would contend, in short, that the question whether or not all governments are absolute is not and cannot be simply a question of observable fact. Conflicting theories of the origin and nature of the state, of civil government, and of sovereignty are always involved in opposed interpretations of political phenomena or experience, so that there are no unmixed questions of fact which can be resolved empirically.

This, at least, is one way of understanding an existential issue about political liberty. To treat it simply as an issue of fact, and one on which the facts are overwhelmingly decisive against the position of Bodin, Hobbes, and Boucher, would be to dismiss it as preposterous and not worth a moment's further consideration. But however much political convictions now widely prevalent would tend to favor that course, such treatment can still be charged with begging the question and with being prejudicial to one of the conflicting points of view involved.

Taking this possible issue seriously in the manner suggested, the debate of it would draw on arguments *pro* and *con* concerning some of the most fundamental points in political theory. That debate could be conducted without reference to freedom in general, or to political liberty in particular, since it is concerned primarily with questions about the political underpinnings of freedom in one form or another. We saw, in the case of the existential issue concerning acquired self-perfection, that the dispute over the validity of the presuppositions of such freedom involves arguments concerning fundamental points in moral and psychological theory; and that the construction of such debate would require us to go far beyond the literature of freedom.[102] So, here too, we would have to go too far afield to construct the debate between the absolutists and the constitutionalists in political theory.

We must be content, therefore, to leave the matter with the observation that if Bodin, Hobbes, and Boucher, to take them as typical representatives of the absolutist point of view, were more than probable opponents of political liberty and were actually to join issue with its adherents, and if the resultant existential issue were treated seriously as one involving fundamental differences in political theory, then the debate of that issue could certainly be constructed, but only as the result of extensive dialectical work on such subjects as the state, government, and sovereignty.

Our situation with respect to the conceptual issue about political liberty is different. This issue in the general controversy turns on the question whether or not what is conceived by the affirmative authors as a distinct form of freedom is freedom in any acceptable sense, i.e., whether or not it conforms to the common understanding or the general idea of freedom. Since we have not found any writers who actually take the negative side of this issue, we can hardly expect to find any evidence of an actual debate of it in the literature. However, we can speculate about the possible lines of argument which might be employed in the debate of this issue.

One writer gives us some indication of how he might argue against political liberty by reference to the idea of freedom itself. According to Hegel, the essence of freedom, in general and in every genuine embodiment, lies in the agency of the self. As his followers, Green, Bradley, and Bosanquet, point out, it always consists in some form of "self-assertion."[103] No act is free which does not flow from the self as the active principle or agent. So far the defenders of political liberty would agree, and such agreement on their part concerning the self as the principle of freedom would provide the necessary ground for genuine debate of the conceptual issue. In that debate, the opposing arguments would stem from divergent views about the self that is the principle of freedom.

According to Hegel, anything which is attributed to the subjective or

---

[102] See Ch. 5, p. 95, *supra.*
[103] See Ch. 5, pp. 112, 124 ff., *supra.*

individual, as distinguished from the objective or universal, self can be at most an illusory freedom, an inadequate moment in the development of the true idea. He probably would make that judgment of political liberty, were he fully cognizant of the terms in which it is conceived by its adherents as a special variant of individual self-realization. In fact, he comes very close to saying precisely this in his remarks about certain false notions of constitutional government and suffrage, even though in that connection he is dealing with these things as if they were the basis for SR(PL) rather than PL as a special variant of self-realization in the political sphere.[104]

On the affirmative side of the debate, the defenders of political liberty might reply by recourse to the same type of argument which such writers as Laski and Hobhouse employ in their rebuttal of the attack, from the Hegelian point of view, on the freedom of self-realization. The only self, they contend, which is or can be the principle of freedom is the individual self, the whole human person in his individuality, not some fictitious real or true self which is identified with the state.[105] In addition, Hobhouse, who is an exponent of PL as well as of SR(PL), might argue against Hegel's objective or universal self, which is offered as the only principle of true freedom in his version of SP(PL), in the same manner in which he argues against Bosanquet's exposition of Hegel's views in his attack on acquired self-perfection, in itself and in its political aspect. That mode of argument would be as cogent in support of the individual self, which is the principle of political liberty, as it is in the case of self-realization, in general or in its political aspect.[106]

The debate of this issue might also include a somewhat different set of opposed arguments.

On the negative side, it might be argued that the individual self is subject to the will of others whenever the individual belongs to a minority that is adversely affected by a political decision or act. The fact that the individual had an opportunity to express his own will about the matter, or even the fact that his exercise of suffrage had some effect upon the political result, does not exempt him from suffering the imposition of a will other than his own. The public will to the formation of which he may have contributed is identical with his own only in some trivial or accidental sense; and in many cases it is quite contrary to his own. But, according to the common understanding of freedom, the individual is free only when and only to the extent that his own will prevails. Hence, the freedom

104 See pp. 158–61, *supra.*
105 See Ch. 4, pp. 81–85, *supra.*
106 See Ch. 5, pp. 120–21, *supra.*

which is attributed to the citizen in virtue of his suffrage or participation in political life is only an accidental aspect of his freedom of self-realization, and not, as the adherents of political liberty insist, a special variant of that freedom and one that is quite distinct from it.

This argument might be broached by such authors as Laski, Knight, and Kelsen. In reply to it, two things might be pointed out by the exponents of political liberty.

In the first place, the argument itself calls attention to the very reason for distinguishing between PL and SR(PL). The defenders of political liberty do not claim that the citizen's exercise of suffrage prevents him from being subject to the will of others; nor, for that matter, do they claim that it exempts him from coercion or constraint by a government which acts contrary to his own wishes. It is precisely because of this that the special form of self-realization enjoyed by the enfranchised citizen must be distinguished from his freedom to follow his own will in all matters on which no contrary legal regulations prevent him from doing so.

In the second place, with regard to the relation of the individual to the public will, it might be argued that the enfranchised citizen accepts the public will, not as his own, but as representative of his own. It is always that procedurally, even when it is substantively opposed to his own will. By his consent to the constitutionally established processes by which the public will is to be formed, the individual citizen regards himself as sponsoring whatever results are reached by due process of law or the established procedures of constitutional government. In addition, the fact that such procedures involve his own participation through suffrage always gives his individual will some efficacy in determining the substance of the results achieved. These two ways in which the public will represents his individual will are quite sufficient for the special form of self-realization that is political liberty.

Chapter 7

THE ISSUES CONCERNING
COLLECTIVE FREEDOM

We turn now to a form of freedom that is held by its exponents to belong to the future. The past contains no trace of it. It had not begun to exist at the time its principal exponents—Comte, Bakunin, Marx, and Engels —were developing their conceptions of it, nor has it come into existence since their day. It will not come to be on earth, they say, until men achieve the ideal mode of association that is the goal of mankind's development, and are able to direct their communal life in accordance with necessary laws discovered by natural and social science. When, in the future, mankind puts such knowledge to social use, and submits to these necessities and these alone, men will be collectively free. Only through mankind's possession of collective freedom will individuals be able to lead free lives.

In the general controversy about the kinds of freedom, we face a number of special difficulties in attempting to construct the issues and the debate about this form of freedom. To construct an existential issue about CF, we must look for opposite predictions about man's freedom in the future, or at least denials of the predictions which the CF authors make. But it is not so much the futurity of the freedom in question as the recency of the authors who predict its future existence, which creates a special problem.

Since the conception of collective freedom was first proposed in the nineteenth century,[1] we must look to authors in the latter part of that century or in our own for evidence of dispute about it. As a matter of fact, it is only in twentieth-century writings that we have found such evidence, i.e., cognizance of collective freedom together with criticisms of it which can be construed as either existential or conceptual denials. And here we meet with an additional difficulty.

Of the three principal versions of collective freedom, only that of Marx and Engels is widely discussed. For the most part, that discussion focuses on their prediction of an ultimate phase of communist society which will

[1] It may have been anticipated in antiquity in the myths of the Golden Age, in the Stoic dreams of the *Civitas Magna,* and in the Christian hope for the Kingdom of God.

be attained only after the state has withered away, and not during the penultimate stage when the dictatorship of the proletariat is necessary. To deny that the state will wither away as predicted is to deny that collective freedom will be achieved in the manner outlined by the Marxists; but that leaves untouched Bakunin's proposal to achieve collective freedom by the direct action of anarchism, as well as Comte's proposal for its achievement by the creation of the positive polity, i.e., a state which is governed in accordance with the principles of the positive philosophy.

These fundamental differences of opinion concerning the route to collective freedom bring the collective-freedom authors into a three-sided dispute in the special controversy on that subject. The issue about ways and means is especially intense so far as the Marxists and Bakunin, or the anarchists, are concerned. Furthermore, Bakunin, as we shall see, in arguing against the withering away of the state, does so on grounds which closely resemble the reasons advanced by other writers such as Hirsch, Belloc, Mannheim, Salvadori, Joad, Djilas, Talmon, and Simon, who attack the Marxist program, but who do not themselves offer an alternative program for achieving collective freedom. It has no place at all in their theories.

With regard to these other writers, we therefore face the problem whether their attacks on the Marxist doctrine should be treated in the special controversy about collective freedom rather than here in the general controversy. By our own principles, the general controversy about CF should be restricted to issues in which the negative side is taken by authors who can be construed as opposing collective freedom in its most general formulation, not just one theory of it. But by the same principles the special controversy about CF should also be restricted to issues in which the opposed parties affirm conceptions of collective freedom, no matter how else they differ about it.

Within this framework, there would seem to be no proper place to treat the writers in question. The solution which recommends itself on pragmatic grounds is to treat them here. Were we to follow the opposite course, we should be left with only two authors—Berdyaev and Maritain—who argue against every variety of collective freedom, not just the Marxist version of it.

But that is not the only consideration. Another is the fact that, of the three major conceptions of collective freedom, the Marxist version is of signal importance today. It has active protagonists in the world of thought and of action, to an extent and in a way that does not obtain in the case of Comte and Bakunin. Nor have the views of Comte and Bakunin elicited as extensive a critical reaction. Even Berdyaev and Maritain who criticize what they regard as the utopianism that is common to Comte and Bakunin, as well as to Marx and Engels, direct their attack mainly against the doctrines of the latter. Hence, we think it advisable to include here, along with them, authors who concentrate their critical attention entirely on the Marxist theory of collective freedom.

This decision does not mean, however, that we shall include all adverse criticisms of socialism or communism, or even all that have some direct relevance to the problems of human freedom. Such writers as Spencer, Hayek, and von Mises, for example, regard the socialist economy as inimical to individual freedom and destructive of a free society. But it is perfectly clear that it is the freedom of self-realization which they think cannot prosper under socialism. Their arguments have no direct bearing on collective freedom.

To speak against socialist measures from the point of view of SR is not to say that CF is a false conception of freedom, nor even to say that the establishment of communist collectivism, through the revolutionary dictatorship of the proletariat, is not a step toward the achievement of collective freedom. Since the communist writers themselves proclaim that collective freedom will come into existence only when the need for the dictatorship has banished, to point out that such freedom does not exist under the strong central government of the socialist state would hardly be to argue against them. It is even less relevant to say that individual freedom of self-realization is greatly curtailed by the political and economic organization of the socialist state.

We shall, therefore, confine our attention to those adverse views of socialism or communism which deny the predicted future existence of the collective freedom that Marx, Engels, and their followers envision as the ultimate goal of the revolution and the ideal that mankind is destined to achieve. Such views, together with the more comprehensive attack by Berdyaev and Maritain on the whole family of CF conceptions, will constitute the negative side of the existential issue about collective freedom in the general controversy, as we shall construct it. In addition, we shall try to construct a conceptual issue, in which the very notion of collective freedom is challenged as a false conception of human freedom. Here we have been able to find some evidence for the negative position in Berdyaev, Maritain, and Talmon.

As this brief preview indicates, the writers who can be construed as parties to these issues are not numerous, nor are there more than a few authors in each case who provide us with *explicit* evidence of genuinely opposed views. Nevertheless, there can be no doubt that there are actual disagreements between the well-known authors mentioned above about CF as a form of freedom. But the debate of these issues is deficient in one very important respect.

We have the statement of the affirmative position, together with such grounds as its adherents deem necessary to offer in its support. On the negative side, we have arguments against collective freedom, either on existential or conceptual grounds. But we do not have any rebuttal of these attacks.

This deficiency may be a deficiency in our research, or it may represent the failure of the CF authors or their followers to take cognizance of these attacks. Perhaps they have not deemed them worthy of reply. In any case, instead of a balanced debate, we shall present the attacks for which we can offer documentary evidence and suggest, in the absence of such evidence, what form the rebuttal might take.

We shall proceed as follows. We shall begin in Section 1 with a brief summary of the views of Comte, Bakunin, Marx, Engels, and Lenin, paying special attention to their prediction of the future advent of collective freedom. Then in Section 2 we shall attempt to formulate the existential and the conceptual issues as precisely as possible and indicate the parties to each of them. Finally, in the third and fourth sections, we shall present the existential and conceptual attacks on collective freedom, so far as these can be evidenced, and suggest further possible arguments, both additional arguments on the negative side and also arguments in rebuttal.

1. THE PREDICTION OF COLLECTIVE FREEDOM

We have elsewhere examined the documentary evidence that Comte, Bakunin, Marx, and Engels hold conceptions of freedom which have certain elements in common.[2] All of them conceive freedom as something which is acquired by men collectively. This fact led us to use the term "collective freedom," a term which, incidentally, they themselves some-times employ.

In their view, no freedom which is individual in the sense that some members of a society may enjoy it while others are deprived of it deserves the name of liberty. As we have seen in the preceding chapters, these writers align themselves on the negative side of the issues in the general controversy about the freedom of self-realization, the freedom of self-perfection, and political liberty.[3]

---

[2] See Ch. 19 in Vol. I, pp. 370–99. Cf. Ch. I in this volume, pp. 10–11, *supra*.

[3] See Ch. 4, pp. 56–61; Ch. 5, pp. 104–9; and Ch. 6, pp. 171–74, *supra*. Being determinists, these writers also reject the freedom of self-determination, as we shall subsequently see. Hence, for them, CF is the only genuine form of human freedom.

While they reject the typical SP conception of freedom, which is personal rather than social and which in its Platonic, Stoic, Christian, and Kantian forms involves the willing obedience of the virtuous man to the moral or the divine law, these authors reveal a certain affinity between their theories of freedom and the views of Spinoza, Rousseau, and Hegel: with Rousseau and Hegel, because they conceive man's acquired freedom as essentially social;[4] with all three, because they conceive man's freedom of self-perfection as ultimately springing from man's knowledge of necessity and his acquiescence in it.[5] These considerations led us to treat collective freedom as a special variant of acquired self-perfection.[6]

That Comte, Bakunin, Marx, and Engels affirm CF as the only genuine form of human freedom indicates plainly where they stand in the general controversy about the kinds of freedom. But when we consider the existential, as distinct from the conceptual, issue about collective freedom, we must note the special way in which they assert the existence of CF. One thing distinctive of their position is, as we have seen, the futurity of the freedom they affirm, together with their confidence in its inevitable realization in the course of human history.

Another distinctive feature of collective freedom is that it involves complete emancipation from the state as that has so far existed throughout history.[7] The authors affirming this view, however, do not agree about the way in which that emancipation will be accomplished. Since the existential issue involves attacks on the predictions of CF, it is necessary to examine this difference of opinion among the CF authors about the path which mankind must follow to bring it into existence. And since it is the Marxist prediction which has been most subject to criticism, we shall be especially concerned with the views of Marx and Engels on the withering away of the state, together with Lenin's commentary on them.

For Comte, man's emancipation from all forms of arbitrary personal dictation does not depend upon either the abolition of the state or its gradual withering away. On the contrary, he maintains that "society can no more exist without a government than government can exist without a society."[8] But the ideal society, which is the ultimate goal of human progress, will have a system of government unlike any that has so far existed. It will come into existence when the positive philosophy, replacing

---

[4] See Vol. I, pp. 291–300.
[5] See *ibid.*, pp. 390–96.
[6] For a detailed statement of the considerations which support this classification of collective freedom, see *ibid.*, pp. 389–90. The affinity between collective freedom and certain elements in acquired self-perfection, as that is conceived by Spinoza, Rousseau, and Hegel, does not imply any acceptance by the CF authors of these SP conceptions.
[7] See *ibid.*, p. 381.
[8] *Positive Polity*, Vol. II, p. 162.

the religious and metaphysical views of all earlier ages, is the organizing genius of the new epoch in which men will enjoy collective freedom. This society, in which government will be based on the knowledge of natural and social necessities obtained by the positive sciences, Comte calls "the positive state."[9]

According to Comte, "the only way to reconcile independence with social union, and thereby reach true liberty,

> lies in obedience to the objective laws of the world, and of human nature. . . . Such will be the complex and incalculable benefit of extending the scientific method to the complex and important phenomena of human nature. Man will no longer be the slave of man; he yields only to external Law, and to this those who demonstrate it to him are as submissive as himself. In such obedience there can be no degradation, even where the laws are inflexible. . . . Our obedience here is no longer passive; it implies the devotion of every faculty of our nature to the improvement of a world of which we are in the true sense masters. The natural laws to which we owe submission furnish the basis of our intervention, they direct our efforts and give stability to our purpose. The more perfectly they are known, the more free will our conduct become from arbitrary command or servile obedience.[10]

In this, and in similar passages, Comte is not describing any actual society. He is envisioning one that mankind is destined to create in its progress from the stages of culture which are dominated by religion and metaphysics to the culture in which positive science reigns supreme.

As applicable to social phenomena, the laws which science will teach us are "within certain limits . . . modifiable by wise action on the part of society."[11] Here then is the mission which humanity is destined to fulfill, as Comte sees it: "To give full effect to the action of the will in modifying, so far as they are modifiable, the conditions to which it is necessarily subject."[12] When that is accomplished, society will be so organized and governed that men will collectively enjoy the "true liberty [which] is nothing else than a rational submission to the preponderance of the laws of nature, in release from all arbitrary personal dictation."[13]

Some aspects of Comte's final philosophy appear to be at variance with this conception of freedom. The religion of humanity which he promulgated in later writings creates an intellectual and moral power that directs

[9] See *Positive Philosophy*, p. 26; and *Positive Polity*, Vol. I, p. 131.
[10] *Positive Polity*, Vol. I, p. 296.
[11] *Ibid.* While "the doctrinal system of Positivism may seem to chain us to external necessities," Comte declares that "in reality it procures us the only possible liberty. . . . Subject to modifiable laws, we are in the truest sense free and moral beings" (*ibid.*, Vol. IV, p. 149).
[12] *Positive Polity*, Vol. IV, p. 35.
[13] *Positive Philosophy*, p. 435.

the proper balance in society between sympathy and self-regard, between love and intellect. It is to this power with its ritual and priests, rather than to "the preponderance of the laws of nature," that we now owe complete submission. Political rights are anti-social and must give way to duties. "Everyone has duties, duties toward all; but rights in the ordinary sense can be claimed by none. . . . In other words, no one has any Right but that of doing his Duty."[14]

Far from withering away, government becomes highly centralized—a kind of popular dictatorship, modified by the influence of the priests and women. It might thus appear that the freedom which was to substitute the rule of science for the authority of man over man has been completely abandoned. However, there is evidence that Comte regarded the submission to this particular religion of humanity, to this particular morality of duty and altruism, and to this particular dictatorship as not only consistent with but the very stuff of liberty. This is because they are to be founded on scientific fact and law, on a rational economy, and on an exhaustive knowledge of history and human nature. By submergence of self in humanity and in duty men become truly human; here is the means to collective freedom.

Although this religious phase of Comte's positivism is contrary to the letter and spirit of Bakunin's philosophy, both men held that freedom lies in the application of scientific knowledge to human affairs, and differed, it might be said, chiefly in the ways and means of the application. "Man's liberty," Bakunin declares, "consists uniquely in this: that he obeys natural laws because he himself has recognized them as such, and not because they were externally imposed on him by a strange will, divine or human, collective or individual."[15] This means, in his view, the elimination of all man-made laws or institutions. It means "the independence of the will of everyone from the will of others."[16]

So long as the state exists, with all its juridical devices for imposing the will of some upon others and thus negating liberty, the collective freedom of mankind cannot be achieved.[17] To bring it about, the juridical state must be abolished by direct action and replaced by an association of men *sans* state or government, i.e., an ideal anarchic community in which men live together in freedom, submitting to no laws except those established by science.

He describes the ideal society he envisions in the following terms.

[14] *Republic of the West; Order and Progress. A General View of Positivism,* pp. 400–1.
[15] *Oeuvres,* Vol. III, p. 51. Cf. *ibid.,* pp. 213–14, 235, 287, 291.
[16] *Ibid.,* Vol. V, p. 158.
[17] *Ibid.,* Vol. I, pp. 143–44, 284; Vol. III, pp. 213–14. "Only when the state has ceased to exist will humanity obtain its freedom" (*Political Philosophy of Bakunin,* p. 299).

It is the triumph of humanity, it is the conquest and accomplishment of the full freedom and full development, material, intellectual and moral, of every individual, by the absolutely free and spontaneous organisation of economic and social solidarity as completely as possible between all human beings living on the earth.[18]

This, in his view, cannot be accomplished by the revolution which sets up a "People's State" under the dictatorship of the proletariat.

The social revolution, as the Latin and Slav toilers picture it to themselves, desire it and hope for it, is infinitely broader than that promised them by the German or Marxian programme. It is not for them a question of the emancipation parsimoniously measured out and only realisable at a very distant date, of the working class, but the complete and real emancipation of all the proletariat, not only of some countries but of all nations, civilised and uncivilised—a new civilisation, genuinely of the people, being destined to commence by this act of universal emancipation.

The immediate goal of this revolutionary emancipation is the full fruition of collective freedom for the human race as a whole,

not that political, bourgeois liberty, so much approved and recommended as a preliminary object of conquest by Marx and his adherents, but *the great human liberty*, which, destroying all the dogmatic, metaphysical, political, and juridical fetters by which everybody today is loaded down, will give to everybody, collectivities as well as individuals, full autonomy in their activities and their development, delivered once and for all from all inspectors, directors, and guardians.[19]

While Bakunin exhorts the workers to engage in the revolutionary action leading to anarchism, he also thinks that inexorable forces are working

[18] *Marxism, Freedom, and the State*, p. 22. "He who wants the triumph of humanity, and the full and complete emancipation of the masses of the people," Bakunin writes, "should also aim toward the destruction of all States and the establishment upon their ruins of a Universal Federation of Free Associations of all the countries in the world" (*Political Philosophy of Bakunin*, p. 225).

[19] *Ibid.*, p. 52. "We already have expressed our abhorrence for the theories of Lasalle and Marx," Bakunin writes, "theories which counseled the workers—if not as their ultimate ideal, at least as their next chief aim—*to form a People's State*, which, according to their interpretation, will only be 'the proletariat raised to the position of a ruling class.'" Bakunin then asks: "If the proletariat is to be the ruling class, over whom will it rule? The answer is that there will remain another proletariat which will be subjected to this new domination, this new State." He sees no hope that the new ruling class will give up its power, and that the state will wither away, as the Marxists predict. "Consequently," he concludes, "there is no other means of emancipating the people economically and politically, or providing them with well-being and freedom, but to abolish the State, all States, and once and for all do away with that which until now has been called *politics*" (*Political Philosophy of Bakunin*, p. 286). Cf. *ibid.*, pp. 287–89.

toward "the supreme end of history," which is the ideal he sets before us. "We, who are Materialists and Determinists just as much as Marx himself," he declares,

> we also recognise the inevitable linking of economic and political facts in history. We recognise, indeed, the necessity, the inevitable character of all events that happen. . . .[20]

The proletariat, he says, "is actuated by a realistic instinct which leads it straight to the right goal. . . .

> There is no power now in the world, there is no political nor religious means in existence, which can stop, among the proletariat of any country . . . the drive toward economic emancipation and toward social equality.[21]

To complete their emancipation, they must also overthrow the State, which is the "negation and annihilation of all liberty."[22]

The masses will be in a position to do this when they come into possession of enough scientific knowledge to direct their own affairs entirely in accordance with natural laws, and so can rid themselves of all subservience to man-made impositions. The "wide diffusion of knowledge" Bakunin maintains, "will lead to full freedom." Once the natural laws pertaining to society "have been recognized, first by science and then by means of an extensive system of popular education and instruction, once they have become part and parcel of the general consciousness—the question of liberty will be completely solved."[23]

That it *will* be solved, Bakunin holds to be the inevitable outcome of the whole course of human history, for collective freedom is the goal mankind is destined to achieve—"the goal of the historic progress of humanity."[24] It does not depend upon any choices men are free to make. "The negation of free will," Bakunin declares, "does not connote the negation of freedom. *On the contrary, freedom represents the corollary, the direct result of natural and social necessity.*"[25] This freedom is not freedom for some. It is the *"individual freedom of every man,* [which] *becomes actual and possible only through the collective freedom of society, of which man constitutes a part by virtue of a natural and immutable law."*[26]

[20] *Ibid.*, p. 21.
[21] *Political Philosophy of Bakunin*, p. 202.
[22] *Ibid.*, p. 268.
[23] *Ibid.*, p. 265.
[24] *Ibid.*, p. 268.
[25] *Ibid.*, p. 339.
[26] *Ibid.*, p. 341.

The classic statement by Marx of mankind's march to collective freedom is, of course, the following oft-quoted passage from the *Communist Manifesto*.

> When, in the course of development, class distinctions have disappeared, and all production has been concentrated in the hands of a vast association of the whole nation, the public power will lose its political character. Political power, properly so called, is merely the organized power of one class for oppressing another. If the proletariat during its contest with the bourgeoisie is compelled by the force of circumstances, to organize itself as a class, if, by means of a revolution, it makes itself the ruling class, and, as such, sweeps away by force the old conditions of production, then it will, along with these conditions, have swept away the conditions for the existence of class antagonism, and of classes generally, and will thereby have abolished its own supremacy as a class.[27]

The prediction that the proletariat, who hold the reigns of political and economic power during the first stage of communist revolution, will abolish "its own supremacy as a class" looks toward the time when "the public power will lose its political character" and the state, as we know it, will wither away.

Four years after the publication of the *Manifesto*, Marx in a letter to Weydemeyer says that there is nothing novel in his account of the class struggle throughout history, but that he does claim novelty for his insight that "the class struggle necessarily leads to the *dictatorship of the proletariat*" and that "this dictatorship itself only constitutes the transition to the *abolition of all classes* and to a *classless society*."[28] Later, in 1875, in his *Critique of the Gotha Programme*, he makes clear that such phrases as "People's State" obscure his picture of the transformation which the state will undergo in the successive stages of the communist revolution.

> Between capitalist and communist society lies the period of the revolutionary transformation of the one into the other. There corresponds to this also a political transition period in which the state can be nothing but *the revolutionary dictatorship of the proletariat.*[29]

With the eventual evanescence of that dictatorship, every vestige of the state will itself disappear.

In this letter to Bebel, at about the same time (March 1875), Engels suggests that the word "community" be substituted for the word "state" in describing the classless society of the future.

[27] *Op. cit.*, p. 343.
[28] *Marx-Engels: Selected Correspondence*, p. 57.
[29] *Op. cit.*, p. 18.

The whole talk about the state should be dropped, especially since the Commune, which was no longer a state in the proper sense of the word. The "people's state" has been thrown in our faces by the anarchists too long, although Marx's book against Proudhon and later the *Communist Manifesto* directly declare that with the introduction of the socialist order of society the state will dissolve of itself and disappear. As, therefore, the "state" is only a transitional institution which is used in the struggle, in the revolution, in order to hold down [*niederzuhalten*] one's adversaries by force, it is pure nonsense to talk of a "free people's state"; so long as the proletariat still *uses* the state, it does not use it in the interest of freedom but in order to hold down its adversaries, and as soon as it becomes possible to speak of freedom the state as such ceases to exist. We would therefore propose to replace the word "state" everywhere by the word *Gemeinwesen* [Community], a good old German word which can very well represent the French *commune*.[30]

In another place, Engels points out that, under the conditions of production which obtained in primitive societies, the state did not exist; nor need it exist in the future, *after* the class-structured economy is destroyed by the abolition of private property in the means of production. The state, he writes,

has not existed from all eternity. There have been societies which have managed without it, which had no notion of the state or state power. At a definite stage of economic development, which necessarily involved the cleavage of society into classes, the state became a necessity because of this cleavage. We are now rapidly approaching a stage in the development of production at which the existence of these classes has not only ceased to be a necessity, but becomes a positive hindrance to production. They will fall inevitably as they once arose. The state inevitably falls with them. The society which organizes production anew on the basis of free and equal association of the producers will put the whole state machinery where it will then belong—into the museum of antiquities, next to the spinning wheel and the bronze ax.[31]

And in still another place, Engels explains that the revolutionary act by which private property in the means of production is abolished, and by which its ownership is transferred to the state, does not abolish the state, but only prepares for its withering away.

[30] *Marx-Engels: Selected Correspondence*, pp. 336–37. Cf. *The German Ideology*, pp. 74–75, where it is pointed out that only the classless society is a true community. "The illusory community, in which individuals have up till now combined, always took on an independent existence in relation to them, and was at the same time, since it was the combination of one class over against another, not only completely illusory community, but a new fetter as well."

[31] *Origin of the Family, Private Property, and the State*, p. 158.

The first act in which the state really comes forward as the representative of society as a whole—the taking possession of the means of production in the name of society—is at the same time its last independent act as a state. The interference of the state power in social relations becomes superfluous in one sphere after another, and then ceases of itself. The government of persons is replaced by the administration of things and the direction of the processes of production. The state is not "abolished," *it withers away*.[32]

From this point on, Engels predicts,

men, with full consciousness, will fashion their own history; it is only from this point that the social causes set in motion by men will have, predominantly and in constantly increasing measure, the effects willed by men. *It is humanity's leap from the realm of necessity into the realm of freedom*.[33]

The collective freedom of mankind will then exist for the first time. "To carry through this world-emancipating act is the historical mission of the modern proletariat."[34]

Published a few months after the Russian Revolution of April 1917, Lenin's *The State and Revolution* comments at length on the points we have just examined in the writings of Marx and Engels. In addition to its value as an elucidation of the Marxist doctrine, this commentary reaffirms the prediction of "humanity's leap from the realm of necessity into the realm of freedom" at a still future date. Lenin tells us that the first phase of the revolution, then in process, must not be interpreted as doing more than preparing for it; nor should the achievement of collective freedom, with the withering away of the state, be expected in the immediate future.

In the *Communist Manifesto*, Lenin remarks, it was predicted that, once the proletariat have seized political power and transformed the bourgeois into the proletarian state, "this proletarian state will begin to wither away immediately . . . because the State is unnecessary and cannot exist in a society in which there are no class antagonisms."[35] But what Marx meant, Lenin explains, is merely that the process of withering away begins. Commenting on Engels' letter to Bebel, he insists that there is no difference between Marx and Engels on this point. "Clearly there can be no question of defining the exact moment of the *future* 'withering away'—the more so since it will obviously be a lengthy process."[36]

[32] *Anti-Duhring*, p. 309. "It is from this standpoint," Engels adds, "that we must appraise the phrase 'free people's state'—both its justification at times for agitational purposes, and its ultimate scientific inadequacy—and also the demand of the so-called anarchists that the state should be abolished overnight" (*ibid.*).

[33] *Ibid.*, p. 312. (Italics added.)

[34] *Ibid.*

[35] *Op. cit.*, p. 42.

[36] *Ibid.*, p. 117.

Lenin further explains why it is only the bourgeois state that can be abolished by direct revolutionary action, and why the proletarian state must be allowed to wither away, contrary to the views of the anarchists who call for the immediate abolition of the state in every form.

> According to Engels, the bourgeois state does not "wither away," but is *"abolished"* by the proletariat in the course of the revolution. What withers away after this revolution is the proletarian State or semi-State.[37]

Precisely because "the political form of the 'State' at that time"—*after* the bourgeois state has been overthrown—"is the most complete democracy," the next step in its evolution is to wither away. "Revolution alone can 'abolish' the bourgeois State. The State in general, i.e., the most complete democracy, can only 'wither away.' "[38]

After describing the transition from capitalism to communism and the first phase of communist society under the dictatorship of the proletariat,[39] Lenin comments on what Marx calls "the higher phase of communist society," in which man's collective freedom will begin to exist, for only then will the state have withered away completely.

> For the State to wither away completely, complete Communism is necessary. . . .
>
> Only now can we appreciate to the full the correctness of Engels' remarks in which he mercilessly ridiculed the absurdity of combining the words "freedom" and "State." So long as the State exists there is no freedom. When there will be freedom, there will be no State.[40]

Lenin then tells us that "it will become possible for the State to wither away completely when society adopts the rule: 'From each according to his ability, to each according to his needs,' i.e., when people have become

---

[37] *Ibid.*, p. 28.

[38] *Ibid.*, p. 29. Cf. *ibid.*, p. 33, where Lenin says: "The supercession of the bourgeois State by the proletarian State is impossible without a violent revolution. The abolition of the proletarian State, i.e., of the State in general, is impossible except through the process of 'withering away.' " See also *ibid.*, p. 124, where he declares: "The expression 'the State *withers away*' is very well chosen, for it indicates both the gradual and the spontaneous nature of the process."

[39] See *ibid.*, pp. 120–32.

[40] *Ibid.*, pp. 132–33. "Politically," Lenin says, "the difference between the first, or lower, and the higher phase of Communism will in time, probably, be tremendous; but it would be ridiculous to take cognizance of this difference now, under capitalism, and only individual anarchists, perhaps, could invest it with primary importance (if there still remain people among the anarchists who have learned nothing from the 'Plekhanovite' conversion of the Kropotkins, the Graveses, the Cornelisens, and other 'stars' of anarchism into social-chauvinists or 'anarcho-trenchists')" (*ibid.*, p. 136). Cf. *ibid.*, pp. 147–48, where "Plekhanov's controversy with the anarchists" is discussed.

so accustomed to observing the fundamental rules of social intercourse and when their labour becomes so productive that they will voluntarily work according to their ability."[41] But the withering process begins

> from the moment all members of society, or even only the vast majority, have learned to administer the State *themselves* . . . from this moment the need for government of any kind begins to disappear altogether. . . . The more democratic the "State" which consists of the armed workers, and which is "no longer a State in the proper sense of the word," the more rapidly does *every form* of State begin to wither away.[42]

Once a state of affairs exists in which "*all* have learned to administer and actually do independently administer social production," Lenin predicts that "the *necessity* of observing the simple, fundamental rules of human intercourse will very soon become a *habit*.

> And then the door will be wide open for the transition from the first phase of Communist society to its higher phase, and with it to the complete withering away of the State.[43]

To this prediction, Stalin adds one important qualification. Declaring that "we now have an entirely new Socialist State without precedent in history and differing considerably in form and functions from the Socialist State of the first phase," he says that "development cannot stop there. We are going on ahead towards Communism." And to the question, "Will our State remain in the period of Communism also?" he gives two answers. On the one hand, he says:

> Yes, it will, unless the capitalist encirclement is liquidated, and unless the danger of foreign military attack has been eliminated.

On the other hand, he says:

> No, it will not remain and will wither away if the capitalist encirclement is liquidated, if it is replaced by a Socialist encirclement.

[41] *Ibid.*, p. 134. "From the bourgeois point of view," he adds, "it is easy to declare that such a social order is 'sheer utopia' and to sneer at the Socialists for promising everyone the right to receive from society, without any control over the labour of the individual citizen, any quantity of truffles, automobiles, pianos, etc. . . . Ignorance— for it has never entered the head of any Socialist to 'promise' that the higher phase of the development of Communism will arrive; whereas the great Socialists, in *fore-seeing* that it will arrive, presuppose not the present productivity of labour and *not the present ordinary* run of people. . . . Until the 'higher' phase of Communism arrives, the Socialists demand the *strictest* control of society *and by the State* of the measure of labour and the measure of consumption; but this control must *start* with the expropriation of the capitalists . . ." (*ibid.*, pp. 134–35).
[42] *Ibid.*, pp. 141–42.
[43] *Ibid.*, pp. 142–45.

At present, he concludes, "That is how the question stands with regard to the Socialist State."[44]

The difference of opinion between the Marxists and the anarchists about the way in which collective freedom will be achieved, so far as the elimination of the state is concerned, and the opposite point of view, which is held by Comte, that there is no need or possibility of eliminating the state, constitute a three-sided disagreement in the special controversy about collective freedom. We shall deal with this later in a chapter devoted to the issues in that special controversy. For the present, however, our interest in these differing predictions of the advent of collective freedom is confined to their bearing on the existential issue in the general controversy. We shall try, in the next section, to clarify that issue.

2. FORMULATION OF THE ISSUES

Let us suppose for a moment that the only theory of collective freedom is that advanced by the Marxists. That theory, as we have seen, involves a prediction of the advent of CF with the withering away of the proletarian state *sometime after* the first or lower phase of communist society has been set up under the dictatorship of the proletariat. According to the theory in question, the dictatorship of the proletariat, which abolishes the bourgeois state, is a necessary step toward the attainment of collective freedom.

Hence, we know the Marxist answer to the question, "Will the first phase of the communist revolution inevitably lead to the second; or, in other words, will the strong central government of the socialist state gradually liquidate itself in favor of the stateless community in which men will enjoy collective freedom?"

To the same question, we have relatively explicit evidence that a number of authors would give a negative answer. Far from being inevitable, they would say, it is highly improbable that the dictatorship of the proletariat, once established, will gradually liquidate itself. It is highly improbable, therefore, that collective freedom will ever come into existence in the way predicted by the Marxists. Denying this prediction, or at least challenging the certitude of it, such authors as Mannheim, Salvadori, Joad, Croce, Djilas, and Talmon oppose the Marxists in the existential issue about CF which is raised by the question stated above.

A quite different question frames the existential issue in another way. It is to this question that at least two authors—Berdyaev and Maritain—

[44] *Problems of Leninism*, p. 606.

would give a negative answer. The question, suggested by the kind of attack these authors make, is as follows: "Is collective freedom ever capable of realization on earth and in the course of human history?" The fact that the Marxists, in giving an affirmative answer to this question, would wish to add that it is not merely realizable but *inevitable* only intensifies their opposition to Berdyaev and Maritain.

The foregoing question, it will be noted, is not restricted in its application to the Marxist theory of the attainment of collective freedom, nor even to the specific Marxist version of what constitutes collective freedom when it is attained. It does not ask whether collective freedom, *as envisioned by the Marxists*, is capable of realization on earth and in the course of human history, *through the dictatorship of the proletariat first and, after that, through the withering away of the proletarian state*. It questions the attainability of collective freedom as that is commonly conceived by any author who predicts that mankind will be free when the state in all its historic forms ceases to exist and when men live together under no direction except that derived from the scientifically established laws of nature and of society.

Not only the Marxists but Bakunin, Comte, and perhaps other writers, such as Fourier, Owen, and Saint-Simon (who envision a community in which the administration of things replaces the government of men), can be placed on the affirmative side of the existential issue raised by this question. Hence, in answering it negatively, Berdyaev and Maritain take issue with CF authors generally, and not just with the Marxists, as do Mannheim, Salvadori, Joad, Croce, Djilas, and Talmon.

In a strict sense, as we have already pointed out, it is only the second of the two questions which raises an issue about the future existence of the freedom envisaged by Comte, Bakunin, Marx, Engels, Lenin, and perhaps also a number of other writers such as Saint-Simon, Owen, and Fourier. Nevertheless, for the reasons already given, we shall also present documentary evidence of the existential issue concerning collective freedom in the specifically Marxist version of its inevitable attainment.[45]

We have now formulated the existential issue concerning collective freedom and indicated the parties who are in disagreement about the

---

[45] It may be asked whether the opposition to the Marxist version of CF, which is based entirely on the way that theory predicts its coming to be, can be generalized, so that it can be construed as implying an opposition to other versions of CF, such as that of Bakunin or of Comte. On the face of it, the answer seems to be "no." The opposition so definitely centers on the withering away of the state as a process which the dictatorship of the proletariat will inevitably bring about that it can hardly be extended to cover Bakunin's program of direct anarchistic action to abolish the state at one fell swoop, and much less to cover Comte's prediction that collective freedom will be brought about by the establishment of the positive polity.

attainabilty of CF as a form of freedom; and we have also formulated an existential issue about the Marxist version of CF and indicated the authors who are in opposition. What remains to be done is the formulation of a conceptual issue about CF in the general controversy.

As in the case of other forms of freedom, a conceptual issue about collective freedom would have to turn on the question whether CF, as it is commonly conceived by its adherents, fits the general understanding or the generic idea of freedom. Its adherents obviously think it does, for in every case they assert it to be the only true form of freedom—the only embodiment of human liberty when that is properly understood.

The nearest to an explicit statement which would place an author on the negative side of the conceptual issue is to be found in a passage in Talmon. Maritain's implied contention that the CF authors are attributing to men a freedom which is appropriate to God but not to man may entail the denial that CF, as conceived by its adherents, is properly a human freedom. But this may only, in effect, repeat his denial that, man being what he is, collective freedom will never be attained in the course of human history. If so, it is an existential rather than a conceptual denial, for it does not reject CF conceptions as departing from the meaning of freedom itself. Finally, there is Berdyaev's repeated insistence that the CF conceptions pervert and falsify the SP meaning of freedom. This can be construed as a conceptual attack on collective freedom only in the context of an argument which contends that acquired self-perfection exemplifies the essence of freedom and that anything which is a false conception of freedom, as measured by the standard it sets up, is no conception of freedom at all.

We shall document the views of Talmon, Maritain, and Berdyaev in Section 4 of this chapter, and in that connection we shall also consider the possibility of other conceptual attacks on collective freedom, together with possible rebuttals of such attacks. But first, in the immediately following section, we must examine the documentary evidence of the two existential attacks—the one that denies the future existence of collective freedom, *without regard to the different ways in which its advent is predicted,* and the one that denies *the Marxist prediction of how it will come to be.* In this connection also, we shall consider possible rebuttals of these attacks.

3. EXISTENTIAL ATTACKS

We shall deal first with the denial of the prediction that the state will inevitably wither away, recognizing that this attack applies only to the Marxist version of collective freedom. Doing so will set the stage for examing the two more general denials, to the effect that collective freedom is now attainable by any means within the bounds of man's earthly destiny.

(a) *Attacks on the Marxist theory of man's inevitable attainment of collective freedom.* Many authors express their disbelief that the socialist ideal of complete communism will ever be realized; but since they do not take cognizance of the collective freedom which Marxists associate with communism in its higher or ultimate phase, they do not exemplify the attack with which we are here concerned.

Thus, for example, Hirsch doubts that the dictatorship of the proletariat will ever be self-liquidating, on the basis of the oft-repeated observation that "no man or body of men was or ever will be fit to exercise absolute power." He thinks that "the members of the socialistic bureaucracy must use their power, as men with even less power have used it in the past, for their own advantage." The bureaucrats of the proletarian state not only have political power concentrated in their hands but, together with that, they also "hold in their hands the whole of the wealth of the country." Contrary to the Marxist prediction that the leaders of the revolutionary movement will ultimately dispossess themselves of their extraordinary power, in order to achieve the communist ideal, Hirsch predicts that they will act like ordinary men, striving to perpetuate themselves in power.

> You can make a picture for yourselves of an ideal man whom you will see standing at the top of Socialism, but when he gets there he will not be an ideal—he will be an ordinary man, probably on horseback with a sword in his hand! I say men are human, and, whatever changes you make in society, will desire to leave their children in as good a position or a better one than they have occupied themselves. Therefore, the officials of Socialism will inevitably try to prevent their children from falling into the ranks of the regulated masses, and will endeavor to get their children to be officials as well. . . . Inevitably the officialdom of the socialized State will become an hereditary caste with a despot at the top, who will be either hereditary or elected exclusively by the members of the official class. Then they will lord it over the subject people, reduced to a degrading equality in poverty, and deprived of every vestige of economic and political independence.[46]

[46] *An Analysis of the Proposals and Conceptions of Socialism*, pp. 51–52. It should be noted that the substance of this book consists of lectures delivered in 1904.

Belloc is another author who, writing before the Russian Revolution of 1917, doubts that socialism will ever achieve the full fruition of its theory. In the light of what he knows of the socialist movement up to 1913, he declares: "I cannot believe that theoretical Collectivism, now so plainly failing, will ever inform a real and living society."[47] And Yves Simon, writing at a much later date, sees nothing in the progress of Russian socialism so far to justify the hope, much less the certitude, that the proletarian state will gradually wither away.[48]

Even though Hirsch, Belloc, and Simon do not refer to collective freedom as the objective of the socialist program,[49] their denial that it can or will realize in practice the theoretical or ideal goals it claims to aim at implicitly includes the socialist ideal of freedom. In contrast, the authors to whom we now turn explicitly say that that ideal cannot be, or probably will not be, achieved by the steps laid down in the Marxist plan for moving toward the collective freedom of mankind.

"Not only has the supposedly 'transitional' dictatorship in Soviet Russia not withered away," Mannheim declares, "but we can presuppose that it never would in any social experiment based upon dictatorship."[50] And he continues:

> No established totalitarian régime, whatever its political creed, can be broken from within; it takes an external war to unseat it. It follows that the utopian hopes of the Communists that their dictatorship would gradually fade away are even more visionary than many of their other over-optimistic expectations.[51]

[47] *The Servile State*, p. 188.

[48] See *Community of the Free*, pp. 146–48. "The promise to substitute 'the administration of things for the government of persons,' according to the Saint-Simonist formula (which was taken over by most schools of socialism) admits of two interpretations," he thinks. "It may mean that the sociability of man is concerned exclusively with economic needs: once economic questions are settled by the proper administration of things, man would be delivered to the absolute initiative of his ego and wander without guidance, help, or restraint, in all domains other than the economic. Or it may not exclude higher forms of sociability; but then it implies that social life, insofar as it extends beyond the field of economic relations, does not need to be organized and directed by a temporal power. Both interpretations are contrary to reason and experience. The first is debasing and silly" (*ibid.*, p. 148).

[49] Simon does refer to the claim, which he calls paradoxical, "that state socialism would foster all liberties and carry on the task of emancipation undertaken by the revolutions of the eighteenth century" (*ibid.*, p. 146). The context suggests that the liberties he has in mind are all forms of the freedom of self-realization, not collective freedom as the Marxists conceive it.

[50] *Freedom, Power and Democratic Planning*, p. 27.

[51] *Ibid.*, pp. 27–28.

In Mannheim's opinion, "the only chance for the ideal of freedom to remain relevant in the minds of rulers lies in the continuance of free institutions and their support."[52]

Joad concedes that "communists do not hesitate to admit that the suppression of liberty would follow the success of their efforts," since they also claim "that such a suppression will be temporary only. . . . When the danger of counter-revolution is over and the building up of a classless community is complete, the State will, in Lenin's phrase, 'wither away,' and the restrictions which have been placed upon liberty during the dictatorship of the proletariat will disappear." But Joad asks,

> Is this likely? Does history afford a single example which would permit us to regard it as likely? Have those who have won power by violence ever been known voluntarily to relinquish power, those who have been above criticism voluntarily to permit criticism?[53]

Referring to the "era of liberty . . . predicted by Marx," together with the withering away of the state, Salvadori writes:

> In theory most things are possible. On the basis of historical evidence, however, this optimistic view of the future of communism seems to be based on a number of misconceptions concerning certain fundamentals, particularly (a) the nature of collectivism, (b) the communist ideology, and (c) the influence of political institutions brought into existence by communism.[54]

"It is possible to imagine," Salvadori goes on, "that, having eliminated all opposition and all dissent, communists might put an end to the use of the coercive powers of the state"; but, in his view, "it is highly unlikely that they will ever abandon the instruments required for the total enforcement of the communist will over the citizens."[55] The dictatorship of the proletariat, he thinks, cannot help being a self-perpetuating oligarchy which makes "the 'withering away' of the state . . . out of the question."[56]

[52] *Ibid.*, p. 28.

[53] *Liberty Today*, pp. 81–82. Talmon similarly stresses "the improbability—confirmed by all history—of men in power divesting themselves of power, because they have come to think themselves superfluous." As he sees it, "the hope of the withering away of the State [is] a chimera"; and, in addition, he declares that "the promise of a state of perfect harmonious freedom to come after the total victory of the transitional Revolutionary dictatorship represents a contradiction in terms" (*Rise of Totalitarian Democracy*, pp. 253–54).

[54] *Liberal Democracy*, p. 114.

[55] *Ibid.*, p. 117.

[56] *Ibid.*, p. 118. "If communist societies continue to exist for some time," Salvadori writes, "it is likely that they will evolve the institution of small and closed . . . self-perpetuating oligarchies—politburos or their equivalents—enforcing political tyranny, intellectual dogmatism, and economic monopoly" (*ibid.*).

In his "Note on the History of Communism as Practical Politics," Croce says that

> Marx fabricated a mythology of historical development as essentially eco-
> nomic, leading up to the reign of equality, which for some reason, perhaps
> in conformity to the spirit of this age, he called liberty. . . .[57]

In terms of that mythology, Marx pointed to "a promised land afar off in which classes would have been abolished and there would be no more need of state machinery or coercion, since all would be in the enjoyment of liberty by free association."[58] Before such collective freedom is attained there would have to be a dictatorship of the proletariat, but since this according to Croce, is in the very nature of the case "not temporary but permanent," the promise or prediction of collective freedom will never be fulfilled. The dictatorship itself, Croce remarks, is

> not of the proletariat, but of a technical and political bureaucracy . . .
> a new class, better paid than its subordinates, which educates its successors,
> sending its children to the universities and preparing them to succeed it in
> the public leadership and administration. . . . Of the "reign of liberty"
> prophesied by Marx the very memory has disappeared, and the "withering
> away of the state" is, by tacit agreement, no longer mentioned.[59]

The "new class" to which Croce refers is the central theme of a book by Djilas, who for a time occupied a high post in the Communist government of Yugoslavia. According to Djilas, the bureaucrats who come into power with the revolutionary dictatorship constitute a new class of rulers and owners in whose hands the whole political and economic power of the communist state is concentrated. The extent and self-perpetuating character of that power turn the ideals of the revolution into bitter illusions. The greatest of these illusions, Djilas says,

> was that industrialization and collectivization in the U.S.S.R., and the
> destruction of capitalist ownership, would result in a classless society[60]

and that, with the withering away of the state, mankind would enjoy, as Marx predicted, a "higher level" or "higher form" of freedom.[61] As Djilas views it, "the Communist revolution cannot attain a single one of the ideals named as its motivating force."[62] Nevertheless, he observes, "those who

[57] *My Philosophy*, p. 105.
[58] *Ibid.*, p. 75.
[59] *Ibid.*, p. 76.
[60] *The New Class*, p. 37.
[61] See *ibid.*, p. 8.
[62] *Ibid.*, pp. 30–31. "Everything happened differently in the U.S.S.R. and other Communist countries, from what the leaders—even such prominent ones as Lenin, Stalin, Trotsky, and Bukharin—anticipated" (*ibid.*, p. 37).

carry out the Communist revolution as well as those among the lower echelons persist in their illusions. . . . Despite oppression, despotism, unconcealed confiscations, and privileges of the ruling echelons, some of the people—and especially the Communists—retain the illusions contained in their slogans."[63]

To overcome these illusions, Djilas thinks that it is necessary to understand that "the essential aspect of contemporary Communism is the new class of owners and exploiters,"[64] not just "a temporary dictatorship and an arbitrary bureaucracy."[65] This new class, he writes,

> instinctively feels that national goods are, in fact, its property, and that even the terms "socialist," "social," and "state" property denote a general legal fiction. The new class also thinks that any breach of its totalitarian authority might imperil its ownership. Consequently, the new class opposes any type of freedom, ostensibly for the purpose of preserving "socialist" ownership.[66]

While "property is legally considered social and national property," Djilas maintains that "in actuality, a single group manages it in its own interest." One consequence of this is that

> the discrepancy between legal and actual conditions continuously results in obscure and abnormal social and economic relationships. It also means that the words of the leading group do not correspond to its actions; and that all actions result in strengthening its property holdings and its political position.[67]

The "disharmony between [its] words and actions," shows that the new class is still trying to hold up ideals that its actions belie and make illusory.

> While promising to abolish social differences, it must always increase them by acquiring the products of the nation's workshops and granting privileges to its adherents. It must proclaim loudly its dogma that it is fulfilling its historical mission of "final" liberation of mankind . . . while it acts in exactly the opposite way.[68]

It would be comforting to hope that the new class would come to perceive that

[63] *Ibid.*, p. 30.
[64] *Ibid.*, p. 58.
[65] *Ibid.*, p. 54.
[66] *Ibid.*, p. 65.
[67] *Ibid.*
[68] *Ibid.*, p. 66.

in the near future there cannot be any talk of the withering away of the
state, or talk of a Communist society—in which everyone will work according to his capabilities and will receive according to his needs.[69]

Then, it might also be hoped, it would either

renounce the current means it is using, [or] renounce the idea that its goals
are within sight and real.[70]

But, Djilas thinks, "there is no prospect of such a development . . . in
any of the Communist countries, least of all in the post-Stalin U.S.S.R.";[71]
though he does think that, in the reaction against Stalin, doubts have been
sowed about the means he used and, consequently, about the ends they
were supposed to serve. His fundamental disbelief in the Marxist prediction of the ideal society in which men will be collectively free turns
on the incompatibility with that ideal of the means that Marxists prescribe
for attaining it.

Throughout history there have been no ideal ends which were attained
with non-ideal, inhumane means, just as there has been no free society
which was built by slaves. . . .

If the end must be used to condone the means, there is something in the
end itself, in its reality, which is not worthy. . . .

Thus, by justifying the means because of the end, the end itself becomes
increasingly more distant and unrealistic, while the frightful reality of
the means becomes increasingly obvious and intolerable.[72]

Without access to the current literature in which communist theoreti-
cians may be answering Djilas, or the quite similar attacks of such writers
as Croce, Salvadori, Joad, and Mannheim, we can only imagine what arguments they might use in rebuttal.

For one thing, they would probably point out that the proletarian state
of communism's first phase constitutes so radical a break with all preceding
history that the records of past dictatorships cannot be used to prove that
the dictatorship of the proletariat will not wither away as predicted.

For another thing, they might call attention to the fact that the arguments of their opponents do not lead to the conclusion that the stateless,
classless society and, with it, collective freedom *cannot* or *will not* come
into existence at some future time. The only conclusion to which they
lead is that the predicted event now *appears to be improbable in the near*

[69] *Ibid.*, pp. 159–60.
[70] *Ibid.*, p. 160.
[71] *Ibid.*
[72] *Ibid.*, pp. 162–63.

uture. The evidence which makes it appear to be improbable in the near
future still does not show that the communist ideals are intrinsically unrealizable, nor can it refute the proposition that their realization is inevitable. Their improbability in the foreseeable future is quite consistent with
their inevitability in the full working out of historical necessities.

Finally, attention might be called to the reason which Stalin gave for a
change in the time schedule of the withering away of the state. Even
though every other motion toward communism in its higher phase takes
place in Russian and other Communist countries, the state must remain
in existence until "the capitalist encirclement is liquidated" and "replaced
by a Socialist encirclement."[73] If that change is not foreseeable in the
immediate future, then neither is the withering away of the state. But as
soon as communism is established on an international basis, embracing
all the peoples of the world, then not only will the final step toward
the realization of the ideal society begin to be taken but also the advent
of collective freedom for mankind will become as concretely foreseeable
as it has always been abstractly inevitable.

(b) *Attacks on the attainability of collective freedom within the bounds
of human history*. What is being attacked here, as we have pointed out, is
not simply the Marxist prediction or even the Marxist conception of
collective freedom. It is rather what these opponents regard as the utopian
ideal of collective freedom itself, which, in their view, is incapable of being
realized on earth and in the course of human history. What Berdyaev
and Maritain have to say on this score applies to collective freedom as
conceived and envisioned by Comte and Bakunin as well as to the Marxist
version of it.

Berdyaev explicitly refers to all of the principal CF authors. He frequently links the names of Comte and Marx, sometimes in the company
of Hegel and Rousseau, and sometimes along with references to Saint-
Simon, Proudhon, and Fourier.[74] He speaks of the "boundless freedom,"
which anarchism promises mankind, and specifically mentions "the pro-
grammes of Bakunin and Kropotkin."[75] In all this, he clearly recognizes
diverse conceptions of collective freedom as well as the elements which
they have in common. However, he takes most explicit cognizance of the
Marxist theory of the leap from the realm of necessity into the realm of
freedom and remarks that this theory "gives a new meaning to freedom."[76]

[73] *Problems of Leninism*, p. 606.
[74] See *The Realm of Spirit and the Realm of Caesar*, pp. 78, 107–9, 129; *The
Meaning of History*, pp. 163–64, 188.
[75] *The Meaning of History*, pp. 171–72, 199.
[76] *Origin of Russian Communism*, p. 151. Cf. *ibid.*, p. 148, and *Towards a New
Epoch*, p. 78.

Against the Marxist theory, and especially its prediction of the withering away of the state sometime after the dictatorship of the proletariat, Berdyaev argues in the same way as Djilas, Croce, Salvadori, and others "Socialism will never create either the perfect society or social equality," he declares.

> It may be that the sinful forms of the exploitation of man by man will disappear, or that classes in the sense that they have been created by the capitalist system will be no more. But there will be formed a new, privileged ruling class, a new bureaucracy. . . .[77]

The abolition of private property does not emancipate men, in his view, if it places the ownership of the means of production in the hands of the state, or of the central government which the new bureaucrats control. The power which this gives the state and its officialdom enables them to become the new "tyrants and exploiters."[78]

After summarizing the theory of the state's transformation and eventual disappearance, as presented by Lenin in *The State and Revolution*, Berdyaev writes:

> [Lenin] believed that a compulsory social organization could create any sort of new man you like, for instance, a completely social man who would no longer need the use of force. Marx believed the same thing, that the new man could be manufactured in factories. This was Lenin's utopianism, but it was a utopianism which could be and was realized. One thing he did not foresee; he did not foresee that class oppression might take an entirely different form, quite unlike its capitalist form. The dictatorship of the proletariat, having increased the power of the State, is developing a colossal bureaucracy which spreads like a network over the whole country and brings everything into subjection to itself. This new Soviet bureaucracy is more powerful than that of the Tsarist regime. It is a new privileged class which can exploit the masses pitilessly. . . . Soviet Russia is a country of state capitalism which is capable of exploitation no less than private capitalism. The transitional period may be drawn out indefinitely. Those who are in power in it acquire a taste for power and desire no changes which are unavoidable for the final realization of communism. The will-to-power becomes satisfying in itself and men will fight for it as an end and not as a means.[79]

These things Lenin failed to take into account; and therein, Berdyaev says, "he was particularly utopian and very naive."[80]

[77] *The Realm of Spirit and the Realm of Caesar*, p. 65.
[78] *The Destiny of Man*, p. 217.
[79] *Origin of Russian Communism*, p. 128. See *ibid.*, pp. 125–27.
[80] *Ibid.*, p. 128.

The foregoing observations are specifically directed against the Marxist-Leninist theory. They give Berdyaev's reasons for not believing that the ideal freedom which the communist movement claims as its ultimate fruition will be achieved by a dictatorship that liquidates itself in order to promote the withering away of the state. But the last passage quoted makes two points which are applicable to other conceptions of collective freedom and other theories of how such freedom must and will be attained. One is the charge of illusory utopianism, which Berdyaev in other places brings against Comte and Bakunin as well as against Marx, Engels, and Lenin. The other is the closely related charge that such utopianism rests on a false view of man, not only of what he is but also of what he can become: it envisions the impossible—the creation of a new man, "a completely social man who would no longer need the use of force."

The emergence of a "new class" bars the way to the classless society prophesied by the Marxists; the non-emergence, the unrealizability, of the "new man," on the other hand, gives the lie to the utopian visions of Comte and Bakunin as well as to those of Marx and Engels. With man as he is and as he is destined to be throughout the whole of history, the collective freedom which these utopian visions project is completely illusory. It is absolutely unattainable, i.e., intrinsically, by reason of its incompatibility with the nature of man, and not just because this or that specific program for its achievement is ineffective.

In arguing thus that collective freedom cannot be realized on earth and within the bounds of human history, Berdyaev rests his case ultimately on his Christian faith that perfect or ideal freedom can exist only in the Kingdom of God or the realm of the spirit, not in the secular societies of this world nor in the realm of Caesar. "The social utopia of Marx, no less than that of Fourier" and other exponents of collective freedom, Berdyaev tells us,

contains the idea of a perfect, harmonious state of society, that is, the faith that the realm of Caesar can be such a state. This is a radical error. Only the Kingdom of God, the realm of Spirit, can be perfect and harmonious, not the realm of Caesar. Such a perfect realm is conceivable only eschatologically. A perfect and harmonious order in the realm of Caesar would annihilate freedom, which means that such an order is not attainable in this world.[81]

He maintains that "there can be no perfect society within this 'earthly' scheme of things, and the expectation of such perfection is merely a utopian illusion." And, he continues:

The Realm of Spirit and the Realm of Caesar, p. 177.

It becomes Christians at any rate to believe that the only kingdom which can achieve success is the Kingdom of God. The Kingdom of God is not merely a matter of expectation: it is being founded, its creation is beginning already here and now. [82]

The apostles of collective freedom, according to Berdyaev, confuse "th realm of Caesar and the Kingdom of God, or even [make] them ider tical,"[83] because their secular prophecies spring from doctrines tha have the guise of new religions. Where the Gospel says, "Ye shall know th truth and the truth shall make you free," Berdyaev maintains that th Marxist communists say: "Know the Marxist-communist truth, and it wi make you free. Outside this truth there is no freedom: everything is fals there is only a formal freedom affirmed in capitalist societies."[84] Comt no less than the Marxists, substitutes a pseuo-religion, with its illusor belief in the "new man," for Christianity and its faith in Christ as th savior and emancipator of man as he is. "The totalitarian system c Auguste Comte," he declares, "might be described as Catholicism withou God."[85] And in another place, Berdyaev writes:

Auguste Comte, in fact, desired to establish a positivist religion to which he adapts various forms of the mediaeval Catholic cult. Thus he would have positivist Saints, a positivist calendar, the religious regimentation of life, a hierarchy of scholars, in brief, a revival of Catholicism without God. His system is therefore based upon Catholicism, but he replaces belief in God by that in a Higher Being—mankind. . . .[86]

[82] *The Beginning and the End*, pp. 221–22.

[83] *The Realm of Spirit and the Realm of Caesar*, p. 78. We meet with this "iden fication of the two realms and the two orders," Berdyaev writes, "in Hegel, Mar Auguste Comte, Spann; in communism and in fascism"; and in "democracy Rousseau and the Jacobins [which] was equally monistic and totalitarian" (*ibid.*

[84] *Ibid.*, p. 107. "As a religion," Berdyaev writes, "Marxism is a secularized for of the idea of predestination. The division of history into two parts is another pseud religious trait of Marxism: the period before the socialist or communist revolutic is only an introduction to history; the period after that is only the beginning of tr history. At the basis of the Marxist religion lies a secularized, if sub-consciou chiliasm. Outside this, the whole pathos of Marxism is meaningless. Marxists alwa get angry when Marxist doctrine is called a theology, but they have never been ab to refute this" (*ibid.*, p. 138).

[85] *Ibid.*, pp. 108–9. To understand this reference to Catholicism, it must be remen bered that Berdyaev is as much opposed to what he regards as the totalitarianism Rome and the mediaeval church, as he is to all secular efforts to impose a dogmat version of the "truth that frees." See *Dream and Reality*, pp. 177–78; *Freedom an the Spirit*, pp. 126–29, 133–35, 152–57.

[86] *The Meaning of History*, p. 163. For Berdyaev's similar interpretation of "th Utopian Socialism of Saint-Simon," who, no less than Auguste Comte, held in hig esteem "Joseph de Maistre, who embodied the mediaeval revival of the nineteent century," see *ibid.*, p. 164; and for Berdyaev's treatment of Bakunin and the anarchist

Precisely because, in his view, all secular utopias tend to be totalitarian, Berdyaev thinks that they are "essentially . . . always hostile to freedom."[87]

A utopia always includes a project for the complete totalitarian ordering of life. . . . Totalitarianism always brings slavery with it. The totalitarianism of the Kingdom of God alone is an affirmation of freedom. But totalitarianism in the world of objectivization [i.e., in the secular, social, external order] is always slavery.[88]

The secular utopias of Comte, Bakunin, and the Marxists are all imbued with a "messianic . . . striving for the Kingdom of God on earth, although without any belief in God."[89] They all involve a "doctrine of progress" which, in Berdyaev's opinion, "has not the slightest scientific, philosophical or moral justification. The doctrine of progress," he insists, "is bound to be a religious faith, since there can be no positive science of progress. . . . This was the faith of Comte, Hegel, Spencer, and Marx."[90]

It is in these terms that Berdyaev reiterates once more his charge that the apostles of collective freedom have confused the realm of Caesar with the realm of Spirit, or the Kingdom of God. "Closely connected with the doctrine of progress," he tells us, is "the Utopia of terrestrial paradise and beatitude," which is "nothing more than a perversion and distortion of the religious faith in the coming of the Kingdom of God on earth. . . . It asserts that the entire historical process has no other function than the preparation for this beatitude." The root of falsehood in such secular prophecies of a "new man" and a "new heaven" on earth lies in the fact that

the Utopia of terrestrial paradise implies an absolute humanity within the transitory relations of terrestrial history.

as also trying to break "the bonds of history" and to realize "the boundless freedom" of the Kingdom of God "within the historical process itself," see *ibid.*, pp. 171–72, 198–99.

[87] *The Realm of Spirit and the Realm of Caesar*, p. 175.
[88] *Slavery and Freedom*, p. 206.
[89] *The Realm of Spirit and the Realm of Caesar*, p. 73. "The philosophy of history taught by Hegel, Marx and Auguste Comte," Berdyaev writes, "is permeated with this messianic and prophetic fervour. When history is divided into three periods, and the last is considered as the beginning of perfection, this always means secularized messianism. . . . The enthusiasm in Marxism comes from the messianic idea of the proletariat, of a liberated humanity. All the qualities of the chosen people of God are transferred to the proletariat. . . . The idea of the proletariat, which does not at all correspond with the real empirical proletariat, is a mystic-messianic idea" (*ibid.*, pp. 129–30).
[90] *The Meaning of History*, pp. 187–88.

But, Berdyaev insists,

> there is no room in terrestrial reality, by its nature strictly confined and
> limited, for an absolute life. Yet the Utopia theory asserts that what has
> been impossible until now will not be so always, that an absolute and con-
> clusive state will sooner or later crown historical relations. It affirms, not
> a transition from limited historical relations to some other plane of be-
> ing . . . but a fourth dimension of absolute life within the very framework of
> three dimensional space. In this lies its fundamental metaphysical antithesis
> and essential instability. Instead of seeing absolute life as the transition
> from terrestrial to celestial history, it presupposes an ultimate solution of
> human destiny within the framework of terrestrial relations, a final inte-
> gration of the three-dimensional world. It desires to humanize that absolute
> perfection and beatitude which can only be attained in the celestial
> reality and only contained in the fourth dimension.[91]

Like Berdyaev, Maritain criticizes the pseudo-religious fantasy that
underlies the messianic prophecy of collective freedom, and, like Berdyaev,
he does so from the point of view of his own religious faith. That he differs
from Berdyaev in the version of Christianity which he expouses does not
matter here; nor does it matter that, unlike Berdyaev, he concentrates his
attack on the Marxist version of collective freedom and its coming-to-be.
Since the crux of his argument, like that of Berdyaev, lies in his denial of
the "new man" who will arise and the "heaven on earth" which will be
created within the bounds of history, it applies to Comte and Bakunin as
well as to Marx.

As Maritain interprets the Marxist doctrine, it prophesies the coming of
the Kingdom of God on earth and the redemption of man, his emancipation from bondage—all to be achieved by the collectivist utopia. "Socialised
man, at the end of this development," he writes, "will be absolute master
of history and the universe."[92] The creator of this new man, and the
mediator of this redemption, is not God, but the proletariat. "If the
theory of the class-war appeared to Marx as a revelation," Maritain says, it
was because, as he conceived it, it essentially implies this element of
Messianism.

> The proletariat is not only free of the original sin of the exploitation of
> man by man; precisely because it has been stripped of everything, because
> it is in the lowest place in history, it is the bearer of human liberation, the
> messianic victim whose triumph will be the final victory over all that op-
> presses humanity, a resurrection, as it were, from the dead. Berdyaev likes
> to point out the presence of this eschatological element in the thought of
> revolutionary communism. . . . In the womb of history will take place the

[91] *Ibid.*, pp. 191–92.
[92] *True Humanism*, p. 44.

advent of a total and final deliverance, which will cut time in two. The step will be taken—from the kingdom of necessity to that of liberty.[93]

Because of the role it assigns to the proletariat, according to Maritain, the Marxist metaphysic itself is no momentary superstructure. . . . It is bound immanent and alive, incarnate in the proletariat and its action. Thus, after the great day of universal revolution,

> we shall see metaphysical and "mystical" values, those for example which are expressed by the words justice and liberty . . . reappear with an almost infinite plenitude of reality and rectitude: for then they will . . . be *lived* in a complete, an integral immanence through and by humanity, in the practical life of humanity liberated by the proletariat.[94]

Here we see "a contradiction which is often pointed out in Marxism: on the one hand, the fundamental process which it recognises, the dialectic process, must needs be a movement which is endless; yet, on the other hand, revolutionary dynamism has its object and aim in a communist society which will mark the end of 'the quarrel between man and nature and between man and man' and the *final* triumph of man over his destiny." It is this second aspect which Maritain thinks is the stronger and which, overcoming the Hegelian logic of perpetual becoming, aims at "the Kingdom of God *in* history, as a part of history."[95] Hence, Marxism,

> despite the theoretic exigencies of its dialectic . . . sees as finally issuing from the conflicts of history a communist humanity which truly seems like the end of history, and in which all things will be reconciled as in the Word of God. . . . The process of this dialectic ends in the Kingdom of God . . . but it is a secularised Kingdom of God, which while bringing history to an end, yet remains *in and a part of* history, realised in terms of the *time of this world*.[96]

[93] *Ibid*. "God is absolutely rejected on principle, in virtue of an absolute metaphysical dogmatism . . . and this in the name of the historical dynamism of the social collectivity, in the name of the collective or collectivised man, in whom and through whom human nature will find its fulfillment. And at the same time, and as a necessary consequence, a social conception imposes itself which can be no other . . than a monism of collective humanity. This," according to Maritain, "is what gives to communism not the value of a relative economic solution, but rather that of an absolute historical exigency, necessary with a metaphysical necessity, by reason of which man raised to the fulness of his social and political life, the collective man who is the truth of man and in whom liberty will finally come to flower, will integrate in an absolute fashion into his being the individual human personality which was hitherto only a transient phase of its dialectic and subject to the play of heteronymous forces" (*ibid*., p. 45).
[94] *Ibid*., pp. 46–47.
[95] *Ibid*., p. 47.
[96] *Ibid*., pp. 51–52.

The Christian is saved from such utopian illusions by his hope for a beatitude that lies beyond the time of this world and his faith in a perfect freedom that cannot be realized in history. From the Christian's point of view, Maritain declares,

> it is a betrayal at once of man and of God not to understand that history is a movement towards the Kingdom of God and not to wish for the coming of that Kingdom. But it is absurd to think that it will come *in and as a part* of history, where good and evil are inextricably intertwined. Prepared by the growth of history, and by the progressive mixing and refining of the human being that it involves, it will come *at the end* of history, at that hour of the resurrection of the dead to which all history leads.[97]

While criticizing the vision of the Marxists, Maritain is not without a revolutionary vision of his own—his concrete historical ideal of a "new Christendom"—a classless society which, he says, assumes "the liquidation of the capitalist regime . . . as a preliminary."[98] In another place, he writes

> The society of which we speak would in effect be a society *sans classes*, that is to say one in which the distinctions between classes which have been heretofore observed in our Western civilisation would have disappeared. . . .[99]

But this "is conceivable only after the dissolution of capitalist society."[100] To this extent, Maritain as a Thomist expresses his sympathy with the Marxist's objectives. "As much as Karl Marx," he tells us,

> St. Thomas is cognizant of the humiliation inflicted on man by what Marx calls the alienation of work for the profit of another, and which St. Thomas called more simply servitude. As much as Marx, he renders intelligible this desire which possesses us, this nostalgia for a state where human work would be liberated and all servitude abolished.[101]

But, unlike the Marxists, Maritain maintains that

> this will not be accomplished by a quick change and a messianic revolution abolishing private property, but by better and more human arrangements of private property.[102]

[97] *Ibid.*, p. 52. For Maritain's contrast between what he calls "a concrete historical ideal" and the socialist utopia, see *ibid.*, pp. 122–25.

[98] *Ibid.*, p. 194. Cf. *ibid.*, pp. 184 ff. Berdyaev also envisions a better society in the future—also a classless society produced by what he calls the Christian form of "personal socialism," in contrast to the communist form of "collective socialism." He, too, looks for the liquidation of capitalism. See *Slavery and Freedom*, pp. 181–89 esp. 185, and 215–19.

[99] *Freedom in the Modern World*, pp. 57–58.

[100] *Ibid.*, p. 56.

[101] *Scholasticism and Politics*, pp. 139–40.

[102] *Ibid.*, p. 140.

The most important difference here, however, is that Maritain does not expect servitude to be completely eliminated from human life and human society within the bounds of human history.

> This [complete] liberation, that is, every form and modality of servitude, of service to another for the peculiar or private good of another, would be abolished for all men *only at the termination of the movement of human history.*[103]

Just as the Christian does not hope for the Kingdom of God on earth, neither does he expect perfect social freedom to be realized within the scope of man's historical development.

We have now examined the attack on collective freedom in general by two authors both of whom argue, from the Christian point of view, that, man being what he is, such freedom is intrinsically incapable of realization in the whole course of human history.[104] We cannot cite any actual rebuttals of these arguments. There may be no followers of Comte and Bakunin who have taken account of the opinions of Berdyaev and Maritain on this subject; nor do we know of any contemporary Marxists who have. It may even be the case that exponents of collective freedom, in any of its principal versions, would not take these attacks seriously, because they rest on religious dogmas which Comte, Bakunin, Marx, and their disciples dismiss as superstitions or as ecclesiastical impositions which serve the purposes of the ruling class.

However, there is one premise in the arguments of Berdyaev and Maritain which would be asserted by them as a matter of fact and which might, therefore, elicit efforts at rebuttal from the adherents of collective freedom, certainly from the Marxists if not from Comte and Bakunin. That is the proposition about man's nature.

According to both Berdyaev and Maritain, it is the finiteness of man and the irremediable imperfection of his nature which make collective freedom intrinsically unrealizable in human life, no matter what institutional developments the future course of human history holds in store. As Berdyaev says, human nature is such that there never will be "a completely social man who would no longer need the use of force," the elimination of

---

[103] *Ibid.* (Italics added.)
[104] This argument finds an echo in the conservative point of view represented by Russell Kirk. He refers to the freedom which the Marxists predict will come into existence after the withering away of the state. See *The American Cause*, pp. 97–98. But in his judgment the ideal of communism "is an illusion; in its 'true' or 'pure' form, it never can be established among men." What "triumphant Communists" bring about when they succeed "is not the promised Heaven upon Earth—which is impossible— but a very real Hell upon Earth" (*ibid.*, p. 131).

which is an essential trait of the collective freedom envisioned by Comte, Bakunin, Marx, and Engels. The utopian illusion of collective freedom, as Maritain sees it, calls for a form of liberty "with an almost infinite plenitude of reality and rectitude," which is utterly beyond the attainment of finite men.

Furthermore, for both Berdyaev and Maritain, human nature is a constant and unchangeable factor in human history. The shape which human institutions and social arrangements will take in the future, as the shape they have taken in the past, is determined by unalterable elements in the nature of man—his needs and his aspirations, together with his weaknesses and limited powers.[105] But it is precisely this view of human nature as a fixed, anterior, and determining cause of human institutions, social arrangements, and all historical developments of human life on earth, which the Marxists challenge and explicitly repudiate.

From their point of view, it is the other way around. The features of man's social environment, the institutions and arrangements under which man lives in any epoch, not only condition human life but also determine the traits which man exhibits under these conditions. History determines man, not man history.[106] What man is in any epoch reflects the determining influence of historical forces and the conditioning effect of the social and economic organization then in existence. Hence, it is invalid to argue from the shape human nature has taken so far in history to the conclusion that collective freedom is unattainable by man. The "new man" required for the realization of such freedom will be the product of history's future course when it brings into existence the "new society" predicted by the CF authors.

Here, then, is a possible argument in rebuttal, and one which is based on actual views held by the collective-freedom authors concerning the conditioning of human nature by the social environment. Marx maintains that "by . . . acting on the external world and changing it, [man] at the same time changes his own nature";[107] and in his theses against

---

[105] That such different philosophers as Aristotle and Hobbes take this view, and that they hold it as a matter of philosophical conviction and not as a consequence of religious faith, shows that this premise in the argument of Berdyaev and Maritain is at least capable of being divorced from Christian dogmas, whether or not Berdyaev and Maritain would regard it as adequately stated out of that context.

[106] In one place, Maritain recognizes this basic tenet in the Marxist doctrine, but nevertheless insists that "man, in Marx's eyes, is not a *passive* product of his surroundings: he is active, he acts on his surroundings to transform them," though he is "*in a sense determined by* economic and social evolution" (*True Humanism*, p. 123).

[107] *Capital*, Vol. I, Part III, Ch. VII, Sect. I, p. 198. In another place, Marx writes: "It is not the consciousness of men that determines their existence, but, on the contrary, their social existence determines their consciousness" (*Critique of Political Economy*, pp. 11–12).

Feuerbach he declares: "The human essence is no abstraction inherent in each single individual. In its reality, it is the *ensemble* of social relations."[108] In Bakunin, we find an even more emphatic declaration that "every child, youth, adult, and even the most mature man is *wholly* the product of the environment that nourished and raised him—an inevitable, involuntary, and consequently irresponsible product."[109] And Comte explicitly expresses the view that the characteristics of man evolve according to a necessary law of progress from one stage of culture to another: "theological man" and "metaphysical man" will inevitably be supplanted by "scientific man" with the dawn of the positive polity.[110]

In these passages, we can see the outlines of a possible debate concerning the future existence of collective freedom, in which the bone of contention is the nature of man.

4. CONCEPTUAL ATTACKS

As we have already pointed out, only three authors provide us with anything that can be construed as a challenge to the conceptual validity of collective freedom.[111] None of these explicitly argues that a freedom which is conceived as involving voluntary acquiescence in the natural and social necessities discovered by science does not conform to the idea of freedom or express an acceptable meaning of the term.

We have already examined conceptual denials of the SP form of freedom which contend that to give the name "freedom" to a voluntary submission to laws of any kind is a travesty of the term.[112] This contention applies to collective freedom insofar as, being a variant of acquired self-perfection, it also involves submission to law (in this case to the scientifically established laws of nature and society, not moral or juridical laws). A number of the self-realization authors who take the negative side of the conceptual issue about the freedom of self-perfection might, therefore, take the negative side of the conceptual issue about collective freedom, *if they were to take cognizance of CF as a variant of SP.* But none satisfies this condition.

---

[108] Appendix to Engels' *Ludwig Feuerbach*, pp. 83–84.

[109] *The Political Philosophy of Bakunin*, p. 153. (Italics added.) Cf. *ibid.*, pp. 153–69.

[110] *Positive Philosophy*, pp. 25–28. Unlike Bakunin and the Marxists, Comte affirms the immutability of the human essence, though he maintains that the fixed potentialities of human nature are realized in three successive stages, of which the last is, in a sense, the most religious, because the ultimate religion is the religion of Mankind. Religion in the traditional sense, of course, belongs only to the "theological stage" of human development.

[111] See pp. 199–200, *supra*.

[112] See Ch. 5, *supra*.

And of the three authors who do criticize collective freedom, two—Berdyaev and Maritain—are themselves exponents of the SP form of freedom, and so they would hardly argue in this way.

The third of these authors, Talmon, flatly says that what the CF authors offer in the name of a perfect or ideal liberty for mankind is utterly devoid of meaning, so far as the common understanding of freedom is concerned. In one place, where he seems to have the Marxist version of collective freedom in mind, he writes:

> The promise of a state of perfect harmonious freedom to come after the total victory of the transitional Revolutionary dictatorship represents a contradiction in terms. . . . Liberty will be offered when there will be nobody to oppose or differ—in other words, when it will no longer be of use. *Freedom has no meaning, without the right to oppose and the possibility to differ.*[113]

But in another place, Talmon makes the same point in a way that appears to be applicable to other versions of collective freedom as well. Here he says:

> Liberty has . . . no meaning without freedom to oppose and without there being anybody to oppose. The vision of an unfettered freedom at the end of the days, and the prophecy of the cessation of the conflict between freedom and duty, in spontaneous obedience without a sense of constraint, turns out to be a fiction. . . .[114]

In other words, the fact that conceptions of collective freedom envisage men as being free in a void, created by the removal of all external and internal opposition, renders these conceptions vacuous or empty of meaning.

Since the generic sense of freedom involves some opposition between self and other, Talmon's criticism of collective freedom appears to be grounded, as are conceptual attacks on other forms of freedom, in the generic meaning of the term.

Another possible attack, which Talmon does not employ, would call attention to the fact that collective freedom is attributed to mankind as a whole, and it would then ask whether humanity is the self that functions as the principle of freedom in this case. If not, in the agency of what self does the freedom inhere?

Let us regard the foregoing double-barreled attack—in terms of both the self and the other—as indicating at least a possible argument on the

[113] *The Rise of Totalitarian Democracy*, pp. 253–54.
[114] *Ibid.*, p. 138. However, it should be noted that this passage is found in a chapter entitled "The Jacobin Improvisation."

negative side of the conceptual issue about collective freedom. How might such an argument be rebutted by those who take the affirmative side of this issue? With regard to the self that is the principle of freedom in the case of CF, its defenders might remind us that, while the form of freedom which they affirm as the only true embodiment of the idea is *collectively* achieved, it is *individually* enjoyed. Individual men will enjoy perfect liberty when mankind is collectively free. In fact, the individual person can be free only when every other person enjoys a corresponding and equal freedom under that ideal mode of association "in which," to use the words of Marx, "the free development of each is the condition for the free development of all."[115] Hence, it might be said that only through a misunderstanding of collective freedom can it be charged that it does not envisage the individual self as a free agent.

The point about the absence of opposition also represents a misunderstanding. The social environment, in all its historic forms or stages *until* the ultimate phase of mankind's historical development is reached, constitutes the *enslaving other* from which men are emancipated when they are collectively free. Hence, it might be pointed out that it is a misunderstanding of the generic idea of freedom on Talmon's part to suppose that struggle against opposing forces must be present when freedom is completely achieved. It cannot be achieved without such struggle, but neither can it be achieved to the full and perfectly enjoyed unless the opposing other is completely overcome or removed. Hence, the defenders of collective freedom might conclude that this part of the argument against their conception is as unfounded as the part which has to do with the self.

In the foregoing argument, by way of rebuttal, one point is made which leads to another attack on the CF conception of freedom. It concerns the perfection, completeness, or even absoluteness which the argument claims for collective freedom by asserting that when such freedom is fully achieved by mankind, no opposing other will remain in existence.

No claim of this sort is made by the adherents of the freedom of self-realization; they recognize that no man can ever do entirely as he wishes, for he is never wholly exempt from interference by, or the threat of, adverse circumstances. Nor do most of the adherents of the freedom of self-perfection claim that even the wisest or most virtuous of men so completely possesses the power to will as he ought that he need make no further effort to overcome inclinations to the contrary.

[115] *The Communist Manifesto*, p. 343. Cf. Bakunin's statement that he is advocating "*the conquest and accomplishment of the full freedom and full development, material, intellectual and moral, of every individual, by the absolutely free and spontaneous organisation of economic and social solidarity as completely as possible between all human beings living on the earth*" (*Marxism, Freedom and the State*, p. 22); and see also *Oeuvres*, Vol. I, pp. 143–44.

In avoiding such claims, both groups of authors, it can be argued, are acknowledging the limited character of the freedom they attribute to man —a finiteness or imperfection that is proportionate to the finiteness and imperfection of human beings. Man is not God, earth is not Heaven, and it is, therefore, a misconception of human freedom to give it attributes which are appropriate only to divine liberty or to the freedom of the saints who are gathered to the bosom of God.

The argument just suggested is, of course, implied in the criticism which Berdyaev and Maritain level against collective freedom as envisioning the Kingdom of God achieved on earth and by earthly means. It is somewhat more explicitly contained in Berdyaev's description of CF as a "boundless freedom,"[116] and in his statement that it tries to "humanize that absolute perfection and beatitude which can only be attained in the celestial reality."[117] What Maritain calls the "freedom of exultation," the perfect freedom of autonomy which is the joy of the blessed in Heaven, is vouchsafed "socialized man" on earth in the Marxist vision of the future.

The critical point here is not only that this "new man" and the social conditions peculiar to collective freedom will never exist but also that it is a divine, and not a human, freedom which socialized man, according to Maritain, will supposedly enjoy when he becomes "the absolute master of history and the universe."[118] The CF authors thus deify man and divinize man's freedom when, "in the place of that real though impeded freedom" which man has in struggling to mold history and his social environment to a pattern more in accord with his aspirations, they seek "for an illusory freedom which is infinitely more ambitious"—the freedom of man "become the God of history, exercising an absolute sovereignty."[119]

To this attack, the CF authors might reply as we have imagined them replying to the existential attack which denies the attainability of collective freedom on the ground that the "new man" or the "heaven on earth" it envisages cannot be produced within the course of historical time. From their point of view, the distinction between the human and the divine, or between earth and heaven, simply begs the question. It assumes the very point which the CF authors deny, namely, that the limitations of human nature and the imperfections of human life are unalterably fixed rather than merely relative to historical conditions as they have so far existed. When these conditions are transcended, man will transcend the limitations under which he has suffered, and human life will be rid of its imperfections.

---

[116] *Meaning of History*, pp. 199–200.
[117] *Ibid.*, p. 192.
[118] *True Humanism*, p. 44.
[119] *Ibid.*, p. 125.

If this is tantamount to saying that men will be as free as gods, what of it? Throughout history, man has been making God in his own idealized image. In history's ultimate consummation, man will become what he has imagined God to be, for, at long last, he will have realized in truth the ideal he falsely projected in his religious fantasies. Human freedom will then be absolute. It is, therefore, no argument against the conception of collective freedom to say that it does not conform to notions about freedom which have had a specious appeal under the enslaving conditions of past and present, especially to those who have found comfort in the illusions foisted on them by the traditional religions. These notions of freedom are the illusory ones, not the conceptions of collective freedom, which represent the only true and perfect embodiment of the idea.

If the CF authors would dismiss as question begging the argument that collective freedom fails to conform, not to the idea of freedom but to mistaken notions of what human freedom must be, how much more irrelevant and presumptuous in their eyes would be Berdyaev's charge that any conception which tries to "objectivize" the freedom of self-perfection falsifies that freedom. For Berdyaev to assert that his own theory of freedom contains the only true conception of it is hardly an argument against collective freedom or, for that matter, against any other conception of it that Berdyaev does not happen to hold.

Three points must be noted about Berdyaev's theory of freedom. First, it includes two conceptions which can be classified as affirmations of man's natural freedom of self-determination and of his acquired freedom of self-perfection.[120] Second, man's freedom of self-perfection cannot be acquired without God's grace: God is freedom and the source of freedom;[121] "apart from Christianity there is no freedom."[122] Third, the freedom of self-perfection is essentially *personal in form*: it is entirely a matter of man's inner and spiritual life; it can neither be increased nor diminished by changes in the external world of objects; it is in no way affected by natural or social forces.[123]

It is the third point which leads Berdyaev to criticize all conceptions of the freedom of self-perfection which treat this freedom as essentially *social*

---

[120] See *Freedom and the Spirit*, pp. 125–33; *The Destiny of Man*, pp. 79–80; *Dream and Reality*, pp. 52–53.

[121] See *The Realm of Spirit and the Realm of Caesar*, p. 41; *Freedom and the Spirit*, pp. 136–41.

[122] *Freedom and the Spirit*, p. 121.

[123] See *The Realm of Spirit and the Realm of Caesar*, p. 42; and *The Fate of Man in the Modern World*, pp. 40–41; and *Towards a New Epoch*, pp. 74, 84; though in *Freedom and the Spirit*, pp. 155–57, Berdyaev asserts that the realization of the Kingdom of God in Christendom will be required to save us from the tyranny of the powers of this world.

in form. His criticism applies to the SP conceptions advanced by Rousseau and Hegel, just as much as it applies to the CF conceptions held by Comte, Bakunin, and Marx, whom, as we have seen, Berdyaev affiliates with Hegel and Rousseau.[124] In his view, all these writers, by trying to make the freedom of self-perfection social in form and thus externalizing it, distort the "true freedom of personality [which] has a spiritual rather than a social origin . . . [and] is rooted in the spiritual rather than the social world."[125] In Hegel and Rousseau, as well as in Comte, Bakunin, and Marx, there is "a tendency . . . to aim at absolute objectification, to arrive at a finally objectified and socialized spirit." But, according to Berdyaev, "spirit is freedom" and "the objectification of spirit is therefore a violation of spirit," which leads to the very opposite of freedom.[126]

Berdyaev's position with respect to the personal as opposed to the social form of the freedom of self-perfection aligns him with the Stoics and with Kant against Rousseau and Hegel in an issue which belongs to the special controversy about SP. This issue has been foreshadowed in our earlier account of basic differences of opinion about the form in which self-perfection should be conceived.[127] Here we are concerned only with the application of Berdyaev's point to collective freedom, and, more specifically, with its relevance to the conceptual issue about that freedom in the general controversy.

It is true that collective freedom, as a variant of SP, has an affinity with Rousseau's and Hegel's conception of self-perfection as essentially social in form, an affinity it does not have with the Stoic, Christian, or Kantian conceptions of it as personal in form. Hence, reasons which were advanced against a socialized freedom of self-perfection could also be used to support an argument against collective freedom. But Berdyaev does not offer such reasons. He merely asserts that man's freedom of self-perfection must be purely personal in form. The CF authors would need do no more than point this out, were they to take cognizance of Berdyaev's criticism of their views.

[124] See p. 41, on pp. 209–10, *supra*.

[125] *The Fate of Man in the Modern World*, p. 35. Cf. *The Destiny of Man*, pp. 159–60. For the same reason, Berdyaev even insists upon a personalist, as opposed to a collectivist, form of socialism. See *Slavery and Freedom*, pp. 208–11; *Spirit and Reality*, pp. 115–16.

[126] *Spirit and Reality*, p. 59. Cf. *Freedom and the Spirit*, pp. 133–34.

[127] See Ch. 16, on the forms of self-perfection, in Vol. I, esp. Sect. 2, pp. 291–306.

Chapter 8

INTRODUCTION TO THE ISSUES
CONCERNING THE FREEDOM
OF SELF-DETERMINATION

Three things distinguish this subject from all others in the general controversy: (1) the large number of authors who dispute the existence of natural self-determination or question its genuineness as a kind of freedom; (2) the extent to which the literature affords evidence of actual debates or at least direct interchanges between authors who take explicit cognizance of each other's views and respond to each other's arguments; and (3) the fact that the differences of opinion are such that we must formulate at least four distinct issues in this part of the controversy.

What is traditionally called "the problem of free will" concerns questions about the existence or genuineness of natural self-determination as a kind of freedom. In the extensive literature on this subject, these are the questions which loom largest and which have received the greatest attention, especially in the last three hundred years. The number of authors who deny natural self-determination, either on existential or on conceptual grounds or on both, matches, if it does not exceed, the number of those who affirm this freedom. In almost every case, that denial is quite explicit. The writers who take a negative stand do so quite plainly, taking cognizance of the subject in question and addressing themselves to the disputed questions about it. In addition, they usually give us some indication of their reasons and often advance fairly elaborate arguments.

In none of the preceding four chapters have we found a single instance of direct confrontation on the part of writers whom we have construed as joining issue and advancing arguments relevant to the issue. In a few instances, we observed that some of the authors on the negative side mention by name adherents of the position they oppose. But in no instance do those writers respond directly to the attack or engage in any interchange with their opponents.[1] It is only in regard to natural self-determination

---

[1] See, for example, Ch. 4, pp. 50–51, *supra.*, where it is pointed out that, in the controversy about circumstantial self-realization, Bosanquet, taking the negative side, mentions Bentham, J. S. Mill, and Spencer on the affirmative side, while on the affirmative side Hobhouse, Laski, and B. Russell refer to Rousseau and Hegel as

that we can report a number of actual disputes in the form of written interchanges between writers who take opposite sides of one or another of the issues in the general controversy about this freedom. To name only the most prominent instances of this sort, there are the Hobbes-Bramhall dispute in the seventeenth century, the Priestley-Price dispute in the eighteenth century, the interchange in the nineteenth century between Mansel and Mill occasioned by Mill's critique of Sir William Hamilton's views, and the interchanges which have been going on in recent years between such writers as Campbell, H. D. Lewis, MacLagan, and L. J. Russell, on the one hand, and such writers as Nowell-Smith, Bradley, Ross, and Hobart, on the other.

The general controversy about natural self-determination involves more issues than does the general controversy about the other kinds of freedom. In the other cases we dealt at most with two issues, one existential and one conceptual. But here it is necessary to formulate three distinct issues concerning the existence of natural self-determination, because of differences in the grounds on which this freedom is denied.[2] Taken together with one conceptual issue, there are four issues to be dealt with here.

We shall treat each of these issues in a separate chapter. In preparation for the four chapters to follow, this introductory chapter will be devoted to a number of preliminary clarifications. It will be helpful, first of all, to have before us a brief summary of the main points shared by the self-determination authors, together with some indication of the principal differences which divide them and determine where they stand on the several issues in this controversy. Then we shall formulate the four issues in the following order: first, the two basic existential issues; second, a subordinate existential issue; and third, the conceptual issue. Finally, we shall, in a series of tables, name the authors whom we shall treat as parties to one or more of these issues and give some indication of the procedure we shall follow in the succeeding chapters.

---

taking the view they oppose. In addition, see *ibid.*, pp. 83 ff., *supra*. Here are attacks on Bosanquet by MacIver, Hobhouse, and Laski. But nowhere in that chapter is there a single pair of authors who directly confront each other in argument. The situation is very much the same in the case of the controversy about acquired self-perfection.

[2] Each of these existential issues will align different groups of authors on its opposite sides, for not only do the opponents of natural self-determination divide according to the grounds on which they attack it but the exponents of it also differ in their defense of it.

1. SUMMARY OF THE TOPICAL AGREEMENT ABOUT SELF-DETERMINATION

We have employed the following descriptive formula to summarize the understanding of self-determination that is shared by authors who affirm man's possession of such freedom. They regard it, we have said, as "a freedom which is possessed by all men, in virtue of a power inherent in human nature, whereby a man is able to change his own character creatively by deciding for himself what he shall do or shall become."[3]

We have further explained that "being able to change one's own character creatively by deciding for one's self what one shall do or shall become" expresses the topical agreement about self-determination only when at least two of the three following points are affirmed:

(i) that the decision is *intrinsically unpredictable*,
i.e., given perfect knowledge of all relevant causes, the decision cannot be foreseen or predicted with certitude;

(ii) that the decision is *not necessitated*,
i.e., the decision is always one of a number of alternative possible decisions any one of which it was simultaneously within the power of the self to cause, no matter what other antecedent or concurrent factors exercise a causal influence on the making of the decision;

(iii) that the decision flows from the *causal initiative of the self*,
i.e., on the plane of natural or finite causes, the self is the uncaused cause of the decision it makes.[4]

These three points, as we shall see, generate three distinct existential issues about man's natural freedom of self-determination. Writers who deny (iii) that, on the plane of natural or finite causes, there are any uncaused causes deny, in consequence, the existence of a freedom the conception of which posits such causes. Writers who deny (ii) that an effect can be caused in a manner which does not necessitate it deny, in consequence, the existence of a freedom the conception of which attributes to the self the power of causing but not necessitating the decisions it makes. The existence of self-determination is also denied by writers who claim (i) that God's omniscience excludes a freedom the conception of which involves the intrinsic unpredictability of decisions that are the product of man's power of self-determination.

[3] See Ch. 1, pp. 6–7, *supra*.
[4] See *ibid.*, p. 7, *supra*.

Among the opponents of SD, there are some who reject it on only one of the grounds indicated above; some who reject it on two; and some on all three. This fact alone would require us to formulate three distinct existential issues. The situation is further complicated by the parallel fact that not all adherents of SD hold conceptions of it which place them on the affirmative side of each of these issues. Some, for example, do not conceive the self as the uncaused cause of the decisions it makes;[5] and some do not regard the decisions the self makes as being intrinsically unpredictable.[6] On the contrary, these authors appear to agree with writers who maintain that there are no uncaused causes or that nothing is unforeseeable by an omniscient deity. Should they, then, be aligned with the opponents of SD on the negative side of the issue that concerns causal initiative or of the issue that concerns intrinsic unpredictability?

We think it would be confusing to group (a) authors who affirm SD on two of the three points involved in the topical agreement about it with (b) authors who do not affirm it at all. The latter are opponents of self-determination, whether they reject it on one count, on two, or on all three. The former, in contrast, are defenders of self-determination, whether they uphold it on all three counts or on only two, and even though they may deny one of these points.

Hence, in constructing the issues in the general controversy about SD, we shall not place an SD author on the negative side even though on the point in question he shares the views held by the opponents of SD. This does not mean, however, that we shall ignore these differences of opinion among the SD authors themselves concerning how the freedom of self-determination should be conceived. In Book II, we pointed out that these disagreements among SD authors constitute issues in the *special* controversy about the freedom of self-determination.[7] It is in that controversy, not here in the *general* controversy, that the negative views of certain SD authors, mentioned above, will be treated.

In the issues of the special controversy about self-determination, the authors who take opposite sides because they hold conflicting conceptions of this freedom are united by a minimal topical agreement, i.e., a common understanding of the subject about which they are disagreeing. They are also united by their common affirmation of the reality or existence of this freedom, in spite of their disagreements about how it should be conceived in detail.

In the existential issues of the general controversy about SD, the authors who take opposite sides are obviously not united by a common affirmation.

[5] See Vol. I, p. 433 fn. 19, 490–94, and 497.
[6] See Vol. I, pp. 447–50 and 497.
[7] See Vol. I, Ch. 25, pp. 546–83, and esp. p. 547 fn. 1.

But, while they divide on the question whether man has or can have any freedom of self-determination, they must at least be united in topical agreement about the subject the existence of which they are disputing. Failing to deal with the same subject, they could hardly join issue.

Since there are three distinct existential issues in the general controversy about SD, the requisite topical agreement will be different for each issue. In each case, it will focus on a different element in the meaning of SD— (i) causal initiative, (ii) causal indeterminacy, and (iii) intrinsic unpredictability. The opponents in the particular issue in which one of these elements is the bone of contention must have some common understanding of that element. We have already presented documentary evidence of such understanding among SD authors with regard to each of these elements.[8] And with regard to each of them we have also attempted to clarify the meaning of the terms involved in that understanding.[9]

In order to ascertain whether writers who question the reality of self-determination on one of the three counts indicated above are denying the existence of that which is being posited by the adherents of SD, we must consult the understanding which unites the latter on the affirmative side of the question. Thus, for example, the opponents of SD in the issue which turns on the existence or non-existence of causal initiative must show signs that they understand what the defenders of SD in that issue mean by causal initiative. They have the burden of coming into topical agreement with the adherents of SD, in order to join issue with them. It can hardly be the other way around. Should the opponents of SD understand causal initiative, for example, in some way that bears little or no resemblance to the understanding of it shared by its adherents, the latter have no further obligation, at least so far as the defense of their position is concerned; though, of course, they may see fit to point out that, since what they contend has not been understood, it has not been challenged.[10]

This being so, preparation for the construction of the three existential issues must include a brief summary of the understanding of each of the three elements in the meaning of SD, on the part of those SD authors who include that element in their conception of this freedom.

(i) *Causal Initiative.* What is meant by causal initiative can be stated in both negative and positive terms.

In negative terms, the self is said to exercise causal initiative in the mak-

---

[8] With regard to their common understanding of causal initiative, see Vol. I, Ch. 23; with regard to causal indeterminacy, see *ibid.*, Ch. 24; and with regard to intrinsic unpredictability, see *ibid.*, Ch. 22.

[9] See *ibid.*, Ch. 21, esp. pp. 429–40.

[10] The point made above about the understanding of causal initiative applies equally to causal indeterminacy and intrinsic unpredictability.

ing of decisions when it acts as the *uncaused* cause of those decisions, or as the *unconditioned* or *independent* cause of them. It operates as a cause which is *not* itself caused to cause that which it causes: its operation as a cause is *not* the effect of some efficient cause outside itself. Before we turn to the positive expression of what is here being said, it is necessary to qualify and explain the foregoing statement of the matter in a number of ways.

(a) Some of the SD authors who posit causal initiative on the part of the self are philosophers or theologians who also attribute causal initiative and, in addition, causal primacy to God. In their view, nothing which exists and no action which occurs is uncaused by God. Nevertheless, they also maintain that, while God alone has causal primacy, man still retains causal initiative when that is understood with the following added qualification; namely, that the self is a finite and, therefore, created cause which has causal initiative on the plane of finite or natural causes, even though it is dependent for its being and operation on the infinite causal power of God, which extends to everything that is or happens. Hence, for these authors the self is an uncaused cause of the decisions it makes only in the sense that no other *finite* cause efficiently causes the self to make those decisions. For other SD writers, who do not hold such theological views, the added qualification can, of course, be removed.

(b) Some of the SD authors distinguish between efficient causes, on the one hand, and formal and final causes, on the other. In their view, the motives or purposes which may be considered by the self in the deliberative process that eventuates in a decision can function as the formal or final cause of that decision, but not as its efficient cause. Hence, while they do not regard the self as the sole cause of the decision it produces, they do maintain that it is the sole efficient cause of it. In the making of the decision, the self may be somehow moved or affected by motives or purposes, but these do not efficiently cause it to act or not to act, i.e., to make or not make whatever decision it makes. If motives were the efficient causes of decisions, and if motives were themselves the effects of other efficient causes, operative on the self from without or even from within its own past, then the cause of a decision would be a caused cause on the plane of finite causes. This is precisely what is being denied by those who attribute causal initiative to the self as the uncaused efficient cause of the decisions it makes, even when they admit the presence of formal and final causes in the making of decisions. The same thing is denied by other SD writers who do not treat motives as formal or final causes but who, nevertheless, attribute causal initiative to the self. For them as well, the presence of motives in the making of decisions does not require us to go outside the self or into its past for the causal origin of the self's action in producing a decision.

(c) Some SD authors attribute causal initiative to the self as a whole, whereas others attribute it to the self in virtue of its having a certain power or faculty, such as will, intellect, reason, mind, consciousness, the power of attention, or the power to suspend judgment. These differences may lead to significant disagreements about how man's power of self-determination should be conceived, but these disagreements belong to the special controversy on that subject. They do not impair the agreement of the authors who, in the general controversy, take the affirmative side of the issue with regard to causal initiative. Whether or not they specify a particular part of the self in virtue of which man exercises causal initiative, and regardless of how those who do may specify this part, these authors all conceive the *present* self as having the power to make decisions without being caused to do so by anything operative out of its own past or by environing circumstances or influences.

(d) One further negative point unites these authors. The decision which the self makes is an act on its part; and, like any other act, it has the character of an event or an occurrence. But, according to these authors, the cause of the decision is *not* another—and antecedent—event or occurrence. They conceive the self as having a continuing or enduring existence which is quite different from the momentary being of events or occurrences. Hence, when they relate the self (as uncaused cause) to the decisions it makes (as effects of that cause), they are not to be understood as saying that one event, an effect, follows another, the cause, but this does not in turn follow any other as an effect. They are saying instead that decisions, which are events and effects, issue from a cause which is not an event and not an effect. Whereas causally related antecedent and consequent events are separate items in a sequence of occurrent entities, the self acting to make a decision and the decision produced are not thus separated. The self as a cause has the power to produce decisions, and the decisions as effects are manifestations of that power's being exercised. The self, in exercising its power to make decisions, thus operates as uncaused cause of its own acts, namely, the decisions made.

(e) Finally, it must be pointed out that when decisions are called "free" this epithet is being transferred to the effect from the cause. While causal initiative means that something is uncaused, it does not mean that the decisions a man makes are uncaused. On the contrary, the position that is being taken is that they are caused, but by a cause which is uncaused, namely, by the self, which, as operating to produce decisions, is not caused to do so by anything extrinsic to itself on the plane of finite causes. It is the self which is a free (i.e., uncaused) cause; the decisions it makes are freely caused (i.e., caused by an uncaused cause).

We turn now to what can be said positively about the meaning of "free cause" and of the causal initiative which that phrase connotes. The word "initiative" suggests one aspect of the matter. To conceive the power of self-determination as involving causal initiative is to conceive that power as the effective starting point, origin, or source of an action which is given its direction by the decision formed. Another way of seeing the positive side of that which so far has been called "uncaused" or "independent" is to contrast the active and the passive, or the active and the reactive. The SD authors who attribute causal initiative to the self ascribe to it, in whole or in part, the possession of an active power, i.e., one which can act without being acted upon, and one which, as operating, does not react to something else but acts from itself alone.

The difficulty of grasping imaginatively or illustratively what such words are intended to convey lies, of course, in the fact that the SD authors are here trying to express what they themselves consider to be a unique phenomenon in the whole world of natural or finite things. As they see it, we have experience, or are in the presence, of a purely active power which is able to initiate results only insofar as we have experience of our own power of self-determination or can detect it in the behavior of other beings. It is their claim that, except for beings thus endowed (whether men alone or other things as well), the finite beings of which we have experience or knowledge act only by reacting or have powers of acting which, in order to become operative, must be acted upon.

The only thing analogous to the causal initiative of self-determination in the realm of finite things—at least according to some SD authors—is the creative power of an infinite being, God. Since that is even more difficult for us to understand in positive terms, the analogy scarcely helps us in our effort to grasp, imaginatively or by means of illustrations, the positive meaning of causal initiative. That is why it is necessary to resort to such negative terms as "uncaused cause" or "independent cause" to state the point about causal initiative which is being denied in one of the existential issues about SD. In contrast, those who deny SD can readily express their contrary view in positive terms by saying that all causes are caused causes, dependent causes, the effects of other causes.

(ii) *Causal Indeterminacy.* For those SD authors who conceive self-determination as involving both causal initiative and causal indeterminacy, the two elements represent different respects in which a self-determined decision is freely caused.

On the side of causal initiative, the decision is freely caused in that the power of producing it is an active power, able to act without being acted upon. On the side of causal indeterminacy, the decision is freely caused in that the power of producing it is not necessitated to produce that one decision or to produce any decision at all. At that moment and under identical conditions, it is able to produce any one of a number of alternative decisions. The self has causal initiative even if it can produce only one decision, *so long as that one is caused by an active power uncaused in its causing*. The self has causal indeterminacy, in addition to causal initiative, if, under identical conditions at a given moment, several alternative decisions can be made, and of these the one that is produced is caused by a power that is not necessitated to cause it rather than some other.

For those SD authors who conceive self-determination as involving causal indeterminacy but not causal initiative, the meaning of causal indeterminacy is the same. It means that the power of self-determination is a power of freely choosing one of several alternative decisions. If C is a cause which has such power, and if E_1, E_2, E_3 . . . E_n comprise the alternative decisions it can effect, then to say that C is not necessitated in its causing is to say that, by itself and under identical extrinsic conditions, C can produce E_1 or E_2 or E_3, etc. No matter which of these decisions is made, it could always have been otherwise even though all the conditions under which it was made remained exactly the same.

SD authors differ among themselves on the question whether a cause can be free in the sense of causal indeterminacy without also being free in the sense of causal initiative. But this disagreement among them belongs to the special controversy about SD. It does not prevent them from standing together on the affirmative side of the issue about casual indeterminacy in the general controversy, though it does affect the way in which they argue the case for freedom of choice and the theory of causation they invoke to defend it.

The following points should be noted to clarify the position that is being attacked by writers who take the opposite side on this issue.

(a) SD authors use the term "choice" in a sense radically different from that attached to the word by those who call themselves determinists. When the latter speak of men as having choice, they usually mean no more than that under circumstances which allow them alternative courses of action, they could have acted differently, *had they chosen to*. From the point of view of the SD authors, the critical question about the character of the choice is whether the man could have chosen otherwise under identical inner and outer conditions, not whether he could have acted otherwise, had he chosen to. To deny that the individual who could have acted otherwise under certain conditions could under the same conditions have also chosen otherwise is to deny that the man's choice is free (i.e., not necessitated by the conditions under which it was made). But this is precisely what the SD authors who affirm causal indeterminacy are asserting, namely, the freedom of a choice among alternatives that is not determined by the inner and outer conditions under which the decision in favor of one alternative rather than another is made.

(b) The foregoing statement of their position is inadequate from the point of view of the SD authors. It makes them appear to say that a free choice is one that is totally undetermined. But that is not their view of the matter. On the contrary, they hold that the making of one rather than another decision is determined by the self, but in a manner that is not necessitated by whatever extrinsic factors may be operative at the moment when the decision is made.

This does not exclude the presence of competing motives, nor of any other influences upon the course of deliberation—influences impinging from without or arising from within as the effects of man's past or of his nature (i.e., his habits, his formed character, his knowledge or opinions, his adherence to certain reasons or principles, his emotional predispositions, his temperamental inclinations, etc.). But to admit the relevance of such factors, or even their causal efficacy, is not to say that the choice of one decision rather than another is completely determined by any one or by a combination of them.

According to the SD authors who affirm causal indeterminacy, free choice falls between two extremes: on the one hand, a free choice is not one that is completely determined by the relative strength among competing motives or other influences operating on the self from within or without; nor, on the other hand, is it totally unaffected by such factors or influences. Confronted by such factors or influences, the self determines which shall prevail when it chooses to make one rather than another of several alternative decisions.

While the range and character of the alternative possible decisions at a given moment may be determined by the individual's past and by his present circumstances, his freedom of choice consists in the fact that none of these influences has the power to determine which of the alternative decisions shall be made. That rests with his power of self-determination which, through its causal indeterminacy, is able to give dominance to one motive or one set of influences rather than another. Far from motives or other influences determining which of several decisions is made, it is the other way around, according to the SD authors: the self determines which motive or set of influences shall be decisive (i.e., which shall find expression in the decision made).

In other words, just as, with regard to causal initiative, it was said that a free decision is not one that is uncaused but one that is freely caused (i.e., by the self which is its uncaused cause), so here, with regard to causal indeterminacy, what is being said is that a free decision is not one that is undetermined, but one that is freely determined (i.e., by the self which determines which decision shall be chosen).

(c) Some SD authors speak of cause and effect as being contingent when the causal nexus involves indeterminacy of the kind described above; that is, they use the word "contingent" as an antonym for "necessary" and contrast the situation in which a cause has the power of producing any one of a multiplicity of alternative effects with the situation in which a cause has the power to produce one and only one effect. In the latter case, given the cause in operation, that one effect necessarily results, whereas in the former case, given the cause in operation, no one effect necessarily results, and whichever effect does result is contingent in the sense that it need not have resulted from the operation of the cause.

Other SD writers, while agreeing that causal indeterminacy is thus distinguished from causal necessity, also distinguish the contingency of that which happens by chance from the contingency of that which is determined by free choice. These two types of contingency, in their view, are alike only in the negative respect that both involve effects that are *not* necessitated by their causes. According to these authors, the threefold distinction of (1) chance, (2) necessity, and (3) freedom corresponds to a threefold classification of causes as (1) deficient, or less than sufficient and, therefore, non-necessitating, (2) sufficient and necessitating, and (3) superabundant, or more than sufficient and, therefore, also non-necessitating.

With respect to a particular effect, a deficient cause is one which is not sufficient by itself for the production of that effect. The occurrence of the effect depends upon the cooperation of other causes; and it is the fact that a coincidence of causes is required to produce the effect that makes the effect contingent and each of the requisite causes deficient.

With respect to a particular effect, a sufficient cause is one which, when operative, is adequate for the production of that effect. No other causes are needed. But if it is merely a sufficient cause, it is adequate for the production of that one effect and that alone. Hence, a merely sufficient cause is one that necessitates the effect it produces, i.e., given such a cause in operation, the effect which it uniquely determines cannot not result.

With respect to a particular effect, a superabundant cause is sufficient in the sense that it is adequate for the production of this one effect; but it is more than sufficient in the sense that its causal power extends to the production of other effects, each of which it is by itself adequate to cause. Hence, while such a cause is sufficient for the production of any one of a number of alternative effects, it does not necessitate whatever effect it produces, i.e., given such a cause in operation, the effect which it in fact determines need not have resulted.

Writers who, in one way or another, acknowledge this threefold classification of causes accordingly contrast a man's freely chosen decisions not only with effects that are necessitated by their causes but also with events that happen by chance or are dependent upon a coincidence of causes. For them, the causal indeterminacy of a free choice is the very opposite of the chance toss of a coin, even though the outcome might be described as "contingent" in either case, when that word is used to mean no more than "non-necessitated."

To express the difference between these two ways in which an effect can be non-necessitated, they sometimes speak of the active indeterminacy or dominating indifference which a superabundant cause (such as man's power of self-determination) exercises with respect to the alternative effects any one of which it is able to produce. In contrast, that which is subject to having one or another alternative imposed upon it, like a lump of wax being shaped by a variety of molds, is passively indeterminate or submissively indifferent with respect to the alternative effects that can be thus produced.

Other SD authors who do not employ the foregoing theory of causes nevertheless do conceive the causal indeterminacy that is involved in free choice as quite different from chance. The power of self-determination is for them always more than a sufficient cause, adequate for the production of one and only one effect; and, *a fortiori*, it is even further removed from the deficiency of a cause that produces a particular effect only if other causes happen to concur.

Even those SD authors who maintain that causal indeterminacy is present in the operation of all causes distinguish it from chance. No cause, in their view, necessitates its effect; nor for them does anything happen by chance. Every cause freely, selectively, or creatively determines the effect it produces, that effect being only one of a number of alternative events within its power to produce. Hence, they, too, in a way acknowledge the conceptual distinction of freedom, necessity, and chance; for, on the one hand, they deny the existence of the merely sufficient and necessitating causes which they regard as the root fallacy of determinism; and, on the other hand, they also deny the existence of the deficient causes which are posited by those who, in their opinon, mistakenly hold that, among events which are not necessitated, some happen by chance.

Furthermore, for all the SD authors who affirm causal indeterminacy, whether or not they also affirm causal initiative, the power of self-determination is the efficient and, in that sense, the active, determining cause of a freely chosen decision. It is not a material cause, like a lump of wax which has the potentiality of taking one shape or another because it is passively indeterminate or submissively indifferent to the variety of shapes which can be imposed upon it. It actively shapes itself by exercising its power over alternative forms, any one of which it can assume.

It is in virtue of this last point that these SD writers maintain that the power of self-determination is a power of self-creation. The creativity which they see in its causal indeterminacy consists in the realization of the possible. No matter what character a man has at a given moment, it is always possible for it to be otherwise, and that possibility can be realized by free choice on his part. With every such realization by choice, a man actively changes himself. He makes himself over, if only in some slight respect. His future is not wholly determined by his past, but emerges from his past by creative choices on his part. Thus, according to some SD authors, the causal indeterminacy of free choice introduces genuine novelty into the world—that which would not be there but for man's elective determination to make it so.

(iii) *Intrinsic Unpredictability.* The foregoing explication of causal indeterminacy indicates the close connection between that element in the meaning of self-determination and this third element, intrinsic unpredictability. However, not all the SD authors who affirm the one also affirm the other. Their disagreement with other SD authors about God's certain foreknowledge of the decisions man will freely choose to make belongs to the special controversy and does not concern us here. Our present interest is in getting clear that which is being denied by those opponents of SD who take the negative side of the existential issue about intrinsic unpredictability.

SD authors who conceive man's power of self-determination as productive of decisions which are intrinsically unpredictable maintain that perfect knowledge of all relevant causes still leaves a future free decision incapable of being foreseen with certitude. The point remains the same whether "perfect knowledge of all relevant causes" expresses a purely hypothetical possibility or is understood to exist in the divine omniscience. In either case what is being asserted is that, given perfect knowledge of all the causes which will operate to produce a freely chosen decision, it is impossible to predict with certitude the particular effect which will result.

This view is shared (a) by authors who hold that the power of self-determination, with its causal initiative and its causal indeterminacy, is the only relevant cause; (b) by authors who hold that, while it is not the only relevant cause, it is the sole efficient cause of a freely chosen decision, at least on the plane of finite causes; (c) by authors who hold that the causal indeterminacy of the power of self-determination, without causal initiative suffices to render a freely chosen decision intrinsically unpredictable; and (d) by authors who attribute causal indeterminacy not only to man's power of self-determination but also to the operation of other causes or even to all causes.

In the view of all these writers, to say that a future event is intrinsically unpredictable is not to say that it is totally unpredictable. If there were anything which happened by chance, where the chance event is conceived as a happening without cause, that would be totally unpredictable. Not even a merely probable prediction of its occurrence could be made. On the other hand, for those who use the word "chance" to refer to future contingent events which result from a coincidence of causes, that which may or may not happen by chance is subject to calculations of probability. Hence, such eventualities are not totally unpredictable, though they are held to be unpredictable with certitude, even given perfect knowledge of all relevant causes.

As we have already pointed out, the SD authors who affirm causal indeterminacy distinguish that which happens freely not only from that which happens necessarily but also from that which happens by chance. Hence, their assertion of the intrinsic unpredictability of the future decisions a man will freely choose to make is unaffected by whatever opinions they or others may hold about the unpredictability of future events in the realm of chance. But their position would be seriously misunderstood if it were interpreted to mean that such future decisions are totally unpredictable.

Their view, as many of them explicitly remark, does not exclude probable predictions of what men will do in that sphere of their conduct which is subject to self-determination. Given knowledge of a man's settled character, his intellectual apparatus, his emotional bent, and his underlying temperament, what he will freely decide to do in an imaginable future situation may be predicted with high probability. But no matter how complete or perfect the knowledge of all these relevant factors, the decision can never be predicted with certitude. This, and this alone, is the contention of those who conceive self-determination as entailing the intrinsic unpredictability of freely chosen decisions.

The foregoing summary of the three elements in the meaning of self-determination prepares us for the formulation of the three existential issues, to which we now turn. This is to be carefully distinguished from the conceptual issue which involves the relation between self-determination and moral responsibility. We shall discuss that issue in Section 3 of this chapter.

2. FORMULATION OF THE EXISTENTIAL ISSUES

If a conception of freedom presupposes certain things, and if the existence of these is questioned, then an existential issue is raised about the freedom itself.

Thus, for example, in the case of the acquired freedom of self-perfection, we saw that, on the one hand, those who affirm such freedom presuppose the existence of a number of things, while, on the other hand, those who deny the validity of these presuppositions (i.e., those who deny the existence of the things presupposed) consequently deny that the conception which involves these things has any reality corresponding to it.[11] The root of the disagreement about the reality of the freedom of self-perfection is thus a disagreement about something else, such as the existence of moral obligations binding on all men. The existence of such universally binding obligations being presupposed by the conception of SP freedom, those who take opposite sides on the question of the reality of such freedom do so in virtue of taking opposite sides about the existence of that which is presupposed, according to the conception of SP held by its adherents. The complex question which covers both points can be phrased as follows: "Is there any reality corresponding to a conception of freedom, such as that of self-perfection, which presupposes the existence of moral obligations binding on all men?"

Of the three existential issues about self-determination, the two principal ones take the same form as the existential issue about self-perfection to which we have just referred. In the first of these, the presupposition being questioned is causal initiative; in the second, it is causal indeterminacy. The third existential issue, which involves intrinsic unpredictability, takes a somewhat different form. We shall deal with that after we have formulated the questions which constitute the first two issues.

In all three cases, we shall use the words "causal initiative," "causal indeterminacy," and "intrinsic unpredictability" with the meanings set forth in the preceding section. It is only as thus understood that these things are involved in conceptions of SD; and, consequently, they must be similarly understood by those who deny the reality of SD by denying the existence of one or another of these presuppositions.

(a) *The existential issue concerning causal initiative.* The question can be formulated in a number of ways: If the existence of a freedom of self-determination for man depends upon his having causal initiative,

[11] See Ch. 5, pp. 93–96, *supra.*

does man really have such freedom? Or, if the conception of a freedom of self-determination involves causal initiative, and if the existence of such a freedom depends upon the existence of causal initiative on man's part, does such freedom exist? Or, is there any reality corresponding to a conception of freedom, such as that of self-determination, which presupposes the existence of causal initiative on man's part?

Of these the last, which is not hypothetical, may be preferred for that reason. It clearly focuses the issue on the validity of the existential presupposition—causal initiative. Writers who are in topical agreement about the meaning of causal initiative and disagree about the validity of this presupposition also disagree about the existence of an SD freedom in human life. More precisely, they come into disagreement in the following manner.

Taking the affirmative side of this issue are authors who hold conceptions of self-determination which involve causal initiative on man's part. They acknowledge that their affirmation of SD presupposes the existence of causal initiative. But they assert the validity of this presupposition, and, therefore, they assert the reality of man's power of self-determination, as they conceive it.

Taking the negative side of this issue are authors who address themselves to conceptions of self-determination which involve causal initiative on man's part. They recognize that the existence of SD as thus conceived presupposes the existence of causal initiative. But they deny the validity of this presupposition, and, therefore, they deny the reality of man's power of self-determination, as conceived by most of its adherents.

(b) *The existential issue concerning causal indeterminacy.* Adopting the phrasing used above, the question at issue here can be put as follows: Is there any reality corresponding to a conception of freedom, such as that of self-determination, which presupposes the existence of causal indeterminacy on man's part? The only difference between this second existential issue and the first described above is the substitution of causal indeterminacy for causal initative as the existential presupposition upon which the issue focuses. Making this substitution, we can see that writers come into disagreement here precisely as they do in regard to causal initiative.

(c) *The existential issue concerning intrinsic unpredictabilty.* Because of the connection between causal indeterminacy and intrinsic unpredictability, writers who deny the one usually deny the other; and also, with few exceptions, as already noted, writers who affirm the one tend to affirm the other. Hence, there is no need for an additional existential issue involving intrinsic unpredictability if that is formulated by the following question: Is there any reality corresponding to a conception of freedom, such as that of self-determination, which presupposes the intrinsic unredictability of the decisions that a man determines by free choice? But here is an additional, if somewhat subordinate, existential issue, which differs in form from the preceding two.

In this third issue those who affirm and those who deny the existence of SD do so in the light of an existential presupposition on which they agree. They agree on the existence of God, conceived as omniscient and, therefore, as having that perfect knowledge of causes which both understand to be relevant to the question about intrinsic unpredictability. Within the framework of such agreement, they disagree about the compatibility of human self-determination, conceived as involving intrinsic unpredictability, with the existence of an omniscient deity.

Hence, the question at issue here can be formulated as follows: Granted the presupposition that an omniscient deity exists, is there any reality corresponding to a conception of freedom, such as that of self-determination, which presupposes the intrinsic unpredictability of the decisions which a man determines by free choice? The conflict focuses on one existential presupposition as being compatible or incompatible with another existential presupposition, about which there is no disagreement, at least not by the parties to this issue. The parties come into disagreement here in the following manner.

Taking the affirmative side of this issue are authors who hold conceptions of self-determination which involve the intrinsic unpredictability of freely chosen decisions. They acknowledge that their affirmation of SD presupposes the existence of such intrinsic unpredictability. But while they affirm the existence of an omniscient deity, they also maintain that the existence of intrinsic unpredictability is compatible with it. Hence, they deny that the existence of an omniscient deity renders the intrinsic unpredictability of self-determination impossible; and since it is for them inseparably connected with the causal indeterminacy which they affirm, they assert the reality of man's power of self-determination, conceived as involving intrinsic unpredictability.

Taking the negative side of this issue are authors who address themselves to conceptions of self-determination which involve the intrinsic unpredictability of free decisions. They recognize that the existence of SD as thus conceived presupposes the existence of such intrinsic unpredictability. But, affirming the existence of an omniscient deity, they maintain that the existence of intrinsic unpredictability is incompatible with it. Hence, they contend that the existence of an omniscient deity renders the intrinsic unpredictability of self-determination impossible; and so, denying the validity of this presupposition, they deny the reality of man's power of self-determination, as conceived by certain of its adherents.

3. FORMULATION OF THE CONCEPTUAL ISSUE

As we have seen in earlier chapters dealing with circumstantial self realization and acquired self-perfection as subjects in the general contro versy, a conceptual issue turns on a question which asks, concerning the freedom under consideration, whether the conception of it conforms to the generic idea of freedom or the generally accepted understanding of it. Where the generic idea of freedom is appealed to as the basis for affirming or denying that what a particular conception, or family of conceptions, pre sents to us is genuinely a kind of freedom, the arguments pro and con pivot on the self as the principle of freedom. For any act to be free, it must proceed from the self; if it does not proceed from the self, it is not free in any sense which fits the generic idea of freedom.

Thus, for example, the conceptual issue about the freedom of self perfection involves the question whether, as that freedom is conceived, the act of willing as one ought flows from the self or, being submissive to duty or obligation, it lacks the spontaneity of a free act. Authors who argue the affirmative side of this issue appeal to the real or true self of the virtuous man, in which is vested the acquired power of being able willingly to will as one ought in conformity to the moral law or in the discharge of moral obligation. Authors who take the negative side dismiss the notion of a real or true self as fictitious and argue that, when the self is identified with the individual as a whole, what the self wishes may or may not happen to conform to moral rules or obligations; but whether they do or not, human acts are free if they realize the individual's wishes, because they then flow from his self, not from externally imposed rules of conduct.

The conceptual issue about the freedom of self-determination similarly involves the question whether, as that freedom is conceived, a freely chosen decision, or the act to which it gives rise, flows from the self.

The negative answer to this question argues that, far from being the basis of responsibility, self-determination, conceived as involving causal indeter minacy or causal initiative or both, nullifies it. According to this notion of responsibility, a man is answerable or accountable only for such acts as are his own (i.e., proceed from his self); and, conversely, whatever acts are his own, he is responsible for. Hence, if free choice, as it is conceived nullifies responsibility, such a conception of freedom does not conform to the generic idea of the free act as one that flows from the self. Or, to put it somewhat differently, the negative side of this issue is taken by writers who contend that self-determination, as conceived by its adherents, is incompatible with responsibility, which in turn shows that it does not conform to the generic idea of freedom.

The SD authors who take the affirmative side of this issue insist on the contrary that, far from being incompatible with responsibility, moral responsibility and responsibility before God are non-existent unless men have the power of self-determination, conceived as involving at least causal indeterminacy and, perhaps also, causal initiative. They often express this point by saying that to deny man's freedom of self-determination is to destroy the foundations of morality and religion. In their view, men can be held responsible only for that which they freely choose to do or to become, because only such things have the self as their decisive, determining principle. Accordingly, they not only maintain that self-determination conforms to the generic idea of freedom but also that no other freedom, neither self-realization nor self-perfection, does conform to the generic idea unless such freedom is rooted in man's power of self-determination.

In the light of the foregoing we can formulate the two questions which together constitute the conceptual issue about SD. Does self-determination, conceived as involving causal indeterminacy or causal initiative or both, provide a basis for responsibility? To this question must be added a second, which calls for the opposed conclusions that follow from the opposed answers to the first question. In view of what is said about self-determination as a basis for responsibility, does self-determination conform to the generic idea of freedom? Unless this second question is asked and answered, the issue, as formulated by the first question alone, is an issue about self-determination and responsibility, not an issue about self-determination as a kind of freedom. And unless we have here an issue about self-determination as a kind of freedom, we do not have one that belongs to the general controversy.

Putting the two questions together, we can indicate the steps by which writers come into disagreement on this conceptual issue about SD.

Taking the affirmative side are authors who hold conceptions of self-determination which involve causal indeterminacy or causal initiative or both. They maintain that a freedom so conceived is the basis of responsibility. This is their answer to the first question. But it is acknowledged that that for which a man can be held responsible is that which proceeds from his self. Hence, they conclude, self-determination, being the basis of responsibility, must have the self as its principle; therefore, it conforms to the generic idea of freedom. This is their answer to the second question.

Taking the negative side are authors who address themselves to conceptions of self-determination which involve causal indeterminacy or causal initiative or both. In answer to the first question, they maintain that something so conceived cannot be the basis of responsibility. But it is acknowledged that that for which a man cannot be held responsible does not proceed from his self. Hence, they conclude, self-determination, not being the basis of responsibility, does not have the self as its principle; therefore it does not conform to the generic idea and is not genuinely a kind of freedom. This is their answer to the second question.

For authors thus to join issue, they must be in topical agreement on a number of points. They must agree on the notion of responsibility, both sides acknowledging that acts for which a man can be held responsible proceed from his self, and, conversely, that acts for which he cannot be held responsible do not. There must be some agreement about the generic idea of freedom, at least to the extent of recognition by both sides that if it can be shown that an act called free does not proceed from the self then that act is not properly called free. Finally, those who attack the genuineness of self-determination as a kind of freedom (on the ground that, as conceived by its adherents, it cannot be the basis of responsibility) must share with its adherents at least a minimal common understanding of SD, the validity of which conception they challenge. Since the question about self-determination in relation to responsibility turns on the attribution of causal initiative or causal indeterminacy or both to the power of self-determination, the meaning of these two elements in conceptions held by the adherents of self-determination must be understood by its opponent in this conceptual issue.

It is this last requirement which, in many cases, makes it difficult to be sure that writers who appear to disagree about self-determination in relation to responsibility are sufficiently in topical agreement actually to join issue. We have seen that, according to the SD authors, the causal indeterminacy which they attribute to the power of self-determination distinguishes free acts not only from necessitated effects but also from chance events. The SD authors would admit that if the causal indeterminacy of self-determination made freely chosen decisions matters of chance, then such decisions could not be ascribed to the self as their cause or principle and hence self-determination could not be the basis of a man's responsibility for the decisions he makes or the acts he decides on. But, as we shall see when we come to this issue in Chapter 12, opponents of SD rest their denial that self-determination can be the basis of responsibility on an interpretation of causal indeterminacy which reduces the so-called "freely chosen" decision or act to a chance event, or to one in which chance plays a significant role.

This divergence in understanding, on the part of the SD authors and their opponents, is usually expressed in terms of the notion of "indifference." Both sides may call self-determination, in virtue of its causal indeterminacy, "a freedom of indifference." But while they may be using the same words, they are not using them with the same meanings if the adherents of SD insist that the power of self-determination exercises an active and dominating indifference over the alternatives from among which a free choice is made, while the opponents regard free choice as involving a passive and submissive indifference in the presence of alternatives. For the latter, the decision chosen is like something which happens to the self by chance; for the former, it is something actively caused by the self, even though not necessitated by it. With the term "indifference" thus ambiguously used, and with the indicated discrepancy in the understanding of causal indeterminacy, the requisite topical agreement would appear to be lacking. If that is the case, then we do not have a genuine issue here about self-determination and responsibility, but only an apparent one based on a misunderstanding.

However, this difficulty may not be insuperable. We shall find that the writers who appear to take opposite sides on the question of self-determination and responsibility do so in virtue of holding opposite views about the relation of causal indeterminacy to chance. In other words, in the debate of the conceptual issue, as we have formulated it so far, the negative side argues that causal indeterminacy is either reducible to chance or involves chance to a significant extent. This is the basic reason it offers for contending that self-determination cannot be the basis of responsibility. On the other hand, the affirmative side argues that causal indeterminacy excludes chance as much as it excludes causal necessity. This is the basic reason it offers for maintaining that self-determination is the basis of a man's being responsible for the decisions he makes, as he would not be if his decisions either were necessitated by his character and circumstances or were products of chance. Furthermore, it is by arguing that causal indeterminacy does not involve chance that SD authors defend self-determination against the attacks brought against it on the ground that causal indeterminacy abolishes responsibility.

The root of the conceptual issue about self-determination thus appears to lie in another conceptual issue, one about causal indeterminacy. That issue can be formulated by the question: Does causal indeterminacy, as conceived by SD authors, either reduce a free choice to a chance event or introduce the element of chance to a significant extent? To this question, an affirmative answer by the opponents of SD leads them to give negative answers to the question about self-determination and responsibility and to the further question about self-determination as a genuine kind of freedom. Correspondingly, a negative answer by the adherents of SD leads to the affirmative answers they give to the other two questions.

The only problem which remains, then, is whether authors actually join issue on the question about causal indeterminacy and chance. This depends, of course, on their being in minimal topical agreement about the meaning of the two critical terms in the question—"chance" and "causal indeterminacy." The opponents of SD are obligated to recognize what its adherents mean by "causal indeterminacy," so that they can show why they think that, *as it is conceived by the SD authors*, causal indeterminacy involves chance. And both sides must share common notions about chance either as that which results from a coincidence of separate causes or as that which happens without any cause at all.

This is not the place to decide whether the requisite topical agreement exist, at lease sufficiently to set up a genuine issue about causal indeterminacy and chance. If that is a genuine issue, it solves the difficulty about the issue concerning self-determination and responsibility. This can be much better decided in the light of the evidence which will be presented in Chapter 12. We are here concerned only to show why the conceptual issue about SD turns into a set of related issues, of which the most fundamental is the one concerning causal indeterminacy and chance, subordinate to which is the issue concerning the relation of responsibility to self-determination (conceived as involving causal indeterminacy). Subtending from these two is a final issue, which, strictly speaking, is the only one that is a conceptual issue about SD. It is the issue concerning the genuineness of self-determination as a kind of freedom, which turns on its conformity to the generic idea of freedom, as that in turn depends on the relation of responsibility to self-determination (conceived as involving causal indeterminacy).

In the foregoing analysis of this related set of issues, we have, for simplicity's sake, concentrated our attention on causal indeterminacy and neglected to mention causal initiative. But the latter is hardly irrelevant to the basic question about the role of chance in self-determination. On the one hand, those who attribute causal initiative to the power of self determination conceive that power as the uncaused cause of its own acts. On the other hand, according to one of the meanings of chance, the chance event is that which happens without any cause at all; and it is this meaning of the term to which opponents of SD frequently appeal. *Hence, the set of related issues, which are set forth in the preceding paragraph, can be duplicated by another set in which the most fundamental issue concern causal initiative and chance, and the one subordinate to that concerns the relation of responsibility to self-determination (conceived as involving causal initiative).*

Whether the set of related issues is formulated with causal indeterminacy as its most critical term, or with causal initiative instead, there are two further points to be noted.

(i) As we have just observed, it is only the last of the three related ssues which is, strictly speaking, a conceptual issue about self-determination that belongs to the general controversy about the kinds of freedom. Conceptual issues about causal indeterminacy or causal initiative and chance, and conceptual issues about responsibility in relation to self-determination (conceived as involving causal indeterminacy or causal initiative), do not, by themselves, belong to this general controversy. They belong to it only in virtue of underlying the issue concerning the conformity of self-determination to the generic idea of freedom, and hence concerning its genuineness as a kind of freedom.

However, authors who appear to engage in the dispute of the two underlying issues seldom go on to take sides on the conceptual issue about SD, as a matter of explicit conclusion from the positions they take on the underlying issues. On the one hand, SD authors are quite explicit about the relation of responsibility to self-determination, but, maintaining this, they take for granted the genuineness of self-determination as a kind of freedom, instead of using their position on self-determination and responsibility as the ground for an explicit conclusion to this effect. On the other hand, opponents of SD also appear to assume that, if they are right in asserting that self-determination cannot be the basis of responsibility, then there must be something wrong about SD conceptions—so wrong, in fact, that what they present resembles chance rather than freedom.

In other words, the writings we shall examine when we come to Chapter 12 will largely, if not wholly, bear on what we have called the two underlying issues. We will find little, if any, evidence which bears directly and explicitly on the question whether self-determination conforms to the generic idea or is a genuine kind of freedom. But in view of what appears to be taken for granted or is assumed in writings which bear directly and explicitly on the underlying issues, we feel justified in treating these issues in a chapter devoted to the conceptual issue about self-determination as a kind of freedom.

(ii) The conceptual issue, as described above, sometimes appears to overlap or merge with the existential issue that involves causal indeterminacy. One reason for this is that the conceptual issue also involves causal indeterminacy as one of its critical terms. Another reason is that the conceptual issue turns on the relation of self-determination to responsibility and to morality.

As we have observed, those who assert that freedom of self-determination is indispensable to moral responsibility and man's responsibility before God also maintain that the denial of SD undermines the foundations of morality and religion. To this fact must be added the fact that one of the classic arguments for the existence of causal indeterminacy rests on the proposition that, if divine commandments and the moral law impose certain obligations on men, then men must be able freely to choose between obeying and disobeying, i.e., "ought implies can." These two facts together account for a tendency to confuse matters which are relevant to the conceptual issue and matters which are relevant to the existential issues concerning freedom of choice.

Though moral responsibility and freedom of choice enter into the debate of both issues, the issues themselves can be kept quite clearly distinct.

On the one hand, the proposition "ought implies can" simply represents one type of argument for the existence of causal indeterminacy of free choice. That argument runs somewhat as follows. (a) Moral obligation, moral responsibility, rewards and punishments, etc., presuppose freedom of choice on man's part, i.e., the causal indeterminacy of man's power of self-determination.[12] (b) But the moral or the divine law exists, and, with it, moral obligations, rewards and punishments. (c) Hence, what is presupposed by such things must exist, namely, the causal indeterminacy of man's power of self-determination whereby he exercises a free choice between willing as he ought and willing as he ought not.

The counter-argument, advanced by opponents of SD, denies the first of the foregoing premises and asserts the contrary. It holds that obligations, responsibility, rewards and punishments remain quite intelligible in the total absence of free choice. In other words, freedom of self-determination (conceived as involving causal indeterminacy) is not necessarily presupposed by the existence of obligations, responsibility, rewards and punishments in human life. Hence, the existence of the latter is not a valid argument for the existence of the former.[13]

On the other hand, the proposition "ought implies can" or equivalent expressions of the same point also play a part in the argument on the affirmative side of the conceptual issue about SD. Here, too, it is asserted

[12] Theologians often express this first premise by saying that God would be unjust to command man and to mete out rewards and punishments if man were not created with freedom to choose between obedience and disobedience. One philosophical expression of the same premise might take the form of declaring that the existence of the moral law is the *ratio cognoscendi* of the existence of freedom, i.e., the freedom of self-determination.

[13] It should be carefully noted that this counter-argument does not directly support the negative side of the existential issue. It does not lead to the conclusion that there is nothing in reality corresponding to a conception of freedom, such as that of self-determination, which involves causal indeterminacy on man's part; for even if obligations, responsibility, rewards and punishments are intelligible quite apart from freedom of choice, such freedom might still exist. All that the counter-argument does is to challenge the validity of the conclusion reached in the affirmative argument by challenging the truth of the proposition "ought implies can," i.e., the thesis that obligation and responsibility presuppose free choice.

hat moral responsibility presupposes freedom of choice. But here that assertion is not at all for the purpose of arguing to the existence of free choice or causal indeterminacy, but rather for the purpose of arguing that, since free choice is the basis of responsibility, freely chosen decisions must have the self for their principle, and so self-determination conforms to the generic idea and is genuinely a kind of freedom.

The counter-argument here is to the opposite effect. The assertion that self-determination, conceived as involving causal indeterminacy, cannot possibly be the basis of responsibility is not for the purpose of arguing that there is no reality corresponding to conceptions of free choice which involve causal indeterminacy; but it is rather for the purpose of arguing that so-called "freely chosen" decisions do not have the self for their principle, and so self-determination is not genuinely a kind of freedom.

Thus we see why it is difficult to disentangle the conceptual issue about self-determination from the existential issue about it which involves causal indeterminacy, for the propositions about the relation of free choice to responsibility occur in the debate of both issues. But as soon as we observe that, in one case, the proposition is being used in arguments for or against SD as genuinely a kind of freedom, and that, in the other case, it is being used in arguments for or against the existence of the causal indeterminacy attributed to SD, the possible confusion is prevented or removed.

4. PARTICIPANTS IN THIS CONTROVERSY

The number of authors who attribute a freedom of self-determination to man or who deny such freedom is very much larger than the number who engage in the dispute of one or more of the four main issues which constitute this controversy. The mere affirmation or denial of SD does not, by itself, enable us to construe an author as a party to one or another of these specifically formulated issues. Only when the affirmation or denial is accompanied by some defense of it is it possible to discern that a particular author is addressing himself to one or another of the questions at issue and taking a definite position on it. Hence, in enumerating the participants in this controversy, we shall confine ourselves to those writers who argue for or against self-determination in such a way that they can be construed as taking the affirmative or negative side on one or more of the issues which we have set forth in the preceding two sections of this chapter.

Nevertheless, it may be of background interest to recall the range and variety of authors who were treated in Volume I either as holding detailed

conceptions of self-determination or at least as affirming man's possession
of such freedom. That enumeration, given in Book II, Chapter 20,[14] is
repeated below.

Aristotle	Burke
Cicero	John Adams
Epicurus	Fichte
Lucretius	Hegel
Philo	De Tocqueville
Augustine	Secrétan
Boethius	Renouvier
Saadia Gaon	Lequier
Anselm	Green
Judah Halevi	Fouillée
Maimonides	James
Aquinas	Meyerson
Duns Scotus	Bergson
Ockham	Dewey
Erasmus	Whitehead
Machiavelli	Santayana
Luther	A. E. Taylor
Calvin	N. Hartmann
Molina	Maritain
Bellarmine	Knight
Suarez	Barth
Descartes	Tillich
Pascal	Marcel
Locke	Demos
Malebranche	Campbell
Leibniz	Hartshorne
Vico	Weiss
Berkeley	Yves Simon
Montesquieu	Castell
Rousseau	Sartre
Adam Smith	Berlin
Kant	

Of these authors, we pointed out that a considerable number merely
attribute self-determination to man, adopting some traditional conception
of such freedom without contributing any theory of their own to the
discussion of it. Among the writers listed above, this is true, for example, of

14 *Loc. cit.*, p. 404.

Cicero, Philo, Anselm, Pascal, Vico, Berkeley, Montesquieu, Adam Smith, Burke, John Adams, De Tocqueville, Santayana, Knight, Isaiah Berlin.

It might be supposed that authors who have to some extent developed their own conception of SD would also be authors who have argued for the reality or genuineness of such freedom. But this is not always the case. Not all the remaining authors listed above can be construed as taking the affirmative side of one or another of the issues with which we are concerned. The enumeration below names in chronological order those who can be so interpreted.

Aristotle	Lequier
Epicurus	T. H. Green
Augustine	Fouillée
Boethius	James
Maimonides	Meyerson
Aquinas	Bergson
Duns Scotus	Dewey
Luther	Whitehead
Calvin	A. E. Taylor
Suarez	N. Hartmann
Descartes	Maritain
Locke	Tillich
Leibniz	Campbell
Rousseau	Hartshorne
Kant	Weiss
Hegel	Yves Simon
Secrétan	Castell
Renouvier	Sartre

However, as we shall see (when, in the chapters to follow, we come to the treatment of particular issues), only some of the foregoing authors contribute to the debate by the original manner in which they argue for the position they take. Some merely repeat arguments which have been advanced by others; and some merely indicate their assertion of this or that point about self-determination, which places them on the affirmative side of this or that issue.

In addition to the foregoing authors, all of whom have been treated in Chapters 20–25 of Volume I, there are a number of other writers whom we have been able to construe as participants in this controversy and, more specifically, as taking the affirmative side on one or more of its issues. The following enumeration names those whose contributions were made prior to the twentieth century. The order is alphabetical.

Bishop Bramhall	C. S. Peirce
William Hamilton	Joseph Price
Rudolph H. Lotze	Thomas Reid
Henry L. Mansel	Frederick Schelling
James Martineau	James Ward
Henry More	Isaac Watts

It is of interest to group together the twentieth-century writers wh◦ argue the affirmative case. For the sake of completeness, the following enumeration includes authors who have been already treated in Volume along with writers not considered there. The names of the former ar◦ placed in parentheses. The list is alphabetical.

Magda Arnold	(William James)
Francis Aveling	N. Lawrence
William Barrett	H. D. Lewis
(Henri Bergson)	N. Lossky
Bernard Bosanquet	J. D. Mabbott
Emile Boutroux	A. C. MacIntyre
(C. A. Campbell)	W. G. MacLagan
Milic Capek	Michael Maher
E. F. Carritt	André Marc
(Alburey Castell)	(Jacques Maritain)
Maurice Cranston	James Martineau
B. Croce	Karl Popper
Lecomte DuNouy	Joseph Rickaby
A. C. Ewing	Josiah Royce
Austin Farrer	L. J. Russell
G. C. Field	(Jean-Paul Sartre)
Phillippa Foot	F. C. S. Schiller
Morris Ginsberg	(Yves Simon)
T. M. Greene	A. K. Stout
Hubert Gruender	(A. E. Taylor)
J. S. Haldane	(Paul Tillich)
(Nicolai Hartmann)	A. G. Van Melsen
(Charles Hartshorne)	(Paul Weiss)
D. J. B. Hawkins	John Wisdom
George T. Hughes	

Turning now to participants in this controversy who take the negative side on one or more of the issues involved, we shall first recall, again as a matter of background interest, authors who were mentioned in Volume I as being opposed to the freedom of self-determination.[15] Named alphabetically, they are as follows: A. J. Ayer, C. D. Broad, Jonathan Edwards, Benjamin Franklin, Sigmund Freud, Thomas Hobbes, L. T. Hobhouse, David Hume, Hans Kelsen, J. S. Mill, Joseph Priestley, Bertrand Russell, Moritz Schlick, Henry Sidgwick, Herbert Spencer, Benedict Spinoza, C. L. Stevenson, François de Voltaire, and the contributors to a work on the subject published by the Philosophy Department of the University of California.

To make the enumeration of the authors on the negative side comparable with the enumeration already given of the affirmative authors, we present the following two listings of their names.

The first mentions writers whose contributions to the controversy were made prior to the twentieth century. The list is alphabetical.

Alexander Bain	T. H. Huxley
Mikhail A. Bakunin	J. S. Mill
Thomas Henry Buckle	F. Nietzsche
Anthony Collins	Joseph Priestley
Jonathan Edwards	Henry Sidgwick
Benjamin Franklin	Herbert Spencer
David Hartley	Benedict Spinoza
Thomas Hobbes	Abraham Tucker
Baron d'Holbach	François de Voltaire
David Hume	

The following enumeration, also alphabetical, lists twentieth-century writers who argue the negative case.

Samuel Alexander	R. D. Hobart
A. J. Ayer	Sidney Hook
Brand Blanshard	L. T. Hobhouse
F. H. Bradley	John Hospers
R. D. Bradley	H. W. B. Joseph
C. D. Broad	Hans Kelsen
Georges Clemenceau	W. T. Matson
Curt J. Ducasse	E. B. McGilvary
Austin E. Duncan-Jones	J. M. E. McTaggert
Phillipp Frank	G. A. Paul
Sigmund Freud	F. Paulsen
W. B. Gallie	Hastings Rashdall
H. L. A. Hart	Sir David Ross

[15] See Vol. I, pp. 218–23 and 411–12.

Bertrand Russell	University of California Associates
Moritz Schlick	Ludwig Von Mises
Susan Stebbing	Gardner Williams
C. L. Stevenson	J. Wilson

The foregoing enumerations are not intended to be exhaustive. They include the major authors prior to the twentieth century, and we feel that they are fairly representative of the wide range of contemporary writers who have taken part in this controversy. Even as exemplary, these enumerations indicate how much more "controversial" self-determination is than any of the other freedoms.

In one respect, our procedure in the chapters to follow will differ from that of the preceding chapters. As we have already pointed out, self-determination is the one subject in the general controversy with respect to which authors who disagree have actually confronted one another in debate by means of written interchanges.[16] Such actual debate may serve to set the stage for the debate that must be constructed from the conflicting opinions of writers who did not in fact address themselves explicitly to the views advanced by other writers and argue against them or reply to their arguments. Hence, wherever it is possible, we shall first report the actual debate of a particular issue and then amplify the picture it gives us by construing other writers as parties to the same dispute.

The detailed order of treatment will, of course, vary from chapter to chapter to fit the exigencies of the materials relevant to the issue being considered in that chapter. Chapter 9 will deal with the existential issue concerning causal initiative; Chapter 10, with the existential issue concerning causal indeterminacy; Chapter 11, with the existential issue concerning intrinsic unpredictability; and Chapter 12, with the conceptual issue about self-determination which turns on the relation of self-determination to responsibility.

[16] See pp. 223–24, *supra.*

Chapter 9

SELF-DETERMINATION:
THE EXISTENTIAL ISSUE
CONCERNING CAUSAL INITIATIVE

We shall be concerned in this chapter with the debate of the issue that is constituted by opposite answers to the question, "Is there any reality corresponding to a conception of freedom, such as that of self-determination, which presupposes the existence of causal initiative on man's part?" As we pointed out in the preceding chapter, writers who are in topical agreement about the meaning of causal initiative and disagree about the validity of this presupposition disagree as a consequence about the existence of a freedom of self-determination in human life.[1]

Those who would take the negative side in this dispute actually join issue only if they understand causal initiative in a manner which corresponds sufficiently to the understanding of it held by authors who take the affirmative side. The burden of coming into topical agreement with the adherents of SD falls on them.[2] They must deny that the self or the will is the uncaused cause of its own acts, i.e., its volitions; or that, in making decisions, it has the power to act without being acted upon by efficient causes outside itself on the plane of finite or natural causes.[3]

Since the issue is raised, in the first place, by the denial of causal initiative, it is appropriate to begin our exposition of the debate by considering first the arguments advanced on the negative side. These, as we shall see, fall into two main types, one more general than the other. The more general attack appeals to the universal principle of causation and argues that there can be no exception to it in the sphere of human action, i.e., in human action, as in all other natural phenomena, there can be no effect without a cause and no cause which is not also the effect of some prior cause. The less general attack, based on a causal analysis of volition itself, argues that a man's character and his motives cause the decisions

---

[1] See Ch. 8, p. 238, *supra*.

[2] See *ibid.*, p. 227, *supra*.

[3] For a more complete summary of the understanding of causal initiative on the part of those SD authors who affirm it, see *ibid.*, pp. 237–40, *supra*.

he makes, and that these causes are themselves all effects of other causes, which were operative in the past or are now operative in the present.

To these attacks the defenders of causal initiative respond by calling attention to their reasons for thinking that both fail. It is important to observe here that the reasons given are, for the most part, to be found in the theories of man's freedom of self-determination which SD authors propound, quite apart from any exigency to defend causal initiative against such attacks. They are not, in other words, invented *ad hoc*. Rather it is as if the defenders of SD were saying to their opponents: "If you will examine the things we have said to explain and support our assertion of causal initiative, you will see why we think your arguments fail. To make them effective, you must deal with the grounds on which our assertion rests, not just with the assertion itself."

Many of the authors on the negative side of the issue do attack the grounds on which certain defenders of SD claim to rest their case. They, too, can be interpreted as saying to their opponents: "We have not overlooked the things you posit as the basis for your assertion of causal initiative; but our position remains the same, for we deny the reality of what you posit, and so we continue to deny the causal initiative which you think can be thus supported or defended."

In that part of the debate which has just been described, it makes no difference whether we regard the reasons given by the adherents of SD as grounds for the *support* of causal initiative or as points made subsequently in its *defense*, i.e., in response to attack. In either case, the reasons are intrinsic to the nature of that which is being defended or supported.

In addition, there are arguments, which the adherents of SD advance, that are quite extrinsic in character. These are usually offered in primary support of their position, rather than defensively. As thus offered, they constitute a challenge to be met by the writers on the opposite side.

There are two main types of argument of this extrinsic sort. One holds that men cannot be held responsible for the actions which flow from their decisions unless their decisions are causally initiated by them. The other rests on the proposition that men *feel* that they make their decisions in a way which either directly testifies to their possession of casual initiative, or warrants an inference to that effect.

To these extrinsic arguments for the existence of causal initiative, writers on the negative side of the issue respond by giving their reasons for thinking that they fail to establish what their proponents claim they do. And here, in a few cases, the proponents have something further to say in defense of the arguments.

The foregoing summary indicates that the whole debate of this issue can be divided into four main parts, two in which reasons given for the denial of causal initiative are countered by reasons which can be offered either in support or in defense of it, and two in which grounds or evidence given for the assertion of causal initiative are countered by criticisms which claim that they fail to establish the affirmative case. We shall, therefore, organize this chapter accordingly, presenting the four parts of the debate in successive sections.

However, not all writers on either the negative or the affirmative side argue for or in defense of the position they take. Some merely deny the existence of causal initiative; some merely assert it. Hence, in Section I, where we shall enumerate the writers who take the affirmative or negative side of this issue, we shall indicate those who, while joining issue, do not engage in debate. Those who do will, of course, be treated more fully in the sections to follow.

Section 2 will deal with that part of the debate which centers on the universal principle of causation. Section 3 will deal with that part which concerns the role of character and motives in the determination of decisions. In both these parts, we shall begin with arguments that are advanced against causal initiative.

Section 4 will treat that part of the debate which turns on the relation of responsibility to causal initiative. Section 5 will treat that part in which the feeling, consciousness, or experience of free decision is central. In both these parts, we shall begin with arguments that are offered in support of causal initiative.

It was pointed out in the preceding chapter that the literature of this subject contains a few outstanding instances of actual debate, i.e., of actual interchanges between authors in which each refers to the other.[4] More numerous, of course, are the instances in which an author refers to other writers as holding opinions which he is criticizing, but where these others do not reply to him. The actual dispute between Hobbes and Bishop Bramhall in the seventeenth century, between Priestley and Price in the eighteenth century, and the interchange in our own day between C. A. Campbell, on the one hand, and P. H. Nowell-Smith and R. D. Bradley, on the other, represent instances of the first sort. Instances of the second sort are afforded by Spinoza's critique of Descrates, Windelband's critique of Kant, and the criticism of C. D. Broad by C. A. Campbell and L. J. Russell.[5]

---

[4] See Ch. 8, pp. 223–24, *supra.*
[5] In the writings of Thomas Aquinas, we find unnamed objectors who oppose the position he takes, to whose objections he, in turn, replies. Even though the actual dispute is here presented by one of the parties, we shall treat these interchanges in the same way as we treat the actual dispute between Hobbes and Bramhall, or between Priestley and Price.

In setting forth each part of the debate (in Sections 2–5), we think it only proper to give prominence to the authors who have actually disputed with one another. Wherever it is possible to do so, we shall let them set the stage for us, before we introduce other writers whose role or contribution to the debate, while drawn from their works, is to some extent a matter of our own construction. The debate presented as a whole is mainly a construction from the literature, since, as a whole, it is implicit in the literature and cannot be reported as actually occurring. Most of the authors who are presented as opposed in argument did not in fact actually confront one another in oral or written interchanges. Nevertheless, it will be instructive to observe that the disputes which did take place do touch most of the lines of argument and counter-argument that are the constructed elements of the debate as a whole.

Throughout, it should be remembered that this issue concerning causal initiative involves points of argument that are also involved in the three other issues which will be considered in subsequent chapters, especially the issue concerning causal indeterminacy to be considered in Chapter 10. The incompleteness of certain arguments here, or even their total absence, which may appear to be deficiencies in the dispute of this issue, results in some instances from the fact that certain matters have been reserved for treatment or fuller development later. These will be duly noted.

1. THE PARTIES TO THE ISSUE AND TO THE DEBATE

In Chapter 8, we enumerated, in several tabulations, the authors whom we interpreted as affirming a freedom of self-determination. The first tabulation repeated the list of authors who had been so classified in Volume I; the second named those among them in whose writings we found a developed theory of such freedom and who can also be construed as arguing the affirmative case in one or another of the four issues about SD; the third listed additional authors of the same sort whose contributions to the debate were made prior to the twentieth century; and the fourth, twentieth-century authors who uphold SD.[6]

Not all of these writers, however, are parties to the particular issue with which we are here concerned. Of the authors treated in some detail in Volume I, only the following can be construed as definitely taking the affirmative side of the question about causal initiative. The enumeration is alphabetical.

[6] See *loc. cit.*, pp. 248–50, *supra*.

Aquinas	Kant
Aristotle	Leibniz
Augustine	Locke
Campbell	Maritain
Cicero	Meyerson
Descartes	Renouvier
Duns Scotus	Rousseau
Epicurus	Sartre
Fouillée	Secrétan
Hegel	Simon
James	Suarez

The evidence for this interpretation of the views of the foregoing authors can be found by consulting the analytical index to Volume I. Of these authors, some do little more than assert causal initiative, e.g., Cicero, Epicurus, Locke, Meyerson, Secrétan. All the rest, in varying degrees, offer reasons which play a part in the debate of this issue. The evidence of this will be found in the sections to follow.

The following alphabetical enumeration lists authors, not treated in Volume I, who can also be construed as definitely taking the affirmative side of the question about causal initiative.

Magda Arnold	Michael Maher
Emile Boutroux	Henry L. Mansel
Borden Parker Bowne	James Martineau
Bishop Bramhall	Harald Ofstad
Benedetto Croce	Joseph Price
Austin Farrer	Joseph Rickaby
Hubert Gruender	Josiah Royce
J. S. Haldane	L. J. Russell
William Ernest Hocking	Frederick Schelling
N. Lossky	F. C. S. Schiller
Hermann Lotze	A. K. Stout
A. C. MacIntyre	Isaac Watts

All of these writers make some contribution to the debate of this issue, some to a much greater extent than others. The part they play will be documented in the sections to follow.

A number of authors who take the negative side of this issue were mentioned as opponents of SD in Volume I, e.g., Hobbes, Spinoza, Hume, Edwards, Priestley, J. S. Mill, Sidgwick, B. Russell, M. Schlick, C. D. Broad, H. Kelsen, A. J. Ayer, and C. L. Stevenson. The following alpha-

betical enumeration, which includes them, completes the picture by adding
the names of others who were not treated in Volume I.

Samuel Alexander	H. W. B. Joseph
A. J. Ayer	Hans Kelsen
Alexander Bain	William McDougall
Mikhail Bakunin	J. S. Mill
Brand Blanshard	F. Nietzsche
F. H. Bradley	P. H. Nowell-Smith
R. D. Bradley	Arthur Pap
C. D. Broad	Friedrich Paulsen
T. H. Buckle	Joseph Priestley
G. Clemenceau	Hastings Rashdall
C. J. Ducasse	Bertrand Russell
Jonathan Edwards	Moritz Schlick
David Hartley	Henry Sidgwick
Carl G. Hempel	Herbert Spencer
E. R. Hobart	B. Spinoza
Thomas Hobbes	C. L. Stevenson
L. T. Hobhouse	Abraham Tucker
Baron d'Holbach	Gardner Williams
David Hume	William Windelband
T. H. Huxley	

The foregoing by no means exhausts the list of authors who deny that man
has a natural freedom of self-determination.[7] It includes only those who
can be interpreted as having considered the question about causal initative
and as having given a negative answer to it.

The documentary evidence of the ways in which these authors argue
against causal initiative, or their reasons for rejecting such arguments as are
offered for it, will be found in the sections to follow.

2. THE DISPUTE ABOUT THE PRINCIPLE OF CAUSATION

Those who base their denial of causal initiative on the principle of
causation regard this principle as stating a universal truth to which there
is no exception. In their view, the exponents of causal initiative appear to
claim that, in human behavior, the self or the will acts in a way that would

[7] For a more complete list, see Ch. 8, pp. 251–52, *supra*.

constitute an exception to the universality of the causal principle. Hence, they argue, that claim cannot be sustained.

Though their reasoning follows this pattern in general, their specific arguments take two somewhat different forms, according to the manner in which the principle of causation is formulated.

One formulation of it is that nothing moves itself to action, i.e., everything which acts does so only as a result of being acted upon by something else. But the exponents of causal initiative claim that the self or the will moves itself to action, i.e., that it acts without being acted upon. Since this claim violates the principle, it must be false.

The other formulation of the principle is that there is no effect without a cause, and no cause which is not itself the effect of some antecedent cause. The chain of causes has no first link. Nothing happens without a cause of its happening or coming to be. But the exponents of causal initiative claim that man's volitions constitute a break in the chain of causes, positing here either an uncaused effect or a cause which is not the effect of any antecedent cause. Since this claim violates the principle, it must be false.

In both formulations of the principle, a cause is either that which acts to produce an effect, or that from which the effect flows or follows. In both cases, the mover or the antecedent has the character of an efficient cause. But the two formulations appear to differ in one significant respect.

The first seems to admit that the stream of causes and effects involves substantive beings (i.e., enduring entities or continuing existences, such as a man, his self or his will) which both act and are acted upon; it simply denies that any such beings act without being acted upon. The second seems to recognize no continuing existences, but only events or occurrences, and puts volitions into the stream of events, regarding them as effects of prior events and as causes of subsequent ones.

The second way of formulating the principle of causation is best exemplified by Hume, and is found in most of the writers who follow him or are influenced by him. In some cases, as, for example, that of Hobbes and Priestley, it is not always clear in which form they are appealing to the principle of causation. On the other hand, the objectors whom Aquinas presents as his opponents talk in terms of substances and powers when they deny that any substance has the power of moving itself to act or that any power can act without being acted upon.

However, in responding to these arguments based on the universal principle of causation, formulated in either way, the defenders of causal initiative adopt, for the most part, that view of the causal nexus which involves enduring beings or their powers. As we pointed out in the preceding chapter, they conceive the self as having a continuing or enduring existence which is quite different from the momentary being of events or occurrences. Hence when they relate the self (as uncaused cause) to the decisions it makes (as effects of that cause), they are not to be understood as saying that one event, an effect, follows another, the cause, but this does not in turn follow any other as an effect. They are saying instead that decisions, which are events and effects, issue from a cause which is not an event and not an effect. Whereas causally related antecedent and consequent events are separate items in a sequence of occurrent entities, the self acting to make a decision and the decision produced are not thus separated. The self as a cause has the power to produce decisions, and the decisions as effects are manifestations of that power's being exercised. The self, in exercising its power to make decisions, thus operates as uncaused cause of its own acts, namely, the decisions made.[8]

One other point must be observed. As we shall see, many of the writers who deny causal initiative as violating the universal principle of causation declare that "an uncaused effect" is self-contradictory or impossible. But as we shall also find, many defenders of causal initiative explicitly reply by saying that they also regard an uncaused effect as self-contradictory or impossible. They insist that if the effect in question is a volition or a decision, it must, as an effect, be caused. But its cause, they go on to declare, is not an effect and not caused; i.e., it acts without being acted upon by causes outside itself on the plane of finite causes.[9]

There would, therefore, seem to be no issue about whether there can be an uncaused effect. Hence, if we were to interpret those who speak of the impossibility of uncaused effects as having this as their sole ground for denying causal initiative, we could not construe them as joining issue with the writers whom they regard as their opponents. But it seems reasonable to suppose that their use of the phrase "uncaused effect" is only their shorthand way of saying not only that there can be no uncaused effect, but also that there can be no cause which is not itself an effect. Interpreted in this way, they clearly do join issue with all the authors who assert that the self or will, in effecting decisions or volitions, acts without being acted upon, i.e., operates as a cause without being efficiently caused to do so by anything extrinsic to itself, at least so far as other finite causes are concerned.

With these points clarified, we turn now to the first phase of the fairly

---

[8] Ch. 8, p. 229, *supra*.

[9] These writers sometimes distinguish, as we shall see, between the existence of the cause and its operation; and, making this distinction, they acknowledge that the will, for example, must be caused to exist even if it is able to act without being caused to act by some other finite cause. They regard the will as a caused effect in the order of existence, but as an uncaused cause in the order of its own operation.

elaborate dispute which involves different understandings of the principle of causation and, consequently, differing views about whether causal initiative is or is not an exception to it. The first phase consists of the opening attack, made by the negative side, against the proposition that the self or the will is the uncaused cause of its own acts, i.e., of its decisions or volitions. Then, in the second phase, we shall consider the direct rejoinders, made by the affirmative side to the various forms of this attack; in the third phase, we shall examine the underlying reasons or grounds to which the affirmative side appeals in making the foregoing rejoinders; and, finally, in the fourth phase, we shall deal with the rejection of these reasons or grounds by the negative side.

First Phase

Typical expressions of the argument against causal initiative, regarded as violating the universal principle of causation, are found in (i) the statement of objections to free will in the writings of Aquinas, in (ii) the objections of Hobbes to Bramhall, and (iii) the objections of Priestley to Price. Somewhat variant expressions of the same general line of argument are also found in (iv) statements by Spinoza and in (v) statements by Hume. To the summary of each of these classic statements, we shall append references to other writers who make essentially the same points.

(i) In Aquinas's *De Malo*, the objector maintains that whatever changes in any respect must be changed by something, because "everything which is moved is moved by something."[10] Citing Augustine as authority for the statement that "nothing by itself is the cause that it is," the objector argues: "By the same reason, nothing is the cause by itself that it is moved. Therefore, the will does not move itself; but it is necessary that it be moved by something, for it begins to act after not acting before."[11]

In the *Summa Theologica*, where the question is "Whether the will moves itself?" the objector appeals to Aristotle's definition of movement as *the act of that which is in potentiality, in so far as it is in potentiality.* Accordingly, the objector argues that since every mover, as mover, must be in act, whereas that which is moved must be in potentiality, it follows that "nothing moves itself," for to do so it would have to be both in potentiality and in act. The will, the objector says, is no exception to this universal rule.[12] Furthermore, the objector points out, the will is not always acting,

---

[10] *Op. cit.*, Q. 6, Objection 17.
[11] *Ibid.*, Objection 20.
[12] *Op. cit.*, Part I–II, Q. 9, A. 3, Objection 1.

but since the will is always present to itself, it would always be moved to action if it moved itself or were the cause of its own action.[13]

(ii) In *The Questions Concerning Liberty, Necessity, and Chance, Clearly Stated and Debated between Dr. Bramhall and Thomas Hobbes,* Hobbes declares it to be a universal principle of change that "nothing taketh beginning from itself, but from the action of some other immediate agent without itself." This, he claims, applies to the action of the will as to everything else: like everything else, the will is "caused by other things whereof it disposeth not."[14] Furthermore, Hobbes points out, it is not only impossible to imagine anything happening, or beginning to be, without a cause, but even if we could imagine a happening without a cause, we could not answer the question why it should occur at one time rather than another.[15] This question resembles the one asked by the objector in Aquinas. Where the objector asks, "Why if the will can cause its own actions, is it not always acting?" Hobbes asks, "If the will can begin to act without a cause extrinsic to itself, why does it act at one time rather than another?"

Jonathan Edwards argues in the same vein against the Arminians, whose doctrine he interprets as maintaining that "the faculty or power of will, or the soul in the use of that power, determines its own volitions; and that it does it without any act going before the act determined."[16] He insists that "if the particular act or exertion of will, which comes into existence, be anything properly determined at all, then it has some cause of its existing . . . which cause is distinct from the effect and prior to it."[17] Hence, he concludes, that cause cannot be "the will exercising a sovereign power over itself, to determine, cause, and excite volitions in itself."[18]

(iii) One of the basic tenets in Joseph Priestley's writings on freedom and necessity, which occasioned his debate with Dr. Price, puts the argument against causal initiative on the part of the will in somewhat different form. Priestley maintains that the universal principle of causation holds "as much in the intellectual, as in the natural world."[19] That every effect has

---

[13] *Ibid.*, Objection 2. Cf. F. H. Bradley's statement that "something like a self-contained cause with an effect within itself . . . surely is illusory. The old difficulties about the beginning of change and its process in time, the old troubles as to diversity in union with sameness—how is any one of these got rid of, or made more tractable?" (*Appearance and Reality*, p. 99).

[14] *Op. cit.*, in *English Works*, Vol. V, pp. 372–73.

[15] *Ibid.*, p. 390.

[16] *Freedom of the Will*, p. 175.

[17] *Ibid.*, p. 178.

[18] *Ibid.*, p. 226.

[19] *The Doctrine of Philosophical Necessity Illustrated; Being an Appendix to the Disquisitions relating to matter and spirit; To which is added an answer to several persons who have controverted the principles of it*, p. 8. In further references to this work, the title will be abbreviated to *The Doctrine of Philosophical Necessity*.

a cause, and that every cause is itself the effect of some prior cause—these "same general maxims apply to them both"; i.e., to events which are voluntarily produced as well as to those which are mechanically produced.[20] Priestley maintains that a scientific approach to the phenomena of human behavior, or to the actions of man's will, will not exempt them from the same general principles which science has so successfully applied to the phenomena of the physical world. "In all investigations relating to human nature," he declares, "the philosopher will apply the same rules by which his inquiries have been conducted upon all other subjects."[21]

(iv) Before we mention the numerous writers who argue, as Priestley does, that the same causal laws apply uniformly to human as to all other natural phenomena, we must consider the somewhat different way in which Spinoza makes essentially the same point. The general proposition which he applies without exception, Spinoza states in the following manner.

Every individual thing, or everything which is finite and has a conditioned existence, cannot exist or be *conditioned to act,* unless it be conditioned for existence *and action* by a cause *other than itself,* which also is finite and *has a conditioned existence;* and likewise this cause cannot in its turn exist, or be *conditioned to act,* unless it be conditioned for existence and action by another cause, which also is finite, and has a conditioned existence, and *so on to infinity.*[22]

On the plane of finite causes and effects, there is nothing which exists or acts that is not caused to exist or act by some other finite thing which must be similarly caused to exist and act by still some other. There can be no break or beginning in the infinite chain of causes and effects.

The will, Spinoza then goes on to declare, is no exception to this universal truth. Treating the will as nothing but "a particular mode of thinking," and thus identifying it with its volitions, Spinoza maintains that "no volition can exist, nor be conditioned to act, unless it be conditioned by some cause other than itself, which cause is conditioned by a third cause, and so on to infinity."[23] In other words, "the mind is determined to wish this or that by a cause, which has also been determined by another cause, and this last by another cause, and so on to infinity."[24]

Other writers assert the existence of an unbroken, endless chain of causes and argue against man's having causal initiative on the ground that it

[20] *Ibid.,* pp. 13–14. See also *A Free Discussion of the Doctrine of Materialism and Philosophical Necessity* (Priestley-Price Controversy), pp. 145–46, where Priestley maintains that man is no more a self-moving agent than a stone is, and for the same reason.
[21] *The Doctrine of Philosophical Necessity,* p. 35.
[22] *Ethics,* Part I, Prop. XXVIII, p. 67. (Italics added.)
[23] *Ibid.,* Prop. XXXII, p. 70.
[24] *Ibid.,* Part II, Prop. XLVIII, p. 119.

requires man, his self, or his will, to be a first cause, a starting point, in the causal series in which his voluntary actions are effects. Thus, for example, T. H. Huxley writes:

> We are conscious automata, endowed with free will in the only intelligible sense of that much-abused term—inasmuch as in many respects we are able to do as we like—but none the less parts of the great series of causes and effects which, in unbroken continuity, composes that which is, and has been, and shall be—the sum of existence.[25]

Similarly, Mikhail Bakunin rejects that "pretended free will" which would "pull man out of the stream of universal causality which determines the existence of everything and makes each depend on all others." We must "reject it as nonsense for nothing can exist outside this causality."[26] And Hans Kelsen declares that "there is no such thing as an end point in causality," such as would be required by conceptions of the free will as a first or uncaused cause.[27] "To conciliate the freedom of will with the universal law of causality is impossible," Kelsen declares, "if freedom of will means exemption from the causality governing natural reality."[28]

Still other writers, while agreeing with Spinoza about the endless chain of cause and effect, place more emphasis on Priestley's point that causal laws apply to the determination of human volition and action in exactly the same way as they apply to the determination of all nonhuman natural phenomena. For example, J. S. Mill asserts that, since the law of causation permits no exception, it applies to volitions in the same way as it does to everything else.[29] According to Herbert Spencer, volitions, as effects, are "as conformable to law as the simplest reflex actions."[30] In Sidgwick's opinion, we must regard "the future actions of ourselves or others . . . as determined by unvarying laws," as is the case with all natural phenomena.[31] Such authors as Friedrich Paulsen, Samuel Alexander, Bertrand Russell, and Georges Clemenceau express views similar to those of Mill, Spencer, and Sidgwick.[32]

(v) Finally, we come to the form in which Hume states the argument against causal initiative. His reasoning can be summarized as follows.

---

[25] *Method and Results*, p. 244.

[26] *Oeuvres*, Vol. I, p. 96.

[27] *What is Justice?*, p. 333.

[28] *Ibid.*, pp. 344–45.

[29] *A System of Logic*, Vol. 1, p. 380 fn. Cf. *ibid.*, Vol. II, p. 409 ff.

[30] *Principles of Psychology*, Vol. I, p. 502.

[31] *Methods of Ethics*, p. 71. Cf. *ibid.*, pp. 63–64.

[32] See Paulsen, *A System of Ethics*, pp. 457–59, 471; Alexander, *Moral Order and Progress*, p. 337; Russell, "Determinism and Morals," in the *Hibbert Journal*, Vol. 7, p. 115; Clemenceau, *In the Evening of My Thought*, pp. 52, 54–55.

Necessity (i.e., the necessitation of the effect by the cause), he tells us, is by definition an essential aspect of causation. But liberty (i.e., a free choice between alternative decisions or volitions) is, again by definition, incompatible with necessity. Consequently, it is also incompatible with causation. Liberty, in his view, is thus reduced to causelessness which, Hume maintains, "is the very same thing with chance." And, he continues, "as chance is commonly thought to imply a contradition, and is at least directly contrary to experience, there are always the same arguments against liberty or free-will."[33]

From the point of view of the arguments of C. D. Broad and C. A. Campbell, which we shall consider later, it is of interest to note that Hume argues that the causal indeterminacy of a free choice presupposes the causelessness of causal initiative on the part of the chooser. Hume thus equates indeterminacy (the absence of necessity) with initiative (the absence of a cause), and then he equates causelessness with chance. We shall subsequently consider what Broad and Campbell have to say about this. For our present purposes, the nub of Hume's argument lies in his treating an "uncaused cause" and an "uncaused effect" as equally self-contradictory. For him, both represent causelessness or, what is the same, chance, i.e., something happening without any cause whatsoever, which is impossible if everything which happens must have a cause or a sufficient reason.

A number of writers argue against causal initiative in a way that adopts Hume's reduction of it to causelessness and chance. Thus, for example, David Hartley says that "if we put for philosophical free-will the power of doing things without a cause, it will be a word of nearly the same import as chance. . . . It will therefore be as unfit to ascribe a real causality to free-will as to chance."[34] According to T. H. Buckle, "The doctrine of Chance in the external world corresponds to that of Free Will in the internal";[35] and this, for Buckle, is sufficient to dismiss the latter along with the former. For Nietzsche, "*causi sui* is the best self-contradiction that has yet been conceived."[36] And for Wilhelm Windelband, a cause of willing which is not itself the effect of another cause not only interrupts

[33] *A Treatise of Human Nature*, Book II, Part III, Sect. I, p. 407. Cf. *An Enquiry Concerning Human Understanding*, Sect. VIII, Part I, Div. 74, pp. 95–96, where Hume writes: "It is universally allowed that nothing exists without a cause of its existence, and that chance, when strictly examined, is a mere negative word, and means not any real power which has anywhere a being in nature"; and, in his view, "liberty, when opposed to necessity, not to constraint, is the same thing with chance, which is universally allowed to have no existence."

[34] *Observations on Man*, p. 364. Cf. Abraham Tucker, *Free Will, Foreknowledge, and Fate*, pp. 52–55, 67–68, 76–77.

[35] *History of Civilization in England*, Vol. I, p. 8.

[36] *Beyond Good and Evil*, p. 21.

the chain of causes, but also introduces the causelessness which is the same as chance.[37] Still other writers, such as H. W. B. Joseph, E. R. Hobart, G. Williams, and C. J. Ducasse, reject causal initiative as self-contradictory or inconsistent with the principle of causation.[38]

SECOND PHASE

We shall consider here the replies which (i) Aquinas makes to the objections raised against causal initiative; the replies (ii) of Bishop Bramhall to Thomas Hobbes and the replies (iii) of Dr. Price to Joseph Priestley; the comment (iv) of Henry Mansel on J. S. Mill, and (v) of Joseph Rickaby on Hobbes, Hume, and Mill.

(i) Before we examine the specific answers which Aquinas makes in the *De Malo* to the objections there raised, we must look first at the statement he makes about the causal initiative of the human will, in the body of Question 6. He maintains that, in the exercise of its power to act, "the will is moved by itself"; but, he immediately declares, it does not follow from this "that the will is both in potency and in act with respect to the same thing." He then explains that it is through being in act with respect to one thing that the will moves itself to act in respect to another; i.e., having a certain actuality in one respect, it is able to reduce itself from potentiality to act in another respect.

Now the respect in which the will is able to move itself to act is the volition of the means. In order to reduce itself from potentiality to act with respect to the means, it must be in act in another respect, namely, with respect to the end. But in this respect, according to Aquinas, the will cannot move itself in the order of exercise. In that act which is the volition of the end, the will must be moved by an exterior agent, namely, God. Nevertheless, though God is the efficient cause of man's will's being in actual operation in the first place (i.e., in its volition of the end, happiness), the will, being thus in act, has the active power to be the cause of its secondary operations (i.e., its volition of the means to happiness). It thus remains unique among created causes; for it is an uncaused cause, inasmuch as it operates without being efficiently caused to do so by any finite agent outside itself.[39]

[37] See *Über Willensfreiheit*, pp. 122–24, 132.

[38] Joseph, *Some Problems in Ethics*, p. 128; Hobart, "Free Will as Involving Determinism and Inconceivable Without It," in *Mind*, Vol. XLIII, No. 169, pp. 3, 6, 7; Williams, "Free Will and Determinism," in *The Journal of Philosophy*, Vol. XXXVIII, No. 26, p. 702; Ducasse, *Nature, Mind, and Death*, pp. 191–93.

[39] *Loc. cit.* Cf. *Summa Theologica*, Part I–II, Q. 9, AA. 3, 4, 6; and *Summa Contra Gentiles*, Book III, Ch. 89.

Appealing to the points just made, Aquinas meets the three objections raised against causal initiative.

Acknowledging the truth of the objector's proposition that everything which moves must be moved by something, Aquinas explains that that which moves the will, when its potentiality for choosing is actualized, is the will itself.[40]

To the further objection that for something to move itself, it must be at once in act and in potency, Aquinas replies that, while nothing can be both potential and actual *in the same respect*, the will, in moving itself, is *not in the same respect* both potential and actual; for it is through being in act with respect to the end that it moves itself, or reduces itself from potentiality to act, with respect to some means.[41]

Finally, to the objection that the will is not always acting, as it might be expected to if it were the cause of its own action, since it is always present to itself, Aquinas makes the following reply.

> The power of the will is always actually present to itself; but the act of the will, by which it wills the end, is not always in the will. But it is by this act that it moves itself. Accordingly, it does not follow that it is always moving itself.[42]

Before we turn to Bishop Bramhall's rejoinders to Hobbes, which are generally similar to those that Aquinas makes to his objector, let us consider a twentieth-century commentary on the position of Aquinas in this debate. The commentator, Yves Simon, is aware of the attacks on causal initiative which have been made from the seventeenth century on. In a chapter on "Free Will and the Principle of Causality," he begins by saying that no sound theory of self-determination can regard "the free act [as] an event without cause."

> If it were true that the free act is, in any sense whatever, an exception to the principle of causality, then nothing . . . would prevent the whole theory of free will from foundering on the absurdities of irrationalism and lawless contingency.[43]

---

[40] *De Malo*, Q. 6, Reply to Objection 17.

[41] *Ibid.*, Reply to Objection 20. Cf. *Summa Theologica*, Part I–II, Q. 9, A. 3, where in Reply to Objection 1, Aquinas writes: "It is not in the same respect that the will moves itself and is moved; and so neither is it in act and in potentiality in the same respect. But in so far as it actually wills the end, it reduces itself from potentiality to act concerning the means, so as to will them actually."

[42] *Summa Theologica*, Part I–II, Q. 9, A. 3, Reply to Objection 2.

[43] *Traité du Libre Arbitre*, Chapter VII, p. 93. Cf. similar declarations by other contemporary Thomists that there is no conflict between free will and the principle of causality: Michael Maher, *Psychology*, pp. 419–20; Hubert Gruender, *Free Will*, pp. 20–25.

Simon then discusses the three essential aspects of the principle of efficient causality. The first he calls the principle of the *altereity* of the cause: that everything which is in motion is moved by *another*.[44] The second he calls the principle of the *actuality* of the cause: that nothing can function as a causative agent unless it is itself something *actual*, i.e., is in act rather than in potency.[45] And the third he calls the principle of resemblance: that every agent produces something which resembles itself.

On this understanding of the principle of causality, which he recognizes may not be the understanding of it on the part of those who deny causal initiative, Simon asks: Does the conception of the will as an active power moving itself to act, violate the law of causality? He undertakes to show (a) that since the will is *not* both mover and moved in the same respect, the will's causal initiative does not violate the principle of altereity;[*] (b) that, when the decision which the will makes to act in a certain way is followed by the carrying out of that action, the principle of resemblance between cause and effect is verified;[48] and (c) that the principle of actuality is satisfied by the fact that the will's active power to move itself to act with respect to the means comes from the actuality of its very nature, i.e., its being by nature in act with respect to the end—the perfect or complete good.[49]

Simon's concluding observation, to which we shall return in another connection, is that the principle of efficient causality, as he understands it in its threefold aspect, is exemplified by what he calls "free causality," on the one hand, and by what he calls "determined causality," on the other. Free causality belongs to a causative agent, such as the will, which has the active power to cause its own acts. Determined causality is found in intrinsically inert things, such as bodies which act as causes only insofar as they are acted upon by causes outside themselves.[50]

(ii) To Hobbes's remark that "nothing taketh beginning from itself but from the action of some other immediate agent without itself," Bramhall responds by making two distinctions.

(a) If Hobbes is talking about the will as a faculty or power of the human soul, then Bramhall thinks he would be right to say that the will does not take its "beginning from itself, but from God, who created and

---

[44] *Traité du Libre Arbitre*, pp. 96–97.
[45] *Ibid.*, pp. 97–98.
[46] *Ibid.*, pp. 98–99.
[47] *Ibid.*, pp. 100–2.
[48] *Ibid.*, pp. 102–5.
[49] *Ibid.*, pp. 105–10.
[50] *Ibid.*, p. 111. "The first part of this division," Simon writes, "constitutes, without doubt, the most intelligible case in itself; but determined causality is less mysterious and, despite certain appearances, more familarly known than free causality" (*ibid.*).

fused the soul into man and endowed it with its power." If, however,
1 distinction from the will as a faculty, Hobbes uses the word "will" to
efer to the act of willing, then Bramhall thinks it is also right to say that
it takes not beginning from itself, but from the faculty or from the power
f willing."[51]

(b) Bramhall then distinguishes between two possible meanings for
taking a beginning." One is "*a beginning of being*"; the other, "*a beginning of working and acting.*" If Hobbes means the first, then, according
o Bramhall, he is quite right to say that nothing—at least nothing on
arth—has the beginning of its being or existence from itself. But if Hobbes
neans the second, then Bramhall thinks he is wrong, since the question
hen concerns the act of willing, not the faculty or power of the will; for
ince one and the same thing can be both mover and moved in different
espects, the active power of the will can be assigned as the cause of
articular acts on the part of the will.[52]

Finally, Bramhall takes up the question which Hobbes had propounded
or him: "How can a man imagine anything to begin without a cause, or
f it should begin without a cause, why it should begin at this time rather
han at that time?" Agreeing with Hobbes that nothing can begin *to be*
vithout a cause, Bramhall reiterates that the will can "*begin to act* of itself
vithout any other cause." But, he continues, since the will is a free cause,
n virtue of having the power to cause its own acts, it also has the power
:o choose the time when it will act, in contrast to a determined cause,
vhich is not only determined to act by extrinsic causes but is also deter-
nined by them *when* to act. This, Bramhall thinks, suffices to answer the
question propounded by Hobbes.[53]

Hobbes, it must be observed in passing, turns the answer back against
Bramhall. To say that the will can begin to act of itself is to say that it
begins to act without a cause outside itself. But Bramhall has conceded
that nothing can begin to be without a cause outside itself. Yet when
something begins to act, the action begins to be. Accordingly, Hobbes

---

[51] *The Questions Concerning Liberty, Necessity, and Chance*, p. 373. In another
place, Bramhall calls attention to the fact that, in his view, Hobbes confuses "the
faculty of the will with the act of volition," when he uses the word "will" to stand
for the act which concludes deliberation and immediately precedes a bodily motion
or other execution of a decision. See *ibid.*, p. 360. We shall subsequently see, in the
fourth phase, that Hobbes replies to this by denying the existence of faculties, and
identifying, as Spinoza does, the will with acts of volition.

[52] *Ibid.*, p. 374.

[53] *Ibid.*, p. 395. As we pointed out earlier, this question resembles a question put to
Aquinas by the objector, namely, why does not the will·always move itself to action,
since, as moving cause of its own acts, the will is always present to itself (*Summa
Theologica*, Part I–II, Q. 9, A. 3, Objection 2). Cf. Aquinas's reply which distinguishes
between the power and the act of the will. See pp. 267–68, *supra*.

points out, this action *"begins to be* without any cause," which Bramhall had said nothing can do," thus "contradicting what he had said but in the line before."[54]

(iii) To Priestley's assertion that the principle of causation applies to volitions as it does to everything else—that the *same* rules of cause and effect are operative in voluntary as in mechanical actions—Dr. Price makes two rejoinders.

First, he calls Priestley's attention to the fact that he talks as if "self determination implies an effect without a cause," which would, of course violate the principle of causation. "But," Price insists, "this cannot be justly said. Does it follow that because I am *myself* the cause, there is no cause?"[55]

Secondly, he distinguishes between two kinds or orders of causation: physical and moral. In the one, physical beings, such as bodies, operate as causes. In the other, states of mind operate as causes. Since the two types of causes are so radically different, they should not be expected to operate in the same way; nor should we try to apply the same rules of causation to them both.[56]

(iv) What is of central interest to us in Henry Mansel's comment on J. S. Mill is Mansel's denial of the universality of the principle of causation, *if* that principle is conceived exclusively in terms of *physical* causes and effects.

Like Price, Mansel maintains that, in human voluntary behavior, the cause is of a radically different type. A volition is not an effect without a cause, but it is the effect of a cause that is not in turn the effect of antecedent phenomena.

> As applied to Physics, the *cause* of a phenomenon is a certain antecedent fact. . . . This notion of cause is gathered from material phenomena, and can only by an imperfect analogy be applied to mental . . . To speak of the determinations of the will as *caused* by phenomena, in the same sense in which the fusion of metal is *caused* by fire, is to give the lie to consciousness for the sake of theory.[57]

In an Appendix devoted to the consideration of Mill's views, Mansel takes up Mill's question, "Are our volitions, like other events, the results of causes?" He understands the question to mean: Are they the results of

---

[54] *Ibid.*, p. 404.
[55] *Priestley-Price Controversy*, p. 136.
[56] *Ibid.*, pp. 139 ff.
[57] *Prolegomena Logica*, pp. 152–53. The reference to consciousness is explained by Mansel's next statement: "On the other hand, if *cause* be interpreted to mean an agent with power, my only positive notion of cause in this sense is derived from the consciousness of myself as determining, not as determined" (*ibid.*).

extrinsic causes, causes other than the will of the individual in whom the volitions occur? Mansel's answer is that they are not, and that, consequently, we must admit "the freedom of the will" even if that requires us to deny "the applicability of the principle of causality [as understood by Mill and others] to human actions."[58]

(v) Rickaby charges Hobbes, Hume, and Mill with ignoring the difference between the types of causes which operate in the spheres of material and mental phenomena. "As men blinded by physics to everything above the physical and material order," he writes, "they ignore a vital difference between beings *conscious of the ego* and beings totally *unconscious,* between *persons* in fact and *things.*"[59] Excluding all causes except those of the physical type, they make, in his view, the simple error of converting the statement that volitions are *not* caused in this way into the statement that violitions are *uncaused.* Speaking specifically of Mill, Rickaby declares:

> I reject, equally with Mill, "the hypothesis of spontaneousness". . . . That is to say, I do not believe an act of the will to come out of nothing, a causeless phenomenon. I hold that the person who wills causes his own volition, under certain motives as conditions. To Mill the person is nobody; that is why he would call a free act "spontaneous," meaning that it has no cause.

It *is* caused, Rickaby insists, but not "in Mill's sense of the term," nor can the same kind of explanation be found for volitions "as for physical events."[60]

One point that is implicit in this criticism of Mill, Rickaby makes explicit in his criticisms of Hobbes and Hume. Not only do these writers ignore the difference between physical and mental causes but, in his view, they also misconceive the nature of causes, physical as well as mental. They reduce causes and effects to antecedent and consequent events in the sequence of phenomena, excluding substantial existences, whether persons or things. But, according to Rickaby, changes take place in enduring substances, and are caused by the action of other substances on them, as in the case of the motions of inert things, or by the subject of the change itself, as in the case of the free actions of persons. In the latter case, the principle of causation, correctly understood, is not violated by the statement that nothing outside the will of a voluntary agent—no antecedent event or extrinsic thing—is the cause of volitions.[61]

---

[58] *Ibid.,* p. 303. We shall return in Section 5 to the reason which Mansel gives at this point: that the opposite view is "at variance with the whole testimony of consciousness and with the experience of every day" (*ibid.*).
[59] *Free Will and Four English Philosophers,* p. 177.
[60] *Ibid.,* p. 197.
[61] See *ibid.,* pp. 67 ff., 148 ff.

THIRD PHASE

In the preceding summary of rejoinders to attacks based on the univers: principle of causation, we saw that the defenders of causal initiative als uphold the universality of causation, certainly to the extent of mai taining that no finite thing exists or happens without an efficient cause c its being or happening. But, in doing so, they differ from their opponents i their conception of causation.

Two of these writers, Simon and Rickaby, both followers of Aquina conceive efficient causes in terms of substances (i.e., enduring beings) an their powers to act. This conception permits them to give a caus: analysis of volition which regards certain acts of the will as effects that th will itself has the active power to cause.

In sharp contrast to this conception is the conception introduced b Hume, and adopted by his followers, according to which the cause is a: antecedent event from which another event, the effect, follows. This vie of cause and effect is usually accompanied by a denial of substances o: as in the case of Hobbes and Spinoza, at least by a denial of substantiv faculties. The will, accordingly, is not a power which can act. There i nothing but this or that particular volition, the cause of which must be a: antecedent event. In the context of this account of causes, to deny tha volitions are the effects of antecedent events is to assert that they ar uncaused.

There is another way in which the defenders of causal initiative, whom we have so far considered, differ from their opponents concerning causation As we have seen, Price and Mansel, together with Simon and Rickaby, insis that, while the principle of causation has the universality claimed for i by their opponents, it embraces two quite distinct modes of causation: o: the one hand, the mode of causation to be found in the realm of materia or physical things; on the other hand, the mode of causation to be found ir the immaterial realm of the human mind or soul and such of its powers o faculties as reason and will. As the one is the realm of determined causation so the other is the realm of free causation.[62] It is only in the latter realm that these writers posit the existence of causal initiative. Hence, as they see it, their opponents' denial of causal initiative stems from their denial o: any type of causation except that exhibited in the world of material things or physical phenomena.[63]

[62] Cf. Emile Meyerson, *Identity and Reality*, p. 47.
[63] A number of other writers, whom we have not yet mentioned, join them in pointing out that the defense of causal initiative requires an attack on an exclusively materialistic

The foregoing reveals two underlying reasons or grounds to which ‹ponents of causal initiative appeal in their defense of it as quite con-
‹stent with the universal principle of causation. Both, as we shall see, are
‹jected by writers who take the negative side of this issue.

The first is the metaphysical doctrine of individual substances, together
‹ith the theory of their powers or faculties, which is connected with the
‹nception of a cause as the action of a substance, and of an effect as the
‹tualization of a potency, either in the same substance or in another. This
‹eory is most fully developed by Aristotle, Aquinas, and their followers.
‹ut there are traces of it in Descartes, Leibniz, Rousseau, and even in
‹ant, for whom the transcendental ego or noumenal self, as contrasted
‹ith the empirical ego or phenomenal self, is a permanent or enduring
‹eing, endowed with certain faculties or powers.[64]

The second reason that underlies the attribution of initiative to certain
‹uses, but not to all, is the metaphysical doctrine that certain beings or
‹owers are immaterial. It is admitted that no purely material being can
‹ct without being acted upon. It is admitted that no change which occurs
‹ the realm of bodies can be a cause without also being an effect. Hence,
‹ is admitted that, if reality includes nothing but bodies or material
‹eings, causal initiative can have no existence in the order of real things.

But those who affirm causal initiative, and defend it against attack, do
‹ot admit that reality includes nothing but bodies or material beings.
‹a ways as various as their metaphysical doctrines, they assert the real

---

‹d mechanistic view of causation. See William James, *The Principles of Psychology*,
‹ol. I, pp. 447–48, 453–54; and Austin Farrer, *The Freedom of the Will*, pp. 48–52,
‹7–88, 93, 96–100.
‹ Kant's distinction between noumena and phenomena underlies his distinction be-
‹ween two modes of causation: free causation in the noumenal realm, in which causes
‹re beings that have the power to initiate or originate effects, and determined causa-
‹on in the phenomenal realm, in which every cause is an event that is the effect of
‹me antecedent cause. See *Critique of Pure Reason*, pp. 300–9; *Fundamental Princi-
‹les of the Metaphysics of Morals*, pp. 77–78. In contrast, for Aquinas and his fol-
‹wers, both free and determined causation involve substances and their powers; in
‹either case are cause and effect conceived as antecedent and consequent occurrences
‹ a sequence of phenomena or events. Hence, where Kant's distinction between deter-
‹ined and free causation involves him in a dichotomy between what he calls "the
‹ealm of nature" (i.e., the realm of sensible phenomena) and what he calls "the realm
‹f freedom" (i.e., the realm of noumenal or purely intelligible beings), no such di-
‹hotomy is involved in the distinction which Aquinas and his followers make between
‹ree and determined causation. Both fall within the realm of nature, the realm of
‹nite substances. The basic difference, as we shall presently see, is connected with the
‹ifference between those (e.g., Kant, Lotze, Schelling, Royce, Croce, Lossky, and
‹aldane) who think that causal initiative belongs only to supra-temporal causes, and
‹hose (e.g., Aquinas, Leibniz, Descartes, Fouillée, Maritain, Simon) who think that the
‹ction of free causes occurs in time.

existence of the immaterial, i.e., of that which is neither a body nor th
action of a body. It is to such things as spirit, spiritual substance, soul, mir
reason, will, the rational or transcendental ego, and consciousness, and on
to these, that causal initiative is attributed.

The following brief summary exemplifies the diversity of doctrines i
which the immateriality of the agent or cause is connected with its havin
causal initiative or being a free cause.

(a) Aristotle conceives reason as the one immaterial power of th
human soul, the only one the acts of which are not the acts of any bodi]
organ.[65] To nature and chance, he adds human reason as a third type c
cause.[66] It is through reason, more specifically desiderative reason, the
"man is a moving principle of [his own] actions."[67]

(b) Aquinas distinguishes between the intellect as a cognitive facult
and the will as an appetitive faculty; but the will, as an intellectual c
rational appetite, is for him, like the intellect itself, an incorporeal powe
of the human soul, i.e., a power the actions of which are not the acts c
bodily organs, as the acts of sensation, memory, and imagination are act
of the sense organs and brain.[68] It is in virtue of its being a spiritua
faculty in this sense that the will, for Aquinas and his followers, cai
exercise causal initiative to the extent of being the "agent cause" of its owi
acts.[69]

(c) For Descartes, the agency of the will is the distinctive characteristi
of mind (or thinking, immaterial substance), as local motion is th
distinctive characteristic of body (or extended, material substance).[*]
Similarly, for Rousseau, man's distinctive power of "free agency" is rootee

---

[65] See De Anima, Book III, Ch. 4, 429ª22–26.

[66] Nicomachean Ethics, Book III, Ch. 3, 1112ª30–32.

[67] Ibid., 1112b31. And in another place Aristotle writes: "The origin of action—it
efficient, not its final cause—is choice, and that of choice is desire and reasoning witl
a view to an end" (ibid., Book VI, Ch. 2, 1139ª31–32). A twentieth-century writer—
A. C. MacIntyre—also maintains that reason cannot be reduced to other causes ane
that the causal analysis which science applies to other phenomena does not apply t
rational behavior. See his article "Determinism," in Mind, Vol. LXVI, No. 261, pp
37–38. But there is nothing in MacIntyre's article to suggest that, like Aristotle, h
regards reason as an immaterial cause.

[68] Summa Theologica, Part I, Q. 75, AA. 2, 3; Q. 76, A. 1; Q. 78, A. 1; Q. 82, AA. ;
4; and see also Truth, Vol. III, Q. 23, A. 1, pp. 95–96.

[69] See Aquinas, Truth, Vol. III, Q. 22, A. 12, p. 79; and cf. Summa Theologica, Par
I–II, Q. 9, A. 4, Reply to Objection 3. See also Simon, Traité du Libre Arbitre, Ch. II
and III; and Maritain, "The Conquest of Freedom," in Freedom, Its Meaning, p. 632
where he says that "pure empiricists . . . cannot understand the existence of free will
because recognizing only sensory sequences, the idea of causality exercised upon a spiri
by itself has no meaning for them."

[70] See Passions of the Soul, Article XLI, in Philosophical Works, Vol. I, p. 350; ani
cf. Article CLII, in ibid., p. 401.

in "the spirituality of his soul."[71] For Leibniz, spontaneity (i.e., acting without being acted upon) belongs to all simple (i.e., spiritual) substances. "The soul," he writes, "is active of itself";[72] like every other simple substance, it "has within itself the principle of all its actions."[73] For Hegel, it is the very essence of spirit to be an independent agent, i.e., not to be dependent on anything external for its existence or actions.[74]

(d) The authors to whom we now come talk in terms of consciousness rather than in terms of spirit or soul, or of the mind and its faculties. Nevertheless, William James does speak of "purely spiritual causation" and "a principle of spiritual activity."

> When we reflect that the turnings of our attention form the nucleus of our inner self; when we see . . . that volition is nothing but attention; [and] when we believe that our autonomy in the midst of nature depends on our not being pure effect but a cause . . . we must admit that the question whether attention involve such a principle of spiritual activity or not is metaphysical as well as psychological.[75]

For Renouvier, however, it is consciousness itself which is the source of man's freedom of self-determination. "When we take ourselves as having what we call self-direction," he writes, "we identify our consciousness above all with those representations which at every moment seem to produce themselves without any efficient antecedent cause, that is, first causing themselves and then determining the others."[76] And for Sartre, only that which is for-itself, which is the same as conscious being, can determine itself from moment to moment, projecting its future without dependence on its past.[77]

---

[71] See *Discourse on Inequality*, p. 208. Rousseau declares that "in the power of willing . . . nothing is to be found but acts which are purely spiritual and wholly inexplicable by the laws of mechanism" (*ibid.*). To which he adds in another place: "The first causes of motion are not to be found in matter" (*Emile*, p. 235); and in still another place: "No material creature is in itself active, [as] I am active" (*ibid.*, p. 242).

[72] *Theodicy*, Part III, Sect. 323, p. 321.

[73] *Ibid.*, Part I, Sect. 65, p. 158. Cf. *ibid.*, Part III, Sect. 291, p. 304.

[74] See *Philosophy of History*, Introduction, p. 17. See also *Logic*, Sect. 35, p. 71, and Sect. 147, p. 268. Cf. Croce, *The Philosophy of the Practical*, pp. 180–86.

[75] *Principles of Psychology*, Vol. I, pp. 447–48. "It is in fact," James adds, "the pivotal question of metaphysics, the very hinge on which our picture of the world shall swing from materialism, fatalism, monism, towards spiritualism, freedom, pluralism—or else the other way" (*ibid.*, p. 448). Cf. *ibid.*, pp. 452–54; and see also *Talks to Teachers*, p. 191, where James says: "After what we have just seen—namely, the part played by voluntary attention in volition—a belief in *free will and purely spiritual causation* is still open to us." (Italics added.) Cf. B. P. Bowne, *Personalism*, pp. 196 ff.

[76] *Psychologie Rationelle*, Vol. I, pp. 191–92. Cf. Charles Secrétan, *Mon Utopie*, p. 164.

[77] See *Being and Nothingness*, pp. 435–39, 496–504.

(e) Finally, we come to Kant and those who hold views similar to his, at least in one important respect. Here, as we observed earlier,[78] two points are involved in Kant's metaphysical theory of causal initiative. The first, in which Kant concurs with the authors treated in paragraphs (a) through (d), is the non-sensuous character of the purely intelligible being—the transcendental ego or noumenal self—which exercises causal initiative by "*spontaneously* originating a series of events."[79] The second point, which is first introduced into the discussion of causal initiative by Kant, is the supra-temporal character of a cause that causes without itself being the effect of antecedent causes. Not only is such a cause a permanent or enduring being rather than a transient event, but, since it is a supra-sensible being, it must also, for Kant, transcend space and time.

While the series of phenomenal effects which it originates occurs in time, the uncaused cause which originates the series acts out of time. "This cause and its causality," Kant declares, "exist therefore out of and apart from the series of phenomena; while its effects do exist and are discoverable in the series of empirical conditions."[80] And, he continues, "this active subject would, in its character of intelligible subject, be subordinate to no conditions of time, for time is only a condition of phenomena, and not of things in themselves."[81] On this point of the supra-temporal as well as non-physical character of the agent which has the power to act without being acted upon, a number of other writers agree with Kant, notably Frederick Schelling,[82] Hermann Lotze,[83] Josiah Royce,[84] Nikolai Lossky,[85] and J. S. Haldane.[86]

FOURTH PHASE

In the first phase of this dispute, the proximate reason for the denial of causal initiative was its supposed incompatibility with the universal principle of causation; and, in the second phase, the proximate defense of causal initiative was the denial of such incompatibility. Here the only existential question concerned the existence of causes that are not effects.

---

[78] See fn. 62 on p. 272, *supra*.
[79] *Critique of Pure Reason*, p. 301.
[80] *Ibid.*, p. 302.
[81] *Ibid.*, p. 303. Cf. *ibid.*, pp. 311 and 450–51. See also *Prolegomena To Any Future Metaphysic*, pp. 91–92.
[82] See *Of Human Freedom*, pp. 63, 66.
[83] See *Microcosmus*, Vol. I, pp. 260–61.
[84] See *The Spirit of Modern Philosophy*, pp. 409–15.
[85] See *Freedom of the Will*, pp. 89–91.
[86] See *Mechanism, Life, and Personality*, pp. 106–8.

Furthermore, in the second phase, a divergent interpretation of the principle of causation emerged as the defenders of causal initiative argued that the principle of causation embraced two distinct modes of causation.

With the third phase, the dispute about causal initiative and the principle of causation moved to the plane of metaphysical theories which provide grounds in support or defense of the affirmative side of this issue. What is common to all these theories is the special character of the agent that exercises causal initiative, together with a distinction between two modes of causation, one exemplified by the action of such agents, and one exemplified by causes that act only insofar as they are moved to action by other causes.

With the distinction in mind, the affirmative authors claim that causal initiative is not inconsistent with the universal principle of causation, at least as they understand it. Since the negative authors contend that all causation is of the same type, and that this type is one in which every cause is also an effect, they remain unpersuaded that causal initiative does not violate the universal principle of causation. The affirmative authors, on the other hand, do not rest their case solely on their reconciliation of causal initiative with the principle of causation. In addition, they base their assertion of causal initiative on their assertion of the reality of immaterial beings or powers, or of supra-sensible and supra-temporal agents, which, in virtue of their special character, can act without being acted upon, as bodies cannot.

Hence, with the third phase, a number of additional existential questions arise. Does reality include individual substances and their substantive powers (i.e., permanent or enduring beings), as well as momentary occurrences or events? Does man, regarded as an individual substance, have faculties or powers, such as reason or will, which are the principles of particular actions on his part, such as judgment or volition? Do such powers have an immaterial mode of existence, in the sense that their actions are not the acts of bodily organs, as seeing is the action of eye and brain? To put the last question more generally, does reality include the existence of the spiritual (i.e., the immaterial or non-physical)? Are there such things as soul, mind, consciousness, or the noumenal self (which is supra-temporal as well as non-physical)?[87]

It would seem as if the fourth phase of the dispute should find the

---

[87] As we saw in the third phase, not all the defenders of causal initiative affirm the existence of individual substances or, in the case of man, such substantive faculties as reason or will. Nor do all maintain that causal initiative involves a supra-temporal agent. But all do concur in positing the existence of something immaterial or spiritual as having the causal initiative which, admittedly, is not to be found in the realm of bodies, material things, or physical phenomena.

negative authors giving negative answers to these existential questions. In part that is the case, as we shall presently see. But the negative authors do not join issue with their opponents on all these questions, not even on the question about the existence of something immaterial, spiritual, or non-physical as having the causal initiative which bodies or physical things do not have. The situation is further complicated by the fact that certain writers on the negative side, who concede the existence of psychic, as distinct from physical, phenomena, or who even affirm the existence of a spiritual self, do not see in this any ground for conceding the existence of causal initiative.[88] From the point of view of the affirmative authors, it nevertheless remains the case that to deny the existence of immaterial causes is to deny causal initiative.

We shall, therefore, proceed in this fourth phase by indicating typical denials of the existential premises which underlie, for one group of authors or another, the affirmation of causal initiative. To this we shall add, in the case of C. D. Broad's attack on Kant's position, the criticisms which his attack elicited from such defenders of causal initiative as C. A. Campbell and L. J. Russell.

Before we turn to (a) the question about substantive powers or faculties, (b) the question about immaterial causes, and (c) the question about supra-temporal causes, it is necessary to explain why we shall not first consider the question about the existence of individual substances, which would seem to be prior to the question about substantive powers or faculties.

On the one hand, the existence of individual substances, acting and being acted on, is an essential point in the causal theory held by Aristotle, Aquinas, and their followers, and it is essential also to their theory of man as an agent who has the power to act without being acted on. On the other hand, we know that the causal theory, formulated by Hume and shared by his followers, involves the denial of substances, or permanent beings, and converts the causal nexus into a sequence of events. But, with one exception, neither Hume nor his followers explicitly argue that, since there is no substantive causation, there can be no causal initiative.

That one exception is C. D. Broad. Distinguishing between what he calls "continuants" (i.e., substances) and "occurrents" (i.e., events), Broad argues that, since there is only occurrent causation, there can be no causal

---

[88] Thus, for example, Hartley, Bain, Spencer, and others in the school of English associationist psychology maintain that the principle of causation applies to states of consciousness in the domain of psychic phenomena, exactly in the same way that it does in the domain of physical phenomena. And Hastings Rashdall, while maintaining that freedom involves the causality of a spiritual self, denies that this involves any undetermined beginnings in the stream of volitions: see *The Theory of Good and Evil*, Vol. II, pp. 308 ff.

nitiative. But his denial of substantive causation rests on the proposition hat a continuant, as cause, must be a supra-temporal cause, i.e., it must act outside of time, even though the effects it produces are temporal events. His attack is thus limited to the Kantian theory of the noumenal self, not merely as a permanent being but as one that is also supra-temporal.

Broad's argument, therefore, does not apply to the Aristotelian or Thomistic theory of substantive causes, none of which, on the plane of inite beings, is supra-temporal or acts out of time. Furthermore, without adopting the Aristotelian or Thomistic theory, L. J. Russell argues that substantive causes can exercise causal initiative without acting in a non-temporal fashion. The Thomists, for their part, have a different answer to Broad, as we shall see. Since this quite special circle of debate takes its origin from Broad's attack on the Kantian position, we shall append it to the third of the three existential questions to which we now turn.

(a) *The question about substantive powers or faculties.* In the dispute between Hobbes and Bramhall, the question arises in the context of the statement by Hobbes that, in the course of deliberation wherein alternative contrary desires pass in succession, "the last [desire] is that which we call he will before the doing of the action. . . . All other appetites to do or o quit, that come upon a man during his deliberation, are usually called ntentions and inclinations, but not wills."[89]

To this statement, Bramhall replies by charging Hobbes with con-ounding "the faculty of will with the action of volition." Further, he points out, Hobbes "makes the intention, which is a most proper and elicit act of the will, or a willing of the end, as it is to be attained by certain means, to be no willing at all, but only some antecedaneous *inclination* or propension." And in consequence of the denial that the will is a faculty and the principle of such things as intentions or volitions which are its particular acts, Hobbes, in Bramhall's opinion, commits "the grossest mistake," i.e., he acknowledges "no act of man's will to be his will, but only the last act, which he calls the last will."[90]

Hobbes meets these charges by reiterating that will is nothing but the volition which makes an action voluntary.

> To confound the faculty of the will with the will, were to confound a *will* with *no will*; for the faculty of the will is not will; the act only, which he [i.e., Bramhall] calls *volition* is the will . . . It is true, I make the will to be the last part of deliberation; but it is that will which maketh the action voluntary, and therefore needs must be the last.[91]

[89] *The Questions Concerning Liberty, Necessity, and Chance,* p. 360.
[90] *Ibid.,* pp. 360–61.
[91] *Ibid.,* pp. 361–62.

In a subsequent passage, referring to Bramhall's contention that the facult of the will is the principle of particular acts of willing, Hobbes declare that, in his view, "the act of willing is not produced by the faculty o willing."[92]

Other writers on the negative side of this issue also reject the notion of the will as a faculty productive of its own acts, and make will identica with willing, i.e., particular acts of volition. Thus, for example, Spinoz denies that there is any "absolute faculty of positive or negative volition." To speak of a faculty of understanding, desiring, or willing, is to speak o fictions, or "merely abstract or general terms, such as we are accustomed t put together from particular things. . . . The intellect and the will stan in the same general relation to this or that idea, or this or that volition, a 'lapidity' to this or that stone." These so-called "faculties of ours," Spinoz concludes, are nothing but "general notions which cannot be distinguishe from the particular instances on which they are based."[93]

(b) *The question about immaterial causes.* We know from the treatis *Concerning Body* in his *Elements of Philosophy* that Hobbes reaffirms th central tenet of ancient atomism—that nothing exists except bodies an the void.[94] Accordingly, for him, the words "incorporeal substance" are a self-contradictory or as insignificant as the words "incorporeal body."[95] Hence, we can readily infer how Hobbes would respond to a defense o causal initiative that rests on a distinction between material and immateria causes. In the case of Priestley, who expresses his indebtedness to Hobbes, no inference is necessary; for, in his dispute with Dr. Price, he argues from his own materialistic premises against Price's contention that states o mind have causal properties different from those found in the realm o material or physical phenomena.[96]

As we have seen, Price argues for different modes of causation on the ground that physical and moral causes are not of the same type, the one consisting of bodily motions, the other, of states of mind.[97] Priestley, on the contrary, insists that "the determinations of what we call the will are, in fact, nothing more than a particular case of the general doctrine of

[92] *Ibid.*, p. 376. Cf. *ibid.*, pp. 359–60, where Hobbes points out the redundancy of such expressions as "the will willeth."

[93] *Ethics*, Part II, Prop. XLVIII, Note, pp. 119–20. For other denial of the will as a faculty, see Priestley, *The Doctrine of Philosophical Necessity*, p. 44; Spencer, *Principles of Psychology*, Vol. I, p. 503; Bain, *The Emotions and the Will*, p. 492.

[94] *Op. cit.*, Ch. VIII, Sect. 1–9.

[95] See *Leviathan*, Part I, Ch. 4, p. 30; and cf. *ibid.*, Ch. 12, pp. 83–84.

[96] The 1792 edition of the Priestley-Price debate bears the title *A Free Discussion of the Doctrine of Materialism and Philosophical Necessity, in a Correspondence between Dr. Price and Dr. Priestley.*

[97] See p. 270, *supra*.

association of ideas, and therefore a perfectly mechanical thing."[98] Advert-
ing to the distinction "that Dr. Price and others make between *moral* and
physical causes and effects," Priestley remarks that, in his view, the only
difference here is that between "*voluntary* and *involuntary* causes and
effects."[99] But the causal connection is no less mechanical in the one
case than in the others.

There is a somewhat parallel opposition between Jonathan Edwards
and Isaac Watts. Watts holds the view that

> all other things besides a Spirit or Being endowed with a Will are, properly
> and philosophically speaking, *passive* Beings . . . But Spirits are Beings of
> an *active* Nature, the Spring of Action is within themselves, and they can
> determine themselves. The Will of God is an active and self-determining
> power; and the Will of Man perhaps in this respect is the chief Image of
> God in this lower world, as it is an *active* Power that can determine itself.[100]

While Edwards does not deny the existence of the human soul or of its
spiritual character, he sees no reason why it should be exempt from the
same law of cause and effect that applies in the case of bodies. "The activity
of the soul," he writes, "may enable it to be the cause of effects; but it
doesn't at all enable or help it to be the subject of effects which have no
cause; which is the thing this author [Watts] supposes concerning acts of
the will."[101]

Other writers base their denial of the will's agency or causal initiative
directly upon their denial of the immaterial (i.e., soul, spirit, or spiritual
force). Thus, for example, Baron d'Holbach asserts that "man is a being
purely physical," and hence he rejects the pretension that "man is a *free
agent*" since that rests on the further pretension that "the *soul* is distin-
quished from the body, is immaterial . . . [and] acts by its own energies."[102] For Bakunin, similarly, the denial of free will is inseparably connected with the denial of the soul.[103]

(c) *The question about supra-temporal causes.* In its bearing on the
present question, Broad's argument can be summarized as follows.

By "occurrent causation," Broad means causation in which events have
as their causal progenitors either other events or causes which include
events as cause-factors. By "non-occurrent causation," he means causation
in which events would "originate from causal progenitors which are con-

[98] *The Doctrine of Philosophical Necessity*, p. 46.
[99] *Ibid.*, pp. 147–48.
[100] *An Essay on the Freedom of the Will in God and His Creatures*, p. 69.
[101] *Freedom of the Will*, p. 187.
[102] *The System of Nature*, Vol. I, p. 88. Cf. *ibid.*, pp. 89–90, 95, 102–3.
[103] See *The Political Philosophy of Bakunin*, pp. 148, 164.

tinuants and not events." Here the "total cause . . . would not be an event and would not contain an event as a cause factor."[104]

As Broad understands what he calls the "Libertarian" position of those who affirm causes that are not the effects of antecedent causes, they are affirming non-occurrent causation. He writes:

> They would like to say that the putting forth of a certain amount of effort in a certain direction at a certain time is completely determined, but is determined in a unique and peculiar way. It is literally determined *by the agent or self*, considered as a substance or continuant, and not by a total cause which contains as factors *events in* and *dispositions of* the agent. If this could be maintained, our puttings-forth of effort would be completely determined, but their causes would neither be events nor contain events as cause-factors.[105]

While Broad does not refer to Kant in thus describing what he takes to be the "libertarian" view, his description, as we have seen, fits the Kantian doctrine that the noumenal—and *supra-temporal*—self, acting outside of time, is the uncaused cause of a series of phenomenal events that occur in time. It does not, as we have also seen, fit other theories of causal initiative which involve substantive (i.e., non-occurrent) causation but do not involve supra-temporal causes.

Having thus described the view which he thinks the defenders of causal initiative are maintaining, Broad then declares that "such a view is impossible" and self-evidently so. His argument is stated in the following passage:

> The putting-forth of an effort of a certain intensity, in a certain direction, at a certain moment, for a certain duration, is quite clearly an event or process, however unique and peculiar it may be in other respects. It is therefore subject to any conditions which self-evidently apply to every event, as such. Now it is surely quite evident that, if the beginning of a certain process at a certain time is determined at all, its total cause *must* contain as an essential factor another event or process which *enters into* the moment from which the determined event or process *issues* . . . In so far as an event *is* determined, an essential factor in its total cause must be other *events*. How could an event possibly be determined to happen at a certain date if its total

---

[104] "Determinism, Indeterminism, and Libertarianism," in *Ethics and the History of Philosophy*, p. 215.

[105] *Ibid.*, pp. 214–15. In another place, Broad gives the following summary of the "Libertarian" position. "This doctrine," he writes, "may be summed up in two propositions. (i) Some (and it may be all) voluntary actions have a causal ancestor which contains as a cause-factor the putting forth of an effort which is not completely determined in direction and intensity by occurrent causation. (ii) In such cases the direction and the intensity of the effort are completely determined by non-occurrent causation, *in which the self or agent, taken as a substance or continuant, is the non-occurrent total cause*" (*ibid.*, p. 217). (Italics added.)

cause contained no factor to which the notion of date has any application? And how can the notion of date have any application to anything that is not an event?[106]

Since Broad thinks that only one answer to these questions is possible, he concludes that "Libertarianism is self-evidently impossible."[107]

Before we turn to the replies which writers who affirm causal initiative have made to Broad, let us first consider other criticisms of the Kantian position by writers who deny causal initiative.

According to Windelband, an uncaused cause may either be an event that is a cause without being an effect, or an agent, a "substantial self" which has "aseity," i.e., which acts from itself alone, without being acted on. The first of these theories of an uncaused cause, Windelband attributes to Epicurus (the "swerve of the atom"); the second, to Kant. Without referring to the supra-temporal character of the noumenal or substantial self which has aseity, Windelband then argues that the "cause-lessness" which is being asserted in either case equally reduces to chance, and so is no basis for the moral responsibility which these authors think must be based on causal initiative.[108]

Hastings Rashdall, on the other hand, makes the supra-temporality of the noumenal self the critical point. Interpreting Kant as asserting "a timeless self [which] is the cause of the series of acts in time," Rashdall asks, "How [can there] be a timeless individual self which is not also uncreated?" He thinks that "the only intelligible sense which can be given to the idea of 'noumenal freedom' is to interpret it as meaning that the individual [i.e., the "timeless self"] is uncreated. . . . But," he adds, "there seems to be no evidence that that is what Kant intended by it."[109] The nub of this argument seems to be not that it is intrinsically impossible for a timeless causal progenitor to originate a series of effects in time, as Broad maintains, but rather that such a cause must be an eternal or uncreated being. We shall return to this point presently when we reconsider the position of Aquinas as it is affected by Broad's argument; for, according to Aquinas, both an eternal, uncreated being (God) and a temporal, created being (the human will) are together the uncaused causes of man's volitions, one out of time and the other in time.[110]

The replies which C. A. Campbell and L. J. Russell make to Broad do

---

[106] *Ibid.*, p. 215.
[107] *Ibid.*, p. 217.
[108] See *Über Willensfreiheit*, pp. 122–24, 127–32. See also *ibid.*, pp. 176–98, where Windelband points out what he regards as an inconsistency between Kant's theory of transcendental freedom in the *Critique of Pure Reason* and his theory of moral freedom in the *Critique of Practical Reason*.
[109] *The Theory of Good and Evil*, Vol. II, pp. 308–9 fn. 1.
[110] See pp. 266–67, *supra*.

not involve any reference to divine action as an essential element in the explanation of man's causal initiative. Both Campbell and Russell approve of Broad's statement of the problem.[111] Both agree that the kind of individual responsibility which they think must be based on the causal initiative or agency of the self is the kind that Broad calls "categorical obligability"; both, furthermore, agree that such causal initiative or agency is impossible if the only kind of causation is the occurrent type of causation which Broad regards as universal. It is with regard to all causation being exclusively occurrent, that both then take issue with Broad. But Campbell argues for another type of causation, which would permit the agency of the self, only on the grounds that such agency is indispensable to moral responsibility and that experience gives us some evidence of the existence of such agency. We shall, therefore, postpone Campbell's dispute with Broad until we come to Sections 3 and 4 of this chapter, where we shall deal with these extrinsic considerations.

Russell, in contrast to Campbell, develops a causal theory which, in his view, provides intrinsic grounds not only in support of causal initiative but also in defense of it against Broad's attack. He distinguishes between what he calls "analytic" and "non-analytic" causation. In analytic causation, universal causal laws can be formulated which connect the determinate properties of one set of events, or states of things, with the determinate properties of another set. It is this type of causation, Russell claims, that Broad has in mind; and, if it were the only type, Broad would be right in ruling out both the causal indeterminacy which is the basis of categorical obligability and the causal initiative or agency which such indeterminacy presupposes.

But, according to Russell, no intrinsic impossibility prevents us from affirming a non-analytic type of causation which involves indefinite causal properties and indeterminate states of things. While such non-analytic causation would be of no use in the natural sciences or in any effort to formulate universal causal laws, it would fit the kind of actions in which men actively determine that which is otherwise indeterminate, i.e., not determined by their nature or character or present circumstances. Such determination of the indeterminate on their part exhibits the kind of agency or causal initiative which Broad dismisses as impossible, because incompatible with universal analytic causation.[112]

---

[111] See C. A. Campbell, *In Defence of Free Will*, pp. 27–31, and *On Selfhood and Godhood*, p. 159; L. J. Russell, "Ought Implies Can," in the *Proceedings of the Aristotelian Society*, Vol. XXXVI, pp. 151–52, 174.

[112] See "Ought Implies Can," in *loc. cit.*, pp. 152–83, especially p. 182, where Russell, referring to the action of a self-determining agent, says: "It seems clear that on the view I am following out it is necessary to accept the conclusion that an 'act' is an 'uncaused cause.'"

Russell challenges the two propositions which he regards as essential to the universality of analytic causation. They are:

(i) every thing has states, all of which can be completely characterized by determinate characteristics, and (ii) the 'nature' of every thing, in so far as it has any nature beyond the actual succession of its states, is completely definable in terms of definite properties.[113]

This challenge leaves him in agreement with Broad on one point. His theory of causation—both analytic and non-analytic—involves continuants as well as occurrents. The total cause of a change or an event is never simply another event, but neither is it ever simply a continuant or substance. The total cause always includes both—an *event* that is the action of or a change in a substance, and the *substance* itself, i.e., an enduring thing. Hence he agrees with Broad in ruling out the possibility of "an agent not in time interfering in the time series."[114]

In this last point, he is joined by other defenders of causal initiative who also maintain that the self or the will, in exercising the agency whereby it acts without being acted upon, does not act timelessly. Thus, for example, Fouillée, while acknowledging his indebtedness to Kant's conception of the will as an uncaused cause,[115] rejects the Kantian view that the action of the will is not in time.[116] And for Aquinas also, the will, in being sole cause of its own act in its volition of the means, exercises its causal initiative at one time rather than another.[117] To this extent at least, Aquinas agrees with Broad that the total cause of an event in time (i.e., the volition effected) includes a cause-factor which is itself an event (i.e., the will's exercise of its causal initiative). For Aquinas as for Russell, that total cause also includes something non-occurrent, i.e., a continuing existence such as the self or the will.

However, where Russell agrees with Broad that a timeless cause of effects that are events in time is an intrinsic impossibility, Aquinas plainly holds a contrary view. As we have seen, the will is, for Aquinas, the cause of its own act *only* when that act is a volition of the means. But when the act is a volition of the end, God is the efficient cause of the will's action.[118] While this leaves the will, even with respect to its volition of the end, an uncaused cause *on the plane of finite causes* (since no finite thing outside the will is the cause of its volition of the end), it also makes the will's

---

113 *Ibid.*, p. 169. Cf. *ibid.*, p. 172.
114 *Ibid.*, p. 172. "I cannot see any way," he writes, "by which the timeless could get variable connexion from time to time with what is in time" (*ibid.*).
115 See *La Liberté et le Déterminisme*, p. 245.
116 See *ibid.*, pp. 119 ff., 217–18.
117 See *Summa Theologica*, Part I–II, Q. 9, A. 3, Reply to Objection 2.
118 See pp. 266–67, *supra*.

volition of the end, *which occurs in time*, the effect of cause which is *timeless and which operates timelessly.* Aquinas finds nothing self-contradictory in such causation; contrary to Broad, he does not think that a timeless cause of effects in time is self-evidently impossible.

This brings us, finally, to a special question which is disputed by only a few authors. Hartley puts the matter bluntly. The infinite power of God would be infringed if man's will had the power to cause a single act in which it is not moved to do so by God. "To suppose that man has a power independent of God," he writes, "is to suppose that God's power does not extend to all things, i.e., is not infinite."[119] If, on the contrary, to ascribe infinite power to God means that nothing happens in this world which is not caused by God, then we cannot ascribe infinite power to God and also claim that man's will is in any sense an uncaused cause of its own acts. Windelband similarly argues that what he calls the "aseity" of the self, i.e., its having the power to act without being acted upon, is incompatible with God's omnipotence.[120] And Clemenceau declares that there cannot be two "first causes" in the universe, which would be the case if causal initiative is attributed both to God and to man.[121]

These authors all represent opposition to Aquinas's attempt to retain some causal initiative for man while at the same time asserting that God must move the will (with respect to the end) before the will is able to move itself (with respect to the means). The objections which Aquinas presents to his own position confront him with the difficulty of reconciling the agency of the will with the agency of God. In the *Summa Theologica,* the objector argues thus: "What is moved by another is not free. But God moves the will. . . ."[122] In another place, the objector points out that it is inadmissible to say "that the human mind is as the principal cause of its own act and God is as the remote cause." On the contrary, the objector argues, "the more a cause influences the effect, the more it stands as the principal cause. But the first cause influences the effect more than the second. . . . Hence the first cause is more the principal cause than the second; and thus our mind is not the principal cause of its own act, but God is."[123] Furthermore, the objector maintains, "Every mover that is moved, moves as an instrument. But an instrument is not free in its action,

[119] *Observations on Man*, p. 363.
[120] See *Über Willensfreiheit*, pp. 165–75.
[121] See *In the Evening of My Thought*, Vol. I, pp. 51–55. Clemenceau writes: "'If man were free,' said the Abbé Galiani, 'God would cease to exist.' That is obvious. How could there be room in the world for two simultaneous omnipotences?" (*ibid.*, p. 55).
[122] *Op. cit.*, Part I, Q. 83, A. 1. Objection 3. Cf. *Truth*, Vol. III, Q. 24, A. 1, Objection 3, pp. 133–34.
[123] *Truth*, Vol. III, Q. 24, A. 1, Objection 4, p. 134.

since it does not act inasmuch as it is used. Since, then, the human mind operates only when moved by God, it does not seem to be endowed with free choice," nor with the causal initiative that free choice presupposes.[124]

To these objections, Aquinas replies in the following manner. He reiterates that "God works in each agent," but adds that God does so always "in accord with that agent's manner of acting."[125] Since God created the will as an active power, able to move itself in the volition of the means, the fact that God moves the will in its volition of the end does not remove its causal initiative with respect to the means.[126] The will is the principal cause in one respect, while God is the principal cause in another.[127] Furthermore, the will, though moved by God, is not an instrument in the same sense in which the saw moved by the carpenter is an instrument. The saw is "wholly without freedom." But the will is an active power, which has the principle of its own action in itself. It is, therefore, the kind of instrument which "can be moved by another and still move itself."[128]

These replies are consistent with Aquinas's view of the will, not as a first or uncaused cause, absolutely speaking, but only as a cause which, when it operates, is not the effect of any other efficient cause *on the plane of finite causes*.

3. THE DISPUTE ABOUT CHARACTER AND MOTIVES

As we pointed out at the beginning, the arguments advanced on the negative side fall into two main types, one more general than the other.[129] We have just considered the more general type of attack. It rests its denial of causal initiative on the universal principle of causation, arguing that, in human behavior as in everything else, there is no cause that is not itself an effect. We turn now to the less general type of attack. It focuses more narrowly on the psychological process of volition; and from the account it gives of how human volitions are actually caused, it argues against any causal initiative on man's part.

The argument runs as follows. A man's motives, purposes, or desires are the proximate, efficient causes of his volitions. But these in turn spring from his character in its reaction to present circumstances. How a man is

---

[124] *Ibid.*, Objection 5, p. 134.
[125] *Ibid.*, Reply to Objection 3, pp. 139–40. Cf. *Summa Theologica*, Part I, Q. 83, A. 1, Reply to Objection 3.
[126] See *Summa Theologica*, Part I–II, Q. 9, A. 4, Reply to Objection 3.
[127] See *Truth*, Vol. III, Q. 24, A. 1, Reply to Objection 4, p. 140.
[128] *Ibid.*, Reply to Objection 5, p. 140.
[129] See pp. 253–54, *supra*.

motivated to act in any particular situation is causally determined by
how his character reacts to the alternatives afforded him; and, should
conflicting motives arise, the one most consistent with his character will
predominate and determine what he wills to do. His character is itself the
product of causes that go back to his inherited traits and dispositions and
to the shaping influence upon them of the circumstances of his life. The
motive which causes the volition of this moment is merely the last link in
the chain of causes that stretches back into the individual's past. Unable
to interrupt that chain of causes at any point or to act against his character,
such as it is at the moment, the individual has no causal initiative, i.e., no
power to cause a volition in a way that makes a causal break with his past.

The foregoing argument, expressed in somewhat different ways by
different writers, constitutes the first phase in this dispute. The second
phase consists in the replies it elicits from authors on the affirmative side,
together with such rebuttals as these in turn call forth. A third and final
phase involves a number of special elaborations on the main arguments,
both pro and con.

First Phase

The argument against causal initiative with which we are here concerned
is advanced (i) by the "objector" whom Aquinas undertakes to answer, (ii)
by Hobbes against Bramhall, and (iii) by Priestley against Price. The
argument is presented in its most typical form by Priestley. It is in this form
that it is most frequently repeated by other writers to whom we shall refer.

(i) In the *Summa Theologica*, the objector appeals to the position
taken by Aquinas on the question whether the intellect moves the will.
Aquinas had made the point that the object to be willed is presented to the
will by the intellect or reason. What Aquinas here refers to as the object
of volition later writers call the reason or motive. As the objector sees the
point, Aquinas is conceding that volitions are caused by the intellect
or reason, considering this or that object to be willed. The objector does
not go on to argue that it is the individual's character that, in such
considerations, gives predominance to one object over another. He thinks
it sufficient to insist that "the will does not move itself"; for if "the will is
moved by the intellect," as has been conceded, and if the will were also
to move itself, then "it would follow that the same thing is at once
moved immediately by two movers, which seems unreasonable."[130]

(ii) Against Bishop Bramhall's avoidance of the proposition that what
a man wills flows directly from "the last dictate of [his] understanding,"

---

[130] *Loc. cit.*, Part I–II, Q. 9, A. 3, Objection 3. Cf. *ibid.*, A. 1, where Aquinas gives his
answer to the question whether the will is moved by the intellect.

Hobbes argues that the Bishop fails to understand the point. The proposition in question means that "the will follows the last opinion or judgment, immediately preceding the action, concerning whether it be good to do it or not; whether he hath weighed it long before or not at all."[131] In those instances in which a man does deliberate, the deliberation terminates with some judgment or opinion about what should be done, and it is this "last opinion or judgment" which is the immediate cause of willing the action to be performed. Where no deliberation takes place, whatever desire happens to prevail supplies the motive of volition and its cause.[132] The last opinion or judgment to prevail, Hobbes points out, is only the proximate cause of the volition, not its whole cause, for "that last dictate of the understanding was produced by causes antecedent."[133] These, he elsewhere explains, go back ultimately to the "appetites and aversions" with which men are born, or those which they acquire "from experience, and trial of their effects upon themselves, or other men."[134]

(iii) According to Priestley, a man's volitions are caused by his state of mind and the view which he takes of things. The latter, says Priestley, "is generally called the *motive*," though under this term some writers comprehend a man's state of mind as well.[135] "In no case whatever," he contends, "can the mind be determined to action, i.e., to a volition, without something that may as well be called a *motive* as be expressed in any other manner. . . . For, exclusive of what necessarily comes under the description either of *motive*, or *state of mind*, the mind itself can no more be the cause of its own determination, than the beam of a balance can be the cause of its own inclination."[136] In another place, Priestley speaks of "*the previous disposition of the mind*," together with the individual's present "*view of the objects*" which elicit his action, as being the two factors that causally determine his volitions.[137] Summing both factors up under the term *motives*, he concludes that "motives [are] the proper causes of volitions and actions. . . . All volitions and actions are preceded by corresponding motives."[138]

131 *The Questions Concerning Liberty, Necessity, and Chance*, p. 317.
132 "When it cometh into a man's mind to do or not to do some certain action, if he have no time to deliberate, the doing or abstaining necessarily followeth the present thought he had of the good or evil consequences thereof to himself. As for example, in sudden anger, the action shall follow the thought of revenge, in sudden fear the thought of escape" (*ibid.*, p. 344).
133 *Ibid.*, p. 323.
134 *Leviathan*, Part I, Ch. 6, p. 40.
135 *The Doctrine of Philosophical Necessity*, p. 13.
136 *Ibid.*, pp. 23–24.
137 *Ibid.*, p. 36.
138 *Ibid.*, p. 38. Cf. *ibid.*, p. 43, where Priestley maintains that "exclusive of everything that comes under the denomination of *motive*, there is really nothing at all left that can produce the determination," i.e., the particular volition.

Similarly, Jonathan Edwards asserts that "every act of the will whatsoever, is excited by some motive" and argues thus:

> If every act of the will is excited by a motive, then that motive is the cause of the act of the will. If the acts of the will are excited by motives, then motives are the causes of their being excited; or, which is the same thing, the cause of their being put forth into act and existence.[139]

From this it follows, in Edward's opinion, that the will does not exercise causal initiative. "The volition which is caused by previous motive and inducement," he concludes, "is not caused by the will exercising a sovereign power over itself, to determine, cause and excite volitions in itself."[140]

According to Herbert Spencer, the self at any moment is nothing but the "aggregate of feelings and ideas which then exists."[141] Furthermore, will is nothing but the feeling or impulse which gains predominance at a given moment and motivates action. "Until there is a *motive* (mark the word)," Spencer declares, "there is no Will."[142]

Other writers argue that the acknowledged predictability of human behavior rests on the fact that a man's volitions flow from his character and motives. This fact excludes free will, as T. H. Buckle understands it, for the causal initiative of a free will, in his view, means "a cause of action residing in the mind, and exerting itself independently of motives."[143] On the contrary, Buckle asserts, "when we perform an action, we perform it in consequence of some motive or motives"; and "those motives are the result of some antecedents," so that, "if we were acquainted with the whole of the antecedents, and with all the laws of their movements, we could with unerring certainty predict the whole of their immediate results."[144]

S. Alexander also equates "the notion of a free-will" with "the idea of the existence of a mysterious power latent in the will which can act independently of motive." In the light of the "general agreement that the will is determined by character and circumstances," Alexander dismisses "the idea of such a free-will . . . [as] a sheer delusion."[145] It violates "the assumption upon which all social intercourse proceeds: we could not deal with our fellow-men unless we could reckon on their acting according to their character."[146] Furthermore, Alexander insists, this very notion of free-will, "though invented to save responsibility . . . renders it inexpli-

---

[139] *Freedom of the Will*, p. 225.

[140] *Ibid.*, p. 226.

[141] *Principles of Psychology*, Vol. I, p. 501.

[142] *Ibid.*, p. 503.

[143] *History of Civilization in England*, Vol. I, p. 13 fn. 16.

[144] *Ibid.*, p. 13.

[145] *Moral Order and Progress*, pp. 336–38.

[146] *Ibid.*, p. 337.

cable; a will independent of motives could never be responsible, because it could not be called to account."[147]

A number of other writers argue in the same vein that the opponents of determinism remove the only basis of responsibility by denying that a man's volitions are caused by his character and motives. We shall be concerned subsequently with the question of responsibility.[148] What is germane here is simply the fact that these writers assert that determinism is not only compatible with responsibility but also indispensable to it.[149] It is not the causal initiative of a will acting independently of motives, but the fact that a man's actions flow from his own character and motives, which makes them "self-determined," in the opinion of these writers.[150]

SECOND PHASE

To the argument that volitions, or acts of the will, are caused by the judgments which reason makes concerning the objects of action, Aquinas replies by distinguishing between two ways in which the will is moved when it acts. The intellect's practical judgment about the object to be willed is not, according to Aquinas, the efficient cause of the will's acting, but only its formal cause. In the exercise of its power to act, the will, he reiterates, moves itself. Though it is not the sole cause of particular volitions, it is the efficient cause. Hence, the fact that the reasons or motives which the intellect's practical judgments supply also cause volitions, in the manner of a formal cause specifying the object willed, does not remove the will's causal initiative in the order of exercise. "The will is moved by itself, as to the exercise of its act, in respect to the end."[151]

---

[147] *Ibid.*, p. 338.
[148] See Sect. 4, *infra*; and also Ch. 12.
[149] See M. Schlick, *Problems of Ethics*, pp. 146 ff.; A. J. Ayer, *Philosophical Essays*, pp. 275 ff.; R. E. Hobart, "Free Will as Involving Determinism and Inconceivable Without It," in *Mind*, Vol. XLIII, No. 169, pp. 3 ff.; P. H. Nowell-Smith, "Free Will and Moral Responsibility," in *Mind*, Vol. LVIII, No. 225, pp. 46 ff.
[150] This last point is made, in a variety of ways, by a number of other writers. See W. Windelband, *Über Willensfreiheit*, p. 76; Hastings Rashdall, *The Theory of Good and Evil*, Vol. II, pp. 327–28; L. T. Hobhouse, *The Elements of Social Justice*, pp. 51–55; and C. J. Ducasse, *Nature, Mind, and Death*, pp. 194–95.
[151] *Summa Theologica*, Part I–II, Q. 9, A. 3, Reply to Objection 3. See also *ibid.*, A. 1; and *Truth*, Vol. III, Q. 22, A. 12, pp. 77–86. The point that the reasons or motives which enter into the formation of volitions are causes, but not the efficient causes of the will's action, is stressed by commentators on the theory of Aquinas or writers in the Thomistic tradition. In the instantaneous act of free choice, the will and intellect exercise mutual causation on one another. See, for example, Gerard Smith, "Intelligence and Liberty," in *The New Scholasticism*, Vol. XV, No. 1, pp. 13–15; R. Z. Lauer, "St. Thomas's Theory of Intellectual Causality in Election," in *The New Scholasticism*, Vol. XXVII, No. 3, pp. 317–19; and Magda Arnold, *The Human Person*, pp. 40–43.

Furthermore, as the followers of Aquinas point out, it is the will that terminates the process of deliberation and, in so doing, it adopts one reason or motive rather than another to specify the object of its volition. The last practical judgment—or what Hobbes refers to as "the last dictate of the understanding"—does not come to be *last* in the process of deliberation except through the power which the will exercises over the intellect as the efficient cause that moves it to act or stop acting. The voluntary termination of deliberation makes one reason or motive prevail over another. Hence, according to these writers, the role of reasons or motives in the formation of volitions, far from nullifying the will's causal initiative, testifies to it.[152]

Other defenders of the will's causal initiative make substantially the same reply to the argument that motives cause volitions. Thus, Dr. Price, in replying to Joseph Priestley, insists that motives are only "the *occasions* of our putting ourselves into motion." In his view, nothing could be "more absurd than to say that *our inclinations act upon us,* and compel us, that our *desires and fears put us into motion,* or *produce our volitions,* i.e., are agents." It is we ourselves who are agents, through the active self-moving power that we have to be the cause (i.e., the efficient cause) of our own volitions.[153]

Against those who say that "the will always follows the last determination of the understanding," Renouvier maintains that it is the will which acts on motives, not motives on the will. As soon as we recognize that "a *motive* is always *willed,* that is, singled out at the moment among other equally possible motives, the argument for determinism is," in his view, "instantly overthrown."[154] Boutroux concedes that motives precede volitions, but denies that they are the "complete cause" of the will's acts. "In the resolve that follows a consideration of motives, there is something more than the motives themselves: the consent of the will to some

---

[152] See Jacques Maritain, *Freedom in the Modern World,* pp. 9–10; *Scholasticism and Politics,* Ch. V, pp. 127–29; "The Conquest of Freedom," in *Freedom, Its Meaning,* p. 634; and Yves Simon, *Traité du Libre Arbitre,* pp. 118–19.

[153] *The Doctrine of Philosophical Necessity,* pp. 55–56. Commenting on these remarks of Dr. Price, Priestley rejects the distinction between motives as merely the occasions and the will as the efficient cause of volitions. He is unimpressed by Price's contention that if motives were the efficient causes of volitions, we ourselves would not be the agents we customarily think ourselves to be. Though "it is the man that is called the agent," nevertheless, "motives [are] the proper causes of human actions . . . since the motives, in all cases, *precede* the actions." And since "the action is ultimately according to the motive, *flows from* it, or *depends* upon it . . . the motive ought to be called the *proper cause* of the action" (*ibid.,* pp. 65–66). Cf. *ibid.,* pp. 145–46. See the similar reaction of Jonathan Edwards to the views of Thomas Chubb who, on this point, takes a position closely resembling that of Dr. Price: *Freedom of the Will,* pp. 226–28.

[154] *Traité de Psychologie Rationelle,* Vol. I, pp. 315–16.

particular motive in preference to some other."[155] According to Boutroux, it is the will which invests one motive with greater force than another and so makes it predominate or prevail.[156] And L. J. Russell, identifying causes with efficient causes, denies that motives are ever causes. They are, in his view, grounds, but not causes.[157]

In somewhat different terms, William James also denies that motives or reasons are by themselves the causes of voluntary actions. Rather it is the effort of attention, which James identifies with will power, that makes one motive prevail over another. "The essential achievement of the will," he tells us, "is to *attend* to a difficult object and hold it fast before the mind."[158] By holding "some one ideal object, or part of an object, a little longer or a little more intensely before the mind," we give what James calls "our voluntary fiat" to one "amongst the alternatives which present themselves as genuine possibles," and make that one effective.[159] Hence, the cause of the voluntary act is not the predominating object or motive, but the energy of the will, i.e., its power to attend to some object or motive and make it predominate. It is this energy or will power which James regards as a cause that is not an effect.[160]

From still another point of view, Harald Ofstad maintains that the individual is not only able to make decisions that are in accord with his character but also, under certain conditions, decisions which run somewhat

---

[155] *Contingency of the Laws of Nature*, p. 140.
[156] *Ibid.*, pp. 140–41. Cf. W. E. Hocking, *The Self: Its Body and Freedom*, pp. 151–153.
[157] Russell writes: "I do not think that when the conclusion 'This is the right act' has been come to, we need explain the decision to do it as supervening on a desire to do it. The perception that an act is right is often the 'ground' of our decision to do it; but it is not to be described as the 'cause' of our decision, or as a cause-factor in our decision. It is we who have to decide; and 'grounds' of decisions are not 'causes'" ("Ought Implies Can," in *Proceedings of the Aristotelian Society*, Vol. XXXVI, p. 184). Cf. A. K. Stout, "Free Will and Responsibility," in *Proceedings of the Aristotelian Society*, Vol. XXXVII, pp. 215–24.
[158] *Principles of Psychology*, Vol. II, p. 561.
[159] *Ibid.*, pp. 576–77.
[160] See *ibid.*, Vol. I, pp. 447–48, 453–54. William McDougall comments on this theory of James that "*the will* exerts itself on the side of the weaker motive and enables it to triumph over its stronger antagonists," and says that it posits the will as "an influx of energy that works on the side of the weaker motive, an influx of energy of whose source, causes, or antecedents we can say nothing" (*An Introduction to Social Psychology*, p. 236). In his own view, "the effort of volition is not the mysterious and utterly incomprehensible process the libertarians would have it to be . . . It involves no new principles of activity and energy, but only a more subtle and complex interplay of those impulses which actuate all animal behavior" (*ibid.*, p. 237). The analysis McDougall then gives of the factors involved in voluntary and non-voluntary behavior reduces the difference between them to one of degree of complexity. See *ibid.*, pp. 243–46. For an extended critique of McDougall's analysis, see Campbell, *Scepticism and Construction*, pp. 145–50.

contrary to it. He calls the former "high-integrated" and the latter "low-integrated" decisions. In making a low-integrated decision, the individual initiates some change in his personality or character. What is germane in this to the present dispute is the compatibility of Ofstad's views with the thesis that decisions always flow from a man's character, or from that and the motives to which his character gives rise.[161]

Third Phase

What we shall treat as a third phase of this dispute does not carry the opposed argumentation, which we have so far considered, to the plane of underlying reasons. The question whether an individual's motives, arising from the established tendencies of his character, are or are not the efficient causes of his volitions is certainly arguable pro and con by authors who hold different theories of causation in general or who employ such theories to give different analyses of the causes of human behavior. But, in the actual literature, such arguments are not advanced on either side of this dispute. Those who deny causal initiative appear content to rest their denial on the assertion that, since, in the psychological process, motives precede volitions, it is the motive, not the will or the self, which is the efficient cause of the volition. And those who defend causal initiative against this attack similarly appear content to rest their defense on the assertion that, while motives play a significant role in the formation of volitions, they do not function as efficient causes.

In the absence of further argument for either of these contrary assertions, we turn to what can be described as a peripheral elaboration of this dispute. It is developed mainly by C. A. Campbell in a number of books and articles in which he attempts to uphold the causal initiative of the self against objections raised by the opponents of this doctrine. One of these opponents, P. H. Nowell-Smith, provides us with some direct response to Campbell's arguments insofar as they bear on the question of character and motives.

In his early writings on the subject of free will, Campbell acknowledged that the causal initiative and causal indeterminacy of self-determination involve a breach in causal continuity, i.e., an interruption of the causal series wherein present volitions are the effects of antecedent factors operative through the established character of the individual.[162] Moritz Schlick,

---

[161] See "Can We Produce Decisions," in *The Journal of Philosophy*, Vol. LVI, No. 3, pp. 90–94.

[162] See *Scepticism and Construction*, pp. 130–32; *In Defence of Free Will*, pp. 13–14; "The Psychology of the Effort of Will," in *Proceedings of the Aristotelian Society*, Vol. XL, pp. 66–70.

one of the authors whom Campbell regards as a prime adversary, subsequently employed the phrase "exemption from causality" to characterize the libertarian view.[163] Commenting on Schlick's language, Campbell substituted the phrase "contra-causal freedom" for "exemption from causality" as a more accurate expression of what he had in mind.[164]

In treating what is germane to the dispute with which we are here concerned, we can use Campbell's phrase "contra-causal freedom" as a shorthand expression of his whole view that, insofar as self-determination involves causal initiative (as well as causal indeterminacy) the free act is not uncaused, but caused by the person's self as distinct from his character. It is "contra-causal" only in the sense that it involves a denial that the person's character is *always* a decisive causal-factor in the production of his voluntary acts. "A contra-causal freedom," Campbell repeatedly affirms, is one that "posits a breach of causal continuity between a man's character and his conduct."[165]

One of the objections to contra-causal freedom, which Campbell deals with, is based on a generally acknowledged fact about human behavior, namely, that an individual's voluntary actions are predictable from our knowledge of his character. "It is the common assumption of social intercourse," Campbell writes, "that our acquaintances will act 'in character'; that their choices will exhibit the 'natural' response of their characters to the given situation. And this assumption seems to be amply substantiated, over a wide range of conduct, by the actual success which attends predictions made on this basis. Where there should be, on the contra-causal hypothesis, chaotic variability, there is found in fact a large measure of intelligible continuity."[166]

This objection, as stated by Campbell, is advanced, as we have seen, by earlier writers, such as T. H. Buckle and S. Alexander.[167] It is to be found in P. H. Nowell-Smith's writings, though it is not there explicitly addressed to Campbell.[168] Campbell's handling of this objection concedes a large measure of truth in it, but simply denies that it states a truth which is without exception.[169]

---

[163] See *Problems of Ethics*, p. 146.
[164] See "Is 'Freewill' a Pseudo-Problem?" in *Mind*, Vol. LX, No. 240, pp. 446, 459–60.
[165] *Ibid.*, pp. 459–60. Cf. *On Selfhood and Godhood*, pp. 149–50, 152–54, 156–57.
[166] "Is 'Freewill' a Pseudo-Problem?" in *loc. cit.*, p. 460.
[167] See pp. 290–91, *supra*.
[168] See "Free Will and Moral Responsibility," in *Mind*, Vol. LVII, No. 225, pp. 47–48.
[169] Unlike both Campbell and Nowell-Smith, Ludwig Wittgenstein holds that "in no way can an inference be made from the existence of one state of affairs to the existence of another entirely different from it" (*Tractatus Logico-Philosophicus*, 5. 135). He writes: "There is no causal nexus which justifies such an inference" (*ibid.*, 5. 136);

Men frequently do act in accord with their characters and, to the extent that they do, human behavior is predictable; but it is not perfectly predictable precisely because they also sometimes exercise their power of self-determination to act "contra-causally," i.e., against their characters.[170] Campbell writes:

> Even in situations where free will does come into play it is perfectly possible, on a view like ours, given the appropriate knowledge of a man's character, to predict within certain limits how he will respond.
>
> But 'probable' prediction in such situations can, I think, go no further than this.[171]

Admitting that there is considerable causal continuity between a man's character and his conduct, but also insisting that it is sometimes interrupted by "contra-causal freedom" on the individual's part, Campbell only denies that human behavior is perfectly predictable or that it is even predictable with high probability in all cases. "I claim, therefore," he writes, "that the view of free will I have been putting forward is consistent with the predictability of conduct on the basis of character over a very wide field indeed. And I make the further claim that that field will cover all the situations in life concerning which there is any empirical evidence that successful prediction is possible."[172]

A second objection which Campbell considers is that, if a man's character and motives do not causally determine his conduct, then his actions are reduced to "accidents" or "products of chance."[173] This objection is advanced by Hume, as we have already observed.[174] It is also raised by Windelband.[175] Confronting it, Campbell denies that an act which "does not flow from the agent's character can only be a matter of 'chance.'" It can be a creative act on the part of the self.[176] This requires Campbell to distinguish between a man's self and his character, which he does in the following manner.

"the freedom of the will consists in the fact that future actions cannot be known now. We could only know them if causality were an *inner* necessity, like that of logical deduction" (*ibid.*, 5. 1362).

[170] See "Is 'Freewill' a Pseudo-Problem?" in *loc. cit.*, pp. 460–61.

[171] *On Selfhood and Godhood*, p. 174.

[172] *Ibid.*, p. 174. *Scepticism and Construction*, pp. 162–65.

[173] See "Is 'Freewill' a Pseudo-Problem?" in *loc. cit.*, pp. 461–62. Cf. *Scepticism and Construction*, pp. 160–61.

[174] See p. 265, *supra*.

[175] See *Über Willensfreiheit*, pp. 76–77.

[176] "Is 'Freewill' a Pseudo-Problem?" in *loc. cit.*, p. 462. Cf. *On Selfhood and Godhood*, p. 178; and *Scepticism and Construction*, pp. 161–62.

. . . the very function of moral effort, as it appears to the agent engaged in the act, is to enable the self to act against the line of least resistance, against the line to which his character as so far formed most strongly inclines him. But if the self is thus conscious here of *combating* his formed character, he surely cannot possibly suppose that the act, although his own act, *issues* from his formed character . . .

What this implies . . . is that the nature of the self is for itself something more than just its character as so far formed. The 'nature' of the self and what we commonly call the 'character' of the self are by no means the same thing, and it is utterly vital that they should not be confused. The 'nature' of the self comprehends, but is not without remainder reducible to, its 'character'; it must, if we are to be true to the testimony of our experience of it, be taken as including *also* the authentic creative power of fashioning and re-fashioning "character."[177]

Criticizing Campbell's position, Nowell-Smith dismisses as unsatisfactory his solution of the difficulty "of distinguishing a 'free' action from a random event." The solution, Nowell-Smith says, is an attempt to offer a third alternative to the indeterminism of chance action and the determinism of action in accord with character. The self-determinism of the free or creative act in which the self acts against character in order to refashion it is that third alternative. But, according to Nowell-Smith, "the difficulty here is to construe 'self-determinism' in such a way that the 'self' can be distinguished from the 'character' without lapsing into indeterminism."[178] And, he continues, "if 'self-determined' is to mean 'determined by the self,' it is necessary to give some account of what the 'self' is."[179]

Nowell-Smith doubts that an intelligible account of what the self is, as distinct from character, can be given. Taking up this problem of "the Self and the Character" in another place, he undertakes to maintain

that the conception of actions which "issue from the self, and yet not from the self regarded as just the unity of its existing conative tendencies" cannot be sustained. It must turn out either to be the repudiated doctrine of indeterminism or to be a doctrine in which the 'self' is identified with the whole or a part of what the determinist calls the "character."[180]

If we try to isolate the self from the character, we have, in Nowell-Smith's opinion, no way of establishing the identity and continuity of the self. "What are the criteria of its identity?" he asks. "Is there any way of

---

[177] *On Selfhood and Godhood*, p. 177. Cf. *ibid.*, pp. 149–50, 152–53. See also "The Psychology of Effort of Will," in the *Proceedings of the Aristotelian Society*, Vol. XL, pp. 69–72.
[178] *Ethics*, p. 282.
[179] *Ibid.*, p. 283.
[180] "Determinists and Libertarians," in *Mind*, Vol. LXIII, No. 251, p. 329.

deciding whether two or more acts are acts of the same self except by showing that they display some sort of consistency or continuity of attributes, that they are 'in character?'" In the absence of answers to these questions, "the 'self' appears to vanish either in the 'character,' as the determinist asserts, or into a series of *disconnected* interventions, irruptions into the 'causal chain,' which is what the indeterminists (if there are any) assert."[181]

Nowell-Smith thus concludes by reasserting the very point that Campbell finds it necessary to deny, namely, that the only alternatives are (a) actions which are causally determined by a man's character and (b) chance or random actions which are contra-causal, that is, represent interruptions in the "causal chain" which connect a man's actions to his character. Campbell, as we have observed, repudiates the indeterminism of "chance actions" as much as he rejects the determinism of "actions determined by character" exclusively. Proposing, as a third alternative, the self-determinism of "contra-causal freedom," he argues that actions can be determined by the self, as distinct from character. Where "contra-causal," as Nowell-Smith uses the term, means that actions which are *not caused* by a man's character are not caused and so *are* chance events, "contra-causal," as used by Campbell, means that actions which are not caused by a man's character are *caused by his self* and so are *not* chance events.

Campbell recognizes that, in order to defend this third alternative, it is necessary to answer Nowell-Smith's question about how the self can be distinguished from the character. In "A Reply to Mr. Nowell-Smith," which is appended to *On Selfhood and Godhood*, he says that he has already answered Nowell-Smith's question in "the extensive treatment [which he has given] to this problem in the present work."[182] That treatment includes the critical point which we have already noted, namely, that, over and above a man's character, which his self comprehends, his self includes "the authentic creative power of fashioning and re-fashioning 'character.' "[183] In other words, a man's self is distinct from his character as a whole is distinct from a part, not as one whole is distinct from another. Though it comprehends the character, the self is not reducible to it, for it includes not only a man's formed character but his creative power to form or reform his own character.

This still leaves the question of the identity and continuity of the self as distinct from the self's character. On this point, Campbell refers the reader to Lecture V in which he discusses "the relation of *self*-identity to *personal* identity (which Nowell-Smith, I think mistakenly, treats as

181 *Ibid.*, p. 330.
182 *Op. cit.*, p. 219.
183 *Ibid.*, p. 177.

ndistinguishable)."[184] Briefly summarizing the conclusion of the argument advanced in that lecture, Campbell says that "a man's *self*-identity can be retained even where there is loss or suspension of *personal* identity —which latter is for me tantamount to identity of *character*, of the self's dominant cognitive, conative and emotive dispositions."[185]

Writing many years earlier, Hobhouse appears to be on the side of Nowell-Smith in his debate with Campbell. The freedom of the will, as he sees it, "does not mean either self-determination or absence of present restraints. It means essentially freedom from the past—its own past included. The will is cause but never effect. It brings events about but is not itself brought about—not even by its own previous being. Essentially, it is a new being every time it acts."[186] This analysis of what he calls the "libertarian principle" leads Hobhouse to say of the will what Nowell-Smith says of the self:

> The will disappears when its continuity is broken. It is replaced by so many separate volitional acts, "free" like beads scattered sparsely on a string, that neither pull nor push one another, but move or rest each "of itself." The "I" which wills this now has nothing to say to the "I" of yesterday or of five minutes hence. Each choice is a new fact arising out of the void and plunging into it again. There is no will which abides, whether changeless or growing by successive acts of self-determination, for there is no self-determination.[187]

In short, if the will or the self interrupts the causal continuity which connects a man's character and his actions, it cannot itself have any continuity as a cause or any enduring identity as a being.

We have already considered Campbell's reply to this argument, which rests on his distinction between identity of self and identity of character. The argument advanced by Hobhouse and Nowell-Smith is one that earlier writers on the affirmative side of this dispute did not explicitly consider as an objection to their position. However, it can be pointed out that the question of the will's enduring identity—and also of its continuity as a power subject to habit formation and change of habit—is implicitly answered by earlier writers, such as Aquinas or Bishop Bramhall, insofar as they assert the substantive character of the will as a power of the human soul.[188] This answer is, of course, rejected by those who, from Hume on,

184 *Ibid.*, p. 219. Cf. *ibid.*, pp. 73–94.
185 *Ibid.*, p. 219.
186 *The Elements of Social Justice*, p. 52.
187 *Ibid.*, p. 53.
188 See pp. 268–69, 272, 278 ff., *supra.*, where these and other writers are mentioned as upholding the substantive character of the will as a cause.

deny the existence of enduring substances, of substantive powers or faculties.[189]

Finally, we come to one other objection that Campbell attempts to meet. "It is constantly objected against the Libertarian doctrine," he writes, "that it is fundamentally *unintelligible*." He, then, elucidates the objection in the following manner.

> Libertarianism holds that the act of moral decision is the *self's* act, and yet insists at the same time that it is not influenced by any of those determinate features in the self's nature which go to constitute its "character." But, it is asked, do not these two propositions contradict one another? Surely, a *self*-determination which is determination by something other than the self's *character* is a contradiction in terms? What meaning is there in the conception of a "self" in abstraction from its "character?" If you really wish to maintain, it is urged, that the act of decision is not determined by the self's character, you ought to admit frankly that it is not determined by the *self* at all.[190]

To this objection, Campbell replies by distinguishing two senses in which the "contra-causal freedom" of the self can be called "unintelligible." He admits that the free act is unintelligible in the sense that it is "inexplicable," i.e., it cannot be deduced in the manner in which a consequence can be inferred from known antecedents.

> If by the "intelligibility" of an act we mean that it is capable, at least in principle, of being inferred as a consequence of a given ground, then naturally my view is that the act in question is "*un*intelligible."[191]

But, according to Campbell, there is another sense of "intelligibility" in which the free act is not unintelligible. From the inner standpoint of the person who is conscious of making an effort to act against his character, the free act is meaningful.

> If we adopt this internal stand-point—surely a proper stand-point, and one which we should be only too glad to adopt if we could in the case of other entities—the situation is entirely changed. We find that we not merely can,

[189] See pp. 271, 278–80, *supra*.

[190] *In Defence of Free Will*, p. 22. For another statement of this objection, see *On Selfhood and Godhood*, p. 175.

[191] *In Defence of Free Will*, p. 24. "The Libertarian," Campbell continues, "often has the experience of being challenged by the critic to tell him *why*, on his view, the agent now decides to put forth moral effort and now decides not to, with the obviously intended implication that if the Libertarian cannot say 'why' he should give up his theory. Such critics apparently fail to see that if the Libertarian *could* say why he would already have given up his theory!" (*ibid.*, pp. 24–25). See also *On Selfhood and Godhood*, p. 175; *Scepticism and Construction*, p. 162.

but constantly do, attach meaning to a causation which is the self's causation but is yet not exercised by the self's character.[192]

In other words, while the free act is unintelligible in the sense that the reason why it occurs cannot be given, it is not unintelligible "in the *further* sense that we can attach no meaning to it." Campbell declares that "if it could really be shown that the Libertarian's 'free will' were unintelligible in this sense of being meaningless . . . Libertarianism would have been conclusively refuted." But, he continues,

> it seems to me manifest that this can *not* be shown. The critic has allowed himself, I submit, to become the victim of a widely accepted but fundamentally vicious assumption. He has assumed that whatever is meaningful must exhibit its meaningfulness to those who view it from the standpoint of external observation. Now if one chooses thus to limit one's self to the rôle of external observer, it is, I think, perfectly true that one can attach no meaning to an act which is the act of something we call a "self" and yet follows from nothing in that self's character. But then *why should we* so limit ourselves, when what is under consideration is a subjective activity? For the apprehension of subjective acts there is *another* standpoint available, that of *inner experience*. . . . If our free will should turn out to be something to which we can attach a meaning from *this* standpoint, no more is required. And no more ought to be expected. For I must repeat that only from the inner standpoint of living experience *could* anything of the nature of "activity" be directly grasped. Observation from without is in the nature of the case impotent to apprehend the active *qua* active . . . It follows that if anyone insists upon taking his criterion of the meaningful simply from the standpoint of external observation, he is really deciding in advance of the evidence that the notion of activity, and *a fortiori* the notion of a free will, is "meaningless." He looks for the free act through a medium which is in the nature of the case incapable of revealing it, and then, because inevitably he doesn't find it, he declares that it doesn't exist![193]

In the foregoing passage, Campbell introduces the evidence of consciousness or inner experience and insists upon its significance for the problem. Critics of his argument, such as Nowell-Smith and R. D. Bradley, deny that the evidence of consciousness or inner experience has the significance which they think Campbell claims for it. However, their exchanges on this point will not be treated here, but in Section 5 in the context of the whole dispute about the consciousness of freedom.

It should also be pointed out that in the present treatment of the dispute about character and motives, we have confined our attention to arguments that bear directly on the denial or defense of causal initiative. The question of the causal influence of a man's character and motives upon

---

[192] *In Defence of Free Will*, p. 23.
[193] *On Selfhood and Godhood*, p. 176.

his choices is also one of the disputed questions in the issue about caus?
indeterminacy, which will be treated in Chapter 10. In addition, it ?
closely connected with the question whether a freedom that involves caus?
initiative and causal indeterminacy can be the basis of responsibility. Thi?
gives rise to the conceptual issue which will be treated in Chapter 12. ?
considerable amount of documentary material, bearing on character an?
motives in relation to self-determination, remains to be examined in thes?
later chapters. Though this section of the present chapter is devoted to th?
dispute about character and motives, that material has been omitted her?
because it does not directly relate to the issue about causal initiative.

What has just been said about the present section applies also to the tw?
sections which immediately follow. Section 4 will deal with the disput?
about the relation of responsibility to causal initiative and to that alone?
and Section 5 will deal with the dispute about the evidence of conscious?
ness or inner experience, again in relation to causal initiative and tha?
alone. Both of these matters—the basis of responsibility and the evidenc?
of consciousness—will be treated again in Chapter 10 in relation to causa?
indeterminacy; and, in addition, the basis of responsibility, which is centra?
to the conceptual issue about self-determination, will be treated muc?
more fully in Chapter 12.

4. THE DISPUTE ABOUT RESPONSIBILITY AND INITIATIVE

In the two preceding disputes, those who take the negative side of the?
issue open the argument by offering grounds for denying the existence of?
causal initiative. Those who affirm its existence respond by giving reasons?
in its defense. In this and also in the one remaining dispute, the affirmative side opens by offering grounds for asserting the existence of causal
initiative. In both cases, the affirmative side gives reasons, but it is important to note the difference in the type of reasons given.

In the two preceding disputes, the affirmative authors argue from grounds
that are intrinsic to the nature or meaning of causal initiative as they
conceive it. In meeting the argument based on the universal principle of
causation, they claim that that principle holds, but not in the same way,
for free and for determined causes; or that causal initiative can be attributed
to immaterial, but not physical, causes. Similarly, in meeting the argument
based on the causal influence of character and motives, they distinguish
between efficient and formal causes, and deny that motives are the efficient
causes of volitions. Such points in the theory of causation itself supply

ntrinsic reasons in support or defense of causal initiative. But to argue or causal initiative by claiming that, in the absence of it, there would be no basis for responsibility (as the affirmative side argues in this dispute); or to argue that our inner experience of freedom warrants the assertion of causal initiative (as the affirmative side argues in the dispute with which we shall deal in Section 5) is to appeal to considerations that are extrinsic o the nature or meaning of causal initiative.

A brief summary of the argument on the affirmative side, which opens he present dispute, reveals this. It runs as follows: (a) it is generally acknowledged that men are responsible, or can properly be held account-ble, for such actions as they freely perform; (b) but unless the actions hey freely perform involve causal initiative on their part, we have no valid basis for holding them responsible or accountable; (c) hence, we must *either* affirm the existence of causal initiative *or* admit that there is no valid basis for holding men responsible for their so-called "free" acts; in other words, to have a valid basis for moral responsibility, we must affirm he existence of causal initiative.

The foregoing summary omits one step in the argument as it is developed by C. A. Campbell, in what is, perhaps, the most explicit statement of it hat the literature affords. That step makes the causal indeterminacy of a free choice the proximate basis of moral responsibility. The contention is hat a man is responsible, not simply if he could have acted otherwise, *had he chosen to act otherwise*, but only *if he had the power to choose otherwise* under identical conditions. But, the argument runs, such free-dom of choice (or the causal indeterminacy it involves) presupposes causal initiative on the agent's part. Hence, the basis of a man's responsibility for he acts he freely performs involves causal initiative as well as causal indeterminacy on his part.[194]

In the presentation of this dispute, we shall deal mainly with the actual interchange between Campbell, on the affirmative side, and Nowell-Smith, on the negative. The position that Campbell takes reflects the views of many other writers on the affirmative side of this issue, from Augustine and Aquinas to Kant, L. J. Russell, and Jacques Maritain. So, too, the position that Nowell-Smith takes reflects the views of many other writers on the negative side, from Hobbes and Hume to Hans Kelsen, C. J. Ducasse, M. Schlick, A. J. Ayer, and C. L. Stevenson. But the lines of his dispute can be effectively sketched by confining our attention, in the

---

[194] Not all self-determination authors hold that causal indeterminacy presupposes causal initiative; and some affirm the one while denying the other. But a large number (e.g., Aquinas, Descartes, Kant, Renouvier, James, Sartre) are with Campbell in holding that only an active power can exercise the kind of active or dominating indifference to alternatives that is involved in free choice. The creativity of choice presupposes an agent with initiative, i.e., one who can act without being acted on.

main, to the actual debate between Campbell and Nowell-Smith, wit
appropriate references here and there to writers who share the views c
one or the other of these disputants.

We shall begin with (i) Campbell's affirmative argument, consider nex
(ii) Nowell-Smith's rejection of it, and conclude with (iii) Campbell
criticism of Nowell-Smith's position.

(i) According to Campbell, the kind of freedom which is the basis c
moral responsibility involves "some breach of causal continuity." A ma
can either act in accord with his character or not; and his having such free
dom of choice ultimately depends on the active or creative power of h
self. As Campbell sees it, the reason why moral responsibility presuppose
"contra-causal freedom" is that the individual can be held responsible onl
where "he could have acted otherwise than he did," that is, could hav
chosen to act otherwise as well as could have carried out whatever choic
he made.[195]

Campbell recognizes that there are two distinct problems here: (a) "th
question 'Is a contra-causal type of freedom implied by moral respons
bility?'" and (b) "the question 'Does a contra-causal type of freedor
anywhere exist?'" In his opinion,

> many philosophers . . . begin their inquiry with so firm a conviction that
> the contra-causal type of freedom nowhere exists, that they find it hard
> to take very seriously the possibility that it is *this* sort of freedom that
> moral responsibility implies. For they are loth to abandon the commonsense
> belief that moral responsibility itself is something real. The implicit reason-
> ing I take to be this. Moral responsibility is real. If moral responsibility
> is real, the freedom implied in it must be a fact. But contra-causal freedom
> is not a fact. Therefore contra-causal freedom is not the freedom implied
> in moral responsibility.[196]

As examples of such philosophers, Campbell explicitly refers to M. Schlic
G. E. Moore, C. L. Stevenson, and P. H. Nowell-Smith. They do nc
abandon the notion of responsibility or claim that it has no valid basis i
fact; but, according to Campbell, they attempt either to alter the meanin
of responsibility or to substitute, as the basis for it, a kind of freedom whic
is not contra-causal, i.e., involves neither causal indeterminacy nor causa
initiative.

We shall presently consider Campbell's criticism of the views of Schlic
Moore, Stevenson, and Nowell-Smith. What is of more immediate inte
est here is Campbell's reference to the position of C. D. Broad, in th
latter's essay "Determinism, Indeterminism, and Libertarianism."

[195] See "Is 'Freewill' a Pseudo-Problem?" in *loc. cit.*, p. 446.
[196] *Ibid.*, p. 450.

In that essay, which we treated earlier in another connection,[197] Broad argues (a) that a contra-causal type of freedom *is* implied by moral responsibility when that is interpreted as "categorical obligability," but (b) that such responsibility has no foundation in fact, because (c) such contra-causal freedom cannot exist. This view of the matter, Campbell points out, sets Broad against those of his contemporaries (e.g., Schlick, Moore, Stevenson, Nowell-Smith) who, agreeing with Broad (a) that a contra-causal type of freedom does not exist, then maintain (b) that moral responsibility can be based on a type of freedom that is not contra-causal, admitting, of course (c) that such responsibility is not categorical, but only conditional. While Campbell disagrees with Broad about the non-existence of contra-causal freedom, he agrees with him that no other type of freedom can serve as a valid basis for categorical obligability, which, as Campbell sees it, must be affirmed to exist if we accept the traditional commonsense notions of moral responsibility.[198]

This last point Campbell argues as follows. To the question "about the *conditions* of moral responsibility, and in particular the question whether freedom of a contra-causal kind is among these conditions," the answer of the common man, Campbell thinks, "is that it most certainly *is* among the conditions. Why does he feel so sure about this?" Campbell's reply is:

> Not . . . because the common man supposes that causal law exercises 'compulsion' in the sense that prescriptive laws do, but simply because he does not see how a person can be deemed morally praiseworthy or blame-worthy in respect of an act which he could not help performing . . . And the common man might not unreasonably go on to stress the fact that we all, even if we are linguistic philosophers, do in our actual practice of moral judgment appear to accept the common view.

Campbell then undertakes to spell out "the argument implicit in the common view, as follows:

> The moral 'ought' implies 'can.' If we say that A morally ought to have done X, we imply that, in our opinion, he could have done X. But we assign moral blame to a man only for failing to do what we think he morally ought to have done. Hence if we morally blame A for not having done X,

[197] See pp. 278–79, 281–83, *supra.*
[198] See *In Defence of Free Will*, pp. 27–31, devoted to Campbell's comments on Broad's essay. See also L. J. Russell's comments on Broad's essay in "Ought Implies Can" (*loc. cit.*, pp. 151–52). Like Campbell, Russell disagrees with Broad about the non-existence of contra-causal freedom, while at the same time agreeing with him that such freedom is required for categorical obligability. "I am in full agreement with Mr. Broad," Russell writes, "as to the two conditions required for the strictly moral use of 'ought' "; namely, causal indeterminacy and causal initiative. "I agree, further," Russell continues, "that if his general view of causation be accepted, it is difficult to see how both conditions can be satisfied" (*ibid.*).

we imply that he could have done X even though in fact he did not. In other words, we imply that A could have acted otherwise than he did. And that means that we imply, as a necessary condition of man's being morally blameworthy, that he enjoyed a freedom of a kind not compatible with unbroken causal continuity.[199]

In another place, Campbell offers the following brief summary of his answer to the "question about the kind of freedom required to justify moral responsibility. It is that a man can be said to exercise free will in a morally significant sense only in so far as his chosen act is one of which he is the sole cause or author, and only if—in the straightforward, categorical sense of the phrase—he 'could have chosen otherwise.' "[200]

From Campbell's point of view, it is not sufficient to say that a man is free in the sense that he "could have acted otherwise *if* [he] had chosen otherwise," nor to say that he is free in the sense that he "could have acted otherwise *if* [he] had been a differently constituted person."[201] While these senses of freedom do not raise any problem about freedom and causality, neither do they, in his opinion, provide an acceptable solution to the problem of freedom and responsibility.

(ii) Nowell-Smith, on the contrary, asserts that these senses of freedom are quite sufficient for ascribing responsibility, as that is commonly understood. He maintains that, in order to hold a man morally blameworthy or responsible for his actions, we need not suppose that

> when we say 'A could have acted otherwise,' we mean that A, being what he was and being placed in the circumstances in which he was placed, could have done something other than what he did.

In fact, Nowell-Smith continues,

> we never do mean this; and if we believe that voluntary action is uncaused action that is only because we believe erroneously that uncaused action is a necessary condition of moral responsibility. The Libertarian believes that an

[199] "Is 'Freewill' a Pseudo-Problem?" in *loc. cit.*, pp. 450–51. That Campbell's statement of the argument conforms to the view of the matter held by earlier writers who are on his side of this dispute can be seen in Augustine's statement that unless man himself—and not God—is the cause of man's wrongdoing, it would be unjust of God to blame or punish him (see *The Problem of Free Choice*, pp. 35–36); in Aquinas' statement that unless man has free choice "counsels, exhortations, commands, prohibitions, rewards and punishments would be in vain" (*Summa Theologica*, Part I, Q. 83, A. 1); and in Kant's statement that "without [absolute transcendental] freedom . . . no moral law and no moral imputation are possible." If man's action were necessitated by mechanical or psychological causes, he would have "nothing better than the freedom of a turnspit, which, when once it is wound up, accomplishes its motion of itself" (*Critique of Practical Reason*, pp. 190–91).
[200] *On Selfhood and Godhood*, p. 164.
[201] *Ibid.*, p. 165.

action cannot be a moral one if the agent could not have acted otherwise, and he takes no account of possible differences in the causes that might have prevented him from acting otherwise. The Determinist, on the other hand, holds that the objective possibility of alternative actions is an illusion and that, if A in fact did X, then he could not have done any action incompatible with X.[202]

If a man need not have been able to choose otherwise than he did in fact choose, what, then, are the conditions which must be present in order to hold him responsible for his actions?

In Nowell-Smith's opinion, the answer is the one given by A. J. Ayer in his explanation of what it means for anyone to say "that I could have acted otherwise."[203] It means, first "that I could have acted otherwise, if I had so chosen"; i.e., that external circumstances did not prevent me from carrying out some other choice than the only one I could have made at the time, my character and situation being what they were. It means, secondly, "that my action was voluntary in the sense in which the actions, say, of the kleptomaniac are not." And it means, thirdly, "that nobody compelled me to choose as I did"; i.e., that the choice I did in fact make flowed from my own character and motives, operative under the circumstances of the case, and was not brought about by fear induced by duress, as, for example, is the choice of a man who complies with some request at gun point.[204]

"Granted that we sometimes act 'freely' in the sense defined by Ayer," Nowell-Smith thinks that it is still necessary to answer another question: "In what sense is it rational or just or moral to praise or blame voluntary actions but not involuntary ones? It is surely not enough to say: 'Actions of such-and-such a kind are given the name "voluntary" and "are praised and blamed; others are not." ' " We need to explain the relation of 'fittingness' that is held to obtain between voluntary actions and moral judgment.[205] In other words, why is it "morally justifiable" to hold a man

---

[202] "Free Will and Moral Responsibility," in *Mind*, Vol. LVII, No. 225, pp. 49–50.
[203] See *ibid.*, p. 52.
[204] See A. J. Ayer, *Philosophical Essays*, pp. 278–82. Ayer's analysis of the meaning of freedom which provides an adequate basis for ascribing responsibility is endorsed not only by Nowell-Smith, but also shared by other writers, probably on all three points but certainly on the first one. See M. Schlick, *Problems of Ethics*, Ch. VII; C. L. Stevenson, *Ethics and Language*, Ch. XIV; G. E. Moore, *Ethics*, Ch. VI. With the exception of Ayer, all of the authors named are considered by Campbell in his argument against this position. There are still other writers who take this position, or one that resembles it in its main contention that a man can be held responsible for actions which are imputable to him because he and not some one or some thing else is their cause. See especially Hans Kelsen, *What is Justice?*, pp. 333–34; and also C. J. Ducasse, *Nature, Mind, and Death*, pp. 181–202; R. E. Hobart, "Free Will as Involving Determinism and Inconceivable Without It," in *Mind*, Vol. XLIII, No. 169, pp. 1–27.
[205] "Free Will and Moral Responsibility," *loc. cit.*, p. 52.

responsible for those actions and only those actions which are "voluntary" or "free" in the sense defined by Ayer?

This question, Nowell-Smith maintains, cannot be answered by firs trying to determine "what classes of actions are voluntary," and then secondly, looking for a "connexion between being voluntary and bein liable to praise and blame." To proceed in this way, he declares, leaves u "in the insuperable difficulty of libertarianism and also leaves the secon problem insoluble."[206] The second problem, that of connecting the vol untary with what is susceptible to praise and blame, should come first. It is he writes,

> simply the empirical problem of deciding what characteristics are alterable; and the solution of this problem then provides the criterion for deciding what actions are voluntary.[207]

Thus, according to Nowell-Smith, of all actions that may be called goo or bad, some are of the kind that can be altered in the future by the influence upon the agent of praise and blame, or reward and punishment Only such actions deserve to be called moral; only such actions shoulc also be called voluntary. Nowell-Smith illustrates the distinction he ha in mind by the example of "cleverness and industriousness . . . both valuable characteristics"; but "the latter is called 'moral' and the forme not, because we know from experience that the former cannot be induced by means of praise and blame, while the latter can."[208] He then sums up hi position on the voluntary in the following passage:

> To say that a man could have acted otherwise is to say that he might have been the sort of person who would have acted otherwise, and to attribute his acting as he did to his moral character, as opposed to some amoral defect, is to say that his action was due to one of the characteristics that can be altered by means of rewards and punishments.[209]

This explains why we punish a man who steals voluntarily but do no punish a kleptomaniac. "The reason," Nowell-Smith writes,

> is that we believe that the fear of punishment will affect the future behavior of the thief but not that of a kleptomaniac.[210]

Being alterable by punishment, being a voluntary agent, and being responsible are thus, in Nowell-Smith's analysis, inseparably connected.

[206] *Ibid.*, p. 58.
[207] *Ibid.*, *pp.* 58–59.
[208] *Ibid.*, p. 59.
[209] *Ibid.*
[210] *Ibid.*, p. 60.

When we are able empirically to determine that a man is capable of being
changed by punishment with respect to a certain type of action, then we
can tell that his acting in that way is voluntary and can regard him as
responsible for such actions. In offering this solution of the problem of
responsibility, Nowell-Smith follows the lead of Moritz Schlick who is, if
anything, more explicit. Schlick writes:

> The question regarding responsibility is the question: Who, in a given
> case, is to be punished?[211]

That question, according to Schlick, is to be answered entirely in terms of
future effects: no one is to be punished whose future conduct cannot be
altered by it. "Punishment," he maintains, "is an educative measure."

> [It] is a means to the formation of motives, which are in part to prevent
> the wrongdoer from repeating the act (reformation) and in part to prevent
> others from committing a similar act (intimidation). Analogously, in the
> case of reward we are concerned with incentive.[212]

What remains to be considered here are Nowell-Smith's objections to
Campbell's position. As he sees it, Campbell's theory is that "most of our
voluntary actions are 'free' only in this sense [i.e., the sense defined by
Ayer] which implies no breach in causal continuity. I choose because my
desires are what they are; and they have been moulded by countless influences from my birth or earlier." But, Nowell-Smith continues, Campbell
holds that "*moral* choices are free in a quite different sense."[213] This
sense involves a categorical as opposed to a hypothetical interpretation of
the statement that a man is responsible only when he could have acted
otherwise.[214]

> Professor Campbell puts the contrast in the following way: "Freewill does
> not operate in those practical situations in which no conflict arises in
> the agent's mind between what he conceives to be his 'duty' and what he

211 *Problems of Ethics*, p. 152.
212 *Ibid.* Schlick also anticipates Nowell-Smith's remark concerning the kleptomaniac,
when he explains that "we do not charge an insane person with responsibility, for the
very reason that he offers no unified point for the application of a motive. It would be
pointless to try to affect him by means of promises or threats, when his confused soul
fails to respond to such influence because its normal mechanism is out of order" (*ibid.*,
p. 153).
213 *Ethics*, p. 279.
214 See *ibid.*, p. 278. The categorical interpretation, as we have seen, asserts that the
individual could have acted otherwise *because* he could have chosen otherwise; whereas
the hypothetical interpretation asserts that he could have acted otherwise *only if* he
could have chosen otherwise, which, given his character and circumstances, was not
possible.

feels to be his 'strongest desire.' It does not operate here because there is just no occasion for it to operate. There is no reason whatever why the agent should here even contemplate choosing any course other than that prescribed by his strongest desire. In all such situations, therefore, he naturally wills in accordance with his strongest desire. But his 'strongest desire' is simply the specific expression of that system of conative and emotive dispositions which we call his 'character.' In all such situations, therefore, whatever may be the case elsewhere, his will is in effect determined by his character as so far formed."[215]

Before considering the objections that Nowell-Smith raises, it is necessary to point out that other exponents of what Campbell and Nowell-Smith call the "libertarian" position do not restrict the operation of free will to those instances in which an individual decides to act in the line of duty and against his "strongest desire" of the moment. In their view, the individual exercises a free choice, involving causal initiative on his part, just as much when he chooses to act in the line of least resistance by yielding to the "strongest desire" of the moment as when he chooses to act in the line of duty or in conformity to some moral principle and against contrary desires on his part.

Campbell, however, insists that it is only the latter choice which deserves to be called a "*moral* choice." He thinks that his "delimitation of the field of effective free will" to such choices "denies to the Libertarian absolutely nothing which matters to him. For it is precisely that small sector of the field of choices which our principle of delimitation still leaves open to free will, . . . that is crucial for moral responsibility." And, he continues, it is "with respect to such situations, and in the last resort to such situations alone, that the agent himself recognises that moral praise and blame are appropriate. . . . If the reality of freedom be conceded *here*, everything is conceded that the Libertarian has any real interest in securing."[216]

However, as Nowell-Smith sees it, Campbell's "delimitation" of free will to cases of "moral choice" raises a serious doubt about the soundness of his position. Calling attention to the fact that Campbell, while accepting a hypothetical interpretation of "he could have acted otherwise" in most cases, insists on a categorical interpretation in the special case of moral choice, Nowell-Smith writes:

It would indeed be remarkable if modal forms which are normally used in a hypothetical way were used categorically in one type of case alone.[217]

[215] *Ibid.*, pp. 279–80. The quotation from Campbell is taken from his article "Is 'Freewill' a Pseudo-Problem?" *loc. cit.*, pp. 460–61.
[216] "Is 'Freewill' a Pseudo-Problem?" *loc. cit.*, p. 461.
[217] *Ethics*, p. 278.

Acknowledging that Campbell supposes that the categorical interpreta-tion is necessary "only in a very small, but very important part of the whole range of human choice," Nowell-Smith then adds:

> And this too is remarkable; for it implies that the words 'free' and 'choose' are logically different in moral and in non-moral cases.[218]

He follows this up with a number of objections, some of which have been considered in another connection.[219] Three are relevant to the present dispute.

Of these, the first is stated in the following manner:

> If it is necessary to decide whether or not a man could have acted other-wise before ascribing responsibility, it is necessary that we should have some criterion for deciding this; and on the libertarian theory such a criterion is quite impossible. For, let us suppose that we know a great deal about his character and also that the temptation which he faced seems to be a fairly easy one for such a man to overcome. On the libertarian hypothesis this in-formation will not be sufficient to enable us to conclude that he could have acted otherwise. If he in fact does the wrong thing, there are three alternative conclusions that we might draw. (a) The action was not against his moral principles at all, so that no conflict between "duty" and "inclina-tion" arose. This is what I have called "wickedness"; (b) he knew it was wrong and could have resisted the temptation but did not (moral weak-ness); (c) he knew it was wrong but the temptation was *too* strong for him; he *could* not overcome it (addiction). Now it is essential to be able to distinguish case (b) from case (c), since (b) is a culpable state while (c) is not. By treating "he could have acted otherwise" in a hypothetical way, the determinist thesis does provide us with a criterion for distinguishing between these cases; but the categorical interpretation cannot provide one, since no one, not even the man himself, could know whether he could have overcome the temptation or not.[220]

The second of the aforementioned objections is stated as follows:

> The libertarian theory involves putting a very special construction on the principle that "ought" implies "can," which it is very doubtful whether it can bear. If we take this principle in a common-sense way it is undoubtedly true. It is no longer my duty to keep a promise, if I literally *cannot* do so. But when we say this we have in mind such possibilities as my being de-tained by the police or having a railway accident or the death of the promisee; and it is possible to discover empirically whether any of these exonerating conditions obtained. But if "cannot" is construed in such a way that it covers my being too dishonest a person or not making the

---

[218] *Ibid.*, p. 279.
[219] See pp. 297–98, *supra*.
[220] *Ethics*, pp. 283–84.

necessary effort, it is no longer obvious that "ought" implies "can." These reasons for failure, so far from exonerating, are just what make a man culpable.[221]

And the last of the three objections which Nowell-Smith raises, he states as follows:

> Even if it were possible to discover whether or not a man could have acted otherwise by attending to the actual occasion, as the categorical interpretation insists, why should this be held relevant to the question whether or not he is to blame?[222]

(iii) In an Appendix to *On Selfhood and Godhood*, Campbell presents "A Reply to Mr. Nowell-Smith" that contains his reactions to the specific criticisms which we have just considered. We shall deal with these first. We shall then turn to another source for his own criticism of the theory of responsibility advanced by Schlick and Nowell-Smith.

Campbell declares that he sees nothing "remarkable" about his shifting from a hypothetical interpretation of "he could have acted otherwise" in the case of non-moral action to a categorical interpretation in the case of moral action.[223] "Even less 'remarkable,'" in his opinion, is the fact that, in consequence of this shift, he attaches different meanings to such words as "free" and "choose" in moral and non-moral cases. He points out that "if there is one word of philosophical significance in the vocabulary of the English language that can beat 'feeling' in the diversity of its usages, it is the word 'free.'" And, he continues,

> to anyone who appreciates the distinctive character of our usage of the word 'free' when we are talking about freedom as a condition of moral responsibility, it will certainly not come as a shock to learn that the 'logic' of the word 'free' is different in moral and in non-moral cases.[224]

To Nowell-Smith's objection that the libertarian theory can offer no criterion for determining whether or not a man could have acted otherwise (i.e., could have chosen otherwise),[225] Campbell replies that he sees no difficulty about the demanded criterion, so far as the libertarian theory is concerned. He writes:

> The libertarian view (based primarily upon the introspective report of the moral agent engaged in the act of moral decision) is that a man in the

221 *Ibid.*, p. 284.
222 *Ibid.*, pp. 284–85.
223 *On Selfhood and Godhood*, pp. 214–15.
224 *Ibid.*, pp. 215–16.
225 See p. 311, *supra.*

situation Nowell-Smith depicts could *always* have acted otherwise; though of course the effort required to rise to duty will be harder in proportion to the strength of the temptation, and corresponding allowances will have to be made in passing moral judgment on the man—a practice which accords perfectly with our more carefully pondered moral assessments of men in ordinary life.[226]

Next, to Nowell-Smith's objection that the libertarian theory involves putting a very special construction on the principle that "ought implies an,"[227] Campbell replies in the following passage:

To me it seems about as obvious as anything can be that 'ought' implies 'can' in a sense of 'can' which goes far beyond the absence of external obstacles to the fulfillment of the duty, which is apparently all that Nowell-Smith (judging from his illustrations) is willing to allow. I do not even believe that any very adroit maieutic would be needed to deliver this truth from 'commonsense.' For if on any grounds whatsoever—scientific, psychological, metaphysical, or religious—one has come to believe that moral choices are all determined in the sense that there only appear to be, and never really are, genuinely open possibilities before a man, so that he *cannot* act otherwise than he does, then it seems every bit as evident nonsense to say that he morally 'ought to act otherwise' as it would be if there were external obstacles such as Nowell-Smith cites preventing his so acting. And of course the 'cannot' here *does* cover 'being too dishonest a person,' since it is implied (in the determinist belief) that he is too dishonest a person because 'that's the way he's made'; and it covers similarly his 'not making the necessary effort,' since it is implied that he *couldn't* make the necessary effort. These 'reasons for failure,' unlike those mentioned earlier, *are* indeed 'just what make a man culpable'; but only on the assumption that 'reasons for failure' here mean '*ways of* failing' and *not* '*conditions necessitating* failure.' Surely we *must* all agree that a man cannot be held morally culpable for that which he can't help doing? It matters not a jot, ethically speaking, whether what prevents him acting otherwise is the strong arm of the law or the metaphysical structure of the universe.[228]

Finally, we come to Nowell-Smith's query why libertarians think that the categorical interpretation of "he could have acted otherwise" (which involves the assertion that *he could have chosen otherwise*), is "relevant to the question whether or not he is to blame."[229] Campbell does not respond to this query directly.[230] However, his response is implied in a

---

[226] *On Selfhood and Godhood*, p. 221.
[227] See pp. 311–12, *supra*.
[228] *On Selfhood and Godhood*, p. 222.
[229] See p. 312, *supra*.
[230] For what amounts to a direct response to Nowell-Smith's query, see C. D. Broad's essay "Determinism, Indeterminism, and Libertarianism" in *Ethics and the History of Philosophy*.

query which he himself puts. "How can a man be morally responsible," the reflective man, according to Campbell, asks himself, "if his choices, like all other events in the universe could not have been otherwise than they in fact were?" The reflective man will answer that he cannot be held responsible. For him, Campbell continues,

> . . . it will in *no* class of cases be a sufficient condition of moral responsibility for an act that one could have acted otherwise *if* one had chosen otherwise—not even in these cases where there *was* some possibility of the operation of 'external constraint.' In these cases he will, indeed, expressly recognise freedom from external constraint as a *necessary condition*, but not as a *sufficient* condition. For he will be aware that, even granted *this* freedom, it is still conceivable that the agent had no freedom to choose otherwise than he did, and he will therefore require that the latter sort of freedom be added if moral responsibility for the act is to be established.[231]

Campbell then goes on to say that "for the unreflective person, 'A could have acted otherwise,' as a condition of moral responsibility, *is* apt to mean no more than 'A could have acted otherwise *if* he had so chosen.' " In his opinion, it is only "for persons at *a tolerably advanced level of reflexion*" that " 'A could have acted otherwise,' as a condition of A's moral responsibility, means 'A could have chosen otherwise.' " Hence, it seems to him that "the view now favoured by many philosophers, that the freedom required for moral responsibility is merely freedom from external constraint, is a view which they share only with the less reflective type of layman."[232]

Futhermore, in Campbell's opinion, the theory of responsibility offered by his opponents is untenable. It is, as we have seen,[233] the theory that an individual is responsible for actions only to the degree that rewards and punishments can alter his future conduct. It makes no difference in their view whether the individual could have chosen to act otherwise *at the time*. The critical point is whether he can, *in the future*, be *made* to act otherwise or even to choose otherwise. If so, then he should be held responsible for his present action, i.e., he should be subject to praise or blame, reward or punishment.

[231] "Is 'Freewill' a Pseudo-Problem?," in *loc. cit.*, p. 456. Cf. *ibid.*, p. 455, where Campbell writes: "The freedom to translate one's choice into action, which . . . is for Schlick the *only* freedom required for moral responsibility, is without doubt *one* of the conditions of moral responsibility." See also *On Selfhood and Godhood*, pp. 162–64.
[232] "Is 'Freewill' a Pseudo-Problem?," in *loc. cit.*, p. 456. In the course of this essay, Campbell names and deals with the philosophers to whom he refers. In addition to Nowell-Smith (see pp. 452–53), there are Schlick (see pp. 442–50) and Stevenson (see p. 454). And in *On Selfhood and Godhood*, p. 162, he refers to the position of Moore and Stevenson.
[233] See pp. 307–9, *supra*.

The first point Campbell makes against this theory is that it does not correspond to "what we mean by 'moral responsibility' in ordinary linguistic usage."

> We do not ordinarily consider the lower animals to be morally responsible. But *ought* we not to do so if Schlick is right about what we mean by moral responsibility? It is quite possible, by punishing the dog who absconds with the succulent chops designed for its master's luncheon, favourably to influence its motives in respect of its future behaviour in like circumstances. If moral responsibility is to be linked with punishment as Schlick links it, and punishment conceived as a form of education, we should surely hold the dog morally responsible. The plain fact, of course, is that we don't. We don't, because we suppose that the dog 'couldn't help it': that its action (unlike what we usually believe to be true of human beings) was simply a link in a continuous chain of causes and effects. In other words, we do commonly demand the contra-causal sort of freedom as a condition of moral responsibility.[234]

Secondly, Campbell points out:

> . . . we do ordinarily consider it proper, in certain circumstances, to speak of a person no longer living as morally responsible for some present situation. But *ought* we to do so if we accept Schlick's essentially 'forward-looking' interpretation of punishment and responsibility? Clearly we cannot now favourably affect the dead man's motives. No doubt they could *at one time* have been favourably affected. But that cannot be relevant to our judgment of responsibility if, as Schlick insists, the question of who is responsible "is a matter only of knowing who is to be punished or rewarded."[235]

Finally, Campbell calls attention to the "paradox in Schlick's identification of the question 'Who is morally blameworthy?' with the question 'Who is to be punished?'" which, he says, "is apt to be partially concealed from us just because it is our normal habit to include in the meaning of 'punishment' an element of 'requital for moral transgression' which Schlick expressly denies to it." Hence, he continues,

> . . . we commonly think of 'punishment,' in its strict sense, as implying moral blameworthiness in the person punished. But if we remember to mean by punishment what Schlick means by it, a purely 'educative measure,' with no retributive ingredients, his identification of the two questions loses such plausibility as it might otherwise have.[236]

234 "Is 'Freewill' a Pseudo-Problem?," in *loc. cit.*, p. 447. In these pages Campbell addresses himself to Schlick's statement of the theory he is criticizing. Nowell-Smith's work, in which he advances the same theory, was published some years after Campbell's article.
235 *Ibid.*
236 *Ibid.*, pp. 448–49.

The foregoing points lead Campbell to the conclusion that it must be admitted "that constantly people do assign moral responsibility where Schlick's theory says they shouldn't, don't assign moral responsibility where Schlick's theory says they should, and assign degrees of moral responsibility where on Schlick's theory there should be no difference in degree."[237]

This completes our examination of the dispute between Campbell and Nowell-Smith, Schlick, and others. With regard to this dispute as a whole, two things should be noted.

(a) Nowell-Smith and Schlick, to mention only these two, insist, on the one hand, that a hypothetical interpretation of "he could have acted otherwise" (i.e., *if* he had chosen otherwise) is a sufficient basis for moral responsibility. On the other hand, they offer as a basis for holding a man responsible for his actions the effect of rewards and punishments on his future conduct with respect to such actions. The first of these two grounds for determining whether a man is responsible directly contravenes Campbell's insistence, on the contrary, that a categorical interpretation of "he could have acted otherwise" (i.e., *because* he could have chosen otherwise) is required as the basis for moral responsibility.

(b) Campbell, on his part, deals with these two grounds in what appear to be opposite ways. On the one hand, he admits that a hypothetical interpretation of "he could have acted otherwise" may fit the unreflective layman's way of thinking and talking about responsibility, but here he denies that it is acceptable to a reflective person. On the other hand, with regard to Schlick's and Nowell-Smith's theory that moral responsibility should be attached only to such actions as can be altered in the future by rewards and punishments, Campbell denies that it fits the ordinary man's way of thinking and talking about responsibility.

5. THE DISPUTE ABOUT THE EVIDENCE OF CONSCIOUSNESS OR INNER EXPERIENCE

Here, as in the dispute dealt with in Section 4, the affirmative side of the issue about causal initiative opens the argument. Here, too, the affirmative authors appeal to an extrinsic, not an intrinsic, reason for asserting the existence of causal initiative.[238] In this case, it is the evidence which consciousness or inner experience affords that man has a freedom of self-determination.

As we shall see in the next chapter, many writers who affirm causal

[237] *Ibid.*
[238] See p. 302, *supra.*

indeterminacy, (i.e., a freedom of choice which consists in being able to choose otherwise under identical conditions) argue that we are directly conscious of our power to choose freely. In fact, the evidence of consciousness or inner experience is more frequently used to support the affirmation of causal indeterminacy than to support the assertion of causal initiative. Nevertheless, some self-determination authors do maintain that we are directly aware of our power to act without being acted upon. Others, who think that we are conscious of exercising a free choice, maintain that such evidence indirectly supports our having causal initiative, since, in their view, causal initiative is presupposed by causal indeterminacy.

The affirmative argument, based on the evidence of consciousness, thus takes two forms: (i) one in which it is argued that our direct experience of causal initiative warrants our asserting its existence; and (ii) one in which it is argued that our direct experience of free choice raises a genuine question, not a "pseudo-problem," about the existence of causal indeterminacy and, with it, the causal initiative that it presupposes. It is important to note here that the second mode of argument differs from the first in two respects, not one: on the one hand, it does not claim that we have any direct experience of causal initiative (i.e., of being able to act without being acted upon); on the other hand, it does not claim that such experience as we have of free choice warrants our asserting the existence of causal indeterminacy or of the causal initiative which some writers think that it presupposes. In this second respect, it claims only that the evidence of consciousness precludes us from dismissing the question about the existence of either causal indeterminacy or causal initiative as an unreal question or "pseudo-problem."

We shall deal with those two modes of argument in the order indicated. In each case, we shall present, along with the argument, the response which it elicits from the opposite side in this dispute. In the first case, we can report only one actual interchange, involving Priestley and Price. In the second case, we shall be concerned chiefly with one actual interchange, involving Campbell, Nowell-Smith, and R. D. Bradley. In the latter case, after we examine what Nowell-Smith and Bradley have to say about Campbell's position, we shall have to consider his reaction to their criticisms.

(i) In the context of describing the will as sovereign among the powers of the mind, because it alone is active as a cause, Descartes declares that "no one, when he considers himself alone, fails to experience the fact that to will and to be free are the same thing."[239] Other writers—Renouvier

---

[239] *Objections and Replies, III*, in *Philosophical Works*, Vol. II, p. 75. Cf. *Passions of the Soul*, Article CLII, in *ibid.*, Vol. I, p. 401.

and Martineau, for example—use man's consciousness of himself as an actively free being to question the assumptions of determinism.[240]

In his debate with Joseph Priestley, Dr. Price maintains that "whatever to the contrary men may say, it is impossible for them, in earnest, to think they have *no active self-moving powers*, and are not causes of their own volitions, or not to ascribe to *themselves* what they must be conscious they think and do." In his opinion, "we have, in truth, the same constant and necessary consciousness of liberty that we have that we *think, choose, will*, or even *exist*."[241]

Henry Mansel presents the argument from consciousness in a somewhat different form. In his *Prolegomena Logica*, to which is appended his criticism of J. S. Mill's views on causality and causal initiative, Mansel writes:

> To speak of the determinations of the will as *caused* by phenomena, in the same sense in which the fusion of metal is *caused* by fire, is to give the lie to consciousness for the sake of theory.

On the contrary, he insists that "if *cause* be interpreted to mean an agent with power, my only positive notion of cause in this sense is derived from the consciousness of myself as determining, not as determined." Furthermore, he argues:

> My notion of causes with power, other than myself, is derived from the primary intuition of myself as a cause, and cannot be made to react upon that intuition, with the fallacy of deducing the known from the unknown.[242]

Like Mansel, F. C. S. Schiller points out that "the conception of causes has entered the world of science from our own direct experience." That direct experience includes our consciousness of choosing and choosing freely between real alternatives. "If choice is real, if there really are alternatives," Schiller argues, "it follows that in choosing between them we are exhibiting our power as real agents, real causes and initiators of new

[240] See Renouvier, *Psychologie Rationelle*, Vol. I, pp. 204–6; Martineau, *Types of Ethical Theory*, pp. 39 ff. Cf. Hocking, *Human Nature and Its Remaking*, p. 11.

[241] *The Doctrine of Philosophical Necessity*, p. 55. Cf. *Priestley-Price Controversy*, pp. 135–36, at which point Price presents what he regards as a demonstrative argument for the agency of the will as an active power that can act without being acted upon.

[242] *Op. cit.*, pp. 152–53. "You are conscious, says the necessitarian, of yourself as a determining cause; therefore you must be a determined effect. By what logic does this follow?" Mansel asks. "If these considerations suggest a limit to the universality of the principle of sufficient reason, so be it. No principle can consistently be allowed so much universality, as to overthrow the intuition from which it had its rise" (*ibid.*, p. 153).

departures in the flow of cosmic change. We thereby prove the existence of free causes." The proof, according to Schiller, rests on our accepting "the verdict of consciousness" concerning "acts of choice [which] are surely about the most vivid, real and important experiences of our lives. . . . It will hardly be disputed," he continues, "that the alternatives in choice *feel* real; that we feel 'free' in choosing, in a way distinct from the feeling which accompanies all our other actions, voluntary and involuntary." It is up to the determinist to show that these feelings are illusory. "Surely the burden of proof lies on those who allege that what seems to be real is not really so."[243]

Hubert Gruender, representing a point of view that is quite common among scholastic philosophers, goes further than the foregoing authors in his explicit formulation of the argument from consciousness. He maintains that we do experience what he calls *"the active interposition of the Ego by which the issues between conflicting motives is settled."*[244] He refers to the carefully controlled observations of such inner experience made by subjects in experiments performed by Ach, Michotte, Prüm, and Wells, but he disagrees with the conclusions they draw from their data.[245] He writes:

> From these data we draw the obvious conclusion that we have the ability to settle the issue between two conflicting motives, equal or unequal, by the active interposition of the Ego. And this ability is what common sense designates as free will. In short, *controlled observation has confirmed the common-sense doctrine of free will.*[246]

Gruender acknowledges that "many are the attempts made to invalidate this simple experimental proof of free will. It has been said that the question of free will cannot possibly be settled by an appeal to the data of introspection. For free will, by its very nature, is an *ability* or a *power*. . . . But introspection does not reveal any ability or power of ours. The object of introspection is *present internal facts*; but no ability or power of ours is a present internal fact."[247]

In Gruender's opinion, this difficulty ("which has been proposed and discussed by the staunchest defenders of free will—the schoolmen") is not insuperable. The scholastic philosophers, he claims, have a satisfactory solution of it. He presents it in the following passage:

---

[243] *Riddles of the Sphinx*, p. 458. Cf. *ibid.*, pp. 445–46; and see also *Studies in Humanism*, pp. 401 ff.
[244] *Experimental Psychology*, p. 428.
[245] See *ibid.*, p. 433.
[246] *Ibid.*, pp. 433–34.
[247] *Ibid.*

We grant, then, that in literal strictness free will is not a matter of immediate experience: it is not a present internal fact. . . . Free will, precisely because it is an *ability* or *power* of ours, can only be a matter of inference. But inference is of two kinds, immediate and mediate. . . . This premised, we admit that in literal strictness *we experience only the fact that here and now we settle the issue between conflicting motives by the active interposition of the Ego.* From this we infer that we have the *ability* to do so. This inference, however, is *immediate* and far removed from that indirect way of arriving at a judgment which alone is designated by the term "reasoning process."[248]

We turn now to the writers on the negative side. Spinoza summarily dismisses the evidence of consciousness. "Men think themselves free," he writes, "inasmuch as they are conscious of their volitions and desires, and never even dream, in their ignorance, of the causes which have disposed them so to wish and desire."[249] Other writers take very much the same view. Samuel Alexander, considering "the testimony of our minds which gives us the consciousness of freedom," i.e., of a will that "can act independently of motive," declares that "the idea of such a free-will is . . . a sheer delusion."[250] To those who say "we feel ourselves to be free," Georges Clemenceau replies, "Well and good; but are we free? That is the kernel of the problem."[251] In the opinion of Brand Blanshard, our intuition that "we can choose our own choice," cannot be relied on to support the case of the libertarian against the determinist.[252] Commenting on Blanshard's handling of our "stubborn feeling of freedom," Carl Hempel writes: "I fully agree with Mr. Blanshard that it cannot count as evidence against determinism, for this kind of feeling can surely be deceptive."[253]

Joseph Priestley and J. S. Mill argue against the consciousness of freedom in a somewhat different manner. Replying to Dr. Price, Priestley maintains that "all that a man can possibly be conscious of" is being able to choose that which he most strongly desires, when nothing external hinders him from making such a choice.[254] In his *Examination of the*

---

[248] *Ibid.*, pp. 434–35. Gruender then goes on to say that "in the language customary in natural science we should rather say that our mode of procedure is in literal strictness *an experimental proof of free will.* If the possibility of a certain phenomenon is questioned, and a scientist succeeds in actually producing that phenomenon in the laboratory, that scientist is said to have proved *experimentally* the *possibility* of that phenomenon (*ibid.*, p. 435).

[249] *Ethics*, Part I, Appendix, p. 75.

[250] *Moral Order and Progress*, p. 338.

[251] *In the Evening of My Thought*, Vol. I, p. 52.

[252] "The Case for Determinism," in *Determinism and Freedom*, pp. 5–7.

[253] "Some Reflections on 'The Case for Determinism,'" in *ibid.*, p. 161.

[254] *The Doctrine of Philosophical Necessity*, pp. 57–58. See also *ibid.*, p. 60, where Priestley says that "the *consciousness of freedom* . . . is an ambiguous expression, and cannot prove any thing in favour of philosophical or metaphysical liberty."

Philosophy of Sir William Hamilton, Mill considers Hamilton's argument that "we are conscious . . . either of our freedom, or at all events . . . of something which implies freedom."[255] In the course of cross-examining "the alleged testimony of consciousness," Mill also refers to Mansel as going further than Hamilton (whom Mansel defended against Mill); for Mansel asserts that "we are directly conscious of free-will."[256] The cross-examination Mill conducts results in the opposite conclusion.

> I ask my consciousness what I do feel, and I find, indeed, that I feel (or am convinced) that I could, and even should, have chosen the other course if I had preferred it; but not that I could have chosen one course while I preferred the other.[257]

Like Priestley, Mill insists that our feeling of freedom is simply our feeling that nothing prevents us from choosing in accordance with our preference or strongest desire. He flatly denies "that we are conscious of being able to act in opposition to the strongest desire or aversion."[258]

Other writers also interpret our consciousness of freedom in a way that rejects it as evidence for the existence of a freedom of self-determination that involves causal initiative and causal indeterminacy. In their view, we are simply aware of our freedom of self-realization, that is, of our being able to carry out our decisions or desires in the absence of external impediments. This view is taken by Friedrich Paulsen. What my consciousness tells me, he writes, is "that I am not moved from without like a cogwheel in a machine."[259] Referring to our "sense of spontaneity," Bertrand Russell says that it arises from our being able to do as we choose, not from our being able to choose independently of all motives.[260]

Moritz Schlick even more plainly declares that "the consciousness of freedom . . . is merely the knowledge of having acted of one's *own* desires." The fact that nothing external compelled me to act as I did rather than in some other way gives rise to the "well-known feeling (usually considered characteristic of freedom; *that* [I] *could also have acted otherwise.*" But, Schlick asks,

> how could such a feeling inform me of anything regarding the purely theoretical question of whether the principle of causality holds or not?

[255] *Op. cit.,* p. 578.
[256] *Ibid.,* p. 580. Mansel, Mill writes, "makes the assertion in the broadest form it is capable of . . . and goes so far as to maintain that our immediate intuition of Power is given us by the ego producing its own volitions" (*ibid.,* p. 580 fn.). Cf. Hamilton, *Lectures on Metaphypics,* Vol II, pp, 614–15.
[257] *Ibid.,* p. 582.
[258] *Ibid.,* p. 585.
[259] *A System of Ethics,* p. 459.
[260] "Determinism and Morals," in *The Hibbert Journal,* Vol. 7, p. 115.

In his view, it cannot. He denies "that from any such fact of consciousness the least follows regarding the principle's validity. This feeling is not the consciousness of the absence of a cause, but of something altogether different, namely, of *freedom*, which consists in the fact that I can act as I desire."[261]

(ii) To understand Campbell's argumentative use of our consciousness of freedom, it is necessary to remember that he distinguishes two closely related questions: (a) "Is a contra-causal type of freedom implied by moral responsibility?" and (b) "Does a contra-causal type of freedom anywhere exist?"[262] It is to the second question that Campbell thinks our inner experience of being able to exert our will power in the line of duty and against our desires is relevant. He thinks it is relevant to the problem of the existence of a contra-causal freedom, i.e., a freedom which involves causal initiative on the part of the self and a break in the causal chain whereby a man's decisions or choices flow entirely from his character as so far formed.

However, Campbell does not regard our inner sense of freedom as having demonstrative force. It does not, in his opinion, prove the truth of an affirmative answer to the question "Does a contra-causal type of freedom anywhere exist?" It only forms the basis of an argument that that question is real or genuine and not a "pseudo-problem."

Campbell's argument is that we have introspective evidence that men believe themselves to be in possession of contra-causal freedom on the basis of their inner experience of being able to make the hard choice against the predominant tendency of their character. He admits that "these beliefs may, of course, be illusory, but that is not at present the point. For the present argument all that matters is whether beliefs of this sort are in fact discoverable in the moral agent in the situation of 'moral temptation.' For my own part," he writes, "I cannot doubt the introspective evidence that they are."[263]

[261] *Problems of Ethics*, pp. 154–55. Cf. Arthur Pap, "Determinism, Freedom, Moral Responsibility, and Causal Talk," in *Determinism and Freedom*, p. 200. Pap writes: "I fail to see why our 'feeling free' calls for explanation if one believes in determinism. Innumerable times in the past I have verified that my decisions were followed by the actions I decided to perform; hence I ascribe to myself the *power* 'to do as I please.' That I feel free just means that I believe, on good grounds that—within limits, of course—I can do as I please" (*loc. cit.*).

[262] See "Is 'Freewill' a Pseudo-Problem?" in *loc. cit.*, p. 450.

[263] See *ibid.*, p. 463. In another place, Campbell writes: "Why do human beings so obstinately persist in believing that there is an indissoluble core of purely *self*-originated activity which even heredity and environment are powerless to affect? There can be little doubt, I think, of the answer in general terms. They do so, at bottom, because they feel certain of the existence of such activity from their immediate practical experience of themselves" (*In Defence of Free Will* p. 13). Cf. *ibid.*, pp. 16–17.

The existence of a widely prevalent belief in contra-causal freedom requires us to face, as a real problem, the question whether that belief is in fact true. Though Campbell admits that the belief may be illusory (i.e., false), he also insists that "in considering the claim to truth of this belief . . . we should begin by noting that the onus of proof rests upon the critic who rejects this belief. Until cogent evidence to the contrary is adduced, we are entitled to put our trust in a belief which is so deeply imbedded in our experience as practical beings as to be, I venture to say, ineradicable from it."[264]

Like Campbell, Yves Simon admits that our inner experience does not prove the existence of free will, but is only evidence of a problem to be solved by further inquiry. He writes:

> The experience of free will is certain, but it is confused in the extreme. Because of this confusion we do not think that appealing to the testimony of consciousness can constitute a special argument in favor of free will; it is very simply the experimental point of departure for rational inquiry. . . .[265]

In his opinion, "the value of the testimony of consciousness as a sign of our free will would be less contested if the mistake of asking more of the inner experience than it can give had not been committed."[266]

On the negative side, we turn now to the criticisms of Campbell's position, which are presented by Nowell-Smith and R. D. Bradley.

Nowell-Smith maintains that we cannot have the experience of contra-causal freedom which Campbell claims that we do have. "When I am conscious of being free," he says, "I am not directly conscious that my actions are uncaused, because absence of causation is not something of which one could be directly aware."[267] And in another place he writes:

> Campbell insists that the question whether choice is 'free' in a contra-causal sense must be settled by introspection. But is this so? To doubt the

[264] *In Defence of Free Will*, p. 18. Cf. F. C. S. Schiller's remarks about the burden of proof being on those who would dismiss our consciousness of freedom: see pp. 318–19, *supra*.

[265] *Traité du Libre Arbitre*, p. 70. Cf. the view expressed by John W. Stafford in "Freedom in Experimental Psychology," in *Proceedings of the American Catholic Philosophical Association*, Vol. XVI, pp. 148–54. Stafford denies that psychology can provide any conclusive evidence with regard to the existence of free will.

[266] *Ibid.*, p. 54. In another place, Simon says that "contrary to the postulates of certain spiritualist philosophies, the intuition of consciousness does not reveal to us, without more effort, the nature of our acts, of our power, and of our substance. . . . It is not intuition which can be substituted for the work of reason and dispense with its difficulties" (*ibid.*, pp. 58–59). C. Lotze, *Outlines of Psychology*, p. 152; and Fouillée, *Liberté et Determinisme*, pp. 81, 88.

[267] "Free Will and Moral Responsibility," in *loc. cit.*, p. 46.

findings of his self-examination may seem impertinent; but the doubt is concerned, not with what he finds, but with the propriety of the language he uses to describe what he finds. The universal negative form of statement ("Nothing caused my decision," "No one could have predicted my decision") does not seem to be a proper vehicle for anything that one could be said to *observe* in self-examination. That I know introspectively what it is like to choose may be true; but I cannot be said to know introspectively that my choice was contra-causal or unpredictable; and this is the point at issue. He represents 'I can rise to duty' as a report of a mental event or, perhaps, a state of mind, not as a statement about a capacity, and 'I could have . . .' as a statement about a past state of mind or mental event. But, if this is really so, it is at least surprising that, in this one context alone, we use the modal words 'can' and 'could have' for making categorical reports. The issue between determinists and libertarians is an issue about the way in which expressions such as 'choose,' 'can,' and 'alternative possibilities' are to be construed; and this is surely an issue which is to be settled not by self-observation but by logical analysis.[268]

According to R. D. Bradley, Campbell is "convinced not only that the free-will question can be answered, but that it has been answered, and that its answer is given by the introspective method."[269] As Bradley sees it, Campbell maintains that "all we need to do is to attend honestly to the deliverances of our practical consciousness and we will *know* forthwith that our wills are really free."[270] And, he continues, "if Campbell is right, further discussion and argument about the free-will problem will clearly be pointless."[271]

Against Campbell Bradley argues, first, that conflicting reports are obtained by the introspective method, and this by itself raises serious doubts about the validity of its findings.[272] In the second place, he points out that "we may, under certain conditions, be able to observe X, but we can never be completely sure that we have observed non-X: it is always possible that we have instead merely not-observed X. Thus, absence of an experience of causality is far from being the same as experience of an absence of causality."[273] In other words, we can never observe that our decision in a par-

---

[268] *Ethics*, pp. 280–81. See Nowell-Smith's comments on introspection versus logical analysis in "Determinists and Libertarians," in *Mind*, Vol. LXIII, No. 251, pp. 322–23. It should be observed here that certain exponents of free will agree that consciousness or experience affords no proof of causal initiative. See, for example, Secrétan, *Mon Utopie*, p. 162.

[269] "Free Will: Problem or Pseudo-Problem," in *Australasian Journal of Philosophy*, Vol. 36, No. 1, p. 38. In the immediately following pages, Bradley refers to various books and articles by Campbell in support of this interpretation of his position. See *ibid.*, pp. 39–40.

[270] *Ibid.*, pp. 38–39.

[271] *Ibid.*, p. 40.

[272] *Ibid.*, pp. 40–41.

[273] *Ibid.*, p. 42.

ticular case is not caused by our character; we can only fail to observe that it is thus caused; and this is no basis for concluding that it is not thus caused. In the third place, Bradley denies "that we can *know* that such propositions as 'My will is contra-causally free,' 'I could (in a categorical sense of "could") have chosen otherwise,' and 'The self has a power of absolute spontaneity or self-origination,' are true . . . if we examine the contents of our consciousness by means of inner perception." This, Bradley argues, "cannot be the case, firstly because the data of introspection do not in fact include *any* propositions, and, secondly, because such propositions cannot even be said to *report* such data, let alone report them correctly."[274]

To Nowell-Smith's attack, Campbell responds by pointing out that his position has been misrepresented.

> What I have insisted upon is that introspection provides highly important evidence for the settlement of the question, not that it can *per se* settle it. . . . Metaphysics, science, epistemology, ethics, and religion have all, I think, something relevant to contribute to a 'settlement.'

Campbell says that he agrees with Nowell-Smith that we cannot know introspectively that our choices are free in a contra-causal sense; then adding: "I think he has failed to appreciate that what I report as discerned in introspection is . . . not a contra-causal activity, but a belief—seemingly ineradicable—that one is contra-causally active."[275]

Campbell's reply to R. D. Bradley even more emphatically calls attention to the misrepresentation of his views. "On account of one basic misunderstanding," Campbell begins, "Bradley—despite his manifest fairmindedness—has comprehensively misrepresented my arguments." Hence, Campbell thinks that Bradley's critical points are "quite irrelevant to anything [he has] ever held."[276]

[274] *Ibid.*, p. 42. To say that we "feel contra-causally free" or "feel spontaneous" or "feel self-originative" can have no bearing, in Bradley's opinion, on the questions whether, in fact, we *are* any of these things, *unless* the criteria for a correct use of such expressions as "I feel free" and "I am free" are identical. See *ibid.*, pp. 43–45.

[275] *On Selfhood and Godhood*, p. 216. This belief is one of the facts in the experience of making a moral decision. Such facts are the primary source of the libertarian's claim that his use of the expression "could have done otherwise" is the proper one. Logical analysis will not tell us what the correct usage is; only the facts will. "And among the relevant facts are those supplied by introspection" (*ibid.*, p. 218).

[276] "Free Will: A Reply to Mr. R. D. Bradley," in *Australasian Journal of Philosophy*, Vol. 36, No. 1, p. 51. To one critical point raised by Bradley, Campbell sees fit to reply directly. Bradley had asked: "What are we to say when the reports of two introspective experimenters conflict, as do, for example, those of Professors Campbell and MacLagan? Both believe in the efficacy of the introspective method, but whereas Campbell reports that our sense of effort in making a difficult moral choice reveals freedom to us, MacLagan denies this and reports rather that he has no intuition of freedom independent of the fact of duty" ("Free Will: Problem or Pseudo-Problem?," in *loc.*

Bradley's misunderstanding, Campbell explains, "concerns the part which I conceive introspection to play in supporting the libertarian doctrine. I do *not* hold, as Bradley thinks, that by introspection we can become aware of 'contra-causal' freedom (as it were) 'in action.' What I *do* hold is that by introspection we can become aware of an *experience* in which a *belief* in 'contra-causal' freedom is an intrinsic element. On the former of these views, introspection, in so far as veridical, would of itself establish free will. But I have never dreamt of crediting introspection with such authority."[277]

Campbell's contention, in short, is that the introspective evidence does at least one thing. By showing the existence of a commonly held belief that we have free will, it brings us face to face with *the problem whether that belief is true or false*. It does not supply us with a full solution of that problem, but it should, Campbell thinks, stop anyone from dismissing the question as a pseudo-problem, or from holding, as Hume does, that "the free-will controversy arises from mere 'verbal' confusion."[278]

It remains only to examine Campbell's reply to two criticisms by Bradley, which he thinks deserve extended comment.

The first of these, Campbell writes, "opens with the statement that my thesis is 'that against all argument it *can be shown* that man has the power to (and often does) interrupt the causal order.' " Campbell's comment here is as follows:

---

cit., p. 40). To which Campbell replies: "Bradley has very properly drawn attention to a seeming conflict between my introspective finding and that of my colleague Professor MacLagan. I think, however, and I have MacLagan's assurance that he agrees, that any difference that remains between us is one of emphasis rather than of substance ("Free Will: A Reply to Mr. R. D. Bradley," in *loc. cit.*, p. 51 fn. 8).

277 *Ibid.*, p. 52. "On several occasions," Campbell adds, "I have expressly acknowledged that the 'belief' element discerned by introspection in the experience of moral decision may be an *illusory* belief, and that a philosophical defence of free will cannot base itself upon this *alone*, but must take into account a large number of other relevant considerations" (*ibid.*). It should, perhaps, also be added that Campbell acknowledges some fault for the misunderstanding that has arisen. "It *is* my view that, *qua* moral agent actually engaged in the situation of moral temptation, one feels an absolute assurance that one is 'contra-causally' free; and it may well be that at times I have spoken of the 'assurance of freedom' without making it as clear as I ought that it was not an assurance *qua* moral philosopher, but only an assurance *qua* moral agent, that I had in mind. If so, I must certainly accept some responsibility. I do not think that, in its context, anything said in my later writings should have created the wrong impression, but I agree that there are ambiguous phrases in *Scepticism and Construction*, from which Bradley quotes; though even in this early work so much is said that is irreconcilable with Bradley's understanding of these phrases that I am a little surprised that they have misled him" (*ibid.*, p. 52–53).

278 *Ibid.*, p. 51. His detailed criticism of what he takes to be Hume's unsound analysis and treatment of the question (see *ibid.*, pp. 47–50) is not relevant here; though it may be relevant to report his suspicion that "the real source of Bradley's confidence in the 'unanswerability' of the free-will question lies, not in any grounds he offers here, but in his belief that David Hume has shown once and for all that the question is at bottom a mere dispute about words" (*ibid.*, p. 47).

I take exception to the word 'shown'; and still more so to the expression "against all argument," if by this is meant that I recognise no need for anything beyond introspective observation. Bradley then goes on to argue that since *no* kind of observation, internal any more than external, can establish a negative existential proposition like 'there is no cause for this event,' I must be wrong in holding that in introspection we directly observe an interruption of the causal order. But of course what we observe in introspection, for me, is not 'an interruption of the causal order,' but a *belief* that one is bringing about such an interruption. Introspection (so far as veridical) establishes not a 'negative existential proposition,' but the positive existential proposition that there exists, in my experience as a moral agent in the situation of moral temptation, a belief of a certain kind. The sense in which, in that situation, one believes that one is interrupting the causal order, I have already explained. It is perhaps worth repeating, however, that it is not a belief that one's moral decision is, without qualification, 'uncaused.' For my experience, "I" cause it; but by a *creative* causality which is incompatible with causal *continuity*.[279]

The second of Bradley's criticisms, Campbell describes as beginning with the remark: "Campbell contends that we can *know* that such propositions as 'My will is contra-causally free' . . . are true . . . if we examine the contents of our own consciousness by inner perception." Campbell's comment here is as follows:

Again my contention is mis-stated. That introspection can provide us with valuable positive evidence for the proposition's truth, I do claim . . . But I do not contend that it *establishes* the proposition in question.[280]

Apart from this mis-statement of his position, Campbell points out that Bradley "in developing [this] criticism . . . raises and discusses a more debatable point, about the meaning of 'feel' in such expressions as 'I feel free,' 'I feel I could (categorically) have acted otherwise,' and the like." But here, once more, he charges Bradley with attributing to him a view he does not hold, namely, that "when—to take the example to which Bradley devotes most attention—I say 'I feel free,' I mean . . . no more and no less than 'I am free.' "[281]

The statement "I am free" is an assertion of objective fact, which cannot be verified or disproved by introspective evidence; but the statement "I feel free," Campbell maintains, expresses a subjective fact, a belief, the

[279] *Ibid.*, p. 53.
[280] *Ibid.*, p. 54. "I agree of course," Campbell continues, "that propositions cannot be included among the data of introspection. I agree also that such a proposition as 'My will is contra-causally free' could not 'report' a datum of introspection, since the data of introspection are experiences, and this proposition does not report an *experience*. But all this does not touch the view I hold" (*ibid.*).
[281] *Ibid.*, p. 54.

existence of which cannot be verified or disproved *except by reference to inner experience*. Hence, in Campbell's judgment, "Bradley's assertion that there is no difference between 'the criteria for the correct use of the expression "I feel free" and the expression "I am free"' seems to me to fly in the face of plain facts."[282]

6. CONCLUDING OBSERVATIONS

We have examined the four ways in which the issue concerning the existence of causal initiative is disputed. Of these, only the first—the dispute about the principle of causation—involves points of argument which do not recur in the context of issues to be treated in subsequent chapters. Since that first dispute revolves around the question whether the existence of an uncaused cause, or of an agent that can act without being acted upon, is compatible with the universal principle of causation, it is confined to points that bear on the existence of causal initiative and on that alone.

The other three disputes—about character and motives, about responsibility, and about the evidence of consciousness—all involve points that bear on other issues as well as on the issue concerning causal initiative. In fact, as we shall see, the issue concerning causal indeterminacy, to be treated in Chapter 10, will involve all three of these disputes; and certain lines of argument, which have appeared only in the background in this chapter, will come to the foreground there. Still other aspects of the dispute about character and motives and the dispute about responsibility will be more fully developed in Chapter 12.[283]

Hence, the completeness of the arguments in these three disputes cannot be fairly judged here. We have already pointed out, for example, that the dispute about the causal role of character and motives does not move to the level of underlying reasons (i.e., reasons for asserting or denying the proposition that motives are efficient causes of volitions).[284] But such grounds will appear in the debate of the issue concerning causal indeterminacy. At that point, we shall be in a better position to assess the adequacy of the arguments that bear on the causal role of character and motives.

However, one critical observation can be made here. It arises from the fact that the actual debate involving C. A. Campbell, P. H. Nowell-Smith, and a few others occupies the center of the stage in the dispute about

282 *Ibid.*, p. 55.
283 Cf. what was said on p. 302, *supra*.
284 See p. 294, *supra*.

responsibility and causal initiative and in the dispute about the evidence of consciousness with regard to causal initiative; and it provides us with much the most extensive argumentation in the dispute about character and motives. In all three of these disputes, we cannot help being struck by the relatively small number of other writers who have addressed themselves to the disputed question, by the paucity of the documentary materials from which we can construct their contribution to the dispute, and by the slender clues that they afford of the reasons to which they appeal in support of their assertions or denials.

The same critical point applies, though perhaps less forcefully, to the dispute about the bearing of the principle of causation on causal initiative. But with respect to the arguments advanced in this dispute, which will not recur in other contexts in later chapters, another critical observation can be justly made. It concerns the inadequacy or deficiency of the argumentation, as measured by the ideal of rational debate, according to which we should expect the disputants to be pushed back until they reach those basic grounds beyond which argument can go no further.

In constructing the dispute about the principle of causation in relation to causal initiative, we marked off a third and a fourth phase in which, as we said, the debate moved to the level of underlying reasons. In the third phase, we presented two or three underlying reasons for the affirmative side's assertion that causal initiative exists and is compatible with the principle of causation: the point about the substantive character of the self or the will as a cause, the assertion of the immateriality of this cause, and the claim that it operates outside of time.[285] Then, in the fourth phase, we presented evidence that authors on the negative side denied one, two, or all of these three underlying reasons in support of man's possession of causal initiative in the sphere of his volitions.[286]

But the dispute of these matters goes no further than the assertion by the affirmative side of the grounds indicated, and the denial of them by the negative side. Since the truth or falsity of the points contested is not self-evident, the disputants in an ideal debate would be expected to get to the bottom of the matter by attempting, on the affirmative side, to argue for the existence of substances or substantive powers, such as the will; for the existence of immaterial beings or powers, and the immateriality of the power concerned with volition; or for the existence of a noumenal ego and the supra-temporal character of its action. And, similarly, on the negative side, the disputants would be expected to argue against the existence of such things. Until such arguments are advanced pro and con, the debate remains incomplete. The underlying reasons are in themselves

[285] See pp. 272 ff., *supra*, and esp. pp. 273–74 and 276.
[286] See pp. 276 ff., *supra*.

ungrounded assertions or denials; and we are left with the question whether or not grounds can be supplied.

To say that that question is not answered within the narrow confines of the literature on freedom is, of course, not to say that no answer can be found in the whole of philosophical literature. On the contrary, we have good reason to believe that it is possible to discover therein arguments for the existence of substances and substantive powers; for the existence of the immaterial and for the immateriality of the power concerned with volition; for the existence of a noumenal ego and for the supra-temporal character of its action. The same holds true for arguments against the existence of these things.

However, we cannot say, with the same assurance, that these opposing arguments get to the bottom of the matter and go as far as argumentation can go in the direction of ultimate reasons. The whole extant literature of philosophy may fail to push the dispute of these matters as far as the ideal of rational debate would demand; or, in the very nature of the case, these matters may not be susceptible of such debate.

Whichever is the case, the fact remains that in the literature on freedom, even in that voluminous portion of it which is devoted to opposing views about man's natural freedom of self-determination, we are left with an inadequately argued or incompletely reasoned debate of the issue concerning causal initiative.

Chapter 10

SELF-DETERMINATION: THE EXISTENTIAL ISSUE CONCERNING CAUSAL INDETERMINACY

The issue to be treated in this chapter closely resembles the one dealt with in Chapter 9. In both cases, those who deny that men have a freedom of self-determination do so because they deny the validity of something presupposed by the adherents of SD—in the one case, that men have causal initiative; in the other, that causal indeterminacy is present in the decisions or choices men make. Both issues, therefore, turn on a question about causation, or, more strictly, a question about the character and operation of causes in the sphere of human behavior.

As we saw, in order to join issue on the question about man's possession of causal initiative, writers must share at least a minimal understanding of the subject in dispute. Those who would take the negative side of that issue have the burden of coming into topical agreement with the adherents of SD who affirm causal initiative. To discharge that burden, they must recognize what the SD authors are affirming; namely, that the self or will is the uncaused cause of its own acts; or that, in making decisions, it has the power to act without being acted upon by efficient causes outside itself on the plane of finite or natural causes.[1]

The same prerequisite applies to the present issue about causal indeterminacy. Writers who would take the negative side of this issue must deny causal indeterminacy as that is affirmed by the adherents of self-determination. They must recognize that what the SD authors are affirming involves the following points: (i) that when the self or will produces a decision, it is not necessitated to produce that one decision or to produce any decision at all; (ii) that at the moment of producing a decision, it is able to produce any one of a number of alternative decisions; and (iii) that, given the identical conditions under which the self or will produces a particular decision, it is also able to produce a contrary decision.[2]

---

[1] See Ch. 9, pp. 253–54, *supra*.
[2] For a more complete summary of the understanding of causal indeterminacy on the part of those SD authors who affirm it, see Ch. 8, pp. 230–35, *supra*.

Though the issue about causal initiative and the issue about causal indeterminacy both turn on questions of causation, there is a significant difference between the questions in the two cases. This can be indicated in the following manner.

Let the effect with which we are concerned in both cases be represented by a particular act, which we will call "volition A." Let us consider the self or the will as the cause of the act which is volition A. The issue about causal initiative is then raised by the question whether, in causing volition A, the self or will is itself uncaused, at least on the plane of finite causes. In contrast, the issue about causal indeterminacy is raised by the question whether, given the very same conditions under which it caused volition A, the self or will could have caused other effects, let us say, volition B, volition C, etc.

In the one case, the question is about the power of a cause to produce a single effect without being caused to do so; in the other case, the question is about the power of a cause to produce any one of two or more effects under identical conditions. In both cases, we are confronted by the relation between a cause and an effect; but in the one case, we ask about other causes (i.e., whether or not the cause is itself caused, and in the other, we ask about other effects (i.e., whether or not this particular effect is the only one that could have been produced by the cause under the given conditions).

The writers who deny causal indeterminacy say in effect that, given the conditions under which volition A is caused, no other volition could have been produced by the will or self. The very opposite is said by the writers who affirm causal indeterminacy; and they in effect go on to say that it is precisely because the will or self can, under identical conditions, produce either volition A or volition B that they attribute to it the power of free choice. The issue about causal indeterminacy can, therefore, be briefly stated in the question: Does man have the power of free choice in the sense just indicated?

The debate of this issue closely parallels the debate concerning causal initiative, as set forth in the preceding chapter. Here, as there, the best way to present the debate as a whole is to divide it into a number of distinct disputes. As in the case of causal initiative, so here we have, on the one hand, arguments against causal indeterminacy, to which the defenders of it reply, and, on the other hand, arguments for causal indeterminacy, to which the opponents of it reply. Again, as in the case of causal initiative, arguments of the first sort give grounds or reasons that are intrinsic to the subject under dispute in that they are directly concerned with the nature and operation of causes; whereas arguments of the second sort appeal to xtrinsic reasons or evidence, such as the connection between free choice nd responsibility or man's consciousness of freely choosing.[3]

So far the two debates have the same general pattern. But there are a umber of respects in which they differ.

(i) While many of the same authors are parties to both issues, some who ppear as disputants in the issue concerning causal initiative do not take ides on the question of causal indeterminacy, and here, on the issue oncerning causal indeterminacy, there are some authors not represented 1 the debate about causal initiative.

(ii) We divided the arguments against causal initiative into a general ttack, based on the universal principle of causation, and a special attack, ased on the causal role of character and motives in the formation of olitions. We find similar general and special attacks on causal indeter-ninacy; but, in addition, there is an attack which argues that science, vith the predictability or uniformity which it posits, precludes indeter-ninacy.

(iii) The arguments for causal indeterminacy that are based on its onnection with moral responsibility or on our consciousness of free choice narallel similar arguments for causal initiative; and these arguments elicit narallel arguments in reply. But here, in the debate about causal indeter-ninacy, there are certain arguments, advanced to support it, which have to parallel in the debate about causal initiative.

The foregoing considerations dictate a division of the debate into five lisputes. In all of these there are arguments on both sides of the issue. In ddition, we must consider the arguments advanced by the adherents of elf-determination to which the opponents of indeterminacy do not reply. since the issue itself is raised by the denial of free choice, we shall place irst the three disputes in which the adversaries of free choice open the rgument. After dealing with these, we shall turn to the two disputes in vhich the exponents of free choice take the initiative. Throughout, we hall give prominence to the authors who have engaged in actual dispute vith one another. Here, as in the debate about causal initiative, they serve o set the stage for us before we introduce other writers whose part in the lebate is to some extent a matter of our own construction.[4]

The present chapter will, therefore, be organized as follows. In Sec-ion 1, we shall enumerate the authors who are opposed on this issue. section 2 will set forth the dispute about indeterminacy that turns on lifferent theories of causation; Section 3 will deal with the dispute that oncerns the compatibility or incompatibility of indeterminacy with

Cf. what is said about this distinction in the types of argument in Ch. 9, *supra.*
Cf. what is said on this score in Ch. 9, p. 256, *supra.*

science and prediction; Section 4 will deal with the dispute that involve questions about the causal role of certain psychological factors in the formation of decisions. Then, in Section 5, we shall turn to the dispute about the connection between moral responsibility and free choice, and in Section 6, to the dispute about the validity of the evidence of ou consciousness that we exercise free choice. Finally, in Section 7, we shal consider the arguments advanced by the defenders of indeterminacy, t which their opponents do not reply. A brief concluding Section 8 will ca attention to other deficiencies or inadequacies in the debate.

1. THE PARTIES TO THE ISSUE AND THE DEBATE

Of the authors who take sides on this issue or who take part in thi debate, some were treated in Volume I and some are introduced in thi chapter for the first time. We shall list them separately.

While all the writers listed can be construed as either affirming or deny ing that man has the power of free choice, not all engage in the debate o this issue by arguing their side of the case. In the tabulations below, we shal place in parentheses the names of those who do not contribute argument to the debate; they are, therefore, not further considered in the sections t follow. Most of these authors are on the affirmative side of the issue. Thei views have been treated in Chapter 24 of Volume I; and the evidenc for our interpretation of their position can be found by consulting the analytical index to that volume.

One other point of interest here is the appearance in this debate o authors who are *not* parties to the issue about causal initiative. We shal place an asterisk after the names of such writers. If the reader is als interested in discovering the writers who are parties to the issue abou causal initiative but who do not take part in the present debate, he can d so by comparing the tabulations below with those given in Chapter 9.[5]

Of the authors treated in some detail in Volume I, the following can b construed as affirming free choice; and, with the exception of those indi cated by parentheses, we shall find occasion to treat them in one or anothe of the disputes that constitute the debate of this issue.

[5] See *loc. cit.*, pp. 257–58, *supra*. Since the tabulations in the preceding chapter and i this one are alphabetically arranged, they are readily comparable.

(Anselm)*	(Hegel)
Aquinas	James
Aristotle	Kant
(Augustine)	(Knight)*
(Barth)*	Lequier*
Bergson*	(Locke)
(Berlin)*	(Luther)*
(Boethius)*	Maritain
Calvin*	Renouvier
Campbell	(Rousseau)
Castell*	Sartre
(Cicero)	Secrétan
Descartes	Simon
(Dewey)*	(Suarez)
(Duns Scotus)	Taylor, A. E.*
(Epicurus)	Tillich*
(Fouillée)	Weiss*
Hartmann	(Whitehead)*

The following tabulation lists authors, not treated in Volume I, who can be construed as affirming free choice. All the authors mentioned also contribute to the debate, some to a much greater extent than others.

Arnold	Lamprecht*
Aveling*	Lewis, H. D.*
Barrett*	Lossky
Bosanquet*	Lotze
Boutroux	Mabbott*
Bowne	MacLagan*
Bramhall	Mansel
Capek*	Marc*
Carritt*	Martineau
Cranston*	Mascall*
Ewing*	More, H.*
Farrer	Peirce*
Field*	Price
Ginsberg*	Reid*
Greene, T. M.*	Rickaby
Gruender	Russell, L. J.
Hamilton, Sir W.*	Schiller, F. C. S.
Hartshorne*	Stout, A. K.
Hawkins*	Taylor, R.*
Hughes*	Watts

A number of authors who take the negative side of the issue about caus: indeterminacy were mentioned as opponents of self-determination ; Volume I, e.g., Hobbes, Spinoza, Hume, Edwards, Priestley, J. S. Mil Sidgwick, B. Russell, Schlick, Broad, Kelsen, Ayer, and Stevenson. Th following enumeration includes them and adds the names of others wh were not treated in Volume I. With a few exceptions, indicated k parentheses, these writers take part in the debate of this issue.

(Alexander)	Kelsen
Ayer	McTaggart*
Bain	Matson*
Bakunin	Mill, J. S.
Blanshard	(Nagel)*
Bradley, F. H.	Nietzsche
Bray*	Nowell-Smith
Broad	Pap
(Chisholm)*	Paulsen
Collins*	Priestley
Ducasse	Ross*
Ebersole*	Russell, B.
Edwards, J.	Schilck
Edwards, P. *	Schopenhauer
Freud*	Sidgwick
Gallie*	Spinoza
Green, T. H.*	Stebbing*
Hartley	Stevenson
Hobart	(University of California Associates)*
Holbach	Voltaire*
Hook*	Von Mises*
Hospers*	Windelband
Hume	

A few of the foregoing authors take part in that special phase of tl debate which concerns the bearing of the principle of indeterminacy quantum mechanics on the issue concerning causal indeterminacy in hum: behavior. Others, not mentioned above, join in this dispute. On t affirmative side, arguing that quantum indeterminacy offers some supp(for man's possession of free choice, are such writers as Bohr, Boi Eddington, and Heisenberg. On the negative side, arguing either th quantum indeterminacy is totally irrelevant to the problem of free choi in man or that, rightly interpreted, it offers no support for the freedom the will, are such writers as Blanshard, Bridgman, Cassirer, Einstei rank, Kelsen, Margenau, Maritain, Planck, Popper, Ross, Schrödinger, ves Simon, and Stebbing.

With the exception of the authors whose names are placed in parenthe-es, the writers listed in the foregoing tabulations will be treated in the sec-ons to follow. Not all, of course, make major or original contributions to ne debate. There is naturally considerable repetition of the arguments ad-anced on either side. We shall try to document only the major or original guments by means of quotation in the body of the text, and merely fer to others, who repeat these arguments, in footnotes.

2. THE DISPUTE ABOUT INDETERMINACY AND CAUSATION

In the view of those whose theories of causation lead them to deny at man has a power of free choice, the causal indeterminacy required for ee choice is self-contradictory and, therefore, impossible. In their view, cause is to determine; that which is caused is causally determined; and, nsequently, it is impossible for something to cause without determining effect, or for something to be an effect without being causally deter-ined.

Many of the writers who hold this view also regard the relation of cause d effect as a necessary connection. That which is caused is also cessitated in the sense that, given the efficacious operation of the cause, e effect cannot fail to occur, nor can anything other than this one effect cur as a result of the cause's efficacious operation. To say that a cause cessitates its effect is to say that it produces, results in, or leads to one d only one effect.

Furthermore, those who regard the relation of cause and effect as a cessary connection also identify determinacy with necessity. In their view, cause an effect, to necessitate it, and to determine it are all one. Being necessary connection, the causal connection is also a determinate relation, ., a relation of one cause, or one set of causal factors, to one effect. ausal necessity" and "causal determinacy" are thus synonymous phrases. To those who hold the foregoing theory of causation, the name "necessi-rians" was once applied; more recently, with equal appropriateness, they ve been called "determinists." Their opponents, in turn, have been lled "indeterminists" and "libertarians," usually without any differentia-n in the connotation of the names. But recently C. D. Broad and hers following him have distinguished between two positions, both of hich they reject, but one of which they call "indeterminism" and the other, "libertarianism." There is, as we shall see, another development of recent years which complicates the matter further. Those who uphold causal indeterminacy now divide into two groups: on the one hand, those who deny only the *universality* of causal determinism; on the other hand, those who reject the theory of causal determinism entirely, maintaining that it never obtains at all. Some clarification of names and positions is, therefore, necessary in order to prepare for an examination of the arguments advanced in this dispute.

From the point of view of the determinists, the only alternative to causal necessity is chance in that sense of "chance" which means "happening without cause."[6] An effect which is not necessitated or determined is, in their view, an effect without a cause and, like an uncaused effect, self-contradictory. Their assertion that nothing happens by chance is the other face of their assertion that everything which happens is caused and, as caused, necessitated.

If we used the word "chance" in the sense indicated above, then those who affirm causal indeterminacy agree that nothing happens by chance and they understand this to mean that everything which happens is caused. But they do not agree that everything which happens, i.e., every effect, is causally necessitated or determined.

As the phrase "causal indeterminacy" suggests, their position either permits or requires the conjunction of causation and indeterminacy.[7] They see nothing self-contradictory in an effect's being caused but not being necessitated or determined by its cause; nor do they see anything impossible about a causal nexus which is indeterminate in the sense that from one cause, or set of causes, any one of several alternative effects may follow.

If we use the term "indeterminist" without qualification to signify the view that some things happen by chance or without cause, then it is misunderstanding on the part of determinists for them to interpret their opponents as indeterminists in the sense just indicated. That such misunderstanding exists will be seen in the numerous statements by determinists that those who affirm a freedom which is incompatible with necessity must be asserting the existence of uncaused or chance events. Nevertheless, in spite of such misunderstanding, issue is joined in the following manner.

The determinists assert two things: (i) that nothing is uncaused or happens by chance; and (ii) that whatever happens is not only caused

---

[6] This conception of chance is not universally shared. Aristotle, for example, conceived a chance event not as one that is totally uncaused but rather as one produced by coincidence of causes. See *Physics*, Book II, Ch. 5.

[7] It is thus the direct opposite of the position of the determinists, for that involves the disjunction of causation and indeterminacy.

ut is also thereby necessitated. Another way of stating the second of these wo propositions is to say that every causal nexus is determinate; i.e., from a given cause, or set of causes, only one effect can follow or result.

Indeterminists would disagree with determinists on the first proposition as well as the second, but "*causal* indeterminists" disagree with them *only* on the second. Since all the writers who affirm man's possession of free choice, conceived as involving causal indeterminacy, take issue with the second of the two propositions asserted by the determinists, a genuine dispute exists between them, even if some determinists mistakenly interpret their opponents as affirming the indeterminism of chance instead of the indeterminacy of causes.

While all writers who affirm man's possession of free choice are opposed to the determinists on the proposition that whatever is caused is thereby necessitated, they do not agree among themselves on the proposition to be affirmed in its place. We have already mentioned this division of opinion among them.[8] We pointed out that, on the one hand, there are those who assert that some effects are necessitated by their causes and some are not, and that, on the other hand, there are those who assert that no effects are necessitated by their causes.

The first group distinguishes between two kinds of causal connection, necessary and contingent; and between two kinds of causal relation, determinate and indeterminate. The second group, like the determinists they oppose, insist that causes are all alike. But whereas the determinists maintain that every causal connection is necessary and that every causal relation is determinate, this second group of their opponents maintains that every causal connection is contingent and that every causal relation is indeterminate.[9]

The introduction of the term "contingency" requires one further point of clarification.

For some writers, the term "contingent," applied to the relation of cause and effect, means that from the efficacious operation of a given cause, or set of causes, any one of a number of different effects may result or follow. Which one does in fact result depends upon a certain selectivity that is inherent in the cause. The cause, in other words, has the power to produce any one of a number of alternative effects.

For other writers, the term "contingent," applied to the relation of cause and effect, has two meanings, not one. In addition to the meaning

---

[8] See pp. 337–38, *supra*.

[9] To identify these two groups, it might be appropriate to call the first group "libertarians" and the second group "causal indeterminists"; for the second group asserts that indeterminacy is present in all causation throughout nature, whereas the first group holds that it is present only or mainly in free choice on man's part.

stated in the preceding paragraph, these authors also use the term to refer to causal connections in which a given effect results from two or more independent causes, each of which is insufficient by itself to produce that effect. Even though one of these causes is operative, the effect may not result because it is contingent upon the cooperation of other causes.[10]

It will be observed that in both senses of "contingency," the causal relation is indeterminate rather than determinate. But the indeterminacy is not the same in both cases. In the first sense of contingency, the causal indeterminacy consists in the relation of one cause to a number of alternative effects, any one of which it is able to produce. In the second sense of contingency, the causal indeterminacy consists in the relation of one effect to a number of independent causes, no one of which by itself is able to produce that effect.

Those who distinguish two senses of contingency and admit that some causes are necessary make a threefold distinction among causes: (i) the contingent cause that is *deficient*, i.e., unable by itself to produce a given effect; (ii) the necessary cause that is *sufficient*, i.e., able by itself to produce one and only one effect; and (iii) the contingent cause that is *more than sufficient*, or *super-abundant*, i.e., able by itself to produce any one of a number of effects.[11] While there is causal indeterminacy in both types of contingent causation, writers who make this threefold distinction conceive free choice as involving only the causal indeterminacy that arises from the operation of super-abundant causes. Accordingly, they distinguish between (a) effects that are not only contingent but also freely caused, and (b) effects that are contingent but not freely caused.[12]

In contrast, writers for whom causal indeterminacy is present only in the relation of one cause to a number of alternative possible effects identify contingency in causation with the operation of what we have just called super-abundant causes. For them, effects which are contingent are also freely caused. If they affirm the existence of causal necessity as well as of causal indeterminacy, they distinguish between necessitating causes, on the one hand, and contingent or free causes, on the other. If, however, they deny the existence of causal necessity, they regard all causation as being of the same type—at once both contingent and free.

A summary of the positions described in the foregoing pages may provide

[10] Authors who employ the term "contingency" in this second sense also use the term "chance" to mean that which results from a *coincidence* of causes. Hence, in their view, what happens by chance is not uncaused. See fn. 6, on p. 338, *supra*.

[11] For other discussions of this threefold distinction, see Ch. 8, pp. 18–21, *supra*; and also Vol. I, Ch. 21, pp. 232–35.

[12] The second type of contingent effect represents what is caused by chance, i.e., by a coincidence of causes. See fn. 10, *supra*. Free causality is thus opposed, on the one hand, to chance causality, and, on the other hand, to necessary causality.

helpful chart of the distinctions considered as well as a guide to the
complex opposition of opinions that we shall find in the dispute about
indeterminacy and causation. For the purposes of this summary, we shall
use the names proposed above as labels for the positions we have distinguished.

1. *The position of the determinist, who takes the negative side in this dis-*
   pute concerning the existence of a freedom of self-determination which
   involves causal indeterminacy.
   A. Nothing happens by chance; which is to say, nothing is causally
      undetermined. If anything is undetermined, it is not caused; if it is
      caused, it is not undetermined.
      NOTE: Some determinists admit that an effect may be produced by
      a composition of independent causes but they do not regard this
      as indeterminacy or contingency.
   B. Whatever happens is caused and, as causally determined, is necessi-
      tated; the cause-effect relation is determinately a one-one relation,
      i.e., given one and the same cause, or *set of composite causes*, one
      and the same effect always results or follows.
2. *The position of the libertarian, who takes the affirmative side in this dis-*
   pute.
   A. Nothing happens by chance, in the sense of "chance" which is
      indicated in 1.A above.
   B. Not everything which is caused is causally determined or necessi-
      tated. The same cause does not always have the same effect (for
      some causes are super-abundant).
      (1) Some things are causally determined or necessitated, in the
          sense of causal determination or causal necessity indicated in 1.B
          above.
      (2) But there are also instances of causation which involve causal
          indeterminacy in the sense that the cause-effect relation is inde-
          terminate, i. e., it is a one-many relation such that, given one and
          the same cause, or set of causes, any one of a number of alterna-
          tive effects may result or follow.
3. *The position of the causal indeterminist, who takes the affirmative side*
   of this dispute.
   A. Nothing happens by chance, in the sense of "chance" which is
      indicated in 1.A above.
   B. Nothing which is caused is causally determined or necessitated, as
      the determinist asserts in 1.B above. No cause-effect relation is
      determinately a one-one relation.
   C. Causal indeterminacy is universal; i. e., in every instance in which
      a given cause or set of causes is efficaciously operative, it is able to
      produce any one of a number of alternative effects.

The foregoing summary plainly indicates that the libertarian holds a
position which is logically contradictory to that of the determinist (2.B vs.

1.B), while the causal indeterminist holds a position which is logicall contrary to that of the determinist (3.B vs. 1.B). Both kinds o opposition constitute a genuine issue, since in neither case can th opposed assertions both be true. The fact that, at one point, the positio of the libertarian contradicts the position of the causal indetermini [2.B (1) vs. 3.C] does not remove the common ground which the share in opposition to the position of the determinist (i.e., their denia of 1.B). However, it will manifest itself in the difference in the argument they advance against the determinist or for the position they hold.[13]

The summary omits any reference to the position of the extreme indete minist who asserts that some things happen by chance (in the sense of total absence of causes). Since the libertarian and the causal indete minist agree with the determinist in rejecting this extreme position, it not really relevant to this dispute, even though some determinists interpre the causal indeterminacy upheld by their opponents as being the same a the indeterminacy of chance.

The summary also omits reference to the subordinate distinction c views concerning contingency, as contrasted with necessity, in causatior As we have seen, there are two subordinate views.

(a) All instances of contingent causation are instances of causal inde terminacy in the sense defined in 2.B (2) and in 3.C above; and, accordingly, there is no distinction between that which is inde terminately caused, that which is contingently caused, and that which is freely caused.

(b) Some instances of contingent causation are instances of causal indeterminacy in the sense defined in 2.B (2) and in 3.C above, and these are the cases in which what is contingently caused is also freely caused. But there are also instances of contingent causation in which the causal indeterminacy is of a different type, i.e., the effect is related to a number of independent causes, no one of which is able by itself to produce that effect, so that the production of the effect depends upon the coincidence of a number of causes, each by itself deficient as a cause in relation to that effect.

View (a) or view (b), with regard to contingency, can be added to th position of the libertarian or the position of the causal indeterminist, with out in any way affecting their opposition to the determinist. However, th inclusion of one or the other of these two views of contingency in th

[13] The disagreement between the libertarian and the causal indeterminist, which is ir dicated above, will be presented as one of the issues in the special controversy abou the freedom of self-determination.

position of the libertarian or the position of the causal indeterminist will affect the manner in which they argue against the position of the determinist or for their own position.

With these matters clarified, we are now prepared to examine the evidence of the dispute about indeterminacy and causation. We shall present, first, the arguments by the exponents of Position 1 against causal indeterminacy; then, second, the arguments for causal indeterminacy by exponents of Position 2, who admit the existence of causal necessity; and third, the arguments for causal indeterminacy by the exponents of Position 3, who do not admit the existence of causal necessity. Included with both types of argument for causal indeterminacy will be replies to the arguments advanced by its opponents.

Arguments against Causal Indeterminacy

The arguments against causal indeterminacy which claim that it is inconsistent with the principle of causation all employ the same fundamental premise. That premise, as we have seen, asserts the identity of *being caused* with *being causally determined* and being *causally necessitated*. When that premise is combined with the assertion that whatever happens is caused, the conclusion follows that nothing can be causally indeterminate.

The fundamental premise is expressed in three slightly different ways. (i) It is said that a sufficient cause, by virtue of its being a sufficient cause, cannot fail to produce its effect. (ii) It is said that it is in the very nature of a cause, when operative, to necessitate its effect. (iii) It is said that, given the same cause, or set of causes, the same effect always follows. We find the first mode of expression used in some of the objections considered by Aquinas, and it is also used by Hobbes. We find the second mode of expression used by Spinoza, Hume, and Priestley. The third is used by Hume, Priestley, and Ross. We shall consider these three forms of the argument in the order just indicated.

(i) In Aquinas's *De Malo*, the objector argues as follows:

> If the will wills anything determinate, there must be some cause which makes it will thus. A cause having been posited, however, it is necessary that the effect also be posited, as Avicenna proves (Book VI of the *Metaphysics*, Ch. 1 and 2), because if, a cause having been posited, it is still possible for the effect *not* to be, there will still be need for something else to reduce it from potency to act; and thus the first was not a sufficient cause.

From which it is concluded that "the will is moved by necessity to will anything."[14]

According to Hobbes, any cause of a particular effect is either its whole (i.e., "entire") cause, or it is a partial cause of that effect (i.e., a part of the total cause, or set of causes). A partial cause, being deficient by itself, can be operative without the effect resulting; but if the entire cause of a given effect is operative, then the effect must result, for "an entire cause is always sufficient for the production of its effect."[15] Hobbes points out that it is self-contradictory to suppose the operation of a sufficient cause together with the non-occurrence of its effect; since the effect can fail to occur only if there is something wanting in the cause, in that case the cause would not be a sufficient cause, as was supposed. A sufficient cause is, therefore, also a necessary cause, that is, one which necessitates the occurrence of its effect. Hobbes writes:

> And seeing a necessary cause is defined to be that, which being supposed, the effect cannot but follow; this also may be collected, that whatsoever effect is produced at any time, the same is produced by a necessary cause. For whatsoever is produced, in as much as it is produced, had an entire cause [a sufficient cause], that is, had all those things, which being supposed, it cannot be understood but that the effect follows; that is, it had a necessary cause.[16]

Whatever effects are produced, including human acts, must have sufficient causes for their occurrence; and, having such causes, the effects are thereby necessitated.[17] When future events or acts are called contingent, this does not import the absence of necessity in their production, but only our ignorance of their sufficient causes.[18] Voluntary acts on man's part are no exception. Unless a voluntary act has a sufficient cause, it will not occur; and if it has, its occurrence is necessitated. "To him that could see the connexion of those causes," Hobbes writes, "the necessity of all men's voluntary actions would appear manifest."[19] Their necessity, however, is consistent with their liberty, since man's freedom in the performance of a voluntary act consists in the absence of coercion or compulsion from

[14] *Op. cit.*, Q. 6, A. 1, Objection 15. Cf. *Truth*, Vol. III, Q. 23, A. 5, Objection 1, where it is said that if the cause is sufficient, then, when it is operative, the effect is necessitated, i.e., it cannot not occur.
[15] *Elements of Philosophy*, p. 95.
[16] *Ibid.*, pp. 95–96.
[17] "Every act that shall be produced," Hobbes declares, "shall necessarily be produced" (*ibid.*, p. 101).
[18] See *ibid.*, pp. 102–3.
[19] *Leviathan*, Part 2, Ch. 21, p. 162.

without, not in the absence of necessity in the causes which operate within him.[20]

In his debate with Bishop Bramhall, Hobbes repeats the foregoing points: that the only sense in which human acts are free is the sense in which they are voluntary, which is to say that they proceed, without external impediment, from a man's own desires and deliberations; that whenever man's will, subsequent to deliberation, is the sufficient cause of his voluntary action, the latter is necessitated; and that the necessary connection between the will as cause and the voluntary action as effect does not remove the liberty of the latter.[21] The nub of the argument is then summarized in the following passage:

> I hold that to be a sufficient cause, to which nothing is wanting that in needful to the producing of the effect. The same is also a necessary cause; for if it be possible that a sufficient cause shall not bring forth the effect, then there wanted somewhat which was needful to the producing of it; and so the cause was not sufficient. But if it be impossible that a sufficient cause should not produce the effect, then is a sufficient cause a necessary cause; for that is said to produce an effect necessarily, that cannot but produce it. Hence it is manifest, that whatever is produced, has had a sufficient cause to produce it, or else it had not been. And therefore also voluntary actions are necessitated.[22]

The argument based on sufficient causes as necessitating causes is later applied by Hartley, when he declares it "absurd at first sight" to suppose that "though there be a desire sufficient to cause the exertion of the will, this exertion may or may not follow."[23]

(ii) For Spinoza, as for Hobbes, the attribution of contingency to things is an expression of our ignorance, not of anything real in the order of nature. "A thing can in no respect be called contingent," Spinoza declares, "save in relation to the imperfection of our knowledge."[24] In reality, everything which exists or happens is conditioned by causes, proximate or ultimate, and whatever is caused is thereby necessitated. Only the infinite substance of God is unconditioned or uncaused, but even God exists from and acts by the necessity of his own nature.[25] Everything else is "conditioned by the necessity of the divine nature, not only to exist, but also to exist and operate in a particular manner, and there is nothing that is

---

[20] See *ibid.*, p. 161.
[21] See *The Questions Concerning Liberty, Necessity and Chance*, pp. 363, 365–67, 373.
[22] *Ibid.*, p. 380. Cf. *ibid.*, pp. 406–7.
[23] *Observations on Man*, p. 357.
[24] *Ethics*, Part I, Prop. 33, Note I, p. 71.
[25] See *ibid.*, Prop. 17, pp. 59–62.

contingent."[26] Furthermore, according to Spinoza, "things could not have been brought into being by God in any manner or in any order different from that which has in fact obtained."[27] God being what he is, and all individual things, including men, being what they are, nothing can ever act otherwise than as it does. This applies, of course, to the will as it does to everything else: the will is a necessary cause, not a free cause, both in the case of God and in the case of man.[28] However, Spinoza does distinguish between the "free necessity" with which God acts (i.e., the necessity of his own nature) and the "constrained necessity" with which all other things act (i.e., their necessitation by extrinsic causes).[29]

For Hume, as for Spinoza, necessitation is inseparable from causation. "According to my definitions," he writes in A *Treatise of Human Nature*, "necessity makes an essential part of causation; and consequently liberty, by removing necessity, removes also causes, and is the very same thing with chance."[30] Whether the actions are those of matter or mind, they are links in a chain of necessary causes and effects.[31] In neither case does anything happen except as it is necessarily determined to happen by its causes.

If, according to Hume, the doctrine of liberty (i.e., of the freedom of the will) involves the will's exemption from necessity in its acts of choice, then such liberty is as non-existent as chance. He writes:

> It is universally allowed that nothing exists without a cause of its existence, and that chance, when strictly examined, is a mere negative word, and means not any real power which has anywhere a being in nature. But it is pretended that some causes are necessary, some not necessary. Here then is the advantage of definitions. Let anyone *define* a cause, without comprehending, as a part of the definition, a *necessary connexion* with its effect; and let him show distinctly the origin of the idea expressed by the definition; and I shall readily give up the whole controversy.

However, Hume continues, "if the definition above mentioned be admitted, liberty, when opposed to necessity, not to constraint, is the same thing with chance; which is universally allowed to have no existence."[32]

---

[26] *Ibid.*, Prop. 29, Proof, p. 68.

[27] *Ibid.*, Prop. 33, Note II, pp. 71–74.

[28] See *ibid.*, Prop. 32, p. 70; and Part II, Prop. 48, pp. 119–20.

[29] See *Correspondence*, Letter LXII, pp. 390–91.

[30] *Op. cit.*, Book II, Part III, Sect. 1, p. 407. Cf. A. J. Ayer's statement, centuries later: "That all causes equally necessitate is indeed a tautology, if the word 'necessitate' is taken merely as equivalent to 'cause': but if . . . it is taken as equivalent to 'constrain' or 'compel' then I do not think that this proposition is true" (*Philosophical Essays*, p. 281).

[31] See *ibid.*, pp. 399–406.

[32] *An Enquiry Concerning Human Understanding*, Sect. VIII, Part 1, Div. 74, pp. 95–96. Cf. *ibid.*, Sect. VI, Div. 46, p. 56; and also A *Treatise of Human Nature*, Book II, Part III, Sect. 1, pp. 404, 411–12.

A number of other authors follow in the footsteps of Hume. Anthony Collins argues that human acts, being caused, are also necessitated; for "whatever has a beginning must have a cause; and every cause is a necessary cause."[33] Similarly, Joseph Priestley argues that the acts of the will are determined by causes, and that such determination "cannot be any other than a *necessary* determination, subject to laws, as strict and invariable as those of mechanics."[34] According to Jonathan Edwards, to hold "the free acts of the will to be contingent events" is tantamount to saying that they are without cause.[35] But, Edwards maintains, "nothing ever comes to pass without a cause."[36] Furthermore, effects are necessarily determined by their causes, in the realm of man's moral acts as well as in the realm of physical nature.

Moral necessity may be as absolute as natural necessity. That is, the effect may be as perfectly connected with its moral cause, as a naturally necessary effect is with its natural cause.[37]

Other writers assert the universality of causal determinism, maintain that it applies to human volitions as to everything else, and conclude, therefore, that the causal indeterminacy required for free choice does not exist.[38]

(iii) That the same causes always produce the same effects is a corollary of the proposition that the relation between causes and effects is a necessary connection. Those who affirm causal indeterminacy say the opposite; namely, that it is possible for the same cause, under the same conditions, to produce any one of several alternative effects. A man, they say, who willed, under certain conditions, to perform a certain act might have willed, under identical conditions, to perform some other act. Hence, we have the argument against causal indeterminacy which is based on the premise that the same causes always produce the same effects. We find this argument employed by some of the writers we have already considered, and by some others as well.

Hume, for example, not only makes necessitation an essential part of causation but also affirms the rule "that the same events will always

---

[33] *A Philosophical Inquiry Concerning Human Liberty*, p. 57.
[34] *The Doctrine of Philosophical Necessity*, p. 83. Cf. *ibid.*, pp. 7–9. Priestley acknowledges his indebtedness to Collins among others: see *ibid.*, Preface, p. xxvi–xxvii.
[35] *The Freedom of the Will*, p. 179. Cf. *ibid.*, pp. 190–91.
[36] *Ibid.*, p. 181.
[37] *Ibid.*, p. 157.
[38] See Sidgwick, *The Methods of Ethics*, pp. 59–64; McTaggart, *Some Dogmas of Religion*, pp. 142–45, 177; Paulsen, *A System of Ethics*, p. 457; Von Mises, *Theory and History*, pp. 76–77. Cf. Pap, "Determinism, Freedom, Moral Responsibility, and Causal Talk," in *Determinism and Freedom*, pp. 200–6; Williams, "Free Will and Determinism," in *The Journal of Philosophy*, Vol. XXXVIII, No. 26, pp. 702–3, 705.

follow from the same causes."[39] Joseph Priestley expands on this point Once we recognize, he says, that "throughout all nature, the same consequences . . . result from the same circumstances," we realize that "no event could have been otherwise than as it *has been, is,* or *is to be.*"[4] Hence, Priestley argues, a man cannot have the power of "*doing several things when all the previous circumstances* (including the *state of his mind,* and his *views of things*) are precisely the same. What I contend for is," he continues,

> that, with the same state of mind (the same strength of any particular passion, for example) and the same views of things (as any particular object appearing equally desirable), he would always, voluntarily, make the same choice, and come to the same determination. For instance, if I make any particular choice today, I should have done the same yesterday, and shall do the same tomorrow, provided there be no change in the state of my mind respecting the object of the choice.[41]

Or, as Schopenhauer says:

> . . . every man, being what he is and placed in the circumstances which for the moment obtain, but which on their part also arise by strict necessity, can absolutely never do anything else than just what at that moment he does do. Accordingly, the whole course of a man's life, in all its incidents great and small, is as necessarily pre-determined as the course of a clock.[42]

Jonathan Edwards points out that the will would be able to produce different acts at different times even though all the circumstances of volition were the same, only if "the *same* cause, the same causal power, force or influence, *without variation in any respect,* would produce

---

[39] *An Enquiry Concerning Human Understanding,* Sect. IX, Div. 83, p. 105. Cf. *ibid.,* pp. 57–58; and also *A Treatise of Human Nature,* Book II, Part III, Sect. I, pp. 401, 403–4.

[40] *The Doctrine of Philosophical Necessity,* p. 9. "The circumstances preceding any change," Priestley writes, "are called the *causes* of that change; and since a determinate event or effect constantly follows certain circumstances, or causes, the connection between the cause and the effect is concluded to be *invariable,* and therefore *necessary*" (*ibid.,* p. 10).

[41] *Ibid.,* pp. 7–8. Cf. *ibid.,* pp. 14–16, 22–25. Following Priestley, Charles Bray argues in a similar vein: "The doctrine of Necessity, in plain language, means that a man could in no case have acted differently from the manner in which he did act, supposing the state of his mind, and the circumstances in which he was placed to be the same; which is merely saying, that the same causes would always produce the same effects (*The Philosophy of Necessity,* p. 23). "Men are prone to suppose that they could have done otherwise," Bray writes, "because, in reviewing their conduct, its consequences—the experience resulting from it—are mixed up with the motives that decided them before, so that if they had to decide over again, different circumstances must be taken into the calculation" (*ibid.*).

[42] "Free Will and Fatalism," in *Complete Essays of Schopenhauer,* p. 57.

different effects at different times."[43] But this, according to Edwards, we know to be impossible. J. S. Mill and Sir William David Ross repeat the same point in somewhat different ways. Mill writes:

> When we think of ourselves hypothetically as having acted otherwise than we did, we always suppose a difference in the antecedents: we picture ourselves as having known something that we did not know, or not knowing something that we did know; which is a difference in the external inducements; or as having desired something, or disliked something, more or less than we did; which is a difference in the internal inducements.[44]

Were all the external and internal inducements the same, Mill implies, we could not have acted otherwise, since the same causes lead always to the same effects.

According to Ross, the universal law of causation will be immediately seen to exclude causal indeterminacy when that law is understood as maintaining that "for every variation between two events, there must be some variation between the antecedent circumstances, without which the variation between the events would not have existed."[45] It is not experience which establishes the universal truth of this law; "only reason or insight can do that."[46] But when, by reason or insight, we know its truth, we also know that "the libertarian belief in its complete form cannot be true"; for the libertarian belief is

> the belief that, the circumstances being what they are, and I being what I am, with that whole system of beliefs, desires, and dispositions which compose my nature, it is objectively possible for me here and now to do either of two or more acts.

"This," Ross argues, "is *not* possible, because whatever act I do, it must be because there is in me, as I am now, a stronger impulse to do that act than to do any other."[47] I could do some other act only if the causes were different, i.e., only if some other impulse were stronger. Or, as Windelband says, no one is able to have acted otherwise than as he did, except in the sense that he could have, had he been another person or had he been different in some significant respect.[48]

There are two lines of argument which do not fit into the pattern of the foregoing attacks on causal indeterminacy. One is advanced by Nietzsche, the other by C. D. Broad.

[43] *The Freedom of the Will*, p. 188.
[44] *Examination of Sir William Hamilton's Philosophy*, p. 583.
[45] *Foundations of Ethics*, p. 214.
[46] *Ibid.*
[47] *Ibid.*, p. 230. Cf. *ibid.*, pp. 234–36.
[48] See *Über Willensfreiheit*, pp. 212–13.

What distinguishes Nietzsche from the writers we have examined so far is his denial of causal necessity or causal determinism. He rejects what he calls "the mechanical interpretation of the world," which is based on the notion of the necessary connection of cause and effect.[49] He dismisses the notions of cause and effect as misleading.[50] But though he is thus opposed to what he calls the "non-free will" doctrine of causal determinism, he is equally opposed to what he calls "the crass stupidity of the celebrated conception of 'free will.' "[51] His reason for rejecting the indeterminacy of free choice—for denying that anything could have ever acted otherwise than as it did—lies in his view that everything is absolutely necessitated, not by its causes, but by its own nature. In holding this view, he regards himself as following Spinoza's theory of an indwelling necessity in the very nature of things, which governs everything inexorably.[52]

"There are no laws," Nietzsche declares; "every power draws its last consequence at every moment. Things are calculable precisely owing to the fact that there is no possibility of their being otherwise than they are."[53] And in another place he writes:

> The fact that something always happens thus or thus, is interpreted . . . as if a creature always acted thus or thus as the result of obedience to a law or a law-giver; whereas apart from the "law" it would be free to act differently. But precisely that inability to act otherwise might originate in the creature itself, it might be that it did not act thus or thus in response to a law, but simply because it was so constituted. It would mean simply that something cannot also be something else; that it cannot be first this, and then something quite different; thus it is neither free nor the reverse, but merely thus or thus.[54]

Though it is based on a necessity that is rooted in the nature of things rather than in the relation of cause and effect, Nietzsche's argument against the indeterminacy of free choice has an obvious affinity with the arguments that are based on the affirmation of causal necessity.

Broad's argument, on the other hand, does not employ the notion of necessity, causal or otherwise, but it does rest on a theory of causation. As we have already seen, Broad interprets what he calls the "libertarian" theory of free choice as requiring an agent or self which is a substantive and supra-temporal cause, i.e., a cause which does *not* contain any temporal

---

[49] See *The Will to Power*, Vol. II, pp. 109–23.
[50] See *ibid.*, pp. 55–59.
[51] *Beyond Good and Evil*, p. 403.
[52] See his postcard to Overbeck, July 30, 1881, as translated by W. A. Kaufmann, in *Nietzsche: Philosopher, Psychologist, Antichrist*, p. 116.
[53] *The Will to Power*, Vol. II, p. 117.
[54] *Ibid.*, Vol. II, p. 116. Cf. *Human, All Too Human*, pp. 121, 125–26.

factors, such as *"events in* and *dispositions of* the agent." According to Broad, the libertarian holds not that the act which is supposed to be freely chosen is causally undetermined, but rather that it is determined by a cause that is totally non-occurrent, i.e., one that is neither an event nor contains events as cause-factors.[55] This, Broad maintains, is impossible: a particular volition is an event, and "in so far as an event *is* determined, an essential factor in its total cause must be other *events."*[56]

Hence, Broad concludes that "Libertarianism is self-evidently impossible."[57] With this conclusion as well as the argument on which it is based, L. S. Stebbing expresses complete agreement.[58]

ARGUMENTS FOR CAUSAL INDETERMINACY

As we have already pointed out, the exponents of causal indeterminacy uphold the principle of causation as universally true.[59] Like their adversaries, they also deny that anything happens without a cause. But unlike their adversaries they deny that every effect is causally determined or necessitated in the sense that, given the operation of the cause, the effect could not have been otherwise. Their arguments for causal indeterminacy are, therefore, based on theories of causation which differ in certain fundamental respects from the principle of causation as that is understood by their opponents. But they also differ among themselves with regard to the theory of causation.

Some of the exponents of causal indeterminacy affirm that it exists either exclusively or pre-eminently in human acts of choice, affirming also that causal necessity exists in nature. Other exponents of causal indeterminacy affirm that it obtains in every relation of cause to effect, denying that causal necessity exists anywhere in nature.[60] Accordingly, there are two main types of argument for causal indeterminacy. These include not only reasons for rejecting the position of the causal determinist but also, at least in certain cases, replies to the arguments advanced by the determinists.

(i) *Arguments for causal indeterminacy by those who admit that some instances of causation involve necessity.* Replying to Objection 15 in the

---

[55] See "Determinism, Indeterminism, and Libertarianism," in *Ethics and the History of Philosophy*, pp. 214–15. Cf. what is said about Broad's theory in Ch. 9, pp. 278–79 and 281–83, *supra.'*

[56] *Ibid.*, p. 215.

[57] *Ibid.*, p. 217.

[58] *Philosophy and the Physicists*, pp. 235–36.

[59] See pp. 338 ff., *supra.*

[60] See pp. 338–39, 340–42, *supra.*

De Malo,[61] Aquinas denies that a sufficient cause always necessitates its effect. He does not say that sufficient causes never operate with necessity, but only that *"not every cause* brings its effect about by necessity, *even though it is a sufficient cause."*[62] In other words, it is possible for a cause to be sufficient for the production of its effect, and yet fail under certain conditions to produce that effect.

The conditions he has in mind are those in which some impediment occurs to interfere with the operation of the cause in question; as, for example, when sunlight, oxygen, nutriment in the soil, etc., the set of causes sufficient to produce plant growth, are present and operative on a plant, but an insect blight prevents the plant from growing. Here the set of factors mentioned remains, in Aquinas's opinion, a sufficient cause, even though it does not always necessarily result in plant growth. The impediment mentioned is an extraneous and accidental condition; it is no part of the total cause of plant growth. Hence, it can be said that a sufficient cause (or a set of causes that is sufficient to produce a particular effect) necessarily produces that effect in the absence of extraneous and accidental conditions which would operate to prevent it from doing so; but it cannot be said that a sufficient cause always operates with necessity, because the operation of a sufficient cause does not exclude the simultaneous operation of impeding conditions or counteracting causes.

Aquinas summarizes this point by saying that natural causes do not always produce their effects by necessity, though they do for the most part, the exceptions being the few times when they are impeded.[63] In his theory of causes, then, a natural cause is a sufficient cause and one that necessarily produces a certain effect, *on condition that no impeding conditions are present and no counteracting causes are operative.* This means that, in the realm of natural phenomena, there are many effects which necessarily result from the operation of causes; but there are also some effects which are contingent, in the sense of being the result of an accidental conjunction of natural causes with impeding conditions, as in the case of the plant whose growth was stunted by an insect blight.

In his reply to Objection 21 in *De Malo*, Q. 6, Aquinas points out that not everything which happens has a natural cause (in the sense in which sunlight, oxygen, etc. are natural causes of plant growth); some things, he says, "which happen by accident, do not happen by any active natural cause."[64] These are the things which happen by chance; they are the

---

[61] For the statement of this objection see pp. 343–44, *supra*.
[62] *Loc. cit.* Q. 6, A. 1. (Italics added.)
[63] See *loc. cit.*
[64] *Loc. cit.*

effects produced by a coincidence of causes rather than by a single cause or by a unified set of related causal factors.

Bishop Bramhall, in his reply to Hobbes on the point that sufficient causes necessitate their effects, gives similar reasons for saying that a cause may be sufficient to produce a certain effect and yet not always do so. Like Aquinas, Bramhall does not deny that, for the most part, effects necessarily result when their sufficient causes are in operation. But he points out that if certain conditions are present or absent, a sufficient cause, actually operating, may fail to produce its effect. "The cause may be sufficient," he writes, "and yet something which is needful to the production of the effect may be wanting"; and so "every sufficient cause is not a necessary cause."[65] He gives the following example of what he has in mind.

> Two horses jointly are sufficient to draw a coach, which either of them singly is insufficient to do. Now to make the effect, that is, the drawing of the coach necessary, it is not only required that the two horses be sufficient to draw it, but also that their conjunction be necessary, and their habitude such as they may draw it. If the owner of one of these horses will not suffer him to draw; if the smith have shod the other in the quick, and lamed him; if the horse have cast a shoe, or be a resty jade, and will not draw but when he list; then the effect is not necessarily produced, but contingently more or less, as the concurrence of the causes is more or less contingent.[66]

Hobbes dismisses this argument by Bramhall, as he would probably have dismissed the similar argument by Aquinas, on the ground that the argument violates the meaning of sufficient cause, as he understands it. "A sufficient cause," he repeats, is "that cause to which nothing is wanting needful to the producing of the effect."[67] If something is wanting, then the causal factors which are present do not constitute a sufficient cause; since they are not what Hobbes calls the "entire cause" of the given effect, but only part of it, they cannot be its sufficient cause.[68] Bishop Bramhall's example is a case in point. The two horses, even when they are together in harness to the coach, are not the entire or sufficient cause of its motion, since other causal conditions must be present, such as their not being lame or halt, the willingness of their owners to let them draw, their being activated to motion, etc. But when all the conditions "needful to the producing of the effect" are present and operative, the effect cannot fail to occur.[69]

[65] *The Questions Concerning Liberty, Necessity and Chance*, p. 382.
[66] *Ibid.*, pp. 380–81. Cf. *ibid.*, pp. 407–16.
[67] *Ibid.*, p. 382.
[68] See pp. 343–44, *supra*.
[69] See *The Questions Concerning Liberty, Necessity and Chance*, p. 383.

If we substitute for the lameness of one of the horses the blighted condition of the plant, in the example given above of what Aquinas means by an impediment to the operation of a sufficient cause, we can see how Hobbes would have dealt with that example. The entire and sufficient cause of plant growth, Hobbes would have said, includes the unimpaired nutritive power of the plant: when this, which is needful, is wanting, all the rest of the natural causes (sunlight, oxygen, nutriment in the soil, etc.) do not constitute the entire and sufficient cause of the effect in question. Hence, those who, like Aquinas and Bramhall, say that sufficient causes may fail to necessitate their effects *under certain conditions* simply fail to see that the conditions which must be present or absent in order for the effect to be produced are not accidental, but essential, and parts of the total or entire cause. Only when all the causal conditions requisite for the production of the effect are present do we have a set of factors that constitutes a sufficient cause; and then, that cause being operative, the effect must result. It cannot fail.

The dispute at this point between Hobbes, on the one hand, and Aquinas and Bramhall, on the other, turns on the definition of a sufficient cause. If, as Hobbes maintains, it consists of *all* the requisite causal conditions for the production of an effect, then, as he insists, it is self-contradictory to say that a sufficient cause does not *always* necessarily produce its effect. But if, as Aquinas and Bramhall maintain, a sufficient cause (whether single or a set of causes) is that which is essential to the production of an effect and *does not include* the absence of certain accidental conditions which, if present, would impede the operation of the cause, then it is hardly self-contradictory to say that sufficient causes *do not always* necessitate their effects. Underlying this difference in the conception of what makes a cause sufficient are two different theories of causes, one of which makes distinctions between the essential and the accidental, and between causes and conditions, which the other does not allow.

Once the definition of sufficient cause that he proposes is understood and accepted, Hobbes sees no further question about liberty and necessity. In his view, a man's will, either by itself or together with other causes either is or is not sufficient to produce a particular decision or it is; if it is, then that decision is necessitated. No other decision could have resulted under the causal conditions which produced this particular one. "I hold," Hobbes writes,

that the ordinary definition of a free agent, namely, that a free agent is that, which when all things are present which are needful to produce the effect, can nevertheless not produce it, implies a contradiction, and is nonsense;

being as much as to say, the cause may be sufficient, that is, necessary, and yet the effect not follow.[70]

Among the things needful to produce the effect, in the case of a voluntary act, Hobbes includes the will to do it, along with all the other causes that dispose the will to this particular decision.[71] He dismisses as nonsense the supposition that, all the other causes being present, the will still has the power not to will this particular decision, or to will some other. Referring to statements by Bramhall, he says:

> These words, "the will hath the power to forbear willing what it doth will"; and these, "the will hath a dominion over its own acts"; and these, "the power to will is present *in actu primo*, determinable by ourselves"; are as wild as ever were any spoken within the walls of Bedlam, and if science, conscience, reason, and religion teach us to speak thus, they make us mad.[72]

However, from the point of view of Aquinas and Bramhall, the acceptance of Hobbes's definition of a sufficient cause does not foreclose all further questions about liberty and necessity. Even if they were to concede that, in the action of all things other than man, every effect is necessitated by its causes and nothing ever happens contingently or by chance, they would still maintain that the human will is one outstanding exception to the reign of causal necessity. They assert that the will is a free rather than a necessary cause, and that its freedom consists in two respects in which it can operate with causal indeterminacy. (a) Confronted in this life with any object to be willed, a man is able either to will it or not will it. This "freedom of exercise," as it is called, means that the action or inaction of the will is never necessitated. (b) Confronted by alternative objects, between which a choice is to be made, a man, if he wills at all, is able to will either one; or, to put it in another way, if under the given conditions, he chooses this one, then, under the same conditions, he could have chosen the other. This "freedom of specification," as it is called, means that no particular choice that is willed is ever necessitated.[73]

Assertion is one thing, argument another. The argument is provided by Aquinas, if not by Bramhall. It is to be found compactly stated in the main body of the article, to which is attached Aquinas's reply to the

[70] *Ibid.*, p. 385. Cf. *ibid.*, p. 424.
[71] See *ibid.*, pp. 387–88; and cf. *ibid.*, *pp.* 426–28.
[72] *Ibid.*, p. 388. The statements quoted from Bramhall are to be found on pp. 386–87, beginning with his statement that "in these words, 'all things needful,' or 'all things requisite' the actual determination of the will is not included." Cf. *ibid.*, pp. 425–26.
[73] For the assertion of these two freedoms of the will, or exemptions from causal necessity, by Aquinas and Bramhall, see (in the case of Aquinas) *De Malo*, Q. 6, and (in the case of Bramhall), *The Questions Concerning Liberty, Necessity, and Chance*, pp. 374–76.

objection based on the definition of a sufficient cause, which the objector draws from Avicenna and which is the same one that Hobbes later employs. In the last sentence of his reply, Aquinas turns from talking about other causes to the consideration of the causes of volitions. He writes:

> A cause, therefore, which makes the will will anything need not do this by necessity; because through the will itself an impediment can be set up, either by removing such consideration as leads it to willing, or by considering the opposite, namely, that which is proposed as good is not good in a certain respect.[74]

This sentence obviously refers back to the point already made about impediments to sufficient causes. But it also refers to points made in the main body of the article, where the argument for the will's causal indeterminacy is stated quite apart from any comment on the operation of sufficient causes, with or without impediment. There, as we now shall see, the will's exemption from causal necessity is not attributed to the contingency of accidental conditions, but to an indeterminacy that is inherent in the very nature of the will as a cause. It is this indeterminacy which makes the will more than a sufficient cause, not less than one.

According to Aquinas, the indeterminacy of the will—its power to act or not act and, when acting, to choose this or that—lies in two things.

The first is that the will, as an active power, moves itself so far as its exercise is concerned. "It is first of all manifest," Aquinas writes, "that the will is moved by itself; for just as it moves other powers, so it moves itself."[75] Here the will is the efficient cause of its own action. But when a man wills this or that, the objects to which he voluntarily directs himself are apprehended not by the will, but by the intellect or reason. Here then, so far as the object which specifies its act is concerned, the will is moved by the reason, but in the manner of a formal, not an efficient, cause. The question, therefore, is whether the object apprehended by reason, functioning as the formal cause of *what* the will wills, necessarily determines what it wills. Is the will disposed by its very nature as an intellectual or rational appetite to will whatever the reason apprehends as an object to be willed?

Aquinas's answer to this question brings us to the second of the two things on which, in his view, the indeterminacy of the will depends. It is the fact that the will, by its very nature, tends toward one object and one alone—the complete or perfect good. Nothing less than that which is completely good—good in all respects and lacking in none—can, ac-

---

[74] *De Malo*, Q. 6, A. 1, Reply to Objection 15.
[75] *Ibid.*, Answer. Aquinas's theory of the will's causal initiative is set forth in Ch. 9, pp. 266–67, *supra*.

cording to Aquinas, completely satisfy our appetite for the good insofar as that appetite is rooted in the intellect's power to apprehend the good in general; i.e., the good universally considered, not just this or that particular good. That alone which can completely satisfy us is the end we naturally seek; and so it is the complete or perfect good which functions as the final cause in every act of willing. When that which we will is something which is good only in some particular respect (i.e., a partial or imperfect good), we will it as a means to the end. It is in willing the means, not the end, that Aquinas places our power of free choice, precisely because the means, unlike the end, are always fragments of the good, not the whole good.

"If anything is apprehended as good and suitable in all respects," he writes, "it will move the will by necessity." It is in this way, he explains, that man wills the happiness which he conceives as consisting in "the perfect state of all goods together," and therefore as the complete good and the ultimate end to be sought. "But if there is a good such that it is not thought to be good in all respects which can be considered, it will not move the will by necessity"; for in this case, Aquinas points out, it is possible "to will the opposite . . . because it is good and suitable in some other respect which may be considered."[76]

In another place, Aquinas gives us the following summary of the argument.

Man does not choose of necessity. And this is because that which is possible not to be, is not of necessity. Now the reason why it is possible not to choose, or to choose, may be gathered from a twofold power in man. For man can will and not will, act and not act; and again, he can will this or that, and do this or that. The reason for this is to be found in the very power of the reason. For the will can tend to whatever the reason can apprehend as good. Now the reason can apprehend as good not only this, viz., *to will* or *to act*, but also this, viz., *not to will* or *not to act*. Again, in all particular goods, the reason can consider an aspect of some good, and the lack of some good, which has the aspect of evil; and in this respect, it can apprehend any single one of such goods as to be chosen or to be avoided. The perfect good alone, which is Happiness, cannot be apprehended by the reason as an evil, or as lacking in any way. Consequently man wills Happiness of necessity, nor can he will not to be happy, or to be unhappy. Now since choice is not of the end, but of the means, as we stated above; it is not of the perfect good, which is Happiness, but of other particular goods. Therefore man chooses not of necessity, but freely.[77]

[76] *Ibid.*, cf. Suarez, *Disputationes Metaphysicae*, XIX, Sect. 6, n. 14.
[77] *Summa Theologica*, Part I–II, Q. 13, A. 6. For the ramifications of this argument, see the following texts: *Summa Theologica*, Part I, Q. 82, AA. 1, 2, 4; Q. 83, A. 1; Part I–II, Q. 9, A. 1; Q. 10, AA. 1, 2; Q. 13, AA. 1, 2, 3, And cf. *Truth*, Q. 22, AA 5, 6, 12, 14, 15; Q. 24. AA. 1, 2.

Only the supreme good, which can completely satisfy our desire, attracts us irresistibly. To say that when we consider the supreme good, we cannot avoid willing it, is to say that when this object is among the causes of the will's action, its action is causally necessitated, so far as what is willed is concerned.[78] The irresistible attraction which the supreme good exercises over the will is not only the source of the causal necessity to which the will is subject but it is also the source of the causal indeterminacy that the will possesses with respect to all other objects. Being less than the supreme good, none of these is attractive in a way that necessitates the will's action with respect to it. When such objects are among the causes of the will's action, any one of several alternative volitions may result (i.e., the choice of this object or the choice of that) from the same set of causes which include the will as efficient cause, the supreme good as final cause, and some particular good as formal cause. It is not that this set of causes fails to necessitate because it is insufficient to produce any effect whatsoever. It fails to necessitate because it is more than sufficient to produce whatever effect it in fact produces; for it could have equally well produced some other.

The followers of Aquinas repeat this argument, emphasizing what they call the active or dominating indifference of the will to particular goods. They are aware that their theory of the causal indeterminacy of the will not only involves a conception of the nature of the will as a rational appetite which their opponents do not share, but also involves an analysis of causation and distinctions among different types of causes, not acknowledged by determinists.[79] They, for their part, do not reject the view that causal necessity obtains in the physical world, but they deny that it obtains universally even there; and, in addition, they insist that the action of such immaterial powers as reason and will involves a type of causality not to be found in the world of bodies.[80] Thus, for example, Rickaby, replying to Hobbes, writes: "Every sufficient mechanical cause is necessary; but a mental cause may be sufficient and yet not necessary."[81] His explanation of this is that an act of the will is sufficiently caused, not only when it is a necessary effect, as is the will's volition of the end (i.e., the

---

[78] We are always able, according to Aquinas, to avoid considering any object, even the supreme good. At any moment, a man "can will not to think of happiness, because the acts of the intellect and will are particulars" (De Malo, Q. 6, A. 1, Reply); i.e., being particulars, they are good only in certain respects, not in all.

[79] See Maritain, Scholasticism and Politics, Ch. V, pp. 119–31, Freedom in the Modern World, pp. 5–20; Simon, Traité du Libre Arbitre, Ch. VI, VII, IX; De Munnynck, "La Démonstration Métaphysique du Libre Arbitre" in Revue Neo-Scholastique de Philosophie, Vol. 20, pp. 32–33, 280–93.

[80] On this point, see Ch. 9, pp. 273–76, supra.

[81] Free Will, p. 16.

supreme good), but also when it is a free effect, as is the will's choice of a particular means (i.e., some partial good).[82]

Other writers, who do not subscribe to the Thomistic explanation of the causal indeterminacy of the will in its acts of choice, also argue against the universality of causal necessity on the ground that the actions of the mind, reason, or will involve a type of causality radically different from that to be found in the physical world. It is in this way, as we have seen, that Price argues against Priestley, and Mansel against Mill.[83] So, too, for Kant, the indeterminacy of the elective will is inseparable from its special character as a cause operating in the noumenal order even though it produces effects in the phenomenal world;[84] and for Reid, necessity obtains only in the mechanical, not in the moral, sphere.[85]

Among writers who distinguish between causes which necessitate and causes which do not necessitate but which, nevertheless, are adequate to produce an effect, some call attention to what they consider a begging of the question on the part of their opponents. In their view, determinists, by equating sufficient with necessary causes, as Hobbes does, or causation in general with necessitation, as Hume does, illicitly demand that a statement of the causes for an effect be equivalent to a rational explanation of that effect. They regard as a rational explanation one which shows that the effect follows from the causes as a conclusion follows from premises that provide its rational ground. To say what its causes are is thus to give the reasons why the effect occurs. Hence, if a free choice is a caused effect and not a matter of chance, it should be possible, according to these determinists, to give the reasons why this particular choice was made rather than that.

The defenders of free choice here interpret their opponents as confronting them with the following dilemma: either tell us the reasons why an individual makes the choices that he does, or, if you admit that in the very nature of the case *such reasons cannot be found*, then cease to claim that the causal indeterminacy of free choice is distinct from the indeterminacy of chance.

Admitting that no rational explanation can ever be given for any choice that is freely made, Yves Simon rejects this dilemma as begging the question whether or not all causes necessitate their effects. He points out that

[82] See *ibid.*, pp. 68–70.
[83] See Ch. 9, pp. 270–71, *supra*.
[84] See *Critique of Pure Reason*, pp. 299–314.
[85] See *Essays on the Active Powers of the Human Mind*, pp. 195–97. Cf. *ibid.*, pp. 186–87. See also Richard Taylor, "Determinism and the Theory of Agency," in *Determinism and Freedom*, p. 216. Cf. Boutroux, *Contingency of the Laws of Nature*, pp. 32, 140–42; Bowne, *Personalism*, pp. 178–97; Lawrence, "Causality, Will, and Time," in *The Review of Metaphysics*, Vol. IX, No. 1, pp. 16–18.

the demand to know *why* this rather than that particular choice was made is legitimate on one meaning of the word "why," and question begging on another. If the "why" asks for causes *without excluding the possibility of causes that do not necessitate*, then it can be answered by an account of how the choice was caused without at the same time eliminating the freedom of the choice. But if the "why" requires the giving of causes that necessitate the choice, and afford a rational explanation of it, then it is already assumed, by the sense of the question, that the choice either is determined and not free or is a matter of chance.[86]

The matter is summed up by MacLagan in the following way.

> We are told that to claim that a man may just as well choose either of his alternatives amounts to saying that, whichever he does choose, his choice is an inexplicable freak.

While saying that there is a sense in which the choice has a reason, Mac-Lagan also says that "a moment's reflection shows that, in another sense, the choice has *not* got a reason." The sense in which it does have a reason "refers only to those facts by virtue of which the alternatives are genuine alternatives; and as soon as you distinguish the question 'What makes them alternatives?' and 'Why, as between these alternatives, did you actually elect the one in preference to the other?' you observe that you have no answer at all to the second." And what is more important, MacLagan maintains, is

> that it is necessary not to find an answer, for if it were found it would exhibit the choice as determined. In this sense a free choice is something by its very nature inexplicable, and it would do the Libertarian cause no good to gloss over that fact.[87]

Two writers—Renouvier and Bergson—remain to be considered. They belong to this first group in that, like the authors whom we have treated so far, they distinguish between the operation of causes in the physical world and in the domain of mind or consciousness. For Renouvier, free choice belongs to man alone; it is a unique attribute of human con-

[86] See *Traité du Libre Arbitre*, Ch. VII, p. 111. Rickaby makes the same point in his reply to Hume, when he says that "though, strictly speaking, no 'explanation' is assignable for a free volition, yet every volition has a cause." See *Free Will*, pp. 147–49. Bergson also points out that every attempt to give a rational explanation for free choice is self-defeating, for the effort assumes a determinism that is incompatible with freedom. See *Time and Free Will*, pp. 219–21; see also his "Letter to Brunschvicq," quoted in Vol. I, p. 512 fn. 56; and cf. Bosanquet, *The Principle of Individuality and Value*, pp. 353–55.

[87] "Freedom of the Will," in *Proceedings of the Aristotelian Society*, Supplementary Vol. XXV, pp. 194–96.

ciousness.[88] For Bergson, free choice is co-extensive with consciousness
s that, in turn, is co-extensive with life; but it is pre-eminently present
n the conscious life of man.[89] Both authors, furthermore, conceive free
hoice as involving causal indeterminacy. According to Renouvier, the
reedom that is characteristic of a human act means that "other acts
xclusive of the first were possible at the same instant."[90] According to
3ergson, "consciousness corresponds exactly to the living being's power
of choice; it is coextensive with the fringe of possible action that surrounds
he real action."[91]

What differentiates these two authors is the special character of the
argument they employ to defend free choice against determinism.

As Renouvier sees it, the notion of a necessary connection between
cause and effect conceives the effect as already pre-existing in the cause, to
be released, as it were, by the action of the cause: "a contained phenomenon which springs out of the containing phenomenon by the release of
a spring (as in children's toys)." To conceive the effect as somehow pre-
existing in the cause, Renouvier insists, is to ignore "the reality of time."
The necessitarian sets before us a completely static universe in which
'*everything is and nothing begins*"—in which there is no process of becoming or change. But, Renouvier argues, the very notion of cause has
meaning only in relation to becoming or change. Whatever difficulties
may attach to a conception of cause which allows for the coming to be of
contingent effects in an indeterminate but real future, the difficulties faced
by the causal determinist are even greater. Causality is "far from being less
obscure in the necessitarian hypothesis than in that of freedom," Renouvier
declares; on the contrary, "we can say that [in the former] it disappears
altogether."[92] The conjunction of causality with necessity, in other words,
falsifies the very meaning of cause as a principle of change or becoming.

Bergson argues in a somewhat similar fashion. He does not deny all
meaning to the words "cause" and "effect" when they are applied to the
tatic relation between phenomena which are subject to the laws of
mechanics. But he does insist that the notion of cause must have a radically different meaning in the inner world of conscious states, where
duration is real and everything is in process of change. "If the causal
relation still holds good in the realm of inner states," Bergson writes,
"it cannot resemble in any way what we call causality in nature. For the
physicist the same cause always produces the same effect: for a psychologist

---

88 See Vol. I, Ch. 23, pp. 483–84.
89 See Vol. I, Ch. 24, pp. 511–12.
90 *Psychologie Rationelle*, Vol. I, p. 317.
91 *Creative Evolution*, p. 287.
92 *Psychologie Rationelle*, Vol. I, pp. 325–26.

who does not let himself be misled by merely apparent analogies, a deep seated inner cause produces its effect once for all and will never repro duce it. . . . The principle of universal determination," Bergson con cludes, "loses every shred of meaning in the inner world of consciou states."[93]

(ii) *Arguments for causal indeterminacy by those who deny that any effect is completely necessitated by its causes.* The writers to whom we now turn share with Renouvier and Bergson the view that a completely necessitarian theory of causation makes time unreal by making the cause- and-effect relation static instead of a process of transition from a temporal antecedent to a temporal consequent. Like Renouvier and Bergson, they argue from the reality of time and process to the reality of an indetermi- nate future, in which effects will occur that are not completely necessitated by the causes that produce them. But Capek, Weiss, and Hartshorne carry this argument further than Renouvier and Bergson. Where the latter employ it to affirm causal indeterminacy only in the realm of psychological and biological processes, Capek, Weiss, and Hartshorne affirm causal indeterminacy throughout the whole of nature. For them, every cause stands in an indeterminate relation to a number of possible effects, any one of which it may produce in the course of its actual operation as a cause.[94]

Whereas the authors we have considered earlier defend man's possession of free choice by arguing against the universality of causal determinism, these writers argue for the universality of causal indeterminacy and treat man's freedom of choice as a special case of it. According to Capek, Weiss, and Hartshorne, it is freedom that is universal: the creativity and selectivity of choice are intrinsic to the very nature of the causal process. All three stress this creativity and the genuinely unpredictable novelties which

---

[93] *Time and Free Will*, pp. 200–1. Cf. Du Nouy, *Human Destiny*, pp. 48–52.

[94] Two other writers who argue in similar fashion are Lamprecht and Macmurray. Lamprecht maintains that time as a genuine process makes all events in nature genuinely contingent. See "Metaphysical Background of the Problem of Freedom" in *Freedom and Authority in our Time*, p. 601. "Man has a measure of freedom," he writes, "because all events in nature are genuinely contingent (*ibid.*, p. 598); that freedom "is the exploitation by rational agents of the contingencies in nature" (*ibid.*, p. 604). Macmurray declares that "the falsity of determinism lies simply in the dogma that the future is already determinate. But if this were so there would be no future; the future would be already past" (*The Self as Agent*, p. 135). Again, he writes: "A determinate future is not a real future. The real future is the indeterminate which is determined in action, and in being determined becomes the past. The physicist's time is not real time; it is time represented as past, without a future" (*ibid.*, p. 139). As he sees it, "to possess free-will is simply to be able to determine the indeterminate, that is, the future. . . . This is implied in the very conception of action. The Agent is the determiner. To deny free-will is to deny the possibility of action" (*ibid.*, p. 134).

emerge in the process.[95] But they differ somewhat in the terms in which they set forth their argument against determinism.

The doctrine of necessity which Capek attacks he finds classically exemplified in the causal theories of Spinoza and LaPlace.[96] According to these theories, Capek declares, the entire future is, as it were, deducible from the past. But just as a conclusion is timelessly contained in and co-present with its premises, so according to these theories the effect is contained in its causes, and is in no sense a temporal consequent. This is tantamount to denying a real temporal succession or transition from cause to effect. "If the future logically pre-exists in the present state of the universe, why," Capek asks, "does it require a certain time to become present?" In his view, no theory of caustion which regards future effects as necessarily determined by past causes can answer this question, for *necessity and temporality are logically incompatible.*[97]

The undeniable reality of the temporal process, Capek argues, requires us to reject the doctrine of causal necessity. But necessity can be rejected without rejecting causation. "When causal connection is *not* conceived as a deductive implication," Capek writes, then it can

> retain its dynamic successive character which appears as a foreign and unaccountable element in the necessitarian scheme. But this implies that *the possibility of the future*, instead of being a simple label for our ignorance, is real in a certain sense; in other words, that the future is only *probably* implied by the present, instead of being mathematically performed in all its individual details.[98]

When we substitute for the static causal nexus, which is as timeless as logical implication, "the temporal continuity of a real process of causation," we are able to acknowledge the reality of a *"growing world with genuine novelties emerging from past antecedents."* Capek writes:

> In such a growing world every present event is undoubtedly caused, though not necessitated, by its own past. For as long as it is not yet present, its specific character remains uncertain for one simple reason: that it is only its presentness which creates its specificity, i.e., brings an end to its uncertainty by eliminating all other possible features incompatible with it. Thus every present event is by its own essence *an act of selection* ending the hesitation of reality between various possibilities. The terms "selection"

[95] On this and related points, all three also express their indebtedness to a number of predecessors, including such authors as Renouvier, Bergson, Boutroux, James, Peirce, and Whitehead.

[96] See "The Doctrine of Necessity Re-Examined," in *The Review of Metaphysics*, Vol. V, No. 1, pp. 40, 49, 53.

[97] See *ibid.*, pp. 31–33.

[98] *Ibid.*, pp. 47–48.

and "hesitation" appear to be metaphorical and even anthropomorphic at first glance; in truth they express nothing but the ambiguous character of the unrealized future as well as its subsequent concrete realization. They describe complementary aspects of every temporal process: its indeterminacy and its creative character.[99]

Capek then asks, "does causality thus redefined affect in any significant way the traditional problem of freedom?" While conceding that opinions differ on this, he aligns himself with Peirce and James, as well as with Renouvier, Bergson, and Boutroux, in holding that the rejection of strict necessitarianism as intrinsically untenable removes the traditional objections to freedom of choice on man's part. Capek argues further that once we recognize that every future effect which comes to be realized is an event selected by its cause from a number of possibilities, we see that the individual man, in exercising choice among future possible courses of action, operates with essentially the same freedom or indeterminacy—the same exemption from necessity—that is to be found in causes generally.[100]

For Weiss, as for Capek, LaPlace represents the classical expression of the view that future effects are completely determined by and completely predictable from their causes.[101] If this were the correct view of causation, then, Weiss points out, "either man is free but is so far not part of a causal world, or he is part of such a world but is so far not free." This dilemma can be avoided by "a correct understanding of the nature of causation."[102] That understanding, he thinks, will not only reveal how the operation of causes in the sphere of human behavior leaves man freedom of choice, but will also show that a similar freedom is present wherever causes operate in nature. He is insistent on this point.

The importance of the problem of ethical responsibility makes most thinkers attend to the question of freedom only as it relates to man. . . . Confident that the world of nature is thoroughly determined (except perhaps in the region of quanta phenomena), they insist that man, at least if ethics is to have any meaning and responsibility a locus, is somehow free. But their position involves the cutting off of man from nature. It is a view that is incompatible with the theory of evolution, and in the end it deals with man as though he were "a kingdom in a kingdom." To be sure, man is different from other beings; he has and can exercise powers denied to them.

[99] *Ibid.*, pp. 50–51. To this paragraph, Capek appends a footnote in which he quotes Whitehead's statement that "whatever is realized in any one occasion of experience necessarily excluded the unbounded welter of contrary possibilities. There are always 'others,' *which might have been and are not*" (*Adventures of Ideas*, p. 356). (The italics are Capek's.)
[100] See *ibid.*, pp. 51 ff.
[101] See *Nature and Man*, pp. 20–21.
[102] *Ibid.*, p. 4.

But the powers that they do have must fall under categories comprehending his, if both he and they are to be parts of the same cosmos.[103]

The critical correction to be made in the theory of causation involves seeing it as a threefold, not a twofold, affair. "The nature of causation has been oversimplified," Weiss writes, "to make it seem as if there were only two factors to consider, the cause and the effect." What is omitted is the process wherein the cause acts to produce the effect.

A cause must precede its effect. That is why history can cover an extensive stretch of time. This means that the cause cannot necessitate the effect. If it did, the effect would exist when the cause did. What is normally termed a cause is only an antecedent condition. The nature of the effect is defined by it, and can often be predicted in the light of what we know of it. But the cause does not produce the effect that in fact ensues. The actual effect comes about as the result of an activity that, taking its start from the cause, ends by producing an instance of the predictable effect. The causal situation, then, has not two, but three components: the cause, the process of production, and the effect. Since freedom is the doing of something beyond the determination by a cause, the process of production is evidently free. An actual effect is freely produced inside a frame that necessarily binds together an antecedent cause and a predictable type of effect.[104]

Weiss's theory of causation does not exclude either the general predictability of the effect in advance or its necessary existence, once it has been produced. But the effect is predictable *only in general*: the nature of the cause enables us to predict the type of effect which such a cause can produce, *not* the particular instance of that type, which in fact will be produced.[105] Since predictability "concerns only kinds of things, the generic features, the merely possible," it "allows for the free occurrence of this or that particular instance"; and, therefore, "predictability is compatible with freedom."[106]

So, too, necessity is compatible with freedom. Weiss writes:

Every effect is necessitated. It must be what it is, because the process started with just those antecedents and ended with just that effect. But though necessitated the effect is freely produced, the outcome of a free course which works its way out here and now in ways impossible to know with surety in advance. Whatever necessities there are, result from the exercise of freedom. A thunderclap, the moving of a billiard ball, an impulsive act or an act

[103] "Common Sense and Beyond," in *Determinism and Freedom*, p. 223.
[104] *Ibid.*, p. 224. Cf. *Nature and Man*, pp. 9–11, 31–34; and *Modes of Being*, pp. 44–45.
[105] See "Common Sense and Beyond," *loc. cit.*, p. 222.
[106] *Ibid.*, cf. *Nature and Man*, pp. 11 ff.

of design are on a par because they are all the outcome of free occurrences by which indeterminate possibilities are made into determinate actualities.[107]

Necessity, in the sense in which Weiss affirms it, is plainly not the causal necessity affirmed by the determinists, for that is a necessity which excludes the causal indeterminacy that is involved in the production by a given cause of any one of a number of possible effects. Such necessity, Weiss maintains, "allows no place for time and thus makes causation impossible. Causation is a temporal phenomenon, a concrete free course linking past 'çauses' with subsequent determinate effects." Necessity, in Weiss's sense, is inseparable from freedom; for every effect is freely produced insofar as until produced, it is only one of a number of effects which the process of causation has the power to bring into existence, as it turns "the indeterminate into the determinate"; and a particular effect is necessary insofar as, when produced, it is the only actually determinate result that can exist at the termination of that particular process of causation.[108]

Weiss applies this analysis of causation in general to the special case of free choice in man. "The reason for choosing an act," he writes, "is produced in the choosing; it is the acceptance of a commitment to a justifying end. The reason for choosing the end is provided at the same time; it is the acceptance of some act as the best possible. In the production of these reasons a man is free."[109]

[107] *Nature and Man*, p. 18. Cf. *Modes of Being*, p. 45, where Weiss declares that "just as there is no inconsistency between the idea of freedom and the idea of prediction . . . so there is no inconsistency between the idea of a freely produced effect and a necessitated actual effect." This point has been overlooked, he explains, "because it has been thought that the transcendence of the process of causation beyond the cause meant that there was no limit to where the process might go and what it might achieve. But a production has definite limits. It makes only possible, predictable, and formally necessary effects into actual, not wholly predictable, existentially necessary ones."

[108] See *Nature and Man*, pp. 10 and 18–19. "A world of necessity without freedom," Weiss declares, "is a world in which logicians dwell. It is a world in which there are logical connections between existents, but no real movement from one to the other. A world in which there is freedom without necessity is a world in which romantics live. There is movement and life in it, but nothing definite and fixed before or after" (*ibid.*, p. 19).

[109] *Modes of Being*, pp. 98–99. "The determinist knows that the various alternative actions have initially different degrees of attractiveness, and that a man *must* choose *just* one of them. His opponent knows that the various alternatives are all equally open to a choice, and that he *could* choose *any* one of them. The first says that the second treats choice as an act of irresponsible caprice; the second says that the first treats choice as a creature of an external amoral pressure. The first charges the second as having no reasons, and he replies that the first has no ethics. Both criticisms are justified. But both make the same mistaken assumptions. Both overlook the fact that choice is an act of providing a reason" (*ibid.*). Cf. *Man's Freedom*, p. 119, where Weiss points out that "free choice would present an insoluble problem were there no middle ground between a necessitating reason and the absence of all reason."

Like Capek and Weiss, Hartshorne affirms the universal truth of the principle of causation while at the same time denying that any cause completely necessitates its effect. "The universal validity of causality," he writes, "is not the same as determinism. The point is simple: there is a deterministic definition and an indeterministic definition of 'cause,' and the difference does not turn upon whether or not 'every event has a cause.' It turns rather upon how causes are thought to be related to their effects, or antecedent conditions to subsequent happenings."[110]

Hartshorne introduces his view of the relation of causes to their effects in the following passage.

> Every event has its cause or causes; so far we nearly all agree. But not every event—indeed some of us would say, not *any* event in its concrete actuality —is fully and absolutely determined by its causes. In other words, an indeterminist . . . rejects a certain definition of "cause," namely that it is a condition, or set of conditions, from which only one outcome is possible, or from which, in principle, or ideally the outcome is wholly predictable.[111]

The causal indeterminist, on the contrary, holds that antecedent conditions

> logically imply not any particular subsequent event as their inevitable outcome, but only a class of "really possible" outcomes . . . The features which *all* the really possible outcomes have in common are then necessary, i.e., they are bound to be actualized whatever happens. This is the meaning of "necessary," namely, "common to all the possibilities." What is common to *most* of the possibilities is probable. Thus temporal succession is quite different from unqualified logical implication: yet there is implication. Something like what happens next was more or less bound to happen—so far, there is a "necessary connection"—but the precise particulars just do happen, quite without necessity or implication.[112]

For Hartshorne as for Weiss, the future is predictable only *in general* insofar as antecedent causes impose certain necessary limits on the range

[10] "Freedom Requires Indeterminism and Universal Causality," in *The Journal of Philosophy*, Vol. LV, No. 19, p. 793. Hartshorne makes plain that by "indeterminism" he means the indeterminacy of causes, not the indeterminism of chance (i.e., uncaused events). To distinguish these two, he refers to causal indeterminacy as a "relative indeterminism." He regards necessitarian determinism, on the one hand, and the indeterminism of chance, on the other, as opposed absolutes. The determinists, in his view, tend to make "the issue one between [these] two absolutes . . . instead of a triadic choice between two absolutistic views and one relativistic view. But if this done," he adds, "then it is arguable that indeterminism is a doctrine no one defends, a fictitious position invented for purposes of controversy" (*ibid.*, pp. 793–94).

[11] *Ibid.*, p. 794.

[12] *Ibid.*, pp. 802–3. Cf. "Causal Necessities: An Alternative to Hume," in *The Philosophical Review*, Vol. LXIII, No. 4, pp. 485–86. See also *Reality as Social Process*, Chapter Five, pp. 86 ff.

of possible outcomes. What is not predictable, because it is not neces
sitated by its antecedents, is the concrete particular outcome which realize
one of the possibilities.[113]

Only when causation is so conceived that it combines the indeterminac
of future particulars with the necessity of the range of real possibilitie
to which they belong does it allow for what Hartshorne calls the "creativ
leap beyond anything made inevitable or predictable by the causal condi
tions."[114] And only when the causal process involves a creative leap
Hartshorne argues, is it genuinely a temporal process at all. Without crea
tivity in causation, without the emergence of novelty, there is no becoming
"If becoming does not create new quality and quantity, new determinate
ness," Hartshorne says, "then, we argue, it creates nothing, and nothin
ever really becomes. . . . In short, creativity is an essential aspect of th
idea of becoming or process."[115] This is the nub of his argument agains
a necessitarian determinism which holds "that conditions unqualifiedl
restrict the outcome to but one wholly definite sort of event, entirel
excluding any creative leap, any novelty not specifiable in advance, give
ideal knowledge of conditions."[116]

The creativity which causal indeterminacy permits is for Hartshorne th
essence of freedom. "Freedom," he writes, "is choice among really possibl
acts, acts possible not only given the external situation but also given th
pre-existing individual with his history and constitution."[117] Since causa
indeterminacy is present at all levels of nature, so, too, is creativity an
freedom. The creativity of free choice on man's part is merely the highes
instance of it. Wherever causes operate, they determine subsequent event
only by limiting "more or less sharply what can happen. . . . Inanimat
nature involves the least scope of alternatives—and here the 'more or les
determined' means 'more'; man involves the widest scope—and here i
means very much 'less.' Thus we need not make man an arbitrary exceptio
to the general principles of nature; he is but the intensive case of the gen
eral principle of creative action, of which causality is an aspect."[118]

We have now presented the arguments for causal indeterminacy an
against causal necessity which are advanced by (i) those who admit tha
some particular events are completely necessitated by their causes, bu

[113] See "Causal Necessities: An Alternative to Hume," *loc. cit.*, pp. 480–81; *Realit*
as Social Process, pp. 86–89, 92–93, 97–99.
[114] "Freedom Requires Indeterminism and Universal Causality," *loc. cit.*, p. 795.
[115] *Ibid.*, p. 796.
[116] *Ibid.*, p. 795.
[117] *Ibid.*, pp. 809–10.
[118] *Ibid.*, p. 795. Cf. *ibid.*, pp. 798–99, 805–6, 808. Cf. *Reality as Social Process*, pp
94–96.

deny that *all* are, and (ii) those who deny that *any* particular event is completely necessitated. Both groups of writers think that these arguments constitute a defense of man's freedom of choice against the denial of such freedom by the determinists. But it will be seen that the arguments in defense respond only to the arguments against free choice which are advanced by such exponents of causal necessity as Hobbes, Spinoza, Hume, Edwards, Priestley, Hartley, Mill, McTaggart, Paulsen, Windelband, and Ross, to mention only some of the outstanding members of this group. At the end of the section devoted to the presentation of the arguments against the causal indeterminacy required for free choice, we mentioned an argument of a different type, that advanced by Broad against the libertarian position.[119] What remains to be considered, therefore, are the counter-arguments to Broad.

The central point in Broad's attack on free choice is that it requires a cause which acts outside of time, one that is totally non-occurrent, i.e., a cause that is neither an event nor contains events as cause factors. This point, as we saw in the preceding chapter, is explicitly denied by L. J. Russell.[120] As we have also seen, it is implicitly denied by Aquinas, who conceives the act of the will in making a free choice as a temporal event.[121] Like Russell, A. C. Ewing explicitly comments on Broad.

According to Ewing, the indeterminist must admit that human actions are at least partially determined.[122] His account of free action, Ewing says, must run somewhat as follows.

> Previous events and causal laws limit the number of alternatives at all possible; they further commonly render one alternative more attractive than the others. Then the causal tendency towards adopting it will be more powerful, and it will be more probable that the agent will adopt it . . . Whatever the probability, provided it falls short of certainty, the action rightly judged beforehand to be more probable may not occur because the agent may will differently after all.[123]

But the indeterminism thus described, Ewing thinks, does not supply a basis for moral responsibility. It is necessary to add that the free act is determined by the self as a substance, independently of its established

[19] See pp. 350–51, *supra*.
[20] See Ch. 9, pp. 284–85, *supra*. Russell's argument is there summarized.
[21] See *ibid*., pp. 55–56, and esp. 59. While Aquinas's conception of God as a cause would, in addition, lead him to deny Broad's premise that a supra-temporal cause of an event in time is self-evidently impossible, this additional point is not essential to his defense of man's freedom of choice against Broad's insistence that that, too, must invoke a supra-temporal cause.
[22] See 'Indeterminism,' in *The Review of Metaphysics*, Vol. V, No. 2, p. 199.
[23] See *ibid*., p. 212.

characteristics and of whatever past events are causally relevant. On thi
point Ewing finds himself in agreement with Broad.[124] He then refers t
Broad's objection to the libertarian view on the ground that "it is obviou
that any event in time must, if it has a cause at all, include in its caus
previous events to fix its beginning in time."

To this objection, Ewing responds by writing:

> I should have thought that most libertarians would have admitted this
> and merely maintained that such previous events and characteristics did
> not constitute *the whole cause*.[125]

In other words, most libertarians conceive the total cause of a free act a
including some events, though they may also include a substantive or nor
occurrent factor, such as the self or one of its powers.[126] The position o
L. J. Russell and of Aquinas and his followers supports Ewing's contentio
that there are libertarians for whom the total cause of a free act include
both occurrent and non-occurrent (or substantive) causal factors. Thi
would seem to suffice as an answer to Broad; but Ewing tells us tha
when he "mentioned this orally to Professor Broad, he said that in tha
case it would be impossible to distinguish libertarianism from any deter
minist view."[127]

Ewing then undertakes to distinguish the two views in a way that woul
fit Broad's acceptance of the determinist and his rejection of the libertaria
position. According to the determinist view, as Ewing sees it, there reall
is no non-occurrent factor in causation, for there is no such thing as
substance "over and above its characteristics." In contrast, according to th
libertarian,

> there would be in free acts a causal factor which could only be stated in
> terms of substance; when we had enumerated all the characteristics that
> could conceivably be enumerated, there would still be left over a factor
> in the effect which could not be accounted for by any characteristics, but
> only by a substance which exercises its causality not through or not only
> through, but to some extent independently of, its characteristics.[128]

[124] See *ibid.*, p. 214. "The indeterminist," Ewing writes, "must adopt the view calle
by Professor Broad *libertarianism* and distinguished by the latter from both dete
minism and indeterminism. . . . Libertarianism, as understood by Professor Broad, i
the view that free acts, though determined, are determined by the self as substanc
and neither by its characteristics nor by past events" (*ibid.*).

[125] *Ibid.*, p. 214. (Italics added.)

[126] As we have already seen, some libertarians, or exponents of free choice, do conceiv
the cause of a free act as supra-temporal; e.g., Kant, Schelling, Lotze, Royce, Lossk
and others. See Ch. 9, pp. 275–76, *supra*.

[127] *Ibid.*

[128] *Ibid.*, pp. 215–16.

Whether or not this correctly represents what Broad has in mind, Ewing himself insists that the libertarian position he has just described must be what indeterminism must come to if it is not to be sheer nonsense."[129] The position described may escape Broad's objection against a supra-temporal cause, but it does not escape other difficulties, such as the difficulty of making "the very sharp separation between a substance and its characteristics" and the difficulty of explaining how the free act can be effected by an individual's characteristics and yet not be completely determined by them.[130]

These difficulties, not raised by Broad, are raised, as we have seen, by Nowell-Smith in his dispute with Campbell.[131] Ewing, as well as Campbell, attempts to solve them. We shall consider these solutions in Section 4, which is concerned with the whole dispute about the causal influence of a man's character, motives, and circumstances upon the determination of his decisions and actions.

3. THE DISPUTE ABOUT INDETERMINACY AND PREDICTABILITY

For certain authors, causal determinism is inseparably connected with the theoretical or intrinsic predictability of all future events. By "theoretical" or "intrinsic" predictability is meant the predictability of future events *with certitude, given adequate knowledge of the causes which determine or necessitate these events as to their effects.* The lack of such knowledge, or even the unattainability of it, in a particular case or even in every case, does not alter the proposition that, were such knowledge possessed, future effects could be predicted with certitude.

Since theoretic predictability implies determinism, these authors conclude that the denial of determinism in some particular sphere entails the denial of theoretic predictability in all spheres. But, as we have seen, only some of the writers on the opposite side maintain that theoretic predictability is impossible in *all* spheres. Some admit that causal necessity obtains in large areas of nature and deny it only or mainly in the sphere of human voluntary behavior. Hence, only the former can be charged by

---

[129] *Ibid.*, p. 216. "The indeterminist holds," Ewing says, "that the self decides how it shall act, and therefore, by implication, that it determines its act, but he denies that they are determined completely by character and circumstances, so he is clearly asserting that the free causality of the self is a causality which is not dependent on the characteristics of the self" (*ibid.*).

[130] See *ibid.*, pp. 217–18.

[131] See Ch. 9, pp. 297–98, *supra.*

determinists with denying that any particular future event is ever com
pletely predictable, even on the basis of adequate knowledge of the cause
The latter, from the point of view of the determinist, merely insist tha
human voluntary behavior is an exception to the general rule that futur
events are theoretically predictable.

In this dispute, the determinists sometimes argue that scientific inquir
and knowledge presuppose the truth of causal determinism and, with i
the uniformity of nature and the theoretical predictability of future event
Hence, to deny theoretical predictability in general is to undermine th
scientific enterprise as a whole; and to insist that certain natural phe
nomena, such as the voluntary acts of man, are not theoretically predictabl
is to preclude the attainment of scientific knowledge in the field of hu
man behavior or to say that the so-called "behavioral sciences" will neve
be able to achieve the results obtained in other fields of scientific inquir
As this form of the argument runs, the acknowledged achievements c
science constitute evidence that causal indeterminacy does not obtain i
nature. If, by extrapolation, it is held that science can extend its achieve
ments to include human behavior, it is then argued that the possibilit
of these future developments of science means that causal determinism i
universal and causal indeterminacy non-existent.

Those who take the negative side sometimes argue that the predictabilit
of future effects is an unquestionable fact, connected, of course, with th
fact that scientific inquiry has succeeded in obtaining the knowledge from
which such predictions can be made. This argument is often extended t
include the predictability of human behavior, either as a matter of fac
and as a result of accomplished scientific knowledge or as a genuine pos
sibility to be realized by further developments in the behavioral science
The asserted predictability of future events, attained or attainable, ther
becomes the premise for the denial of the causal indeterminacy which i
thought to be incompatible with it.

Before we turn to what is said on the opposite side of this dispute, w
must note two things about the foregoing arguments.

One is the contention, usually explicitly stated, that human behavic
or voluntary acts do not constitute an exception—a field of phenomena i
which science cannot hope to achieve what it has achieved elsewhere. W
have already observed, in the preceding dispute, that determinists see n
ground for regarding the voluntary acts of man as an exception limitin
the universality of the causal principle, conceived as involving a necessar
connection of cause and effect. Just as they maintain there that causatio
is essentially the same in the psychological or moral order as in th
physical, so they maintain here that predictability is the same in the spher

f human behavior as it is in the rest of nature; and so causal indeterminacy must be excluded from the one as it is from the other.

The other thing to be noted about these arguments is that they are formulated without reference to the comparatively recent problem of the significance of indeterminacy in quantum mechanics or sub-atomic physics. In this context, the intrinsic unpredictability of certain future phenomena is admitted by a large number of writers, though not by all.[132] But the prior question is whether this unpredictability and the indeterminacy that goes along with it have significance for the issue about free choice on man's part and for the causal indeterminacy that it involves. We shall, therefore, postpone the consideration of this area of the dispute until we have examined the arguments on both sides of the dispute about predictability and indeterminacy in general, which is carried on without reference to the "new physics."

Those who defend causal indeterminacy, either in general or in the particular case of human free choice, argue in one of the following ways. i) They maintain, as a matter of fact, that no particular future effect is theoretically predictable; and in so doing, they deny the premise from which their opponents argue against causal indeterminacy in general. ii) Or they maintain that, as a matter of fact, though human behavior is to a certain extent predictable with probability, it is never wholly predictable with certitude; and here again they deny the premise from which their opponents argue against causal indeterminacy in human behavior. (iii) Or they point out that scientific inquiry and scientific knowledge do not require an unqualified acceptance of causal determinism and its corollaries –the complete uniformity of nature and theoretical predictability; and thus, arguing that science only presupposes a high degree of uniformity and of probability in prediction, they maintain that the achievements of science, present and promised, do not establish or require the universal reign of causal necessity. (iv) Or they point out that the uniformity of nature is only a postulate, useful in science and limited to certain areas of scientific inquiry; and thus, arguing that the uniformity of nature is not an established truth, nor one of universal applicability, they maintain that the assertion of causal indeterminacy, expecially if it is limited to the sphere of human behavior, does not conflict with the principles of science nor undermine scientific inquiry in general.

With this sketch of the arguments and counter-arguments before us, we are prepared to examine the evidence of this dispute. We shall first present

---

[132] A few, as we shall see, maintain that the unpredictability in this case results from certain unavoidable limitations on our knowledge rather than from an actual indeterminacy in the behavior of particles.

evidence of the arguments against causal indeterminacy based on the a sertion of theoretical predictability. We shall then present evidence of th arguments against theoretical predictability which are employed in th defense of causal indeterminacy, either in general or in human behavic in particular. Finally, we shall examine the arguments and counter-argu ments in the dispute about the significance of indeterminacy in quantun mechanics or sub-atomic physics.

<h3 style="text-align:center">ARGUMENTS AGAINST CAUSAL INDETERMINACY BASED ON THE ASSERTION OF THEORETICAL PREDICTABILITY</h3>

To those who point out that "human conduct is irregular and uncer tain," whereas in actions governed by necessity, everything "is regular an certain," Hume says: "I reply, that in judging of the actions of men w must proceed upon the same maxims, as when we reason concernin external objects."[133] In the behavior of men, he maintains, "the sam uniformity and regular operation of natural principles are discernible Like causes still produce like effects; in the same manner as in the mutua action of the elements and powers of nature."[134] Since "there is no know circumstance that enters into the connexion and production of the action of matter, that is not to be found in all the operations of the mind," Hum concludes that "we cannot, without a manifest absurdity, attribute neces sity to the one, and refuse it to the other."[135]

It makes no difference, Hume declares, whether we define necessity i terms of the "constant union and conjunction of like objects" or in term of "the inference of the mind from the one to the other."[136] In bot senses, it applies to human acts exactly as it does to the motions of bodies When we recognize this, and in so doing exclude the operation of chanc from the one as from the other, we also recognize that any uncertaint about future effects arises solely from our ignorance or limited knowledg of the causes.[137]

According to J. S. Mill, the facts of experience provide a clear warran for asserting that the same kind of uniformity and predictability obtain in the sphere of human behavior as in the rest of nature. He writes:

---

[133] *Treatise of Human Nature,* Book II, Part III, Sect. 1, p. 403.
[134] *Ibid.,* p. 401.
[135] *Ibid.,* p. 404.
[136] *Ibid.,* p. 409.
[137] See *ibid.,* pp. 403–4. See also *Enquiry Concerning Human Understanding,* Sect VIII, Part I, pp. 88–91. Cf. Charles Bray, *The Philosophy of Necessity,* pp. 31–37

What experience makes known, is the fact of an invariable sequence between every event and some special combination of antecedent conditions, in such sort that wherever and whenever that union of antecedents exists, the event does not fail to occur. Any *must* in the case, any necessity, other than the unconditional universality of the fact, we know nothing of.[138]

The "so-called Necessitarians," Mill then says, "demand the application of the same rule of judgment to our volitions. They maintain that there is he same evidence for it. They affirm, as a truth of experience, that volitions do, in point of fact, follow determinate moral antecedents with the same uniformity, and (when we have sufficient knowledge of the circumstances) with the same certainty, as physical effects follow their physical causes."[139]

Mill dissociates himself from the necessitarian position only insofar as it insists upon some meaning of necessity over and above the experienced facts of uniformity and predictability. His own opinion is that "a volition is a moral effect which follows the corresponding moral causes as certainly and invariably as physical effects follow their physical causes." To which he adds:

> Whether it *must* do so, I acknowledge myself to be entirely ignorant, be the phaenomenon moral or physical; and I condemn, accordingly, the word Necessity as applied to either case. All I know is, that it always *does*.[140]

As McTaggart states the argument against what he calls "indeterminism," it takes a somewhat different form. He begins by pointing out that

> the indeterminist admits that on his theory there can be no certainty of prediction. For all practical purposes the determinist must admit the same, since only an omniscient person could be quite certain what causes were at work and with what strength. The indeterminist, however, thinks that his theory admits of statements of probability as to volitions.[141]

But he contends that if the indeterminist's position is true, then "there is no justification whatever for making any statement as to the probability

---

[138] *Examination of Sir William Hamilton's Philosophy*, p. 576.
[139] *Ibid.*, pp. 576–77. "The cases in which volitions seem too uncertain to admit of being confidently predicted," Mill adds, "are those in which our knowledge of the influences antecedently in operation is so incomplete, that with equally imperfect data there would be the same uncertainty in the predictions of the astronomer and the chemist" (*ibid.*, p. 577).
[140] *Ibid.*, p. 578.
[141] *Some Dogmas of Religion*, p. 182. "The indeterminist, like everyone else," McTaggart writes, "assumes that it is possible to predict with some probability, though not with absolute certainty, how men will act under particular circumstances. To reject this would render impossible all trade, all government, and all intercourse with our fellow men" (*ibid.*).

of future volitions. The indeterminist theory assumes that in every case the choice between motives is undetermined. There cannot then be the slightest probability that this choice will be of one motive rather than another."[142] This, according to McTaggart, is not the main argument against indeterminism.[143] But it does reveal what McTaggart thinks is an important inconsistency "in the position of the average indeterminist" who "attaches some value to expectations that men will, under certain circumstances, act in certain ways."[144]

Bertrand Russell tends to follow Mill's line of reasoning and P. H. Nowell-Smith that of McTaggart. In Russell's view,

> the principle of causality—that every event is determined by previous events, and can (theoretically) be predicted when enough previous events are known—appears to apply just as much to human actions as to other events.[145]

And he tells us that "the grounds in favor of determinism"—so conceived— "appear to me overwhelming."[146] As Nowell-Smith understands the position of the determinist, "*moral* choices are free" in a sense which is "incompatible with their being predictable." This unpredictability, he says,

> is an essential feature in the categorical interpretation of 'he could have acted otherwise'; for, if anyone could predict what I am going to do, I should not really be choosing between genuinely open alternatives, although I might think I was.[147]

But, Nowell-Smith argues, well-attested facts support the predictability of human choices and thus preclude their indeterminacy.

> In calling a man 'honest' or 'brave' we imply that he can be relied on to act honestly or bravely, and this means that we predict such actions from him. This does not mean that we can predict human actions with the same degree of assurance as that with which we predict eclipses. Psychology and the

---

[142] *Ibid.*, pp. 182–83. "According to the indeterminist theory our choice between motives is not determined by anything at all. And thus it follows that all ground for predicting the action of any man, so far as it depends on his volition, vanishes altogether" (*ibid.*, p. 183).

[143] "The main argument against it," he writes, "is that which proceeds by establishing the universal validity of the law of Causality, and so showing that volitions, like all other events, must be completely determined" (*ibid.*, p. 177).

[144] *Ibid.* Cf. *ibid.*, pp. 183–84.

[145] "Determinism and Moral," in *The Hibbert Journal*, Vol. VII, p. 115.

[146] *Ibid.*, p. 113. In another place, Russell admits that the case for determinism is not proved: see *Mysticism and Logic*, pp. 194–96.

[147] *Ethics*, p. 279. Cf. *ibid.*, pp. 281–83.

social sciences have not yet succeeded in establishing laws as reliable as those that we have established in some of the natural sciences, and maybe they never will.[148]

Nevertheless, the highly probable prediction of voluntary actions is sufficient warrant for the rejection of a theory which, as Nowell-Smith sees it, provides no basis for their predictability in any degree.

A number of other writers, who take the determinist's side in this issue, concur with McTaggart and Nowell-Smith in thinking that the determinist need not assert the complete predictability of human actions in order to argue against the causal indeterminacy that is involved in free choice. Von Mises, while admitting that we do not and, perhaps, cannot know enough about the causes of human behavior to predict human acts as we can predict physical events, nevertheless, maintains that "the determinists are right in asserting that everything that happens is the necessary sequel of the preceding state of things." This applies to human behavior. "What a man does at any instant of his life is entirely dependent on his past, that is, on his physiological inheritance as well as of all he went through in his previous days."[149] Gallie goes further than this. He sees no reason why "determinism in science should be connected with prediction, or even with predictable (i.e., future) events at all." In his view,

all that Determinism requires . . . is the deducibility of later from earlier, not of future from present or past events. We could therefore say, if we wished, that it requires not prediction or predictability, but prediction-*like* inference or inferribility.[150]

The case against causal indeterminacy is fully made, in other words, if we can show that any *later* event is deducible from *earlier* ones, whether or not that later event, when it was still future, could have been predicted.[151]

[148] "Freewill and Moral Responsibility," in *Mind*, Vol. LVII, No. 225, p. 47.
[149] *Theory and History*, p. 77. See also *ibid.*, p. 78. Cf. Richard von Mises, *Positivism*, pp. 326–27.
[150] *Free Will and Determinism Yet Again*, pp. 14–15. Cf. the statement by A. J. Ayer: "That my actions should be capable of being explained is all that is required by the postulate of determinism" (*Philosophical Essays*, p. 282).
[151] See *ibid.*, p. 27. Cf. Ducasse, "Determinism, Freedom, and Responsibility," in *Determinism and Freedom*, pp. 148–54; and also *Nature, Mind, and Death*, pp. 175–80, 202–4, 211–16.

ARGUMENTS AGAINST THEORETICAL PREDICTABILITY

As we have already seen, authors such as Capek, Weiss, and Hartshorne, who hold that the reality of time and of the future involves causal indeterminacy, also deny that the future in its full concreteness is theoretically predictable. What they are denying, they explain, is the LaPlacean view that perfect knowledge of causes would enable us to predict the future with certitude, down to the last detail; for, in their theory of causation, particular effects are not implicitly present in and deducible from their causes, as conclusions are from premises.

According to their theory, the future is predictable *in general:* certain types of effects can be foreseen to follow from certain types of causes. But just as no particular effect is ever necessitated by its causes, so no particular future event is ever predictable from them. Hence, whereas the theoretical or complete predictability which they deny would be incompatible with a freedom that involves causal indeterminacy, the limited predictability they affirm is quite compatible with it. As Weiss says, since predictability "concerns only kinds of things, the generic features, the merely possible," it "allows for the free occurrence of this or that particular instance."[152]

Another group of authors, who hold that causation in the sphere of consciousness or mind is radically different in type from causation in the sphere of bodies, deny the theoretical predictability of certain future events, but not of all. The causal indeterminacy which such writers as Renouvier, Bergson, Maritain, and Simon attribute to the conscious self or the human will in its acts of choice excludes the possibility of foreknowing free acts, even granted the most perfect knowledge of all their causes.[153]

So far there would appear to be disagreement but no debate between those who, on the one hand, assert theoretical predictability without qualification, and those who, on the other hand, either deny it entirely or deny

[152] "Common Sense and Beyond," in *Determinism and Freedom,* p. 222. For the report already given of the views of Capek, Weiss, and Hartshorne, see pp. 54–64, *supra.* See also the report of Whitehead's similar views about causation and predictability in Vol. I, pp. 456–57.

[153] For the views of Renouvier on this point, see Vol. I, pp. 450–51. For the views of Bergson, see *ibid.,* pp. 458–59, and also *Time and Free Will,* pp. 183–90. For the views of Maritain, see Vol. I, pp. 446–47; and for the views of Simon, see *ibid.,* p. 460. In this connection, see also the report of Meyerson's views, *ibid.,* p. 459. The problem of the predictability of future contingent events is first raised by Aristotle in his *De Interpretatione,* Ch. 9.

it in part. These contrary assertions about the possibility of foreseeing future effects from perfect knowledge of past and present causes follow as strict corollaries from contrary theories of causation. If, on the one hand, the necessitarian theory is true, then theoretical predictability obtains universally and free choice is excluded. If, on the other hand, the theory is not true, there remain two possibilities. (a) If the causal indeterminism of Weiss, Capek, and Hartshorne is right, freedom obtains universally, and no particular future event is theoretically predictable. (b) If libertarians such as Renouvier, Bergson, Maritain, and Simon are right, freedom obtains only for conscious or voluntary behavior, and some future events are not theoretically predictable.

The dispute about theoretical predictability in relation to freedom achieves the form of rational debate only to the extent that the disputants advance arguments for or against the conflicting theories of causation that provide the basic premises here. We have examined such arguments in the preceding section, which presented evidence of the dispute about indeterminacy and causation. In the final section of this chapter, we shall consider the adequacy of the argumentation there presented. Whatever assessment of that is made will also measure the extent to which reasons are given for asserting or denying theoretical predictability.

Precisely because the predictability in question is theoretical, it cannot be settled by any appeal to facts. Those who affirm theoretical predictability acknowledge that it may not be attainable in fact because the conditions for its attainment may never be actually present, namely, complete or perfect knowledge of all the relevant causes. Hence, those who deny it do not claim that it is refuted by the mere fact that we never do achieve certitude in foretelling particular future events.

However, those who deny causal indeterminacy do argue that scientific prediction is an accomplished fact. Such prediction may have only high probability instead of certitude; and it may not completely realize the ideal of theoretical predictability; but the undeniable success of science in prediction is, nevertheless, thought to constitute empirical evidence for the theory of causation that would at least make theoretical predictability a genuine possibility. This is the tenor of the argument as it is presented by Hume and Mill.[154]

Furthermore, these writers, and others such as McTaggart and Nowell-Smith, point out, again as a matter of fact, that human behavior is also predictable to a great extent and with fairly high probability, though it is not and may never be, in fact, as predictable as physical events are. Now since the position of the libertarian or the indeterminist, as they under-

[154] See pp. 374–75, *supra*.

stand it, excludes even the predictability of free acts as probabilities, they think that the facts of successful prediction—of human behavior as well as of the course of other events—tend to refute the views held by their opponents, or at least to reveal their inconsistency.[155]

To this argument against their views, the exponents of causal indeterminacy reply by pointing out that their position has been misinterpreted. While they reject theoretical predictability, either entirely or in part, they do not deny that future events are predictable, in general if not in detail, and with probability if not with certitude. Nor do they deny that human behavior is also thus predictable. Such predictability as exists is not incompatible with the existence of causal indeterminacy and free choice unless these are identical with chance. The identification of causal indeterminacy with the indeterminism of chance constitutes the misunderstanding which, in their view, renders the argument of their opponents irrelevant. Properly understood, causal indeterminacy or free choice, they assert, is quite consistent with all the predictions that have succeeded and with all the predictability that is possible.

An early indication of this type of response is to be found in Thomas Reid, who writes:

> It is true that we reason from men's motives to their actions, and, in many cases, with great probability, but never with absolute certainty. And to infer from this, that men are necessarily determined by motives, is very weak reasoning.
>
> For, let us suppose for a moment, that men have moral liberty. I would ask, what use may they be expected to make of this liberty? It may surely be expected, that of the various actions within the sphere of their power, they will choose what pleases them most for the present, or what appears to be most for their real, though distant good. When there is a competition between these motives, the foolish will prefer present gratification; the wise, the greater and more distant good.
>
> Now, is not this the very way in which we see men act? Is it not from the presumption that they act in this way, that we reason from their motives to their actions? Surely it is. Is it not weak reasoning, therefore, to argue that men have not liberty, because they act in that very way in which they would act if they had liberty? It would surely be more like reasoning, to draw the contrary conclusion from the same premises.[156]

[155] See pp. 375–77, *supra*.
[156] *Essays on the Active Powers of the Human Mind*, p. 194. "Nor," Reid continues, "is it better reasoning to conclude that, if men are not necessarily determined by their motives, all their actions must be capricious" (*ibid.*). He then points out that, while virtuous men often follow the line of duty rather than yield to animal motives, they do not *always* do so, as we would expect them to if their actions *necessarily followed* from their virtuous characters.

More recently, C. A. Campbell replies in the same manner to Nowell-Smith who, like McTaggart, as we have seen, argues that the predictability of human behavior is inexplicable on the libertarian theory. He writes:

> Even in situations where free will does come into play it is perfectly possible, on a view like ours, given the appropriate knowledge of a man's character, to predict within certain limits how he will respond.
>
> But 'probable' prediction in such situations can, I think, go no further than this.[157]

While denying that human behavior is perfectly predictable or that it is even predictable with high probability in all cases, Campbell claims that

> the view of free will I have been putting forward is consistent with predictability of conduct on the basis of character over a very wide field indeed. And I make the further claim that that field will cover all the situations in life concerning which there is any empirical evidence that successful prediction is possible.[158]

Other writers argue in a similar vein. Gruender, for example, writes:

> We admit that it is indeed impossible to foretell the future free actions of our fellow men with *absolute* certainty. We can, however, do so, frequently at least, with that degree of assurance which is required for prudent action. Such an assurance is known as *moral certainty in the wider sense of the term*. It does not exclude the *possibility* of error, but only its *probability*. It is such a certainty on which society is built and this certainty is in perfect accord with the doctrine of free will.[159]

And Hawkins points out "that not all volitions are free in the full sense of the word" and "that, where there is freedom, it is always freedom within a certain range of possibilities, sometimes wider, sometimes narrower. Consequently," he continues,

> there is plenty of room for approximate and statistical generalizations about human conduct. Our position would be affected only if all conduct could be brought under general laws and if it were always true that, with complete knowledge of the antecedent situation, human choices could be predicted with certainty.

---

[157] *On Selfhood and Godhood*, p. 174.
[158] *Ibid.* Cf. *Scepticism and Construction*, pp. 162–65. Like Reid, Campbell also points out that the causal indeterminacy which is part of his conception of free will is quite distinct from the indeterminism of chance. On this point, see Ch. 9, pp. 296 ff., *supra*.
[159] *Experimental Psychology*, pp. 438–39.

But, Hawkins maintains, "there is no ground at all for making such assertions. Indeed, it is notoriously more difficult to arrive at generalizations about human behavior than about physical events, and generalizations about human behavior seem on the face of them to be approximate." This difference "between the physical and the human sciences is," in Hawkins' opinion, "a consideration in favor of the freedom of the will."[160]

In addition to the foregoing, it must also be recalled that such authors as Capek, Weiss, and Hartshorne affirm the predictability of future events in a way and to an extent which they maintain is quite compatible with causal indeterminacy and freedom. The same holds true of such authors as Renouvier, Bergson, Maritain, and Simon. In short, none of the writers whom we have treated so far see any challenge to their position in the acknowledged fact of scientific prediction or in any assertion of predictability, even in the field of human behavior, which does not claim completeness and certitude. The writers to whom we now turn take a somewhat different approach to the matter.

These writers—Barrett, Ewing, Cranston, and Popper—cannot be construed as defending the libertarian position, or as offering positive arguments for causal indeterminacy and free choice. They content themselves with raising difficulties which they think that determinists cannot answer. To this extent, at least, they give aid and comfort to the opponents of determinism.

According to Barrett, the truth of determinism cannot be asserted without claiming that theoretical predictability obtains universally. "For determinism," he writes, "predictability in general is not enough; it has to assert (and prove, if it can) predictability down to the last detail—lock, stock, and barrel, and even down to the last scratch on the barrel. Anything less than this, and the thesis of determinism must crumble."[161] But the assertion about predictability which the determinist cannot help making, goes too far, Barrett maintains, certainly far beyond anything which has been proved. He questions the extent of predictability in four specific fields—mathematics, physics, artistic and intellectual creation, and history —in the light of the contingencies met with in those fields. And he concludes by saying that he does not regard the considerations he has adduced as proof, but "only as a reminder to the determinist that the spheres in which determinism has so far been established are restricted." Of all the

---

160 "Free Will and Right Action," in *The Modern Schoolman*, Vol. XXVI, No. 4, pp. 290–91. Again, like Reid and Campbell, Hawkins charges his opponents with erroneously identifying "freedom with caprice." They hold, he says, "an undetermined choice . . . to be equivalent to an unmotivated choice, and consequently a free volition is thought to be an unintelligible caprice which would have no relation to the character of the agent. . . . Thus Hume identifies liberty with chance" (*ibid.*, p. 291).
161 "Determinism and Novelty," in *Determinism and Freedom*, p. 32.

objections to determinism, he thinks that "the simplest, most direct, and . . . most overriding objection" is "that as a total thesis determinism simply remains to be proved."[162]

In Ewing's opinion, "the proposition that every event is predictable before it happens" means that

> all characteristics of the event predicted would have to be inferable from characteristics of events which had already occurred and of actually existing things.

He points out that, "on the libertarian view" this is, of course, "impossible in the case of free acts."[163] Without defending the libertarian view, Ewing then argues for a less radical indeterminism and against traditional determinism. If we look at a man's character "as a set of laws determining his actions," then, "on the ordinary determinist view these laws would be deducible from more general psychological and physical laws as applied to the particular circumstances determining the origin and development of the individual man in question." But, on the indeterminist view he is proposing, Ewing maintains that "they would not be thus deducible."[164] He writes:

> Though a man's act would theoretically be deducible from the laws together with his antecedents in the sense that propositions specifying them would follow logically from these and could be deduced if we knew them, the laws could never be known in advance of the acts to which they applied, because they are not deducible from any other laws, and therefore the prediction could never be effected at all. The last part does not specify a merely human limitation such as the most rigid determinist would have to admit, but something, on this view, intrinsically impossible for any mind.[165]

Cranston goes further than Ewing and Barrett, for he tells us that his views on prediction and predictability lead him to "end on the side of the libertarian against the determinist." As he sees it,

> the theory of the freedom of the will is not dogmatic, as determinism is. The libertarian theory admits 'a large measure of determinism' in the sense that it admits a large measure of predictability. Determinism can admit nothing of the libertarian claim, since it upholds total and comprehensive predictability.[166]

[162] *Ibid.*, p. 39.
[163] "Indeterminism," in *The Review of Metaphysics*, Vol. V, No. 2 p. 217.
[164] *Ibid.*, p. 220.
[165] *Ibid.*, p. 221. "I must admit," Ewing adds, that this view "does not go far enough completely to satisfy the indeterminist [i.e., the libertarian], for it does not leave it possible for us ever to have acted differently, our character and circumstances being what they are" (*ibid.*).
[166] *Freedom, A New Analysis*, p. 169.

In Cranston's opinion, "there is nothing sinister in the hospitality which libertarianism affords to a large measure of predictability . . . for no intelligent advocate of the freedom of the will has thought he could dispense with causal explanation altogether. . . . Certainly the libertarian cannot be said to deny that actions have motives or to imply that all actions are capricious."[167] Nevertheless, Cranston thinks that the libertarian case cannot be established by positive proofs.[168] While he concludes by saying that there is a "residual uncertainty as to whether the libertarian case holds good," he also says that "the weight of the argument is strongly against determinism."[169]

Karl G. Popper also makes a case for indeterminism without committing himself to libertarianism. He argues that classical mechanics as well as quantum physics is inconsistent with determinism, if determinism is taken to imply that all future events are predictable. Because of the well-known difficulty of determining simultaneously the position and momentum of a particle, quantum physics "implies that, however full and precise the initial information obtained, and however well isolated the system in question, there are certain physical events which cannot be predicted, although it is possible to predict the frequency of their occurrence under like conditions."[170]

More unusual is Popper's contention that classical mechanics is also inconsistent with a determinism calling for complete predictability. The central phase of his argument is to the effect that a calculator, by transmitting information about its own state, is apt to alter this state so much as to falsify the prediction based on this information. Self-information is thus incomplete. If there are two calculating machines C and C+, C could of course get information about its own states from C+, but the trouble here is that "C's state is strongly interfered with if it is given any information by C+."[171] But could not C+ foresee this interference and make allowance? This is apparently impossible, for the self-information C can furnish about its states will not be complete enough to permit the corrected predictions. "C's self-information of its state at t_1, in order to be correct and up to date, would have to contain, as one of its parts, a physical description of that very self-information."[172] This cannot be done. The calculator cannot predict future events which are too close to the present, because the interval of time required for the necessary calculations will

[167] *Ibid.*
[168] *Ibid.*, p. 170.
[169] *Ibid.*, p. 172.
[170] "Indeterminism in Quantum Physics and in Classical Physics," in *The British Journal of the Philosophy of Science*, Vol. I, No. 2, p. 127.
[171] *Ibid.*, Vol. I, No. 3, p. 190.
[172] *Ibid.*

sometimes be greater than the interval which separates these events from the present.

A number of other writers—Peirce, James, and Schiller—call attention to the fact that the determinist's principle of the uniformity of nature is only a postulate or assumption, and one that, while useful in science, does not need to be treated as having universal application.

Commenting on the proposition "that every fact in the universe is precisely determined by law," which is advanced as a " 'presupposition' or postulate of scientific reasoning," Peirce expresses doubt as to its validity and questions the notion that science depends upon our making this unlimited assumption.

> To say, for instance, that the demonstration by Archimedes of the property of the lever would fall to the ground if men were endowed with free will is extravagant; yet this is implied by those who make a proposition incompatible with the freedom of the will the postulate of all inference.[173]

According to James,

> the most that any argument can do for determinism is to make it a clear and seductive conception, which a man is foolish not to espouse, so long as he stands by the great scientific postulate that the world must be one great unbroken fact and that prediction of all things without exception must be ideally, even if not actually, possible.[174]

Over against this scientific postulate, James sets what he calls the "moral postulate" that ought implies can, i.e., that men are free to choose between duty and contrary desires. Confronted with the conflicting postulates of necessity and freedom, James writes:

> When scientific and moral postulates war thus with each other and objective proof is not to be had, the only course is voluntary choice, for scepticism itself, if systematic, is also voluntary choice. If, meanwhile, the will *be* undetermined, it would seem only fitting that the belief in its indetermination should be voluntarily chosen from amongst other possible beliefs. Freedom's first deed should be to affirm itself.[175]

---

[173] *Collected Papers*, Vol. VI, p. 31. In this connection, see *ibid.*, p. 108, where Peirce writes: "No mental action seems to be necessary or invariable in its character. . . . The truth is, the mind is not subject to 'law' in the same rigid sense that matter is. It only experiences gentle forces which merely render it more likely to act in a given way than it otherwise would. . . ."

[174] *Principles of Psychology*, Vol. II, p. 573.

[175] *Ibid.*, p. 573. Cf. *Collected Essays*, pp. 32–35, where James expresses his indebtedness to Renouvier for this approach to the problem. In the essay on Bain and Renouvier, which was written in 1876, James also says: "The argumentation of Bain that as a matter of fact men always do expect each other to act with predictable uniformity is —*sit venia verbo*—rubbish" (*op. cit.*, p. 31).

In addition to stressing the fact that a conflict of postulates demands a
choice on our part, whether that is a choice in favor of necessity or in favor
of freedom, James points out that the postulate of necessity—of uniformity
and theoretical predictability—need not be extended in its application
beyond those fields of science in which it works usefully. Science, he
declares,

> must be constantly reminded that her purposes are not the only purposes
> and that the order of uniform causation which she has use for, and is
> therefore right in postulating, may be enveloped in a wider order, on which
> she has no claims at all.[176]

F. C. S. Schiller's treatment of the conflict between "the Scientific
Postulate of Determinism and the Ethical Postulate of Freedom" is like
that of James.[177] Like James, too, he acknowledges the usefulness to
science of the postulate of determinism, while at the same time insisting
that it must not be extended beyond the sphere of its usefulness.

> Determinism, clearly, cannot and ought not to give up its status as a scien-
> tific principle. We cannot renounce the right of looking for a determinate
> connexion between events, for that is the deepest postulate of scientific
> method. But we need not claim for it absolute and ultimate validity. It
> is enough if we are entitled always to treat events *as if* they were determined,
> and if that treatment is true enough to the facts to be useful.[178]

Other writers make the same point. Saying that the "fruitfulness of science
(as contrasted with its theoretical validation) depends not on the supposition of necessity but on that of uniformity," MacLagan adds:

> And, as regards uniformity even, [it requires] not that it should be unbroken
> but only that it should not be broken too much . . . The uniformity comes
> nowhere near precluding, and there is no possibility that it ever will be
> found to preclude, that degree of "looseness" in the sequences of history
> that moral decisions involve.[179]

Similarly, Meyerson maintains that "to suppose the existence of free
phenomena entirely detached from the domination of law and from our
prevision in no way assails the principles of science"; for, to the extent that
science limits "its activity to what is capable of being foreseen," it is not
affected by what it itself omits from the domain of its investigations.[180]

---

[176] *Principles of Psychology*, Vol. II, p. 576.
[177] See *Studies in Humanism*, pp. 394 ff.; and cf. *The Riddle of the Sphinx*, Appendix
1 on Free Will and Necessity, pp. 439 ff.
[178] *The Riddle of the Sphinx*, Appendix II on Choice, p. 457.
[179] "Freedom of the Will," in *Proceedings of the Aristotelian Society*, Supplementary
Vol. XXV, p. 200.
[180] *Identity and Reality*, p. 26. See also Aveling, *Personality and Will*, p. 204; Maher,
Psychology, p. 420.

THE SIGNIFICANCE OF INDETERMINACY IN QUANTUM PHYSICS

The "uncertainty principle" or "principle of indeterminacy," which was formulated by Heisenberg in sub-atomic physics, has occasioned two divisions of opinion among physicists and philosophical commentators on physics.

One is the difference between those, on the one hand, who think that the Heisenberg principle should be interpreted as asserting a real or objective indeterminacy in sub-atomic phenomena and those, on the other hand, who think that it merely points to a subjective uncertainty which cannot be overcome because of insuperable difficulties in measuring the phenomena.

The first group holds the view that the causal determinism of classical or Newtonian mechanics is no longer universally valid. As Heisenberg puts it, "Pure determinism had to be abandoned"; "atomic physics has moved ever further away from the concept of determinism."[181] The reason for this abandonment, Louis de Broglie tells us, is that

we can never assume that both the position and the initial momentum of a corpuscle are known simultaneously.[182]

Through this principle of indeterminacy "nature . . . provides that knowledge of one-half of the world will ensure ignorance of the other half."[183] Other writers affirm the reality of the indeterminacy thus indicated.[184]

The second group holds the view that the principle of strict causality and causal determinism still applies to all events in nature. In a letter to Max Born, Einstein charges him with believing in a "dice-playing god." Einstein himself declares his belief "in the perfect rule of law." He contends that even "the great initial success of quantum theory cannot convert him to believe in that fundamental game of dice."[185] A similar view is voiced by Max Planck who maintains that he has "not been able to find the slightest reason, up to now, which would force us to give up the assumption

---

[181] *The Physicist's Conception of Nature*, pp. 39 and 49.
[182] *Matter and Light*, p. 246.
[183] A. S. Eddington, *The Nature of the Physical World*, p. 308.
[184] See Bohr, "On the Notions of Causality and Complementarity," in *Science*, January 20, 1950, Vol. 111, No. 2873, pp. 51–54; Born, *Natural Philosophy of Cause and Chance*, pp. 126–27; Bridgman, "Determinism in Modern Science," in *Determinism and Freedom*, pp. 43–63; Margenau, *The Nature of Physical Reality*, pp. 321–23, 362–63, 387. See also Karl Popper, whose view was discussed on pp. 384–85, *supra*.
[185] Cited in Born, *Natural Philosophy of Cause and Chance*, p. 122.

of a strictly law-governed universe."[186] Referring to the disagreement among the scientists, Brand Blanshard concludes "with much hesitation" that the new physics "provides no good evidence for indeterminism . . . in the physical world."[187]

It would seem that this second group of authors must deny that the will is free. For the most part we do find this expected denial. An exception, however, is Planck who affirms freedom of choice, on the ground that the action of the will can be viewed in two ways:

> In other words, we might say that looked at from outside (objectively) the will is causally determined and that looked at from inside (subjectively) it is free.[188]

The first group of authors, since they abandon the causal determinism of classical or Newtonian mechanics, also repudiate the LaPlacean ideal of the theoretical predictability of all events. It is this ideal, as we have seen, which is employed in the argument against causal indeterminacy in general and against human freedom of choice in particular. But though the indeterminacy of quantum mechanics precludes the "LaPlacean argument" *against* free will, there is a division of opinion as to whether it constitutes positive evidence *for* human freedom of choice.

Eddington, for example, is emphatic in saying that it does. We have quoted him extensively in Volume I; here we only summarize. "If we wish to emancipate mind"—namely from determinism—"we must to some extent emancipate the material world also." The new indeterminism of quantum theory provides this emancipation. In order to explain volition we must

> attribute to the mind power not only to decide the behaviour of atoms individually but to affect systematically large groups—in fact to tamper with the odds on atomic behaviour.

[186] *The New Science*, p. 58.
[187] "The Case for Determinism," in *Determinism and Freedom*, p. 7. A similar view is expressed by Ross, who agrees that it follows from quantum mechanics that the law of causality cannot be established inductively. Since, however, he "regards the law of causality as self-evident and needing no proof, inductive or of any other kind," his belief in strict causality is not shaken. See *The Foundations of Ethics*, pp. 217–18.
[188] *The New Science*, pp. 253–54. Planck's resolution of the conflict between necessity and freedom by finding each valid from a certain point of view resembles Bohr's "principle of complementarity" as a way of affirming incompatible formulations in atomic physics. See Planck's *Scientific Autobiography*, pp. 69–75. Bohr himself does not make use of the principle of complementarity to affirm free will; nor, according to Phillipp Frank, would such use of the principle be justified. See *Modern Science and Its Philosophy*, pp. 165 ff.

This admission, Eddington concedes, "involves a genuine physical difference between inorganic and organic (or, at any rate, conscious) matter." He adds that he "would prefer to avoid this hypothesis, but it is necessary to face the issue squarely."[189]

Most of those who believe that indeterminism is implied by quantum mechanics, however, do not claim that it constitutes an argument for freedom of the will. Stebbing takes direct issue with Eddington. She refers to his admission that inorganic and organic matter behave differently.

> This cleavage may not do 'violence to physics' but it seems to me to leave the problem of free will just where it was before physicists became indeterminists.[190]

And she adds, a few lines later,

> I cannot help thinking that Eddington is on the wrong track in trying to rest any part of the case for the freedom of man upon the present acceptance of indeterminism in physics.[191]

The fact that Planck, a determinist, and Eddington, an indeterminist, both affirm human freedom of choice, Stebbing thinks indicates that this problem is not susceptible to resolution by scientific evidence. "Scientific theories may in part guide but cannot decide our philosophies."[192]

Other writers, such as Cassirer, Born, Shrödinger, Margenau, Maritain, Yves Simon, P. Frank, Kelsen, and Blanshard, agree with Stebbing against Eddington. They maintain that quantum indeterminacy and statistical laws do not provide any grounds whatsoever for affirming freedom of choice.[193]

---

[189] *The Nature of the Physical World*, pp. 310, 313. Cf. Vol. I, pp. 461–63.
[190] *Philosophy and the Physicists*, p. 216.
[191] *Ibid.*
[192] *Ibid.*, p. 221.
[193] The views of Cassirer, Born, and Shrödinger are reported in Vol. I, pp. 461–66. For the views of the others mentioned above, see Blanshard, "The Case for Determinism," in *Determinism and Freedom*, pp. 9–10; Frank, *Philosophy of Science*, pp. 249–59; Kelsen, *What is Justice?*, pp. 340–45; Margenau, "Physical Versus Historical Reality," in *Readings in the Philosophy of Science*, pp. 567–69; Maritain, *Degree of Knowledge*, 2nd edition, p. 189; Simon, *Trávaux d' Approche pour une Théorie du Déterminisme.*

4. THE DISPUTE ABOUT MOTIVES AND CHOICE

In the preceding chapter, where we dealt with the issue concerning causal initiative, we distinguished two disputes: one in which the attack on causal initiative appealed to the universal principle of causation, and one in which the denial of causal initiative rested on a psychological analysis of how volitions are caused. We pointed out that the second of these attacks made a specific application of the general principle employed in the first. Where the first argued that every volition is the effect of a cause which is itself the effect of antecedent causes, the second argued that volitions are caused by motives which, in turn, are caused by the individual's character in reaction to present circumstances.[194]

Here, in the debate of the issue concerning causal indeterminacy, we find two disputes that are similarly related. One is the dispute considered in Section 2, in which the attack on causal indeterminacy is based on a general theory of causation, a theory that interprets the cause-and-effect relation as a necessary connection.[195] The other dispute, to be considered in this section, applies that theory of causation in explaining how an individual's character and desires, judgments or motives, determine his choices.

The argument takes three closely related forms. All of them reach the same conclusion: that, under a given set of conditions, a man is able to make only one choice. He cannot choose otherwise under those conditions, though he might have chosen otherwise had the conditions been different, i.e., had his motives, his desires, his character, or the circumstances been different.

One form of the argument asserts that men always choose with an eye to what is best for them, or what is better rather than worse. They naturally seek the good and whatever they will they necessarily will under the aspect of the good. Confronted with conflicting objects or alternatives that solicit or motivate their will, they always choose that which appears best or most desirable to them. In each case, the choice they make is necessitated by the object which has, in their judgment, paramount goodness or desirability. The judgment they make of the alternatives will itself be determined by their character. Hence, being what they are, they could not have

194 See Ch. 9, pp. 287 ff., *supra.*
195 The fundamental premise, we saw, took one of three forms: (i) sufficient causes cannot fail to produce their effects; (ii) all causes necessitate their effects; (iii) given the same cause, or set of causes, the same effect always follows. See pp. 343–44, *supra.*

chosen otherwise, for they could not have judged otherwise with regard to the objects or alternatives confronting them.

A second form of the argument asserts that a man's desires determine his choices. When only one desire is present and operative, a man has no deliberative choice at all: he simply wills that which he desires. But when several desires conflict, a process of deliberation may occur in which competing desires are represented. That process ends when the strongest desire predominates over the rest and determines the choice. What makes one desire strongest at a given moment and in relation to these circumstances is to be accounted for by the whole history of the individual. Hence, constituted as he is, the individual could not have chosen otherwise in any particular case, for no other desire could have prevailed to determine his choice.

A third form of the argument asserts that motives are related to acts of choice as causes are to effects. Just as the same causes will always produce the same effects, so, too, the same motives will always determine the making of the same choices, given the same circumstances. What a man's controlling motive is in a particular case is itself determined by his character in relation to the circumstances of that case. Hence, given his character, the circumstances of the case, and the motive to which these give rise, the choice he makes is necessitated. In that case, he could not have chosen otherwise. Were the elements of the case different, his choice would have been different, though no less necessarily determined by the altered elements.

There are some minor variations on the argument summarized above; and, in the case of two of its three forms, there are some elaborations of it, introducing considerations not mentioned above. We will note these when we come presently to the actual expression of reasons or grounds given for denying that a man could ever have chosen otherwise than the way he did in fact choose under a given set of conditions.

The foregoing argument in its three forms, together with their variations and elaborations, constitutes the first phase in this dispute. The second phase consists of the responses it elicits from authors who affirm free choice and the causal indeterminacy involved in it. Here we shall also present the psychological analysis of the act of choice by authors who hold that choice is free, i.e., that it could have been otherwise under identical conditions.

The argument is advanced in its first form by the "objector" whom Aquinas undertakes to answer, and also by Priestley and Holbach. It is advanced in its second form by Hobbes, Edwards, Voltaire, J. S. Mill, Nietzsche, and Bain; and in its third form by Hume, Priestley, Ross, Alexander, and Nowell-Smith.

(i) In the *Summa Theologica*, the "objector" argues as follows: "If two or more things are available, of which one appears to be more desirable, it is impossible to choose any of the others. Therefore that which appears to be best is chosen of necessity. But every act of choosing is in regard to something that seems in some way better. Therefore every choice is made necessarily."[196]

This argument is supported by a number of other considerations to which attention is called in other objections. It is pointed out that "the will tends of necessity to the good which is proposed to it."[197] It is also pointed out that since all men seek happiness as their ultimate end, "each man necessarily wills to be happy." But "just as the end is the object of the will, so also is that which is a means toward this end. . . . If, therefore, the will is moved by necessity toward the end, it seems that it is also moved by necessity toward that which is a means to the end."[198]

Taken together, these objections amount to saying that the will is necessitated in all its acts, since the object of the will is either the ultimate end, happiness, or some means to it. The reason why the will has no freedom of choice at all is the one stated in the first objection cited. No one is free to choose between what he deems to be his happiness and something contrary to it. And, willing necessarily whatever he deems to be his happiness, a man also necessarily wills that which appears to him to be the best means of achieving it.

The argument as stated does not consider what makes one thing appear to be best, or better than another. It is tacitly assumed that the way things

---

[196] *Op. cit.*, Part I–II, Q. 13, A. 6, Objection 3.

[197] *Ibid.*, Part I, Q. 82, A. 2, Objection 1. *De Malo*, Q. 6, A. 1, Objection 6, where it is said: "The object of the will is the good. Therefore the will cannot will anything except the good. Hence it wills the good from necessity and does not have free choice of either good or bad." See also *Truth*, Vol. III, Q. 22, A. 5, Objections 12, 13, pp. 50–51.

[198] *De Malo*, Q. 6, A. 1, Objection 8. Cf. *Summa Theologica*, Part I–II, Q. 10, A. 2, Objection 3 and Q. 13, A. 6, Objection 1. See also *Truth*, Vol. III, Q. 22, A. 5, Objections 1, 11, pp. 48–49; and Q. 24, A. 1, Objection 20, p. 136.

appear to a man is determined by his character, his state of mind, his past experience. That being so, no man can choose otherwise among things than as they appear to him to be better and worse.

Priestley presents the whole argument in the following manner.

> Man is a being of such a make, that when certain things, two kinds of fruit, for instance, are proposed to him, they become the objects of desire in different degrees, according to his experience of their different qualities, their wholesomeness, the pleasure they give to his taste, and various other considerations. As the *desirableness*, in this case, is complex, and the impression that each circumstance belonging to it makes upon the mind is also various, depending upon the momentary state of it, the presence or absence of other ideas, etc., it is possible that the comparative desirableness of the two fruits may vary much in a short space of time, sometimes the one, and sometimes the other, having the ascendant. But, provided the man were obliged to make a choice at any one moment of time, it will not be denied that he would certainly choose that which appeared to him, for that moment, the more desirable.

And, Priestley adds, "There is always some *reason* for any object appearing desirable or preferable: a reason existing either in a man's own *previous disposition of mind*, or in his *idea of the things* proposed to him."[199] This reason is what Priestley calls the controlling motive in the case, i.e., the motive which determines and necessitates the choice he makes between the objects before him.[200] Since the reason why a man regards one thing as more desirable than another is determined by his character and his state of mind in reaction to present circumstances, and since that reason is the motive which determines his choice in the present case, he could not have chosen otherwise than he did.

Holbach repeats the same argument in slightly different language. "Man, then, is not a free agent in any one instant of his life," he maintains.

> He is always guided necessarily by the real or fictitious advantages which he attaches to the objects which arouse his passions. These passions are necessary in a being who tends unceasingly toward his own happiness.[201]

And, Holbach continues, his action, "always being the effect of his will once determined, and as his will cannot be determined but by a motive which is not in his own power, it follows that he is never the master of the determination of his own peculiar will."[202] The motive which deter-

---

[199] *The Doctrine of Philosophical Necessity*, pp. 56–57.
[200] See *ibid.*, pp. 58–59.
[201] *The System of Nature*, p. 95.
[202] *Ibid.*, p. 92.

mines his choice "is always either the immediate or ultimate advantage he finds, or thinks he finds, in the action of which he is persuaded."[203]

An additional argument for the complete necessitation of the will i found among the objections which Aquinas raises. It is based on a comparison of the will and the intellect. The intellect, it is said, cannot but assent to that which appears to be true. But the good stands to the will as the true stands to the intellect. Hence, if the intellect is necessitated in its judgments, so is the will in its volitions. Furthermore, the "objector" calls attention to the similarity of intellect and will, in that each "is a power separate from matter." In view of this, the fact that "the intellect is moved with necessity by its object: for man is forced with necessity to assent to any truth," leads him to conclude that "by the same reason the will is also necessarily moved by its object."[204]

Again, we find Priestley restating the same argument. "Another argument for the necessary determination of the will," he writes, "may be drawn from the analogy it bears to the *judgment*. It is universally acknowledged," he continues,

> that the judgment is necessarily determined by the perceived agreement or disagreement of ideas. Now the *will* is but a kind of judgment, depending upon the perceived *preferableness* of things proposed to the mind, which apparent preferableness results as necessarily from the perception of the ideas themselves. . . . The faculties of the mind, as the ancients have well observed, are only different modes in which the same principle acts; the judgment being the *mind judging,* and the will the *mind willing;* and it would be very extraordinary, indeed, if the same mind should not be determined in a *similar manner* in these two very similar cases.[205]

This leads Priestley to conclude that the will is "necessarily determined by the circumstances the mind is in."[206]

There is one further argument, advanced by the "objector" in *De Malo,* which is not to be found in Priestley. It relates to the special char-

[203] *Ibid.,* p. 91.
[204] *De Malo,* Q. 6, A. 1, Objection 10. Cf. *ibid.,* Objection 12; and see also *Summa Theologica,* Part I–II, Q. 10, A. 2, Objections 1 and 2; *Truth,* Vol. III, Q. 22, A. 5, Objections 3, 8, 9, 10, pp. 49–50; *ibid.,* Q. 24, A. 1, Objection 18, p. 136.
[205] *The Doctrine of Philosophical Necessity,* pp. 43–44.
[206] *Ibid.,* p. 45. Cf. Ross, *Foundation of Ethics,* p. 223: "We certainly cannot choose what conclusion we shall draw from the premises; if we see their truth and notice their relevance to one another we cannot but see the truth which by the laws of logic follows from them. It is only acts where *choice* is involved that can with any plausibility be said to escape the law of causation. And while there might conceivably be some plausibility in making the law of causation apply to all physical and to no mental events, it is very unplausible to make it apply to all physical and some mental but not to other mental events."

acter of the will as an active power. For the will to be able to choose either one of two conflicting alternatives, it would have to be disposed to contraries. But, the objection points out, if the will, which is an active power, were simultaneously disposed toward contraries, "two opposites would be simultaneously, which is impossible. Therefore, it is not disposed to opposites, but of necessity is determined to one."[207]

(ii) The classical statement of the second form of the argument that the act of choice is always necessitated occurs in Hobbes's analysis of volition. The will, for Hobbes, is nothing but a name for particular acts of desire. To say that a man wills this or that is to say no more than that he desires it. The volition to perform a certain action is nothing but the desire to do it. Now action is sometimes preceded by what is called deliberation and choice, sometimes not. Deliberation occurs when competing desires vie with one another for the control of action. What terminates deliberation is the predominance of one desire over all the rest. We do not choose between the competing desires; on the contrary, the desire which is strongest and which prevails over all the others determines our action. And it is that desire or volition which we refer to as a choice on our part simply because it terminates a process of deliberation in which conflicting desires were present.

Actually, the cause of our action is the same whether we deliberate or not: it is always the dominant desire that determines how we act, whether that dominant desire is the only one present or is that one of several which happens to prevail over the others, because it is the strongest. What makes one desire prevail over the others on a particular occasion is, of course, the totality of antecedents in the life of an individual, including his inherited nature or temperament, his experiences, his habits, and so on. The individual being what he is, he can never choose otherwise than as he does under particular circumstances; for, under those circumstances, his action is determined by that one desire which his whole past causes to become dominant at the moment.[208]

Those who follow Hobbes usually epitomize this analysis in brief statements to the effect that our choices are always determined by the strongest desire of the moment, or that they are always determined by the predominant influence of the moment, or that the strongest desire or motive decides for us what we shall do.

Thus, Jonathan Edwards remarks that "there is no great difficulty in shewing . . . that the mind must be influenced in its choice by something

[207] *Op. cit.*, Q. 6, A. 1, Objection 16. Cf. *ibid.*, Objection 19.
[208] See *Leviathan*, pp. 39–41, 46–47, 162.

that has a preponderating influence upon it."[209] That, of course, is th
dominant motive of the moment; and when conflicting motives compete
for dominance, Edwards goes on to say, we cannot choose which one wil
prevail. That is determined for us by our own particular past as it emerge
in our present state of mind.[210]

Voltaire presents the same argument in the following concrete form:

> It is proposed to you that you mount a horse, you must absolutely make
> a choice, for it is quite clear that you either will go or that you will not go.
> There is no middle way. It is therefore of absolute necessity that you wish
> yes or no. Up to there it is demonstrated that the will is not free. You
> wish to mount the horse; why? The reason, an ignoramus will say, is be-
> cause I wish it. This answer is idiotic; nothing happens or can happen with-
> out a reason, a cause; there is one therefore for your wish. What is it?
> the agreeable idea of going on horseback which presents itself in your brain,
> the dominant idea, the determinant idea. But, you will say, can I not resist
> an idea which dominates me? No, for what could be the cause of your
> resistance? None. By your will you can obey only an idea which will
> dominate you more.
>
> Now you receive all your ideas; therefore you receive your wish, you wish
> therefore necessarily.[211]

And Nietzsche summarizes the argument in his observation that though
we talk of "soul-struggles . . . in which one is torn this way and that by
contending motives until one finally decides in favor of the strongest,"
the fact is that "it is the strongest motive that decides for us."[212]

To those who say that we are sometimes conscious of being able to act
against strong desires, even the strongest, J. S. Mill replies:

> I . . . dispute altogether that we are conscious of being able to act in
> opposition to the strongest present desire or aversion. The difference be-
> tween a bad and a good man is not that the latter acts in opposition to his
> strongest desires; it is that his desire to do right, and his aversion to doing
> wrong, are strong enough to overcome, and in the case of perfect virtue, to
> silence, any other desire or aversion which may conflict with them.[213]

In short, Mill rejects entirely the supposition, which he attributes to the
libertarians, that we have an "ability to will in opposition to our strongest

[209] *Freedom of the Will*, p. 198.
[210] *Ibid.*, pp. 225–27, 304–5. See also *ibid.*, pp. 203–12, where Edwards argues
against the possibility of a state of indifference, in which motives are equally
balanced and call upon us to give predominance to one.
[211] *Philosophical Dictionary*, pp. 142–43. Cf. *ibid.*, pp. 187–90.
[212] *Human, All Too Human*, p. 133.
[213] *Examination of Sir William Hamilton's Philosophy*, p. 585.

reference."[214] And in another place he connects this account of volition with the general theory of causal necessity by saying that, "given the motives which are present to an individual's mind, and given likewise the character and disposition of the individual, the manner in which he will act may be unerringly inferred: that if we know the person thoroughly, and knew all the inducements which are acting upon him we could foretell his conduct with as much certainty as we can predict any physical event."[215] Arguing in the same way, Bain declares that "various motives— present or prospective pleasures and pains—concur in urging me to act; the result of the conflict shows that one group is stronger than another, and that is the whole case."[216] In Bain's view, to speak of man's self-determining power is "merely another, and not a good, expression for the ordinary course of the will, as I understand it." He adds:

> If any acts can be pointed out as unconnected with motives, or antecedents, of the character that we have recognized throughout our inquiry into the will, the exception ought to be made good, and admitted as a new element of voluntary determination.[217]

But Bain denies that such acts can be found.

(iii) The third form of the argument introduces only a slight variation. It stresses the character of the individual, which has been formed by all the causal influences that have operated in his life. As shaped by his past, the individual's character reacts to present circumstances and produces his motives for acting in one way or another in response to them. The motive, if there is only one, or the strongest motive, if there are several, is, according to the argument, the cause of the individual's volition. Hence, the argument runs, given the character of the individual, the circumstances

[214] *Ibid.*, p. 586. Cf. *ibid.*, pp. 600–6, in which Mill comments on the contrary views of Mansel. He sums up his position by saying: "Even if the strongest motive meant only the motive which prevails, yet if there is a prevailing motive—if, all other antecedents being the same, the motive which prevails today will prevail to-morrow and every subsequent day—Sir W. Hamilton was acute enough to see that the free-will theory is not saved. I regret that I cannot, in this instance, credit Mr. Mansel with the same acuteness" (*ibid.*, p. 605).
[215] *A System of Logic*, p. 410. See also *ibid.*, pp. 410–16. Cf. also *Examination of Sir William Hamilton's Philosophy*, p. 583, where Mill says: "When we think of ourselves hypothetically as having acted otherwise than we did, we also suppose a difference in the antecedents: we picture ourselves as having known something that we did not know, or not having known something that we did know; which is a difference in the external inducements; or as having desired something or disliked something, more or less than we did; which is a difference in the internal inducements."
[216] *The Emotions and the Will*, p. 488. Cf. *ibid.*, pp. 408–11.
[217] *Ibid.*, p. 493; see also pp. 490–500.

of the present case, and the motive for action that results therefrom, the individual could not have chosen otherwise, for the same causes alway produce the same effects.

This form of the argument is to be found in Hume and Priestley. "No union can be more constant and certain," Hume declares, "than that of some actions with some motives and characters."[218] In the context of saying that "like causes produce like effects," Hume has no hesitancy in saying that he can "prove from experience that our actions have a constant union with our motives, tempers, and circumstances."[219] And in another place he maintains that "the conjunction between motives and voluntary actions is as regular and uniform as that between the cause and the effect in any part of nature."[220]

Like Hume, Priestley holds to the principle that the same causes always produce the same effects. To apply this principle to human behavior, and to conclude therefrom that the choices men make are necessitated, we need only see that a man's character and motives are the causes of his volitions—his choices or decisions. "Whenever any person makes a choice, or comes to any resolution," Priestley writes, "there are two circumstances which are evidently concerned in it." One is his character or "what we call the *previous disposition of the mind*." The other is his reason or motive for deciding among the objects presented for choice, that is, his "*view of the objects* which the choice or resolution respects."[221]

Saying that "all volitions and actions are preceded by corresponding motives," Priestley then summarizes the argument as follows:

> In all *regular deliberations* concerning any choice, every reason or motive is distinctly attended to, and whatever appears to be the stronger, or the better reason, always determines us. In these cases, the *choice* and the *motive* correspond precisely to an *effect* and its *cause*. In cases that do not require a formal deliberation, i.e., in cases similar to those in which I have often determined before, the moment I perceive my situation, I determine instantly, without attending distinctly, as before, to all the motives or reasons. But this *instantaneous determination* cannot be said not to be produced by motives, because it is, in fact, only the same *mental process abridged.*[222]

Hence, Priestley concludes, "since every *deliberate choice* is regulated by motives, we ought, as philosophers, to take it for granted, that *every choice*

---

[218] *Treatise of Human Nature*, Book II, Part III, Sect. 1, p. 404.
[219] *Ibid.*, p. 401.
[220] *An Enquiry Concerning Human Understanding*, Sect. VIII, Part I, Div. 69, p. 88. "It seems almost impossible . . . to engage either in science or action of any kind," Hume writes, "without acknowledging the doctrine of necessity, and this *inference* from motive to voluntary actions, from characters to conduct" (*ibid.*, p. 90).
[221] *The Doctrine of Philosophical Necessity*, p. 36.
[222] *Ibid.*, p. 38.

s made in the same manner, and is subject to the same rules, and therefore
determined by motives."[223] Such determination "must be directed by
certain invariable laws, depending upon the previous state of mind, and
he ideas present to it at the moment of forming any resolution: so that,
in no case whatever, could they have been otherwise than they actually
were."[224]

With attention to what he calls the "free-will controversy," at least as it
s carried on by Locke, Kant, and Hegel, T. H. Green dismisses any
solution that regards "the will as independent of motives, as a power of
deciding between motives without any motive to determine the deci-
ion."[225] In his view,

> to ask whether a man has power over determinations of his will, or is
> free to will as he is to act, as the question is commonly understood . . .
> is to ask whether, the man being what at any time he is, it is still uncertain
> (1) whether he will choose or forbear choosing between certain possible
> courses of action, and (2) supposing him to choose one or other of them,
> which he will choose.

"We must admit," Green says, "that there is really no such uncertainty. The
appearance of it is due to our ignorance of the man and the circumstances."[226] And in another place Green asserts the truth of the proposition
that there is a necessary connexion between character and motive, and
between motive and act."[227] Hence, Green argues, "given the man and
his object as he and it at any time are, there is no possibility of the will
being determined except in one way, for the will is already determined,
being nothing else than the man as directed to some object."[228]

Ross repeats the same argument in slightly different language. "The
libertarian belief," he tells us, "is the belief that, the circumstances being
what they are, and I being what I am, with that whole system of beliefs,
desires, and dispositions which compose my nature, it is objectively possible
or me here and now to do either of two or more acts. This is *not*
possible," he maintains,

> because whatever act I do, it must be because there is in me, as I am now,
> a stronger impulse to do that act than to do any other.[229]

[23] *Ibid.*, p. 39.
[24] *Ibid.*, p. 53. Bray closely follows Priestley's line of reasoning. See *The Philosophy
f Necessity*, pp. 29–30.
[25] *Principles of Political Obligation*, p. 12.
[26] *Ibid.* Cf. pp. 12–14.
[27] *Prolegomena to Ethics*, p. 115.
[28] *Principles of Political Obligation*, p. 14.
[29] *Foundations of Ethics*, p. 230. "If my nature and condition and the circumstances are such and such," Ross declares, "I shall set myself to produce one
change; if they are different, I shall set myself to produce another" (*ibid.*, p. 234).

Among these impulses, Ross explains, may be "a desire to do one's duty adding that "duty is done when and only when that desire is strong than all those with which it has to contend."[230] But it is not one isolate desire vying with another that determines the choice we make in particular case. "What choice depends upon, and reveals," Ross maintain "is . . . the trend of the whole character, of the whole system of mo or less permanent desires, including of course the desire to do one duty."[231]

For Ross, as for Hume and Priestley, the whole argument hinges on th understanding of the law of causation, that the same causes always produc the same effects.[232] The causes of human behavior are a man's whol character and the desire or motive which emerges from his character dominant in the particular case. Hence, in a particular case, the caus conditions being what they are, only one action can take place, i.e., onl one effect can result from the given causes. I may, of course, not kno all these conditions, in which case I can say "that there are no existin conditions *known to me* with which my doing A is incompatible, an none with which my doing B is incompatible," where A and B a themselves contrary or incompatible courses of action. But "what th libertarian says," Ross points out, "is that *all* the conditions, known an unknown, are compatible with my doing the one action, and also wit my doing the other; and this cannot be true."[233]

A number of other writers—Alexander, Ducasse, Nowell-Smith—asse that a man's choice in a particular case is completely determined by wha

---

[230] *Ibid.*, pp. 227–28.

[231] *Ibid.*, p. 228. "In the deliberation which precedes choice," Ross writes, "w set ourselves, more or less thoroughly according to our character, to choose n between isolated objects of desire but between acts each of which is thought involve a whole set of consequences, and it is one act with all its expected cons quences that is chosen in preference to all others with all *their* expected co sequences. The choice is thus determined not by the strength of the isolated desir as they were before the process of deliberation, but by the strength of the appe which one act, with all that it is expected to involve, makes on us, as compare with the appeal which the alternatives make. Thus what is resolved on may b and often is, very different from what would have been done if deliberation an choice had not intervened" (*ibid.*).

[232] "The law may be formulated," Ross says, "in various ways." His way of form lating it is to say, "for every variation between two events, there must be som variation between the antecedent circumstances, without which the variation betwee the events would not have existed" (*ibid.*, pp. 213–14).

[233] *Ibid.*, p. 239. Similarly, Ross explains, there is the hypothetical sense in whic it is true to say that I can do this, *if I wish to*, and I can also do that, *if I wis to*; but this does not mean that, at the moment of action, I can do the opposit of what all the relevant causes make the stronger of the two wishes. See *ibid* pp. 240–43.

ever motive (or desire or preference) his character, in reaction to the circumstances of that case, causes to dominate or control his behavior.[234] These writers and others whom we have mentioned—Priestley and Ross —follow Hume in reinforcing this line of argument with one additional consideration, which they present in the form of a dilemma: *either* a man's choices and his chosen actions are causally determined by his character and motives *or* they are entirely matters of chance. Thus, for example, Ross says that a belief "in occasional or even in universal indeterminacy . . . is equivalent to a belief in blind chance";[235] Ducasse argues that "pure fortuity—absolute chance—is the only strict contradictory of complete determination";[236] and Nowell-Smith maintains that it is impossible for the libertarian to distinguish "a 'free' action from a random event."[237] F. H. Bradley must also be mentioned in this connection, for he, too, asserts that "freedom means chance" when "Free-will means Non-determinism."[238] The added force which this additional consideration gives to the main argument derives, of course, from the asserted impossibility or unreality of chance. Chance being non-existent, the dilemma must be resolved in favor of the first alternative, namely, that a man's choices and his chosen actions are causally determined by his character and motives, and determined in such a way that he cannot ever choose otherwise than as he does.

Second Phase

The arguments in defense of free choice, which concern themselves with the role played by a man's motives and character, involve two points which are sometimes combined and sometimes made separately.

(a) One is the proposition that the motives or reasons which a man has for the decisions he makes do not by themselves cause him to make

---

[234] See Alexander, *Moral Order and Progress*, pp. 336–41. "What motive is chosen," Alexander writes, "is perfectly fixed and dependent upon the character, which cannot choose otherwise than it does" (*ibid.*, p. 340). See also Ducasse, *Nature, Mind, and Death*, pp. 196, 203–4, 214; Nowell-Smith, "Determinists and Libertarians," in *Mind*, Vol. LXIII, No. 251, pp. 329–30, and *Ethics*, pp. 273–85.

[235] *Foundations of Ethics*, p. 223.

[236] *Nature, Mind, and Death*, p. 192. Cf. *ibid.*, p. 213.

[237] *Ethics*, p. 281.

[238] *Ethical Studies*, p. 11. "If we always can do anything, or nothing, under any circumstances, or merely if, of given alternatives, we can always choose either, then," Bradley says, "it is always possible that any act should come from any man. If there is 'no real, no rational connexion between the character and the actions . . . then, use any phrases we please, what it comes to is this, that volitions are contingent. In short, the irrational connexion, which the Free-will doctrine fled from in the shape of external necessity, it has succeeded only in reasserting in the shape of chance" (*ibid.*, pp. 11–12).

those decisions. This proposition is expressed in various ways: sometime by saying that the motives or reasons—the objects of choice or the judg ments of the mind concerning them—*occasion, but do not cause* choice and sometimes by saying that the objects of choice or the practical judg ments about them are only the *formal, not the efficient, causes* of choice.

(b) The other proposition is that the act of choice itself makes one motive stronger than another. Far from choice being determined by the dominant motive, it is the act of choice which, favoring one motive against others, gives it the strength to become dominant. Neither the objects of choice, nor the judgments which the mind makes about them, reflecting the past experience and character of the person, have in themselves the power to dictate the decision that shall be made with respect to them. That which appears best to a man, or most desirable, is that which he himself by choosing it, endows with the superior attractiveness it has for him in the particular case.

Each of these propositions by itself negates the central thesis advanced by the opponents of free choice. Taken together, they fully support the contrary thesis. The opposition of arguments and conclusions can be briefly sketched as follows.

If, on the one hand, a man's character, in reaction to the circumstances of a particular case, determines the dominant motive or desire of the moment, and if that, in turn, determines the course of action he chooses under these circumstances, then under these circumstances, the individual being what he is, could not have chosen otherwise. But if, on the other hand, motives do not causally determine acts of choice, or if it is the act of choice itself which makes one motive or desire dominant over others, then the self or will is not caused but free in choosing one motive over another. Thus, under the same circumstances and with the same character the individual could have chosen otherwise.

It must be noted that, for both sides of the dispute, the choice is motivated, not motiveless. Both say that a reason enters into the choice that is made. But according to the argument against freedom of choice, the motive produces the choice, as an efficient cause produces its effects given the same cause, the same effect necessarily follows. According to the argument for freedom of choice, the act of choice takes unto itself one of several competing motives or reasons, and by causing which of these shall prevail, it determines itself and thus is free.

Hence, the latter argument concludes, while a man's character may deter mine the various motives or reasons which will occur to him under the circumstances of a particular case, it is his own choice that determines which motive or reason shall prevail; and so, with a given character and with the same set of competing motives for acting in a particular case, the

ndividual who in fact chooses to act in one way could have chosen to act
otherwise. The individual's self or will, which is the efficient cause of the
choice, has the power to produce any one of several alternative effects (i.e.,
different particular choices), all other causal influences being the same at
the moment of choice.

Once the choice is made, of course, one motive or reason is seen to
have predominated. Had a different choice been made, a different motive
or reason would have prevailed. The motive for the act which was chosen
is never the same as the motive for the act that might have been chosen
instead. But these different motives, together with different choices of
which they are the reasons, constitute the variety of possible effects which
it is within the power of the same cause to produce.

The argument for freedom of choice, outlined above, takes three forms,
all of which attempt to answer the argument from the opposite side, in
one or another of its forms: (i) a form which combines both the two
central propositions—(a) and (b)—stated above and which asserts them
in the context of an elaborate theory of the separate but related powers of
the intellect and the will, together with an analysis of their appropriate
objects, their natural tendencies, and their causal interaction;[239] (ii) a
form in which either (a) or (b) is stressed and the other is left unstated
but implied; here the theoretical underpinnings of the argument are
usually left implicit;[240] and (iii) a form which condenses (a) and (b)
into the single statement that the self acts independently of character and
motives in the making of moral choices; this form of the argument usually
includes a subsidiary point, to the effect that such free action by the self,
while quite contrary to the determinism of action caused by an individual's
character and motives, is also quite contrary to the indeterminism of
chance.[241]

In presenting evidence of the argument in its several forms, we shall
follow the order indicated above. In the course of this, we shall find explicit
attempts to meet the argument from the opposite side, on the part of
Aquinas in reply to objections he himself sets forth; on the part of Price
to the argument as stated by Priestley and thus also to the argument as
stated by Hume; on the part of Mansel to the argument as stated by Mill

[39] This form of the argument is to be found in Aquinas and in the school of
thought which includes many authors from his day to the present time. Echoes
of it are to be found in other writers who are not Thomists, such as Henry More,
Isaac Watts, A. E. Taylor, and Austin Farrer.

[40] This form of the argument is to be found in a large number of authors, from
Joseph Price, Thomas Reid, Henry Mansel, Herman Lotze, Charles Renouvier, and
Charles Secrétan, to Emile Boutroux, C. S. Peirce, Jean-Paul Sartre, and Paul
Weiss.

[41] This form of the argument is to be found in Immanuel Kant, James Martineau,
Bernard Bosanquet, Nikolai Lossky, and C. A. Campbell.

and thus also to the argument as stated by Hobbes; on the part of Gruende
and Rickaby, who are followers of Aquinas, to the argument as stated b
Jonathan Edwards and Mill and thus also to the argument as stated b
Hobbes; on the part of G. E. Hughes and G. C. Field to the argument a
stated by Ross and thus also to the argument as stated by Hume; and o
the part of C. A. Campbell to the argument as stated by Nowell-Smith

(i) The theory of the will and intellect, in terms of which Aquina
answers objections to freedom of choice and argues for it, has been sum
marized in other connections.[242] Of the points made in other context
those particularly germane to the present argument are the following.

(a) The will is the efficient cause of its own activity or inactivity a
well as of the activity or inactivity of other powers. Whether, on a give
occasion, we think or do not think about a certain object, look at it or not
move toward it or not, our doing so or not doing so is voluntary. So, too
on a given occasion, whether we exercise our will or refrain from exercisin
it—willing or not willing—is caused by the will.

(b) While, so far as its exercise is concerned, the intellect is moved b
the will in the manner of an efficient cause, the intellect also moves th
will in the manner of a formal cause. The will, by its very nature, tend
toward the good; but in its particular acts it tends toward the good a
apprehended by reason or intellect. The rational apprehension of some
thing as good takes the form of a practical judgment that something shoul
be sought or done. Where other writers talk about particular desires o
motives as the causes of volitions, Aquinas substitutes the practical judg
ment that something apprehended as good is desirable. Such judgment
provide the motives or reasons for acts of the will. But where other writer
say that the sole cause of a particular volition is the dominant motive of th
moment, Aquinas says that the practical judgment which prevails at th
moment of volition is only one of the causes of that volition. It i
the formal cause of the volition—that which specifies the act of will to b
the volition of the particular object judged good. Of that same volition
the efficient cause is the will itself, since, in regard to any object appre
hended as good by the intellect, the will causes itself to act or not to act.

(c) The will, by its natural inclination toward the good, is irresistibl
attracted only by that which is completely or perfectly good and is clearl
apprehended as such. To such an object, and to such alone, it adheres o
necessity: it cannot turn away. Confronted with an object that is appre
hended as not wholly good, but good only in part, the will need not adher
to it. It can turn away from any object that cannot be apprehended a

---

[242] In the present chapter, see pp. 355–59, *supra*. See also Ch. 9, pp. 266–67, 288–8g
supra. Cf. Vol. I, pp. 500–2.

completely good by virtue of its power to turn the attention of the mind to the respects in which the object lacks goodness. Hence, Aquinas argues that the will is indeterminately related to any object that is not perfectly good and apprehended as such: it can either adhere to it or turn away from it, according as it is apprehended in one way or another, i.e., as good in one respect or as lacking goodness in another.

The three foregoing points include the point that motives do not by themselves cause volitions and that they function only as formal, not efficient, causes of volitions. But this is only one of the two propositions which are central to Aquinas's defense of free choice against the various objections he himself considers. The other is the proposition that, when various motives or reasons occur in deliberation prior to choice, it is the act of choice itself which makes one motive stronger than others and makes it prevail as the formal cause of the decision that terminates deliberation. This proposition is crucial to Aquinas's answer to the objection which ran as follows:

> If two or more things are available, of which one appears to be more desirable, it is impossible to choose any of the others. Therefore that which appears to be best is chosen of necessity. But every act of choosing is in regard to something that seems in some way better. Therefore every choice is made necessarily.[243]

Aquinas admits that we always choose that which appears to be better or best when we are confronted with a number of objects, each of which is something less than perfectly good. So far, he agrees with the objector. But he does not admit that, therefore, every choice is made necessarily, because he does not admit that the judgment of one object as better than another, or best among several, is determined by our mind, as influenced by our past experience, our habitual desires, our character, *independently of our will.*

If that were so, then the choice among the objects would not be free, but completely determined and thus necessitated by whatever judgment the mind came to as a result of the causes operating on it. We should have to choose that which, independently of our will, appeared to be best, which is another way of saying that our choice would always be determined by the dominant motive or desire of the moment. But if it is our will that causes one thing to be judged better than another, or best, then our choice is not necessitated, for it could have been otherwise if we had willed to make a contrary judgment, i.e., to regard something else as better or best. In that case, one object is more attractive than another only

---

[243] *Summa Theologica*, Part I–II, Q. 13, A. 6, Objection 3.

because we choose to think of it that way; we do not choose it because w
cannot help thinking of it as more attractive.

In either case, we always choose that which we judge to be better or besⁱ
but the question is, which causes which? The choice the judgment, c
the judgment the choice? Aquinas's answer, as we have already seen, i
that each causes the other, but not in the same way. The act of choice i
the efficient cause of that particular judgment's being made. The judgment
simultaneously, is the formal cause of that very same act of choic
specifying what it is a choice of, i.e., giving it the object chosen and th
reason or motive for choosing it, namely, its being apprehended as goo
and judged better than the other alternatives which were considered.

What ground does Aquinas have for giving this answer? One part of it ha
just been indicated: the simultaneous interaction of intellect and will
operating on each other as causes, but as different kinds of causes. To thi
must be added the point that the will is the efficient cause of its ow
activity as well as of the intellect's being exercised, and the point tha
nothing except the complete or perfect good, clearly apprehended as such
attracts the will irresistibly. These three points, set forth in (a), (b), an
(c) above, constitute a large part of the argument, but, to complete it
two further points must be made.[244]

(d) When, voluntarily exercising our intellects, we think about some
thing, the judgment we form of it is sometimes determined by the objec
of thought, and sometimes not. It is thus determined when the proposition
being considered is *either* something necessarily true, the opposite of which
is impossible, *or* a conclusion which necessarily follows from premise
that are necessarily true. Confronted with such propositions, we ar
compelled to judge them true. We can choose to think about them or not
but if we choose to think about them, we cannot help assenting to them
We are powerless to think otherwise. Our thinking about them is voluntary
but what we think about them—whether we assent or dissent and asser
their opposites—is not. But when the proposition being considered i
contingently true, the opposite of which is also contingently true, our assen
is not necessitated or compelled by the object of our thought. If the objec
does not cause assent on our part, what does? Aquinas's answer is tha
where the intellect's assent is required, the intellect is moved to assen
either by its object (as it is in the case of what he calls "scientific knowl
edge") or by desire on the part of the will (as it is in the case of what he
calls "opinions"). When we affirm an opinion, we assent to something

[244] The textual documentation of the three points already made has been given
in earlier pages, as mentioned in fn. 240, p. 403, *supra*. However, the capital texts
can be cited again here. They are as follows: *Summa Theologica*, Part I, Q. 82
AA. 2, 5; Part I–II, Q. 9, AA. 1, 3; Q. 10, A. 2; Q. 13, A. 6; *De Malo*, Q. 6
A. 1; *Truth*, Vol. III, Q. 22, AA. 6, 12, pp. 56–60, 77–80.

which may or may not be true, because we wish to. We could have voluntarily made the opposite judgment. In this sense, an affirmed opinion is a *willful* or *arbitrary* judgment on the part of the intellect, because in that act of assent the intellect is moved by the will, not by its object.[245]

(e) Volitions are either of the end or of the means thereto. Only a good which is completely satisfying can be the end in an ultimate sense. The end is, therefore, the complete or perfect good. All particular goods, being partial and imperfect, are means. Since, according to Aquinas, choice is always of the means, choice is always concerned with particular goods. Furthermore, since a particular good is imperfect, it may be judged in opposite ways, either in respect of its goodness or in respect of its lacking goodness. Hence, the judgments we make about particular goods are like contingent propositions, which we can assert, or deny and assert the opposite. Which judgment we make is determined not by the object being considered, but by our will, according as we choose to think of the particular object as attractive or unattractive, or as more or less attractive than some other. The practical judgment about some particular action to be done or avoided, being itself voluntarily made (i.e., chosen), it follows that our choice is free; or, as it is sometimes said, the practical judgment which enters into a choice as its formal cause is a free or arbitrary judgment (*liberum arbitrium*), in that it is not caused by the object being considered, but by the will.

This becomes especially clear in cases where we deliberate about alternative means. During the process of deliberation, conflicting practical judgments are entertained (i.e., reasons or motives for contrary actions are considered). But no one of these judgments can prevail over the others by virtue of its evident truth, or by anything like a demonstration of its truth, for they are all judgments about particular goods and, as such, are like opinions. Hence, the only way deliberation can be terminated is by an act of the will, an act which causes one of the competing judgments as the one to prevail. It is this last practical judgment which then becomes the formal cause—the reason or motive—of the choice which we make between the several alternative objects or actions that we have been considering in the course of deliberation.[246]

With this last point, we complete Aquinas's argument for the proposition that it is the act of choice itself which makes one motive stronger than

---

[245] See *Summa Theologica*, Part I, Q. 82, A. 2; Part II–II, Q. 1, A. 4; Q. 2, AA. 1, 2. See also *Truth*, Vol. II, Q. 14, A. 1, pp. 207–13.
[246] See *Summa Theologica*, Part I–II, Q. 13, A. 3; Q. 14, AA. 2, 6; Q. 15, A. 3; Q. 17, AA. 5, 6. Cf. Maritain, *Scholasticism and Politics*, Ch. V, pp. 126–27; and Simon, *Traité du Libre Arbitre*, Ch. VII, pp. 104–10. See also de Finance, *Existence et Liberté*, p. 17.

others. Said another way, the object that appears to be most desirable is the one to which we voluntarily attach the greatest desire; for when we choose it in preference to others, by voluntarily judging it to be best, we endow it with the attractiveness of the end, toward the attainment of which we have chosen it as a means.[247] That choice is, therefore, free since it is within the power of our will to have chosen otherwise, given exactly the same circumstances, the same background of antecedents, the same habits of mind and of character. All of these do no more than produce the various and, perhaps, conflicting motives that may occur to us as we deliberate, no one of which can become the reason for our decision unless and until we choose to make it so.[248]

The argument, in its full statement, provides the basis for the answers to the other objections that Aquinas poses for himself.[249]

To the objection that the will tends of necessity to the good which is proposed to it, Aquinas replies:

> The will can tend to nothing except under the aspect of good. But because the good is of many kinds, for this reason the will is not of necessity determined to one.[250]

[247] See Maritain, *Scholasticism and Politics*, pp. 128–29: "In the act of freedom the will goes out to meet half-way an attraction which is incapable of quite reaching it by itself; and this is because the free act is a gratuitous answer, which has sprung forth from the very depths of the will, toward a powerless solicitation of a finite good." Cf. *Freedom in the Modern World*, pp. 7–10. See also Simon *Traité du Libre Arbitre*, Ch. VII, pp. 108–9: "To put one's happiness in a particular good is to give to a particular good the additional quantity of goodness it needs in order to make itself desirable, absolutely speaking, to the rational appetite. But from where do I draw the power of adding to the goodness of things, to their desirability? In technical language, I draw this power from my adherence to the universal essence of good. In more familiar language, the question would be: How does it happen that I can put my happiness where I will? and the answer: I can put my happiness where I will *because I will to be happy.* If it is true, in other words, that the will desires happiness necessarily, and if it is true that all concrete goods that are presented to it are particular goods mixed with non-goodness, then it follows that the voluntary agent has the power of putting his happiness where he pleases, or, what comes to the same thing, of adding to the desirability of a particular good to the point of making it into an absolutely desirable good."
[248] "To be free," Maritain writes, "means to be master of one's judgment. The will is master of the very judgment which determines it, and *thus* has full mastery of its own actions" (*Scholasticism and Politics*, p. 128). And in another place, he says: "The indetermination which is identical with free will is . . . an *active and dominating* indetermination. It consists in *the mastering by the will of the practical judgment which determines it*" (*ibid.*, p. 125). It is in this context also that Maritain observes "in what sense it is correct to say with M. Bergson . . . that 'our motives are what we make them' " (*ibid.*, p. 128). Cf. Simon, *Traité du Libre Arbitre*, Ch. VI.
[249] See pp. 391–92, 394–95, *supra.*
[250] *Summa Theologica*, Part I, Q. 82, A. 2, Reply 1. Cf. *De Malo*, Q. 6, A. 1. Reply 6; *Truth*, Vol. III, Q. 22, A. 5, Replies 12, 13, pp. 54–55.

To the objection that every one necessarily wills his ultimate good, happiness, and, consequently, he necessarily wills all the means that are needed to achieve it, Aquinas replies:

> The end does not always necessitate in man the choosing of the means, because the means are not always such that the end cannot be gained without them; or, if they be such, they are not always considered in that light.[251]

Additional light is thrown on this reply by the argument in the body of the article, which runs as follows:

> There are certain individual goods which have not a necessary connection with happiness, because without them a man can be happy: and to such the will does not adhere of necessity. But there are some things which have a necessary connection with happiness, by means of which things man adheres to God, in Whom alone true happiness consists. Nevertheless, until through the certitude produced by seeing God the necessity of such connection be shown, the will does not adhere to God of necessity, nor to those things which are of God.[252]

To the objection, that the will and the intellect, both being immaterial powers, operate in the same way, and that, therefore, since the intellect is necessitated by the true, so is the will necessitated by the good, Aquinas replies:

> Just as the will is moved by necessity by an object that is in all respects good, but not by an object that can be taken as in some aspect bad, so the intellect is also moved by necessity by a necessary truth that cannot be taken as false, but not by a contingent truth, which can be taken as false.[253]

Finally, to the objection that if the will, being an active power, is disposed toward contraries, opposites would exist simultaneously, which is impossible, Aquinas replies that though the will is an active power and disposed toward opposites, "it does not follow that the opposites exist simultaneously; for even though each of the opposites to which the power

251 *Summa Theologica*, Part I–II, Q. 13, A. 6, Reply 1. Cf. *ibid.*, Q. 10, A. 2, Reply 3; and also *De Malo*, Q. 6, A. 1, Reply 8; *Truth*, Vol. III, Q. 22, A. 5, Replies 1, 11, pp. 53–54; Q. 24, A. 1, Reply 20, pp. 143–44.
252 *Summa Theologica*, Part I, Q. 82, A. 2. Commenting on this point, Maritain writes: ". . . it must be made clear that not only particular and partial goods, offered us by the finite world, but all the concrete goods which we may love and desire in this life, are thus the object of the will's free choice. Even the noblest good, even the divine good, is thus, and for the same reason, the object of the will's free choice" (*Scholasticism and Politics*, Ch. V, p. 122).
253 *De Malo*, Q. 6, A. 1, Reply 10. Cf. *Summa Theologica*, Part I–II, Q. 10, A. 2, Reply 2; and *Truth*, Q. 22, A. 5, Replies 3, 8, 9, 10; Q. 24, A. 1, Reply 18.

is disposed is possible, still one is incompossible with the other."[254] This reply is reminiscent of Aristotle's argument concerning rational potency, which is, for him, the power to "produce contrary effects." He observes that "if they produced their effects necessarily they would produce contrary effects at the same time; but this is impossible." Hence, he concludes, "there must, then be something else that decides; I mean by this, desire or will."[255]

A large number of writers regard themselves as followers of Aquinas, or at least manifest their indebtedness to him for the main points in this argument in support of free choice. In view of the length of the list, which extends from the fourteenth century to the present day, we shall confine ourselves to a sampling of contemporary authors.[256] Of these, two address themselves explicitly to arguments advanced by opponents of free choice whom we have already considered. Commenting on Jonathan Edwards' contention that "the will always follows the greater seeming good," Hubert Gruender analyzes the sense in which it is true that we always choose that which appears best, and the sense in which this is false, namely, that the judgment of what is best imposes itself upon the will, instead of being determined by it.[257] Joseph Rickaby proceeds in a similar fashion to analyze what is true and false in J. S. Mill's contention that we cannot act against our strongest desire or exercise our will in opposition to our strongest preference.[258]

In addition, a number of writers who are not professedly Thomists argue in a Thomistic manner against the proposition that choice is determined by the strongest motive in a manner that renders it unfree. Book III, Chapter II, in Henry More's *An Account of Virtue* takes up "two principal objections against Free-Will. Of these, one is based on God's foreknowledge; the other is that "the Will evermore inclines to the Good

---

[254] *De Malo*, Q. 6, A. 1, Reply 16. Cf. *ibid.*, Reply 19.

[255] *Metaphysics*, Book IX, Ch. 5, $1048^a8–9$. See also *ibid.*, $1048^a9–24$.

[256] Reference has already been made to the writings of Jacques Maritain and Yves Simon. In addition, attention is called to the following: Magda Arnold, *The Human Person*, pp. 38–40; Francis Aveling, *Personality and Will*, pp. 193–208; Roland Dalbiez, "Le Moment de la Liberté" in *Revue Thomiste*, Vol. XLVIII, Nos. 1–2, pp. 180–87; D. J. B. Hawkins, "Free Will and Right Action," in *The Modern Schoolman*, Vol. XXVI, No. 4, pp. 287–91; Bernard Lonergan, *Insight*, pp. 607–21; André Marc, *Psychologie Réflexive*, Vol. II, pp. 109–11, 137–39, 144–49; F. de Munnynck, "La Demonstration Metaphysique du Libre Arbitre," in *Revue Neo-Scholastique*, Vol. 20, pp. 32–33, 280–93; Joseph Scully, "The Initial Freedom," in *The Concept of Freedom*, pp. 48–54; Gerard Smith, "Intelligence and Liberty," in *The New Scholasticism*, Vol. XV, No. 1, pp. 3–15.

[257] *Free Will*, pp. 67–72. Cf. *Experimental Psychology*, pp. 399–401, 428–29.

[258] *Free Will and Four English Philosophers*, pp. 201–5, 218–19. Rickaby also argues against the view of Hobbes that our will is determined by the last dictate of the understanding, which represents our strongest desire; see *ibid.*, pp. 50–53.

that is most apparent." More's reply to this latter objection reflects the Thomistic analysis of the will as a rational appetite.[259] Isaac Watts employs the Thomistic distinction between active and passive indifference to support his argument that the will is not determined by the greatest apparent good or by the dominant motive.[260] Among contemporary writers, A. E. Taylor, confronting the problem of how choice is free though determined by motives, declares: "St. Thomas's explanation seems to me to go to the root of the matter."[261] And in Austin Farrer's treatment of that problem, many traces of Thomistic thought are implicit.[262]

(ii) In the interchange between Price and Priestley, we find the question of the role of motives in relation to choice disputed in a somewhat different manner. To Priestley's contention that motives are the causes of volitions exactly as gravity is the cause of motion in freely falling bodies,[263] Price replies:

> A man choosing to follow his judgment and desires, or his actually doing what he is inclined to do, is what we mean when we say *motives determine him*. At the same time, it is very plain that motives can have no concern in effecting his determination, or that there is no *physical connection* between his judgment and views, and the actions consequent upon them. What must be more absurd than to say that *our inclinations act upon us, and compel* us, that our *desires and fears put us in motion*, or *produce our volitions*, i.e., are *agents*; and yet what is more conceivable than that they may be the *occasions* of our putting ourselves into motion?

Price makes the distinction between *occasions* and *causes* the nub of his argument. "What sense would there be in saying," he asks, "That the situation of a body, which may properly be the *occasion* . . . is the *efficient* [cause] *of its motion, or its impeller?*"[264]

---

[259] *Op. cit.*, pp. 181–90.
[260] See *An Essay on the Freedom of the Will in God and His Creatures*, pp. 17–20, 69–73, 76–77, 98.
[261] "The Freedom of Man," in *Contemporary British Philosophy*, p. 283. Cf. *ibid.*, p. 282 and pp. 285 ff., where Taylor applies the Thomistic analysis in his criticism of the views of T. H. Green and F. H. Bradley.
[262] See *The Freedom of the Will*, pp. 117–21; also pp. 168, 176–77, and esp. pp. 217–22.
[263] *The Doctrine of Philosophical Necessity*, pp. 37–38. Cf. *ibid.*, pp. 43–46.
[264] *Ibid.*, pp. 55–56. Commenting on this, Priestley says, "I do not think that this objection to the doctrine of necessity can be expressed in a stronger or better manner"; but he, nevertheless, sees nothing in it to make him refrain from repeating that a man, having to make a choice at a given moment, "would certainly choose that which appeared to him, for that moment, the more desirable" (*ibid.*, pp. 56–57). According to Priestley, the distinction between occasions and causes is an "arbitrary and verbal distinction"; and, he continues, "It makes no difference to say, that the motive does not *immediately* produce the action. It is enough if it necessarily produce the immediate

Furthermore, Price argues, if motives were the efficient causes of voli
tions, the self would not be the agent in our voluntary actions. "Asserting
self-determination with a regard to motives (and no one ever yet asserted
the contrary)," Price writes, "is asserting *self-determination*, and therefore,
it is the same with asserting liberty." And, he continues,

> supposing a power of self-determination to exist, it is by no means necessary
> that it should be exerted without a regard to any end or rule . . . All that
> should be avoided here is the intolerable absurdity of making our reasons
> and ends in acting the physical *causes* or *efficients* of action. This is the
> same with ascribing the action of walking, not to the feet . . . but to
> the eye, which only *sees the way*. The perception of a reason for acting,
> or the judgment of the understanding, is no more than seeing the
> way. It is the eye of the mind, which informs and directs, and whatever
> *certainty* there may be that a particular determination will follow, such de-
> termination will be the *self-determination* of the mind, and not any change
> of its state stamped upon it, over which it has no power, and in receiving
> which, instead of being an *agent*, it is merely a *passive subject* of agency.[265]

Price tries to derive further support for his view of motives from the
distinction between physical and moral causes.[266] "To ascribe a necessary
and physical efficiency to motives," he writes, "is . . . the same with saying
that *an abstract notion can strike a ball*."[267]

Like Joseph Price, Thomas Reid holds that the conception of man as
an agent is incompatible with the view that he must necessarily do what
the strongest motive moves him to, for that would render him merely
passive.[268] He maintains, again like Price, that motives influence, but do
not cause our actions; but, in addition, he declares that some actions are
capricious and proceed without motives, and that it is even possible to act

---

cause of the action, or the cause of the immediate cause, etc. . . . For contrive as
many mediums of this kind as you please, it will still follow, that the action is *ultimately* according to the motive, *flows from it*, or *depends upon it*; and, therefore . . .
the motive ought to be called the *proper cause* of the action" (*ibid.*, pp. 63–66).

[265] *Ibid.*, pp. 137–38. Cf. *ibid.*, p. 136. Priestley here replies: "If the will is as invariably influenced by motives as the stone is influenced by gravity, it may just as
well be said that the stone moves itself, though always according to the laws of
gravity, as that the will or the mind, moves itself, though always according to the
motives. . . . The perception of reasons or motives, Dr. Price calls 'the eye of the
mind, which informs and directs'; but if the determination of the mind, which follows
upon it, be invariably *according* to that perception, I must conclude that the nature of
the mind is such, as that it *could not* act otherwise, and therefore it has no self-determination properly so called" (*ibid.*, pp. 146–47).

[266] *Ibid.*, pp. 139 ff.

[267] *Ibid.*, p. 140. Priestley rejects this distinction, too. See *ibid.*, pp. 147–48, where he
says that it amounts to no more than a distinction between involuntary and voluntary
actions.

[268] See *Essays on the Active Powers of the Human Mind*, pp. 186–88.

against the strongest motive. He explains this last point by distinguishing between what he calls "animal" and "rational" motives, according as they are "addressed either to the animal or to the rational part of our nature."[269] One animal motive may be stronger than another; similarly, in the case of diverse rational motives. The measure of their strength is different for these two kinds of motives. Hence, Reid argues, "a motive which is the strongest, according to the animal test, may be, and very often is, weakest according to the rational."[270] It is in this sense that men may act against the strongest motive—virtuous men against the strongest animal motive, and vicious men against the strongest rational motive.

In his criticism of J. S. Mill's dictum concerning the strongest desire or motive, Henry Mansel takes a somewhat different position. Like Price, he, too, distinguishes between material and mental causes. "As applied to Physics," he writes, "the *cause* of a phenomenon is a certain antecedent fact, which being repeated, the phenomenon will recur." But, in his opinion, "this notion of cause . . . can only by an imperfect analogy be applied to mental [phenomena]. In this sense, motives addressed to the will are not causes."[271] Mansel recognizes that, against this view, writers such as Mill maintain that "the conduct of a man . . . is the invariable consequent of motives present to his mind; so that, given the motives and the man's character, we could certainly predict the action."

This theory, he thinks, gets its plausibility "from an ambiguity in the term *motive*." If the strongest motive is simply the one on which I do, in fact, act, then Mill's statement that we cannot act contrary to the strongest motive is a truism; but if motives are considered apart from their relation to the will, i.e., without regard to the will's choice of the motive for a given action, then it is impossible to tell which is the strongest motive.

> The so-called motives are either a set of phenomena viewed in their relation to the will or viewed out of that relation. If the former, the argument has long ago been refuted by Reid. The strongest motive prevails, but I only know the strength of motives in relation to the will by the test of ultimate prevalence; so that this means no more than the prevailing motive prevails.[272]

---

[269] *Ibid.*, p. 192.
[270] *Ibid.*, p. 193.
[271] *Prolegomena Logica*, p. 152. Mansel then goes on to say that "in every act of volition, I am fully conscious that I can at this moment act in either of two ways, and that, all the antecedent phenomena being precisely the same, I may determine one way today and another way tomorrow" (*ibid.*).
[272] *Ibid.*, pp. 300–2. Mill's comment on this argument is as follows: "Those who say that the will follows the strongest motive, do not mean the motive which is strongest in relation to the will, or in other words, that the will follows what it does follow. They mean the motive which is strongest in relation to pain and pleasure; since a motive, being a desire or aversion, is proportional to the pleasantness, as conceived by

It is with Sir W. D. Ross in mind that G. E. Hughes offers still another analysis of the problem of motives in relation to choice.[273] He admits that, in certain cases, motives may be the efficient causes of action. But, he maintains, "those cases in which my motive is simply the efficient cause of my act are not cases of fully deliberate or *willed* action. . . . In the case of a fully deliberate act, or an act which we *will*," he continues, "it seems more appropriate to speak of the motives as the *reason* for the act, or as our reason for acting, than as the cause of act."[274] But then the question is, "How do I make such a desire, emotion, or belief"—the things Ross calls motives—"a *reason?*" The answer Hughes gives is that they are, initially, only potential motives, and that in voluntary, as contrasted with involuntary, action, a potential motive does not become an actual motive, or the reason for my action, "unless I *make* it my reason." He explains this as follows:

> In order to make a potential motive my reason for acting I select it from the others and "adopt" or "sanction" or "recognise" it; and in so doing I confer upon it an entirely new status. . . . There is a great difference in status between say a desire which, although I am aware of it as *my* desire, I am "considering" i.e., deliberating whether to accept or reject—and a desire which I have accepted or recognised and made the basis of my acting. . . . When a potential motive is thus accepted and the act is performed, the potential motive becomes the *actual motive* of that deliberate act.[275]

G. C. Field, also writing in criticism of Ross, takes a similar view. "In any sense in which we can choose what action we shall do," he declares, "we can choose what motive we shall act from."[276] And H. D. Lewis, reviewing the critical essays directed against Ross's position, sides with Hughes and Field.[277]

---

us, of the thing desired, or the painfulness of the thing shunned. . . . This is the first answer to Mr. Mansel. The second is, that even supposing there were no test of the strength of motives but their effect on the will, the proposition that the will follows the strongest motive would not, as Mr. Mansel supposes, be identical and unmeaning. . . . Even if the strongest motive meant only the motive which prevails, yet if there is a prevailing motive . . . the free-will theory is not saved" (*An Examination of Sir William Hamilton's Philosophy*, p. 605). See also *ibid.*, pp. 600–4.

[273] For an account of Ross's position, see pp. 399–400, *supra*.

[274] "Motive and Duty," in *Mind*, Vol. LIII, No. 212, p. 316.

[275] *Ibid.*, p. 317. Hughes follows this with an analysis of four types of cases in which we choose our motives. See *ibid.*, pp. 319–22. In the light of this, he writes: "My conclusion is, therefore, that in very many cases at least it is within the control of our will to act from one motive rather than another" (*ibid.*, p. 322).

[276] "Kant's First Moral Principle," in *Mind*, Vol. XLI, No. 161, p. 33.

[277] "Moral Freedom, in Recent Ethics," in *Readings in Ethical Theory*, pp. 580–85. Summarizing the analysis presented by Hughes, Lewis says, "the substance of Hughes's contention seems beyond dispute" (*ibid.*, p. 582). For his comments on Field, see *ibid.*, p. 584. In the same volume, see also G. A. Paul's critique of the paper by Lewis,

A wide range of writers, from diverse points of view, subscribe to the proposition that we choose the motives which, after being chosen, become the reasons for our actions, as against the proposition that our motives, determined by our antecedents and our characters, determine our choices. Charles Renouvier maintains that, in deliberate action, "a *motive* is always *willed*, that is, singled out at the moment among other equally possible motives."[278] In the act of decision "that follows a consideration of motives," Emile Boutroux declares, "there is something more than in the motives themselves: the consent of the will to some particular motive in preference to some other. The motive, therefore, is not the complete cause of the action."[279] E. F. Carritt holds that "voluntary actions . . . have no motive in the proper sense of a desire which compels to either choice. We may be said," he continues,

> to have two 'incentives' or 'grounds,' our belief in an obligation and a contrary desire, between which we choose, and the one chosen is loosely called our motive. If we speak thus, we may say, rather absurdly, that we have 'made it our motive' by adopting it.[280]

Paul Weiss, in the context of an elaborate analysis that has been summarized elsewhere,[281] argues that the appeal that one of several alternatives has for us, at the moment we select it, depends upon the attractiveness with which we help endow it at that moment. If "the alternative with the greatest appeal is the alternative we always select," he tells us, this

> would preclude our being free to select any other alternative, were it not possible for us to add freely to the appeal which an alternative initially possesses. An alternative possessing an initial slight or even negative appeal can have its appeal increased until it is greater than the appeal of any other alternative. The increase is due to us and us alone, the outcome of the creative exercise of native freedom.[282]

---

in which he contends that Lewis's views do not really square with the libertarian or indeterminist doctrine that is espoused by Hughes and Field: *loc. cit.*, pp. 625 ff.

[278] *Psychologie Rationelle*, Vol. I, p. 316. Cf. Secrétan, *Mon Utopie*, p. 164.

[279] *The Contingency of the Laws of Nature*, p. 140. C. S. Peirce takes a more qualified position on the point in question. In his view, "that every act of will is determined by the strongest motive . . . has never been proved." And he also says: "Unless there is a perfect regularity as to what is the strongest motive with me, to say that I act from the strongest motive is mere tautology" (*Collected Papers*, Vol. V, p. 210 fn. 1).

[280] *Ethical and Political Thinking*, p. 138. "My reason for this conclusion," Carritt writes, "is my conviction that when I obey or disobey my conscience I could have chosen otherwise, and that I could not blame myself for disobeying it when it was contrary to desire if I thought I were determined to follow the strongest desire" (*ibid.*).

[281] See Vol. I, pp. 515–17.

[282] *Man's Freedom*, p. 65. "The act of adopting a possibility and thereby turning it into a goal," Weiss adds, "is an act inseparable from that in which the appeal of the

And Jean-Paul Sartre, against the background of a quite different analysis,[283] reaches the same conclusion. "Causes and motives," he declares, "have only the weight which my project—the free production of the end and of the known act to be realized—confers upon them."[284]

(iii) We come finally to that form of the argument for freedom of choice which turns on the proposition that the self acts independently of character and motives in the making of moral choices, especially those choices in which one alternative is to do one's duty and the other is to follow the contrary promptings of desire. To say that the self acts independently of character and motives is to say that it has the power to choose between acting in accord with or against the dominant tendencies of the moral character as so far formed. It can act against the strongest desire by investing the injunction of duty with even greater strength. Hence, the position taken here is clearly opposed to the other side in this dispute, which maintains that a man's choices are completely determined by his character as formed and, in a particular case, by whatever motive is made dominant by that character in reaction to the present circumstances.

This opposition is represented in an interchange between P. H. Nowell-Smith and C. A. Campbell. Nowell-Smith advances an argument with which we are already familiar—the argument we have examined in the writings of Hume, Priestley, Ross, and others.[285] Campbell, on the other hand, offers two reasons for the proposition he defends, neither of which have been mentioned so far. They are extrinsic reasons, in the sense that neither appeals to a general theory of causation to explain the causal indeterminacy involved in free choice and neither applies a theory of causation to the psychological process of deliberation and choice.

One of these extrinsic reasons is that moral responsibility presupposes free choice in a sense that involves causal indeterminacy and causal initiative (what Campbell calls "contra-causal freedom"). The other is that we are, introspectively, aware of such freedom: we have experienced situations in which we were conscious of deciding against the trend of our character. Nowell-Smith challenges both of these reasons, arguing to the contrary that moral responsibility does not depend on free choice contra-causally conceived and that the evidence of consciousness is incapable of establishing the existence of "contra-causal freedom."

---

goal is added to the appeal of presented alternative. . . . It is always up to us freely to determine just which alternative is to be made most appealing by the goal" (*ibid.*). See also *ibid.*, pp. 118–20. Cf. *Modes of Being*, pp. 98–99.

283 For a summary of this see Vol. I, pp. 517–20.

284 *Being and Nothingness*, pp. 450–51. Cf. *ibid.*, pp. 437–39, 449–50.

285 See pp. 397–400, *supra.*

These arguments and counter-arguments belong to disputes which we shall consider in the next two sections, which are concerned with the question about moral responsibility and the evidence of consciousness. Apart from these arguments and counter-arguments, what remains of the interchange between Campbell and Nowell-Smith focuses on two points: (a) Nowell-Smith's denial that there is any meaning or reality in the notion of a self that is completely independent of the individual's formed character, and Campbell's attempt to give that notion meaning and reality; (b) Nowell-Smith's assertion, following Hume, that our choices are either causally determined by our character and motives or they are purely chance or random events, and Campbell's insistence that a self-determined free choice is a genuine third alternative, distinct from both a character-determined choice that is not free and a causally undetermined choice that is a chance event.

In view of the fact that we have already examined in some detail what Nowell-Smith and Campbell have to say on both of these points, we shall not offer any further documentation here.[286] But to complete the picture, it is necessary to mention a number of authors whose theories of free choice place them on Campbell's side. The most eminent of these, to whom Campbell expresses his indebtedness, is Immanuel Kant. For Kant, the transcendental or noumenal self exercises freedom of choice through its faculty of election, which Kant calls *Willkür* or "elective will." The alternatives between which it chooses are the imperatives of duty under the moral law, on the one hand, and the inclinations of sensuous desire, on the other. The choice results in the determination of the will by a maxim of action (i.e., a kind of motive), which is adopted by the will. Thus, the transcendental ego or self has the power to act either in the line of duty or to yield to the promptings of desire; it either confirms the moral character as formed or departs from it. And while the consequences of the free choice comprise a series of effects that occur in the temporal order of phenomena, the act of choice is supra-temporal and its cause—the transcendental ego's elective will—is a timeless or noumenal entity.[287]

A number of other writers—James Martineau, Bernard Bosanquet, and Nicholai Lossky, to mention only those who are not professedly Kantians—hold conceptions of the self as having a power of choice that involves its

---

[286] See Ch. 9, pp. 296–301, *supra*.

[287] The documentation for this brief summary of Kant's theory has already been given in detail. See Vol. I, pp. 525–29; and also pp. 480–83. It may be useful to observe here that it is the Kantian theory of free choice which C. D. Broad identifies with the libertarian position, the impossibility of which he argues on the ground that events in time cannot be the effects of a supra-temporal or timeless cause. See Ch. 9, pp. 278–79, 281–83, *supra*.

independence of all past and present influences upon decision among available alternatives. Of these authors, Lossky, like Kant, conceives that self as a supra-temporal being.[288] Two contemporary writers—L. J. Russell and C. E. Ewing—who deny that free choice involves a supra-temporal agent, nevertheless, do maintain that it involves a substantive agent, such as the self, with the power to act independently of past and present influences.[289]

One point in the interchange between Nowell-Smith and Campbell consists in their opposite opinions on the question whether the indeterminacy of free choice is identical with the indeterminism of chance. On this point, some of the authors just mentioned explicitly indicate that they are on Campbell's side. Like Campbell, they maintain that *self*-determination does not involve the absense of a cause, but rather the action of a cause that is indeterminately related to a range of possible effects, any one of which it has the power to produce, even though all other conditions are the same. Choice for them is not like the toss of a coin to decide between alternatives that are absolutely indifferent; nor, in their view, does the statement that a man could have chosen otherwise, with the same character and with the same motives to choose from, amount to saying that how he chooses must then be a matter of chance.[290]

[288] See Martineau, *Types of Ethical Theory*, pp. 38–43; Bosanquet, *The Principle of Individuality and Value*, pp. 354 ff.; Lossky, *Freedom of the Will*, pp. 76–98. Another writer who bears comparison to Kant and who argues for freedom of choice in the realm of moral values is Nicholai Hartmann. For a detailed summary of his views, see Vol. I, Book II, Ch. 23, pp. 484–86; and Ch. 24, pp. 529–31.

[289] See Russell, "Ought Implies Can," in the *Proceedings of the Aristotelian Society*, Vol. 36, pp. 152–83; and also the summary of Russell's arguments given in Ch. 9, pp. 283–85, *supra*. See Ewing, "Indeterminism," in *The Review of Metaphysics*, Vol. 5, No. 2, pp. 212–22, esp. pp. 214–15, 217, 221. Both Russell and Ewing take issue with Broad's statement of the libertarian position as being narrowly restricted to the Kantian theory of free choice, and both offer alternative theories which they think escape Broad's attack by explaining how the self, as agent, can act independently of antecedents in the life of the individual.

[290] See Kant, *Introduction to the Metaphysic of Morals*, pp. 282–83; Lossky, *The Freedom of the Will*, Ch. IV; Bosanquet, *The Principle of Individuality and Value*, p. 356. See also Alburey Castell, *Science as a Goad to Philosophy*, pp. 64–67. These writers, together with Campbell, are not the only ones who think that Hume poses a false dilemma when he maintains that the only alternatives are causal necessity or chance. See pp. 83, 86 fn. 160, 123 fn. 241.

5. THE DISPUTE ABOUT FREE CHOICE AND RESPONSIBILITY

In the current literature of this controversy, it is frequently said by those who take the determinist side of the issue that the two main arguments for free choice are the one that regards it as the indispensable condition of moral responsibility and the one that appeals to our consciousness or experience of its existence.

There is a tendency to ignore the affirmative arguments set forth in the three preceding sections or to dismiss them as of insufficient weight. Although assessments of their weight or validity differ, these arguments must certainly be taken into account. More than that, in a logical approach to the controversy, they take precedence over the arguments based on responsibility, just as the arguments against free choice which are based on theories of causation, on the scientific ideal of theoretical predictability, or on psychological analyses of choice as affected by character and motives take precedence over arguments that attempt to rebut the point about responsibility.

We have elsewhere called attention to a logical difference between arguments of the first sort (i.e., those based on theories of causation, etc.) and arguments of the second sort (i.e., those concerned with responsibility or introspective evidence).[291]

The reasons advanced in the first type of argument, we said, are intrinsic to the point under dispute: since what is under dispute is the existence of causal indeterminacy in free choice, diverse theories of causation or diverse psychological accounts of the role of motives in relation to choice supply reasons for affirming or denying free choice that go to the heart of the matter. We pointed out that, in contrast, the reasons advanced in the second type of argument are extrinsic: what is in dispute here is the connection between free choice and responsibility, or the import and validity of introspective observations.

We also called attention to a difference between disputes involving arguments of the first type and disputes involving arguments of the second type. In the first case, the dispute is initiated by arguments against man's possession of a freedom of self-determination: it is the determinist who attacks the libertarian doctrine. In the second case, the dispute is initiated by arguments for the existence of a freedom of self-determination: it is the libertarian who attacks the position of the determinist.

[291] See Ch. 9, pp. 302–03, *supra*.

In the preceding chapter, we examined the dispute about the bearing of responsibility on the existence of causal initiative. We saw there that the libertarian argument does not proceed directly from the notion of responsibility to the existence of causal initiative, but connects responsibility directly with free choice and then points out that causal indeterminacy presupposes causal initiative.[292] Because of this, the present dispute—the one about responsibility and free choice—involves many more authors on both sides than the one treated in the preceding chapter. Most writers on this subject consider responsibility in relation to free choice, not in relation to causal initiative.[293]

The number of authors on both sides of this dispute attests to the importance that has been attached to the point at issue. This dispute, furthermore, is complicated by the fact that the writers on the determinist side do not agree with one another on the conclusion they reach about responsibility in the light of their denial of free choice. The dispute has two sides only in the sense that, on the one hand, there are libertarians who argue that free choice is the *sine qua non* of responsibility, while, on the other hand, there are the determinists who argue that free choice does not exist. But some of them then go on to say that responsibility still remains in a significant sense; and some, on the contrary, say that the notion of responsibility must be completely given up.

Recently, a distinction, first proposed by William James, has come into vogue. It is the distinction between hard and soft determinists, i.e., respectively, between (a) determinists who, denying free choice, also deny responsibility, and (b) determinists who, denying free choice, assert that responsibility remains. The hard determinists are thus seen to agree with the libertarians about the dependence of responsibility on free choice, while also agreeing with the soft determinists—against the libertarians—that free choice does not exist. In view of this, we shall present the materials of this dispute in the following manner.

In the first phase, we shall present the libertarian arguments which initiate the dispute. In the second phase, we shall deal with the counter-arguments on the part of the soft determinists, in which they set forth a conception of responsibility that is based on circumstantial freedom of self-realization (i.e., the freedom of being able to act as one wishes) and so deny that the notion of responsibility must be given up by those who reject free choice. In the third phase, we shall consider the rebuttals to these

[292] See *ibid.*, pp. 303–4, *supra.*
[293] Our treatment of the dispute about responsibility in Ch. 9 dealt mainly with the interchange between C. A. Campbell and P. H. Nowell-Smith: see pp. 304–16, *supra.* Other writers, who were there mentioned only in passing, will be treated more fully here.

counter-arguments, in which the libertarians criticize the notion of responsibility proposed by the soft determinists and explain why, in their opinion, responsibility, properly conceived, depends upon free choice. Finally, in the fourth phase, we shall take up the criticisms of the soft determinists by the hard determinists. Here, too, other differences of opinion on the part of those who deny free choice will be considered insofar as they bear on the whole problem of freedom and the moral life.

FIRST PHASE

In documenting the argument for freedom of choice which rests on the proposition that man's possession of it is indispensable to his moral life (responsibility, praise and blame, rewards and punishments), we shall divide the affirmative authors into three groups. We shall treat, first, those whose theories of self-determination we examined in detail in Volume I; second, those who have figured in the actual debates or interchanges on this subject; and third, a sampling of other writers, most of them comparatively recent or contemporary.

(i) Augustine tells us that Cicero affirmed freedom of choice, even if this required him to deny divine foreknowledge, because unless man has free choice "the whole economy of human life is subverted." Unless man has free choice, Augustine continues, speaking for himself as well as for Cicero, "in vain are reproaches, praises, chidings, exhortations had recourse to; and there is no justice whatever in the appointment of rewards for the good, and punishment for the wicked."[294] Boethius argues similarly that without free choice on man's part, all rewards and punishments are without justification; and, furthermore, he points out that man's crimes as well as his good deeds must then be attributed to God, "the author of all good."[295]

Referring to the view that man does not have freedom of choice, Aquinas says flatly, "This opinion is heretical, because it does away with the ground of merit and demerit in human actions. For it does not seem to be meritorious or demeritorious that someone does by necessity what he cannot avoid. . . . If we are moved by necessity in willing," he continues, "then deliberation, exhortation, precept and punishment, praise and

---

[294] *City of God*, Vol. I, Book V, Ch. 9, p. 191. Cf. *ibid.*, Ch. 10, p. 196. See also *The Problem of Free Choice*, pp. 35–36.
[295] *The Consolation of Philosophy*, Book V, pp. 106–7.

blame—in which things moral philosophy consists—are all done away with."[296] In another place, he spells this out.

> Commands and prohibitions should be imposed only upon one who can do or not do; otherwise they would be imposed in vain. But prohibitions and commands are divinely imposed upon man. It is therefore in man's power to do or not to do, and so he is endowed with free choice.
>
> No one should be punished or rewarded for something which it is not in his power to do or not to do. But man is justly punished and rewarded by God for his deeds. Therefore man can do and not do; and so he is endowed with free choice.[297]

Scholastic philosophers, writing in the tradition of Aquinas, reiterate these points.[298]

Descartes omits reference to divine commands and prohibitions, rewards and punishments, and states the argument entirely in terms of praise and blame. Man's having free will, he says, "is what renders him deserving of either praise or blame. . . . For we do not praise automatic machines although they respond exactly to the movements which they were destined to produce, since their actions are performed necessarily. We praise the workman who has made the machines because he has formed them with accuracy and has done so freely and not of necessity."[299]

With Kant the argument takes a slightly different turn, and one that is followed by many writers who come after Kant. It is often repeated in the condensed statement: *ought implies can.* Expanded, this means that, since a man is subject to the moral law, which categorically commands him to perform certain actions and to avoid others, he must be able freely to choose between the actions he ought to perform and the actions he ought not to perform.[300] For Kant, this argument contains the only reason for

[296] *De Malo*, Q. 6, A. 1. Cf. Judah Halevi, *Kitab Al Khazari*, Part V, pp. 280–81; and Maimonides, *Eight Chapters on Ethics*, Ch. VII, pp. 86–89; *The Guide for the Perplexed*, Part III, Ch. XVII, pp. 285–88.
[297] *Truth*, Vol. III, Q. 24, A. 1, To the Contrary, ※5', 6', pp. 133–44. See also *Summa Theologica*, Part I, Q. 83, A. 1.
[298] See, for example, Gruender, *Free Will*, pp. 59–64; Maher, *Psychology*, p. 418; Ryan, "Religion as the Basis of the Postulates of Freedom," in *Freedom, Its Meaning*, p. 476; Hawkins, "Free Will and Right Action," in *The Modern Schoolman*, Vol. XXVI, No. 4, pp. 281 ff.
[299] *Principles of Philosophy*, Principle XXXVII, in *Philosophical Works*, Vol. I, pp. 233–34. Cf. *The Passions of the Soul*, Part Third, Articles CLIII–CLIV, in *ibid.*, pp. 401–2.
[300] As C. A. Campbell puts it, since we are morally obligated to do our duty in spite of the inclination of contrary desires, we must be able to exercise a free choice between the imperatives of duty and the solicitations of desire. It is also worth noting here that C. D. Broad's distinction between what he calls "categorical" and "conditional" obligability is based on Kant's argument that duty presupposes free choice. As

assuming the existence of a freedom that involves causal indeterminacy and causal initiative. Such freedom, he tells us, "is the *ratio essendi* of the moral law, while the moral law is the *ratio cognoscendi* of freedom. For had not the moral law been previously distinctly thought in our reason, we should never consider ourselves justified in *assuming* such a thing as freedom, although it be not contradictory."[301]

Renouvier argues in a similar vein. "When the notions of right, of duty, and of justice . . . come into conflict with other passions whose impulse would carry man elsewhere, the moral law makes itself heard." But if, of the two courses of action, "only one were possible in reality, the moral law which, at this point, would command that which necessarily *will be* and forbid that which necessarily *will not be*, or command that which *will not be* and forbid that which *will be*, such a moral law would be a purposeless injunction, ridiculous, bizarre, and odious." Renouvier, therefore, argues that "since consciousness cannot help putting down this law as both serious and real, it then affirms real freedom in the same stroke."[302] Secrétan contends that determinism destroys the moral life. If determinism is true, he says, "The notions of merit and demerit are empty notions, and these words ought to be struck from the dictionary."[303] And N. Hartmann, like Kant, maintains that freedom of the will has "ontological possibility" and "ethical necessity," i.e., only its possibility, not its reality, can be argued on metaphysical grounds, but its real existence can be seen in the fact that it is necessary for the moral life.[304]

From a quite different point of view, Sartre asserts the inseparability of freedom and responsibility. "Man, being condemned to be free," he writes, "carries the weight of the whole world on his shoulders; he is responsible for the world and for himself as a way of being."[305] And from still another point of view, Weiss tells us that "the denial that a man is free to decide means that he is not responsible for the course he adopts."[306]

Broad sees it, it is the unconditional ought of the categorical imperatives of duty, and that alone, which requires free choice; a conditional imperative (which, in effect says "Do this *if* you can") requires only a circumstantial freedom of self-realization, i.e., that external conditions should permit him to do this, if he wishes to, but not that he should be free to wish or not to wish doing it.

[301] *Critique of Practical Reason*, p. 88 fn. 1. Cf. *ibid.*, p. 119, where Kant says that a man judges that "he can do a certain thing because he is conscious that he ought, and he recognizes that he is free, a fact which but for the moral law he would never have known." See also *Critique of Pure Reason*, pp. 299–301.

[302] *Psychologie Rationelle*, Vol. II, pp. 246–47. Cf. *ibid.*, Vol. I, pp. 306–7. Cf. William James, *Principles of Psychology*, Vol. II, p. 573.

[303] *Mon Utopie*, pp. 188–89. Cf. *ibid.*, pp. 182–86.

[304] *Ethics*, Vol. III, pp. 246–47.

[305] *Being and Nothingness*, p. 553. See whole section on Freedom and Responsibility, in *ibid.*, pp. 553–56. Cf. Tillich, *Systematic Theology*, Vol. I, p. 184.

[306] *Man's Freedom*, p. 233. Cf. *ibid.*, pp. 61–63. Here Weiss declares: "We are free

(ii) In his debate with Thomas Hobbes, Bishop Bramhall contends that the denial of free will would "overthrow all societies and commonwealths in the world." He points out that laws "which prohibit that which a man cannot possibly shun" are unjust. Furthermore, "all consultations are vain, if every thing be either necessary or impossible. . . . It is to no more purpose to admonish men of understanding than fools, children, or madmen, if all things be necessary. Praises and dispraises, rewards and punishments, are as vain as they are undeserved, if there be no liberty."[307]

Joseph Priestley quotes Dr. Price as arguing, in similar vein, that free choice is indispensable to the moral life. Without it, virtue is meaningless.[308] "It has always been the general, and it has evidently been the natural sense of mankind," he writes, "that they cannot be accountable for what they have no power to avoid. Nothing can be more glaringly absurd than applauding or reproaching ourselves for . . . what it was no more possible for us to prevent than the return of the seasons or the revolutions of the planets."[309]

The interchange between Mansel and Mill is provoked by Mill's examination of Sir William Hamilton's views on free will and necessity. In his affirmation of free choice, Hamilton relies exclusively on the indispensability of such freedom to morality. In his view, "the assertion of absolute necessity . . . is virtually the negation of a moral universe."[310] And in another place he states the argument in the following manner:

> Man is a moral agent only as he is accountable for his actions,—in other words, as he is the object of praise or blame; and this he is, only inasmuch as he has prescribed to him a rule of duty, and as he is able to act, or not to act, in conformity with its precepts. The possibility of morality thus depends on the possibility of liberty; for if man be not a free agent, he is not the author of his actions, and has, therefore, no responsibility,—no moral personality at all.[311]

---

to select any alternative, yet there are reasons for our selecting what we do. We can intend otherwise than we now do, but we do intend as men who are, want, and have undergone specific things. We are neither free from all conditioning nor inexorably bound. We have neither too much nor too little freedom. We have just enough to be responsible."

[307] The Questions Concerning Liberty, Necessity, and Chance, p. 150.
[308] See The Doctrine of Philosophical Necessity, p. 67.
[309] Ibid., pp. 74–75.
[310] Lectures on Metaphysics, Vol. I, p. 410.
[311] Ibid., Vol. II, p. 33. Hamilton maintains, however, that free will, conceived as involving causal initiative and causal indeterminacy, is clearly inconsistent with the principle of causality, and therefore unintelligible. He affirms it only because, in his view, causal determinism makes morality and responsibility unintelligible. See Lectures on Metaphysics, Vol. II, pp. 410–11, 623–25; and cf. J. S. Mill, An Examination of Sir William Hamilton's Philosophy, pp. 573–75.

We have already examined the position of C. A. Campbell on free choice and moral responsibility.[312] The central point for him is that, according to the generally accepted view of moral responsibility, a man is not properly subject to praise and blame, or rewards and punishments, unless he could have chosen to act otherwise as well as have been able to act in accordance with that choice. It is not enough to say that external circumstances would have permitted him to act otherwise, had he chosen so to act, if it is then added that he could not have chosen otherwise, given his character, his antecedents, and the circumstances of the case.

Campbell makes this point in a number of books prior to his dispute with P. H. Nowell-Smith; and in that dispute he maintains it against Nowell-Smith's contention that responsibility can be meaningfully attributed to a man who, under the circumstances, could have acted otherwise even if he could not have chosen to act otherwise.[313] On this point, he finds himself partly in agreement and partly in disagreement with C. D. Broad.[314] Even though Broad denies the existence of free choice, he does support Campbell's thesis that without free choice there is no basis for moral responsibility in the generally accepted sense of that term. The man who could have acted otherwise *if* he had chosen otherwise is only hypothetically obligable or responsible. To be categorically obligable for his actions, a man must have been able to choose otherwise as well as to act in accordance with his choice; and, in Broad's view, it is categorical obligability and that alone which moralists have in mind when they attribute responsibility to a man.[315]

(iii) The essence of the foregoing argument is given a variety of expressions by a number of other writers in the nineteenth and twentieth centuries. Before we examine their statements of the case for free choice,

[312] See Ch. 9, pp. 305–7, *supra*.

[313] See *Scepticism and Construction*, pp. 120–21, 167; *In Defence of Free Will*, pp. 8–9; *On Selfhood and Godhood*, pp. 162–64; and "Is Freewill a Pseudo-Problem?" in *Mind*, Vol. LX, No. 240, pp. 446–58.

[314] See *In Defence of Free Will*, pp. 27–31.

[315] See "Determinism, Indeterminism, and Libertarianism," in *Ethics and History of Philosophy*, pp. 204–5, 214–17. Other writers, like Campbell, find support in Broad for their own view that free choice is essential to moral responsibility, properly conceived, while they take issue with Broad's reasons for denying the existence of such freedom. See L. J. Russell, "Ought Implies Can," in the *Proceedings of the Aristotelian Society*, Vol. 36, pp. 151–52, 168; and A. C. Ewing, "Indeterminism," in the *Review of Metaphysics*, Vol. V, No. 2, pp. 214–17. Although Campbell groups G. E. Moore with writers such as Nowell-Smith, Schlick, and Stevenson who take the opposite point of view, there is one passage in Moore's writings that suggests his agreement with Broad's identification of moral responsibility with the categorical sense of "could have acted otherwise." See "A Reply to My Critics," in *The Philosophy of G. E. Moore*, p. 624.

let us consider one seventeenth- and one eighteenth-century author in order to observe that the argument, while varying in style, remains the same in substance over the centuries.

"To what purpose," Henry More asks, "do we reprehend some men for what they act, pardon others, and have pity on the rest, if Mankind be destitute of *Free-Will*; if it be not given him to turn away from what is vile and to embrace what is laudable and just?"[316] Thomas Reid tells us that he means by "moral liberty" the liberty of moral agents who can choose between "acting well or ill, wisely or foolishly"; and by "necessity" he says he understands "the want of that moral liberty which I have above defined."[317] He then points out that moral approbation and disapprobation rest on moral liberty. The man who is either good or bad *"because he could not be otherwise"* does not deserve praise or blame.[318] And he concludes his analysis of the relation between freedom and accountability with the following statement:

> If we adopt the system of necessity, the terms *moral obligation* and *accountableness*, *praise* and *blame*, *merit* and *demerit*, *justice* and *injustice*, *reward* and *punishment*, *wisdom* and *folly*, *virtue* and *vice*, ought to be disused, or to have new meanings given them when they are used in religion, in morals, or in civil government; for upon that system, there can be no such things as they have always been used to signify.[319]

The point which Reid here makes about the commonly accepted meanings of these terms and the new meanings which might be given to them is also made by other writers on both sides of this dispute. Among those who deny the existence of free choice, there are, on the one hand, the "soft determinists" who propose new meanings for these terms, to replace the traditional meanings which involve the affirmation of free choice; and, on the other hand, there are the "hard determinists" who do not accept these new meanings as substitutes for the older ones and, therefore, advocate abandoning the basic terms of morality. Among the adherents of free

[316] *An Account of Virtue*, p. 180. "We might in point of justice," More writes, "insist upon it, that if Men are ty'd to Sin, and do it by *Necessity*, and cannot otherwise act, there is both Pardon and Commiseration due unto them" (*ibid.*, pp. 180–81).
[317] *Essays on the Active Powers of the Human Mind*, p. 174.
[318] See *ibid.*
[319] *Ibid.*, p. 211. See *ibid.*, pp. 208–10. It is interesting to note that Reid regards the argument from responsibility as one of three arguments for moral liberty. "The arguments to prove that man is endowed with moral liberty, which have the greatest weight with me," he writes, "are three: 1st, Because he has a natural conviction or belief, that, in many cases, he acted freely; 2dly, Because he is accountable; and 3dly, Because he is able to prosecute an end by a long series of means adapted to *it*" (*ibid.*, p. 201).

choice, a number of recent authors recognize the possibility of giving these terms meanings which do not involve free choice, but also point out that these new meanings do not satisfy the requirements of moral thought or action.

Thus, for example, James Martineau, after declaring that "either free-will is a fact, or moral judgment a delusion," considers the notion that, even if men do not have free-will, it may still make sense to praise or blame them for what they do in order to influence their future conduct. This notion may lead some to think that "it may be judicious, with a view to benefits to come, to commit the absurdity of praising what is not praiseworthy, and censuring what is not to blame." But, in Martineau's view, "to reduce the moral sentiments to a policy providing for the future, instead of a sentence pronounced upon the past, is simply to renounce them; and amounts to a confession that they cannot coexist with a theory of necessary causation."[320]

J. D. Mabbott and H. D. Lewis, after reviewing the writings of the "soft determinists," in which new meanings for responsibility, praise and blame, etc., are proposed, come to the same conclusion. Telling us that he is not satisfied with the attempts to connect determinism with responsi-bility, Mabbott writes:

> I remain convinced that moral responsibility requires that a man should be able to choose alternative actions, everything in the universe prior to the act, including his self, being the same.[321]

And Lewis, also after examining the proposed new meanings, declares that

> we can only retain the ideas of obligation and guilt as properly ethical ideas, if we can also believe in actions which could have been otherwise than they were, even though everything else in the universe had remained the same.[322]

We shall return, in a later phase of this dispute, to the specific criticisms which adherents of free choice level against the theories of the "soft determinists." There we shall see why Mabbott and Lewis, together with Campbell, Cranston, and Schiller, reject the new meanings for traditional moral terms which are proposed by such writers as Hobart, Schlick, Stevenson, Nowell-Smith, Russell, and Ayer.

The authors to whom we now turn do not engage in this special dispute with the "soft determinists." They simply take the view that determinism

---

[320] *Types of Ethical Theory*, pp. 41–42.

[321] "Free Will and Punishment," in *Contemporary British Philosophy*, Third Series, p. 301. Cf. *ibid.*, pp. 292–300.

[322] "Moral Freedom in Recent Ethics," in *Readings in Ethical Theory*, pp. 615–16. Cf. *ibid.*, pp. 594–95, 610.

of any variety is incompatible with the generally accepted notions of responsibility, praise and blame, rewards and punishments. Thus, according to Lotze, "these conceptions have always appeared meaningless to the ordinary reflection, unless it might be presupposed that the conduct which has occurred could just as well have been left unperformed."[323] In Lossky's opinion, "another conception for which determinism leaves no room is the conception of the *ought* as qualitatively distinct from the *is*" and he goes on to say that "such a conception of duty presupposes freedom"—the kind of freedom that involves the indeterminacy of choice.[324] W. G. MacLagan writes:

> I am unable to find any way of avoiding Libertarianism if duty be admitted as a fact and any reason for holding it except the admission of duty as a fact.[325]

Like MacLagan, T. M. Greene also adopts the Kantian argument, rephrasing it as follows:

> We experience a sense of duty directly, and we are unable to dismiss it as illusory; it, in turn, tells us directly that we are free because without freedom duty would be illusory.[326]

And E. F. Carritt, considering the cases of conflict between desire and duty, tells us that "when I obey or disobey my conscience I could have chosen otherwise, and . . . I could not blame myself for disobeying it when it was contrary to desire if I thought I were determined to follow the strongest desire."[327]

[323] *Practical Philosophy*, p. 35. The conduct in question, Lotze explains, has moral quality only if "it is not the necessary consequence of our spiritual states, but has originated through a free act of the will" (*ibid.*).
[324] *Freedom of the Will*, pp. 38–39. Cf. *ibid.*, pp. 41–44.
[325] "Freedom of the Will, "in *Proceedings of the Aristotelian Society*, Suppl. Vol. XXV, p. 193. MacLagan expresses his agreement with Kant's statement "that it is morality that first discovers to us the notion of freedom" (*ibid.*). Cf. G. C. Field, "Kant's First Moral Principle," in *Mind*, Vol. XLI, No. 161, pp. 32–33.
[326] *Liberalism, Its Theory and Practise*, p. 85.
[327] *Ethical and Political Thinking*, p. 138. See also Austin Farrer, *The Freedom of the Will*, pp. 259–62; Alburey Castell, *Science as a Goad to Philosophy*, pp. 72–74; Morris Ginsberg, *On the Diversity of Morals*, pp. 81–82. A. E. Taylor, "The Freedom of Man," in *Contemporary British Philosophy*, Second Series, pp. 290–94; A. K. Stout, "Free Will and Responsibility," in *Proceedings of the Aristotelian Society*, Vol. XXXVII, pp. 213–30; and R. Taylor, "Determinism and the Theory of Agency," in *Determinism and Freedom*, pp. 212–18.

Second Phase

We turn now to authors who deny that moral responsibility, praise and blame, rewards and punishments presuppose the causal indeterminacy of free choice.

All the authors with whom we are here concerned fall into the category of "soft determinists," as that epithet is currently used. They admit that to hold men responsible or accountable for their actions in some meaningful way and to praise or blame them, reward or punish them for the acts does presuppose that the acts in question are free. But, in their view, freedom of action unaccompanied by freedom of choice is quite sufficient as a basis for responsibility and punishment. An act is free if it is voluntary (i.e., if it executes the individual's own volition or desire) or if, under the circumstances, the individual could have acted otherwise if he had chosen to, even if he could not have chosen otherwise. In other words, an adequate basis of responsibility is provided by SR freedom—the circumstantial freedom of self-realization.

Hence, these authors contend, the denial of SD freedom (i.e., the natural freedom of self-determination which involves freedom of choice) does not remove responsibility, praise and blame, reward and punishment, from the lexicon of meaningful terms. But they also recognize that the significance of these terms is altered by the change in the mode of freedom that is implicated in their meaning. When men are praised or blamed, rewarded or punished for acts that are free only in the SR sense, the intention is forward looking or prospective. The sole aim is to influence their future conduct. Any intention that is purely retrospective or retributive is excluded; for a retrospective or retributive application of praise and blame, rewards and punishments, is justified, it is held, only if an individual's responsibility rests upon his having freedom of choice (in the SD sense). Since on this view men do not have such freedom, they are not responsible in the sense that is claimed by the SD authors. But this does not mean that they cannot be held responsible or accountable in some other sense of the term.

The argument, as outlined above, is expressed in a variety of ways from Hobbes and Hume to P. H. Nowell-Smith, A. J. Ayer, Schlick, and B. Russell in the present day. We shall begin with (i) writers such as Hobbes, Priestley, and J. S. Mill, who respond to arguments advanced on the affirmative side of this dispute, and then treat (ii) writers such as Hume, F. H. Bradley, B. Russell, who argue the negative case without reference to specific opponents.

(i) In reply to Bishop Bramhall, Hobbes dismisses the contention that unless men have freedom of choice, they cannot be justly punished or blamed for their acts. Insofar as their actions are voluntary (i.e., are the uncoerced and unconstrained expression of their own desires or volitions) there is some use to praising or blaming them for what they do, and some justification for rewarding or punishing them. The fact that voluntary actions are necessitated by causes that operate within the individual does not remove his responsibility or render him unpunishable, so long as no external circumstances operate to prevent him from acting as he wills. "From the necessity of a voluntary action," Hobbes declares, "cannot be inferred the injustice of the law that forbiddeth it, or of the magistrate that punisheth it."[328] And in another place, he writes: "It is enough to the judge that the act he condemneth be voluntary. The punishment whereof may, if not capital, reform the will of the offender; if capital, the will of others by example."[329]

The justification of punishment, in short, is its utility—either the reformation of the wrongdoer himself or the deterrence of others. Insofar as a man's action is voluntary, it proceeds from his own will, not that of another, and so punishment, operating as one of the causes that affect his future volitions, may alter his voluntary conduct in the future. Hobbes applies the same reasoning to praise and blame. They, too, are useful as affecting a man's future voluntary conduct. Like reward and punishment, he says, "praise and dispraise . . . do by example make and conform the will to good or evil."[330] That, too, is the reason why we admonish men: by "telling a man the good and evil consequences of his actions," we hope to influence him to will one sort of action rather than another.[331]

To the Bishop's observation that this purely prospective and utilitarian conception of praise and blame, rewards and punishments may be fitting in the case of beasts, but not in the case of men, Hobbes replies:

> For my part, I am too dull to perceive the difference between those rewards used to brute beasts, and those that are used to men. If they be not properly called rewards and punishments, let him give them their proper name.

Hobbes refers to the fact that Bramhall has said that the means whereby setting dogs, and coy ducks, and parrots are taught to do what they do "is by their backs, by their bellies, by the rod, or by the morsel, which have indeed a shadow or resemblance of rewards and punishments"; but, the

[328] *The Questions Concerning Liberty, Necessity, and Chance*, p. 153.
[329] *Ibid.*, p. 181.
[330] *Ibid.*, p. 155.
[331] See *ibid.*, pp. 190–91.

ishop added, "we take the word here properly, not as it is used by vulgar
eople, but as it is used by divines and philosophers." Hobbes then asks:

> Does not the Bishop know that the belly hath taught poets, and historians,
> and divines, and philosophers, and artificers, their several arts, as well as
> parrots? Do not men do their duty with regard to their backs, to their necks,
> and to their morsels, as well as setting-dogs, coy-ducks, and parrots? Why
> then are these things to us the substance, and to them but the *shadow* or
> *resemblance* of rewards or punishments?[332]

Joseph Priestley, like Hobbes, argues that freedom of action, accom-
anied by the necessitation rather than the freedom of the will, supports
sponsibility, rewards and punishments, etc.; but, like Hume, he also
rgues that freedom of the will renders responsibility unintelligible. The
cond of these two arguments will be considered later.[333] Here we are
oncerned only with the first. He summarizes it in the following passage.

> Since motives have a certain and necessary influence on the mind of A, I
> know that the prospect of good will certainly incline him to do what I
> recommend to him, and the fear of evil will deter him from any thing that
> I wish to dissuade him from. . . . Every promise and every threatening,
> every reward and every punishment, judiciously administered, works to my
> end.[334]

ccordingly, Priestley declares that "there is all the foundation that we
an wish for a proper *accountableness*, and for *praise* and *blame*, upon
ie doctrine of necessity, and not so much as a shadow of any real founda-
ion for them upon any other supposition."[335]

In his *Examination of Sir William Hamilton's Philosophy*, J. S. Mill
ebuts the argument that "on the theory of Necessity . . . a man cannot
elp acting as he does; and it cannot be just that he should be punished
or what he cannot help."[336] His response to this is very much like that
f Hobbes and Priestley. Equating a man's being responsible with his
eing justly punishable,[337] Mill declares that

> there are two ends which, on the Necessitarian theory, are sufficient to
> justify punishment: the benefit of the offender himself, and the protection
> of others. The first justifies it, because to benefit a person cannot be to do
> him an injury. . . . In its other aspect, punishment is a precaution taken by

[32] *Ibid.*, pp. 195–96.
[33] See Ch. 12, *infra.*
[34] *The Doctrine of Philosophical Necessity Illustrated*, pp. 86–87.
[35] *Ibid.*, p. 90. Cf. *ibid.*, p. 97.
[36] *Op. cit.*, p. 591.
[37] *Ibid.*, p. 586.

society in self-defence. . . . Used to protect the just rights of others against unjust aggression by the offender, it is just. . . . Free-will or no free-will, it is just to punish so far as is necessary for this purpose, as it is just to put a wild beast to death (without unnecessary suffering) for the same object.[338]

The utility of punishment in exerting a causal influence upon future conduct justifies it; but, according to Mill, on the Necessitarian theory of responsibility, there is no justification for punishment that is purely retributive or retaliatory in purpose.[339] Hence, he concludes by telling us that it seems to him

that a person holding what is called the Necessitarian doctrine should on that account *feel* that it would be unjust to punish him for his wrong actions [is] the veriest of chimeras. . . . If the criminal was in a state capable of being operated upon by the fear of punishment, no metaphysical objection, I believe, will make him feel his punishment unjust. Neither will he feel that because his act was the consequence of motives, operating upon a certain mental disposition, it was not his own fault. For, first, it was at all events his own defect or infirmity, for which the expectation of punishment is the appropriate cure. And, secondly, the word fault, so far from being inapplicable, is the specific name for the kind of defect or infirmity which he has displayed—insufficient love of good and aversion to evil. The weakness of these feelings or their strength is in every one's mind the standard of fault or merit, or degrees of fault and degrees of merit.[340]

Like Mill, P. H. Nowell-Smith maintains, in his dispute with C. A. Campbell, that being alterable by punishment and being morally responsible are inseparably connected. We have already reported in considerable detail Nowell-Smith's argument to this effect, as well as his specific criticisms of Campbell's contrary view that responsibility, as that is commonly understood, can be attributed only to the man who could have chosen otherwise, not to one who could have acted otherwise if he had chosen to do so, even if he could not have chosen otherwise.[341] A number of other writers, cited by Nowell-Smith and Campbell in their interchange, espouse the view that insofar as a man's conduct is alterable, it is voluntary, and he is properly subject to praise or blame, rewards and punishments; for

[338] *Ibid.*, pp. 592–94. Like Priestley, Mill also combines this with the counter-argument. "Punishment," he writes, "proceeds on the assumption that the will is governed by motives. If punishment had no power of acting on the will, it would be illegitimate however natural might be the inclination to inflict it. Just so far as the will is supposed free, that is, capable of acting *against* motives, punishment is disappointed of its object, and deprived of its justification" (*ibid.*, p. 592).
[339] See *ibid.*, pp. 597–98.
[340] *Ibid.*, pp. 599–600.
[341] See Ch. 9, pp. 306–12, *supra*.

ch things then have a utility which justifies them. This is the position
A. J. Ayer, M. Schlick, and C. L. Stevenson.[342]
We must also mention here the criticism leveled by Calvin against the
ew held by Aquinas, by Spinoza against the position of Descartes, and
Jonathan Edwards against the doctrine of the Arminians. Calvin insists
at punishments are "justly inflicted on us, from whom the guilt of sin
oceeds . . . whether sin be committed with a judgment free or enslaved,
it be committed with the voluntary bias of the passions."[343] And in
nother place, treating of predestination, he writes:

> The reprobates wish to be thought excusable in sinning, because they can-
> not avoid a necessity of sinning; especially since this necessity is laid upon
> them by the ordination of God. But we deny this to be a just excuse; be-
> cause the ordination of God, by which they complain that they are destined
> to destruction, is guided by equity, unknown indeed to us, but indubitably
> certain. Whence we conclude, that they sustain no misery that is not in-
> flicted upon them by the most righteous judgment of God.[344]

ejecting the Cartesian argument that virtue and vice require freedom of
hoice and that if everything happened from predestined necessity and
othing from free will, all wickedness would be excusable, Spinoza main-
ains that "wicked men are not less to be feared, and are not less harmful,
hen they are wicked from necessity," and so they should be treated
ccordingly.[345] And Edwards argues that moral responsibility is quite con-
istent with the fact that an individual is necessitated to choose certain
cts, or unable to choose others, so long as he is free to act on whatever
hoice he makes.[346]

(ii) Though Hume does not refer specifically to any exponent of the
iew he rejects, he does castigate in general the view that morality and
eligion are destroyed by the denial of free will. "There is no method of
easoning more common," he writes, "and yet none more blameable, than
n philosophical disputes, to endeavor the refutation of any hypothesis,
y a pretense of its dangerous consequences to religion and morality."[347]
Ie then proceeds to argue that universal causal necessity, together with
iberty conceived as freedom of action (i.e., the absence of coercion or

[42] See A. J. Ayer, *Philosophical Essays*, pp. 274–77; M. Schlick, *Problems of Ethics*,
p. 149–58; C. L. Stevenson, *Ethics and Language*, pp. 298–318. Stevenson explicitly
xpresses his indebtedness to Hobbes, Hume, and Mill.
[43] *Institutes of the Christian Religion*, Vol. I, p. 343.
[44] *Ibid.*, Vol. II, p. 209. Cf. *ibid.*, pp. 205–10.
[45] *Chief Works*, Vol. II, p. 392. Cf. Waxman, *The Philosophy of Don Hasdai
Crescas*, pp. 127–38; and Neumark, *Essays in Jewish Philosophy*, pp. 315–16.
[46] See *Freedom of the Will*, pp. 156–62, 302–11, 320–27, 357–71.
[47] *Enquiry Concerning Human Understanding*, Sect. VIII, Part II, Div. 75, p. 96.

constraint), "are not only consistent with morality, but are absolutely essential to its support."[348] On the one hand, he tells us that

> actions are, by their very nature, temporary and perishing; and where they proceed not from some *cause* in the character and disposition of the person who performed them, they can neither redound to his honor, if good; nor infamy, if evil. The actions themselves may be blameable; they may be contrary to all the rules of morality and religion: but the person is not answerable for them; and as they proceeded from nothing in him that is durable and constant, and leave nothing of that nature behind them, it is impossible he can, upon their account, become the object of punishment or vengeance. According to the principle, therefore, which denies necessity, and consequently causes, a man is as pure and untainted, after having committed the most horrid crime, as at the first moment of his birth, nor is his character anywise concerned in his actions, since they are not derived from it, and the wickedness of the one can never be used as a proof of the depravity of the other.[349]

A man is responsible, blameworthy, and properly punishable only for such actions as necessarily flow from his character and motives. On the other hand, he is responsible, blameworthy, and properly punishable only for such actions as are free in the sense of being caused by him rather than external forces. Such freedom, Hume declares,

> is also essential to morality, and . . . no human actions, where it is wanting, are susceptible of any moral qualities, or can be the objects either of approbation or dislike. For as actions are objects of our moral sentiment, so far only as they are indications of the internal character, passions, and affections; it is impossible that they can give rise either to praise or blame, where they proceed not from these principles, but are derived altogether from external violence.[350]

In these passages, Hume does not comment on the shift in the meaning of responsibility when it is rooted in freedom of action rather than freedom of choice, though in the pages which immediately follow them he does consider the question whether God, and not man, is responsible for human misdeeds, on the supposition that God initiates the chain of causes which inevitably leads to a particular wrongful act. Here, as W. I. Matson, a critic of Hume, points out, Hume appears to acknowledge a meaning of responsibility that is different from the one which he defends as consistent with causal necessity.

We shall examine this point presently when we take up the objections

[348] *Ibid.*, p. 97.
[349] *Ibid.*, Div. 76, p. 98.
[350] *Ibid.*, Div. 77, p. 99.

:o soft determinism that are raised by the hard determinists.[351] Here let us turn to a number of writers who, following Hume and in some cases with indebtedness to Hobbes and Mill as well, stress the altered meaning of the basic terms when responsibility is conceived in terms of freedom of action rather than freedom of choice (i.e., SR freedom rather than SD freedom).

Charles Bray asks us to replace one meaning of responsibility by another. "If a man's actions," he writes, "are determined necessarily by the previous state of his mind, and the circumstances or influences to which he is exposed, and if, consequently, no action of his life could possibly have been different from what it actually was, in the circumstances—responsibility, in the sense in which it is generally used, is without meaning. . . . Is then man not accountable for his actions?" Bray thinks that "most certainly he is, for he can never get away from their consequences, and these are made pleasurable or painful as the actions are right or wrong. All true responsibility," he explains, "must have reference to the future, never, as is commonly supposed, to the past."[352]

According to J. M. E. McTaggart, "The argument from the judgment of obligation is perhaps the most usual argument for free will. It seems to me," he adds, "that it is also the strongest, though I cannot regard it as satisfactory."[353] His reasons are as follows. For one thing, he holds that the validity of judgments of obligation are quite consistent with determinism.[354] For another, he maintains that men are responsible and punishable for such voluntary conduct as can be affected by considerations of pleasure and pain.[355] "The expectation of . . . rewards and punishments," he declares, "may encourage right volitions and discourage wrong volitions"; and, consequently, "my responsibility to my fellow men for my volitions consists in the fact that it is reasonable for them to reward and punish me for my volitions, and in that fact only."[356] But, in McTaggart's view, the punishment must be utilitarian and with an eye to future effects, not retrospective and vindictive.[357]

Henry Sidgwick is also of the opinion that "on the Determinist theory, 'responsibility,' 'desert,' and similar terms, have to be used, if at all, in new

[351] See p. 446, *infra.*
[352] *The Philosophy of Necessity*, pp. 39–40.
[353] *Some Dogmas of Religion*, p. 151.
[354] See *ibid.*, pp. 152–59.
[355] See *ibid.*, pp. 159–64.
[356] *Ibid.*, p. 161.
[357] See *ibid.*, pp. 162–64. It should be noted that McTaggart regards vindictive or retributive punishment as unjustifiable on the basis of free will, as well as unjustifiable on the basis of determinism. Cf. Rashdall, *The Theory of Good and Evil*, Vol. II, Book III, Ch. iii, pp. 328–37, 348–50.

significations. On the other hand," he continues, "it seems to me no les
undeniable that the Determinist can give to these terms perfectly clea
and definite meanings: that the distinctions thus obtained give us a pract
cally sufficient basis for criminal law: and that on the Determinist view
the ordinary moral sentiments are seen to be appropriate and useful, as
part of the natural adaptation of social man to his conditions of life."[358]
Bertrand Russell goes further, though no further than Hume's classi
statement of the case. Russell writes:

> Praise and blame, rewards and punishments, and the whole apparatus of
> the criminal law, are rational on the deterministic hypothesis, but not on
> the hypothesis of free will, for they are all mechanisms designed to cause
> volitions that are in harmony with the interests of the community, or what
> are believed to be its interests.[359]

It is in this context that he also remarks that "the conception of 'sin' i
only rational on the assumption of free will." It is appropriate, in Russell'
view, not to a rational ethic, "but only to the vindictive ethic that justifie
hell and holds that 'sin' should be punished regardless of any good tha
punishment may do."[360]

Finally, we come to a number of authors for whom the conception o
responsibility requires, or can have, no basis other than freedom of actior
(SR freedom). Thus, for example, Voltaire declares that "it is a vair
witticism . . . to say that without the pretended liberty of the will, al
pains and rewards are useless." On the contrary, when a brigand goes to
the scaffold, his accomplice, witnessing this, may be deterred. "His com
panion's punishment becomes useful to him and insurance for society only
so long as his will is not free."[361] Using the phrase "popular liberty" for
SR freedom, in contrast to SD freedom which he calls "philosophica
liberty," David Hartley asserts that popular liberty affords "sufficient foun

---

[358] The Methods of Ethics, pp. 65–66. Sidgwick goes on to say that "the Determinis
allows that, in a sense, 'ought' implies 'can,' that a man is only morally bound to do
what is 'in his power,' and that only acts from which a man 'could have abstained'
are proper subjects of punishment or moral condemnation. But he explains 'can' and
'in his power' to imply only the presence of no obstacle that may not be overcome by
sufficient motive" (ibid.). In other words, he explains these terms in an SR not ar
SD, sense of freedom. Consequently, Sidgwick points out, "the meaning of punishmen
is altered: it can no longer be regarded as strictly retributory, but rather as reformatory
and deterrent" (ibid.). Cf. C. J. Ducasse, Nature, Mind and Death, pp. 193–94
199–200; and also "Determinism, Freedom, and Responsibility," in Determinism and
Freedom, pp. 156–57.
[359] Human Society in Ethics and Politics, pp. 79–80.
[360] Ibid., p. 80. Cf. "Determinism and Morals," in The Hibbert Journal, Vol. VII,
Oct., No. 8, pp. 113–21. See also Charles Baylis, "Rational Preference, Determinism,
and Moral Obligation," in The Journal of Philosophy, Vol. XLVII, No. 3, pp. 61–63.
[361] Philosophical Dictionary, pp. 144–45.

lation for commendation and blame, for the difference between virtue and vice, and for the justice of punishing vice."[362] And Hans Kelsen argues that, far from imputing responsibility to men because they are free, we regard human beings as free only insofar as "we impute reward, penance, or punishment, as consequence, to human behavior, as condition, not because human behavior is not determined by causal laws but in spite of the undeniable fact that it is determined by causal laws."[363]

F. H. Bradley stands apart from all the writers whom we have so far considered by reason of his insistence that neither the doctrine of free will nor the doctrine of necessity accords with what he calls the "vulgar" or popular notion of responsibility. On the one hand, he appears to agree with the authors that we have been examining when he points out that the vulgar notion of responsibility, which holds a man accountable for acts that are determined by his character and motives, is quite consistent with the doctrine of necessity and, indeed, untenable without it.[364] On the other hand, Bradley argues that responsibility and liability to punishment are strictly correlative notions, and hence no theory can account for responsibility that cannot justify punishment; but, in his view, the correct as well as the popular view of punishment is that it is essentially retributive, not reformative or deterrent; and here the doctrine of necessity fails, for it can only justify punishment for utilitarian or forward-looking purposes, not punishment that is retrospective and retributive.[365] Bradley, therefore, concludes that "neither the one nor the other of our 'two great philosophical modes of thought' "—the theory of free will and the doctrine of necessity—"does in any way theoretically express the moral notions of the vulgar mind, or fail in some points to contradict them utterly."[366]

THIRD PHASE

In replying to the arguments of the soft determinists, the libertarians do not deny that their opponents can give some meaning to responsibility, praise and blame, rewards and punishments, but they maintain that the interpretation placed upon these terms is inadequate. It fails, in their

[362] *Observations on Man*, p. 359. Cf. *ibid.*, pp. 355–65. Cf. W. Windelband; *Über Willensfreiheit*, pp. 209–11, 220–21; and see also F. Paulsen, *A System of Ethics*, pp. 460–65.
[363] *What is Justice?*, p. 334. Cf. pp. 344–47.
[364] *Ethical Studies*, pp. 1–26. Cf. R. E. Hobart, "Free Will as Involving Determination and Inconceivable Without It," in *Mind*, Vol. XLIII, No. 169, pp. 1–14. See also A. E. Duncan-Jones, "Freedom: An Illustrative Puzzle," in *Proceedings of the Aristotelian Society*, Vol. XXXIX, pp. 107 ff.
[365] *Ethical Studies*, pp. 26–32.
[366] *Ibid.*, p. 33.

view, to account for the moral judgments which men make about themselves and other men *without reference to future conduct*. Nor, as they
see it, does the altered meaning given these terms accord with the common understanding of them that is traditional in philosophical thought
and current in everyday discourse. Thus do Hawkins and Rickaby argue
against Hobbes and J. S. Mill; and, similarly, Campbell, Lewis, Cranston
and Mabbott against Nowell-Smith, Schlick, and Stevenson.

Hobbes and Mill miss the point, D. J. B. Hawkins declares, when they
"insist that, apart from free will, punishment would still be justified by the
purposes of reformation and deterrence." In his opinion,

> the question is not whether praise and blame, reward and punishment, would
> have any meaning or function if determinism were true, but what is their
> actual meaning and function in the moral sphere. If all volition were neces-
> sitated, they would still undoubtedly have the uses attributed to them by
> Hobbes and Mill; but they would not have the place which they in fact
> hold in the estimation of men.

Without denying that reformation and determination are of "great importance in any account of punishment," Hawkins insists that "they are
not the whole account"; retribution must also be included.[367] We may
reward and punish animals and small children for purely corrective or
educative purposes, but in our treatment of adult human beings, whom
we regard as morally responsible, Hawkins maintains that we proceed
differently: the merit or fault of the person, and not future effects, is
central.[368]

In a similar vein, Joseph Rickaby acknowledges that Hobbes can justify
inflicting pain on an offender to correct his future conduct or deter others
from like conduct; but, according to Rickaby, if the offender's action was
causally necessitated, "there is . . . no ground for visiting him with any
moral disapprobation: you may call him names, significant of moral reproach, as stimulants corrective of his will, but in your heart you cannot
reproach him, for what else could he have done?"[369] Attacking the
utilitarianism of Mill, Rickaby writes:

> To punish is not simply to pain: it is to pain and to blame together. Though
> it be sometimes just, for a man's own benefit and for the protection of oth-
> ers, to make him suffer pain for what he cannot help, it can never be just
> to blame him for what he cannot help. The castigations which we inflict on
> children and brute animals are only styled punishments in an improper
> sense of the term, inasmuch as they are not accompanied with moral re-

[367] "Free Will and Right Action," in *The Modern Schoolman*, Vol. XXVI, No. 4,
p. 282.
[368] *Ibid.*, p. 283.
[369] *Free Will and Four English Philosophers*, pp. 23–24.

proach. It is from an exclusive study of this improper sense that utilitarians have evolved their theory of punishment, a theory which supposes that a wicked man, a 'naughty boy,' and a restive horse, are all on a level as objects of punishment. A moment's consideration destroys this supposition. Man, boy, and horse receive stripes alike; but the man is blamed severely, the boy perhaps slightly, the horse not at all. The blame is an essential portion of the man's punishment.

And blame, Rickaby maintains, "supposes that the delinquent could and ought to have done otherwise."[370]

We have elsewhere reported in full C. A. Campbell's objections to the theory of responsibility, blame, and punishment advanced by Nowell-Smith, Schlick, Stevenson, and others.[371] As we have seen, Campbell admits that the freedom to translate one's choice into action is one of the conditions of moral responsibility; but he insists that, while necessary, it is not sufficient. Furthermore, a conception of responsibility that is based solely on freedom of action (SR freedom) does not accord with "what we mean by 'moral responsibility' in ordinary linguistic usage." For one thing, we do not ordinarily consider animals to be morally responsible, but there is no reason why we should not, Campbell says, if responsibility is equated with punishability on utilitarian grounds. For another thing, we ordinarily consider it proper to speak of a person no longer living as morally responsible for some present situation; but, Campbell points out, we should not do so if we accept the forward-looking interpretation of punishment and responsibility. These difficulties, according to Campbell, result from omitting the retributive ingredient in punishment which, in turn, results from trying to conceive responsibility without reference to freedom of choice (SD freedom).[372]

M. Cranston points to the same difficulties in Nowell-Smith's view of responsibility, blame, and punishment. "It allows us," he says, "to praise and blame where praise and blame are *effective* instead of where praise and blame are *deserved*."[373] Though Cranston expresses his own distaste for the retributive theory of punishment, he nevertheless feels that the utilitarian theory cannot avoid two serious difficulties. They are as follows.

(1) Since blame and punishment *does not* affect the behaviour of the hardened criminal, the hardened criminal cannot be said to be morally responsible for his misdeeds.

---

[370] *Ibid.*, pp. 210–11. Cf. *ibid.*, 207–10, 211–16.
[371] See Ch. 9, pp. 255–60, *supra*.
[372] Cf. H. D. Lewis's similar criticisms of the views of Nowell-Smith and Stevenson: "Guilt and Freedom," in *Readings in Ethical Theory*, pp. 610–14.
[373] *Freedom, A New Analysis*, p. 155. In other words, "it simply substitutes *pragmatic* blame for 'backward-looking' blame (together with reformative and deterrent punishment for retributive punishment)" *ibid.*, p. 154.

(2) Since punishment *does* affect the behavior of many cats and dogs and other animals, many cats and dogs and other animals must be said to be morally responsible for their misdeeds.[374]

Neither of these propositions, according to Cranston, "is consistent with the familiar, the almost universal notion of what moral responsibility is. And while Nowell-Smith has successfully persuaded us that determinism is consistent with ethical judgments, it is consistent only with ethical judgments of a strange, strained kind." In Cranston's opinion; "We can give a better, more commonsense account of ethical judgments if we accept the libertarian case."[375]

To the foregoing criticisms of the views of Nowell-Smith, Schlick, and others, J. D. Mabbott adds a number of further objections. He calls attention to the fact that sometimes the utilitarian theory regards men as responsible only where actual punishment will alter their future behavior and sometimes it includes fear of punishment as a factor.[376] He challenges the assumption that either punishment or fear of punishment reforms the moral character of the culprit.[377] He points out that "the act which is affected by blame or punishment is not the act *for which* the blame or punishment is awarded."[378] Furthermore, Mabbott insists "the effect of punishment on the criminal is wholly irrelevant to its justification."[379] And in another place he says that "it is often thought that this [utilitarian] view of punishment . . . is modern and humane compared with the retributive theory, which is primitive and barbaric. But the essential point about retributive punishment is that it treats the criminal as a man."[380] And he concludes:

> For all these reasons I am not satisfied by this latest attempt to connect determinism with responsibility. I remain convinced that moral responsibility requires that a man should be able to choose alternative actions, everything else in the universe prior to the act, including himself, being the same.[381]

[374] *Ibid.*, p. 155.
[375] *Ibid.* See also *ibid.*, pp. 156–59.
[376] "Free Will and Punishment," in *Contemporary British Philosophy* (Third Series) p. 296.
[377] *Ibid.*, p. 297.
[378] *Ibid.*, p. 298.
[379] *Ibid.*, p. 299.
[380] *Ibid.*, p. 303. "To be punished for reform reasons," Mabbott writes, "is to be treated like a dog" (*ibid.*).
[381] *Ibid.*, p. 301. Cf. *ibid.*, pp. 292–95, in which Mabbott criticizes the views of F. H. Bradley and R. E. Hobart. It should be noted that Mabbott is of the opinion that "the defence of freewill must always be . . . an attempt to refute deterministic arguments rather than a positive argument itself" (*ibid.*, p. 302).

The libertarian argument against the soft determinists is summarized by James Martineau in the following statement: "To reduce the moral sentiments to a policy providing for the future, instead of a sentence pronounced upon the past, is simply to renounce them; and amounts to a confession that they cannot coexist with a theory of necessary causation."[382]

FOURTH PHASE

In the last phase of this dispute concerning responsibility and freedom of choice, we come to the position of those who, denying man's possession of free choice, also deny that there is any basis for attributing moral responsibility to men. This is the position which has come to be called "hard determinism," in contrast to the "soft determinism" of those who try to make responsibility, blame, and punishment—in some sense—consistent with causal necessity.[383] In this dispute, therefore, the hard determinists side with the libertarians against the soft determinists, though, along with the soft determinists, they oppose the libertarians in the dispute about the existence of causal indeterminacy.

Bakunin and Nietzsche offer classic statements of the hard-determinist point of view. For Bakunin, the negation of free will entails the negation of the right of society of punish: no one is responsible, "since every individual, with no exception whatever, is but an involuntary product of natural and social environment."[384] Saying that "everything is necessity," Nietzsche declares that "all is guiltlessness, and knowledge is the way to insight into this guiltlessness."[385] And in another place he writes:

> The absolute irresponsibility of man for his acts and his nature is the bitterest drop in the cup of him who has knowledge, if he be accustomed to behold in responsibility and duty the patent of nobility of his human na-

[382] *Types of Ethical Theory*, p. 42. Cf. T. M. Greene's statement to the effect that determinism restricts us "to corrective blame and praise, punishment and reward designed exclusively to modify future behavior, as animals and small children are punished and rewarded not to even the score or because they merit such treatment but only to train them for the future. In short, radical determinism completely negates our moral differentiation between responsible adults and infants, the senile, and the mentally deranged" (*Liberalism, Its Theory and Practise*, p. 78). See also A. K. Stout, "Free Will and Responsibility," in *Proceedings of the Aristotelian Society*, Vol. XXXVII, pp. 225–27.
[383] The epithets are borrowed from William James who used them in a somewhat different sense. See "The Dilemma of Determinism," in *The Will to Believe*, p. 149.
[384] *The Political Philosophy of Bakunin*, p. 338.
[385] *Human, All Too Human*, p. 134.

ture. All his estimates, preferences, dislikes are thus made worthless and
false . . . He may no longer praise, no longer blame, for it is irrational to
blame and praise nature and necessity.[386]

As compared with such writers as Bakunin and Nietzsche, C. D. Broad
is a hard determinist in a qualified sense. As we have seen, he wins agreement from such libertarians as Campbell, Ewing, and L. J. Russell by his
acknowledgment that, unless man has free choice, he is not categorically
obligable or responsible. The agreement is on the proposition that the
denial of SD freedom entails the denial of responsibility, as that is traditionally understood in moral philosophy, with a retrospective and retributive application of blame and punishment and a sharp distinction between
men and brute animals with regard to the manner in which they should be
judged and treated for their acts. But C. D. Broad also holds that there
is another sense of responsibility in which men are conditionally or hypothetically obligable, the condition being that they were able to act otherwise, if they had so chosen to act. To this extent, Broad allows for the
altered sense of responsibility proposed by the soft determinists on the
basis of the SR freedom which is to be found in a hypothetical interpretation of "could have done otherwise." But, unlike them, he does not think
that the fundamental conceptions of ethics are saved by the substitution
of the hypothetical for the categorical interpretation of "could have done
otherwise."[387] Broad denies that there is categorical substitutability and
therefore denies responsibility.

Paul Edwards and John Hospers go further than Broad, in that they not
only acknowledge the dependence of responsibility, as traditionally understood, upon freedom of choice but also flatly reject the altered sense of
responsibility proposed by the soft determinists. In their view, freedom of
action (SR freedom) provides no basis at all for moral responsibility; and
since they deny the existence of freedom of choice (SD freedom), they
accept the conclusion of hard determinism that the notion of responsibility
must be completely abandoned.

According to Edwards, the soft determinism of Hobbes, Hume, J. S.
Mill, Schlick, Ayer, Stevenson, and Nowell-Smith is, in the language of
William James, a "quagmire of evasion."[388] In his view, C. A. Campbell
is right, as against Nowell-Smith, Schlick, Stevenson, and other soft determinists, in insisting that the SD sense of freedom (i.e., the categorical

---

[386] *Ibid.*, p. 132.
[387] See "Determinism, Indeterminism, and Libertarianism," in *Ethics and the History of Philosophy*, pp. 201–5. Cf. G. E. Moore, "A Reply to My Critics," in
The Philosophy of G. E. Moore, p. 624. For a rejection of Broad's view as "mainly
retrospective," see Stebbing, *Philosophy and the Physicists*, p. 246.
[388] See "Hard and Soft Determinism," in *Determinism and Freedom*, pp. 105–8.

interpretation of "could have done otherwise" which involves the assertion that the individual *could have chosen otherwise*) is required for responsibility.[389] "What Campbell calls the reflective sense of 'moral responsibility,'" Edwards declares, "is the only one that qualifies as a properly moral use of the term."[390] But since Edwards does not also agree with Campbell's rejection of determinism, his conclusion is that men "are never morally responsible."[391]

Concurring with Edward's attack on soft determinism,[392] Hospers, like him, denies that we are morally responsible for our actions since they are all inevitably determined by our character and antecedents.[393] "As with responsibility," he says, "so with deserts. Someone commits a crime and is punished by the state; 'he deserved it,' we say self-righteously—as if we were moral and he immoral, when in fact we are lucky and he is unlucky —forgetting that there, but for the grace of God and a fortunate early environment, go we."[394]

Understanding Edwards and Hospers to assert that, if determinism is true, there can be no meaningful attribution of responsibility, or praise and blame, Sidney Hook, Ernest Nagel, and others criticize their argument against soft determinism. According to Hook, "To say, as Professor Hospers does, that 'It's all a matter of luck' is no more sensible than saying: 'Nothing is a matter of luck'—assuming 'luck' has a meaning in a world of hard determinism."[395] He calls attention to the inconsistency of Edwards and Hospers in expressing "concern about the injustice of blaming the morally innocent. . . . If *moral responsibility is a vacuous expression*," Hook writes, "*then moral innocence and guilt are too.*"[396] According to Nagel, Edwards and Hospers simply fail to understand the way in which the phrase "morally responsible" is normally used. He says:

> Moral responsibility is correctly ascribed to individuals who possess certain capacities; and it is correct to make the ascription for the sufficient reason that this is just the way the phrase 'morally responsible' is used. The fact that possessing these capacities is contingent on a variety of conditions, most of which are perhaps beyond the control of an individual, is irrelevant to the analysis of what we do mean by the phrase as well as to the grounds on

[389] See *ibid.*, pp. 109–11.
[390] *Ibid.*, p. 113.
[391] *Ibid.* Cf. Richard Taylor, "Determinism and the Theory of Agency," in *Determinism and Freedom*, pp. 212–14, 217–18.
[392] See "What Means This Freedom?" in *Determinism and Freedom*, p. 113 ff.
[393] See *ibid.*, pp. 119–20, 123–24.
[394] *Ibid.*, p. 127. Cf. "Free Will and Psychoanalysis," in *Readings in Ethical Theory*, pp. 573–74.
[395] "Necessity, Indeterminism, and Sentimentalism," in *Determinism and Freedom*, p. 179.
[396] *Ibid.*, p. 175.

which the ascription is rightly made. . . . Professors Edwards and Hospers can sustain their thesis only by radically altering the customary conception of what it means for anyone to be morally responsible.[397]

There remain to be considered three authors who, while plainly opposed to the causal indeterminacy of free choice, cannot be classified as either hard determinists or soft determinists.

One is Sir David Ross, who comes close to being a soft determinist, though he does not wholly embrace that position. "I am far from contending," Ross writes, "that the whole of our ordinary thought about moral action is reconcilable with the doctrine of Determinism. But," he also says, "it is worth while to point out that it is by no means true that *all* the arguments drawn from the moral consciousness tell in favour of Libertarianism, and only the metaphysical argument tells in favour of Determinism."[398] He then examines the utilitarian view of responsibility, praise and blame, reward and punishment, which is based on the imputation of an act to an individual when that action proceeds from him, i.e., when he is free to do as he wishes.[399] The view he espouses is somewhat different. He states it as follows:

> . . . holding fast to Determinism, I am inclined to think that the only account we can give of responsibility is this: that bad acts can never be forced on any one in spite of his character; that action is the joint product of character and circumstances and is always therefore to some extent evidence of character; that praise and blame are not (though they serve this purpose also) mere utilitarian devices for the promotion of virtue and the restraint of vice, but are the appropriate reactions to action which is good or is bad in its nature just as much if it is the necessary consequence of its antecedents as it would be if the libertarian account were true; that in blaming bad actions we are also blaming and justifiably blaming the character from which they spring; and that in remorse we are being acutely aware that, whatever our outward circumstances may have been, we have ourselves been to blame for giving way to them where a person of better character would not have done so. I cannot pretend that this satisfies the whole of our natural thought about responsibility, but I think that in claiming more, in claiming that a moral agent can act independently of his character, we should be claiming a metaphysical impossibility.[400]

[397] "Some Notes on Determinism," in *Determinism and Freedom*, pp. 187–88. See also the comments on Edwards and Hospers by Arthur Pap, "Determinism, Freedom, Moral Responsibility, and Causal Talk," in *Determinism and Freedom*, p. 203; and by Roderick Chisholm, "Responsibility and Avoidability," in *ibid.*, pp. 145–47.
[398] *Foundations of Ethics*, p. 246.
[399] See *ibid.*, pp. 247–48.
[400] *Ibid.*, pp. 250–51. See H. D. Lewis's critique of Ross's position: "Guilt and Freedom," in *Readings in Ethical Theory*, pp. 614 ff.

The other two authors—F. Ebersole and W. I. Matson—propose solutions of the moral problem which, they claim, are unaffected by the alternatives of indeterminism and determinism. Ebersole points out that free choice is required for responsibility and punishment only when the latter are conceived retrospectively and retributively.[401] He rejects these conceptions, along with free choice.[402] He then proposes a reformatory theory of punishment and states three factual conditions for regarding acts as condemnable or punishable. The act, Ebersole says, must be imputable to the person; it must be the kind of act the person could have chosen or else it must result from desire which could have been subject to choice; and it must not be such as to be caused by the environment and organism of the person without acting through his personality.[403] This leads him to the following conclusion.

> If we confine ourselves to the factual conditions for justifiable condemnation, the question of whether the condemned action is determined or undetermined is irrelevant. If all our actions were completely caused by our desires, and they by past actions, desires, attitudes, thoughts, etc., which were, in turn, completely caused by our heredity and environment, there would remain exactly the same reason for condemnation that would be present if they were not so caused. Either way will do for moral purposes.[404]

Matson admits that "the necessitarian theory cannot ascribe 'moral responsibility' to anyone" unless it uses the term "responsible" merely for those on whom it is probably expedient to inflict punishment.[405] He does not think that the attempt to base responsibility on freedom, when the freedom is simply that of a voluntary but causally necessitated action, succeeds in removing the hard moral consequences of the necessitarian theory. He agrees with Campbell that moral responsibility cannot be saved by what he calls Hume's ploy, which has become so fashionable among Hume's positivist followers.[406] But Matson does not agree with Campbell that the libertarian theory succeeds where the necessitarian theory fails.

---

[401] "Free-Choice and the Demands of Morals," in *Mind*, Vol. LXI, No. 242, p. 239.

[402] See *ibid.*, p. 250.

[403] See *ibid.*, pp. 253–54.

[404] *Ibid.*, p. 255. Cf. *ibid.*, pp. 256–57. Mabbott, in his criticism of Ebersole, points out that Ebersole, with minor variations, adopts the utilitarian theory of blame and punishment that is concerned only with their future effects and so, in spite of his conclusion, he holds a position which very closely resembles the soft determinism of Nowell–Smith and others. See "Free Will and Punishment," in *Contemporary British Philosophy* (Third Series), pp. 295–302.

[405] "On the Irrelevance of Free-Will to Moral Responsibility, and the Vacuity of the Latter," in *Mind*, Vol. LXV, No. 260, p. 491.

[406] See *ibid.*, pp. 492–94. "Hume's ploy," Matson writes, "was intended to take in the vulgar, but it has beguiled the learned in our time" (*ibid.*, p. 493).

As he sees it, "The consequences of necessitarianism and libertarianism for moral responsibility are *precisely the same.*"[407] Moral responsibility is thus left without any foundation, a result which recommends itself to Matson, for, in his view, "the concept refers to a very prevalent mode of moral thinking which [he considers] pernicious."[408]

In the course of his analysis, Matson calls attention to the fact that Hume, having argued that an individual can justly be held responsible for his voluntary (i.e., uncoerced) acts even though they are causally necessitated, then "pondered whether, if necessity is universal, we must not impute all human sin ultimately to God."[409] Hume concluded that this is a mystery which reason cannot fathom. Matson interprets this conclusion, "in accordance with canons of Humean exegesis," to mean "that we must indeed impute sin to God."[410] But he also recognizes that Hume's question (concerning God's responsibility for human misdeeds if He is their free cause and man their necessary cause) acknowledges a meaning of responsibility which is compatible with free choice, but not with causal necessity.

6. THE DISPUTE ABOUT THE EVIDENCE OF CONSCIOUSNESS

In the preceding chapter, which dealt with the issue concerning causal initiative, we pointed out that the evidence of consciousness is more frequently used to support the affirmation of causal indeterminacy than to support the assertion of causal initiative. However, in many cases, the two arguments are merged: experience of free choice is said to be the grounds not only for the reality of causal indeterminacy but also for causal initiative insofar as the former presupposes the latter. Some of the documentation presented in the preceding chapter, therefore, covered both points, especially the report given of the actual disputes between Price and Priestley, Mansel and J. S. Mill, Campbell, Nowell-Smith, and R. D. Bradley.[411]

We also pointed out in the preceding chapter that affirmative argument,

407 *Ibid.*, p. 496. For the argument leading up to this conclusion, see *ibid.*, pp. 494–96.
408 *Ibid.*, p. 497.
409 *Ibid.*, p. 493. The passage in Hume to which Matson is here referring is in the *Enquiry Concerning Human Understanding*, Sect. VIII, Part II, Div. 78–81, pp. 99–103.
410 *Ibid.*
411 For the Price-Priestley dispute, see Ch. 9, pp. 317–21, *supra*; for the Mansel-Mill dispute, see *ibid.*, pp. 317–18, 320–21, *supra*; and for the dispute involving Campbell, Nowell-Smith, and R. D. Bradley see *ibid.*, pp. 321–28, *supra*.

based on the evidence of consciousness, takes two forms. In one form, our direct experience of free choice is said to be evidence of a genuine, not a pseudo-problem about the real existence of "contra-causal freedom," involving both causal indeterminacy and causal initiative. It is in this form that Campbell argues that our experience supports a belief in free choice, which in turn confronts us with a genuine problem about the validity of that belief. Nowell-Smith and R. D. Bradley argue against him that the introspective evidence does not validate the existence of contra-causal freedom; and Campbell, in reply, points out that he admits that the validity of the belief in free choice is not established by the introspective evidence, though that evidence does give rise to the belief.[412]

With the exception of Campbell, the affirmative authors employ the second form of argument, in which it is said that our direct experience of free choice warrants us in asserting the existence of causal indeterminacy. The validity of this argument is denied on several counts, by a few authors who affirm the existence of causal indeterminacy as well as by a considerable number who deny it. In documenting this dispute, we shall, therefore, proceed as follows: (i) we shall examine the arguments that are advanced by affirmative authors who have not already been fully treated in the preceding chapter; (ii) we shall then consider the criticism of such arguments by writers who themselves affirm free choice; and (iii) finally, we shall turn to the rebuttal of the affirmative arguments by writers who deny the existence of free choice, again limiting ourselves to those who have not been fully treated in Chapter 9.

(i) Descartes reports the objection raised by Hobbes that "the freedom of the will has been assumed without proof."[413] To this, Descartes replies as follows: "I made no assumption concerning freedom which is not a matter of universal experience; our natural light makes this most evident."[414] He is here repeating what he laid down as a proposition in, *The Principles of Philosophy*, namely, that "freedom of the will is self-evident."[415] And, in replying to another objection, he reasserts this proposition.

---

[412] See J. D. Mabbott's statement that he agrees "entirely with Nowell-Smith's rejection of Professor C. A. Campbell's view that we are directly aware in certain cases that our choice is undetermined": "Free Will and Punishment," in *Contemporary British Philosophy* (Third Series), p. 302. Campbell would regard Mabbott as sharing the same misunderstanding with which he charges Nowell-Smith. See also M. Arnold's critique of Freud's analysis of our belief in free choice: *The Human Person*, pp. 19–24.

[413] *Objections and Replies*, III, in *Philosophical Works*, Vol. II, p. 74.

[414] *Ibid.*, p. 75.

[415] *Op. cit.*, in *Philosophical Works*, Vol. I, p. 234. Cf. *Meditation IV*, in *ibid.*, pp. 173–75.

You . . . deny certain truths about the indeterminateness of the will; and although they are in themselves quite evident, I refuse to undertake to prove them before your eyes. For these matters are such that anyone ought to experience them in himself rather than be convinced of them by ratiocination.[416]

Lequier and Fouillée, like Descartes, express the conviction that our freedom is immediately evident to us in our experience.[417]

Lequier describes the experience somewhat more fully than Descartes. "At the moment when I decide," he writes, "I have the idea that I have the power of willing otherwise. Since I do not make use of this power, I ought to see that I have not an actual sense of it, but a presentiment: the presentiment of something which is as though it were not, since I do not make use of it at the moment when I am actually willing."[418] So, too, for Henry More, "it is manifest that we sometimes act so, as that to have willed and acted otherwise was in our power."[419] In N. Lossky's opinion, "the naive reference to the immediate consciousness of freedom is, like many naive judgments, an expression of a primitive but sound sense of truth and merely needs philosophic elaboration." He then goes on to say that "the possibility of acting differently may . . . be established by a *direct* proof, i.e., by the immediate observation of a single action."[420]

Other writers combat the suggestion that our experience of free choice may be illusory. "Is the feeling or experience of free self-determination in the dynamic states of resolution and choice," Aveling asks, "a direct intuition of a free person, or is it an illusion?"[421] His answer is that "if any experience is real, surely this is real."[422] Castell's approach is somewhat different. It is only the belief in determinism which leads us to suspect that our experience of freedom is illusory. "Aside from the demands of determinism," he asks, "how do we get to know that the experience of freedom is illusory?" As he sees it, "We must believe that our experience of voluntariness is illusory because, and only because, determinism requires it."[423] F. C. S. Schiller argues in a similar vein.

There is always a risk in taking appearances to contain ultimate truth. But it is not so serious as to take them as containing no truth at all. And to our

---

[416] *Objections and Replies*, V, in *Philosophical Works*, Vol. II, pp. 224–25.
[417] See Lequier, *La recherche d'une première vérité* p. 141; Fouillée, *La liberté et le déterminisme*, p. vii.
[418] *La recherche d'une première vérité*, pp. 119–20.
[419] *An Account of Virtue*, p. 179.
[420] *Freedom of the Will*, p. 123.
[421] *Personality and Will*, p. 203.
[422] *Ibid.*, p. 204.
[423] *Science as a Goad to Philosophy*, p. 72. Cf. *ibid.*, pp. 70–71.

Humanism it will naturally seem a better risk to take to trust appearances than to invalidate them for no sufficient reason.[424]

MacLagan also confronts the problem of whether our belief in free choice, based on experience, may not be an "inescapable illusion." In his view, "One is certainly tempted to say that our freedom is, after all, a matter of immediate apprehension."[425] But he feels called upon to qualify this statement in the following manner. The question whether the experience is real or illusory would never arise, MacLagan thinks, if we approached the matter either exclusively from the viewpoint of the moral agent observing himself from within or exclusively from the viewpoint of the spectator observing the conduct of others from without. "The problem," he writes, "is constituted by the collision of affirmations proper to these two standpoints respectively, and no solution of it accordingly can fall within the purview of either of them separately. The solution must in the nature of the case take the form of a verdict on the relative status, as vantage grounds of insight, of the two standpoints themselves."[426] The solution MacLagan then proposes gives primacy to the introspective evidence in support of freedom, since from the other standpoint we are not required to assert the universal reign of necessity, but only a uniformity of nature, as he puts it, "that is not broken too much"; in other words, a degree of uniformity that does not preclude freedom.[427]

A similar approach to the problem is also to be found in the writings of Max Planck and Niels Bohr. From the standpoint of the introspective observer, free choice is a fact of experience; from the standpoint of the objective observer, everything is causally necessitated. These two ways of looking at things are, according to Bohr, complementary rather than contradictory, since the phenomena cannot be approached in both ways at once.[428] Tolstoy, on the other hand, sees a profound contradiction in the fact that human behavior, observed from without, is subject to law and necessity, while, observed from within, it involves freedom. "In this contradiction," he writes, "lies the problem of free will." Whether that problem can be solved or not, Tolstoy maintains that we have an "unshakable, irrefutable consciousness of freedom."[429]

---

[424] *Studies in Humanism*, p. 408. See also *ibid.*, pp. 401–8.
[425] "Freedom of the Will," in *Proceedings of the Aristotelian Society*, Suppl. Vol. XXV, pp. 197–98.
[426] *Ibid.*, p. 199.
[427] See *ibid.*, pp. 199–200.
[428] See Bohr, "On the Notions of Causality and Complementarity," in *Science*, Vol. III, No. 2873, p. 54. Cf. Planck, *Scientific Autobiography*, pp. 69–75; *The New Science*, pp. 59–63, 287–88; *The Universe in the Light of Modern Physics*, pp. 99–100.
[429] See *War and Peace*, Second Epilogue, Ch. VIII. For Tolstoy's solution of the problem, within the framework of his philosophy of history, see *ibid.*, Ch. IX.

(ii) Three authors who affirm freedom of choice nevertheless maintain that our conscious experience does not establish its existence. According to Secrétan, "The pretension of proving freedom from immediate consciousness is an illusion which reflection dispels easily."[430] According to Boutroux, freedom, "of which the contingency of things is here regarded as the outer sign, is not and cannot be, either directly or indirectly, given or set forth in experience."[431] According to N. Hartmann, the argument from the consciousness of free choice to the existence of it lacks cogency in the same way that the ontological argument for God's existence does. It begs the question, which is "whether there corresponds to the consciousness of freedom a freedom of consciousness or not."[432] While Hartmann admits that "the consciousness of self-determination must of course have its ground," he points out that "the ground need not be the real existence of self-determination," and so the inference cannot be validly made from consciousness to existence.[433]

(iii) On the negative side of this dispute, authors such as Spinoza and Hume briefly dismiss the consciousness or feeling of freedom that is thought to reveal its existence. In a letter about his disagreement with Descartes concerning free will, Spinoza says that when men boast of their possession of freedom, "[they] are conscious of their own desire, but are ignorant of the causes whereby that desire has been determined."[434] Referring to the "false sensation or seeming experience which we have, or may have, of liberty or indifference, in many of our actions," Hume says that "however we may imagine we feel a liberty within ourselves, a spectator can commonly infer our actions from our motives and character."[435]

Paulsen quotes Sidgwick's statement "that against the formidable array of cumulative evidence offered for Determinism, there is but one argument of real force: the immediate affirmation of consciousness in the moment

---

[430] *Mon Utopie*, p. 162. It should be noted that he also says that "the pretension of establishing its impossibility is only a confusion of the same kind and less pardonable" (*ibid.*).

[431] *Contingency of the Laws of Nature*, p. 173.

[432] *Ethics*, Vol. III, p. 119. But from the fallacy of the argument, according to Hartmann, "it by no means follows that there is no freedom of the will, just as little as the non-existence of God follows from it" (*ibid.*, p. 120).

[433] *Ibid.*, p. 148. Gruender and Simon offer what purport to be answers to the type of criticism here advanced by Hartmann. See Ch. 9, pp. 116–17 and 123–24, *supra*. Cf. Suarez, *Disputationes Metaphysical*, XIX, Sect. 2, N. 15; *De Finance, Existence et Liberté*, pp. 10–12; and Keith Lehrer, "Can We Know That We Have Free Will by Introspection?" in *Journal of Philosophy*, Vol. LVII, No. 5, pp. 145–57.

[434] *Chief Works*, Vol. II, p. 390.

[435] *Enquiry Concerning Human Understanding*, Sect. VIII, Part I, p. 94 fn. 1. Cf. *ibid.*, Div. 71, pp. 92–93.

of deliberate action."[436] Paulsen admits that "everyone has an immediate feeling of certainty that he is not moulded into what he is from without, that everything would have happened otherwise if he had willed otherwise. . . . Is this an illusion?" he asks. "Certainly not," he replies. "Self-consciousness does not deceive us. But what does it say?" His answer is that it reveals nothing but our sense that our action follows from our own wishes or inclinations, not that we are free in determining which of our wishes or desires shall prevail.[437]

A number of other writers make the same point, namely, that our feeling of freedom is simply the feeling that we can do as we wish, not an awareness of our being able to choose what we shall wish. Referring "to the argument from that feeling of freedom which we experience in action," McTaggart writes: "To prove that we have this sense of freedom an appeal must be made to introspection, and thus this argument is apt to be confounded with the assertion . . . of an immediate certainty of the proposition that the will is not completely determined." McTaggart does not question that we feel free when we act as we wish instead of being subject to coercive forces; but, in his view, the reality of our "freedom of self-direction" (i.e., our SR freedom) explains this feeling, and so "there is no necessity to accept freedom in the sense of indetermination."[438] Ross tells us that "in considering the intuition of freedom, we shall do well to consider separately the two questions of the freedom to choose, or decide, or resolve, and of freedom to do what we have resolved upon."[439] In his view, it is only the latter freedom of which we are directly aware; there is no intuition of freedom of choice.[440]

Blanshard, on the other hand, thinks that the matter cannot be so easily disposed of. "The feeling of freedom that is relevant as evidence," he writes, "is the feeling of an open future as regards the choice itself. After the noise of argument has died down, a sort of intuition stubbornly remains that we can not only lift our hand if we choose, but that the choice itself is open to us. Is this not an impressive fact?"[441] In Blanshard's opinion, its impressiveness is removed by the following consideration.

[436] *A System of Ethics*, p. 459 fn. 1. (The quoted statement is from Sidgwick's *Methods of Ethics*, p. 64.)
[437] *Ibid.* Cf. Bain's handling of Sidgwick's argument in *The Emotions and the Will*, pp. 493–96.
[438] *Some Dogmas of Religion*, pp. 146–47. "My sense of freedom," he says in another place, "is proportionate to the extent to which my action is determined by my will. And I maintain that it is quite accounted for by the fact that the action is determined by the will, and that there is no need to hold the determining volition is itself undetermined" (*ibid.*, p. 148).
[439] *Foundations of Ethics*, pp. 223–24.
[440] See *ibid.*, pp. 224–30.
[441] "The Case for Determinism," in *Determinism and Freedom*, p. 5.

. . . when we are making a choice our faces are always turned toward the future, toward the consequences that one act or the other will bring us, never toward the past with its possible sources of constraint. Hence these sources are not noticed. Hence we remain unaware that we are under constraint at all. Hence we feel free from such constraint.[442]

Hence, "to the objection that we always feel free," Blanshard answers "that it is natural to feel so, even if we are determined, since our faces are set toward results and not toward causes, and the causes of present action always elude us."[443] Commenting on Blanshard's argument, Pap remarks that he fails "to see why our 'feeling free' calls for explanation if one believes in determinism." In his opinion, "that I feel free just means that I believe, on good grounds, that—within limits of course—I can do as I please."[444]

Finally, we must consider Hans Kelsen's criticism of Planck's argument which distinguishes between the subjective evidence of freedom and the objective evidence of causal necessity.[445] Kelsen writes:

There is, of course, no contradiction between the law of causality, that is, the statement that all phenomena are causally determined, and a man's statement that he has a feeling which induces him to think that his will is not causally determined, which is a statement about a fact. However, from the fact that a man has a feeling which induces him to think that his will is free, does not follow that this thought is true. For there is certainly a contradiction between the law of causality and the content of the man's thought, and it is precisely the content of the man's thought that refers to the question of the freedom of will.[446]

As Kelsen sees it, Planck tries to demonstrate that

the freedom of will, that is, its being not causally determined—and not man's feeling to be free—is compatible with the universal law of causality assumed by natural science. He declares that "the question as to whether the will is or is not causally determined is, in truth, a question of the viewpoint from which one approaches the problem, that is, the question of the supposition with which one judges an act of will." He admits that "the human will, viewed from an objective scientific standpoint, is causally determined," but, he asserts, "viewed from the subjective standpoint of individual self-consciousness, the human will is free."[447]

[442] *Ibid.*
[443] *Ibid.*, p. 15.
[444] "Determinism, Freedom, Moral Responsibility, and Causal Talk," in *Determinism and Freedom*, p. 200. "It seems to me," Pap adds, "that what requires explanation is not the feeling of freedom but the fallacious belief that a caused decision is not really a decision."
[445] See p. 388, *supra*.
[446] *What is Justice?*, p. 336.
[447] *Ibid.*, p. 337.

But, Kelsen argues,

> this means that one and the same question may be answered in different ways if it is asked from different points of view. But if the question of free will—as Planck supposes—is the question as to whether the human will is or is not subjected to the law of causality, and that means, a question of the validity of the law of causality, it is by its very nature a question of objective science, and not of subjective self-consciousness. If, however, the question which arises from the point of view of the individual self-consciousness is the question as to what man is feeling at the moment of an act of will, or the question whether he is aware of the cause of this act, it is a question different from that of the free will, and the answer to the former questions is no answer to the latter. And then it is not the same question namely, the question as to whether the will is or is not causally determined, which may be answered in different ways from different points of view.[448]

Consequently, in Kelsen's opinion, the scientific principle of complementarity cannot be applied here.

> In physics, one and the same question: as to whether the sun is moving and the earth is at rest, or whether the earth is moving and the sun at rest, is answered in different ways according to the system of reference chosen. However, it is not the same question which is answered from the objective point of view of science in a way different from that in which it is answered from the subjective point of view of the individual self-consciousness. There are two questions. The first one is the question as to whether the human will is or is not causally determined; and the answer is that it is causally determined. The second one is the question as to whether the individual can understand his future act of will as causally determined; and the answer is that he cannot. This, however, does not mean that his act of will is not causally determined.[449]

7. SPECIAL AND UNANSWERED ARGUMENTS

In the controversy about free choice, as we have examined it so far, arguments against causal indeterminacy have been met by replies or counter-arguments in its favor, and the defense of free choice by libertarians has been criticized and challenged by determinists. But now we come to arguments advanced by libertarians to which no reply can be found on the part of determinists. These fall into two groups. The first attempts to show that determinism undermines its own validity. The second asserts that neither causal determinism nor causal indeterminacy can be proved, and

---

[448] *Ibid.*
[449] *Ibid.*, p. 339. Kelsen's arguments apply to Bohr's principle of complementarity as well as to Planck's use of this principle. See fn. 428, p. 449, *supra*.

454 The General Controversy

asks us to recognize, therefore, that both are postulates between which we can and must choose—freely. The first type of argument, as we shall see, makes a point which has some relevance for the second, but this goes unnoticed by the writers who advance the second.

(i) According to M. Ginsberg, the very process of scientific inquiry would be undermined if every judgment of the mind were causally necessitated, as the determinists maintain. "If it be maintained," he writes, "that a man's judgments are themselves completely determined, that he cannot help making the judgments he makes, the answer is that this makes nonsense of all knowledge." For, he explains,

> if all judgments were causally necessitated, they would all be on the same level and it would be impossible to distinguish some as true and others as false. Sense and nonsense would all be equally necessitated. The whole notion of going by the evidence would lose all its meaning, if in forming a judgment we were completely unable to resist the violence of present desire, the effects of past habits, the persistence of ancient prejudices or the forces of the unconscious.

Furthermore, he points out, there could be nothing like a rational debate of this issue, for "there would be no sense in arguing about determinism or indeterminism if all our arguments were rigidly determined in advance." We should be determined by our character and antecedents to be either determinists or indeterminists, and all our arguments would be a pretense at rationalization rather than an offer of genuine reasons. But, Ginsberg concludes, "if we admit that we can sometimes eliminate bias, that we can sometimes act on the basis of a judgment we form of the facts and of the relative value of the alternatives between which we have to choose, we have the minimum freedom required for moral accountability or responsibility."[450]

Paul Weiss also maintains that determinism is self-defeating.

> The determinist's theory allows one to say that there is nothing wrong or right in holding to the theory and nothing wrong or right in opposing it. The formulation of the theory and the acceptance or rejection of it are, by that theory itself, predetermined, unavoidable expressions of an external force, and any supposed comment or evaluation of them, favorable or unfavorable, is also predetermined by the alien power.[451]

The determinist who willingly asserts his theory to be true acknowledges implicitly his own freedom. "If a determinist is willing to affirm that his

450 *On the Diversity of Morals*, p. 82.
451 *Nature and Man*, p. 25.

theory is true," Weiss writes, "he must affirm that it is something which can be freely considered and responsibly adopted, and thus that those who know it are so far not determined by an alien power."[452] No determinism can be so complete as to leave out "the fact that someone is making a responsible judgment of its merits." For, Weiss continues,

> if a determinist . . . denies that he freely considers and responsibly adopts his position, he denies that he has a view which opposes others; his view is then acknowledged to be but one verbal fact among a multitude, no better or worse, no more or less important, than any other.[453]

E. L. Mascall similarly contends that "a radical determinism about our mental processes is self-stultifying," when, in all consistency, it is "applied not only to our volitions and our attitudes, but to our reasoning processes as well."[454] His argument for this conclusion is very much like that of Ginsberg and Weiss. "Suppose, for example, it was the case," he writes, "that the necessary and sufficient condition for me to be convinced that an argument which I was considering was valid was that an event of some particular type A should occur in my cerebral cortex, and that the necessary and sufficient condition for me to be convinced that an argument which I was considering was invalid was that an event of some other particular type B should occur in the cortex." Now, he continues, if the events in question are causally necessitated by my character and past antecedents, that an event of type A should occur rather than the event of type B is just as likely whether the argument was in fact valid or invalid. Hence, "my conviction that an argument which I had been considering was valid would provide no evidence for the argument's validity, but only for the occurrence of a type A event."[455]

As Mascall sees it, when the determinist position is thus stated, it is self-destructive in the sense that "the mere statement of the position deprives it of any claim for acceptance"; for the position asserts "that my conviction that an argument is valid is no evidence of its validity." And, he continues, if the theory of determinism is true,

> then no arguments against it have any force. But then, if it is true, no arguments in its favour have any force either. It is pretty clear that no one in normal society in fact holds this position in its fullness, for its consistent adoption would lead to insanity. What, I think, frequently happens is that it is held in a mitigated form. The second half of the position, which denies that acts which seem free are really free, is asserted, while the first half,

---

[452] *Ibid.*
[453] *Ibid.,* p. 26.
[454] *Christian Theology and Natural Science,* p. 216.
[455] *Ibid.,* p. 213.

which denies that arguments which seem valid are really valid, is not. This, however, seems very arbitrary, for it is difficult to see why one type of mental operation should be held to bear genuine credentials if another type is held to bear forged ones.[456]

In other words, the doctrine of determinism, if carried out with rigorous consistency, would not only deny free choice in the sphere of human action but also independent intellectual decisions in the sphere of human thought; and so it would result in so thoroughgoing a skepticism that it could not rationally argue the truth of its own position.

Another formulation of the same attack on determinism is offered by Alburey Castell in the following passage, which is here quoted in full.

> Suppose it is said that no one ever could do other than he did do, and we ask, "What reason is there for believing that that statement is true?" Our question here invites the speaker to do some reasoning, to go through some reasoning processes, to consider some facts as premises and show how you can reason from them to the conclusion that no one ever could do other than he did do. Now, what about these reasoning processes? Do they, too, fall under the ban of "could not have done otherwise?" When a man is reasoning, are we to understand that each step taken by his mind is as rigidly necessitated as the sequence of steps by which a stone rolls down a hill? Is a man reasoning no more "in charge" of what he is doing than, say, when he is falling through the air from a roof top? If he is "in charge" of acts performed with his mind (e.g., reasoning) but not "in charge" of acts performed with his body (e.g., striking some one over the head), then we seem to have a break in the rule about "could not have done otherwise." Is determinism prepared to acknowledge such an exception to itself? If so, why? If not, if a person is no more "in charge" in the one case than in the other, then is the reasoning trustworthy? Are we to say that a mental process is trustworthy simply because each stage is causally necessitated by what precedes it? If so, the processes of a sick or crazed or over-fatigued mind are as trustworthy as the processes of a healthy, alert, sensitized mind, since in both cases (the claim is) each stage is causally necessitated by what precedes it. But if the processes of a sane mind are no more trustworthy than the processes of an insane mind, why do we trust the man who reasons in support of the theory that no one ever could do other than he does do? His reasoning processes are no more binding than a series of hiccoughs. Does this amount to saying that you cannot give a reason for determinism which would *justify* a person in accepting it? If so, the theory is pricing itself out of the market. It is hoist on its own petard.[457]

According to Paul Tillich, the argument boils down to the fact that "the determinist does not see that the very affirmation of determinism as true

[456] *Ibid.*, p. 214.
[457] *Science as a Goad to Philosophy*, pp. 74-75.

presupposes the freedom of decision between true and false."[458] What is left implicit in this statement is the *a fortiori* inference that if we have freedom of decision between true and false, we also have it between good and bad. Hence, if the affirmation of determinism as true presupposes that we are free to decide between the opposed theories in the light of all available evidence and reasons, then it also presupposes that we are free to decide between alternative sources of action in the light of our thinking about their advantages and disadvantages. But if that is so, then the affirmation of determinism as true leads to the affirmation of a freedom that makes determinism untrue.

The connection between this type of attack on determinism and the argument to which we shall presently turn can be indicated by the following considerations. It might be said by the determinist that at least some truths are necessary, in the sense that their opposite are impossible to assert because patently self-contradictory. It makes no difference here whether such necessary truths are conceived as self-evident axioms, as purely analytic propositions, or even as tautologies. The point is that, in the presence of a necessary truth, we are not free to decide between it and its opposite: our judgment is itself necessitated by the proposition being considered. But since no one claims that all propositions are necessary truths, there remain all those matters which, by their very nature, do not compel the mind's assent or dissent.

Now in these cases, either the proposition can be demonstrated or it cannot be. If it can be, then again our judgment is necessitated—on condition, of course, as the determinist might add, that our intellectual character is such that we are habitually predisposed to think rationally, i.e., to follow the argument to its conclusion and yield to the weight of the evidence. But if the proposition—or its contrary—cannot be demonstrated (if such evidence and reasons as are available are *inconclusive*), then whatever position we adopt, we must take *voluntarily*. Since the necessity of the proposition or the evidence in its favor does not make up our minds for us, we must make up our own minds by a decision that stems from our will. In short, if our intellectual judgments are not determined *objectively* by the objects we are considering (i.e., the propositions themselves or the evidence and reasons for them), then they must be determined *subjectively*, in which case they are voluntary in the sense of stemming from our will, desires, wishes, etc.

It is at this point that the arguments against determinism, which we have been examining, have some bearing on the second type of argument, to which we shall now turn. The latter, as we shall see, maintains that neither

---

[458] *Systematic Theology*, Vol. I, pp. 200–1.

determinism nor its opposite can be proved. It regards the proposition which asserts the universal reign of causal necessity and the proposition which asserts causal indeterminacy in man's acts of choice as assumptions, i.e., as postulates which, by their very nature as postulates, require an act of will on our part. We must make up our own minds voluntarily whether to adopt the postulate of determinism or the postulate of freedom. Since we are free to decide, the best use of this freedom, so the argument runs, is to decide in favor of freedom.

(ii) The classic statement of this argument is to be found in William James, though it has precursors in the writings of Renouvier and Lequier.

Renouvier declares that "the thesis of freedom is not logically demonstrable, any more than that of necessity is."[459] According to Lequier, the "dogma of necessity cannot be demonstrated"; but, he points out, "freedom, real though it be, cannot be demonstrated either."[460] Both are postulates. It may be noted in passing that a number of determinists agree that their position cannot be proved. Nagel, for example, tells us that determinism must be postulated as a useful regulative principle;[461] Bertrand Russell says that "the reasons for supposing volitions to be determined are strong but not conclusive";[462] and A. J. Ayer refers to "the postulate of Determinism."[463] On the other hand, a number of libertarians also admit that their position cannot be proved. Thus, Lotze says that free will is a postulate of the practical reason;[464] N. Hartmann maintains that all we can establish is the possibility of free choice, not its actuality;[465] and M. Cranston tells us that the theory of free will cannot be established by positive argument, but only defended negatively.[466] But these writers do not argue, as Renouvier, Lequier, and James do, that the logical situation created by conflicting postulates opens the door for a free affirmation of freedom itself.

In an essay on Bain and Renouvier, James states that argument in the following manner.

The "assumption" of a fixed law in natural science is . . . an intellectual *postulate*, just as the assumption of an ultimate law of indetermination might be a moral postulate in treating of certain human deliberations. Is

[459] *Psychologie Rationelle*, Vol. I, p. 328.
[460] *La recherche d'une première vérité*, p. 134.
[461] See "Some Notes on Determinism," in *Determinism and Freedom*, p. 187.
[462] *Mysticism and Logic*, p. 196.
[463] "Freedom and Necessity," in *Philosophical Essays*, p. 282.
[464] See *Practical Philosophy*, p. 50.
[465] See *Ethics*, Vol. III, pp. 137–40.
[466] See *Freedom, A New Analysis*, p. 170. Cf. J. D. Mabbott, "Free Will and Punishment," in *Contemporary British Philosophy* (Third Series), p. 302.

each assumption true in its sphere, or is determinism universal? Since no man can decide empirically, must one remain for ever uncertain, or shall one anticipate evidence and boldly choose one's side?

Questions of this sort, James then points out, lead "M. Renouvier to a most vigorous and original discussion of the ultimate grounds of certitude, of belief *in general,* from which he returns to make his decision about this particular point." As James reports Renouvier's view, it is that "in every wide theoretical conclusion we must seem more or less arbitrarily to *choose* our side. Of course the choice may at bottom be predetermined in each case, but also it may not. This brings us back to our theoretical dilemma about freedom, concerning which we must now bow to the necessity of making a choice; for suspense itself would be a choice, and a most practical one, since by it we should forfeit the possible benefits of boldly espousing a possible truth."[467]

In this situation, Renouvier, says James, "boldly avows the full conditions under which alone we can be right if freedom is true, and says: 'Let our liberty pronounce on its own real existence.'"[468] James adopts Renouvier's argument in *The Principles of Psychology,* where he gives his own version of it.

When scientific and moral postulates war thus with each other and objective proof is not to be had, the only course is voluntary choice, for scepticism itself, if systematic, is also voluntary choice. If, meanwhile, the will *be* undetermined, it would seem only fitting that the belief in its indetermination should be voluntarily chosen from amongst other possible beliefs.

James therefore recommends that "freedom's first deed should be to affirm itself. We ought never to hope for any other method of getting at the truth if indeterminism be a fact."[469]

A slightly different version of this argument is to be found in F. C. S. Schiller.

Methodological postulates as such cannot be refuted; they can only be disused. And metaphysical dogmas also, that is, ultimate attitudes of thought, cannot be refuted; they can only be chosen or rejected; for they form the foundations on which our demonstrations rest.

Of determinism, he then says that its status as a metaphysical creed "reduces . . . like all such ultimate assumptions, to a matter of free choice.

[467] "Bain and Renouvier," in *Collected Essays and Reviews,* pp. 32–34.
[468] *Ibid.,* p. 34. James quotes Renouvier's statement that "I prefer to affirm my liberty and to affirm it by means of my liberty" (*ibid.*).
[469] *Op. cit.,* Vol. II, p. 573. Cf. "The Dilemma of Determinism," in *The Will to Believe,* pp. 146–48.

And herein, in this case, lies a paradox, perhaps; for as we cannot vindicate our freedom unless we are determined to be free, so we cannot compel those to be free who are free to be determined, and prefer to think it so."[470]

The foregoing style of argument for indeterminacy will, of course, not be acceptable to those libertarians who hold that man's possession of free choice is immediately evident or demonstrable, either from an analysis of causes or from the fact of moral responsibility. This includes such traditionally famous defenders of man's free will as Aquinas, Descartes, and Kant, as well as such contemporary proponents of it as Campbell, Weiss, and Hartshorne. Nor, of course, will the argument advanced by Renouvier, James, and Schiller have much weight for those determinists, such as Hobbes, Spinoza, Hume, Priestley, McTaggart, Ross, and Hobart, who hold that the doctrine of causal necessity is self-evidently true or that it can be demonstrated either by an appeal to the facts of nature or by the impossibility of holding men morally responsible unless their acts are fully determined.

8. CONCLUDING OBSERVATIONS

Three of the disputes that we have examined in this chapter parallel disputes that were treated in the preceding chapter. In the debate of this issue concerning causal indeterminacy, as in the debate of the issue concerning causal initiative, there is a dispute about the role of character and motives in the determination of volitions, a dispute about the relation between the freedom in question and moral responsibility, and a dispute about the evidence of consciousness or inner experience. In all three of these cases, as we pointed out at the end of the preceding chapter, lines of argument which appear in the debate about causal initiative become more fully developed in the debate about causal indeterminacy, and in addition new arguments are introduced in the latter debate.[471]

Nevertheless, certain inadequacies or deficiencies can still be pointed out. Measured by the ideal of rational debate, the literature of this controversy falls short of what we might hope for.

The most obvious example of this is in the dispute about responsibility and freedom. Here we find the disputants appealing to two quite different conceptions of responsibility, praise and blame, reward and punishment —one that is exclusively prospective and utilitarian in intent, and one that

[470] *Studies in Humanism*, pp. 405–6.
[471] See Ch. 9, p. 328, *supra*.

involves retrospective and retributive intent without necessarily excluding reference to the production of future effects. Now if the utilitarian conceptions represent the common understanding of the moral matters involved and if, in addition, they leave no problems of moral philosophy incapable of being satisfactorily solved, then the proponents of this set of conceptions would appear to be right in their contention that the denial of free choice has no regrettable consequences for ethical thought or action. But if, on the other hand, the retributive conceptions represent the generally prevalent understanding of the moral matters involved and if, in addition, they are the set of conceptions which the moral philosopher must employ or fail to solve his problems, then the proponents of this set would appear to be right in their contention that the denial of free choice renders much of ethical thought and action unfounded and unintelligible.

As the dispute is carried on in the literature of freedom, the adversaries for the most part go no further than to assert, on the one hand, that the denial of free choice has no regrettable consequences *because* the utilitarian conceptions can be substituted for the retributive; and to assert, on the other hand, that the denial of free choice makes many moral judgments and actions meaningless *because* the retributive conceptions cannot be replaced by the utilitarian.[472] To go further, the opposed parties would have to argue more fully the question of the substitutability of the utilitarian conceptions for the retributive. To do this, the opponents of free choice would have to give reasons for dismissing, as invalid or meaningless, a large body of traditional moral philosophy; and the defenders of free choice would have to meet this challenge by giving reasons of an opposite tenor. This is not done. Such argumentation would, of course, involve fundamental questions both in and about moral philosophy and so, perhaps, the deeper level of this dispute, which is not reached in the literature of freedom, may be found in literature devoted to the basic problems of moral philosophy. We have some reason to doubt that that literature contains better examples of rational debate than does the literature of freedom; but whether or not it does, it remains the case that the dispute about moral responsibility and freedom, as surveyed in this and the preceding chapter, fails to carry the argument to fundamentals.

The inadequacy of the dispute about the role of character and motives in the determination of volitions is of similar origin. Here the adversaries approach the issue from radically divergent viewpoints or theories in psychology. The parties to the dispute who argue for the proposition that a man's choice is always determined by the motive which, as a result of

---

[472] They also engage in the counter-assertions that the utilitarian or retributive conceptions exclusively represent the commonly accepted understanding of responsibility, praise and blame, reward and punishment.

that man's character and background, becomes dominant at the moment appeal to a psychological theory in which desires or motives operate like competing forces of changing magnitude. On the other hand, the parties who argue for the proposition that it is the act of choice itself which makes a particular motive dominant and, in a man of the same character and background, could have made some other motive dominant under the same circumstances appeal to a psychological theory in which the power of will is conceived as having a certain agency in relation to the judgments of the mind.

It is not necessary to detail all the critical differences between the two psychological theories in order to make the point that the dispute would reach the level of fundamental reasons, *pro* and *con*, only by arguing the exclusive validity of one of these psychological theories as against the other. Such argumentation may be found elsewhere, but it is not found in the literature of freedom; and so the dispute about the role of character and motives, as reported in these chapters, does not get down to fundamentals.

In addition, it should be pointed out, that the proponents of free choice introduce causal distinctions—as between efficient causes, on the one hand, and formal causes, on the other—in order to assert that motives are never the efficient causes of volitions, but only their formal cause. Their opponents, on the other hand, assert that motives are efficient causes. These contrary assertions are crucial in the dispute; but to support either one against the other would require the parties to defend one theory of causes against the other. They do not, however, go beyond making the contrary assertions.

This last point brings us to what is, perhaps, the most serious deficiency —the deficiency in the dispute about indeterminacy and causation. Here, for example, we found that one party advanced a theory of sufficient causes, or of causes in general, which entailed the truth of the proposition that if anything is caused at all, it is necessitated. Hence, indeterminacy, being the absence of necessity, must be one with causelessness or chance. A second party advanced a contrary theory of sufficient causes, or of causes in general, which entailed the truth of the proposition that while some causes necessitate their effects, others do not, but operate with causal indeterminacy, which is quite different from chance.[473] And a third party advanced still another contrary theory of causation which supported the conclusion that no cause necessitates the effect it produces.

Each of the three parties to this dispute gave us some indication of the reasons for the causal theory which he advanced. To this extent, the argument reached a fundamental level. But what, ideally at least, one

[473] See pp. 354 ff., *supra*.

would wish, in order to see this dispute carried to bedrock, would be some indication, on the part of each of the major adversaries, that he understood the causal theories of his opponents and, in the light of that understanding, could give clear reasons for rejecting them. With few and slight exceptions, such understanding and rational criticism is not indicated.

A thoroughly developed debate about the principle of causation may, of course, be found elsewhere in the literature of philosophical thought. It would involve disputes about a number of fundamental matters that are integrally involved in any theory of causation, such things as substance, powers, material and immaterial substances or powers, events, time, the reality of the future, and so on. We can observe the dim presence of these disputed matters in the rival causal theories which are advanced in support or denial of causal indeterminacy or free choice. But the argument, on one side or another, proceeds without ever bringing these fundamentals to the forefront and making them the center of the dispute. Yet they are central, and the merely peripheral argumentation, therefore, remains seriously inadequate.

Chapter 11

THE THEOLOGICAL ISSUE
CONCERNING MAN'S FREEDOM
OF SELF-DETERMINATION

Like the issues treated in the two preceding chapters, the issue with which we are here concerned is an existential one. Man's possession of a freedom of self-determination is denied by those who, affirming the existence of an omnipotent and omniscient deity, argue that that precludes the existence of free will on man's part. They are opposed by those who affirming the existence of God, also affirm the existence of human free will, arguing that self-determination on man's part is not thereby precluded.

On the negative side of this issue, we find mainly writers who not only deny that human self-determination is compatible with God's foreordination and foreknowledge but who also affirm the existence of an omnipotent and omniscient deity and who, therefore, deny the existence of free will in man. However, the incompatibility of human free will with God's providence is sometimes asserted by writers who do not commit themselves on the question of God's existence. They do so for the purpose of arguing in the following hypothetical fashion. If you believe that an omnipotent and omniscient God exists, they say to their opponents, you cannot also affirm that man has free will; that is precluded by God's foreordination and foreknowledge of everything that happens, including all the actions of men.

On the affirmative side of this issue, we naturally find writers who affirm the existence of an omnipotent and omniscient deity. It would be possible for writers who do not commit themselves on the question of God's existence to argue, in hypothetical fashion, that even if God exists, man can also have free will, because the one does not preclude the other. But there is little or no evidence of such argumentation in the literature of freedom. However, we later cite an author who, while denying man's possession of free will, argues hypothetically that even if free will existed it would not be incompatible with the existence of an omnipotent and omniscient deity.

In what follows, we shall be concerned mainly with the dispute between authors who disagree about the existence of free will in man while agreeing about the existence of God. The issue is, therefore, properly called "theological," since it is argued categorically only by writers who dispute the existence of free will within a common framework of theological assertions, namely, that God exists, that nothing happens contrary to God's will or to his decrees, and that nothing can happen which would render God's knowledge inadequate or erroneous. The common theological framework does not extend further than this. As we shall see, the authors who take opposite sides of this issue do so in virtue of different views of the relation of God's will and knowledge to the actions of man. It is on the basis of such theological differences that some of them assert that freedom of choice on man's part is precluded by God's omnipotence and omniscience, while others assert that free choice is compatible with an all-powerful and all-knowing God.

The separate issues treated in the two preceding chapters dealt respectively with (a) the existence of self-determination insofar as it is conceived as involving causal initiative on man's part, and (b) the existence of self-determination insofar as it is conceived as involving causal indeterminacy on man's part. In view of this, the theological dispute with which we are here concerned might, conceivably, be twofold: on the one hand, it could turn on the question whether, since God is the cause of everything which happens, man's will can be the uncaused cause of its own acts; on the other hand, it could turn on the question whether, since God wills and knows everything which happens, man's will can ever choose otherwise than as it does. Were this the case, we should have here two distinct theological issues, running parallel to the two issues treated separately in Chapters 9 and 10. But, for whatever reason, it is only the second of these two theological issues—the issue about God's all-embracing providence and man's free choice—which is disputed to any great extent as an issue in the general controversy.

In Chapter 9, we found a few authors—Hobbes, Hartley, Windelband, and Clemenceau—who argued that causal initiative on man's part is inconsistent with God's being first cause of all that happens. Aquinas also proposes this objection and answers it by explaining that, while God moves the human will in all its acts, he moves it in such a way as to leave it the sole cause of its own acts on the plane of natural causes.[1] Other theologians differ with Aquinas about how God moves the human will so as not to deprive it of the causal initiative that is thought to be indispensable to its freedom.[2] But such disagreement constitutes a theological issue in the

[1] See Ch. 9, pp. 286–87, *supra*.
[2] Molina, for example, offers a different explanation of the operation of the divine causality in relation to the human will. See his *Concordia*, Q. 14, A. 13, Disp. 26 and 35.

special controversy about free will. It is not relevant to the general controversy since the parties on both sides concur in affirming the existence of a freedom that involves causal initiative on man's part.

So far as the general controversy is concerned, it is the causal indeterminacy of free choice, not the causal initiative of the will, that is the focus of theological dispute. It is, furthermore, the intrinsic unpredictability of the freely chosen act that appears to be irreconcilable with God's foreknowledge. That is why most of the authors on the negative side of this dispute appeal to God's omniscience as the ground for their denial of free choice. But many of them also rest their case on God's omnipotence—that nothing happens except it be willed or decreed by God and that what God wills or decrees must necessarily happen. In their view, this leaves no room for indeterminacy. A few writers, notably Luther and Calvin, employ the term "foreordination" to cover both God's willing and God's knowing all that is to take place.

It is also God's foreknowledge that most of the affirmative authors recognize as the nub of the issue. They recognize its *apparent* irreconcilability with free choice, in view of their own conception of the freely chosen act as intrinsically unpredictable even by a mind which possesses perfect knowledge of all relevant causes. However, here as in the case of the negative authors, the consideration of God's will and providence also enters into the picture. How certain human acts can be exempt from necessitation and yet, like everything else, be subject to God's will must be explained. But explanations are not offered by all the affirmative authors. Some accept the apparent irreconcilability of man's free choice with God's omniscience and omnipotence as a mystery beyond human comprehension.

We have, therefore, a threefold division of authors: (i) writers such as Crescas, Luther, Calvin, Hobbes, Edwards, Collins, Hartley, Priestley, Paulsen, and Rashdall, who maintain that God's foreknowledge or foreordination necessitates all that happens; (ii) writers such as Ockham, Descartes, Reid, Price, Hamilton, Mansel, and Campbell, who maintain that we must affirm free choice together with God's omnipotence and omniscience even if we cannot explain how they are reconcilable; and (iii) writers such as Augustine, Boethius, Ibn Daud, Maimonides, Gersonides, Aquinas, Bramhall, Watts, Henry More, Lequier, William James, Lossky, Weiss, Hartshorne, and Tillich, who attempt to show that the irreconcilability is only apparent and who thus try to counter the arguments advanced by the opponents of free choice.

Accordingly, we shall present the evidence of this dispute in three sections, beginning with the representatives of the negative position, proceeding then to those who take the affirmative side but do not reply to the arguments of their opponents, and finally coming to those on the affirmative side who attempt to defend that position.

1. THE NEGATIVE POSITION

Cicero is described by Augustine as holding the view that the freedom of the will is irreconcilable with God's complete foreknowledge of the future. But, according to Augustine, he rejected the foreknowledge of future things rather than freedom of choice, on the ground that to reject the latter would subvert the whole of human life by removing justice from rewards and punishments and making exhortations vain and praise or blame meaningless.[3] Hence, Cicero, though concerned with the problem, cannot be cited as an early representative of the negative position. Nor can Evodius, a character in Augustine's dialogue, *The Problem of Free Choice*. Evodius poses the problem, but does not categorically argue for the solution which, in effect, maintains that God's omniscience precludes man's free choice. After saying that God foreknows our sins, but "in such a way that our will remains free," Evodius, questioned further by Augustine, replies: "I do not yet see how these two, God's foreknowledge of our sins and our free will in sinning, do not contradict one another."[4]

The problem is also posed by Boethius in his *Consolation of Philosophy*. "There seems to me to be," he writes, ". . . incompatibility between the existence of God's universal foreknowledge and that of any freedom of judgment. For if God foresees all things and cannot in anything be mistaken, that which His Providence sees will happen, must result. Wherefore if it knows beforehand not only men's deeds but even their designs and wishes, there will be no freedom of judgment."[5] However, Boethius, like Cicero, recoils from this conclusion because it makes all rewards and punishments both unfair and vain.[6] Nor is he willing, like Cicero, to save man's free will by denying God's omniscience. Instead, as we shall see in Section 3, Boethius works out a solution of the problem which satisfies him, that man's freedom of choice can be reconciled with God's foreknowledge.

The problem, as stated by Augustine's Evodius and by Boethius, confronts all later theologians in the Judaeo-Christian tradition, as well as philosophers whose thought takes account of accepted religious beliefs.

[3] See *City of God*, Vol. I, Book V, Ch. 9, p. 191; and cf. Cicero, *De Divinatione*, Book II.
[4] *Op. cit.*, p. 149.
[5] *Op. cit.*, p. 104.
[6] See *ibid.*, p. 107.

Hasdai Crescas, a Jewish philosopher of the fourteenth century, is one of the first to offer what may, on the surface, appear to be an affirmative solution. But, in effect, it amounts to a denial of free choice, as that is commonly understood by the SD authors. As we shall see, earlier Jewish and Christian philosophers or theologians of the Middle Ages attempt, like Augustine and Boethius before them, to find some solution of the problem which will save both man's freedom and God's foreknowledge.

For Crescas, both God's omniscience and man's free will are "Principles of Torah," i.e., fundamental dogmas of the Jewish religion. But while both must therefore be affirmed, Crescas holds that it is possible to do so only by acknowledging that divine foreknowledge necessitates the acts of the will, so far as they are considered in relation to their causes, and leaves them free only insofar as in themselves they are mere possibilities. Any particular act of the will is such that its opposite is possible (i.e., not self-contradictory), and in this fact lies the sense in which the act is free (i.e., not necessitated). But when that same act is viewed in relation to its causes, stemming ultimately from God as the omnipotent and omniscient cause of everything, it is necessitated and not free. Free choice, as involving causal indeterminacy, is therefore precluded by the causal necessity which God's foreknowledge and foreordination imposes on everything that happens.[7]

A century earlier, the argument from God's foreknowledge is given its full force by an "objector" in the writings of Aquinas.

> Whatever God foreknows must necessarily come about, since God's foreknowledge cannot be in error. But God foreknows all human acts. They therefore come about of necessity, and so man is not endowed with free choice in his action.[8]

In another place, a parallel argument is stated in terms of God's omnipotence.

> It would seem that the will is moved of necessity by God. For every agent that cannot be resisted moves of necessity. But God cannot be resisted, because His power is infinite. . . . Therefore God moves the will of necessity.[9]

---

[7] See Meyer Waxman, *The Philosophy of Don Hasdai Crescas*, pp. 107–11, 124–30, 136–38; and cf. David Neumark, *Essays in Jewish Philosophy*, pp. 313–15. As we shall see presently, Leibniz's attempt to save "free will" while admitting that the causal indeterminacy of free choice is incompatible with divine foreknowledge also reduces the freedom of a particular choice to the fact that the opposite choice, metaphysically considered, is always possible, and therefore the particular choice is not metaphysically necessitated.

[8] *Truth*, Vol. III, Q. 24, A. 1, Objection 13, p. 135.

[9] *Summa Theologica*, Part I–II, Q. 10, A. 4, Objection 1.

And in still another place we find the following argument.

> It is impossible that the will of man should be in discord with God's will.
> . . . But the will of God is unchangeable; therefore so also is man's will.
> Thus all human choices proceed from invariable choice.[10]

For Luther, the negative position is inescapable. "For if we believe it to be true," he writes,

> that God foreknows and foreordains all things; that He can not be deceived
> or obstructed in His foreknowledge and predestination; and that nothing
> happens but at His will (which reason itself is compelled to grant), then
> on reason's own testimony, there can be no free will in man, or angel, or
> in any creature.[11]

Luther adds one qualification to this statement when he says: "I confess that mankind has a free-will, but it is to milk kine, to build houses, etc., and no further."[12] The interpretation of this statement would appear to be that in matters which are morally indifferent and have no merit for salvation, man is free to choose. Whether there are such matters and whether, if there are, they come within the purview of divine foreordination and foreknowledge, Luther does not discuss. In any case, he reiterates his fundamental position that man has no self-determination in the sphere of his moral life.[13]

Calvin's position differs from Luther's by reason of the emphasis which he places on God's foreordination. It is that, rather than God's foreknowledge, which precludes free choice on man's part. The salvation and damnation of particular men, he tells us, "are acts of God's will, rather than of his foreknowledge. If God simply foresaw the fates of men, and did not also dispose and fix them by his determination, there would be room to agitate the question, whether his providence or foresight rendered them at all necessary. But," Calvin argues, "since he foresees future events only in consequence of his decree that they shall happen, it is useless to contend about foreknowledge, while it is evident that all things come to pass rather by ordination and decree."[14]

Calvin is aware that those who attempt to reconcile free choice with

---

[10] *De Malo*, Q. 6, A. 1, Objection 5. Cf. Boethius, *The Consolation of Philosophy*, p. 119, where a similar difficulty is set forth in terms of the unchangeableness of God's knowledge.

[11] *The Bondage of the Will*, p. 317.

[12] "Of Free-Will," in *The Table Talk of Martin Luther*, p. 165. Cf. *Luther's Works*, Vol. 31, pp. 58–59.

[13] See *ibid.*, pp. 159–60; and cf. *Luther's Works*, Vol. 31, pp. 48–49, 317.

[14] *Institutes of the Christian Religion*, Vol. II, Book III, Ch. XXIII, pp. 206–7.

divine omniscience make the point that nothing is future to God and so his "foreknowledge" must be understood without any temporal reference

> When we attribute foreknowledge to God, we mean that all things have ever been, and perpetually remain, before his eyes, so that to his knowledge nothing is future or past, but all things are present; and present in such a manner, that he does not merely conceive of them from ideas formed in his mind, as things remembered by us appear present to our minds, but really beholds and sees them as if actually placed before him. And this foreknowledge extends to the whole world, and to all the creatures.[15]

But this does not alter the case, since it is "predestination by which God adopts some to the hope of life, and adjudges others to eternal death." To recognize this is to avoid the "many cavils" of "those who make foreknowledge the cause of it."[16]

Like Luther, Calvin considers the question of the liberty man possesses "in those actions which in themselves are neither righteous nor wicked, and pertain rather to the corporeal than to the spiritual life. . . . Some have admitted him in such things to possess a free choice; rather, as I suppose, from a reluctance to dispute on a subject of no importance than from an intention of positively asserting that which they concede.' But, even in such external things, Calvin thinks that "the hearts of men are governed by the Lord"; and "that God, whenever he designs to prepare the way for his providence, inclines and moves the wills of men even in external things," so that "their choice is not so free, but that its liberty is subject to the will of God."[17] Certainly, insofar as human action has any moral quality whatsoever, it is entirely subject to God's will and man is without freedom to choose between good and evil.[18]

As we have already pointed out,[19] Leibniz, like Crescas, holds that man's actions are free in the sense that they are not *metaphysically necessitated*, i.e., a particular action is possible rather than necessary, since some other action in its place is not impossible. But the particular action is possible in this sense only when it is viewed in itself as something which may or may not exist. When it is viewed in relation to its causes, or as flowing from the individual nature of the agent, it is necessitated. Given a man of that nature, no other action could have been chosen by him at that moment.[20] All of man's future actions are, therefore, capable of being

---

15 *Ibid.*, Book III, Ch. XXI, pp. 175–76.
16 *Ibid.*, p. 175.
17 *Ibid.*, Vol. I, Book II, Ch. IV, pp. 339–40.
18 *Ibid.*, Chs. II–III, pp. 286, 327–28, 331–33.
19 See fn. 7, p. 468, *supra*.
20 For an extended exposition of Leibniz's views about free will, see Vol. I, pp. 539–45. It will there also be seen why we described Leibniz's position as one that affirms man's self-determination but denies his having free choice, conceived as involving causal indeterminacy. See also *ibid.*, pp. 549–51.

foreseen with certitude by a mind that has adequate knowledge of the agent's individual nature. Hence, for Leibniz, an omniscient deity, knowing the natures of individual men, foresees all the choices they will make. These, then, remain free choices only in the sense already indicated.[21]

In his debate with Bishop Bramhall, Hobbes reserves for the end his concluding argument about the "inconvenience of denying necessity," which is that "it destroys both the decrees and prescience of God Almighty." Hobbes writes:

> . . . whatsoever God hath purposed to bring to pass by man as an instrument, or foreseeth shall come to pass, a man, if he have liberty, such as he [Bramhall] affirmeth from necessitation, might frustrate and make not to come to pass; and God should either not foreknow it and not decree it, or he should foreknow such things as shall never be, and decree that which shall never come to pass.[22]

Jonathan Edwards argues in similar fashion.

> To suppose the future volitions of moral agents not to be necessary events; or, which is the same thing, events which it is not impossible but that they may not come to pass; and yet to suppose that God certainly foreknows them, and knows all things, is to suppose God's knowledge to be inconsistent with itself. For to say, that God certainly, and without all conjecture, knows that a thing will infallibly be, which at the same time he knows to be so contingent that it may possibly not be, is to suppose his knowledge be inconsistent with itself; or that one thing that he knows is utterly inconsistent with another thing that he knows.[23]

Edwards goes on to point out that the relation between events and God's foreknowledge is the same as that between events and God's decrees: they are equally necessitated in both cases.[24] To those who insist that God's prescience has no influence on our actions, Edwards replies:

> . . . what is said about knowledge, its not having influence on the thing known to make it necessary, is nothing to the purpose, nor does it in the least affect the foregoing reasoning. Whether prescience be the thing that *makes* the event necessary or no, it alters not the case. Infallible

---

[21] See *Discourse on Metaphysics*, Ch. XIII, pp. 19–23.

[22] *The Questions Concerning Liberty, Necessity and Chance*, pp. 428–29. Cf. *Leviathan*, Book II, Ch. 21, p. 162.

[23] *Freedom of the Will*, p. 260. "There is no geometrical theorem or proposition whatsoever, more capable of strict demonstration," Edwards declares, "than that God's certain prescience of the volitions of moral agents is inconsistent with such a contingence of these events as is without all necessity" (*ibid.*, pp. 268–69).

[24] "The connection between the event and certain foreknowledge is as infallible and indissoluble, as between the event and an absolute decree. That is, 'tis no more impossible that the event and decree should not agree together, than that the event and absolute knowledge should disagree" (*ibid.*, p. 261).

foreknowledge may *prove* the necessity of the event foreknown, and yet not be the thing which *causes* the necessity. If the foreknowledge be absolute, this *proves* the event known to be necessary.[25]

Priestley acknowledges his debt to Hobbes, and also to Collins and Hartley, for his views on the subject.[26] If men had freedom of choice Priestley contends, "the Divine Being could not possibly foresee what would happen in his own creation, and therefore could not provide for it which takes away the whole foundation of *divine providence*, and moral government, as well as all the foundation of *revealed religion*, in which *prophecies* are so much concerned."[27] Furthermore, Priestley argues,

if man be possessed of a power of proper *self-determination*, the Deity himself cannot control it (as far as he interferes, it is no self-determination of the man), and if he does not *control* it, he cannot *foresee* it.[28]

That which is contingent or uncertain, as future acts of free choice are thought to be, cannot, according to Priestley, be the object of divine foreknowledge. This, in his view, must lead Christians to reject free will since "if there be any truth in the Scriptures, the Divine Being certainly foresees every determination of the mind of man."[29]

Other writers assert the incompatibility of free will and divine omniscience without entering into the argument. Paulsen, for example, simply refers to the "purely theological objections [to free will] . . . based upon the omnipotence and omniscience of God.[30] Asserting the irreconcilability of free choice with God's foreknowledge, Rashdall goes on to say that "a doctrine of Free-Will which involves a denial of God's Omniscience

---

25 *Ibid.*, p. 263. Cf. *ibid.*, pp. 264–65; and see also *ibid.*, pp. 245–46, 248.

26 See *The Doctrine of Philosophical Necessity*, pp. xxiv–xxvii. According to Collins, "A fourth argument to prove Man a necessary Agent shall be taken from the consideration of the divine Prescience. . . . For if any things future were contingent, or uncertain, or depended on the liberty of Man, that is, might or might not happen, their certain existence could not be the object of the divine prescience" (A *Philosophical Inquiry Concerning Human Liberty*, pp. 82–83). Hartley asserts that "the natural Attributes of God, or his infinite Power and Knowledge, exclude the Possibility of Free-will in the philosophical sense." See his *Observations on Man*, pp. 363–65, where Hartley argues for this conclusion in a manner that closely resembles the arguments of Hobbes and Edwards.

27 *The Doctrine of Philosophical Necessity*, p. 28. "The whole history of revelation shows," Priestley adds, "that every determination of the mind of man is certainly fore-known by the Divine Being" (*ibid.*, p. 31).

28 *Ibid.*, pp. 30–31.

29 *Priestley-Price Controversy*, p. 155. "I think it hardly possible," he writes, "that a person who believes in *contingencies* can have a steady faith in the doctrine of *divine prescience*" (*ibid.*, p. 164).

30 A *System of Ethics*, p. 455.

cannot claim any superiority over such a theistic Determinism as I have defended on the score of avoiding a limitation of the divine Omnipotence."[31] And Schrödinger, the physicist, sees the theological problem as the analogue of the scientific problem concerning free will: "the part of the Law of Nature," he writes, "is taken by the omniscient and almighty God."[32] Schrödinger's further statement that the religious attitude toward this problem is that "we are here confronted with a deep mystery into which we cannot penetrate" does not, as we shall see, apply to all the authors on the affirmative side of this issue. But it does describe the position of the writers to whom we now turn.

2. THE AFFIRMATIVE SIDE

William of Ockham recognizes the difficulty of affirming both man's free will and God's foreknowledge of man's free acts, in view of the fact that they represent future contingencies. On the one hand, he says, "it must be held that God certainly and clearly knows all future contingent things." But, on the other hand, he admits that "to make this clear and to express the manner in which he knows all future contingents is impossible for any intellect in the present state."[33] Nevertheless, Ockham affirms both man's free will and God's foreknowledge of future contingents without resolving the difficulty that he sees in this.[34]

In his *Principles of Philosophy*, Descartes asks "how the freedom of the will may be reconciled with Divine pre-ordination" and frankly acknowledges that the answer to this question is beyond our comprehension.[35] We must remember, Descartes tells us, that "our thought is finite, and that the omnipotence of God, whereby He has not only known from all eternity that which is or can be, but also willed and pre-ordained it, is infinite." Thus we will recognize, he explains, that

[31] *The Theory of Good and Evil*, Vol. II, Book III, pp. 343–44. "Omniscience," Rashdall adds, "need not involve Omnipotence, but Omnipotence (in the popular sense) certainly includes Omniscience" (*ibid.*, p. 344).

[32] *Science and Humanism*, pp. 59–60.

[33] *Ordinatio*, Dist. 38, in *Tractatus de Praedestinatione et de Praescientia Dei et Futuris Contingentibus*, p. 99. Cf. *ibid.*, pp. 14–15.

[34] Another way of stating the difficulty is to ask how the free act is genuinely contingent if, in view of God's foreknowledge of it, it is not intrinsically unpredictable.

[35] It should be observed that before Descartes considers this question, he asserts, as a fundamental principle, that "the freedom of the will is self-evident." See *The Principles of Philosophy*, Principles XXXIX and XLI, in *The Philosophical Works of Descartes*, Vol. I, pp. 234–35.

we may have intelligence enough to come clearly and distinctly to know that this power is in God, but not enough to comprehend how He leaves the free action of man indeterminate; and, on the other hand, we are so conscious of the liberty and indifference which exist in us, that there is nothing that we comprehend more clearly and perfectly.

Hence, he concludes, "it would be absurd to doubt that of which we inwardly experience and perceive as existing within ourselves, just because we do not comprehend a matter which from its nature we know to be incomprehensible."[36]

Like Ockham and Descartes, Thomas Reid maintains that the actions which flow from man's free choice are genuinely contingent, and yet also that they are foreseen by God. With regard to the proposition "that it is impossible that any free action can be certainly foreseen," he observes "that every man who believes the Deity to be a free agent must believe that this proposition not only is incapable of proof, but that it is certainly false."[37] He refers to Priestley's attempt to prove the contrary, namely, that there cannot be a greater absurdity or contradiction than to maintain that a future contingent event should be the object of certain knowledge. But while Reid thinks that the attempt fails, he also thinks that we cannot understand how God foresees the future free acts of man. "The prescience of the Deity . . . must be different not only in degree, but in kind, from any knowledge we can attain of futurity"; but "though we can have no conception how the future free actions of man may be known to the Deity, this is not a sufficient reason to conclude that they cannot be known."[38] Dr. Price's response to Priestley's argument is less complete. Admitting that "the foreknowledge of a contingent event [carries] the appearance of a contradiction," he admits that this "is indeed a difficulty"; but, while saying "I do not pretend to be capable of removing it," he does not withdraw his affirmation of man's power of free choice or of God's omniscience.[39]

According to Sir William Hamilton, the failure to explain rationally how man's free will can be reconciled with God's foreknowledge and foreordination does not exempt a Christian from believing in both. Hamilton quotes Augustine as saying that the problem is "a most difficult question, intelligible only to a few"; and then adds: "Had he denounced it as a fruitless question, and (to understanding) soluble by none, the

---

[36] *Ibid.*, Principle XLI, p. 235. Cf. *The Passions of the Soul*, Part Second, Article CXLVI, in *The Philosophical Works of Descartes*, Vol. I, p. 397.

[37] *Essays on the Active Powers of the Human Mind*, p. 225. "The Deity," Reid writes, "foresees his own future free actions, but neither his foresight nor his purpose makes them necessary" (*ibid.*, p. 224).

[38] *Ibid.*, p. 227.

[39] *Priestley-Price Controversy*, pp. 175–76.

world might have been spared a large library of acrimonious and resultless disputation." In Hamilton's opinion, the conciliation is possible when the things to be reconciled are regarded as "things to be believed," but not when they are taken as things to be understood.[40]

In his defense of Hamilton's position on free will against the attack of J. S. Mill, Henry Mansel says that he has "purposely avoided touching on a subject alluded to by Mr. Mill, the compatibility of man's free-will with God's foreknowledge. This question," Mansel confesses, "is insoluble, because we have nothing but negative notions to apply to it. . . . In this, as in all other revelations of God's relation to man, we must be content to believe without aspiring to comprehend."[41] The fact that we cannot solve the problem in a rational manner does not, for Mansel, lead to the rejection of either man's free will or of God's omnipotence and omniscience. C. A. Campbell is of the same opinion. Like Mansel, he says: "I propose to ignore . . . the type of criticism of free will that is sometimes advanced from the side of religion, based upon religious postulates of Divine Omnipotence and Omniscience. So far as I can see," he declares,

> a postulate of human freedom is every bit as necessary to meet certain religious demands (e.g., to make sense of the 'conviction of sin'), as postulates of Divine Omniscience and Omnipotence are to meet certain other religious demands.[42]

That being so, both doctrines, from the religious point of view, must be affirmed, even if, from the philosophical point of view, their compatibility cannot be understood.

3. THE AFFIRMATIVE POSITION DEFENDED

In an early work, *The Problem of Free Choice*, Augustine declares that it does not follow that because "God has foreknown my future will [and] because nothing can happen contrary to his foreknowledge, [therefore] I must necessarily will what he has foreknown."[43] To defend this position, Augustine first points out that "our will would not be a will, if it were not in our power. Moreover, since it is in our power, it is free." He then argues as follows:

[40] *Discussion on Philosophy and Literature Education and University Reform*, pp. 626–27.
[41] *Prolegomena Logica*, pp. 304–5. Mill's allusion to the problem, mentioned by Mansel, occurs in his *System of Logic*, Book VI, Ch. II, Sect. 2.
[42] *On Selfhood and Godhood*, pp. 171–72.
[43] *Op. cit.*, p. 148.

Since He has foreknowledge of our will, that will must exist, of which he has the foreknowledge. It will be a will, because He has foreknowledge of a will. Nor could it be a will, if it were not in our power. So He has foreknowledge also of our power over it. My power is not taken away by His foreknowledge, but I shall have it all the more certainly because He whose foreknowledge is not mistaken has foreknown that I shall have it.[44]

Therefore, Augustine concludes, there is no need to deny that God has foreknowledge of all future events, because we freely will what we will.[45]

Later, in *The City of God*, criticizing Cicero's denial of divine foreknowledge in order to affirm freedom of choice for man, Augustine says that "the religious mind . . . maintains both by the faith of piety."[46] He repeats, in slightly different form, the argument already given.

It does not follow that, though there is for God a certain order of causes, there must therefore be nothing depending on the free exercise of our own wills, for our wills themselves are included in that order of causes which is certain to God, and is embraced by His foreknowledge, for human wills are also causes of human actions; and He who foreknew all the causes of things would certainly among those causes not have been ignorant of our wills.[47]

From the very nature of our wills, of which God is the cause and of which he has knowledge, "it is necessary that when we will, we will by free choice," but this does not "subject our wills . . . to a necessity which destroys liberty."[48] Hence, he concludes,

it is not the case . . . that because God foreknew what would be in the power of our wills, there is for that reason nothing in the power of our wills. For he who foreknew this did not foreknow nothing . . . Therefore we are by no means compelled, either, retaining the prescience of God, to take away the freedom of the will, or, retaining the freedom of the will, to deny that He is prescient of future things, which is impious.[49]

---

[44] *Ibid.*, pp. 148–49.

[45] To this argument, Augustine adds the further consideration that foreknowledge does not *cause* what is foreseen. Addressing Evodius, he says: "You would not necessarily compel a man to sin by foreknowing his sin, though undoubtedly he would sin; otherwise you would not foreknow that this would happen. Therefore, these two are not contradictory, your foreknowledge and someone else's free act. So too God compels no one to sin, though He foresees those who will sin by their own will" (*ibid.*, p. 150).

[46] *Op. cit.*, Vol. I, Book V, Ch. 9, p. 191. "Against the sacrilegious and impious darings of reason," Augustine declares, "we assert both that God knows all things before they come to pass, and that we do by our free will whatsoever we know and feel to be done by us only because we will it" (*ibid.*, p. 192).

[47] *Ibid.*, p. 193. Cf. *ibid.*, pp. 194–95.

[48] *Ibid.*, Ch. 10, p. 196.

[49] *Ibid.*

Boethius repeats and expands upon Augustine's argument. Like Augustine, he maintains a threefold division of causes: some things are necessitated by their causes; some happen by chance or by the coincidence of causes; and some result from the free judgments that men make.[50] He then argues that if all things, as caused, do not happen by necessity, then the fact that God has foreknowledge of everything cannot be interpreted to mean that everything happens by necessity; for God, foreknowing, foresees that only some things will happen by necessity, whereas others will happen by chance, and still others will result from free choice on man's part. The way things happen depends upon the way in which they are caused, not upon God's foreknowledge which, being knowledge of the way things are caused, comprehends things that happen by free choice and by chance as well as things that happen by necessity.[51]

What Boethius adds to Augustine's argument is a clarification of the meaning of "*fore*knowledge" when that is attributed to God. For both God and man, foreknowledge refers to future events. But whereas future events for man are those things which are still to come to pass, they are all co-present to God's eternal vision. The things we experience happening successively in time, God sees in the eternal present and sees each thing as occurring in accordance with its own nature or character whether as cause or effect.[52] Boethius then calls attention to the fact that we also see certain things happening in our temporal present, but this does not affect the way in which they happen.

> For instance, when you see at the same time a man walking on the earth and the sun rising in the heavens, you see each sight simultaneously, yet you distinguish between them, and decide that one is moving voluntarily, the other of necessity.[53]

[50] See *The Consolation of Philosophy*, pp. 101–3.

[51] See *ibid.*, pp. 108–9. It should be noted here that Boethius, like Augustine, also makes the point that "foreknowledge cannot be held to be a cause for the necessity of future results, and therefore free will is not in any way shackled by foreknowledge" (*ibid.*). In other words, God's foreknowledge neither causally necessitates all future events, nor signifies that all are necessitated by their own causes. This is also the view of the Renaissance philosopher Lorenzo Valla who asks rhetorically, "You know it is now day; because you know it, is it on that account also day? Or, conversely, because it is day, do you for that reason know it is day?" He concludes that, "if the foreknowledge of man is not the cause of something occurring, neither is the foreknowledge of God" (*Dialogue of Free Will*, in *The Renaissance Philosophy of Man*, pp. 163–64). Writing in opposition to Luther, Erasmus remarks that the difficulties about God's foreknowledge have not been explained "more felicitously in my opinion than [by] Lorenzo Valla" (*Diatribe Concerning Free Will* in *Opera*, T. IX, Co. 1231A). Erasmus then repeats the distinction between knowing something will happen and causing it to happen.

[52] See *ibid.*, pp. 115–16.

[53] *Ibid.*, pp. 117–18.

The fact that you see both things happening does not prevent one from happening by necessity and the other from happening by free choice. "In like manner," Boethius maintains, "the perception of God looks down upon all things without disturbing at all their nature, though they are present to Him but future under the conditions of time." If among these things are some that happen by man's free choice, God both knows that such events are occurring and knows that they are not occurring of necessity.[54]

Still it may be objected that "what God sees about to happen, cannot but happen, and that what cannot but happen is bound by necessity." To this objection, the reply is that "there are two kinds of necessities; one is simple: for instance, a necessary fact 'all men are mortal'; the other is conditional; for instance, if you know that a man is walking, he must be walking; for what each man knows cannot be otherwise than it is known to be." Nevertheless, Boethius points out, the conditional necessity is not followed by the simple and direct necessity; "for there is no necessity to compel a voluntary walker to proceed, though it is necessary that, if he walks, he should be proceeding. In the same way, if Providence sees an event in its present, that thing must be, though it has no necessity of its own nature."

Hence, Boethius argues, when "God looks in His present upon those future things which come to pass through free will," they have a conditional necessity (i.e., "they come to pass of necessity under the condition of divine knowledge"); but these same things, "viewed by themselves . . . do not lose the perfect freedom of their nature. Without doubt then," he concludes,

> all things that God foreknows do come to pass, but some of them proceed from free will; and though they result by coming into existence, yet they do not lose their own nature, because before they came to pass they could also not have come to pass.[55]

With the notable exception of Crescas, whom we have already treated, the Jewish philosophers of the Middle Ages take the affirmative side of

[54] *Ibid.*, p. 118.

[55] *Ibid.*, p. 118. If it is still objected that free acts are as much "bound by necessity" as events which are causally necessitated, "since they result under all circumstances as by necessity, on account of the condition of divine foreknowledge," Boethius replies once again: "Take the sun rising and a man walking; while these operations are occurring, they cannot but occur: but the one was bound to occur before it did, the other was not so bound. What God has in His present, does exist without doubt; but of such things some follow by necessity, others by their authors' wills. Wherefore I was justified in saying that if these things be regarded from the view of divine knowledge, they are necessary, but if they are viewed by themselves, they are perfectly free from all ties of necessity" (*ibid.*, pp. 118–19).

this issue. But while they affirm man's possession of free choice and do so within the framework of the religious dogmas concerning God's omnipotence and omniscience, they do not all fit the one into the other in the same way.

Saadia Gaon and Judah Halevi maintain that God has foreknowledge of man's free acts, but argue that God's omniscience does not interfere with man's freedom. According to Saadia Gaon, those who doubt that man can have free will because God foreknows with certainty what he will do make the mistake of supposing that "the Creator's foreknowledge of things is the cause of their coming into being." But this, says Saadia, is "an erroneous assumption," the untenability of which "is made clear by the realization that if God's foreknowledge of anything could be the cause of its coming into being, then all things would have to be eternal, having existed always since God has always known them."[56] Judah Halevi argues similarly that "the knowledge of events to come is not the cause of their existence, just as is the case with the knowledge of things which have been."[57] He, therefore, also concludes that God's omniscience does not preclude man's freedom.

According to Maimonides, "the theory of man's perfectly free will is one of the fundamental principles of the Law of our Teacher Moses, and of those who follow the Law."[58] Since, in his view, God's providence goes no further than the universal laws of nature which were established once and for all at creation, God does not pre-determine the particular events which happen in accordance with these laws. This is especially true in the case of man, whom God created with free will. Man's free actions are thus pre-ordained to be free.[59]

When he comes to the problem of man's freedom and God's foreknowledge, Maimonides, affirming God's omniscience, explains that the perplexity we face here results from our failure to recognize that God's knowledge is totally unlike human knowledge. His knowledge is identical with His essence. "We cannot comprehend God's knowledge," Maimonides writes,

[56] *The Book of Beliefs and Opinions*, p. 191. "What we profess, therefore," Saadia writes, "is that God has a knowledge of things as they are actually constituted. He also knows before anything happens to them that it will happen. Furthermore, He is cognizant of what man's choice will be before man makes it" (*ibid.*). But this, in Saadia's opinion, does not preclude man's choice from being free.
[57] *Kitab Al Khazari*, p. 282. While God's omnipotence, for Halevi, means that God is the cause of everything that happens, Halevi explains that only some things are caused directly by God, and some are caused indirectly through the operation of intermediate causes, among which are the free wills of men. See *ibid.*, pp. 279–86.
[58] *Guide for the Perplexed*, Part III, Ch. XVII, p. 285. Cf. *ibid.*, Ch. XLVIII; and see also *The Eight Chapters of Maimonides on Ethics*, Ch. VIII, esp. pp. 86–88, 92.
[59] See *Guide for the Perplexed*, Part III, Ch. XVII, pp. 285–88.

"our minds cannot grasp it at all, for He is His knowledge and His knowledge is He."[60] Since we cannot comprehend God's knowledge, it is not surprising that we cannot understand how God has foreknowledge of future contingencies, including the free acts of man.[61]

Abraham Ibn Daud and Gersonides propose a different solution of the problem. Where Maimonides, unwilling to limit God's knowledge in any respect, places God's foresight of the contingent beyond our understanding, they place the contingent beyond even the power of God's knowledge. Future contingencies, including the free choices that men will make, are intrinsically unpredictable or unforeseeable. This being so, they argue that God's inability to foresee future contingencies imposes no limit on God's omniscience. Omniscience consists in knowing all that is knowable; it is unaffected by the failure to know that which is intrinsically unknowable.[62]

For Aquinas, as for other writers whom we have considered, the problem is twofold: it relates to God's omnipotence, on the one hand, and to God's omniscience, on the other.

With regard to God's omnipotence, Aquinas holds the divine providence "moves all things in accordance with their conditions; so that from necessary causes through the Divine motion, effects follow of necessity; but from contingent causes, effects follow contingently. Since, therefore," he continues,

> the will as an active principle is not determinate to one thing, but having an indifferent relation to many things, God so moves it, that He does not determine it of necessity to one thing, but its movement remains contingent and not necessary. . . .[63]

To the objection that, since "God cannot be resisted, because His power is infinite," it must follow that "the will is moved of necessity by God," Aquinas replies that "it would be more repugnant to the Divine motion, for the will to be moved of necessity, which is not fitting to its nature, than for it to be moved freely, which is becoming to its nature."[64] And

[60] *The Eight Chapters of Maimonides on Ethics*, Ch. VIII, p. 101.
[61] See *Guide for the Perplexed*, Part III, Chs. XX–XXI, pp. 292–96.
[62] For a summary of Ibn Daud's views, see Husik, *History of Mediaeval Jewish Philosophy*, pp. 228–31; and for a summary of the argument of Gersonides, see *ibid.*, pp. 340–46. See also Husik, *Philosophical Essays*, pp. 45–46, 59–60, 180–82; and Waxman, *The Philosophy of Don Hasdai Crescas*, Ch. III, pp. 92–93.
[63] *Summa Theologica*, Part I–II, Q. 10, A. 4. Cf. *ibid.*, Part I, Q. 19, A. 8; and Q. 83, A. 1, Reply 3. See also *Truth*, Q. 24, Vol. III, A. 1, Reply 3, pp. 139–40, where Aquinas writes: "God works in each agent, [but] in accord with that agent's manner of acting. . . . [Hence] by the fact . . . that God is a cause working in the hearts of men, human minds are not kept from being the cause of their own motions themselves."
[64] *Ibid.*, Objection 1 and Reply 1.

to the objection that since God's will is unchangeable, and nothing can be in discord with the divine will, man's will cannot be variable in its choices, Aquinas replies that "with respect to the mode of willing it is not needful that the will of man conform to God's will, because God wills everything eternally and infinitely, but man does not."[65]

A number of other writers resemble Aquinas in the general manner of his reconciliation of man's freedom with God's omnipotence.

Responding to the argument advanced by Hobbes that, if man have liberty from necessitation, he may frustrate the decrees of God, Bishop Bramhall points out that it is "his decree that man should be a free agent," and "so free actions do proceed as well from the eternal decree of God, as necessary."[66] Bishop Bossuet argues similarly that we are free by divine decree; far from there being any incompatibility between man's freedom and God's will, the one is established by the other.[67] And Lequier maintains that though God's power is such that whatever he wills has to occur, including what we shall choose; nevertheless, if God wills that we choose freely, then our choice will be free.[68]

Let us return to Aquinas in order to examine his handling of man's free choice in relation to God's omniscience. He proposes two solutions, (a) one which closely resembles that offered by Boethius and (b) one which resembles that offered by Gersonides and Abraham Ibn Daud. Aquinas comes to these two solutions by distinguishing two ways in which future events can be known: either (a) *as present and in their actually existing natures* or (b) *as future and through their causes.*[69] Whereas future events that are contingent can be apprehended by man only in the second way (and then only with uncertainty), they are perfectly known by God in the first way.

(a) The first solution, therefore, maintains that contingent things, including man's free choices, are infallibly known by God when they are known as present and as they actually are in themselves. "Although contingent things become actual successively," Aquinas writes, "nevertheless God knows contingent things not successively . . . but simultaneously. The reason is that His knowledge is measured by eternity, as is also His being; and eternity, being simultaneously whole, comprises all time. . . .

---

[65] *De Malo*, Q. 6, A. 1, Objection 5 and Reply 5. Cf. Boethius, *The Consolation of Philosophy*, p. 119.

[66] *The Questions Concerning Liberty, Necessity, and Chance*, pp. 429–30.

[67] See *Traité du Libre Arbitre in Oeuvres Completes*, Vol. 9, pp. 197–98.

[68] See *La recherche d'une première vérité*, pp. 235, 243. Cf. *ibid.*, pp. 311–14. See also Bernard Lonergan, "St. Thomas' Theory of Operation," in *Theological Studies*, Vol. 3, No. 4, pp. 544–47; Austin Farrer, *The Freedom of the Will*, pp. 310–11; and Gerard Smith, "Luther and Free Choice," in *The Modern Schoolman*, Vol. XX, No. 2, pp. 87–88.

[69] See *Summa Theologica*, Part I, Q. 14, A. 13.

Hence all things that are in time are present to God from eternity . . . because His glance is carried from eternity over all things as they are in their presentiality. Hence it is manifest that contingent things are infallibly known by God, *inasmuch as they are subject to the divine sight in their presentiality.*"[70]

Boethius anticipates this argument, as we have already noted. It is repeated by a number of writers who come after Aquinas. We find it, expressed in slightly different ways, in Bramhall,[71] Lequier,[72] Lossky,[73] Guitton,[74] Rickaby,[75] Lonergan,[76] and Scully.[77]

(b) The second solution offered by Aquinas maintains that when contingent things are known as future and through their causes, they are "not subject to any certain knowledge."[78] Stated another way, they are not intrinsically predictable with certainty, even given perfect knowledge of their causes, such as that possessed by an omniscient God. In saying that "whoever knows a contingent effect in its cause only, has merely a conjectural knowledge of it,"[79] Aquinas does not make God an exception. In another place, he explicitly declares that future contingencies "can be known as future by no cognition that excludes all falsity and the possibility of falsity; and since there is no falsity or possibility of falsity in the divine knowledge, it would be impossible for God to have knowledge of future contingents if He knew them as future."[80] The impossibility here mentioned concerns only infallible and certain knowledge, which even God cannot have with respect to contingent things, considered as future and in terms of their causes. But since God "knows all contingent

[70] *Ibid.* (Italics added.) Cf. *Truth*, Vol. III, Q. 24, A. 1, Reply 13, p. 141.
[71] See *The Questions Concerning Liberty, Necessity, and Chance*, pp. 430–32. For Hobbes' rejoinder to this argument, as advanced by Bishop Bramhall, see *ibid.*, pp. 432–33. "He would have me conceive eternity to be *nunc stans*," Hobbes writes, "that is, an instant of time, and that instant of time to be God; which neither he nor I can conceive. . . . But that anything can be foreknown which shall not necessarily come to pass, which was not granted, he proveth no otherwise than by his assertion, 'that every instant of time is God'; which is denied him." See also Jonathan Edwards' rejection of this type of argument from the eternity of God's knowledge, in *Freedom of the Will*, pp. 266–67.
[72] *La recherche d'une première vérité*, p. 199.
[73] *Freedom of Will*, pp. 115–18. In these pages, Lossky refers to Boethius's theory of the supra-temporality of God's knowledge; he also criticizes what he thinks is Hobbes's misunderstanding of the eternal present as if it were a single unchanging instant of time, a *nunc stans*.
[74] "Predestination et Liberté" in *La liberté*, p. 143.
[75] *Free Will and Four English Philosophers*, pp. 167–69.
[76] "St. Thomas' Theory of Operation" in *Theological Studies*, Vol. 3, No. 4, p. 544.
[77] "The Initial Freedom" in *Concept of Freedom*, pp. 53–54.
[78] *Summa Theologica*, Part I, Q. 14, A. 13.
[79] *Ibid.*
[80] *Commentary on the Sentences*, Book I, Dist. 38, Q. 1, A. 5.

things, not only as they are in their causes, but also as each one of them is actually in itself,"[81] he has, in the second respect, infallible and certain knowledge of them as present, even though he does not have infallible and certain *fore*knowledge of them as future. In short, precisely because man's free choices, as contingent, are intrinsically unpredictable, it is impossible—for God or man—to foresee them infallibly or with certitude when, *as future*, they can be known *only in their causes*.[82]

For Aquinas, as for Ibn Daud and Gersonides, the divine omniscience is in no way diminished by the fact that God does not have infallible foresight with regard to future contingent events when these are known as future and through their causes. It is no defect not to know that which is unknowable. As Maritain points out, "To foresee or foreknow is to see or recognize a thing *in its cause* before it actually happens; but when the cause is of such a kind that it fails to make known with certitude the thing to which it is preordained, such a thing is not in itself capable of being foreseen with certitude."[83] And, he continues,

> for this reason, God, though possessing a fully comprehensive knowledge of created wills, nevertheless does not know free decisions in their created causes, that is to say, in the previous disposition of these wills themselves; nor in any other created cause.[84]

What a man's free choice will be, according to Maritain, is a secret even from the man himself, "a secret which he will learn only at the very moment when he makes his decision. . . . Even with a 'super-comprehension of the causes,' however perfect it may be supposed, you cannot foresee this act. Even God cannot do this."[85]

Weiss and Hartshorne take a different view of God's omniscience. They hold that contingent future particulars are intrinsically unpredictable, and, therefore, that the failure to foresee them with certitude is not a defect that diminishes God's omniscience. "His omniscience," writes Weiss, "is the power to know all that *can* be known." It does not consist in "the power to know what cannot be known." What cannot be known by any-

---

[81] *Summa Theologica*, Part I, Q. 14, A. 13.
[82] Molina's solution differs from that of Aquinas. He requires us to distinguish a threefold knowledge in God—*scientia libera*, *scientia naturalis*, and *scientia media*. It is in terms of *scientia media* that Molina explains how God foreknows man's free choices in such a way as to leave them contingent. For the documentation of Molina's position, see Vol. I, pp. 448–49.
[83] "Reflections on Necessity and Contingency," in *Essays in Thomism*, p. 34.
[84] *Ibid.*, p. 34. Maritain here adds that God does know "free decisions in their state of always being *present* to His divine Vision. And so He knows them with certitude."
[85] *Scholasticism and Politics*, Ch. V, pp. 129–30. Cf. *Existence and the Existent*, Ch. 4, pp. 85–87. See also M-J. Nicolas, "La Liberté Humaine et le Problème du Mal," in *Revue Thomiste*, Vol. 48, No. 1–2, pp. 192–209.

one, according to Weiss, is the future in its concrete particularity, and this is unknowable to God and man alike.[86]

Hartshorne maintains that "omniscience does not imply a knowledge 'above time.'"[87] He, therefore, rejects the doctrine that "God knows the future not as future to him but as belonging to all times in a single eternal present." "This doctrine," he writes,

> is not deducible from the mere idea of omniscience, or the knowing of all reality as it is, until or unless it has been demonstrated that that which to us is future possesses objectively the same reality as that which to us is present or past; and this is a quite special and by no means self-evident doctrine about time, not in the least implied by any essential religious idea.[88]

Holding that the future is indeterminate, and that "there is real freedom between alternatives, any one of which *can* happen," Hartshorne argues that "the true way to know the future is as undetermined, unsettled. To know just what 'is to happen' is to know falsely if there is in fact no definite thing which is to happen." This, in Hartshorne's opinion, holds true for God as well as for man; nor is this any limitation on the perfection of God's knowledge, "for if the future is in fact unsettled, indeterminate, it would not be ignorance to see it as such, but, rather, true knowledge."[89] Omniscience, Hartshorne declares, "is all the knowledge that is possible, which by definition is perfect knowledge, but . . . since some truths about the future could not be known at present, omniscience does not know them."[90]

A scattering of other writers remains to be considered. They offer divergent solutions of the theological problem. Of these, one, Abraham Tucker, does not take the affirmative side of this issue, for, on other grounds, he denies the existence of free choice in man. Nevertheless, he argues, hypothetically, that if free choice did exist, it would be reconcilable with God's foreknowledge.

"The difficulties we make," Tucker writes, "spring from our conceiving too narrowly of the divine prescience; we consider God as foreknowing an event separately, without knowing, or without contemplating, the causes

[86] *Nature and Man*, p. 13. Unlike Maritain, Weiss does not add that all things, even contingencies and free decisions, are completely known to God *as present*, if not as future. See fn. 85 on p. 483, *supra*.
[87] *Man's Vision of God*, p. 104.
[88] *Ibid.*, p. 98.
[89] *Ibid.*, pp. 98–99. See *ibid.*, p. 139, where Hartshorne attributed to Gersonides the "earliest statement" of the principle "that omniscience sees the future as it is, that is, as partially indeterminate."
[90] *Ibid.*, p. 140. Cf. *ibid.*, pp. 328–30.

giving it birth. . . . But the prescience of God is universal as well as absolute; when he knows what will come to pass, he knows the causes he himself has provided for accomplishing it, nor can anybody who considers the matter at all imagine him ever ignorant or forgetful of either."[91]

According to Henry More, the omniscience and the omnipotence of God extend to everything that is possible—possible to know and possible to do. What is impossible (i.e., self-contradictory), God can neither know nor do, without any loss of omniscience or omnipotence. His argument then proceeds as follows.

> We say that the fore-knowledge of contingent effects, which proceed from a free principle of acting, does either imply a contradiction, or it does not. If it does imply a contradiction, then such effects are not the objects of God's omniscience. . . . But if it does not imply a contradiction, then we actually confess that Divine Prescience and man's free-will are not inconsistent, but that both of them may fitly stand with each other.[92]

Since More finds nothing self-contradictory about free choice, he dismisses, as unreal, the supposed difficulty about free choice in relation to an omnipotent and omniscient God.

Posing the problem in terms of Providence, William James maintains that "the belief in free-will is not in the least incompatible with the belief in Providence, provided you do not restrict the Providence to fulminating nothing but *fatal* decrees."[93] James explains what he means in the following passages:

> If you allow him [i.e., Providence] to provide possibilities as well as actualities to the universe, and to carry on his own thinking in those two categories just as we do ours, chances may be there, uncontrolled even by him, and the course of the universe be really ambiguous; and yet the end of all things may be just what he intended it to be from all eternity.

> . . . Suppose him to say, I will lead things to a certain end, but I will not *now* decide on all the steps thereto. At various points, ambiguous possibilities shall be left open, *either* of which, at a given instant, may become actual. But whichever branch of these bifurcations become real, I know what I shall do at the *next* bifurcation to keep things from drifting away from the final result I intend.[94]

[91] *Free-will, Foreknowledge, and Fate*, pp. 125–26.
[92] *An Account of Virtue*, p. 183.
[93] "The Dilemma of Determinism," in *The Will to Believe*, p. 180.
[94] *Ibid.*, pp. 180–82. At the italicized word *"now"* in the second passage quoted above, James drops a footnote in which he says: "This of course leaves the creative mind subject to the law of time. And to any one who insists on the timelessness of that mind I have no reply to make. A mind to whom all time is simultaneously present must see all things under the form of actuality, or under some form to us unknown. If he thinks certain moments as ambiguous in their content while future, he

On this view of the matter, James tells us that "the creator's plan of the universe would thus be left blank as to many of its actual details, but all possibilities would be marked down. . . . So the creator himself would not need to know *all* the details of actuality until they came; and at any time his own view of the world would be a view partly of facts and partly of possibilities, exactly as ours is now."[95]

Paul Tillich offers us a somewhat similar interpretation of Providence, and one that also allows for all the intrinsically unpredictable novelties that are produced by the creative freedom of God's creatures, especially by that of man. "Providence," he writes, "means a fore-seeing (*pro-videre*) which is a fore-ordering ('seeing to it'). This ambiguity of meaning," he tells us, "expresses an ambiguous feeling toward providence, and it corresponds to different interpretations of the concept." Tillich goes on:

> If the element of foreseeing is emphasized, God becomes the omniscient spectator who knows what will happen but who does not interfere with the freedom of his creatures. If the element of fore-ordering is emphasized, God becomes a planner who has ordered everything that will happen "before the foundations of the world"; all natural and historical processes are nothing more than the execution of this supratemporal divine plan. In the first interpretation the creatures make their world, and God remains a spectator; in the second interpretation the creatures are cogs in a universal mechanism, and God is the only active agent.

According to Tillich, "both interpretations of providence must be rejected." The correct view, in his opinion, is as follows.

> Providence is a permanent activity of God. He never is a spectator; he always directs everything toward its fulfillment. Yet God's directing creativity always creates through the freedom of man and through the spontaneity and structural wholeness of all creatures. Providence works through the polar elements of being. . . . Providence is not interference; it is creation. It uses all factors, both those given by freedom and those given by destiny, in creatively directing everything toward its fulfilment.[96]

---

must simultaneously know how the ambiguity will have been decided when they are past. . . . Is not, however, the timeless mind rather a gratuitous fiction? And is not the notion of eternity being given at a stroke to omniscience only just another way of whacking upon us the block-universe, and of denying that possibilities exist?—just the point to be proved" (*ibid.*, p. 181).

[95] *Ibid.*, p. 182.

[96] *Systematic Theology*, Vol. I, pp. 266–67. See also *ibid.*, p. 269, where Tillich writes: "Creation is the creation of finite freedom; it is the creation of life with its greatness and its danger. God lives, and his life is creative. If God is creative in himself, he cannot create what is opposite to himself; he cannot create the dead, the object which is merely object. He must create that which unites subjectivity and objectivity—life, that which includes freedom and with it the dangers of freedom. The creation of finite freedom is the risk which the divine creativity accepts."

Tillich thus takes a position in theology which more closely resembles the theory of William James than it does the position of Luther and Calvin, or, for that matter, the doctrines of Augustine and Aquinas.[97]

[97] For Tillich's comments on traditional theological views of man's freedom in relation to providence and predestination, see *The Protestant Era*, pp. 129, 172–73.

Chapter 12

A POSSIBLE CONCEPTUAL ISSUE CONCERNING SELF-DETERMINATION: CHANCE, RESPONSIBILITY, AND FREEDOM

In the general controversy about man's freedom of self-determination, there are two distinct disputes about such freedom in relation to moral responsibility. We have already treated one of these in great detail.[1] A schematic summary of it follows.

A. *The dispute is initiated by the proponents of SD.*
   1. They assert that moral responsibility presupposes a freedom that involves causal initiative or causal indeterminacy or both.
   2. From this premise they argue to the conclusion that anyone who wishes meaningfully to employ the notion of responsibility *must affirm the existence of SD* in order to do so.
   3. In other words, they present their opponents with the dilemma: *either abandon the notion of moral responsibility or affirm the existence of self-determination.*

B. *This argument is met by the opponents of SD in the following manner.*
   1. The "hard determinists" accept the dilemma as stated, and, therefore, *abandon the notion of moral responsibility,* since they deny the existence of self-determination.
   2. The "soft determinists" reject the dilemma as stated, and, therefore, *see no reason to abandon the notion of moral responsibility,* even though the existence of self-determination is denied.
      a. They assert that responsibility is tenable in the total absence of self-determination, and that it can be given meaning by reference to man's circumstantial freedom of self-realization.
      b. They do not conclude from this that the non-existence of SD is demonstrated, but only that the argument advanced by its adherents fails: its existence need not be affirmed in order to attribute responsibility to men.

The following schematic summary of the second dispute about self-determination and responsibility will plainly show the way in which it differs from the one outlined above.

[1] See Ch. 9, Sect. 4, pp. 302–16; and Ch. 10, Sect. 5, pp. 418–46, *supra.*

A. *The dispute is initiated by the opponents of SD.*
1. They assert that moral responsibility *precludes* a freedom that involves causal initiative or causal indeterminacy or both.[2]
2. To reach this conclusion, they argue from three premises:
   a. First, that causal initiative or causal indeterminacy makes the free act or the free choice *equivalent to a chance event;*
   b. Second, that what a man does by chance *cannot be imputed to him as his own act or his own choice;*[3]
   c. Third, that if an act or choice cannot be imputed to a man, *he cannot be held morally responsible for it.*
3. Hence, they present their opponents with the dilemma: *either deny the existence of self-determination or abandon the notion of moral responsibility.*

B. *This argument is met by the proponents of SD in the following manner.*
1. They reject the dilemma as stated and, with it, the conclusion that moral responsibility precludes a freedom that involves causal initiative or causal indeterminacy or both.[4]
2. They do so on the following basis:
   a. First, they assert that self-determination is the *very opposite of chance* and *involves no element of chance;*
   b. Second, they maintain that, far from precluding imputability, it is the indispensable basis of it;
   c. Third, they conclude that since the free act or the free choice can be imputed to a man as its agent or cause, *he can be held morally responsible for it.*

We have seen intimations of this second dispute in earlier chapters.[5] Its arguments, pro and con, are often so merged with the arguments of the first dispute that it would have been impossible to give detailed documentary evidence of the first dispute, as we did, without also including some passages which relate to the second. Nevertheless, many texts bearing directly on this second dispute remain to be considered. We shall present them in this chapter; but, before doing so, we must ask what this second dispute adds to the first, as far as the general controversy about the kinds of freedom is concerned.

The first answer that suggests itself interprets the argument against self-determination in the second dispute as amplifying the position taken by the opponents of SD in the first dispute. It is as if they were to say:

[2] Whereas in the first dispute some of the opponents of SD contend that responsibility is tenable without self-determination, here the opponents contend that it is not tenable on the basis of self-determination.

[3] An action is commonly said to be imputable to a man if it can be seen to proceed from him as its cause.

[4] Whereas in the first dispute the proponents of SD contend that self-determination must be affirmed by those who attribute responsibility to men, here they contend that responsibility can be affirmed by those who attribute self-determination to men.

[5] See Ch. 9, pp. 290–91; and Ch. 10, pp. 430–31, 433–34, 436–37, *supra.*

we have already shown that we are not obliged to affirm the existence of self-determination in order to attribute responsibility to men in some meaningful way; now, in addition, we are showing you why we are obliged to deny the existence of it in order to attribute responsibility to men. Two things must be pointed out about this interpretation of what the second dispute adds to the first.

(i) It makes the second dispute existential in import, just as the first is. In both cases, the opposed propositions about SD and responsibility are premises in an existential argument. Thus, in the first dispute, the proposition *responsibility presupposes* SD leads to the conclusion that SD *exists*; and the proposition *responsibility does not presuppose* SD enables the other side of the dispute to say that that conclusion is unproved. In the second dispute, the proposition SD *precludes responsibility* leads to the conclusion that SD *does not exist*; and the proposition SD *does not preclude responsibility* enables the other side of the dispute to say that that conclusion is unproved.

Hence, from the point of view of the opponents of SD, the argument by which they initiate the second dispute goes further than the argument which they advance in order to rebut the position of the adherents of SD in the first dispute. In the first dispute, they merely conclude that the argument advanced by the adherents of SD *fails*, which merely leaves the existence of SD *unproved*, whereas, in the second dispute, they argue that the nonexistence of SD *is proved*.

From the point of view the adherents of SD, the picture is somewhat different. The argument which they advance in order to rebut the opponents of SD in the second dispute merely confirms the argument by which they initiate the first dispute. In the first dispute, they regard themselves as proving the conclusion that SD exists, because *responsibility presupposes* SD. In the second dispute, they regard themselves as confirming that conclusion, by showing that their opponents fail to prove the opposite conclusion. This is the effect of their denying their opponents' assertion that SD *precludes responsibility*.

From both points of view, then, the second dispute, like the first, bears on the existential issues concerning SD. But it is only from the point of view of the opponents of SD that the second dispute is more conclusive than the first. When we appraise the second dispute in this way, we must observe that it contains two arguments, not one, against the existence of SD.

(ii) To make this clear, let us look at the basic premise employed by the opponents of SD in the second dispute in order to prove that SD does not exist. That premise is: SD *either is nothing but chance or involves an element of chance*. Now, by adding the proposition that chance does not exist, we get the first and simplest argument against the existence of SD. It is as follows:

Argument I
   (a) SD involves chance.[6]
   (x) Chance does not exist.

Conclusion: Therefore, SD does not exist.

The second argument against the existence of SD requires the addition of a number of other propositions, as follows:

Argument II
   (a) SD involves chance.
   (b) Chance precludes imputability.
   (c) The absence of imputability entails the absence of responsibility.

First conclusion: (d) Therefore, SD precludes responsibility.
   (e) But responsibility can be attributed to men.

Second conclusion: Therefore, SD does not exist.

The first part of this argument, which ends with the conclusion that *SD precludes responsibility*, involves two points with which the adherents of SD agree. They agree that what an individual does by chance does not proceed from him as cause, and so cannot be imputed to him as agent, i.e., proposition (b). They also agree that, according to the common understanding of responsibility, a man cannot be held responsible for an act that is not imputable to him, i.e., proposition (c). But they deny proposition (a), that self-determination involves chance.[7] They assert the contrary of this, for they hold that the self or the will is the cause of the decisions a man makes by self-determination. The acts which follow from such decisions can, therefore, be imputed to him. Hence, arguing from the contradictory of proposition (a), they conclude that a man can be held responsible for the actions that flow from his free decision. If they could not maintain that SD excludes chance, they would have to admit the cogency of the argument which yields the conclusion that SD precludes responsibility;

[6] Proposition (a) has the same force in this argument whether it asserts merely that SD involves an element of chance or asserts more strongly that SD is nothing but chance.

[7] They deny chance in the sense in which they understand that term to be used by their opponents, namely, to signify causelessness. It should also be noted here that their opponents reject self-determination as they understand that to be affirmed by its adherents, namely, as involving causal initiative or causal indeterminacy or both. We shall discuss later these two points of mutual understanding.

for if self-determination involves chance, then what is done by self-deter
mination is not imputable, and, in consequence, is something for which a
man cannot be held responsible.

Now let us return to our question about what the second dispute con
cerning self-determination and responsibility adds to the first as far as the
general controversy about the kinds of freedom is concerned. As we have
just seen, one answer to that question is that, from the point of view of the
opponents of SD, it adds two arguments in support of the conclusion that
SD does not exist. But since one of these (i.e., Argument I) has already
been noted in earlier chapters, and since, moreover, it involves no refer
ence to SD and responsibility, we need not be concerned any further with
it here.[8] And while Argument II does involve the premise that SD pre
cludes responsibility, it, too, has exclusively existential import and so really
belongs with the materials covered in Chapters 9 and 10 rather than here
where we are concerned with the conceptual issues about self-determina
tion.

Let us recall the distinction between existential and conceptual issues
in the general controversy. Authors disagree existentially when one affirms
and the other denies the reality of a freedom which is conceived in a
certain way.[9] They disagree conceptually when one affirms and the other
denies that a freedom which is conceived in a certain way conforms to
the generic idea of freedom or to the common understanding of it.[10]

Hence, if the opponents of SD employ the proposition that SD pre
cludes responsibility in order to argue that SD does not exist (as in Argu
ment II), then that argument is not germane to a conceptual issue about
SD in the general controversy. Its relevance is to the existential issues
treated in Chapters 9 and 10, and it belongs with the other arguments
advanced there by the opponents of SD. But it was not presented there as
a distinct argument, nor was documentary evidence given of its expression
by the writers who advance it.[11] This requires a word of explanation.

When, in Section I of this Chapter, we present Argument II as it is
expressed by the opponents of SD, it will be seen that it stops with what
we have called its "first conclusion," (that *SD precludes responsibility*).

[8] For documentary evidence of Argument I, see Ch. 9, pp. 264–66, 297–98; and Ch.
10, pp. 346–47, 400–1, *supra*. For evidence of the reply to it by the defenders of SD,
see Ch. 9, pp. 297–98; and Ch. 10, pp. 362–69, 382, 416–18, *supra*.

[9] Thus, Ch. 9 and 10 deal with existential issues about self-determination, i.e., dis
agreements about the reality of SD conceived as involving causal initiative or causal
indeterminacy.

[10] Thus, Ch. 4 deals with the conceptual issue about the circumstantial freedom of
self-realization. One side affirms that SR conforms to the common understanding of
freedom, and the other side denies that it does.

[11] As we pointed out on p. 489, *supra.*, some intimations of this argument were given
in both Ch. 9 and 10.

The authors quoted do not go on to draw the "second conclusion" (that SD *does not exist*). The intention to make this further point may be implicit in their assertion that SD precludes responsibility, but it is not explicit.

The foregoing not only explains why Argument II was treated only in an incidental fashion in Chapters 9 and 10;[12] it also enables us to see the way in which Argument II is, *implicitly at least,* germane to a conceptual issue concerning SD in the general controversy about the kinds of freedom. To see this, we need only remember that the generic idea of freedom involves the notion of the self as somehow the cause or principle of the action said to be free. In other words, according to the common understanding of freedom, nothing can properly be called free that does not somehow proceed from the self.[13] But this is also tantamount to saying that if an action or decision cannot be imputed to a person (as somehow flowing or proceeding *from him*), neither can it properly be called free.

This last proposition calls our attention to the common element in the notion of imputability and in the generic idea of freedom, namely, that both can be applied only to "that which proceeds from the self as cause or agent." By substituting this proposition, which we shall call proposition (y), for proposition (c) in Argument II, we reach a conclusion that constitutes the negative side of the conceptual issue about SD in the general controversy.[14] Let us call the argument that results from this substitution Argument III. It runs as follows.

Argument III
    (a) SD involves chance
    (b) Chance precludes imputability.
    (y) But that which cannot be imputed to a man cannot properly be called free (i.e., does not conform to the generic idea of freedom).

Conclusion: Therefore, SD does not conform to the generic idea of freedom.

12 It appeared there as an aspect of the effort by the opponents of SD to rebut the argument for its existence, advanced by the adherents of SD. Since the latter base their argument on the proposition that responsibility presupposes SD, the former can rebut that argument in two ways: first, by denying that responsibility presupposes SD (since it can be given meaning by reference to SR); second, by asserting that SD precludes responsibility. If SD precludes responsibility, it can hardly be the case that responsibility presupposes SD.

13 For the exposition of the generic idea of freedom see Vol. I, Ch. 27, esp. pp. 608–16.

14 It does not answer the question whether self-determination, as conceived, exists, but rather the question whether self-determination, as conceived, signifies anything that can be recognized as genuinely a form of freedom.

By looking back at Argument II, we can see the relation between th "first conclusion" there drawn and the conclusion here drawn in Argu ment III.

In Argument II, the middle premise (b), by equating that which a man does by chance with that which is not imputable to him, connect the first premise (a), which makes that which a man does by self-deter mination equivalent to chance, with the conclusion (d), that SD preclude responsibility. The other link needed to make this connection is provide by premise (c), which equates that which is not imputable to a man with that for which he cannot be held responsible, according to the common understanding of responsibility.

In Argument III, the same middle premise (b), by equating that which a man does by chance with that which is not imputable to him connect the same first premise (a), which makes that which a man does by self determination equivalent to chance, with the conclusion that SD does no conform to the generic idea of freedom. Here the other link needed to make this connection is provided by premise (y), which equates that which is not imputable to a man with that which cannot properly be called free, according to the common understanding of freedom.

Here, as in the case of Argument II, the adherents of SD deny only proposition (a).[15] They assert the contradictory of it, namely, that self determination excludes chance. In their view, the self or the will is the cause of the decisions a man makes by self-determination. Hence, the actions that flow from such decisions are imputable to him and conform to the common understanding of the free act as one that proceeds from the self. Thus a conclusion is reached which constitutes the affirmative side of the conceptual issue about SD in the general controversy.

In the view of the evidence already presented, there can be no doubt that SD authors would assert the propositions needed to defend this con clusion against the attack presented in Argument III.[16] But, as we shall see when we come to Section 3, the SD authors there presented as taking part in this dispute do not argue in this way. They argue against the con clusion that SD precludes responsibility (which is the first conclusion reached in Argument II), not against the conclusion that SD fails to con form to the generic idea of freedom (which is the conclusion reached in Argument III). The probable reason for this is that it is only the "first

[15] Cf. pp. 491–92, *supra.*

[16] We have seen how many of them explicitly deny that any element of chance is involved in SD. And from the fact that so many of them explicitly argue that SD is required as the basis of moral responsibility, we can safely infer that, in their view, the actions which flow from free decisions can be imputed to the self or will that causes such decisions.

conclusion" of Argument II (that *SD precludes responsibility*) which is ever explicitly argued by the opponents of SD.

Nevertheless, we have seen how the conclusion that SD does not conform to the generic idea of freedom is implicit in Argument II. By substituting proposition (y) for proposition (c), we transform Argument II into Argument III. We have every reason to believe that the opponents of SD, as well as the defenders of it, would assert proposition (y): that acts which cannot be imputed to man, because they do not proceed from him as their cause or agent, also cannot properly be called free, according to the common understanding of freedom. Hence, there seems to be justification for constructing a conceptual issue about self-determination, even though that issue is not present in the literature as is the issue about whether SD does or does not preclude responsibility.

In the course of the preceding chapters, we have constructed many issues that are only implicitly present in the literature, in the sense that some, if not all, the authors involved have to be construed as taking sides on the question at issue. What they do say explicitly warrants our interpreting them as answering the question in opposite ways. But in the case of the conceptual issue with which we are here concerned, our construction involves an additional step. Here, from what the authors do say, we must infer what they would say to a related question.[17] We are, therefore, constructing a possible issue, yet one that is implicit in an issue that is actually and plainly present in the literature.[18]

The inference involved in this construction is supported, at least for the opponents of SD, by the fact that they make the reduction of SD to chance the basic premise in their argument. Only a few of the authors who defend SD against the charge that SD precludes responsibility explicitly deny that basic premise. The rest attempt to rebut the charge by attacking other aspects of the argument on which it rests. Nevertheless, the fact that they defend SD against this charge and argue that it can be the basis of responsibility shows that a denial that SD is chance must be at least implicit in their argument; otherwise they could not make it the basis of responsibility, for, if free decisions were matters of chance, they would not give rise to acts that could be imputed to the men who do them.

---

[17] Argument II and the reply to it are present in the literature. As Sect. 2 and 3 to follow will show, the issue whether SD does or does not preclude responsibility is explicitly joined and disputed. But, as we have seen, Argument II can be transformed into Argument III by construing the authors who assert proposition (c) or its contrary, as also asserting proposition (y) or its contrary. This amounts to inferring how authors who answer the question about SD and responsibility would also answer the question about SD and the generic idea of freedom.

[18] The necessity for constructing this possible issue was discussed in Ch. 8, pp. 240–47, *supra*. See esp. pp. 243–46.

In Chapter 4, where we dealt with the conceptual issue about the free dom of self-realization, we found writers who explicitly reject SR as a kind of freedom or treat it as an illusory or counterfeit freedom. We also found writers who plainly enough assert that SR is truly freedom, even the only true freedom. Hence, there the conceptual issue was explicitly joined and could be documented as actually present in the literature. But here we find no writers at all on the negative side who, in addition to denying the existence of self-determination, also maintain that, even if it did exist, it could not be regarded as a genuine form of freedom. What we find instead are writers who assert that self-determination, as conceived, makes responsibility impossible, and, replying to them, writers who assert that self-determination is the basis of responsibility.

Nevertheless, the possible conceptual issue about self-determination is implicitly present in the dispute about whether SD precludes responsibility. That is the only justification for presenting in this chapter the documentary evidence of the latter dispute. We are, in effect, asking the writers whose arguments are reported in Sections 1 and 2 a question which they do not appear to have asked themselves; namely, *Can self-determination be properly regarded as a kind of freedom?* The topical agreement that is needed for joining issue on this question is provided by the common understanding of freedom, according to which the self is the principle of every genuine form of freedom and whatever does not somehow flow from the self cannot properly be regarded as a free act. Given such topical agreement about the question, we are justified in inferring the positions which the opposed authors would take, were they to answer this question.

We shall proceed as follows. In Section I, we shall present various formulations of the first part of Argument II (i.e., the part which concludes that *SD precludes responsibility*). These are all advanced by writers who reject SD as non-existent. In Section 2, we shall present evidence of the attempts to rebut this argument. These attempts are made by writers who affirm the existence of SD and who also maintain that it is the indispensable basis of responsibility. Then, in Section 3, we shall construct the conceptual issue about self-determination that is implicit in this dispute about its relation to responsibility; and we shall attempt to show that, underlying it, is another conceptual issue—the one which is constituted by opposed answers to the question, *Does self-determination involve chance, conceived as causelessness?*

This last issue underlies the existential issues about self-determination as well as the conceptual issue about whether it is or is not a genuine form of freedom. It is probably the most fundamental issue in the whole controversy about self-determination. Hence, it is of great importance to discover how certain authors can hold that self-determination either is nothing but chance or involves an element of chance, whereas other writers deny that any element of chance is involved in self-determination.

Let us suppose, for the moment, that both groups of authors conceive self-determination in the same way (i.e., are in topical agreement about the meaning of SD as involving causal initiative or causal indeterminacy) and that both groups conceive chance in the same way (i.e., are in topical agreement about the meaning of chance as being that which happens without cause). If this supposition is not correct, then, in the absence of the requisite topical agreement about the basic terms involved, we do not have a genuine issue here, but only an apparent one that conceals a misunderstanding. But if this supposition is correct and, in consequence, we do have a genuine issue, then we must ask what fundamental differences between the two groups of authors can be found to explain the opposite views they hold about SD and chance.

The attempt that we shall make to answer this question in Section 3 seems to us a fitting conclusion not only to the present chapter but also to the earlier chapters that deal with the issues about causal initiative and causal determinacy. If it is ever possible to resolve, one way or the other, the issue about self-determination and chance, that would go a long way toward resolving the issues about the existence of causal initiative and of causal indeterminacy. The same thing is true of the conceptual issue about SD and the generic idea of freedom. That, too, would be resolved by a resolution of the issue concerning SD and chance. Hence, if we can find the reasons why opposite sides are taken on this issue, we have the key to most, if not all, of the disputes about self-determination.

1. FREE WILL PRECLUDES RESPONSIBILITY

It is not always possible to ascertain the original expression of an argument which, once expressed, gets repeated again and again. But in this case there can be little doubt that Hume is the author of the argument with which we are here concerned and which is many times repeated by writers who come after him. Furthermore, the original statement of the argument by Hume is so complete that, apart from variations in expression, little is added in the subsequent repetitions. For the sake of completing the record, however, we shall document the appearance of the argument in later writers and observe the minor variations that occur.

Hume's first statement of the argument is in his early work, *The Treatise of Human Nature.* It occurs in a section immediately following the one which concludes with the statement that "liberty, by removing necessity, removes also causes and is the very same thing with chance."[19] The argument opens with the observation that causal necessity—and with it th whole determinist view that a man's character and motives determine hi choices and actions—is required for both religion and morality. Hum writes:

> This kind of necessity is so essential to religion and morality, that without it there must ensue an absolute subversion of both, and . . . every other supposition is entirely destructive to all laws both *divine* and *human*. 'Tis indeed certain, that as all human laws are founded on rewards and punishments, 'tis supposed as a fundamental principle that these motives have an influence on the mind, and both produce the good and prevent the evil actions. We may give to this influence what name we please; but as 'tis usually conjoined with the action, common sense requires it should be esteemed a cause, and be looked upon as an instance of that necessity, which I would establish.[20]

The argument then goes on to point out that free will (which Hum thinks he has shown to be synonymous with chance) would, if it existed render it impossible to impute to an individual his freely willed action and, therefore, impossible to hold him responsible for them. Referring t the connection of a man's actions with his character and motives, Hum says:

> . . . according to the doctrine of liberty or chance, this connexion is reduced to nothing, nor are men more accountable for those actions which are designed and premeditated, than for such are the most casual and accidental. Actions are by their very nature temporary and perishing; and where they proceed not from some cause in the characters and disposition of the person who performed them, they infix not themselves upon him, and can neither redound to his honour, if good, nor infamy, if evil. The action itself may be blameable; it may be contrary to all the rules of morality and religion. But the person is not responsible for it; and as it proceeded from nothing in him, that is durable or constant, and leaves nothing of that nature behind it, 'tis impossible he can, upon its account, become the object of punishment or vengeance. According to the hypothesis of liberty, therefore, a man is as pure and untainted, after having committed the most horrid crimes, as at the first moment of his birth . . . 'Tis only upon the principles of necessity, that a person acquires any merit or demerit from his actions, however the common opinion may incline to the contrary.[21]

[19] *Op. cit.*, Book II, Sect. 1, p. 407. Hume immediately calls attention to the existential import of the statement that liberty (in the SD sense) is the same thing as chance; for he says that the same arguments apply to liberty or free will as apply to chance, namely, that, being self-contradictory, it cannot exist.

[20] *Ibid.*, Sect. 2, p. 410. This statement is later repeated almost verbatim in the *Enquiry Concerning Human Understanding*, Sect. VIII, Part II, Div. 76, pp. 97–98.

[21] *Treatise of Human Nature*, Book II, Sect. II, p. 411. See *ibid.*, pp. 411–12. These pages are also repeated almost verbatim in the *Enquiry*, on pp. 98–99. In the *Enquiry*,

It is important to note that, for Hume, the lack of causal connection between a man's character and his acts makes the latter not *his* acts at all, but products of chance. To say that free will means that a man's decisions are not determined by his character and motives is to say that free will reduces to chance; for to exclude character and motives as the causal determinants of the so-called "free" decision is to leave it totally without causal determination. This is true not only for Hume but also for his followers. As we have seen in Chapters 9 and 10, the argument against the existence of causal initiative or causal indeterminacy which is based on the proposition that a man's decisions are causally determined by his character and motives is merely a special form of the argument which appeals to the universal principle of causation. The evidence presented in those chapters plainly shows that there are not two quite distinct arguments here. In both, the reduction of SD to chance is the basic premise on which the denial of its existence rests.[22]

In the half century following Hume's publication of the *Treatise* in 1739, a number of other eighteenth-century writers repeat Hume's argument in part or whole. Equating free will with what he calls a "liberty of indifference" instead of with chance, Jonathan Edwards argues that, as the source of human actions, indifference, like chance, if it existed, would be inconsistent with morality, i.e., with responsibility, praise and blame, rewards and punishments.[23] Similarly, David Hartley declares that "religion does not presuppose Free-Will in the philosophical sense, i.e., it does not presuppose a power of doing different things, the previous circumstances remaining the same." In his opinion, free will, "so far from being

---

Hume adds one further point, namely, that liberty, not in the sense of free will, but in the sense of absence of impediment to doing as one pleases, is "essential to morality, and . . . no human actions, where it is wanting, are susceptible of any moral qualities, or can be the objects either of approbation or dislike. For as actions are objects of our moral sentiments, so far only as they are indications of the internal character, passions, and affections, it is impossible that they can give rise either to praise or blame, where they proceed not from these principles, but are derived altogether from external violence" (*ibid.*, p. 99).

22 It is also the basic premise in every argument which concludes that SD precludes responsibility, though sometimes it is explicitly stated and sometimes it is merely implicit in the assertion that SD precludes the determination of a man's acts by his character and motives. As Nowell-Smith points out in his debate with C. A. Campbell, such human behavior as is not causally determined by character and motives is not causally determined at all, i.e., is a random or chance event. Campbell's proposal of a third alternative (namely, "causally determined by the self, independently of character and motives"), Nowell-Smith dismisses as devoid of meaning. See Ch. 9, pp. 297–98, *supra*. In rejecting "self-caused" as a genuine alternative to "caused by character and motives," Nowell-Smith represents the views of Hume and his followers, for whom there is no alternative to "caused by character and motives" except chance.

23 See *Freedom of the Will*, Part III pp. 303–4, 320–21, 326.

required [by religion] . . . is inconsistent" with it.[24] But it is not until we come to Joseph Priestley toward the end of the century that we come upon a writer who not only repeats Hume's argument in all its detail but also acknowledges his indebtedness to Hume for it.[25]

In his debate with Dr. Price, Priestley points out, first of all, that, so far as he can understand what Price means by a *self-determining power*, "the determination, though dignified with the appellation of *self*, cannot be anything but a mere *random decision* . . . like the chance of a die"; and, therefore, he remarks, it "cannot possibly be of a nature to be entitled to praise or blame, merit or demerit, reward or punishment."[26] The reason for this he attempts to make clear by calling Dr. Price's attention to the fact that, since "self-determined" decision is nothing but a chance event, the action which follows from it cannot be imputed to the self who made the decision in this random manner. He asks Dr. Price to consider

> in what sense a determination of his mind can be said to be more *his own*, on account of its not having been produced by *previous motives*, but in a manner independent of all motives, or reasons, for choice. . . . If nothing in the preceding state of his mind (which would come under the description of motive) contributed to it, how did *he* contribute to it? and, therefore, in what sense can he call it *his*? If he reject a determination produced by motives, because motives are *no part of himself*, he must likewise give up all claim to a determination produced without motives, because that also would be produced without the help of any thing belonging to himself.[27]

Like Hume, he therefore concludes that, far from being incompatible with morality, the idea of responsibility, and just rewards and punishments, the doctrine of necessity is indispensable to them.[28] "In short," he writes, "where the proper *influence of motives* ceases, the proper foundation of

[24] *Observations on Man*, p. 357. Cf. Abraham Tucker, *Freewill, Foreknowledge and Fate*, pp. 71–73. One other writer, Anthony Collins, should be mentioned in this connection. His *Inquiry Concerning Human Liberty*, published in 1715, antedates Hume's *Treatise*. While it does not contain Hume's argument insofar as the essential premise in it is the identification of free will with chance, Collins's book does offer, as a fifth argument to prove "Man a necessary agent," the reason that if he were not, "there would be no foundation for rewards and punishments" (*op. cit.*, p. 86). To this, he adds a sixth argument to the effect that "if Man was not a necessary Agent determined by pleasure and pain, he would have no notion of *morality*, or motive to practise it; the distinction between morality and immorality, virtue and vice, would be lost, and Man would not be a moral Agent" (*ibid.*, p. 88).
[25] See *The Doctrine of Philosophical Necessity*, pp. 101–2, where Priestley quotes one of the passages from Hume's *Enquiry*, mentioned above. Priestley also quotes (see *ibid.*, pp. 104–8) another version of the same argument from a work by Lord Kaims (Henry Home), his *Sketches of the History of Man*, published in 1774.
[26] *The Doctrine of Philosophical Necessity*, pp. 81–82.
[27] *Ibid.*, pp. 82–83.
[28] See *ibid.*, pp. 84–85.

praise and blame disappears with it; and a *self-determining power*, supposed to act in a manner independent of motive, and even contrary to every thing that comes under that description, is a thing quite foreign to every idea that bears the least relation to praise or blame."[29]

Toward the end of the nineteenth century, F. H. Bradley revives Hume's argument, but also gives it his own special twist. In his famous essay, "The Vulgar Notion of Responsibility in Connexion with the Theories of Free-Will and Necessity," Bradley, like Hume, equates the freedom of a free will with chance. "Free-will," he says, "means Non-determinism." Pointing out that "the will is not determined to act by anything *else*; and further, it is not determined to act by anything *at all*," he insists that "the *libertas arbitrii* is no more . . . than *contingentia arbitrii*. Freedom means *chance*; you are free, because there is no reason which will account for your particular acts, because no one in the world, not even yourself, can possibly say what you will, or will not, do next."[30]

But with the freedom of self-determination reduced to chance, we face, according to Bradley, the paradox that "[we] are 'accountable' . . . because [we] are wholly 'unaccountable' creature[s]."[31] Far from saving responsibility, the theory of free will destroys it. So far, Bradley stands with Hume. He writes:

> A man is responsible, *because* there was no reason why he should have done one thing rather than another thing. And that man, and *only* that man, is responsible, concerning whom it is impossible for any one, even himself, to know what in the world he will be doing next. . . . So far is such an account from saving responsibility (as we commonly understand it), that it annihilates the very conditions of it.[32]

But Bradley departs from Hume at the next step. While, in his opinion, the doctrine of necessity is more consistent with responsibility, since it permits us to impute to the individual the voluntary acts he performs which are determined by his character and motives, nevertheless, it, too, fails in one respect. It cannot justify retributive punishment; and retribution, according to Bradley, is part of the vulgar notion of responsibility.[33]

---

[29] *Ibid.*, p. 93. See also *ibid.*, pp. 91–93, 95–99.

[30] *Op. cit.*, in *Ethical Studies*, p. 11. "In short," Bradley adds, "the irrational connexion, which the Free-will doctrine fled from in the shape of external necessity, it has succeeded only in reasserting in the shape of chance" (*ibid.*, p. 12).

[31] *Ibid.*, p. 11.

[32] *Ibid.*, p. 12.

[33] See *ibid.*, pp. 26–32. This leads Bradley to the conclusion that "neither the one nor the other of our 'two great philosophical modes of thought' . . . does in any way theoretically express the moral notions of the vulgar mind, or fail in some points to contradict them utterly" (*ibid.*, p, 33). And in another place, he says that "for both alike responsibility (as we believe in it) is a word altogether devoid of signification

The fact that Bradley finds certain difficulties with the determinist view in connection with responsibility does not weaken his attack on free will as totally incapable of providing a basis for imputability, because it involve chance.[34] The same holds true of the positions taken by Hastings Rash dall, J. M. E. McTaggart, and Sir David Ross. They find some difficulty in reconciling determinism with a retributive theory of punishment, but tha does not temper their unqualified rejection of indeterminism as totally irreconcilable with the requirements of morality, the notion of responsi bility, and the utilitarian justification of punishment.

Rashdall, for example, tells us that "if the true object of punishment be retribution, there might be something to be said for the suggestion tha Determinism would make it unjust."[35] But if we exclude retribution, a Rashdall thinks we should, that difficulty is removed. "The notion o merit," he writes, "in so far as it does not involve the retributive view o punishment in no way presupposes the theory of Indeterminism."[36] On the contrary, he maintains, the theory of indeterminism removes all meaning from the notions of merit and demerit.

> Not only is Determinism not inconsistent with responsibility, but it may even be maintained with much force that it is Indeterminism which really undermines responsibility. A free act is, according to the Indeterminist, an absolutely new beginning, not springing from, or having any necessary connection with the past. The question may be raised, What is the meaning of holding me 'responsible' for some past act of mine if that act did not really proceed from and reveal the true nature of the self which I still am?[37]

In other words, indeterminism undermines responsibility because it re moves the ground for imputing the free act to the self. And the reason for this, Rashdall explains, is that

---

and impossible of explanation" (*ibid.*, pp. 40–41). Two more recent writers concu with Bradley in thinking that neither determinism nor libertarianism can account for responsibility. One is W. I. Matson, whose views are reported in Ch. 10, pp. 445–46 *supra.* But Matson, in addition to saying that the consequences of necessitarianism and libertarianism are precisely the same so far as responsibility is concerned, also dismisse responsibility as a notion that moral philosophy would be well rid of. The other writer is A. E. Duncan-Jones, who explicitly assimilates his own position to that of Bradley's essay. See "Freedom: An Illustrative Puzzle," in *Proceedings of the Aristotelian Society* Vol. XXXIX, pp. 107–8.

[34] Failing this, it also makes it impossible, in Bradley's view, for us to regard man as a moral agent. "We have seen that responsibility (on the usual understanding of it)," he writes, "can only exist in a moral agent. And, if it be true of any man, that his actions are matters of chance, and his will in a state of equilibrium disturbed by contingency, then I think that the question whether such a being is a moral agent, is a question answered as soon as raised" (*Ethical Studies*, p. 13).

[35] *The Theory of Good and Evil*, Vol. II, Book III, p. 334.

[36] *Ibid.*, p. 332.

[37] *Ibid.*, p. 335. See also *ibid.*, pp. 335–36, and cf. pp. 318–32.

insofar as we believe in events undetermined by causes we believe in pure chance. . . . Pure chance is as irrational and unthinkable an idea as Fate. . . . And if there were such things as human acts determined by pure chance, they could not with any reasonableness be regarded as acts for which any particular person is responsible.[38]

McTaggart differs from Rashdall on one point. In his view, vindictive or retributive punishment, if it can be justified at all, is no more impossible for the determinist to justify than for the indeterminist. "But they are not on a level as to other sorts of punishment." The indeterminist, McTaggart maintains, "is quite inconsistent in supporting either deterrent or reformatory punishment."[39] And furthermore, he argues, the fact that indeterminism provides no basis for imputability makes "indeterminism . . . inconsistent with the validity of morality," for it does not entitle us to pass "from the volition to the person who makes it."[40] Ross similarly argues that if a man were capable of doing either of two acts indifferently, "the doing of either could have no moral value."[41] The reason, for Ross as for others, is that a belief in indeterminism is "equivalent to a belief in blind chance."[42]

In contrast to the authors whom we have just considered, such writers as Samuel Alexander, L. T. Hobhouse, and Bertrand Russell take the position that responsibility can be attributed to men, and rewards or punishments justified, *only* on a deterministic view of human action. "Punishment, and with it responsibility," Alexander writes, "would be unmeaning except for the fact that, in face of institutions which demand from him a certain course of conduct, an agent, in virtue of his character, pursues a different course."[43] The other face of the same picture, according to Alexander, is that indeterminism precludes responsibility. "Though invented to save responsibility," he says, "free-will renders it inexplicable; a will independent of motives could never be responsible, because it could not be called to account."[44] Hobhouse similarly points out that the argument by which the libertarian theory tries to support itself can be turned against it.

[38] *Ibid.*, p. 337.
[39] *Some Dogmas of Religion*, pp. 163–64. Cf. *ibid.*, pp. 166–67.
[40] *Ibid.*, pp. 177–78. See also *ibid.*, pp. 168–69, 178–82. Cf. Charles Baylis, "Rational Preference, Determinism, and Moral Obligation," in *The Journal of Philosophy*, Vol. XLVII, No. 3, pp. 62–63.
[41] *Foundations of Ethics*, p. 230. But cf. *ibid.*, pp. 250–51, where Ross confesses some doubt about the success of attempts "to reconcile responsibility with Determinism."
[42] *Ibid.*, p. 223.
[43] *Moral Order and Progress*, p. 341. See *ibid.*, p. 335.
[44] *Ibid.*, p. 338.

It is held that I cannot be responsible for my acts if they grow out of my past, and my past ultimately out of my ancestry and my circumstances. It must be replied that I cannot be held responsible unless I am the same agent that did the deed. If the doer was a will which popped up out of nothing, it was not the "I" of this moment whom you accuse, but the fleeting disconnected "I" of *that* moment, which you should blame. The "I" of this moment is free and might take a quite contrary line. Responsibility implies continued self-determination.[45]

Such self-determination, Hobhouse explains, involves the determination of volitions by character and motives and is thus the very opposite of "conceptions of freedom which require in each act of choice a breach with the past."[46] Bertrand Russell, in the same fashion, contends that "it is not determinism but free-will that has subversive consequences" for morality.[47] And in a much later work he confirms his earlier stand: "Praise and blame, rewards and punishment, and the whole apparatus of the criminal law, are rational on the deterministic hypothesis, but not on the hypothesis of free will."[48]

In his debate with C. A. Campbell, P. H. Nowell-Smith represents a point of view that is shared by others in the group of contemporary analysts. As we have seen in earlier reports of this debate, Nowell-Smith maintains that it is impossible for the libertarian to distinguish "a 'free' action from a random event." For him, there is no third alternative to the indeterminism of chance action and the determinism of action in accord with character.[49] Accordingly, he concludes that responsibility requires causal determinism and is impossible without it.[50] We find the same reasoning in A. J. Ayer. Asking how it is that I come to make my choice, Ayer says:

Either it is an accident that I choose to act as I do or it is not. If it is an accident, then it is merely a matter of chance that I did not choose otherwise; and if it is merely a matter of chance that I did not choose otherwise, it is surely irrational to hold me morally responsible for choosing as I did.

[45] *The Elements of Social Justice*, p. 53.
[46] *Ibid.*, p. 55. Cf. *ibid.*, pp. 51–52, 54.
[47] "Determinism and Morals," in *The Hibbert Journal*, Vol. 7, p. 121. "If we really believed that other people's actions did not have causes," Russell writes, "we could never try to influence other people's actions"; and, in consequence, "almost all the actions with which morality is concerned would become irrational" (*ibid.*, p. 120).
[48] *Human Society in Ethics and Politics*, p. 79. See also *ibid.*, p. 80.
[49] See Ch. 9, pp. 297–98, *supra*.
[50] See "Freewill and Moral Responsibility," in *Mind*, Vol. LVII, No. 225, pp. 45–52. It should be noted that since, for Nowell-Smith, the basis for attributing freedom to men must be the same as the basis for attributing responsibility to them, he also holds that "freedom, so far from being incompatible with causality, implies it" (*ibid.*, p. 46). In a footnote at this point, he cites R. E. Hobart's essay "Freewill as Involving Determinism and Impossible Without It," in *Mind*, Vol. XLIII, No. 169, pp. 1–25. The argument in Hobart's essay is, of course, to the same effect.

But if it is not an accident that I choose to do one thing rather than another then presumably there is some causal explanation of my choice, and in that case we are led back to determinism.[51]

Arguing that "if man's choice was not determined, it was theoretically unpredictable," C. L. Stevenson goes on to say that, since "the man himself could not have foreseen his choice, nor taken any steps to prevent it," it follows that "it would not have sprung from his personality, but from nothing at all." This being so, Stevenson asks, "what room is there here for an ethical judgment?"[52]

A number of other writers remain to be considered. All make the same point, and make it for the same reasons. Charles Baylis, for example, writes that indeterminism, in the sense of choice not determined by motives, "would result in complete lack of responsibility. For," he continues, "if our choices be independent of every aspect of our character, they are capricious, and entirely outside of our control." They are then entirely accidental, and "to say that there is not cause is to say nothing was responsible."[53] C. J. Ducasse, as we have already noted, maintains that "pure fortuity—absolute chance—is the only strict contradictory of complete determination."[54] Hence, it follows for him that free will, when it is conceived in such a way that it amounts to pure fortuity, cannot support imputability or responsibility. Not only is moral responsibility "not incompatible with determinism, but on the contrary [it] presupposes determinism."[55] And L. S. Stebbing gives us still one more version of the same in the following passage:

Suppose . . . that my acts of choice, i.e., my decisions, are spontaneous, uncaused, in no sense springing from what I am. How then can I be said to be responsible for that which issues from that choice? It would, indeed, be a straining of language to say either that it was 'an act of choice' or that it was 'mine.'[56]

[51] "Freedom and Necessity," in *Philosophical Essays*, p. 275. See also *ibid.*, pp. 275–76. Cf. M. Schlick, *Problems of Ethics*, pp. 151–53.
[52] "Ethical Judgments and Avoidability," in *Readings in Ethical Theory*, pp. 551–52. By similar reasoning, the University of California Associates in Philosophy come to the conclusion that "responsibility . . . implies determination, rather than indetermination" (*Knowledge and Society*, p. 173).
[53] "Rational Preference, Determinism, and Moral Obligation" in *The Journal of Philosophy*, Vol. XLVII, No. 3, p. 62.
[54] *Nature, Mind, and Death*, p. 192. See *ibid.*, pp. 198–202.
[55] "Determinism, Freedom, and Responsibility," in *Determinism and Freedom*, p. 157.
[56] *Philosophy and the Physicists*, p. 239. Cf. E. B. McGilvary, "Freedom and Necessity in Human Affairs," in *The International Journal of Ethics*, Vol. XLV, No. 4, p. 396; and W. McDougall, *An Introduction to Social Psychology*, pp. 237–40. "The argument from moral responsibility," McDougall concludes, "is . . . altogether on the side of the determinist. It is the advocate of freewill who would undermine moral responsibility" (*ibid.*, p. 240).

2. FREE WILL DOES NOT PRECLUDE RESPONSIBILITY

A relatively small number of authors explicitly defend self-determination against the charge that it provides no basis for imputability and, therefore no ground for attributing responsibility to men.

Two followers of Aquinas—Joseph Rickaby and D. B. J. Hawkins—address themselves to Hume's statement of the charge and criticize hi argument. C. A. Campbell answers Nowell-Smith's version of Hume' argument and also comments on certain aspects of it not mentioned by Nowell-Smith. Reviewing the development from Hume to Hobart, Ayer and Nowell-Smith, Phillippa Foot attempts the rebuttal of the somewhat different versions of the argument which they advance; and J. D. Mabbot attempts to answer the versions of the argument to be found in Bradley and in Hobart. A. C. Ewing, W. G. MacLagan, M. Cranston, and H. D Lewis make efforts which employ the same general pattern of reasoning while A. K. Stout undertakes a different approach to the problem.

The number of authors who argue affirmatively that freedom of choice is required to make sense of moral responsibility, praise and blame, reward: and punishments is very much larger.[57] Clearly, authors who hold that attribution of responsibility to man depends on his possession of free choice would also deny that free choice destroys responsibility. In fact almost every SD author enumerated in Chapter 8[58] can be construed as an opponent of Hume's thesis that free will is identical with chance.[59] Since that thesis is an essential premise in Hume's argument, as well as in the reasoning of those who follow him, the fact that almost all SD authors reject it means that, if they were to consider Hume's whole argument they would reject it also. Yet, except for the writers mentioned at the beginning of this section, the SD authors do not engage in the dispute with Hume and his followers by explicitly criticizing the reasoning which leads them to the conclusion that self-determination precludes responsibility.[60]

[57] See Ch. 10, Sect. 5, pp. 418–28, 437–46, supra.
[58] See loc. cit., pp. 48–51.
[59] We have in earlier chapters indicated that the repudiation of chance or causelessness is an element in the common understanding of causal initiative or causal indeterminacy on the part of those who affirm it. See Ch. 8, pp. 227–36; Ch. 9, pp. 267–68, 270, 271, 296–98; Ch. 10, pp. 337–43, 362–69, 380, 403, 417–18, supra.
[60] We cannot say why this is the case for those who come after Hume. It may be inadvertence or neglect; or it may be that they thought their repudiation of his basic premise, equating free will with chance, sufficed by itself to dismiss the whole problem.

Referring to Hume's argument, Rickaby remarks with some surprise that it "is still current; I have myself heard it on the lips of an eminent lecturer in the University of Oxford."[61] But, as he sees it, the argument does not touch "one single defender of free will. We all allow," Rickaby explains,

> that character has a vast influence on conduct; we only deny that it has an absolutely determining influence upon every single point of premeditated action. . . . Character is more or less permanent; but there is something still more permanent than character: that is the "person, or creature endowed with thought and consciousness," a definition which I thankfully take from Hume. Free will in act is eminently a personal act: it is the rational creature's outpouring of its own vitality.[62]

Hawkins refers to the attack on free will that is based on "an identification of freedom with caprice. . . . Thus Hume identifies liberty with chance" and "Bradley declares that such a power of free choice would make a man not accountable for his actions, but wholly unaccountable." He finds "the persistence of this type of objection . . . curious" because "the difference between free choice and chance or caprice seems very evident." He continues as follows:

> The objection would hold only if free choice were unmotivated, and no defender of free will maintains such an absurdity. We speak of chance or accident when an event occurs with no apparent ground, and, if there could be an instance of real or absolute chance, it would be an event which really occurred without any ground. Such an event would certainly be a monstrosity; but in a free choice there is a sufficient although not a necessitating motive for whichever alternative is chosen, and it is necessary also that a choice should be made. The will is motivated; but, since there is a conflict of motives, the choice is free. This choice—as proceeding not from antecedent determination, but from the spontaneous agency of the subject —belongs not less but more to the self. So far from being without intelligible relation to the self, it is precisely that sort of manifestation of the self, which, since it is freely adopted, belongs most completely and exclusively to the self, and for which the self is strictly accountable. Free will involves a genuine indeterminacy, but it is plainly distinct from chance or caprice.[63]

We have elsewhere reported in detail the debate between Campbell and Nowell-Smith, in which Campbell answers the charge that, if a man's actions are not causally determined by his character, then they are chance or random actions for which he cannot be held responsible.[64] Before we

---

[61] *Free Will and Four English Philosophers*, p. 157.
[62] *Ibid.*, p. 158.
[63] "Free Will and Right Action," in *The Modern Schoolman*, Vol. XXVI, No. 4, p. 291.
[64] See Ch. 9, pp. 296–98, *supra*.

summarize his answer here, it is worth quoting his own formulation of the charge to indicate not only his understanding of it, but also that he, like Rickaby and Hawkins, feels it to be wide of the mark.

The "standard objection" raised against the libertarian doctrine, Campbell writes, is "that if the person's choice does not . . . flow from his *character*, then it is not *that person's* choice at all." Of all the objections raised, this is "the one which is generally felt to be the most conclusive. For," he continues,

> the assumption upon which it is based, *viz.*, that no intelligible meaning can attach to the claim that an act which is not an expression of the self's *character* may nevertheless be the *self*'s act, is apt to be regarded as self-evident. The Libertarian is accordingly charged with being in effect an *Inde-terminist*, whose 'free will,' in so far as it does not flow from the agent's character, can only be a matter of 'chance.'[65]

The libertarian, Campbell tells us, "invariably repudiates this charge," for he maintains that the self can choose to act in a way that either confirms its character or alters it. Either way, the self's act is creative; either way, the choice which the self makes is not uncaused or undetermined, but self-determined.

This, in short, is Campbell's answer: as between a character-determined choice that is not free, on the one hand, and a causally undetermined choice that is a chance event, on the other, there is a genuine third alternative—a self-determined free choice. Campbell, speaking for the libertarian position, repudiates the indeterminism of "chance actions" as much as he rejects the determinism of "actions wholly determined by character." The libertarian's answer, he thinks, not only invalidates Hume's conclusion that free will precludes responsibility but also meets his objection that a liberty which is opposed to necessity has no meaning.

Campbell develops this second point. Addressing himself to the reader, he says:

> I invite him . . . to imagine a situation of moral temptation, and then to ask himself whether, as engaged in that situation, he can *help* believing (a) that his moral decision is *not* necessitated by his character as so far formed (how *could* it be, when the very essence of the decision is, for the agent, whether or not to *oppose* his character as so far formed, in its manifestation as 'strongest desire?'); and (b) that his decision is nevertheless not just 'uncaused'—a mere 'chance' phenomenon—but is a decision which *he* makes and for which *he* is responsible.
>
> My own finding is that, as engaged in the situation, I cannot help believing both (a) and (b). And since (a) and (b) conjointly involve a liberty which

is opposed both to necessity and to chance, it is for me impossible to accept Hume's view that a liberty of this kind is without meaning.[66]

In another place, Campbell admits that free choice is "unintelligible" in the sense that it is "inexplicable." While we have no difficulty in attaching meaning to causation by the self as distinct from character as so far formed, we cannot assign a *reason why* one choice rather than another is made by the self. "If by the 'intelligibility' of an act," Campbell writes, "we mean that it is capable, at least in principle, of being inferred as a consequence of a given ground, then naturally my view is that the act in question is '*uni*ntelligible.' "[67]

This point, as we have noted earlier, is also made by Yves Simon, Joseph Rickaby, and W. G. MacLagan.[68] Its importance in the present connection is that it constitutes an answer to the contention that if a choice is made without a reason which fully explains its being made and which necessitates that choice as premises necessitate a conclusion, then it must be an act of chance. The defenders of free will argue that to demand this kind of reason for a free choice, in order to make it intelligible and not an act of chance, is to beg the question. As Paul Weiss puts it, "Free choice would present an insoluble problem were there no middle ground between a necessitating reason and the absence of all reason."[69] The middle ground is a reason that is itself then and there produced; such a reason suffices to distinguish choice from chance and yet also leaves it free, i.e., not necessitated.

The argument that a choice not fully determined by reasons would not be the action of a rational agent is one of the three arguments which Phillippa Foot attempts to answer.[70] What concerns us here, however, are her answers to the other two arguments, as these are advanced by Hume, Ayer, Nowell-Smith, and Hobart.

To Hume's point that if a person acted from free choice he could not be held responsible for his action, because it would not flow from anything "durable and constant" in his nature, Miss Foot replies:

[66] "Free Will: A Reply to Mr. R. D. Bradley," in *Australasian Journal of Philosophy*, Vol. 36, No. 1, p. 50.
[67] *In Defence of Free Will*, p. 24. If the libertarian could say why a particular choice was made, Campbell observes, "he would have already given up his theory" (*ibid.*, p. 25).
[68] See Ch. 10, pp. 358 ff., *supra*.
[69] *Man's Freedom*, p. 119.
[70] See "Free Will as Involving Determinism," in *The Philosophical Review*, Vol. LXVI, No. 4, p. 447. Her answer to this argument repeats a point made by many other SD authors, namely, that while a free choice is not made without reasons or motives, these are not the efficient cause of the choice. See *ibid.*, pp. 443–45.

Hume is surely wrong in saying that we could not praise or blame, punish or reward, a person in whose character there was nothing "permanent or durable." As he was the first to point out, we do not need any *unchanging* element in order to say that a person is the same person throughout a period of time, and our concept of merit is framed to fit our concept of personal identity.[71]

To Ayer's point (which is also made by Hume) that if my choice is not causally determined, it must be an accident for which I cannot be held responsible, Miss Foot replies:

> It is not at all clear that when actions or choices are called "chance" or "accidental" this has anything to do with the absence of causes, and if it has not we will not be saying that they are in the ordinary sense a matter of chance if we say that they are undetermined.[72]

Finally, she attempts to deal with Hobart's and Nowell-Smith's point that if an individual's actions were not determined by his character and motives, they could not be imputed to him; they would be as inexplicable as chance events, i.e., things which happened to the individual but which he could not be said to *have done*. She writes:

> It is hard to see why a man who does something inexplicably does not really *do* it. . . . In any case, to explain an action is not necessarily to show that it could have been predicted from some fact about the agent's character —that he is weak, greedy, sentimental, and so forth. We may if we like say that an action is never *fully* explained unless it has been shown to be covered by a law which connects it to such a character trait; but then it becomes even more implausible to say that an action must be explicable if we are to admit it as something genuinely *done*.[73]

In his article on free will in the Encyclopaedia Britannica, J. D. Mabbott reports "various attempts . . . to show that moral responsibility, far from requiring indeterminism or free will, really requires determinism." Without referring to Hume as their source, he points out that those who regard "choice [as] equivalent to chance, caprice or chaos," maintain that choice, so regarded, precludes responsibility, because the actions for which we hold men responsible must be imputable to them, as issuing "from the self or character."[74] In another essay, Mabbott says that "Bradley was

[71] *Ibid.*, p. 448. Furthermore, she continues, we praise people for past actions, irrespective of what they will do in the future.
[72] *Ibid.*, p. 449. In her view, a choice is properly called "accidental" when something about it is unintentional, but this does not mean that the choice or the action was uncaused. See *ibid.*, p. 450.
[73] *Ibid.*, pp. 442–43.
[74] *Loc. cit.*, Fourteenth Ed., 1958, Vol. 9, p. 747.

the first to make a powerful case for this view."[75] But he thinks that Bradley also provides us with at least part of the answer to his own argument, when he himself calls our attention to the fact that "character is alterable and alterable by a man's own acts. . . . Character," Mabbott continues, "is the system of formed and relatively permanent dispositions. But there are elements in my self which are not part of my character because not so systematized."[76] Bradley seems to admit this, according to Mabbott, when he speaks of a volition as resulting "not merely from the habituated or principled self, but from that plus a new force."[77] But to admit this, Mabbott argues, is to admit that the action is not necessitated, and to accept indeterminism.[78]

The arguments advanced by Foot and Mabbott, which we have just examined, are attempts to show flaws in their opponents' reasoning or to turn it against itself. They do not directly challenge the basic premise which equates choice with chance and which grounds the denial of imputability. The writers to whom we now turn, especially A. C. Ewing, meet the attack in somewhat more direct fashion.

Ewing clearly states the objection that he thinks must be answered. If my will "does something wrong without this following from my character," he says, "Why should I be to blame for it any more than if the action had been done by somebody else?" Again: How can the free act "be said to be done by me at all if it is not determined by something in me? If it is done by me, it is caused by me: and if it is caused by me, it must be determined by my nature." And again: "The doer must determine what is done. And, in so far as the acts are not determined by the self, how is the self responsible for them? What responsibility seems to require is not that my acts of will should be undetermined but that I should determine them, and if and in so far as they do not follow from my characteristics, do I determine them any more than if they followed from somebody else's characteristics?"[79]

The objection thus stated is fully met, in Ewing's opinion, by any defender of free will who holds a position akin to that proposed by C. D. Broad as the only basis for what he calls "categorical obligability" (i.e., unconditional responsibility). As phrased by Ewing, the position is "that free acts, though determined, are determined by the self as substance

---

[75] "Freewill and Punishment," in *Contemporary British Philosophy*, Third Series, p. 292.

[76] *Ibid.*, p. 293.

[77] The words Mabbott quotes from Bradley are to be found in *Ethical Studies*, p. 54.

[78] For Mabbott's consideration of Hobart's version of the same argument, see his essay in *Contemporary British Philosophy*, Third Series, pp. 293–95.

[79] "Indeterminism," in *The Review of Metaphysics*, Vol. V, No. 2, pp. 213–14.

and neither by its characteristics nor by past events."[80] It will be observed at once that this is the position which Campbell takes in his reply to Nowell-Smith.[81] If one eliminates from it the special point which Broad adds, and which applies only to some theories of self-determination (namely, that the substantive agent is supra-temporal and acts supra-temporally), the position formulated by Broad can be taken as fairly representative of the libertarian point of view. Its central assertion is that the self (a substance) or the will (a substantive power) is the cause of the free decision, and its power as a cause is such that, given the same character, antecedents, and present circumstances, it could have caused some other decision. Referring to what Broad calls "libertarianism," Ewing says that this is what the defender of free will "has really had in mind all along."[82]

Of all the attacks on libertarianism, "the unkindest cut, considering the grounds of the theory, is," in the opinion of W. G. MacLagan, "the suggestion that it actually makes nonsense of moral experience." He recognizes the reason for this destructive suggestion. Those who make it argue as follows: to say "that a man may just as well choose either of his alternatives amounts to saying that, whichever he does choose, his choice is [an] inexplicable freak"; hence "such indeterminism, even if admissible in the natural world, is impossible in moral action; freak or chance can carry no moral significance whatsoever."[83] To this difficulty, the only solution that MacLagan has to offer is one that we mentioned earlier.[84] It consists in pointing out that the libertarian is not forced to choose between the hard alternatives of "determinism or chance" because he is not able to answer the question, "Why did you choose this, *rather than* that?" The failure to answer this question does not reduce choice to chance. If an answer could be found, MacLagan says, "it would exhibit the choice as determined. In this sense a free choice is something by its very nature inexplicable, and it would do the Libertarian cause no good to gloss over that fact."[85]

[80] *Ibid.*, p. 214.

[81] See pp. 508–9, *supra*.

[82] *Op. cit.*, p. 214. With regard to Broad's argument against libertarianism, on the ground that any event in time must, if it has a cause at all, include in its cause previous events to fix its beginning in time, Ewing says: "I should have thought that most libertarians would have admitted this and merely maintained that such previous events and characteristics did not constitute the whole cause" (*ibid.*). It should also be noted that Ewing proposes an alternative to the libertarian position, which he himself prefers. See *ibid.*, pp. 219–22; or Ch. 10, pp. 383–84, *supra*, where it is discussed. "We have thus two alternative theories which differ from strict determinism," he says, "and may be thought to make possible a more satisfactory account of responsibility than this gives" (*ibid.*, p. 222).

[83] "Freedom of the Will," in *The Proceedings of the Aristotelian Society*, Supplementary Vol. XXV, pp. 193–94.

[84] See p. 509, *supra.*, and cf. Ch. 10, pp. 359 ff., *supra*.

[85] *Op. cit.*, pp. 195–96. MacLagan goes on to point out that, though free choice

M. Cranston and H. D. Lewis add little to what has gone before. Cranston refers to the "fantastic allegation" made by Bradley and echoed by Ayer that libertarians "deny that actions have motives" or "imply that all actions are capricious."[86] He dismisses this with the comment that "no intelligent advocate of the freedom of the will has thought he could dispense with causal explanation altogether when he has said that motives and choices are not always effects."[87] Similarly, Lewis points out that "in so far . . . as it is assumed that the indeterminist repudiates all connection between conduct and a continuous character, it is most understandable that he should usually be dismissed with contempt. But," Lewis adds, "he need not hold anything so foolish, and he rarely does so today. His position only requires that there should be genuine choice *within limits*, the limits prescribed by conscience and character."[88]

Finally, we come to the somewhat different approach that A. K. Stout makes to the problem of free will and responsibility. As he sees it, the difficulty to be solved is as follows:

> If there is nothing in the nature of the self as a voluntary agent which determines it to decide in one way rather than another, the decision cannot properly be attributed to it; it does not really decide. It has no inducement to intervene in favour of one course rather than another. Where the connexion between it and its so-called decision ought to come in, there is a gap. Since it is not really the author of the volition, it cannot be held responsible for it.[89]

---

defies "*causal* explanation," in the sense that such explanation would necessitate the result as premises necessitate their conclusion, this does not "rule out freedom as an absurdity" (*ibid.*, p. 196). Like Campbell, he suggests that, though inexplicable in this sense, free choice may, nevertheless, be quite "*intelligible per se* in the actual experience of choosing" (*ibid.*, p. 197). But like Campbell, and unlike Yves Simon, Jacques Maritain, Paul Weiss, Charles Hartshorne, and others, he does not offer a positive theory of free causation which explains why a free choice cannot be given the kind of "causal explanation" that is demanded by those who ask for the necessitating reasons why a particular choice is made.

[86] *Freedom, a New Analysis*, p. 169. "Ayer's statement," Cranston writes, "is doubly unfortunate in that it implies (1) that accidents are uncaused, and (2) that every happening that is not explicable as an effect is an accident" (*ibid.*, p. 170).

[87] *Ibid.*, p. 169.

[88] "Moral Freedom in Recent Ethics" in *Readings in Ethical Theory*, p. 592. Lewis's point is exemplified by Paul Weiss's statement: "We are both conditioned and free. . . . We have neither too much nor too little freedom. We have just enough to be responsible" (*Man's Freedom* pp. 62–63). See also the statement by Michael Maher who writes in the tradition of Aquinas. Referring to the influence which a man's character and motives exert upon his choices, he says: "The most thoroughgoing libertarian allows that man's will is *influenced*, though not *inexorably constrained*, by these forces" (*Psychology*, p. 418).

[89] "Free Will and Responsibility," in *The Proceedings of the Aristotelian Society*, Vol. XXXVII, p. 216.

The only way of solving this difficulty, in Stout's opinion, "is to deny that determination by motives and determination by the self are in principle opposed and mutually exclusive." And, he continues,

> action from motives . . . is free action inasmuch as the motives belong to the nature of the self and are not external forces acting upon it. I do not mean by this that the self which wills is identical with this or that special motive or group of motives *taken separately*—not even with that which in the end prevails as the motive for the voluntary decision. The self is rather the complex whole within which alone the several motives can exist at all and interact with each other. It is only as related to each other within the unity of the self that the motives are motives for a self at all.[90]

To understand what Stout has in mind, we must observe the two senses in which he thinks it can be said that our decisions are "not pre-determined by our past history and present character."

The first is that a decision is "not so determined independently of the actual process of making up our minds on the practical question before us." A man, Stout writes,

> has to go through the process of coming to a decision before he knows what that decision is going to be. . . . Even if he admits that the decision *will* be an outcome of his character as brought to bear on the practical issue, yet he does not know what his character in this regard is till he has developed it through the actual process of deliberating and deciding. He is right, therefore, in saying that apart from this process and its result his voluntary decision is not predetermined. . . . He has only the general presumption that what he shall decide is dependent on the process of deciding. But from the nature of the case this may have one or other of various alternative results. Hence it is clear that in *this* sense he is bound to recognize that he may decide in favour either of one alternative or the other.[91]

This, according to Stout, "is a very essential part, if not the whole, of the reason why in the process of willing we may adopt one or other of two alternative courses, and why in retrospect we say that we might have adopted one or other of them. But . . . there is still something more to be said."[92]

This additional point is the second sense in which "we are free to do otherwise"; namely,

> that the self from which the decision proceeded is only a partial and imperfect and transitory phase of a fuller self—a self more coherent or more comprehensive, or both. It is the more fully developed self which we recog-

[90] *Ibid.*
[91] *Ibid.*, pp. 218–19.
[92] *Ibid.*, p. 219.

nize as the true self or real self. This may sound mysterious but its meaning is really contained in the expression "the appeal from Philip drunk to Philip sober."[93]

Insisting that "a man is held to be responsible for what he wills only so far as he is free in willing it," Stout then observes that "since there are various degrees in which [a man] may be held responsible for the same act, it follows that there must be correspondingly various degrees of freedom." Such variation, Stout thinks, is provided by the sense in which "freedom . . . consists in the degree in which the volition of the moment proceeds from and expresses the self as a whole."[94]

3. INTERPRETATION AND CONSTRUCTION

The issue explicitly disputed in the preceding pages plainly enough concerns self-determination and responsibility. Furthermore, as constituted by the opposed propositions—SD *precludes responsibility* and SD *does not preclude responsibility*—it is a conceptual issue, not an existential one. Whether or not self-determination precludes responsibility, as these two things are conceived, remains a genuine question even if SD does not exist. In fact, as we know, many of the authors who argue that SD *precludes responsibility* are writers who, independently of this point, deny the existence of SD.

But while this issue is conceptual, it is not a conceptual issue in the general controversy about freedom. To answer the question whether or not SD precludes responsibility is not to answer the question whether or not SD conforms to the generic idea or common understanding of freedom; and it is the latter question, and that alone, which raises a conceptual issue about SD which belongs to the general controversy about the kinds of freedom. While there is no dispute of that question in the preceding

---

[93] *Ibid.*
[94] *Ibid.*, pp. 220–21. Stout's theory bears some resemblance to that of Paul Tillich. A man's acts, Tillich writes, "are determined neither by something outside him nor by any part of him but by the centered totality of his being. Each of us is responsible for what has happened through the center of his self, the seat and organ of his freedom" (*Systematic Theology*, Vol. I, p. 184). Such freedom, Tillich says in another place, is not "the freedom of indeterminacy," by which he means a freedom of passive indifference. "That would make every moral decision an accident, unrelated to the person who acts. . . . Freedom is the possibility of a total and centered act of the personality, an act in which all the drives and influences which constitute the destiny of man are brought into the centered unity of decision. None of these drives compels the decision in isolation. (Only in states of disintegration is the personality determined by compulsions.) But they are effective in union and through the deciding center" (*ibid.*, Vol. II, pp. 42–43).

pages, the dispute presented there (i.e., the dispute of the question about SD and responsibility) involves assertions and counter-assertions from which we can infer how the disputants would answer the question about SD in relation to the generic idea of freedom.

Before we make the interpretations and inferences necessary to construe the disputants as parties to the issue about SD as a genuine form of freedom, let us recall the general form of the argument that is advanced by the opponents of SD to support the conclusion *SD precludes responsibility*. It is as follows.

(a) Self-determination either is chance or involves an element of chance.
(b) What a man does by chance cannot be imputed to him.
(c) If something cannot be imputed to a man, he cannot be held responsible for it.

Conclusion: Therefore, if a man does anything by self-determination, he cannot be held responsible for it.

Now, of the authors opposed to SD whom we examined in the preceding pages, the following explicitly assert propositions (a), (b), and (c).

Hume	Ross
Edwards	Nowell-Smith
Hartley	Ayer
Priestley	Baylis
Bradley	Ducasse
Rashdall	Stebbing
McTaggart	

The remaining opponents of SD, whom we considered, do not explicitly assert proposition (a), but they do argue that acts which do not flow from a man's character and motives cannot be imputed to him. As we have seen, the basic premise in their reasoning, even when unexpressed, is that acts which are not causally determined by a man's character and motives cannot be attributed to him as their cause, i.e., are products of chance.[95] We, therefore, construe the following authors as holding proposition (a), implicitly at least.

Alexander	Hobart
Hobhouse	Stevenson
B. Russell	

[95] See pp. 498–99, *supra*.

To show that all the writers mentioned can also be construed as implicitly holding that SD does not conform to the generic idea of freedom, we restate here the argument which would lead to that conclusion. It is as follows.

(a) Self-determination either is chance or involves an element of chance.
(b) What a man does by chance cannot be imputed to him.
(y) If an act cannot be imputed to man (because it does not flow from his self as cause or agent), then neither can it properly be regarded as free (for the same reason), according to the generic idea of freedom.

Conclusion: Therefore, if a man does anything by self-determination, that act cannot properly be called free; or, in other words, self-determination does not conform to the generic idea of freedom.

Hence, to construe the writers in question as holding the above conclusion, we need only assume their assent to proposition (y). This assumption seems to be justified by the fact that the generic idea of freedom and the generally accepted notion of imputability have one point in common, namely, that for an act to be imputable and for an act to be free it must somehow *proceed from the self as its cause or agent*. Making this assumption, we can interpret all the writers mentioned as taking the negative position on the issue about SD and the generic idea of freedom.

We turn now to the writers who rebut the charge that SD precludes responsibility. Let us examine them in the light of the argument by which that charge can be rebutted. It runs as follows.

(a^1) Self-determination is not chance nor does it involve any element of chance.
(b^1) What a man does by self-determination is caused by him and so can be imputed to him as his deliberate act.
(c^1) If something can be imputed to a man as his deliberate act, he can be held responsible for it.

Conclusion: Therefore, if a man does something by self-determination, he can be held responsible for it.

Of the authors whom we have found attempting to defend SD against the charge that it precludes responsibility, the following explicitly assert propositions (a^1), (b^1), (c^1).

Rickaby	Yves Simon
Hawkins	MacLagan
Campbell	Cranston

The remaining defenders of SD, whom we have considered, do not explicitly assert proposition (a^1), but the way in which they criticize the argument advanced to show that SD precludes responsibility indicates that they definitely hold views opposite to those expressed in propositions (b) and (c). Hence, it is reasonable to infer that they would also deny that a man's acts of self-determination are like chance happenings, for, if that were so, they could not be imputed to him and he could not be held responsible for them. We, therefore, construe the following authors as holding proposition (a^1), implicitly at least.

Foot	Lewis
Mabbott	Stout
Ewing	Weiss

Now to show that both groups of writers just mentioned above can also be construed as implicitly holding that SD does conform to the generic idea of freedom, we need only look at the argument which would lead to that conclusion. It is as follows.

(a^1) Self-determination is not chance nor does it involve any element of chance.

(b^1) What a man does by self-determination is not done by chance, but is caused by him and so can be imputed to him.

(y^1) If an act be imputed to man (because it flows from his self as cause or agent), then it can also be properly regarded as free (for the same reason), according to the generic idea of freedom.

———————

Conclusion: Therefore, if a man does anything by self-determination, that act can properly be called free; or, in other words, self-determination conforms to the generic idea of freedom.

Here as before, in order to construe the writers in question as holding the above conclusion, we need only assume their assent to proposition (y^1). That assumption has the same justification here as it does in the case of the writers on the opposite side of this issue. Making it, we can interpret all the writers under consideration as taking the affirmative position on the issue about SD and the generic idea of freedom. In addition, we can add to their number most of the other SD authors, even though they are not parties to this particular dispute.[96]

[96] As we have pointed out, almost every SD author can be construed as an opponent of Hume's thesis that free will is identical with chance. See Sect. 2, p. 506, *supra*. Furthermore, all of the SD authors who take the affirmative side on the question whether free choice is indispensable to moral responsibility can certainly be interpreted as denying that it precludes responsibility, from which we

By making the foregoing inferences and interpretations, based on the documentary evidence set forth in Sections 1 and 2, we have constructed a conceptual issue about SD, on one side of which are those writers who hold, implicitly at least, that self-determination does not conform to the common understanding of freedom, and on the other side those who hold, also implicitly, that it does. It remains only to note two things about this issue, the first of minor, the second of major, importance.

(i) The proposition *SD precludes responsibility* is not a premise in the argument for the conclusion that SD does not conform to the generic idea of freedom; nor is the contradictory of that proposition a premise in the argument for the opposite conclusion. As we have seen, *SD precludes responsibility* and *SD does not conform to the generic idea of freedom* are the conclusions of arguments that have two of their three premises in common but differ in their third.[97] But the fact that *SD precludes responsibility* is not needed as a premise to prove that *SD fails to conform to the generic idea of freedom* should not be interpreted to mean that there is no logical connection between the two conclusions.

On the contrary, they are related by the common premises in the arguments which, respectively, establish each of them; and also by the fact that wherever imputability is denied (because the act in question cannot be seen as flowing from the self), two other things must be denied: on the one hand, that a man can be held responsible for an act that is not imputable to him; on the other hand, that a man can properly be called free in respect to an act that is not imputable to him. This makes the two propositions—*SD precludes responsibility* and *SD does not conform to the generic idea of freedom*—equivalent, in the sense that if either one is true, so is

---

can infer that they would also hold that a man's free decisions are imputable to him as their cause. That being so, they are properly called free, and SD conforms to the generic idea of freedom.

97 The point being made here indicates a difference between the conceptual issue about SD as a genuine form of freedom and the conceptual attack on SP, which was discussed in Ch. 5, pp. 130–33, *supra*. In the latter case, the argument ran as follows: acquired self-perfection does not conform to the generic idea of freedom because the possession of it is in no way the basis of attributing moral responsibility to men. The bad men who lack SP and the good men who possess it are equally responsible for their acts, or equally devoid of responsibility. In other words, there is no connection between their having acquired self-perfection and their being responsible. But since the self is the principle of both freedom and responsibility, the spheres of freedom and responsibility should be co-extensive; and from this it is argued that acquired self-perfection does not conform to the common understanding of freedom. The disconnection between SP and responsibility is thus a premise in the argument that SP fails to conform to the generic idea of freedom, whereas the disconnection between SD and responsibility is not a premise in the argument that SD fails to conform.

the other. Since if either one is false, the other is, too, the contradictories of these two propositions (i.e., *SD does not preclude responsibility* and *SD conforms to the generic idea of freedom*) are also equivalent.

The importance of this point is that it justifies an inference which we have made to interpret certain authors as, implicitly at least, taking sides on the conceptual issue about SD and the generic idea of freedom. The convertibility of the propositions mentioned above warrants our construing any writer who denies that responsibility can be based on man's exercise of free choice, as an author who also denies that such self-determination conforms to the generic idea of freedom. We usually have additional reasons for construing writers as being on this side of the issue, e.g., their assertion that SD is chance or involves chance. But, on the other side of the issue, there are a great many authors who can be construed as maintaining that self-determination does conform to the generic idea of freedom *only* on the basis of their explicit insistence that man's possession of free choice is indispensable to his being morally responsible.

What holds true of the inference from *the connection between free choice and moral responsibility* to *the relation of SD to the generic idea of freedom* also applies to another inference that is of critical significance. Since responsibility presupposes the imputability of the act for which an individual is thought to be responsible, and since the act would not be imputable if it were a chance event, but only if it is somehow caused by the individual, it follows that any writer who maintains that a man is responsible for his free decisions, or the actions consequent upon them, can also be interpreted as denying, implicitly at least, that free choice is the same as chance. And writers who assert that free choice precludes responsibility because it precludes the causal determination of a man's choices by his character and motives also either explicitly assert or at least imply that free choice is the same as chance.

In short, the two disputes about the relation of SD and responsibility (the one that has been examined in this chapter, and the one that was examined in Chapters 9 and 10) provide us with the basis for interpreting most of the adherents of SD and most of its opponents as being in fundamental disagreement about SD and chance. While many writers express themselves explicitly on this matter, not all do. Yet for those who do not, but do express themselves on the subject of SD and responsibility, we now see the ground for construing their views on the fundamental question concerning SD and chance.

(ii) Let us suppose that the following statement is true or closely approximates the truth: that all the authors who are opposed to SD either explicitly hold or maintain by implication that self-determination involves chance; and that all the authors who defend SD either explicitly deny or deny by implication that there is any element of chance in self-determination. If that is the case, we find them arrayed on opposite sides of the most fundamental issue in the controversy about SD, for, as we pointed out earlier, it underlies all but one of the issues that we have considered in the preceding chapters.[98] If the issue about SD and chance could be resolved, it would be a critical, perhaps the decisive, step toward resolving the other issues.

On the one hand, if the opponents of SD are right in thinking that causal initiative and causal indeterminacy reduce to chance, and if they could show that this is so, then they should have little difficulty in getting the adherents of SD to yield on the existential and conceptual issues about it. Since the adherents of SD are as unqualified as the opponents of it in denying the existence of chance events, conceived as totally uncaused or without any causal determination, it follows that they should concede the non-existence of self-determination, conceived as involving causal initiative or causal indeterminacy, if these involve chance. Furthermore, since the adherents of SD agree with the opponents of it that what happens by chance cannot properly be called free, according to the common understanding of freedom, they should also concede that self-determination does not conform to the generic idea of freedom.

On the other hand, if the adherents of SD are right in thinking that causal initiative and causal indeterminacy do not involve chance, and if they could show that this is so, then they, too, should have little difficulty in getting the opponents of SD to yield on the other issues. Since the most fundamental reason which the opponents of SD advance for denying the existence of self-determination, conceived as involving causal initiative or causal indeterminacy, is that it violates the universal principle of causation (which is another way of saying that it reduces to chance conceived as causelessness), they should concede its existence, or at least be compelled to find other reasons for denying it, if it could be shown that it is not "contra-causal" in the sense in which chance is. Similarly, if SD does not involve chance, the reason for thinking that it does not conform to the generic idea of freedom is removed; and so the opponents of SD should concede that it does, or find some other reason for still denying it.

However, one further condition must be satisfied in order to assure us that the foregoing analysis of the situation is sound. The opponents of SD and the adherents of it must be in minimal topical agreement about the critical terms in the issue, i.e., they must have enough common understanding of the terms "causal initiative," "causal indeterminacy," and

---

[98] That one exception is the theological issue about man's free will and God's foreknowledge, treated in Ch. 11.

"chance," to be in genuine disagreement on the question, *Does self-determination* (which, it will be remembered, involves causal initiative or causal indeterminacy or both) *also involve chance, conceived as causelessness?* Let us consider the possibilities here.

There seems to be no difficulty about the understanding of "chance." When the opponents of SD assert that it involves chance and the adherents of SD deny this, they both use the term "chance" to signify that which happens without cause.[99] We turn, therefore, to the other two critical terms in the issue. To what extent are these commonly understood by those who appear to disagree about SD and chance? There are three alternatives here.

(a) The first is that there is not enough common understanding to provide the minimal topical agreement requisite for real disagreement. If that is the case, then none of the issues which we have treated in the preceding chapters is genuine. But from all evidence we have examined, dispute after dispute, we feel justified in concluding that that is not the case.[100]

(b) The second alternative carries us to the opposite extreme. It is that the opponents and adherents of SD do not differ at all in their understanding of "causal initiative" and "causal indeterminacy." If this is the case, then it is difficult, if not impossible, to see how they can disagree about whether SD does or does not reduce to chance. All the evidence we have examined tends to show that the adherents of SD

[99] It is true that some of the adherents of SD use the term "chance" as a synonym for that which happens contingently (i.e., by a coincidence of causes or through the operation of counteracting causes). But it is also clear that this meaning of "chance" does not enter into the present issue, nor would the recognition of it alter the case. There are two reasons for this. In the first place, that which happens through a coincidence of causes or through the operation of counteracting causes is something which, while contingent from one point of view, can also be regarded as necessitated when it is viewed in the framework of the total complex of causes in the universe. Hence, the opponents of SD would not regard causal initiative or causal indeterminacy as equivalent to chance *in this sense.* And, in the second place, those adherents of SD who use the term "chance" in this sense (which is quite distinct from "chance" as causelessness) also sharply distinguish the contingency of free choice from the contingency of chance. In their view, free choice involves "chance" in neither sense.

[100] We considered this possibility in Ch. 8, pp. 242–43, *supra.* We said there that "this is not the place to decide whether the requisite topical agreements exist, at least sufficiently to set up a genuine issue about causal indeterminacy and chance"; and, we added, "this can be much better decided in the light of the evidence which will be presented in Ch. 12" (*loc. cit.* pp. 511–12). But it is not merely the evidence presented in this chapter that helps us to decide; all the evidence we have examined in Ch. 9 and 10 tends to show that there is sufficient topical agreement about "causal initiative" and "causal indeterminacy" for the issues disputed in those chapters to be considered genuine disagreements. In this connection, see Ch. 8, pp. 229–30, 237, 242–43, *supra.*

understand "causal initiative" and "causal indeterminacy" in such a way that neither violates the principle of causation, *as they conceive it;* both signify a certain type of causality rather than a total absence of causes. Hence, if the opponents of SD were perfectly to share *this* understanding of these critical terms, their identification of self-determination with chance would become unintelligible. The same point can be made in the opposite direction. All the evidence we have examined tends to show that the opponents of SD understand "causal initiative" and "causal indeterminacy" in such a way that both violate the principle of causation, *as they conceive it;* one connotes an uncaused cause, the other an effect which, not being necessitated, is not causally determined in any way. Hence, if the adherents of SD were perfectly to share *this* understanding of these critical terms, their refusal to admit the identity of self-determination and chance would become unintelligible.[101]

(c) The third alternative is the only one which can lead us to the middle ground between merely apparent disagreement, on the one hand, and complete agreement, on the other. That middle ground is obviously achieved by something in-between the lack of sufficient common understanding to provide real disagreement and the presence of such perfect common understanding that real disagreement becomes unintelligible. To make this intermediate condition definite, we must be able to say what points of common understanding are present (to supply what is requisite for real disagreement) and also in what respects common understanding is lacking (in order to make real disagreement intelligible). We propose the following hypothesis, not only as one which, if true, would provide a solution of this problem but also as one which appears to be true in the light of all the evidence we have examined.

The points of common understanding are the negative notes in the conceptions of causal initiative and causal indeterminacy.

Those who affirm the existence of causal initiative conceive the self or he will as a cause that is *not* caused by other finite causes when it produces a free decision. This negative point is understood by the opponents of SD: what they are denying is that, in the order of finite causes, there is any *uncaused* cause, i.e., any cause which is *not* itself the effect of some other finite cause.

Those who affirm the existence of causal indeterminacy conceive the self or the will as a cause which is not necessitated to produce one and only one effect; i.e., it is able to produce some other effect, all other conditions

---

[101] The reader will observe that the second alternative stated above involves two quite divergent conceptions of the principle of causation. Yet it remains the case that if the opponents and adherents of SD were to share either one of these, their disagreement about SD would be unintelligible.

being identical. This negative point is understood by the opponents of SD: what they are denying is that, in the order of finite causes, there is any indeterminate cause, i.e., any cause which is not necessitated to produce one and only one effect.

But, for the adherents of SD, the negative notes mentioned above do not adequately convey their conceptions of causal initiative and causal indeterminacy. In each case, their conception includes positive points as well. Thus, their conception of causal initiative goes beyond understanding that the self or the will is *not* caused to operate by other finite causes; it includes the understanding that the self or will is an active power, able to cause its own acts without being caused to do so. So, too, their conception of causal indeterminacy goes beyond the understanding that the self or will is not subject to necessitation in the production of its decisions; it includes the understanding that the self or will has the power to cause any one of a number of alternative decisions, all other relevant factors being the same.

As these positive points are understood by the adherents of SD, they constitute a sufficient ground for denying that causal initiative and causal indeterminacy reduce to the causelessness of chance. Those who affirm causal initiative maintain, as we have seen, that there are two radically different types of causes: the *caused cause* and the *free cause*. The free decision or the free act is not uncaused, but freely caused; and, in their view, the universal principle of causation is not violated by the fact that the free cause is not itself an effect of some other finite efficient cause.[102] Those who affirm causal indeterminacy maintain either that all causes or that at least some causes (e.g., the self or will) are able to produce any one of a number of alternative effects, all other conditions being the same. The effects produced are not uncaused, even though they are not necessitated; and so, the universal principle of causation, as they understand it, is not violated.

As the opponents of SD see these same matters, the positive points either add nothing to the negative points or do not alter the significance of the latter. To say that the self or will is the cause of its own acts does not remove the fact that, as causing its own acts, it is *not* caused by other finite causes. But, according to their understanding of causation, there can be no finite cause which is not in turn the effect of some other finite cause. Hence, it still remains the case for them that causal initiative violates the universal principle of causation and reduces, therefore, to the causelessness of chance. Similarly, to say that the self or the will is able to produce

---

[102] In certain SD authors, it will be recalled, the free volition is caused in the order of formal causality (i.e., by motives), though not in the order of efficient causality (except by God).

any one of a number of alternative effects, other conditions being the same, is to say no more than that the self or will does *not* necessitate the decisions it produces. But, according to their understanding of causation, there can be no cause which does not necessitate its effects. Hence, it still remains the case for them that causal indeterminacy violates the universal principle of causation and reduces to the causelessness of chance.[103]

Thus we see that the root of the real disagreement about self-determination and chance lies in conflicting theories of causation. This, of course, merely confirms the insight which has been expressed in earlier chapters.[104] But it also explains how there can be enough common understanding present to make all the basic issues in this controversy genuine, and yet not enough to make such disagreements unintelligible.

If the parties to these issues shared the same theory of causation, their common understanding of causal initiative and causal indeterminacy would be such that they could not disagree (not rationally at least) about whether or not self-determination exists and about whether or not it is genuinely a form of freedom, for they could not disagree about whether or not it reduces to chance. Precisely because they hold quite disparate theories of causation, their understanding of causal initiative and causal indeterminacy is sufficiently different to explain their disagreement on all these issues, and yet not so different that their disagreement is merely apparent rather than real.

The conclusion we reach, therefore, is that the basic issues in the controversy about self-determination cannot be resolved unless the basic issues in another controversy can be resolved first—the issues arising from conflicting theories of causation. But until a dialectical clarification of the vast literature concerning causation is undertaken, we cannot be sure that those issues are really joined and rationally debated in such a way that their resolution lies within the bounds of possibility.

[103] The determinist's understanding of the principle of causation can also be stated thus: "having a cause" implies "being an instance of a universal causal law." Accordingly, if the effect varies, so must the cause, and conversely. Such an understanding of causation obviously excludes causal indeterminacy.

[104] See Ch. 9, Sect. 6, pp. 329–30; and Ch. 10, Sect. 8, pp. 461–63, *supra*.

PART III

The Special Controversies

Chapter 13

INTRODUCTION

Each of the five freedoms, which we have identified as a distinct subjec of discussion, is or can be a subject of controversy in two ways. (i) It real existence or its genuineness as a form of human freedom may b affirmed or denied. Such existential or conceptual issues make it a subjec in the general controversy. (ii) Those who accept it as a kind of freedom existent and genuine, may disagree about it in other respects. The issue that are constituted by such disagreements make it the subject of a specia controversy. There are or can be as many special controversies as there ar distinct freedoms. There is only one general controversy.[1]

It is important to emphasize one thing which differentiates each of th special controversies from the general controversy. In addition to th topical agreement that is the pre-requisite for the formation of issues i any controversy, general or special, categorical agreement is required o the parties to the special controversies. The parties to the special con troversy about circumstantial self-realization, for example, must not only b in topical agreement about that subject (i.e., share a minimal commo understanding of it); they must also be in categorical agreement on th reality of such freedom and on its genuineness as a kind of freedom.

These two points of categorical agreement are precisely the points o

---

[1] The unity of the general controversy, embracing as it does issues about each o the five freedoms, derives from the one question that ties all these issues togethe In each case, the question is whether that which is in issue is a kind of freedom See Vol. I, Book I, Ch. 4, pp. 33–34; and, in this volume, Ch. 3, *supra*.

existential and conceptual disagreement in the general controversy. Thus, in the conceptual issue about SR in the general controversy, opposite sides are taken by writers who maintain that SR does or does not conform to the generic idea of freedom; and in the existential issues about SD, opposite sides are taken by writers who maintain that SD does or does not exist; whereas in any of the issues about SR or SD, in the special controversies about these subjects, opposite sides are taken by writers all of whom can be called SR authors or SD authors because they affirm such freedom.[2]

What was accomplished in Volume I, Book II, is relevant in one way to the construction, in the present volume, of the general controversy, and in another way to the construction of the special controversies. Book II did two things. (i) It identified the five freedoms that are distinct subjects of discussion and can be subjects of controversy.[3] (ii) In the case of each of the three main freedoms—circumstantial self-realization, acquired self-perfection, and natural self-determination—it also surveyed the variety of forms it took, or the diversity of opinions about it, in the theories of it advanced by different writers.[4] The accomplishment of the first of these tasks prepared the way for the construction of both the general and the special controversies, since the minimal topical agreements required for the construction of their constituent issues were expressed in neutral terms in the course of identifying each of the five subjects. But the accomplishment of the second task prepared the way for the construction of issues in the special controversies only. The differences of opinion which divide SR authors, for example, may set them on opposite sides of issues in the special controversy about SR, but such differences do not prevent them from standing together on the same side of the issues about SR in the general controversy.[5]

[2] One further restriction must be added. The group of authors who can become parties to issues in the special controversy about SR is restricted to writers who, in addition to affirming SR as a distinct freedom or as a distinguishable aspect of freedom, also hold divergent views about it which are *not* affected by its relation to other kinds of freedom. Thus, for example, in the conceptual issue about SR in the general controversy, there are writers who maintain, on the one hand, that SR is the only freedom and writers who maintain, on the other, that SR is a genuine form of human freedom only when it is subordinate to and circumscribed by the acquired freedom of self-perfection. But if a particular question about SR is not affected by this point of disagreement, writers of both sorts can become parties to the issue raised by that question.
[3] This was accomplished in Ch. 4, 6, 8, 12, 15, 18, 19, 20–24.
[4] This was accomplished in Ch. 5, 7, 9, 13, 16, 17, 25. Such differences of opinion as exist about political liberty and collective freedom were exhibited in Ch. 18 and 19, in the process of identifying these two special variants.
[5] In the preceding chapters, where we constructed the issues in the general controversy, we paid no attention to the fact that writers who defend a particular

An examination of the chapters in Book II which survey the differences of opinion to be found in a certain group of authors (the SR authors, for example) may raise the following question in the reader's mind. Since these differences of opinion have been systematically set forth, what now remains to be done in order to construct the special controversy about SR? Are not the disagreements which divide the SR authors already plain enough for us to see the issues in this controversy?

If the answer to that last question were affirmative, the only thing which would remain to be done would be to report or construct the dispute of these issues, to whatever extent arguments and counter-arguments can be found in the literature.[6] But the answer is negative. A careful reader of Book II will observe that, in the course of surveying the diversity of opinions about each of the five freedoms, we always labeled them as such; i.e., we always spoke of "differences of opinion," never of "disagreements." Our reason for this caution was simply that we had not yet taken the steps that are required in order to show that the differences of opinion which we discovered in the literature constitute real disagreements. Upon further examination, we can now observe that only some of these differences of opinion turn into genuine issues. Others do not. They represent non-agreement, or a mere difference of opinion, rather than disagreement.[7]

What remains to be done, therefore, is, first of all, to show, for the subject of each special controversy, what the real disagreements about it are. All the differences of opinion about it which have already been surveyed can be looked upon as potential issues. Taking these, we must determine which ones only *appear* to involve disagreement, and which ones *really* do. In some cases, there may not even be the appearance of a disagreement. Hence, we are obliged to make a threefold distinction separating the real issues from the apparent issues, on the one hand, and from differences of opinion which do not even simulate disagreement, on the other.

A controversy, in the full sense of that term, does not consist solely or principally in the joining of issues. Controversy primarily connotes debate which consists in the dispute of issues by arguments *pro* and *con*. But, as we shall see, the issues in the special controversies, where they exist, are seldom disputed. In most cases, no arguments can be found on either side of an issue. Hence, in setting forth issues in the special controversies, we are obliged to distinguish between the issues which are and are not

freedom disagree among themselves about it in ways that do not affect their defense of it against those who reject it for one reason or another.

[6] In addition, perhaps, we might add references to writers who, for one reason or another, were not treated in Vol. I.

[7] See Vol. I, Book I, Ch. 2, on the conditions of agreement and disagreement.

disputed, and to use "controversy" in a sense that includes *disputable* issues
as well as *disputed* ones.

The task of setting forth issues, reporting them where they are explicitly
present in the literature and constructing them where they are only implicit, involves the same steps in the special controversies as it did in the
general controversy. In both cases, the possibility of disagreement rests on
minimal topical agreement among a certain group of authors. The authors
must all have the same subject in mind, with enough common understanding of it to identify it as the same subject for all. But this is not enough.
They really disagree about that common subject *only* if, in addition, they
answer the same question about it in opposite ways. But to do that they
must have the same question in mind; i.e., they must share a common understanding of the terms in which the question is asked. Only then are they
in complete topical agreement, and only then do they really disagree when
they give opposite answers. In the absence of complete topical agreement,
a difference of opinion (about SR, let us say) may give the appearance of
disagreement; but it will be recognized that the disagreement is apparent
rather then real as soon as it is shown that divergent views are not answers
to the same question, commonly understood by the writers concerned.

In the special controversies, as in the general, it is sometimes possible
to find writers who are *explicitly* in disagreement. This occurs whenever
two authors not only assert opposite opinions about the same subject
but also indicate by what they say that they recognize the question at
issue and the answer to it with which they disagree. Explicit disagreement
is much less frequent in the special controversies than in the general
controversy. There will accordingly be more instances in which we do not
find, but must *construe*, writers as disagreeing.

The one condition to be satisfied, in order to construct disagreements
that are only implicitly present in the literature, is as follows: for a given
pair of writers, it must be the case that they hold opinions which can be
interpreted as opposite answers to the same question. Thus, for example,
if one writer asserts A *is* B, and the other asserts A *is not* B, and if it is
sufficiently clear that the terms "A" and "B" have the same meaning for
both, then we can construe them as answering the same question, namely,
whether or not A *is* B. Since they answer it in opposite ways, they can
further be construed as being in real disagreement. It may not always be
the case that the propositions are explicitly asserted in so many words. It
may be necessary to interpret what an author does say as *implying* his
opinion that A is B, or is not B. If this can be done, it is still possible to
construe the two writers as being in disagreement, even though they do
not explicitly assert the propositions which constitute opposite answers
to the same question, and even if what they do say indicates no explicit

recognition of that question or of writers who give an opposite answer t
it.[8]

Where issues are not disputed and where the documentary evidenc
on the basis of which authors can be construed as parties to issues ha
already been presented in Volume I, we shall do no more than formulat
the issues, list the writers who are parties to it, and refer back to th
evidence on the basis of which they are thus construed. Some writer
not treated in Volume I will make their appearance in the followin
chapters. Wherever that occurs, the interpretation of their positions wil
of course, be documented. And wherever writers explicitly indicate o
implicitly suggest their reasons for taking one side or another of a particula
issue, their contribution to the dispute of that issue will also be docu
mented.

From the point of view of documentation, the chapters to follow wi
go beyond the evidence already presented only insofar as authors ar
added to those already treated and insofar as arguments which are german
to the issues of the special controversies can be found in the literature. A
compared with the chapters dealing with the general controversy, th
chapters to follow are slight. The chief reason for this is that so few of th
issues in the special controversies are disputed.

Our main effort, in the case of the issue constituting the general con
troversy, was to present the arguments and counter-arguments by whic
those issues are disputed. It is that which accounts for the length of th
chapters, especially those dealing with the issues about self-determination
In the case of other subjects, such as self-realization and self-perfection, o
political liberty and collective freedom, we called attention to the relativ
paucity of argumentation. Yet in every case we could find evidence that a
least some of the writers who join issue express or suggest their reason
for taking one side or the other. But for most of the disagreements that w
shall be able to authenticate as genuine issues in the special controversies
no evidence of argumentation is discoverable.

The difference between the general controversy and the special con
troversies in this respect lies in the fact that, with one exception, th
issues in the general controversy are explicitly joined.[9] As we have alread
pointed out, this occurs when authors who hold opinions that place then
on one side of an issue take explicit cognizance of the opinions which plac
other writers on the opposite side, often even referring to the latter b
name. In the case of the issues concerning the freedom of self
determination, we found a large number of writers who explicitly joir
issue in this way; and while in the case of the issues concerning the freedon

[8] Cf. the fuller exposition of these points in Ch. 2, pp. 17–18, 20–28, *supra*.
[9] The one exception is in the case of political liberty.

of self-realization, the freedom of self-perfection, and collective freedom, we found fewer authors who thus explicitly join issue, we always found some.

It is the writers just referred to, and these alone, who debate an issue; taking cognizance of the position of their opponents, they argue against it or in defense of their own position against attack. This is not true of authors whom we construe as being on one side or the other of a possible issue, but who do not indicate any awareness of the opposite side or do not make any reference to authors who take it. Though they may offer reasons for the position they hold, they do not turn those reasons into an argument either against the opposite position or in defense of their own against attack.

Few of the issues in the special controversies are explicitly joined in this sense. Therefore, few are disputed; and in the case of those which are, the number of writers who engage in the dispute is very small. Hence, if we were to confine our attention to the disputed issues in the special controversies, we could present the relevant materials in short order.[10]

Where debate is not present, the formulation of issues that are only implicitly joined adds very little to the differences of opinion that were set forth in Book II. Nevertheless, even the bare statement of issues which can be authenticated as genuine, accompanied by the enumeration of representative authors who are parties to them, does add something. For one thing, it answers a question that we left unanswered in Book II, namely, which of all these differences of opinion constitute real disagreements? For another thing, it enables us to ask a question that should be considered: why are these issues not explicitly joined and not disputed?

While our main task is to exhibit and clarify the disputes about freedom, so far as they exist, we are also concerned to show the extent to which writers about freedom have either failed to join issue at all, or have failed to do so explicitly and with argumentation. That is in one way as revelatory of the state of controversy in this field as the presentation of the debate is in another way. Together, they enable us to form some estimate of the rational achievements and the rational possibilities which we have inherited from twenty-five centuries of discussion devoted to this subject.

[10] Such a procedure would be justified by the fact that we are here concerned, in Book III, with the *controversies* about freedom. The bare statement of issues that are implicitly joined and not disputed exhibits potential rather than actual controversy. While real disagreement is the *sine qua non* condition of controversy, it is certainly not sufficient by itself. Debate through opposing arguments is needed. Hence where it is present, as in the general controversy, our presentation of issues and disputes adds substantially to the materials covered in Vol. I where, in Book II, we confined ourselves to identifying the various subjects discernible in the discussion of freedom and the diversity of views about each of those subjects.

We shall, therefore, proceed as follows. The chapters to follow will deal successively with issues about circumstantial self-realization, acquired self-perfection, collective freedom, and natural self-determination.[11] For each of these subjects, we shall try to indicate the state of the controversy by separating the real issues from the apparent ones, by calling attention to those differences of opinion which do not even take on the appearance of disagreements, and by presenting such debate as there is of those issues which are disputed. Here, as in the case of the general controversy, it may also be instructive to call attention to the possibility of real issues, even where they have not been joined, or to the possibility of arguments for or against a certain position, even where they have not been made. Having done these things, we shall then devote a concluding chapter to the question that we said should be considered. We can at least speculate about why these possibilities have not yet been realized in the special controversies about freedom.

[11] The issue about political liberty will be treated in connection with the special controversy about freedom of self-realization.

Chapter 14

THE CONCEPTUAL ISSUES
CONCERNING THE FREEDOM
OF SELF-REALIZATION

It was pointed out in Volume I that a great many differences of opinion exist among authors who maintain that men are free whenever circumstances are such that they can act as they wish, realize their desires, or carry out their plans.[1] The different things which writers say about this freedom are not always incompatible; the authors are often merely considering different aspects of the subject, or talking about it in different connections, or trying to stress some particular point which they regard as important or overlooked. In short, those differences of opinion which *appear* to represent conflicting points of view, do not always do so.

What follows is a summary of those differences of opinion about circumstantial self-realization which may or may not turn out to be issues in this controversy. We shall, therefore, refer to them for the time being as "possible issues." In this chapter and the two chapters to follow, one of our main concerns will be to show which of these possible issues turn out to involve actual disagreements. The following summary, therefore, merely classifies the possible issues according to type (i.e., according to whether they are conceptual, existential, or normative) and does not indicate which are genuine issues:

(i) *Conceptual issues.* In the general controversy, a conceptual issue is always raised by the question whether something regarded as a form of human freedom is truly that. We ask such questions about SR when we ask whether it conforms to the generic idea or common understanding of what freedom is in general. Since that question is answered affirmatively by *all* parties to *any* issue in the special controversy about SR, conceptual issues in the special controversy must necessarily originate in a different way.

The SR authors not only concur in thinking that circumstantial self-realization is a genuine form of human freedom; being in topical agree-

[1] See Vol. I, Book II, Ch. 4–5, 12–14, esp. Ch. 5, 13, and 14.

ment about it, they also share a minimal common understanding of it. They all agree that it is a freedom which men possess only under certain circumstances, and not under other conditions; they all agree that it consists in an individual's being able, under favorable circumstances, to realize his desires. To this extent at least, they can all be said to hold the *same conception* of it.

If that conception answered all questions about what such freedom consists in, it would be obviously impossible for SR authors to be divided by conceptual disagreements of any sort. But that conception represents only the minimal common understanding of SR. This is sufficient to identify it as the same subject for all these writers; but it leaves quite open questions which they may answer in opposite ways when they try to define SR more precisely, or set forth what they would regard as the right way to conceive it.

In other words, the identification of SR, as expressed by the minimal common understanding of it, is not a definition; on the contrary, it designates a *definiendum*—something which needs definition. Hence, conceptual disagreements about SR take the form of definitional disagreements. Such disagreements arise when authors who share the minimal common understanding needed to identify a common subject of discussion such as SR then attempt to give a more complete or precise account of what it consists in and do this in ways that bring them into conflict with one another.[2]

There appear to be four conceptual issues, or definitional disagreements, in this controversy. They can be briefly described as follows.

(1) A possible issue about whether fear induced by threatening circumstances results in a loss of SR freedom.
(2) A possible issue about whether SR freedom is wholly circumstantial or partly dependent on non-circumstantial factors.
(3) A possible issue about whether SR freedom depends solely on the absence of external impediments or also requires the presence of certain enabling means.
(4) A possible issue about whether SR freedom consists not only in an individual's being able to do as he wishes at the moment but also in his being able to carry out one or more alternative courses of action.

The foregoing formulations are intentionally vague. We shall become more precise as we deal with each of these issues in the process of determining which of them involves a genuine disagreement among the SR authors. But in advance of a more exact formulation of the real issues in this

[2] The nature of definitional disagreements and some problems concerning them are disscussed in Vol. I, Book I, Ch. 3.

controversy, we can give some indication of what is at stake in each of the possible issues stated above.

Issue (1): On one side, we should expect to find authors who hold that *only* physical impediments to action remove a man's freedom of self-realization. On the other side, we should expect to find authors who hold that a man is also deprived of SR freedom by the fear which results from threatening circumstances. According to the latter view, the individual who does not perform an act through fear of the consequences is as unfree as one who is forcefully prevented from performing that act.

Issue (2): On one side, we should expect to find authors who maintain that a man's freedom of self-realization is impaired only by external circumstances, whether these take the form of physical impediments or exert duress through the inhibiting effect of the fear which they induce. On the other side, we should expect to find authors who maintain that certain states of mind, not induced by present external circumstances, can also deprive a man of SR freedom. On this view, for example, the kleptomaniac who obeys his inner compulsion to steal is not free.

Issue (3): On one side, we should expect to find authors who hold that the *only* condition requisite for the freedom of self-realization is the *absence* of impediments to doing as one wishes, whether these impediments take the form of physical coercion or the form of psychological duress, such as fear. On the other side, we should expect to find authors who hold that, *in addition*, certain other conditions have to be present, such as having at one's disposal the means needed to perform the desired act, whether such means are physical instrumentalities or mental equipment, such as knowledge or skill.

Issue (4): On one side, we should expect to find authors who think that a man enjoys freedom of self-realization if he can enact whatever desire happens to be dominant at the moment. On the other side, we should expect to find authors who think that that is not sufficient; in addition to being able to realize a particular desire, the individual must also be able to realize alternative and even contrary desires, though such desires may not be actual at the moment of action.

For the sake of brevity, we shall employ the following shorthand designations for the foregoing issues: (1) the issue about fear; (2) the issue about states of mind; (3) the issue about enabling means; and (4) the issue about alternatives.

(ii) *Existential issues.* Like the conceptual issues, the existential issues change character as we go from the general to the special controversy. In the general controversy, existential issues are always raised by the question whether a freedom that is conceived in a certain way has reality or existence. But that question is answered affirmatively by *all* parties to *any* issue in one of the special controversies. Hence, if there are any existential issues in the special controversy about SR, they will be raised by questions about the conditions under which such freedom exists.

To ask, for example, what circumstances increase the number of men in a given society who enjoy a fuller measure of the freedom of self-realization is to ask an existential question about SR. Similarly, to ask what conditions increase the amount of such freedom that an individual enjoys is to ask an existential question. Underlying both questions is an assumption on which all SR authors agree, namely, that, in any society, all men have such freedom to some degree. But some may have very little of it, while others have it in ampler amounts.

There appear to be seven possible issues of this sort. They can be briefly described as follows.

(1) A possible issue about whether there is more SR freedom in a primitive culture than in a highly civilized society.

(2) A possible issue about whether SR freedom is greater in a state of nature (or anarchy) than in civil society and under government.

(3) A possible issue about the relation of SR freedom to equality.

(4) A possible issue about the relation of SR freedom to security.

(5) A possible issue about SR freedom in relation to civil law and government.

(6) A possible issue about the effect of political democracy on SR freedom.

(7) A possible issue about the effect of economic factors, institutions, or policies on SR freedom.

Again, for brevity of reference, we shall employ the following shorthand designations for these issues: (1) the issue about primitive culture; (2) the issue about the state of nature; (3) the issue about equality; (4) the issue about security; (5) the issue about law; (6) the issue about democracy; and (7) the economic issue.

Issues (1) and (2) need no further explication. In the issue about equality, (3), we should expect one side to be taken by authors who maintain that freedom and equality are incompatible, and the other side by authors who maintain that equality promotes freedom. In the issue about security, (4), we should similarly expect one side to be taken by authors who think that freedom and insecurity are incompatible, and the other side by authors who think that freedom does not have to be sacrificed for the sake of security.

In the issue about law, (5), the opposition can be expected to arise in the following manner. One side will be taken by authors who hold that whenever a man complies with a rule of conduct prescribed by the state, he is to that extent not free; and, in consequence, the extent of his SR freedom diminishes as the number of laws he is obliged to obey increases. The other side will be taken by authors who hold that, even when a man complies with a law of the state, it is still possible for him to be free, on condition that what the law requires him to do is something which he himself wishes to do anyway. Consequently, the writers on this side hold that the extent to which a man enjoys SR freedom is not diminished by the total number of laws he is obliged to obey, but only by the number of laws which prescribe conduct that happens to be contrary to his own desires.

In the issue about democracy, (6), the point is not simply whether political democracy increases SR freedom, but whether it augments SR freedom for the whole population, for most men, or only some. Similarly in the economic issue, (7), the crucial point is whether certain economic factors increase SR freedom for all or only some of the persons affected by the economic system in question.

(iii) *Normative issues.* There are no issues of this type in the general controversy. Nor is it clear that there are any normative issues in the special controversies about acquired self-perfection or natural self-determination. It is, perhaps, only in the case of circumstantial self-realization and its special variant—political liberty—that we meet with issues of this type. The reason for this will be seen in a moment.

A normative issue arises when men disagree about the worth of the freedom in question, or disagree about the persons upon whom it *should* be conferred, either by right or by just desert. In the special controversy about SR, normative issues are thus raised by questions of value or questions of policy. There appear to be four possible issues of this type. They can be briefly described as follows.

(1) A possible issue about whether every man has a natural right to SR freedom.
(2) A possible issue about whether SR freedom should be conferred on all members of society or only on some.
(3) A possible issue about whether SR freedom is intrinsically good.
(4) A possible issue about whether political liberty should be granted to all men or only to some.[3]

As before, we shall employ shorthand labels to refer to these issues: (1) the issue about natural rights; (2) the issue about who should have SR

---

[3] While this fourth issue is not about SR freedom, we have chosen to treat it in connection with the special controversy about SR, because political liberty is a variant of circumstantial self-realization, and because this is the only issue about political liberty which is discoverable in the literature.

freedom; (3) the issue about the value of SR freedom; and (4) the issue about who should have political liberty.

The foregoing brief statement of these four normative issues indicates plainly enough the directions that must be taken by opposed answers to the questions at issue. It can now be seen why such questions can be asked about the circumstantial freedom of self-realization, but not about the acquired freedom of self-perfection, nor about the natural freedom of self-determination. In the case of SP, the very conception of the freedom as one that is acquired by the wise or virtuous man precludes any question about its intrinsic moral worth as well as any question about who should have it or how much of it anyone should have. Similarly, in the case of SD, the very conception of it as the inherent possession of all men prevents us from asking questions about its worth or how widely it should be distributed among men.

Because of the number of issues in the special controversy about circumstantial self-realization, and the length or complication of the treatment required by some of them, we cannot deal with issues of all three types in a single chapter. We shall devote Chapter 15 to the treatment of the existential issues and Chapter 16 to the treatment of the normative issues. In this chapter, we shall examine the four possible conceptual issues—the issue about fear, the issue about states of mind, the issue about enabling means, and the issue about alternatives.

1 . THE ISSUE ABOUT FEAR

The question at issue here is whether the circumstances which prevent a man from being able to do as he wishes are exclusively physical impediments to the desired action or whether they include external conditions which inhibit action indirectly by arousing fear of the consequences that will follow from taking the action desired. Is a man unfree when, fearful of being apprehended and punished, he refrains from violating a law that prohibits an action he wishes to perform? Or is he unfree only when he is physically restrained from the action by the coercive intervention of a police officer?

The proponents of one conception of SR freedom maintain that only physical impediments render a man unfree. Unless he is physically coerced or constrained, he is free to do as he wishes, even though the circumstances may incline him to substitute one wish for another. He is doing as he wishes if he disobeys the law and risks the consequences of arrest; and he is also doing as he wishes if, fearful of those consequences, he obeys the law. While it is true that his desire to perform the action which complies with the law stems solely from his fear of the consequences of disobeying it, nevertheless it is his desire under those circumstances. The fact that, *but for those circumstances,* he would not wish to perform the action in question does not alter the fact that his action is voluntary and free.

Diametrically opposed to this conception is the view that a man's freedom of self-realization is as effectively removed by circumstances which inhibit or compel action through fear as by circumstances which coerce or constrain action through physical violence. In neither case is the man able to do as he wishes. Since what he does or does not do through fear is something he would have no desire to do or refrain from doing *except for those circumstances,* that desire is foisted on him from without. It is not his own; the action to which it gives rise does not proceed from his self, and, therefore, the act in question is no more free, in the SR sense, than an act he performs under physical coercion.

These conflicting conceptions of what the circumstantial freedom of self-realization consists in constitute a genuine definitional disagreement about such freedom. They place authors on opposite sides of an issue which is precisely formulated by the following question: Is a man free (in the SR sense) when the desire he carries out in action is itself something which he would not have wished to do under other circumstances, i.e., in the absence of circumstances that induce fear of the consequences?

A clearly affirmative answer is given by Hobbes.

> Fear, and liberty are consistent; as when a man throweth his goods into the sea for *fear* the ship should sink, he doth it nevertheless very willingly, and may refuse to do it if he will: it is therefore the action, of one that was *free:* so a man sometimes pays his debt, only for *fear* of imprisonment, which, because no body hindered him from detaining, was the action of a man at liberty.

He immediately goes on to consider the case of the man who, as in our example, is kept from lawbreaking by the fear of punishment.

> And generally all actions which men do in Commonwealths, for *fear* of the law, are actions, which the doers had *liberty* to omit.[4]

Hobbes stands alone in the affirmation that fear and liberty are consistent. What is even more striking is that he takes the negative as well as the affirmative side of this issue.

"If we take liberty in the proper sense, for corporal liberty," he writes, then it consists solely in "freedom from chains, and prison."[5] Fear cannot

---

[4] *Leviathan,* Part II, Ch. 21, p. 162.
[5] *Ibid.,* p. 163.

deprive a man of corporal liberty, for such freedom is taken away *only* by "external impediments of motion."[6] But Hobbes also offers us another conception of freedom, which he calls "civil liberty" or the "liberty of subjects" in a commonwealth. According to this conception, the laws of the commonwealth are "artificial chains" which take away the liberty of subjects.[7] They are artificial chains precisely because they bind through fear; it is only in the actual enforcement of the laws that corporal liberty is taken away by physical coercion or constraint.

Hence, when Hobbes says that the "liberty of a subject lies . . . only in those things, which in regulating their actions, the Sovereign has praetermitted," or left unregulated, he is plainly espousing a conception of freedom according to which a man is unfree when he obeys a law solely from fear of the consequences of violating it. This is confirmed by the following passage from an earlier chapter of the *Leviathan.*

> Rights consist in liberty to do, or to forbear; whereas Law determines and binds to one of them; so that Law and Right differ as much as Obligation and Liberty; which in one and the same matter are inconsistent.[8]

And, in still another place, Hobbes declares:

> There is great difference . . . between *law* and *right*. For law is *a fetter*, right is *freedom*; and they differ like contraries.[9]

The two conceptions of liberty which Hobbes advances—that which he calls "corporal liberty" and that which he calls "civil liberty"—are conceptions of circumstantial self-realization, for in both cases freedom is conceived as being able to do as one wishes. But the two conceptions offer apparently conflicting definitions of that freedom. When SR freedom is defined as Hobbes conceives corporal liberty, it is only the actual enforcement of the law (by police officers, prison bars, or chains) which can deprive a man of freedom; but when SR freedom is defined as Hobbes· conceives civil liberty, then freedom consists in exemption from law, i.e., in being able to do as one wishes in matters on which the law is silent. According to the first definition, SR freedom is consistent with fear, whether that is fear of the consequences of disobeying a law or fear induced by other threatening circumstances. According to the second definition, fear removes freedom, for it is precisely through fear of punishment that

[6] *Ibid.*, p. 161.
[7] See *ibid.*, p. 162.
[8] *Op. cit.*, Part I, Ch. 14, p. 99.
[9] *Philosophical Rudiments*, in *English Works*, Vol. II, Ch. XIV, Sect. 3, p. 186.

the law operates as a "fetter" upon freedom, binding men by "artificial chains."[10]

With the single exception of Hobbes, and then only so far as he conceives the freedom of self-realization as "corporal liberty," SR authors hold the view that fear curtails freedom. However, they do not all agree about the *extent* to which psychological duress exerts repressive force, preventing a man from doing as he wishes.

At one extreme, the University of California Associates in Philosophy maintain that fear removes freedom as completely as physical coercion does. In fact, they consider the constraint exerted by fear as the most usual example of constraint.

> Acts are . . . always constrained when they *must* be performed; that is, when a failure to observe some command or injunction incurs the risk of punishment.[11]

A man may not feel constrained when that which he must do also happens to be that which he wants to do, but, in their view, it does not matter how the individual *feels* about it. He is not free when his failure to perform the action would incur the risk of punishment. He is not only unfree but also feels the constraint when the action runs counter to his wishes.

> When I perform the act with reluctance, or when it is necessary to secure my compliance by overcoming my resistance by threats of punishment, I experience the constraint as compulsion.[12]

Some authors agree with Hobbes that physical constraint is the primary and most obvious obstacle to freedom. Nevertheless, they maintain that it is not the only way in which men suffer the loss of freedom. "Where does constraint begin?" Durkheim asks, and answers his own question by saying: "It does not consist solely in the direct use of violence, for indirect violence suppresses liberty quite as well."[13] The example of indirect violence which he offers is that of extortion accomplished by the threat of death.

Ayer similarly asserts that, in order for someone to constrain me, it is not necessary "that he should make it physically impossible for me to go against his will." The constraint may be exerted indirectly.

[10] When, in Ch. 16, we come to the existential issue about law, we shall see that Hobbes is ambivalent on that issue, as the inevitable result of his holding these two conflicting conceptions of SR freedom.
[11] *Knowledge and Society*, p. 238.
[12] *Ibid.*
[13] *The Division of Labor*, p. 382.

It is enough that he should induce me to do what he wants by making it clear to me that, if I do not, he will bring about some situation that I regard as even more undesirable than the consequences of the action that he wishes me to do. Thus, if the man points a pistol at my head I may still choose to disobey him: but this does not prevent its being true that if I do fall in with his wishes he can legitimately be said to have compelled me.[14]

Writing somewhat earlier, Schlick makes the same point as Ayer and illustrates it in the same way.

[A man] is unfree when he is locked up, or chained, or when someone forces him at the point of a gun to do what otherwise he would not do.[15]

A man is free, Schlick adds, "if no such external compulsion is exerted upon him."[16] Schlick is here clearly using the term "external compulsion" to cover the duress that is exerted indirectly through the psychological mechanism of fear as well as the coercion that is exerted directly by physical means.

Some authors apparently do not think that freedom is *completely* removed by fear. They seem to think that freedom is diminished when fear makes a man substitute one desire for another, or inclines him to restrict my desires. However, it is not entirely clear whether these writers really differ from Ayer and Schlick or whether the difference is merely a matter of phraseology. We cannot be sure how such authors as Sidgwick, Laski, and Tawney would answer the question whether fear ever completely removes freedom, or only diminishes the degree of it that a man possesses.

Sidgwick declares that freedom is opposed not only to "physical constraint" but also "to the moral restraint placed on inclination by the fear of painful consequences resulting from the action of other human beings."[17] He follows this up by saying that "my liberty is impaired by the restraint on volition caused by fear of the acts of human beings generally."[18] The word he uses here—"impaired"—may mean a diminution in the amount or degree of freedom, or it may mean the total curtailment of it.

In one statement, Laski says that fear destroys freedom, but in another he says that it diminishes its value. When he is demanding democratic

---

[14] *Philosophical Essays*, p. 279. Two other familiar examples of a threat that removes freedom are given by Isaiah Berlin, who writes: "If in a totalitarian state I betray my friend under threat of torture, perhaps even if I act from fear of losing my job, I can reasonably say that I did not act freely." (*Two Concepts of Liberty*, p. 15 fn. 1).

[15] *Problems of Ethics*, p. 150.

[16] *Ibid.*

[17] *Elements of Politics*, p. 45.

[18] *Ibid.*, p. 46.

organization of industry and advocating the play of individual initiative, he writes:

> A system built upon fear is always fatal to the release of the creative faculties, and it is therefore incompatible with liberty.[19]

But in another context, where he is deploring the effects that fear, especially economic insecurity, has upon men, he writes:

> Those who know the normal life of the poor, its perpetual fear of the morrow, its haunting sense of impending disaster, its fitful search for a beauty which perpetually eludes, will realize well enough that, without economic security, liberty is not worth having. Men may well be free and yet remain unable to realize the purposes of freedom.[20]

Tawney appears to share the view expressed in the second of these two statements by Laski. He tells us that "of all emotions the most degrading and the least compatible with freedom is fear."[21] The words "least compatible" suggest that fear impairs freedom to a high degree, but does not totally destroy it.[22]

Two other writers remain to be considered. They are Aristotle and Aquinas. The introduction of them in this context requires a word of explanation.

It will be recalled from Volume I that Aristotle is not an SR author and that Aquinas accepts self-realization as a genuine human freedom only insofar as it is subordinate to and circumscribed by the freedom of self-perfection.[23] Nevertheless, both authors address themselves to the problem of the effect of fear upon voluntary action. Neither of them thinks that voluntariness is identical with freedom in the full human sense. But what they have to say about fear in relation to voluntariness is relevant to the present issue, because the kind of action called "voluntary" by Aristotle and Aquinas is the kind of action called "free" by Hobbes and other SR authors. In fact, beginning with Hobbes, many of these writers use the terms "free" and "voluntary" as synonyms.

Aristotle and Aquinas take what seems to be a middle position between the view that fear and voluntariness are completely compatible (as Hobbes maintains with respect to "corporal liberty") and the view that they are

[19] *A Grammar of Politics*, pp. 148–49.
[20] *Liberty in the Modern State*, p. 51.
[21] *The Attack and Other Papers*, p. 90.
[22] That also is the interpretation to be placed upon the following statement by Heald: "Neither individualism nor freedom can flourish in an atmosphere of anxiety" (*A Free Society*, p. 476).
[23] See Vol. I, pp. 593–94; and cf. Ch. 4, pp. 42–44, 59–62, *supra*.

completely incompatible (as Ayer, Schlick, and others contend). "With regard to the things that are done from fear of greater evils," Aristotle tells us "it may be debated whether such actions are involuntary or voluntary."[24] He then considers the example of the captain of a ship beset by storms, the very same example later used by Hobbes. In fear of shipwreck, the captain may be impelled to throw his goods overboard to lighten his ship. But, Aristotle points out, in the abstract, or apart from such threatening circumstances, "no one throws goods away voluntarily." Yet "any sensible man" will do so "on condition of its securing the safety of himself and his crew." According to Aristotle, "Such actions . . . are mixed, but are more like voluntary actions."[25] They are, in one respect, voluntary, and, in another respect, involuntary. They are voluntary in the sense that the captain himself wills to throw his goods overboard, but involuntary in the sense that he would not will such an action, *except for the circumstances which inspire him with fear.*[26]

Substituting the words "free" and "unfree" for "voluntary" and "involuntary," we can express Aristotle's position by saying that fear causes a "mixed act," i.e., one that is partly free and partly unfree. Yet in saying that the mixed act is "more like voluntary actions" than like involuntary ones, Aristotle tends in the direction of the view which Hobbes holds in regard to "corporal liberty," namely, that such freedom is compatible with fear. But he also gives some support to the view that there is an impairment of freedom (in Aristotle's terms, some involuntariness) in actions inspired by fear.

Aquinas develops Aristotle's theory of the mixed act. Asking "whether fear causes involuntariness simply" he answers that "such things as are done through fear are of a mixed character." But, he adds,

> if the matter be considered rightly, such things are voluntary rather than involuntary; for they are voluntary simply, but involuntary in a certain respect.[27]

He explains this as follows:

> That which is done through fear is voluntary in so far as it is here and now, that is to say, in so far as, under the circumstances, it hinders a greater evil which was feared; thus the throwing of the cargo into the sea becomes voluntary during the storm, through fear of the danger.[28]

[24] *Nicomachean Ethics*, Book III, Ch. 1, 1110[a]4–8.
[25] *Ibid.*, pp. 1110[a]8–12.
[26] See *ibid.*, pp. 1110[a]18–19.
[27] *Summa Theologica*, Part I–II, Q. 6, A. 6.
[28] *Ibid.*

The action becomes involuntary only when we consider it not as it is done here and now, but in so far as it is contrary to what the man in general desires and hopes for. He writes:

> . . . if we consider what is done through fear as being outside this particular case, and according as it is repugnant to the will, this is merely a consideration of our mind. And consequently what is done through fear is involuntary, considered in that respect, that is to say, outside the actual circumstances of the case.[29]

2. THE ISSUE ABOUT STATES OF MIND

The phrase "states of mind" is here used to signify internal or psychological factors, as contrasted with external, physical impediments. The question raised in the preceding issue, whether fear curtails a man's freedom of self-realization, would, therefore, appear to be a question about the effect of a state of mind. But, as the formulation of that issue indicates, the state of mind with which the authors are there concerned is one immediately induced by external circumstances, e.g., the threatening pistol or perilous storm. The authors who maintain that fear curtails freedom attribute that curtailment to circumstances which exert a psychological effect.

The states of mind with which we are concerned in the present issue do not represent the direct psychological impact of external circumstances. The SR authors who contend that such states of mind interfere with a man's freedom are, therefore, saying that internal factors, unrelated to existing circumstances, can render a man unfree by preventing him from doing as he himself wishes. But, being SR authors, they recognize that external circumstances must also be favorable. To be free in the SR sense, the individual must be exempt not only from interfering states of mind but also from impeding circumstances.

Hence, the question at issue here can be stated as follows: Does the freedom of self-realization depend wholly upon external circumstances, or only partly upon circumstances and partly on inner or non-circumstantial factors, such as states of mind?

Only a few authors—Ayer, Schlick, Mannheim, and Laski—address themselves to this question. They answer it by affirming the partial role played by non-circumstantial factors. In the case of most of the other SR writers, it is difficult to construe the position that they would take, were they to consider the question. But in the case of one author, Hobbes, we do have

[29] *Ibid.*

some ground for interpreting him as taking the opposite view—that nothing but external circumstances can affect a man's freedom of self-realization. Hobbes, of course, does not address himself to the question at issue, and so an issue exists here only if we are correct in construing Hobbes as holding a view which puts him into disagreement with Ayer, Schlick, Mannheim, and Laski.

According to Ayer, the things which deprive a man of freedom go beyond physical coercion and constraint, and even beyond the inhibiting effect of fear inspired by threatening circumstances. If "another person has obtained an habitual ascendancy over me," that, in Ayer's opinion, can result in my doing as he wishes rather than as I wish, in which case I am not free.

> I have acquired so strong a habit of obedience that I no longer go through any process of deciding whether or not to do what the other person wants. About other matters I may still deliberate; but as regards the fulfillment of this other person's wishes, my own deliberations have ceased to be a causal factor in my behaviour. And it is in this sense that I may be said to be constrained.[30]

In this example, a mental state—habitual obedience—constrains the individual and renders him unfree in a certain area of his behavior. Should he succeed in ridding himself of his subserviency to the person who has ascendancy over him, he would become able to do certain things which he cannot now do, on condition, of course, that external circumstances would also be favorable to such actions.

Ayer offers us another example, that of the kleptomaniac who cannot, or does not, deliberate about whether or not to steal. His mental illness is such that he is compelled to steal when external circumstances make it possible.[31] To that extent, according to Ayer, he is not free.

For Schlick also "a person who is mentally ill" is one whom we do not consider "free with respect to those acts in which the disease expresses itself, because we view the illness as a disturbing factor which hinders the normal functioning of his natural tendencies."[32] Nor, in Schlick's opinion, is a man free if he acts "under the influence of alcohol or a narcotic."[33] Though the mental state in these cases may itself be caused by an external factor, such as a drug, it is not the drug but the mental condition induced by the drug which interferes with his freedom.

[30] *Philosophical Essays*, pp. 279–80.
[31] See *ibid.*, p. 280.
[32] *Problems of Ethics*, pp. 150–51. Cf. Mannheim's statement that freedom is equally curtailed "by physical force or by psychological compulsion, for instance, by hypnosis" (*Man and Society*, pp. 370–71).
[33] *Ibid.*

Like Ayer, Laski sees a man's freedom lost when other men gain habitual ascendancy over him. That is the way the serf loses freedom in relation to his master, or the peasant in relation to his landlord.

The English agricultural labourer lived for so long in an atmosphere of frustrated impulse that, when he was raised to the status of citizenship, he rarely, in general, knew how to take advantage of his opportunities.[34]

Even when the peasant was stirred up to revolt, Laski writes, "he was too habituated to uncritical inertia to persist when opposition came."[35] Though the outer circumstances changed to permit freedom, the mental inertia of the peasants prevented them from taking advantage of it. As Laski sees it,

men who see others selected to govern by a principle other than their own choice tend, over a period, to believe that these have come to govern by nature. They will lose both the will and the power to act for themselves. . . . Whenever men accept, their habits, sooner or later, come to be formed at the will of others. They lose the ability to realise their own good.[36]

As against Ayer, Schlick, and Laski, Hobbes can be construed as maintaining that nothing but physical impediments to bodily motion interfere with freedom. He tells us that

liberty, or freedom signifies (properly) the absence of opposition; (by opposition I mean external impediments to motion); and may be applied no less to irrational, and inanimate creatures, than to rational.[37]

Insofar as the freedom he is talking about is not specifically human freedom, but is attributable in a univocal sense to inanimate bodies and irrational creatures as well, it cannot be dependent on states of mind. Hence, if, for Hobbes, man's freedom of self-realization is identical with what he calls "corporal liberty" (i.e., the liberty of bodies to move without hindrance from other bodies), it follows that he would disagree with Ayer, Schlick, and Laski, were he to answer the question concerning states of mind as obstacles to freedom.

Hobbes does say that "when the words *free*, and *liberty*, are applied to anything but *bodies*, they are abused";[38] and that "if we take liberty in the proper sense," it is "corporal liberty."[39] But, as we have already noted in the preceding section, Hobbes holds another conception of SR

---

[34] *A Grammar of Politics*, p. 149.
[35] *Ibid.*
[36] *Ibid.*
[37] *Leviathan*, Part II, Ch. 21, p. 161.
[38] *Ibid.*
[39] *Ibid.*, p. 163.

freedom, which is exclusively applicable to man, and which he calls civil liberty or "the liberty of the subject" in a commonwealth.[40] In the light of what Hobbes has to say about that conception of SR freedom, we cannot tell where he would stand on the question at issue. Hence, we must conclude that we have a real disagreement here between Hobbes and the others only in terms of a conception of SR freedom which identifies it with "corporal liberty."

3. THE ISSUE ABOUT ENABLING MEANS

Unlike the two preceding issues, the disagreement with which we are here concerned involves a number of authors who more or less explicitly take opposite sides on the question at issue. They do not use the phrase "enabling means." That is our term to signify the set of factors about whose relevance to freedom they differ. But, as we shall attempt to show, that term accurately—and neutrally—covers what is at stake in this issue.

As the issue makes its appearance in the literature of freedom, it is sometimes expressed in terms of the negative and positive aspects of freedom. Certain writers maintain that the freedom of self-realization depends solely on the *absence* of unfavorable circumstances, i.e., the absence of coercion, constraint, duress, or any other forces that interfere with a man's being able to do as he wishes. Other writers maintain that, *in addition* to these negative conditions, SR freedom depends on the *presence* of favorable circumstances, i.e., the presence of the instrumentalities or means which a man needs in order to be able to do as he wishes. For these writers, such things as wealth, education, health, skill, or other implements of action constitute the positive conditions of freedom. It should be noted that the authors who hold this view regard the positive aspect as supplementary to the negative: the absence of the negative conditions is necessary, but not sufficient without the presence of the positive factors where these are needed. The authors on the opposite side regard SR freedom as entirely negative: nothing more is required than the absence of unfavorable circumstances which thwart the enactment of desires.

The same disagreement is also sometimes expressed in terms of "Freedom *from*" and "freedom *to*." On the one hand, those who hold that nothing more is required than the absence of unfavorable circumstances conceive self-realization entirely as exemption from impediments to doing as one pleases. On the other hand, those who hold that freedom has a positive as well as a negative aspect conceive self-realization as involving

[40] See Sect. 1, pp. 539–41, *supra*.

not only exemption from impediments to action but also as depending on possession of whatever means may be needed to make possible the individual's realization of his desires.

One other expression of the disagreement is to be found in the literature. The authors who conceive SR freedom as entirely negative, as "freedom from," charge their opponents with confusing freedom and power. In their view, a man may have the freedom to do as he wishes when nothing *prevents* him from realizing his desires, and yet he may still be unable to do as he wishes because he lacks the power to do so, for want of whatever means are needed to implement his carrying out his purposes. But for the authors on the opposite side freedom is power, not only the power to act when nothing stands in the way but also the power to act that is provided by whatever means are needed to support action.

The phrase "enabling means" serves as shorthand for the variety of positive factors insisted upon by certain writers, just as "impediments" serves as shorthand for all the negative factors which other authors regard as sufficient. By "enabling means," we understand whatever is needed, over and above the absence of impediments, to enable a man to realize his desires. They may be either external conditions, such as wealth, status, social position, physical instrumentalities, etc., or internal conditions, i.e., states of body or mind such as health, physical strength, knowledge, skill, etc. Similarly, so far as this issue is concerned, the impediments may be either external or internal: either physical obstacles to action or mental states, such as the fear that is inspired by threatening circumstances.

With these basic terms clarified, we can now formulate the question at issue: Does SR freedom depend upon the presence of enabling means, as well as upon the absence of impediments?

The affirmative side of this issue is taken by those who insist that freedom has a positive as well as a negative aspect, that it is "freedom to" as well as "freedom from," or that a man's freedom consists in his power to act where the power comes from his *having the means* to act as well as from his *not having* obstacles in his way.[41]

The negative side is taken by those who insist that freedom is entirely negative, that it is simply "freedom from," or that it is quite distinct from power, consisting solely in the ability to act which the absence of obstacles confers. To ask for enabling means beyond this is to ask for power, not freedom.

We shall present, first, documentary evidence of the affirmative position;

[41] Insofar as the enabling means are states of body or mind, such as health or knowledge, the authors on the affirmative side of this issue can be construed as taking the affirmative side in the preceding issue since they are asserting that SR freedom depends, in part, on non-circumstantial factors.

and then turn to the writers who explicitly express their disagreement with that position.

R. H. Tawney epitomizes the affirmative position in his remark that a man is not free to dine at the Ritz if he does not have the money to pay for his dinner, though nothing else bars his way.[42] To think otherwise, Tawney says, is to think of freedom in the abstract. But it is not an abstract thing. "It involves a power of choice between alternatives . . . which exist in fact, not only on paper."[43] A society, he writes,

> is free in so far, and only in so far, as all the elements composing it are able in fact, not merely in theory, to make the most of their powers, to grow to their full stature, to do what they conceive to be their duty, and—since liberty should not be too austere—to have their fling when they feel like it.[44]

It is from the same point of view that Hale declares: "Inequalities of fortune, based ultimately on governmental assignment and protection of property rights and enforcement of contracts, are inequalities in individual liberty."[45]

Dewey is emphatic on the proposition that human freedom is not properly conceived in exclusively negative terms. Rightly viewed, it involves the power of enabling means.

> For freedom from restriction, the negative side, is to be prized only as a means to a freedom which is power: power to frame purposes, to judge wisely, to evaluate desires by the consequences which will result from acting upon them; power to select and order means to carry chosen ends into operation.[46]

That the enabling means essential to freedom are a combination of internal power (given by intelligence and knowledge) and external power (given by money) is a constantly recurrent theme in Dewey's writings. In *Human Nature and Conduct*, he lists both kinds of means as among the elements that make up freedom.[47] And in an article in *The Social Frontier*, he tells us that "the liberties that any individual actually has depend upon the distribution of power or liberties that exist, and this dis-

[42] *The Attack and Other Papers*, p. 83.
[43] *Ibid.*
[44] *Ibid.*, p. 84.
[45] *Freedom Through Law*, p. 385.
[46] *Experience and Education*, p. 74. It is necessary to point out that for Dewey man possesses a single, unitary freedom which has several aspects, one of which is circumstantial self-realization. See Vol. I, p. 594. Dewey is, therefore, in sufficient topical agreement with the SR authors to participate in the special controversy about SR freedom.
[47] See *op. cit.*, pp. 303–4.

tribution is identical with actual social arrangements, legal and political—
and, at the present time, economic, in a peculiarly important way."[48]

In a passage which is typical of many others, Malinowski sums up his
view that freedom can be lost for lack of enabling means.

> Real freedom is neither absolute nor omni-present and it certainly is not
> negative. It is always an increase in control, in efficiency, and in the power
> to dominate one's own organism and the environment, as well as artifacts
> and the supply of natural resources.[49]

Two other writers insist upon the positive as well as the negative aspect
of SR freedom. For Perry, it is both "a freedom *from* and a freedom
to. . . . The opening of prison doors does not make a man free unless he
chooses to walk, and has the necessary leg power; unless he has somewhere
to go and is able to go there."[50] For Ben Zion Bokser,

> Freedom is positive and it is negative. It means the presence of those con-
> ditions, economic, social, cultural, which govern the growth of man toward
> his uniqueness as a person.[51]

In the opinion of Barbara Wootton, the distinction between "freedom
from" and "freedom to" is often nothing more than emphasis upon the
negative or the positive factors involved in freedom. Nevertheless, she
insists upon both aspects of freedom. To be free, a man must be exempt
from obstacles to action and possess the means required. She writes:

> The question whether emphasis is laid upon the obstacles, or upon the use
> to be made of the freedom, is a question which of the two, in the circum-
> stances of the moment, happens to loom larger. It has nothing to do with
> the qualitative nature of different freedoms, or the purpose to which they
> are put. A hungry man is unlikely either to play a good game of football or
> to make an effective political organizer, and lack of money prevents a man
> equally from buying pamphlets and from buying drinks. But so does im-
> prisonment.[52]

[48] "Liberty and Social Control," *loc. cit.*, Nov. 1935, p. 41.
[49] *Freedom and Civilization*, p. 59. Cf. Salvadori, who tells us that *"liberty exists
in the measure in which individuals can reach decisions through the use of their
own critical reasoning powers, and in the measure in which they can act on the
basis of the decisions reached"* (*Liberal Democracy*, p. 33).
[50] "What Does It Mean To Be Free?" in the *Pacific Spectator*, Vol. VII, No. 2, p.
125. Elsewhere Perry calls "poverty and ignorance" the chief enemies of freedom,
indicating the need for both kinds of enabling means. See "Liberty in a Democratic State," in *Freedom, Its Meaning*, p. 269.
[51] "Freedom and Authority" in *Freedom and Authority*, p. 489.
[52] *Freedom Under Planning*, p. 15.

A number of other writers hold views which make it impossible to place them squarely on either side of this issue. But their sympathies are clearly with the affirmative rather than the negative position. Laski, for example, insists that we must not "confound liberty with certain other goods *without which it has no meaning.*" While he tells us that "economic security is not liberty," he also maintains that "it is a condition *without which liberty is never effective.*"[53] Hence, while Laski does not say that the lack of enabling means renders a man unfree, he certainly appears to say that the lack of such means makes the freedom that a man does have meaningless, ineffective, and not worth having. Nevertheless, if in Laski's view meaningless or worthless freedom has all the essentials of freedom, such as the absence of impediments to action, then he cannot be construed as agreeing with writers who insist upon enabling means as essential to a proper conception of SR freedom.

Simons, Viereck, and Rossiter express views similar to Laski's. According to Henry Simons, "Freedom without power, like power without freedom, has no substance or meaning."[54] According to Viereck, "unbearable poverty . . . makes a sham of civil liberties."[55] And, according to Rossiter,

> No man can be expected to give much thought to liberty if liberty gives him nothing but exhausted privation. . . . The free society needs a surplus of wealth to provide education, information, leisure, and culture for its citizens. Economic well-being makes neither men nor nations free, but it does provide the stable foundation on which they can wrestle with the other disciplines of liberty and have some hope of victory.[56]

We turn now to the authors on the negative side of this issue: Thomas Hobbes, Karl Mannheim, Frederick Hayek, Frank Knight, Isaiah Berlin, and Dorothy Fosdick.

In a single statement which distinguishes between freedom (absence of external impediments) and power (possession of enabling means), Hobbes aligns himself on the negative side.

> When the impediment of motion is in the constitution of the thing itself, we use not to say it wants the liberty, but the power to move; as when a stone lies still, or a man is fastened to his bed by sickness.[57]

In the same vein, Mannheim writes:

[53] *Liberty in the Modern State*, p. 50. (Italics added.) "Without economic security," he also says, "liberty is not worth having" (*ibid.*, p. 51).
[54] *Economic Policy for a Free Society*, p. 6.
[55] *Shame and Glory of the Intellectuals*, p. 192.
[56] *Aspects of Liberty*, p. 26.
[57] *Leviathan*, Part II, Ch. 21, p. 161.

Nature poses obstacles, but no one would be called unfree because illness hampered his activities.[58]

Hayek and Knight even more explicitly insist upon the distinction between freedom and power. "To the great apostles of political freedom," Hayek writes,

the word had meant freedom from coercion, freedom from the arbitrary power of other men, release from the ties which left the individual no choice but obedience to the orders of a superior to whom he was attached. The new freedom promised, however, was to be freedom from necessity, release from the compulsion of the circumstances which inevitably limit the range of choice of all of us, although for some very much more than for others. Before man could be truly free, the "despotism of physical want" had to be broken, the "restraint of the economic system" relaxed.[59]

These advocates of the "new freedom," in Hayek's judgment, are not talking about freedom at all. As he sees it, "Freedom in [their] sense is, of course, merely another name for power or wealth."[60]

For Knight, as for Hayek, freedom is "essentially a negative concept; it means freedom from interference in individual activity."[61] Consequently, freedom (the absence of such interference) must be distinguished from power (the presence of enabling means). To be free means not to be interfered with in the use of such power as one has.[62] He recognizes that what men desire is not merely freedom in the sense of absence of coercion; and we find him even saying that "power is what freedom as a desideratum really means."[63] Nevertheless, Knight maintains that freedom and power are two different things, in spite of the fact that men never desire freedom without also desiring power. He writes:

It is difficult to see how reasonably accurate communication is possible unless such independent variables as freedom and power are kept separate by different names. As a minimum departure from usage it may at least be suggested that such terms as "formal freedom" and "effective freedom" would

[58] *Freedom, Power, and Democratic Planning*, p. 275.
[59] *The Road to Serfdom*, pp. 25–26.
[60] *Ibid.*, p. 26. In a footnote, he criticizes John Dewey as one of the leading exponents of the "new freedom," and charges him with confusing power and freedom. Hayek reaffirms his position on this issue in his most recent book, *The Constitution of Liberty*. See pp. 16–17.
[61] "The Ideal of Freedom," in *Philosophy of American Democracy*, p. 91.
[62] See *Freedom and Reform*, p. 55. "The fatal defect in the utilitarian doctrine of maximum freedom as a goal of social policy," Knight writes, "is its confusion of freedom and power" (*ibid.*, p. 4).
[63] "The Meaning of Freedom," in *Philosophy of American Democracy*, p. 68.

be less question begging and misleading than "positive" and "negative" freedom.[64]

While recognizing, as Knight does, that the power to carry out their wishes is important to men, Berlin does not think that the lack of power makes a man unfree. "I am normally said to be free," he says, "in the degree to which no human being interferes with my activity."[65] When, for example, an individual lacks the requisite wealth or education to realize certain desires, he is not being directly constrained by other men, and so he is not unfree, even though he may be powerless to use his freedom. "You lack political liberty or freedom," Berlin declares, "only if you are prevented from attaining your goal by human beings. Mere incapacity to attain your goal is not lack of political freedom."[66]

According to Berlin, the tendency to regard the poor man as unfree for lack of certain economic advantages arises from the fact that his poverty is thought to be due to conditions which other human beings have imposed upon him. But, he says,

> if my poverty were a kind of disease, which prevented me from buying bread . . . as lameness prevents me from running, this inability would not naturally be described as lack of freedom at all. . . .[67]

It is a widely accepted theory, Berlin admits, that lack of enabling means is due to the action and conspiracy of other human beings. Such a theory, of course, implies that lack of enabling means is a lack of freedom. "The best-known version of this theory," Berlin writes, is "the Marxist conception of social laws." He adds that it also "forms a large element in some Christian and utilitarian, and all socialist, doctrines."[68]

Dorothy Fosdick refers to many of the writers with whom we have already dealt on the affirmative side of this issue. These writers, she says, claim that freedom involves "the presence of means to do something, or of some special power by which to effect it." In her judgment, they fail

---

[64] *Ibid.*, p. 79. We interpret this passage as saying that, according to the formal definition of freedom, nothing more is required than the absence of coercion or constraint; but such freedom may not be effective unless a man also possesses the power to carry out his wishes. This echoes the point made by Laski. See pp. 551–52, *supra.*
[65] *Two Concepts of Liberty*, p. 7.
[66] *Ibid.*
[67] *Ibid.*, p. 8.
[68] *Ibid.*, fn. 1. Berlin points out that the Marxist theory calls for the enlargement of human freedom by giving men more power, i.e., an ampler supply of enabling means. Though both Hayek and Berlin attribute the confusion of freedom and power to socialists or Marxists, the leading Marxists have not been included in this chapter because the freedom they seek for mankind is not SR freedom, but collective freedom. See Vol. I, Ch. 19.

to see that "means and liberty must be distinguished."[69] Arguing against these writers, she points out that it is quite possible to be provided with enabling means and yet not be free because impediments stand in the way.[70] Admitting that "what one *can do* depends as much on the presence of means as on the absence of restraint," she nevertheless concludes that "freedom itself consists in not being prevented from doing what one already has the means at hand to do."[71]

4. THE ISSUE ABOUT ALTERNATIVES

In Volume I we pointed out that, for certain authors, it is not enough that circumstances should permit or enable a man to do the one particular thing which at the moment he wishes to do. In their view, the individual is not free unless the circumstances also permit or enable him to do the very opposite or anything else he may happen to desire. John Locke offers us the first clear statement that having alternative courses of action open is essential to the freedom of self-realization. J. S. Mill, John Dewey, Harold Laski, Frank Knight, and the University of California Associates in Philosophy share his conception of SR freedom as involving "circumstantial indeterminacy," according to which the circumstances permit the individual not only to perform a particular act, but also to forbear from doing it or to perform some other.

The position of the writers mentioned has already been sufficiently documented.[72] But two authors, not quoted on this point in Volume I, must be treated here. One is R. H. Tawney, the other, Dorothy Fosdick.

Tawney declares that whatever else freedom may or may not imply, "it involves a power of choice between alternatives—a choice which is real, not merely nominal, between alternatives which exist in fact, not only on paper." If freedom does not mean both the ability to do and also to refrain from doing, "it means nothing at all."[73] Similarly, Fosdick insists that

liberty involves the continued existence of unclosed possibilities of choice even after one has been taken, allowing a person to continue to do what he wants even if he changes his mind.[74]

[69] *What is Liberty?* p. 12.
[70] *Ibid.*, pp. 74–76. It must be noted here that Miss Fosdick fails to see that the writers whom she is criticizing do not say that enabling means by themselves suffice to produce freedom; on the contrary, they say that the absence of impediments is necessary, though it may not be sufficient: enabling means may be required in addition. See p. 548, *supra*.
[71] *Ibid.*, p. 78.
[72] See Vol. I, Book II, Ch. 4, pp. 115–17. Cf. *ibid.*, Ch. 13, pp. 208–10.
[73] *The Attack and Other Papers*, p. 83.
[74] *What is Liberty?* p. 11.

And later she reiterates:

> When all present and potential alternatives of choice are closed by con-
> straint men are not free. Liberty implies an absence of restraint
> both on what a man does and on what he may incline to do. Having
> liberty is necessarily dependent on an external situation offering a continu-
> ous succession of alternative possibilities of action.[75]

Fosdick and Tawney, together with Locke, Mill, Dewey, Laski, and
Knight, hold a conception of SR freedom which necessitates an affirmative
answer to the following question: Does SR freedom depend upon circumstances such that the individual not only can do as he wishes at the
moment but also can forbear from such action or can do other things
which he might wish to do? In other words, does it involve always
having alternatives open, even if, at the moment, there is only one thing
that a man wishes to do and nothing prevents him from doing it?

Against their affirmative answer to this question, only two authors stand
opposed. They are Hobbes and Hayek. One passage in Hayek is quite
explicit in its denial of the relevance to freedom of alternative courses of
action. No similar passage is to be found in Hobbes. Our interpretation
of his position rests mainly on his conception of SR freedom as "corporal
liberty." According to that conception, physical coercion and nothing but
physical coercion can interfere with an individual's freedom. While Hayek,
as we shall see, does not fully agree with Hobbes' conception of "corporal
liberty," he does agree that nothing but coercion can infringe on a man's
freedom. It is this point which clearly places Hayek on the negative side
of this issue. Our interpretation of Hobbes is complicated by his having
another conception of SR freedom (i.e., "civil liberty"), in terms of which
his position on this issue is not so clear.

Insofar as he conceives corporal liberty as consisting solely in the
unhindered motion of bodies, Hobbes, we have reason to think, would not
regard alternative possibilities as an essential part of freedom. A body
(human or otherwise) in motion or tending to move in a certain direction
is free if it is not stopped or diverted. No other course need be open to it.
Thus, for example, a freely falling body, as contrasted with a projectile,
represents for Hobbes a body at liberty, since nothing interferes with the
tendency of its own gravity. Attributing corporal liberty, in an identical
sense, to men as well as to stones, Hobbes would, therefore, say that a
man is free, if tending or wishing to move in a certain way, no exterior
force prevents him from doing so, whether or not any other path of
motion or course of action is open to him. This is the sense of his statement

[75] *Ibid.*, p. 24.

that "a free-man is he, that in those things, which by his strength and wit he is able to do, is not hindered to do what he has a will to."[76]

In another passage, Hobbes envisages degrees of liberty. "Every man," he writes, "has more or less *liberty*, as he has more or less space in which he employs himself: as he has more *liberty*, who is in a large, than he that is kept in a close prison." He then adds: "The more ways a man may move himself, the more *liberty* he has. And herein consists civil *liberty*."[77] It would, therefore, appear that in his conception of civil liberty, as well as in his conception of corporal liberty, Hobbes does not make the having of alternatives essential to freedom; for the "more ways a man may move himself" merely affects the degree of liberty he has, not the possession or lack of it. In other words, the text just quoted can be interpreted as saying that a man who can move himself *in only one way* (i.e., has no alternative possible motions open to him) has the *least degree of liberty*. Nevertheless, he is free to that minimum degree rather than unfree. Hence, circumstantially present alternatives are not essential to SR freedom, whether it is conceived as corporal liberty or as civil liberty.

On the other hand, when he explains more fully his conception of civil liberty, Hobbes tells us that in those matters on which the law is silent, the subject is free to do as he wishes, i.e., to act or to forbear acting in a certain way.[78] Furthermore, even in those matters where a man is subject to the sovereign's commands, and may be motivated to obey the law by fear of the consequences of transgressing it, he is free whether he obeys or disobeys. "All actions which men do in commonwealths for *fear* of the law," Hobbes says, "are actions which the doers had *liberty* to omit."[79] These remarks at least suggest that, in the case of civil liberty if not in that of corporal liberty, Hobbes conceives SR freedom as including alternative courses of action. Yet Hobbes nowhere explicitly insists upon alternatives as essential to liberty, any more than he explicitly denies their relevance.

With regard to that version of SR freedom which Hobbes calls "civil liberty," it is difficult to choose between the contrary interpretations—the one which would place Hobbes on the affirmative side of this issue and the one which places him on the negative side. But if we take what Hobbes calls "corporal liberty" to be his primary conception of SR freedom, then we can, with some assurance, interpret him as denying the relevance of alternatives.

Whereas, in Hobbes' view, a man's "corporal liberty" can be infringed by purely physical impediments which are not put in his way by the wills

[76] *Leviathan*, Part II, Ch. 21, p. 161.
[77] *Philosophical Rudiments*, in *English Works*, Vol. II, p. 120.
[78] See *Leviathan*, Part II, Ch. 21, pp. 162–63.
[79] *Ibid.*, p. 162.

of other men, Hayek maintains that freedom "refers solely to a relation of men to other men, and the only infringement on it is coercion by other men. This means, in particular," he continues, "that the range of physical possibilities from which a person can choose at a given moment has no direct relevance to freedom. The rock climber on a difficult pitch who sees only one way out to save his life is unquestionably free, though we would hardly say he has any choice."[80]

The absence of a choice between alternative courses of action does not deprive a man of freedom, so long as other men do not prevent him from doing what, at the moment, he wants to do. "Whether he is free or not," Hayek writes, "does not depend on the range of choice but on whether he can expect to shape his course of action in accordance with his present intention, or whether somebody else has the power so to manipulate the conditions as to make him act according to that person's will rather than his own."[81] And in another place he says:

> Whether or not I am my own master and can follow my own choice and whether the possibilities from which I must choose are many or few are two entirely different questions. The courtier living in the lap of luxury but at the beck and call of his prince may be much less free than a poor peasant or artisan, less able to live his own life and to choose his own opportunities for usefulness.[82]

These passages, taken together, seem to make it sufficiently clear that Hayek does not regard having alternatives as essential to SR freedom. We, therefore, have a genuine issue here, even if Hayek is the only author on the negative side, though we do have some grounds for thinking that Hobbes is on that side, too.

5. CONCLUDING COMMENTS

Of the four issues set forth in the preceding pages, two of them—the issue about fear and the issue about states of mind—would not exist were it not for the fact that Thomas Hobbes conceives SR freedom as "corporal liberty," i.e., the liberty enjoyed by bodies in motion when they are not impeded or diverted from their course by other bodies. As we have seen when Hobbes conceives SR freedom as "civil liberty," i.e., the liberty of the subject in relation to the laws of the commonwealth, he does not disagree with the SR authors who hold that fear induced by threatening

[80] *The Constitution of Liberty*, p. 12.
[81] *Ibid.*, p. 13.
[82] *Ibid.*, p. 17.

circumstances abrogates freedom or who hold that a man's freedom can be destroyed by certain non-circumstantial factors, such as pathological states of mind.

This is not to say that all SR authors agree on the two points just mentioned. In fact, a large number of them say nothing which would indicate what position they take on the points in question. Their conceptions of SR freedom simply do not specify how such freedom is affected by circumstantially inspired fear or by non-circumstantial factors. Hence, were it not for Hobbes, there would be no disagreements here, i.e., no issues joined explicitly or even inferentially.

What is even more remarkable about this fact is that Hobbes joins issue on these two counts only by virtue of a conception of SR freedom which defines it in a way that applies equally and univocally to inanimate bodies, lower organisms, and man. Far from being a specifically or characteristically human freedom, the "corporal liberty" which is not affected by fear or by other states of mind is a freedom not peculiar to man. Since the subject under discussion is *human* freedom, it can, therefore, be argued that Hobbes' conception of circumstantial self-realization as "civil liberty" is relevant, but not his conception of SR as "corporal liberty." If we adopt that restriction, then the two conceptual issues which we have been considering would remain mere possibilities of definitional disagreement about SR.

We should then be left with two real issues, the one about enabling means and the one about alternatives. With regard to the latter, we have found only two writers—Hobbes and Hayek—who take the negative position, and only Hayek does so with an awareness of the point of view against which he is contending. Furthermore, since the position of Hobbes on this issue is largely based on his conception of a freedom that is common to men, animals, and inanimate things (i.e., "corporal liberty"), only Hayek denies the relevance of alternatives to a freedom that is conceived as specifically human.

With regard to the issue about enabling means, we have found a number of writers on each side, writers whose conceptions are relevant to specifically human freedom and who more or less explictly take cognizance of the opposite point of view. This is particularly true of the authors who take the negative side of this issue and criticize their opponents as confusing freedom with power. It is less true of the authors on the affirmative side. In fact, we cannot call attention to a single affirmative author who explicitly answers the charge that freedom is erroneously confused with power when it is made to depend on the presence of enabling means as well as on the absence of external impediments to action.

This fact leads us to two further observations with regard to the issue about enabling means.

The first concerns the relation between the issue about enabling means and the issue about the non-circumstantial aspect of SR freedom. The writers who maintain that, in order to be free, a man must have the means he needs to carry out his plans, as well as be exempt from hindrances to their enactment, either explicitly or tacitly include both internal and external factors among the requisite enabling means, i.e., such things as health, bodily strength, knowledge, or skill, on the one hand, and such things as wealth, implements, or other physical accessories, on the other. The latter are, of course, circumstantial factors, but knowledge or skill and even such things as health or bodily strength, would not usually be classified as external circumstances. They may, of course, depend upon external circumstances, e.g., a man's knowledge or skill upon his educational opportunities, a man's health upon the conditions under which he lives or works. But neurotic anxieties or compulsions may also have some origin in pathogenic circumstances. Hence, if writers are justified in regarding such states of mind as non-circumstantial factors, they would be equally justified in regarding internal enabling means in the same way. It follows, therefore, that authors who take the affirmative side of the issue about enabling means should also take the affirmative side of the issue about the non-circumstantial aspect of SR freedom. But they do not do so. The connection between the two issues is nowhere explicitly recognized nor even indirectly intimated.

The second observation has to do with almost total absence of argumentation by either side in the issue about enabling means.

The negative side might have attempted to show that in ordinary usage the word "freedom" refers only to the absence of impediments to action or that, according to the common understanding of freedom as being able to do as one wishes, the only ability involved is the one conferred by permissive circumstances. While these authors do say that freedom must be kept distinct from power, they also recognize that some power or ability is involved in freedom, i.e., the power or ability which the individual has to do as he wishes when no impediments prevent him. Hence, to defend their position they should explain why such power or ability constitutes freedom, but not the power or ability which comes from having the means necessary for carrying out one's plans.

As we have already noted, the affirmative side does not even take cognizance of the charge that their insistence upon enabling means results in a confusion of freedom with power. These authors may be assuming, tacitly at least, that the common understanding of freedom, or the ordinary usage of the term, justifies their view that a man lacks the power or ability to do as he wishes whenever he lacks *anything* required for the execution of his desires. But they do not make this point explicitly, nor do they argue, as they might, that the generic idea of freedom makes power an essential element in freedom. In no sense, therefore, can we regard the disagreement about enabling means as a disputed issue.

We are left with the general impression that there is little evidence of explicit disagreement among the SR authors, and even less evidence of dispute about points on which they differ. While their conceptions of SR differ, the differences, as we remarked at the beginning of this chapter, may be largely matters of emphasis or of divergent interest. That some writers fail to mention factors which occupy the attention of others leaves quite open the question whether they would agree or disagree if both groups were to address themselves explicitly to the same considerations. The possibility of controversy still remains, of course, but it is difficult to estimate the extent to which real disagreement and debate about circumstantial self-realization will ever develop, so far as conceptual issues are concerned.

Chapter 15

THE EXISTENTIAL ISSUES
CONCERNING THE FREEDOM
OF SELF-REALIZATION

It is generally acknowledged by the SR authors that all men have the freedom of self-realization to some degree. Circumstances are never so unfavorable throughout the lifetime of an individual that he cannot in any respect or on any occasion act as he wishes. But the amount of SR freedom that an individual has during the course of his life will depend on the circumstances under which he lives. Hence, the question naturally arises: "Under what circumstances will any individual be more or less free?" When attention is turned from the individual to the multitude, there is also the question, "Under what social, political, or economic conditions, will *all* men or *most* have a fuller measure of the freedom of self-realization?"

As we pointed out in Chapter 14, questions of this type raise existential issues in the special controversy about SR freedom if the divergent answers given to them satisfy the requirements for genuine disagreement.[1] That SR authors give divergent answers to questions of this type has already been amply documented.[2] But such evidence must be more closely examined in order to determine whether, with regard to one or another specific condition or set of conditions affecting the measure of SR freedom that men possess, genuine disagreement exists.

Writers may differ about whether men living under certain circumstances (e.g., in a democracy, under a system of free enterprise, in a primitive society) have more SR freedom than those living under other circumstances (e.g., in an oligarchy, under a system of socialism, in a highly civilized society). But while they are all concerned with SR freedom, they may not define it in the same way. For example, some may maintain that the lack of enabling means deprives men of the power to do as they wish and so curtails their freedom; while others may hold that such lack of power involves no loss of freedom. If their conceptual disagreement or

[1] See *loc. cit.*, pp. 535–37, *supra.*
[2] See Vol. I, Book II, Ch. 5, 13, 14.

this point affects the answers they would give to an existential question about SR, then they are not in sufficient topical agreement to join issue on that question. They can disagree about the conditions under which freedom exists or does not exist only if they are talking about freedom in the same sense, i.e., as defined in the same way.[3]

Even supposing that two authors are talking about SR freedom in the same sense, they may not have the same understanding of the other terms in the question, i.e., such terms as democracy, socialism, free enterprise, primitive society, civilization, etc. Unless they do, they will not be in complete topical agreement and cannot join issue.

Further, it may be that some authors are interested in the amount of freedom that one individual possesses under certain circumstances, while other writers are interested in the number of men who have a substantial measure of freedom under the same circumstances. In that case also, the apparently contrary opinions which they may hold cannot be construed as answers to the *same question*, and so no issue will result.

At the beginning of Chapter 14, we enumerated seven *possible* existential issues about SR freedom.[4] We shall now examine each in an effort to discover whether there is any real disagreement among authors whose opinions appear to conflict. Of these issues, all but one can be regarded as political in the sense that the critical factors involved are political institutions or arrangements, the operation of the laws of the state, or the forms of government. The one exception concerns the economic factors which affect SR freedom. However, two issues—the issues about equality and about security—can also be regarded as in part economic, insofar as the equality or security in question is economic rather than political.

---

[3] It is only in the case of the conceptual issues in the special controversies that the requisite topical agreement about the subject under consideration is provided by an identifying formulation which represents the common understanding of that subject. See Ch. 14, pp. 533–34, *supra*; and cf. Vol. I, Book I, Ch. 4, pp. 31–32.

[4] These are issues about culture or civilization, the state of nature, equality, an issue about security, an issue about law, democracy, and economics. See Ch. 14, pp. 536–37, *supra*.

1. THE ISSUE ABOUT CULTURE
OR CIVILIZATION

The possibility of an issue here is indicated in the following statement by Hobhouse.

> How Liberty withers under civilization, how the individual is lost in the crowd and smothered under the vast apparatus of modernity, how he sighs for the simple life and untrammelled self-dependence of the savage is an old story. It is also an old illusion. One of the few generalizations that emerge clearly from the study of archaic cultures and of the simpler peoples is that in "primitive" society men are unfree.[5]

Unfortunately, Hobhouse does not name the writers who hold what, in his view, is the illusory opinion that primitive societies allow more freedom than modern, civilized ones.

Nor can the typical exponents of SR freedom be interpreted as holding this opinion. On the basis of our survey, therefore, one side of the issue cannot be documented.

Certain statements by Malinowski and Freud appear to place them in opposition. Malinowski says that "freedom is a gift of culture";[6] and that "culture implies directly and immediately an initial installment in freedom."[7] Freud, on the other hand, says that "the liberty of the individual is not a benefit of culture. It was greatest before any culture."[8]

What appears, verbally at least, to be a disagreement here turns out not to be a real one. Freud is not concerned with the difference between primitive and civilized societies, or the difference between early and later stages of human civilization. He uses the words "culture" or "civilization" to signify all modes of organized social life, as contrasted with man's pre-cultural existence in a wild and isolated condition. Culture begins, he tells us, when men associate with one another and attempt to regulate their social relationships.[9] "Had no such attempt been made," Freud

---

[5] *Elements of Social Justice*, pp. 90–91. Hobhouse explains that men in primitive societies "may not be servants of a master, but they are in bondage to custom and, as a rule, to complex and minute codes of custom." Furthermore, he adds, "they do not know that freedom of the spirit which would prompt them to the reorganization of their customs for the betterment of their lives" (*ibid.*, p. 91).

[6] *Freedom and Civilization*, p. 29.

[7] *Ibid.*, p. 31. Cf. *ibid.*, pp. 37–38, 52, 110.

[8] *Civilization and Its Discontents*, p. 60.

[9] *Ibid.*, p. 58. ". . . the first attempt ever made to regulate these social relations already contained the essential element of civilization" (*ibid.*, pp. 58–59). Freud

writes, "these relations would be subject to the wills of individuals: that is to say, the man who was physically strongest would decide things in accordance with his own interests and desires."[10] Unless such a man met with one who was in turn stronger than he, he would have more freedom of self-realization than any individual has when, with the beginning of organized social life, "a number of men unite together in strength superior to any single individual and remain united against all single individuals." And, Freud continues,

> this substitution of the power of a united number for the power of a single man is the decisive step towards civilization. The essence of it lies in the circumstance that the members of the community have restricted their possibilities of gratification, whereas the [isolated] individual recognized no such restrictions.[11]

Since "civilization is built up on renunciation of instinctual gratifications,"[12] it follows, according to Freud, that "liberty has undergone restrictions through the evolution of civilization."[13] In saying this, Freud has in mind the taboos and regulations of primitive cultures as well as the laws and customs of more advanced, civilized societies.

Malinowski, on the other hand, after saying that "culture implies directly and immediately an initial installment in freedom," goes on to say:

> This initial installment of freedom becomes then gradually developed, and increases into that extensive control of environment, the manipulation of natural forces, and the development of physical and mental faculties which have now made man into the master of the globe.[14]

Since modern societies are technologically much more advanced than primitive cultures, men now have greater power at their disposal for the realization of their desires. As freedom for Malinowski is "neither more nor less but full success in action" and is, therefore, facilitated by the possession of enabling means, modern civilized man, in his view, has more freedom than his primitive ancestors had.[15]

---

describes culture as "the sum of the achievements and institutions which differentiate our lives from those of our animal forebears and serve two purposes; namely, that of protecting humanity against nature and of regulating the relations of human beings among themselves" (*ibid.*, pp. 49–50).

[10] *Ibid.*, p. 59.

[11] *Ibid.*

[12] *Ibid.*, p. 63.

[13] *Ibid.*, p. 60.

[14] *Freedom and Civilization*, p. 31.

[15] See *ibid.*, p. 39. Malinowski does not think that culture increases freedom in every respect. He calls our attention to the ways in which culture "provides the

Mannheim gives the same reason for thinking that "the man of today has far more freedom in the determination of his destiny" than the man of the past.[16] He writes:

> At an earlier date complete subjection to the caprices of nature was regarded as essential to individual freedom. Uncivilized man feels that his freedom is threatened when a doctor saves him from the blind forces of an epidemic by inoculation. It cost a tremendous effort to convince men at the stage of chance discovery that they could be free if they would make full use of technical devices to challenge the powers of nature; and it will require a thorough re-education to convince them that to combat the blindness of the social forces by the help of human regulation will make man freer than he has been before.[17]

Malinowski and Mannheim would thus appear to agree with Hobhouse that the advance from primitive to civilized society is attended by an increase in human freedom. But the reasons they give are different, for Hobhouse sees this increase as a result of a less stringent regulation of the individual's conduct by the community, whereas Malinowski and Mannheim see it as a result of the technological advances which give men more power to realize their desires.

Since Freud does not discuss the dependence of SR freedom on the possession of enabling means, we cannot tell whether or not he would agree with Malinowski and Mannheim that modern civilized man has more freedom in this respect than his primitive forebears. And since he does not compare the degree to which man is subject to social regulation—by custom or by law—in primitive and in civilized society, we cannot tell whether Freud would agree with Hobhouse that civilized society interferes less with individual self-realization. Hence, we have no issue here on which we can construe the writers considered as being in real disagreement.

---

means for its annihilation" (*ibid.*, p. 110). He writes: "Cultures organized for the pursuit of collective violence; cultures economically founded on slavery; cultures chronically or occasionally facing crises, especially war crises, imply a type of constitution where freedom does not flourish" (*ibid.*, p. 28).

[16] *Man and Society*, p. 381.

[17] *Ibid.*, p. 376. Cf. *ibid.*, p. 369.

2. THE ISSUE ABOUT THE STATE OF NATURE

As the term "state of nature" is used by such authors as Hobbes, Locke, Montesquieu, and Rousseau, it signifies a condition of human life in which men are not socially organized and are not subject to civil government or its coercively enforced laws. Though these authors differ about other aspects of the state of nature, it represents for all of them a condition of anarchy, i.e., the total absence of civil government with the power to apply and enforce the laws it makes.

We know that a number of SR authors—Hobbes, Bentham, Spencer, Hale, Hayek, for example—hold the view that every law encroaches upon human freedom and limits the extent to which the individual, living in civil society, can do as he pleases.[18] It might be expected, therefore, that such writers would also hold that man's freedom of self-realization is greatest in a state of nature or anarchy or in the total absence of social regulations and positive law.

Hobbes does appear to take this position. The state of nature, he tells us, is one in which "every man has a right to every thing."[19] This means that man has unlimited liberty, for, according to Hobbes, "law is *a fetter,* right is *freedom,* and they differ like contraries."[20] In a state of nature, then, "the *laws* being removed, our *liberty* is absolute."[21]

Another writer who appears to share this view is Freud. Using the term "culture" to stand for any organized society in which men are subject to social regulations enforced by the power of the group, Freud declares that liberty is restricted by society and that "it was greatest before any culture," i.e., before men came to live together under some form of government.[22]

On the other hand, we find a number of SR authors who appear to take the opposite point of view. Though man in a state of nature is not subject to civil authority and regulation, he is, according to Locke, subject to violence on the part of other men. "Who could be free," Locke asks, "when every other man's humour might domineer over him" as would be the case in a state of nature? Civil government protects the individual from such aggressions. "Liberty," he says, "is to be free from restraint and violence from others; which cannot be where there is no law."[23] A state of affairs in which the stronger man enjoys his freedom by depriving

---

[18] See Vol. I, Book II, Ch. 14, pp. 232–36.
[19] *Leviathan*, Part I, Ch. 14, p. 99.
[20] *Philosophical Rudiments*, Ch. XIV, Sect. 3, *English Works*, Vol. II, p. 186.
[21] *Ibid.*
[22] *Civilization and Its Discontents*, p. 60.
[23] *Civil Government*, Ch. VI, Sect. 57, p. 37.

other men of theirs does not secure the greatest freedom for mankind as a whole. "Since it is impossible for every individual . . . simultaneously to be stronger than his neighbours, it is a truism," Tawney declares, "that liberty, as distinct from the liberties of special persons and classes, can exist only in so far as it is limited by rules, which secure that freedom for some is not slavery for others."[24] For the same reason, Bertrand Russell maintains that "the greatest degree of liberty is not secured by anarchy."[25]

In view of the texts quoted, we might conclude that a real issue exists here. It would be formulated by the question, "Does man have a greater degree of SR freedom in a state of nature or anarchy than in civil society and under positive law?" Hobbes and Freud seem to answer this question in the affirmative, Locke, Tawney, and Russell in the negative. Other writers might be cited on the negative side, but that is not necessary if the only problem with which we are concerned for the moment is whether the issue as formulated really exists.

The solution of the problem is to be found in the qualifications which Hobbes and Freud place on their affirmative answers.

After saying that the liberty of the individual was greatest before the advent of organized society, Freud immediately adds that "it had little value at that time, because the individual was hardly in a position to defend it."[26] The implication seems to be that the freedom men have in society is better in the sense that it is more secure, even if it is also subject to certain limitations.[27]

Hobbes makes this implication quite explicit. Since, for him, the state of nature is "a condition of war of every one against every one,"[28] he recognizes that the "absolute liberty" men enjoy in a state of nature is highly precarious. "As long as this natural right of every man to every thing endureth," Hobbes writes, "there can be no security to any man (how strong or wise soever he be)."[29] What Hobbes says of the life men lead in a state of nature applies equally to the liberty they enjoy in that state: it is "nasty, brutish, and short."[30] He, therefore, thinks they are bet-

---

[24] *Equality*, p. 220.

[25] *Political Ideals*, p. 28. Cf. *The Impact of Science on Society*, p. 41; *Roads to Freedom*, pp. 121–23; *Skeptical Essays*, p. 173.

[26] *Civilization and Its Discontents*, p. 60.

[27] "The strength of this united body [i.e., society]," Freud writes, "is then opposed as 'Right' against the strength of any individual, which is condemned as 'brute force.'" With the establishment of justice, Freud continues, we arrive at "a state of law to which all . . . have contributed by making some sacrifice of their own desires, and which leaves none . . . at the mercy of brute force" (*ibid.*, pp. 59–60).

[28] *Leviathan*, Part I, Ch. 14, p. 99.

[29] *Ibid.*, pp. 99–100.

[30] *Ibid.*, Ch. 13, p. 97.

ter off living in a commonwealth and under government. Though the freedom granted to them in civil society is limited, they enjoy it securely throughout their lives, as compared with the unlimited freedom they so precariously possess and enjoy for so short a time in the state of nature. Hobbes can, therefore, be interpreted as saying that, seen in the perspective of a whole lifetime, the total amount of freedom for the individual is probably greater in civil society than in the state of nature.

On the foregoing interpretation of Hobbes and Freud, they cannot be construed as taking the affirmative position on the issue as formulated. Nor can any other SR writer. None thinks that anarchy affords optimum freedom.

We have already seen this to be true of Locke, Tawney, and Russell. It is also true of such writers as Bentham, Spencer, Hale, and Hayek. Though they regard every coercive law as an encroachment upon liberty, they nevertheless recognize that men are saved from extra-legal forms of violence, aggression, and coercion by the enforcement of law. Since, in their view, more liberty is gained than lost, they do not advocate anarchy or lawlessness, but accept government and law as the way to maximize SR freedom.[31]

Hence, what at first appeared to be an issue turns out not to be one. All of the SR authors whom we have examined agree that men enjoy a greater freedom in civil society than they would in a state of nature or under conditions of lawlessness and anarchy. Their reasons for taking this view are generally alike—that while law and government limit freedom, they increase the total amount of it by securing the individual from interference or intimidation by other men.

It is necessary to comment briefly on Locke, Montesquieu, and Rousseau in this connection. Locke and Hobbes would appear to see eye to eye. Locke's remark that no one is free in a state of nature wherein "every other man's humour might domineer over him" echoes the statement by Hobbes that for men to seek the anarchic freedom which consists in total exemption from laws is to ask for "that liberty by which all other men may be masters of their lives."[32] But we must remember that Locke and Hobbes do not hold the same conception of SR freedom. For Locke,

[31] For the documentation of the views of Bentham, Spencer, Hale, and Hayek, see Vol. I, Book II, Ch. 14, pp. 234–36. See *ibid.*, pp. 226–27 for the documentation of similar views on the part of Laski and Knight. Still other writers, not treated in Vol. I, can be mentioned as viewing the matter in the same way. See Burke, *Reflections on the Revolution in France, Works*, Vol. IV, pp. 64–65; Heald, *A Free Society*, p. 32; Harper, *Liberty, A Path to Its Recovery*, p. 59; McIver, "The Meaning of Liberty and Its Perversions," in *Freedom, Its Meaning*, p. 281; and Sidgwick, *Elements of Politics*, p. 46.
[32] *Leviathan*, Part II, Ch. 21, p. 163.

just laws do not curtail the freedom of reasonable men; in obeying the law, such men are free in the SP sense and they are also free in the SR sense with regard to all matters not regulated by law. On Locke's conception of the freedom of self-realization as subordinate to and circumscribed by the freedom of self-perfection, law is in no way antithetical to freedom. Hence, he looks upon the hypothetical liberty which men might have in a state of nature as a freedom which, strictly speaking, is that of brutes rather than of men. "The end of law," Locke writes, "is not to abolish or restrain, but to preserve and enlarge freedom." For all "beings capable of laws, where there is no law there is no freedom."[33]

Like Locke, Montesquieu affirms man's freedom of self-realization only as subordinate to and circumscribed by his freedom of self-perfection.[34] According to him, men in a state of nature enjoy independence, not true freedom. When men gave up "their natural independence to live under political laws," Montesquieu tells us, "they acquired liberty."[35]

Rousseau even more emphatically repudiates the SR freedom which men are thought to have in a hypothetical state of nature. Like Montesquieu, he distinguishes between man's anarchic independence and his liberty under law. Only the latter is truly human freedom. The transition from a state of nature to civil society is not a calculated exchange of one kind of freedom for another. For Rousseau, it is the elevation of man from a brutish to a human condition. He thereby acquires that liberty, at once civil and moral, "which alone makes him truly master of himself, for the mere impulse of appetite is slavery, while obedience to a law which we prescribe to ourselves is liberty."[36]

3. THE ISSUE ABOUT EQUALITY

Much has been written, especially in the last hundred years, on the relation of liberty to equality. The liberty referred to is always the circumstantial freedom of self-realization; the equality, always an equality in the circumstances which affect the behavior of men, not an equality in their natures, talents, or virtues. The question being discussed is whether equality —or inequality—promotes freedom; or, as it is sometimes put, whether equality and freedom are compatible. Opposite answers to this question

---

[33] *Civil Government*, Ch. VI, Sect. 57, pp. 36–37. For a fuller account of Locke's theory of freedom under law, see Vol. I, Book II, pp. 245–49, 323–27.
[34] See Vol. I, Book II, Ch. 17, pp. 321–23.
[35] *The Spirit of Laws*, Book XXVI, Ch. 13, p, 570.
[36] *The Social Contract*, Book I, Ch. 8, p. 19. For a fuller account of Rousseau's SP conception of man's liberty in civil society, see Vol. I, Book II, pp. 292–97.

would give rise to an existential issue about self-realization: one answer would assert that equality of circumstances is favorable to the existence of SR, the other, that inequality, not equality, is favorable.

We find such apparently conflicting statements being made, often in the extreme form that equality destroys freedom countered by the opposite extreme that equality is essential to freedom.[37] But when statements of this sort are read in context, they are seen to be not really in conflict. To perceive this, we need only keep one question in mind as we read the authors who appear to be in disagreement. Whose freedom are they concerned about? Freedom for the privileged or fortunate few who have more of it under conditions of inequality? Or freedom for the many whose freedom would be augmented if equality replaced inequality?

On the one hand, authors who assert that equality promotes freedom do not deny that the removal of inequality would also take away the special liberties or reduce the amount of liberty possessed by those who enjoy a superior station in society. In fact, they advocate equalization of circumstances precisely because they wish to see freedom more widely and equally distributed among the members of society. Hence, they implicitly acknowledge that equality will diminish the freedom possessed by the privileged or fortunate few, which is what the advocates of inequality contend.

On the other hand, authors who assert that inequality safeguards freedom do not deny that the establishment of equality would augment the freedom of those who do not have it by virtue of their inferior condition. They, too, acknowledge, for the most part implicitly, that if the underprivileged or less fortunate members of society had the means or power possessed by their betters, some increase of freedom might be theirs in consequence. These writers oppose the establishment of equality precisely because they wish to preserve the freedom, or the amount of freedom, enjoyed by those who now have it under conditions of inequality.

When the advocates of equality or inequality are thus interpreted, there is no real disagreement between them, that is, not on the effect of circumstantial equality or inequality on circumstantial freedom. The reason for the mistaken impression that a real disagreement exists is twofold.

(i) The writers stress one side of the picture, and seldom if ever explicitly refer to the other. The advocates of inequality dwell mainly on the loss of freedom that they think will result from the establishment of equality and do not wish to call attention to the spread of freedom which might result from it. Similarly, the advocates of equality concentrate their at-

---

[37] It is also sometimes said that inequality is essential to freedom, and this is then countered by the statement that inequality destroys freedom.

tention on the gains in freedom or its extension and ignore the freedom which will be taken away or reduced with the removal of inequality.[38]

(ii) A real disagreement does exist between the advocates of equality and the advocates of inequality, but it is not a disagreement about the circumstantial factors favorable or unfavorable to the existence of freedom (for some or for all); it is rather a disagreement about who should have freedom, or the greater amount of it—the few or the many, some or all. The disagreement, in other words, gives us a normative, not an existential, issue in the special controversy about SR freedom. The fact that the merely apparent disagreement on the existential question involves a real disagreement on the normative question is partly responsible for the erroneous impression that there is a genuine existential issue here.[39]

Before we turn to the literature in order to document the foregoing interpretation of what is said about equality and inequality in relation to freedom, one further point must be observed. Circumstantial equality or inequality consists largely in an equality or inequality of the conditions under which men live, work, and act.[40] Translated into terms that are significant for SR freedom, such equality or inequality bears either on the possession of enabling means or on having a range of alternatives open. Thus, for example, the man who has more wealth than another has at his call or disposal more of the means that he may need in order to do what he wishes; he may also have a wider range of alternatives. And as between the man who has certain political rights and privileges and one who lacks them, the former has power and opportunities which the latter does not have. In general, then, equality of condition means equality of opportunity, equality in the possession or accessibility of enabling means, or equality in power.[41]

[38] Robert Hale, however, sees both parts of the picture. While he is exclusively concerned with economic equality and inequality, the insight he expresses applies generally to other factors affecting the circumstantial equality or inequality of men. ". . . legislation which tends to equalize wealth," Hale writes, "may diminish the economic liberty of those who have least it it is so unwisely drawn that it decreases greatly the total output of society . . . If it accentuates economic inequality it will, unless it causes a sufficient increase of the total output of society, reduce the liberty of the least fortunate while enhancing that of the more fortunate. If it mitigates inequality it will reduce the liberty of the more fortunate, and it may, by reducing production, diminish the liberty of all. If wisely drawn, on the other hand, it may greatly increase the liberty of those whose freedom is now the most restricted" (*Freedom Through Law*, pp. 542–43).

[39] Ch. 16 will treat the normative issues in this controversy, and we shall deal there with the disagreement that involves equality and inequality.

[40] These conditions may be social (e.g., equality or inequality of social class), political (e.g., equality or inequality of political status or civil rights), or economic (e.g., equality or inequality in wealth).

[41] It follows, therefore, that writers who maintain that SR freedom depends solely on the absence of impediment to action, can have little interest in equality or inequality

Such writers as Laski and Tawney who regard equality as essential to liberty are concerned mainly with the extension of freedom to the multitude and think of this as something which can be accomplished by equalizing the conditions, particularly the economic conditions, under which men live. They are joined in this opinion by Hobhouse, Simons, and Knight. After examining their expression of this point of view, we shall turn to writers, such as Calhoun and Sumner, who maintain that attempts to equalize conditions will restrict the freedom of the more able members of society or take away the freedom that they have already attained through their success in acquiring power, position, and wealth.

In saying that "great inequalities of wealth make impossible the attainment of freedom,"[42] Laski leaves no doubt as to whose freedom is impaired. He writes:

> . . . if the form of social organization is a pyramid, men are bound to struggle toward its apex. . . . The freedom that the poor desire in a society such as this is the freedom to enjoy the things their rulers enjoy. The penumbra of freedom, its purpose and its life, is the movement for equality.[43]

Inequality, as Laski sees it, gives some men the power to interfere with the freedom of others. The man with more power has a "differential advantage to hinder another from the opportunity to be the best he can." Aiming at the widest extension of freedom, Laski therefore recommends "the enforcement of equality by the State" in order to prevent "the private person from the exercise of force for his own ends."[44] Hence, when he says that liberty and equality are not antithetic but complementary, and that "in the absence of certain equalities no freedom can ever hope for realization," we know that he has in mind the freedom of the many, not the freedom of the few.

Remarking that "liberty and equality have usually in England been considered antithetic," Tawney points out that "freedom for the pike is death for the minnows," and hence that "it is possible that equality is to be contrasted, not with liberty, but only with a particular interpretation of it."[45] For, if liberty means "that every individual shall be free, according to his opportunities, to indulge without limit his appetite for [wealth and power]," and if equality means "the prevention of sensational extremes of

---

of conditions, since these mainly affect the positive factors on which SR freedom is thought by other writers to depend. As we shall see, the authors who deal with the problem of equality and inequality are those who conceive SR freedom as involving enabling means.

[42] *A Grammar of Politics*, Ch. 4, Sect. III, p. 161.
[43] *Liberty in the Modern State*, Ch. 3, Sect. I, p. 172.
[44] *A Grammar of Politics*, Ch. 4, Sect. V, p. 170.
[45] *Equality*, pp. 219–20.

wealth and power by public action for the public good," then, Tawney declares, liberty

> is clearly incompatible, not only with economic and social, but with civil and political, equality, which also prevent the strong exploiting to the full the advantages of their strength.[46]

But, he goes on,

> when liberty is construed realistically, as implying not merely a minimum of civil and political rights, but securities that the economically weak will not be at the mercy of the economically strong, and that the control of those aspects of economic life by which all are affected will be amenable, in the last resort, to the will of all, a large measure of equality so far from being inimical to liberty, is essential to it.[47]

Considering especially gross inequalities in wealth and economic power as they affect individual liberties, Tawney concludes that "the existence of the former is a menace to the latter, and the latter is most likely to be secured by curtailing the former."[48]

A number of other authors share the point of view expressed by Laski and Tawney. Hobhouse declares that "liberty without equality is a name of noble sound and squalid result."[49] As he sees it, "the freedom of man

[46] *Ibid.*

[47] *Ibid.*, p. 226. "Inequality of power," Tawney says in another place, "is not necessarily inimical to liberty. On the contrary, it is the condition of it. Liberty implies the ability to act, not merely to resist . . . But, while inequality of power is the condition of liberty . . . it is also a menace to it, for power which is sufficient to use is sufficient to abuse. Hence in the political sphere, where the danger is familiar, all civilized communities have established safeguards, by which the advantages of differentiation of function, with the varying degrees of power which it involves, may be preserved, and the risk that power may be tyrannical, or perverted to private ends, averted or diminished" (*ibid.*, pp. 220–21). Yves Simon similarly maintains that freedom "excludes the particular kind of inequality which obtains between exploiter and exploited" (*Community of the Free*, p. 169).

[48] *Ibid.*, p. 229. "As long as liberty is interpreted as consisting exclusively in security against oppression by the agents of the State, or as a share in its government, it is plausible, perhaps, to dissociate it from equality"; but it ceases to be plausible, Tawney points out, when we look at the economic side of the picture. ". . . political arrangements may be such as to check excesses of power, while economic arrangements permit or encourage them"; hence, a society "may be both politically free and economically the opposite" (*ibid.*, p. 225). In such circumstances, Tawney adds, "the conventional assertion that inequality is inseparable from liberty is obviously . . . unreal and unconvincing" (*ibid.*, p. 229).

[49] *Liberalism*, p. 86. "Just as government first secured the elements of freedom *for all*," Hobhouse writes, "when it prevented the physically stronger man from slaying, beating, despoiling his neighbours, so it secures a larger measure of freedom *for all* by every restriction which it imposes with a view to preventing one man from making use of any of his advantages to the disadvantage of others" (*ibid.*, p. 91). The italics added plainly

in society . . . is always conditioned by the equal claims of others."[50] In the absence of such equality, one man's freedom is identical with power over others and the loss of freedom to them.[51] Simons similarly declares that "save as the bride of liberty, equality is pale and deadly dull, if not revolting. But the ultimate liberty obviously is that of men equal in power."[52] And Knight makes the same point in the following manner.

> The content of freedom is relative to what one wishes to do . . . and is also dependent on the possession of *power* to act. In exchange relations, moreover, effective freedom requires power not too far inferior to that possessed by the other party to any transaction; hence general freedom implies some limitation on inequality.[53]

We turn now to two writers—Calhoun and Sumner—who epitomize what seems to be the opposite point of view—that equality (or, more specifically, equality of condition) destroys liberty. But what they say on the subject immediately makes it clear that the liberty which is threatened by equality and requires inequality is the freedom of the stronger or more fortunate segment of mankind. Hence, they do not really disagree with those who think that it is the freedom of the weaker and less fortunate which requires equality of condition and of opportunity.

Calhoun concedes that the "equality of citizens, in the eyes of the law, is essential to liberty in a popular government." But, he immediately adds, "to go further, and make equality of *condition* essential to liberty, would be to destroy both liberty and progress." He explains how this would come about.

> Now, as individuals differ greatly from each other, in intelligence, sagacity, energy, perseverance, skill, habits of industry and economy, physical power, position and opportunity . . . the necessary effect of leaving all free to exert themselves to better their condition, must be a corresponding inequality between those who may possess these qualities and advantages in a high degree,

---

indicate that, for Hobhouse, it is the general freedom of the multitude, not the special freedom of the privileged few, which calls for equality (i.e., equality of condition and of opportunity, not merely equality before the law).

[50] *Elements of Social Justice*, p. 186.
[51] Speaking of freedom of contract as implying "substantial equality between the parties," Hobhouse maintains that "where no such equality exists one party acts under a degree of compulsion" (*ibid.*, p. 75).
[52] *Economic Policy for a Free Society*, p. 7.
[53] *Freedom and Reform*, p. 201. It will be recalled that, in the conceptual issue concerning enabling means, Knight distinguishes between freedom and power. See Ch. 14, pp. 553–54, *supra*. However, he does concede that it is only "formal freedom" which must be distinguished from power (i.e., the power provided by enabling means); for what Knight calls "effective freedom," power is required.

and those who may be deficient in them. The only means by which this result can be prevented are, either to impose such restrictions on the exertions of those who may possess them in a high degree, as will place them on a level with those who do not; or to deprive them of the fruits of their exertions. But to impose such restrictions on them would be destructive of liberty.[54]

On the other hand, while Calhoun tacitly admits that the establishment of equality of conditions might increase the freedom of the many, he denies that they would be able to retain it for long.

Liberty . . . when forced on a people unfit for it, would, instead of a blessing, be a curse; as it would, in its reaction, lead directly to anarchy . . . the greatest of all curses. No people, indeed, can long enjoy more liberty than that to which their situation and advanced intelligence and morals fairly entitle them.[55]

Like Calhoun, Sumner believes that equality before the law is essential to freedom. This means, for him, "that a man shall not be interfered with while using his own powers for his own welfare. . . . Liberty, therefore, does not by any means do away with the struggle for existence."[56] In that struggle, "nature," Sumner maintains, "is entirely neutral; she submits to him who most energetically and resolutely assails her. She grants her rewards to the fittest, therefore, without regard to other considerations of any kind."[57]

The system of nature constantly forces the student of political philosophy to recognize "the antagonism of equality and liberty."[58] We can understand this in Sumner's terms by seeing that, in his view, "the object of equality before the law is to make the state [like nature] entirely neutral," leaving "each man to run the race of life for himself as best he can." Hence, it follows for him that "equality of possessions or of rights [i.e., equality of condition or of opportunity] and equality before the law are diametrically opposed to each other."[59] And similarly opposed are equality of possessions or of rights and the liberty which thrives on equality before the law, i.e., the liberty of the stronger to win out in the race of life. If such liberty exists, then, Sumner argues, men will wrest from the world what their efforts deserve.

[54] "Disquisition on Government," in *Calhoun: Basic Documents*, pp. 64–65.
[55] *Ibid.*, pp. 63–64.
[56] "The Challenge of Facts," in *The People Shall Judge*, Vol. II, p. 86.
[57] *Ibid.*, p. 85.
[58] *Ibid.*, p. 89. "Socialists," Sumner remarks, "are filled with the enthusiasm of equality. Every scheme of theirs for securing equality has destroyed liberty" (*ibid.*).
[59] *Ibid.*

Such is the system of nature. If we do not like it, and if we try to amend it, there is only one way in which we can do it. We can take from the better and give to the worse. We can deflect the penalties of those who have done ill and throw them on those who have done better. We can take the rewards from those who have done better and give them to those who have done worse. We shall thus lessen the inequalities. We shall favor the survival of the unfittest, and we shall accomplish this by destroying liberty. Let it be understood that we cannot go outside of this alternative: liberty, inequality, survival of the fittest; not-liberty, equality, survival of the unfittest. The former carries society forward and favors all its best members; the latter carries society downwards and favors all its worst members.[60]

We have so far omitted reference to De Tocqueville. He is, of course, greatly concerned with the problem of freedom and equality. But his approach to the problem differs from that of either group of authors whom we have so far considered.

While, on the one hand, he agrees with Calhoun and Sumner in thinking that equality of condition will necessarily destroy the liberty enjoyed by the favoured members of society, he does not, like them, oppose the establishment of such equality. He looks upon the tendency toward the development of equality of condition as a providential and, therefore, irresistible fact.[61] He is persuaded that "all who attempt, in the ages upon which we are entering, to base freedom upon aristocratic privilege will fail."[62] Hence, for him, the only practical question with which we should be concerned is whether, as democratic equality replaces aristocratic privilege, the liberty of all will be attendant upon their equal status or condition, as the liberty of the few was a consequence of their superior rank and advantages.

Confronting this question, De Tocqueville, on the other hand, does not agree with Laski, Tawney, and Hobhouse in thinking that equality of condition will necessarily increase the total amount of freedom by extend-

---

[60] *Ibid.*, p. 85. We cannot find in Sumner, as in Calhoun, even the tacit admission that equality may confer a certain freedom on the weak, while taking away the liberty of the strong. On the contrary, Sumner's linking of equality with the negation of liberty would seem to imply that he really opposes those who maintain that equality promotes the spread of liberty. Nevertheless, the context indicates that when he says that equality destroys freedom, Sumner is always thinking of the liberty of those who, in his opinion, should have it in the fullest degree because they can make the most of it. To give all men the relatively ineffective liberty that they would have under an equality of conditions would be to destroy the effective liberty that equality before the law gives to the stronger. Cf. Hayek, *The Constitution of Liberty*, p. 85: "Equality of the general rules of law and conduct . . . is the only kind of equality conducive to liberty and the only equality which we can secure without destroying liberty. Not only has liberty nothing to do with any other sort of equality, but it is even bound to produce inequality in many respects."

[61] See *Democracy in America*, Vol. I, p. 6.

[62] *Ibid.*, Vol. II, p. 322.

ing it to the multitude, though each may have less of it than the privileged few once had. Freedom, in his view, is not the distinguishing characteristic of democracy. It is equality of condition that is the "peculiar and preponderant fact" about the democratic societies which De Tocqueville observed replacing the *ancien régime*. Furthermore, he tells us, "the taste which men have for liberty and that which they feel for equality are, in fact, two different things; and, I am not afraid to add that among democratic nations they are two unequal things."[63] The love of equality is so much stronger that it can even lead to the relinquishment of freedom if that is necessary to secure equality. De Tocqueville says:

> I think that democratic communities have a natural taste for freedom; left to themselves, they will seek it, cherish it, and view any privation of it with regret. But for equality their passion is ardent, insatiable, incessant, invincible; they call for equality in freedom; and if they cannot obtain that, they still call for equality in slavery. They will endure poverty, servitude, barbarism, but they will not endure aristocracy.[64]

Thus, while De Tocqueville maintains that the passion for equality is now so great that "in our age freedom cannot be established without it," he does not hold the view that equality will necessarily increase the freedom of men in general, or preserve such freedom as they may have. On the contrary, he thinks that equality of condition can lead to a totalitarian form of democracy—a despotism so extreme as to extinguish all traces of freedom from society.[65] He does not think that this is inevitable any more than he thinks that liberty will necessarily thrive under equality of conditions. As De Tocqueville sees it, remedies are available to prevent democratic societies from becoming totalitarian (i.e., with all political and economic power concentrated in the hands of a central government), but whether men will make use of them he leaves to their wisdom and free choice. "The nations of our time," he concludes, "cannot prevent the conditions of men from becoming equal, but it depends upon themselves whether the principle of equality is to lead them to servitude or freedom. . . ."[66]

All of the authors whom we have so far considered are largely concerned with equality of condition or of opportunity. They do not exclude political equality (since that involves equality of status, power, and privilege), but they do not emphasize it or treat it as a special term in relation to freedom. However, other writers do discuss the problem of liberty and equality

[63] *Ibid.*, p. 95.
[64] *Ibid.*, p. 97.
[65] See *ibid.*, pp. 316–30.
[66] *Ibid.*, p. 334.

almost exclusively in political terms. A brief examination of their views will show that they do not alter the picture.

When political equality is understood to mean simply equality before the law, it is generally agreed that such equality fosters freedom. As we have seen, such arch opponents of equality of condition as Calhoun and Sumner advocate equality before the law in the interests of freedom.

When political equality is attributed to men who have (through the equal rights of citizenship, including equal suffrage) an equal voice in public affairs, then there can be no disagreement about the relation of such equality to political liberty, conceived as a special variant of self-realization.[67] Since the possession of political liberty, as understood by the few authors who hold this special conception of it, depends on the one favorable circumstance of being enfranchised, it must follow, for anyone who holds this conception, that universal and equal suffrage distributes political liberty as widely as possible. Hence, the political equality of all achieved through universal suffrage establishes political liberty for all; and, contrariwise, the political inequality which obtains in a society that is divided into a disfranchised subject class and an enfranchised ruling class necessarily confers political liberty only on the few and denies it to the many.

One further question remains. Still conceiving political equality in terms of an equality of political rights and powers, such as belong to enfranchised citizens, it has been asked whether the extension of the franchise from the few to the many jeopardizes or promotes freedom. We can find what appear to be opposite answers to this question, but here as before the context reveals at once that the authors are not really opposed on existential grounds, though they are opposed normatively or as a matter of policy.

Thus, for example, Chancellor Kent declares that "the tendency of universal suffrage is to jeopardize the rights of property and the principles of liberty."[68] The liberty that Kent thinks is threatened by universal suffrage is the liberty of the propertied class. While he argues that men of substantial property and they alone should have a full measure of SR freedom, because they alone have the virtue and wisdom to use it well, he does not deny that the extension of the franchise would give more

[67] See Vol. I, Book II, Ch. 18, for the distinction between political liberty, as consisting in the freedom which suffrage gives a man, and self-realization, as consisting in doing as one pleases. It is there made quite clear that a man can have political liberty and yet, on many occasions and in many connections, lack the freedom of self-realization because of the impediments or restrictions imposed on his conduct by the government and laws under which he lives, and, conversely, a man can have SR freedom in relation to government and law and yet lack political liberty.
[68] See "Debate in the New York Convention," in *The People Shall Judge*, Vol. I, p. 569.

freedom to the motley mob and take some freedom away from their betters. In fact, this is precisely what Kent fears.[69]

Lecky and Berlin, on the other hand, simply express some doubts that political equality ensures a great measure of freedom for all. "A tendency to democracy," Lecky writes, "does not mean a tendency to parliamentary government, or even a tendency towards greater liberty." In fact, he adds, "the strongest democratic tendencies are distinctly adverse to liberty." But when Lecky explains why he says this, we see that his view of the matter closely resembles that of Sumner. He writes:

> Equality is the idol of democracy, but, with the infinitely various capacities and energies of men, this can only be attained by a constant, systematic, stringent repression of their *natural development. Whenever natural forces have unrestricted play, inequality is certain to ensue.*[70]

An enforced equality, in other words, diminishes the liberty of those who are most gifted by nature to make the best use of it. The other side of the same picture, according to Berlin, is that the multitude, under conditions of political equality, do not have "more than a modicum of individual liberty."[71]

Since the authors to whom we now turn are exponents of democracy (which they conceive in terms of universal suffrage), we know that they have the freedom of all in mind when they say that liberty is promoted by political equality. "There is no liberty," Laski writes, "if special privilege restricts the franchise to a portion of the community."[72] Certainly, the few who have the franchise when it is restricted also have liberty, just as surely, in Laski's opinion, as the disfranchised many lack it. Laski tacitly acknowledges this when he writes: "Freedom . . . will not be achieved for the mass of men save under special guarantees. It can never . . . exist in the presence of special privilege. Unless I enjoy the same access to power as others, I live in an atmosphere of contingent frustration."[73]

According to Knight, a man's freedom in society "requires equal participation in the activities of law-making," and so only those who are thus politically equal—whether they are the few or the many—are also free.[74] It is the freedom of all that Knight has in mind, as he plainly indicates when he writes:

[69] See *ibid.*, pp. 570–72.
[70] *Democracy and Liberty*, Vol, I, Ch. III, p. 212. (Italics added.) Lecky also points out that democracy tends "to impair the efficiency and authority of parliaments, which have hitherto proved the chief organs of political liberty" (*ibid.*).
[71] *Two Concepts of Liberty*, p. 53.
[72] *Liberty in the Modern State*, Ch. III, p. 159.
[73] *A Grammar of Politics*, Ch. 4, Sect. II, p. 149.
[74] *Freedom and Reform*, p. 391.

The free individual must live in a free society . . . itself made free by the free and equal participation of all members of society, and representing an intellectual-moral consensus as to the content of rights and obligations.[75]

Similarly, Kelsen maintains that "the view that the degree of freedom in society is proportionate to the number of free individuals implies that all individuals are of equal political value." Hence, for him, "the idea of democracy, is a synthesis of the ideas of freedom and equality."[76]

The real disagreement between the pro-democratic and anti-democratic authors is thus seen to be a normative, not an existential, issue. They disagree, as a matter of fundamental principle and policy, about whether the privileged liberty of the few should be preserved by maintaining the political inequality of a ruling and subject class or whether freedom should be increased for all by the democratic abolition of such inequality and special privilege. They do not disagree, as a matter of fact, about the effect of political equality and inequality on the freedom of the many and the few.

4. THE ISSUE ABOUT SECURITY

The discussion of security in relation to freedom divides into the consideration of two quite separate problems, according as one or the other of two quite distinct meanings of "security" is involved.

(i) *Security of the individual's person and property.* Authors who use "security" in this sense have in mind the protection of the individual from violence, aggression, and injury by other individuals or groups. They think that such protection is to be provided by the state and by the enforcement of its laws. While they recognize that the laws of the state restrict the individual's freedom, they think that, on balance, more freedom is preserved than lost through the use of legal coercion to prevent all forms of extra-legal coercion and intimidation of individuals by other individuals.

We have already seen in Section 2 that there is no disagreement among SR writers on this point. Even those, such as Hobbes, Bentham, Spencer, Hayek, and Hale, who hold that every coercive law curtails freedom, nevertheless maintain that the individual probably has more freedom under law and government than if he were to live in a state of nature—a state of lawlessness or anarchy. As Hobbes points out, the individual has no

---

[75] "The Ideal of Freedom," in *The Philosophy of American Democracy*, p. 91.
[76] *General Theory of Law and the State*, p. 287. See also his *Vom Wesen und Werte der Demokratie*, pp. 9–10. Cf. Hobhouse, *Elements of Social Justice*, pp. 88, 185; and Joad, *Liberty Today*, pp. 22, 35, 74–75.

security in a state of nature: his anarchic freedom is precarious and short-lived. Neither he nor any other SR author thinks that freedom in the total absence of the personal security which government and law provides is superior—either in quality or quantity—to the combination of freedom and security which men enjoy in civil society.[77]

(ii) *Economic security.* What writers who use "security" in this sense have in mind is the individual's secure hold on the economic goods which constitute enabling means for his freedom, e.g., his secure hold on the means of subsistence or his livelihood, on his job, on sufficient income to support him during sickness or unemployment or in old age. Economic security, thus conceived, includes the protection by the state of such property as the individual has legally acquired, but it goes far beyond this. It calls for the promotion of the general economic welfare by the state— for the widest dissemination to individuals and families of the wherewithal that is needed for a decent human life.

This sense of security, when considered in relation to freedom, raises a question on which SR authors appear to disagree. Are economic security and individual freedom compatible? The writers who answer this question negatively hold the view that the economic programs or welfare measures which achieve security do so and can do so only with substantial loss of freedom to the individual, as a result of the state's control and regulation of the economy to achieve the economic welfare of all. On the other hand, there are those who maintain that more freedom is gained than lost by these efforts.

Since this difference of opinion, when fully expressed, involves opposed views about quite divergent economic proposals in relation to SR freedom, we think it better to deal with this problem of security and freedom in the context of the economic considerations that will be treated in Section 7 to follow.

5. THE ISSUE ABOUT LAW

We have already seen that certain SR authors maintain that every law curtails freedom, and that men living in civil society have more or less individual liberty to do as they please according as their conduct is subject

[77] In addition to the writers treated in Sect. 2, a number of others can be cited as expressing the same point of view, and do so explicitly in terms of the relation of freedom to security. See Calhoun, "Disquisition on Government," in *Calhoun: Basic Documents*, pp. 62–63; Sidgwick, *Elements of Politics*, p. 47; Hobhouse, *Liberalism*, p. 62, and *Elements of Social Justice*, p. 62; de Madariaga, "Rights of Man or Human Relations?" in *Human Rights*, pp. 50–51; Heald, *A Free Society*, pp. 377–78.

to less or more extensive regulation by the laws of the state. The principal authors who advance this view are Hobbes, Bentham, Spencer, Hayek, and Hale. Since we have elsewhere sufficiently documented their espousal of this position, we shall not repeat the evidence here.[78]

We have also seen that a number of other SR writers generally adopt the same point of view, but do so with a single qualification on the word "every." Such writers as J. S. Mill, Hobhouse, Laski, Knight, Tawney, and Kelsen insist upon one exception to the proposition that every law curtails freedom. The exception occurs when there happens to be a coincidence between what the law requires and what the individual wishes to do anyway. As these writers see it, the individual is free in relation to law if he wishes to do what the law commands, or does not wish to do what it prohibits. In all other cases, in which the law comes into conflict with the individual's desires, his obedience to the law involves some loss of freedom on his part.[79]

Is there a real issue here? Do these two groups of SR authors really disagree on the question, "Is the individual free in civil society *only* in regard to those parts of his conduct which are not subject to legal regulation by the state?" Or, to put the question another way, "Does every law, *without exception*, curtail individual freedom?"

There is no difficulty or uncertainty about attributing a negative answer to Mill, Hobhouse, Laski, Knight, Tawney, Kelsen, and Fosdick. But to be sure that Hobbes, Bentham, Spencer, Hayek, and Hale join issue with them, we must be able to interpret them as giving the affirmative answer. They do explicitly say that *every* law curtails freedom; they do explicitly say that it is *only* in matters on which the law is silent that the individual is free. But, so far as we can see, they have never faced the question whether they would defend their unqualified statement of the case against the one exception proposed by the other SR writers.

The exception may have occurred to them and they may have dismissed it as unwarranted and thought there was no reason ever to mention it. Or the exception may never have occurred to them, in which case we cannot be certain whether they would have accepted or rejected it. If we take their emphasis on "every" and "only" to express their firm adherence

---

[78] See Vol. I, Book II, Ch. 14, pp. 232–36.

[79] The position of these authors has also been sufficiently evidenced in Vol. I. See Book II, Ch. 14, pp. 237–44. To the writers there treated, one other author can now be added. Dorothy Fosdick, considering Bentham's remark that "all coercive laws . . . are, as far as they go, abrogative of liberty," says that "it does not follow, however, from the fact that the law restrains some liberties that law restrains liberty itself." She then points out that "in so far as men are not inclined to do what the law forbids, the law is no curtailment of their freedom" (*What is Liberty?* p. 145). Miss Fosdick does not explicitly say that men are also free when they wish to do what the law commands, but that would seem to be implied in her statement.

to a position which, in their view, brooks no qualification, then they do join issue with the writers who accept that position, but only as qualified by the added exception. If we have any doubt about that interpretation of Hobbes, Bentham, Spencer, Hayek, and Hale, then we cannot be sure that they would disagree with Mill, Hobhouse, Laski, Knight, Tawney, Kelsen, and Fosdick.

We have so far omitted reference to the position taken on this issue by the University of California Associates in Philosophy. They provide us with the *only* statement on the affirmative side which *explicitly takes cognizance of the exception proposed and rejects it*. In their view, "I am free when my conduct is under my own control," by which they mean that "it is determined by my own desires, motives, and intentions." I am unfree "when my conduct is controlled by someone else," i.e., "when it is determined by the desires, motives, and intentions of someone else." The "someone else" can certainly be interpreted to stand either for another individual, a group, or the community itself, which acts through the institutions of law and government. Accordingly, when these writers say that my conduct is "not under my own control even when my own desires and intentions are in agreement with those of another person who seeks to control my conduct," they can also be interpreted to mean that I am not free when certain conduct is required of me by law, *even though that conduct happens to conform to my own desires or intentions.*[80]

Here, then, we have the affirmative position stated in such a way that it takes account of the qualification which the negative side insists upon, and at the same time explicitly rejects the qualifying exception. Hence, there is no doubt that the University of California Associates join issue with Mill, Hobhouse, Laski, etc. But when we examine the reason which the University of California Associates give for rejecting the qualification proposed by Mill, Hobhouse, Laski, etc., we are faced with a new problem about the issue with which we are here concerned.

The University of California Associates argue against the qualifying exception in the following manner. Suppose, they say, that I had "desires and intentions which did not agree" with the desires and intentions of someone else—either another individual, a group, or the government in power. In that case, "I should have . . . been free only had I been able to seek the realization of my own."[81] But if having alternatives, and especially contrary courses of action, open to me is essential to my freedom of self-realization, then a rule of law always—without exception—curtails my freedom, for it *either* prevents me from doing as I wish when what it commands is contrary to my desire, *or* it takes away the possibility of my

[80] See *Knowledge and Society*, p. 156.
[81] *Ibid.*

enacting an alternative or contrary desire when what it commands happens to coincide with my desire. Hence, I am not free in either case.

The argument for this conclusion is set forth as follows:

> My act is constrained when I am obliged to perform it, when, having performed it, there was nothing else I could do in its stead. Acts are therefore always constrained when they *must* be performed, that is, when a failure to observe some command or injunction incurs the risk of punishment. Acts that I must perform are constrained even when they have my approval. . . . What is essential to constraint is . . . the limitation of the possible alternatives of action by a command or injunction. An act of mine is free when there has been no restriction to the number of possible acts I *could* have performed; it is constrained when a command or injunction prevents me from performing one or more of the possible acts. Whether I approve or disapprove of the limitation of alternatives is irrelevant to the question of whether my act is constrained or not.[82]

We might attribute this argument against the qualifying exception to such writers as Hobbes, Bentham, Spencer, Hayek, and Hale if they, too, maintained that the availability of alternative courses of action is essential to SR freedom. But none of these writers takes that position on the conceptual issue concerning alternatives.[83] In fact, as we have already shown, two of these writers, Hobbes and Hayek, deny the relevance of alternatives to SR freedom.[84] Hence, if the only reason that can be given for asserting that every law curtails freedom (with no exception for those laws which concur with an individual's own desire) is that even such laws remove alternatives, then Bentham, Spencer, and Hale do not appear to give any reason for being on the affirmative side of the issue about law, and Hobbes and Hayek would have a reason for taking the opposite side.

When we turn to the writers who are on the opposite side, we find that, among them, Mill, Laski, Knight, Tawney, and Fosdick (i.e., all except Hobhouse and Kelsen) are authors who clearly can be construed as holding the view that having alternatives open is essential to SR freedom.[85] We do not have any evidence which would show, one way or the other, how Hobhouse and Kelsen stand on the conceptual issue concerning alternatives. Hence, they may have some defense of their position on the issue about law, against the argument advanced by the University of California Associates. But since Mill, Laski, Knight, Tawney, and Fosdick agree with the University of California Associates that alternatives are essential, one

---

[82] *Ibid.*, p. 238.

[83] See Ch. 14, Sect. 4, pp. 555–57, *supra*.

[84] See *ibid.*, pp. 556–57, *supra*. As we pointed out there, Hobbes denies the relevance of alternatives on the basis of his conception of SR freedom as "corporal liberty."

[85] See *ibid.*, pp. 555–56, *supra*. Cf. Vol. I, Book II, Ch. 4, pp. 115–17, and Ch. 13, pp. 206–10.

would expect that they would agree with them also that every law, without exception, curtails freedom. Since they fail to agree with them, one naturally looks for some defense of the exception they propose, by answering the argument that even laws which coincide with an individual's desires remove alternatives. But, so far as we can see, that is not to be found.

6. THE ISSUE ABOUT DEMOCRACY

Much of the literature on democracy and freedom (and it is vast and varied), defeats the kind of analysis that we are here attempting for the sake of clarification. We meet with statement after statement that democracy is the bulwark of freedom, that democracy is the enemy of freedom, that democracy increases freedom, that democracy diminishes freedom, that democracy is the free society, or that there is no connection between democracy and freedom. But in too many instances to count or cite, neither the statement itself nor the context reveals in what sense the terms "democracy" and "freedom are being employed, whose freedom is being considered—that of the few or of the many—and the reason for the statement. We are simply left with the impression that the word "democracy" is being used eulogistically or dyslogistically, that "freedom" is an honorific term, and that the writer is for or against the one by virtue of some relation to the other which he regards as too evident to need explanation.

If any real disagreement can be found in all this, it is a normative, not an existential, issue. It turns on the question about who should have freedom (either SR freedom or political liberty in the special sense in which that is a variant of SR freedom). Writers who think that freedom (in either sense) should be restricted to the few are *against* democracy; writers who think that freedom should be extended to the many or to all are *for* it.

Implicit in such conflicting attitudes toward democracy, of course, is an agreement rather than a disagreement about the existential connection between democracy and freedom. The writers who are thus opposed concur in thinking that democracy tends to spread SR freedom, or in thinking that it confers political liberty on more men than does any other form of government. They share this common ground for their rejection of democracy in the interest of preserving the freedom of the few or for their espousal of democracy in the interest of extending freedom to the many.[86]

---

86 The real disagreement indicated above will be treated in Ch. 17 on the normative issues. There it will be seen that the crux of the issue lies in opposite opinions about who should have SR freedom or political liberty.

Are there any authors who deny the existential premise concerning democracy and freedom, which is implicit in and presupposed by both sides of the normative issue about who should have freedom? To answer this question, it is necessary to deal separately with the two senses of freedom that may be involved—political liberty, on the one hand, and the freedom of self-realization, on the other.

(i) *The existential connection between democracy and political liberty.* A relatively small number of SR authors affirm political liberty as a freedom that is distinct from the freedom of self-realization.[87] They conceive political liberty as resting solely in the individual's ability, through citizenship with suffrage, to have his wishes represented in the formation of the public will—in the laws that are made or the policies that are followed by the government in whose sovereignty he shares as a citizen. They see that the possession of political liberty does not by itself guarantee the individual that he will be able to do as he himself pleases, for, in matters regulated by law, he may be coerced or restrained even if he has political liberty in the special sense indicated.

Many writers who talk about democracy and freedom use the term "political liberty," but it is impossible to tell whether they mean political liberty in this special sense, or the freedom of self-realization as that is seen in the realm of political life (i.e., in relation to government and law), or, for that matter, the acquired freedom of self-perfection (also in relation to civil government and positive law). Since we cannot identify the specific freedom they are talking about, we cannot construe these authors as parties to an issue about democracy and freedom, even were we able to determine, as is seldom the case, the precise meaning with which they use the term "democracy."[88] Whether we have a genuine disagreement here depends on a precise definition of both terms.

On one definition of democracy, we can see at once that no disagreement is possible about the relation of it to political liberty, as distinct from SR freedom. If democracy is conceived as constitutional government with

[87] They are principally Hobhouse, Sidgwick, and Barbara Wootton. Of the remaining writers who affirm political liberty as a distinct freedom, Aristotle and Kant, as we have seen, deny the genuineness of SR freedom. Aquinas, Locke, Montesquieu, Maritain, and Simon affirm SR freedom only as subordinate to and circumscribed by man's acquired freedom of self-perfection. Marsilius, Hamilton, and Jaspers do not express themselves definitely enough with regard to SR freedom to be classified one way or the other. For the documentary evidence on all these points see Vol. I, Book II, Ch. 18; and also, in this volume, Ch. 6, esp. pp. 152–56, *supra.*

[88] The same holds true of the many authors who use the term "freedom" rather than "political liberty" in talking about democracy. In addition, there are writers who use the term "democratic liberty" as a term of praise without making clear whether they mean SR freedom or political liberty in the special sense, and without explaining what is democratic about the freedom they are praising.

universal suffrage and with operating procedures which make that suffrage effective as a means of obtaining the consent of the governed, and if political liberty is enjoyed by all men who are enfranchised citizens in a constitutional state, *then it necessarily follows* that democracy confers political liberty on more men than does any other form of constitutional government with a more restricted franchise.[89] On the other hand, *if* the term "democracy" is used in any sense which does not include the active participation of citizens in the formation of the public will and, directly or indirectly, in the acts of government, and *if* political liberty is conceived as belonging only to those who, through citizenship with suffrage, are participants in self-government, *then* what basis is there for saying that democracy either does or does not confer political liberty on men?

Is there, then, no possibility at all of disagreement about democracy and political liberty? What about those who think that democracy can be totalitarian government, a dictatorship acquiesced in by the masses, mob rule, or even a constitutional state in which suffrage does not really operate as it is supposed to, either because gross economic inequalities frustrate the exercise by the poor of an independent voice or because the franchise itself is so constituted as to be a sham rather than a functioning reality? Lecky, for example, says that "a tendency to democracy does not mean a tendency to parliamentary government, or even a tendency towards greater liberty. On the contrary, strong arguments may be adduced, both from history and from the nature of things, to show that democracy may often prove the direct opposite of liberty."[90] Henry George also observes that

> to turn a republican government into a despotism the basest and most brutal, it is not necessary formally to change its constitution or abandon popular elections . . . forms are nothing when the substance has gone, and the forms of popular government are those from which the substance of freedom may most easily go. Extremes meet, and a government of univer-

[89] On another definition of democracy, disagreement about its relation to political liberty is also impossible. *If* democracy is conceived as any form of constitutional government in which the enfranchised citizens comprise the ruling class, then, regardless of whether the suffrage is more or less restricted, democracy confers political liberty on more men than does any form of non-constitutional government in which there are no enfranchised citizens at all (e.g., an absolute monarchy, a despotic dictatorship, etc.).

[90] *Democracy and Liberty*, Vo. I, Ch. III, p. 212. Lecky adds: "A despotism resting on a plebiscite is quite as natural a form of democracy as a republic, and some of the strongest democratic tendencies are distinctly adverse to liberty" (*ibid.*). Similarly, Moley points out that "farsighted men realized that a broad franchise and popular political institutions might allow a popular tyranny even more sinister than that of royal absolutism or aristocratic privilege" (*How to Keep Our Liberty*, pp. 20–21). Cf. Kuehnelt-Leddihn, *Liberty or Equality*, p. 9.

sal suffrage and theoretical equality may, under conditions which impel the change, most readily become a despotism.[91]

And Bertrand Russell, who thinks that "if a government is not to be tyrannical, it must be democratic . . ." nevertheless says that "it is only by a mystical identification of the majority with the community that democracy can be held to involve liberty. It is a means to liberty if the majority are lovers of liberty; if not, not."[92]

We see here, of course, the possibility of real disagreements about what democracy is or should be. In any case, its relations to political liberty will be self-evident (or tautological): that it is favorable to political liberty cannot be denied if it is conceived as providing for the existence and effective operation of suffrage; that it is unfavorable cannot be denied if it is conceived as excluding, attenuating, or frustrating the effective participation of citizens in their own government.

(ii) *The existential connection between democracy and the circumstantial freedom of self-realization.* Here as before we must pass over writers who do not enable us to tell whether they are talking about SR freedom, or political liberty as distinct from self-realization, or the acquired freedom of self-perfection. That leaves a certain number of authors concerning whom we can be sure that, in talking about democracy, they have in mind only the individual's ability to do as he wishes.

It is necessary to narrow this group further by excluding those, such as Burke, Calhoun, Chancellor Kent, and other conservative writers, who are against democracy on normative, not existential, grounds, i.e., who wish to see the freedom of the privileged or the virtuous few preserved and who think that democracy, in its tendency to give a greater measure of freedom to the multitude, will encroach upon the special liberties enjoyed by the aristocratic classes in society. The disagreement between the liberals and conservatives, or between the proponents of democracy and of aristocracy, is a disagreement about who should have freedom, not about the existential conditions under which the few or the many possess it more fully.

Turning, then, to writers who wish to see SR freedom enjoyed by as many men as possible and in as full a measure as possible, what differences of opinion can we expect to find among them concerning the relevance of democracy to their policy on the spread of freedom? To answer this question, let us follow the same kind of analytical procedure we employed

[1] *Progress and Poverty*, Book X, p. 530.
[2] "Freedom and Government," in *Freedom, Its Meaning*, pp. 252–53.

in the case of political liberty. The possibilities we shall consider all stem from different specifications of the term "democracy."

(a) Let the term "democracy" be specified to mean that organization of society in which equality of conditions prevails or is best approximated. This way of conceiving democracy takes us back at once to the question about the existential relation between freedom and equality. As we have seen, there is no real disagreement on this existential question among SR authors. Hobhouse, Laski, Tawney, Knight, Simons, Kelsen, and Hale all agree that the establishment of an equality of condition promotes the spread of freedom to more men and the enlargement of the freedom that each individual enjoys. Among SR writers who are in favor of the extension of freedom to the multitude, the only dissenting voices are those of De Tocqueville and Berlin. But even they do not *deny* that equality of condition can have this effect; they merely *doubt* that the result necessarily follows.[93]

Now if democracy is conceived as involving a greater degree of equality than any other form of society has, then SR authors who so conceive it will generally agree that democracy gives more men the freedom of self-realization (and also, perhaps, more of it) than do societies in which inequality prevails. De Tocqueville and Berlin separate themselves from the rest by the expression of doubts about the necessary connection between equality and freedom; but that does not constitute an issue about democracy and freedom, any more than it constitutes an issue about equality and freedom.

One possibility of real disagreement here still remains to be considered. Democracy may be conceived in exclusively political terms; it may be thought to establish political equality by giving all men the equal status of enfranchised citizens, with all the rights, power, privileges, and immunities appertaining thereto. But political democracy, so conceived, may not obliterate social classes, or remove or attenuate economic inequalities. On the other hand, democracy may be conceived as a society which is not only politically but also socially and economically, classless, i.e., one in which equality of condition is not confined to political equality, but includes social and economic equality as well.

Among the SR writers who deal with the problem of freedom and equality, we know that almost all of them definitely express the view that mere political equality is not enough for the full measure of freedom which as many individuals as possible should enjoy.[94] Hence, they would

[93] See Sec. 3, pp. 570–81, esp. pp. 572–75, 577–79 and 579–80, *supra.*
[94] Thus, for example, Laski asserts that "political equality, therefore, is never real unless it is accompanied by virtual economic equality." He points out that "great inequalities of wealth make impossible the attainment of freedom" (A *Grammar of Politics*, Ch. V, Sect III, pp. 161–62). Cf. Tawney, *Equality*, p. 226.

disagree with writers who maintain that democracy promotes SR freedom by establishing political equality, regardless of any other inequalities—social or economic—that may exist in a politically democratic community. But we cannot find definite expressions of the latter point of view.

Furthermore, even if that view were expressed, it would give rise to an issue about how democracy should be conceived (i.e., narrowly, in terms of political equality or more comprehensively, in terms of social and economic as well as political equality). So far as the question about democracy and SR freedom reduces to a question about the relation between equality and freedom (by virtue of conceiving democracy in terms of equality), there would still be no disagreement among authors who specified the meaning of democracy in the same way.[95]

(b) Let the term "democracy" be specified to mean a form of government in which universal suffrage exists and in which, therefore, all members of society can exercise some influence on the content of the laws under which they live. This takes us back at once to the issue about law. Certain SR writers, we observed, maintain that men are free in obeying laws when, and *only* when, the conduct which law requires of them consists of actions which they wish to perform anyway.[96] Of these writers, we also know that Mill, Laski, Knight, Kelsen, and Tawney definitely maintain that the democratic institution of universal suffrage increases the likelihood, for more men, that the laws under which they live will reflect their own desires.[97] Hence, they feel justified in concluding that democracy tends to increase the individual's freedom in relation to law.

The foregoing conclusion rests on two premises: the first states the qualifying exception to the proposition that every law curtails freedom; the second asserts that universal suffrage makes it more likely that what the law requires will coincide with the desires or wishes of a large number of men. Hence, authors who hold that every law, without exception, curtails freedom would see nothing gained by universal suffrage, since it makes no difference to the individual's freedom whether his wishes do or do not coincide with the prescriptions of law.

But, as we have pointed out in Section 5, we cannot be sure that Hobbes,

---

[95] Those who think of democracy in purely political terms and who also think that political equality by itself suffices, would agree with one another about the relation of democracy to SR freedom. And those who think of democracy more comprehensively and who also think that a general equality of condition is necessary, would also agree with one another about the relation of democracy to SR freedom. The two groups would disagree, first, on the question whether political equality suffices or whether other equalities of condition are necessary; and, second, on the question of how democracy should be conceived.

[96] They are J. S. Mill, Hobhouse, Laski, Knight, Tawney, Kelsen, and Fosdick. See Sect. 5, pp. 582–83, *supra*.

[97] For the documentation of this point, see Vol. I, Book II, Ch. 14, pp. 237–44.

Bentham, Spencer, Hayek, and Hale, who do assert that every law curtails freedom, would also deny the exception proposed by other SR authors.[98] Hence, we cannot infer from their position about freedom in relation to law how they would stand on the question of democracy in relation to freedom, given the specification of "democracy" as a form of government which establishes universal suffrage. Even in the case of the University of California Associates in Philosophy, who do explicitly deny the exception proposed, we cannot infer that they must also deny the proposition that democracy increases individual freedom in relation to law, since the denial of a premise does not logically necessitate the denial of the conclusion.

Hence, the position that these authors take on the issue about law does not help us to ascertain the position they take on the question about democracy in relation to freedom, when democracy is conceived in terms of universal suffrage.

What was pointed out earlier in connection with democracy and political liberty applies here to the relation of democracy and the freedom of self-realization. We saw there that democracy may be conceived as involving universal suffrage and at the same time be thought of also as involving obstacles to its effective operation.[99] In that case, of course, the existence of universal suffrage would not tend to increase the likelihood of a coincidence between what the law requires and what a large number of individuals wish.[100] Writers who took this point of view about democracy might, therefore, say that even if democracy is conceived in terms of universal suffrage, and even if men are free in relation to law when legal prescriptions do not conflict with their own desires, it does not follow that democracy tends to increase the individual's freedom in relation to law. But they would then be disagreeing with Mill, Laski, Knight, Kelsen, and Tawney about how democracy in fact operates, not about how it affects freedom when it operates in the way they imagine.[101]

(c) Let the term "democracy" be specified to mean a form of government or an organization of society which imposes a minimum of legal regulation upon the conduct of individuals; or which interferes least in the private

[98] See *loc. cit.*, pp. 582–84, *supra*.
[99] See pp. 587–89, *supra*.
[100] Commenting on indirect or representative democracy, Belloc says that "delegation destroys freedom. Parliaments everywhere have proved irreconcilable with democracy. They are not the people. They are oligarchies" (*Restoration of Property*, p. 23). Belloc gives us no indication of whether he thinks that individuals are free when they obey laws that coincide with their desires. But even if he did think so, the passage quoted would mean in effect that an indirect democracy only increases the freedom of a minority (the lawmaking parliament), not of the majority of the citizens.
[101] Conversely, Mill, Laski, Knight, Kelsen, and Tawney would not disagree with the anti-democratic writers that, if democracy operated as they suppose it to, it would hardly serve to increase the individual's liberty in relation to law.

affairs of men; or which creates the greatest security of the individual's person and property against encroachments by other individuals or groups through extra-legal forms of coercion or intimidation; or which subjects men least to the arbitrary wills of other men; or which provides the individual with the widest range of alternatives.

On any one of the various specifications mentioned above, we can infer what SR writers who take that view of democracy would think about its relation to freedom.

Since all SR authors hold that an individual has more freedom if he is subject to fewer legal regulations, it follows that SR authors who think that men in a democratic society are subject to less regulation or less interference by government would also think that democracy increases the individual's freedom. The fact that certain authors see no connection between democratic government and the number of laws or the amount of interference to which individuals are subject results in a difference of opinion about what democracy is or should be, but not in a disagreement about democracy in relation to freedom.[102]

Since all SR authors who deal with the problem hold that security of person and property serves the cause of freedom, it follows that SR authors who think that men are more secure in their persons and property when they live in a democracy would also think that democracy increases the individual's freedom. Similarly, since SR authors agree that the individual's freedom consists in exemption from the arbitrary wills of other men as well as from physical coercion, it follows that SR authors who think that democracy, more than any other form of government, exempts men from arbitrary rule would also think that democracy is more favorable to individual freedom than is any other political form. In both instances, other writers may differ about what democracy is or should be. However, this does not constitute a disagreement about democracy's bearing on freedom when democracy is thought of in the two ways indicated above.

Finally, we come to the point about enabling means. Not all SR authors agree that the possession of enabling means is essential to freedom.[103] Hence, not all would agree that freedom is promoted by democracy even if democracy does provide men with a larger measure of enabling means than does any other form of government or organization of society. But this

---

[102] On the one hand, we find Russell saying that "democracy is a device—the best so far invented—for diminishing as much as possible the interference of governments with liberty" (*Political Ideals*, p. 30). On the other hand, Berlin tells us that he sees "no necessary connexion between individual liberty and democratic rule. The answer to the question 'Who governs me?' is logically distinct from the question 'How far does government interfere with me?'" (*Two Concepts of Liberty*, p. 14).

[103] See Ch. 14, Sect. 3, pp. 548 ff., *supra*.

fact would point to a conceptual issue about the freedom of self-realization not to an existential issue about democracy in relation to such freedom.[104]

The foregoing does not claim to exhaust the possible statements that can be made about the relation of democracy (conceived in a certain way) to the freedom of self-realization (conceived in a certain way). No need it be exhaustive; for it amply illustrates the point that authors who disagree about what democracy is or should be or about how SR freedom should be conceived are not in sufficient topical agreement to join issue about democracy in relation to freedom. And where they share the same conception of democracy and the same conception of SR freedom, they are almost bound to agree about the relation between the two.

Hence, it is not necessary to present documentary evidence of the opinions expressed on this subject in order to support our conclusion that no existential issue about democracy and freedom exists in the literature.[105]

7. THE ECONOMIC ISSUE

During the last hundred years, a great deal has been written about the economic conditions which promote or impair the individual's freedom, specifically his freedom of self-realization. The literature abounds with assertions that freedom is fostered and augmented by capitalism or socialism, free enterprise or the planned economy, private property or public ownership, fewer or more extensive government controls; and it is also filled with assertions to the contrary, that one or another economic system or organization diminishes or destroys freedom. One would, therefore, expect

---

[104] Similarly, it might be said that democratic institutions promote freedom because, more than any other social arrangements, they afford the individual with a greater range of alternatives. However, not all SR authors agree that having alternatives is essential to freedom. (See Ch. 14, Sect. 4, pp. 555 ff., *supra*.) Hence, not all would agree that freedom is promoted by democracy even if democracy does provide men with an enlarged range of alternatives. But this fact would point to a conceptual issue about SR freedom, not to an existential issue about democracy in relation to it.

[105] As we pointed out at the beginning of this section, the literature on this subject is so full of statements which defy precise interpretation that much of the documentation would consist of an attempt to show how few statements about democracy and freedom are clear enough to permit anyone to disagree with them. That would not only prove tiresome but it would hardly help to clarify the situation. In our opinion, the analysis of the possibilities, presented in this section, not only helps to clarify what has been written on this subject but also indicates real issues (about democracy or about freedom) even if there is none about democracy in relation to freedom.

to find a number of issues concerning the existential bearing of economic conditions on SR freedom. But what at first may appear to be issues turn out, upon careful examination, not to be issues at all, at least not existential issues about freedom.

The explanation of why this is so involves the same reasons which, in the preceding section, served to explain why, in all the discussion of democracy and freedom, we found no genuine existential issues. The two cases are quite similar. In both, we find that writers who are for or against a particular political or economic system disagree about who should have freedom rather than about the conditions which promote anyone's having it. And in both we also find disagreements about the political or economic institutions in question, but not about freedom. Let us briefly illustrate these two points with regard to the discussion of the economic aspects of freedom.

(i) It has been said again and again that property is essential to freedom.[106] Writers who have advocated the restriction of citizenship or suffrage to the propertied class have done so on the ground that the exercise of political liberty requires the economic independence which is conferred on men by their possession of income-producing property. Other writers whose concern has been with SR freedom rather than political liberty have maintained that property exempts a man from dependence on the wills of other men, that it enlarges the range of his opportunities for personal satisfaction, gives him a wider choice of alternatives to pursue, and in general enables him more fully to realize his desires.[107]

It has also been said that the institution of private property is inimical to freedom.[108] We know, of course, that such authors as Bakunin, Marx, and Engels call for the abolition of all private ownership of the means of production as an indispensable part of the revolutionary program that is

---

[106] See Hobhouse, *Elements of Social Justice*, pp. 154–55; Belloc, *Restoration of Property*, p. 18; Maritain, *Freedom in the Modern World*, Appendix I, p. 201; Simon, *Philosophy of Democratic Government*, pp. 247–48; Lippmann, *The Method of Freedom*, p. 100; Kirk, *The American Cause*, p. 108; R. J. S. Hoffman, *The Will to Freedom*, p. 77; F. A. Harper, *Liberty, A Path to Its Recovery*, pp. 33–34; Lecky, *Democracy and Liberty*, Vol. II, pp. 187–88; Simons, *Economic Policy for a Free Society*, pp. 27–28.

[107] See Salvadori, *Liberal Democracy*, pp. 39, 41; Jones, *The New Society*, pp. 45, 219. See also Cox, *Economic Liberty*, pp. 25, 200–1; Hirsh, *Democracy vs. Socialism*, pp. 244–45; *An Analysis of the Proposals and Conceptions of Socialism*, pp. 25, 43; Kirk, *The Intelligent Woman's Guide to Conservatism*, p. 107; Simon, *Philosophy of Democratic Government*, pp. 246–48, *Community of the Free*, p. 166.

[108] See Laski, *Liberty in the Modern State*, p. 38; Vail, "The Socialist Movement," in *The People Shall Judge*, Vol. II, pp. 114, 117, 121; Thomas, *After the New Deal, What?* pp. 180–81.

directed toward the establishment of the ideal society and collective freedom. But there are also SR authors who maintain that the rights of men must take precedence over the rights of property and that encroachments on the power and privileges of the propertied class in society are required for the sake of freedom.[109]

Hence, excluding authors who are talking about collective freedom, it would appear that we have a clear division of opinion about the relation of private property to SR freedom or to political liberty. But upon closer examination we find that the basic opposition here is on the question of who should have freedom, not on the question of property in relation to freedom. This can be shown as follows.

In the first place, we find that writers who advocate the preservation of property as essential to freedom fall into two groups. On the one hand, there are those who accept the existing division of society into men of property and the laboring classes and are concerned only with the freedom of the propertied few. To safeguard their liberties, these writers advocate the protection of their property rights.[110] On the other hand, there are those who are concerned with the freedom of all men and who, therefore, advocate the widest possible diffusion of private property. Agreeing that the possession of income-producing property contributes to an individual's freedom, they wish to see property in the hands of as many men as possible. In addition, they argue that such diffusion of property diffuses economic power and supports the diffusion of political power, which they regard as necessary for a free society. In their opinion, the concentrated ownership of property, either by a small class in society or by the state itself, concentrates both political and economic power in the hands of the few and subjects the rest to their will.[111]

If there is any disagreement between these two groups of writers, it is on the question of the distribution of freedom—whether it should be restricted to the few or extended to all. They do not disagree about property as an existential condition of freedom. Agreeing about that, they differ

---

[109] See Laski, *Liberty in the Modern State*, pp. 171–73, and *Grammar of Politics*, p. 149; Thomas, *After the New Deal, What?* p. 182; Vail, "The Socialist Movement," in *The People Shall Judge*, Vol. II, pp. 111–12.

[110] See Sumner, "The Challenge of Facts," in *The People Shall Judge*, Vol. II, p. 90. See also Chancellor Kent's remarks in the "Debate in the New York Constitutional Convention, 1821," in *ibid.*, Vol. I, p. 569.

[111] See Belloc, *Restoration of Property*, pp. 14, 17, 20–21, 27, 100, and *The Servile State*, pp. 7, 14; Simons, *Economic Policy for a Free Society*, pp. 7, 27–28, 105; Salvadori, *Liberal Democracy*, p. 40; Kirk, *The Intelligent Woman's Guide to Conervatism*, p. 72; Lippmann, *The Method of Freedom*, pp. 99–100, 103; Hewes, *Decentralize for Liberty*, p. 36; Mann, "The Importance of Universal, Free Public Education," in *The People Shall Judge*, Vol. I, pp. 591–92.

about whether the existing distribution of property should be preserved or modified.

In the second place, we find that writers who look upon property as inimical to freedom do not deny that the propertied class in society enjoy a freedom, or a degree of freedom, not shared by their less fortunate fellow men. They are, therefore, not denying that property contributes to the freedom of the individuals who are fortunate enough to possess it. But they are concerned with the freedom of all men, not the freedom of the fortunate few.

In this respect, they agree *normatively* with those defenders of property who advocate the widest possible diffusion of it for the sake of securing the freedom of all. But instead of advocating the diffusion of property (which they may not think feasible or which may not have occurred to them), they call for or endorse encroachments on the rights of property not only to reduce the power in the hands of the propertied few but also to secure the economic welfare of the working classes. While allowing property to remain in the hands of the few, they advocate the various welfare measures by which the non-propertied classes in society come to enjoy in some degree the economic advantages which property confers on the few. It is through the widest possible diffusion of these economic advantages that they hope to see the freedom of all promoted.

Here, then, we see a basic normative issue between those who think that freedom should be the exclusive privilege of the few (or that some should have much more freedom than others) and those who think that freedom should be the possession of all (or that all should enjoy freedom equally). That there is no existential issue concerning property as a condition of freedom can be seen in the universal agreement that the possession of property is one of the circumstances favorable to the possession of freedom. This is agreed upon by those who seek to defend the freedom of the propertied few and by those who wish to extend freedom to the propertyless many; and among the latter, it is agreed upon by those who advocate the diffusion of property as a means of diffusing freedom in society and by those who advocate encroachments on property as essential to the welfare program by which those without property will enjoy economic conditions as favorable (or almost as favorable) to freedom as property is.

The foregoing analysis applies to other economic factors. If we turn from property to such things as the free-enterprise system or the planned economy we find that a basic normative disagreement prevents us from aligning authors as opposed to one another on existential issues concerning these economic systems in relation to freedom. Authors who favor the free-enterprise system, with more or less unrestricted competition in the market, and authors who attack this system do not disagree *existentially* if the former are concerned only with the freedom of the few who, under competitive conditions, succeed in rising to the top of the economic heap, whereas the latter are concerned with the freedom of all, and therefore wish to introduce regulations and restrictions that will tend to equalize economic opportunities and advantages. Similarly, authors who favor the planned or controlled economy (as contrasted with a relatively unrestricted system of free enterprise) do not disagree *existentially* if the former advocate economic planning and controls for the sake of spreading freedom to all, and the latter opposes such measures because they will infringe on the freedom of the few to whose advantage unrestricted competition redounds.

But, it may be asked, can we not find existential issues among authors who agree on the normative question, i.e., who concur in the policy of freedom for all? We have seen, for example, that among authors who share this policy some advocate the widest possible diffusion of property and others advocate welfare measures which encroach on existing property rights. Is this not a disagreement about the function that property plays in the promotion of freedom? Similarly, among authors who agree that the ultimate goal is freedom for all, some think that the system of free enterprise rather than the planned economy serves best to achieve this end and others think the very opposite. Is this not a disagreement about which of these rival systems most effectively promotes SR freedom for all?

The answer to these questions and to others like them is negative. When we deal with authors who consider alternative economic policies or systems from the point of view of their efficacy in securing freedom for all, we find that their disagreement is about the way in which a particular economic system or policy works rather than about its effect on freedom. If they were to agree about the way it works, they would agree about its effect on freedom. Hence, such disagreements are primarily about the operation of the economic factors under consideration, and only secondarily about freedom. This brings us to the second of the two reasons why we have not been able to find any existential issues about the economic aspects of SR freedom. We turn now to a few clear illustrations of this second point.

(ii) We have already observed that authors who seek to promote the freedom of all differ in their approach to the problem of private property and its rights. On the one hand, there are those who think that the most widely diffused ownership of productive property will tend to secure the economic conditions of freedom for most men. On the other hand, there are those who think that the same goal is better served by the widest distribution of welfare benefits, to achieve which they unhesitatingly recommend whatever invasions on the rights of property may be necessary.

If the proponents of "welfare benefits" tell the proponents of "diffused property" that they doubt the possibility of diffusing property so that, in effect, every citizen is also a capitalist, the disagreement between them is about the feasibility of widespread ownership, not about the desirability of it, could it be achieved. We find in the literature nothing that even suggests a denial of the proposition that the diffusion of property (were it achievable) would be desirable for the sake of diffusing economic power and spreading freedom with it.

However, we do find among very recent writers grave doubts not only about the possibility of widespread ownership but even more basically about the importance or even reality of property under present conditions of technically advanced corporate capitalism. There is talk of a parapropri-etal society, i.e., one which has largely dispensed with the institution of property.[112] But if this raises a genuine issue, it is an issue about property and its place in our economy, not about property in relation to freedom. For these two propositions are not incompatible: (a) that, in a paraproprietal society (if one exists), freedom can be secured without reference to property; and (b) that, in a proprietary society of the kind that has existed, property contributes to the freedom of whatever individuals possess it.

Another illustration involves what at first appear to be incompatible propositions about socialism in relation to freedom. On both sides of this apparent issue are authors who hold that the political institutions of democracy are conducive to freedom for all. These writers are in agreement, furthermore, that no economic system can serve the cause of freedom unless it preserves and strengthens democratic institutions and processes. The question on which they divide, then, is whether socialism preserves and strengthens democracy, or weakens and destroys it.

They understand socialism to involve the public or state ownership and operation of all the means of production. It is this aspect of socialism which leads one group of writers to maintain that the consequent concentration of economic and political power in a central government, or its bureaucrats, must inevitably militate against democracy.[113] They are met with denials by those who think that democratic socialism is quite possible, in other words, that the public ownership of the means of production

---

[112] See Harbrecht, *Pension Funds and Economic Power*. Cf. also Berle, *Power Without Property*.
[113] See Hirsch, *Democracy vs. Socialism*, pp. 244–45, and *An Analysis of the Proposals and Conceptions of Socialism*, pp. 25, 54. Simons, *Economic Policy for a Free Society*, pp. 43–44, 52; Knight, *Freedom and Reform*, p. 203.

permits the citizens to avail themselves of democratic processes in regard to their common economic interests.[114]

The disagreement here is thus primarily about the way in which socialism functions politically. If all the writers with whom we are concerned were to agree that, as a matter of fact, socialism always leads to totalitarian government and cannot operate without it, they would also agree that socialism is inimical to SR freedom and destructive of political liberty. If, on the other hand, they were all to take the opposite view about socialism (that, as a matter of fact, it can be united with democracy), then they would also take the opposite view about the relation of socialism to SR freedom and political liberty. The disagreement about how socialism functions politically thus leads to a disagreement about its bearing on freedom; but the latter issue is derivative and inseparable from the former, and the former is not an issue about the existential conditions of freedom but about how socialism in fact operates.

In certain European circles there has recently appeared a tendency to revise the principles of socialism. The most striking departure from orthodox doctrine is the modification of the principle of public ownership or nationalization of *all* the means of production. Socialism, it is said, can permit some private ownership of capital and even allow private profits to be made from its operation. It requires only that private enterprises be controlled in such a way that they contribute to the general economic welfare. And socialism thus constituted, it is said, avoids that excessive concentration of economic power in the central government which endangers democracy.[115]

If those who are opposed to orthodox socialism were to consider this revised version of it, and if, furthermore, they were to agree that socialism, thus constituted, can operate democratically, they would then have to change their minds about the relation of socialism to freedom. If they continued to oppose socialism in the interests of freedom, the focus of their disagreement with the proponents of socialism would be on questions of fact about how socialism—of any variety—works out in practice.

Sometimes the problem of socialism vs. capitalism is not discussed in terms of public and private ownership of the means of production, but rather in terms of the planned or centrally operated economy, on the one hand, and the free enterprise or competitive economy, on the other. This affords us another and somewhat different illustration of the reason why

---

114 See Laski, *Liberty in the Modern State*, pp. 178, 184; Soule, *The Future of Liberty*, pp. 174–75; Clark, "Forms of Economic Liberty," in *Freedom, Its Meaning*, edited by Anshen, p. 322; Thomas, *The Future: Socialism?*, p. 156; Strachey, *Contemporary Capitalism*, pp. 313, 344–45, 350–52.
115 See C. A. R. Crosland, "The Future of the Left," in *Encounter*, Vol. 78, March 1960, pp. 3–12; F. R. Allemann, "Farewell to Marx," in *ibid.*, pp. 67–69.

these differences in economic points of view do not lead to existential issues about freedom.

In Chapter 14 we dealt with a number of conceptual issues about self-realization. We saw that there is some disagreement about whether the possession of enabling means is essential to an individual's freedom. A number of writers insist that a man is unfree only when he is coercively prevented from doing what he wishes; in the absence of external coercion or constraint he remains free even if he lacks the means he needs to carry out his purposes. Hence, when, in economic discussions, the question is raised whether the free enterprise or the planned economy is more effective in the production and distribution of goods, the significance of that question for freedom is seen in terms of enabling means.

Which economic system provides more men with an ampler supply of the economic means they need to satisfy their desires? This question can hardly lead to a disagreement about freedom between (a) authors who think that freedom depends on the possession of enabling means and (b) authors who think that it is unaffected by the lack of them. It can only lead to a disagreement between authors who agree that the possession of enabling means is essential to freedom. But even when we confine our attention to such authors, we find that their primary disagreement is about the way in which a free enterprise or a planned economy operates.

Those who think that the free-enterprise system is more effective in the production and distribution of economic goods will also think that it is more favorable to individual freedom than the planned or centrally managed economy is.[116] The proponents of the planned economy simply reverse the picture. For them it is the centrally managed economy that is more effective in the production and distribution of goods, with obvious consequences for freedom.[117]

A similar analysis can be made of differences of opinion about these two types of economic organization in relation to the range of economic alternatives—occupational or consumer choices—which they afford the members of a society.[118] Here, again, any disagreement must be confined to SR authors who maintain that having alternatives is essential to freedom. But when we restrict our attention to such authors, we find, here as before, that the primary disagreement is about how the two types of

[116] See Von Mises, *Socialism*, p. 195.
[117] See Laski, *Liberty in the Modern State*, p. 40; Soule, *The Future of Liberty*, p. 149; Thomas, *After the New Deal, What?* pp. 157, 183.
[118] For the position that a planned economy offers more alternatives, see Soule, *The Future of Liberty*, pp. 168–69; Thomas, *After the New Deal, What?* For the contrary view that a free-enterprise economy offers more alternatives, see Hayek, *The Road to Serfdom*, pp. 60–61, 92–94, 95, 199, 203; Simons, *Economic Policy for a Free Society*, pp. 3–4, 16, 41, 43.

economic organization operate with regard to this matter of economic alternatives. The question at issue is whether the planned economy or the free-enterprise system provides the greater range of alternatives to workers, producers, and consumers. If that question of fact could be settled, there would be no disagreement about which system is more favorable to freedom.

Chapter 16

THE NORMATIVE ISSUES
CONCERNING THE FREEDOM
OF SELF-REALIZATION

In Chapter 14, we enumerated four possible issues which are normative in the sense that they turn on questions of value or of policy with regard to freedom, i.e., questions about the *goodness* of freedom or about who *should* have it.[1] The four possible issues can be briefly indicated by the following questions.

(1) Do men have a natural right to freedom—either the freedom of self-realization or of political liberty?

(2) Should freedom of self-realization be conferred on all members of society or only on some?

(3) Is freedom of self-realization one of the basic human goods?

(4) Should political liberty be granted to all men or only to some?

Since political liberty is a special variant of SR freedom, we shall treat the issues concerning it along with the two issues—the second and third—which are exclusively about the freedom of self-realization.

Our aim here, as in the preceding chapters, is to determine which of these possible issues is real. Where real disagreement does exist, we shall present documentary evidence of it.

1. THE ISSUE ABOUT NATURAL RIGHTS

In all the great statements about the natural or inalienable rights of men, liberty is always included among the rights enumerated. This is true of enumerations that merely name a few exemplary rights as well as of those that try to be exhaustive. In the former case, it is sometimes property or estates that are conjoined with life and liberty or, as in the Declaration of Independence, it is the pursuit of happiness; but the right to liberty, like the right to life itself, is always mentioned.

[1] See *loc. cit.*, pp. 537–38, *supra*.

Hence, among authors who maintain that men have certain natural or inalienable rights, there is no disagreement about man's right to freedom. The fact that writers differ in their theories of natural law and natural rights (as do Hobbes and Locke, for example) leaves this point unchanged. To construct a real issue here, we would have to find authors who affirm the existence of natural rights, but who nevertheless deny that men are by nature entitled to freedom. What we find instead are writers who deny the existence of natural rights, for one reason or another.[2]

It is far from clear that the understanding of natural rights, on the part of those who affirm and those who deny their reality, is sufficiently alike for genuine disagreement in every case. But even if we may suppose that, as between certain authors at least, topical agreement does exist on the subject of natural rights, the resultant issue would be about natural rights in general, not about the right to freedom in particular.

Nevertheless, the positions which authors take on natural rights, among which the right to freedom is pre-eminent, have some significance for the three normative issues which remain to be considered.[3] Those who affirm that freedom belongs to man as a matter of natural right also hold that justice requires a society to confer freedom on all men. On the other hand, among the authors who maintain that a society would be well advised to give freedom only to some, we find writers who also deny that freedom belongs to any man by natural right. Similarly, among authors who regard freedom as an unqualified good, we find writers who regard freedom as one of the basic natural rights of man, and among authors who question the intrinsic goodness of freedom are writers who see nothing inherently unjust in witholding freedom from men. The position these authors take on the existence of natural rights provides part of the underlying reason for the answers they give to the normative questions about the value of freedom or about the just or wise policy for a society to follow in conferring freedom upon its members.[4]

In what has so far been said, we have used the word "freedom" without attempting to specify whether the freedom in question is the SR freedom which consists in a man's being able to act as he wishes, or the political liberty which consists in a man's being able to have his individual judgment

---

[2] Among these are two authors who specifically deny man's natural right to freedom. See Knight, *Freedom and Reform*, p. 305; and von Mises, *Socialism*, p. 194.

[3] As we shall see, authors can be found whose views are clearly enough in disagreement to make each of these possible issues real.

[4] In the sections to follow, we shall call attention to the views that authors hold on natural rights, wherever they are relevant to the positions writers take on the normative issue there being considered. As we shall see, not all authors who disagree about who should have freedom or whether it is a basic human good also express themselves on the subject of natural rights.

represented, through suffrage, in the formation of the public will—in the shaping of public policy or in the making of laws. Which of these freedoms is intended is seldom clear in that part of the literature which deals with natural rights. Sometimes, as when Hamilton refers to man's "inviolable right to personal liberty," or when Maritain speaks of "the right to personal freedom," the word "personal" suggests that the freedom obtains in the sphere of man's private life rather than in the sphere of his political activity. Sometimes, when we find the discussion of man's right to freedom imbedded in the context of a debate about the restriction or extension of suffrage, we may be justified in inferring that the freedom in question is political liberty, not the freedom of self-realization. But such inferences are at best precarious, and in most cases it is simply not possible to tell whether one or both freedoms are being declared man's by natural right.

However, we do know which authors have a conception of political liberty as a freedom that is quite distinct from being able to act as one wishes.[5] Hence, we shall look to them and them alone when we come, in Section 4, to construct the normative issue about who should have political liberty—all men or only some. And we shall confine our attention to authors who are concerned exclusively with SR freedom when, in Sections 2 and 3, we deal with the other two normative issues about freedom.

2. WHO SHOULD HAVE SR FREEDOM?

Issue is joined on this question by those, on the one hand, who say that society should aim at giving freedom to all, and by those, on the other hand, who say that society should confer freedom only upon those members of society who are worthy of it and will use it well. These conflicting policies represent the traditional positions of the liberal and the conservative with respect to the distribution of freedom, insofar as it is within the power of society to bestow it upon its members or to withhold it from them.

Adherents of each position introduce certain qualifications. The liberal usually recommends giving, not unlimited freedom to all without exception, but as much freedom to each as is consistent with giving the same measure of freedom to others; and he would make exceptions in the case of the insane, criminals, infants, etc. The conservative, in recommending that a full measure of freedom should be given only to those who are virtuous or wise enough to use it well, does not propose that all the rest be totally

[5] See Vol. I, Book II, Ch. 18; and see also, in this volume, Ch. 15, Sect. 6, pp. 587 ff., *supra*.

deprived of freedom, but only that they should be subject to direction or control, as children are, in all matters where they would be better off as wards of society than as masters of themselves.

These qualifications are variously expressed in the statements of the liberal and conservative points of view, to which we now turn. We shall present the conservative position first, and then the liberal position.[6]

(i) *The conservative position.* According to Burke, liberty is a blessing only to those who know how to use it; for the rest, it is a curse. "The effect of liberty to individuals," he writes, "is, that they may do what they please: we ought to see what it will please them to do, before we risk congratulations, which may be soon turned into complaints."[7] Far from being an unqualified boon to all men, liberty, in Burke's view, "without wisdom, and without virtue . . . is the greatest of all possible evils; for it is folly, vice, and madness, without tuition or restraint."[8] Burke's answer to the question, Who should have liberty? is clearly implied. He states it for us explicitly in the following passage:

> Men are qualified for civil liberty in exact proportion to their disposition to put moral chains upon their own appetites; in proportion as their love

[6] To the question, Who should have SR freedom? a third answer is, of course, possible. Against both those who say that all should have it and those who say that only some should, it can be contended that the ideal is for no one to be free. This view is, in fact, advanced by George Fitzhugh, who is as singular as he is extreme in his espousal of universal slavery as the ideal that best fits human nature and best serves the social welfare. By "slavery," Fitzhugh means the condition of being duty-bound and governed in all the major affairs of life. "Good men," he tells us, "obey superior authority, the laws of God, of morality, and of their country; bad men love liberty and violate them" (*Sociology for the South*, p. 30). "The world wants good government and plenty of it—not liberty" (*ibid.*). "We use the term 'free society,'" he goes on, "for want of a better; but, like the term 'free government,' it is an absurdity: those who are governed are not free—those who are free are not social" (*ibid.*, p. 33). Hence, he concludes, that "with thinking men, the question can never arise: Who ought to be free? Because no one ought to be free. All government is slavery" (*ibid.*, Ch. XVII, p. 170). It is worth noting here that Fitzhugh attacks the Declaration of Independence and the Virginia Bill of Rights for disseminating the false doctrine of natural rights. In his view, "Men are not created or born equal"; nor are they " 'born entitled to equal rights!' It would be far nearer the truth to say that 'some were born with saddles on their backs and others booted and spurred to ride them'—and the riding does them good. They need the reins, the bit, and the spur. No two men by nature are exactly equal or exactly alike. No institutions can prevent the few from acquiring rule and ascendancy over the many. Liberty and free competition invite and encourage the attempt of the stronger to master the weak and insure their success" (*ibid.*, p. 179). Accordingly, Fitzhugh recommends that government replace freedom for all—for the strong as well as the weak, to restrain the one and to direct the other.

[7] *Reflections on the Revolution in France*, in *The Works of Burke*, Vol. IV, p. 9.
[8] *Ibid.*, p. 272.

to justice is above their rapacity; in proportion as their soundness and so-
briety of understanding is above their vanity and presumption; in proportion
as they are more disposed to listen to the counsels of the wise and good, in
preference to the flattery of knaves.[9]

Like Burke, Calhoun recommends that liberty should be conferred only
on the few. "It is a reward to be earned," he writes, "not a blessing to be
gratuitously lavished on all alike—a reward reserved for the intelligent,
the patriotic, the virtuous and deserving—and not a boon to be bestowed
on a people too ignorant, degraded and vicious, to be capable either of
appreciating or of enjoying it."[10] Like Burke also, Calhoun is opposed to
the doctrine of natural rights, which proclaims all men equal in their
fundamental rights, among which is the right to freedom. "Instead . . . of
all men having the same right to liberty and equality, as is claimed by
those who hold that they are all born free and equal, liberty," according
to Calhoun, "is the noblest and highest reward bestowed on mental and
moral development, combined with favorable circumstances."[11]

Other writers echo the sentiments of Burke and Calhoun. Chancellor
Kent, for example, says that "liberty, rightly understood, is an inestimable
blessing, but liberty without wisdom, and without justice, is no better than
wild and savage licentiousness."[12] When he opposes universal suffrage on
the grounds that it jeopardizes "the rights of property and the principles
of liberty," he seeks to protect and preserve the liberties enjoyed by the
few, the propertied class, who alone, in his opinion, can be trusted with

[9] *Letter to a Member of the National Assembly, ibid.*, Vol. IV, p. 319. While
Burke maintains that only the virtuous few should be allowed the freedom to do
as they wish, he also speaks of freedom in another sense, which consists in being
protected by law, and this, he says, belongs by right to all. Referring to a proposed limitation on the applicability of *Habeas Corpus*, Burke writes: "liberty,
if I understand it at all, is a *general* principle, and the clear right of all the subjects within the realm, or of none. Partial freedom seems to me a most invidious
mode of slavery" (*A Letter to the Sheriffs of Bristol, ibid.*, Vol. III, p. 248).
There is no inconsistency here: freedom to do as one pleases requires virtue;
freedom in the sense of being protected by law does not. All are entitled to
the second kind of freedom, and to take it away from some endangers it for
all. It is just the other way around in the case of what is typically SR freedom: to
allow all to do as they please endangers the freedom of the few who deserve to
have it in the fullest measure.
[10] *Disquisition on Government,* in *Calhoun: Basic Documents,* pp. 63–64. To
attempt "to elevate a people in the scale of liberty, above the point to which
they are entitled to rise," Calhoun declares, "must ever prove abortive, and end
in disappointment., The progress of a people rising from a lower to a higher point
in the scale of liberty, is necessarily slow—and, by attempting to precipitate, we either
retard, or permanently defeat it" (*ibid.*).
[11] *Speech on the Oregon Bill, ibid.*, p. 294.
[12] *Debate in the New York Constitutional Convention,* 1821, in *The People Shall
Judge,* Vol. I, p. 570.

freedom.[13] Sumner, as we have seen in another connection, argues that to try to set up conditions of equality is to restrict the freedom of those who can use it best to get ahead in the competitive struggle of life. His advocacy of inequality clearly follows from his judgment that it is essential to freedom—not the freedom of all, but the freedom of the few who, by their virtues, talents, and industry, alone deserve to have it.[14] As Rossiter points out, this is typical of the conservative point of view, for "the conservative . . . when he is forced to choose between liberty and equality . . . throws his support unhesitatingly to liberty."[15] The position which the conservative takes on the issue about freedom and equality always reflects his underlying judgment that only the few deserve to have a full measure of freedom.[16]

(ii) *The liberal position*. In his essay *On Liberty*, J. S. Mill lays down the principle of universal liberty as one which calls for securing freedom of self-realization for every man to whatever extent that is compatible with an equal freedom on the part of all others. Society, according to Mill, is warranted in restricting the individual's liberty of action only "to prevent harm to others."[17] All of us, he says, should be free to pursue "our own good in our own way, so long as we do not attempt to deprive others of theirs, or impede their efforts to obtain it."[18] As later commentators observe, the liberal point of view is summed up "in the proposition that each individual should be free to think, speak, and act as he pleased, provided he did not thereby interfere with the like freedom on the part of anyone else."[19]

Mill adds a number of qualifications to his statement of the liberal principle. It is

> meant to apply only to human beings in the maturity of their faculties. We are not speaking of children, or of young persons below the age which the law may fix as that of manhood or womanhood. Those who are still in a state to require being taken care of by others, must be protected against their own actions as well as against external injury.[20]

[13] See *ibid.*, pp. 569–71.
[14] Ch. 15, Sect. 3, pp. 576–77, *supra*. It should be noted here that Sumner, like Burke and Calhoun, decries the notion of natural rights. See "The Challenge of Facts," in *The People Shall Judge*, Vol. II, p. 88.
[15] *Conservatism in America*, p. 24.
[16] See Ch. 15, Sect. 3, pp. 571–72, *supra*.
[17] *Loc. cit.*, Ch. I, p. 73.
[18] *Ibid.*, p. 75.
[19] University of California Associates in Philosophy, *Knowledge and Society*, p. 269. The ideal, they go on to say, envisages that "everyone should be free, provided he does not infringe upon the like freedom of others" (*ibid.*, p. 270).
[20] *On Liberty*, Ch. I, p. 73.

Furthermore, he continues,

> For the same reason, we may leave out of consideration those backward
> states of society in which the race itself may be considered as in its nonage.
> . . .. Liberty, as a principle, has no application to any state of things anterior
> to the time when mankind have become capable of being improved by free
> and equal discussion.[21]

Then, however, "compulsion, either in the direct form or in that of
pains and penalties for non-compliance, is no longer admissible as a
means to their own good, and justifiable only for the security of others."[22]

Other liberal writers advocate freedom for all on the grounds that each
individual is secure in his freedom only when all are. Hobhouse, for
example, declares that "if any are to be truly and morally free, all must be
free."[23] According to Laski, "There is no liberty if special privilege restricts
the franchise to a portion of the community."[24] Freedom cannot exist, he
maintains "in the presence of special privilege," which is "incompatible
with freedom because [freedom] belongs to all alike in their character as
human beings."[25] Similarly, Tawney points out that the rights which are
essential to freedom must be such as to secure the liberties of all, not
merely of a minority. A society is free, he tells us, "only in so far as all the
elements composing it are able in fact, not merely in theory, to make the
most of their powers, to grow to their full stature, to do what they conceive
to be their duty, and—since liberty should not be too austere—to have
their fling when they feel like it."[26]

As we have seen, Hobhouse, Laski, and Tawney are among the writers
who maintain that inequality is incompatible with freedom precisely be
cause they espouse the view that all men are equally entitled to be free.[27]
In this connection, Max Hirsch's statement of the "law of equal freedom"
must be noted: that "everyone shall be free to exercise such of his faculties
as he pleases . . . provided his resulting activities do not infringe the equal
rights of others."[28] The connection between freedom and equality has
been so often reiterated in the last hundred years that, in the opinion of E.
H. Carr, "hardly anyone openly contests any longer . . . that freedom
means freedom for all and therefore equality."[29]

---

[21] *Ibid.* Cf. *Representative Government*, Ch. I, pp. 178–79.
[22] *On Liberty*, pp. 73–74.
[23] *Elements of Social Justice*, p. 185.
[24] *Liberty in the Modern State*, Ch. III, Sect. I, p. 159.
[25] *A Grammar of Politics*, Ch. IV, pp. 149–50.
[26] "We Mean Freedom," in *The Attack*, p. 84.
[27] See Ch. 15, Sect. 3, pp. 572–75, *supra*. Simons and Knight share this view. See
ibid., p. 575, *supra*. However, Knight denies that freedom is a natural right. See
Freedom and Reform, p. 305.
[28] *Democracy vs. Socialism*, Part III, Ch. VIII p. 244.
[29] *The New Society*, p. 108.

Advocacy of freedom for all is not limited, however, to the liberal tradition of the last hundred years. In a sense, it goes back to Hobbes and Locke, for whom it follows from their doctrine of natural rights.[30] And in still another tradition we find Jacques Maritain and Msgr. John A. Ryan claiming personal freedom for all men as a matter of natural right.[31]

3. IS SR FREEDOM A BASIC HUMAN GOOD?

Certain authors, as we have seen in another connection, condemn or deplore the notion that it is good to be able to act as one wishes. In their view, indulging one's desires or giving vent to one's inclinations is morally reprehensible. It would appear, therefore, that for such writers as Plato, Aristotle, Spinoza, Rousseau, Kant, and Hegel, the freedom of self-realization, far from being a basic human good, is intrinsically evil. But we must remember that for these authors—and for other writers who think that man's freedom consists in being able to will or act as he ought, not to do as he pleases—self-realization is not truly freedom. The sharp line which they draw between liberty and license, or between true freedom and the counterfeit of it, says in effect that self-realization has no claim to the honorific title of freedom. They do not say that it is truly freedom and, at the same time, detrimental or injurious to those who possess it. Hence, these authors are not parties to an issue about the value of SR freedom in the special controversy about that subject.[32]

Since the term "freedom" is generally honorific, it might be supposed that any writer who regards self-realization as genuine freedom would also

[30] For Hobbes, the most fundamental "right of nature . . . is the liberty which each man has, to use his own power, as he will himself, for the preservation of his own nature; that is to say, of his own life (*Leviathan*, Part I, Ch. 14, p. 99). The individual never surrenders this natural right, nor is it abrogated by his becoming a member of the commonwealth. Locke similarly believes that men are "by nature all free, equal, and independent," and have "a title to perfect freedom" and a right to "life, liberty, and estate" (*Civil Government*, pp. 56, 63). And Hayek says that "the argument for the freedom of some . . . applies to the freedom of all" (*The Constitution of Liberty*, p. 32).

[31] See Maritain, *The Rights of Man and Natural Law*, pp. 71, 79–80; Ryan, "Religion as the Basis of the Postulates of Freedom," in *Freedom, Its Meaning*, pp. 479–81. Cf. also "Forms of Economic Liberty and What Makes Them Important," in *ibid.*, p. 317, where John M. Clark declares that "there is much to be said for the contention that liberty of some sort *is* a natural right in the sense that it is such a vital need of humanity that it cannot be denied without serious or even disastrous social consequences."

[32] They are parties to an issue about SR freedom in the general controversy, for they deny that circumstantial self-realization is admissible as a kind of human freedom. See Ch. 4, *supra*.

regard it as good for men to possess. Were that the case, there would be no disagreement about the value of SR freedom in human life. But we have found one author—Fitzhugh—who seems to have no other meaning for "freedom" except "doing as one pleases" and who, at the same time, condemns such freedom as wholly destitute of value for man.[33] And we have found other writers, such as Burke, Calhoun, and Sumner, who also conceive freedom in the SR sense of that term, but do not look upon it as an unqualified good. The picture is completed by a fairly large number of SR authors who praise such freedom as unquestionably good.

Hence, it would appear that we have a three-sided issue here, constituted by the following answers to the question whether SR freedom is good for men: (i) No, not at all; (ii) Yes, under certain conditions; and (iii) Yes, without qualification. But a moment's consideration also reveals that these three answers are connected with the three answers given to the question, Who should have SR freedom? (i) Fitzhugh says that no one should have it; (ii) conservatives, such as Burke, Calhoun, and Sumner, maintain that only the virtuous or wise should have it; and (iii) liberals, such as J. S. Mill, Hobhouse, Laski, and others, contend that freedom should be given to all.[34]

The connection between the two issues—this one and the one treated in the preceding section—is plain. The way in which an author evaluates SR freedom constitutes the reason for his answer to the question about who should have it. If such freedom is wholly evil, then, of course, no one should have it. If it is good, but only with the qualification that it be in the hands of those who have enough virtue or wisdom to use it well, then, similarly, it follows that society would be well-advised to confer such freedom, in full measure, on only the virtuous or wise. Finally, if it is good without qualification, then a benevolent or just society could hardly adopt any policy except one of promoting freedom for all.

Sufficient documentation has already been given of Fitzhugh's extreme position and also of the conservative position exemplified in the views of Burke, Calhoun, and Sumner. Their answer to the question about the value of SR freedom is intermingled with their answer to the question about who should have it. Other conservative writers might be quoted as sharing the view so eloquently set forth by Burke, but their general agreement with Burke is too well known to need lengthy documentation.[35]

[33] "Liberty," he declares, "is an evil which government is intended to correct" (*Sociology for the South*, p. 170). Liberty, according to Fitzhugh, degrades men, while slavery saves them from such degradation. See *ibid.*, p. 37.

[34] See Sect. 2, pp. 608–10, *supra*.

[35] In the writings of contemporary conservatives, one of the clearest statements reflecting Burke's views is that of Russell Kirk: "*Freedom* as an abstraction is the liberty in whose name crimes are committed. Freedom, as realized in the prescriptive,

The situation is very much the same in the case of the liberals. We find that certain authors praise freedom as an end in itself as well as a means to other goods.[36] In contrast, some writers think that the goodness of freedom consists solely in its serving as a means in the pursuit of happiness or in the fullest development of the individual.[37] But this difference of opinion does not affect their common judgment that freedom is, without qualification, good for men to possess, and, hence, that every man should have access to the fullest measure of it which is compatible with the good of all and the welfare of society.[38]

4. WHO SHOULD HAVE POLITICAL LIBERTY?

The question with which we are here concerned parallels the one treated in Section 2. As that issue was constituted by the conflicting recommendations that SR freedom should be reserved for the few or extended to all, so this issue is constituted by a similar conflict in policies. There are authors who have the view that only some men, whose competence is marked by social or economic position in society, should be admitted to the status of enfranchised citizens, for only they can be trusted to exercise the political liberty which suffrage confers upon men who, as citizens, can

---

separate, limited, balanced, well-defined rights of persons and groups, operating within a state governed by moral principle, is the quality which makes it possible for men to become truly human" (*Commonweal*, Jan. 13, 1956, p. 373). Kirk also asserts that "the freedom of the few who really deserve freedom—and they are fewer in our time than ever they were before, I am inclined to believe—is infinitely precious; and in the long run, the security and contentment of the whole of humanity depend upon the survival of that freedom for a few" (*ibid.*, p. 373). Cf. Rossiter, *Conservatism in America*, p. 58.

[36] Bertrand Russell, for example, declares in one place that "freedom is the greatest of political goods" (*Roads to Freedom*, p. 121); and in another, that "liberty . . . must always remain a *sine qua non* of other political goods" ("Freedom and Government," in *Freedom, Its Meaning*, p. 260). Cf. Laski, *Liberty in the Modern State*, pp. 88, 95; Hobhouse, *Elements of Social Justice*, pp. 71, 87; Knight, *Freedom and Reform*, pp. 4, 174, 190, 340, 372–73; Joad, *Liberty Today*, pp. 75–76, 117–18; Beard, "Freedom in Political Thought," in *Freedom, Its Meaning*, pp. 300–1; Jones, *The Challenge of Liberty*, p. 6.

[37] Thus, J. S. Mill considers liberty as "the only unfailing and permanent source of improvement" (*On Liberty*, Ch. III, p. 128); and he maintains that "genius can only breathe freely in an *atmosphere* of freedom (*ibid.*, p. 122). See *ibid.*, *passim*; and cf. Sidgwick, *Elements of Politics*, p. 44; Malinowski, *Freedom and Civilization*, pp. 29, 335; Belloc, *The Restoration of Property*, pp. 21–22, 27; Hayek, *The Road to Serfdom*, p. 240, *The Constitution of Liberty*, pp. 3, 6; Cox, *Economic Liberty*, p. 1; Adam Smith, *The Wealth of Nations*, p. 634; Hoffman, *The Will to Freedom*, p. 76.

[38] Not all of the authors mentioned in fn. 36 and 37, *supra.*, explicitly express themselves on the question of who should have SR freedom; but their position on that question is certainly implied by their unqualified estimate of the goodness of such freedom.

actively participate in self-government. Other writers believe that, with the exception of those disqualified by immaturity, pathological condition, or criminal turpitude, all human beings, regardless of wealth, sex, color, or creed, should be admitted to citizenship and given the political liberty that flows from suffrage.

Not all writers who take opposite positions on the question of restricting or extending the franchise affirm political liberty as a distinct and separate freedom. Those who are usually classified as conservatives do not of necessity espouse the view that political liberty is a privilege to be enjoyed only by some men; and those who are usually classified as liberals do not necessarily espouse the opposite view that it is the right of all. But while conservatives generally advocate or defend a restricted franchise, many of them do not think of suffrage as conferring a special freedom, distinct from the freedom of self-realization. The same holds true of liberals who, for the most part, advocate extensions of the franchise. Only a few of them see suffrage as the source of a freedom that is distinct from a man's ability to act as he wishes.[39]

Furthermore, not all authors who hold a conception of political liberty, and conceive it as quite distinct from SR freedom, also explicitly take a position on the question of suffrage. Aquinas, Marsilius, Locke, and Montesquieu, for example, do not speak out either for a definitely restricted franchise *or* for universal suffrage. Nevertheless, there may be other indications of where they stand on the question of who should have political liberty.

It is necessary, therefore, to deal primarily with the few writers who, in addition to being PL authors, also address themselves to the question of who should have political liberty and recommend a restricted franchise or universal suffrage because they wish to reserve such freedom for the few or grant it to all. As for the remaining PL authors, we shall try to indicate, so far as we can, on which side of this issue their sympathies tend to align them. Using the terms "oligarchical" and "democratic" to name the opposed positions, we shall first present the oligarchical view, and then the democratic.

(i) *The oligarchical position.* The classic statement of this point of view about political liberty is to be found in Aristotle's *Politics.* We know, of course, that Aristotle makes a sharp distinction between those who are intended by nature to be free and those who are intended by nature to be slaves.[40] We also know that he regards women, even those who are

---

[39] See Vol. I, Book II, Ch. 17; and see also, in this volume, Ch. 6, *supra.*, esp. pp. 160 ff.
[40] See *op. cit.*, Book I, Ch. 3–7.

freeborn, as the political inferiors of men.[41] From the point of view of modern democrats, these two points alone suffice to identify Aristotle as an opponent of universal suffrage. But, in his advocacy of restricting citizenship to the wellborn and wealthy, even among those males who are intended by nature to be free, Aristotle identifies himself as a prime exponent of the oligarchical position in politics.

In the context of defining the status and the virtues of citizenship, Aristotle deals with the question about laborers, mechanics, and the lower classes generally. Even if they are not resident-aliens or foreigners, he sees "no more absurdity in excluding them than in excluding slaves and freedmen." In his own view, "the best form of state will not admit them to citizenship." Their occupations, he explains, prevent them from acquiring the virtues requisite for citizenship as he conceives it. "Our definition of the virtue of a citizen," he says, "will not apply . . . to every free man as such, but only to those who are freed from necessary services." Only those who have enough property to exempt them from toil also have enough free time to develop the requisite virtues; they alone can engage in the leisure activity of politics. As for the rest, Aristotle simply says that "we cannot consider all those to be citizens who are necessary to the existence of the state." He mentions children as among those who are necessary to the existence of the state, but some of them, after all, will grow up to be citizens. By "the necessary people," he mainly has in mind those who never will nor can become citizens—"either slaves who minister to the wants of individuals, or mechanics and labourers who are the servants of the community."[42]

Toward the end of his treatise, Aristotle returns to the problem of the ideal state. In that context, he again considers the proper qualifications for citizenship. He repeats the point that "husbandmen, craftsmen, and labourers of all kinds are necessary to the existence of states," but they are not parts of it, i.e., not participants in it as citizens, not members of its ruling class.[43] Under "the best form of government," he tells us, "the citizens must not lead the life of mechanics or tradesmen, for such a life is ignoble and inimical to virtue. Neither must they be husbandmen, since leisure is necessary both for the development of virtue and the performance of political duties."[44] They have neither the free time nor the competence to take part in ruling and being ruled in the manner appro-

---

[41] See *ibid.*, Book I, Ch. 2, 1252ª24–ᵇ8; Ch. 5, 1254ᵇ13–16; Ch. 12.

[42] *Ibid.*, Book III, Ch. 5, 1278ª1–12. Cf. *ibid.*, Book I, Ch. 7, 1255ᵇ35–37, where Aristotle says: "Those who are in a position which places them above toil have stewards who attend to their households while they occupy themselves with philosophy or with politics."

[43] *Ibid.*, Book VII, Ch. 9, 1329ª35–36.

[44] *Ibid.*, 1328ᵇ35–1329ª2.

priate to politically free men. As Aristotle views the world in which he lives, both the leisure and the virtue requisite for citizenship are accessible only to men of property. "The ruling class," he therefore declares, "should be the owners of property, for they are citizens, and the citizens of a state should be in good circumstances; whereas mechanics or any other class which is not a producer of virtue have no share in the state."[45]

Those who advocate a widely extended franchise or universal suffrage always do so with certain exceptions which they regard as justifiable on grounds of incompetence: the immature, the feeble-minded or insane, and convicted felons are not qualified for active participation in political life. The argument for a restricted franchise, as stated by Aristotle, similarly makes incompetence the reason for excluding a large number of human beings from citizenship. Those who are by nature slaves are by nature unfit for political liberty; women, too, are intended by nature to be ruled; the laboring classes—the artisans, mechanics, and husbandmen—may include men who are not by nature slaves, but their servile occupations and the exhaustion of their time and energies in toil render them unable to take part in political affairs. In other words, political liberty must be withheld both from those whose natural inferiority makes them incompetent and from those whose conditions of life and work have the same effect.

We pointed out earlier that a number of authors who have some conception of political liberty as the freedom which men have when they participate in self-government do not explicitly address themselves to the question of suffrage. Nevertheless, we can use Aristotle's statement of the oligarchical position to determine on which side of this issue their sympathies lie. Thus, if we use the disfranchisement of women as a sign, we need have no hesitation in inferring where such PL authors as Aquinas, Marsilius, Locke, Montesquieu, and Hamilton stand. In the case of Aquinas and Montesquieu, we have further evidence of a discrimination between those portions of mankind who are qualified for political liberty and those who are not. Aquinas distinguishes between people who are in a condition to be free (i.e., "able to make their own laws") and people who are not in that condition.[46] And Montesquieu emphatically declares that the Oriental peoples, as contrasted with those of Europe, are slavish by nature, unfit for political liberty, and in need of despotic government.[47] Finally, if we use insistence on a property qualification for citizenship, or other means of excluding the laboring classes from suffrage, we have sufficient evidence in the writings of Alexander Hamilton to classify

[45] *Ibid.*, 1329ª18–22.
[46] *Summa Theologica*, Part I–II, Q. 97, A. 3, Reply 3.
[47] *The Spirit of Laws*, Book XVIII, Ch. 6, p. 321.

him as an oligarch by that test, as well as by reference to his views on women and slaves.[48]

Another PL author—Kant—remains to be considered before we turn to writers who take the other side of this issue. He presents us with a difficult problem of interpretation.

On the one hand, Kant appears to favor a restricted franchise: he excludes from active citizenship all those whose economic or social status makes them dependent on others.

> The apprentice of a merchant or a tradesman, a servant who is not in the employ of the state, a minor (*naturaliter vel civiliter*), all women, and generally everyone who is compelled to maintain himself not according to his own industry, but as it is arranged by others (the state excepted) are without civil personality, and their existence is only, as it were, incidentally included in the state.[49]

Such human beings, Kant writes, are "mere subsidiaries of the commonwealth and not active members of it, because they are of necessity commanded and protected by others, and consequently possess no political self-sufficiency in themselves." They are "not qualified to exercise the right of suffrage under the constitution and to be full citizens of the state." As "mere passive subjects under its protection," they are without political liberty.[50]

On the other hand, Kant holds that "the laws of natural freedom and equality" require us to look forward to a time when all human beings (except, perhaps, minors and the pathologically disabled) will possess the economic, social, or cultural advantages which fit them for the political equality and liberty that should belong to all as a matter of natural right. For the present, however, all that the disadvantaged classes in society have "a right in their circumstances to claim" is that "whatever be the mode in which the positive laws are enacted, these laws must not be contrary to the natural laws that demand the freedom of all the people and the equality that is conformable thereto." In other words, natural law imposes upon society the duty to make it "possible for them to raise themselves from this passive condition in the state to the condition of active citizenship."[51] When, in the course of time, economic and social conditions

[48] See, for instance, *The Basic Ideas of Alexander Hamilton*, pp. 104–5; *The Mind of Alexander Hamilton*, pp. 114–15.
[49] *Science of Right*, p. 437.
[50] *Ibid.* Though such individuals are "entitled to demand to be treated by all the other citizens according to the laws of natural freedom and equality, as *passive* parts of the state . . . it does not follow," Kant maintains "that they ought themselves to have the right to deal with the state as active members of it, to recognize it, or to take action by way of introducing certain laws" (*ibid.*).
[51] *Ibid.*

are progressively amelioriated, man's natural right to political liberty and political equality may be fully realized.

Since he asserts that all human beings are entitled to political liberty as a matter of natural right, Kant is in principle a democrat. But he also asserts that under certain conditions, such as those existing in his own day, natural right must be denied to persons who, lacking independence in their economic and social relations, are not in a position to exercise political liberty. To this extent, he would appear to side with Aristotle. But Aristotle thinks that some men and all women are unalterably inferior in nature. In contrast, Kant thinks that no one is unalterably inferior in nature, but only that some individuals must, as a matter of political prudence, be deprived of political liberty by reason of inferior conditions. Furthermore, where Aristotle gives us no indication that he regards the inferior condition of the working classes as remediable, Kant plainly indicates that he looks upon the dependent condition of women and of certain types of workers as essentially alterable, i.e., capable of progressive amelioration and eventual elimination.

In view of these differences, it seems reasonable to construe Kant as a democrat, with the qualification that he is a gradualist. He looks upon a restricted suffrage as a temporary expedient, justified by circumstances which prevent certain classes in society from being able to make good use of political liberty. He calls for the alteration of these circumstances so that all human beings can have the political liberty which is everyone's by natural right.

If we take Kant as a democrat, with this qualification added, then, perhaps, J. S. Mill deserves to be treated in the same way. Whether Mill affirms a political liberty as a freedom distinct from self-realization is, as we have seen, somewhat doubtful.[52] But if we resolve the doubt in favor of his affirming the two freedoms as quite distinct, then there can be no question about where he stands on this issue. He is for universal suffrage, for the extension of the franchise to women and to the working classes in society, even though he also recommends the safeguard of a graduated suffrage which would give superior men more weight in public affairs.[53] Nevertheless, he looks upon his proposal of a universal though unequal suffrage as one which would secure the political liberty of all—the minority who would be outvoted unless they have plural votes, as well as the majority who do not need plural votes because they have the weight of numbers.[54]

[52] See Vol. I, Book II, Ch. 18, pp. 337–58 and 367 fn. 121.
[53] See *Representative Government*, Ch. VIII.
[54] See *ibid.*, p. 288, where he speaks of "the emancipation of those who already have votes, but whose votes are useless, because always outnumbered."

So far, Mill is clearly a democrat in his view on the question of who should have political liberty. But he is also a gradualist, though not in the same way as Kant. Where Kant temporarily excludes certain classes in a particular society from active citizenship and looks to their eventual emancipation, Mill recommends despotic government as a temporary expedient for whole peoples who are still in a barbarous or primitive condition. At the same time, he thinks it is the despot's duty to exercise a benevolent tutelage that will eventually raise his subjects to the point where they can be safely trusted with self-government. Hence, Mill, like Kant, envisages a time when political liberty will be as universal as mankind.[55]

(ii) *The democratic position.* Construing Kant and Mill as PL authors who think that all men should eventually have the political liberty that is rightfully theirs by nature, we must now add, on this side of the issue, the names of Maritain, Simon, Sidgwick, Hobhouse, and Jaspers.[56]

The strongest statement of the argument for universal suffrage and, therewith, the bestowal of political liberty upon all is to be found in Jacques Maritain. "The right of suffrage for all adult citizens," according to Maritain, is based on the fact "the human person as such is called upon to participate in political life."[57] This, in his opinion, is the interpretation which must be placed upon "the famous saying of Aristotle that man is a political animal." It does not mean merely "that man is naturally made to live in society"; it means "that man naturally asks to lead a political life and to participate actively in the life of the political community. It is upon this postulate of human nature that political liberties and political rights rest, and particularly the right of suffrage."[58]

Maritain continues:

[55] See *ibid.*, Ch. II, pp. 197–99. That Mill regards even the most benevolent despotism as, at best, a temporary expedient, he makes quite clear when he says of the notion that the rule of a wise despot is ideal: "I look upon this as a radical and most pernicious misconception of what good government is" (*ibid.*, Ch. III, p. 202).

[56] Tom Paine should be mentioned also, for he regards suffrage as a primary human right, and says that "the only ground upon which the exclusion from the right of voting is consistent with justice would be to inflict it as a punishment for a certain time upon those who should propose to take away that right from others" (*Dissertation on First Principles of Government*, p. 165). However, it is doubtful whether, in the eighteenth century, Paine would have recommended the extension of the franchise to women. It is even more doubtful that Major Rainborough and Sir John Wildman had women in mind when, in 1643, they proposed to General Cromwell and Colonel Ireton that, after their victory over King Charles, universal manhood suffrage should be established in England.

[57] *Christianity and Democracy*, pp. 69–70.

[58] *The Rights of Man and Natural Law*, p. 84.

For if it is true that political authority has as its essential function the direction of free men towards the common good, it is normal for these free men to choose by themselves those who shall have the function of leading them: this is the most elementary form of active participation in political life. That is why universal suffrage, by means of which every adult human person has, as such, the right to make his opinion felt regarding the affairs of the community by casting his vote in the election of the people's representatives and the officers of the State—that is why universal suffrage has a wholly fundamental political and human value and is one of those rights which a community of free men can never give up.[59]

In somewhat the same vein, Hobhouse declares that "a community is regarded as politically free on condition, not only that it is independent of others, but that its own constitution rests on a wide if not a universal suffrage.[60] His reason is simply that "political freedom is . . . the right of every man bound by decisions to contribute whatever it is in him to contribute to the making and remaking of those decisions."[61] Hence, a politically free society is one in which every member "is called on for [his] contribution, and no decision is taken till [each] has made [himself] heard and felt."[62] Jaspers similarly insists that every member of society has a "right to participate in the life of the whole." Hence, in his view, "free conditions are . . . possible only through *democracy*, that is, where it is possible for everyone to play a part in forming the collective will."[63]

Sidgwick and Yves Simon are a little more qualified in their endorsement of universal suffrage. Agreeing that only those who are governed with their own consent are politically free, Sidgwick adopts the principle of universal suffrage with a number of qualifications. "When we speak of the consent of 'the governed,'" he says, "we never mean to imply that all the human beings governed are to have a voice in the matter. The most ardent democrat does not wish to give votes to lunatics, criminals, or infants." Sidgwick then refers to the fact, true in his day, that "the modern movement towards democracy has, in the main, stopped short of enfranchising women." But, in his own opinion, "this latter exclusion . . . is hardly defensible except on grounds that would justify limitations going much further."[64] Sidgwick himself proposes a number of other exclusions, each of which he thinks is justified by the special circumstances of the

---

[59] *Ibid.*, p. 85. Cf. *Ransoming the Time*, pp. 46–47, 50; *Scholasticism and Politics*, Ch. IV, pp. 107–8, 112–13; *Man and the State*, pp. 25–26, 59, 101; and "The Conquest of Freedom" in *Freedom, Its Meaning*, p. 642.

[60] *The Elements of Social Justice*, p. 88.

[61] *Ibid.*

[62] *Ibid.*, p. 186. Cf. *Liberalism*, pp. 235–36.

[63] *The Origin and Goal of History*, p. 161.

[64] *Elements of Politics*, p. 611. Cf. *ibid.*, pp. 385 ff.

case.[65] He argues against the disqualification of individuals on the grounds of poverty or ignorance,[66] but he also thinks that exclusion from citizenship on the basis of race may be justified; and that voluntary disfranchisement should be allowed.[67] These things raise some doubt about whether Sidgwick's sympathies are wholly on the democratic side of this issue; and that doubt seems to be strengthened by his flat rejection of the doctrine that citizenship, suffrage, and political liberty belong to everyone as a matter of natural right.[68]

For Yves Simon, the citizen is a politically free man, for he "retains, in his relation to authority, the character of an autonomous agent."[69] Though he tells us that "taken by itself, universal suffrage does not constitute a sufficient guaranty of democratic freedom," he also acknowledges that "the principle of universal suffrage has won an almost axiomatic position in the political conscience of peoples."[70] But, in his opinion, "the decisive argument in favor of universal suffrage [is] the need for a distribution of power to those who enjoy no distinction apart from their having number on their side." Unless the power of self-government is placed in the hands of the people as a whole, the many will be at a disadvantage, and political freedom, which should be every man's by natural right, will be the privilege of the few.[71]

[65] See *ibid.*, pp. 377–94.
[66] See *ibid.*, p. 383.
[67] See *ibid.*, pp. 387–88. On the second of these two points, cf. *ibid.*, p. 379.
[68] See *ibid.*, p. 377.
[69] *Philosophy of Democratic Government*, p. 75.
[70] *Ibid.*, p. 77.
[71] See *ibid.*, p. 98.

Chapter 17

THE ISSUES CONCERNING
THE FREEDOM OF SELF-PERFECTION

A large number of authors affirm a freedom which is possessed by those alone whose state of mind or character enables them to will as they ought or to live in accordance with an ideal that befits the nature of man. We have, in various places, listed these authors and presented documentary evidence that they are in topical agreement about the freedom thus identified.[1]

That they differ in a multitude of respects will be obvious at once to anyone acquainted with the philosophical or theological doctrines which they represent, for the doctrines include such radically diverse points of view as those advanced by Plato, Spinoza, and Freud; by Kant, Hegel, Whitehead, and Dewey; by Leibniz, Rousseau, Bradley, and Russell; by neo-Platonists such as Plotinus and Boethius; by Roman Stoics such as Seneca, Epictetus, and Marcus Aurelius; and by Christian theologians of different persuasions, such as Augustine and Aquinas, on the one hand, and Luther and Calvin, on the other.[2] The fundamental differences which divide these authors concern the principles of morality, the nature of man, and the relation of man to God and to the state; but, as we have pointed out, these differences do not affect the common understanding of the acquired freedom of self-perfection which these authors share.[3] They do result, however, in a number of differences in the theories advanced by these authors concerning SP freedom.

We have surveyed these differences in Volume I, and there given docu-

[1] See Vol. I, Book II, Ch. 6 and 15. Enumerations of SP writers can be found there on pp. 134, 250–51, and 592–94. In the present volume, a number of additional SP authors were mentioned: see Ch. 5, pp. 106–7, *supra*. The list can undoubtedly be even further extended, as, for example, by the inclusion of Kierkegaard in this company. See *Works of Love*, pp. 32–33; *Either/Or*, Vol. II, pp. 179–81; *Journals*, ⁂1051, pp. 371–72; *Stages on Life's Way*, p. 323.

[2] Still other divergent points of view are represented by such authors as Epicurus, Anselm, Maimonides, Locke, Montesquieu, T. H. Green, Kierkegaard, Santayana, Maritain, Barth, Tillich, Marcel, Croce, and Berdyaev.

[3] See Vol. I, Book II, Ch. 6, 15, and esp. 16.

mentary evidence of them. On the basis of that evidence, it is possible to construct three issues about SP. To do so, we must formulate the questions to which we can find opposite answers given by SP authors. The authors themselves show no awareness that they are taking one side or the other on the questions at issue. Each presents his own theory of man's acquired freedom of self-perfection without any indication that he is acquainted with conflicting theories of the same freedom. He does not refer to other writers with whom he disagrees on this point or that; and it follows, 'of course, that he does not argue for his own view and against that of others.

We can illustrate what has just been said by taking one point on which the evidence clearly enough shows that SP authors do disagree. The point concerns the relation of favorable circumstances to man's enjoyment of SP freedom. The question can be posed in the following way: Does a man's freedom of self-perfection depend on external circumstances which affect his being able to execute what he wills? Is it diminished or removed by circumstances which prevent him from enacting his will; or is the good man, who is able to will as he ought, just as free even though external circumstances prevent him from acting in accordance with his will?

The question arises from the fact that a number of SP authors plainly indicate that man's freedom of self-perfection is entirely beyond the influence of external circumstances. In the view of such writers as Philo, Plotinus, the Roman Stoics, and Kant, the only thing that matters is the internal state of mind or character which is indispensable to a man's being able to will as he ought. It makes no difference whether he can, in addition, carry out his will in overt action. We can be reasonably sure that, if they were asked the question whether SP freedom depended in any way on external circumstances, they would answer, "No, not at all." A number of other writers—notably Rousseau, Hegel, and Dewey—say things which warrant our inferring that, if they were asked the same question, they would answer it by saying that, in order to be free, the good man must not only be able to will as he ought but also able to act as he wills. Hence, in their view favorable circumstances permitting the execution of virtuous intentions are essential to the existence of SP freedom. And there is a third group of authors, including Aquinas, Spinoza, and Montesquieu, who would answer it by saying that, while favorable circumstances are not essential, the freedom of the virtuous man is made more complete by his being able to act as he wills, in addition to willing as he ought.[4]

Here then is a three-sided disagreement on an existential issue about SP freedom. When we say that this issue is wholly constructed by us, we

[4] For the documentary evidence on which we base our inferences concerning the answers, different groups of SP authors would give to the question as posed, see Vol. I, Book II, Ch. 16, pp. 306–12.

are simply calling attention to the fact that the writers whom we construe as parties to it do not give any indication whatsoever that they themselves are aware of being in disagreement with other writers on the point. The disagreement is, of course, no less real in consequence; but it might also have been a disputed one, had the authors explicitly entered into it, recognized their adversaries, and tried to argue for their own position or against that of others. As matters stand, however, we can do no more than report the disagreement and refer the reader to Volume I for the evidence which justifies our construction of this issue.

There is another existential issue which we can construct in the same way. The question here can be phrased as follows. Does the character of the political community or state in which the individual lives affect his possession of the freedom of self-perfection? Can a man have the moral character requisite for living as he should if he does not live in a well-constituted society? Three writers—Rousseau, Hegel, and Dewey—take the position that individuals can attain the virtue requisite for freedom only in societies which have a certain moral structure. A larger number of SP authors (including Philo, Plotinus, the Roman Stoics, the Christian theologians, Spinoza, Leibniz, Kant, and Maritain) take the opposite view. They hold that it is possible for men to achieve the virtue or wisdom which makes them free even in societies that do not honor these qualities or definitely discourage the pursuit of them.[5]

Finally, we can construct one conceptual issue about SP. Kant asserts that the free man is absolutely autonomous: the moral law which he obeys is a law that is the product of his own reason. Other writers, such as Rousseau and Hegel, also speak of the free man as obeying a law he gives himself; but they do not, like Kant, conceive the freedom of self-perfection as consisting in absolute autonomy, for, as we pointed out above, they see the free man as dependent upon the state. The rule of life which Dewey and Freud regard as the basis of SP freedom is also one that the sound or healthy man imposes on himself; but, from Kant's point of view, it would involve some heteronomy rather than complete autonomy since it rests on the empirical nature of man instead of being a pure *a priori* judgment of the reason. The remaining SP authors conceive man's freedom of self-perfection as a willing obedience to the law of God or an acquiesence in the necessities of nature. Accordingly, for such writers as the Christian theologians, on the one hand, or the Roman Stoics and Spinoza, on the other, the free man has only a relative, not an absolute, autonomy.[6]

5 For the evidence which supports the construction of this issue, see Vol. I, Book II, Ch. 16, pp. 291–306.
6 For the relevant evidence here, see Vol. I, Book II, Ch. 16, pp. 282–91.

If, then, we pose the question, "Should man's freedom of self-perfection be conceived as consisting in absolute autonomy?" we have an issue or which Kant alone takes the affirmative side and is opposed by all the rest. This is a satisfactory disposition of the matter on condition that we also recognize certain differences among the writers on the negative side. While all of them conceive man's freedom in relation to laws which come from God, nature, or the state, they differ about the degree of autonomy possessed by the free man when, by his willing compliance, he makes the law he obeys the rule of his own life. For Dewey and Freud the free man has more autonomy than for Rousseau and Hegel; and he has more for Rousseau and Hegel than he does for the Stoics, Augustine, Aquinas, Calvin, Luther, Spinoza, Leibniz, Maritain, and Yves Simon.

One other division of opinion among the SP authors remains to be mentioned. It concerns the role which divine grace plays in the individual's acquirement of rectitude of will. For Christian theologians such as Augustine, Aquinas, Luther, and Calvin, and for Christian philosophers such as Maritain, Marcel, Berdyaev, and Simon, fallen man cannot attain the virtue requisite for freedom without God's saving grace. We know, therefore, how such authors would answer the question about the role of grace in man's freedom of self-perfection. It is difficult to say how such pagan authors as Plato, Plotinus, Seneca, Marcus Aurelius, and Epictetus would answer it, supposing that it could be made an intelligible question for them. On the other hand, we can be reasonably sure that modern writers whose theories of freedom do not take account of original sin and the fallen nature of man (e.g., Spinoza, Rousseau, Kant, Hegel, Whitehead, Russell, Dewey, and Freud) would either dismiss the question or answer it negatively.[7]

In view of what has just been said, we do not think that it is meaningful to construct an issue here and place certain writers on one side of it by imputing to them a view that is so remote from the whole texture of their thought. However, if we confine our attention exclusively to Christian theologians and philosophers, the problem of grace may raise an issue in a different way. Disagreements concerning grace in relation to freedom are generally recognized by commentators on the history of Christian thought. The classic example of such disagreement is, of course, the famous Pelagian controversy. If we take that as representative of other disagreements, we are brought to the conclusion that the issues here directly concern man's freedom of self-determination, and only indirectly his freedom of self-perfection.

[7] See, for instance, Dewey's criticism of the view that human nature is corrupt, in "Antinaturalism in Extremis," in *Naturalism and the Human Spirit*, pp. 9, 14. Cf. *Reconstruction in Philosophy*, Introduction, pp. xxix–xxxi.

The question which Pelagius and Augustine answer in opposite ways has to do with fallen man's freedom of choice. Can man, without God's grace, will the good or choose to act in a manner that has merit before God? There is also the question whether man, by the exercise of his free will, can act in such a way as to deserve God's grace or can predispose himself to receive it. These and similar questions relate directly to the effect of original sin on man's power of free choice. But indirectly they bear on man's ability to make the virtuous choices that will establish in him the habitual rectitude of will which constitutes his freedom of self-perfection.[8]

If, as Pelagius maintains, man unredeemed by God's grace has, by his natural freedom of will, the power to choose between obeying and disobeying God, then of course man does not need God's grace in order to acquire the virtue whereby his will is conformed to God's. If, on the other hand, as Augustine maintains, man needs God's grace in order to make a single good (i.e., meritorious) choice, then it also follows that, without God's grace, he cannot attain the virtue requisite for freedom.

This suffices to indicate how theological differences concerning the effect of original sin on man's freedom of will and concerning the need for grace to restore man's power of choice also divide theologians on the role of grace in relation to man's attainment of the freedom of self-perfection.

[8] In Augustine's view, man receives from God the grace to will freely that which he ought; this in turn gives him "liberty," by which Augustine means what we have called freedom of self-perfection. See *On the Spirit and the Letter*, esp. pp. 172, 184, 189, 211, 219, 223. Cf. *On Grace and Free Will; On Nature and Grace, Against Two Letters of the Pelagians*. Augustine bases his position on Pauline texts, such as *Romans* 9:15–16, where St. Paul says that God's mercy is due not to any work "of him that willeth, nor of him that runneth, but of God that sheweth mercy"; and *Philippians* 2:13, where St. Paul says that "it is God which worketh in you both to will and to do of his good pleasure." Pelagius dismisses the first text by claiming it is not St. Paul who is speaking. With regard to the second text, he says that God does not work in men by grace, as Augustine claims, but on man's will "through persuasion and by promising rewards." God gets men to do what they ought, Pelagius asserts, "by saying 'he who perseveres unto the end will be saved.'" See *Expositions of Thirteen Epistles of St. Paul*, pp. 75–76, 400.

Chapter 18

THE ISSUES CONCERNING
COLLECTIVE FREEDOM

The conception of collective freedom, which we have found most fully developed in the writings of Comte, Bakunin, and Marx, Engels and Lenin, is a special variant of the acquired freedom of self-perfection.[1]

These authors maintain that this is the only true or the ideal freedom. They see it as a freedom which will be acquired by mankind only when human life and social organization is directed by man's knowledge of natural and social necessities. It does not involve man-made rules or coercive force of any sort. It is, therefore, a freedom that belongs to the future. However else they differ on this point or on matters related to it, these authors agree that collective freedom cannot begin to exist until the state or political community, as we know it in history and at present, has ceased to exist.[2]

It is, however, in relation to this very point that the only clear issue among the collective freedom authors emerges. In Chapter 7 of this volume, which dealt with the general controversy about collective freedom, we projected this issue as the principal one in the special controversy on this subject. We said there that it is constituted by a three-sided disagreement which separates Comte from both Bakunin and the Marxists, on the one hand, and separates the Marxists from Bakunin, on the other.[3]

Upon closer examination of this threefold difference of opinion, we find that the disagreement can be more clearly presented by dividing it into two distinct issues. Bakunin together with the Marxists stand opposed to Comte on one question, while to a quite different question, the Marxists and Bakunin give opposite answers.

Before we examine these two issues, it is important to remember that there is a question to which all these writers give the same answer. *Can collective freedom exist in a state or political community in which men*

---

[1] See Vol. I, Ch. 19.
[2] See Vol. I, Ch. 19, p. 381. Cf. in this volume Ch. 1, pp. 9–11, *supra*.
[3] See *loc. cit.*, pp. 15–16, *supra*.

are subject to the arbitrary authority of other men and are governed by man-made laws, coercively enforced? All the principal CF authors answer this question emphatically and unqualifiedly in the negative. If the word "anarchy" were used to mean "the abolition of the state and political government as it has existed historically and still exists at present," then all the collective freedom authors, by virtue of their answer to this question, could properly be called "anarchists."

But in the usual sense of the word, only Bakunin can be called an anarchist. In still another sense, it might be proper to call the Marxists as well as Bakunin anarchists. In neither of these senses can Comte be so denominated. The two questions to which we now turn will reveal the differences that separate them in spite of their common rejection of all historic and currently existing states as the enemy of freedom.

The first of these questions can be formulated as follows: *Is collective freedom compatible with some form of state in which a central government exercises political power?* This is a question about the conditions under which collective freedom can exist. On the existential issue raised by it, only Comte takes the affirmative position. The others take the negative.

We have already given documentary evidence of Comte's position on this issue. In the *Positive Polity*, we have found Comte asserting that "society can no more exist without a government than government can exist without society."[4] What Comte envisages is not the abolition of the state or political government as such, but rather the transformation of the state into the positive polity in which men will no longer be subject to the arbitrary commands of other men. In the positive polity, men will be governed only by scientifically, not politically, determined rules of conduct.[5]

Nevertheless, positivism, according to Comte, also teaches "that true liberty is impossible at present without the vigorous control of a central power."[6] Not only in the transition to the positive polity is a strong central government needed but also, after it is established, the union of

---

[4] *Op. cit.*, Vol. II, p. 162.
[5] "The only way to reconcile independence with social union, and thereby reach true liberty," Comte explains, "lies in obedience to the objective laws of the world, and of human nature" (*ibid.*, Vol. I, p. 296). When man submits only to the objective laws which scientific knowledge teaches him, "man will no longer be the slave of man; he will [yield] only to external Law; and to this, those who demonstrate it to him [will be] as submissive as himself." And, Comte adds, "the more perfectly [the natural laws to which we owe submission] are known, the more free will our conduct become from arbitrary command or servile obedience" (*ibid.*). See also *Positive Philosophy*, p. 435. For a fuller exposition of Comte's views, see Vol. I, Ch. 19, pp. 371–73, 391–92; and in this volume, Ch. 7, pp. 188–90, *supra*.
[6] *A General View of Positivism*, p. 138.

"Liberty and Public Order" will always require the existence of the state and the operation of political institutions. Temporal power will continue, but it is to be guided and modified by a spiritual authority. As is well known, Comte's system of positivism culminated in "the religion of Humanity" which, "could human life be freed from the pressure of material wants, would suffice for its guidance." This new religion becomes possible only as society enters into its industrial phase and material problems approach solution. The aim of positivism, according to Comte,

> is so to regenerate our political action, as to transform it ultimately into a practical worship of Humanity; Morality being the worship rendered by the affections, Science and Poetry that rendered by the intellect. Such is the principal mission of the Occidental priesthood, a mission in which women and the working classes will actively cooperate.[7]

Such an ideal of future society seems clearly inconsistent with Comte's view that freedom involves emancipation from the arbitrary authority of man over man. It was Comte's belief, however, that since the authority will rest upon science, rational economy, and the laws of human nature, not upon metaphysics, it will be neither arbitrary nor coercive. His expectation was that moral suasion and voluntary cooperation would prevail in the operation of political institutions, and it is this element in his program which reconciles it, theoretically, with his ideal of collective freedom.

Bakunin and the Marxists take the opposite point of view. The fact that they disagree about the transition from the present oppressive political order to the ideal association of men when the state will have ceased to exist in any form does not affect their stand on this issue. Bakunin advocates the immediate overthrow of the state. The Marxists call for the proletarian state as a transitional step to the anarchic condition which will exist when that state has withered away. But they agree that the collective freedom of mankind does not begin to exist until the state and political government are completely abolished, whether that is to come about all at once by the anarchist revolution or, gradually, by the communist revolution, which first sets up the dictatorship of the proletariat.

Here, as in the case of Comte, documentary evidence of the relevant views of Bakunin, on the one hand, and of the Marxists, on the other, has been amply given in earlier chapters.[8] "If there is a State, there must necessarily be domination, and therefore slavery," Bakunin asserts again

[7] *Republic of the West; Order and Progress. A General View of Positivism*, pp. 399–400.
[8] For the views of Bakunin, see Vol. I, Book II, Ch. 19, pp. 373–75, 393–95; and in this volume, Ch. 7, p. 11 ff. *supra*. For the Marxist theory of the withering away of the state, see Vol. I, Ch. 19, pp. 375–79, 395–98; and, in this volume, Ch. 7, pp. 193–98, *supra*.

and again.[9] Engels, in a letter written in 1875, admits that "so long as the proletariat still *uses* the state"—as it must in order to prepare for the state's withering away—"it does not use it in the interests of freedom, but in order to hold down its adversaries."[10] Yet to the extent that the proletarian state prepares the way for the truly classless and stateless society of the future, freedom is the ultimate objective of the dictatorship of the proletariat.[11] "Only now," wrote Lenin many years later, "can we appreciate to the full the correctness of Engels' remarks in which he mercilessly ridiculed all the absurdity of combining the words 'freedom' and 'State.' So long as the State exists there is no freedom. When there will be freedom, there will be no State."[12]

This last statement by Lenin echoes Bakunin's declaration that "where the State begins, liberty ceases, and vice versa."[13] But, as we have already pointed out, Bakunin and the Marxists disagree about the route to freedom and anarchy. The question to which they give opposed answers can be formulated as follows: *Is some form of state necessary as a means and transitional phase in the process of attaining the collective freedom men will enjoy when they can live and work together without the political apparatus of the state and government?* The Marxists, think that the revolution for freedom requires two steps: first, the overthrow of the bourgeois state and its replacement by the proletarian state, sometimes called the "people's state"; second, the gradual withering away of the proletarian state and the coming to be of that classless and stateless association of men "in which the free development of each is the condition for the free development of all." Bakunin holds, on the contrary, that the revolution to establish mankind's freedom can and must be accomplished all at once.[14]

The first issue, which sets Comte against the other collective-freedom authors, is not actually disputed. The opponents do not take cognizance of each other's views and engage in argument. But the second issue, which sets Bakunin against the Marxists, elicits an actual interchange in which the opponents refer to each other. What follows is an illustrative sampling of passages in which Bakunin rejects the revolutionary tactics of the

---

[9] *The Political Philosophy of Bakunin*, p. 287. Cf. *ibid.*, 207, 211, 224, 240, 409–10; and see also *Oeuvres*, Vol. I, pp. 143–44.

[10] *Marx-Engels, Selected Correspondence*, p. 337. Engels goes on to say: ". . . as soon as it becomes possible to speak of freedom, the state as such ceases to exist" (*ibid.*).

[11] This doctrine is compactly stated in the concluding paragraph of Ch. II of the *Manifesto of the Communist Party*.

[12] *The State and Revolution*, p. 133.

[13] *Oeuvres*, Vol. I, p. 143.

[14] We have indicated where the documentation of these opposed views can be found in earlier chapters. See fn. 7 on p. 628, *supra*.

Marxists and in which the Marxists attack the revolutionary action called for by Bakunin.

Bakunin not only sees no need for the first step in the Communist program but also definitely opposes it as likely to prevent the final stage from ever being reached. In this respect, as we have already pointed out, Bakunin shares the views of those who, in the general controversy about collective freedom, argue that the dictatorship of the proletariat, once established, will perpetuate itself and that the proletarian state, therefore, will never wither away.[15]

"Dictatorship cannot beget freedom," Bakunin declares. "No dictatorship can have any other aim but that of self-perpetuation."[16] The Marxists, according to Bakunin,

> say that the only care and aim of this [transitional] government will be to educate and uplift the people—economically and politically—to such an extent that no government will be necessary, and that the State, having lost its political character, that is, its character of rule and domination, will turn all by itself into an altogether free organization of economic interests and communes.

But, in his opinion, this is "an obvious contradiction." As he sees it,

> if their State is going to be a genuine people's State, why should it then dissolve itself—and if its rule is necessary for the real emancipation of the people, how dare they call it a people's State?

From Bakunin's point of view, "Every state, their own people's State included, is a yoke, which means that it begets despotism on one hand and slavery on the other. . . . Freedom can be created only by freedom, that is by a universal rebellion on the part of the people and free organization of the toiling masses from the bottom up."[17]

Writing to an American labor leader, Philip Van Patten, Engels answers his inquiry "regarding Karl Marx's attitude toward the anarchists in general." He begins by saying that "since 1845 Marx and I have held the

---

[15] See Ch. 7, pp. 184–85, *supra;* and see also *ibid.,* pp. 201–07, *supra.*

[16] *The Political Philosophy of Bakunin,* pp. 287–88.

[17] *Ibid.* "It is this point," Bakunin tells us, "which mainly divides the Socialists or revolutionary collectivists from the authoritarian Communists, the partisans of the absolute initiative of the State. . . . Hence the two different methods. The Communists believe that it is necessary to organize the forces of the workers in order to take possession of the political might of the state. The revolutionary Socialists organize with the view of destroying, or if you prefer a more refined expression, of liquidating the State. The Communists are the partisans of the principle and practice of authority, while revolutionary Socialists place their faith only in freedom" (*ibid.,* p. 300). Cf. Bakunin, *Marxism, Freedom, and the State, passim.*

view that one of the ultimate results of the future proletarian revolution will be the gradual dissolution of the political organizations known by the name of state." To do this, "the working class must first take possession of the organized political power of the state and by its aid crush the resistance of the capitalist class and organize society anew. This is to be found as early as the Communist Manifesto of 1847, Chapter II, conclusion."

The anarchists, according to Engels, fail to understand the reason for this. He writes:

> The anarchists stand the thing on its head. They declare that the proletarian revolution must *begin* by abolishing the political organization of the state. But the only organization that the proletariat finds ready to hand after its victory is precisely the state. This state may require very considerable alterations before it can fulfill its new functions. But to destroy it at such a moment would mean to destroy the only organism by means of which the victorious proletariat can assert its newly conquered power, hold down its capitalist adversaries, and carry out that economic revolution of society without which the whole victory must end in a new defeat and in a mass slaughter of the workers similar to that after the Paris Commune.[18]

In an earlier letter to Cuno, Engels says that "Bakunin has a singular theory, a potpourri of Proudhonism and communism, the chief point of which is, first of all, that he does not regard capital, and hence the class antagonism between capitalists and wage earners which has arisen through social developments, as the main evil to be abolished, but instead the *state*." Against this, Engels argues that

> the abolition of the state is nonsense without a previous social revolution: the abolition of capital *is* the social revolution and involves a change in the whole mode of production. However, since for Bakunin the state is the main evil, nothing must be done that can keep alive the state, *i.e.*, any state, republic, monarchy, or whatever it may be. Hence, *complete abstention from all politics*.[19]

The state in its final form (i.e., the proletarian state needed for the liquidation of bourgeois capitalism), is, according to Engels, "not 'abolished,' *it withers away*. It is from this standpoint that we must appraise the phrase 'free people's state'—both its justification at times for agitational purposes, and its ultimate scientific inadequacy—and also the demand of the so-called anarchists that the state should be abolished overnight."[20]

Commenting at length on Engel's whole theory of revolutionary tactics

---

[18] *Letters to Americans*, pp. 137–38.
[19] *Ibid.*, pp. 96–97.
[20] *Anti-Dühring*, p. 309.

(the overthrow of the bourgeois state and the withering away of the proletarian state), Lenin says that "the most remarkable thing in this argument of Engels is the way he states the case against the anarchists. . . . The anarchist idea of the abolition of the State is muddled and *non-revolutionary*—that is how Engels puts it. It is precisely the revolution in its rise and development, with its specific tasks in relation to violence, authority, power, the State, that the anarchists do not wish to see."[21] And, in another place, Lenin writes:

> We are not utopians, we do not indulge in "dreams" of dispensing *at once* with all administration, with all subordination; these anarchist dreams, based upon a lack of understanding of the tasks of the proletarian dictatorship, are totally alien to Marxism, and, as a matter of fact, serve only to postpone the Socialist revolution until people are different.[22]

One other difference of opinion, which divides the principal collective-freedom authors, suggests a possible issue in this special controversy. It concerns the primacy of economic factors in the revolution for freedom. Is a radical reorganization of the economic system and the transformation of all existing economic relationships indispensable to the creation of that free association of men in which the regulation of human affairs will be devoid of everything arbitrary and oppressive?

To this question, the Marxists give an affirmative answer.[23] Bakunin joins them in this. He is no less insistent than they are that the overthrow of capitalism and the emancipation of the workers must occupy a primary place in the revolutionary program.[24] Only Comte appears to take the opposite point of view.

In enumerating the points of doctrine shared by the collective-freedom authors, we called attention to the fact that Comte does not say, as the others do, that freedom involves emancipation from compulsory toil, degrading poverty, economic servitude and exploitation, i.e., from organizations of production in which the conditions of work are determined by a master class who own the means of production, and in which the fruits of work are alienated from the workers to the benefit of their masters.[25]

The evidence for our interpretation of Comte's position on this issue

[21] *The State and Revolution*, pp. 88–89.
[22] *Ibid.*, pp. 69–70.
[23] See Marx, *Critique of Political Economy*, pp. 11–12, *Capital*, Vol. III, pp. 954–55; Engels, *Anti-Dühring*, p. 32, *Ludwig Feuerbach*, pp. 52–54, 59; Marx-Engels, *German Ideology*, pp. 14–15, 70; Marx-Engels, *Selected Correspondence*, p. 475; Lenin, *Selected Works*, Vol. XI, p. 5.
[24] See *The Political Philosophy of Bakunin*, pp. 187–88, 213.
[25] See Vol. I, Book II, Ch. 19, fn. 32, on p. 381.

lies mainly in his unmistakable lack of concern about the economic institutions on the alteration of which the others lay primary emphasis. However, we do have some positive confirmation of it in Comte's general thesis that "ideas govern the world."[26] For him, the attainment of collective freedom is to be brought about primarily by the overthrow not of historic and existing economic systems, but of the religious and metaphysical systems of the past and present, and by the enthronement of science and the positive philosophy in their place.[27]

[26] *Positive Philosophy*, p. 36.
[27] See, for example, *The Positive Polity*, Introduction, pp. 25–26, 28, where Comte discusses the movement of the human race from the theological state to the metaphysical state to the positive polity, which is brought about by a change in modes of thought. Cf. also *ibid.*, Book I, p. 264; Book II, p. 65.

Chapter 19

THE ISSUES CONCERNING THE
FREEDOM OF SELF-DETERMINATION

We saw in Chapter 17 that, while writers who affirm an acquired freedom of self-perfection can be construed as disagreeing on a number of points about that freedom, they do not confront one another as opponents on these possible issues. Each of the major authors expounds his own theory of SP freedom, but does so without taking cognizance of the conflicting theories of other writers. Consequently, he does not undertake to argue against other points of view nor to defend his own against them. The differences that divide the SP authors are sufficiently clear to warrant us in saying that controversy is possible; but none actually exists.

The state of affairs is very much the same in the case of the natural freedom of self-determination. Here, too, we find that writers who affirm SD freedom conceive that freedom in the context of radically divergent philosophical and theological doctrines. The major theories of free will or self-determination are, in consequence, so diverse that we found it necessary to expound each of them individually in our effort to document their agreement on this or that point in the understanding of SD[1]

While our main interest is in their agreements and disagreements, the primary concern of each of the principal authors is to persuade us of the truth of his own theory, and of his philosophy as a whole, in which his theory of man's freedom of self-determination is imbedded. With a few exceptions to be noted subsequently, the major SD authors do not take cognizance of the differences which divide them and place them in opposition on issues about which they might conceivably engage in dispute with one another. Here, as in the case of the freedom of self-perfection,

[1] See Vol. I, Book II, Ch. 22–24. In Ch. 25, where we dealt with the forms of self-determination, we pointed out that the extensiveness of the treatment required in the preceding chapters resulted from the fact that "each of the major authors had to be treated individually. Evidence that he shared the common, neutrally formulated understanding of self-determination had to be given in terms of his own theory of the matter. . . . In most cases, an author's theory of self-determination could not be stated without some indication of the fairly elaborate metaphysical—and sometimes theological—doctrine in which he couched it" (*loc. cit.*, p. 546).

controversy is certainly possible; but except for the exceptions just mentioned, which, as we shall see, consist solely of arguments for one side of a possible issue, no controversy actually exists.[2]

We have elsewhere noted and documented the main differences of opinion about how man's freedom of self-determination should be conceived. These can be recalled by remembering the three points that we employed to set forth the common meaning of self-determination: (i) intrinsic unpredictability, (ii) causal initiative, and (iii) causal indeterminacy.[3] We explained the first by saying that, given perfect knowledge of all relevant causes, a free decision cannot be foreseen or predicted with certitude from such knowledge, not regarding even God's omniscience as an exception. We explained the third by saying that a free decision is always one of a number of alternative possible decisions any one of which is simultaneously within the power of the self to cause, no matter what other antecedent or concurrent factors exercise a causal influence on the making of the decision. And to say that the decision flows from the causal initiative of the self, we explained, means that, on the plane of natural or finite causes, the self is the uncaused cause of the decision it makes.[4] In formulating the common understanding of other freedoms, such as SR or SP, we were able to say that all the elements of meaning involved entered into the topical agreement which unites the SR authors or the SP authors. But we found this impossible to do in the case of SD. Here we had to be satisfied with a topical agreement that rests on at least two of the three points set forth. We were able to show that, with the exception of Leibniz, all the SD authors affirm at least two of the three points; and that the great majority of them affirm all three.[5] In other words, while the preponderance of SD authors hold that a free decision is intrinsically unpredictable, not all do; while almost all of them regard causal indeterminacy as an essential ingredient in self-determination, some exclude it wholly or in

---

[2] The absence of controversy among SD writers contrasts strikingly with the extent to which these same authors participate in the general controversy about SD. There, as we have seen in Ch. 9–11, *supra.*, exponents of SD explicitly join issue with those who deny this freedom and argue, often at great length, in defense of their position or against the criticisms and objections raised by their opponents. A much larger number of the SD authors are parties to the general controversy about SD than is the case with the SP authors, only a few of whom actually participate in the general controversy about that subject. But though the SD authors are more generally inclined to recognize the controversial nature of the freedom which they espouse, when the controversy is about the existence of that freedom, they remain aloof from controversy when it involves conflicting theories about SD itself.

[3] See Vol. I, Book II, Ch. 21, esp. pp. 433–39.

[4] See Ch. 8 *supra.*, p. 225; and for a fuller exposition of each of these three points, see *ibid.*, pp. 227–36.

[5] See Vol. I, Book II, Ch. 22, p. 438; and Ch. 24, p. 497. Cf. in this volume Ch. 8, p. 225, *supra.*

part; and while most of them also maintain that causal initiative on the part of the self is indispensable, some deny this aspect of self-determination while still insisting on causal indeterminacy and intrinsic unpredictability. In these divisions of opinion, we have the source of three conceptual issues which might conceivably be debated in the special controversy about man's freedom of self-determination, were that controversy to take place.

There are, in addition, three other matters about which the SD authors differ significantly. In these three cases, as before, we find that one view of the matter is taken by a great preponderance of the authors, with only a few dissenting voices on the other side. Most of the SD writers hold that the freedom of self-determination is to be found in man alone, but a few maintain that other things—either other living organisms or all physical processes—exhibit that freedom in some degree. The great majority of them hold that self-determination is a limited freedom, circumscribed in scope, but a few regard it as infinite, transcending all limitations. For almost all of the SD authors, the act of self-determination involves elements of both rationality and arbitrariness; but for one writer, it is purely arbitrary, and for two others, it is purely rational. These divisions of opinion give us three more issues concerning which dispute is possible.

The fact that debate is lacking for the most part does not make these six issues any the less real. They represent genuine disagreements. In each case, we can formulate a question which certain authors would answer in one way, and others in the opposite way. But though the issues are thus genuine, they are also constructed in the sense that we do not find them explicitly present in the literature.

With a few exceptions, the authors whom we construe as being opposed do not themselves actually join issue by explicitly acknowledging the question which divides them, or by explicitly setting their own position against the position they reject. They simply make their own position clear. Nevertheless, insofar as we are able to assure ourselves that their views are incompatible on points about which they have enough in common to be in disagreement, we can discover issues that are implicitly present in the literature, even if they are not explicitly present.

In stating the six issues that have been alluded to above, we shall proceed as follows. In each case, we shall first formulate the question which covers the opposition of views that we have found in the literature. We shall then name only the authors who can be construed as giving a negative answer to this question, for these in each case are the few dissenting voices who take a stand against all the rest.[6] Documentary evidence to support our

---

[6] It would be burdensome to repeat each time what would be for the most part the same long list of affirmative authors. For a complete list of the SD writers whom we treated in Vol. I, see Book II, Ch. 20, p. 404 of that volume; and for additional SD

attribution of the negative or the affirmative answer to certain writers has already been given in Volume I, or in earlier chapters of the present volume; and so, instead of repeating it here, we shall give references to the pages where such documentation can be found. Finally, where the statement of the question at issue does not catch all the critical differences between the authors who take opposite sides, we shall comment briefly on these further ramifications which, in some cases, lead to subordinate or related issues.

(1) *Does man's freedom of self-determination result in acts which are intrinsically unpredictable?* For the authors who answer this question negatively, a more apt phrasing of the question would be: *Are the decisions which men reach by the exercise of free choice unforeseeable even by God who has perfect knowledge of all the causes operative in the making of such decisions?* To the question thus phrased, Ockham, Molina, Luther, Descartes, Thomas Reid, Sir William Hamilton, Henry Mansel, and C. A. Campbell reply by affirming free choice on man's part and also attributing to divine omniscience the power of foreseeing the future choices men will make, *that foresight being derived from God's perfect knowledge of all the operative causes.*[7] Hence, man's free decisions are not intrinsically unpredictable even though they are causally indeterminate, i.e., not necessitated by their causes. Of the authors mentioned above, Luther alone wavers between denying free choice to man and granting him such freedom in a very limited sphere, i.e., only in matters that are totally devoid of moral quality. It should also be pointed out that, of these authors, only Molina proposes, through his theory of *scientia media*, a way of reconciling man's free choice with God's foreknowledge of the future choices he will make. All the rest acknowledge the incompatibility of the two things they feel bound to affirm and regard the whole truth here as beyond our human comprehension.

(2) *Does man's freedom of self-determination involve the causal indeterminacy of free choice?* When the question is thus put, Leibniz is the

---

writers who are treated in the present volume as parties to the general controversy about SD, see Ch. 8, pp. 249–51, *supra*.

[7] See Vol. I, Book II, Ch. 22, pp. 447–49; and in this volume Ch. 11, pp. 467–69, 473–75, *supra*. For evidence of Calvin's position on this question see *ibid.*, pp. 469–70, *supra*. Though Leibniz also denies the intrinsic unpredictability of man's free acts, he is not included among the authors on the negative side of this issue because his conception of man's self-determination does not involve the causal indeterminacy of free choice. See Vol. I, Book II, Ch. 22, pp. 449–50; Ch. 24, pp. 539–45; and in this volume Ch. 11, pp. 470–71, *supra*. For documentary evidence of the affirmative position on this issue, as taken by such authors as Augustine, Boethius, Aquinas, and Maritain, Weiss, Hartshorne, Tillich, and others, see Vol. I, Book II, Ch. 22, pp. 442–47, 450–59; and in this volume Ch. 11, pp. 475 ff., *supra*.

only author who must be interpreted as negative; for though he regards a free decision as something which is not metaphysically necessitated (i.e., the opposite decision is not impossible), he also regards it as an act that is causally necessitated (i.e., any other decision is impossible, given the individual agent's character and antecedents).[8] We have, in consequence, treated Leibniz's conception of self-determination as atypical in the extreme, since it reduces man's natural freedom to an unimpairable spontaneity.[9]

To elicit the views of two other writers, we must revise the question by asking whether man's freedom of self-determination is ever operative in the absence of free choice. Or, to put the question another way, *Is the exercise of free choice essential to man's freedom of self-determination?* Only Hegel and Fouillée answer this question negatively by maintaining that, while self-determination involves free choice at an imperfect stage of its development, it transcends the contingency and arbitrariness of choice when it attains its fullest perfection. Unlike Leibniz, Hegel and Fouillée do not exclude free choice entirely; but neither do they regard it as an essential element in man's freedom of self-determination. On the contrary, for them, that freedom is possessed in its highest and truest form only when there is no longer any need for choice.[10] But in its highest form, when it transcends choice, man's freedom of self-determination becomes one with his freedom of self-perfection. To other writers, what Hegel and Fouillée call self-determination may appear to be indistinguishable from the acquired freedom of being able to will as one ought; but the element of causal initiative or independence, upon which they lay great stress, might justify their insistence that, at the acme of its development, human freedom combines self-determination with self-perfection.[11]

Finally, we must ask still another question to distinguish the position of Aquinas from that of Hegel and Fouillée. Does every act of self-determination on man's part involve free choice? Aquinas answers this question negatively only in order to make an exception of two very special acts—in this life, the act by which a man necessarily wills his happiness; in the life to come, the act by which the blessed, vouchsafed the vision of God, necessarily love and adhere to God. Except for those two acts, every other act of self-determination, according to Aquinas, involves freedom of choice on the part of the will, both as to exercise and as to specification; and, in this life, freedom of choice is retained even with regard to happiness

[8] See Vol. I, Book II, Ch. 24, pp. 539–45.
[9] For a fuller discussion of this reduction which makes natural self-determination indistinguishable from natural self-realization, see Vol. I, Book II, Ch. 25, pp. 549–51.
[10] See Vol. I, Book II, Ch. 24, pp. 531–39.
[11] For a fuller discussion of this point, see Vol. I, Book II, Ch. 25, pp. 551–52.

so far as willing or not willing is concerned. These two exceptions aside, Aquinas, unlike Hegel and Fouillée, makes the causal indeterminacy of free choice an essential aspect of man's freedom of self-determination. Furthermore, so far as this life is concerned, there is no act of self-determination from which freedom of choice is completely absent, whereas, for Hegel and Fouillée, man attains the highest form of self-determination in this life only by transcending freedom of choice.[12]

Hence, if we were to ask the question, *Does man's freedom of self-determination, as exercised in this life in its normal or typical form, always involve the causal indeterminacy of free choice?*, only Leibniz, Hegel, and Fouillée would take the negative position, with Leibniz maintaining that causal indeterminacy is never involved, and with Hegel and Fouillée restricting free choice to an imperfect or incomplete stage of self-determination. Aquinas together with all the rest of the SD authors would take the affirmative side of the issue thus formulated.[13]

Attention must be called to one other issue which concerns the role of free choice in self-determination. Aquinas, as we have seen, holds the view that, in the presence of God, the blessed retain their freedom of self-determination even though they do not exercise free choice, for they cannot not will to love God. Aquinas is opposed by Duns Scotus who maintains, on the contrary, that even in the presence of God, the blessed can refrain from willing, i.e., they can choose between willing and not willing, even though, willing, they cannot choose but to love God and adhere to Him.[14]

This issue, on which Aquinas and Scotus most eminently represent the opposite points of view, has significance beyond the question about free choice in the very special act by which the blessed will their love of God in His presence. The position of Scotus on this issue is traditionally taken to exemplify a voluntarism which insists upon the supremacy or sovereignty of the will, never dominated by reason, not even when reason is perfected by the enjoyment of the beatific vision. As the prime exponent of such voluntarism, Scotus is thought to be the precursor of Descartes and, in a later day, of such existentialists as Sartre. Though Aquinas opposes Scotus with regard to choice on the part of the blessed, he cannot be taken as representing the opposite extreme of a rationalism that insists upon the supremacy of the reason over the will. It is Hegel rather than Aquinas who can be taken as the exponent of a rationalism diametrically opposed to the voluntarism of Scotus. The perfection of self-determination for Hegel lies in the most

---

[12] See Vol. I, Book II, Ch. 25, pp. 552–54.
[13] See Vol. I, Book II, Ch. 24, pp. 495–531; and, in this volume, Ch. 10, pp. 335, 351–71, 401–18, *supra*.
[14] See Vol. I, Book II, Ch. 24, p. 504.

complete submission to rational necessity: the free will is the completely rational will, one from which all arbitrariness has been removed by its being no longer subject to the blind contingencies of choice.

(3) *Does man's freedom of self-determination involve causal initiative on his part?* To this question, a number of modern SD authors reply in the negative. Bergson, Dewey, Whitehead, and Weiss hold the view that, in the natural order, every cause has causal antecedents, that there is nothing which is an independent or first cause, a cause which acts without being acted upon. As they see it, the causal indeterminacy whereby a cause is able to produce any one of a number of alternative effects does not require that cause to be itself an uncaused cause. The fact that it is itself caused to operate does not, when it operates, determine it or necessitate it in the production of its own effects. It remains a free cause, in the sense of not being necessarily bound to produce one and only one effect, while, at the same time, it is a caused cause.[15]

On the opposite side of this issue are the great majority of SD authors who, affirming the causal indeterminacy of free choice, maintain that such causal indeterminacy is inseparable from causal initiative. As they see it, for the self or the will to be actively indeterminate in the production of its effects, it must have or be an active power, in the sense of being able to act without being acted upon (except by God). This does not mean that the self or the will is uncaused in its existence, but only that, in its operation, it is not efficiently moved by antecedent causes in a temporal nexus or chain of causes and effects.[16]

When we said earlier that, for the most part, the SD authors who can be construed as disagreeing on this point or that merely assert their own position and do not take explicit cognizance of the opposite view (the denial of which is implied by the position they take), we also said that there were several exceptions. We meet with one of them here. Bergson, Dewey, Whitehead, and Weiss are clearly aware that they are rejecting the traditional "free-will doctrine" which insists upon the causal initiative of the will. They recognize that they are, in a sense, occupying a middle ground; for while siding with the traditional libertarians against the determinists with respect to the existence of causal indeterminacy, they also find themselves in the company of the determinists who deny that there are any uncaused causes in the natural order. Their theories of causation are such that they find it possible to defend man's freedom of choice against the determinist doctrine

[15] See Vol. I, Book II, Ch. 21, p. 433 fn. 19; Ch. 23, pp. 490–94; Ch. 24, p. 497; and cf. in this volume Ch. 8, p. 231, *supra.*
[16] See Vol. I, Book II, Ch. 23, pp. 469–90; and in this volume Ch. 9, pp. 266–76, 291–94, 303–7, *supra.*

of causal necessity, while at the same time disagreeing with the libertarian or "free-willist" doctrine of causal initiative.

It is not difficult to see why the situation remains one-sided. The SD authors who, prior to the twentieth century, affirm causal initiative as essential to the freedom of self-determination could hardly be aware of the dissenting SD theories advanced by Bergson, Dewey, Whitehead, and Weiss. On the other hand, the twentieth-century followers of Aquinas, such as Maritain and Simon, or of Kant, such as Campbell, might conceivably have adverted to the opponents in their own camp as well as to those among the determinists. Furthermore, William James and F. C. S. Schiller were in a position to question this aspect of Bergson's theory of free will, with which they must have been acquainted. But, for whatever reason, these writers content themselves with defending causal initiative against the determinists and do not join issue with those among their contemporaries who part company from them on this point.

The affirmation of causal initiative raises another issue on which SD authors are divided. It concerns the relation of the divine causality to the causality of the will. As we have seen, Aquinas attributes causal initiative to the human will *only* on the plane of natural causes. The free acts of the will, like all other occurrences in nature, are caused by God, but, according to Aquinas, the acts of the will are so caused by God that they remain free acts on the part of the will.[17] However, in scholastic circles, other philosophers and theologians (e.g., Molina and Suarez) disagree with Aquinas on subtle points concerning how God moves the human will in a manner that still leaves it the cause of its own acts and free.[18] On these points, the followers of Aquinas, on the one hand, and of Molina and Suarez, on the other, have joined issue and engaged in debate; but since the matters disputed mainly concern the way in which God moves the human will, and not whether the will retains the causal initiative which is essential to its freedom, we do not think it appropriate to treat such issues here.[19]

(4) *Is the freedom of self-determination uniquely the property of man among all natural things, belonging to him alone in virtue of the causal power possessed by his whole self or by such of his faculties as his reason or will?* With the exception of John Dewey, we find the same authors on the negative side here as in the preceding issue. For Bergson, the power of self-determination, involving causal indeterminacy but not causal initiative, is

[17] See Vol. I, Book II, Ch. 23, pp. 471–72; and in this volume Ch. 9, pp. 266–67, 286–87; Ch. 11, pp. 480–81, *supra*.
[18] See Vol. I, Ch. 22, pp. 448–49; Ch. 23, p. 472 fn. 20; and in this volume Ch. 11, p. 465 fn. 2, *supra*.
[19] See Garrigou-Lagrange, *La Prédestination des saints et la grâce*, Part 3, Ch. IX; Maritain, *Existence and the Existent*, Ch. IV.

to be found in all conscious living things; for Whitehead and Weiss, it is to be found in every natural process.[20] Capek and Hartshorne must also be mentioned as holding theories similar to that of Weiss, according to which causal indeterminacy, and something like a free or creative choice, is to be found in the operation of every cause.[21]

On the opposite side of this question are all the writers from Aristotle on who attribute rationality and free will to man alone. They differ among themselves in their detailed psychological theories concerning the faculties of man, and especially about the precise relation of his reason and will, but they concur in thinking that only a being equipped with such faculties can have the power of creative self-determination through free choice.[22] However, it must be observed that not all the writers who attribute self-determination to man alone accept the traditional doctrine of faculties. Some of them, such as Locke, James, Dewey, and Sartre, explicitly reject that doctrine and speak instead of the self-determining power inherent in the human mind as a whole, or in consciousness, or in human nature.[23] On the other hand, it is significant that of the authors who deny that man alone has the power of self-determination or free choice, none, in treating of human freedom, locates that power in the special functioning of man's reason or will. For Bergson, Whitehead, Weiss, Tillich, and the others, it is consciousness, or mind, or the very structure of the personality or self that, in man's case, is the seat or center of his freedom of self-determination.

(5) *Is man's freedom of self-determination limited in scope, either by external and internal factors, or by the absence of other freedoms?* We find only three authors who clearly take the negative side of this issue. For Sartre, Hegel, and Fouillée, man's freedom of self-determination is one of absolute independence, subject neither to limiting external conditions nor to internal impairment or defect. For Sartre, there is no other freedom, such

---

[20] See Vol. I, Book II, Ch. 8, pp. 152–54; Ch. 21, p. 438 fn. 30; Ch. 22, pp. 453–57. For Dewey's affirmative stand on this issue, see *ibid.*, Ch. 8, pp. 151–52; Ch. 22, pp. 452–53; Ch. 24, pp. 508–10. Paul Tillich can also be grouped with Whitehead and Weiss as holding that there is at least an analogue of human self-determination in infra-human things: see *ibid.*, Ch. 8, pp. 153–54; and Ch. 9, p. 160.

[21] See Ch. 10, pp. 362–69, *supra*; and cf. *ibid.*, p. 340 fn. 12. The dissenting authors here constitute the second of the two exceptions mentioned earlier; for here, as in the case of the preceding issue, they are aware that the position they take separates them from the traditional SD view. Writers such as Weiss, Hartshorne, and Capek, for example, advance a theory of causation which explicitly challenges the view that the power of free choice is to be found only in man. That challenge is not met, largely for the same reason here as that given in the case of the preceding issue. Hence, the issue is not explicitly joined.

[22] See Vol. I, Book II, Ch. 9, p. 158.

[23] See *ibid.*, pp. 159–60.

as self-realization or self-perfection, the absence of which could limit the scope of man's self-determination or render this freedom incomplete.[24] For Hegel and Fouillée, the freedom of self-determination is imperfect and limited only at the stage when it still involves the element of choice; but when that is transcended and man is no longer dependent on anything external for the content of his freedom, his freedom becomes infinite—at once a freedom of self-determination and of self-perfection.[25]

A number of other writers—Descartes, Hartmann, and Weiss—regard man's freedom of self-determination as infinite or unlimited in certain respects, but none of these authors goes so far as to maintain that it is a freedom of complete or absolute independence.[26] The rest of the SD authors, at least those whose theories of self-determination touch on matters relevant to the question at issue, answer that question affirmatively. For some of them, a man's freedom of self-determination is imperfect or incomplete when circumstances curtail his freedom of action and prevent him from executing his free decision.[27] For some of them, internal psychological factors, affecting the process of deliberation and choice, can, in certain extreme instances, deprive man of his freedom of choice and, in other cases, limit the degree of his freedom.[28] And for a large number of them who affirm self-determination and self-perfection as distinct freedoms, or distinct aspects of freedom, not only the Christian theologians and philosophers but also such writers as Rousseau, Kant, and Dewey, a man's freedom of choice is amplified by his virtue or wisdom (i.e., his acquired ability to choose as he ought), though it is also always limited by the moral law.[29]

Only the Christian theologians dwell on the reverse side of this picture—the case of the man who, lacking the freedom of self-perfection because still in bondage to sin, also lacks the power to choose the good or to act meritoriously. According to the fundamental dogma of original sin, sin does not deprive man of his inherent freedom of self-determination. But

24 See Vol. I, Book II; Ch. 24, pp. 513–14, 517–20; Ch. 25, pp. 558–59, 560, 576.
25 See *ibid.*, Ch. 24, pp. 532–39; Ch. 25, pp. 566–67, 576–78.
26 For evidence bearing on Descartes' views, see *ibid.*, Ch. 24, p. 522; Ch. 25, pp. 558, 560–61, 569, 579. For Hartmann's views, see *ibid.*, Ch. 24, pp. 530–31, 555, 560, 578–79. For Weiss's views, see *ibid.*, Ch. 24, pp. 513, 515–17; Ch. 25, pp. 570, 578, 579–80.
27 For an examination of the diverse views that SD writers hold on the relation of freedom of choice and freedom of action, see *ibid.*, Ch. 25, pp. 555–59. Cf. *ibid.*, pp. 571–72, and also Ch. 20, pp. 409–10.
28 See *ibid.*, Ch. 25, pp. 571–73.
29 For evidence of the views of the Christian theologians and philosophers on this point, see *ibid.*, Ch. 20, pp. 413–19; Ch. 25, pp. 559, 561–62. For the views of Rousseau, Kant, and Dewey, see *ibid.*, pp. 563–66. Cf. *ibid.*, p. 571.

his freedom of choice is stringently limited in scope until he is redeemed from sin by God's sanctifying grace.

An ancient and continuing dispute centers on issues which concern the precise effect of original sin and of God's grace on man's freedom of choice. It begins in the fifth century with Augustine's condemnation of the Pelagian doctrine as heresy; and at this stage the issue is framed by the question whether fallen man is able, without God's grace, to choose good as against evil and so merit salvation. On this question, the affirmative answer of Pelagius and the negative answer of Augustine are diametrically opposed. In the later Middle Ages, the theological controversy shifts to related issues, one concerning man's freedom so to choose that he is able to move himself, predispositively at least, toward receiving God's grace, and another concerning the degree of freedom that man retains or enjoys with different degrees of grace. The dispute continues to the present day in the conflicting views about these matters on the part of Catholic and Protestant theologians.[30]

While these issues are explicitly joined and extensively disputed, the arguments and counter-arguments turn mainly on different theological interpretations of the fundamental dogmas concerning the effects of original sin, the prerequisites of salvation, and the indispensability and efficacy of grace. These differences of opinion do not significantly alter the position that is common to Christian philosophers and theologians, namely, that man's freedom of self-determination is not an infinite, but a limited freedom. Furthermore, with the exception of the Pelagian doctrine in its most extreme form, it is generally agreed that the will of fallen man, unredeemed by grace, is radically restricted in the choices open to it, so far as their moral quality is concerned. Hence, in connection with the issue about the infinite or limited character of self-determination, we do not think it is appropriate to treat further the Pelagian and neo-Pelagian controversies, just as we saw no need to treat the dispute between the followers of Aquinas and of Molina concerning the way in which God moves the human will and yet allows it to retain its causal initiative.[31]

(6) *Does man's freedom of self-determination exhibit both rationality and arbitrariness in some degree of admixture?* The three negative authors here—Sartre, on the one hand, and Hegel and Fouillée, on the other—do not really stand together except in opposing the great majority of SD writers who would answer this question affirmatively. For Sartre, free choice is the

---

[30] For some indication of this division of opinion, see Vol. I, Book II, Ch. 15, pp. 279–80; Ch. 20, pp. 414–18; Ch. 25, p. 562. See also, in this volume, Ch. 18, pp. 629–31, *supra*.

[31] See pp. 641–42, *supra*.

core of self-determination, and free choice is wholly arbitrary—totally without reason or, in the very nature of the case, manifestly absurd.[32] While Hegel and Fouillée admit that choice introduces the element of arbitrariness into man's freedom of self-determination, they also, for that very reason, regard choice as a blemish or defect in such freedom. For them, self-determination reaches perfection only at the stage when it no longer involves choice, and then it is a purely rational freedom, devoid of all arbitrariness whatsoever.[33]

The affirmative answer to the question at issue here is given by the many SD authors who maintain that free choice is usually grounded in reasons, but that, when conflicting reasons are present to motivate the will, the one which prevails is itself elected by the will; and to that extent at least the rationally grounded choice is also willful or arbitrary.[34] These writers must be construed as being in disagreement with Sartre on one count, and with Hegel, Fouillée, and Leibniz on another. They stand opposed to Sartre because they deny the total arbitrariness of self-determination insofar as it involves free choice. They might agree with Hegel, Fouillée, and Leibniz that arbitrariness can be eliminated from self-determination along with choice, but they still reject the notion that self-determination is, either always or in its highest form, purely rational *because* it does not involve free choice.

We have now completed a brief summary of the six main issues in the special controversy about the freedom of self-determination. As we have already observed, these issues are not debated. Each of the major authors expounds his own theory of self-determination, but does so without taking cognizance of the conflicting theories of other writers. In advancing his

[32] See Vol. I, Book II, Ch. 24, pp. 517–18; Ch. 25, pp. 575–76. For evidence of the extent to which Hartmann's views on this subject tend in the direction of Sartre's extreme position, see *ibid.*, p. 578.

[33] See *ibid.*, Ch. 24, pp. 534–36, 537–39; Ch. 25, pp. 574–78. Insofar as Leibniz holds a theory of self-determination, in which what he calls a free choice is always determined by a sufficient reason (i.e., the individual's judgment of that which appears to be best), he should be mentioned here as an SD author for whom there is nothing of the arbitrary in self-determination. But neither is there any genuine element of choice, as that is understood by all the other SD authors. See *ibid.*, Ch. 24, pp. 539 ff. esp. 542–43.

[34] See *ibid.*, Ch. 24, pp. 500–12, 515–17, 521–29; Ch. 25, pp. 574, 579–83; and in this volume Ch. 10, pp. 401–16, *supra*. John Dewey must be mentioned here as holding a divergent view, at least to the extent that he sides with the determinists in thinking that an individual's choices are not only motivated but also determined by his character and antecedents. The other writers (Bergson, Whitehead, Weiss) who, like Dewey, deny causal initiative on the part of the self or the will, do not go that far. For them, as for the great majority of the SD authors, the motivation of choice does not preclude a free choice among the motives that an individual's character and antecedents make available to him at a given moment.

own view on a particular question, he may give reasons for his position, but he does not argue against other points of view nor does he defend his own against them.

In the general controversy about the freedom of self-determination, we have reported a number of disputed issues in which determinists and libertarians argue against one another. In some cases these disputes are explicitly present in the literature in actual interchanges between opposing authors. In other cases we constructed them, but that construction was based on arguments which the authors actually advance even though they do not do so in interchanges with opposing authors.

These arguments in the general controversy go beyond the reasons which authors have for their own positions. They consist in arguments against views which they reject or arguments in defense of their own views against attack. Hence, even when two authors do not refer to one another, it is possible to construe them as opponents in a debate insofar as each takes cognizance of the position held by the other and advances an argument that represents either an attack on the position of the other or a reply to that argument in defense of his own position.

But while the disagreements between the determinists and the libertarians are argued in this manner, such argumentation does not occur with regard to the disagreements that place SD authors on opposite sides of the six main issues in the special controversy about self-determination. The situation here is like the one we found in the special controversy concerning the freedom of self-perfection. In neither case are there, even implicitly in the literature, the indications of argument and counter-argument, which we should need in order to construct a dispute of the issues. To attempt to imagine the shape such argumentation might take, on the basis of the theoretical grounds which the major authors give for their own positions, would require us not only to go far beyond the evidence available but also to deal with many fundamental issues in philosophy and theology which underlie the issues about freedom. That, in turn, would require extensive dialectical work to be done on other subjects (e.g., causation), comparable to the effort we have made with respect to freedom.

One need only mention the names of Aquinas and Dewey, Descartes and Kant, Aristotle and Whitehead, Leibniz and Sartre, Hegel and Bergson, to appreciate the difficulty of constructing disputes between them which would involve the underlying presuppositions of their conflicting views about self-determination—presuppositions to be found in their elaborately developed views on substance and causation, on necessity and contingency, on mind and body, on the nature and faculties of man, the order of nature, and the relation of man and the world to God.

The point just made is not restricted to the special controversy about self-determination, or to the one about self-perfection. It also explains the inadequacies to which we have called attention in the debate between determinists and libertarians about causal initiative and causal indeterminacy in the general controversy.[35]

One exception remains to be mentioned. In their arguments against causal initiative, Bergson,[36] Dewey,[37] Whitehead,[38] and Weiss[39] clearly have in mind those theories of self-determination which maintain that the self or will operates as an uncaused cause, independent of causal antecedents on the plane of natural causes. Their arguments would be pointless against determinists who insist that every cause is an effect of prior causes. On the other hand, precisely because Bergson, Dewey, Whitehead, and Weiss are SD authors who defend the causal indeterminacy and intrinsic unpredictability of free choice against the denial of these things by determinists, their arguments against causal initiative are far from being identical with the arguments against causal initiative advanced by determinists. The former undertake to do what the latter have no interest in doing, namely, to preserve all the essentials of self-determination other than causal initiative, to accommodate the phenomena that the hypothesis of causal initiative attempts to explain, and to account for them in other ways.

Consequently, we cannot construct the other side of this dispute by availing ourselves of the arguments which the adherents of causal initiative employ in defense of it against the determinists. We cannot assume that the followers of Aquinas, Kant, or Renouvier would argue against Bergson, Dewey, Whitehead, and Weiss as they have argued against Hobbes, Hume, Priestley, and Nowell-Smith. Furthermore, we cannot fail to see that the opponents on this issue in the special controversy differ in their theories of causation and their theories of the mind and its powers almost as radically as the defenders of causal initiative in the general controversy differ from the out-and-out determinists. But to recognize this is also to recognize that, even were we able to imagine how this dispute might begin, we could not carry it to the point where the basic presuppositions of wholly divergent philosophical systems come into play.

[35] See Ch. 9, pp. 327–30; and Ch. 10, pp. 460–63, *supra.*
[36] See *Creative Evolution*, p. 8; *Matter and Memory*, p. 296; *Time and Free Will*, pp. 165–66, 172–73.
[37] See *Human Nature and Conduct*, Part IV, Sect. III, p. 311; *Ethics*, Part II, Ch. XV, Sect. 5, p. 339; *Experience and Nature*, Ch. III, pp. 99–100, Ch. VII, pp. 273–74; *Philosophy and Civilization*, pp. 273–74.
[38] See *Process and Reality*, Part II, Ch. I, Sect. IV, pp. 75–76; *ibid.*, Ch. III, Sect. I, p. 135; *ibid.*, Ch. VI, Sect. III, p. 228. Cf. *Adventures of Ideas*, Part III, Ch. XIII, Sect. IV, pp. 251–52, Sect. VII, p. 255.
[39] See *Nature and Man*, p. 33; *Man's Freedom*, pp. 62–64.

PART IV

Epilogue

Chapter 20

CONCLUDING OBSERVATIONS

If we understand controversy to consist in the dispute of issues by arguments *pro* and *con*, then we must conclude that only a few instances of controversy can be found in the literature of freedom. The best example is the controversy about self-determination as a kind of freedom. In this one case, we were not only able to construct a debate that involved a large number of authors on the opposite sides of each issue but we could also report actual interchanges in which writers engaged in dispute with one another. Here we did not have to distinguish between possible issues and issues that were really joined; nor did we have to separate the real issues into those which were and those which were not disputed.

It will be recalled that we found it necessary to point out certain deficiencies even in this debate. The arguments failed to attack or defend the fundamental premises or assumptions of the opposed views.[1] Nevertheless, the dispute of the various issues concerning self-determination offers us an approximation to the ideal of rational debate. It is far from being a close approximation, as measured by what one might expect in a full realization of the ideal, but it comes much closer than anything else we have treated in this book.

As compared with it, all the other disputes in the general controversy about the kinds of freedom are strikingly deficient in many respects. In none of them did we find authors who engaged in actual interchanges with one another. Such debate as we could present had to be entirely con-

[1] See Ch. 9, pp. 327–30, Ch. 10, pp. 460–63, and Ch. 12, pp. 520–25, *supra.*

structed by us from the indications of argument and counter-argument in the literature; and, in some instances, where arguments were lacking on one side or the other, we had to supply them by imagining what might have been said.

Furthermore, even where we found in the literature the materials from which we could construct a dispute cf the issues about self-realization, self-perfection, and collective freedom, the number of authors involved in the disputes were relatively small. Many could be interpreted as joining issue about self-realization or self-perfection as kinds of freedom but few offered any argument for the position they took or against the one they rejected.

Yet, as we have said, the general controversy about the kinds of freedom does qualify as a controversy in that sense of the word which connotes debate.[2] But when we turn to what we have called the special controversies about freedom, the word "controversy" is applicable only if it can be used for a set of issues which are *disputable*, even is they are *not* disputed. With a few very slight exceptions, we found no disputes here at all.[3] Furthermore, in many cases we had to call attention to possible issues that had not been joined, and to apparent issues which, upon closer examination, turned out not to be real ones. However, we were able to point to a number of real disagreements in the case of each of the five freedoms; and so, even though we did not find anything here that is comparable to the disputed issues in the general controversy, we can at least see in these disagreements, insofar as they are disputable issues, the possibility of a more fully developed set of special controversies about freedom.

There may be considerable difference of opinion about whether the state of the controversies about freedom is what might have been expected in view of the nature of the philosophical enterprise as a whole, and the generally recognized defects of discussion when it deals with difficult subjects. But if the idea of rational debate is appropriate to the philosophical enterprise, as we think it is, then it would be hard to gainsay the fact that what has been accomplished in twenty-five centuries of Western thought about freedom is a very poor performance, indeed.

Individual thinkers have presented us with elaborate theories and have told us, with clarity and cogency, the reasons for the conclusions they have reached about freedom. There has been no dearth of theoretical insights,

[2] Of the five subjects the reality or genuineness of which as a kind of freedom can be questioned, there was only one—political liberty—with regard to which the best we could do was to indicate a few authors who would probably reject it. In every other case, we were able to show the existence of real issues; and, in addition, we found some dispute of these issues.

[3] The exceptions occurred with respect to several of the normative issues about self-realization and with respect to the issue about collective freedom; and in the latter case, we did find some evidence of actual argument between Bakunin and the Marxists.

no lack of originality or variety. Century after century, great intellectual resources have been lavished on the discussion of freedom. The signal contributions of individual genius have started new ways of thinking about the subject and enriched or deepened others. Yet the fact remains that the profound disagreements which have emerged from all this intellectual effort have not become well-disputed issues in a sustained and rationally conducted series of controversies about freedom.

What explanation can be given for this? For those who deny that philosophy is a rational process of inquiry competent to advance man's knowledge of the fundamental truths, no explanation is needed. In their view, the diversity of philosophical systems, like the diversity of great poetic works or other works of the imagination, should not be treated like conflicting hypotheses or formulations in the empirical sciences. It is an illusion to suppose that they can be so juxtaposed logically that they can be seen to disagree on this or that proposition wrenched from the systematic context in which it is embedded. That thinkers differ in their theories of freedom cannot be denied, but in all these differences of opinion there are no genuine disagreements which are capable of being resolved by any logical process. If, then, we should not look for real issues in the philosophical discussion of a subject like freedom, why should we be surprised to find that there is no debate?

Against this point of view, we offer these two volumes as overwhelming evidence to the contrary. We think that they establish beyond question the existence of a large number of genuine disagreements about freedom. Of these real issues, many are clearly disputable and some have in fact been disputed to a greater or less extent. Hence, we are justified in wondering why dispute has not taken place where it was possible and why, where it has taken place, it is less fully developed than it might have been. Some explanation is called for.

Perhaps the best explanation is that philosophers have been content to state their own theories of freedom, to present them as clearly as they could, to argue for their truth, and to deal with such objections as have occurred to them. This, it would appear, has been accepted as the philosophical task, and the best philosophers have discharged it admirably. But not even the best philosophers have thought it necessary to engage in controversy by disputing, point by point, the various issues on which they are opposed.

They have somehow assumed that their own position, in all its controversial bearings, would be understood and would ultimately be judged, *vis-à-vis* all competing theories, by some ideal board of review. Even if they had recognized the need to participate in full-scale debate, they might have been deterred by the difficulty of that undertaking. The time and effort required of them just to become acquainted with all the issues in which they were involved would have constituted too great a distraction from what they considered their primary or main task.

It was precisely for this reason that we proposed, in Book I, a division of labor in the philosophical enterprise as a whole.[4] Creative philosophical thought is one kind of work; it is quite another task to review the whole discussion of a particular subject in order to discover the basic issues which have arisen and the extent to which they have been disputed. The latter task, we said, should be undertaken by the dialectician and specifically for the sake of helping the creative philosopher. But while the dialectician can provide the philosopher with a clarification of the agreements and disagreements that exist in a particular field of thought, and while he can show the extent to which issues have been disputed, either actually or implicitly, he cannot do more than this.

The dialectician cannot play successively the role of opposed philosophers, jumping from one side of an issue to the other in order to create a debate where none has occurred, or to enrich one where it is poorly developed. In our judgment, no one but the philosopher himself can argue for his own point of view on a particular issue, or argue against the positions he rejects. He can be helped to do this by having the preparatory dialectical work done for him, so that he is as fully informed as possible about the state of the issue. He can then see clearly where he stands in opposition to others, who his opponents are, and what reasons have so far been given for any of the positions in conflict. With this information provided by the dialectician, it should then become a legitimate and feasible task for the philosopher to improve the state of the controversy by engaging in the dispute of issues to which he is a party by virtue of the theories he holds.

We are saying, in effect, that with this dialectical work on the idea of freedom completed, it is reasonable to expect the philosophers of subsequent generations to dispute the issues about this subject more explicitly and extensively than their predecessors have done. If the ideal of rational debate were, in consequence, more fully approximated in the various controversies about freedom, that might lead to the resolution of some age-old issues or at least enable us to see why they are irresolvable. In either case, an advance would have been made.

The dialectician's contribution to the pursuit of philosophical truth lies solely in the clarification of a field of thought for the sake of progress in that field. The progress itself must be made by the philosophers, not merely by the creative effort which adds new theories or insights but also by the equally creative effort to supply the arguments and counter-arguments that

---

[4] See Vol. I, Book I, Part II, Ch. 7, pp. 57–60.

are called for by the issues which exist and either have not been disputed at all or have been inadequately debated.

We hope that this dialectical work on the idea of freedom will serve as a first step toward greater progress in man's thinking about this subject. Whether or not it effectively serves the purpose for which it is intended can be fairly and accurately judged only by those who try to make use of it to advance human thought about freedom. Should they find it of substantial assistance to them in that task, our labors will have been duly rewarded. In addition, others may be encouraged to undertake similar dialectical labors in the field of other basic ideas.

BIBLIOGRAPHIES

Vols. I and II

BIBLIOGRAPHY OF WORKS REFERRED TO

Acton, Lord Dalberg
   Essays on Freedom and Power. Boston: The Beacon Press, 1948
Adams, John
   The Selected Writings of John and John Quincy Adams. Ed. by Adrienne
   Koch and William Peden. New York: Alfred A. Knopf, 1946
Adler, Mortimer J.
   Dialectic. New York: Harcourt, Brace & Co., 1927
Alexander, Samuel
   Moral Order and Progress: An Analysis of Ethical Conceptions. Second
   Edition. London: K. Paul, Trench, Trubner & Co., 1891
Allemann, F. R.
   "Farewell to Marx" in *Encounter*, Vol. XIV, No. 3, March 1960
Ambrose
   Letters. Trans. by Sister Mary Melchior Beyenke, O.P. In Vol. 26, *Fathers
   of the Church*. New York: Fathers of the Church, 1954
Anselm of Canterbury
   De Libertate Arbitrii. In Vol. I, *Opera Omnia*. Ed. by F. S. Schmitt,
   O. S. B. Edinburgh: Thomas Nelson & Sons, 1946
   Proslogium; Monologium; An Appendix in Behalf of the Fool by Gaunilon;
   and *Cur Deus Homo*. Trans. by Sidney Norton Deane. La Salle, Ill.: The
   Open Court Publishing Co., 1939
Aquinas, Thomas
   (*Commentary on St. John*) *Sancti Thomae Aquinatis in Joannem Evange-
   listam Expositio*. In Vol. X, *Opera Omnia*. New York: Musurgia Pub-
   lishers, 1949
   (*Commentary on the Sentences*) *Scriptum super Libros Sententiarum*.
   Ed. by P. Mandonnet, O.P., and M. F. Moos, O.P. 4 vols. Paris:
   P. Lethielleux, 1929–1947
   DeMalo. In Vol. II, *Quaestiones Disputatae et Quaestiones Duodecim
   Quodlibetales*. Turin—Rome: Marietti, 1931
   DePotentia Dei. In Vol. I, *ibid*.
   (*Summa Contra Gentiles*) *On the Truth of the Catholic Faith*. Book I
   trans. by Anton C. Pegis; Book II trans. by James F. Anderson; Book
   III trans. by Vernon J. Bourke; Book IV trans. by Charles J. O'Neil.
   New York: Hanover House, 1955–1957
   Summa Theologica. Trans. by Fathers of the English Dominican Province.
   3 vols. New York: Benziger Brothers, 1947–1948

Truth. Vol. I trans. by Robert W. Mulligan, S.J.; Vol. II trans. by James V. McGlynn, S.J.; Vol. III trans. by Robert W. Schmidt, S.J. Chicago: Henry Regnery Co., 1952–1954

ARISTOTLE

(*Eudemian Ethics*) *Ethica Eudemia.* trans. by J. Solomon. In Vol. IX, *The Works of Aristotle.* Ed. by W. D. Ross. Oxford University Press, 1940

(*Metaphysics*) *Metaphysica.* Trans. by W. D. Ross. In Vol. VIII, *ibid.*

(*Nicomachean Ethics*) *Ethica Nicomachea.* Trans. by W. D. Ross. In Vol. IX, *ibid.*

(*On Interpretation*) *De Interpretatione.* Trans. by E. M. Edghill. In Vol. I, *ibid.,* 1937

(*On the Soul*) *De Anima.* Trans. by J. A. Smith. In Vol. III, *ibid.,* 1931

(*Physics*) *Physica.* Trans. by R. P. Hardie and R. K. Gaye. In Vol. II, *ibid.,* 1930

(*Politics*) *Politica.* Trans. by B. Jowett. In Vol. X, *ibid.,* 1921

ARNOLD, MAGDA B.

"Basic Assumptions in Psychology" in *The Human Person, An Approach to an Integral Theory of Personality.* Ed. by Magda B. Arnold and John A. Gasson. New York: Ronald Press Co., 1954

AUGUSTINE

Admonition and Grace. Trans. by John Courtney Murray, S.J. In Vol. 2, *Fathers of the Church.* New York: Fathers of the Church, 1950

The City of God. Trans. by Marcus Dods. 2 vols. Edinburgh: T. & T. Clark, 1891

The Confessions of St. Augustine. Trans. by E. B. Pusey. Everyman's Library, New York: E. P. Dutton & Co., 1945

(*Enchiridion*) *Faith, Hope and Charity.* Trans. by Bernard M. Peebles. In Vol. 2, *Fathers of the Church.* New York: Fathers of the Church, 1950

The Free Choice of the Will (*De Libero Arbitrio*). Trans. by Francis E. Tourscher. Philadelphia: The Peter Reilly Co., 1937

(*On the Gospel According to St. John*) *Lectures or Tractates on the Gospel According to St. John.* 2 vols. Trans. by James Innes. Edinburgh: T. & T. Clark, 1884

On Grace and Free Will. Trans. by P. Holmes. In *Basic Writings of St. Augustine.* Ed. by Whitney J. Oates. New York: Random House, 1948

The Happy Life. Trans. by Ludwig Schopp. In Vol. 1, *Fathers of the Church.* New York: Cima Publishing Co., 1948

De Moribus Ecclesiae Catholicae. In *Oeuvres de St. Augustin.* 1re Série: Opuscules. I. La Morale Chrétienne. Paris: Desclée de Brouwer et Cie., 1949

On Nature and Grace. Trans. by Peter Holmes. In *The Works of Aurelius Augustine,* Vol. IV, "The Anti-Pelagian Works of Saint Augustine, Vol. I." Ed. by Marcus Dods. Edinburgh: T. & T. Clark, 1892

The Problem of Free Choice. Trans. by Dom Mark Pontifex. Ancient Christian Writers, No. 22. Westminster, Md.: Newman Press, 1955

On the Spirit and the Letter. Trans. by Peter Holmes. In *The Works of Aurelius Augustine,* Vol. IV, "The Anti-Pelagian Works of Saint Augustine, Vol. I." Ed. by Marcus Dods. Edinburgh: T. & T. Clark, 1892

AVELING, FRANCIS
   Personality and Will. Cambridge University Press, 1931
AYER, A. J.
   Philosophical Essays. London: Macmillan & Co., 1954
BAIN, ALEXANDER
   The Emotions and the Will. London: Longmans, Green & Co., 1875
BAKUNIN, MIKHAIL ALEKSANDROVICH
   Marxism, Freedom and the State. Trans. and ed. by K. J. Kenafick.
   London: Freedom Press, 1950
   Oeuvres. 6 vols. Paris: P. V. Stock, 1895–1913
   The Political Philosophy of Bakunin: Scientific Anarchism. Ed. by
   G. P. Maximoff. Glencoe, Ill.: The Free Press, 1953
BARRETT, WILLIAM
   "Determinism and Novelty" in *Determinism and Freedom.* Ed. by Sidney
   Hook. New York: New York University Press, 1958
BARTH, KARL
   The Doctrine of the Word of God. Trans. by G. T. Thomson. In 2 half
   vols. New York: Charles Scribner's Sons, 1955–1956
   Dogmatics in Outline. Trans. by G. T. Thomson. New York: Philosoph-
   ical Library, 1947
BAYLIS, CHARLES
   "Rational Preference, Determinism, and Moral Obligation" in *Journal
   of Philosophy*, Vol. XLVII, No. 3, February 2, 1950
BEARD, CHARLES A.
   "Freedom in Political Thought" in *Freedom, Its Meaning.* Ed. by Ruth
   Nanda Anshen. New York: Harcourt, Brace & Co., 1940
BELLOC, HILAIRE
   The Restoration of Property. New York: Sheed & Ward, 1936
   The Servile State. London: Constable & Co., 1927
BENTHAM, JEREMY
   The Theory of Legislation. Trans. from the French of E. Dumont by
   Richard Hildreth. Ed. by C. K. Ogden. London: Routledge & Kegan
   Paul, 1950
   The Works of Jeremy Bentham. Ed. by J. Bowring. 11 vols. Edinburgh:
   William Tait, 1838–1843
BERDYAEV, NICOLAS ALEXANDROVITCH
   The Beginning and the End. Trans. by R. M. French. New York: Harper
   & Brothers, 1952
   The Destiny of Man. Trans. by Natalie Dudlington. London: Geoffrey
   Bles, 1948
   Dream and Reality, An Essay in Autobiography. Trans. by Katherine
   Lampert. New York: The Macmillan Co., 1951
   The Fate of Man in the Modern World. Trans. by Donald Lowrie. New
   York: Morehouse Publishing Co., 1935
   Freedom and the Spirit. Trans. by O. F. Clarke. London: Geoffrey
   Bles, 1948

The Meaning of History. Trans. by George Reavey. London: Geoffrey Bles, 1949

The Origin of Russian Communism. Trans. by R. M. French. London: Geoffrey Bles, 1948

The Realm of Spirit and the Realm of Caesar. Trans. by Donald Lowrie. London: Victor Gollancz, 1952

Towards a New Epoch. Trans. by O. F. Clarke. London: Geoffrey Bles, 1949

BERGSON, HENRI

Creative Evolution. Trans. by Arthur Mitchell. Modern Library, New York: Random House, 1944

"Letter to Brunschvicg" in *Bulletin de la Société Française de Philosophie*, Vol. III. Paris: Armand Colin, 1903

Matter and Memory. Trans. by N. M. Paul and W. S. Palmer. London: George Allen & Unwin, 1950

Time and Free Will. Trans. by F. L. Pogson. London: George Allen & Unwin, 1950

Two Sources of Morality and Religion. Trans. by Audra and Brereton. New York: Henry Holt & Co., 1935

BERKELEY, GEORGE

Alciphron or The Minute Philosopher. In Vol. III, *The Works of George Berkeley, Bishop of Cloyne.* Ed. by A. A. Luce and T. E. Jessop. London: Thomas Nelson & Sons, 1950

BERLE, ADOLF A., JR.

Power Without Property, A New Development in American Economy. New York: Harcourt, Brace & Co., 1959

BERLIN, ISAIAH

Historical Inevitability. London: Oxford University Press, 1955

Two Concepts of Liberty. Oxford: Clarendon Press, 1958

BIDNEY, DAVID

"The Problem of Freedom and Authority in Cultural Perspective" in *Freedom and Authority in Our Time* (Twelfth Symposium of the Conference on Science, Philosophy and Religion). Ed. by Lyman Bryson, Louis Finkelstein, R. M. MacIver, Richard McKeon. New York, London: Harper & Brothers, 1953

BIRD, OTTO

"Dialectic in Philosophical Inquiry" in *Dialectica*, Vol. 9, No. 35/36, 1955

BLANSHARD, BRAND

"The Case for Determinism" in *Determinism and Freedom.* Ed. by Sidney Hook. New York: New York University Press, 1958

BODIN, JEAN

Six Books of the Commonwealth. Abridged and trans. by M. J. Tooley. Oxford: Basil Blackwell, no date

BOETHIUS

The Consolation of Philosophy. Trans. by W. V. Cooper. Modern Library, New York: Random House, 1943

(*Second Commentary on Aristotle's De Interpretatione*) *In Librum Aristotelis De Interpretatione Libri Sex*. Editio Secunda, seu Majora Commentaria. In Vol. 64, *Patrologia Latina*. Ed. by J. P. Migne. Paris: 1860

BOHR, NIELS
"Discussion with Einstein on Epistemological Problems in Atomic Physics" in *Albert Einstein: Philosopher-Scientist*. Ed. by Paul A. Schilpp. Evanston, Ill.: The Library of Living Philosophers, 1949
"On the Notions of Causality and Complementarity" in *Science*, Vol. 111, No. 2873 (reprinted in *Dialectica*, Vol. 2, No. 7/8, 1948)

BOKSER, BEN ZION
"Freedom and Authority" in *Freedom and Authority in Our Time* (Twelfth Symposium of the Conference on Science, Philosophy and Religion). Ed. by Lyman Bryson, Louis Finkelstein, R. M. MacIver, Richard McKeon. New York, London: Harper & Brothers, 1953

BORN, MAX
Natural Philosophy of Cause and Chance. Oxford: Clarendon Press, 1949

BOSANQUET, BERNARD
The Philosophical Theory of the State. London: Macmillan & Co., 1930
The Principle of Individuality and Value. London: Macmillan & Co., 1912

BOSSUET, JACQUES BENIGNE
Traité du Libre Arbitre. In Vol. IX, *Oeuvres Complètes*. 12 vols. Paris: Blond et Barral, no date

BOUCHER, JONATHAN
A View of the Causes and Consequences of the American Revolution, In Thirteen Discourses. London: G. G. and J. Robinson, 1797

BOURASSA, FRANÇOIS, S.J.
"La Liberté sous la loi" in *Enquête Sur La Liberté* (Féderation Internationale des Societés de Philosophie). Publié avec le concourse de l'U.N.E.S.C.O. Paris: Hermann & Cie., 1953

BOUTROUX, EMILE
Contingency of the Laws of Nature. Trans. by Fred Rothwell. Chicago: The Open Court Publishing Co., 1916

BOWNE, BORDEN PARKER
Personalism. Boston: Houghton Mifflin & Co., 1908

BRADLEY, FRANCIS HERBERT
Appearance and Reality. Oxford: Clarendon Press, 1951
Ethical Studies. Second Edition. Oxford: Clarendon Press, 1927

BRADLEY, R. D.
"Free Will: Problem or Pseudo-Problem?" in *Australasian Journal of Philosophy*. Vol. 36, No. 1, May 1958

BRANDEIS, LOUIS D.
"True Americanism" in *Freedom, Its Meaning*. Ed. by Ruth Nanda Anshen. New York: Harcourt, Brace & Co., 1940

BRAY, CHARLES
The Philosophy of Necessity. New York: Longmans, Green & Co., 1889

BRIDGMAN, PERCY W.
"Determinism in Modern Science" in *Determinism and Freedom*. Ed. by Sidney Hook. New York: New York University Press, 1958

BROAD, C. D.
Ethics and the History of Philosophy. New York: Humanities Press, 1952

BROGLIE, LOUIS DE
Matter and Light. Trans. by W. H. Johnston. New York: Dover Publications, Inc., 1946

BUCHANAN, SCOTT
Possibility. New York: Harcourt, Brace & Co., 1927

BUCKLE, HENRY THOMAS
History of Civilization in England. 2 vols. New York: Hearst's International Library, 1913

BURKE, EDMUND
The Works of the Right Honourable Edmund Burke. 6 vols. The World's Classics, London: Humphrey Milford, Oxford University Press, 1925

BURTT, EDWIN A.
"The Generic Definition of Philosophic Terms" in *The Philosophical Review*, Vol. LXII, No. 1, January 1953

CALHOUN, JOHN C.
Calhoun: Basic Documents. Ed. by John M. Anderson. State College, Pa.: Bald Eagle Press, 1952
Works of John C. Calhoun. 6 vols. Ed. by Richard K. Cralle. Charleston, S.C.: Steam Power-Press of Walker and James, 1851; "Disquisition on Government" in Vol. I; "Speech on the Oregon Bill" in Vol. IV

CALVIN, JOHN
Institutes of the Christian Religion. Trans. and ed. by John Allen. 2 vols. Grand Rapids, Mich.: Wm. B. Eerdmans Publishing Co., 1949
Ioannis Calvini Opera. Ed. by Guielmus Baum, Eduardus Cunitz, Eduardus Reuss. 59 vols. Same as *Corpus Reformatorum*, Vols. 29–87. Brunsvigae, apud C. A. Schwetschke et Filium, 1863–1900. (The texts cited are translated by W. E. Stuerman, *A Critical Study of Calvin's Concept of Faith*, Tulsa, 1952, pp. 264, 267)

CAMPBELL, CHARLES A.
In Defence of Free Will. Glasgow: Jackson, Son & Co., 1938
"Free Will: A Reply to Mr. R. D. Bradley" in *Australasian Journal of Philosophy*, Vol. 36, No. 1, May 1958
"Is 'Freewill' a Pseudo-Problem?" in *Mind*, Vol. LX, No. 240, October 1951
On Selfhood and Godhood. London: George Allen & Unwin, 1957
"The Psychology of the Effort of the Will" in *Proceedings of the Aristotelian Society*, Vol. XL, 1939–1940. London: Harrison & Sons, 1940
Scepticism and Construction. London: George Allen & Unwin, no date

CAPEK, MILIC
"The Doctrine of Necessity Re-Examined" in *The Review of Metaphysics*, Vol. V, No. 1, September 1951

CARNAP, RUDOLF
Logical Foundations of Probability. Chicago: University of Chicago
Press, 1950

CARR, EDWARD HALLETT
The New Society. London: St. Martins Press, 1957

CARRITT, EDGAR F.
Ethical and Political Thinking. London: Oxford University Press, 1947

CASSIRER, ERNST
Determinism and Indeterminism in Modern Physics. Trans. by O. Theo-
dor Benfey. New Haven: Yale University Press, 1956

CASTELL, ALBUREY
Science as a Goad to Philosophy. Philosophy Institute Publication. Vol.
III. Stockton: College of the Pacific, 1953

CHISHOLM, RODERICK W.
"Responsibility and Avoidability" in *Determinism and Freedom*. Ed. by
Sidney Hook. New York: New York University Press, 1958

CHRISTOFF, DANIEL
Recherche de la liberté. Paris: Bibliothèque de Philosophie Contempo-
raine, 1957

CICERO, MARCUS TULLIUS
De Divinatione. In *De Senectute, De Amicitia, De Divinatione*. Trans.
by William A. Falconer. Cambridge, Mass.: Harvard University Press,
1953
De Fato. In *De Oratore*, 2 vols., Book III together with *De Fato, Para-
doxa Stoicorum, De Partitione Oratoria*. Trans. by H. Rackham. Loeb
Classical Library, Cambridge, Mass.: Harvard University Press, 1948
(Laws). In *De Re Publica, De Legibus*. Trans. by Clinton W. Keyes.
Loeb Classical Library, Cambridge, Mass.: Harvard University Press,
1948
Offices, Essays and Letters. Offices trans. by Thomas Cockman. Every-
man's Library, New York: E. P. Dutton & Co., 1949
Paradoxa Stoicorum. In *De Oratore*, 2 vols., Book III together with *De
Fato, Paradoxa Stoicorum, De Partitione Oratoria*. Trans. by H. Rack-
ham. Loeb Classical Library, Cambridge, Mass.: Harvard University
Press, 1948
(Republic). In *De Re Publica, De Legibus*. Trans. by Clinton W. Keyes.
Loeb Classical Library, Cambridge, Mass.: Harvard University Press, 1952

CLARK, JOHN M.
"Forms of Economic Liberty and What Makes Them Important" in
Freedom, Its Meaning. Ed. by Ruth Nanda Anshen. New York: Harcourt,
Brace & Co., 1940

CLEMENCEAU, GEORGES
In the Evening of My Thought. Trans. by Thompson & Heard. Vols.
I and II. New York: Houghton Mifflin & Co., 1929

COLLINS, ANTHONY
A Philosophical Inquiry Concerning Human Liberty. London: R. Robinson, 1717

COMPTON, ARTHUR HOLLY
  The Freedom of Man. New Haven: Yale University Press, 1935
COMTE, AUGUSTE
  A General View of Positivism Or, Summary Exposition of the System of Thought and Life. London: George Routledge & Sons, Ltd., 1910
  Positive Philosophy. Trans. by Harriet Martineau. New York: Calvin Blanchard, 1855
  (Positive Polity). System of Positive Polity. 4 vols. Trans. by J. H. Bridges et al. London: Longmans, Green & Co., 1875–1877
Concept of Freedom. Ed. by Carl W. Grindel. Chicago: Henry Regnery Co., 1955
Contemporary British Philosophy: Personal Statements. Second Series. Ed. by J. H. Muirhead. New York: The Macmillan Co., 1953. (First and Second Series bound as one)
Contemporary British Philosophy: Personal Statements. Third Series. Ed. by H. D. Lewis. New York: The Macmillan Co., 1956
COX, HAROLD
  Economic Liberty. New York: Longmans, Green & Co., 1920
CRANSTON, MAURICE
  Freedom, A New Analysis. London: Longmans, Green & Co., 1953
CROCE, BENEDETTO
  My Philosophy, and Other Essays on the Moral and Political Problems of Our Time. Selected by R. Klibansky and trans. by E. F. Carritt. London: George Allen & Unwin, 1951
  The Philosophy of the Practical, Economic and Ethic. Trans. by Douglas Ainslie. London: Macmillan & Co., 1913
CROSLAND, C. A. R.
  "The Future of the Left" in *Encounter*, Vol. XIV, No. 3, March 1960
DALBIEZ, ROLAND
  "Le Moment de la Liberté" in *Revue Thomiste*, Vol. XLVIII, Nos. 1–2
DANTE ALIGHIERI
  (De Monarchia) On World Government or De Monarchia. Trans. by Herbert W. Schneider. New York: Liberal Arts Press, 1949
DEMOS, RAPHAEL
  "Human Freedom—Positive and Negative" in *Freedom, Its Meaning.* Ed. by Ruth Nanda Anshen. New York: Harcourt, Brace & Co., 1940
DESCARTES, RENÉ
  Oeuvres de Descartes. 12 vols. Ed. by Charles Adam and Paul Tannery. Paris: Leopold Cerf, 1897–1910
  (Philosophical Works) The Philosophical Works of Descartes. 2 vols. Ed. and trans. by Haldane and Ross. Cambridge University Press, 1931–1934
    Arguments. In Vol. II, *ibid.*
    Discourse on the Method. In Vol. I, *ibid.*
    Meditation IV. Ibid.
    Objections and Replies. In Vol. II, *ibid.*
    Passions of the Soul. In Vol. I, *ibid.*

The Principles of Philosophy. Ibid.
Determinism and Freedom In the Age of Modern Science. A philosophical symposium. Ed. by Sidney Hook. New York: New York University Press, 1958

DEWEY, JOHN
"Antinaturalism in Extremis" in *Naturalism and the Human Spirit.* Ed. by Y. Krikorian. New York: Columbia University Press, 1948
Democracy and Education: An Introduction to the Philosophy of Education. New York: The Macmillan Co., 1917
Ethics (with Tufts). Revised Edition. New York: Henry Holt & Co., 1952
Experience and Education. New York: The Macmillan Co., 1950
Experience and Nature. Chicago: The Open Court Publishing Co., 1925
Freedom and Culture. New York: G. P. Putnam's Sons, 1939
How We Think. New York: D. C. Heath & Co., 1910
Human Nature and Conduct: An Introduction to Social Psychology. Modern Library, New York: Random House, 1922
Knowing and the Known (with Bentley). Boston: The Beacon Press, 1949
Philosophy and Civilization. New York: Minton, Balch & Co., 1931
The Quest for Certainty: A Study of the Relation of Knowledge and Action. New York: Minton, Balch & Co., 1929
Reconstruction in Philosophy. New American Library, New York: Mentor Book 53, 1950

DIOGENES LAERTIUS
Lives of Eminent Philosophers. Trans. by R. D. Hicks. 2 vols. Loeb Classical Library, Cambridge, Mass.: Harvard University Press, 1950

DJILAS, MILOVAN
The New Class. New York: Frederick A. Praeger, 1957

DOSTOYEVSKY, FYODOR
The Brothers Karamazov. Trans. by Constance Garnett. Modern Library, New York: Random House, no date

DU-BOIS-REYMOND, ÉMIL
Reden (Scr. 1). Leipzig, 1886. (Quoted by Cassirer, *Determinism and Indeterminism in Modern Physics,* New Haven, 1956, pp. 4–7 passim)

DUCASSE, CURT J.
"Determinism, Freedom, and Responsibility" in *Determinism and Freedom.* Ed. by Sidney Hook. New York: New York University Press, 1958
Nature, Mind and Death. La Salle, Ill.: The Open Court Publishing Co., 1951

DUNCAN-JONES, A. E.
"Freedom: An Illustrative Puzzle" in *Proceedings of the Aristotelian Society,* Vol. XXXIX, 1938–1939. London: Harrison and Sons., 1939

DUNS SCOTUS, JOHN
Commentaria Oxoniensia. Ed. by P. Marianus Fernandez Garcia. 2 vols. Quaracchi, 1912–1914
Quaestiones Quodlibetales. In *Opera Omnia Joannis Duns Scoti.* Paris: Vivès, 1894
Reportata Parisiensia. Ibid.

DURKHEIM, EMILE

The Division of Labor in Society. Trans. by George Simpson. Glencoe, Ill.: The Free Press, 1949

The Rules of Sociological Method. Trans. by Sarah A. Solovay and John H. Mueller. Glencoe, Ill.: The Free Press, 1950

Sociology and Philosophy. Trans. by D. F. Pocock. Glencoe, Ill.: The Free Press, 1953

Suicide: A Study in Sociology. Trans. by John A. Spaulding and George Simpson. London: Routledge & Kegan Paul, 1952

EBERSOLE, FRANK B.

"Free Choice and the Demands of Morals" in *Mind,* Vol. LXI, No. 242, April 1952

EDDINGTON, ARTHUR STANLEY

The Nature of the Physical World. New York: The Macmillan Co., 1928

New Pathways in Science. Cambridge University Press, 1935

EDWARDS, JONATHAN

Freedom of the Will. Ed. by Paul Ramsey. New Haven: Yale University Press, 1957

EDWARDS, PAUL

"Hard and Soft Determinism" in *Determinism and Freedom.* Ed. by Sidney Hook. New York: New York University Press, 1958

EINSTEIN, ALBERT

"Remarks to the Essays Appearing in this Collective Volume" in *Albert Einstein: Philosopher-Scientist.* Ed. by Paul A. Schilpp. Evanston, Ill.: The Library of Living Philosophers, 1949

Albert Einstein: Philosopher-Scientist. Ed. by Paul A. Schilpp. Evanston, Ill.: The Library of Living Philosophers, 1949

Encyclopaedia Britannica. Eleventh Edition. 29 vols. New York: Encyclopaedia Britannica, 1910–1911

Encyclopaedia Britannica. Fourteenth Edition. 24 vols. New York: Encyclopaedia Britannica, 1959

Encyclopaedia Britannica. Ninth Edition. 25 vols. New York: Samuel L. Hall, 1878–1889

Encyclopaedia of the Social Sciences. 15 vols. Ed. by Edwin R. Seligman and Alvin Johnson. New York: The Macmillan Co., 1935

ENGELS, FRIEDRICH

(Anti-Dühring) Herr Eugen Dühring's Revolution in Science. Trans. by Emile Burns. Ed. by C. P. Dutt. London: Lawrence & Wishart, 1934

The Conditions of the Working-Class in England in 1844. Trans. by Florence Kelley Wischnewetzky. London: George Allen & Unwin, 1950

Letters to Americans, 1848–1895: A Selection. Trans. by Leonard E. Mine. New York: International Publishers Co., 1953

Ludwig Feuerbach and the Outcome of Classical German Philosophy. Ed. by C. P. Dutt. New York: International Publishers Co., 1941

Enquête Sur La Liberté. (Fédération Internationale des Sociétés de Philosophie). Publié avec le concourse de l'U.N.E.S.C.O. Paris: Hermann & Cie., 1953

EPICTETUS
(*Discourses*) *Arrian's Discourses of Epictetus.* Trans. by P. E. Matheson. In *The Stoic and Epicurean Philosophers.* Ed. by W. J. Oates. New York: Random House, 1940

EPICURUS
Letter to Herodotus. Trans. by C. Bailey. In *The Stoic and Epicurean Philosophers.* Ed. by W. J. Oates. New York: Random House, 1940
Letter to Menoeceus. Trans. by C. Bailey. *Ibid.*

ERASMUS, DESIDERIUS
De Libero Arbitrio Diatribe. In *Opera Omnia.* Ed. by J. Clericus. 10 tomes in 11 vols. Lugduni Batavorum, 1703–1706

Essays in Thomism. Ed. by Robert E. Brennan. New York: Sheed & Ward, 1942

Essays on Logic and Language. Ed. by A. G. N. Flew. New York: Philosophical Library, 1951

EWING, A. C.
"Indeterminism" in *The Review of Metaphysics,* Vol. V, No. 2, December 1951

FARRER, AUSTIN
The Freedom of the Will. London: Adam & Charles Black, 1958

FEUER, LEWIS SAMUEL
Spinoza and the Rise of Liberalism. Boston: Beacon Press, 1958

FICHTE, JOHANN GOTTLIEB
The Vocation of Man. Trans. by William Smith. La Salle, Ill.: The Open Court Publishing Co., 1946

FIELD, G. C.
"Kant's First Moral Principle" in *Mind,* Vol. XLI, No. 161, January 1932

FITZHUGH, GEORGE
Sociology for the South, or the Failure of Free Society. Richmond, Va.: A. Morris, 1854

FOOT, PHILIPPA
"Free-Will as Involving Determinism" in *The Philosophical Review,* Vol. LXVI, No. 4, October 1957

FOSDICK, DOROTHY
What is Liberty? A Study in Political Theory. New York: Harper & Brothers, 1939

FOUILLÉE, ALFRED
La Liberté et le déterminisme. Quatrième Edition. Paris: Felix Alcan, 1895

FRANK, PHILIPP
Modern Science and Its Philosophy. Cambridge, Mass.: Harvard University Press, 1941
Philosophy of Science. Englewood, N. J.: Prentice-Hall, 1957

FRANKLIN, BENJAMIN
A Dissertation on Liberty and Necessity, Pleasure and Pain. New York: The Facsimile Text Society, 1930

Freedom and Authority in Our Time (Twelfth Symposium of the Conference on Science, Philosophy and Religion). Ed. by Lyman Bryson, Louis Finkelstein, R. M. MacIver, Richard McKeon. New York, London: Harper & Brothers, 1953

Freedom in the Modern World. Ed. by Horace M. Kallen. New York: Coward-McCann, Inc., 1928

Freedom, Its Meaning. Ed. by Ruth Nanda Anshen. New York: Harcourt, Brace & Co., 1940

FREUD, SIGMUND
Civilization and Its Discontents. Trans. by Joan Riviere. Chicago: University of Chicago Press, no date (reprinted from edition published by Hogarth Press). In Vol. II: *Civilization and Its Discontents*. Trans. by Joan Riviere. New York: Jonathan Cape & Harrison Smith, 1930
Collected Papers. Trans. by Joan Riviere et al. 5 vols. London: Hogarth Press and the Institute of Psycho-Analysis, 1950
The Ego and the Id. Trans. by Joan Riviere. Fourth Edition. London: Hogarth Press, 1947
General Introduction to Psycho-Analysis. Authorized trans. by Joan Riviere. New York: Garden City Publishing Co., 1943
New Introductory Lectures on Psycho-Analysis. Trans. by W. J. H. Sprott. New York: W. W. Norton & Co., 1933
"The Origin and Development of Psychoanalysis" in *Outline of Psychoanalysis*. Ed. by J. S. Van Teslaar. New York: Boni & Liveright, 1924
An Outline of Psychoanalysis. Trans. by James Strachey. New York: W. W. Norton & Co., 1949

FROMM, ERICH
Escape from Freedom. New York: Rinehart & Co., 1941
Man For Himself, An Inquiry into the Psychology of Ethics. New York: Rinehart & Co., 1947

GALILEO GALILEI
(*Two New Sciences*) *Dialogues Concerning Two New Sciences*. Trans. by Henry Crew and Alfonso de Salvio. New York: The Macmillan Co., 1914

GALLIE, W. B.
"Free Will and Determinism Yet Again" (Lecture). Marjory Boyd: Printer to the Queen's University of Belfast, 1957

GEIGER, L. B.
"De la liberté. Les conceptions fondamentales et leur retentissement dans la philosophie pratique" in *Revue des Sciences philosphiques et théologiques*, Vol. XVI (1957), pp. 601–631

GENTILE, GIOVANNI
Che cosa è il fascismo. Firenze: Vallechi, 1924
"The Philosophic Basis of Fascism" in *Foreign Affairs*, Vol. 6, No. 2, January 1928

GEORGE, HENRY
Progress and Poverty. New York: Robert Schalkenbach Foundation, 1942

GILSON, ETIENNE
Jean Duns Scot. Paris: J. Vrin, 1952

La Philosophie au moyen âge. Paris: Payot, 1952
The Unity of Philosophical Experience. New York: Charles Scribner's Sons, 1957

GINSBERG, MORRIS
On the Diversity of Morals. Vol. I of *Essays in Sociology and Social Philosophy.* New York: The Macmillan Co., 1957

GREEN, THOMAS HILL
Lectures on the Principles of Political Obligation. New York: Longmans, Green & Co., 1950
Prolegomena to Ethics. Ed. by A. C. Bradley. Oxford: Clarendon Press, 1890

GREENE, THEODORE MEYER
Liberalism, Its Theory and Practice. Austin: University of Texas Press, 1957

GRUENDER, HUBERT
Experimental Psychology. Milwaukee: Bruce Publishing Co., 1932
Free Will. St. Louis: B. Herder, 1911

GUITTON, JEAN
"Prédestination et Liberté" in *La Liberté.* Neuchâtel: Baconnière, 1949

HALDANE, J. S.
Mechanism, Life and Personality: An Examination of the Mechanistic Theory of Life and Mind. London: John Murray, 1929

HALE, ROBERT L.
Freedom through Law: Public Control of Private Governing Power. New York: Columbia University Press, 1952

HALEVI, JUDAH
Kitab Al Khazari. Trans. from the Arabic with an Introduction by Hartwig Hirschfeld. London: Routledge & Sons, 1905

HAMILTON, ALEXANDER
The Basic Ideas of Alexander Hamilton. Ed. by Richard Morris. New York: Pocket Books Inc., 1957
The Mind of Alexander Hamilton. Arranged and with an Introduction by Saul K. Padover. New York: Harper & Brothers, 1958

HAMILTON, ALEXANDER (with JOHN JAY and JAMES MADISON)
The Federalist. Ed. by Henry Cabot Lodge. New York: G. P. Putnam's Sons, 1888

HAMILTON, SIR WILLIAM
Discussion on Philosophy and Literature, Education and University Reform. Second Edition. London: Longman, Brown, Green & Longmans, 1853
Lectures on Metaphysics. Fifth Edition. 2 vols. Ed. by Rev. H. L. Mansel and John Veitch. Edinburgh, London: William Blockwood & Sons, 1870

HARBRECHT, PAUL P.
Pension Funds and Economic Power. New York: Twentieth Century Fund, 1959

HARPER, FLOYD ARTHUR
    Liberty, A Path to Its Recovery. Irvington-on-Hudson, N. Y.: Foundation for Economic Education, 1949
HART, H. L. A.
    "The Ascription of Responsibility and Rights" in *Essays on Logic and Language.* Ed. by A. G. N. Flew. New York: Philosophical Library, 1951
HARTLEY, DAVID
    Observations on Man. Sixth Edition. London: T. Tegg & Son, 1834
HARTMANN, NICOLAI
    Ethics. Trans. by Stanton Coit. 3 vols. (Vol. III, *Moral Freedom*) New York: The Macmillan Co., 1951
HARTSHORNE, CHARLES
    "Causal Necessities: An Alternative to Hume" in *The Philosophical Review*, Vol. LXIII, No. 3, October 1954
    "Freedom Requires Indeterminism and Universal Causality" in *The Journal of Philosophy*, Vol. LV, No. 19, September 11, 1958
    Man's Vision of God. New York: Harper & Brothers, 1941
    Reality as Social Process. Glencoe, Ill.: The Free Press, 1953
HAWKINS, D. J. B.
    "Free Will and Right Action" in *The Modern Schoolman*, Vol. XXVI, No. 4, May 1949
HAYEK, FRIEDRICH A.
    Individualism and Economic Order. Chicago: University of Chicago Press, 1948
HEALD, MARK M.
    A Free Society. New York: Philosophical Library, 1953
HEGEL, GEORG WILHELM FRIEDRICH
    The Logic of Hegel. Trans. by W. Wallace. Second Edition. London: Oxford University Press, G. Camberlege, 1950
    The Phenomenology of Mind. Trans. by J. B. Baillie. Second Edition. New York: The Macmillan Co., 1949
    The Philosophy of History. Trans. by J. Sibree. New York: Willey Book Co., 1944
    Philosophy of Mind. Trans. by W. Wallace. Oxford: Clarendon Press, 1894
    (*Philosophy of Religion*) *Lectures on the Philosophy of Religion.* Trans. by E. B. Speirs and J. B. Sanderson. 3 vols. London: K. Paul Trench, Trübner, 1895
    Philosophy of Right. Trans. by T. M. Knox. Oxford: Clarendon Press, 1945
HEISENBERG, WERNER
    The Physicist's Conception of Nature. Trans. by Arnold J. Pomerans. New York: Harcourt, Brace & Co., 1958
HEITLER, WALTER
    "The Departure from Classical Thought in Modern Physics" in *Albert Einstein: Philosopher-Scientist.* Ed. by Paul A. Schilpp. Evanston, Ill.: The Library of Living Philosophers, 1949

HELMHOLTZ, H.
  Popular Lectures on Scientific Subjects. Trans. by E. Atkinson. London: Longmans, Green & Co., 1873

HEMPEL, CARL
  "Some Reflections on 'The Case for Determinism' " in *Determinism and Freedom.* Ed. by Sidney Hook. New York: New York University Press, 1958

HEWES, THOMAS
  Decentralize for Liberty. New York: Richard R. Smith, 1945

HIRSCH, MAX
  An Analysis of the Proposals and Conceptions of Socialism. New York: B. W. Huebsch, 1920
  Democracy Versus Socialism. Third Edition. New York: Henry George School of Social Science, 1939

HOBART, R. E.
  "Free Will as Involving Determinism and Inconceivable Without It" in *Mind,* Vol. XLIII, No. 169, January 1934

HOBBES, THOMAS
  Elements of Philosophy Concerning Body. In *Hobbes Selections.* Ed. by F. J. E. Woodbridge. New York: Charles Scribner's Sons, 1930
  The English Works of Thomas Hobbes. Ed. by W. Molesworth. 11 vols. London: John Bohn, 1839–1845
    (*Liberty, Necessity and Chance*) *The Questions Concerning Liberty, Necessity, and Chance.* In Vol. V, *ibid.*
    Philosophical Rudiments Concerning Government and Society. In Vol. II, *ibid.*
  Leviathan. Oxford: Clarendon Press, 1929

HOBHOUSE, L. T.
  The Elements of Social Justice. London: George Allen & Unwin, 1949
  The Metaphysical Theory of the State. London: George Allen & Unwin, 1959

HOCKING, WILLIAM E.
  Human Nature and Its Remaking. New Haven: Yale University Press, 1918
  The Self: Its Body and Freedom. New Haven: Yale University Press, 1928

HOFFMAN, R. J. S.
  The Will to Freedom. New York: Sheed & Ward, 1935

HOLBACH, BARON D'
  The System of Nature: or, Laws of the Moral and Physical World. Trans. by H. D. Robinson. 2 vols. in 1. Boston: J. P. Mendum, 1868

HOLCOMBE, ARTHUR N.
  The Foundations of the Modern Commonwealth. New York: Harper & Brothers, 1923

HOOK, SIDNEY
  "Necessity, Indeterminism, and Sentimentalism" in *Determinism and Freedom.* Ed. by Sidney Hook. New York: New York University Press, 1958

HOSPERS, JOHN
"Free-Will and Psychoanalysis" in *Readings in Ethical Theory*. Ed. by Wilfrid Sellars and John Hospers. New York: Appleton-Century-Crofts, Inc., 1952
"What Means This Freedom?" in *Determinism and Freedom*. Ed. by Sidney Hook. New York: New York University Press, 1958

HUGHES, G. E.
"Motive and Duty" in *Mind*, Vol. LIII, No. 212, October 1944

HUME, DAVID
Enquiry Concerning Human Understanding. In *Enquiries Concerning the Human Understanding and Concerning the Principles of Morals*. Ed. by L. A. Selby-Bigge. Oxford: Clarendon Press, 1951
A Treatise of Human Nature. Ed. by L. A. Selby-Bigge. Oxford: Clarendon Press, 1896

HUSIK, ISAAC
A History of Medieval Jewish Philosophy. Philadelphia: The Jewish Publication Society of America, 1940
Philosophical Essays. Oxford: Basil Blackwell, 1952

HUSSERL, EDMUND
Méditations Cartésiennes. Paris: Armand Colin, 1931

HUXLEY, THOMAS HENRY
Method and Results. New York: D. Appleton & Co., 1898

JAMES, WILLIAM
Collected Essays and Reviews. New York: Longmans, Green & Co., 1920
Essays in Radical Empiricism and *A Pluralistic Universe*. New York: Longmans, Green & Co., 1947
Pragmatism. New York: Longmans, Green & Co., 1949
Principles of Psychology. 2 vols. New York: Henry Holt, 1907
Some Problems of Philosophy. New York: Longmans, Green & Co., 1948
Talks to Teachers on Psychology. New Edition. Introduction by John Dewey and William H. Kilpatrick. New York: Longmans, Green & Co., 1949
The Will To Believe. New York: Longmans, Green & Co., 1917

JASPERS, KARL
The Origin and Goal of History. London: Routledge & Kegan Paul, 1953

JOAD, C. E. M.
Liberty Today. London: Watts and Co., 1934

JOHN OF ST. THOMAS
Cursus Theologicus. Ed. by L. Vivès. Paris: 1886

JONES, ROBERT VERNON
The Challenge of Liberty. Chicago: The Heritage Foundation, 1956

JOSEPH, H. W. B.
Some Problems in Ethics. Oxford: Clarendon Press, 1931

JOURDAN, PASCUAL
Anschauliche Quantentheorie. Berlin: Springer, 1936

KANT, IMMANUEL
(*Critique of Practical Reason*) *Critical Examination of Practical Reason*.

In *Kant's Critique of Practical Reason and Other Works on the Theory of Ethics*. Trans. by Thomas Kingsmill Abbot. Sixth Edition. London: Longmans, Green & Co., 1948
Critique of Pure Reason. Trans. by J. M. D. Meiklejohn. Revised Edition. New York: Willey Book Co., 1943
First Part of the Philosophical Theory of Religion. In *Kant's Critique of Practical Reason and Other Works on the Theory of Ethics*. Trans. by Thomas Kingsmill Abbot. Sixth Edition. London: Longmans, Green & Co., 1948
Fundamental Principles of the Metaphysic of Morals. Ibid.
Introduction to the Metaphysic of Morals. Ibid.
Preface to the Metaphysical Elements of Ethics. Ibid.
Prolegomena to Any Future Metaphysics. Ed. by Lewis Beck. New York: Liberal Arts Press, 1951
The Science of Right. Trans. by W. Hastie. In Vol. 42, *Great Books of the Western World*. Chicago: Encyclopaedia Britannica, 1952

KAUFMANN, W. A.
Nietzsche: Philosopher, Psychologist, Antichrist. Princeton: Princeton University Press, 1950

KELSEN, HANS
General Theory of Law and State. Trans. by A. Wedberg. Cambridge, Mass.: Harvard University Press, 1949
Vom Wesen und Werte der Demokratie. Tubingen: J. C. B. Mohr (Paul Siebeck), 1929
What is Justice? Berkeley: University of California Press, 1957

KENT, CHANCELLOR
"Debate in the New York Constitutional Convention, 1821" in *The People Shall Judge*, Vol. I. Ed. by the Staff, Social Sciences I, The College of the University of Chicago. Chicago: University of Chicago Press, 1953

KIERKEGAARD, SÖREN AABYE
Either/Or. Trans. by Walter Lowrie. 2 vols. Princeton: Princeton University Press, 1949
Journals. Ed. and trans. by Alexander Dru. London: Oxford University Press, 1951
Stages on Life's Way. Trans. by Walter Lowrie. Princeton: Princeton University Press, 1945
The Works of Love. Trans. by David F. Swenson and Lillian Mervin Swenson. Princeton: Princeton University Press, 1941

KIRK, RUSSELL
The American Cause. Chicago: Henry Regnery Co., 1957
"Conditions of Freedom" in *The Commonweal*, January 13, 1956
The Intelligent Woman's Guide to Conservatism. New York: Devin-Adair, 1957

KNIGHT, FRANK H.
Freedom and Reform. New York: Harper & Brothers, 1947
"The Ideal of Freedom" in *The Philosophy of American Democracy*. Ed. by Charner M. Perry. Chicago: University of Chicago Press, 1943
"The Meaning of Freedom," *ibid.*

KUEHNELT-LEDDIHN, ERIK VON
Liberty or Equality, The Challenge of Our Time. Caldwell, Id.: The Caxton Printers Ltd., 1952

LALANDE, ANDRÉ
Vocabulaire technique et critique de la philosophie. Paris: Presses Universitaires de France, 1947

LAMPRECHT, STERLING P.
"Metaphysical Background of the Problem of Freedom" in *Freedom and Authority in Our Time* (Twelfth Symposium of the Conference on Science, Philosophy and Religion). Ed. by Lyman Bryson, Louis Finkelstein, R. M. MacIver, Richard McKeon. New York, London: Harper & Brothers, 1953

LANGFORD, C. H.
"The Notion of Analysis in Moore's Philosophy" in *The Philosophy of G. E. Moore.* Ed. by Paul Schilpp. Second Edition. New York: Tudor Publishing Co., 1952

LASKI, HAROLD J.
A Grammar of Politics. Second Edition. New Haven: Yale University Press, 1931
"Liberty" in *Encyclopaedia of the Social Sciences*, Vol. IX. Ed. by Edwin R. A. Seligman and Alvin Johnson. New York: The Macmillan Co., 1935
Liberty in the Modern State. Harmondsworth, Middlesex: Penguin Books, 1937
The State in Theory and Practice. New York: The Viking Press, 1935

LAUER, ROSEMARY Z.
"St. Thomas's Theory of Intellectual Causation in Election" in *New Scholasticism*, Vol. XXVIII, No. 3, January 1954

LAWRENCE, NATHANIEL
"Causality, Will and Time" in *Review of Metaphysics*, Vol. IX, No. 1, September 1955

LECKY, WILLIAM E. H.
Democracy and Liberty. 2 vols. London: Longmans, Green & Co., 1896

LEIBNIZ, GOTTFRIED WILHELM
Discourse on Metaphysics, Correspondence with Arnauld, and Monadology. La Salle, Ill.: The Open Court Publishing Co., 1950
New Essays Concerning Human Understanding. Trans. by A. G. Langley. Third Edition. La Salle, Ill.: The Open Court Publishing Co., 1949
The Philosophical Works of Leibniz. Trans. by G. M. Duncan. Second Edition. New Haven: Tuttle, Morehouse & Taylor Co., 1908
Die philosophischen Schriften von G. W. Leibniz. Ed. by C. J. Gerhardt. 7 vols. Berlin: Weidmannsche Buchhandlung, 1875–1890. (The passage cited is quoted by B. Russell, *The Philosophy of Leibniz*, London, 1951, pp. 193–194, fn. 2)
Theodicy. Trans. by E. M. Huggard. Ed. by A. Farrer. New Haven: Yale University Press, 1952
"Von dem Verhängnisse," *Hauptschriften zur Grundlegung der Philosophie.* Ed. by E. Cassirer and A. Buchenau. Leipzig, 1924. (The passage cited is quoted by E. Cassirer, *Determinism and Indeterminism in Modern Physics*, New Haven, 1956, pp. 11–12)

LENIN, VLADIMIR ILYICH
  Selected Works. New York: International Publishers Co., 1943
  The State and Revolution. Moscow: Foreign Languages Publishing House, 1949
LEQUIER, JULES
  La recherche d'une première vérité. Paris: Armand Colin, 1924
LEWIS, H. D.
  "Guilt and Freedom" in *Readings in Ethical Theory*. Ed. by Wilfrid Sellars and John Hospers. New York: Appleton-Century-Crofts, Inc., 1952
  "Moral Freedom in Recent Ethics," *ibid.*
La Liberté (Actes du IVᵉ Congrès des Sociétés de Philosophie de Langue Française). Neuchâtel: Baconnière, 1949
LIPPMANN, WALTER
  The Method of Freedom. New York: The Macmillan Co., 1934
LOCKE, JOHN
  (*Civil Government*) *Treatise of Civil Government and a Letter Concerning Toleration*. Ed. by C. L. Sherman. New York: D. Appleton-Century Co., 1937
  An Essay Concerning Human Understanding. Ed. by A. C. Fraser. 2 vols. Oxford: Clarendon Press, 1894
LONERGAN, BERNARD
  Insight, A Study of Human Understanding. New York: Philosophical Library, 1958
  "St. Thomas' Theory of Operation" in *Theological Studies*, Vol. 3, No. 4, September 1942. New York: The America Press, 1942
LOSSKY, NIKOLAI
  Freedom of Will. Trans. by Natalie Duddington. London: Williams and Norgate, 1932
LOTZE, HERMAN
  Microcosmus. Trans. by Elizabeth Hamilton and E. E. Constance Jones. 2 vols. Edinburgh: T. & T. Clark, 1885
  Outlines of Psychology. Boston: Ginn & Co., 1886
  (*Practical Philosophy*) *Outlines of Practical Philosophy*. Ed. and trans. by George Ladd. Boston: Ginn & Co., 1885
LOVEJOY, ARTHUR O.
  "On Some Conditions of Progress in Philosophical Inquiry" in *The Philosophical Review*, Vol. XXVI, No. 2, March 1917
  The Revolt against Dualism. New York: W. W. Norton & Co., 1931
LUCRETIUS
  On the Nature of Things. Trans. by H. A. J. Munro. In *The Stoic and Epicurean Philosophers*. Ed. by W. J. Oates. New York: Random House, 1940
LUTHER, MARTIN
  A Commentary on St. Paul's Epistle to the Galatians. Trans. by Philip S. Watson. London: James Clarke & Co., 1953
  Luther's Works. Vol. 31. *Career of the Reformer*, I. Ed. by Harold J.

Grimm; Gen. Ed., Helmut T. Lehmann. Philadelphia: Muhlenberg Press, 1957
On the Bondage of the Will. Trans. by Henry Cole. Grand Rapids, Mich.: Wm. B. Eerdmans Publishing Co., 1931. In Vol. II: *The Bondage of the Will.* A new translation of *De Servo Arbitrio* (1525) by J. I. Packer and O. R. Johnston. London: James Clarke & Co., 1953
Reformation Writings of Martin Luther. 2 vols. Trans. by Bertram Lee Woolf. London: Lutterworth Press, 1952
The Table Talk of Martin Luther. Ed. by T. S. Kepler. New York: The World Publishing Co., 1952

MABBOTT, J. D.
"Free Will" in the *Encyclopaedia Britannica,* Fourteenth Edition. Vol. 9, 1959
"Free Will and Punishment" in *Contemporary British Philosophy,* Third Series. Ed. by H. D. Lewis. London: George Allen & Unwin, 1956

McDOUGALL, WILLIAM
An Introduction to Social Psychology. Thirteenth Edition. Boston: John W. Luce & Co., 1918

McGILVARY, E. B.
"Freedom and Necessity in Human Affairs" in *International Journal of Ethics,* Vol. XLV, No. 4, July 1935

MACHIAVELLI, NICCOLO
The Prince and the Discourses. Modern Library, New York: Random House, 1950

MacINTYRE, A. C.
"Determinism" in *Mind,* Vol. LXVI, No. 261, January 1957

MacIVER, ROBERT M.
"The Meaning of Liberty and Its Perversions" in *Freedom, Its Meaning.* Ed. by Ruth Nanda Anshen. New York: Harcourt, Brace & Co., 1940

McKEON, RICHARD
Freedom and History, The Semantics of Philosophical Controversies and Ideological Conflicts. New York: Noonday Press, 1952

MacLAGAN, W. C.
"Freedom of the Will" in *Proceedings of the Aristotelian Society,* Supplementary Vol. XXV, 1951

MACMURRAY, JOHN
Freedom in the Modern World. New York: D. Appleton-Century Co., 1938
"Freedom in the Personal Nexus" in *Freedom, Its Meaning.* Ed. by Ruth Nanda Anshen. New York: Harcourt, Brace & Co., 1940
The Self as Agent. New York: Harper & Brothers, 1958

McTAGGART, JOHN McTAGGART ELLIS
Some Dogmas of Religion. London: Edward Arnold, 1906

MADARIAGA, DON SALVADOR DE
"Rights of Man or Human Relations" in *Human Rights: Comments and Interpretations.* UNESCO symposium with introduction by Jacques Maritain. London: Allan Wingate, 1950

MAHER, MICHAEL
Psychology: Empirical and Rational. New York: Longmans, Green &
Co., 1925

MAIMONIDES (MOSES BEN MAIMON)
The Eight Chapters of Maimonides on Ethics. Ed. and trans. by Joseph
I. Gorfinkle. New York: Columbia University Press, 1912
The Guide for the Perplexed. Trans. by M. Friedlander. London: George
Routledge & Sons, 1928

MALINOWSKI, BRONISLAW
Freedom and Civilization. London: George Allen & Unwin, 1947

MANN, HORACE
"The Importance of Universal, Free Public Education" in *The People
Shall Judge,* Vol. I. Ed. by The Staff, Social Sciences I, The College
of the University of Chicago. Chicago: University of Chicago Press, 1953

MANNHEIM, KARL
Freedom, Power, and Democratic Planning. London: Routledge & Kegan
Paul, 1951
*Man and Society in an Age of Reconstruction: Studies in Modern Social
Structure.* Trans. by E. Shils. London: Kegan Paul, Trench, Trübner &
Co., 1946

MANSEL, HENRY
Prolegomena Logica. Oxford: William Graham, 1851

MARC, ANDRÉ
Psychologie Réflexive. 2 vols. Paris: Desclée de Brouwer, 1949

MARCEL, GABRIEL
The Mystery of Being. 2 vols. Chicago: Henry Regnery Co., 1950–1951

MARCUS AURELIUS
The Meditations of Marcus Aurelius Antoninus. Trans. by G. Long. In
The Stoic and Epicurean Philosophers. Ed. by W. J. Oates. New York:
Random House, 1940

MARGENAU, HENRY
"Einstein's Conception of Reality" in *Albert Einstein: Philosopher-Scien-
tist.* Ed. by Paul A. Schilpp. Evanston, Ill.: The Library of Living Philos-
ophers, 1949
The Nature of Physical Reality: A Philosophy of Modern Physics. New
York: McGraw-Hill Book Co., Inc., 1950
"Physical Versus Historical Reality" in *Philosophy of Science,* Vol. XIX,
No. 3, July 1952

MARITAIN, JACQUES
Christianity and Democracy. Trans. by D. C. Anson. New York: Charles
Scribner's Sons, 1950
"The Conquest of Freedom" in *Freedom, Its Meaning.* Ed. by Ruth
Nanda Anshen. New York: Harcourt, Brace & Co., 1940
Degrees of Knowledge. Second Edition. New translation directed by
Gerald B. Phelan. New York: Charles Scribner's Sons, 1959
Existence and the Existent. English version by L. Galantière and G. B.
Phelan. New York: Pantheon Books, 1949

Freedom in the Modern World. Trans. by R. O'Sullivan. New York: Charles Scribner's Sons, 1936

Man and the State. Chicago: University of Chicago Press, 1951

Ransoming the Time. Trans. by Harry L. Binsse. New York: Charles Scribner's Sons, 1948

"Reflections on Necessity and Contingency" in *Essays in Thomism.* Ed. by Robert E. Brennan. New York: Sheed & Ward, 1942

The Rights of Man and Natural Law. Trans. by D. C. Anson. New York: Charles Scribner's Sons, 1951

St. Thomas and the Problem of Evil. Milwaukee, Wis.: Marquette University Press, 1942

Scholasticism and Politics. Ed. by M. J. Adler. New York: The Macmillan Co., no date

True Humanism. Trans. by M. R. Adamson. New York: Charles Scribner's Sons, 1950

MARSILIUS OF PADUA

Defensor Pacis, The Defender of the Peace. 2 vols. Study and trans. by Alan Gewirth. New York: Columbia University Press, 1951 and 1956

MARTINEAU, JAMES

Types of Ethical Theory. 2 vols. New York: The Macmillan Co., 1886

MARX, KARL

Capital: A Critique of Political Economy. 3 vols. Ed. by Frederick Engels. Vol. I trans. by Samuel Moore and Edward Aveling. Vols. II and III trans. by Ernest Untermann. Chicago: Charles H. Kerr & Co., 1906–1909

Critique of the Gotha Programme. With appendices by Marx, Engels, and Lenin. Ed. by C. P. Dutt. New York: International Publishers Co., 1938

(*Critique of Political Economy*) *A Contribution to the Critique of Political Economy.* Trans. by N. I. Stoke. Calcutta: Bharati Library, 1904

MARX, KARL, and ENGELS, FRIEDRICH

The Communist Manifesto. In *Capital, The Communist Manifesto and Other Writings of Karl Marx.* Ed. by Max Eastman. Modern Library, New York: Random House, 1932

The German Ideology. Parts I and III. Ed. by R. Pascal. New York: International Publishers Co., 1947

Letters to Americans, 1848–1895, A Selection. Trans. by Leonard E. Mins. New York: International Publishers Co., 1953

Selected Correspondence: 1846–1895. Trans. by Dona Torr. New York: International Publishers Co., 1942

MASCALL, E. L.

Christian Theology and Natural Science. New York: The Ronald Press Co., 1956

MATSON, WALLACE I.

"On the Irrelevance of Free-Will to Moral Responsibility, and the Vacuity of the Latter" in *Mind,* Vol. LXV, No. 260, October 1956

MAYDIEU, A. J.

Le Désaccord. Paris: Presses Universitaires de France, 1952

MELANCHTHON, PHILIPP
Opera Quae Supersunt Omnia. 28 vols. Same as *Corpus Reformatorum*,
Vols. 1–28. Ed. by Carolus G. Bretschneider. Halis Saconum, apud C.
A. Schwetschke et Filium, 1834–1860

MEYERSON, EMILE
Identity and Reality. Trans. by K. Loewenberg. New York: The Macmillan Co., 1930

MILL, JOHN STUART
An Examination of Sir William Hamilton's Philosophy. Fifth Edition.
London: Longmans, Green, Reader and Dyer, 1878
Principles of Political Economy. London: Longmans, Green & Co., 1909
*A System of Logic, Ratiocinative and Inductive, being a connected view
of the Principles of Evidence, and the Methods of Scientific Investigation.*
2 vols. Fourth Edition. London: John W. Parker and Son, 1856
Utilitarianism, Liberty, and Representative Government. Everyman's Li-
brary, New York: E. P. Dutton & Co., 1944

MISES, LUDWIG VON
Socialism: An Economic and Sociological Analysis. Trans. by J. Kahane.
New Haven: Yale University Press, 1951
Theory and History, An Interpretation of Social and Economic Evolution.
New Haven: Yale University Press, 1957

MISES, RICHARD VON
Positivism, A Study in Human Understanding. New York: George Brazil-
ler, Inc., 1956

MOLEY, RAYMOND
How to Keep Our Liberty. A Program for Political Action. New York:
Alfred A. Knopf, 1952

MOLINA, D. LUDOVICO
*Concordia Liberi Arbitrii cum gratiae donis, divina praescientia, provi-
dentia, praedestinatione et reprobatione.* Paris: P. Lethielleux, 1876

MONTESQUIEU, BARON DE
The Spirit of the Laws. Trans. by Thomas Nugent. Revised by J. V.
Prichard. New York: D. Appleton & Co., 1912

MOORE, GEORGE EDWARD
"A Defence of Common Sense" in *Contemporary British Philosophy:
Personal Statements.* Second Series. Ed. by J. H. Muirhead. New York:
The Macmillan Co., 1953 (First and Second Series bound as one)
Ethics. Home University Library, London: Oxford University Press, 1949
"A Reply to My Critics" in *The Philosophy of G. E. Moore.* Ed. by
Paul Schilpp. The Library of Living Philosophers Series, New York: Tudor
Publishing Co., 1942

MORE, HENRY
(*An Account of Virtue*) The English translation of *Enchiridion Ethicum.*
London: Benjamin Tooke, 1690. Reproduced by The Facsimile Text
Society, New York: 1930

MUNNYNCK, P. DE
"La Démonstration Metaphysique de Libre Arbitre" in *Revue Neo-Scho-*

lastique de Philosophie. Vol. 20 (1913). Louvain: Institute Superior de Philosophie

NAGEL, ERNEST
"Some Notes on Determinism" in *Determinism and Freedom.* Ed. by Sidney Hook. New York: New York University Press, 1958

NEUMARK, DAVID
Essays in Jewish Philosophy. Vienna: Central Conference of American Rabbis (printed by A. Holzhausen's Successors), 1929

NICOLAS, M. J.
"La Liberté Humaine et le Problème du Mal" in *Revue Thomiste,* Vol. 48, Nos. 1–2

NIETZSCHE, FRIEDRICH
Beyond Good and Evil. In *The Philosophy of Nietzsche.* Trans. by Helen Zimmern. The Modern Library, New York: Random House, 1927
Human, All Too Human. Trans. by Alexander Harvey. Chicago: Charles H. Kerr & Co., 1908
The Twilight of the Idols. Trans. by Anthony M. Ludovici. London: T. N. Foulis, 1911 (Vol. 16, *Complete Works of Friedrich Nietzsche.* Ed. by Dr. Oscar Levy)
The Will to Power. Trans. by Anthony M. Ludovici. 2 vols. London: T. N. Foulis, 1914 (Vols. 14–15, *ibid.*)

NOWELL-SMITH, P. H.
"Determinists and Libertarians" in *Mind,* Vol. LXIII, No. 251, July 1954
Ethics. Baltimore: Penguin Books, 1954
"Free Will and Moral Responsibility" in *Mind,* Vol. LVII, No. 225, January 1948

OCKHAM, WILLIAM OF
The Tractatus de Praedestinatione et de Praescientia Dei et de Futuris Contingentibus of William of Ockham. Ed. by Philotheus Boehner. St. Bonaventure, N.Y.: The Franciscan Institute, 1945

OFSTAD, HARALD
"Can We Produce Decisions?" in *The Journal of Philosophy,* Vol. LVI, No. 3, January 1959
Outline of Psychoanalysis. Ed. by J. S. Van Teslaar. New York: Boni & Liveright, 1924

PAINE, THOMAS
Common Sense and Other Political Writings. Ed. by Nelson F. Adkins. The American Heritage Series, New York: Liberal Arts Press, 1953
Dissertation on First Principles of Government. In *Common Sense and Other Political Writings.* Ed. by Nelson F. Adkins. New York: Liberal Arts Press, 1953

PAP, ARTHUR
"Determinism, Freedom, Moral Responsibility, and Causal Talk" in *Determinism and Freedom.* Ed. by Sidney Hook. New York: New York University Press, 1958

PARETO, VILFREDO
The Mind and Society (Trattato di Sociologia generale). Ed. by Arthur

Livingston. Trans. by Andrew Bongiorno and Arthur Livingston. 4 vols. New York: Harcourt, Brace & Co., 1935

PASCAL, BLAISE
Pensées. Provincial Letters. Modern Library, New York: Random House, 1941

PAUL, G. A.
"H. D. Lewis on the Problem of Guilt" in Readings in Ethical Theory. Ed. by Wilfrid Sellars and John Hospers. New York: Appleton-Century-Crofts, Inc., 1952

PAULSEN, FRIEDRICH
A System of Ethics. Trans. by Frank Thilly. New York: Charles Scribner's Sons, 1911

PEIRCE, CHARLES SAUNDERS
Collected Papers of Charles Saunders Peirce. Ed. by Charles Hartshorne and Paul Weiss. 6 vols. Cambridge, Mass.: Harvard University Press, 1931

PELAGIUS
Expositions of Thirteen Epistles of St. Paul. Vol. IX, No. 2 in Texts and Studies: Contributions to Biblical and Patristic Literature. Ed. by J. Armitage Robinson, D.D. London: Cambridge University Press, 1926

The People Shall Judge. Ed. by The Staff, Social Sciences I, The College of the University of Chicago. 2 vols. Chicago: University of Chicago Press, 1953

PERRY, RALPH BARTON
The Thought and Character of William James. 2 vols. Boston: Little, Brown & Co., 1936
The Thought and Character of William James. Briefer version. Cambridge, Mass.: Harvard University Press, 1948
"What Does It Mean to Be Free?" in Pacific Spectator, Vol. VII, No. 2, Spring, 1953

PHILO
Every Good Man Is Free. In Vol. IX, Philo. Trans. by F. H. Colson. 10 vols. (and 2 supplementary vols.). The Loeb Classical Library, Cambridge, Mass.: Harvard University Press, 1954
On the Unchangeableness of God. In Vol. III, ibid. Trans. by F. H. Colson and G. H. Whitaker.

The Philosophy of American Democracy. Ed. by Charner M. Perry. Chicago: University of Chicago Press, 1943

The Philosophy of G. E. Moore. Ed. by Paul Schilpp. Second Edition. New York: Tudor Publishing Co., 1952

PLANCK, MAX
The New Science. New York: Meridian Books Inc., 1959
Scientific Autobiography and Other Papers. Trans. by Frank Gaynor. New York: Philosophical Library, 1949
The Universe in the Light of Modern Physics. Trans. by W. H. Johnston. New edition with a new section on Free-Will. London: George Allen & Unwin, 1937
Where is Science Going? In The New Science. Trans. by James Murphy. New York: Meridian Books Inc., 1959

PLATO
> *Meno.* In Vol. I, *The Dialogues of Plato.* Trans. by B. Jowett. 2 vols.
> *Republic. Ibid.*

PLEKHANOV, GEORGE
> *Fundamental Problems of Marxism.* Ed. by D. Riazanov. Marxist Library, New York: International Publishers, 1929

PLOTINUS
> *The Enneads.* 5 vols. Trans. by Stephen McKenna. London: Philip Lee Warner, 1917–1930

POLANYI, MICHAEL
> "Passion and Controversy in Science" in *Bulletin of the Atomic Scientists,* Vol. XIII, No. 4, April 1957

POPPER, KARL R.
> "Indeterminism in Quandum Physics" in *The British Journal of the Philosophy of Science,* Vol. I, Nos. 2 and 3, August and November 1950

PRIESTLEY, JOSEPH
> *The Doctrine of Philosophical Necessity Illustrated.* London, 1782

PRIESTLEY, JOSEPH, and PRICE, RICHARD
> *A Free Discussion of the Doctrine of Materialism and Philosophical Necessity, in a Correspondence between Dr. Price and Dr. Priestley.* London, 1778

RASHDALL, HASTINGS
> *The Theory of Good and Evil.* 2 vols. Oxford: Clarendon Press, 1907

REID, THOMAS
> *Essays on the Active Powers of the Human Mind.* In Vol. III, *The Works of Thomas Reid.* New York: Duyckinck, Collins, Hannay, Bliss and White, 1822

RENOUVIER, CHARLES
> (*Psychologie rationnelle*) *Traité de psychologie rationnelle.* 2 vols. (*Essais de critique générale,* deuxième essai.) Paris: Armand Colin, 1912

RICKABY, JOSEPH
> *Free Will and Four English Philosophers.* London: Burns & Oates, 1906

ROSS, W. DAVID
> *Foundations of Ethics.* Oxford: Clarendon Press, 1939

ROSSITER, CLINTON
> *Aspects of Liberty.* Essays presented to Robert E. Cushman. Ed. by Milton R. Konvitz and Clinton Rossiter. Ithaca, N.Y.: Cornell University Press, 1958
> *Conservatism in America.* New York: Alfred A. Knopf, 1955

ROUSSEAU, JEAN JACQUES
> *A Discourse on the Origin of Inequality.* In *The Social Contract and Discourses.* Trans. by G. D. H. Cole. Everyman's Library, New York: E. P. Dutton & Co., 1950
> *Emile,* or *Education.* Trans. by Barbara Foxley. Everyman's Library, New York: E. P. Dutton & Co., 1950
> (*Letters from the Mountain*) *Lettres écrites de la montagne.* In Vol.

VII, *Oeuvres complètes de J. J. Rousseau*. Ed. by P. R. Auguis. Paris: Dalibon, 1824
(*Political Economy*) *A Discourse on Political Economy*. In *The Social Contract and Discourses*. Trans. by G. D. H. Cole. Everyman's Library, New York: E. P. Dutton & Co., 1950
The Social Contract. *Ibid*.

ROYCE, JOSIAH
The Spirit of Modern Philosophy. Boston, New York: Houghton Mifflin Co., 1892

RUSSELL, BERTRAND
Authority and the Individual. New York: Simon and Schuster, 1949
"Determinism and Morals" in *The Hibbert Journal*, Vol. VII, 1908–1909
"Freedom and Government" in *Freedom, Its Meaning*. Ed. by Ruth Nanda Anshen. New York: Harcourt, Brace & Co., 1940
Human Society in Ethics and Politics. New York: Simon and Schuster, 1955
The Impact of Science on Society. New York: Simon and Schuster, 1953
Mysticism and Logic and Other Essays. London: Penguin Books, 1953
Political Ideals. New York: The Century Co., 1917
Roads to Freedom. Third Edition. London: George Allen & Unwin, 1949
Sceptical Essays. London: George Allen & Unwin, 1952

RUSSELL, L. J.
"Ought Implies Can" in *Proceedings of the Aristotelian Society*, Vol. XXXVI, 1935–1936. London: Harrison and Sons, 1936, pp. 151–186

RYAN, JOHN A.
"Religion on the Basis of the Postulates of Freedom" in *Freedom, Its Meaning*. Ed. by Ruth Nanda Anshen. New York: Harcourt, Brace & Co., 1940

SAADIA GAON
The Book of Beliefs and Opinions. Trans. by Samuel Rosenblatt. New Haven: Yale University Press, 1951

SAINT-SIMON
Doctrine de Saint-Simon. Exposition. Première année (1829). Ed. by C. Bouglé and Elie Halévy. Paris: Rivière, 1924. (The passage cited is quoted by Y. Simon, *Philosophy of Democratic Government*, p. 288, fn. 7)

SALVADORI, MASSIMO
Liberal Democracy. New York: Doubleday & Co., 1957

SANTAYANA, GEORGE
Dominations and Powers. New York: Charles Scribner's Sons, 1951

SARTRE, JEAN-PAUL
Being and Nothingness. An Essay on Phenomenological Ontology. Trans. by Hazel E. Barnes. New York: Philosophical Library, 1956
Existentialism. Trans. by Bernard Frechtman. New York: Philosophical Library, 1947

SCHELLING, FRIEDRICH WILHELM VON
Of Human Freedom. Trans. by James Gutman. Chicago: The Open Court Publishing Co., 1936

SCHILLER, F. C. S.

Riddles of the Sphinx, A Study in the Philosophy of Humanism. New and revised edition. New York: The Macmillan Co., 1910

Studies in Humanism. London: Macmillan & Co., 1907

SCHLICK, MORITZ

Problems of Ethics. Trans. by D. Rynin. New York: Prentice-Hall, 1939

SCHOPENHAUER, ARTHUR

"Free-Will and Fatalism" in *Complete Essays of Schopenhauer.* Trans. by T. Bailey Saunders. New York: Willey Book Co., 1942

SCHRÖDINGER, ERWIN

Science and Humanism. Cambridge University Press, 1951

What is Life? Cambridge University Press, 1951

SCULLY, JOSEPH G.

"The Initial Freedom" in *Concept of Freedom.* Ed. by Carl W. Grindel. Chicago: Henry Regnery Co., 1955

SECRÉTAN, CHARLES

Mon utopie. Lausanne: F. Payot, 1892

SENECA, LUCIUS ANNAEUS

Moral Essays. Trans. by J. W. Basore. 3 vols. The Loeb Classical Library, Vol. I, New York: G. P. Putnam's Sons, 1928; Vols. II and III, Cambridge, Mass.: Harvard University Press, 1935

SIDGWICK, HENRY

The Elements of Politics. Fourth Edition. London: Macmillan & Co., 1919

The Methods of Ethics. Fourth Edition. London: Macmillan & Co., 1906

SIMON, YVES

Community of the Free. Trans. by W. R. Trask. New York: Henry Holt & Co., 1947

Nature and Functions of Authority. Milwaukee, Wis.: Marquette University Press, 1940

Philosophy of Democratic Government. Chicago: University of Chicago Press, 1951

Prévoir et savoir. Montreal: Editions de l'Arbre, 1944

Traité du libre arbitre. Liège: Sciences et Lettres, 1951

Travaux d'Approche pour une Théorie du Déterminisme.

SIMONS, HENRY C.

Economic Policy for a Free Society. Chicago: University of Chicago Press, 1951

SMITH, ADAM

The Theory of Moral Sentiments. London: A. Millar, 1767

(Wealth of Nations) An Inquiry into the Nature and Causes of the Wealth of Nations. Ed. by Edwin Cannan. Modern Library, New York: Random House, 1937

SMITH, GERARD

"Intelligence and Liberty" in *New Scholasticism*, Vol. XV, No. 1, January 1941

"Luther and Free Choice" in *The Modern Schoolman*, Vol. XX, No. 2, January 1943

SOULE, GEORGE
The Future of Liberty. Norwood, Mass.: Norwood Press Linotype, Inc., 1936

SPENCER, HERBERT
"The Man versus the State" in *A Collection of Essays by Herbert Spencer*. Ed. by Truxtun Beale. New York: Mitchell Kennerley, 1916
In Vol. II:
The Man versus the State. Intro. by Albert Jay Nock. Caldwell, Id.: The Caxton Printers Ltd., 1954
The Principles of Ethics. 2 vols. New York: D. Appleton & Co., 1898
The Principles of Psychology. 3 vols. New York: D. Appleton & Co., 1897

SPINOZA, BENEDICT DE
The Correspondence of Spinoza. Trans. and ed. by A. Wolf. London: George Allen & Unwin, 1928
Ethics. In Vol. II, *The Chief Works of Benedict de Spinoza*. Trans. by R. H. M. Elwes. Vols. I and II bound as one. New York: Dover Publications, 1951
A Political Treatise. In Vol. I, *ibid*.
Theologico-Political Treatise. *Ibid*.

STAFFORD, JOHN W.
"Freedom in Experimental Psychology" in *Proceedings of the American Catholic Philosophical Association*, Vol. XVI, 1940

STALIN, JOSEPH
Problems of Leninism. New York: International Publishers Co., 1934

STARR, MARK
"Freedom and Authority in Labor Unions" in *Freedom and Authority in Our Time* (Twelfth Symposium of the Conference on Science, Philosophy and Religion). Ed. by Lyman Bryson, Louis Finkelstein, R.M. MacIver, Richard McKeon. New York, London: Harper & Brothers, 1953

STEBBING, SUSAN
Philosophy and the Physicists. New York: Dover Publications, 1958

STEVENSON, CHARLES L.
"Ethical Judgments and Avoidability" in *Readings in Ethical Theory*. New York: Appleton-Century-Crofts, Inc., 1952
Ethics and Language. New Haven: Yale University Press, 1950
The Stoic and Epicurean Philosophers. Ed. by W. J. Oates. New York: Random House, 1940

STOUT, A. K.
"Free Will and Responsibility" in *The Proceedings of the Aristotelian Society*, Vol. XXXVII, 1936–1937. London: Harrison & Sons, 1937

STRACHEY, JOHN
Contemporary Capitalism. New York: Random House, 1956

STURMTHAL, ADOLF F.
"Workers' Control: Freedom and Authority in the Plant" in *Freedom*

and Authority in Our Time (Twelfth Symposium of the Conference on Science, Philosophy and Religion). Ed. by Lyman Bryson, Louis Finkelstein, R. M. MacIver, Richard McKeon. New York, London: Harper & Brothers, 1953

SUAREZ, FRANCIS
Disputationes Metaphysicae. In Vols. XXV and XXVI, *Opera Omnia.* 28 vols. Paris: Vivès, 1856–1878

SUMNER, WILLIAM GRAHAM
"The Challenge of Facts" in *The People Shall Judge,* Vol. II. Ed. by The Staff, Social Sciences I, The College of the University of Chicago. Chicago: University of Chicago Press, 1953

TALMON, J. L.
The Rise of Totalitarian Democracy. Boston: Beacon Press, 1952

TARTARKIEWICZ, LADISLAS
"The History of Philosophy and the Art of Writing It" in *Diogenes,* No. 20, Winter, 1957

TAWNEY, RICHARD HENRY
The Acquisitive Society. New York: Harcourt, Brace & Co., 1920
The Attack and Other Papers. New York: Harcourt, Brace & Co., 1953
Equality. New York: Harcourt, Brace & Co., 1931

TAYLOR, A. E.
"The Freedom of Man" in *Contemporary British Philosophy: Personal Statements.* Second Series. Ed. by J. H. Muirhead. New York: The Macmillan Co., 1953 (First and Second Series bound as one)

TAYLOR, RICHARD
"Determinism and the Theory of Agency" in *Determinism and Freedom.* Ed. by Sidney Hook. New York: New York University Press, 1958

THOMAS, NORMAN
After the New Deal, What? New York: The Macmillan Co., 1936

TILLICH, PAUL
"Freedom in the Period of Transformation" in *Freedom, Its Meaning.* Ed. by Ruth Nanda Anshen. New York: Harcourt, Brace & Co., 1940
The Protestant Era. Trans. by J. L. Adams. Chicago: University of Chicago Press, 1951
Systematic Theology. Vol. I. Chicago: University of Chicago Press, 1951

TOCQUEVILLE, ALEXIS DE
Democracy in America. Ed. by Phillips Bradley. 2 vols. New York: Alfred A. Knopf, 1951

TOLSTOY, LEO
War and Peace. Trans. by Louise and Aylmer Maude. New York: Simon and Schuster, 1942

TUCKER, ABRAHAM
Free Will, Foreknowledge and Fate: A Fragment. By Edward Search (pseudonym). London: R. and J. Dosdley, 1763

UNIVERSITY OF CALIFORNIA ASSOCIATES
Knowledge and Society. New York: D. Appleton-Century Co., 1938

VAIL, CHARLES H.
"The Socialist Movement" in *The People Shall Judge*, Vol. II. Ed. by The Staff, Social Sciences I, The College of the University of Chicago. Chicago: University of Chicago Press, 1953

VICO, GIAMBATTISTA
The New Science of Giambattista Vico. Trans. by Max H. Fisch and Thomas G. Bergin. Ithaca, N.Y.: Cornell University Press, 1948

VIERECK, PETER
Shame and Glory of the Intellectuals. Boston: The Beacon Press, 1953

VOLTAIRE, FRANÇOIS DE
A Philosophical Dictionary. 10 vols. In *The Works of Voltaire*. Trans. by William F. Fleming. 42 vols. Paris: E. R. Dumont, 1901. In Vol. II: *Voltaire's Philosophical Dictionary*. Selected and trans. by H. I. Woolf. London: George Allen & Unwin, 1924

WATTS, ISAAC
An Essay on the Freedom of the Will in God and His Creatures. London: J. Roberts, 1732

WAXMAN, MEYER
The Philosophy of Don Hasdai Crescas. New York: Columbia University Press, 1920

WEISS, PAUL
"Common Sense and Beyond" in *Determinism and Freedom*. Ed. by Sidney Hook. New York: New York University Press, 1958
Man's Freedom. New Haven: Yale University Press, 1950
Modes of Being. Carbondale: Southern Illinois University Press, 1958
Nature and Man. New York: Henry Holt & Co., 1947

WEYL, HERMANN
The Open World. New Haven: Yale University Press, 1932
Philosophy of Mathematics and Natural Science. Trans. by Olaf Helmer. Princeton: Princeton University Press, 1949

WHITEHEAD, ALFRED NORTH
Adventures of Ideas. New York: The Macmillan Co., 1952
"Aspects of Freedom" in *Freedom, Its Meaning*. Ed. by Ruth Nanda Anshen. New York: Harcourt, Brace & Co., 1940
The Function of Reason. Princeton: Princeton University Press, 1929
Process and Reality. New York: The Macmillan Co., 1941

WILLIAMS, GARDNER
"Free Will and Determinism" in *The Journal of Philosophy*, Vol. XXXVIII, No. 26, December 1941

WINDLEBAND, WILHELM
Über Willensfreiheit. Tubingen und Leipzig: C. B. Mohr (Paul Giebeck), 1904

WINTHROP, JOHN
The History of New England, from 1630–1649. Ed. by James Savage. 2 vols. Boston: Thomas B. Wait & Son, 1826

WITTGENSTEIN, LUDWIG
Tractatus Logico-Philosophicus. London: Routledge & Kegan Paul, 1958

Wootton, Barbara
Freedom Under Planning. Chapel Hill: University of North Carolina Press, 1945
Zilboorg, Gregory
Sigmund Freud. His Exploration of the Mind of Man. New York: Charles Scribner's Sons, 1951

LIST OF OTHER WORKS EXAMINED

I. BOOKS

ACTON, LORD DALBERG
Essays on Church and State. Ed. by Douglas Woodruff. London, 1952
The History of Freedom. London, 1909

ADAMS, BROOKS
The Law of Civilization and Decay: An Essay on History. New York, 1943
The Theory of Social Revolutions. New York, 1913

ADAMS, HENRY BROOKS
The Degradation of the Democratic Dogma. Ed. by B. Adams. New York, 1920

ADAMS, JOHN
A Defence of the Constitutions of Government of the United States. 3 vols. Philadelphia, 1797
Discourses on Davila. Boston, 1805
The Works of John Adams. 10 vols. Boston, 1852–1865

ALLPORT, GORDON W.
Becoming: Basic Considerations for a Psychology of Personality. New Haven, 1955

AQUINAS, THOMAS
Commentaria in Aristotelis Libros Perihermeneias. In Vol. I, Opera Omnia. Editio Leonina. Rome, 1882
In Metaphysicam Aristotelis Commentaria. Ed. by M. O. Cathala, O. P. Turin, 1935
In Octo Libros Politicorum Aristotelis. Editio Lavallensis. Quebec, 1940

ARNOLD, MAGDA, and GASSON, JOHN A.
The Human Person. New York, 1954

ARNOLD, MATTHEW
Culture and Anarchy, An Essay in Political and Social Criticism. London, 1882
Mixed Essays, Irish Essays and Others. New York, 1904

ASCOLI, MAX
The Power of Freedom. New York, 1949

AUGUSTINE
The City of God. 3 vols. Trans. by Zema and Walsh. New York, 1950

AVERROES
Tahafut al-Tahafut, Incoherence of the Incoherent. 2 vols. Trans. by Van den Bergh. London, 1954

AVICENNA
Avicenna's Psychology. An English translation of *Kitab al-Najat* Book II, Ch. VI by F. Rahman. London, 1952
Le Livre de Science. Trans. by M. Achena and Henri Masse. 2 vols. Paris, 1955–1958

AYER, A. J.
Foundations of Empirical Knowledge. London, 1951
Language, Truth and Logic. London, 1949

BABBITT, IRVING
Democracy and Leadership. New York, 1953

BAGEHOT, WALTER
The English Constitution. London, 1955
Physics and Politics. New York, 1948

BAIN, ALEXANDER
Moral Science: A Compendium of Ethics. New York, 1869

BALFOUR, ARTHUR JAMES
Essays Speculative and Political. London, 1920

BANTOCK, G. H.
Freedom and Authority in Education. Chicago, 1952

BARRETT, WILLIAM
Irrational Man, A Study in Existential Philosophy. Garden City, N.Y., 1958

BARTH, KARL
Credo. London, 1937
The Doctrine of the Word of God. Volume I, Part I of *Church Dogmatics.* Trans. by G. T. Thanson. New York, 1949
The Epistle to the Romans. Trans. from Sixth edition by Edwyn C. Hoskyns. London, 1953

BARZUN, JACQUES
Of Human Freedom. Boston, 1939

BASTIAT, FRÉDÉRIC
Economic Sophisms. Trans. by P. J. Stirling. Edinburgh, 1873

BAUER, RAYMOND A.
The New Man in Soviet Psychology. Cambridge, 1952

BAY, CHRISTIAN
The Structure of Freedom. Stanford, 1958

BECKER, CARL
The Declaration of Independence. New York, 1922
New Liberties for Old. New Haven, 1941

BELLARMINE, ROBERT
De Controversiis Christianae Fidei. 5 vols. Venice, 1721

BENETT, WILLIAM
Freedom and Liberty. New York, 1920

BERDYAEV, NICOLAS ALEXANDROVITCH
The Divine and the Human. Trans. by R. M. French. London, 1949
The End of Our Time. Trans. by Donald Attwater. London, 1935
Slavery and Freedom. Trans. by R. M. French. New York, 1944
Spirit and Reality. Trans. by George Reavey. London, 1946

BERGSON, HENRI
The Creative Mind. Trans. by Mabelle Andison. New York, 1946
Note on "Liberté." In *Vocabulaire technique et critique de la philosophie.*
Ed. by André Lalande. Fifth Edition. Paris, 1947

BERKELEY, GEORGE
The Works of George Berkeley, Bishop of Cloyne. Ed. by A. A. Luce
and T. E. Jessop. 9 vols. London, 1948–1957

BERLE, ADOLF A., JR.
Economic Power and the Free Society. New York, 1957

BERMAL, J. D.
The Freedom of Necessity. London, 1949

BERNDSTON, CARL ARTHUR E.
The Problem of Free Will in Recent Philosophy. Chicago, 1942

BERNSTEIN, EDWARD
*Cromwell and Communism: Socialism and Democracy in the Great English
Revolution.* London, 1930

BLANSHARD, BRAND
The Nature of Thought. 2 vols. London, 1948

BODIN, JEAN
The Six Books of a Commonweale. Trans. by R. Knolles. London, 1606

BOSANQUET, BERNARD
Psychology of the Moral Self. London, 1904
The Value and Destiny of the Individual. London, 1923

BOUTROUX, ÉMILE
The Contingency of the Laws of Nature. Trans. by Fred Rothwell. Chicago, 1916
Historical Studies in Philosophy. Trans. by Fred Rothwell. London, 1912

BOWNE, BORDEN PARKER
Metaphysics: A Study in First Principles. New York, 1882

BRADLEY, FRANCIS HERBERT
Collected Essays. 2 vols. Oxford, 1935

BRENNAN, ROBERT EDWARD
Thomistic Psychology. New York, 1941

Brett's History of Psychology. Edited and abridged by R. S. Peters. New York, 1953

BROGAN, D. W.
The Free State. New York, 1945

BROGLIE, LOUIS DE
The Revolution in Physics. New York, 1953

BROWNSON, ORESTES
The American Republic. New York, 1866

BRUNER, EMILE
   Man in Revolt, A Christian Anthropology. London, 1953

BUNGE, MARIO
   Causality. The Place of the Causal Principle in Modern Science. Cambridge, Mass., 1959

BURCKHARDT, JAKOB
   Force and Freedom, Reflections on History. Ed. by J. H. Nichols. New York, 1943

BURGESS, JOHN W.
   Reconciliation of Government with Liberty. New York, 1915

BURKE, EDMUND
   Correspondence of the Right Honourable Edmund Burke. 4 vols. Ed. by William and Bourke. London, 1833

BURLAMAQUI, J. J.
   The Principles of Natural and Politic Law. Trans. by Nugent. Philadelphia, 1859

BURNS, EDWARD McNALL
   Ideas in Conflict. New York, 1960

BURY, JOHN
   A History of Freedom of Thought. New York, 1913

BUTTERFIELD, HERBERT
   Liberty in the Modern World. Toronto, 1952

BYE, RAYMOND T.
   Principles of Economics. Fifth Edition. New York, 1956

CAMPBELL, CHARLES A.
   "Self-Activity and its Modes" in *Contemporary British Philosophy.* Third Series. Ed. by H. D. Lewis. London, 1956

CAMUS, ALBERT
   The Myth of Sisyphus. New York, 1955

CARLYLE, ALEXANDER J.
   Political Liberty, A History of the Conception in the Middle Ages and Modern Times. Oxford, 1941

CARLYLE, R. W. and CARLYLE, A. J.
   A History of Mediaeval Political Theory in the West. Six vols. New York, n.d.

CARLYLE, THOMAS
   Past and Present. London, 1950

CARR, EDWARD H.
   The Soviet Impact on the Western World. New York, 1947

CASSIRER, ERNST
   An Essay on Man. New Haven, 1944
   Freiheit and Form. Berlin, 1918
   The Myth of the State. New Haven, 1950
   The Question of Jean Jacques Rousseau. New York, 1954

CECIL, LORD HUGH
   Conservatism. London, 1919

Liberty and Authority. London, 1910

CHAFEE, ZECHARIAH, JR.
Free Speech in the United States. Cambridge, 1941

CLARK, JOHN MAURICE
Economic Institutions and Human Welfare. New York, 1957

CLARK, MARY T.
Augustine, Philosopher of Freedom. New York, 1959

COHEN, MORRIS RAPHAEL
The Faith of a Liberal. New York, 1946
Law and the Social Order: Essays in Legal Philosophy. New York, 1933

COLLINGWOOD, ROBIN GEORGE
Idea of History. Oxford, 1951
The New Leviathan. Oxford, 1947

The Conservative Tradition. Ed. by R. J. White. London, 1950

COOPER, JAMES F.
The American Democrat. New York, 1931

CRESCAS, CHASDAI BEN ABRAHAM
Or Adonai. Book I, ed. and trans. by H. A. Wolfson. Cambridge, Mass., 1929

CROCE, BENEDETTO
History as the Story of Liberty. Trans. by S. Sprigge. New York, 1941
Politics and Morals. Trans. by S. J. Castiglione. New York, 1945

CROPSEY, JOSEPH
Polity and Economy: An Interpretation of the Principles of Adam Smith. The Hague, 1957

CUDWORTH, RALPH
A Treatise on Freewill. Ed. by J. Allen. London, 1838
The True Intellectual System of the Universe. London, 1678

CUMMINGS, HOMER S.
Liberty under Law and Administration. New York, 1934

DALY, JEANNE JOSEPH
The Metaphysical Foundations of Free Will as a Transcendental Aspect of the Act of Existence in the Philosophy of St. Thomas Aquinas. Washington, D.C., 1958

DARBON, ANDRÉ
Philosophie de la Volonté. Paris, 1951

DAUDIN, HENRI
La Liberté de la Volonté: Signification des Doctrines Classiques. Paris, 1950

DAVENPORT, RUSSELL
The Dignity of Man. New York, 1955

DAVIDSON, DONALD and SUPPES, PATRICK
Decision Making, An Experimental Approach. In collaboration with Sidney Siegel. Stanford, 1957

DAWSON, CHRISTOPHER
Beyond Politics. New York, 1939

Religion and the Modern State. New York, 1937

DEFOE, DANIEL
 An Essay on the Regulation of the Press. Oxford, 1948

The Democratic Spirit. A Collection of American Writings from the Earliest Times to the Present Day. Ed. by Bernard Smith. New York, 1941

DEWEY, JOHN
 Ethical Principles Underlying Education. Third Yearbook Hobart Society, 1897
 "Freedom of Will" in A *Cyclopaedia of Education*, Vol. II. New York, 1911
 Individualism Old and New. New York, 1930
 Liberalism and Social Action. New York, 1935
 The Public and Its Problems. New York, 1927

DICKINSON, GOLDSWORTHY LOWES
 Justice and Liberty: A Political Dialogue. New York, 1908

Dilthey's Philosophy of Existence. Translation of an Essay with an Introduction by William Kluback and Martin Weinbaum. New York, 1957

DOBZHANSKY, THEODOSIUS
 The Biological Basis of Human Freedom. New York, 1956

DODDS, E. R.
 The Greeks and the Irrational. Berkeley, 1951

DONDO, M. M.
 The French Faust: Henri de Saint Simon. New York, 1955

DRUCKER, PETER F.
 The New Society. New York, 1949

DUCASSE, CURT J.
 Causation and the Types of Necessity. Seattle, 1924
 A Philosophical Scrutiny of Religion. New York, 1953

DUGUIT, LEON
 Le Droit social. Paris, 1911
 Law in the Modern State. Trans. by F. and H. Laski. New York, 1919
 Souveraineté et liberté, leçons faites à l'Université Columbia. Paris, 1922

DUNAYEVSKAYA, RAYA
 Marxism and Freedom. New York, 1958

EDDINGTON, SIR ARTHUR
 The Philosophy of Physical Science. Cambridge, 1939

ENGELS, FRIEDRICH
 Dialectics of Nature. Trans. and ed. by Clemens Dutt. New York, 1940
 "Introduction to the Address on the Question of Free Trade" in *The Poverty of Philosophy*. Ed. by C. P. Dutt and V. Chattopadhyaya. New York, n.d.
 The Origin of the Family, Private Property and the State. New York, 1942

Essays on Logic and Language. Second Series. Ed. by A. G. N. Flew. Oxford, 1953

EWING, A. C.
 The Fundamental Questions of Philosophy. New York, 1951
 The Morality of Punishment. London, 1929

FANFANI, AMINTORE
Catholicism, Protestantism and Capitalism. New York, 1955

FERGUSON, JOHN
Pelagius. Cambridge, 1956

FEUERBACH, LUDWIG
The Essence of Christianity. Trans. by Marian Evans. London, 1854

FICHTE, JOHANN GOTTLIEB
The Science of Rights. Trans. by A. E. Kroeger. London, 1889

FICINO, MARSILIO
"Five Questions Concerning the Mind" in The Renaissance Philosophy of Man. Chicago, 1950

FILMER, SIR ROBERT
Patriarcha and Other Political Works. Ed. by Peter Laslett. Oxford, 1949

FINANCE, JOSEPH DE
Etre et Agir. Paris, 1945
Existence et Liberté. Paris, 1955

FISKE, JOHN
Outlines of Cosmic Philosophy: Based on the Doctrine of Evolution with Criticisms on the Positive Philosophy. 2 vols. London, 1874

FONSEGRIVE, GEORGE
"Déterminisme" in Dictionaire Théologie Catholique. Essai sur le Libre Arbitre, sa Théorie et son Histoire. Paris, 1896

FOUILLÉE, ALFRED JULES EMILE
La Psychologie de Idées-Forces. Paris, 1912

FOURIER, FRANÇOIS MARIE CHARLES
Selections from Works of Fourier. Trans. by Julia Franklin. London, 1901

FRANK, JEROME
Fate and Freedom: A Philosophy for Free Americans. Revised Edition. Boston, 1953

FRANK, PHILIPP
Between Physics and Philosophy. Cambridge, Mass., 1941
Foundations of Physics. Chicago, 1946

Freedom and Reason. Studies in Philosophy and Jewish Culture in Memory of Morris Raphael Cohen. Ed. by Baron, Nagel and Pinson. Glencoe, Ill., 1951

FREUD, SIGMUND
"Psychopathology of Everyday Life" in Basic Writings of Sigmund Freud. New York, 1938

GALBRAITH, JOHN KENNETH
The Affluent Society. Boston, 1958

GAY, PETER
The Dilemma of Democratic Socialism. Eduard Bernstein's Challenge to Marx. New York, 1952

GEORGE, HENRY
The Science of Political Economy. New York, 1953

GILSON, ÉTIENNE
La Liberté chez Descartes et la Théologie. Paris, 1913

GODKIN, EDWIN L.
Problems of Modern Democracy. New York, 1896
Reflections and Comments. New York, 1895
Unforeseen Tendencies of Democracy. Boston and New York, 1898

GODWIN, WILLIAM
An Enquiry Concerning Political Justice, and Its Influence on General Virtue and Happiness. 2 vols. London, 1842

GOSNELL, HAROLD F.
Democracy, the Threshold of Freedom. New York, 1948

GREEN, THOMAS HILL
Works of T. H. Green. Ed. by R. L. Nettleship. 3 vols. London, 1885–1888

GRENE, MARJORIE
Dreadful Freedom. Chicago, 1948

GRUENDER, HUBERT
Psychology Without a Soul. St. Louis, 1911

GURVITCH, GEORGES
The Bill of Social Rights. New York, 1946

HACKER, LOUIS M.
Politics and the Corporation. New York, 1958

HALDANE, J. S.
The Sciences and Philosophy. Garden City, N.Y., 1929

HAMILTON, ALEXANDER
Alexander Hamilton and the Founding of the Nation. Ed. by Richard B. Morris. New York, 1957

HAND, LEARNED
Liberty. Stamford, Conn., 1941
The Spirit of Liberty. New York, 1954

A Handbook of Marxism. A Collection of Extracts from Marx, Engels and the Greatest of their Followers. Ed. by Emile Burns. New York, 1935

HAYEK, FRIEDRICH A.
The Constitution of Liberty. Chicago, 1960
Freedom and the Economic System. Public Policy Pamphlet No. 29. Chicago, 1939

HAZLITT, HENRY
The Free Man's Library. Princeton, 1956

HEGEL, GEORG WILHELM FRIEDRICH
Naturphilosophie. Second Part of Encyklopadie der Philosophischen Wissenschaften. Ed. by Karl Rosenkranz. Berlin, 1870
Science of Logic. Trans. by W. H. Johnston and L. G. Struthers. 2 vols. New York, 1951

HEIDEGGER, MARTIN
Existence and Being. Chicago, 1949

HERRICK, C. JUDSON
Fatalism or Freedom. New York, 1926

HOBBES, THOMAS
The Elements of Law. Ed. by Ferdinand Tönnies. Cambridge, 1928
Of Liberty and Necessity. In Vol. IV, *The English Works of Thomas Hobbes.* Ed. by W. Molesworth. 11 vols. London, 1839–1845

HOCKING, WILLIAM E.
Freedom of the Press. Chicago, 1947
Man and the State. New Haven, 1926
The Spirit of World Politics. New York, 1932

HODGSON, SHADWORTH HOLLWAY
Philosophy and Experience. London, 1885

HOFFMAN, ROSS
The Spirit of Politics and the Future of Freedom. Milwaukee, 1951

HOOK, SIDNEY
Determinism and Freedom in the Age of Modern Science. New York, 1958
From Hegel to Marx. New York, 1950
Heresy, Yes; Conspiracy, No. New York, 1953
The Hero in History. New York, 1950
Reason, Social Myths and Democracy. New York, 1940
Toward the Understanding of Karl Marx. New York, 1933

HOOKER, RICHARD
Hooker's Works. 2 vols. Oxford, 1885
On the Laws of Ecclesiastical Polity. New York, 1907

HOOVER, CALVIN
The Economy, Liberty and the State. New York, 1959

HORTEN, MAX JOSEPH
Die Metaphysik des Averroes. Halle, 1912

HUNT, R. N. CAREN
Marxism, Past and Present. New York, 1955

HURST, JAMES WILLARD
Law and the Conditions of Freedom. Madison, 1956

HUSSERL, EDMUND
Ideas. General Introduction to Pure Phenomenology. Trans. by W. R. B. Gibson. London, 1952
Logische Untersuchungen. Halle, 1900–1921

JAMES, WILLIAM
Essays on Faith and Morals. Selected by R. B. Perry. New York, 1949

JASPERS, KARL
Existentialism and Humanism. Trans. by E. B. Ashton. New York, 1952
Man in the Modern Age. Trans. by E. C. Paul. London, 1933
The Perennial Scope of Philosophy. Trans. by R. Manheim. New York, 1949
The Philosophy of Karl Jaspers. Ed. by Paul A. Schilpp. New York, 1957

JEFFERSON, THOMAS
The Complete Jefferson. Ed. by Saul K. Padover. New York, 1943
Democracy. Ed. by S. K. Padover. New York, 1939
Thomas Jefferson on Democracy. Ed. by Saul K. Padover. New York, 1946

The Writings of Thomas Jefferson. Ed. by Paul L. Ford. 10 vols. New York, 1892

JOAD, C. E. M.
 Guide to the Philosophy of Morals and Politics. New York, 1937

JOLIVET, REGIS
 Les Doctrines Existentialistes de Kierkegaard à J. P. Sartre. Saint-Wandrille, 1948

JOUVENEL, BERTRAND DE
 Power, the Natural History of its Growth. Trans. by J. F. Huntington. London, 1952
 Sovereignty, An Inquiry into the Political Good. Trans. by J. F. Huntington. Chicago, 1957
 The Ethics of Redistribution. Cambridge, 1951

KALLEN, HORACE M.
 The Liberal Spirit. New York, 1948
 A Study of Liberty. Yellow Springs, Ohio, 1959

KAUTSKY, KARL
 The Class Struggle. Chicago, 1910
 Social Revolution. Trans. by A. M. and M. W. Simons. Chicago, 1905

KELSEN, HANS
 Law and Peace. Oliver Wendell Holmes Lectures, 1940–1941. Cambridge, Mass., 1942
 Society and Nature: A Sociological Inquiry. Chicago, 1943

KIRK, RUSSELL
 Academic Freedom. Chicago, 1955
 The Conservative Mind. Chicago, 1954
 Program for Conservatives. Chicago, n.d.

KIERKEGAARD, SÖREN AABYE
 Concluding Unscientific Postscript. Trans. by David F. Swenson and Walter Lowrie. Princeton, 1944
 Philosophical Fragments. Trans. by David F. Swenson. Princeton, 1946

KRONER, RICHARD
 Culture and Faith. Chicago, 1951

KROPOTKIN, PETER A.
 Ethics: Origin and Development. Trans. by L. S. Friedland and J. R. Piroshnikoff. New York, 1947
 Kropotkin's Revolutionary Pamphlets. Ed. by Roger N. Baldwin. New York, 1927

KUEHNELT-LEDDIHN, ERIK VON
 Liberty or Equality. Caldwell, Id., 1952

KUHN, HELMUT
 Freedom, Forgotten and Remembered. Chapel Hill, N.C., 1943

LA METTRIE, JULIEN OFFRAY DE
 Man a Machine. Chicago, 1927

LANE, ROSE WILDER
 The Discovery of Freedom. New York, 1943

LASKI, HAROLD
  Dilemma of our Times. London, 1952
  Problems of Sovereignty. New Haven, 1917
  Strategy of Freedom. New York, 1941
LEFF, GORDON
  Bradwardine and the Pelagians. Cambridge, 1957
LENIN, VLADIMIR ILYICH
  Imperialism: The Highest Stage of Capitalism. In *A Handbook of Marx-*
  ism. Ed. by Emile Burns. New York, 1935
  Karl Marx. In Vol. XI, *Selected Works.* New York, 1943
  Marxism on the State. In *Critique of the Gotha Programme* by Karl
  Marx. Ed. by C. P. Dutt. New York, 1938
  Materialism and Empirio-Criticism: Critical Comments on a Reaction-
  ary Philosophy. In Vol. XI, *Selected Works.* New York, 1943
  The Proletarian Revolution and Renegade Kautsky. New York, 1934
  Religion. New York, 1933
  The State. In Vol. XI, *Selected Works.* New York, 1943
  What Is to Be Done? In *A Handbook of Marxism.* Ed. by Emile Burns.
  New York, 1935
LENZEN, VICTOR
  Causality in Natural Science. Springfield, Ill., 1954
LINDSAY, ALEXANDER D.
  The Modern Democratic State. New York, 1947
LIPPMANN, WALTER
  The Good Society. Boston, 1937
  An Inquiry into the Principles of the Good Society. Boston, 1950
  The Public Philosophy. Boston, 1955
LOCKE, JOHN
  Letter on Toleration. Oxford, 1946
LOTTIN, O. D.
  Psychologie et Morale aux XII^{e}et XIII^{e}Siècles. 3 Tomes in 4 vols. Louvain,
  1942–1949
LOTZE, HERMANN
  Metaphysic. Trans. by B. Bosanquet. Oxford, 1884
LUTHER, MARTIN
  "Lectures on Genesis" in Vol. I, *Luther's Works.* Ed. by J. Pelikan.
  St. Louis, 1958
  A Treatise on Christian Liberty in *Three Treatises.* Philadelphia, 1947
McCOSH, JAMES
  An Examination of Mr. J. S. Mill's Philosophy; being a defence of fun-
  damental truth. London, 1880
McGILL, V. J.
  Emotions and Reason. Springfield, Ill., n.d.
McKEON, RICHARD (with MERTON, ROBERT K., and GELLHORN, WALTER)
  The Freedom to Read. New York, 1957
MACMURRAY, JOHN
  Conditions of Freedom. Toronto, 1949

MAINE, HENRY
  Popular Government: Four Essays. London, 1897
MAISTRE, JOSEPH DE
  Essay on the Generative Principle of Constitutions, 1810
  Oeuvres du Comte J. de Maistre. Paris, 1862
MALEBRANCHE, NICOLAS
  Dialogues on Metaphysics and on Religion. Trans. by M. Ginsberg. New York, 1923
MALINOWSKI, BRONISLAW
  A Scientific Theory of Culture. Chapel Hill, N.C., 1944
MALLOCK, WILLIAM H.
  The Limits of Pure Democracy. London, 1918
  Social Equality: A Short Study in a Missing Science. London, 1882
  Social Reform. New York, 1915
MANNHEIM, KARL
  Diagnosis of Our Time. New York, 1944
  Essays on Sociology and Social Psychology. Ed. by P. Kecskemeti. London, 1953
  Essays on the Sociology of Knowledge. Ed. by P. Kecskemeti. New York, 1952
  Ideology and Utopia. Trans. by L. Wirth and E. Shils. New York, 1949
MANSEL, HENRY LONGUEVILLE
  The Philosophy of the Conditioned. Comprising some remarks on Sir Wm. Hamilton's philosophy, and on Mr. J. S. Mill's examination of that philosophy. London, 1866
MARC, ANDRÉ
  Dialectique de l'Agir. Paris, 1949
MARCEL, GABRIEL
  Being and Having. Trans. by Katharine Farrer. Westminster, 1949
  Homo Viator: Introduction to a Metaphysic of Hope. Chicago, 1951
  Metaphysical Journal. Trans. by Bernard Wall. Chicago, 1952
  The Philosophy of Existence. Trans. by Manya Harari. New York, 1949
MARCUSE, HERBERT
  Soviet Marxism, A Critical Analysis. New York, 1958
MARITAIN, JACQUES
  On the Philosophy of History. Ed. by Joseph Evans. New York, 1957
MARSHALL, ALFRED
  Principles of Economics. London, 1910
MARTIN, EVERETT DEAN
  Liberty. Norton, 1930
MARX, KARL
  Address to the Communist League (1850). In *A Handbook of Marxism.* Ed. by Emile Burns. New York, 1935
  The Civil War in France. Introd. by Frederick Engels. New York, 1940
  Letters to Dr. Kugelmann. New York, 1934
  "On the History of French Materialism." An appendix in *Ludwig Feuer-*

bach and the Outcome of Classical German Philosophy by Frederick Engels. Ed. by C. P. Dutt. New York, 1941

The Poverty of Philosophy. Introd. by Frederick Engels. Ed. by Eleanor Marx Aveling. London, 1952

Revolution and Counter-Revolution; or Germany in 1848. Ed. by Eleanor Marx Aveling. London, 1952

Theories of Surplus Value. Selections. Trans. by G. A. Bonner and Emile Burns. New York, 1952

"Theses on Feuerbach." An appendix in *The German Ideology* by Marx and Engels. Parts I and III. Ed. by R. Pascal. New York, 1947

MEAD, GEORGE HERBERT

Mind, Self, and Society: From the Standpoint of a Social Behaviorist. Ed. by Charles W. Morris. Chicago, 1934

The Philosophy of the Act. Ed. by Charles W. Morris. Chicago, 1938

The Philosophy of the Present. Ed. by Arthur E. Murphy. Chicago, 1932

MENCZER, BELA

Catholic Political Thought, 1789–1848. Westminster, Md., 1952

MERLEAU-PONTY, MAURICE

Phénoménologie de la perception. Paris, 1945

Sens et Non-Sens. Paris, 1948

MILL, JAMES

Analysis of the Phenomena of the Human Mind. Second Edition. 2 vols. London, 1878

Law of Nations. In *Essays on Government, Jurisprudence, Liberty of the Press, and Law of Nations.* Ed. by Philip Wheelwright. Garden City, N.Y., 1935

Liberty of the Press. Ibid.

On Government. In *The English Philosophers from Bacon to Mill.* Ed. by E. A. Burtt. New York, 1939

MILLER, DAVID L.

Modern Science and Human Freedom. Austin, 1959

MILLS, C. WRIGHT

The Sociological Imagination. New York, 1959

MILTON, JOHN

Areopagitica. In Vol. IV, *The Works of John Milton.* Ed. by F. A. Patterson. 18 vols. New York, 1931–1938

Civil Power. In Vol. VI, *ibid.*

The Readie and Easie Way to Establish a Free Commonwealth. Ibid.

MISES, LUDWIG VON

Planning for Freedom. South Holland, Ill., 1952

MONNEROT, JULES

Sociology of Communism. Trans. by J. Degras and R. Rees. London, 1953

MONTAGUE, FRANCIS CHARLES

The Limits of Individual Liberty. London, 1885

MOORE, GEORGE EDWARD

Philosophical Studies. New York, 1951

Principia Ethica. Cambridge, 1948

MULLANEY, THOMAS U.
    Suarez on Human Freedom. Baltimore, Md., 1950
MULLER, HERBERT J.
    Issues of Freedom, Paradoxes and Promises. New York, 1960
MUNN, ALLEN M.
    Free Will and Determinism. Toronto, 1961
MYRDAL, GUNNAR
    Beyond the Welfare State. New Haven, 1960
NEMESIUS OF EMESA
    A Treatise on the Nature of Man. In *Knowledge and Value.* Ed. by
    Sprague and Taylor. New York, 1959
NEUMANN, FRANZ
    The Democratic and the Authoritarian State. Glencoe, Ill., 1957
NIEBUHR, REINHOLD
    Faith and History. New York, 1951
    Moral Man and Immoral Society. New York, 1949
    The Nature and Destiny of Man, A Christian Interpretation. 2 vols.
    New York, 1941–1943
NOCK, A. J.
    Our Enemy, the State. Caldwell, Id., 1950
OFSTAD, HARALD
    *An Inquiry into Freedom of Decision. An Analytical Approach to a
    Classical Problem.* 4 vols. Oslo, 1953–1955
ORIGEN
    Contra Celsum. Trans. by Henry Chadwick. Cambridge, 1953
ORTEGA Y GASSET, JOSÉ
    Revolt of the Masses. New York, 1932
ORTON, WILLIAM AYLOTT
    *The Liberal Tradition: A Study of the Social and Spiritual Conditions
    of Freedom.* New Haven, 1945
PAINE, THOMAS
    *The Rights of Man: Being an Answer to Mr. Burke's Attack on the
    French Revolution.* New York, 1915
PAP, ARTHUR
    Elements of Analytic Philosophy. New York, 1949
PARETO, VILFREDO
    The Ruling Class in Italy before 1900. Ed. by Giuseppe Prezzolini. New
    York, 1950
    Systèmes socialistes. 2 vols. Paris, 1902
PAVLOV, IVAN PETROVITCH
    Conditioned Reflexes and Psychiatry. Trans. and ed. by W. H. Gantt.
    New York, 1941
    Lectures on Conditioned Reflexes. Trans. and ed. by W. H. Gantt. New
    York, 1941
PENN, WILLIAM
    Three Letters . . . for Universal Liberty of Conscience . . . (1668)

PERCY OF NEWCASTLE, LORD
  The Heresy of Democracy. Chicago, 1955
PERRY, RALPH BARTON
  The Citizen Decides. Bloomington, 1951
  General Theory of Value. New York, 1926
  Puritanism and Democracy. New York, 1944
PICO DELLA MIRANDOLA, GIOVANNI
  Oration on the Dignity of Man. In *The Renaissance Philosophy of Man.*
  Chicago, 1950
PLANCK, MAX
  Determinismus oder Indeterminismus? Leipzig, 1948
PLEKHANOV, GEORGE
  The Materialist Conception of History. New York, 1940
  The Role of the Individual in History. New York, 1940
POLANYI, MICHAEL
  The Logic of Liberty. Chicago, 1951
POMPONAZZI, PIETRO
  Libri Quinque de Fato, De Libero Arbitrio et de praedestinatione. Ed. by
  Richard LeMay. Lucani, 1957
POPPER, KARL
  The Logic of Scientific Discovery. Trans. by Julius and Lan Freed. New
  York, 1959
  The Open Society and Its Enemies. Princeton, 1950
PRICE, RICHARD
  A Review of the Principal Questions in Morals. Ed. by D. Daiches
  Raphael. Oxford, 1948
PROUDHON, PIERRE JOSEPH
  Le Droit au Travail et le Droit de Propriété. Paris, 1848
  System of Economical Contradictions or the Philosophy of Misery. Bos-
  ton, 1888
PUFENDORF, SAMUEL
  Elements of Universal Jurisprudence. 2 vols. Trans. by W. A. Oldfather.
  Oxford, 1931
  (The Law of Nature and of Nations) De Jure Naturae et Gentium.
  Trans. by C. H. and W. A. Oldfather. English text in Vol. II. New
  York, 1934
RANKIN, K. W.
  Choice and Chance. Oxford, 1961
RASHDALL, HASTINGS
  Ethics. London, 1913
REINER, HANS
  Freiheit, Wollen und Aktivität. Halle, 1927
RICE, PHILIP BLAIR
  On the Knowledge of Good and Evil. New York, 1955
RICHARDSON, C. A.
  Happiness, Freedom and God. London, 194*

RITCHIE, DAVID G.
  Natural Rights, a Criticism of Some Political and Ethical Conceptions.
  London, 1903
  Principles of State Interference. 1896

ROBBINS, LIONEL
  The Theory of Economic Policy. London, 1952

ROSS, W. DAVID
  The Right and the Good. Oxford, 1930

ROSSITER, CLINTON L.
  Seedtime of the Republic. New York, 1953

ROSTOW, EUGENE V.
  Planning for Freedom, The Public Law of American Capitalism. New
  Haven, 1959

ROUSSEAU, JEAN JACQUES
  Oeuvres Complètes de J. J. Rousseau. 27 vols. Ed. by P. R. Auguis.
  Paris, 1824–1825

ROYCE, JOSIAH
  The World and the Individual. New York, 1901

RUSSELL, BERTRAND
  Education and the Social Order. London, 1932
  Freedom versus Organization, 1814–1914. New York, 1934
  Power, A New Social Analysis. London, 1948
  The Practice and Theory of Bolshevism. London, 1951

RUSSELL, WILLIAM H.
  Liberty versus Equality. New York, 1936

RYAN, JOHN A.
  A Living Wage in *The People Shall Judge*, Vol. II. Ed. by The Staff,
  Social Sciences I, Chicago, 1953

RYLE, GILBERT
  The Concept of Mind. New York, 1949
  Dilemmas. Cambridge, 1954

SALVADORI, MASSIMO
  The Economics of Freedom. New York, 1959

SANTAYANA, GEORGE
  The Life of Reason or the Phases of Human Progress. 5 vols. New
  York, 1932–1935
  The Winds of Doctrine. New York, 1913

SCHELER, MAX F.
  Die Stellung des Menschen im Kosmos. Munich, 1949

SCHLEIERMACHER, FRIEDRICH
  The Christian Faith. Ed. by H. R. Mackintosh and J. S. Stewart.
  Edinburgh, 1948

SCHMIDT, JOHANN KASPAR
  The Ego and His Own. By Max Stirner (pseudonym). Trans. by
  Steven T. Byington. London, 1912

SCHOPENHAUER, ARTHUR
Die beiden Grundprobleme der Ethik. Leipzig, 1881
On the Fourfold Root of the Principle of Sufficient Reason. London, 1889
The World as Will and Idea. Trans. by R. B. Haldane and J. Kemp.
3 vols. New York, 1950

SCHUMPETER, JOSEPH A.
Capitalism, Socialism and Democracy. New York, 1942
Imperialism and Social Classes. Trans. by H. Norden. New York, 1955

SERTILLANGES, R. P.
Le Problème du Mal. La Solution. Paris, 1951

SIDGWICK, HENRY
The Methods of Ethics. Third Edition. London, 1901
Miscellaneous Essays and Addresses. London, 1904
Principles of Political Economy. London, 1901

SIMON, YVES
The March to Liberation. Trans. by V. Hamm. Milwaukee, 1942

SIMONS, HENRY C.
"A Political Credo" in *The People Shall Judge*, Vol. II. Ed. by The
Staff, Social Sciences I, Chicago, 1953

SMITH, GERARD
The Truth That Frees. Milwaukee, 1956

SMITH, T. V.
Constructive Ethics with Contemporary Readings. New York, 1948

SOREL, GEORGES
Reflections on Violence. Trans. by T. E. Hulme and J. Roth. Glencoe,
Ill., 1950

Sources of Our Liberties. Documentary Origins of Individual Liberties in
the United States Constitution and Bill of Rights. Ed. by Richard L.
Perry. Chicago, 1959

SPIER, J. M.
Christianity and Existentialism. Trans. by D. Freeman. Philadelphia, 1953

SPRADING, CHARLES T.
Freedom and Its Fundamentals. Los Angeles, 1923
Liberty and the Great Libertarians. Los Angeles, 1913

STALIN, JOSEPH
Dialectical and Historical Materialism. New York, 1940
Foundations of Leninism. New York, 1939
The October Revolution. In *A Handbook of Marxism.* Ed. by Emile
Burns. New York, 1935

STEPHEN, J. F.
Liberty, Equality, Fraternity. London, 1873

STRACHEY, JOHN
The Coming Struggle for Power. New York, 1933

SUAREZ, FRANCIS
De Legibus. In *Selections from Three Works of Francisco Suarez, S.J.*
2 vols. Ed. by James Brown Scott. Oxford, 1944

TAUBE, MORTIMER
Causation, Freedom and Determinism. London, 1936
TAWNEY, RICHARD HENRY
Religion and The Rise of Capitalism. New York, 1926
THOMAS, NORMAN
The Choice Before Us; mankind at the crossroads. New York, 1934
THOMSON, DAVID
Equality. Cambridge, 1949
THOREAU, HENRY DAVID
Civil Disobedience. In Walden and Other Writings of Henry David Thoreau. Ed. by B. Atkinson. New York, 1937
THURBER, JAMES
Further Fables for Our Time. New York, 1956
TILLICH, PAUL
The Courage to Be. New Haven, 1952
TOCQUEVILLE, ALEXIS DE
L'Ancien Régime et la Révolution. Paris, 1856
Correspondences and Conversations with Nassau W. Senior. London, 1872
The Recollections of Alexis de Tocqueville. Trans. by A. T. Mattos. Ed. by J. P. Maxer. New York, 1949
TÖNNIES, FERDINAND
Communauté et Société. Paris, 1944
TOULMIN, STEPHEN
An Examination of the Place of Reason in Ethics. Cambridge, 1950
The Philosophy of Science. London, 1953
Truth and Freedom. By Louis de Raeymaeker and other Professors of the University of Louvain. Pittsburgh, 1955
UTLEY, THOMAS EDWIN
Essays in Conservatism. London, 1949
VALLA, LORENZO
Dialogue on Free Will in The Renaissance Philosophy of Man. Chicago, 1948
VAN LAER, P. HENRY
Philosophico-Scientific Problems. Pittsburgh, 1957
VEBLEN, THORSTEIN
The Theory of the Leisure Class. New York, 1926
VENABLE, VERNON
Human Nature: the Marxian View. New York, 1945
VIERECK, PETER
Conservatism from John Adams to Churchill. Princeton, 1956
Conservatism Revisited: The Revolt against Revolt, 1815–1949. New York, 1950
The Unadjusted Man: A New Hero for Americans. Boston, 1956
Vision and Action: Essays in Honor of Horace M. Kallen. New Brunswick, N.J., 1953
VOEGLIN, ERIC
The New Science of Politics. Chicago, 1952

WAHL, JEAN
 The Philosopher's Way. New York, 1948
 Traité de métaphysique. Paris, 1953

WARNOCK, G. J.
 "Every Event Has a Cause" in *Logic and Language* (Second Series).
 Ed. by Antony Flew. Oxford, 1953

WARRENDER, HOWARD
 The Political Philosophy of Hobbes. His Theory of Obligation. Oxford,
 1957

WEBER, MAX
 From Max Weber: Essays in Sociology. Ed. and trans. by H. H. Gerth
 and C. Wright Mills. New York, 1946
 The Methodology of the Social Sciences. Trans. and ed. by Edward A.
 Shils and Henry A. Finch. Glencoe, Ill., 1949
 The Protestant Ethic and the Spirit of Capitalism. Trans. by Talcott
 Parsons. New York, 1952
 The Theory of Social and Economic Organization. Trans. by A. M.
 Henderson and Talcott Parsons. New York, 1947

WHEWELL, WILLIAM
 Elements of Morality, Including Polity. Cambridge, 1864

WILD, JOHN
 Human Freedom and Social Order, An Essay in Christian Philosophy.
 Durham, N.C., 1959

WILLIAMS, ROGER J.
 Free and Unequal, The Biological Basis of Individual Liberty. Austin,
 Texas, 1953

WILSON, FRANCIS
 The Case for Conservatism. Seattle, 1951

WILSON, WOODROW
 The New Freedom. New York, 1913

WISDOM, JOHN
 Problems of Mind and Matter. Cambridge, 1934

WITTFOGEL, KARL A.
 Oriental Despotism. A Comparative Study of Total Power. New Haven,
 1957

WOODBRIDGE, F. E.
 An Essay on Nature. New York, 1940

WRISTON, HENRY M.
 Challenge to Freedom. New York, 1943

II. ANTHOLOGIES

CONCEPT OF FREEDOM. Ed. by Rev. Carl W. Grindel. Chicago:
 Henry Regnery Co., 1955
 BURNS, JOHN V. "The Proper Concept of Freedom in Individual Acts"
 CARLO, WILLIAM E. "Introduction: Freedom and Human Knowledge"

CONNELL, FRANCIS J. "Freedom and Theology"

CZAJKOWSKI, CASIMIR J. "The Acts of Freedom"

FARRELL, EDWARD P. "Freedom of Thought"

GRINDEL, CARL W. "Freedom of Autonomy—The Terminal Freedom"

KOVACS, ARPAD F. "Economic Systems and the Individual"

MCNIECE, HAROLD F. "Freedom and the Law"

O'REGAN, DENIS K. "Freedom in Relation to the Expression of the Beautiful"

RE, EDWARD D. "Freedom in the International Society"

SCULLY, JOSEPH G. "The Initial Freedom"

SULLIVAN, DANIEL C. "Freedom and Education"

WILLIAMS, IRVING G. "Freedom and Government"

WILLIGAN, WALTER L. "Freedom and Labor"

DETERMINISM AND FREEDOM IN THE AGE OF MODERN SCIENCE. A philosophical symposium. Ed. by Sidney Hook. New York: New York University Press, 1958

BARRETT, WILLIAM. "Determinism and Novelty"

BEARDSLEY, ELIZABETH JANE. " 'Excusing Conditions' and Moral Responsibility"

BLACK, MAX. "Make Something Happen"

BLANSHARD, BRAND. "The Case for Determinism"

BRANDT, RICHARD. "Determinism and the Justifiability of Moral Blame"

BRIDGMAN, PERCY W. "Determinism in Modern Science"; "Determinism and Punishment"

CHISHOLM, RODERICK W. "Responsibility and Avoidability"

DUCASSE, C. J. "Determinism, Freedom, and Responsibility"

EDWARDS, PAUL. "Hard and Soft Determinism"

HART, H. L. A. "Legal Responsibility and Excuses"

HEMPEL, CARL G. "Some Reflections on 'The Case for Determinism' "

HINTZ, HOWARD H. "Some Further Reflections on Moral Responsibility"

HOOK, SIDNEY. "Necessity, Indeterminism, and Sentimentalism"

HOSPERS, JOHN. "What Means This Freedom?"

LANDÉ, ALFRED. "The Case for Indeterminism"

LERNER, ABBA. "Punishment as Justice and as Price; On Randomness"

MUNITZ, MILTON K. "The Relativity of Determinism"

NAGEL, ERNEST. "Some Notes on Determinism"

NORTHROP, F. S. C. "Causation, Determinism, and the 'Good' "

PAP, ARTHUR. "Determinism, Freedom, Moral Responsibility, and Causal Talk"

SCHULTZ, ALFRED. "Some Equivocation of the Notion of Responsibility"

SCIAMA, DENNIS W. "Determinism and the Cosmos"; "Observations"

TAYLOR, RICHARD. "Determinism and the Theory of Agency"

WEISS, PAUL. "Common Sense and Beyond"

WILSON, H. VAN R. "On Causation"

ENQUETE SUR LA LIBERTÉ (Fédération Internationale des Sociétés de Philosophie). Publié avec le concourse de l'U.N.E.S.C.O. Paris: Hermann & Cie., 1953

BARIÉ, E. "La libertà"

BAUDOUIN, CHARLES. "Deux dimensions de la liberté: du choix 'horizontal' ou choix 'vertical' "

BLACKHAM, H. J. "The Question of Liberty"

BOURASSA, FRANÇOIS, S. J. "La liberté sous la loi"

BRÉHIER, EMILE. "Enquête sur la liberté"

BRIGHTMAN, EDGAR S. "Response to the Enquiry on Freedom"

CARDONE, DOMENICO ANTONIO. "La libertà come liberazione e la sua norma suprema"

DÍEZ-ALEGRIA, JOSÉ MARIA. "Libertad y valores"

FARBER, MARVIN. "Freedom and the Concept of Equality"

GARCÍA TUDURÍ DE COYA, MERCEDES. "Libertad y sociedad"

GARCÍA TUDURÍ DE COYA, ROSAURA. "Libertad y necesidad"

HAESAERT, JEAN. "Mesure et démesure des libertés"

HAHN, GEORGES A. "Le débat autour de la liberté"

HARTSHORNE, CHARLES. "Politics and the Metaphysics of Freedom"

HENDERSON, EDGAR H. "Footnotes to Freedom"

HERSCH, JEANNE. "Notes marginales"

KOVALEVSKY, PIERRE. "Liberté et rééducation"

LACHIÈZE-REY, PIERRE. "Liberté et autonomie"

LANDGREBE, LUDWIG. "Freiheit von Angst"

LEDRUT, RAYMOND. "Dialectique de la liberté"

LIDDELL, ANNA FORBES. "Freedom and Society"

McKEON, RICHARD. "Philosophic Differences and the Issues of Freedom"

METZ, ANDRÉ. "La Liberté humaine et la 'disponibilité' du monde physique"

MINKOWSKY, DR. E. "Liberté, responsabilité, déterminisme"

MIRKINE-GUETZÉVITCH, B. "Réflexions sur la crise de l'état libre"

MIROGLIO, ABEL. "Liberté économique et liberté spirituelle"

MOTTIER, GEORGES. "Devoir et liberté"

MOUNIN, G. "Marxisme, liberté, talent"

PECHAIRE, JULIEN, C.S.Sp. "Réponse à l'enquête sur la liberté"

PEMARTIN, JOSÉ. "Communicación a la U.N.E.S.C.O. en son encuesta sobre la libertad"

PETERS, PROF. DR. J., C.S.S.R. "Le Sens dernier de la liberté"

PIGUET, HENRI. "Contribution à l'enquête sur la liberté"

POGGI, ALFREDO. "Riflessioni sulla libertà"

POS, H. J., "Rapport sur l'enquête sur la liberté"

QUIRÓS, MIGUEL A. "Crítica de la libertad"

REYMOND, MARCEL. "Liberté structurée"

RIABOUCHINSKY, DIMITRI. "Quelques considérations sur le problème de la liberté"

RUEFF, JACQUES. "Le Concept de liberté"

SALOMAA, J. E. "De la liberté"

SOLAGES, BR. DE. "Liberté humaine et progrès social"

SOMERVILLE, JOHN. "The Relativity of Freedom"

SPECTORSKY, EUGÈNE. "Freedom and Determinism"

VAN DANTZIG, PROF. DR. D. "Footnotes on the Concept of Liberty"

VAN DEN BERG, PROF. DR. I. J. M. "Liberté et dépendance"

VAN LEEUWEN, DR. IR. A. F., S.J. "Liberté et moralité"

WEIL, ERIC. "Réflexions sur la liberté, le contentement et l'organisation"

ZARAGUETA, JUAN. "A propos de la liberté"

FREEDOM AND AUTHORITY IN OUR TIME (Twelfth Symposium of the Conference on Science, Philosophy and Religion). Ed. by Lyman Bryson, Louis Finkelstein, R. M. MacIver, Richard McKeon. New York, London: Harper & Brothers, 1953

ALLERS, RUDOLF. "The Dialectics of Freedom"

BIDNEY, DAVID. "The Problem of Freedom and Authority in Cultural Perspective"

BOKSER, BEN ZION. "Freedom and Authority"

BRIGHTMAN, EDGAR S. "Autonomy and Theonomy"

BRYSON, LYMAN. "Notes on a Theory of Advice"

BURKE, KENNETH. "Freedom and Authority in the Realm of the Poetic Imagination"

CAHN, EDMOND N. "Authority and Responsibility"

COHEN, JULIUS. "The Relation of Law to Freedom and Authority"

CONSTABLE, WILLIAM G. "Problems of Freedom and Authority in the Arts"

DEUTSCH, KARL W. "Communication in Self-Governing Organizations: Notes on Autonomy, Freedom, and Authority in the Growth of Social Groups"

DORSEY, GRAY LANKFORD. "The Necessity of Authority to Freedom"

EBY, KERMIT. "Labor's Emerging Role in the Political Economy"

FEIBLEMAN, JAMES K. "Freedom and Authority in the Structure of Cultures"

FERRE, NELS F. S. "Authority and Freedom"

FRANK, PHILIPP. "The Role of Authority in the Interpretation of Science"

FRANKEL, CHARLES. "Freedom, Authority, and Orthodoxy"

FRIED, JOHN H. E. "The Universal Declaration of Human Rights: An International Effort at a Synthesis of Freedom and Authority"

GINZBERG, ELI. "Work and Freedom"

GRAUBARD, MARK. "Persecution as the Pathology of Freedom and Authority"

GREENBERG, SIMON. "An Outline for a Comprehensive Inquiry into the Problem of Authority and Freedom"

HARRIS, LOUIS, and WOODWARD, JULIAN L. "The Exercise of Freedom"

HARTNETT, ROBERT C., S.J. "Liberty and Authority: Constitutional Aspects of the Problem"

HENDEL, CHARLES W. "Freedom and Authority as Functions of Civilization"

HOXIE, R. GORDON. "Freedom and Authority, Retrospect and Prospect"

IINO, DAVID N. "Freedom and Authority in the Realization of Values"

JOHNSON, F. ERNEST. "The Nature of Personal Freedom"

KADISH, MORTIMER R. "The Location and Dislocation of Freedom"

KAPLAN, MORDECAI M. "Authority as the Validation of Power"

KILPATRICK, WILLIAM H. "The Supposed Conflict between Moral Freedom and Scientific Determinism"

KOHN, HANS. "Freedom and Authority in International Relations"

KUBIE, LAWRENCE S. "Psychiatry in Relation to Authority and Freedom"

LA FARGE, JOHN, S.J. "A Case Study in Freedom through Authority"

LAMPRECHT, STERLING P. "Metaphysical Background of the Problem of Freedom"

LANGER, SUSANNE K. "World Law and World Reform"

LANGROD, GEORGE S. "Liberty and Authority"

LEE, DOROTHY D. "Freedom and Authority as Integral to Culture and Structure"

MARSHALL, JAMES. "Spirit and Function of Organization"

MERCIER, LOUIS J. A. "The Problem of Authority and Freedom and the Two Fundamental Alternatives of Thought"

MONTAGUE, WILLIAM PEPPERELL. "Altruism and Masochism"

NEGLEY, GLENN. "Legal Imperative and Moral Authority"

NEJELSKI, LEO. "Authority and Freedom in Industry"

NEUMANN, FRANZ L. "The Concept of Political Freedom"

OVERSTREET, HARRY A. "Freedom and the Authoritarian Personality"

PATTERSON, EDWIN W. "Freedom and Legal Authority: The Kinds of Authority of Law"

RECASENS-SICHES, LUIS. "Individual Freedom under the Law"

ROHRLICH, GEORGE F. "Social Security: Freedom from Want without Want of Freedom"

SCHRECKER, PAUL. "The Freedom of Civilization"

SELLARS, ROY WOOD. "Ethics and Politics"

SILVING, HELEN. "Freedom and Citizenship"

SIMMONS, ERNEST J. "Some Thoughts on the Soviet Concept of Authority and Freedom"

SMITH, T. V. "Methodological Equality and Functional Idealism"

STARR, MARK. "Freedom and Authority in Labor Unions"

STURMTHAL, ADOLF F. "Workers' Control: Freedom and Authority in the Plant"

ULICH, ROBERT. "Freedom and Authority in Education"

VANCE, RUPERT B. "Freedom and Authority in the Social Structure: A Problem in the Inter-Relation of Institutions"

VON GRUNEBAUM, GUSTAVE E. "Government in Islam"

WEIGEL, GUSTAVE, S.J. "Authority: Intellectual and Political"

WRIGHT, QUINCY. "Freedom and Authority in International Organization"

FREEDOM IN THE MODERN WORLD. Ed. by Horace M. Kallen. New York: Coward-McCann, Inc., 1928

BENT, SILAS. "Freedom of Speech, Conscience and the Press"

CHAFEE, ZECHARIAH, JR. "Liberty and Law"

DARROW, CLARENCE. "Personal Liberty"

DEWEY, JOHN. "Philosophies of Freedom"

EASTMAN, MAX. "Political Liberty"

FOAKES-JACKSON, F. J. "The Protestant View of Freedom"

HAMILTON, WALTON H. "Freedom and Economic Necessity"

JASTROW, JOSEPH. "Freedom and Psychology"

KALLEN, HORACE M. "What Is Real and What Is Illusory in Human Freedom; Why Freedom Is a Problem"

LOVETT, ROBERT MORSS. "Freedom in the Fine Arts"

RYAN, JOHN A., D.D. "How a Catholic Looks at Freedom"

FREEDOM, ITS MEANING. Ed. by Ruth Nanda Anshen. New York: Harcourt, Brace & Co., 1940

ADAMS, JAMES TRUSLOW. "Freedom in America"

BEARD, CHARLES A. "Freedom in Political Thought"

BERGSON, HENRI. "Freedom and Obligation"

BERNSTEIN, FELIX. "The Balance of Progress of Freedom in History"

BIRKHOFF, GEORGE D. "Intuition, Reason, and Faith in Science, and Man's Freedom"

BOAS, FRANZ. "Liberty among Primitive People"

BRANDEIS, LOUIS D. "True Americanism"

BRIDGMAN, P. W. "Freedom and the Individual"

BRIGHTMAN, EDGAR SHEFFIELD. "Freedom, Purpose, and Value"

CLARK, JOHN M. "Forms of Economic Liberty and What Makes Them Important"

CONKLIN, EDWIN GRANT. "Intellectual Freedom"

CORWIN, EDWARD SAMUEL. "Liberty and Juridical Restraint"

CROCE, BENEDETTO. "The Roots of Liberty"

DEMOS, RAPHAEL. "Human Freedom—Positive and Negative"

DEWEY, JOHN. "The Problem of Freedom"

EINSTEIN, ALBERT. "Freedom and Science"

GERARD, RALPH W. "Organic Freedom"

GILSON, ETIENNE. "Medieval Universalism and Its Present Value in the Concept of Freedom"

HALDANE, J. B. S. "A Comparative Study of Freedom"

HU SHIH. "The Modernization of China and Japan: A Comparative Study in Cultural Conflict and a Consideration of Freedom"

JOHNSON, ALVIN. "Academic Freedom"

KINGDON, FRANK. "Freedom for Education"

MACIVER, ROBERT M. "The Meaning of Liberty and Its Perversions"

MACMURRAY, JOHN. "Freedom in the Personal Nexus"

MANN, THOMAS. "Freedom and Equality"

MARITAIN, JACQUES. "The Conquest of Freedom"

MILLIKAN, ROBERT A. "Science, Freedom, and the World of Tomorrow"

MONTAGUE, WILLIAM PEPPERELL. "Freedom and Nominalism"

MORRIS, CHARLES. "The Mechanism of Freedom"

PERRY, RALPH BARTON. "Liberty in a Democratic State"

PHELPS, WILLIAM LYON. "Freedom and Literature"

RIEZLER, KURT. "What Is Freedom?"

RUSSELL, BERTRAND. "Freedom and Government"

RYAN, JOHN A. "Religion as the Basis of the Postulates of Freedom"

SALVEMINI, GAETANO. "Democracy Reconsidered"

SCHNEIDER, HERBERT W. "The Liberties of Man"

SHOTWELL, JAMES T. "Freedom—Its History and Meaning"

STEFANSSON, VILHJALMUR. "Was Liberty Invented?"

TILLICH, PAUL. "Freedom in the Period of Transformation"

WALLACE, HENRY A. "The Genetic Basis for Democracy and Freedom"

WERTHEIMER, MAX. "A Story of Three Days"

WHITEHEAD, ALFRED NORTH. "Aspects of Freedom"

LA LIBERTÉ (Actes du IVᵉ Congrès des Sociétés de Philosophie de Langue Française). Neuchâtel: Baconnière, 1949

BALTHASAR, NICOLAS. "Intrinsécisme du devoir et optimisme existentiel"

BARZIN, MARCEL. "Les deux déterminismes"

BASTIDE, GEORGES. "Les sosies de la liberté"

BERGER, GASTON. "La liberté et le temps"

CARRÉ, JEAN-RAOUL. "Qu'une liberté, source de commencements absolus, est très probable encore qu'inconnaissable"

CAUSSIMON, JEAN. "Repentir et liberté"

CHAIX-RUY, JULES. "Fondement ontologique de la liberté"

CHRISTOFF, DANIEL. "Liberté, responsabilité, innocence"

CRISTOL, HORACE. "Le couple antagoniste liberté-volupté dans les fonctions vitales psychophysiologiques"

DAVID, MADELEINE. "Le fait babylonien et l'autonomie de l'agent"

DELPECH, LÉON. "Perspectivisme spirituel, audrographie et problème de la liberté"

DEPREUX, PAUL. "Étude expérimentale de la liberté"

DEVIVAISE, CHARLES. "Charles Secrétan et le spiritualisme français"

DE WAELHENS, ALPHONSE. "Linéaments d'une interprétation phénoménologique de la liberté"

DUCASSÉ, PIERRE. "Loisir et liberté"

DUPRÉEL, EUGÈNE. "La liberté dans la philosophie des valeurs"

FOREST, AIMÉ. "La liberté existentielle"

FRANCK, ADOLPHE. "De l'indétermination particulaire à la liberté humaine"

FRÈRE, HUBERT. "Illusion et réalité de la libération morale"

GAGNEBIN, SAMUEL. "Réflexions sur le possible"

GEX, MAURICE. "Liberté, nouveauté et détermination dans le monadisme"

GRUA, GASTON. "Recherches de Leibniz sur la liberté divine d'après des textes nouveaux"

GUÉRIN, PIERRE. "La liberté comme valeur religieuse"

GUILLEMAIN, BERNARD. "Technique scientifique et liberté"

GUITTON, JEAN. "Prédestination et liberté"

HAHN, GEORGES. "Le malaise dans la liberté"

HAYEN, ANDRÉ. "L'évidence dynamique de la liberté et son intentionnalité"

HERSCH, JEANNE. "Liberté sans choix"

HUMBERT, PIERRE. "Sur le problème de la liberté dans la recherche scientifique"

HUSSON, LÉON. "Les aspects méconnus de la liberté bergsonienne"

ISAYE, GASTON. "Logique, dialectique et liberté"

JANKÉLÉVITCH, VLADIMIR. "La liberté et l'ambiguïté"

JANSON, FERNAND. "Déterminisme et morale"

JOLIVET, RÉGIS. "La preuve psychologique de la liberté morale"

LACROZE, RENÉ. "Les sentiments de liberté"

LEFEBVE, MAURICE-JEAN. "Ambiguïté de la notion de liberté"

LEROY, ANDRÉ. "La liberté de spontanéité chez David Hume"

LE SENNE, RENÉ. "Caractère, liberté, valeur"

MAIRE, GILBERT. "La liberté et les instants privilégiés"

METZ, ANDRÉ. "La structure du monde physique et la liberté"

MIÉVILLE, HENRI-L. "La notion de liberté absolue comme concept-limité"

MINKOWSKI, EUGÈNE. "Liberté, liberté cherie!"
MIROGLIO, ABEL. "La libre obéissance et la libre discipline"
MOREAU, JOSEPH. "Volonté et liberté"
MOTTIER, GEORGES. "Liberté et participation"
MULLER, MAURICE. "Langage et liberté"
NÉDONCELLE, MAURICE. "La liberté se communique-t-elle?"
PALIARD, JACQUES. "Structure d'équivoque et liberté spirituelle"
PERELMAN, CHAÏM. "Liberté et raisonnement"
PIGUET, J. -CLAUDE. "Liberté et normes artistiques"
POLIN, RAYMOND. "Remarques sur la doctrine de la liberté chez Karl Marx"
PROT, E. -MARCEL. "Analyse psychologique de la notion de liberté"
PUCELLE, JEAN. "La liberté comme agent de transmutation des valeurs"
RENAULD, JEANNE-FRÉDÉRIQUE. "Irrationnel et liberté"
REVERDIN, HENRI. "Les philosophes de la Suisse romande au XIXᵉ siècle et la liberté"
REYMOND, ARNOLD. "Quelques aspects de la liberté"
REYMOND, MARCEL. "Incoordonnable et liberté dans la philosophie de Jean-Jacques Gourd"
RICHARD, GUSTAVE. "La liberté vue par un psychanalyste"
ROCHE, CLAUDE. "La liberté dans la philosophie et la cosmologie de l'Extrême-Orient"
ROCHEDIEU, EDMOND. "La liberté et la grâce"
SAVIOZ, RAYMOND. "Choix et liberté"
SECRÉTAN, CHARLES. "Lettre inédite de Charles Secrétan à Felix Ravaisson"
STERN, AXEL-L. "La liberté et sa dialectique"
THÉVENAZ, PIERRE. "L'expérience réflexive de la liberté"
TROUILLARD, JEAN. "La liberté chez Plotin"
VAN BREDA, HERMAN-LÉO. "Husserl et le problème de la liberté"
VIAL, JEANNE. "Aperçus sur une phénoménologie de la liberté"
VIRIEUX-REYMOND, ANTOINETTE. "La philosophie de la liberté de Charles Secrétan et le Portique"
VIVIER, ZÉNITTA. "Causalité, déterminisme, libre arbitre, probabilité"
WAHL, JEAN. "Le problème de la liberté à partir des philosophes de l'existence"

III. PERIODICALS

ABBAGNANO, N.
   "Contemporary Science and Freedom" in *The Review of Metaphysics*, Vol. V, No. 3, March 1952
ALBRITTON, ROGERS
   "Present Truth and Future Contingency" in *The Philosophical Review*, Vol. XLVI, No. 1, January 1957
AUSTIN, JOHN L.
   "Ifs and Cans" in *Proceedings of the British Academy*, Vol. XLII, 1956
BARKER, SIR ERNEST
   "Elections in the Ancient World" in *Diogenes*, No. 8, Autumn, 1954

BAYLIS, CHARLES A.
"Rational Preference, Determinism, and Moral Obligation" in *The Journal of Philosophy*, Vol. XLVII, No. 3, February 2, 1950

BEARDSLEY, ELIZABETH L.
"Determinism and Moral Perspectives" in *Philosophy and Phenomenological Research*, Vol. XXI, No. 1, September 1960

BRADLEY, M. C.
"A Note on Mr. MacIntyre's *Determinism*" in *Mind*, Vol. LXVIII, No. 272, October 1959

BRADLEY, R. D.
"Must the Future Be What It is Going to Be?" in *Mind*, Vol. LXVIII, No. 270, April 1959

BROAD, C. D., EDDINGTON, A. S., and BRAITHWAITE, R. B.
"Indeterminacy and Indeterminism" in *Indeterminism, Formalism, and Value*, Aristotelian Society. Supplementary Vol. X. London: Harrison and Sons, 1931

BRONFENBRENNER, MARTIN
"Two Concepts of Economic Freedom" in *Ethics*, Vol. LXV, No. 3, April 1955

BROTHERTON, BRUCE WALLACE
"The Conception of Responsibility" in *The International Journal of Ethics*, Vol. XXXIX, July 1929

BROWN, STUART M., JR.
"Does Ought Imply Can?" in *The International Journal of Ethics*, Vol. LX, No. 4, July 1950

BROWNING, DOUGLAS
"Acts" in *The Review of Metaphysics*, Vol. XIV, No. 1, September 1960

CAPEK, MILIC
"The Doctrine of Necessity Re-Examined" in *The Review of Metaphysics*, Vol. V, No. 1, September 1951

CHAPPELL, V. C.
"The Concept of Choice" in *The Journal of Philosophy*, Vol. LVII, No. 24, November 24, 1960

CLAPP, JAMES GORDON
"Freedom as Fulfillment" in *Philosophy and Phenomenological Research*, Vol. VIII, No. 4, June 1948

COLEMAN, WINSON R.
"Knowledge and Freedom in the Political Philosophy of Plato" in *Ethics*, Vol. LXXI, No. 1, October 1960

COLLINGWOOD, R. G.
"On the So-Called Idea of Causation" in *Proceedings of the Aristotelian Society*, Vol. XXXVIII, 1937–1938. London: Harrison and Sons, 1938

CRISSMAN, PAUL
"Freedom in Determinism" in *The Journal of Philosophy*, Vol. XXXIX, No. 19, September 1942

CROCKER, JOHN R.
"The Freedom of Man in Plotinus" in *The Modern Schoolman*, Vol. XXXIV, No. 1, November 1956

DANIELS, ROBERT VINCENT
"Fate and Will in the Marxian Philosophy of History" in *Journal of the History of Ideas*, Vol. XXI, No. 4, October–December 1960

DANTO, ARTHUR C.
"The Paradigm Case Argument and the Free Will Problem" in *Ethics*, Vol. LXIX, No. 2, January 1959

DANTO, ARTHUR, and MORGENBESSER, SIDNEY
"Character and Free Will" in *Journal of Philosophy*, Vol. LIV, No. 16, August 1, 1957

DEWEY, JOHN
"Liberalism and Civil Liberties" in *Social Frontier*, Vol. II, February 1936
"Liberalism and Equality," *ibid.*
"The Meaning of Liberalism" in *Social Frontier*, Vol. II, December 1935
"Voluntarism in the Roycean Philosophy" in *The Philosophical Review*, Vol. XXV, May 1916

DUGUIT, LEON
"The Law and the State" in *Harvard Law Review*, Vol. XXXI, No. 1 (Special number), November 1917

DUHAMEL, JOSEPH S.
"Moral and Psychological Aspects of Freedom" in *Thought*, Vol. XXXV, No. 137, Summer, 1960

EBERSOLE, FRANK B.
"Free-Choice and the Demands of Morals" in *Mind*, Vol. LXI, No. 242, April 1952

ERMATINGER, CHARLES J.
"Averroism in Early Fourteenth Century Bologna" in *Mediaeval Studies*, Vol. XVI, 1954

EWING, A. C.
"Indeterminism" in *The Review of Metaphysics*, Vol. V, No. 2, December 1951

FARRELL, P. M.
"Freedom and Evil" in *The Australasian Journal of Philosophy*, Vol. XXXVI, No. 3, December 1958

FLEW, A. G. N.
"Determinism and Rational Behavior" in *Mind*, Vol. LXVIII, No. 271, July 1959

FOOT, PHILIPPA
"Free Will as Involving Determinism" in *The Philosophical Review*, Vol. LXVI, No. 4, October 1957

FRANKS, O. S.
"Choice" in *Proceedings of the Aristotelian Society*, Vol. XXXIV, 1934–1935

GALBERT, M. R.
"Moral Freedom" in *The Journal of Philosophy*, Vol. XXIV, No. 17, August 18, 1927

GARVIN, LUCIUS
"Libertarianism and Responsible Agency" in *The Journal of Philosophy*, Vol. LVII, No. 24, November 24, 1960

GEACH, PETER T.
"Ascriptivism" in *The Philosophical Review*, Vol. LXIX, No. 2, April 1960

GLASGOW, W. D.
"The Concept of Choosing" in *Analysis*, Vol. XX, No. 3, January 1960

GLEASON, ARTHUR E.
"A Critique of Kantian Autonomy" in *The New Scholasticism*, Vol. VIII, No. 3, July 1934

GRAY, J. GLENN
"Heidegger Evaluates Nietzsche" in *Journal of the History of Ideas*, Vol. XIV, No. 2, April 1953

GRUEN, WILLIAM
"Determinism, Fatalism, and Historical Materialism" in *The Journal of Philosophy*, Vol. XXXIII, No. 23, November 5, 1936

HAMPSHIRE, S. and HART, H. L. A.
"Decision, Intention and Certainty" in *Mind*, Vol. XLVII, No. 265, January 1958

HAMPSHIRE, S., MACLAGAN, W. G., and HARE, R. M.
"The Freedom of the Will" in *Freedom, Language, and Reality*, Aristotelian Society. Supplementary Vol. XXV. London: Harrison and Sons, 1951

HANCOCK, ROGER
"Ideas of Freedom" in *Ethics*, Vol. LXIX, No. 4, July 1959

HANDY, ROLLO
"Determinism, Responsibility, and the Social Setting" in *Philosophy and Phenomenological Research*, Vol. XX, No. 4, June 1960

HARDIE, W. F. R.
"My Own Free Will" in *Philosophy*, Vol. XXXII, No. 120, January 1957

HARTNACK, JUSTUS
"Free Will and Decision" in *Mind*, Vol. LXII, No. 247, July 1953

HARTSHORNE, CHARLES
"Freedom Requires Indeterminism and Universal Causality" in *Journal of Philosophy*, Vol. LV, No. 19, September 11, 1958

HAWKINS, D. J. B.
"Free Will and Right Action" in *The Modern Schoolman*, Vol. XXVI, No. 4, May 1949

HAWORTH, LAWRENCE
"The Free Society" in *Ethics*, Vol. LXVII, No. 2, January 1957

HAY, WILLIAM H.
"Free Will and Possibilities" in *Philosophy of Science*, Vol. XXIV, No. 3, July 1957

HAYEK, F. A.
"Freedom, Reason, and Tradition" in *Ethics*, Vol. LXVIII, No. 4, July 1958

HERBST, P.
"Freedom and Prediction" in *Mind*, Vol. LXVI, No. 261, January 1957

HOBART, R. E.
"Free Will as Involving Determinism and Inconceivable without It" in *Mind*, Vol. XLIII, No. 169, January 1934

HOOK, SIDNEY
"Moral Freedom in a Determined World" in *Commentary*, Vol. 27, No. 10, May 1958

HOSPERS, JOHN
"Meaning and Free Will" in *Philosophy and Phenomenological Research*, Vol. X, No. 3, March 1950

JASPERS, KARL
"Freedom and Authority" in *Diogenes*, No. 1

JESSOP, T. E.
"Evaluation, Causality, and Freedom" in *Proceedings of the Aristotelian Society*, Vol. XXXVII, 1936–1937. London: Harrison and Sons, 1937

KALLEN, HORACE M.
"The Discipline of Freedom" in *Philosophy and Phenomenological Research*, Vol. VIII, No. 4, June 1948

KING-FARLOW, JOHN
"Mr. Bradley and the Libertarians" in *Australasian Journal of Philosophy*, Vol. XXXVII, No. 3, December 1959

KNIGHT, THOMAS S.
"Negation and Freedom" in *The Review of Metaphysics*, Vol. XIII, No. 3, March 1960

LADD, JOHN
"Free Will and Voluntary Action" in *Philosophy and Phenomenological Research*, Vol. LII, No. 3, March 1952

LAUER, ROSEMARY Z.
"Bellarmine on Liberum Arbitrium" in *The Modern Schoolman*, Vol. XXXIII, No. 2, January 1956
"St. Thomas's Theory of Intellectual Causality in Election" in *New Scholasticism*, Vol. XXVIII, No. 3, July 1954

LAWRENCE, NATHANIEL
"The Dialectical Analysis of Freedom" in *The Review of Metaphysics*, Vol. XII, No. 4, June 1959

LEHRER, KEITH
"Can We Know that We Have Free Will by Introspection?" in *The Journal of Philosophy*, Vol. LVII, No. 5, March 3, 1960

LEVI, ALBERT WILLIAM
"The Value of Freedom: Mill's Liberty (1859–1959)" in *Ethics*, Vol. LXX, No. 1, October 1959

LEWIS, H. D.
"Does the Good Will Define Its Own Content: A Study of Green's

Prolegomena" in *The International Journal of Ethics*, Vol. LVIII, No. 3, Part I, April 1948
"Freedom and Immortality" in *The Hibbert Journal*, Vol. LIX, No. 2, January 1961
"Moral Freedom in Recent Ethics" in *Proceedings of the Aristotelian Society*, Vol. XLVII, 1946–1947. London: Harrison and Sons, 1951

LILLIE, RALPH S.
"Biological Causation" in *Philosophy of Science*, Vol. VII, No. 3, July 1940

LUCAS, H. W.
"Dr. Bain and Free Will" in *The Month*, July 1875

McGILL, V. J.
"Conflicting Theories of Freedom" in *Philosophy and Phenomenological Research*, Vol. XX, No. 4, June 1960
"Two Concepts of Freedom," *ibid.*, Vol. VIII, No. 4, June 1948
"Sartre's Doctrine of Freedom" in *Revue internationale de philosophie*, No. 9, June 1949

McGILVARY, E. B.
"Freedom and Necessity in Human Affairs" in *The International Journal of Ethics*, Vol. XLV, No. 4, July 1935

MacINTOSH, D. C.
"Responsibility, Freedom and Causality: Or the Dilemma of Determinism and Indeterminism" in *The Journal of Philosophy*, Vol. XXXVII, No. 2, January 1940

MacKAY, D. M.
"On the Logical Indeterminacy of a Free Choice" in *Mind*, Vol. LXIX, No. 273, January 1960

McKEON, RICHARD
"Philosophy and Freedom in the City of Man" in *Ethics*, Vol. LIX, No. 3, April 1949

MANDLEBAUM, MAURICE
"Determinism and Moral Responsibility" in *Ethics*, Vol. LXX, No. 3, April 1960

MAYS, W.
"Determinism and Free Will in Whitehead" in *Philosophy and Phenomenological Research*, Vol. XV, No. 4, June 1955

MEANS, B. W.
"Freedom, Indeterminacy, and Value" in *The Journal of Philosophy*, Vol. XXXIII, No. 4, February 1936

MEIKLEJOHN, DONALD
"Kantian Formalism and Civil Liberty" in *The Journal of Philosophy*, Vol. LI, No. 25, December 9, 1954

MELDEN, A. I.
"Willing" in *The Philosophical Review*, Vol. LXIX, No. 4, October 1960

MERCIER, LOUIS A. J.
"Freedom of the Will and Psychology" in *The New Scholasticism*, Vol. XVIII, No. 3, July 1944

MISH'ALANI, JAMES K.
"Can Right Acts Be Voluntary?" in *Analysis,* Vol. XX, No. 3, January 1960

MONAHAN, EDWARD J.
"Human Liberty and Free Will According to John Buridan" in *Mediaeval Studies,* Vol. XVI, 1954

MOORE, GEORGE EDWARD
"Freedom" in *Mind,* Vol. XXIII, 1898

MOULDS, HENRY
"John Locke's Four Freedoms Seen in a New Light" in *Ethics,* Vol. LXXI, No. 2, January 1961

MURPHY, ARTHUR E.
"Jonathan Edwards on Free Will and Moral Agency" in *The Philosophical Review,* Vol. LXVIII, No. 2, April 1959

NICOL, EDUARD
"Liberty as a Fact, Freedom as a Right" in *Philosophy and Phenomenological Research,* Vol. VIII, No. 4, June 1948

NOWELL-SMITH, P. H.
"Determinists and Libertarians" in *Mind,* Vol. LXII, No. 251, July 1954

O'CONNOR, D. J.
"Possibility and Choice" in *Proceedings of the Aristotelian Society.* Supplementary Vol. XXXIV, 1960. London: Harrison and Sons, 1960

O'NEIL, CHARLES J.
"Aristotle's Natural Slave Reexamined" in *The New Scholasticism,* Vol. XXVII, No. 3, July 1953

OPPENHEIM, FELIX E.
"Evaluating Interpersonal Freedoms" in *The Journal of Philosophy,* Vol. LVII, No. 12, June 9, 1960

PAPANOUTSOS, E. P.
"Freedom and Causality" in *Philosophy,* Vol. XXXIV, No. 130, July 1959

PEGIS, ANTON C.
"Necessity and Liberty" in *The New Scholasticism,* Vol. XV, No. 1, January 1941

PERRY, RALPH BARTON
"What Does It Mean to Be Free?" in *The Pacific Spectator,* Vol. VII, No. 2, Spring, 1953

PETERS, R. S., McCRAKEN, D. J. and URMSON, J. O.
"Motives and Causes" in *Men and Machines,* Aristotelian Society. Supplementary Vol. XXVI. London: Harrison and Sons, 1952

PIEPER, JOSEF
"Knowledge and Freedom" in *The Review of Politics,* Vol. 19, No. 2, April 1957

PITCHER, GEORGE
"Hart on Action and Responsibility" in *The Philosophical Review,* Vol. LXIX, No. 2, April 1960

RAAB, FRANCIS V.
"Free Will and the Ambiguity of 'Could'" in *The Philosophical Review,*
Vol. LXIV, No. 1, January 1955
"History, Freedom and Responsibility" in *Philosophy of Science,* Vol.
XXVI, No. 2, April 1959

RANKIN, K. W.
"Doer and Doing" in *Mind,* Vol. LXIX, No. 275, July 1960

RAPHAEL, D. DAICHES
"Causation and Free Will" in *The Philosophical Quarterly,* Vol. II, No.
6, January 1952

RORETZ, KARL
"Modern Physics and the Freedom of the Will" in *The Journal of Philosophy,* Vol. LV, No. 2, January 16, 1958

ROSSITER, CLINTON
"The Political Theory of the American Revolution" in *The Review of
Politics,* Vol. 15, No. 1, January 1953

RUSSELL, L. J.
"Ought Implies Can" in *Proceedings of the Aristotelian Society,* Vol.
XXXVI, 1935–1936. London: Harrison and Sons, 1936

SALMON, C. V.
"The Notion of Responsibility" in *The International Journal of Ethics,*
Vol. LX, No. 1, October 1949

SCANLAN, JAMES P.
"J. S. Mill and the Definition of Freedom" in *Ethics,* Vol. LXVIII, No.
3, April 1958

SCOTT, K. J.
"Conditioning and Freedom" in *The Australasian Journal of Philosophy,*
Vol. XXXVII, No. 3, December 1959

SELLARS, ROY WOOD
"Guided Causality, Using Reason, and 'Free-Will'" in *The Journal of
Philosophy,* Vol. LIV, No. 16, August 1957

SIMON, YVES R.
"On the Foreseeability of Free Acts" in *The New Scholasticism,* Vol.
XXII, No. 4, October 1948

SMITH, GERARD
"Luther and Free Choice" in *The Modern Schoolman,* Vol. XX, No. 2,
January 1943
"The Nature and Uses of Liberty" in *The New Scholasticism,* Vol. XXVI,
No. 3, July 1952

STALLKNECHT, NEWTON P.
"Methodology and Experience" in *The Review of Metaphysics,* Vol. VI,
No. 3, March 1953

STALLKNECHT, NEWTON P., WADE, FRANCIS C., and EARLE, WILLIAM
"Freedom and Existence: A Symposium" in *The Review of Metaphysics,*
Vol. IX, No. 1, September 1955

TAFT, ROBERT A.
"The Republican Party" in *Fortune,* Vol. XXXIX, No. 4, April 1949

TAYLOR, RICHARD
"The Problem of Future Contingencies" in *The Philosophical Review*, Vol. LXVI, No. 1, January 1957

TROISFONTAINES, ROGER
"Death: A Test for Love, A Condition of Freedom" in *Cross Currents*, Vol. VII, No. 3, Summer, 1957

VEATCH, HENRY
"A Note on the Metaphysical Grounds for Freedom, with Special Reference to Professor Lovejoy's Thesis in *The Great Chain of Being*" in *Philosophy and Phenomenological Research*, Vol. VII, No. 3, March 1947

WAHL, JEAN
"Freedom and Existence in Some Recent Philosophies" in *Philosophy and Phenomenological Research*, Vol. VIII, No. 4, June 1948

WASSAMER, THOMAS A.
"Freedom, Responsibility and Desire in Kantian Ethics" in *The Thomist*, Vol. XXI, No. 3, July 1958

WEAVER, WARREN
"Statistical Freedom of the Will" in *Reviews of Modern Physics*, Vol. 20, No. 1

WEIGEL, GUSTAVE
"Theology and Freedom" in *Thought*, Vol. XXXV, No. 137, Summer, 1960

WEISSMANN, HANS ASRIEL
"'Freedom' in Ethics—A Transcausal Concept" in *Philosophy and Phenomenological Research*, Vol. XIX, No. 3, March 1959

WEINPAHL, PAUL D.
"Concerning Moral Responsibility" in *Analysis*, Vol. 13, No. 6 (New Series No. 36), June 1953

WILLIAMS, C. J. F.
"Logical Indeterminacy and Free Will" in *Analysis*, Vol. 21, No. 1, October 1960

WILLIAMS, GARDNER
"Free Will and Determinism" in *The Journal of Philosophy*, Vol. XXXVIII, No. 26, December 1941

WILSON, H. VAN RENSSELAER
"Causal Discontinuity in Fatalism and Indeterminism" in *The Journal of Philosophy*, Vol. LII, No. 3, February 3, 1955

WILSON, J.
"Freedom and Compulsion" in *Mind*, Vol. LXVII, No. 265, January 1958

WILSON, R.
"The New Physics—Does It Vindicate Free Will?" in *The New Scholasticism*, Vol. XI, No. 4, October 1937

WOLFF, PETER
"Necessary and Contingent Effects" in *The Review of Metaphysics*, Vol. XI, No. 2, December 1957

"Truth, Futurity, and Contingency" in *Mind*, Vol. LXIX, No. 275, July 1960

WORKMAN, ROLLIN W.
"Is Indeterminism Supported by Quantum Theory?" in *Philosophy of Science*, Vol. XXVI, No. 3, July 1959

XENAKIS, JASON
"Free Will, A 'Negative' Concept" in *The Journal of Philosophy*, Vol. LIV, No. 3, January 31, 1957

ANALYTICAL
TABLE OF CONTENTS

ANALYTICAL TABLE OF CONTENTS

PART I. INTRODUCTION AND RECAPITULATION   3–31

Identification of the five subjects of controversy   4–11
Classification of the theories of freedom   11–13
Distinction between the general and the special
    controversies   14–15
The general idea or common understanding of
    freedom   15–16
The construction of issues and arguments   17–20
Difficulties in the formulation of questions at issue   20–28
Difficulties in the construction of debate   29–31

PART II. THE GENERAL CONTROVERSY   32–526

The structure of the general controversy about the kinds
    of freedom   32–34
The issue concerning the circumstantial freedom
    of self-realization   35–90
Why only a conceptual issue here   35–36
Preliminary clarification of that issue: the distinction
    between liberty and license   36–44
Construction of the question at issue   45–49
The parties to the issue   49–63
The debate of the issue   64–85
Critique of the debate   85–90

The issues concerning the acquired freedom of
    self-perfection   91–134
Both an existential and conceptual issue here   91–93
Construction of the existential issue   93–99
Parties to the existential issue   100–4
Construction of the conceptual issue   104–6
Parties to the conceptual issue   106–11
The debate of the conceptual issue   111–29

Critique of the debate   130–34

The issues concerning political liberty   135–83
  Preliminary clarification of views about freedom in
    relation to the state and government   135–39
  The problem of distinguishing between political liberty
    and other freedoms in relation to the state and
    government   139–41
  The difficulty of constructing an issue here   142–48
  Recapitulation of the conception of political
    liberty as a distinct freedom, together with
    an enumeration of its proponents   149–56
  Probable opponents of political liberty   156–75
  Difficult problems of interpretation   175–79
  The arguments which might be advanced in
    the debate of the possible issues here   179–83

The issues concerning collective freedom   184–222
  Preliminary clarification of the subject   184–87
  Recapitulation of the theory of the future
    existence of collective freedom   187–98
  The formulation of both an existential and
    a conceptual issue about collective freedom   198–200
  The existential attacks on collective freedom   201–15
  Possible rebuttal of these attacks   215–17
  Conceptual attacks on collective freedom   217–19
  Possible rebuttal of these attacks   219–20
  One other conceptual attack on collective
    freedom   220–22

Introduction to the issues concerning the natural
  freedom of self-determination   223–52
  Topical agreement about the natural freedom
    of self-determination   225–36
    What is meant by causal initiative   227–30
    What is meant by causal indeterminacy   230–35
    What is meant by intrinsic unpredictability   235–36
  Formulation of the existential issues   237–39
  Formulation of the conceptual issue   240–47
  Participants in this controversy   247–52

The existential issue concerning causal initiative   253–330
  Structure of the issue   253–56

Parties to the issue and to the debate 256–58

The dispute about the principle of causation 258–87

Preliminary clarification: formulation and
interpretation of the principle of causation 258–61

First phase of the dispute: attacks on the proposition
that the self or the will is an uncaused cause 261–66

Second phase of the dispute: replies to
these attacks 266–71

Third phase of the dispute: elaboration
of the philosophical grounds underlying the defense of causal initiative 272–76

Fourth phase of the dispute: the rejection of
these grounds 276–87

The dispute about character and motives 287–302

First phase: development of the view that volitions
are always determined by character and motives 288–91

Second phase: criticism and rejection
of this view 291–94

Third phase of the dispute: elaboration of the
arguments for and against this view 294–302

The dispute about responsibility and initiative 302–16

The dispute about the evidence of consciousness or
inner experience 316–30

The existential issue concerning causal indeterminacy 331–463

Similarities and differences between this issue and
the issue concerning causal initiative 331–34

The parties to the issue and the debate 334–37

The dispute about indeterminacy and causation 337–71

The differentiation of determinists, libertarians,
and indeterminists 337–43

Arguments against causal indeterminacy 343–51

Arguments for causal indeterminacy 351–71

Libertarians' arguments for 351–62

Indeterminists' arguments for 362–71

The dispute about indeterminacy and predictability 371–89

Definition of theoretical predictability and
introduction to arguments against it 371–74

Arguments against causal indeterminacy based
on the assertion of theoretical
predictability 374–77

Arguments against theoretical predictability 378–86

The significance of indeterminacy
in quantum physics 387–89

The dispute about motives and choice 390–418

Introduction to the dispute 390–91

First phase: arguments that choice is always
determined by strongest desire or motive 392–401

Second phase: replies to these arguments 401–18

The dispute about free choice and responsibility 419–57

Introduction to the dispute: "hard" and "soft"
determinists distinguished 419–21

First phase: the libertarian argument that free
choice is necessary if responsibility is to have
any meaning 421–28

Second phase: the "soft" determinist argument
that responsiblilty can be based on freedom
of action without freedom of choice 429–37

Third phase: libertarian replies to the argument
of the "soft" determinists 437–41

Fourth phase: the "hard" determinist argument
that there is no freedom of choice and
hence no basis for responsibility 441–46

The dispute about the evidence of consciousness 446–53

Special and unanswered arguments 453–60

Concluding observations: critique of the
foregoing disputes 460–63

The theological issue concerning man's freedom of
self-determination 464–87

Introduction to the issue 464–67

The negative position: free will irreconcilable
with God's foreknowledge 467–73

Assertion of affirmative position 473–75

The affirmative position defended 475–87

A possible conceptual issue about self-determination:
chance, responsibility, and freedom 488–525

Recapitulation of arguments concerning
responsibility 488–97

Free will precludes responsibility 497–505

Free will does not preclude responsibility 506–15

Interpretation and construction of the
conceptual issue 515–25

PART III. THE SPECIAL CONTROVERSIES 526–647

Introduction 526–32
Distinction between the special controversies
and the general 526–27
Construction of the special controversies 527–32

The special controversy concerning the circum-
stantial freedom of self-realization 533–61
Classification of the issues in this controversy 533–38
Conceptual issues 533–35
Existential issues 535–37
Normative issues 537–38
The conceptual issues examined 538–61
The issue about fear 538–45
The issue about states of mind 545–48
The issue about enabling means 548–55
The issue about alternatives 555–58
Concluding comments on the conceptual issues 558–61
The existential issues examined 562–602
The issue about culture or civilization 564–66
The issue about the state of nature 567–70
The issue about equality 570–81
The issue about security 581–82
The issue about law 582–86
The issue about democracy 586–94
The economic issue 594–602
The normative issues examined 603–20
Is freedom a natural right? 603–5
To whom should freedom be granted? 605–10
Is freedom a basic human good? 610–12
On whom should political liberty be conferred? 612–20

The special controversy about the acquired freedom
of self-perfection 621–25

The special controversy about collective freedom 626–33

The special controversy about the natural freedom
of self-determination 634–47
Formulation of six issues 634–37
Does the natural freedom of self-determination
result in acts which are intrinsically
unpredictable? 637

Does the natural freedom of self-determination
involve the causal indeterminacy of
free choice?   637–40

Does the natural freedom of self-determination
involve causal initiative?   640–41

Is the natural freedom of self-determination
uniquely the property of man?   641–42

Is the natural freedom of self-determination
limited in scope?   642–44

Does the natural freedom of self-determination
exhibit both rationality and arbitrariness?   644–46

Critique of this controversy   646–47

PART IV. EPILOGUE   648–52

Concluding Observations   648–52

INDICES

INDEX OF AUTHORS IN THE
GENERAL CONTROVERSY

ACH, NARCISS
Freedom of self-determination: the existential issue concerning causal initiative, 319
ADAMS, JOHN
Classification: 248, 249
ALEXANDER, SAMUEL
Freedom of self-determination: the existential issue concerning causal initiative, 264, 290, 295, 320; the existential issue concerning causal indeterminacy, 392, 400 f.; a possible conceptual issue, 503–4. Classification: 251, 258, 336, 516
AMBROSE
Freedom of self-realization: 70–71. Freedom of self-perfection: 116. Classification: 6, 12, 50
ANSELM OF CANTERBURY
Classification: 6, 7, 13, 50, 100, 106, 248, 249, 335
AQUINAS, THOMAS
Freedom of self-realization: 42, 46, 59–60. Freedom of self-perfection: 112, 133. Collective freedom: 214. Political liberty: 138–39, 139, 143, 146–47, 154, 166, 177. Freedom of self-determination: the existential issue concerning causal initiative, 255 fn. 5, 259, 261, 266–67, 269 fn. 53, 272, 273, 274, 278, 283, 285–86, 286–87, 288, 291–92, 299, 303, 306 fn. 199; the existential issue concerning causal indeterminacy, 343–44, 351–58, 369, 370, 392, 394, 394–95, 403 fn. 239, 403–10, 421–22, 433, 460; the theological issue, 468–69, 480–83, 487; a possible conceptual issue, 506. Classification: 5, 6, 7, 9, 13, 14, 27, 50, 100, 106, 155, 248, 249, 257, 335, 466. See also: 7 fn. 1, 20–21, 61, 87, 102 fn. 14, 118 fn. 58, 133 fn. 98, 136 fn. 1, 513 fn. 88
ARISTOTLE
Freedom of self-realization: 37, 52. Freedom of self-perfection: 100,

118 fn. 58. Political liberty: 136, 138, 140, 141 fn. 9, 151, 180. Freedom of self-determination: the existential issue concerning causal initiative, 261, 273, 274, 278; the existential issue concerning causal indeterminacy, 338 fn. 6, 378 fn. 153, 410. Classification: 7, 10, 13, 14, 155, 248, 249, 257, 335. See also: 90 fn. 156, 99 fn. 12, 136 fn. 1, 147, 163–64, 166, 168–69, 170, 174–75, 176, 216 fn. 105
ARNOLD, MAGDA
Freedom of self-determination: the existential issue concerning causal initiative, 291 fn. 151; the existential issue concerning causal indeterminacy, 410 fn. 256, 447 fn. 412. Classification: 250, 257, 335
AUGUSTINE
Freedom of self-perfection: 112. Freedom of self-determination: the existential issue concerning causal initiative, 261, 303, 306 fn. 199, 421; the theological issue, 467–68, 474, 475–77, 487. Classification: 6, 7, 13, 50, 100, 106, 248, 249, 257, 335, 466
AURELIUS, MARCUS
Classification: 6, 12, 49, 100, 106. See also: 90 fn. 156
AVELING, FRANCIS
Freedom of self-determination: the existential issue concerning causal indeterminacy, 386 fn. 180, 410 fn. 256, 448. Classification: 250, 335
AVICENNA
Freedom of self-determination: the existential issue concerning causal indeterminacy, 356
AYER, A. J.
Freedom of self-realization: 62–63. Freedom of self-perfection: 108, 109. Political liberty: 143. Freedom of self-determination: the existential issue concerning causal initiative, 291 fn. 149, 307–8, 309; the existential issue concerning causal indeterminacy, 346 fn. 30, 377 fn. 150, 429, 433,

442, 458; a possible conceptual issue, 504–5, 506, 509–10, 513. *Classification:* 5, 12, 50, 107, 251, 257–58, 336, 516. *See also:* 20–21, 26–27, 90 fn. 156, 427

BAIN, ALEXANDER
Freedom of self-determination: the existential issue concerning causal initiative, 278 fn. 88; the existential issue concerning causal indeterminacy, 385 fn. 175, 392, 397, 451 fn. 437, 458. *Classification:* 251, 258, 336

BAKUNIN, MIKHAIL
Freedom of self-realization: 53, 56–58. *Freedom of self-perfection:* 104, 108, 109. *Political liberty:* 171 fn. 78, 173–75. *Collective freedom:* 184–88, 190–93, 199, 207, 209–11, 212, 215, 217, 219 fn. 115, 221–22. *Freedom of self-determination:* the existential issue concerning causal initiative, 264, 281; the existential issue concerning causal indeterminacy, 441–42. *Classification:* 10, 12, 104, 107, 251, 258, 336. *See also:* 90 fn. 156, 114 fn. 51

BARRETT, WILLIAM
Freedom of self-determination: the existential issue concerning causal indeterminacy, 382–84. *Classification:* 250, 335

BARTH, KARL
Classification: 6, 7, 13, 50, 248, 335

BAYLIS, CHARLES
Freedom of self-determination: the existential issue concerning causal indeterminacy, 436 fn. 360; a possible conceptual issue, 503 fn. 40, 505. *Classification:* 516

BELLARMINE, ROBERT
Classification: 6, 7, 13, 50, 248

BELLOC, HILAIRE
Collective freedom: 185, 202

BENTHAM, JEREMY
Freedom of self-realization: 40, 41 fn. 23, 47, 62, 73–74, 78. *Freedom of self-perfection:* 108, 111, 113, 118–19. *Political liberty:* 137, 139, 144, 147. *Classification:* 5, 12, 14, 50, 51 fn. 44, 107. *See also:* 54, 55, 124 fn. 83, 223 fn. 1

BERDYAEV, NICHOLAS
Collective freedom: 185–87, 198–200, 207–12, 214 fn. 98, 215, 216, 220, 222. *See also:* 107

BERGSON, HENRI
Freedom of self-determination: the existential issue concerning causal indeterminacy, 360 fn. 86, 360–62, 364, 378–79, 382, 408 fn. 248. *Classification:* 7, 12, 14, 50, 248–49, 250,

335. *See also:* 7 fn. 1, 363 fn. 95

BERKELEY, GEORGE
Classification: 7, 12, 248–49

BERLIN, ISAIAH
Classification: 248–49, 335. *See also:* 103 fn. 17

BLANSHARD, BRAND
Freedom of self-determination: the existential issue concerning causal initiative, 320; the existential issue concerning causal indeterminacy, 388, 389, 451–52. *Classification:* 251, 258, 336

BODIN, JEAN
Political liberty: 161–64, 165–67, 174–75, 179–81. *See also:* 164, 171

BOETHIUS
Freedom of self-determination: the existential issue concerning causal indeterminacy, 421; the theological issue, 467, 469 fn. 10, 477–78, 481 fn. 65, 481–82. *Classification:* 6, 7, 13, 50, 248, 249, 435, 466

BOHR, NIELS
Freedom of self-determination: the existential issue concerning causal indeterminacy, 387 fn. 184, 388 fn. 188, 449, 453 fn. 449. *Classification:* 336

BORN, MAX
Freedom of self-determination: the existential issue concerning causal indeterminacy, 387, 389. *Classification:* 336

BOSANQUET, BERNARD
Freedom of self-realization: 53–56, 73–76, 80–84. *Freedom of self-perfection:* 114, 118, 120, 122–23, 123 fn. 82, 124, 128–30. *Freedom of self-determination:* the existential issue concerning causal indeterminacy, 360 fn. 86, 403 fn. 241, 417–18. *Classification:* 6, 12, 50–51, 51 fn. 44, 106, 250, 335. *See also:* 106, 115 fn. 54, 130, 133, 181, 182, 223 fn. 1

BOSSUET, BISHOP JACQUES BENIGNE
Freedom of self-determination: the theological issue, 481

BOUCHER, JONATHAN
Freedom of self-realization: 38, 43, 52. *Political liberty:* 164–66, 174–75, 179–81. *Classification:* 49. *See also:* 90 fn. 156, 166–67, 171–72

BOURASSA, FRANÇOIS
Freedom of self-realization: 40 fn. 16

BOUTROUX, EMILE
Freedom of self-determination: the existential issue concerning causal initiative, 292–93, 415; the existential issue concerning causal indeterminacy, 359 fn. 85, 364, 403 fn. 240, 450.

Classification: 250, 257, 335. *See also:* 363 fn. 95

BOWNE, BORDEN PARKER
Freedom of self-determination: the existential issue concerning causal initiative, 275 fn. 75; the existential issue concerning causal indeterminacy, 359 fn. 85. *Classification:* 257, 335

BRADLEY, FRANCIS H.
Freedom of self-realization: 54, 54 fn. 52, 56 fn. 60, 73. *Freedom of self-perfection:* 112. *Freedom of self-determination:* the existential issue concerning causal initiative, 262 fn. 13; the existential issue concerning causal indeterminacy, 401, 429, 437; a possible conceptual issue, 501–2, 506, 507, 510–11, 513. *Classification:* 6, 12, 106, 251, 258, 336, 516. *See also:* 106, 115 fn. 54, 181, 411 fn. 261, 440 fn. 381

BRADLEY, R. D.
Freedom of self-determination: the existential issue concerning causal initiative, 255–56, 301, 317, 324–28; the existential issue concerning causal indeterminacy, 446–47. *Classification:* 251. *See also:* 224, 509 fn. 66

BRAMHALL, BISHOP JOHN
Freedom of self-determination: the existential issue concerning causal initiative, 255, 261, 262, 268–70, 279–80, 288, 288–89, 299–300; the existential issue concerning causal indeterminacy, 345, 353–56, 424, 430–31; the theological issue, 471, 481, 481–82. *Classification:* 250, 257, 335, 466. *See also:* 29, 224, 266, 267

BRAY, CHARLES
Freedom of self-determination: the existential issue concerning causal indeterminacy, 384 fn. 41, 374 fn. 137, 399 fn. 224, 435. *Classification:* 336

BRIDGEMAN, PERCY W.
Freedom of self-determination: the existential issue concerning causal indeterminacy, 387 fn. 184. *Classification:* 336

BROAD, C. D.
Freedom of self-determination: the existential issue concerning causal initiative, 255, 265, 278–79, 281–86, 305, 313 fn. 230; the existential issue concerning causal indeterminacy, 337, 349–51, 369–71, 417 fn. 287, 418 fn. 289, 422 fn. 300, 425, 442; a possible conceptual issue, 511–12. *Classification:* 251, 258, 336

BROGLIE, LOUIS DE
Freedom of self-determination: the existential issue concerning causal indeterminacy, 387

BUCKLE, THOMAS HENRY
Freedom of self-determination: the existential issue concerning causal initiative, 265, 290, 295. *Classification:* 251, 258

BUKHARIN, NIKOLAI IVANOVICH
Collective freedom: 204 fn. 62

BURKE, EDMUND
Freedom of self-realization: 62–63. *Freedom of self-perfection:* 108. *Political liberty:* 145 fn. 13. *Classification:* 5, 7, 13, 50, 107, 248–49. *See also:* 90 fn. 156, 99 fn. 12

CALHOUN, JOHN C.
Freedom of self-realization: 41 fn. 23, 62. *Freedom of self-perfection:* 108. *Classification:* 50, 107. *See also:* 90 fn. 156

CALIFORNIA ASSOCIATES
Freedom of self-determination: a possible conceptual issue, 505 fn. 52. *Classification:* 251, 252, 336. *See also:* 24 fn. 10, 25 fn. 11

CALVIN, JOHN
Freedom of self-realization: 37–38. *Freedom of self-determination:* the existential issue concerning causal indeterminacy, 433; the theological issue, 466, 469–70, 487. *Classification:* 6, 7, 13, 50, 100, 106, 248, 249, 335, 466

CAMPBELL, CHARLES A.
Freedom of self-determination: the existential issue concerning causal initiative, 255, 265, 278, 283–84, 293 fn. 160, 294–301, 303–6, 307 fn. 204, 309–11, 312–16, 317, 322–28, 328–29; the existential issue concerning causal indeterminacy, 371, 381, 403 fn. 241, 404, 416–18, 422 fn. 300, 425, 432, 438, 439, 442–43, 445, 446–47, 460; the theological issue, 475; a possible conceptual issue, 499 fn. 22, 504, 506, 507–9, 512, 512 fn. 85. *Classification:* 248, 249, 250, 257, 335, 466, 517. *See also:* 29, 382 fn. 160, 224, 420 fn. 293, 427

CAPEK, MILIC
Freedom of self-determination: the existential issue concerning causal indeterminacy, 362–64, 367, 378–79, 382. *Classification:* 250, 335

CARRITT, E. F.
Freedom of self-determination: the existential issue concerning causal in-

determinacy, 415, 428. *Classification:* 250, 335

CASSIRER, ERNST
Freedom of self-determination: the existential issue concerning causal indeterminacy, 389. *Classification:* 336

CASTELL, ALBUREY
Freedom of self-determination: the existential issue concerning causal indeterminacy, 418 fn. 290, 428 fn. 327, 448, 456. *Classification:* 248, 249, 250, 335

CHISHOLM, RODERICK
Freedom of self-determination: the existential issue concerning causal indeterminacy, 444 fn. 397. *Classification:* 336

CHUBB, THOMAS
Freedom of self-determination: the existential issue concerning causal initiative, 292 fn. 153

CICERO, MARCUS TULLIUS
Freedom of self-realization: 53, 68–69, 71. *Freedom of self-perfection:* 112, 116, 119–20. *Freedom of self-determination:* the existential issue concerning causal indeterminacy, 421; the theological issue, 467, 476. *Classification:* 6, 7, 13, 49, 106, 248, 249, 257, 335. *See also:* 69

CLEMENCEAU, GEORGES
Freedom of self-determination: the existential issue concerning causal initiative, 264, 286, 320. *Classification:* 251, 258

COLLINS, ANTHONY
Freedom of self-determination: the existential issue concerning causal indeterminacy, 346–47; the theological issue, 472; a possible conceptual issue, 500 fn. 24. *Classification:* 251, 336, 466

COMTE, AUGUSTE
Freedom of self-perfection: 108. *Political liberty,* 171 fn. 78, 172 fn. 79. *Collective freedom:* 184–87, 188–90, 198, 199, 207, 209–11, 212, 215–17, 222. *Classification:* 10, 12, 107. *See also:* 58 fn. 72, 90 fn. 156

CRANSTON, MAURICE
Freedom of self-determination: the existential issue concerning causal indeterminacy, 382–84, 438–40, 458; a possible conceptual issue, 506, 513. *Classification:* 250, 335, 517. *See also:* 427

CRESCAS, DON HASCAI
Freedom of self-determination: the existential issue concerning causal indeterminacy, 433 fn. 345. the theo-

logical issue, 468, 470. *Classification:* 466. *See also:* 478–79, 480 fn. 62

CROCE, BENEDETTO
Collective freedom: 198–99, 204, 206, 208. *Freedom of self-determination:* the existential issue concerning causal initiative, 273 fn. 64, 275 fn. 74. *Classification:* 250, 257. *See also:* 107

DALBIEZ, ROLAND
Freedom of self-determination: the existential issue concerning causal indeterminacy, 410 fn. 256

DAUD, IBN
Freedom of self-determination: the theological issue, 480, 481, 483. *Classification:* 466

DEMOS, RAPHAEL
Classification: 248

DESCARTES, RENÉ
Freedom of self-perfection: 108. *Freedom of self-determination:* the existential issue concerning causal initiative, 255, 273, 274–75, 303 fn. 194, 317; the existential issue concerning causal indeterminacy, 422, 433, 447–48, 450, 460; the theological issue, 473–74. *Classification:* 7, 12, 14, 107, 248, 249, 257, 335, 466

DEWEY, JOHN
Freedom of self-realization: 42 fn. 26, 62. *Freedom of self-perfection:* 99 fn. 10, 105, 106 fn. 22. *Classification:* 5, 6, 7, 13, 248, 249, 335. *See also:* 7 fn. 1, 99 fn. 12, 103 fn. 16

DJILAS, MILOVAN
Collective freedom: 185, 198–99, 204–6, 208

DUCASSE, CURT J.
Freedom of self-determination: the existential issue concerning causal initiative, 266, 291 fn. 150, 303, 307 fn. 204; the existential issue concerning causal indeterminacy, 377 fn. 151, 400–1, 436 fn. 358; a possible conceptual issue, 505. *Classification:* 251, 258, 336, 516

DUNCAN-JONES, AUSTIN E.
Freedom of self-determination: the existential issue concerning causal indeterminacy, 437 fn. 364; a possible conceptual issue, 501 fn. 33. *Classification:* 251

DUNOÜY, LECOMTE
Freedom of self-determination: the existential issue concerning causal indeterminacy, 362 fn. 93. *Classification:* 250

DUNS SCOTUS, JOHN
Classification: 6, 7, 13, 248, 249, 257, 335

EBERSOLE, F.
Freedom of self-determination: the existential issue concerning causal indeterminacy, 445. *Classification*: 336

EDDINGTON, A. S.
Freedom of self-determination: the existential issue concerning causal indeterminacy, 387 fn. 183, 388–89. *Classification*: 336

EDWARDS, JONATHAN
Freedom of self-realization: 47, 62. *Freedom of self-perfection*: 109, 110, 113. *Freedom of self-determination*: the existential issue concerning causal initiative, 262, 281, 290, 292 fn. 153; the existential issue concerning causal indeterminacy, 347, 348–49, 392, 395–96, 404, 410, 433; the theological issue, 471; a possible conceptual issue, 499. *Classification*: 5, 12, 14, 50, 107, 251, 257, 258, 336, 466, 516. *See also*: 24, 26, 90 fn. 156, 369

EDWARDS, PAUL
Freedom of self-determination: the existential issue concerning causal indeterminacy, 442–44. *Classification*: 336

EINSTEIN, ALBERT
Freedom of self-determination: the existential issue concerning causal indeterminacy, 387. *Classification*: 336

ENGELS, FRIEDRICH
Freedom of self-realization: 53, 56–58. *Freedom of self-perfection*: 104, 108–9. *Political liberty*: 171 fn. 78, 172–73, 174–75. *Collective freedom*: 184–87, 187–88, 193–96, 199, 209, 260. *Classification*: 10, 12, 104, 107. *See also*: 90 fn. 156, 114 fn. 51

EPICTETUS
Freedom of self-realization: 48, 53, 69–70. *Freedom of self-perfection*: 112, 116, 118, 122. *Classification*: 6, 12, 49, 100, 106

EPICURUS
Freedom of self-determination: the existential issue concerning causal initiative, 283. *Classification*: 6, 7, 13, 248, 249, 257, 335. *See also*: 99 fn. 12

ERASMUS, DESIDERIUS
Freedom of self-determination: the theological issue, 477 fn. 51. *Classification*: 248

EWING, A. C.
Freedom of self-determination: the existential issue concerning causal indeterminacy, 369–71, 382–83, 418, 425 fn. 315, 442; a possible conceptual issue, 506, 511–12. *Classification*: 250, 335, 518

FARRER, AUSTIN
Freedom of self-determination: the existential issue concerning causal initiative, 272 fn. 63; the existential issue concerning causal indeterminacy, 403 fn. 239, 411, 428 fn. 327; the theological issue, 481 fn. 68. *Classification*: 250, 257, 335

FEUER, LEWIS
Freedom of self-perfection: 110 fn. 37

FEUERBACH, LUDWIG
Collective freedom: 216–17

FICHTE, JOHANN G.
Classification: 7, 12, 248

FIELD, G. C.
Freedom of self-determination: the existential issue concerning causal indeterminacy, 404, 414, 428 fn. 325. *Classification*: 250, 335

FILMER, SIR ROBERT
Freedom of self-realization: 43

FOOT, PHILLIPPA
Freedom of self-determination: a possible conceptual issue, 506, 509–10. *Classification*: 250, 518

FOSDICK, DOROTHY
Freedom of self-realization: 41 fn. 22, 79 fn. 125. *Freedom of self-perfection*: 108 fn. 29, 111, 113, 117, 118, 121 fn. 73, 122–23, 127 fn. 91. *Political liberty*: 170 fn. 77. *See also*: 130

FOUILLÉE, ALFRED
Freedom of self-determination: the existential issue concerning causal initiative, 273 fn. 64, 285, 323 fn. 266; the existential issue concerning causal indeterminacy, 448. *Classification*: 6, 7, 13, 50, 248, 249, 257, 335. *See also*: 7 fn. 1

FOURIER, ALFRED
Collective freedom: 199, 207, 209

FRANK, PHILLIPP
Freedom of self-determination: the existential issue concerning causal indeterminacy, 388 fn. 188, 389. *Classification*: 251, 337

FRANKLIN, BENJAMIN
Classification: 251

FREUD, SIGMUND
Freedom of self-realization: 62–63. *Freedom of self-perfection*: 105. *Freedom of self-determination*: the existential issue concerning causal indeterminacy, 447 fn. 412. *Classification*: 5, 6, 13, 14, 50, 106, 251, 336. *See also*: 90 fn. 156, 99 fn. 10 and fn. 12, 103 fn. 16

FROMM, ERICH
Freedom of self-perfection: 110 fn. 37

GALLIE, W. B.
Freedom of self-determination: the existential issue concerning causal indeterminacy, 377. *Classification:* 251, 336

GERSONIDES
Freedom of self-determination: the theological issue, 480, 481, 483, 484 fn. 89. *Classification:* 466

GEWIRTH, ALAN
Political liberty: 153 fn. 22

GINSBERG, MORRIS
Freedom of self-perfection: 110 fn. 37. *Freedom of self-determination:* the existential issue concerning causal indeterminacy, 428 fn. 327, 454–55. *Classification:* 250, 335

GREEN, T. H.
Freedom of self-perfection: 114, 118, 120, 122, 123–29. *Freedom of self-determination:* the existential issue concerning causal indeterminacy, 399. *Classification:* 6, 7, 13, 50, 106, 248, 249, 336. *See also:* 56, 63 fn. 95, 130, 133, 181, 411 fn. 261

GREENE, T. M.
Freedom of self-determination: the existential issue concerning causal indeterminacy, 428, 441 fn. 382. *Classification:* 250, 335

GRUENDER, HUBERT
Freedom of self-determination: the existential issue concerning causal initiative, 267 fn. 43, 319–20; the existential issue concerning causal indeterminacy, 381, 404, 410, 422 fn. 298, 450 fn. 433. *Classification:* 250, 257, 335

GUITTON, JEAN
Freedom of self-determination: the theological issue, 482

HALDANE, J. S.
Freedom of self-determination: the existential issue concerning causal initiative, 273 fn. 64, 276. *Classification:* 250, 257

HALE, ROBERT L.
Freedom of self-realization: 41, 62–63. *Freedom of self-perfection:* 108. *Classification:* 5, 12, 50, 107. *See also:* 90 fn. 156

HALEVI, JUDAH
Freedom of self-determination: the existential issue concerning causal indeterminacy, 422 fn. 296; the theological issue, 479. *Classification:* 248

HAMILTON, ALEXANDER
Political liberty: 153. *Classification:* 155. *See also:* 136 fn. 1, 147

HAMILTON, SIR WILLIAM
Freedom of self-determination: the existential issue concerning causal initiative, 321; the existential issue concerning causal indeterminacy, 396 fn. 214, 397 fn. 215, 424, 431–32; the theological issue, 474–75. *Classification:* 250, 335, 466. *See also:* 224, 349 fn. 44, 375 fn. 138, 413 fn. 273

HART, H. L. A.
Classification: 251

HARTLEY, DAVID
Freedom of self-determination: the existential issue concerning causal initiative, 265, 278 fn. 88, 286; the existential issue concerning causal indeterminacy, 345, 436–37; the theological issue, 472; a possible conceptual issue, 499–500. *Classification:* 251, 258, 336, 466, 516. *See also:* 369

HARTMANN, NICOLAI
Freedom of self-realization: 62–63. *Freedom of self-perfection:* 104, 108–9. *Freedom of self-determination:* the existential issue concerning causal indeterminacy, 418 fn. 288, 423, 450, 458. *Classification:* 5, 7, 13, 50, 104, 107, 248, 249, 250, 335. *See also:* 90 fn. 156, 114 fn. 51

HARTSHORNE, CHARLES
Freedom of self-determination: the existential issue concerning causal indeterminacy, 362–63, 367–68, 378–79, 382, 460; the theological issue, 483–84; a possible conceptual issue, 512 fn. 85. *Classification:* 248, 249, 250, 335, 466

HAWKINS, D. J. B.
Freedom of self-determination: the existential issue concerning causal indeterminacy, 381–82, 410 fn. 256, 422 fn. 298, 438; a possible conceptual issue, 506–7. *Classification:* 250, 335, 517

HAYEK, FRIEDRICH A.
Freedom of self-realization: 42 fn. 26. *Freedom of self-perfection:* 103, 109. *Political liberty:* 137. *Collective freedom:* 186. *Classification:* 5, 12, 50, 104. *See also:* 114 fn. 51

HEGEL, GEORG W. F.
Freedom of self-realization: 39–40, 42, 48, 52–53, 71–72, 81. *Freedom of self-perfection:* 112, 118–20, 121–22, 123–24. *Political liberty:* 138, 139–40, 144–47, 157–61, 174–75, 181–83. *Collective freedom:* 207, 210 fn. 83, 211, 222. *Freedom of self-determina-*

tion: the existential issue concerning causal initiative, 275, 399. *Classification:* 6, 7, 13–14, 49, 50–51, 100, 106, 248, 257, 335. *See also:* 7 fn. 1, 54, 56 fn. 60, 57, 63 fn. 95, 73, 75, 79 fn. 122, 87, 164, 171, 178, 188, 223 fn. 1

HEISENBERG, WERNER
Freedom of self-determination: the existential issue concerning causal indeterminacy, 387. *Classification:* 336

HEMPEL, CARL G.
Freedom of self-determination: the existential issue concerning causal initiative, 320. *Classification:* 258

HIRSCH, MAX
Collective freedom: 185, 201–2

HOBART, R. E.
Freedom of self-determination: the existential issue concerning causal initiative, 266, 291 fn. 149, 307 fn. 204; the existential issue concerning causal indeterminacy, 437 fn. 364, 460; a possible conceptual issue, 504 fn. 50, 506, 509–10, 511 fn. 78. *Classification:* 252, 258, 336, 516. *See also:* 224, 427, 440 fn. 381

HOBBES, THOMAS
Freedom of self-realization: 47, 62. *Freedom of self-perfection:* 103, 109–10, 113, 114, 116–17. *Political liberty:* 137, 139, 143–44, 146, 166–69, 174–75, 179–81. *Freedom of self-determination:* the existential issue concerning causal initiative, 255–56, 259, 261, 262, 268–270, 271, 272, 279–80, 288–89, 292, 303; the existential issue concerning causal indeterminacy, 343–45, 353, 354–56, 395–96, 404, 410 fn. 258, 424, 429–31, 438, 442, 447, 460; the theological issue, 471–72, 481, 482 fn. 71 and 73. *Classification:* 5, 12, 14, 27, 50, 104, 107, 251, 336, 466. *See also:* 23–26, 29, 54, 90 fn. 156, 164 fn. 57, 171, 216 fn. 105, 224, 266, 267, 358–59, 369, 435

HOBHOUSE, L. T.
Freedom of self-realization: 42 fn. 26, 62, 63, 78, 81–84. *Freedom of self-perfection:* 103, 107, 109, 111, 113–14, 117, 118, 120. *Political liberty:* 136–38, 140, 141 fn. 9, 145–46, 147–48, 151–52. *Freedom of self-determination:* the existential issue concerning causal initiative, 291 fn. 150, 299; a possible conceptual issue, 503–4. *Classification:* 5, 9, 13, 50, 51 fn. 44, 104, 107, 155, 251, 516. *See also:*

103 fn. 17, 115 fn. 55, 130, 136 fn. 1, 154, 159, 169, 176, 178, 223 fn. 1

HOCKING, WILLIAM ERNEST
Freedom of self-determination: the existential issue concerning causal initiative, 293 fn. 156, 318 fn. 240. *Classification:* 257

HOLBACH, BARON D'
Freedom of self-determination: the existential issue concerning causal initiative, 281; the existential issue concerning causal indeterminacy, 392, 393–94. *Classification:* 251, 258, 336

HOME, HENRY (See Kaims, Lord)

HOOK, SIDNEY
Freedom of self-determination: the existential issue concerning causal indeterminacy, 443. *Classification:* 252, 336

HOSPERS, JOHN
Freedom of self-determination: the existential issue concerning causal indeterminacy, 442–44. *Classification:* 252, 336

HUGHES, GEORGE T.
Freedom of self-determination: the existential issue concerning causal indeterminacy, 404, 414. *Classification:* 250, 335

HUME, DAVID
Freedom of self-realization: 62. *Freedom of self-perfection:* 109–11, 113–14, 116–17. *Freedom of self-determination:* the existential issue concerning causal initiative, 259–61, 264–65, 271–72, 278, 296, 299, 303, 326; the existential issue concerning causal indeterminacy, 346–48, 374, 382 fn. 160, 392, 398, 400, 403, 418 fn. 290, 429, 431, 433–34, 442, 446, 450, 460; a possible conceptual issue, 497–99, 500 fn. 24, 500–1, 506–7, 509–10. *Classification:* 5, 12, 14, 27, 50, 107, 251, 257, 336. *See also:* 90 fn. 156, 266, 359, 367 fn. 112, 368 fn. 113, 369, 416, 500, 516

HUSIK, ISAAC
Freedom of self-determination: the theological issue, 480 fn. 62

HUXLEY, THOMAS HENRY
Freedom of self-determination: the existential issue concerning causal initiative, 264. *Classification:* 251, 258

JAMES, WILLIAM
Freedom of self-perfection: 108. *Freedom of self-determination:* the existential issue concerning causal initiative, 272 fn. 63, 275, 293, 303 fn. 194; the existential issue concerning causal indeterminacy, 364, 385–86,

420, 423 fn. 302, 441 fn. 383, 442, 458–60; the theological issue, 485–87. *Classification:* 7, 12, 14, 107, 248, 249, 250, 257, 335, 466. *See also:* 363 fn. 95

JASPERS, KARL
Political liberty: 153–54. *Classification:* 155. *See also:* 136 fn. 1, 147

JOAD, C. E. M.
Collective freedom: 185, 198–99, 203, 206

JOHN OF ST. THOMAS
Freedom of self-realization: 60 fn. 79

JOSEPH, H. W. B.
Freedom of self-determination: the existential issue concerning causal initiative, 266. *Classification:* 251, 258

KAIMS, LORD (Henry Home)
Freedom of self-determination: a possible conceptual issue, 500 fn. 25

KANT, IMMANUEL
Freedom of self-realization: 38 fn. 10, 48, 52–53, 71, 72–73. *Freedom of self-perfection:* 110, 112, 120 fn. 68, 123. *Political liberty:* 136, 138, 140, 141 fn. 9, 147, 149–51, 177. *Collective freedom:* 222. *Freedom of self-determination:* the existential issue concerning causal initiative, 255, 273, 276, 278, 282–83, 285, 303, 306 fn. 199; the existential issue concerning causal indeterminacy, 359, 403 fn. 241, 417–18, 422–23, 428 fn. 325, 460. *Classification:* 6, 7, 9, 13, 14, 27, 49, 100, 106, 155, 248, 249, 257, 335. *See also:* 54, 56 fn. 60, 63 fn. 95, 87, 136 fn. 1, 147, 174, 176–77, 370 fn. 126, 399, 414 fn. 276

KELSEN, HANS
Freedom of self-realization: 47–49, 62–63. *Freedom of self-perfection:* 108. *Political liberty:* 137, 139, 175–78, 183. *Freedom of self-determination:* the existential issue concerning causal initiative, 264, 303, 307 fn. 204; the existential issue concerning causal indeterminacy, 389, 437, 452–53. *Classification:* 5, 12, 50, 107, 251, 258, 336–37. *See also:* 90 fn. 156, 170

KIRK, RUSSELL
Collective freedom: 215 fn. 104

KNIGHT, FRANK H.
Freedom of self-realization: 41, 42, 47, 62–63. *Freedom of self-perfection:* 103, 108, 109–10. *Political liberty:* 137, 139, 175–78, 183. *Classification:* 5, 7, 13, 50, 104, 107, 248, 249, 335. *See also:* 24–25, 26, 90 fn. 156, 114 fn. 51, 170

LAMPRECHT, STERLING P.
Freedom of self-determination: the existential issue concerning causal indeterminacy, 362 fn. 94. *Classification:* 335

LA PLACE, PIERRE
Freedom of self-determination: the existential issue concerning causal indeterminacy, 363, 364

LA SALLE, FERDINAND
Collective freedom: 191 fn. 19

LASKI, HAROLD J.
Freedom of self-realization: 41 fn. 23, 47, 62, 78, 81, 84–85. *Freedom of self-perfection:* 103–4, 107–8, 109, 111, 113–14, 117–21. *Political liberty:* 137, 139, 140, 145–46, 176–78, 182. *Classification:* 5, 12, 50–51 and fn. 44, 104, 107. *See also:* 103 fn. 17, 115 fn. 55, 130, 170, 223–24 fn. 1

LAUER, ROSEMARY Z.
Freedom of self-determination: the existential issue concerning causal initiative, 291 fn. 151

LAWRENCE, NATHANIEL
Freedom of self-determination: the existential issue concerning causal indeterminacy, 359 fn. 85. *Classification:* 250

LEHRER, KEITH
Freedom of self-determination: the existential issue concerning causal indeterminacy, 450 fn. 433

LEIBNIZ, GOTTFRIED W.
Freedom of self-perfection: 112. *Freedom of self-determination:* the existential issue concerning causal initiative, 273, 275; the theological issue, 468 fn. 7, 470–71. *Classification:* 6, 7, 13, 50, 100, 106, 248, 249, 257. *See also:* 7 fn. 1

LENIN, VLADIMIR I.
Political liberty: 172 fn. 79. *Collective freedom:* 187, 188, 195–98, 199, 203, 204 fn. 62, 208–9

LEQUIER, JULES
Freedom of self-determination: the existential issue concerning causal indeterminacy, 448, 458; the theological issue, 481–82. *Classification:* 12, 248, 249, 335, 466

LEWIS, H. D.
Freedom of self-determination: the existential issue concerning causal indeterminacy, 414, 427, 438, 439 fn. 372, 444 fn. 400; a possible conceptual issue, 506, 513. *Classification:* 250, 335, 518. *See also:* 224

LOCKE, JOHN
Freedom of self-realization: 38, 42, 43,

46, 59–60. *Political liberty:* 138, 141 fn. 9, 144, 147, 151, 177, 180–81. *Classification:* 5, 6, 7, 8–9, 14, 27, 50, 106, 155, 248, 249, 257, 335. *See also:* 54, 60, 61, 87, 102 fn. 14, 133 fn. 98, 136–37 fn. 1, 159, 165, 174, 399

LONERGAN, BERNARD
Freedom of self-determination: the existential issue concerning causal indeterminacy, 410 fn. 256; the theological issue, 481 fn. 68, 482

LOSSKY, NIKOLAI
Freedom of self-determination: the existential issue concerning causal initiative, 273 fn. 64, 276; the existential issue concerning causal indeterminacy, 403 fn. 241, 417–18, 427–28, 448; the theological issue, 482. *Classification:* 250, 257, 335, 466. *See also:* 370 fn. 126

LOTZE, HERMAN
Freedom of self-determination: the existential issue concerning causal initiative, 273 fn. 64, 276, 323 fn. 266; the existential issue concerning causal indeterminacy, 403 fn. 240, 427–28, 458. *Classification:* 250, 257, 335. *See also:* 370 fn. 126

LUCRETIUS
Classification: 7, 12, 248

LUTHER, MARTIN
Freedom of self-determination: the theological issue, 469–70, 477 fn. 51, 481 fn. 68, 487. *Classification:* 6, 7, 13, 50, 100, 106, 248, 249, 335, 466

MABBOTT, J. D.
Freedom of self-determination: the existential issue concerning causal indeterminacy, 427, 438, 440, 445 fn. 404, 447 fn. 412, 458 fn. 466; a possible conceptual issue, 506, 510–11. *Classification:* 250, 335, 518

McDOUGALL, WILLIAM
Freedom of self-determination: the existential issue concerning causal initiative, 293 fn. 160; a possible conceptual issue, 505 fn. 56. *Classification:* 258

McGILVARY, E. B.
Freedom of self-determination: a possible conceptual issue, 505 fn. 56. *Classification:* 251

MACHIAVELLI, NICCOLO
Classification: 248

MACINTYRE, A. C.
Freedom of self-determination: the existential issue concerning causal initiative, 274 fn. 67. *Classification:* 250, 257

MACIVER, ROBERT M.
Freedom of self-realization: 41 fn. 22, 79–81. *Freedom of self-perfection:* 108 fn. 29, 111, 117, 118, 121–22. *See also:* 130, 223–24 fn. 1

MACLAGAN, W. C.
Freedom of self-determination: the existential issue concerning causal initiative, 325–26 fn. 276; the existential issue concerning causal indeterminacy, 360, 386, 428, 449; a possible conceptual issue, 506, 509, 512. *Classification:* 250, 335, 517. *See also:* 224

MACMURRAY, JOHN
Freedom of self-realization: 62, 63. *Freedom of self-perfection:* 108, 109–10. *Freedom of self-determination:* the existential issue concerning causal indeterminacy, 362 fn. 94. *Classification:* 5, 50, 107. *See also:* 90 fn. 156

McTAGGART, JOHN McTAGGART ELLIS
Freedom of self-perfection: 106 fn. 23. *Freedom of self-determination:* the existential issue concerning causal indeterminacy, 347 fn. 38, 375–77, 379–80, 381, 435, 451, 460; a possible conceptual issue, 502–3. *Classification:* 106, 251, 336, 516. *See also:* 369

MAHER, MICHAEL
Freedom of self-determination: the existential issue concerning causal initiative, 267 fn. 43; the existential issue concerning causal indeterminacy, 386 fn. 180, 442 fn. 298; a possible conceptual issue, 513 fn. 88. *Classification:* 250, 257

MAIMONIDES, MOSES
Freedom of self-determination: the existential issue concerning causal indeterminacy, 422 fn. 296; the theological issue, 479–80. *Classification:* 6, 7, 13, 50, 248, 249, 466

MAISTRE, JOSEPH DE
Collective freedom: 210 fn. 86

MALEBRANCHE, NICOLAS
Classification: 248

MALINOWSKI, BRONISLAW
Freedom of self-realization: 41. *Freedom of self-perfection:* 108, 111, 113, 118–20. *Classification:* 5, 12, 50, 107. *See also:* 130

MANNHEIM, KARL
Freedom of self-realization: 62. *Collective freedom:* 185, 198, 199, 202–3, 206. *Classification:* 5, 12, 50. *See also:* 90 fn. 156

MANSEL, HENRY
Freedom of self-determination: the existential issue concerning causal in-

itiative, 270–71, 272, 318, 321; the existential issue concerning causal indeterminacy, 359, 397 fn. 214, 403–4, and fn. 240, 413, 424, 446; the theological issue, 475. *Classification:* 250, 257, 335, 466. *See also:* 224, 266

MARC, ANDRÉ
Freedom of self-determination: the existential issue concerning causal indeterminacy, 410 fn. 256. *Classification:* 250, 335

MARCEL, GABRIEL
Classification: 6, 7, 13, 50, 248

MARGENAU, HENRY
Freedom of self-determination: the existential issue concerning causal indeterminacy, 387 fn. 184, 389. *Classification:* 337

MARITAIN, JACQUES
Freedom of self-realization: 60. *Freedom of self-perfection:* 112, 118, 132, 133. *Political liberty:* 138, 139, 151, 177. *Collective freedom:* 185–87, 198–200, 207, 212–16, 218, 220. *Freedom of self-determination:* the existential issue concerning causal initiative, 273 fn. 64, 274 fn. 69, 292 fn. 152, 303; the existential issue concerning causal indeterminacy, 358 fn. 79, 378–79, 382, 389, 407 fn. 246, 408 fn. 247 and fn. 248, 409 fn. 252, 410 fn. 256; the theological issue, 483; a possible conceptual issue, 512–13 fn. 85. *Classification:* 5, 6, 7, 9, 13, 14, 50, 100, 155, 248, 249, 250, 257, 335, 337. *See also:* 42, 87, 102 fn. 14, 110, 133 fn. 98, 136–37 fn. 1, 147

MARSILIUS OF PADUA
Political liberty: 153. *Classification:* 155. *See also:* 136–37 fn. 1, 147

MARTINEAU, JAMES
Freedom of self-determination: the existential issue concerning causal initiative, 317–18; the existential issue concerning causal indeterminacy, 403 fn. 241, 417–18, 427, 441. *Classification:* 250, 257, 335

MARX, KARL
Freedom of self-realization: 53, 56–58. *Freedom of self-perfection:* 104, 108, 109. *Political liberty:* 171 fn. 78, 172 fn. 79, 174. *Collective freedom:* 184–87, 187–88, 191, 193–94, 195, 196, 199, 203, 204, 207, 208–11, 212, 214, 215–17, 219, 222. *Classification:* 10, 12, 104, 107. *See also:* 90 fn. 156, 114 fn. 51, 174, 195

MASCALL, E. L.
Freedom of self-determination: the

existential issue concerning causal indeterminacy, 455–56. *Classification:* 335

MATSON, WALLACE I.
Freedom of self-determination: the existential issue concerning causal indeterminacy, 434, 445–46; a possible conceptual issue, 501–2 fn. 33. *Classification:* 251, 336

MEYERSON, EMILE
Freedom of self-determination: the existential issue concerning causal initiative, 272 fn. 62; the existential issue concerning causal indeterminacy, 378 fn. 153, 386. *Classification:* 248, 249, 257

MICHOTTE, A.
Freedom of self-determination: the existential issue concerning causal initiative, 319

MILL, JOHN STUART
Freedom of self-realization: 41, 47, 62, 73–75. *Freedom of self-perfection:* 103, 109, 111, 113. *Political liberty:* 175–78. *Freedom of self-determination:* the existential issue concerning causal initiative, 264, 270–71, 318, 320–21; the existential issue concerning causal indeterminacy, 349, 359, 374–75, 392, 396–97, 403–4, 410, 413, 424, 429, 431–32, 438–39, 442, 446; the theological issue, 475. *Classification:* 5, 12, 14, 50, 51 fn. 44, 104, 107, 251, 257, 336. *See also:* 54, 55, 124 fn. 83, 223 fn. 1, 224, 266, 369, 435

MISES, LUDWIG VON
Collective freedom: 186. *Freedom of self-determination:* the existential issue concerning causal indeterminacy, 377. *Classification:* 252, 336

MISES, RICHARD VON
Freedom of self-determination: the existential issue concerning causal indeterminacy, 377 fn. 149

MOLINA, D. LUDOVICO
Freedom of self-determination: the theological issue, 483 fn. 82. *Classification:* 248

MONTAIGNE, MICHEL DE
Freedom of self-perfection: 100

MONTESQUIEU, BARON DE
Freedom of self-realization: 42, 44, 46, 60–61. *Freedom of self-perfection:* 120. *Political liberty:* 138, 141 fn. 9, 144, 147, 151, 177. *Classification:* 5, 6, 7, 9, 13, 14, 50, 106, 155, 248, 249. *See also:* 87, 102 fn. 14, 133 fn. 98, 136–37 fn. 1, 159, 174

MOORE, GEORGE EDWARD
Freedom of self-determination: the existential issue concerning causal initiative, 304–5, 314 fn. 232; the existential issue concerning causal indeterminacy, 425 fn. 315, 442 fn. 387

MORE, HENRY
Freedom of self-determination: the existential issue concerning causal indeterminacy, 403 fn. 239, 410–11, 426, 448; the theological issue, 485. *Classification:* 250, 335, 466

MUNNYNCK, P. DE
Freedom of self-determination: the existential issue concerning causal indeterminacy, 358 fn. 79, 410 fn. 256

NAGEL, ERNEST
Freedom of self-determination: the existential issue concerning causal indeterminacy, 443–44, 458. *Classification:* 336

NEUMARK, DAVID
Freedom of self-determination: the existential issue concerning causal indeterminacy, 433 fn. 345; the theological issue, 468 fn. 7

NICOLAS, M. J.
Freedom of self-determination: the theological issue, 483 fn. 85

NIETZSCHE, FRIEDRICH
Freedom of self-determination: the existential issue concerning causal initiative, 265; the existential issue concerning causal indeterminacy, 349–50, 392, 396, 441–42. *Classification:* 251, 258, 336

NOWELL-SMITH, P. H.
Freedom of self-realization: 62. *Freedom of self-perfection:* 108. *Freedom of self-determination:* the existential issue concerning causal initiative, 255, 291 fn. 149, 292, 295, 297–99, 301, 303–4, 306–16, 317, 323–24, 328–29; the existential issue concerning causal indeterminacy, 371, 376–77, 379–80, 381, 392, 400–1, 404, 416–18, 425, 429, 432–33, 438, 439–40, 442–43, 446–47; a possible conceptual issue, 499 fn. 22, 504, 506, 507, 509–10, 512. *Classification:* 5, 12, 107, 258, 336, 516. *See also:* 29, 90 fn. 156, 224, 420 fn. 293, 427, 445 fn. 404

OCKHAM, WILLIAM OF
Freedom of self-determination: the theological issue, 473, 474. *Classification:* 248, 466

OFSTAD, HARALD
Freedom of self-determination: the

existential issue concerning causal initiative, 293–94. *Classification:* 257

OWEN, ROBERT
Collective freedom: 199

PAP, ARTHUR
Freedom of self-determination: the existential issue concerning causal initiative, 322 fn. 261; the existential issue concerning causal indeterminacy, 347 fn. 38, 444 fn. 397, 452. *Classification:* 258, 336

PARETO, VILFREDO
Freedom of self-realization: 62. *Freedom of self-perfection:* 108. *Classification:* 5, 12, 50, 107. *See also:* 90 fn. 156

PASCAL, BLAISE
Classification: 248, 249

PAUL, G. A.
Freedom of self-determination: the existential issue concerning causal indeterminacy, 414–15 fn. 277. *Classification:* 251

PAULSEN, FRIEDRICH
Freedom of self-determination: the existential issue concerning causal initiative, 264, 321; the existential issue concerning causal indeterminacy, 347 fn. 38, 450–51; the theological issue, 472. *Classification:* 251, 258, 336, 466. *See also:* 369

PEIRCE, CHARLES SANDERS
Freedom of self-determination: the existential issue concerning causal indeterminacy, 364, 385, 403 fn. 240, 415 fn. 279. *Classification:* 250, 335. *See also:* 363 fn. 95

PHILO
Freedom of self-realization: 48, 53, 55 fn. 57, 70–71. *Freedom of self-perfection:* 112, 115–16. *Classification:* 6, 7, 13, 49, 100, 106, 248, 249

PLANCK, MAX
Freedom of self-determination: the existential issue concerning causal indeterminacy, 387–88, 389, 449, 452–53. *Classification:* 336–37

PLATO
Freedom of self-realization: 36–37, 52. *Freedom of self-perfection:* 100, 112, 118 and fn. 58, 119, 122, 123–24. *Classification:* 12, 14, 27, 49, 100, 106. *See also:* 54, 56 fn. 60, 75, 90 fn. 156

PLOTINUS
Classification: 6, 12. *See also:* 90 fn. 156

POPPER, KARL
Freedom of self-perfection: 110 fn.

37. *Freedom of self-determination:* the existential issue concerning causal indeterminacy, 384–85, 387 fn. 184. *Classification:* 250, 336–37

PRICE, JOSEPH
Freedom of self-determination: the existential issue concerning causal initiative, 255, 261, 262, 270, 272, 280–81, 288, 292, 317–18, 320–21; the existential issue concerning causal indeterminacy, 359, 403 and fn. 240, 411–12, 424, 446; the theological issue, 474; a possible conceptual issue, 500. *Classification:* 250, 257, 335, 466. *See also:* 224

PRIESTLEY, JOSEPH
Freedom of self-realization: 62. *Freedom of self-perfection:* 109, 111, 113, 114–15, 116, 117. *Freedom of self-determination:* the existential issue concerning causal initiative, 255, 259, 261, 262–63, 264, 270, 280 fn. 93, 280–81, 288, 289, 292, 317–18, 320–21; the existential issue concerning causal indeterminacy, 347, 348, 359, 392, 393, 394, 398–99, 400, 403, 411–12, 424, 429, 431–32, 446, 460; the theological issue, 472, 474; a possible conceptual issue, 500. *Classification:* 5, 12, 14, 50, 107, 251, 258, 336, 466, 516. *See also:* 29, 90 fn. 156, 224, 266, 369, 416

PROTAGORAS
Freedom of self-perfection: 100

PROUDHON, PIERRE JOSEPH
Collective freedom: 194, 207

PRUM, E.
Freedom of self-determination: the existential issue concerning causal initiative, 319

RASHDALL, HASTINGS
Freedom of self-determination: the existential issue concerning causal initiative, 278 fn. 88, 283, 291 fn. 150; the existential issue concerning causal indeterminacy, 435 fn. 357; the theological issue, 872–73; a possible conceptual issue, 502–3. *Classification:* 251, 258, 466, 516

REID, THOMAS
Freedom of self-determination: the existential issue concerning causal indeterminacy, 359, 380, 403 fn. 240, 412–13; the theological issue, 474. *Classification:* 250, 335, 466. *See also:* 381 fn. 158, 382 fn. 160

RENOUVIER, CHARLES
Freedom of self-perfection: 108. *Freedom of self-determination:* the exis-

tential issue concerning causal initiative, 275, 292, 303 fn. 194, 317–18; the existential issue concerning causal indeterminacy, 360–62, 364, 378–79, 382, 385 fn. 175, 403 fn. 240, 415, 423, 458–59. *Classification:* 7, 12, 107, 248, 249, 257, 335. *See also:* 363 fn. 95

RICKABY, JOSEPH
Freedom of self-determination: the existential issue concerning causal initiative, 271, 272; the existential issue concerning causal indeterminacy, 358–59, 360 fn. 86, 403–4, 410, 438–39; the theological issue, 482; a possible conceptual issue, 506–8, 509. *Classification:* 250, 257, 335, 517. *See also:* 266

ROSS, SIR DAVID
Freedom of self-determination: the existential issue concerning causal indeterminacy, 349, 388 fn. 187, 392, 394 fn. 206, 400–1, 404, 414, 444, 451, 460; a possible conceptual issue, 502–3. *Classification:* 251, 336–37, 516. *See also:* 224, 369, 416

ROUSSEAU, JEAN JACQUES
Freedom of self-realization: 38–39, 44, 48, 52, 71–72, 81. *Freedom of self-perfection:* 112, 118–19, 119–20, 121–22. *Political liberty:* 137, 138, 139, 140, 144, 145, 175–78. *Collective freedom:* 207, 210 fn. 83, 221–22. *Freedom of self-determination:* the existential issue concerning causal initiative, 273, 274–75. *Classification:* 6, 7, 13, 49, 50–51 and fn. 44, 100, 106, 248, 249, 257, 335. *See also:* 54, 57, 73, 75, 87, 188, 223–24 fn. 1

ROYCE, JOSIAH
Freedom of self-determination: the existential issue concerning causal initiative, 273 fn. 64, 276. *Classification:* 250, 257. *See also:* 370 fn. 126

RUSSELL, BERTRAND
Freedom of self-realization: 47. *Freedom of self-perfection:* 105. *Freedom of self-determination:* the existential issue concerning causal initiative, 264, 321, 376, 429, 436, 458; a possible conceptual issue, 504. *Classification:* 5, 6, 13, 50–51 and fn. 44, 251, 257, 336, 516. *See also:* 99 fn. 10 and fn. 12, 103 fn. 16, 223–24 fn. 1, 427

RUSSELL, L. J.
Freedom of self-determination: the existential issue concerning causal initiative, 255, 278, 279, 283–86, 293, 303, 305 fn. 198; the existential issue

concerning causal indeterminacy, 369, 370, 418, 425 fn. 315, 442. *Classification:* 250, 257, 335. *See also:* 224

RYAN, MSGR. JOHN A.
Freedom of self-determination: the existential issue concerning causal indeterminacy, 422 fn. 298

SAADIA GAON
Freedom of self-determination: the theological issue, 479. *Classification:* 248

SAINT PAUL
Freedom of self-perfection: 118, 122, 123. *See also:* 56 fn. 60

SAINT-SIMON, CLAUDE HENRI
Collective freedom: 199, 207, 210 fn. 86

SALVADORI, MASSIMO
Collective freedom: 185, 198, 199, 203, 206, 208

SANTAYANA, GEORGE
Classification: 6, 7, 13, 248, 249. *See also:* 99–100 fn. 12

SARTRE, JEAN-PAUL
Freedom of self-perfection: 104, 108, 109. *Political liberty:* 143–44. *Freedom of self-determination:* the existential issue concerning causal initiative, 275, 303 fn. 194; the existential issue concerning causal indeterminacy, 403 fn. 240, 416, 423. *Classification:* 7, 12, 14, 104, 107, 248, 249, 250, 257, 335. *See also:* 114 fn. 51

SCHELLING, FRIEDRICH WILHELM VON
Freedom of self-determination: the existential issue concerning causal initiative, 273 fn. 64, 276. *Classification:* 250, 257. *See also:* 370 fn. 126

SCHILLER, F. C. S.
Freedom of self-determination: the existential issue concerning causal initiative, 318–19, 323 fn. 264; the existential issue concerning causal indeterminacy, 385, 386, 448–49, 459–60. *Classification:* 250, 257, 335. *See also:* 427

SCHLICK, MORITZ
Freedom of self-realization: 47, 62, 63. *Freedom of self-perfection:* 108, 109. *Freedom of self-determination:* the existential issue concerning causal initiative, 291 fn. 149, 294–95, 303, 304, 307 fn. 204, 309, 312, 314 fn. 231 and fn. 232, 315–16, 321; the existential issue concerning causal indeterminacy, 425 fn. 315, 429, 433, 438, 442; a possible conceptual issue, 505 fn. 51. *Classification:* 5, 12, 25, 50, 107, 251, 257, 336. *See also:* 23–

24, 24–25, 26, 90 fn. 156, 427, 439, 440

SCHOPENHAUER, ARTHUR
Freedom of self-determination: the existential issue concerning causal indeterminacy, 348. *Classification:* 336

SCHRODINGER, ERWIN
Freedom of self-determination: the existential issue concerning causal indeterminacy, 389; the theological issue, 473. *Classification:* 336–37

SCULLY, JOSEPH G.
Freedom of self-determination: the existential issue concerning causal indeterminacy, 410 fn. 256; the theological issue, 482

SECRÉTAN, CHARLES
Freedom of self-determination: the existential issue concerning causal initiative, 275 fn. 76, 324 fn. 268; the existential issue concerning causal indeterminacy, 403 fn. 240, 415 fn. 278, 423, 450. *Classification:* 7, 12, 248, 249, 256–57, 335

SIDGWICK, HENRY
Freedom of self-realization: 42 fn. 26, 47. *Political liberty:* 136, 147–48, 152, 154–55. *Freedom of self-determination:* the existential issue concerning causal initiative, 264; the existential issue concerning causal indeterminacy, 347 fn. 38, 435–36, 450–51. *Classification:* 155, 251, 257, 336. *See also:* 23, 25, 136–37 fn. 1, 147, 159, 169, 176, 178

SIMON, YVES
Freedom of self-realization: 60. *Freedom of self-perfection:* 112, 132, 133. *Political liberty:* 138, 139, 140, 151, 177. *Collective freedom:* 185. *Freedom of self-determination:* the existential issue concerning causal initiative, 267–68, 272, 273 fn. 64, 274 fn. 69, 292 fn. 152, 323; the existential issue concerning causal indeterminacy, 358 fn. 79, 359, 378–79, 382, 389, 407 fn. 246, 408 fn. 248, 410 fn. 256, 450 fn. 433; a possible conceptual issue, 509, 512–13 fn. 85. *Classification:* 5, 6, 7, 8–9, 13, 14, 50, 106, 155, 248, 249, 250, 257, 335, 336–37, 517. *See also:* 42, 87, 133 fn. 98, 136–37 fn. 1, 147.

SMITH, ADAM
Freedom of self-realization: 41 fn. 23, 62, 63. *Classification:* 5, 7, 13, 50, 248, 249. *See also:* 90 fn. 156

SMITH, GERARD
Freedom of self-determination: the existential issue concerning causal ini-

tiative, 291 fn. 151; the existential issue concerning causal indeterminacy, 410 fn. 256; the theological issue, 481 fn. 68

SPANN, OTHMAR
Collective freedom: 210 fn. 83

SPENCER, HERBERT
Freedom of self-realization: 42, 47, 62, 63, 73–75. *Freedom of self-perfection:* 108. *Political liberty:* 137, 139, 144–48, 169–70, 174. *Collective freedom:* 186, 211. *Freedom of self-determination:* the existential issue concerning causal initiative, 264, 278 fn. 88, 290. *Classification:* 5, 12, 50–51 and fn. 44, 107, 251, 257–58. *See also:* 54, 55, 90 fn. 156, 124 fn. 83, 171, 223–24 fn. 1

SPINOZA, BENEDICT DE
Freedom of self-realization: 37 fn. 6, 48, 52. *Freedom of self-perfection:* 112. *Political liberty:* 175–78. *Freedom of self-determination:* the existential issue concerning causal initiative, 255, 261, 263–64, 272, 280, 320; the existential issue concerning causal indeterminacy, 345–46, 350, 363, 433, 450, 460. *Classification:* 6, 12, 14, 49, 100, 106, 251, 257, 336. *See also:* 57, 90 fn. 156, 188, 269 fn. 51, 369

Stafford, John W.
Freedom of self-determination: the existential issue concerning causal initiative, 323 fn. 265

STALIN, JOSEPH
Collective freedom: 197, 204 fn. 62, 206, 207

STEBBING, SUSAN
Freedom of self-determination: the existential issue concerning causal indeterminacy, 351, 389, 422 fn. 387; a possible conceptual issue, 505. *Classification:* 251, 336, 337, 516

STEVENSON, CHARLES L.
Freedom of self-realization: 62. *Freedom of self-perfection:* 108. *Freedom of self-determination:* the existential issue concerning causal initiative, 303, 304, 307 fn. 204, 314 fn. 232; the existential issue concerning causal indeterminacy, 425 fn. 315, 432–33, 438, 442; a possible conceptual issue, 505. *Classification:* 5, 12, 50, 107, 251, 258, 336, 516. *See also:* 90 fn. 156, 427, 439

STOUT, A. K.
Freedom of self-determination: the existential issue concerning causal initiative, 293 fn. 157; the existential

issue concerning causal indeterminacy, 428 fn. 327, 441 fn. 382; a possible conceptual issue, 506, 513–14. *Classification:* 250, 257, 335, 518

SUAREZ, FRANCIS
Freedom of self-determination: the existential issue concerning causal indeterminacy, 450 fn. 433. *Classification:* 6, 7, 13, 50, 248, 249, 257, 335

TALMON, J. L.
Collective freedom: 185, 186, 198, 199, 200, 203 fn. 53, 218–19

TAWNEY, RICHARD HENRY
Freedom of self-realization: 42 fn. 26, 47, 62. *Freedom of self-perfection:* 108. *Political liberty:* 178–79. *Classification:* 5, 12, 50, 107. *See also:* 23–24, 25, 90 fn. 156

TAYLOR, A. E.
Freedom of self-determination: the existential issue concerning causal indeterminacy, 403 fn. 239, 411, 428 fn. 327. *Classification:* 248, 249, 250, 335

TAYLOR, RICHARD
Freedom of self-determination: the existential issue concening causal indeterminacy, 359 fn. 85, 428 fn. 327, 443 fn. 391. *Classification:* 335

TILLICH, PAUL
Freedom of self-determination: the existential issue concerning causal indeterminacy, 423 fn. 305, 456–57; the theological issue, 486–87; a possible conceptual issue, 515 fn. 94. *Classification:* 6, 7, 13, 50, 248, 249, 250, 335, 466

TOCQUEVILLE, ALEXIS DE
Classification: 248, 249

TOLSTOY, LEO
Freedom of self-determination: the existential issue concerning causal indeterminacy, 449

TROTSKY, LEON
Collective freedom: 204 fn. 62

TUCKER, ABRAHAM
Freedom of self-determination: the existential issue concerning causal initiative, 265 fn. 34; the theological issue, 484–85; a possible conceptual issue, 500 fn. 24. *Classification:* 251, 258

VALLA, LORENZO
Freedom of self-determination: the theological issue, 477 fn. 51

VAN MELSEN, A. G.
Classification: 250

VICO, GIAMBATTISTA
Classification: 248, 249

VOLTAIRE, FRANÇOIS DE

Freedom of self-realization: 62. *Freedom of self-perfection:* 109, 111, 113, 114–15, 116, 117. *Freedom of self-determination:* the existential issue concerning causal indeterminacy, 392, 396, 436. *Classification:* 5, 12, 50, 107, 251, 336. *See also:* 90 fn. 156

WARD, JAMES
Classification: 250

WATTS, ISAAC
Freedom of self-determination: the existential issue concerning causal initiative, 281; the existential issue concerning causal indeterminacy, 403 fn. 239, 411. *Classification:* 250, 257, 335, 466

WAXMAN, MEYER
Freedom of self-determination: the existential issue concerning causal indeterminacy, 433 fn. 345; the theological issue, 468 fn. 7, 480 fn. 62

WEISS, PAUL
Freedom of self-determination: the existential issue concerning causal indeterminacy, 362–63, 364–67, 378–79, 382, 403 fn. 240, 415, 423, 454–55, 460; the theological issue, 483–84, 509; a possible conceptual issue, 509, 512–13 fn. 85 and fn. 88. *Classification:* 7, 12, 248, 249, 250, 335, 466, 518. *See also:* 7 fn. 1, 367

WELLS, H. M.
Freedom of self-determination: the existential issue concerning causal initiative, 319

WHITEHEAD, ALFRED N.
Freedom of self-determination: the existential issue concerning causal indeterminacy, 364 fn. 99, 378 fn. 152. *Classification:* 6, 7, 13, 248, 249, 335. *See also:* 363 fn. 95

WILLIAMS, GARDNER
Freedom of self-determination: the existential issue concerning causal initiative, 266. *Classification:* 252, 258

WILSON, J.
Classification: 252

WINDELBAND, WILHELM
Freedom of self-determination: the existential issue concerning causal initiative, 255, 265–66, 283, 286, 291 fn. 150, 296; the existential issue concerning causal indeterminacy, 349, 437 fn. 362. *Classification:* 258, 336. *See also:* 369

WINTHROP, JONATHAN
Freedom of self-realization: 38 fn. 10

WISDOM, JOHN
Classification: 250

WITTGENSTEIN, LUDWIG
Freedom of self-determination: the existential issue concerning causal initiative, 295–96 fn. 169

WOOTTON, BARBARA
Freedom of self-realization: 79. *Freedom of self-perfection:* 108 fn. 29, 111, 113, 118–19. *Political liberty:* 154 fn. 28. *Classification:* 155. *See also:* 136 fn. 1

INDEX OF AUTHORS IN THE
SPECIAL CONTROVERSIES

ALLEMAN, F. A.
Freedom of self-realization: the existential issues, 600 fn. 115
AMBROSE
Classification: 6, 12
ANSELM OF CANTERBURY
Freedom of self-perfection: 621 fn. 2. Classification: 6, 7, 13
AQUINAS, THOMAS
Freedom of self-realization: the conceptual issues, 543, 544; the existential issues, 587 fn. 87; the normative issues, 613, 615. Freedom of self-perfection: 621, 622, 624. Freedom of self-determination: 465, 637 fn. 7, 638, 639, 641, 646, 647. Classification: 5, 6, 7, 9, 13, 27. See also: 7 fn. 1, 20–22, 644
ARISTOTLE
Freedom of self-realization: the conceptual issues, 543–45; the existential issues, 587 fn. 87; the normative issues, 610, 613–16, 617, 618. Freedom of self-determination: 642, 646. Classification: 7, 8–9, 13
AUGUSTINE
Freedom of self-perfection: 621, 624, 625. Freedom of self-determination: 637 fn. 7, 644. Classification: 6, 7, 13
AURELIUS, MARCUS
Freedom of self-perfection: 621, 624. Classification: 6–7, 12
AYER, A. J.
Freedom of self-realization: the conceptual issues, 541–42, 545–47. Classification: 5, 12, 14. See also: 20–21, 26, 542, 543–44
BAKUNIN, MIKHAIL
Freedom of self-realization: the existential issues, 595. Collective freedom: 626–27, 628–31, 632. Classification: 10, 12
BARTH, KARL
Freedom of self-perfection: 621 fn. 2. Classification: 6, 7, 13
BEARD, CHARLES A.
Freedom of self-realization: the nor-

mative issues, 612 fn. 36
BELLARMINE, ROBERT
Classification: 6, 7, 13
BELLOC, HILAIRE
Freedom of self-realization: the existential issues, 592 fn. 100, 595 fn. 106, 596 fn. 111; the normative issues, 612 fn. 36
BENTHAM, JEREMY
Freedom of self-realization: the existential issues, 567, 569, 581–82, 583 and fn. 79, 585, 591–92. Classification: 5, 12, 14
BERDYAEV, NICHOLAS
Freedom of self-perfection: 621 fn. 2, 624
BERGSON, HENRI
Freedom of self-determination: 640–41, 641–42, 645 fn. 34, 646–47. Classification: 7, 12. See also: 7 fn. 1
BERKELEY, GEORGE
Classification: 7, 12
BERLE, ADOLPH A., JR.
Freedom of self-realization: the existential issues, 599 fn. 112
BERLIN, ISAIAH
Freedom of self-realization: the conceptual issues, 542 fn. 14, 552, 554; the existential issues, 580, 590, 593 fn. 102
BOETHIUS
Freedom of self-perfection: 621. Freedom of self-determination: 637 fn. 7. Classification: 6, 7, 13
BOKSER, BEN ZION
Freedom of self-realization: the conceptual issues, 551
BOSANQUET, BERNARD
Classification: 6, 12
BRADLEY, FRANCIS H.
Freedom of self-perfection: 621. Classification: 6, 12, 49
BURKE, EDMUND
Freedom of self-realization: the existential issues, 569 fn. 31, 589; the normative issues, 606–8, 611. Classification: 5, 7, 13

CALHOUN, JOHN C.
Freedom of self-realization: the existential issues, 573, 575–76, 582 fn. 77, 589; the normative issues, 607–8, 611. *See also:* 577 fn. 60

CALIFORNIA ASSOCIATES
Freedom of self-realization: the conceptual issues, 541, 555; the existential issues, 584–85, 585–86, 592; the normative issues, 608 fn. 19. *See also:* 24 fn. 10, 25 fn. 11

CALVIN, JOHN
Freedom of self-perfection: 621, 624. *Freedom of self-determination:* 637 fn. 7. *Classification:* 6, 7, 13

CAMPBELL, CHARLES A.
Freedom of self-determination: 637, 641. *See also:* 29

CAPEK, MILIC
Freedom of self-determination: 641–42

CARR, E. H.
Freedom of self-realization: the normative issues, 609

CICERO, MARCUS TULLIUS
Classification: 6, 7, 13

CLARK, JOHN M.
Freedom of self-realization: the existential issues, 600 fn. 114; the normative issues, 610 fn. 31

CLEMENCEAU, GEORGES
Freedom of self-determination: 465

COMTE, AUGUSTE
Collective freedom: 626–28, 632–33. *Classification:* 10, 12

COX, HAROLD
Freedom of self-realization: the existential issues, 595 fn. 107; the normative issues, 612 fn. 37

CROCE, BENEDETTO
Freedom of self-perfection: 621 fn. 2

CROSLAND, C. A. R.
Freedom of self-realization: the existential issues, 600 fn. 115

CUNO, THEODORE FRIEDRICH
Collective freedom: 631

DESCARTES, RENÉ
Freedom of self-determination: 637, 639, 643, 646. *Classification:* 7, 12

DEWEY, JOHN
Freedom of self-realization: the conceptual issues, 550, 553 fn. 60, 555–56. *Freedom of self-perfection:* 621, 622, 623–24. *Freedom of self-determination:* 640–41, 641–42, 643, 645 fn. 34, 646–47. *Classification:* 5, 6, 7, 13. *See also:* 7 fn. 1

DUNS SCOTUS, JOHN
Freedom of self-determination: 639–40. *Classification:* 6, 7, 13

DURKHEIM, EMILE
Freedom of self-realization: the conceptual issues, 541

EDWARDS, JONATHAN
Classification: 5, 12. *See also:* 24–25, 26

ENGELS, FRIEDRICH
Freedom of self-realization: the existential issues, 595–96. *Collective Freedom:* 626, 628–29, 631–32 and fn. 23. *Classification:* 10, 12

EPICTETUS
Freedom of self-perfection: 621, 624. *Classification:* 6, 12

EPICURUS
Freedom of self-perfection: 621 fn. 2. *Classification:* 6, 7, 13

FICHTE, JOHANN G.
Classification: 7, 12

FITZHUGH, GEORGE
Freedom of self-realization: the normative issues, 606 fn. 6, 611

FOSDICK, DOROTHY
Freedom of self-realization: the conceptual issues, 552, 554–55; the existential issues, 583 fn. 79, 583–86, 591 fn. 96

FOUILLÉE, ALFRED
Freedom of self-determination: 638–39, 642–43, 644–45. *Classification:* 6, 7, 13. *See also:* 7 fn. 1

FREUD, SIGMUND
Freedom of self-realization: the existential issues, 564–65, 566, 567–69. *Freedom of self-perfection:* 621–24. *Classification:* 5, 6, 13, 14

GARRIGOU-LAGRANGE, REV. REGINALD
Freedom of self-determination: 641 fn. 19

GEORGE, HENRY
Freedom of self-realization: the existential issues, 588–89

GREEN, T. H.
Freedom of self-perfection: 621 fn. 2. *Classification:* 6, 7, 13

HALE, ROBERT L.
Freedom of self-realization: the conceptual issues, 550; the existential issues, 567, 569, 572 fn. 38, 581–82, 583–85, 590, 591–92. *Classification:* 5, 12

HAMILTON, ALEXANDER
Freedom of self-realization: the existential issues, 587 fn. 37; the normative issues, 604–5, 615

HAMILTON, SIR WILLIAM
Freedom of self-determination: 637

HARBRECHT, PAUL P.
Freedom of self-realization: the existential issues, 599 fn. 112

HARPER, F. A.
Freedom of self-realization: the existential issues, 579 fn. 31, 595 fn. 106

HARTLEY, DAVID
Freedom of self-determination: 465

HARTMANN, NICOLAI
Freedom of self-determination: 643, 645 fn. 32. *Classification:* 5, 7, 13

HARTSHORNE, CHARLES
Freedom of self-determination: 637 fn. 7, 641–42

HAYEK, FRIEDRICH A.
Freedom of self-realization: the conceptual issues, 552–53, 554 fn. 68, 556, 557–58, 559; the existential issues, 567, 569, 577 fn. 60, 581–82, 582–83, 583–85, 591–92, 601 fn. 118; the normative issues, 610 fn. 30, 612 fn. 37. *Classification:* 5, 12

HEALD, MARK M.
Freedom of self-realization: the conceptual issues, 543 fn. 22; the existential issues, 569 fn. 31, 582 fn. 77

HEGEL, GEORG W. F.
Freedom of self-realization: the normative issues, 610. *Freedom of self-perfection:* 621, 622, 623–24. *Freedom of self-determination:* 638–40, 642–43, 644–45, 646. *Classification:* 6, 7, 13. *See also:* 7 fn. 1, 54, 56 fn. 60, 57, 63 fn. 95, 87, 171–72

HEWES, THOMAS
Freedom of self-realization: the existential issues, 596 fn. 111

HIRSCH, MAX
Freedom of self-realization: the existential issues, 595 fn. 107, 599 fn. 113; the normative issues, 609

HOBBES, THOMAS
Freedom of self-realization: the conceptual issues, 539–41, 545–46, 547–48, 552–53, 556–58, 558–59; the existential issues, 567, 568–70, 581–82, 582–83, 583–86; the normative issues, 610. *Freedom of self-determination:* 465, 647. *Classification:* 5, 12, 14, 27. *See also:* 23, 24, 25, 26, 29, 543, 544

HOBHOUSE, L. T.
Freedom of self-realization: the existential issues, 564–66, 573, 574–75, 577–78, 581 fn. 76, 582 fn. 77, 583–86, 587 fn. 87, 590, 591 fn. 96, 595 fn. 106; the normative issues, 609, 611, 612 fn. 36, 618–19. *Classification:* 5, 8–9, 13, 14

HOFFMAN, R. J. S.
Freedom of self-realization: the existential issues, 595 fn. 106; the normative issues, 612 fn. 37

HUME, DAVID
Freedom of self-determination: 647. *Classification:* 5, 12, 14, 27

JAMES, WILLIAM
Freedom of self-determination: 641, 642. *Classification:* 7, 12

JASPERS, KARL
Freedom of self-realization: the existential issues, 587 fn. 87; the normative issues, 618–19

JOAD, C. E. M.
Freedom of self-realization: the existential issues, 581 fn. 76; the normative issues, 612 fn. 36

JONES, ROBERT VERNON
Freedom of self-realization: the existential issues 595 fn. 107; the normative issues, 612 fn. 36

KANT, IMMANUEL
Freedom of self-realization: the existential issues, 587 fn. 87; the normative issues, 610, 616–18. *Freedom of self-perfection:* 621–24. *Freedom of self-determination:* 641, 643, 646, 647. *Classification:* 6, 7, 8–9, 13, 27

KELSEN, HANS
Freedom of self-realization: the existential issues, 581, 583–86, 590, 591–92. *Classification:* 5, 12

KENT, CHANCELLOR
Freedom of self-realization: the existential issues, 579–80, 589, 596 fn. 110; the normative issues, 607–8

KIERKEGAARD, SÖREN
Freedom of self-perfection: 621 fn. 2. *Classification:* 621 fn. 1

KIRK, RUSSELL
Freedom of self-realization: the existential issues, 595 fn. 106 and fn. 107, 596 fn. 111; the normative issues, 611–12 fn. 35

KNIGHT, FRANK H.
Freedom of self-realization: the conceptual issues, 552–54, 555–56; the existential issues, 569 fn. 31, 573, 575, 580–81, 583–86, 590, 591–92, 599 fn. 113; the normative issues, 604 fn. 2, 609 fn. 27, 612 fn. 36. *Classification:* 5, 7, 13. *See also:* 24–25, 26

KUEHNELT-LEDDIHN, ERIK VON
Freedom of self-realization: the existential issues, 588 fn. 90

LASKI, HAROLD J.
Freedom of self-realization: the conceptual issues, 542–43, 545–46, 547, 552, 555–56; the existential issues, 569 fn. 31, 573, 577–78, 580, 583–86, 589–90 and fn. 94, 591–92, 595 fn. 108, 596 fn. 109, 600 fn. 114,

601 fn. 117; the normative issues, 609, 611, 612 fn. 36. *Classification:* 5, 12, 14. *See also:* 554 fn. 64, 574–75

LECKY, WILLIAM E. H.
Freedom of self-realization: the existential issues, 580, 588–89, 595 fn. 106

LEIBNIZ, GOTTFRIED W.
Freedom of self-perfection: 621–24. *Freedom of self-determination:* 637 fn. 7, 638, 639, 645 fn. 33, 645, 646. *Classification:* 6, 7, 13. *See also:* 7 fn. 1, 635–36

LENIN, VLADIMIR I.
Collective freedom: 626, 629, 631–32

LEQUIER, JULES
Classification: 12

LIPPMANN, WALTER
Freedom of self-realization: the existential issues, 595 fn. 106, 596 fn. 111

LOCKE, JOHN
Freedom of self-realization: the conceptual issues, 555; the existential issues, 567, 568, 569–70, 587 fn. 87; the normative issues, 610, 613, 615. *Freedom of self-perfection:* 621 fn. 2. *Freedom of self-determination:* 642. *Classification:* 5, 6, 7, 8–9, 14, 27

LUCRETIUS
Classification: 7, 12

LUTHER, MARTIN
Freedom of self-perfection: 621–24. *Freedom of self-determination:* 637. *Classification:* 6, 7, 13

MacIVER, ROBERT M.
Freedom of self-realization: the existential issues, 569 fn. 81

MACMURRAY, JOHN
Classification: 5, 12

MADARIAGA, DON SALVADOR DE
Freedom of self-realization: the existential issues, 582 fn. 77

MAIMONIDES, MOSES
Freedom of self-perfection: 621 fn. 2. *Classification:* 6, 7, 13

MALINOWSKI, BRONISLAW
Freedom of self-realization: the conceptual issues, 551; the existential issues, 564–66; the normative issues, 612 fn. 37. *Classification:* 5, 12

MANN, HORACE
Freedom of self-realization: the existential issues, 596 fn. 111

MANNHEIM, KARL
Freedom of self-realization: the conceptual issues, 545–46, 552–53; the existential issues, 566. *Classification:* 5, 12

MANSEL, HENRY
Freedom of self-determination: 637

MARCEL, GABRIEL
Freedom of self-perfection: 621 fn. 2, 624. *Classification:* 6, 7, 13

MARITAIN, JACQUES
Freedom of self-realization: the existential issues, 587 fn. 87, 595 fn. 106; the normative issues, 605, 610, 618–19. *Freedom of self-perfection:* 621 fn. 2, 623–24. *Freedom of self-determination:* 637 fn. 7, 641 and fn. 19. *Classification:* 5, 7, 8–9, 14

MARSILIUS OF PADUA
Freedom of self-realization: the existential issues, 587 fn. 87; the normative issues, 613, 615

MARX, KARL
Freedom of self-realization: the existential issues, 595–96. *Collective freedom:* 626–27, 628–31, 631–32. *Classification:* 10, 12

MILL, JOHN STUART
Freedom of self-realization: the conceptual issues, 555–56; the existential issues, 583–86, 591–92; the normative issues, 608–9, 611, 612 fn. 37, 617–18. *Classification:* 5, 12, 14

MISES, LUDWIG VON
Freedom of self-realization: the existential issues, 601 fn. 116; the normative issues, 604 fn. 2

MOLEY, RAYMOND
Freedom of self-realization: the existential issues, 588 fn. 90

MOLINA, D. LUDOVICO
Freedom of self-determination: 465 fn. 2, 637, 641. *See also:* 644

MONTESQUIEU, BARON DE
Freedom of self-realization: the existential issues, 567, 569–70, 587 fn. 87; the normative issues, 613, 615. *Freedom of self-perfection:* 621 fn. 2, 622. *Classification:* 5, 6, 7, 8–9, 13

NOWELL-SMITH, P. N.
Freedom of self-determination: 647. *Classification:* 5, 12. *See also:* 29

OCKHAM, WILLIAM OF
Freedom of self-determination: 637

PAINE, THOMAS
Freedom of self-realization: the normative issues, 618 fn. 56

PARETO, VILFREDO
Classification: 5, 12

PELAGIUS
Freedom of self-perfection: 624–25. *Freedom of self-determination:* 644

PERRY, RALPH BARTON
Freedom of self-realization: the conceptual issues, 551

PHILO
Freedom of self-perfection: 622, 623.
Classification: 6, 7, 13
PLATO
Freedom of self-realization: the normative issues, 610. Freedom of self-perfection: 621, 624. Classification: 12, 27
PLOTINUS
Freedom of self-perfection: 621, 622, 623, 624. Classification: 6, 12
PRICE, JOSEPH
See also: 29
PRIESTLEY, JOSEPH
Freedom of sell-determination: 647. Classification: 5, 12. See also: 29
RAINBOROUGH, MAJOR
Freedom of self-realization: the normative issues, 618 fn. 56
REID, THOMAS
Freedom of self-determination: 637
RENOUVIER, CHARLES
Freedom of self-determination: 647. Classification: 7, 12
ROSSITER, CLINTON
Freedom of self-realization: the conceptual issues, 552; the normative issues, 608, 611–12 fn. 35
ROUSSEAU, JEAN JACQUES
Freedom of self-realization: the existential issues, 567, 569–70; the normative issues, 610. Freedom of self-perfection: 621, 622, 623–24. Freedom of self-determination: 643. Classification: 6, 7, 13
RUSSELL, BERTRAND
Freedom of self-realization: the existential issues, 568, 569, 589, 593 fn. 102; the normative issues, 612 fn. 36. Freedom of self-perfection: 621, 624. Classification: 5, 6, 13, 14
RYAN, MSGR. JOHN A.
Freedom of self-realization: the normative issues, 610
SAINT PAUL
Freedom of self-perfection: 625 fn. 8
SALVADORI, MASSIMO
Freedom of self-realization: the conceptual issues, 551 fn. 49; the existential issues, 595 fn. 107, 596 fn. 111
SANTAYANA, GEORGE
Freedom of self-perfection: 621 fn. 2. Classification: 6, 7, 13
SARTRE, JEAN-PAUL
Freedom of self-determination: 639, 642–43, 644–45, 646. Classification: 7, 12
SCHILLER, F. C. S.
Freedom of self-determination: 641

SCHLICK, MORITZ
Freedom of self-realization: the conceptual issues, 542, 545–46, 547. Classification: 5, 12, 25. See also: 23–24, 24–25, 26, 544, 547
SECRÉTAN, CHARLES
Classification: 7, 12
SENECA, LUCIUS ANNAEUS
Freedom of self-perfection: 621, 624. Classification: 6, 12
SIDGWICK, HENRY
Freedom of self-realization: the conceptual issues, 542; the existential issues, 569 fn. 31, 582 fn. 77, 587 fn. 87; the normative issues, 612 fn. 37, 618, 619–20. See also: 23, 25
SIMON, YVES
Freedom of self-realization: the existential issues, 574 fn. 47, 587 fn. 87, 595 fn. 106 and fn. 107; the normative issues, 618, 619–20. Freedom of self-perfection: 624. Freedom of self-determination: 641. Classification: 5, 6, 7, 8–9, 14
SIMONS, HENRY
Freedom of self-realization: the conceptual issues, 552; the existential issues, 573, 575, 590, 595 fn. 106, 596 fn. 111, 599 fn. 113, 601 fn. 118; the normative issues, 609 fn. 27
SMITH, ADAM
Freedom of self-realization: the normative issues, 612 fn. 37. Classification: 5, 7, 13
SOULE, GEORGE
Freedom of self-realization: the existential issues, 600 fn. 114, 601 fn. 117 and fn. 118
SPENCER, HERBERT
Freedom of self-realization: the existential issues, 567, 569, 581, 583–86, 591–92. Classification: 5, 12, 14
SPINOZA, BENEDICT
Freedom of self-realization: the normative issues, 610. Freedom of self-perfection: 621, 622, 623–24. Classification: 6, 12
STEVENSON, CHARLES L.
Classification: 6, 12
STOICS, THE ROMAN
Freedom of self-perfection: 623–24
STRACHEY, JOHN
Freedom of self-realization: the existential issues, 600 fn. 114
SUAREZ, FRANCIS
Freedom of self-determination: 641
SUMNER, WILLIAM GRAHAM
Freedom of self-realization: the existential issues, 573, 575, 576–77, 580,

596 fn. 110; the normative issues, 608, 611

TAWNEY, RICAHARD H.
Freedom of self-realization: the conceptual issues, 542–43, 550, 555–56; the existential issues, 568, 569, 573–74, 577–78, 583–86, 590 and fn. 94, 591–93; the normative issues, 609. *Classification:* 5, 12, 14. *See also:* 23, 24, 25

THOMAS, NORMAN
Freedom of self-realization: the existential issues, 595 fn. 108, 596 fn. 109, 600 fn. 114. 601 fn. 117 and fn. 118

TILLICH, PAUL
Freedom of self-perfection: 621 fn. 2. *Freedom of self-determination:* 637 fn. 7, 642 and fn. 20. *Classification:* 6, 7, 13

TOCQUEVILLE, ALEXIS DE
Freedom of self-realization: the existential issues, 577–78, 590

VAIL, CHARLES H.
Freedom of self-realization: the existential issues, 595 fn. 108, 596 fn. 109

VAN PATTON, PHILIP
Collective freedom: 630

VIERECK, PETER
Freedom of self-realization: the conceptual issues, 552

VOLTAIRE, FRANÇOIS DE
Classification: 5, 12

WEISS, PAUL
Freedom of self-determination: 637 fn. 7, 640, 641–42, 643, 645 fn. 34, 647. *Classification:* 7, 12. *See also:* 7 fn. 1

WHITEHEAD, ALFRED N.
Freedom of self-perfection: 621, 624. *Freedom of self-determination:* 640–41, 641–42, 645 fn. 34, 646–47. *Classification:* 6, 7, 13

WILDMAN, SIR JOHN
Freedom of self-realization: the normative issues, 618 fn. 56

WINDELBAND, WILHELM
Freedom of self-determination: 465

WOOTTON, BARBARA
Freedom of self-realization: the conceptual issues, 551; the existential issues, 587 fn. 87